BAPTISM IN THE EARLY CHURCH

SPRINGDALE COLLEGE
TOGETHER IN MISSION
ROWHEATH PAVILION
HEATH ROAD
BIRMINGHAM B30 1HH

BAPTISM IN THE EARLY CHURCH

History, Theology, and Liturgy in the First Five Centuries

Everett Ferguson

WILLIAM B. EERDMANS PUBLISHING COMPANY
GRAND RAPIDS, MICHIGAN / CAMBRIDGE, U.K.

© 2009 Everett Ferguson
All rights reserved

Published 2009 by
Wm. B. Eerdmans Publishing Co.
2140 Oak Industrial Drive N.E., Grand Rapids, Michigan 49505 /
P.O. Box 163, Cambridge CB3 9PU U.K.

Printed in the United States of America

19 18 17 16 15 14 13   9 8 7 6 5 4 3

Library of Congress Cataloging-in-Publication Data

Ferguson, Everett, 1933-
    Baptism in the early church: history, theology, and liturgy in the first five centuries/
Everett Ferguson.
       p.   cm.
    Includes bibliographical references.
    ISBN 978-0-8028-7108-4 (pbk: alk. paper)
    1. Baptism — History — Early church, ca. 30-600.   I. Title.
BV803.F47   2009
234'.16109015 — dc22
                                                          2008030617

www.eerdmans.com

*To the three special persons
who married into our family
and made it better.*

Contents

Preface	xix
Acknowledgments	xxi
1. **Introduction: Survey of Literature**	1
Comprehensive Surveys	1
Studies with Liturgy as the Theme	5
Topical Studies	11
Collections of Sources	20

Part One — Antecedents to Christian Baptism

2. **Washings for Purification in Greco-Roman Paganism**	25
General Usage for Purification	25
Washings in the Mystery Religions	28
Bathing Practices	34
A Special Case from Mythology	36
3. **Words from the *Bapt-* Root in Classical and Hellenistic Greek**	38
βάπτω, βαπτός	38
Literal Usage	38
Metaphorical Usage (Secondary Meanings)	42
Jewish Usage	46
βαπτίζω, βαπτισμός	47
Literal Usage	48
Metaphorical Usage	52

Usage in Pagan Religious and Magical Contexts	55
Jewish Usage	56
Conclusion	59

4. Jewish Washings, Baptismal Movements, and Proselyte Baptism — 60
The Background in the Jewish Scriptures	61
Ceremonial Cleansing	61
Events Seen as Prefiguring Baptism	62
Mishnah and *Mikvaoth*	63
Other References to Jewish Washings	65
Essenes and Dead Sea Scrolls	68
Baptismal Movements	71
Proselyte Baptism	76

5. John the Baptizer — 83
John in Relation to Jewish Immersions	84
New Testament Texts about John's Baptism	89
The Meaning of John's Baptism	93
The Manner of John's Baptism	95

Part Two — Baptism in the New Testament

6. Baptism of Jesus—I — 99
New Testament Texts	99
Early Noncanonical Accounts of the Baptism of Jesus	104

7. Baptism of Jesus—II — 113
Later Christian Interpretation of the Baptism of Jesus: Texts	113
Later Christian Interpretation of the Baptism of Jesus: Art	123

8. Other References to Baptism in the Gospels — 132
Matthew	132
Mark	138
Luke	141
John	142

9. Baptism in the Pauline Epistles — 146
Galatians	147
1 and 2 Corinthians	149
Romans	155

Colossians	158
Ephesians	161
Titus	162
Summary	164
10. The Acts of the Apostles	**166**
Acts 1–2	166
Acts 8:4-25	170
Acts 8:26-40	172
Acts 9:1-19; 22:3-21	173
Acts 10:1–11:18	175
Acts 16:12-15	179
Acts 16:16-34	179
Acts 18:8	180
Acts 18:24–19:7	180
Baptism in(to) the Name of Jesus	182
The Holy Spirit and Baptism	183
Summary on Baptism in Acts	184
11. Baptism in the Rest of the New Testament and Summary	**186**
Hebrews	186
James	188
1 Peter 3:21	189
1 John	193
Revelation	196
Summary of New Testament Information on Baptism	196

Part Three — The Second Century

12. Apostolic Fathers	**201**
Didache	201
1 Clement	206
2 Clement	207
Ignatius	209
Epistle of Barnabas	210
Hermas	214

13. Christian Pseudepigrapha and Apocrypha — 221
   Some Pseudepigrapha — 221
   Odes of Solomon — 222
   Apocalypse of Peter — 225
   Epistle of the Apostles and Baptism of the Righteous Dead — 225
   Acts of Peter — 228
   Acts of Paul — 229
   Acts of John — 232
   Acts of Andrew — 232
   Other Later Apocryphal Acts — 234
   Physiologus — 236

14. Apologists — 237
   Justin Martyr — 237
   Melito of Sardis — 245
   Tatian — 246
   Theophilus of Antioch — 246

15. The Pseudo-Clementines and Jewish Christianity — 248
   Washings for Purification — 249
   Initiatory Baptism — 251
   Baptismal Doctrine — 255
   Epiphanius on the Ebionites — 263
   Observations — 264

16. Jewish and Christian Baptisms — 266
   Justin Martyr — 267
   Oxyrhynchus Papyrus 840 — 269
   Pseudo-Cyprian, *Against the Jews* — 271
   Tertullian, *An Answer to the Jews* — 272
   Cyprian, *Testimonies against the Jews* — 272
   Didascalia — 273
   Epiphanius on the Samaritans and Others — 274
   Conclusion — 275

17. Marcionites, Those Called Gnostics, and Related Groups — 276
   Marcionites — 276
   Valentinians — 278

Sethians	290
Others	299
18. Irenaeus	303
19. Clement of Alexandria	309
Terminology and the Meaning of Baptism	309
Jesus' Baptism	313
Faith and Repentance	314
Ceremony of Baptism	315
Jewish and Pagan Antecedents	317
Clement and Those Called Gnostics	318
The Baptism of the Apostles	319
Postbaptismal Sin	320
Concluding Comments	320

Part Four — The Third Century to Nicaea (325)

20. Writings Attributed to Hippolytus	325
Commentary on Daniel	326
On Christ and Antichrist	326
Against Noetus	326
Apostolic Tradition	327
On the Holy Theophany	333
21. Carthage: Tertullian	336
Antecedents to Christian Baptism	336
Faith and Repentance	338
Ceremony of Baptism	340
Doctrine of Baptism	346
22. Carthage: Cyprian	351
Ceremony of Baptism	351
Sickbed Baptism	355
Doctrine of Baptism	357
23. Origin and Early Development of Infant Baptism	362
Tertullian	363
The *Apostolic Tradition*	366
Origen	367

Cyprian	370
Inscriptions	372
What Was the Origin of Infant Baptism?	377
Conclusion	379

24. The Controversy over "Rebaptism" in the Third Century — 380

Early Statements	380
Novatian	381
Stephen of Rome	383
Anonymous, *On Rebaptism*	385
Cyprian	388
Judgements of the Eighty-seven Bishops	392
Firmilian	394
Dionysius of Alexandria	396
Later Developments	398

25. Origen — 400

Old Testament Foreshadowings of Baptism	401
The Baptisms of John the Baptist and Jesus	405
The Eschatological Baptism of Fire	408
Theology of Baptism	410
Martyrdom	417
Catechumenate and Prerequisites for Baptism	419
Liturgy	423

26. Syria in the Third Century — 429

Acts of Thomas	429
Acts of Xanthippe and Polyxena	435
Didascalia	436
The Baptistery at Dura Europus	440
The Mime/Martyr Gelasinus	443

27. Sources at the Turn to the Fourth Century — 444

Porphyry	444
Lactantius	445
Methodius	447
Eusebius of Caesarea	449
Council of Nicaea, 325	451

Part Five — The Fourth Century

28. Egypt in the Fourth Century — 455
Athanasius — 455
Some Later Athanasian *Spuria* — 458
Serapion — 460
Canons of Hippolytus — 465
Didymus the Blind (?), *On the Trinity* — 467
Papyrus Prayers — 471

29. Jerusalem in the Fourth Century — 473
Cyril of Jerusalem — 473
  Procedures and Ceremony — 474
    Final Instruction and Preparation for Baptism — 475
    Pre-Immersion Rites — 477
    The Baptism Proper — 478
    Postbaptismal Rites — 479
  Meaning and Effects of Baptism — 481
Egeria — 487

30. Writers in Syriac in the Fourth Century: Aphrahat — 489

31. Writers in Syriac in the Fourth Century: Ephraem the Syrian — 499
Typology of Baptism — 499
Baptism of Christ — 502
Faith and Repentance — 505
Ceremony of Baptism — 506
Meaning of Baptism — 509
Hymns on Epiphany Attributed to Ephraem — 513

32. The School of Antioch: Theodore of Mopsuestia — 519
The Process of Initiation — 520
The Doctrine of Baptism — 526

33. The School of Antioch: John Chrysostom—I — 533
Nontechnical Word Usage — 534
Administration of Baptism — 536

34. The School of Antioch: John Chrysostom—II — 547
Christ's Baptism — 547
Images of Baptism — 548

Grace, Faith, and Repentance	550
Doctrinal Meaning of Baptism	552
Death, Burial, and Resurrection	552
New Creation	553
Regeneration	555
Forgiveness of Sins	556
Holy Spirit and Baptism	559
Seal and Circumcision	559
Enlightenment	560
Clothing with Christ	561
Moral Consequences and Faithfulness	562
35. Miscellaneous Sources: Church Orders and "Eunomian" Baptism	**564**
Apostolic Constitutions	564
Baptismal Ceremony	565
Doctrine of Baptism	570
The Nicaeno-Constantinopolitan Creed	573
Council of Laodicea and the Origin of a Postbaptismal Anointing in the East	574
Eunomian Baptism	575
Asterius the Homilist	577
Opus Imperfectum in Matthaeum	579
Testament of the Lord	579
36. Cappadocia: Basil the Great	**582**
Nontechnical Word Usage	583
Baptismal Ceremony	583
Baptismal Theology	585
37. Cappadocia: Gregory of Nazianzus	**592**
Baptismal Ceremony	593
Baptismal Theology	596
38. Cappadocia: Gregory of Nyssa	**603**
Baptismal Ceremony	603
Baptismal Theology	608

39.	**The Delay of Baptism: Sickbed Baptism, Believers' Baptism, and Infant Baptism**	617
	Sickbed Baptism	618
	Basil the Great	618
	Gregory of Nazianzus	620
	Gregory of Nyssa	621
	John Chrysostom	622
	Marcianus the Ascetic	624
	Epiphanius of Salamis	625
	A Report by Socrates	625
	Inscriptions	626
	Sponsors and Instruction	626
	Believers' Baptism in Christian Families	626
	Infant Baptism: The Fourth Century and Beyond	627
40.	**Milan: Ambrose**	634
	Baptismal Ceremony	635
	Baptismal Typology	641
	Baptismal Theology	642
41.	**Other North Italians**	648
	Zeno of Verona	648
	Maximus of Turin	651
	Chromatius of Aquileia	656
	His Writings	656
	Archaeological Evidence	660
42.	**Spain**	663
	Council of Elvira	663
	Gregory of Elvira	665
	Pacian of Barcelona	666
	Some Later Developments in Spain	668
43.	**Some Other Latin Authors**	671
	Hilary of Poitiers	671
	Optatus of Milevis	674
	Jerome	677
	Paulinus of Nola	683

Part Six — The Fifth Century

44. Egypt: Cyril of Alexandria and the Coptic Rite — 687
  Cyril of Alexandria — 687
  A Prebaptismal Anointing Formula — 693
  Der Balyzeh Papyrus — 693
  An Epiphany Hymn — 694
  The Coptic Rite — 695

45. Writers and Writings in Syriac and Armenian — 700
  Syriac Acts of John — 700
  Narsai — 702
  The Teaching of Saint Gregory — 708
  Armenian Ritual of Baptism — 712
  Later Syrian Baptismal Liturgies — 713

46. Greek-Speaking Syria — 715
  Theodoret — 715
  Mark the Deacon, *Life of Porphyry* — 719
  Pseudo-Dionysius the Areopagite — 720

47. Baptism in the Messalian Controversy — 724
  Messalianism — 724
  Pseudo-Macarius: A Moderate Voice — 728
  Diadochus of Photice: A Later Moderate Voice — 732
  Hieronymus (Jerome) of Jerusalem: A Messalian Voice? — 735
  Mark the Monk: An Anti-Messalian Voice — 738

48. Asia Minor and Constantinople — 745
  Theodotus of Ancyra — 745
  Pseudo-Gregory Thaumaturgus, *On the Holy Theophany* — 747
  Socrates on Paul the Novatian — 748
  Proclus — 748
  Barberini Euchologion — 752

49. Ravenna and Rome — 756
  Peter Chrysologus of Ravenna — 756
  Baptisteries of Ravenna — 758
  Siricius of Rome — 760
  Innocent I and Gelasius — 760

Leo I	761
John the Deacon	766
Gelasian Sacramentary	768
The Lateran Baptistery in Rome	769
50. Gaul and North Africa: Gennadius of Marseilles, Some African Councils, and Quodvultdeus of Carthage	**770**
Gennadius of Marseilles	770
Some African Councils	770
Quodvultdeus	771
51. North Africa: Augustine of Hippo — I	**776**
Augustine's Own Experience with Baptism	776
Baptismal Ceremony in Hippo	778
Augustine's Traditional Baptismal Theology	790
52. North Africa: Augustine of Hippo — II	**795**
The Donatists and the Indelible Character of Baptism	795
Pelagianism, Infant Baptism, and Original Sin	803

Part Seven — Baptisteries

53. Baptismal Fonts: East	**819**
Introduction to Baptismal Fonts	819
Israel	821
West Jordan and Jordan	823
Syria and Lebanon	824
Egypt and Libya	825
Turkey	826
Cyprus	827
Greece	828
Balkans	833
54. Baptismal Fonts: West	**836**
Italy	836
Tunisia	841
Algeria	842
France	843
Switzerland	845

  Austria, Lichtenstein, Germany, and England   846
  Spain   847
  Evaluation of the Evidence of Baptismal Fonts   849

55. **Conclusions**   853
  Origin of Baptism   853
  Doctrine of Baptism   853
  Baptismal Ceremony/Liturgy   855
  Origin and Progress of Infant Baptism   856
  Mode of Baptism: Immersion with Exceptions   857

Index of Biblical Passages   861
Index of Greek and Roman Authors and Writings   873
Index of Jewish Authors and Writings   880
Index of Non-Canonical Christian Authors and Writings   884
Index of Modern Authors   934
Index of Subjects   946

Preface

I have attempted to be as complete as possible on the first three centuries but have been content to be progressively less so on the fourth and fifth centuries (where the sources are more abundant) yet still to be full enough for the work to be representatively comprehensive. My training is in the literary sources, but I have tried to become knowledgeable on the art and archaeological sources.

The subject of baptism has been the source of debates between denominations but has also been of concern in ecumenical endeavors. My own intention is to be historically objective. Readers will judge my degree of success. In spite of the theological disagreements of the past and learned differences still in the present, I find wide agreement in regard to the historical facts from scholars representing a wide spectrum of backgrounds. I may have pushed the areas of consensus further than many might. Nonetheless, disputes mostly arise on the interpretation of the facts. Putting different specialties and periods together in a synthesis may be the basis for further conversation.

The introduction surveys scholarly works that have a broad scope and are not often noted in my particular topics; their contents, however, do set the issues for my fresh examination. The reader not interested in the history of scholarship on baptism may choose to skip it and go directly to the meat of my own work. Some readers may want to use the treatment of particular periods, persons, writings, or topics for reference purposes.

Unacknowledged translations are my own.

Thanks are due to many without whom the book could not have been written. I must mention especially my wife, who has provided compatibility and intellectual stimulation as well as making my work possible and pleasant through the years. I have learned much from association with colleagues through their writings and in conversation. The notes do not begin to acknowledge this indebtedness. A special word of appreciation is due to the libraries at Harvard University (Widener and Andover-Harvard) and Abilene Christian University, particularly the interlibrary loan services of the latter. The publisher's readers — Robin Jensen, Maxwell Johnson, and David Wright — while not always agreeing with the author, have improved his work in various ways.

EVERETT FERGUSON

Acknowledgments

The author and publisher hereby gratefully acknowledge permission to reprint the following:

Quotations from various volumes of the Church Fathers series Used with Permission: The Catholic University of America Press. Washington, DC.

Quotations from *The Nag Hammadi Library in English,* 3rd, completely revised edition by James M. Robinson, General Editor. Copyright © 1978, 1988 by E. J. Brill, Leiden, The Netherlands. Reprinted by permission of HarperCollins Publishers.

Quotations from E. C. Whitaker, *Documents of the Baptismal Liturgy,* Liturgical Press.

Excerpts reproduced from *New Testament Apocrypha* by Wilhelm Schneemelcher. © 1992 Westminster John Knox Press. Used by permission of Westminster John Knox Press.

Quotations from Barkhuizen, *Acta Patr. et Byz.,* vol. 14, Jan Barkhuizen and Australian Catholic Univ. Press.

Excerpts from the following, all published by Paulist Press, Inc., New York/Mahwah, NJ. Reprinted by permission of Paulist Press, Inc. www.paulistpress.com:

Pseudo-Macarius: The Fifty Spiritual Homilies and the Great Letter, translated, edited, and introduced by George A. Maloney, SJ. Copyright © 1992 by George A. Maloney, SJ.

Ephrem the Syrian: Hymns, translated and introduced by Kathleen E. McVey. Copyright © 1989 by Kathleen E. McVey.

Quodvultdeus of Carthage: The Creedal Homilies, translation and commentary by Thomas Macy Finn. Copyright © 2004 by Thomas Macy Finn.

Origen: Treatise on the Passover, Dialogue with Heraclides, translated and annotated by Robert J. Daly, SJ. Copyright © 1992 by the New England Province of the Society of Jesus.

The Sermons of St. Maximus of Turin, translated and annotated by Boniface Ramsey, OP. Copyright © 1989 by Boniface Ramsey, OP.

St. John Chrysostom: Baptismal Instructions, translated and annotated by Paul W. Harkins, PhD, LLD. Copyright © 1963 by Rev. Johannes Quasten and Rev. Walter Burghardt, SJ.

St. Irenaeus: Proof of the Apostolic Preaching, translated and annotated by Joseph P. Smith, SJ. Copyright © 1952 by Johannes Quasten and Joseph C. Plumpe.

St. Augustine: Faith, Hope, and Charity, translated and annotated by Louis A. Arand, SS, STD. Copyright © 1974 by Johannes Quasten and Joseph C. Plumpe.

The Letters of Cyprian of Carthage, Vols. 1, 2, 3, 4, translated and annotated by G. W. Clarke. Copyright © 1984 by Rev. Johannes Quasten, Rev. Walter J. Burghardt, SJ, and Thomas Comerford Lawler.

1. Introduction: Survey of Literature

Specialized studies of topics and ancient authors will be noted at their appropriate place. This survey is limited to some of the major studies that are broader in scope.

Comprehensive Surveys

Two older works from Great Britain set the context of discussion in the English-speaking world. William Wall, *History of Infant Baptism,* was first published in 1705 (second edition 1707, third in 1720). It was reissued with supplementary writings in four volumes by Oxford University Press, 1834-1836, and in two volumes in 1862. This large work set forth the viewpoint that was standard among advocates of infant baptism before modern studies began to chip away at details and suggest a different way of putting the evidence together. Darwell Stone, *Holy Baptism* (London: Longmans, Green, 1917 [after earlier editions]), defended baptismal regeneration, which, to be more precise, should be described as regeneration in baptism.

Some articles in older reference works are still useful: Kirsopp Lake, "Baptism (Early Christian)," and H. G. Wood, "Baptism (Later Christian)," in James Hastings, *Encyclopedia of Religion and Ethics* (New York: Charles Scribner's Sons, 1918), Vol. 2, pp. 384-390, 390-398 (up to eighth century); E. Fascher, "Taufe," in *Paulys Real-Encyclopadie* (Stuttgart: J. B. Metzlersche, 1932), Second Series, Vol. 8, cols. 2501-2518.

Two comprehensive works in French canvass in a wide historical frame the issues that are still discussed. Jules Corblett, *Histoire dogmatique, liturgique, et archéologique du sacrement de baptême* (Paris, 1881), 2 volumes, organizes the material topically, then treats its development historically with a very complete listing of references from the church fathers on all subjects with an effort to include the evidence of baptisteries and art as well as the literary texts. As an example of the thoroughness attempted, Corblett treats the following figures of baptism: Jewish aspersions, circumcision, the deluge, waters of creation, rivers of paradise, blood and

1

water from the side of Christ, water in general, washing of Naaman, axe of Elijah, bronze laver at the temple, sea of glass in Revelation, water struck from the rock by Moses, Israel crossing the Red Sea and the Jordan, Jesus healing the blind man at the pool of Siloam, Jesus healing the paralytic at Bethsaida, purification of lepers, serpent of brass set up by Moses in the wilderness, the tomb of the Savior (Book I, chap. 5). Iconography offers partially overlapping figures of baptism: lamb, ark of Noah, man born blind, the bath of the infant Jesus, jar of water, deer, dolphin, stars, rivers, Jordan, Moses striking the rock, passage of the Red Sea, healing of paralytic, fish, and fisherman (Book XVIII, chap. 1).

On the mode of baptism (Book IV, chap. 2) Corblett states that *mergere, mergitare, in aquas mittere* guarantee immersion in the first centuries but not later, for *baptizare = plonger* became figurative. Baptisteries and iconography lead to the conclusion that in the West baptism was ordinarily a partial immersion completed by effusion of water over the head in the same epoch as the writers speak of a total immersion. This viewpoint has had a wide currency. He summarizes (pp. 248-249) that in the East a total submersion was usual; but in the West in the fourth-eighth centuries there was partial immersion in baptisteries with the addition of infusion, in the eighth-eleventh centuries a vertical (based on the shape of the fonts) and complete immersion of children in vats (is the eleventh-century picture of an immersion of an upright body and a bishop pouring out of a small cup over the head not a combination of immersion and infusion but an immersion followed by the post-baptismal anointing?), in the eleventh-thirteenth centuries horizontal and complete immersion of children in vats, in the thirteenth-fourteenth centuries both complete immersion and partial immersion with infusion but rarely infusion alone (in the fourteenth century the first incontestable example of aspersion — p. 264), in the fifteenth-sixteenth centuries rarely complete immersion, and in the seventeenth-eighteenth centuries infusion reigned. That vertical fonts preceded horizontal fonts for infant baptism would argue that the immersion of adults too was first in the upright position, but that raises the problem of the relatively shallow fonts unless the candidate was in a kneeling or crouching position, for which he says no text leads us to suppose.

On the subjects of baptism (Book VII) Corblett states that except when there was danger of death children were baptized only at the age of two or three, when they could answer for themselves, then at one year of age in vertical vats, and only in the eleventh century did the custom of baptizing the newborn within a few days prevail. Volume 2, Book XIV, gives a comprehensive synthesis of preliminaries to baptism, the baptism itself, and subsequent ceremonies.

Eighty years later came another comprehensive work by T. Maertens, *Histoire et pastorale du rituel du catéchuménat et du baptême,* Paroisse et liturgie collection de pastorale liturgique 56 (Bruges: Biblica, 1962). This generally excellent work follows a historical order beginning with Old Testament ablutions, proselyte baptism, the Essenes, and John's baptism (pp. 26-30) as a prelude to the definitive ablution in the Spirit. He has a Roman Catholic framework of interpretation and follows primarily the Western development through the Middle Ages with comments pertaining to the pastoral situation of his day. He represents a heavy dependence on the *Apostolic Tradition* ascribed to Hippolytus for Roman practice beginning in the late second century.

There are problematic elements in the presentation. Maertens argues for pouring of water on the head as a primitive practice (p. 38) and that the connection of Christian ablution with the death and resurrection of Christ did not mean it was done by immersion (p. 47). He also reads a considerable baptismal ritual into New Testament texts (pp. 47-54).

On the positive side Maertens correctly notes that the word and faith were intimately connected with New Testament baptism (pp. 43-46). In the early centuries the action of God, liberty of the candidate, and participation of the community were held together in the baptismal ceremonies, but in the Middle Ages with the practice of infant baptism the free choice by the candidate was suppressed and the community elements either disappeared or were reinterpreted so that these two aspects were absorbed in ritualism (pp. 185-194).

Maertens makes several significant points. Because of the decadence of the catechumenate, Augustine had to place last the moral instruction that came first in the *Apostolic Tradition* (pp. 115-118). The delivery and recitation of the Creed added a declarative formula to the earlier practice of an interrogatory confession at baptism, but this indicative confession was now more of an examination of the faith taught (pp. 131ff.). In early times the emphasis was on the psychological choice between two Masters (renunciation of the devil and adherence to Christ), but by the fifth century the scrutinies placed the emphasis on the theological truth that Satan is not driven out apart from the coming of the Lord (pp. 146ff.). With the emphasis given in the fourth century to baptism as death in a tomb, water became less a symbol of life and more of death, and so an even greater interest was given to the blessing of the water. In the early practice the name of Jesus was proclaimed and professed and baptism was in his name; with the benediction of the water one now also invoked his name (pp. 158-166). Infant baptism, instead of producing a new ritual, "infantilized" the ritual of adults.

Lothar Heiser, *Die Taufe in der orthodoxen Kirche: Geschichte, Spendung, und Symbolik nach der Lehre der Väter* (Trier: Paulinus, 1987), concentrates on the Greek Fathers up to the establishment of the present Orthodox rite, essentially complete in the sixth century and preserved unchanged since then. He covers the evidence of pictures and baptisteries (with good color plates) as well as the principal patristic texts. He emphasizes the patristic interpretation of the baptism of Jesus as the pattern for Christian baptism, of baptism as part of the renewal of humanity according to the pattern of paradise at creation, and of the biblical images of baptism. The differences between the Latin and Byzantine churches in the administration of baptism became acute in the competition for the allegiance of the Bulgars in the ninth century.

Two recent works in English give briefer but comprehensive surveys. Maxwell E. Johnson, *The Rites of Christian Initiation: Their Evolution and Interpretation* (Collegeville: Liturgical, 1999), offers a textbook on the history of the rites of initiation. His approach is textual, historical, and theological (p. xiii) with an ecumenical perspective. He quotes extensively from the relevant texts and notes the current status of scholarship on controverted points.

Johnson begins with the New Testament origins, affirming that Christian practice reflects considerable variety. Chapter 2 discusses Christian initiation in the pre-Nicene period, distinguishing eastern and western practices. In the East the sequence was anointing, baptism, and eucharist; Jesus' baptism in the Jordan and John 3:5 were central. In the West the sequence was baptism, anointing, handlaying, and eucharist; in Rome there was an added anointing after the handlaying. In the West the primary metaphor for baptism was provided by Romans 6. In the East the prebaptismal rites were oriented to reception of the Holy Spirit, but in the West to the expulsion of evil spirits.

Chapters 3 and 4 discuss initiation in the Christian East and the Christian West respectively. A lengthy catechumenate was more a concern of the fourth century than of the third. In contrast to earlier Syriac tradition the prebaptismal rites were transformed from a pneumatic to an exorcistic emphasis. He says that the the gift of the Spirit migrated from prebaptismal anointing (Syria) to the baptismal act (Chrysostom) to postbaptismal anointing. Such a neat progression may be questioned; a preferable view would be that the gift of the Spirit was associated with the rite as a whole and different authors identified it with different moments for various reasons. Western sources began to speak of the bishop "completing," "perfecting," or "confirming" baptism performed by presbyters or deacons, but this was a matter of pastoral oversight and not a sacramental ministry. Augustine was responsible for a loss of sacramental and liturgical richness in favor of a concern for sacramental validity.

Chapter 5 discusses baptismal preparation and the origin of the forty days of Lent. Chapters 6 on initiation in the Middle Ages, 7 on the Protestant and Catholic reforms of the sixteenth century, 8 on initiation in the churches today, and 9 on the implications of a baptismal spirituality for the present move beyond the chronological limits of this study.

Bryan D. Spinks, *Early and Medieval Rituals and Theologies of Baptism: From the New Testament to the Council of Trent* (Aldershot: Ashgate, 2006), offers a brief but thorough survey (a second volume will cover *Reformation and Modern Rituals and Theologies of Baptism*). On the early sources he gives more on the theology (e.g., on Augustine), but he also gives variant views on disputed questions of ritual practice; on the later sources, where liturgies are preserved, the proportions are reversed. Spinks quotes translations that occur in collections (especially Whitaker and Finn — below) and seldom gives the original source references, with the result that the reader who wants to pursue a document further must have the collection he cites. A further limitation for the general reader, for whom the work seems intended, is that there is no list of abbreviations used.

Following a chapter on the New Testament foundations, Spinks organizes the material geographically within a chronological framework. He prefers variety over efforts at harmonization of liturgical practices. The different ritual patterns generated different theological emphases in the various authors, who did not start with a general theology of baptism. Spinks does not discuss the origin of infant baptism, first mentioning it incidentally in regard to Augustine, but then giving attention to it in later developments, as in the East Syrian defense of infant baptism on the grounds of the largess of God's mercy (p. 74). In the West after Augustine baptism "came to be a baptism from something (original sin) more than a baptism into something (the eschatological community of God)" (p. 67). Instead of focusing only on Western developments, Spinks gives full attention also to East and West Syrian developments and to the Armenian, Coptic, and Ethiopic rites as well as the Byzantine liturgy in the sixth century and after.

Spinks concludes that "all rites look back to the [baptism of Jesus in the] Jordan, and ritualize baptism in the conviction that what happened there once, still hapens now in every baptism" (p. 157). The essential elements were "dipping (Christological), naming (trinitarian), and gestures to symbolize the descent of the Spirit (pneumatological) and adoption into an eschatological community (ecclesiological)" (p. 157).

Studies with Liturgy as the Theme

Two works in German, one by a Roman Catholic and the other by a Protestant (Lutheran), have set the framework for study of the liturgy of baptism: Alois Stenzel, S.J., *Die Taufe: Eine Genetische Erklärung der Taufliturgie* (Innsbruck: Felizian Rauch, 1958); and Georg Kretschmar, *Die Geschichte des Taufgottesdienstes in der alter Kirche*, in *Leiturgia*, Vol. 5, 31-35 (1964-1966).[1]

Stenzel's introduction identifies his interest as liturgy, not theology or parallels from the history of religions, and primarily the Latin development leading to the medieval Roman liturgy. The New Testament writings show little of a ritual of baptism. Infant baptism is not demonstrable from the New Testament, but it is not against the practice (p. 17). The sequence was proclamation, faith, and baptism. Nothing supports the idea that faith made baptism unnecessary; repentance also was necessary. Confession of the Lord Jesus and baptism in his name was the core rite; the "word" accompanying the water in Ephesians 5:26 may be a prayer, an epiclesis, or a "formula," but there was an accompanying word (pp. 18-19). A full immersion is not excluded, but Stenzel brings up many "hinderances" to assuming such (pp. 20-22), yet he finds no evidence for a baptizand standing in the font when sprinkling or pouring was employed (pp. 108-110). A confession of faith was employed at baptism,

---

1. Georg Kretschmar, "Recent Research on Christian Initiation," *Studia Liturgica* 12 (1977): 87-106 concludes that it is hard to speak of a single original and normative form of baptism; unity is provided by Christ's saving work.

but what form it took and what words were spoken by the administrator are controversial, for the New Testament gives no clearly recognizable trinitarian confessional formula (pp. 23-29, 36).

Stenzel seeks the first indications in the second century of elements that became common later. Ideas associated with baptism began to be translated into ritual expression (p. 44). Justin knew no organized, normative ritual, no institutional catechumenate, no *disciplina arcani,* no anointing, but recognized no difference between his homeland and Rome (pp. 47-50).

Stenzel takes the *Apostolic Tradition* of Hippolytus as representing the practice at Rome; as the first constructed baptismal ritual it is the point of departure for his discussion of each item in the baptismal liturgy. Although it was a private and not an official work, it represents what was already traditional and so must reflect practices of c. 170 (p. 55). The catechumenate meant that instruction was now official and not just private. In contrast to earlier times, the *Apostolic Tradition* put a strong emphasis on preparation for baptism and a ritual strengthening of demonological moments (pp. 56-69). Although Tertullian gives no prayers and mentions no baptismal exorcism, which became integral to the baptismal liturgy for Cyprian, he has many agreements with the ritual in Hippolytus (pp. 70-75). Tertullian emphasizes the ideas of covenant and vow. The baptismal ceremony in the early third century shows the essential role of faith and its confession (p. 76, n. 70).

The chapter on the development of individual rites in the East treats the following: (1) The baptismal confession belongs to the core rite next to the baptismal act. Interpretations of baptism "in the name of Jesus" include a distinction from the baptism of John, liturgical words by the administrator, and a profession of faith by the one baptized. Neither liturgical documents nor the correspondence of Cyprian confirms a baptism in the name of Jesus as church usage, but that such was known at the time of the rebaptism controversy appears not unjustified. The Symbol was a product of the insitutional catechumenate, but the eastern witnesses to baptismal questions and answers are numerous (pp. 77-98). (2) The denial of Satan usually included three elements and was part of the baptismal confession negatively formulated (perhaps better described as a verbalized repentance). It was part of the original distinction made between two lords. The form of words was originally assertive but later was interrogatory in parallel with the interrogatory confession. A dramatizing occurred with the candidate taking an active role by turning west, stretching out the hand, and breathing out or spitting. A prebaptismal anointing was introduced between the time of Justin and Hippolytus and did not belong to the core rite (pp. 98-104). (3) The verbal adhesion to Christ is provable only in the East; the West was more conservative in juxtaposing the renunciation and the baptismal confession. This act created a new pairing of *apotaxis* and *syntaxis* (pp. 104-108). (4) The baptismal act was not always an immersion. The number "three" was not required by the New Testament; its fundamental symbolism was trinitarian, and the association with Jesus' three days in the grave was secondary (pp. 108-111). (5) The first express witness for the present western formula "I baptize you . . ." is at the end of the eighth century. The first eastern witnesses to a declarative baptismal formula (end of fourth and fifth centuries) have the passive form, "So and so is baptized." The adoption of a declarative formula represents the tendency for formulas to take over the speech of Scripture. Many texts use the word "Symbol" to refer to the baptismal questions and answers (pp. 111-125). (6) The word σφραγίς, *signum*, in the rites after baptism at the beginning was not a technical term for confirmation (pp. 125-132). (7) Rites of the catechumenate (admission to it, classes of catechumens, the "rule of secrecy," exorcisms, delivery of the creed) receive extensive treatment (pp. 132-164). The period of three years is an indication of the weight put on moral formation.

The treatment of individual rites in the West before Augustine mainly depends on Ambrose: *effeta*, renunciation and adhesion, with the consecration of the water between the renunciation and the baptismal confession, the baptismal act, foot washing (of limited spread and short duration), anointing after baptism (the West up to Innocent I knew no anointing at confirmation), the catechumenate (the West had a fixed Symbol delivered to candidates before the East did; Rome took over a delivery of the "Our Father" from Africa) (pp. 165-177).

A special concern of Stenzel is the rite of the scrutinies (Part III). He, like other students of the baptismal liturgy, gives much attention to the eighth-century *Gelasian Sacramentary* (pp. 207-234). (This is understandable because of the importance and influence of Rome, the absence of anything comparably early for Rome, and its inclusion of earlier material; but I omit it as outside my chronological boundaries.) Part IV continues with the development from baptismal rite to baptismal ordo in the Middle Ages.

Kretschmar consciously includes much of theology along with liturgy. In setting forth his methodology he notes that in the third century baptism (and not the Lord's supper) was the central liturgical act of the church (p. 5). Limiting this summary to only his treatment of the first four centuries is sufficient to illustrate the richness of his contribution.

As to the setting for the early Christian practice, he concludes that rabbinic instructions and the practice of Jewish baptizing sects make it probable that Christian baptism was an immersion (p. 9). We know of no single action in early Christian baptismal rites that must have been taken over from Hellenistic mystery cults (p. 53). In contrast to Qumran and John the Baptist, the church not only understood baptism as an eschatological cleansing rite and as reception into the eschatological community but found its special meaning in relation to the person and history of Jesus (p. 16). He throughout finds an interchange between eschatology and Christology in the baptismal understanding of the early church (e.g., pp. 113, 143).

The relation to Jesus as resurrected Lord was expressed by the phrase "in the name of." It meant one was now "transferred to Christ" or assigned to him (see James 2:7 — chap. 10), but this theological expression gave no direction for how this was done in the liturgy. The relation to Christ may have been spoken by the administrator in prayer before, during, or after the baptism, or in a word accompanying the act, or in a confession by the one baptized (p. 18). The meaning "calling on the name of Jesus" may be correct throughout, and the same would apply to the "name of Father, Son, and Holy Spirit" (p. 32).

The book of Acts knows three forms of the relation of Holy Spirit to baptism: received after baptism, received before baptism, or not connected with baptism (pp. 19-25). His suggestion of the possible liturgical sequence of anointing, baptism, and eucharist in the New Testament is doubtful (see comments on 1 John 5:8 in chap. 10). Anointing is used for the theological meaning of baptism in 2 Corinthians 1:21 and 1 John 2:24, 27 but not in reference to a ritual action (p. 27). In some Gnostic circles oil displaced water baptism. The widespread use of oil in the orthodox baptismal ritual at the end of the second century puts its origin not later than the middle of the century (p. 30).

"Seal" was the commonest baptismal designation in the second century. Some texts show the seal clearly as a mark of ownership and protection. For Christian usage in relation to baptism there are two lines of thought — an eschatological and a juristic. There is a close relation of seal and name in the second and third centuries so that "seal" and "baptismal formula" are close together. Indeed "seal" is no separate baptismal rite but an interpretation of the baptismal bath (pp. 36-41).

Another understanding of baptism was as a vow and legal act, expressed liturgically in the renunciation of Satan (p. 42). The designation of baptism as a bath or washing (λουτρόν) was consistent with and perhaps contributed to widespread use of affusion in the third and fourth centuries (this study will express reservations about the extent of affusion). Since running water in the early spring of the year was cold, rubbing the whole body with oil before baptism was understandable. The church's allowance of warm water was against Jewish or Jewish-Christian-Gnostic sects (as the Elkesaites) who expressly advocated cold water (pp. 45-48). Affusion had in its favor that it was "water from above," but in comparison with bathing customs Christian baptism in its essence was not a washing and was a purification bath only in the same sense as one may say it is an anointing, sealing, or priestly consecration. Baptism was no symbolic action, but individual rites were throughout given symbolic meanings (p. 48).

The word and faith were closely connected with baptism, which was the goal of the mission preaching (p. 49). The unity of baptism lay not in the rite, or even in the common theological formulations, but in the saving work of Christ, which provided the ground for the "once for all" nature of baptism (pp. 55-56).

The development of the catechumenate (pp. 63-80) involved a kind of delay of baptism. A precondition of organizing the catechumenate was a decline in the eschatological understanding of baptism. Repentance was expressed in acts of penance. Although the catechumens were brought into some relation with the church, they were distinct from the *fideles*. They were not yet "pure" enough to go to baptism. The renunciation and the exorcisms were the active and passive sides of freeing from the power of demons.

In the fourth century there was the custom of enrolling a child as a catechumen and administering baptism later. Kretschmar thinks both infant and adult baptism existed side by side (p. 85). The practice of others answering for infants shows that the Credo was not a vow of individuals but the confession and pledge of the church (p. 100).

In keeping with the prevailing view at the time he wrote, Kretschmar gives much attention to the rite in the *Apostolic Tradition*, to which we give some references in Chapter 19. Where there was the use of pure running water, a consecration of the water was unnecessary. Although Tertullian had a prayer over the water, his baptismal theology emphasized the oath (answers to questions) and not the water as purifying the soul (in distinction from the flesh — *On the Resurrection of the Flesh* 48.11).

By the baptismal questions and answers in Hippolytus and Tertullian faith and baptism were inseparably bound together (p. 96). The renunciation of Satan and the baptismal questions are bound together for Tertullian. The three-member renunciation always has Satan at the head as the opponent of Christ; then may come pomp, works, worship, angels, or world (p. 97). Hippolytus gives a declaratory renunciation. Kretschmar's interpretation that in the *Apostolic Tradition* baptism is no more the boundary between the church and the world but is set within the church (p. 99) seems to go against the whole tenor of the instructions.

In the rebaptism crisis of the third century (pp. 107-108) Cyprian and associates in effect had the church legitimating faith and baptism rather than growing out of them.

Kretschmar develops the distinctive practices of the Syrian and Greek East, especially the anointing of the whole body that preceded baptism with no postbaptismal rite except the eucharist (pp. 116-133). According to the *Acts of Thomas* and Ephraem the Syrian, the anointing and the Spirit are close together. The anointing is the seal in other Syriac sources; it was the line between the church and non-church.

The baptismal questions were unknown in Syria, but the administrator pronounced one of the divine names with each of the three dippings (p. 123). A full immersion, he says, appears not to have been performed in Syria according to the evidence of archaeology (p. 123). The concepts of consecration developed in relation to blessing the elements of the Lord's supper were transferred to the oil and to the water; in reverse the three-member baptismal formula was the model for consecration of oil and of bread (p. 124).

How widespread was the Syrian sequence of only one anointing, and that before baptism and the use of the declarative baptismal formula? He argues for this sequence in Cappadocia and Egypt (pp. 133-136), but the interrogations are attested, although sometimes with a declarative creed as well.

Victor Saxer, *Les rites de l'initiation chrétienne du IIe au VIe siècle: Esquisse historique et signification d'après leur principaux témoins* (Spoleto: Centro italiano di studi sull'alto medioevo, 1988), may be treated under the rubric of liturgy. Saxer is interested in initiation as a whole, not just its separate parts, and notes its two aspects — moral and ritual. He gives more attention to the rites associated with the catechumenate and the preparation for baptism, less on baptism proper and the postbaptismal rites. He treats the significance of the different rites (especially the preparatory rites) but has little on the doctrinal meaning of baptism.

Part One on the patristic origins in the second century discusses the *Didache, Barnabas,* Hermas, Justin, and Clement of Alexandria. The blessing of the water and the use of oil of anointing appear to have been innovations of Gnostic origin (p. 102). The most common theme in regard to baptism in the second century was remission of sins. Baptism was preceded by repentance and was a new birth, associated with Israel's exodus from Egypt. "Seal" was used of baptism itself as the mark of Christ and sign of new spirit. Baptism was the rite of initiation. Preparatory and complementary rites emerged by the end of the second century.

Part Two is the heart of the book, the golden age of Christian initiation from the third to the fifth century. Works are grouped chronologically and geographically with separate chapters on the *Apostolic Tradition* (definitely Roman and likely by Hippolytus — p. 662), Tertullian and the *Passion of Perpetua,* Cyprian, Origen, Cyril of Jerusalem, Egeria, the Syrian liturgy, John Chrysostom, Theodore of Mopsuestia, the three great Cappadocians, Proclus of Constantinople, Ambrose, Chromatius and Rufinus of Aquileia, Nicetas of Remesiana, Augustine, and Quodvultdeus. The rites in the third century must be distinguished from those of the fourth and fifth centuries. There are significant lacunae in our sources for Egypt, Rome, and Spain (pp. 417-419). The classic forms of Christian initiation were a dramatization of the catechesis given to new converts and were the result of the interaction of ritual elaboration, theological reflection, and the large number of new converts (p. 662).

The Third Part concerns the period of changes in the sixth century. The sources are again treated chronologically by regions: Dionysius the Areopagite, Severus of Antioch, Egyptian sources of the fourth to sixth century, Gaul from the baptism of Clovis to the death of Gregory of Tours, Spain from fourth to sixth century, Rome to the end of the sixth century (with special attention to John the Deacon and the *Gelasian Sacramentary,* whose baptismal ritual is in direct continuity with baptismal usages of the golden age; the subjects of its rites were no more adults newly converted from paganism but infants born to Christian families — pp. 598, 602, 605). Hence, there was not a real catechumenate in the sixth century (p. 626), and its rites became ritualized and their accompanying formulas acquired more and more an apotropaic and prophylactic character (p. 633). The educational and moral aspects were directed to the godparents. The same ritual scheme for the nucleus of the baptismal rite may be discerned in all regions, but each region had its own variations (p. 642). The detachment of confirmation as a separate rite was made at different moments in different places in this period (p. 643). The usage in Gaul, Spain, and Milan was for one chrismation on the forehead by the celebrant of baptism, with the bishop conferring the Holy Spirit by imposition of hand; the Roman practice, which came to prevail, was for a double chrismation, the second on the forehead by the bishop was accompanied by his imposition of hand to confer the Holy Spirit (p. 646).

Saxer's method is to let each document speak for itself. He frequently cautions against filling in silence in a source with information in other sources, so he leaves many questions in liturgical history open. The interpretation of the rites of initiation was less changed than the rites themselves. The interpretation of baptism was oriented to John 3:5 and Romans 6:3-11. The latter interpretation came from the baptismal rite of an immersion as total as the death of Christ and from the theology of the redemptive death of Christ (p. 659).

Topical Studies

Per Lundberg, *La typologie baptismale dans l'ancienne église* (Uppsala: Lorentz, 1942), begins his study with the baptismal liturgies of the ancient church. The frequency with which Psalm 74:13 is placed in rapport with the baptism of Jesus and Christian baptism proves the early church interpreted Jesus' baptism as a *descensus ad inferos* in which he crushed Satan (the dragon). The prayers for the blessing of the water contained as biblical types of transformation the sweetening of the bitter waters of Mara, Elisha making the water of Jericho wholesome, Jesus turning the water to wine at Cana, and the baptism of Jesus. Types of deliverance were the flood in the days of Noah, Israel crossing the Red Sea, Moses drawing water from the rock, and the contest of Elijah with prophets of Baal on Mt. Carmel. Other motifs in the liturgies (confirmed by patristic references) taken from the Bible reinforce the themes of deliverance from the kingdom of death and baptism as a *descensus*.

In ancient Near Eastern mythology the sea was the domicile of monsters and its demonic character was personified as a dragon or a serpent. In the early church the realm under the earth was the home of the dead and also of demonic powers. These views provided the cosmological bases for the deluge as a baptismal paradigm (ark is the church), crossing the Red Sea as a type of baptism, and associating the Jordan with the sea of death.

The cross constituted the very center of baptism. The baptism of Jesus and his cross are closely connected. They are linked by the theme of the *descensus,* and the connection is illustrated by the patristic interpretation of baptismal types as equally figures of the cross. Patristic authors give many types of the wood. The "importance of the cross for the primitive Christian notion of baptism has not been sufficiently observed." It is by baptism that the cross becomes effective (p. 200).

Lundberg uses the *descensus* theme to interpret several New Testament passages. For instance, the ease with which 1 Peter 3 moves from the *descensus* of Jesus to baptism illustrates how firmly connected in the tradition were the two ideas. On Romans 6 he states that Paul's thought focuses on the crucifixion and resurrection of Christ; the mention of burial is taken from a tradition in the church that Paul has received, according to which baptism produces the death, burial, and *descensus* of the baptized. In baptism the death of Christ is actualized sacramentally.

Othmar Heggelbacher, *Die christliche Taufe als Rechtsakt nach dem Zeugnis der frühen Christenheit* (Freiburg, Switzerland: Universitäts Verlag, 1953), after a historical overview of the question, devotes the main body of his study to "Christian Baptism as a Legally Significant Sacramental Act." Topics covered initially include norms for the water employed in baptism (pp. 34-38), norms for the words accompanying the baptismal act (pp. 38-44), requirements for the administrator and sponsors (pp. 44-55), requirements for the recipient *(intentio, instructio, attritio)*. Baptism meant belonging to a community (pp. 72-74) and was the rite of initiation into the church (pp. 79-90). Its necessity was considered binding (pp. 77-78). Especially notable was the understanding of baptism as an oath to God, a contract (Tertullian) (pp. 90-99), and a seal (pp. 101-104). Baptism established the church's personality (pp. 99-105) and was named in the third question of the Symbol from about 200 (p. 104). Duties flowed from baptism — the *lex fidei* (pp. 105-110) and the *lex disciplinae* (submission to church law, pp. 110-112) — but rights accompanied these laws (pp. 127-165). Heggelbacher's final unit places church membership in its *heilgeschichtlichen* context (pp. 166-180).

J. Ysebaert, *Greek Baptismal Terminology: Its Origins and Early Development* (Nijmegen: Dekker & Van de Vegt, 1962), is a linguistic and historical study. He groups his material into four categories: "Washing and Immersion," "Renewal, Recreation, and Rebirth," "Enlightenment," and "Imposition of Hands, Anointing, and Sealing." In each category he presents usages of the terms in pagan antiquity, in the Old Testament and Judaism, in the New Testament, and in early Christian literature. The book is a rich resource, providing historical context for the concepts and detailed examination of the terminology to express them.

P. T. Camelot, *La spiritualité du baptême: Baptises dans l'eau et l'Esprit* (Paris: Cerf, 1963; 2nd ed., 1993), gives a topical treatment of the Fathers' praise of baptism. In part 1, baptism is the sacrament of faith with separate chapters on baptism as profession of faith (pp. 25ff. — page numbers are to the 2nd ed.), as an engagement by faith (pp. 45ff.), baptism and the church (pp. 61ff.), and baptism as "illumination" (pp. 85ff.). Part 2 has separate chapters on baptism as death to sin (pp. 111ff.) and as resurrection to new life (pp. 136ff.), with an excursus on baptism and the return to paradise (pp. 165ff.). Part 3 is on baptism and the Holy Spirit — baptized in the Holy Spirit (pp. 169ff.), the unction and seal (pp. 191ff.), baptism and confirmation (pp. 225ff.), with an excursus on the pouring out of the Spirit (pp. 242ff.). The final chapter (pp. 245-266) is on the baptism of Christ and the baptism of the Christian (see my chap. 6 for a summary).

The relation of baptism to what the Roman Catholic church later distinguished as the separate sacrament of confirmation has much exercised Catholic, Orthodox, and Anglican students of the sacraments. A Roman Catholic view, especially in finding anticipations of the later recognition of confirmation as an independent sacrament, is Burkhard Neunheuser, *Baptism and Confirmation* (New York: Herder & Herder, 1964), translation of *Taufe und Firmung,* Handbuch der Dogmengeschichte, IV.2 (Freiburg: Herder, 1964). Since Neunheuser gives much attention to baptism up to the modern period, his work is an earlier counterpart to the work by Heiser (above) from the Greek Orthodox perspective.

Neunheuser begins with separate chapters on the scriptural doctrine of baptism and then of confirmation. Baptism was a full submersion (pp. 5-7). He considers the baptism in obedience to Matthew 28:19 to be the baptism with the Holy Spirit and fire prophesied by John the Baptist (p. 8), an unlikely interpretation. He understands baptism "in the name of Jesus" to be baptism in obedience to Jesus in the manner prescribed by him. Neither it nor Matthew 28:19 was a "formula"; the latter was an epiclesis, meaning that the Godhead was present in effective power and the baptizand entrusted oneself to them (pp. 14-15). Repentance, faith, and the immersion bath are an undivided unity (p. 20). Ephesians 5:26 makes not just the individual but the church the subject of baptism (p. 22). Who baptizes is irrelevant (1 Cor. 1:13-17), because the efficacy is in the divine name. The interpretation of 1 Peter 3:20-21 is that baptism is a request, and a request granted (pp. 33-35). Baptism in the New Testament is always in proximity to repentance and a confession of faith, so it is always adult baptism, but tradition shows that nothing in the New Testament proves infant baptism is contrary to Scripture (p. 38).

Neunheuser finds the laying on of hands for imparting the Holy Spirit after the water bath in Acts 8:4-20; 19:1-7; and Hebrews 6:1-6. The baptismal bath in the name of Jesus is the first imparting of the Spirit; a complementary imparting of the Spirit by the laying on of hands together with the bath makes up the full initiation into the Christian life (pp. 46, 18-19). "Seal" in Paul is the immersion and the laying on of hands (p. 50); Paul uses "anointing" figuratively (pp. 50-51).

With reference to the noncanonical sources, Neunheuser sees the catechizing and fasting in the *Didache* as a development of the summons to repent; it is the only evidence before the mid-third century of baptism by infusion (p. 54). Justin, Tertullian, and the *Apostolic Tradition* provide testimony to the ritual of baptism (pp. 55-60). Theological reflection is found as well in *Barnabas,* Hermas, and Clement of Alexandria. Faith and regeneration are central ideas; human cooperation is required, but the divine action is the decisive element (pp. 65-66). Three dangers cause Origen to emphasize the moral side of baptism: a magical conception of the mysteries, the Gnostic tendency to turn grace into a natural and cosmological process, and the abuse in the church of performing baptism without understanding its significance (p. 67). The innate blemish Origen mentions in justification of infant baptism is not deduced from the sin of Adam (pp. 70-71). The second century adds illumination and the seal (as spiritual circumcision) to the concepts of baptism (pp. 80-81). The complementary stages by which the Spirit is imparted were not yet distinguished conceptually; there was a rich symbolism associated with anointing, which was probably literally done in this period. Tertullian, *On Baptism,* brings the theological statements into a single picture but without appeal to original sin (pp. 84-91).

Sacramentum and μυστήριον were first used for Christian ceremonies at the end of the second century; a technical consolidation of their usage occurred in the third century (pp. 93-99). The controversy over heretic baptism provides a rich picture of baptismal theology in the third century (pp. 104-106). The mystery of initiation was made up of the water bath in the name of the Trinity and the concluding "anointing with chrism or the laying on of hands for the imparting of the Spirit" (p. 106); Neunheuser leaves an ambiguity in regard to the latter two rites.

The sacramental life of the church developed into a more splendid liturgy in the fourth and fifth centuries (p. 107). Optatus in opposing the Donatists distinguished heretic and schismatic baptism, but his view of heretic baptism was contrary to the teaching of the church (p. 110 — read Roman Catholic church). In comparison to his full description of the mystery of baptism, Ambrose speaks rather briefly about the spiritual seal, but his "seal of the Spirit" is asserted to be clearly distinguished from the water bath in the Spirit (p. 114). Apart from the Donatist and Pelagian controversies on the subject of baptism Augustine moves entirely in a traditional framework (p. 115). He uses *sacramentum* in a broad sense, but he is also familiar with a narrow sense, especially for baptism and the eucharist (p. 116). Sacraments are *signa* that are what they signify; the power of the sacraments depends on the *significatio,* which occurs through the *verbum* (p. 117). Against the Donatists Augustine asserts that a sacrament can be validly performed but without efficacy for salvation (p. 119), and baptism can be stolen from its rightful owner without thereby losing its value (p. 121). Against the Pelagians he fully presented his conception of infant baptism (pp. 124-127). Augustine could not assume that the sign has any actual power to effect grace (in the sense claimed by Scholastic theology); baptism remains merely the prerequisite for grace (p. 127). In North Africa, in contrast to eastern liturgies, the anointing immediately after the bath is followed by giving a white garment and only then the laying on of hands (p. 128). Hence, for Augustine the anointing belonged to the structure of baptism in the strict sense and is the beginning of the giving of the Holy Spirit, and the laying on of hands is a clearly separate rite (p. 130). In Augustine's time what a later age distinguished as two sacraments (baptism and confirmation) constituted one act of initiation (pp. 131-132). Leo and Pacian assign the giving of the Holy Spirit to the anointing (pp. 132-133). The order of rites is that customary at Rome and North Africa since antiquity — water bath, anointing, laying on of hands, and *consignatio* without anointing (p. 134).

Different customs prevailed in the East in regard to rebaptism, but in general the East required rebaptism of genuine heretics, defined as those who did not accept the Nicene doctrine of the Trinity (pp. 135-138). Cyril of Jerusalem provides the basic picture for eastern baptismal practice (pp. 138-146). The historical reality of Christ's death and resurrection is the original in which the believer shares through the sacramental image (p. 141). It is not clear from Cyril whether the power of baptism comes from naming the three divine names, from a separate consecration of the water, or from Christ's baptism (p. 143). No less important than the water was the chrism: as the water was the antitype of Christ's passion, the myrrh was the antitype of the Holy Spirit (pp. 143-144). The whole action is called "baptism" or "seal," but the anointing with chrism was something quite independent (p. 145). The necessity of baptism for salvation was the tradition of the primitive church (p. 145). Cyril does not seem to recognize infant baptism or a baptism of desire (p. 146).

The other Greek Fathers coined long lists of names for baptism (p. 146). The imparting of the Spirit was the conclusion and completion of baptism (p. 148). The principal contribution of the Greek Fathers is bringing out two themes to interpret the essence of baptism — baptism in Jesus' death (pp. 148-149) and filling the water with sanctifying power (pp. 149-151). (The exposition of their thought in this book will conclude that the essence of baptism for them lay elsewhere.) Theodore of Mopsuestia has an anointing before but not after the baptism; "signing" is "what we today call confirmation" (p. 158).

Neunheuser concludes the patristic period by looking at the rite of the Byzantine church, Pseudo-Dionysius, and John of Damascus for the East and the *Sacramentarium Gelasianum, Ordo Romanus* (XI), Gregory the Great, and Isidore of Seville for the West. In the East the intimate unity of the bath and the anointing is shown by the fact that the baptismal service concluded only after the latter (p. 164). The two Roman rites provide information on the period of transition from adult to infant baptism (p. 164). The link between baptism and confirmation was so close that Pseudo-Dionysius has no separate chapter on "confirmation" but merely on "consecration of the myrrh," which had a transcending importance in its own right (pp. 171-172). Gregory the Great recognized single or triple immersion (p. 177). Isidore had chapters on baptism itself, on chrism, and on the imposition of hands or confirmation (pp. 178-180).

Neunheuser continues with chapters on baptism and confirmation in the Carolingian period and early Scholasticism, in high and late Scholasticism, in the Council of Trent and the modern period, and the full recognition of confirmation as an independent sacrament.

Ernst Dassmann, *Sündenvergebung durch Taufe, Busse, und Märtyrerfürbitte in den Zeugnissen frühchristlicher Frömmigkeit und Kunst* (Münster: Aschendorff, 1973), despite its preliminary nature, became a classic work. The aim of the study was to explain whether and how forgiveness of sins left traces in the pre-Constantinian iconographical witnesses. He finds sin and forgiveness to have been at the heart of Christian piety in the period 250-350 and the key to the interpretation of the earliest Christian art. Many patristic texts are cited on each point along with reference to the pictorial motifs (illustrated by fifty-one plates).

With reference specifically to the iconological aspect (chap. 2) Dassmann sees the baptism of Jesus as the pattern of Christian baptism (pp. 99-103). Martyrdom was a second baptism for forgiveness (pp. 153-162). Chapter 3 is his exegesis of the pictorial motifs presented in early Christian art as found in the literature of the second and third centuries. Old Testament motifs are Abraham and Isaac (pp. 184-196), water from the rock by Moses (pp. 196-208), Noah (pp. 208-222), Jonah (pp. 222-232), the fall (seldom mentioned in the earliest literature — pp. 232-258), Daniel and the three youths (pp. 258-270), Susannah (pp. 270-273), Job (pp. 273-279), and the ascension of Elijah (pp. 279-282). The New Testament scenes that are introduced in the earliest Christian art have also in the literature the most marked exegesis. These include the resurrection of Lazarus (pp. 283-287), the Samaritan woman at the well (pp. 289-298), miracles of healing — lame, blind, woman with issue of blood (pp. 298-313) — miracle of wine at Cana (pp. 313-316), and adoration of the magi (p. 316). Dassmann gives special attention to the picture of the Shepherd in literature.

Dassmann's chapter 4 gives an inconographic evaluation. Pages 348 to 352 introduce the specific theme of baptism. In addition to direct pictures of baptism, indirect baptismal pictures and baptismal compositions include especially a fisherman. Biblical motifs of forgiveness are the Shepherd, the Jonah cycle (pp. 385-397), the fall (pp. 397-405), the resurrection of Lazarus (pp. 405-411), and Noah (pp. 411-419). Dassmann's conclusion warns against imposing a dogmatic meaning on the art or overvaluing the case he has made. He notes that it is often difficult to distinguish baptismal and penitential forgiveness (pp. 448-449).

August Jilek, *Initiationsfeier und Amt: Ein Beitrag zur Struktur und Theologie der ämter und des Taufgottesdienstes in der frühen Kirche* (Frankfurt: Peter Lang, 1979), deals only with the *Apostolic Tradition*, Tertullian, and Cyprian. The special concern is the function of the officers in baptism, but Jilek covers much more, especially about the offices and about the baptismal liturgy. Notable is the treatment of the church as the bearer of baptismal authority according to Cyprian (pp. 254-265). For Cyprian water and the laying on of hands are central actions of the ceremony of baptism, corresponding to the forgiveness of sins and gift of the Spirit. By sharply separating these two, Jilek makes the debatable (or at least overly precise) claim that Cyprian's statements about receiving the Spirit by baptism (*Letters* 63.8; 74.5) are not an expression of the means but the origin of the gift of the Spirit (p. 266 — see my comments on these texts in chap. 21).

Henry Ansgar Kelly, *The Devil at Baptism: Ritual, Theology, and Drama* (Ithaca: Cornell University Press, 1985) examines initiation rites in their conceptual and dramatic aspects as they pertain to the devil and demons. The struggle with Satan was ritualized and liturgized (pp. 11-12). The baptismal service at first was simple and had no reference to evil spirits, but at the beginning of the third century it was transformed into an elaborate ritual (p. 10).

Part one of Kelly's book presents the background on evil spirits and conversion in the New Testament (chap. 1), Jewish precedents (chap. 2), sin demons and their removal in the early church (chap. 3), and antidemonic initiation rites in Gnostic groups (chap. 4). Many of the antidemonic rituals that came into Christian communities are first attested among Egyptian Gnostics (p. 17).

Part two takes up early mainstream developments, beginning with the *Apostolic Tradition* (chap. 5). Two activities were important in freeing the candidates from demons — exorcism and renunciation (chap. 6); and later postbaptismal rituals were given an apotropaic interpretation to prevent the return of demons. These three elements of rescue, reversal of allegiance, and armament against renewed attack are noted in the sources for Africa and Europe from Tertullian to John the Deacon (chap. 7). In the East there was a nonexorcistic tradition, beginning with the Pseudo-Clementines, in which "baptism itself was thought to effect the expulsion of the unclean spirits" (p. 124), and continuing to Pseudo-Dionysius (chap. 8). In documents derived from the *Apostolic Tradition* and other sources exorcisms are present (chap. 9). Narsai stressed the prophylactic aspects of the signing and anointing (p. 153).

Part three discusses the formation of modern rituals: Byzantine and West Syrian (chap. 10), Armenia and Egypt (chap. 11), the Roman-Frankish liturgy (chap. 12), Milanese, Gallican, and Spanish rites (chap. 13), and Western reforms in the sixteenth and twentieth centuries.

Peter Cramer, *Baptism and Change in the Early Middle Ages c. 200-c. 1150* (Cambridge: Cambridge University Press, 1993), discusses the social context of liturgy and the (pre-)history of the meaning of sacraments. He begins with Hippolytus of Rome (pp. 9-45), for whom baptism is a crisis, a decisive choice that involves a rejection of pagan society. For Tertullian and Ambrose (pp. 46-86) conversion was not a state of being but of becoming, a transition or translation. In the Bible, according to Tertullian, there is an "ideal water," a *genus* of which the difference of species is irrelevant (p. 60). *Sacramentum* in Tertullian combines the juridical sense of oath and the Greek sense of "mystery" (p. 63). Whereas Tertullian appeals to the mind, Ambrose does to the emotions (p. 64); for Ambrose (as for Cyril of Jerusalem) the actions come before theology (p. 69). The discussion of the *Passion of Perpetua* explores the psychological connection of baptism, martyrdom, and dream (pp. 73-86).

Cramer sees Augustine as concerned with the relation of baptism to the subsequent Christian life (pp. 87-129). Yet the combined effect of the doctrine of original sin and the practice of infant baptism appeared to make the candidate an involuntary being and made baptism an exorcism, a rite that lost its ethical color (pp. 113-114). The necessity of infant baptism rather than its possibility or desirability was the most obvious legacy of Augustune to the Middle Ages (p. 125). Yet this was not his last word. His *Letter* 98 to Boniface shows baptism as a matter of the authenticity of the will and not of the logic of dogma, for the sacrament of faith (baptism) is faith. In what follows Augustine we see how the notion of a social will (expressed in infant baptism) became not only the society of the Spirit but the political society of this world (p. 129).

Cramer's following chapters consider "From Augustine to the Carolingians" (pp. 130-178), "The Diminishing of Baptism" (pp. 179-220), and "The Twelfth Century" (pp. 221-266). For Cramer infant baptism focused the tension between sacrament as an objective functional act and sacrament as an act of will with ethical demands. Although the priest became the broker of ritual power (p. 142), in another dimension the community saw itself in its children, and the child was led through the forms of an adult experience (pp. 173-178). The separation of confirmation from baptism arose from the practical situation in which bishops could not get out into the countryside to baptize all who need it, so he confirmed or finished off the baptism given by a deacon or priest. Alongside the objectification of the sacraments, the wealth of literature about them in the Carolingian age stressed the moral more than the sacramental aspects.

Kilian McDonnell and George T. Montague, *Initiation and Baptism in the Holy Spirit: Evidence from the First Eight Centuries* (Collegeville: Liturgical, 1991), uses "baptism in the Holy Spirit" primarily in the modern Pentecostal sense and is concerned to show an expectation to receive charisms in connection with Christian initiation. The authors use "prophetic charisms" to include tongues and healing in addition to prophecy and in contrast to nonmiraculous charisms. They treat every bestowal of the Spirit as "baptism in the Holy Spirit," a usage that ignores distinctions in terminology in the biblical texts and abolishes the imagery of immersion in the phrase. They seek a middle way blending later Catholic sacramentalism with Pentecostal charismatic interpretation. The last chapter shows that the examination of the history serves a modern doctrinal and pastoral viewpoint.

George Montague writes part one on the New Testament evidence. Although carefully differentiating the viewpoints of different authors, he offers these conclusions on the New Testament evidence (pp. 76-80): the rite of initiation always involves water baptism in the name of Jesus and the gift of the Holy Spirit; the manner in which the baptismal union with Jesus was imaged varied in different authors; many texts assume an experiential dimension to initiation; there was an expectation of a charismatic expression on the part of the receiver but no evidence that any one gift was always expected, and some gifts might manifest themselves later; the inital gift of the Spirit was meant to grow; one should expect the experience of the Spirit; and charisms are of great variety and are for building up the church and for evangelization.

Kilian McDonnell writes part two on the early postbiblical evidence, which treats Tertullian, Hilary of Poitiers, Cyril of Jerusalem, the *Apostolic Constitutions*, John Chrysostom, Philoxenus, and later Syrians (concluding with Joseph Hazzayah in the eighth century). Tertullian concludes his account of baptism with the candidates praying in church for the charisms (*Baptism* 20). Hilary had much to say about experience of the charisms at initiation; for him the charisms of first rank are wisdom, knowledge, and faith, but there are miraculous charisms such as prophecy. Cyril of Jerusalem considered miraculous charisms to be possible for the church and urged candidates to prepare themselves to receive the heavenly charisms, but he never recommended the faithful to be open to tongues (foreign languages for him). The compiler of the *Apostolic Constitutions* placed restraints on prophets and concentrated the charisms in the bishop. John Chrysostom and Theodore of Mopsuestia considered the charisms to belong to the apostolic age and not to be possible for the life of their church. With Philoxenus and other Syrians, when infant baptism had become the norm, the charisms were a second baptism given to those who became perfect in the practice of asceticism.

McDonnell raises the question of a correlation between the paradigm shift from baptism as modelled on the baptism of Jesus in the Jordan to baptism as entering the death and resurrection of Jesus and a decline in expectation of receiving prophetic charisms at baptism. How the church ritualized the imparting of the Spirit in initiation varied, but the imparting of the Spirit is a constant (p. 317). There are multiple reasons for the breakup of the link between Christian initiation and the charisms: infant baptism becoming the norm; concern with Montanism (but his authors are too late to support this connection); close of the canon leading to a dispensationalist view; solidification of hierarchical power (already in the *Didache*). Although recognizing the varied uses of the word *charisma*, the authors are too quick to see prophetic charisms in it, fail to fully acknowledge the tendency of preachers to collapse the difference between biblical text and their own situation, and give inadequate historical contextualizing to the texts examined.

Simon Légasse, *Naissance du baptême* (Paris: Cerf, 1993), after a chapter on the origin of a vocabulary, discusses the baptism by John, Jesus' baptism, the baptizing activity of Jesus, the doubtful influence of the baptism of proselytes, and the meaning of the first Christian baptisms. Baptism "in the name of Jesus" was the absolute novelty by which Christian baptism radically broke with the baptism of John (p. 120). The unique Pauline formulation in Romans 6:3-4 is connected to early Christian tradition by the formula "into name of Christ," which equals "into Christ," and by the connection of baptism with the forgiveness of sins that came from the redemptive death of Christ at Calvary (pp. 127-132).

Legasse concludes that Christian baptism cannot be rooted historically in a word of institution by Jesus, in the baptism of Jesus by John, nor in proselyte baptism. However, Christian baptism reproduced the characteristics of John's baptism — it was passive, nonrepeatable, and for forgiveness of sins. Jesus received John's baptism and himself practiced baptism at the beginning of his ministry. These facts would predispose the early community to adopt the same rite of admission, but we must not mask the gaps in our knowledge between Jesus' ministry and the first attestations of Christian baptism. Christian baptism differed from John's in the realization that salvation had already commenced (p. 133).

Thomas M. Finn, *From Death to Rebirth: Ritual and Conversion in Antiquity* (New York: Paulist, 1997), might have been treated under liturgy, but it more properly belongs here as a topical study centered on the idea of conversion in its ritual aspects. The book builds on Finn's earlier collection of sources (below). Finn begins with a linguistic study of the word "conversion" (chap. 1). Then he characterizes Greco-Roman paganism (chap. 2) before citing examples of conversion in the pagan mysteries and philosophy (chap. 3). Two chapters cover conversion in Judaism — in the second temple period (chap. 4) and in the rabbinic period (chap. 5). Conversion in Christianity is likewise studied chronologically — the first and second centuries (chap. 6) and the third century in various regions (chap. 7). For the fourth century the focus is on Jerusalem (chap. 8) and Milan (chap. 9). Among Finn's conclusions is the importance of the images of death and rebirth and of enlightenment for the transformation involved in conversion (pp. 253-257).

Gerard-Henry Baudry, *Le baptême et ses symboles: Aux sources du salut* (Paris: Beauchesne, 2001), discusses the symbols of water, burial in a tomb with Christ, oil, light, the sun, white clothing, food, the two ways, and seal. His method is to describe the cultural and religious background which explains and justifies the use of each symbol. These symbols had biblical origins yet were accessible to converts from paganism. There was a tendency to find a symbolic significance for each necessary act in the ceremony. Concrete acts in the ritual made metaphors of salvation actual and had a pedagogical purpose. The point of departure for symbols was theological reflection on the significance of Christian baptism.

Water in the ancient world was a symbol of life, a symbol of death, and a symbol of purification. Baptisteries sometimes took the form of a sarcophagus (as at Dura). Anointing with oil had royal, priestly, and prophetic significance; the diversity of practice (before baptism, after it, or both) forbids the thought of a uniform model. The primitive scheme of teaching marked a change from darkness to light. White clothing was interpreted by the Fathers as signifying the change from sin to innocence, from darkness to light, from slavery to Satan to liberation by Christ, from banishment from paradise to return to paradise, as the way to celestial beatitude, and assumption of the royal priesthood. The cup of pure water given at the first eucharist symbolized the eternal life given by Christ; the cup of milk and honey combined the themes of the food of the promised land, food of infants, and God or Christ as a mother nourishing her child. Salt purified and was used in exorcism. The theme of the two ways included the renunciation of Satan and the attachment to Christ. The seal (which in Greek and Latin meant both the object and its imprint) indicated ownership; it signified the confession of the Trinitarian faith and engagement to follow Christ, belonging to the people of God (a spiritual circumcision), and eschatological participation in the glory of the Resurrected One (who gave the firstfruits of the Spirit).

I have given preliminary treatment in *Restoration Quarterly* to some of the topics examined more fully in this book: "Baptism from the Second to the Fourth Century," 1 (1957): 185-197;[2] "Baptismal Motifs in the Ancient Church," 7 (1963): 202-216 (repr. in E. Ferguson, ed., *Conversion, Catechumenate, and Baptism in the Early Church*, Studies in Early Christianity 11 [New York: Garland, 1993], pp. 352-366) — identifying motifs of conversion (faith and repentance), the motif of cleansing (washing), the Christian victory (death and the devil), motifs of the new life (resurrection and rebirth) and motifs associated with the Holy Spirit (seal and illumination); and "The Typology of Baptism in the Early Church," 8 (1965): 41-52 — covering creation and paradise, the flood, the exodus and the promised land, and the Jordan and baptism.

Collections of Sources

The standard collection of sources, *Documents of the Baptismal Liturgy* by E. C. Whitaker (London: SPCK, 1960; 2nd edition 1970), has been updated, expanded, and made more useful by Maxwell E. Johnson, 3rd edition (Collegeville, MN: Liturgical Press, 2003). The collection begins with relevant selections from the Ante-Nicene

---

2. Some of the same ground was covered later in the same journal by Jack P. Lewis, "Baptismal Practices of the Second and Third Century Church," *Restoration Quarterly* 26 (1983): 1-17.

Church, starting with the *Didache*. The material is then arranged by geographical areas: Syria, the Assyrian Church of the East, Armenia, Syrian Orthodox Church, Maronite rite, Byzantine rite, Egypt, North Africa, Spain, Milan, Rome, Gallican documents, and concluding with the Sarum Rite from England. The volume thus has baptismal documents well into the Middle Ages going beyond the chronological limits of this book.

H. F. Stander and J. P. Louw, *Baptism in the Early Church* (Pretoria: Didaskalia, 1988), although more than a collection of texts, aims primarily "to make the ancient writings on [baptism] accessible to the English reader in an objective way" (preface) and so contains extensive quotations of the sources from the Apostolic Fathers through Chrysostom and Theodore of Mopsuestia with an added chapter on early Christian art. The authors have a special concern with infant baptism but also give attention to the mode of baptism, normally immersion but "the method of administering baptism was never an issue" (p. 168), as clinical or emergency baptism shows. The washing away of sins and regeneration were key concepts, but as an emphasis on what was done at baptism increased many other benefits were ascribed to it. Symbolic actions underscored theological aspects. "It is remarkable that the link between baptism and circumcision became relevant only when the issue of the age of the one to be baptized became crucial" (p. 168). The modern claim that adult baptism entailed a missionary situation cannot be sustained, for it continued long after Christianity was well established, and infant baptism is first attested after Christianity was widespread.

T. M. Finn compiled a useful collection in two volumes, *Early Christian Baptism and the Catechumenate: West and East Syria* and *Early Christian Baptism and the Catechumenate: Italy, North Africa, and Egypt*, Message of the Fathers of the Church 5 and 6 (Collegeville: Liturgical Press, 1992). A feature of the collection is more attention to Syriac and eastern sources than is typical. Finn accompanies his selections with brief introductions and bibliographies. The quotations are arranged by geographical region and within each in chronological order: West (Greek-speaking) Syria (from the *Didache* to the *Ordo of Constantinople* and Dionysius the Pseudo-Areopagite); East Syria (from the *Odes of Solomon* to Jacob of Serugh [Syriac] and the *Teaching of St. Gregory* [Armenian]); Italy (from the *Shepherd of Hermas* to selections from the Gelasian and Gregorian Sacramentaries); North Africa (from Tertullian to Augustine); and Egypt (from the *Excerpts of Theodotus* and Clement of Alexandria to selections from the Coptic Rite).

André Hamman's prolific literary output included *Le baptême d'après les Pères de l'Église* (Paris: Grasst, 1962), which appeared in an English translation by Thomas Halton, *Baptism: Ancient Liturgies and Patristic Texts* (Staten Island: Alba House, 1967), and now is in a new revised edition (Paris: Migne, 1995). His introduction briefly mentions the first witnesses to baptism and the explanations the Fathers gave to the names for baptism, its rites, and the biblical figures of baptism. The collection, instead of including many shorter texts, features whole or nearly whole texts of a few major writers. For the early Latin church there are Tertullian, *On Baptism;* Cyprian,

Letters 69 and 70; Zeno of Verona, *Seven Invitations to the Baptismal Font;* and Pacian of Barcelona, *Sermon on Baptism.* For baptism in the Greek church there are Basil, *Protreptic on Holy Baptism;* Gregory of Nazianzus, *Sermon on Holy Baptism;* Gregory of Nyssa, *Sermon on the Feast of Lights;* and four sermons from John Chrysostom. For the Latin golden age are four sermons and one letter from Augustine and Leo the Great, *To the Bishops of Sicily.* A companion volume, *L'initiation chrétienne* (Paris: Grasset, 1963), presented the major mystagogical catecheses of the ancient church: Cyril of Jerusalem, Ambrose *(On the Mysteries),* Chrysostom *(Sermon to Neophytes),* Theodore of Mopsuestia, Narsai, and Maximus the Confessor.

The series Traditio Christiana, #9, contains an important collection of pre-Nicene texts: André Benoît and Charles Munier, *Le baptême dans l'église ancienne/ Die Taufe in der Alten Kirche (Ier-IIIe siècles)* (Bern: Peter Lang, 1994). The format of the series prints Greek and Latin texts on the lefthand page and the French (or German, depending on the edition) translations on the righthand page. Texts not in Greek or Latin are given in English and French translations. The generally excellent sixty-five pages of introduction devotes thirty-three pages to the theology of baptism. The description of the baptismal rite in the *Apostolic Tradition* inexplicably says that the administrator pours a dash of water on the head of the one being baptized (p. xxx), contrary to the explicit wording of the Latin and French (p. 130). There are nineteen pages of bibliography, brief notes on the texts, and full indices. The 218 selections begin with background texts from Qumran and other Jewish sources and continue from the *Didache* through the Council of Nicaea (325) and selected early funerary inscriptions that mention baptism.

A briefer collection of key texts on the ceremony and doctrine of baptism, infant baptism, and immersion and its alternatives is found in Everett Ferguson, *Early Christians Speak,* 3rd edition (Abilene: ACU Press, 1999; 1st edition 1971), pp. 29-64. The texts quoted are mostly from the second and third centuries, but they are accompanied by commentary and notes.

PART ONE

Antecedents to Christian Baptism

2. Washings for Purification in Greco-Roman Paganism

The use of water as a means of purification is widespread in religions of the world. It was common in the religious activities of Greeks and Romans in the period surrounding the rise of Christianity.[1] Sacred sites had fountains or other source of water to be used for the ceremonial cleansing of worshipers and officiants at the sanctuary.

General Usage for Purification

An early reference to a dipping for purification occurs in Herodotus. In explaining that Egyptians considered pigs an unclean animal, he says that "If an Egyptian touched a pig, he went to [ἐς] the river and dipped [ἔβαψε] himself in his clothes" (*Histories* 2.47). He further attributed to the Egyptians introduction of the practice, then followed by Greeks, of not entering a temple after intercourse unwashed (ἄλουτοι) (2.64).

The washings were so common that they were taken for granted and seldom commented on, and where they were mentioned, often little or no detail was given as to how one performed the ablutions. For example, the rules of purity for those coming to the temple of Athena at Pergamum (after 133 B.C.) stated that "Whoever wishes to visit the temple of the goddess ... must complete the required lustrations

---

1. Johannes Leipoldt, *Die urchristliche Taufe im Lichte der Religionsgeschichte* (Leipzig: Dörffling & Franke, 1928), pp. 38-56, including summaries of the initiation rites of the principal mystery religions (below); Arthur Darby Nock, "Early Gentile Christianity and Its Hellenistic Background," in A. E. J. Rawlinson, ed., *Essays on the Trinity and the Incarnation* (London: Longmans, Green & Co., 1928), pp. 111-120; reprinted in Zeph Stewart, ed., *Arthur Darby Nock: Essays on Religion and the Ancient World* (Oxford: Oxford University Press, 1972), pp. 97-104; Albrecht Oepke, "βάπτω, βαπτίζω (et al.)," in Gerhard Kittel, ed., *Theological Dictionary of the New Testament*, tr. Geoffrey W. Bromiley (Grand Rapids: Eerdmans, 1964), Vol. 1, pp. 530-535; J. Ysebaert, *Greek Baptismal Terminology* (Nijmegen: Dekker & Van de Vegt, 1962), pp. 12-20.

[sprinkling]."[2] The means of contact with the water could vary, and the application of water often was part of other ritual requirements: at Lindos (second century A.D.), "You are purified on the same day by a lustral sprinkling and anointing with oil"; at the sanctuary of Men Tyrannus at Sunion (second/third centuries A.D.), "You may go in the same day after washing with water poured over your head."[3]

Latin sources too speak of these preliminary purifications. Virgil has Aeneas say after warfare, "It were a sin to handle sacred things until I have washed myself in a running stream [*flumine vivo abluero*]."[4] Ovid had absorbed some of the moral criticism of merely outward washings.[5]

Preliminary purification by washing occured not only at temples of the ordinary civic cults but also at healing and oracle sanctuaries, before receiving visions, in magic, and in the Mystery Religions.

A source of water for purification was a requirement for healing sanctuaries. The ancient reports concerning the healing god Asclepius mention the patient bathing and offering a sacrifice before incubation.[6] Bathing was also sometimes prescribed by the god as part of the procedure for a cure. Aelius Aristides mentioned that during his treatment at the Asclepius sanctuary in Pergamum, "I washed at the Sacred Well."[7] Excavations at the site have revealed several sources of water, including fountains and pools for bathing.[8]

Purification by water occurred at oracle sites. Famous was the Castalian Spring at Delphi, where the officials of the temple of Apollo and pilgrims visiting the site purified themselves.[9] The Delphic Oracle also promoted a spiritual view of purity. The Pythia was reported to have said:

---

2. W. Dittenberger, *Sylloge Inscriptionum Graecarum*, 3rd ed. (Leipzig, 1920), Vol. 3, no. 982; English translation in F. C. Grant, *Hellenistic Religions* (New York: Liberal Arts Press, 1953), p. 6.

3. Dittenberger, *SIG* 983 and 1042. Cited by A. D. Nock, "Early Gentile Christianity and Its Hellenistic Background," in A. E. J. Rawlinson, ed., *Essays on the Trinity and the Incarnation* (London: Longmans, Green & Co., 1928), pp. 69-70; reprinted in Zeph Stewart, ed., *Arthur Darby Nock: Essays on Religion and the Ancient World* (Oxford: Oxford University Press, 1972), pp. 63-64.

4. Virgil, *Aeneid* 2.717-720; cf. 9.815-818.

5. See quotation on p. 28.

6. Emma J. and Ludwig Edelstein, *Asclepius: A Collection and Interpretation of the Testimonies* (Baltimore: Johns Hopkins University Press, 1945), pp. 148-149, 153 on the bathing, with reference to Aristophanes, *Plutus* 656-657 ("we bathed [ἐλοῦμεν] him") and Pausanias, *Description of Greece* 5.13.3 (one may not go up to the temple of Asclepius [Pergamum] before bathing [λουτροῦ]).

7. *Sacred Orations* 48.71. He devoted one of his orations, number 39 (Keil), to this well. Cf. 48.74-76 for mud baths followed by washing. Edelstein, *Asclepius*, pp. 247-248, cites with text and translation Aristides, *Oration* 48.80 and *Inscriptiones Graecae* IV.1 #126 (c. A.D. 160).

8. Ekrem Adurgal, *Ancient Civilizations and Ruins of Turkey* (Istanbul, 1973), pp. 107-109. These were preserved in the second-century rebuilding of the sanctuary under Hadrian — Adolf Hoffmann, "The Roman Remodelling of the Asklepieion," and Christopher Jones, "Aelius Aristides and the Asklepieion," in Helmut Koester, ed., *Pergamon: Citadel of the Gods* (Harrisburg: Trinity Press International, 1998), pp. 45, 51; 71-72.

9. Euripides, *Ion* 94-97: "You Delphian servants of Apollo, to the silvery streams of Castalia, and

Come, stranger, pure in mind, to the precinct of the pure god, after touching your hand in the stream of the nymphs [ἁψάμενος νάματος]. For a tiny drop suffices for a good man, but the whole ocean shall not cleanse a wicked man with its streams [νίψαι νάμασιν].[10]

Among the inscriptions (late first to mid-third century) at the temple to the god whose hellenized name was Mandulis at Talmis in Nubia was a hymn by the decurion Maximus. In it he described a dream in which he was washing in the waters of the Nile when Mandulis gave him the impulse to write the hymn. Nearby is another inscription, author unidentified, which identifies Mandulis with the sun:

I had a vision and found rest for my soul. For thou didst grant my prayer and show me thyself going through the heavenly vault; then washing thyself in the holy water of immortality [ἁγίῳ τῷ τῆς ἀθανασίας ὕδατι λουσάμενος] thou appearedst again. . . . Then I knew thee, Mandulis, to be the Sun.

The allusion is to the belief that the sun set in the ocean, bathed in it, and arose new in the morning.[11]

An immersion is part of a magical ceremony described in the large magical papyrus in Paris. "Then jump into the river [Nile]. Immerse [βαπτισάμενος] yourself in the clothes you have on, walk backwards out of the water, and, after changing to fresh garments, depart without turning around."[12] The papyrus identifies the ceremony as an "initiation" (τελετή), but A. D. Nock, noting the use of the word in magic for "a ceremony that makes an object suitable for use in working a charm," in this case putting "yourself in a right condition for procuring an oracle from a daemon," considers the immersion to be "something preliminary" to obtaining the magical purpose.[13] Plutarch's description of superstitious practices speaks of calling "an old woman who performs magic purifications," such as "immerse [βάπτισον] yourself in the sea, and sit down on the ground for a whole day," and includes "immersions" [βαπτισμούς] among the things done because of superstition.[14]

Philosophers, like Plutarch, could be critical of merely outward purifications. Theophrastus began his characterizion of the superstitious person as one who will

---

when you have bathed in the pure waters [καθαραῖς δρόσοις ἀφυδρανάμενοι], return to the temple." He also relates that the temple itself was sprinkled with this water.

10. *Greek Anthology* 14.71; cf. 14.74, also from Delphi: "The holy places of the gods are open to the good, nor have they need of purifying [καθαρμῶν]; no defilement touches virtue. Whoever is evil at heart, depart; for never by wetting [διαινόμενον] your body shall you wash clean [ἐκνίψει] your soul."

11. A. D. Nock, "A Vision of Mandulis Aion," *Harvard Theological Review* 27 (1934): 53-104; reprinted in Stewart, *Essays*, pp. 337-400 (inscription of Maximus, p. 60 [362-363]; text and translation, pp. 63-64 [365-366]; commentary, p. 76 [375-376]). Another example from Orpheus, *Argonautica*, is cited in chap. 3. For a Christian appropriation of this solar mythology, see on Melito of Sardis in chap. 14.

12. *PGM* IV, 43-45. Tr. by Hubert Martin Jr., in Hans Dieter Betz, ed., *The Greek Magical Papyri in Translation* (Chicago: University of Chicago Press, 1986), p. 37.

13. Nock, "Early Gentile Christianity," p. 114 (= Stewart, *Essays*, p. 99).

14. Plutarch, *Superstition* 3 [= *Moralia* 166A].

not go out for the day without "washing clean [ἀπονιψάμενος] the hands and besprinkling [purifying] himself [περιρρανάμενος]," and near the end says, "He would seem to be one of those who anxiously besprinkle themselves [ἐπιμελῶς περιρραινομένων] at the sea."[15] But some included outward purifications along with inward qualities. Thus Pythagoras in his teachings said, "Purity is through cleansings [καθαρμῶν], washings [λουτρῶν, baths], and lustrations [περιρραντηρίων, vessels for sprinkling]" along with various abstinences.[16]

It was not only philosophers who sounded a moral note about the ritual purifications. The Latin poet Ovid noted that "Our elders believed every sin and cause of evil could be wiped away by purgation." He said that Greece set the example that the guilty could rid themselves of their crimes by lustrations *(lustratos)*. Citing notorious examples, he declared, Fools "think murder's gruesome stain could be washed away by river water."[17] The very criticism shows that the lustrations were being viewed as going beyond their previous ceremonial function.

Jews like Philo knew the pagan purifications and shared the criticism by philosophers, sounding the note of the Hebrew prophets:

> They cleanse their bodies with washings [λουτροῖς] and purifications, but they neither wish nor attempt to wash off from their souls the passions by which life is defiled. (*Cherubim* [28] 95)
>
> It is foolish to forbid entrance to temples to a person who has not previously washed [λουσάμενος] and cleansed his body but undertakes to pray and sacrifice with a mind still soiled and spotted. (*The Unchangeableness of God* [2] 8)[18]

The Christian apologist Justin Martyr attributed such pagan practices to the influence of demons based on Isaiah 1:16-20:

> The demons, having heard of the washing [λουτρὸν] announced through the prophet, arranged that those approaching and going to enter their temples in order to perform libations and burnt offerings sprinkle [ῥαντίζειν] themselves. And they arrange for them to wash themselves [λούεσθαι] completely as they approach before entering the temples where their images are set up. (*1 Apology* 62.1)

Washings in the Mystery Religions

Particular interest attaches to washings with water in initiation to the Mystery Religions, because some have associated these with the practice of Christian baptism. The Mysteries did occasionally express ideas of forgiveness, rebirth after a mystic

---

15. Theophrastus, *Characters* 16.2, 13.
16. Diogenes Laertius, *Lives of Philosphers* 8.33.
17. *Fasti* 2.35-38, 45-46.
18. The context twice uses ἐκνίψασθαι (from ἐκνίζω), "to wash off" (7 and 9) and περιρραντηρίοις, "sprinklings for purification."

death, eternal life, and illumination, but these ideas were associated with the ceremony as a whole and not primarily with the purification by water. The latter was a preliminary preparation for the initiation and had the same purpose of ritual purification as in the other cults treated above. Those who have paralleled the use of water in the Mystery Cults with Christian baptism have either blended the preliminary baths with the effects of the initiation itself, misinterpreted texts, or relied on late Christian writers who Christianized the significance of the ceremonies. There was a significant difference in the use of water for purification in the Mysteries and its use in Christianity. The washing in the Mysteries was a preliminary preparation for the initiation; in Christianity it was the center of initiation into the church.[19]

Whether Orphism was properly a "mystery religion" may be debated, but I note it here because it represents some ideas associated with the Mysteries. The Orphics were characterized by purifications, which removed more than ceremonial impediments. For instance, a work from late antiquity ascribed to Orpheus says, "You are not able to approach your homeland before you have washed away [ἐκνίφησθε] your stain in the sacred purifications [καθαρμοῖς] thanks to Orpheus" (Orpheus, *Argonautica* 1230-1233).

The washings in the Mysteries were not part of the secret rites and were well known. Thus the philosopher Epictetus says with particular reference to the mysteries of the goddess Demeter at Eleusis that one comes "with a sacrifice, with prayers, having been purified beforehand."[20]

There were three levels of initiation into the Eleusinian Mysteries. The Lesser Mysteries were performed in February/March on the banks of the Illisos River outside the walls of Athens. They included a sprinkling or bathing in the Illisos. The ceremonies associated with the Greater Mysteries in September lasted for ten days.[21] On the third day the candidates went to the sea between Athens and Eleusis to be washed. They each took a pig to be washed with the self,[22] and the pig was then sacrificed to Demeter. The bathing in the sea and the sacrifice of the pig were preliminary purifications. The night of the seventh day was the initiation experience proper. The highest grade of initiation, *Epopteia*, could be received a year later and repeated the Greater Mysteries with the addition of a further revelation.

---

19. Nock, "Early Gentile Christianity," pp. 111-120 (= Stewart, *Essays*, pp. 97-104); see also his "Hellenistic Mysteries and Christian Sacraments," *Mnemosyne*, Ser. 4.5 (1952): 177-213 = Stewart, *Essays*, pp. 791-820; Günther Wagner, *Pauline Baptism and the Pagan Mysteries* (Edinburgh: T&T Clark, 1967). A conjectural reading in Theophrastus says, "They bathe [or dip, βάπτονται] their hands and heads when being initiated into the mysteries" (*Enquiry into Plants* 3.13.6); even if correct, the reading gives no indication of the cult referred to and likely is a general reference to the preliminary purifications that were common knowledge.

20. Arrian, *Discourses of Epictetus* 3.21.14; W. A. Oldfather in the Loeb Classical Library translates, "after a preliminary purification." Cf. 3.21.16, "without sacrifices, without purity [or purification]."

21. Walter Burkert, *Greek Religion* (Cambridge: Harvard University Press, 1985), pp. 285-290, describes the sequence of events with references to the original sources; Everett Ferguson, *Backgrounds of Early Christianity*, 3rd ed. (Grand Rapids: Eerdmans, 2003), pp. 256-259.

22. Plutarch, *Phocion* 28.3, refers to an initiate washing a pig in the harbor of Peiraeus.

There was a fountain near the entrance to the sanctuary that may have served for ablutions by visitors. Near the Greater Propylaea, the large entrance gate to the sanctuary, is the Callichoros Well, where the women of Eleusis danced and chanted praise to the goddess.[23]

The museum at Eleusis contains a large relief of the fourth century B.C. from the site that depicts Persephone (Kore, the daughter of Demeter) purifying a boy initiate. Persephone is twice the height of the boy, according to the convention of depicting a deity larger than a human being, and the boy is nude. Persephone holds a shell above the head of the initiate, apparently for pouring water. This scene may represent an additional purification of a candidate immediately preceding the initiation proper. The relief has been thought to be pertinent for the background of Christian baptism because in Christian art the baptizand is similarly shown nude and smaller than the baptizer. However, in Christian art the hand of the baptizer is on the head of the one being baptized.[24] The scene at Eleusis is meant to show symbolically the purification and may not be a realistic depiction of how this was done.[25]

Initiation into the mysteries of Dionysus likewise included a preliminary washing. The mother of Pulius Aebutius claimed to have made a vow "to initiate him into the Bacchic rites," and she explained to him "that he would have to observe continence for ten days; at the end of that period she could conduct him to a banquet, then, after ceremonial washing [*pure lautum*], to the shrine" for the initiation proper.[26] The women of Tanagra before the orgies of Dionysus "went down to the sea for purifications [καθαρσίων] and were attacked by Triton while they were swimming [νηχομέναις]."[27] The Villa Item (House of the Mysteries) outside Pompeii contains one room with frescoes around the walls depicting Dionysiac scenes.[28] Interpretations of details as well as of the whole scheme of the paintings vary considerably, but it is widely assumed that the pictures have to do with an initiation into the Dionysiac Mysteries. On the left wall as one enters the room one scene shows a standing woman pouring a small pitcher over the right hand of a seated woman. The seated woman may be offering a sacrifice, and the pouring could be a libation, but the positioning of the pitcher makes a lustration possible, particularly since sacrifice and ablutions often went together in purifications for an initiation.

---

23. The name means "lovely dance" — Pausanias, *Description of Greece* 1.38.6. The *Homeric Hymn to Demeter* 98-107 refers to a spring Parthenion, where maidens went to draw water that may be in the same place. The ancient sources do not indicate any use of this well in connection with the mysteries. Mysteries of Demeter and Kore were also celebrated at Andania, and Pausanias, *Description of Greece* 4.33.4, refers to water rising from a spring close to the statue of Kore.

24. See chap. 7.

25. See the comments by Leipoldt, *Taufe*, pp. 38-39.

26. Livy, *History of Rome* 39.9.4.

27. Pausanias, *Description of Greece* 9.20.4.

28. G. Zuntz, "On the Dionysiac Fresco in the Villa dei Misteri at Pompeii," *Proceedings of the British Academy* 49 (1963): 177-201.

Juvenal, in satirizing superstitious practices by women, cites as an example a devotee of the Mother of the Gods (Cybele):

> In winter she shall go down to the river in the morning, break the ice, and plunge [*mergetur*] three times into the Tiber, dipping [*abluet*] her trembling head even in its whirling waters, and crawling out thence naked and shivering.[29]

Juvenal does not explain whether this was done as an act of asceticism, to gain the favor of the goddess, or in response to her command in order to please her. This was apparently an annual rite. The account is notable as background to Christian baptismal practice for the nudity and the triple dipping.

The most nearly circumstantial account of an initiation to come down to us concerns the initiation of "Lucius" into the cult of Isis at Corinth. The description comes from Apuleius, *Metamorphoses* (or *Golden Ass*), written in the third quarter of the second century.[30] The preliminaries could be spoken about openly:

> At the time that the priest had appointed as most suitable, surrounded by a crowd of devotees, I was led to the Baths [*balneas*]. There, after delivering me to the usual bath [*sueto lavacro*], Mithras [high priest of the cult of Isis at Corinth] invoked the pardon of the gods, and sprinkling water over me [*circumrorans*], he cleansed me [*abluit*] most purely.

There followed ten days of fasting. Then, without betraying the secrets of the rite, Apuleius gives details that initiates would recognize but the rest of us can only speculate about:

> I approached the confines of death. I trod the threshold of Proserpine [goddess of the underworld]; and borne through the elements I returned. At midnight I saw the Sun shining in all his glory. I approached the gods below and the gods above, and I stood beside them, and I worshiped them.

This was the initiation proper. When morning arrived, Apuleius, clothed in linen and holding a torch, was presented to the view of the crowd. He celebrated this "festal day of initiation as if it were a birthday."[31] A sacred meal three days later concluded the initiation ceremonies. Later at Rome Apuleius received initiation into

---

29. Juvenal, *Satires* 6.522-525.

30. J. Gwyn Griffiths, *Apuleius of Madauros, The Isis-Book (Metamorphoses, Book XI): Introduction, Translation and Commentary*, Études préliminaires aux religions orientales dans l'empire romaine 39 (Leiden: Brill, 1975).

31. Apuleius, *Metamorphoses* 11.23-24. The translations are from Jack Lindsay, *Apuleius: The Golden Ass* (Bloomington: Indiana University Press, 1962) but modified in the section on the washing. See the summary in Griffiths, *The Isis-Book*, pp. 51-55, and the commentary, pp. 286-320, especially for parallels in ancient Egyptian religion, and the summary and appreciation ("the high-water mark of the piety which grew out of the mystery religions") by A. D. Nock, *Conversion* (Oxford: Clarendon Press, 1933), pp. 138-155.

Osiris and then into the priesthood. In the account Apuleius twice (11.16 and 21) speaks of himself as "reborn" *(renatus)* and the rite of dedication as "performed in the manner of a voluntary death and of a life obtained by grace" (11.21).

Apuleius's preliminary purification included both a bath and an aspersion. Other sources mention repeated washings[32] and sprinkling of the faithful at the daily opening of the temples. Isis temples that have been excavated on Delos and at Pompeii show crypts connected with water systems.[33]

The Latin Christian writer Tertullian of Carthage (c. 200) referred to the use of water in the religions of Isis and Mithras: "In certain sacred rites [the gentiles] are initiated by means of a bath [*lavacrum*] to [belong to] perhaps Isis or Mithras."[34] Tertullian is either using "initiated" in a broad sense to cover the whole complex of ceremonies associated with initiation (assuming he knew that much about them) or was speaking accommodatively to bring out the parallel and contrast with Christian rites (for everything else we know about the Mystery Religions indicates the use of water served for a preliminary purification — as in the Isis initiation described above). He continues by referring to other uses of water for purification by pagans:

> Also they carry their gods out for washings [*lavationibus*]. Moreover, they ritually purify their country and town house, their temples, and whole cities, by carrying water about and sprinkling [*aspergine*] it. Certainly at the Apollinarian and Pelusian games they are immersed [*tinguuntur*] wholesale, and suppose they are doing this with a view to regeneration [*regenerationem*] and release from their broken oaths. Among the ancients, one who had infected himself with homicide looked about for purifying waters. So then, if because cleansing is a particular characteristic of water, they seek favors of an idol as agent of purification, how much more truly shall water convey that benefit by the authority of the God by whom every one of its attributes has been appointed? (*On Baptism* 5)

The passage describes the cleansing or purifying effects generally ascribed in antiquity to water. The last sentence quoted leads into Tertullian's point, namely that if pagans ascribe such power to water, how much more effective is water in the service of the living God. These pagan uses are demonic imitations of what God intended in baptism. Hence, he exaggerates the similarities, even saying the devil "practices baptism [*baptismum*] among his own."[35]

Tertullian is one of the few literary sources about initiation into the mysteries of

---

32. Tibullus, *Poems* 1.3.25, refers to a woman who bathed *(lavari)* in clean water as part of dutiful observance of the rites of Isis.

33. Griffiths, *The Isis-Book*, pp. 276, 286.

34. Tertullian, *On Baptism* 5.1. In this and the following quotations I use but modify Ernest Evans, *Tertullian's Homily on Baptism* (London: SPCK, 1964), text and translation, pp. 12-13, commentary, pp. 61-66.

35. See A. D. Nock's discussion of the passage, "Pagan Baptisms in Tertullian," *Journal of Theological Studies* 28 (1927): 289-290. Cf. Tertullian, *Prescription of Heretics* 40, "[The devil] baptizes some — that is, his own believers and faithful followers; he promises the putting away of sins by a laver."

Mithras, for which most of our knowledge comes from archaeological remains. An invaluable pebble floor mosaic from the Mithraeum of Felicissimus in Ostia depicts the seven grades of initiation in Mithraism.[36] The sections for each grade are preceded by a panel that shows a large vase, perhaps an allusion to a preliminary purification by water before one entered on the series of initiations. The frescoes in the Mithraeum under Santa Prisca in Rome depict each grade of initiation with the paintings commending those in each rank to the protection of the different planetary gods.[37] The frescoes in the Mithraeum at Capua Vetere show the initiate naked. A graffito from the Santa Prisca Mithraeum indicates the understanding of initiation as a rebirth: "Born at first light" with a date equivalent to November 20, 202.[38] "Baptisteries" large enough for an immersion bath have been identified off the cult rooms of the Mithraea at Salzburg and Trier.[39]

Belonging to the practice of purification by blood instead of water, but sometimes brought into consideration as pagan background to Christian baptism, is the taurobolium in the cult of Cybele and Attis. A person entered an underground pit over which was laid wood in a lattice design. A bull was brought to stand over the pit and was killed with a spear. Blood ran through the openings in the lattice work, and the person in the pit held up his face to be covered with the blood and to drink from it.[40] Apart from this late fourth-century account by Prudentius, most information on the taurobolium comes from inscriptions dated from the second to the fourth century.[41] The taurobolium evidently went through an evolution, and only in its last stage in the fourth century do we know that the rite involved a blood bath for purification. The early inscriptions for the most part indicate that the rite was done for the benefit of others or oneself; the later inscriptions refer primarily to an act of consecration or dedication. A few inscriptions speak of the person as "reborn," usually for a period of twenty years. One, dated A.D. 376, has gained much attention, because it speaks of the person as "reborn for eternity" *(in aeternum renatus)*.[42] The taurobolium had in common with Mystery initiations the promise of divine favors, yet these could be for others as well as for oneself, and to be in some cases perhaps a preparation for the afterlife. On the other hand, it was a form of sacrifice, could be public and was not secret, and could be repeated. Therefore, it was noninitiatory and not part of the Mysteries of Cybele.

---

36. Maria Floriani Squarciapino, *I Culti Orientali ad Ostia* (Leiden: Brill, 1962), pp. 52-54, from the style of the mosaic and the type of brickwork dates the Mithraeum to the second half of the third century.

37. Manfred Clauss, *The Roman Cult of Mithras: The God and His Mysteries* (Edinburgh: Edinburgh University Press, 2000), pp. 131-140, interprets the seven grades as representing seven ranks of priests and not seven degrees of initiation.

38. Clauss, *The Roman Cult of Mithras*, pp. 103-105.

39. Leipoldt, *Taufe*, p. 44.

40. Prudentius, *On the Martyrs' Crowns* 10.1006-1050; a translation is in Maarten J. Vermaseren, *Cybele and Attis: The Myth and the Cult* (London: Thames and Hudson, 1977), pp. 102-103.

41. R. Duthoy, *The Taurobolium, Its Evolution and Terminology* (Leiden: Brill, 1969); Vermaseren, *Cybele and Attis*, pp. 101-107.

42. *Corpus Inscriptionum Latinarum* 6.510.

Was a washing or plunging in water part of the initiation itself in any cult? The fifth-century-B.C. comic poet Eupolis wrote a play βάπται that appears to have been a satire on the worshippers of the Thracian goddess Cotyto.[43] J. Hubaux presents the hypothesis that the subterranean basilica near the Porta Maggiore in Rome was dedicated to this deity (corresponding to Cybele) and served as the meeting place of her worshippers, the *Baptae,* at Rome.[44] He interprets the bas relief on the wall in the apse of the basilica as representing a real plunging and proposes that the initiatory rite consisted of a plunge.[45] The proposal is intriguing, but the scenes on the walls and function of the basilica are open to many interpretations, none of which claims a general consensus.

A sanctuary of the Cabiri at Thebes contains two basins, the western one of which has a depth of 1.4 meters, and there is a canal 1.4 meters high and about 40 centimeters wide.[46] The basins and tunnel appear to have been part of an enclosure for cultic baths and ceremonies, but the nature of these is unknown.

An inscription about the Korybantes refers to a washing of those being initiated,"[47] but it is not clear whether the washing was preliminary to the initiation or part of the initiation itself.

Bathing Practices

Eduard Stommel in an influential article has argued that bathing customs in the Greco-Roman world provided a pattern for the Christian administration of baptism.[48] He points to the parallel in both practices of anointing the whole body with oil and to baptism from the New Testament forward being first of all regarded as a cleansing or purification, and purification rites in the Old Testament and in pagan cults could be by sprinkling (pp. 6-7). (Stommel's other arguments for pouring as the normal mode of Christian baptism from the beginning will be dealt with in the relevant sections of this study and in the last chapter.) Stommel's contention is that in antiquity the bather undressed and while standing poured, or had poured on himself, water (p. 8). The data are too limited for generalizations. Plato referred to an orator who "poured a flood of words (καταντλήσας) over our ears like a bath at-

---

43. The testimonia and quotations from the play are collected in R. Kassel and C. Austin, eds., *Poetae Comici Graeci,* Vol. 5 (Berlin: Walter de Gruyter, 1986), pp. 331-342. One of the references to the play is Lucian, *The Ignorant Book-Collector* 27.

44. Referred to by Juvenal, "the secret torchlight orgies of the Baptae wearied the Athenian Cotytto" (*Satires* 2.91-92), and Horace, "with impunity divulge the rites of Cotytia" (*Epode* 17.56-57).

45. J. Hubaux, "Le plongeon rituel," *Musée Belge* 27 (1923):5-81.

46. Gerda Bruns, "Kabirenheiligtum bei Theben: Vorläufiger Bericht über di Grabungskampagnen 1964-1966," *Archäologischer Anzeiger* 1967 (Berlin: de Gruyter, 1967/68):228-273 (p. 245).

47. H. Engelmann and R. Merkelbach, *Die Inschriften von Erythrai und Klezomenai* (1972-73), p. 206.

48. Eduard Stommel, "Christliche Taufriten und antike Badesitten," *Jahrbuch für Antike und Christentum* 2 (1959):5-14.

tendant."⁴⁹ The earlier Greek representations of an external application of water to the bather show a variety of methods. Vase paintings from classical Greece show water poured over a crouching figure, women standing under sprays of water flowing from sprouts above their shoulders, athletes washing with water from sprouts above them, and men gathered around a basin and scooping out water.⁵⁰ In Greek hip-baths from the third century B.C. the bathers sat while hot water was poured over them.⁵¹

During the Roman period large and small bathing establishments, public and private, with sizeable pools for dipping and swimming multiplied. Roman bathing procedures followed a general pattern that could be called a ritual.⁵² By early afternoon the men's workday was concluded. The procedure was for the body to be oiled, to take light exercise, to have a bath, and then to take the main meal of the day. The typical order of the baths was a warm bath, a hot bath, and a cold plunge, and the baths had separate rooms for each: the *tepidarium,* the *caldarium,* and the *frigidarium.* Anointing the body with oil (and sometimes perfumes) might occur before or after (or both) the bath.⁵³ The fullest description comes from a Roman schoolboy's account preserved in the *Hermeneumata* from the third century A.D., here summarized:

> Arriving at the baths, preferably with an escort (slave, servant carrying bathing gear and garments); paying a fee, undressing, and storing clothes and belongings; having the body oiled and anointed (possibly in a special room); taking a sweat bath followed by being immersed in a hot tub; going (outside?) to the cold pool and swimming in it; scraping the body with a strigil and having it dried thoroughly with a towel by an attendant . . . ; dressing . . . ; concluding wishes upon bathing and thanking the bath master for a good bath and going home.⁵⁴

The medical writer Celsus in the early first century, in speaking of the health benefits of the baths, specifies that in some cases the patient should be fully immersed in a tub or take a partial bath to the hips. In other cases he gives this sequence of bathing:

---

49. *Republic* 1.17, 344D.
50. Fikret Yegül, *Baths and Bathing in Classical Antiquity* (New York: The Architectural History Foundation; Cambridge: The MIT Press, 1992), pp. 17-21, figures 19-21.
51. Jaanet DeLaine, "Baths," in Simon Hornblower and Anthony Spawforth, eds., *The Oxford Classical Dictionary,* 3rd edition (Oxford: Oxford University Press, 1996), p. 236.
52. Yegül, *Baths and Bathing,* pp. 33-40; G. G. Fagan, *Bathing in Public in the Roman World* (Ann Arbor: University of Michigan Press, 1999), esp. p. 10.
53. Yegül, *Baths and Bathing,* pp. 38, 354-355.
54. Yegül, *Baths and Bathing,* p. 429, n. 35. He cites also Pliny the Younger, *Epistles* 9.36, "I am oiled, I take my exercise, I have my bath" (p. 33) and the *Augustan History, Alexander Severus* 30.4ff., where the sequence is reading, exercise, being rubbed with oil, bathing in a swimming pool for an hour, drinking cold water, and taking a meal.

[The patient] should first sweat for a while in the tepidarium . . . then undergo anointing in the same room; next pass into the caldarium; after a further sweat he should not go down into the hot bath [he should not take a total immersion in the hot tub], but have himself sluiced freely from head downwards, first with hot, next with tepid, then with cold water . . . (*De medicina* 1.4.3)[55]

Earlier customs continued. Pictures in the House of Menander in Pompeii illustrate bathing at home by a person pouring water from a jug over another or at a fountain by one person pumping water for another.[56]

The practices of nudity and anointing of the body with oil in Christian baptism possibly had as one factor in their development ancient bathing customs. Even in these cases, other factors were present. Jewish immersions would have been a more immediate precedent for nude baptism, and it is possible that the anointing entered the mainstream of the church from rival Christian groups. Whether the Christian mode of baptism derived from bathing customs is much less likely. Even if one can generalize that the essential part of the bath was water being poured over the bather (which seems debatable), there remains the question of what was the likely precedent for Christian baptism. Much more likely is that the action was influenced by Jewish ritual washings, mediated and transformed by John the Baptist. This makes Stommel's argument for the manner of Jewish proselyte baptism (p. 9) of crucial importance (except for this point, his reliance on pagan bathing customs to the neglect of Jewish religious washings is a serious inadequacy). The subject is discussed in chapter 4, but in anticipation it may be said that the Jewish washings were by self-immersion. With the change to an administered immersion, the actions in the baptisms of John and Christians were likely still the ducking of the head of the standing baptizand into the water, an action that we shall see has some support from Christian art (chap. 7) and the size of baptisteries (chaps. 53–54) as well as literary references.

A Special Case from Mythology

A late form of the myth of the goddess Thetis and her mortal son Achilles (hero of the Trojan War) tells of a dipping for a special purpose. In order to make her son invulnerable, Thetis dipped him in the River Styx of the underworld. Her holding him by the heel left that part of his body unprotected. The earliest allusion to this version of the story is found in the Latin poet Statius of the late first century A.D. Thetis says, "Bearing my son . . . to dip *(mergere)* again in the waters of Styx" (*Achilleid* 1.134); "If I armed you at birth with the stern Stygian river (and would it had been all of you!)"

---

55. The translation is by W. G. Spencer in Loeb Classical Library, but I quote from the excerpts in Yegül, Baths and Bathing, p. 354, who mistakenly puts him in the first century B.C.

56. Pictures reproduced in Yegül, *Baths and Bathing*, p. 126.

(1.269-270).[57] The story illustrates the need in this case and in a pagan context for a complete immersion, and its use in the period of the writing of the New Testament of the usual Latin term for "to plunge, dip, immerse" *(mergere)* may introduce the word study of Greek terminology in the next chapter.

---

57. English translation by D. R. Shackleton Bailey, Statius, Vol. 3, Loeb Classical Library (Cambridge: Harvard University Press, 2003). Other references by Escher in G. Wissowa, ed., *Paulys Realencyklopädie der classischen Altertumswissenschaft* (Stuttgart: Alfred Druckenmuller, 1893), Vol. 1, col. 225.

3. Words from the *Bapt-* Root in Classical and Hellenistic Greek

The verbs βάπτω and βαπτίζω are common enough in literal and metaphorical usage to establish their meaning with some degree of confidence.[1] The nouns βάπτης, βαπτισμός, and βαπτιστήριον and the adjective βαπτός appear occasionally. The usage of these words in a religious sense is rare apart from Judaism and Christianity. Without being exhaustive I will cite enough examples to show representative usage.

βάπτω, βαπτός[2]

Literal Usage

The basic meaning of βάπτω is "to plunge," "to dip" in a yielding medium, usually a liquid. From this basic sense comes a use that emphasizes the result, "to wet." Special

---

1. The nineteenth century saw major compilations of their word usage: notably, T. J. Conant, *The Meaning and Use of* Baptizein *Philologically and Historically Investigated* (New York: American Bible Union, 1864). James W. Dale's volumes, ΒΑΠΤΙΖΩ: *Classic Baptism* (1867); *Judaic Baptism* (1869); *Johannic Baptism* (1898); *Christic Baptism and Patristic Baptism* (2nd ed. 1874), have been reprinted (Wauconda, IL: Bolchazey-Carducci; Phillipsburg, NJ: Presbyterian & Reformed Publishing Co., 1989, 1991, 1993, and 1995 respectively); the usefulness of Dale's large collection of source material is marred by use of outdated editions, repetitious polemic, and a tendentious effort to impose secondary and derived meanings on the usage of the words. For the twentieth-century understanding of βάπτω = "to dip in or under" and βαπτίζω as its intensive see the summary by Albrecht Oepke, "βάπτω, βαπτίζω (et al.)," in Gerhard Kittel, ed., *Theological Dictionary of the New Testament*, tr. Geoffrey W. Bromiley (Grand Rapids: Eerdmans, 1964), Vol. 1, pp. 529-546; J. Ysebaert, *Greek Baptismal Terminology* (Nijmegen: Dekker & Van de Vegt, 1962), pp. 12-83, on the terms for washing and immersion (pp. 41-83 on the New Testament and early Christian literature).

2. John Chadwick, *Lexicographica Graeca: Contributions to the Lexicography of Ancient Greek* (Oxford: Clarendon Press, 1996), pp. 59-62, enlarges on and modifies Henry George Liddell, Robert Scott, Henry Stuart Jones et al., *A Greek-English Lexicon with Supplement* (Oxford: Clarendon Press, 1968).

uses are to plunge a weapon into a person and to dip a container in a liquid in order to draw it up. The secondary meaning "to dye" (initially because this was a result of dipping) in time virtually supplanted the primary meaning.

Baptō occurs near the beginning of Greek literature in Homer, *Odyssey* 9.392, "And as when a smith dips [βάπτῃ] a great axe or adze in cold water [εἰν ὕδατι ψυχρῷ] to temper it."

The classical Greek playwrights reflect both literal and metaphorical usage (see more below). Aeschylus, *Prometheus* 863, "dipping [βάψασα] a two-edged sword in his blood," seems to be literal but may also have the connotation of "dyeing" the sword in the blood. Sophocles may express a similar ambiguity (or double meaning): "Is it well you dipped [or stained — Ἔβαψας] your sword with [πρὸς — into?] the army of the Argives?" (*Ajax* 95).

Euripides' usage, however, is always, it seems, literal. "Old servant, Take a vessel, dip [βάψας] in sea water, and bring here" (*Hecuba* 610). Likewise, he speaks of a "stream into which pitchers are dipped [βαπτὰν]" (*Hippolytus* 123).[3] "For a ship too, if its sheet is too vigorously tightened, goes under [ἔβαψεν]" (*Orestes* 707).[4] Similar to his predecessors' usage in reference to a sword, Euripides says, "Taking a bronze blade she thrust [plunged, ἔβαψεν] it into her flesh" (*Phoenician Maidens* 1578).

Although Aristophanes usually has the derived meaning of "dye," he does have the literal meaning. "Having taken this torch, I will dip [ἐμβάψω] in [the lustral water]" (*Peace* 959-960). "Taking the flea, he dipped [ἐνέβαψεν] its foot into [εἰς] the wax" (*Clouds* 150).

The large corpus of medical writings ascribed to Hippocrates (fifth/fourth century B.C.) has scores of uses of *baptō* and its compounds, most in the literal sense. I give a sampling of several of the common expressions.[5] These include "dipping [βάπτων] in cold water" (*De affectionibus interioribus,* 7, 13-14 [twice]); "dipping [βάπτων] sponges in [dative] hot water and applying them" (*De moribus,* book 2, 22, 5) or "dipping [βάπτων] sponges into [ἐς] hot water" (*De moribus,* 2, 26, 18). Other liquids named include: "dipping into [βάπτων ἐς] honey" (*De moribus,* 2, 43, 9); "dipping into [βάπτων ἐς] boiling olive oil" (*De affectionibus interioribus* 28, 34); "dipping into [βάπτων ἐς] gall" (*De affectionibus interioribus* 30, 27); "having dipped [βάψας] in ointment . . . dip [βάπτειν] again into [ἐς] a woman's milk and Egyptian myrrh" (*De mulierum affectibus* 74, 49-51). Sometimes the construction, as in the case of sponges, names the object dipped and the liquid into which it is dipped: "dipping [βάπτων] a cloth in cold water" (ibid. 39, 23); "dipping [βάπτων] a linen cloth into [ἐς] water and applying it to breast and back" (*De moribus,* book 2.54, 26).

---

3. The translation is that of Kovacs in Loeb Classical Library, *Euripides,* Vol. 2 (Cambridge: Harvard University Press, 1995).

4. *De mulierum affectionibus,* Vol. 5 (2002). Babrius, a second-century-A.D. writer of fables, speaks of "ships . . . dipping [βάπτουσαν] . . . in a swelling wave" (71.2).

5. Citation is by title of the work and section and line given in the *Thesaurus Linguae Graecae,* based on the edition by É. Littré, *Oeuvres complètes d'Hippocrate* (Paris: Baillière, 1839-1853; repr. Amsterdam: Hakkert, 1961-1973).

Two passages employing a compound of the verb may be quoted for their description of treatments: "to wash out the ears with clean water, and dipping [ἐμβάπτων] a sponge in honey, he is to apply it" (*De moribus,* 2, 14, 17); "to anoint the body and head with much heat and then making to recline to dip [ἐμβάπτειν] the flesh" (*De affectionibus interioribus* 52, 12).[6]

Plato has the statement, "After that, he dips [βάπτει] it into [εἰς] water" (*Timaeus* 73e). The phrase illustrates that most often the element into which an object is dipped is water, although it may be many things, and the preposition used with the verb is commonly εἰς, "into." Aristotle provides an example of both features in a passage where the verb is used intransitively with the sense of dipping oneself: "If eels plunge [βάπτωσιν] into [εἰς] cold [water]" (*History of Animals* 7[8].2, 592a.18).

Of course, the verb βάπτω says nothing about the element into which something is dipped. Aristotle has a phrase about if anyone should dip (βάψειέ) something into (εἰς) wax (*On the Soul* 3.12, 435a.2). Nor does the verb in itself say "to draw out" as well as "to dip," although this was often implied. Aristotle makes the actions explicit and in doing so gives synonyms: It is necessary to dip (βάψαι) and to draw up (ἑλκύσαι); it can easily be let down (καθιέναι) but difficult to lift up (αἴρειν) (*Mechanical Problems* 28, 357a). In discussing the treatment of elephants, Aristotle speaks of dipping (βάπτοντες) the fodder into (εἰς) honey and giving them to eat (*History of Animals* 7[8].26, 605a.29).

Aristotle's pupil Theophrastus illustrates the common usage of *baptō* for dipping in order to draw water and distinguishes it from another action: A person "goes to the hot-water tanks of the baths, draws a ladle full [βάψας ἀρύταιναν] and rinses himself [pours it over himself, καταχέασθαι]" (*Characters* 9.8). The character says of his action that he has washed himself (λέλουται).[7] The literal sense is implicit in the phrase "covered [ἐπίβαπτα] with a juice" (*Enquiry into Plants* 3.7.4). Another compound form occurs in the description of a certain soft stone that, when dipped (ἀποβαφῇ) in oil, becomes black and hard (*On Stones* 42).

Theocritus, bucolic poet of the early third century B.C., was from Syracuse. He like Theophrastus shows the extension of *baptō* to the subsequent (and often implicit) drawing of the object out of the liquid into which it was dipped. "May the maid in the morning draw [dip, βάψαι] a honeycomb instead of water for my cup" (*Idyl* 5.127).

Aratus, whose poetry popularized a Stoic worldview, also wrote in the third cen-

---

6. ἐνβάπτων and ἀποβάπτων are frequent: ἐμβάπτων ἐς cold water (*De moribus,* book 2, 26, 30) and ἐμβάπτων ἐς hot water (ibid., 2, 31, 4); ἐμβάπτεται, as in coldest water (*De humidorum usu,* 5, 5); hot loaves that are dipped into (ἐμβαπτόμευσα ἐς) sour wine (*De diaeta acutorum,* 79, 9); ἀποβάπτων in honey (*De affectionibus interioribus,* 9, 23); ἐναποβάπτειν in cold water (*De capitis vulneribus,* 21, 14 and 19).

7. Translation by Jeffrey Rusten in Loeb Classical Library 225 (Cambridge: Harvard University Press, 2002). Antiphanes, a fourth-century-B.C. comic writer, also refers to drawing water by dipping a bucket (25). A late example of this usage, distinguishing like Theophrastus both dipping and washing from sprinkling (or pouring), comes from Iamblichus (c. 250-325), "It is not proper to dip [ἐμβάπτειν] into [εἰς] the vessel for sprinkling water, nor be washed in a bath" (*Life of Pythagoras* 18).

tury B.C. He writes of being dipped (or washing oneself, ἐβάψατο) from head to shoulders in the river (*Phaenomena* 951). The word occurs in a passage that might be considered metaphorical, but in view of the cosmology of the time may not inappropriately be treated as literal: the cloudless sun "dips [βάπτοι] in the western ocean" (ibid., 858).[8]

Coming to authors at the time which provides the context for the rise of Christianity, we note Strabo's description of arrows "dipped [and so "imbued" — βεβαμένοις] in the gall of serpents" (*Geography* 16.4.10). Near the same time Dionysius of Halicarnassus spoke of "plunging [or thrusting, piercing, burying — βάψας] a spear into [εἰς] the side" (*Roman Antiquities* 5.15.2).

A century later, Plutarch at the beginning of the second century provides an unusual usage when he speaks of dipping (βάψας) a wreath of flowers in perfume (*Artaxerxes* 22 = *Lives* 1022B). He offers a transition to metaphorical usages by his phrase, "bravery has been dipped [βέβαπται] by reason" (*On the Control of Anger* 10 = *Moralia* 458E).

Lucian of Samosata, second century, refers to a sporting activity in the baths: "The rest were ducking their heads like dolphins in the cold plunge [ψυχροβαφές]" (*Lexiphanes* 5).

The first-century medical writer Dioscorides in a variant reading refers to coral "being dipped [βαπτόμενον] or hardened" (*Medical Matters* 5.121). The whole statement may refer to hardening as a result of being alternately exposed to the air and then covered with water again or to the dipping being equivalent to its effect, the hardening (see below on Aristophanes for another instance of the act identified with its result).

The abundant medical writings of the second-century physical Galen make frequent use of *baptō* and its compounds, most often in a literal sense in a variety of applications and so demonstrating that the metaphorical use had not completely taken over.[9] Several references are to dipping a body in cold water as a medical treatment. Galen was asked about the custom of Germans who dipped (βάπτοντας) bodies into (εἰς) cold water to harden them, as was done to red hot iron (*De sanitate tuenda*, 6, 51, 15).[10] Some were dipped (ἐμβάπτοντας) in cold to quench the heat (*De methodo medendi*, 10, 718, 16).[11] There is also reference to dipping (ἀποβάπτων) in a hot bath (*De compositione medicamentorum*, 12, 813, 13). Many of Galen's uses have to do with dipping foods, as into vinegar and sauce (ἀποβαπτομένων — *De alimentorum facul-*

---

8. The same picture occurs in the Christian Melito of Sardis (chap. 14), but he uses βαπτίζω.

9. The works used from Galen will be cited here and below by the title of the work followed by volume, page, and line number in C. G. Kühn, *Claudii Galeni opera omnia* (Leipzig: Knobloch, 1821-1830; repr. Hildesheim: Olms, 1964-1965).

10. Galen makes the same comparison in *De methodo medendi*, 10, 717, 7-11: entering the *frigidarium* of baths is like the dipping (βαφῇ) of iron; "we are made cold and braced up like the iron, since having become red hot it is dipped [ἐμβάπτηται] in the cold [water]."

11. Other references are "unless you should dip [βάπτοις] into [εἰς] the cold [water]" (*De methodo medendi*, 10, 722, 6); and the warning, "no one dares to dip [βάπτειν] the feeble into the cold" (*De methodo medendi*, 10, 722, 15).

tatibus, 6, 538, 1).¹² He also speaks of dipping (βάπτων) the finger in olive oil (*De compositione medicamentorum*, 12, 407, 16) and dipping (βάπτων) an instrument into the prepared medicine (*De compositione medicamentorum*, 12, 603, 11).¹³ He refers to dipping (ἀποβάπτων) a sponge into the sea (*De compositione medicamentorum*, 12, 814, 1) or into sharp brine (line 2). A special use was for wrapping (βάπτων) a wound with a bandage around it (*De compositione medicamentorum*, 13, 733, 4).¹⁴ There are other references that I have not attempted to classify.¹⁵

Perhaps because of the frequent use of *baptō* for "to dye," *embaptō* became common for dipping, but the usage is older. The antiquarian Athenaeus quotes Hipponax (late sixth century), "not soaking [ἐμβάπτων] fried cakes in honey" (*Learned Banquet* 14, 645c) and Crantinus (fifth century B.C.), "dipping [ἐμβάπτων] in pickle juice" (*Learned Banquet* 9, 385d).

For the use of *baptō* in reference to Jewish baptism, see Arrian, *Discourses of Epictetus* 2.9.20, quoted in chapter 4.

Metaphorical Usage (Secondary Meanings)

One common usage of dipping in water was to temper metals (found already in Homer, cited above), and in some cases this purpose, "to temper," may be the way to translate *baptō*. A character in Aeschylus's *Agamemnon* says, "I know nothing . . . of dipping [tempering — βάψας] bronze" (612). Sophocles uses the comparison, "tempered as iron by dipping [βαφῇ]" (*Ajax* 651). Aristotle compared cities to iron, literally: "They are like iron that is dipped, when at peace," but the meaning is, "Like iron, they lose temper [βαφὴν] when at peace" (*Politics* 7.14, 1334a). Theophrastus speaks of "whatever dulls the temper [βαφήν] of iron" (*De causis plantarum* 1.22.5).

---

12. Other instances are ἐναποβάπτοντες in (dative) sauce (*De alimentorum facultatibus*, 6, 539, 2); same verb in vinegar and sauce (*De alimentorum facultatibus*, 6, 636, 2); dipping (ἀποβάπτοντες) the flesh of fish and eating it (*De alimentorum facultatibus*, 6, 716, 14); mixing vinegar with cold water for dipping (βάπτειν) (*De marcore*, 7, 698, 2); dipping (ἐμβάπτοντας) into vinegar (*De compositione medicamentorum*, 13, 357, 4); not dipping (ἐμβάπτοντας) frequently in sour vinegar (*De venae sectione*, 11, 215, 1); dipping (ἀποβάπτων) into honey (*De compositione medicamentorum*, 12, 991, 14 and 12, 999, 5); "dipping [βάπτων] a little twig of dry herb into hot olive oil" (*De compositione medicamentorum*, 12, 863, 3); "Dip [ἀπόβαπτε] into hot olive oil" (*De compositione medicamentorum*, 12, 875, 4); "Let him eat hot loaves dipping [ἀποβάπτων] from dark wine and olive oil" (*In Hippocratis*, 15, 890, 11; same as Hippocrates, *De diaeta acutorum*, 20, 9).

13. Cf. dipping (καταβάπτων) into the medicine (*De compositione medicamentorum*, 12, 694, 10).

14. Elsewhere Galen uses καταβάπτουσα for covering the place treated (*De compositione mendicatorum*, 12, 958, 15); the same compound form is used more literally for dipping (καταβάπτων) a piece of wool and rolling it up like a lamp wick (*De compositione medicamentorum*, 13, 858, 1).

15. "Dipping [βάπτων] again and again often he does the same, leaving it for no length of time" (*De compositione medicamentorum*, 12, 603, 15); "dipping [βάπτων] twice a day" (*De compositione medicamentorum*, 12, 645, 10); "being dipped [ἀποβαπτόμενος] into sea water" (*De compositione medicamentorum*, 12, 809, 2); "dipping [ἀποβάπτων] these things slightly into hot water" (*De compositione medicamentorum*, 12, 817, 6); ἐμβάπτεται in *De compositione medicamentorum*, 12, 622, 14.

The tempering of iron (σίδερος) by dipping in water is a favorite image with Plutarch: "iron plunged [βαπτόμενον] (in water)" (*Principle of Cold* 2 = *Moralia* 946C); "cool air imbued [βεβάμμενον, or dipped] with [in] earthly power, as iron plunged [βαφῇ] (in water)" (*Principle of Cold* 20 = *Moralia* 954C); "iron dipped [or tempered, βαπτόμενον]" (*Advice about Keeping Well* 25 = *Moralia* 136A).[16]

The principal metaphorical use of *baptō* was for dyeing. Since a common practice was to dye by dipping an object in the coloring agent, a secondary meaning of *baptō* was "to dye," and this meaning almost replaced the primary meaning. This development, I think, came about not because of the effect replacing the act but because of the frequent use of the act for this purpose leading to the secondary meaning. Nevertheless, the secondary meaning took over to such an extent that *baptō* could be used for "dye" whatever the means employed.

A passage in Aeschylus has the meaning of dyeing in association with the action of dipping or plunging: Aegisthus's sword dyed (ἔβαψεν) the robe red (*Libation Bearers* 1011). Sophocles already represents the simple secondary meaning, "I dyed [ἔβαψα] his garment" (*Women of Trachis* 580). He further shows how the secondary meaning could itself be used metaphorically: "Poison dyed [ἔβαψεν] my blood" (*Women of Trachis* 574). The comic poet Eupolis (fifth century B.C.) has the line "to dye [βάπτειν] beautiful garments for the goddess."[17]

Aristophanes has many uses of *baptō* in the sense "I dye." One passage keeps in mind the origin of the secondary sense: "They dye [or dip — βάπτουσι] their wools in the warm [liquid]" (*Ecclesiazusae* 216).[18] In this usage with the dative case the emphasis is on the result of the immersion, "to make wet." In another passage we note that the noun from the same root has the meaning of the "dye" itself: "Lest I dye [βάψω] you with the dye [βάμμα] of Sardis" (i.e., red, the color of blood) (*The Acharnians* 1.112). A different but related usage is *Knights* 523, where an actor is described as acting like Lydians, "being dyed [smeared — βαπτόμενος] with frog-colored dye." Aristophanes uses the adjective βαπτός for a brightly colored bird (*Birds* 287).[19] The secondary sense is the basis of a metaphor, "dyed in the dye [βέβαπται βάμμα] of Cyzicus," that is, is a coward (*Peace* 1176).

Herodotus represents the common use for dyed (βεβαμμένα) garments (*Histories* 7.67). Plato illustrates how the literal action led to the meaning "dye":

Dyers [βαφεῖς], when they want to dye [βάψαι] wool, . . . [after preparation] thus they dip it [or dye it, βάπτουσι]; and what in this manner of dying [βαφῇ] be-

---

16. Also *Obsolescence of Oracles* 41 = *Moralia* 433A (βαφῇ).

17. Fragment 363 in R. Kassel and C. Austin, eds., *Poetae Comici Graeci*, Vol. 5 (Berlin: Walter de Gruyter, 1986), p. 501. Eupolis used βάπτρια for a feminine baptizer or dyer (?) in fragment 434 (p. 526). See chap. 2 for his play *Baptae*, apparently about a group of women who used dipping in religious rituals.

18. Other passages about dyeing garments: *Plutus* 530 (βαπτῶν); *Lysistrata* 51 ("I'll use the saffron colored dye [βάψομαι κροκωτόν]").

19. The adjective βαπτός is most often used with the meaning "dyed."

comes dyed [or, fast colored, βαφέν], washing [πλύσις] will not take away the color. (*Republic* 4.429D-E)[20]

Aristotle, however, shows that the secondary meaning could take over and be used regardless of the manner in which the dyeing or staining was effected: "Being pressed, it dyes [moistens, βάπτει] and colors the hand" (*History of Animals* 5.15, 547a). The medical writings ascribed to Hippocrates contain the secondary meaning quite in contrast to the literal meaning: "When it drops upon the garments, they are dyed [βάπτεται]" (*De mulierum affectibus*, 122, 4).

Theophrastus has numerous uses of *baptō* with the meaning dye. Some of these are the following: "gall with which they dye [βάπτουσιν] wool" (*Enquiry into Plants* 3.8.6);[21] "dyes [βάπτει] hides" (ibid. 3.14.3); "tanners dye [βάπτουσι] white leather" with this tree (ibid. 3.18.5).

In Menander, *Anger*, a character says, "I will dye [βάψομαι] (my hair)."[22] Strabo uses *baptō* normally in the sense of dyeing. "The water at Hierapolis is marvelously suited for dyeing [βαφῆς] of wool, so that wool dyed [βαπτόμενοι] with the roots . . ." (*Geography* 13.4.14).[23] He also speaks of men who dyed (βάπτεσθαι) their beards (15.1.30). Plutarch, *Sayings of Kings and Commanders* 23 (= *Moralia* 178F), too speaks of dyed (βαπτόμενον) beard and hair.

Most often garments are the objects of dyeing, as in Diodorus Siculus, *Library* 5.30.1 (βαπτοῖς). This usage is common in Plutarch.[24] He could also recall a poet who said βάψαι ("to dye") is "to soak" (διῆναι) (*Table Talk* 8.5 = *Moralia* 725C).

Second-century authors continued the common derivative usage and extended its range. The novelist Achilles Tatius says, "They dye [βάπτουσιν] the robe of Aphrodite" (*Leucippe and Cleitophon* 2.11.4), but in a tertiary sense, "the blood dyes [βάπτει] the jaw" of the dog (ibid. 2.11.5).[25] In the medical writer Galen we find, "to dye [βάπτειν] black or yellow" (*De compositione medicamentorum*, 12, 437, 7).[26]

---

20. Cf. Plato, *Laws* 8, 847C, "purple and whatever dyed (βαπτὰ) colors."

21. Other references to dyeing wool are *Enquiry into Plants* 4.6.5, "they dye [βάπτουσι] wool and clothes," in a passage that refers to porphyry dye (βαφή), and 4.6.8, "for dyeing [βαφὴν] wool."

22. Fragment 303.4 in the edition by Koerte for Teubner, Vol. 31.2; Fragment 363.4 in Kock's edition.

23. Other references to dyeing garments are "garments dyed [βαπτάς] in colors" (*Geography* 4.4.5) and "colored [βάπτεσθαι] garments" (15.1.58).

24. "Cloaks dyed [βαπτοῦ]" (*Agesilaus* 30.3 = *Lives* 612d); the steeping of fabrics to be dyed (βαπτομένων) (*Table Talk* 6.2 = *Moralia* 688F; *Phocion* 28.3 = *Lives* 754C); cf. the coverings of couches dyed purple (*Philopoemen* 9.3 = *Lives* 360F).

25. Among his many uses of the noun, "discovers a treasury of dye [βαφῆς]" (*Leucippe and Cleitophon* 2.11.8).

26. Cf. soaking the head continually in pink (dye) like wool or a rag by plunging (ἀποβάπτων) into the pink (dye) (*De compositione medicamentorum*, 12, 502, 8); "the hands of those peeling the nuts are dyed [βάπτονται]" (*De compositione medicamentorum*, 12, 906, 10); dyeing (βάπτων) hands in iris-oil (*De compositione medicamentorum*, 13, 987, 17); "wools dyed [βαπτομένοις] by those called dyers" (*In Hippocratis*, 16, 581, 3); tongues dyed (βαπτόμεναι) by the pale yellow gall (*In Hippocratis*, 17b, 271, 13).

Athenaeus uses *baptō* for glazing earthen vessels: cups are dyed [βάπτονται] to look like silver (*Learned Banquet* 11, 480e). Lucian often refers to dyes, or hues of color.[27] Marcus Aurelius's figurative usages are closely related to the primary and secondary meanings. The soul is imbued (βάπτεται) by (dipped in or dyed by) thoughts; imbue (βάπτε) it therefore by (dip or dye it in) the habitude of such thoughts (*Meditations* 5.16.1); "imbued [dyed, βεβαμμένον] by righteousness to the bottom" (3.4.3); "Beware of Caesarism, lest you be imbued [stained, dyed, βαφῇ] by it" (6.30.1); "even if it is thrown in the mud or dunghill, it will quickly scatter these things and will wash them out and will no more be stained [βαφήσεται]" (8.51.1).

Some of these metaphorical uses led to the argument that *baptō* meant "sprinkle, or color by sprinkling," with no idea of submerge or immerse.[28] The passages cited are: (1) the Homeric poem *The Battle of the Frogs and Mice* v. 220 — One is thrust so severely that the surface of the lake is sprinkled with drops of blood (ἐβάπτετο δ' αἵματι λίμνη, which I would translate, "The lake was dyed with blood") (2) Lucian, *True Story* 17 — Monsters fought in the air and blood dropped on the clouds, and then comes the clause that should be translated, "so that they were dyed [βάπτεσθαι] and appeared red"; and (3) *Iliad* 18.329 — Achilles bewails the death of Patroclus: he and his friend will stain the same soil with their blood, which the Scholiast explains by the word βάπτω. I would reply that Scott confuses the result (dyeing) with the method of application; in each case the secondary meaning "dye" calls attention to the result. A reply to the article in the same journal makes my point: in each passage the meaning of the word is "dye, stain, color," and this meaning resides in the result rather than in the means by which this is effected.[29] The respondent calls attention to Apollonius Rhodius, *Argonautica* 4.156ff., where the action of *baptō* is distinguished from sprinkling: "With a spray of juniper Medea dipped [βάπτους'] the drugs from the witch broth and sprinkled [ῥαῖνε] them on the serpent's eyes."

We may conclude this section with some epigrams in the *Greek Anthology* that preserve both the literal and metaphorical meanings. From Leonidas of Tarentum in the third century B.C., "The cup which I dipped [βαψάμενος] in your stream to quench my thirst" (*Epigram* 9.326).[30] From Lucillius in the first century A.D., "Some say you dye [βάπτειν] your hair" (*Epigram* 11.68).[31] The secondary meaning "dye" could then be used metaphorically: "Dyer [βαφεῦ], who dyes [βάπτων] all things

---

27. *Hall* 11; *Fisherman* 6; *Trials by Jury* 8.
28. John A. Scott, "The Meaning of the Verb βάπτω, βαπτίζω," *Classical Journal* 16 (1920): 53-54.
29. Thomas Macartney, "On a Meaning of βάπτω," *Classical Journal* 16 (1921): 497-498.
30. Translations are by W. R. Paton in *The Greek Anthology* (Loeb Classical Library; Cambridge: Harvard University Press, 1948), sometimes modified. Another literal use refers to weapons that "all have been dipped [βέβαπται] in fire" (9.440, line 29, Moschus).
31. Other references using *baptō* for dyeing hair are 11.67, 4 (βάπτε), 11.398, 1 and 3 (βάπτων and βάφευς, "dyer"), 11.408 ("You dye [βάπτεις] your hair, but you will never dye [βάφεις] your old age" — Lucian). "To dye" is the most common usage in the *Greek Anthology*: "dyed "βαπτὸν] with sea purple" (6.206, 4 — Antipater of Sidon); a "quill dyed "βαπτῇ] with purple" (6.229, 2 — Crinagoras).

and changes them with your colors, you dyed [βάψας] your poverty too and became a rich man" (*Epigram* 11.42, line 3).[32]

Jewish Usage

In the Greek translation of the Hebrew Bible βάπτω, *baptō*, most often translates the Hebrew טבל, *ṭabal*, "to dip." The word often appears in a religious context but always with the simple meaning of "dip." The influence of Hebrew idiom is seen in the wording of the requirement to dip hyssop in blood and place the blood on the lintel and doorposts of the houses on the night of the first Passover (Exod. 12:22). The phrase "dip from [βάψαντες ἀπὸ] the blood" calls attention to the withdrawing as well as the plunging of the object dipped. The priest's dipping his finger "from the blood" is distinguished from the subsequent action of sprinkling it as part of the sin offering for himself and for the people: "The priest shall dip [βάψει] his finger from the blood of the bull and shall sprinkle [ῥανεῖ] it seven times before the LORD" (Lev. 4:17).[33] The normal Greek construction occurs in the parallel statement (Lev. 4:6) where the same contrast of actions is observed (but with another form of the verb for "sprinkle"): "The priest shall dip [βάψει] his finger into [εἰς] the blood and shall sprinkle [προσρανεῖ] (some) of [ἀπὸ] the blood seven times before the LORD."[34] The ceremony of purification for persons and things involved with a dead body required, instead of a priest dipping a finger in blood, a clean person dipping hyssop in water and sprinkling the objects affected: "A clean person shall dip [βάψει] hyssop into [εἰς] water and shall sprinkle around [περιρρανεῖ]" (Num. 19:18).

Baptō occurs in a nonritual context still with its primary meaning of "dip." At the crossing of the Jordan into the Promised Land, "The feet of the priests . . . were dipped into [ἐβάφησαν εἰς] part [the edge] of the water of the Jordan" (Josh. 3:15). Boaz invited Ruth to eat bread, and said, "You will dip [βάψεις] your morsel in [ἐν] vinegar" (Ruth 2:14). King Saul's son Jonathan "dipped [ἔβαψεν] the tip of his staff into [εἰς] the honeycomb" (1 Sam. 14:27). Hazael killed the Syrian king Benhadad by taking bed covering, dipping (ἔβαψεν) it in water, and covering his face to suffocate him (2 Kings 8:15). A nonliteral use occurs in Moses' blessing of Asher, where "He will dip [βάψει] his foot in [ἐν] oil" (Deut. 33:24) is a metaphor for his prosperity. Particularly notable is the metaphorical use in Job 9:31, "You plunged [ἔβαψας] me in [ἐν] filth" (meaning "you overwhelmed me with adversity").

In three passages the Greek Old Testament uses *baptō* where *ṭabal* is not in the

---

32. Another metaphorical use of the meaning "dye": "You dye the lips purple with your discourse" (9.214, 2 — Leo the philosopher).

33. Cf. "He shall dip [βάψει] his right finger from [ἀπὸ] the oil . . . and shall sprinkle it seven times" (Lev. 14:16).

34. "He dipped [ἔβαψεν] his finger into [εἰς] the blood" (Lev. 9:9); "He shall dip [βάψει] them into [εἰς] . . . into the blood . . . and shall sprinkle around [περιρρανεῖ]" (Lev. 14:6-7); "He shall dip [βάψει] it into [εἰς] the blood . . . and shall sprinkle around [περιρρανεῖ]" (Lev. 14:51).

underlying Hebrew. The literal meaning occurs in the statement: "Every vessel . . . will be dipped [βαφήσεται] into [εἰς] water" (Lev. 11:32). A nonliteral sense is conquest described as bathing (dipping) feet in the blood of enemies: "so that you may bathe [dip, βαφῇ] your foot in [ἐν] blood" (Psalm 67:24; Eng. 68:23). Somewhat harder to classify is Daniel 5:21 (Theodotion) about Nebuchanezzar, whose body, while he lived in his madness as a wild animal, was "bathed [ἐβάφη] from [ἀπὸ] the dew of heaven." Here the result, being covered with water, is described by the word for the action that usually produced it, a usage perhaps facilitated by the fact that bathing often involved a dipping.

The only use for "dyed" in the Greek Old Testament may be with the adjective (βαπταὶ) for the tiaras of the Babylonians (Ezek. 23:15).[35]

By way of contrast to the usage of the Greek Old Testament, βάπτω occurs in Josephus exclusively in its secondary meaning of "to dye": Herod's dyed (βαπτομένῳ) hair (*Jewish War* 1.490 [24.7]), dyed (βαμμένων) mantles (*Jewish War* 4.563 [9.10]), and the dyed (βεβαμμένας) fabrics in the tabernacle (Exod. 35:5ff. — *Antiquities* 3.102 [36.1]). Josephus's rewriting of the law of Numbers 19:17-20 (*Antiquities* 4.81 [4.4.6]) concerning the purification of persons polluted by contact with a corpse substitues βαπτίζω for the LXX's βάπτω. He says, "They put a little of the ashes into running water [πηγήν] and, dipping [βαπτίσαντες] hyssop into the running water, they sprinkled [ἔρραινον]" it on them. It is to be noted that Josephus preserves the distinction between the actions of dipping and sprinkling. He represents the tendency for βαπτίζω to replace βάπτω, perhaps because he used βάπτω for dyeing, but his usage is nonetheless significant for the understanding of the meaning of the words.

βαπτίζω, βαπτισμός

The form βαπτίζω would properly have a causative sense ("I cause to dip"), but it seems rarely to have carried this force in the literature of this study. Rather, it does appear to have had a certain intensive force, for the meaning ("I dip," "I plunge," "I overwhelm") often was found more suitable to refer to rather thorough immersions (drowning or sinking), but even this intensive force is not always evident and was weakened in time. The -ίζω form tended to replace βάπτω, in accord with the tendency in languages for strengthened forms of words to replace the root form and to lose their intensified meaning, in this case a development likely related also to *baptō* being ordinarily used for "to dye." Where there was a difference, *baptizō* involved a more thorough and lasting submersion than *baptō*. In some cases βαπτίζω refers to a condition of being under or surrounded (covered) by something (usually a liquid) regardless of the action that brought about the state or condition (as, for example, when the sea flows over a ship or person). This is especially so in the metaphorical

---

35. The NRSV translates the Hebrew as "flowing turbans."

uses. Ordinarily the word refers to being placed in the object that covers, but however the condition occurs, the result is the same — being covered or overwhelmed.

Βαπτίζω was the verb used for the Christian rite of baptism, but Christians favored βάπτισμα over βαπτισμός for the noun (see subsequent chapters).

Literal Usage

As a transition from *baptō* to *baptizō* note may be taken of an epigram on Eupolis's play *Baptae* (see chap. 2). Alcibiades, who had been satirized by Eupolis, threw him into the sea, saying: "You [Eupolis] dipped [βάπτες] me [Alcibiades] in plays, but I immersing [βαπτίζων] you in waves of the sea will destroy you with waves more bitter."[36] *Baptō* may be used in a metaphorical sense — "painted, colored, dyed" — but the choice of this word for the parody on Alcibiades set up the use of *baptizō* in an intensive sense for a literal drowning.

Aesop's *Fables* offer several examples of the literal use of βαπτίζω and the typical contexts in which it occurred. These contexts illustrate the intensive meaning of a thorough submerging. There is reference to a ship in danger of being sunk (βαπτίζεσθαι) (*Fable* 223 [= 275 = 311 = 207 in different collections], *Shepherd and the Sea*, version 3, line 5). A dolphin kills an ape that has been riding on his back by diving below the surface and drowning (βαπτίζων) him (*Fable* 75 [= 363 = 324 = 305 = 73], *The Dolphin and the Ape*, version 1, lines 14-15). A gardener's dog fell into a well, and when the gardener went down into the well to rescue him, the dog thought he had come to make sure he was drowned (βαπτίζεσθαι) (*Fable* 122 [= 77 = 34 = 120], *The Gardener and His Dog*, version 1, line 3).

Pindar uses the negative form of the adjective formed from *baptizō* and thereby illustrates the meaning of the verb: "Like a cork, I shall go undipped [ἀβάπτιστος] over the surface of the brine" (*Pythian Odes* 2.80).

The medical writings ascribed to Hippocrates (fifth/fourth century B.C.?) make far more use of *baptō* than *baptizō*, but two references are significant for the meaning of the latter. He writes of "one who causes a ship to sink [βαπτίσαντα] by too much weight and then blames the sea" (*Epistulae* 17, line 243). Another reference is to a woman breathing as divers breathe after having been immersed (βεβαπτίσθαι) (*De moribus* 5.63, line 5).

Demosthenes uses a strengthened form of the verb that referred to a dipping match in which swimmers engaged and gives it a metaphorical meaning: For orators know how to thoroughly immerse (διαβαπτίζεσθαι) another, that is, "play the dipping match with him" (*Aristogeiton* 1.41, 782).

Aristotle shows the meaning by a synonym he uses with *baptizō*. He reports about "seaweeds which were not submerged [βαπτίζεσθαι] when the tide ebbed, but

---

36. Preserved in a scholium on Aelius Aristides, *Oration* 3.8, quoted in Kassel and Austin, *Poetae Comici Graeci*, Vol. 5, p. 332.

were covered [swamped, κατακλύζεσθαι] when the tide was full" (*On Marvellous Things Heard* 136.844a). Although *baptizō* often occurs with reference to thorough immersions that were destructive (drowning or a ship sinking), this passage is a reminder that there was nothing destructive in the word itself.

Menander (fourth-third century B.C.) has a line in his play *Epitrepontes (The Arbitrants)* where the context does not make the sense clear, but because of the mention of a body of water I take the meaning to be literal. "You saw the pond. . . . I'll make an end of you, ducking [βαπτίζων] you all night long until I compel you to think as I do" (Act III, line 861).

Polybius in the second century B.C. has several occurrences of *baptizō*, all in a literal sense. In one passage a shaft of a spear falls into the sea, and its oaken part is immersed (βαπτίζομενα) or sinks (*History* 34.3.7). In another passage the foot soldiers crossed a river with difficulty, "being immersed [βαπτιζόμενοι] to the breasts" (i.e., the water was breast high) (3.72.4). A synonym reinforces the meaning in the statement about "[The army] plunging [βαπτιζόμενοι] and sinking [καταδύνοντες] in the pools [τέλμασιν]" of the marsh (5.47.2). Polybius's principal usage is with reference to ships sinking. "[They] rammed the vessels and sank [ἐβάπτιζον] many of them" (1.51.6-7). Similarly he speaks of a ship having been rammed by a hostile vessel and being sunk (or sinking, βαπτιζομένην) (16.6.2). Or again, "[Ships] being submerged [βαπτιζόμενα, i.e., went under water] became full of the sea" (8.6[8].4).

Diodorus Siculus has both literal and metaphorical uses of *baptizō*. Literal in the sense of being drowned is the statement: "Many animals cut off [surrounded] by the river perish, being immersed [overwhelmed, βαπτιζόμενα]" (*Library* 1.36.9). Soldiers attempting to swim with their armor on perished (ἐβάπτιζε) (16.80).

Strabo uses *baptizō* slightly more often than *baptō*, illustrating the tendency for the strengthened form to replace the root form of the verb. He refers to lakes in which those who cannot swim are not immersed (do not sink, βαπτίζεσθαι) but float on the surface like wood (*Geography* 6.2.9). Similar is his description of the Dead Sea, "No one who walks into it is immersed [βαπτίζεσθαι] but is raised afloat" because of the nature of the water (16.2.42). Strabo also describes a lake where the salt water solidifies readily around everything immersed (βαπτισθέντι) into (εἰς) it (12.5.4). There was a place where the force of the water resisted so strongly that a javelin let down into it could scarcely be immersed (βαπτίζεσθαι) (12.2.4). Strabo describes a spear shaft made of two kinds of wood: if it falls into the water, it is not lost, for although the oak end sinks ("is immersed," βαπτιζόμενον) because of its weight, the rest stays afloat (1.2.16). He reports on Alexander's troops marching "all day in water immersed [submerged] to the waist" (14.3.9). Since the usual usage was for complete submerging, Strabo qualifies the extent of covering by the water.

Pliny the Younger at the turn to the second century, although writing in Latin, gives an indirect testimony to a common Greek usage. In describing his villa and its baths, he states that the cooling room (*frigidarium*) had two *baptisteria* (basins or swimming baths — *Epistles* 2.17.11). Another passage describing a villa mentions a "large *baptisterium*" or pool in the *frigidarium* of a bath complex but distinct from the *piscina* or swimming pool (*Epistles* 5.6.25). He Latinizes the Greek word βαπτιστήριον, which must have been the common word for a basin or pool in the bath complexes.

Soranus, a physician in the first or second century, describes plunging (βαπτίζειν) a scalpel into (εἰς) a foetus (*Gynaeciorum* 4.11.5).

Epictetus preserves a common usage for being drowned in a shipwreck:

> Just as they would not any more prefer to be drowned [βαπτίζεσθαι] in a large ship elegantly and richly adorned with gold, neither would they like to suffer distress while living in an immense and expensive house.[37]

Lucian in the second century also uses *baptizō* for being drowned. He portrays the misanthrope as saying:

> If the river in winter sweeps someone off his feet and he extends his hands begging me to assist, I am to push his head down, plunging [βαπτίζοντα] him so as not to be able to come up again. (*Timon* 44)

In a fanciful account he describes those with cork feet: "We were amazed to see that they were not immersed [did not go under, βαπτιζομένους] but stayed on top of the waves" (*True Story* 2.4).

The second-century physician Galen maintains the literal sense of *baptizō*, as he does in his use of *baptō* and with no apparent difference in meaning: "when he was more completely immersed [βαπτίσθεντος]" (*De methodo medendi*, 10, 447, 1); "surgical instruments called ἀβάπτιστα [undipped] on account of their not having been dipped [βαπτίζεσθαι]" (*De methodo medendi*, 10, 447, 10-11); someone placed in the hot pool "and so when the body is wholly immersed [βαπτιζομένου] except the face" (*De compositione medicamentorum*, 12, 588, 14); "wool dipped [βαπτισθὲν] in butter" (*De compositione medicamentorum*, 12, 645, 10).

The second-century novelist Achilles Tatius offers several examples of *baptizō* in both literal and metaphorical uses. Two instances of the literal meaning have to do with ships under water. One passage speaks of passengers moving to the part of a boat that was highest out of the water in hopes that their weight would raise up the immersed (βαπτιζόμενον) part of the boat (*Leucippe and Clitophon* 3.1.3). Similarly, "The ship is almost sent under water [βαπτίζεται]" (3.1.5). Other literal usages having to do with water are plunging (or thrusting, βαπτίζουσι) a pole into (εἰς) the water (2.14.4) and a character "dipping [βαπτίσας] the hollow of the hand and filling it with water" (4.18.6). He also writes of a sword plunged (thrust, βαπτίζεσθαι) down against a body (3.21.4).

Also in the second century Polyaenus, in describing a water game, demonstrates the use of different words for the actions of dipping and sprinkling. A certain Philip

---

37. Fragment from Stobaeus, *Gnomologium* 47 (82), translated from the text in H. Schenkl, *Epicteti Dissertationes* (Stuttgart: Teubner, 1965), p. 480.

"dunking [διαβαπτιζόμενος] with the pancratist and splashing [ῥαινόμενος] in his face" (*Stratagems* 4.2.6).

Athenaeus represents mainly metaphorical uses, but he employs derived words that show the literal sense. "You immerse [soak, ἐμβάπτισον] turnips in sharp brine" (*Learned Banquet* 4[11], 133d). In a religious context, "they took a brand from the altar dipped [ἀπέβαπτον] in this water and sprinkled [περιρραίνοντες] the bystanders" (9, 409b).

Heliodorus's third-century novel *Ethiopian Story* illustrates the use of *baptizō* with reference to a boat sinking. "They killed some on land, and some they plunged [sank, βαπτιζόντων] with the boats and their cabins into [εἰς] the lake" (1.39.3). The word is associated with but distinguished from the result of sinking in the phrase, "Already being overwhelmed [βαπτιζομένων] and ready to sink [καταδῦναι]" (5.27.5).

Dio Cassius too shows how *baptizō* had become a common word for the sinking of a ship and those on it, and some of his statements could represent a causative meaning, "caused to sink." Anchored ships were submerged or sunk (caused to sink, βαπτισθῆναι) by a storm (*Roman History* 37.58.3). Some persons perished (went down or sank — βαπτισθέντες) with the vessels by reason of the latter being overloaded (41.42.5). "How should he fail to get sunk [βαπτισθείη] by the multitude of our oars [creating waves] or be sent to the bottom [καταποντωθείη] when shot at by our warriors on our decks" (50.18).[38] Some persons leaped into the sea and drowned; others struck by their enemies were submerged (ἐβαπτίζοντο) (50.35.3).[39]

A work of late antiquity loosely connected with the Orphic literature (but ascribed to Orpheus) gives a mythological use that might be considered metaphorical but by many of the ancients would have been taken as literal. It speaks of "When Titan [= Helios, the sun] was plunged [βαπτίζετο] into [ἐς] the Ocean current [ῥόον]" (Orpheus, *Argonautica* 512).[40]

I have saved Plutarch (after A.D. 50 to after 120) for last, because his frequent use of *baptizō* gives abundant illustration of classical usage in proximity to early Christian times.[41] He represents the common usage in reference to ships: the stern of a ship was submerged or plunged (ἐβάπτιζον) (*Marcellus* 15.2 = *Lives* 306). This usage applied to persons as well: "Agamemnon plunging [βαπτίζων] himself into [εἰς] [or, "gave himself a bath in"] lake Copais" (*Beasts Are Rational* 7 = *Moralia* 990E).[42] Sig-

---

38. Other passages about ships sinking: ships would sink (ἐβαπτίζοντο) (50.32.6); sinking (βαπτίζοντες) ships by stones and engines (50.32.8).

39. A similar passage relates that of those "attempting to flee in some way, some were caused to sink [ἐβαπτίζοντο] by the wind . . . others were destroyed utterly when seized by their enemies" (74.13.3). "Like sailors tempest tossed, if they make the slightest mistake, they are sure to sink [or be wholly submerged, βαπτίζονται]" (38.27.2).

40. See chap. 2 and chap. 14 (Melito of Sardis) for the ancient mythology to which this refers.

41. Plutarch's use of *bapt*- words in a literal sense in a religious context is covered in chap. 2.

42. The two uses are in a way combined in the metaphorical comparison of a person who succeeds in one difficult thing but fails in another to being "dashed against a promontory [and escaping alive] but get[ting] a ducking [βαπτίζεται] all the same" (*Precepts of Statecraft* 27 = *Moralia* 820C).

nificant for the meaning of the word is a passage about Julius Caesar, who threw himself in the sea and escaped with great difficulty by swimming:

> It was said that he was holding many papers and would not let them go, although missiles were flying at him and he was immersed [βαπτιζόμενος] in the sea; but holding them above the water in one hand he swam with the other. (*Caesar* 49.4 = *Lives* 731)

Another usage, for which Plutarch's predecessors employed *baptō*, is a person "dipping [βαπτίσας] his hand into [εἰς] his blood" and writing (*Greek and Roman Parallel Stories* 3 = *Moralia* 306C). Another instance of *baptizō* replacing *baptō* is a reference to "dipping [βαπτίζοντες] out of great wine jars" (*Alexander* 67.2 = *Lives* 702C). As a variation on the practice of tempering wine by diluting it with water, Plutarch refers to "pouring [παραχέουσι] sea water into wine" because an oracle said to "dip [βαπτίζειν] Dionysus in [πρὸς] the sea" (*Causes of Natural Phenomena* 10 = *Moralia* 9114D).[43]

In one passage Plutarch contrasts *baptizō* (submerge) with drowning: a wineskin may be submerged (βαπτίζῃ) but not permitted to sink (δῦναι) (*Theseus* 24.5 = *Lives* 11). In another passage the submersion was more lasting: he refers to armor and weapons found immersed (ἐμβαπτισμένας) in the pools (*Sulla* 21.4 = *Lives* 466). In a negative sense, Plutarch refers to the halcyon's nest that cannot be overturned or immersed (sunk — ἀβάπτιστον) (*Cleverness of Animals* 35 = *Moralia* 983C).

In a work now generally regarded as not by Plutarch, *baptizō* in a figurative sense is parallel to literal drowning in a passage important for the word meaning:

> As plants are nourished by moderate amounts of water, but are drowned [πνίγεται] by much water, in the same way the soul grows by measured tasks but is submerged [βαπτίζεται] by those that are excessive. (*Education of Children* 13 = *Moralia* 9B).

Since being under water was associated with drowning or sinking, many of the uses of βαπτίζω are in a context of (potential) destruction, but destruction does not inhere in the word itself, as is shown by the metaphorical uses.

Metaphorical Usage

Continuing with Plutarch, we find that he represents classical usage of *baptizō* not only in a literal sense with reference to ships sinking, persons drowning, objects submerged, and dipping in a liquid (water, blood, or wine), but also in a metaphorical sense of being overwhelmed whether with drunkenness, affairs of life, or debts.

---

43. Note that the pouring is not equated with the dipping, for the wine = Dionysus, which/who is not poured into the sea but rather is overwhelmed by the sea; the point of comparison is the mixture of the two elements, a practice that according to custom involved more water than wine.

Plutarch's most frequent metaphorical usage of *baptizō* is with reference to drunkenness. As might be expected, this usage occurs in his *Table Talk*: a body not sodden with (or under the influence of — ἀβάπτιστον) wine (6 int. = *Moralia* 686B); a body not yet soaked (intoxicated — βεβαπτισμένον) (3.8.2 = *Moralia* 656D). Plutarch writes of "those soused [βεβαπτισμένοις] by yesterday's debauch" (*Cleverness of Animals* 23 = *Moralia* 975C). In a quotation from an abridgement of an otherwise lost work by Aristophanes we find the phrase, "he soused [dipped — ἐβάπτισεν] the stewards" (*Summary of a Comparison between Aristophanes and Menander* 1 = *Moralia* 853B).

Plutarch furthermore writes of "those immersed [overwhelmed, βαπτιζομένους] by affairs" (*Sign of Socrates* 24 = *Moralia* 593f) and a person "immersed [overwhelmed, βεβαπτισμένον] in debts" (*Galba* 21.2 = *Lives* 1062c). In these figurative uses the point of comparison is not the manner of application of the element that overwhelms but the completeness of the effect or result. The use of *baptizō* does emphasize a total submersion, in the metaphorical sense no less than in the literal.

The metaphorical use of *baptizō* for the effects of drunkenness began quite early, if we may trust the reading of the *Greek Anthology*'s epigram attributed to Evenus (fifth century B.C.): if wine is too strong, "it plunges [βαπτίζει] to a sleep that is neighbor to death" (11.49).[44]

Plato includes a quotation showing the metaphorical use of *baptizō* for drunkenness: "I am myself one of those who yesterday was drunk [βεβαπτισμένων]" (*Symposium* 176B).[45] Plato has another figurative use — "I, knowing the youth was being overwhelmed [getting into deep water, βαπτιζόμενον] in the argument" — used next to the image of being overthrown (covered over) in a wresting match (*Euthydemus* 7, 277D).

A papyrus of the mid-second century B.C. (Papyrus Parisianus 47) was interpreted as representing sacral-cultic speech, but *baptizō* here has a secular use and is not a witness to an Egyptian "baptism."[46] Whether the usage is literal or metaphorical depends on whether ὕλην is literal ("mud") or metaphorical, as I have taken it.

> They [gods] have thrown us into a great morass and therein we could die, and if you [in a dream] have seen that we are going to be saved [from it], at the time we are overwhelmed [βαπτιζώμεθα].

Diodorus Siculus includes a metaphorical use expressing a sentiment with which modern readers can identify: Good rulers "do not overwhelm [swamp, βαπτίζουσι] private citizens by taxes" (*Library* 1.73.6).

---

44. Literal uses in the *Greek Anthology* include "a float that does not sink [ἀβάπτιστον] in the water" (6.192, line 5, Archias) and, alluding to the practice of dipping into the wine bowl, "I dipped [ἐβάπτις'] Eros [Love] into the wine" (16.388, line 4).

45. Cf the translation "got such a soaking" by W. R. M. Lamb in *Plato,* Vol. 5 (Loeb Classical Library; Cambridge: Harvard University Press, 1953).

46. Franz J. Dölger, "Die Bedeutung von βαπτίζεσθαι in einem Papyrustext des Jahres 152/151 v. Chr.," *Antike und Christentum* 2 (1930): 57-62, responding to a claim by R. Reitzenstein.

Lucian represents the usage for the effects of drink: "When an old man drinks and Silenus takes possession of him, . . . he resembles one overwhelmed (sodden, βεβαπτισμένῳ") (*Dionysus* 7).[47]

Achilles Tatius offers several examples in a variety of contexts. One statement picks up on a common literal usage (and thereby shows the basic meaning) but gives a figurative application: "Floods [περικλύζον] the brain and drowns [βαπτίζει] the source of reason" (*Leucippe and Clitophon* 4.10.1). Strictly metaphorical but showing the basic meaning of the word are the following: "Overwhelmed [overcome, βαπτισθῆναι] by such a multitude of evils" (3.10.1); "Fates befalling us overwhelm [βαπτίζουσι] us" (7.2.1);[48] "Love overwhelmed [βεβαπτισμένος] by anger sinks [καταδύεται] [in its flood]" (6.19.5). The strengthened compound form *katabaptizō* also occurs metaphorically: "Disasters astound the soul and overwhelm [κατεβάπτισε] it" (1.3.3); "Overwhelmed [stupefied, καταβαπτίσας] with the same drug" (2.31.2).

These passages show that the metaphorical use of *baptizō* involved a derived sense "to influence," but a particular kind of influence. The verb expresses that something exercises a controlling influence that brings about a change of condition. This derived metaphorical sense does not mean that *baptizō* came to mean "to influence controllingly however that was effected." Rather, the point of departure for the metaphorical usage was the completeness or thoroughness of the action expressed in submersion.

Athenaeus, again as appropriate for the setting of a drinking party, employs *baptizō* for the state of drunkenness: "soused [overwhelmed, βεβαπτίσθαι] in unmixed wine" (*Learned Banquet* 5, 221a).[49] He quotes a line from the fourth-century-B.C. comic writer Aristophon's play *Philinides*, "My master . . . having soused [βαπτίσας] me thoroughly, set me free" (11, 472d). This may also be the sense of his quotation from Eubulus, also a fourth-century-B.C. comedy writer, in his play *Nausikla*: "This is now the fourth day he has been soaking himself [βαπτίζεται], wearing out the fasting life" (Fragment 68 in Athenaeus 7, 307f). Drinking wine might not seem appropriate to the image of immersion, but the point of comparison is being overwhelmed by the influence of the liquid.

The early Greek novelist Chariton of Aphrodisias, of uncertain date but probably between the first century B.C. and second century A.D., has only the metaphorical use of *baptizō*, but these keep the literal sense close at hand in their imagery. A figurative description states, "We saw a vessel wandering in fair weather — capsized [overwhelmed, βαπτιζόμενον] in a calm because filled with its own tempest" (*Chaereas and Callirrhoë* 3.4.6). Another figurative usage, drawn from bathing customs, reads, "Dionysus, an educated man, anointed by stormy weather and dipped

---

47. Other translations include "drugged," "heavyheaded," or simply "drunk."

48. "Waters of fate are closing over my head" is the translation of S. Gaselee in Loeb Classical Library (Cambridge: Harvard University Press, 1947).

49. The verb is parallel to κολυμβήσας — plunged in the large wine jar (πίθος).

[ἐβαπτίζετο] in soul, nevertheless tried to emerge as from a mighty wave of passion" (*Chaereas and Callirrhoë* 3.2.6). There is a similar description of being overcome by passion: "Indeed, overwhelmed [βαπτιζόμενος] by passion, a high minded man he tried to bear up," and he "emerged as from a wave" (*Chaereas and Callirrhoë* 2.4.4).

Heliodorus describes a city which midnight plunged (ἐβάπτιζον) in sleep (*Ethiopian Story* 4.17.3). He most often uses *baptizō* metaphorically for being immersed in troubles. One passage illustrates Jesus' usage of the verb in reference to his death (chap. 7): "absorbed in despair and overwhelmed [βεβαπτισμένον] in (by) calamity" (2.3.4). Other uses are comparable: "Since circumstances overwhelmed [ἐβάπτιζεν] you" (5.16.2); "Let us not be engulfed [submerged, συμβαπτιζώμεθα] in his distress" (4.20.1).

Alexander of Aphrodisias, philosopher of the late second and early third century, has two uses of the phrase "soul submerged [βεβαπτισμένην] in body" (*Problems* 1.28 and 1.38), a figure of speech that keeps close to the literal meaning. He uses the strengthened form καταβαπτίζει in a more obviously metaphorical sense for the fright that "overwhelms the vital warmth of the heart" (*Problems* 1.16) and in the statement "sensation, when it experiences great pain, overwhelms nature and all their powers" (*Problems* 2.38). The same compound form occurs in the common image of the abundance of wine that immerses a person (*Problems* 1.17).

I conclude this sampling with the philosopher Plotinus. He speaks of a "mind swamped [overwhelmed, βαπτισθεὶς] either by illness or magical arts" (*Enneads* 1.4.9). He describes the soul as immersed in the body: "Soul yet plunged [βεβαπτισμένη] in the body is to sink [καταδύναι] in matter and be filled with it" (1.8.13). "Part of us is held by the body, as one has his feet in water but the rest of the body above it, we lift ourselves up by the part that is not submerged [βαπτισθέντι] in the body" (6.9.8). This statement from a third-century writer shows that the literal meaning of immersion (and that in water) was not far away even in the metaphorical uses.

Usage in Pagan Religious and Magical Contexts

For dipping in a river for religious purification, see Herodotus, *Histories* 2.47, quoted in chapter 2. For the use of words from the *bapt-* root in the magical papyri and in reference to superstitious religious practices by Plutarch see chapter 2. In general it can be said that βαπτίζω was not used by Greek writers in a technical sense for a religious bath of purification as it was used by Christians.

The *Corpus Hermeticum* uses βαπτίζω in a metaphorical sense for the religious experience of receiving the revelation of Hermes. It is helpful to quote enough of the context to see the philosophical/religious thought. Hermes speaks to Tat:

> "[God] filled a great mixing bowl with mind [distinguished in the context from reason] and sent it below, appointing a herald whom he commanded to make the following proclamation to human hearts: 'Immerse yourself [βάπτισον σεαυτήν] in the mixing bowl if your heart has the strength, if it believes you will rise up

again to the one who sent the mixing bowl below, if it recognizes the purpose of your coming to be.'

"All those who heeded the proclamation and immersed themselves in mind participated in knowledge and became perfect people because they received mind. . . ."

"I too wish to be immersed, my father."

"Unless you first hate your body, my child, you cannot love yourself, but when you have loved yourself, you will possess mind, and if you have mind, you will also have a share in the way to learn."[50]

The passage is one of the rare uses of βαπτίζω outside Judaism and Christianity for something like a ritual bath, but the word is used metaphorically and the passage gives no indication of a technical sacral sense for the verb. The literal meaning of "immerse" is the basis of the metaphorical use of being completely overwhelmed with "mind," which entails a realization of one's spiritual potential and is the means of perfection. The imagery was perhaps suggested by the use of βαπτίζω and βάπτω noted above for dipping a cup in a mixing bowl. There is no indication of a literal immersion bath in the passage.

The magical papyri demonstrate the continuation of the literal meaning of βαπτίζω in popular usage.[51] Note the fourth-century magical papyrus quoted in chapter 2. A restraining rite dated third/fourth century includes the directions: "When you have washed [λουσάμενος] and immersed yourself [βαπτισάμενος], go up to your own [room] and rest" (*PGM* VII.441-442; Betz, p. 129). "Washed" and "immersed" may be used synonymously, or if there is a difference (as is likely), "washed" is the general word and "immersed" is the specific action of dipping. In this and in the preceding passage the middle voice indicates a self-immersion.[52] A spell (fourth century?) contains an example of *baptizō* for a sunken ship. It instructs that one anoint the right eye with water from a shipwreck, but "If you cannot find water from a shipwreck, then from a sunken [βεβαπτισμένον] skiff" (*PGM* V.66-68; Betz, p. 102).

Jewish Usage

Did the βαπτ- words, especially βαπτίζω, acquire a special technical sense among Jews, distinct from their etymological background? Surviving Greek literature gives a negative answer to the question.

---

50. *Corpus Hermeticum* 4.4, 6. Translation by Brian P. Copenhaver, *Hermetica* (Cambridge: Cambridge University Press, 1992), pp. 15-16.

51. I cite the magical papyri by the numbers in K. Preisendanz and A. Henrichs, *Papyri Graecae magicae: Die griechischen Zauberpapyri*, 2 vols., 2nd edition (Stuttgart: Teubner, 1973-1974), and quote the translation in Hans Dieter Betz, ed., *The Greek Magical Papyri in Translation* (Chicago: University of Chicago Press, 1986).

52. *Baptō* is used in the instructions to "dip [βάπτε]" a leaf of metal "3 times into fire" (*PGM* XII.197; Betz, p. 161).

Baptizō is rarer in the Greek Old Testament than *baptō*, but the occurrences are significant for the word's meaning and usage. Notable is the account of the cleansing of Naaman from leprosy by washing in the Jordan River (2 Kings 5:1-14), an event not used in the New Testament as a type of Christian baptism but one that some Christians later saw as illustrating the action of baptism, its application to Gentiles, and the necessity of obedience. Naaman was a Syrian military commander afflicted with a skin disease. The prophet Elisha commanded him to wash seven times in the Jordan River. Naaman at first objected that there were better rivers in Damascus, but his servants persuaded him that if he would have done something difficult at the prophet's command, then how much more should he follow the command to "wash and be clean." When he immersed himself seven times in the Jordan, he came up with his flesh restored to that of his youth. The Greek translation uses λούω ("wash yourself," λοῦσαι) for Elisha's command with the promise that he would be purified (καθαρισθήσῃ), but βαπτίζω ("he immersed [or dipped] himself," ἐβαπτίσατο) for his compliance with the command.[53] It will be noted in the discussion of Christian usage that "wash" (λούω) often was understood as equivalent to "baptize" (βαπτίζω) and was carried out by a dipping.

The tendency toward a greater use of βαπτίζω is perhaps indicated by Aquila using it in Job 9:31, where the Old Greek used βάπτω (see above). Symmachus uses the word in rendering Psalm 68:3 (Eng. 69:2), "I was plunged [ἐβαπτίσθην] into bottomless pits," and Jeremiah 38 (Gk. 45):22, "They submerged [ἐβάπτισαν] your feet into [εἰς] the swamp." Βαπτίζω is used in a metaphorical sense in Isaiah 21:4, where the translators read a different text from the standard Hebrew, "Lawlessness overwhelms [βαπτίζει] me."

Baptizō also occurs in two deuterocanonical texts. Both refer to Jewish ritual immersions for purification. "If one is immersed [βαπτιζόμενος] after touching a corpse and touches it again, what does he profit from his washing [λουτρῷ]?" (Sir. 34:30[25]).[54] The other text refers to Judith's practice of nightly going out to purify herself and pray: "She went out [of the tent] each night to the valley of Bethulia and immersed herself [ἐβαπτίζετο] at the spring of water in the camp" (Jdt. 12:7). These two texts from the deuterocanonical writings provide early attestation for the means of purification by immersion described in the Mishnah (chap. 4).

Philo, who does not use βάπτω, employs βαπτίζω exclusively in a metaphorical sense. In accord with his classical counterparts he writes of some "before they are completely overwhelmed [βαπτισθῆναι]" with intoxication (*Contemplative Life* 5.46). More often he speaks philosophically: "The river of the senses that drowns [ἐπικλύζοντα] and overwhelms [βαπτίζοντα] the soul in the corruption of passions" (*Allegorical Laws* 3.[6].18). The senses "drown [overwhelm, βαπτίζῃ] the mind" (*Migration of Abraham* 37.204). Immoralities "plunge [βαπτίζοντα] the soul in disasters"

---

53. 2 Kings 5:10, 14.
54. This verse provides an example of the use of "washing" in reference to an immersion.

(*The Worse Attacks the Better* 48.176). "Reason is drowned [overwhelmed, βαπτι-ζομένου]" by food and drink.[55]

Josephus, apart from a rewriting of a law on purification in the Torah (*Antiquities* 4.81 [4.4.6] — chap. 4) and employing the nouns "Baptist," "baptism," and "baptizing" with reference to John the Baptist (*Antiquities* 18.116-117 [5.2] — Chap. 5), uses the βαπτ- family of words in accordance with classical and Hellenistic precedents. Thus βάπτω occurs exclusively in its secondary meaning of "to dye," as listed above. Βαπτίζω occurs more often, and the usage is both literal and metaphorical.

Josephus used βαπτίζω primarily in a literal sense with reference either to sinking a ship or drowning a person, both of which were rather thorough submersions. His most frequent use was in regard to a sinking ship. In retelling the story of Jonah Josephus refers to "the ship being about to sink [βαπτίζεσθαι]" because of the storm (*Antiquities* 9.212 [9.10.2]). Or, from another perspective, "the exceedingly high wave overwhelmed [or was sinking, ἐβάπτιζεν]" some ships (*Jewish War* 3.423 [9.3]). Josephus recounted his own experience, "When our ship foundered [or sank, βαπτισθέντος]) in the midst of the Adriatic Sea, our company of six hundred swam all night" (*Life* 3.15). He compares a coward to a ship's pilot, "who, fearing a tempest, deliberately sinks [ἐβάπτισεν] his ship prior to the thunderstorm" (*Jewish War* 3.368 [3.8.5]). The image of a sinking ship is the basis of the reverse comparison: Many distinguished Jews abandoned the city "as if it were a sinking [βαπτιζομένης] ship" (*Jewish War* 2.556 [20.1]).

Two passages connect a ship's sinking with the occupants drowning or almost so. Jews in their boats attempted to attack Romans on rafts, but "they were submerged ['sent to the bottom' or drowned, ἐβαπτίζοντο] with their boats" (*Jewish War* 3.525 [10.9]). The sinking involved in this usage of *baptizō*, however, did not always involve drowning, for in the same context we read: "When those who had been sunk [immersed, βαπτισθέντων] came up to the surface," the enemy shot arrows at them (*Jewish War* 3.527 [10.9]).

Josephus's other uses of *baptizō* for a person drowning are in his two accounts of King Herod the Great having one of his sons, Aristobulus, whom he saw as a potential center of revolt against his rule, put to death: "The boy was sent by night to Jericho, and there according to the king's command being plunged [drowned, βαπτιζόμενος] in a swimming-bath [κολυμβήθρᾳ] he died" (*Jewish War* 1.437 [1.22.2]). His later account in *Antiquities* 15.55 (3.3) gives more detail: Some of Aristobulus's friends, acting under Herod's orders, "kept pressing him down and submerging [βαπτίζοντες] him as if in sport while he was swimming, and they did not cease until they completely suffocated him." The Hellenistic usage, continued by Josephus, of *baptizō* for drowning perhaps facilitated its use by the Gospel writers (chap. 8) for Jesus's death.

Another literal use by Josephus that has precedent in classical usage was plunging a sword into a person in order to kill. A certain Simon committed suicide: "He

---

55. *On Providence* 67, quoted by Eusebius, *Preparation for the Gospel* 8.14 (399a).

plunged [ἐβάπτισεν] his whole sword [i.e., 'up to the hilt'] into [εἰς] his own throat" (*Jewish War* 2.476 [18.4]).

The picture of waters overwhelming a ship or a person provides the basis of a metaphorical use, only in this instance the people themselves do the flooding: Crowds pouring (ἐπιχεομένους) into Jerusalem at the time of the revolt against Rome "in the end overwhelmed [ἐβάπτισεν] the city" (*Jewish War* 4.137 [3.3]). Here is an instance where the manner (pouring) in which a medium (in this instance people) fill a container (a city) is distinct from the result (immersion or overwhelming), a distinction to be kept in mind in regard to some Christian texts. A figurative use, not far from the literal meaning, involves the compound ἐπιβαπτίζω: "This was, as it were, the final storm that overwhelmed [submerged, ἐπεβάπτισεν] the tempest-tossed youths" (*Jewish War* 1.535 [1.27.1]). Similar is the use of the same compound in the imagery of Josephus's flight from Jotapata having the result of "sinking [wrecking, ἐπιβαπτίσειν] it" (*Jewish War* 3.196 [3.7.15]). Josephus further represents the Hellenistic use of immersion as a metaphor for drunkenness: "Observing him in this condition, plunged [sunken, βεβαπτισμένον] by drunkenness into [εἰς] unconsciousness and sleep" (*Antiquities* 10.169 [10.9.4]).

Conclusion

Baptizō meant to dip, usually a thorough submerging, but it also meant to overwhelm and so could be used whether the object was placed in an element (which was more common) or was overwhelmed by it (often in the metaphorical usages). The secular usage for "destroy" or "perish," as in a person drowning or a ship sinking, did not make this the primary connotation; such was the effect of the submerging and one could substitute the effect for the act, but that was a secondary application. As will be seen, Christian sources maintained the basic meaning of the word. Pouring and sprinkling were distinct actions that were represented by different verbs, and this usage too continued in Christian sources. When the latter speak of the pouring out of the Holy Spirit or the sprinkling of blood, they do not use *baptizō* for these actions.[56]

---

56. I. Howard Marshall, "The Meaning of the Verb 'Baptize,'" in Stanley E. Porter and Anthony R. Cross, *Dimensions of Baptism: Biblical and Theological Studies* (London: Sheffield Academic Press, 2002), pp. 8-24, argues from the promise that Jesus would baptize with the Holy Spirit and the statement that the Spirit was poured out, among other considerations, that the meaning was "drench" or "purify" and that affusion was practiced and was a more fitting symbol of the gift of the Spirit. This conclusion emphasizing the result rather than the mode of the action neglects the basic resultant characteristic that the person (or object) was covered, submerged, or overwhelmed. See the subsequent discussion of the New Testament texts.

4. Jewish Washings, Baptismal Movements, and Proselyte Baptism

Jewish concepts and practices provide a more likely immediate context for Christian baptism than any other antecedents.[1] Ideas of purity among the Jews, however, were similar to those in their surrounding cultures. First-century Judaism, moreover, saw considerable influence from Hellenism. There was considerable variety in the purification practices among Jews and the application of water in those rites.[2]

Our main concern is background information relevant to Christian baptism and hence words of the *bapt-* root, but here we note some generalizations about usage of some other words. Λούω is to wash the whole body; νίπτω is to wash parts of the body (especially hands — Philo preferred the compound ἐκνίπτω); πλύνω is to wash inanimate things; ἀπολούω is a strengthened form stressing the complete removal of dirt; λουτρόν is the place for a bath, a bathhouse, water for a bath, or the bath itself; ῥαίνω is to sprinkle (an aspersion).[3]

---

1. F. Gavin, *The Jewish Antecedents of the Christian Sacraments* (repr. New York: KTAV, 1969), claims too much in this regard, especially in regard to proselyte baptism. N. A. Dahl, "The Origin of Baptism," in N. A. Dahl and A. S. Kapelrud, eds., *Interpretationes ad Vetus Testamentum pertinentes Sigmundo Mowinckel septuagenario messae* (Oslo: Land og kirke, 1955), pp. 36-52.

2. J. Ysebaert, *Greek Baptismal Terminology* (Nijmegen: Dekker & Van de Vegt, 1962), pp. 21-39; Jonathan D. Lawrence, *Washing in Water: Trajectories of Ritual Bathing in the Hebrew Bible and Second Temple Literature* (Atlanta: Society of Biblical Literature, 2006), discusses washing in the Hebrew Bible, Second Temple literature, and the Dead Sea Scrolls and archaeological evidence for ritual baths. He divides the uses of washing terminology into three categories: ritual (general, priestly, preparatory for a theophany, and other), metaphorical, and initiatory.

3. G. R. Beasley-Murray, "Baptism," in Colin Brown, ed., *Dictionary of New Testament Theology* (Grand Rapids: Zondervan, 1978), Vol. 3, pp. 150-154.

The Background in the Jewish Scriptures

Ceremonial Cleansing

The Law of Moses provided for ceremonial applications of water for purposes of purification and included a degree of detail lacking in Greco-Roman sources.[4] This practice applied to human beings and to inanimate objects: "Whoever touches the carcass of any [unclean animal] shall be unclean until the evening, and whoever carries any part of the carcass of any of them shall wash [πλυνεῖ][5] his clothes and be unclean until the evening."[6] Any "article of wood, cloth, skin, or sacking" on which a dead unclean animal falls "shall be dipped into water [εἰς ὕδωρ βαφήσεται], and it shall be unclean until evening."[7]

Uncleanness attached also to a person who touched the dead body of a human being, making that person unclean for seven days. On the third and seventh days a clean person poured running water [ὕδωρ ζῶν] into a vessel containing the ashes of a burnt purification offering, dipped [βάπτω] hyssop into the water mixed with ashes, and sprinkled it on whoever touched the corpse or the grave:

> The clean person shall sprinkle [περιρρανεῖ] the unclean ones on the third day and on the seventh day, thus purifying him on the seventh day. Then he shall wash [πλυνεῖ] his clothes and bathe himself in water [λούσεται ὕδατι], and at evening he shall be clean.[8]

Other occasions of ceremonial defilement required the use of water in purification. A man after a discharge of semen and a woman after the discharge of her monthly period were ceremonially unclean and had to wash their clothes and bathe in water; so did anyone who touched them, their clothing, or their bedding.[9]

A distinction was made in the vocabulary employed for washing clothes and bathing, and between dipping an object and pouring and sprinkling various substances. This is illustrated by the account of the cleansing of a person cured of a skin disease:

> [The priest] shall take the living bird with the cedarwood and the crimson yarn and the hyssop, and dip [βάψει] them and the living bird in the blood of the bird

---

4. A. Y. Collins, "The Origin of Christian Baptism," *Studia Liturgica* 19 (1989): 28-46, finds both Christian and Rabbinic baptism rooted in the washings in Leviticus.

5. Since most Christians read the Jewish Bible in the Greek of the Septuagint translation, I give its readings as relevant for Christian usage.

6. Lev. 11:24; also 11:28, 39-40.

7. Lev. 11:32. On the word usage here and in subsequent passages see chap. 3.

8. Num. 19:17-20. The person who was not sprinkled with the "water of cleansing" [ὕδωρ τοῦ ῥαντισμοῦ, "sprinkling"] remained unclean — 19:20. For Josephus's rewriting of this law (*Antiquities* 4.81 [4.4.6]) see chap. 3 under βάπτω.

9. Lev. 15:5-13, 16-18, 19-27. An additional word, νίπτω, is also used in this context for washing or rinsing hands and objects — Lev. 15:11-12.

that was slaughtered over the fresh water. He shall sprinkle [περιρρανεῖ] it seven times upon the one who is to be cleansed of the leprous disease; then he shall pronounce him clean. . . . The one who is to be cleansed shall wash [πλυνεῖ] his clothes, and shave off all his hair, and bathe [λούσεται] himself in water, and he shall be clean. . . .

The priest shall take some of the . . . oil and pour [ἐπιχεεῖ] it into the palm of his own left hand, and dip [βάψει] his right finger in the oil that is in his left hand and sprinkle [ῥανεῖ] some oil with his finger seven times before the Lord.[10]

These passages are representative of the use of βάπτω in the Greek Old Testament. For a complete listing see chapter 3. It most often translates the Hebrew טבל, *ṭabal*, "to dip." The Hebrew and the Greek maintain different word usage for bathing and washing from dipping or immersing *(ṭabal, baptō)*. The use of "living" (ζῶν), "running," water is specified in Numbers 5:17; 19:17; Leviticus 14:5, 50-53.

The ritual requirements of the Law provided the imagery and vocabulary for the prophetic description of God's future purification of his people. Thus Ezekiel quotes God: "I will sprinkle [ῥανῶ] clean water upon you, and you shall be clean from all your uncleannesses, and from all your idols I will cleanse you. A new heart I will give you, and a new spirit I will put within you."[11]

Events Seen as Prefiguring Baptism

The Jewish scriptures recorded events that the New Testament and later Christian writers saw as types foreshadowing Christian baptism. The two most popular were the flood and the crossing of the Red Sea, both so interpreted already in the New Testament. The flood in the days of Noah covered the earth with water and by destroying all human life except the immediate family of Noah removed wickedness temporarily from the world.[12] This event was viewed as a type of baptism that saves.[13] Israel's crossing of the Red Sea on dry land brought their deliverance from slavery in Egypt.[14] The walls of water on each side and the cloud overhead gave a picture of baptism that brings deliverance.[15] Another event, not used in the New Testament as

---

10. Lev. 14:6-8, 15-16. Shaving, washing clothes, and bathing were repeated on the seventh day — 14:9; the instructions about the oil are also in 14:26-27. Cf. 14:51 for the cleansing of a house by dippping the same materials in blood and fresh water and then sprinkling the house.

11. Ezek. 36:25-26. Cf. Isa. 1:16-17; Ps. 51:6-11. See further in chap. 5 on the prophetic background to John the Baptist's baptism.

12. Gen. 6:1–8:22.

13. First in 1 Pet. 3:20-21. The grammatical problems in the passage (whether the antecedent is the ark or the water, and whether the salvation was by water or through water) will be discussed in chap. 11.

14. Exod. 14:1–15:21.

15. 1 Cor. 10:1-2. The imagery and the meaning to be derived from it are discussed in chap. 9. F. J. Dölger, "Der Durchzug durch das Rote Meer als Sinnbild der christlichen Taufe: Zum Oxyrhynchos-Papyrus Nr. 840," *Antike und Christentum* 2 (1930): 63-69, gives many references to this interpretation,

a type of Christian baptism, that some Christians later saw as illustrating the action of baptism, its application to Gentiles, and the necessity of obedience was the cleansing of Naaman from leprosy by washing in the Jordan River.[16]

Mishnah and *Mikvaoth*

The Mishnah is a codification of the oral law of the Pharisees and scribes. It was compiled under the leadership of Rabbi Judah the Prince about A.D. 200. The Mishnah gives an abstract and idealized picture of the Jewish law, but as drawing on earlier material it often contains information contemporary with New Testament times.

The division of the Mishnah on "Purity," *Tohoroth*, details regulations for the ceremonies prescribed for purification in the Law and sampled above. These regulations preserve the distinctions in the Law between the actions and occasions for sprinkling, pouring, and dipping.[17] The correct intention must accompany each immersion, for an immersion without special intention was as though a person had not immersed himself.[18] The prescriptions understand the washing or bath for purification required in the Law as an immersion. These were particularly stringent for the priests. For example, the high priest on the Day of Atonement immersed himself five times; he removed his clothes, immersed himself, dried himself, and put on the priestly garments.[19]

One tractate, *Mikw(v)aoth* (or "Immersion-Pools"), is devoted to the water to be used for the cleansing baths.[20] The tractate begins (1.1-8) by distinguishing six

---

pointing out that it was natural to apply this meaning to entering and exiting the baptismal pool. Oxyrhynchus Papyrus 840 is discussed in chap. 13. A companion article by idem, "Der Durchzug durch den Jordan als Sinnbild der christlichen Taufe," *Antike und Christentum* 2 (1930): 70-79, sees the crossing of the Red Sea as negative (destruction of evil forces) and crossing the Jordan as positive (entrance into the promised land).

16. 2 Kings 5:1-14. Discussed in chap. 3.

17. Note especially the tractates *Nega'im* (e.g. 14.10 — pouring oil into the hand, dipping the finger in it, and sprinkling the oil) and *Parah* (e.g. 12.11 — dipping the hyssop and then sprinkling what adheres to it as distinct from immersing the body). In *Berakoth* 3.5 a person goes down to immerse himself, but if the water is foul, he pours clean water into it.

18. *Hagigah* 2.6. The rabbis too gave a spiritualizing interpretation of the Law. For instance, Rabban Johanan ben Zakkai (died c. 80) was quoted as saying that a corpse did not defile and water did not purify, but it is an ordinance of the King of Kings (*Pesiqta* 40b; Herman L. Strack and Paul Billerbeck, *Kommentar zum Neuen Testament aus Talmud und Midrasch*, third edition [Munich: C. H. Beck, 1961], Vol. 1, p. 719).

19. *Yoma* 3.3-4.

20. I follow the translation and notes of Herbert Danby, *The Mishnah* (London: Oxford University Press, 1933), pp. 732-745. Jacob Neusner, *A History of the Mishnaic Law of Purities*, Vol. XIII, *Miqvaoth: Commentary* (Leiden: Brill, 1976); Vol. XIV, *Miqvaoth: Literary and Historical Problems*; repr. *The Judaic Law of Baptism: Tractate Miqvaot in the Mishnah and the Tosefta* (Atlanta: Scholars, 1995) (includes a literal translation). Neusner identifies four stages in the development of the tractate: before 70, Yavneh, Usha, and post-Usha (pp. 99-109). He summarizes the four major topics of the tractate as:

grades among pools of water according to their degree of purity. In ascending order of excellence they are the water in a small pond, the water in a pond while rain is falling in it, the water in a pond containing forty seahs or more of water (estimates range from 77 to 140 gallons or 292 to 532 liters, which was sufficient for a total immersion of a person), a well whose water can be increased by drawn water, smitten waters (i.e., salty like the Mediterranean Sea or from a hot spring), and (most excellent of all) "living waters" (flowing water, which could serve for all occasions of immersion, for sprinkling of lepers, and for mixing with the ashes of the sin offering.[21]

The requirements of the tractate *Mikwaoth* clearly point to a total submersion.[22] For a valid immersion, water had to touch all parts of the body.[23] Detailed regulations covered the size of an artificial immersion pool to permit a complete immersion and what constituted clean water to fill it. The size once again had to be sufficient to hold the forty seahs of water and to have a depth to permit a grown person to cover the body in it.[24] Two pools could be connected by a pipe so that clean water from one could flow into the other and so purify its water (clean water purified other water).[25] The Talmud makes provision for throwing nine kabs of water over a person as an alternative to immersion.[26]

Excavations have revealed hundreds of mikvaoth in Israel, over 150 from the first century in Jerusalem alone (including those adjoining the temple mount) as well as many at Jericho, Gamla, Masada, and Herodium from the period before the destruction of the temple.[27] These come in two types: (1) most of the early mikvaoth

---

(1) An immersion pool is formed by rainwater, which is still and not flowing; (2) drawn water (passing through a utensil) spoils the water; (3) water mingles and takes on the character of the predominant element; (4) one must allow the water to touch all parts of the body or utensil (Vol. XIV, p. 178).

21. Cf. the discussion of various waters in *Mikwaoth* 5 and *Parah* 8.8-11.

22. C. F. Rogers, "How Did the Jews Baptize?" *Journal of Theological Studies* 12 (1911): 437-445, argued that the requirement was to bathe the whole body without a stress on submersion. I. Abrahams, "'How Did the Jews Baptize?'" replied in the same journal (609-612) with the evidence for a complete immersion. Later discoveries and studies have supported Abrahams's conclusion.

23. *Mikwaoth* 8.5; 9.1-4; b. *'Erubin* 4b.

24. *Mikwaoth* 2.2 and passim. b. *'Erubin* 14b reckons a minimum size of one cubit by one cubit square and three cubits high.

25. *Mikwaoth* 6.7-9.

26. b. *Berakoth* 22a.

27. Lawrence, *Washing in Water*, pp. 155-183; 251-268, charts the information on the 286 possible *miqva'ot* identified by Ronny Reich in his dissertation in Hebrew at the Hebrew University in Jerusalem, 1990, plus some discovered later, with additional literature. See also Ehud Netzer, "Ancient Ritual Baths *(Miqvaot)* in Jericho," in Lee I. Levine, ed., *The Jerusalem Cathedra*, Vol. 2 (Detroit: Wayne State University Press, 1982), pp. 106-119 (many are Hasmonean and quite large); William L. LaSor, "Discovering What Jewish Miqva'ot Can Tell Us about Christian Baptism," *Biblical Archaeology Review*, January-February 1987, pp. 52-59, with corrections by Ronny Reich in the July-August issue, pp. 59-60; E. P. Sanders, *Jewish Law from Jesus to the Mishnah* (Philadelphia: Trinity Press International, 1990), pp. 214-227 (everyone agreed there should be pools and that they should be large enough for immersion, but there was no uniformity on how much water and what constituted pure water); Y. Magen, "The Ritual Baths *(Miqva'ot)* at Qedumim and the Observance of Ritual Purity among the Samaritans," in F. Manns, ed., *Early Christianity in Context: Monuments and Documents* (Jerusalem: Franciscan, 1993),

were of the single-pool variety (those below the level of a spring and fed from it by an aqueduct would have met Pharisaic requirements for pure water; in others water was probably changed by hand); (2) some have a double pool, one for storing the pure water (the later Hebrew name was *'otsar*) and another for the actual immersion, and this type later became standard. Nearly every excavated stepped mikveh exceeded the minimum rabbinic requirement of one cubit (about 46 centimeters) by one cubit, with a height of three cubits (138 centimeters or just over four and one-half feet). These show that the requirements of the Mishnah about the size and construction of mikvaoth, if not the details of rabbinic decisions about purity regulations, rest on earlier practice and that many people kept the purity laws.

Other References to Jewish Washings

Forms of λούω were the most common for complete washing or bathing in Jewish purifications. Thus, after handling a dead body, Tobit said, "I washed myself" (ἐλουσάμην).[28] One manuscript (E) of the *Testament of Levi* in the *Testament of the Twelve Patriarchs*, containing information not in the other manuscripts but supported in part by the Aramaic fragments from Qumran, says: "Then I washed my clothes and cleansed them in pure water, and I wholly washed myself in living water [ἐλουσάμην ἐν ὕδατι ζῶντι], and I made all my ways straight."[29] All the Greek manuscripts of the *Testament of Levi* elsewhere refer to Levi's washing as part of his consecration to the priesthood.[30] The work gives the instructions, "Before entering into the holies, bathe [λούου]; while sacrificing, wash [νίπτου]; and again when the sacrifice is completed, wash [νίπτου]."[31]

Philo noted the requirement of the Law that a priest who touched an impure object or had a nocturnal emission must bathe himself (λουσάμενος) and be impure until evening.[32] His word usage is evident where, following the vocabulary of the Greek Bible, he distinguishes "washings [λουτροῖς] and sprinklings [περιρραν-

---

pp. 181-192 (six mikvaoth found at Qedumim — showing the concern with ritual purity among the Samaritans — one arguably from the first century, all of the single-pool type holding more than forty seahs of water, and identical to those found around Jerusalem); Ronny Reich, "Design and Maintenance of First-Century Ritual Immersion Baths," *Jerusalem Perspective* 56 (1999):14-19; Ronny Reich, "They Are Ritual Baths," *Biblical Archaeology Review*, March-April 2002, pp. 50-55 (On Sepphoris).

28. Tobit 2:5.

29. *Testament of Levi* 2.3 B1-2, in a passage expressing cleansing from sin and conversion to God. See the discussion in Robert L. Webb, *John the Baptiser and Prophet* (Sheffield: JSOT Press, 1991), pp. 116-120.

30. *Testament of Levi* 8.5, "The second person washed me with pure water [ἔλουσέ με ὕδατι καθαρῷ]." Philo, *Life of Moses* 2.143 (28.157), makes a similar statement about the consecration of priests: "He washed them with the purest and most living spring water [λούει . . . ὕδατι πηγῆς τῷ καθαρωτάτῳ καὶ ζωτικωτάτῳ]."

31. *Testament of Levi* 9.11.

32. *On Special Laws* 1.24.119.

τηρίοις]," and points out that the sprinkling required by the Law did not employ "unmixed water" but water poured (ἐπιφέρειν) over ashes. "The priests then dipped [βάπτοντας] branches of hyssop in the mixture and sprinkled [ἐπιρραίνειν] those being purified."[33] Philo could have been speaking for Greeks as well as for Jews when he said, "Men are sanctified when washed with water, while the water itself (is sanctified) by the divine foot."[34]

Josephus refers to the requirement of Leviticus 15:18 that after intercourse between husband and wife, a bath was required; he strengthens the Septuagint's λούσονται ("they shall wash themselves") to ἀπολούσασθαι (his usual word for ceremonial washings).[35] Elsewhere he interprets the purification for a nocturnal emission (Lev. 15:16) as requiring "going down into cold water,"[36] indicative of an immersion.

The book of *Jubilees* does not survive in Hebrew or Greek, but the Ethiopic version uses the terminology of washing. The book's rewriting of Genesis pushes the requirements of the Law back into the time of the patriarchs. Thus Abraham commands Isaac:

> And at all the (appointed) times be pure in your body and wash yourself with water before you go to make an offering upon the altar. And wash your hands and your feet before you approach the altar. And when you have completed making the offering, wash your hands and feet again.[37]

The Jewish *Sibylline Oracles*, in praising the Jewish manner of life, refers to daily water purifications by Jews: "At dawn from their bed they lift holy arms to heaven, always purifying their flesh with water."[38] The work refers to the current belief that the sun, when it set, was dipped [βαπτισθείη] in the water of the ocean.[39] It also contains a call to conversion involving a close parallel to the baptism of repentance preached by John the Baptist:

---

33. *On Special Laws* 1.48.261–1.49.263; he notes that "almost all other people [non-Jews] sprinkle [περιρραίνονται]" with unmixed water taken from the sea, rivers, or springs. *On Special Laws* 3.10.63 uses the same combination of λουτροῖς and περιρραντηρίοις for the purifications by husbands and wives after intercourse; so also 1.48.257-258.

34. *Questions and Answers on Genesis* 4.5; tr. Ralph Marcus in Loeb Classical Library, *Philo: Supplement I* (Cambridge: Harvard University Press, 1953), p. 277. The reference to "foot" comes from the fact that Philo is commenting on Gen. 18:4.

35. Josephus, *Against Apion* 2.24.203. Cf. 2.23.198 for "purifications [ἁγνείας] after a funeral, child-birth, intercourse with one's wife, and many other occasions."

36. Josephus, *Antiquities* 3.263 (3.11.4).

37. *Jubilees* 21.16. Translation by O. S. Wintermute in James H. Charlesworth, ed., *The Old Testament Pseudepigrapha*, Vol. 2 (Garden City: Doubleday, 1985), p. 96.

38. *Sibylline Oracles* 3.591-593. The reading "flesh" is found in the quotation by Clement of Alexandria, *Exhortation* 6.70, instead of the manuscripts' "hands." "Flesh" would allow the meaning of a bath instead of only washing hands.

39. *Sibylline Oracles* 5.478. The passage refers to the eschatological disappearance of the sun, "setting never to rise again."

Miserable mortals, change these things, ... and wash [λούσασθε] your whole bodies in ever flowing rivers. Stretch out your hands to the sky and ask forgiveness for your previous deeds. ... God will grant repentance and will not destroy.[40]

It is not clear whether this is a call to the nations to receive proselyte baptism, whether it reflects Essene influence, whether it is an extension of usual purification washings by Jews to include a promise of forgiveness of sins, or whether it reflects a semi-sacramental rite by a Jewish baptizing group similar to others to be discussed below.[41] The language reflects Jewish usage of λούω for a complete bath or immersion. The reference in one passage to "illumined by waters, born from above [γεννηθέντες ἄνωθεν]" is part of a Christian insertion in a Jewish passage.[42]

According to the *Life of Adam and Eve* 6-7 (= *Apocalypse of Moses* 29.11-13), the presumed Hebrew original of which may come from the late first century A.D., Eve stood in the Tigris River with the water to her neck and Adam in the Jordan River. Although a requirement for a ritual bath was that the water reach to one's neck (*b. Yoma* 87a) and in proselyte baptism a woman was in the water to her neck for decency (*b. Yebamoth* 47b — see below), Eve and Adam's standing in the water was an act of penitence (she undertook to stand there 37 days, Adam 40 days) and seems unrelated to ritual purification. The Greek *Life of Adam and Eve* (= *Apocalypse of Moses*), in a passage for which there is no counterpart in the Latin, says of Adam after his death: "One of the six-winged seraphim came and carried Adam off to [εἰς] the Lake of Acheron and washed [ἀπέλουσεν] him three times in the presence of God" (37.3).[43] Adam was then taken to "Paradise, the third heaven," and his body was buried in the earthly paradise. The washing "three times" is missing in some manuscripts and may be a Christian addition.[44]

---

40. *Sibylline Oracles* 4.162-170, dated A.D. 80.

41. This last is the view of Joseph Thomas, *Le mouvement baptiste en Palestine et Syrie (150 av. J.-C.-300 ap. J.-C.)* (Gembloux: J. Duculot, 1935), pp. 46-59, who suggests that the bath represents the thought of Isaiah 1:15-16, except taken literally and not as a metaphor.

42. *Sibylline Oracles* 1.339-341. See J. J. Collins, "The Sibylline Oracles," in James H. Charlesworth, *The Old Testament Pseudepigrapha* (Garden City: Doubleday, 1983), 1:341-343; he dates the Christian insertion c. 150 (p. 332). As will become evident in later chapters, illumination and begetting from above were characteristic Christian descriptions of baptism.

43. Translation by M. D. Johnson, "Life of Adam and Eve," in James H. Charlesworth, ed., *The Old Testament Pseudepigrapha* (Garden City: Doubleday, 1985), Vol. 2, pp. 289, 291. The passage is studied by Marinus de Jonge and L. Michael White, "The Washing of Adam in the Acherusian Lake (Greek *Life of Adam and Eve* 37.3) in the Context of Early Christian Notions of the Afterlife," in John T. Fitzgerald et al., eds., *Early Christianity and Classical Culture: Comparative Studies in Honor of Abraham J. Malherbe* (Leiden: Brill, 2003), pp. 609-635.

44. That the passage is Christian is argued by Marinus de Jonge and L. Michael White (preceding note). If it was part of the Jewish original, then there would be a Jewish background for the baptism of the righteous dead in Hermas (chap. 12) and the *Apocalypse of Peter* (chap. 13).

Essenes and Dead Sea Scrolls[45]

Josephus's description of the Essenes includes the information that after one year of probation a candidate for membership in the sect was allowed to "share in the purer kind of waters for purity," but only after two more years of testing was he received into the meetings of the society. He adds this information about the Essenes' daily routine:

> They work strenuously until the fifth hour and again assemble in one area. After girding their loins with linen cloths, they bathe [ἀπολούονται] the body in cold water. After this purification, they assemble in a private room, which no one who is not of their sect is permitted to enter.

He further notes that after defecation, "They make it a rule to wash themselves [ἀπολούεσθαι] as if defiled." A senior member of the Essenes had to take a bath (ἀπλούεσθαι) if touched by a lesser member or by a foreigner. There were both celibate and married Essenes, and in reference to the latter Josephus informs us that "In the bath [λουτρά] the women wear a dress and the men a loincloth."[46] Such concern for modesty was in contrast to the Greek and Roman custom of nude bathing. Josephus says that he studied three years with an ascetic in the wilderness named Bannus, who may have been an Essene. Bannus "washed himself [λουόμενον] for purity frequently by day and night in cold water."[47]

The Dead Sea Scrolls offer comparable information.[48] I concur with the judgment of the majority of scholars that the community at Qumran responsible for the Dead Sea Scrolls were Essenes or a branch of the Essenes. The information in Josephus indicates that the baths of the Essenes were a strict application of the purifications of Judaism. The Dead Sea Scrolls are consistent with this but may indicate an extension of the imagery of cleansing and an intensification of the practices current in Judaism, including perhaps an effort to extend priestly purity to the whole community.

The *Community Rule* declares of the wicked, who shall not enter the community:

> He shall not be reckoned among the perfect; he shall neither be purified by atonement, nor cleansed by purifying waters, nor sanctified by seas and rivers, nor washed clean with any ablution. Unclean, unclean shall he be. . . .

---

45. Robert L. Webb, *John the Baptiser and Prophet*, pp. 133-162, on ablutions at Qumran; Hermann Lichtenberger, "Baths and Baptism," in *Encyclopedia of the Dead Sea Scrolls*, ed. L. H. Schiffman and J. C. VanderKam (Oxford: Oxford University Press, 2000), pp. 85-89; further bibliography in chap. 5 on John the Baptist's possible connections with Qumran.

46. Josephus, *The Jewish War* 2.138 (8.7), 129 (8.5), 149 (8.9), 150 (8.10), 161 (8.13).

47. Josephus, *Life* 11 (2).

48. Todd S. Beall, *Josephus' Description of the Essenes Illustrated by the Dead Sea Scrolls* (Cambridge: Cambridge University Press, 1988), pp. 55-57, for commentary on Josephus's passage about the daily bath compared with the Dead Sea Scrolls. Lawrence, *Washing in Water*, pp. 81-154, discusses washing in the Dead Sea Scrolls.

> When his flesh is sprinkled with purifying water and sanctified by cleansing water, it shall be made clean by the humble submission of his soul to all the precepts of God.

A righteous life (repentance), therefore, was necessary for the bath and other rituals to be effective. The "sprinkled water" in reference to the novices coincides with the cleansing for corpse impurity in what became normative Judaism.[49] The document continues, contrasting those who "enter the covenant of God" with "men of injustice who walk in the way of wickedness" by saying of the latter:

> They shall not enter the water to partake of the pure meal of the men of holiness, for they shall not be cleansed unless they turn from their wickedness, for all who transgress His word are unclean.[50]

In between these statements the document says:

> [God] will cleanse him of all wicked deeds with the spirit of holiness; like purifying water he will shed upon him the spirit of truth (to cleanse him) of all abomination and injustice. And he shall be plunged into the spirit of purification.[51]

The document uses the biblical language of purification for a cleansing that is both spiritual and physical. Daily baths for purification are implied. In keeping with Josephus's description, a bath preceded the community meal, to which only the full members of the community in a requisite state of purity could partake.[52] The description of those who enter the community stresses the oath to observe the Law of Moses according to the understanding of its members and to separate from all others,[53] and this oath seems to have been central to the initiation. The mention of entering the water in this connection may imply that the first bath had a special meaning, but on our present knowledge this cannot be proved.[54] The Qumran covenanters did link their cleansing by water with moral purity.

---

49. Pointed out by Jodi Magness, *The Archaeology of Qumran and the Dead Sea Scrolls* (Grand Rapids: Eerdmans, 2002), pp. 137-142. She notes the phrase "sprinkling waters" also in 4Q284, 5 and that sprinkling occurred at Qumran (as in biblical texts) after an immersion for other types of impurity — e.g., in *Temple Scroll* (11Q19) xlix-li (portions cited below). The sprinkled water was mixed with the ashes of a red heiffer.

50. 1QS iii.4-9 and v. 13. Translation by Geza Vermes, *The Complete Dead Sea Scrolls in English* (New York: Penguin, 1997), pp. 100-101. The fragment named *Ordinances c* (4Q514) 1.i.5-7 also says that one may not eat sacred food until washed for purification. For strong condemnations of wickedness see 1QS ii.4-10, ii.25-iii.4.

51. 1QS iv.21-22.

52. Cf. Mishnah *Hagigah* 2.6 for an immersion before eating.

53. 1QS v.8-11.

54. L. Cerfaux, "Le baptême des Esséniens," *Recherches de science religieuse* 19 (1929): 248-265, before the discovery of the Dead Sea Scrolls, deduced from Josephus's account a bath different from the daily baths (pp. 250-257); the latter were comparable to the sacrifices at the temple. Otto Betz, "Die Proselytentaufe der Qumransekte und die Taufe im Neuen Testament," *Revue de Qumran* 1 (1958): 213-

Most of the passages in the Dead Sea Scrolls on purification, and it is impressive how many there are, repeat or interpret the biblical instructions.[55] The *Temple Scroll* contains the procedures for purification for touching a corpse,[56] and for purification after a nocturnal emission and sexual intercourse (including "bathe his whole body in running water").[57] The fragments of *Purification Rules A* require the person with a skin disease and a woman after menstruation to bathe in water and wash her clothes.[58] The *Halakic Letter* contains the provision in the ceremony of the sacrifice of the heifer for a sin offering that "the pure man may sprinkle upon the impure one."[59] There is also the provision for the leper to be shaved and washed for his purification.[60]

The Dead Sea Scrolls maintain the distinctions in the Old Testament in terminology for washing, bathing, sprinkling, and immersing.[61] A ruling in 4QMMT B55-58 indicates a rejection of the position taken by the rabbis later that water from a pure source purified impure water (as in the miqvaoth with double pools).

One of the fragments of the *Damascus Document* refers to the sprinkling of a garment or vessel defiled by a corpse.[62] A "hybrid text" similar to the *Rule of the Community* and to the *Damascus Document* says not to sprinkle purifying water on the Sabbath.[63] The *Damascus Document* requires that no one entering the house of

---

234, argued that the bath in the *Community Rule* was initiatory and different from the daily baths described by Josephus but comparable to proselyte baptism (pp. 216-220); Joachim Gnilka, "Die essenischen Tauchbäder und die Johannestaufe," *Revue de Qumran* 3 (1961): 185-207, responded with a thorough study, concluding that the first bath was not different from other baths and was not similar to proselyte baptism (p. 191), although the whole framework of the community was oriented to conversion and the coming wrath of judgment (p. 192); the basis of the Qumran covenanters' practices was an extension of the priestly purifications of the Pentateuch (pp. 193, 195) but with a recognition that true purification came from God's Spirit and must await the end-time (pp. 194, 196). Webb, *John the Baptiser and Prophet*, pp. 159-162, argues from 1QS ii.25-iii.9, vv. 7-15 for a special initiatory immersion at Qumran. Joan E. Taylor, *The Immerser: John the Baptist within Second Temple Judaism* (Grand Rapids: Eerdmans, 1997), pp. 76-88, rejects the idea that immersion was initiatory at Qumran and Webb's claim that Qumran's washings cleansed a person from inner defilement (p. 79). Todd S. Beall, *Josephus' Description of the Essenes*, p. 57, finds no evidence of a sacramental meaning in Essene baths: "Both in Josephus and Qumran literature, the washings were performed for reasons of ritual purity." Lawrence, *Washing in Water*, pp. 135-141, surveys the debate over an initiatory bath by the community of the Dead Sea Scrolls and concludes that bathing was part of the initiation even though never explicitly stated.

55. Such is the case with 4Q514 (Vermes, p. 499).

56. 11Q19 *(Temple)* xlix.16-21.

57. 11Q19 *(Temple)* xlv.7-15. Other references to "running" (literally "living") water are found in Lawrence, *Washing in Water*, pp. 84, 87, 132-134.

58. 4Q274 i.1-9 (Vermes, pp. 230-231).

59. 4QMMT (4Q395) 14-17 (Vermes, p. 223).

60. 4Q397 (Vermes, p. 226).

61. Lawrence, *Washing in Water*, pp. 84, 110-111, 142, 146 with reference to 4Q274, 2.1.1-9; 4Q265.7. 3.8-9; 4Q414, 13.1-10.

62. CD, 4Q271, fr. 2.

63. 4Q265, fr. 7. ii.

worship shall come unclean and in need of washing.[64] It also contains requirements for the water to be used in the ceremonial bath similar to those recorded later in the Mishnah:

> No man shall bathe in dirty water or in an amount too shallow to cover a man. He shall not purify himself with water contained in a vessel. And as for the water of every rock-pool too shallow to cover a man, if an unclean man touches it he renders its water as unclean as water contained in a vessel.[65]

The intention is clearly that the bath involve the covering the body with water. Such accords with the size of the immersion pools found at Qumran. Although some of the elaborate water works at the site were to fill cisterns for the storage of water, some of the pools were designed primarily for the ritual bathing.[66]

Baptismal Movements

A work identifying a distinctive "baptismal movement" makes the point that in pagan religion and Judaism baths that symbolized interior purity were unknown and this goes even more so for baths that would positively produce this effect, but this view did emerge among certain Jewish groups around the beginning of the Christian era.[67] Whether the existence of such a movement can be established before John

---

64. CD xi.21 (Vermes, p. 110).
65. CD x.10-14 (Vermes, pp. 108-109); cf. xi.1-2.
66. B. G. Wood, "To Dip or Sprinkle? The Qumran Cisterns in Perspective," *Bulletin of the American Schools of Oriental Research* 256 (1984): 45-60, who concludes the Qumran community most certainly dipped, which accords with what we know of the practice codified in the Mishnah; Magness, *The Archaeology of Qumran and the Dead Sea Scrolls*, pp. 142-147, gives the archaeological evidence for miqva'ot (immersion pools) of the Second Temple Period, and on pp. 147-158, she describes the pools at Qumran — those for purification by immersion being distinguished by steps and plaster. Reich, "Design and Maintenance of First-Century Ritual Immersion Baths," 14-19, notes that of the ten stepped chambers at Qumran six are similar to excavated mikvaoth and that the stepless water installations would have contained sufficient water to support 200 people. Lawrence, *Washing in Water*, pp. 173-179, including a chart on the characteristics of the ten mikvaoth at Qumran.
67. Thomas, *Le mouvement baptiste*, p. 350. For information on these groups, see pp. 34-45. He identifies the following characteristics of the baptist movement: a bath of incorporation into the sect, other baths for purity and sometimes healing, a high estimate of water, especially "living water," and the baths attaining the level of worship as the central act of cult and focus of the religious life, and a rejection of animal sacrifice — pp. 274-284. For a more recent comprehensive survey, Kurt Rudolph, *Antike Baptisten: Zu den Überlieferungen über frühjudische und -christliche Taufsekten*, Sitzungsberichte der Sachsischen Akademie der Wissenschaft zu Leipzig 121.4 (Berlin: Akademie, 1981), pp. 5-37. He gives as their characteristics the use of flowing water, repetition of ritual washings, rejection of sacrifice and the temple cult, and a tendency to syncretism. The presupposition for their development was Jewish washings (as Lev. 15); they represent a radicalizing and a strengthened desire for purity linked with ascetic tendencies, a spiritualizing of cult, and eventually a divinizing (Elchasai) of water as purifying (pp. 21-23). Earlier Cerfaux, "Le baptême des Esséniens," pp. 264-265, identified the

the Baptist is problematical. Other than the Essenes (above and chap. 5) and the solitary ascetic Bannus reported by Josephus, Jewish groups for whom baptizing was a prominent or even central feature are known only for the post-70 period. The positing of an earlier date for the groups discussed below is based on their inclusion among lists by Christian heresiologists of Jewish sects along with those that are pre-Christian (Sadducees, Pharisees) but without an express indication of their date or the nature of their baptismal practice.[68]

Hegesippus in the latter part of the second century listed seven sects among the Jews, one of which were the Hemerobaptists (Ἡμεροβαπτισταί).[69] The name means those who practice daily baptisms. The name occurs in a similar but different listing of seven Jewish sects in Epiphanius, who ascribes to the rite the washing away of sins.[70] The *Apostolic Constitutions* says of them, "Unless they wash, they do not eat" and "unless they cleanse their beds, tables, platters, cups, and seats" they do not make use of them.[71] A Jewish-Christian source in the Pseudo-Clementines uses the word of John the Baptist but also implies he held gnosticizing ideas, because he esteemed Simon Magus as his foremost disciple. The information is suspect, unless some of John's disciples later added some of these practices and ideas, for the description reflects sharp antagonism of some Jewish-Christians against them.[72] It is possible that the Hemerobaptists are the same as the "Baptists" (Βαπτιστῶν) mentioned by Justin, who includes them similarly in a list of seven Jewish sects.[73] The rabbinic references to "Morning Baptists" may refer to them.[74] Nothing beyond what can be inferred from their name is known of them. A reasonable conjecture is

---

Essenes as only the most important branch of a heterodox Judaism given to daily baptism in running water. I have not seen the still earlier work by Wilhelm Brandt, *Die jüdischen Baptismen* (Giessen: Töpelmann, 1910).

68. The nearest to giving a pre-Christian date to them is Epiphanius, *Panarion* 1.19.5.4-7, who says that of four sects bewitched by Elxai (Elchasai — see below, period of Trajan) two came after him (Ebionites and Nazoraeans) and two before (Ossaeans and Nasaraeans), and that the Ossaeans "persisted till the coming of Christ" and after the fall of Jerusalem it and other sects dispersed — "Sadducees, Scribes, Pharisees, Hemerobaptists, Ossaeans, Nasareans, and Herodians." He says nothing of baptismal practices by the Ossaeans before their contact with Elchasai, but he implies the contemporaneous existence of the Hemerobaptists.

69. Eusebius, *Church History* 4.22.7. Rudolph, *Antiken Baptisten,* between pp. 16-17 has a foldout chart of lists of Jewish sects according to Josephus and eight church fathers.

70. Epiphanius, *Ancoratus* 17; *Anacephalaiosis* 1.17 — one cannot obtain eternal life without being baptized every day; *Panarion* 1.17.1.2-3 (he uses βαπτίζεσθαι and βαπτίζοιτό τις ἐν ὕδατι, ἀπολουόμενος to describe their practice). In *Panarion* 1.17.2.1-2 Epiphanius finds their daily baptisms not efficacious or they would not need to be repeated. His listing of waters — ocean, rivers, seas, perennial streams, and brooks (*Panarion* 1.17.2.3) — may reflect the practice of washing in running ("living") water.

71. *Apostolic Constitutions* 6.6.5.

72. Pseudo-Clement, *Homilies* 2.23. The suggestion of antagonism between two small Jewish sects is made by Thomas, *Le mouvement baptiste,* pp. 127-132.

73. Justin, *Dialogue* 80.4.

74. *t. Yadaim* 2.20 (they charged the Pharisees with pronouncing the name of God in the morning without bathing); *b. Berakoth* 22a; 52a (bathing after a nocturnal emission); *y. Berakoth* 3.6c.

that the daily baths originated in a concern for strict observance of purity regulations such as the Essenes had and at some undetermined date (unless the association with forgiveness of sins is a later Christian interpretation of their rites) were ascribed greater power and significance.

Even less can be said of the Masbotheans[75] and Sebueans.[76] They occasion mention because their names can be derived from the Aramaic צבע, "to baptize."

Elchasai claimed to receive revelations from a male angel, the Son of God, accompanied by a female angel, the Holy Spirit, both of enormous height. These revelations were recorded in a book, including that "there was preached to humanity a new remission of sins in the third year of Trajan's reign" (A.D. 100/101).[77] Hippolytus took interest in Elchasai because a follower named Alcibiades appeared in Rome at a time when the Roman church was divided over the forgiveness of postbaptismal sins and on the basis of Elchasai's book preached a forgiveness of sins by means of a second baptism. According to Alcibiades' preaching, a believer who has been converted, obeyed the book, and believed it "receives remission of sins by baptism."[78]

This remission of sins was specified to include bestiality, homosexuality, incest, adultery, and fornication. It was received by those who desired to receive forgiveness and listened to his book. They were exhorted "to be baptized a second time [after a first Christian baptism? — βαπτισάσθω ἐκ δευτέρου] in the name of the Great and Most High God and in the name of his Son the Great King," to be purified and cleansed.[79] They were also exhorted to call as witnesses the seven witnesses described in the book — heaven, water, the holy spirits (winds?), the angels of prayer, oil, salt, and the earth. The baptism was administered in a river or spring, wherever there was a deep spot, while the persons were fully clothed. The persons being baptized prayed to God "in faith of heart" and testified to the seven witnesses, "I will sin no more."

Modern scholars usually treat the Elchasaites as a gnosticizing Jewish-Christian sect. Elements identified as "gnostic" do not seem, on the basis of surviving evidence,

---

75. Hegesippus in Eusebius, *Church History* 4.22.7; cf. Basmotheans in *Apostolic Constitutions* 6.6.4. Rudolph, *Antike Baptisten*, p. 7, identifies them with the "Baptists" mentioned by Justin.

76. Epiphanius, *Panarion* 11, lists these among the Samaritan sects.

77. Hippolytus, *Refutation of All Heresies* 9.13.4 (9.8); the first set of numbers is that of the critical edition by Miroslav Marcovich, *Hippolytus Refutatio omnium haeresium*, Patristische Texte und Studien 25 (Berlin: Walter de Gruyter, 1986); the latter is that in *Ante-Nicene Fathers*, Vol. 5. Origen reported that the book was said to have fallen from heaven and that Elchasai offered a forgiveness other than that which Christ Jesus offered — Eusebius, *Church History* 6.38. Epiphanius discusses Elxai as part of and representative of the Ossaeans (*Panarion* 19.1.4–19.5.1) and says the Elchasaites in his time were known as Sampsaeans (*Panarion* 19.2.1; 30.3.2; *Anacephalaiosis* 53.1.1-9, who "make use of some baptisms [βαπτισμοῖς]"). For the Elchasaites, see A. F. J. Klijn and G. J. Reinink, *Patristic Evidence for Jewish-Christian Sects* (Leiden: Brill, 1973), pp. 54-67; Rudolph, *Antiken Baptisten*, pp. 13-17.

78. Hippolytus, *Refutation of All Heresies* 9.13.4 (9.8).

79. Hippolytus, *Refutation of All Heresies* 9.15 (9.10). J. Ries, "Le rite baptismal elchasaïte et le symbolisme manichéen de l'eau," *Aevum inter utrumque: Mélanges offerts à Gabriel Sandes* (The Hague: Nijhoff, 1991), pp. 367-378.

constitutive of the group. How much connection Elchasai himself had with Christianity is not clear. The Jewish element is clear, but whether this is because Elchasai was himself a Jew or due to his adopting Jewish views is not clear. Some elements are shared with the Jewish-Christian Ebionites (chap. 15).[80] The sect illustrates the great variety of combinations possible from Judaism, Christianity, and Gnosticism.

Elchasai maintained that believers should observe circumcision and live by the Law. He said that Christ was born a man like all others, that he did not come for the first time from a virgin but had been born previously and would be born often in the future. The Elchasaites rejected Paul. Elchasai was also alleged to have indulged in various magical practices. He prescribed other baptisms as well — those with certain ailments and those possessed by demons were to be baptized in cold water forty times during seven days.[81] A reference perhaps to another washing practiced by Elchasai is found in the Cologne Mani Codex, which demonstrated that Mani came from an Elchasaite group. Mani is speaking:

> If you accuse me concerning baptism, see, again I show you from your Law and from what had been revealed to your leaders that it is not necessary to be baptized [or to baptize oneself, βαπτίζεσθαι]. For this is shown by Alchasaios the founder of your Law. When he came to wash himself [λούσασθαι] in the water, a vision appeared to him of a man in the fountain of waters. . . . Whereupon Alchasaios was moved and did not wash himself in the waters.[82]

Epiphanius adds the information that the Elchasaites were obligated to marry, rejected sacrifices, and venerated water.[83]

Because of their survival to the present with their own literature, much more is known about the Mandaeans, the only surviving ancient Gnostic sect.[84] There is no certain evidence of a pre-Christian origin of the movement, and the claim to a connection with John the Baptist seems to be a late secondary development.[85] The

---

80. For the tenuousness of the connection with Jewish-Christianity, see Klijn and Reinink, *Patristic Evidence for Jewish-Christian Sects*, pp. 65-67.

81. Hippolytus, *Refutation of All Heresies* 9.14 and 16 (9.9, 11); cf. 10.29.1-3 (10.25).

82. *Kölner-Codex* 94,1-95,14, ed. Henrichs-Koenen in *Zeitschrift für Papyrologie und Epigraphik* 5.2, pp. 135-136. Gerard P. Luttikuizen, "Elchasaites and Their Book," in Antti Marjanen and Petri Luomanen, eds., *A Companion to Second-Century Christian "Heretics"* (Leiden: Brill, 2005), pp. 335-364 (354-363), doubts that the Jewish-Christian baptists of Mani's youth were Elchasaites.

83. Epiphanius, *Panarion* 19.1.7; 19.3.6; *Anacephalaiosis* 53.1.7.

84. Much of this account is taken from Thomas, *Le mouvement baptiste*, pp. 184-267. For the Mandaeans in later history and in the present, see Edmondo Lupieri, *The Mandaeans: The Last Gnostics* (Grand Rapids: Eerdmans, 2002; Italian original 1993), and Jorunn Jacobsen Buckley, *The Mandaeans: Ancient Texts and Modern People* (Oxford: Oxford University Press, 2002). Kurt Rudolph, *Gnosis* (San Francisco: Harper & Row, 1983), pp. 343-366, summarizes his extensive publications on the Mandaeans; also his *Antiken Baptisten*, pp. 17-18. He considers them a Gnostic sect of Jewish and pre-Christian origin, rooted in the same milieu as early Judaism's fringe, an offshoot of Jewish baptismal sects.

85. Simon Légasse, *Naissance du baptême* (Paris: Cerf, 1993), p. 27, asserts that no scholar today any longer affirms the Mandaeans have their origin among the disciples of John.

Mandaeans presumably began in the Jordan valley early in the Christian era, incorporating elements from Judaism, Christianity, and Gnosticism. They later migrated to Mesopotamia and survived in southern Iraq and southwest Iran, from whence some have been dispersed elsewhere. Whenever the sect originated, some of the ceremonies with water may be older. Their water purifications have a kinship with Jewish baptismal groups and also with ancient Babylonian and Persian rituals. The Mandaeans have a high regard for flowing (living) water as a symbol of life and of purification.

The frequent ceremonial lustrations of the Mandaeans are of three kinds.[86] The *rishama* is performed daily before sunrise with covered head, after defecation, and before other religious ceremonies. It does not require the presence of a priest, and each person recites the prayers accompanying it. The *tamasha* is a triple complete immersion, also not requiring a priest. It is performed by women after menstruation and childbirth and by men after touching a dead body, emission of semen, and touching an unclean person. Particular importance attaches to the *masbuta* received at initiation but renewed each Sunday ("first day of the week") and other special occasions (so not properly initiatory itself) under the direction of an officiating priest, who must be married. The baptizer immerses himself as a preliminary purification. An elaborate ceremony of prayers, hymns, and ritual actions accompanies the whole event, which lasts about two hours. Children (but not infants), women, and men are baptized separately. The person, wearing a white robe, dips him/herself three times in the "Jordan" (the name given to every river in which sacred baths are taken). There is a series of responses between the priest and the candidate. With the person kneeling in the water, the priest dips the person's forehead three times in the water and "signs" the candidate with water by passing his hand three times across his/her forehead from right to left. Sacred names are pronounced over the initiate, who is crowned with a myrtle wreath and given a drink of water three times out of the right hand of the priest. The water rites are done individually, but after the initiate emerges from the water, there are communal rites of great importance. The persons wash their bared right arms in the pool by splashing the water upwards with the right hand, not touching the water with the left hand. The priest gives a triple anointing with oil on the forehead, a handclasp, a wafer to eat and water to drink, a laying of the hand lightly on the head, a formula to be repeated word for word calling on the elements as witnesses, and a final handclasp.

In Arabic sources the Mandaeans are also called *Moughtasilas* ("those who bathe themselves") and *Sabaeans* ("baptizers"). Although claiming to originate in Palestine, they are hostile to Jews and abandoned circumcision and sabbath observance. The customs of the Mandaeans, however, show contact with other Jewish sects. They praise "living water," and they wash when coming from the market and

---

86. The following simplified and abbreviated account is drawn from E. S. Drower, *The Mandaeans of Iraq and Iran* (Leiden: Brill, 1962 reprint), pp. 100-123. See also E. Segelberg, *Masbuta: Studies in the Ritual of the Manaean Baptism* (Uppsala: Almquist & Wiksell, 1958).

after sexual intercourse and menstruation. They dress in white for their rituals. They opposed animal sacrifice. Their literature is also hostile to Christianity, regarding Jesus as a false Messiah inferior to John the Baptist, who is not considered to be the Messiah or founder of the group but as typifying the Mandaean ideal. In their literature John was married and was not killed but was taken from the earth.

The Jewish-Christian Ebionites are discussed in chapter 15.

Proselyte Baptism[87]

Many scholars have found the origin of Christian baptism in Jewish proselyte baptism.[88] According to rabbinic literature there were three requirements for a Gentile converting to Judaism: circumcision, immersion *(tebilah)*, and sacrifice.[89]

Circumcision was the crucial step for a Gentile man in becoming a proselyte to Judaism.[90] This was commanded of all male children of the descendants of Abraham as the sign of participation in God's covenant (Gen. 17:9-14). It was, therefore, required in the Law also for aliens who wished to become part of the Israelite community (Exod. 12:48-49).

The date for the origin of proselyte baptism cannot be determined.[91] It is nota-

---

87. Brandt, *Die jüdischen Baptismen;* Herman L. Strack and Paul Billerbeck, *Kommentar zum Neuen Testament aus Talmud und Midrasch* (Munich: C. H. Beck, 1926; reprint 1961), Vol. 1, pp. 102-112; Johannes Leipoldt, *Die urchristliche Taufe im Lichte der Religionsgeschichte* (Leipzig: Dörffling & Franks, 1928), pp. 1-25; B. J. Bamberger, *Proselytism in the Talmudic Period* (Cincinnati: Hebrew Union College, 1939; reprint New York: KTAV, 1968), pp. 38-52; Shaye J. D. Cohen, "The Rabbinic Conversion Ceremony," *Journal of Jewish Studies* 41 (1990):177-203 = *The Beginnings of Jewishness: Boundaries, Varieties, Uncertainties* (Berkeley: University of California Press, 1999), pp. 198-238.

88. Most aggresively by Joachim Jeremias, "Der Ursprung der Johannestaufe," *Zeitschrift für die neutestamentliche Wissenschaft* 28 (1929):312-320; "Proselytentaufe und des Neues Testament," *Theologische Zeitschrift* 5 (1949):418-428; *Infant Baptism in the First Four Centuries* (Philadelphia: Westminster, 1960); *The Origins of Infant Baptism* (London: SCM, 1963). His arguments are reviewed and answered by Derwood Smith, "Jewish Proselyte Baptism and the Baptism of John," *Restoration Quarterly* 25 (1982):13-32. A full rejection of an influence from the baptism of proselytes on Christian baptism is made by Légasse, *Naissance du baptême*, pp. 89-106, which largely reproduces and updates but without all the reference to secondary literature his article "Baptême juif des prosélytes et baptême chrétien," *Bulletin de littérature ecclésiastique* 77 (1976):3-40.

89. b. Kerithoth 8b-9a. The argument was that the Jewish fathers entered the covenant at Sinai by circumcision, immersion, and the sprinkling of blood. Circumcision was based on Josh. 5:5; the sprinkling of blood (necessary for entering the congregation and partaking of consecrated things) on Exod. 24:5, 8; and immersion on the principle that there is no sprinkling of blood without immersion (cf. Exod. 19:10). Making proselytes was still possible, even though there are "no sacrifices today," on the basis of Num. 15:14-15 ("There shall be for both you and for the resident alien a single statute, a perpetual statute throughout your generations").

90. *Pesaḥim* 8.8; *b. Kerithoth* 9a; *t. Shabbath* 15.9; *t. 'Avodah Zara* 3.12; *Sifre Numbers* 108.

91. L. Finkelstein, "The Institution of Baptism for Proselytes," *Journal of Biblical Literature* 52 (1933):203-211; T. M. Taylor, "The Beginnings of Jewish Proselyte Baptism," *New Testament Studies* 2 (1955/56):193-198; Karen Pusey and John Hunt, "Jewish Proselyte Baptism," *Expository Times* 95 (1984):

ble that no mention of it occurs in Philo, Josephus,[92] or *Joseph and Aseneth*. In the last the activities of Aseneth related to her conversion to Judaism are described in some detail, including her washing her hands and face with "living water" after a period of repentance in sackcloth and ashes and of prayer,[93] but there is no mention of a bath, not even the nuptial bath. A conversion recorded in Judith 14:10 mentions only believing in God and being circumcised.

Many have found the first reference to the practice of proselyte baptism in a dispute between the school of Shammai and the school of Hillel in the latter part of the first century. This dispute was taken note of in rabbinic literature because the subject was one of the few instances in which the school of Shammai took the more lenient interpretation. Rabbi Jose reports the difference of opinion:

> According to the School of Shammai they may immerse themselves in a rain-stream, and the School of Hillel say that they may not do so. The School of Shammai say: If a man became a proselyte on the day before Passover, he may immerse himself and consume his Passover-offering in the evening. And the School of Hillel say: He that separates himself from his uncircumcision is as one that separates himself from the grave.[94]

The dispute had to do with the degree of impurity. The significance of the quotation from the school of Hillel is that purification from touching a dead body required being sprinkled on the third and seventh day before the bath that completed the purification (Num. 19:14-20). The school of Shammai understood the immersion to be the same as that required in other cases of impurity when the person was clean the next evening (e.g., Lev. 11:24; 15:16). Recent study has concluded that the interpretation of the debate between the houses of Shammai and Hillel on immersion before eating Passover as applying to proselyte baptism is almost certainly wrong.[95] Other immersions are possible, and the Shammaite view likely concerns an immersion separate from and later than the act of conversion intended either to remove some minor impurity or to mark a transition in the convert's status with respect to the temple and

---

141-145. Webb, *John the Baptiser and Prophet*, pp. 122-130 — proselyte immersion probably post-70; Rudolph, *Antiken Baptisten*, p. 13, dates its beginning about 80.

92. Not even in the story of the conversion of King Izates of Adiabene, where what was involved in conversion to Judaism was at issue (*Antiquities* 20.34-53 [2.3-5]). The passage is often cited because his teacher seems to suggest that one could be a Jew without circumcision, but the real contention is not this but that omission of circumcision was pardonable (and so culpable) — see Bamberger, *Proselytism in the Talmudic Period*, p. 49.

93. *Joseph and Aseneth* 14.12, 15 (17); cf. 18.8-9 (pure water from the spring).

94. *'Eduyyoth* 5.2 (Danby, p. 431). The same dispute over whether he could eat the Passover is recorded in *Pesaḥim* 8.8; *t. Pesaḥim* 7.13 (167) (with the added statement that all the same are a male Gentile who was circumcised and a slave-woman who was immersed); *b. Pesaḥim* 92a; and *y. Pesaḥim* 8.36b.

95. Shaye J. D. Cohen, "Is 'Proselyte Baptism' Mentioned in the Mishnah? The Interpretation of *m. Pesaḥim* 8.8 (= *m. 'Eduyyot* 5.2)," in John C. Reeves and John Kampen, eds., *Pursuing the Text: Studies in Honor of Ben Zion Wacholder* (Sheffield: JSOT Press, 1994), pp. 278-292 (p. 282).

its cult. This immersion required by the Shammaites perhaps led to the immersion that became integral to the conversion ritual.[96]

The earliest literary account of the rabbinic conversion ceremony in the Babylonian Talmud is probably a *beraita*, that is, a source of Palestinian origin, probably from the second century.[97] The practice may have been earlier, but how early is an assumption and so far lacking in definite proof. Immersion in the ceremony of making a proselyte probably derives from the other ceremonial washings practiced by the Jews and so meant initially cleansing from impurity. This act and the subsequent offering at the temple were in origin, therefore, not so much prerequisites of becoming a proselyte as conditions for acquiring the purity necessary for participation in the Jewish community, but of course that was what being a proselyte meant.

The inclusion of a sacrifice at the temple illustrates the abstract nature of many rulings in the Mishnah and Talmud as based on interpretations of the Law apart from the possibility of actually carrying the rulings out. Exegetical and halakic texts, therefore, are problematic for historical purposes. "R. Eliezer b. Jacob says: A proselyte's atonement is yet incomplete until the blood [of his offering] has been tossed for him [against the base of the altar]."[98] Since the sacrifice was pre-70 in practice, there is a presumption that the immersion was too. When this washing was formalized as part of the process of becoming a proselyte, however, cannot be determined; when its meaning was extended beyond a ceremonial purification is apparently a yet later development.

An important early Gentile reference to Jewish baptism seems to indicate that the centrality of this act to becoming a Jew was recognized by non-Jews. Epictetus illustrates the need to live by as well as adopt the principles of philosophers:

> Why do you act the part of a Jew when you are a Greek? . . . Whenever we see someone halting between two opinions, we are accustomed to say, "He is not a Jew, but he pretends to be one." Whenever he adopts the attitude of mind of the one who has been dipped [βεβαμμένου] and has made his choice, then he both is in reality and is called a Jew. So also we are "false baptists" [παραβαπτισταί, imposters], in word Jews but in deed something else.[99]

---

96. Cohen, "Is 'Proselyte Baptism' Mentioned in the Mishnah?" p. 291.

97. So Shaye J. D. Cohen, *Beginnings of Jewishness: Boundaries, Varieties, Uncertainties* (Berkeley: University of California Press, 1999), pp. 209-211. The texts are *b. Yebamoth* 47a-b and the post-talmudic tractate *Gerim* 1.1. These two texts differ in their present form principally in that circumcision is central, followed by immersion, in *Yebamoth*, whereas the immersion is central in *Gerim*.

98. *Kerithoth* 2.1. On this basis *b. Kerithoth* 8b affirms the necessity of the sacrifice before partaking of consecrated things. Bamberger, *Proselytism in the Talmudic Period*, p. 45, notes that the sacrifice was a burnt offering on the analogy of the covenant sacrifice of Israel; *Gerim* 2.5 allows that one of the three requirements could be omitted, perhaps to cover the circumstance that sacrifice was no longer possible.

99. Arrian, *Discourses of Epictetus* 2.9.19-21. The absence of a reference to circumcision is notable, unless πάθος is a euphemism for circumcision.

The last sentence is unclear.[100] A greater difficulty for our present topic is the possibility that Epictetus is referring to Christians under the name Jews, since Greek and Roman writers before the mid-second century often did not distinguish Christians from Jews. The reference to making a choice and the illustration of manner of life indicate that some kind of conversion is implied and not the frequent washings for purification. A reference in Juvenal of about the same date certainly speaks of Jews but not so clearly of a baptism: "Conducting none but the circumcised to the desired fountain."[101]

In the absence of any definite evidence that the baptism of proselytes preceded Christian baptism, many argue that the former must have been earlier, for Jews would not have borrowed or copied a Christian rite.[102] The argument is specious, however, for Jews had other precedents than Christianity for adopting a bath for proselytes, not least their own purificatory practices, from which the immersion of proselytes probably derived, whenever its origin.

It seems that the immersion of proselytes developed from a purificatory rite to become a symbol of a new life. Beginning likely as an act of cleansing, it became also an initiatory act.[103] The Mishnah refers to the change of status with reference to the Law for the proselyte.[104] Talmudic sources give the first explicit statements that are preserved indicating reflection on what was involved in the change of state for a proselyte. "A proselyte is like a child newly born."[105] When a woman "adopts the Jewish faith she becomes a different person."[106] A slave "performed ritual ablution for the purpose of acquiring the status of a freed man,"[107] because conversion to Judaism brought manumission to a slave owned by a Jew. And, so, there was a new beginning.[108] After the ablution one was an Israelite in all respects.[109] Israel constituted the children of God and the beloved of God.[110] The language of becoming a child does not seem to carry the idea of an inner rebirth, for the concept had more a legal than an ethical meaning.[111] Nor does rabbinic literature customarily associate the

100. Rudolph, *Antiken Baptisten*, p. 13, suggests that παραβαπτισταί could refer to a sectarian strain of Judaism.

101. *Satires* 14.104.

102. E.g., Albrecht Oepke, "βάπτω, βαπτίζω (et al.)," in Gerhard Kittel, ed., *Theological Dictionary of the New Testament*, tr. Geoffrey W. Bromiley (Grand Rapids: Eerdmans, 1964), Vol. 1, p. 535 — but these are not the only two options.

103. Bamberger, *Proselytism in the Talmudic Period*, p. 44, asserts that proselyte baptism was both initiatory and purificatory.

104. *Shebi'ith* 10.9; *Ḥullin* 10.4; but the situation of children of a proselyte was different — *Yebamoth* 11.2.

105. *b. Yebamoth* 22a; also 62a. Quotations from the Babylonian Talmud are taken from I. Epstein, ed., *The Babylonian Talmud* (London: Soncino Press, 1935-1952).

106. *b. Yebamoth* 23a.

107. *b. Yabamoth* 46a.

108. *b. Shabbath* 145b-146a.

109. *b. Yebamoth* 47b.

110. *Gerim* 1.1.

111. Leipoldt, *Urchristliche Taufe*, p. 22; the phrase is "strictly halakic," referring to a new legal sta-

immersion with forgiveness of sins, although this idea does occur.[112] Repentance and a change of life were parts of the understanding: "She no longer lived to the world . . . and they do not return [to their evil ways]."[113]

Since women were immersed but not circumcised, the rabbis discussed which act marked the transition from being a Gentile to being a proselyte.[114] R. Hiyya b. Abba stated in the name of R. Johanan:

> A man cannot become a proper proselyte unless he has been circumcised and has performed ritual ablution; when therefore no ablution has been performed he is regarded as an idolater.[115]

R. Eliezer b. Hyrcanus, on the other hand, said one circumcised but not bathed was a proper proselyte.[116] R. Joshua b. Hananiah countered that one bathed but not circumcised, as was the case with women, was a proper proselyte.[117] The decision of the sages was that for men both were required: "If one has taken the bath without circumcision, or circumcision without the bath, he is not a proselyte, and he will be one only at the moment when he has received the one and the other."[118] This dispute in c. A.D. 90 is the first indication of baptism as a conversion rite in Judaism, not just purification, and the controversy shows that the connection of circumcision and the first bath of a proselyte was not yet established.

Questions were asked of the candidate in order to discourage the half-hearted. Two men gave instructions in the commandments to the candidate. Acceptance of

---

tus — R. J. Zwi Werblowsky, "A Note on Purification and Proselyte Baptism," in *Christianity, Judaism, and Other Greco-Roman Cults: Studies for Morton Smith at Sixty*, Vol. 3 (Leiden: Brill, 1975), pp. 200-205 (203).

112. Forgiveness of sins is stated with reference to becoming a proselyte — *y. Bikkurim* 3.3; R. Judah concluded that since the proselyte became as a newborn child, his previous sins were cancelled — *Gerim* 2.5.

113. *Midrash Rabbah to Ecclesiastes* 1.8.4. Translation by A. Cohen, *Midrash Rabbah* (London: Soncino, 939), pp. 28-29. Forgiveness is not expressed.

114. That the rabbis' disagreement was not over whether one or the other rites was dispensable but over the point at which the transition from Gentile to Jew took place is suggested by Oskar Skarsaune, *In the Shadow of the Temple* (Downers Grove: InterVarsity Press, 2002), p. 355, n. 6, and affirmed by Bamberger, *Proselytism in the Talmudic Period*, p. 51 (discussion of the controversy on pp. 45-51).

115. *b. Yebamoth* 46a; also quoted in 47a.

116. *b. Yebamoth* 71a also cites R. Eliezer's position that a man circumcised and unimmersed is a proselyte.

117. No examples are cited, and Cohen, *Beginnings of Jewishness*, pp. 219-221, argues that the position was invented by the compiler of the Babylonian Talmud and was never a real option in Jewish law. Bamberger, *Proselytism in the Talmudic Period*, p. 46, favors the reading of the Palestinian Talmud according to which R. Eliezer made circumcision alone necessary, but R. Joshua made baptism and circumcision necessary.

118. *b. Yebamoth* 46a-b; the dispute is also cited in *b. Yebamoth* 71a and *y. Qiddushin* 3.13 (64d). The rule requiring both circumcision and the bath is cited in *b. ʿAbodah Zara* 59a. Both Eliezer b. Hyrcanus and Joshua b. Hananiah flourished c. A.D. 80-120.

the commandments was the essence of conversion to Judaism. If the person accepted the commandments, he was circumcised. When he healed, he proceeded to his immersion.[119] He was in water high enough to cover his genitals while receiving instruction in the commandments and then was immersed.[120] Proselyte baptism required two or three men as witnesses (something not required in the ordinary lustrations) and could not be performed at night, so it was not a private affair.[121] Since the requirement was that all parts of the body must be in contact with the water (hence nude),[122] in the immersion of women (presumably to preserve modesty), women assisted women, who were up to their necks in the water, and two learned men who gave the instructions in the commandments stood outside.[123]

Children conceived in holiness (i.e., by Jewish parents) were born in holiness.[124] Hence, children of Jewish parents and children of proselytes received circumcision on the eighth day, even if it was a Sabbath, and were washed and sprinkled.[125] If a pregnant Gentile woman converted to Judaism, her son was born a Jew, received circumcision, and had no need for ritual immersion.[126] Minors of parents who converted were treated as their parents and were immersed. This practice has been claimed as a support for the practice of infant baptism in the church.[127] The argument is problematic, not only because of the uncertain date of the origin of proselyte baptism, but also because the practice applied only to the family converting and not to subsequent generations. Another difficulty with the argument is that these minor children had the right to protest what their father did and not be bound by it yet without being treated as apostates.[128]

Proselyte baptism involved a change of status or condition for the convert. However, this was due more to becoming a proselyte than to the bath itself. The rabbinic conversion ceremony lacked the features of an initiation ritual: "It therefore bears little resemblance to Christian baptism rituals."[129] Proselyte baptism was like other washings in Judaism in being a full immersion and in being self-administered.

---

119. *b. Yebamoth* 47a-b, the first unequivocal linking of circumcision and immersion in the making of a proselyte.
120. *Gerim* 1.1.
121. *b. Yebamoth* 46b-47b.
122. *Mikwaoth* 8.5-9.7; *b. Baba Qamma* 82a-b.
123. *b. Yebamoth* 40b; 47a-b (the first record of the requirement of immersion for women proselytes); *Gerim* 1.1.1-4.
124. *b. Yebamoth* 97b.
125. *Shabbath* 18.3-19.6; 9.3.
126. *b. Yebamoth* 78a, quoting Raba.
127. Notably by Joachim Jeremias, n. 88.
128. *b. Kethuboth* 11a: "A minor [under the age of 13] proselyte is immersed by the direction of the court [when he had no father to act for him] . . . R. Joseph said, When they have become of age they can protest [against their conversion] . . . [A woman proselyte], when she has become of age, too, can protest and go out — As soon as she was of age one hour, and did not protest, she cannot protest any more."
129. Cohen, *Beginnings of Jewishness*, p. 236.

Unlike these other washings, in its developed form, proselyte baptism required witnesses and involved receiving instruction in the Jewish way of life.

The baptism of proselytes, in spite of some superficial similarities, had basic differences from Christian baptism. Proselyte baptism required witnesses but was self-administered; baptism by John and Christians had an administrator. In proselyte baptism the candidate was freed from pagan impurity; in Christian baptism one received pardon and regeneration as divine grace. The heart of the rabbinic conversion ceremony was circumcision, not baptism; baptism was the central act in Christian conversion. Proselyte baptism was for Gentiles; Christians baptized Jews as well as Gentiles. These differences are significant, even if the chronological difficulty can be overcome.[130]

---

130. Légasse, *Naissance du baptême*, pp. 101-105.

5. John the Baptizer

Christian sources consistently saw the antecedent to Christian baptism in the practice of John the Baptizer.[1] They applied the same distinctive terminology, βάπτισμα (other dippings were designated by the word βαπτισμός), and the same purpose, "forgiveness of sins," to John's baptism as they did to their own. Whether the early disciples of Jesus adopted the terminology of John's disciples or later applied their own terminology to John's practice, the distinctive word usage and description of the ceremony point to where Christians saw the origins of their practice.[2] Indeed, the act of baptism was what gave John his identifying title. He was known as the "Baptist" (βαπτιστής)[3] or "the Baptizer" (ὁ βαπτίζων, "the one immersing").[4]

Scholars, in studying John's baptism, have looked behind him for antecedents to

---

1. For John the Baptist, see C. H. H. Scobie, *John the Baptist* (Philadelphia: Fortress, 1964); idem, "John the Baptist," in Matthew Black, ed., *The Scrolls and Christianity* (London: SPCK, 1969); Robert L. Webb, *John the Baptiser and Prophet* (Sheffield: JSOT Press, 1991); E. F. Lupieri, "John the Baptist in New Testament Traditions and History," *Aufstieg und Niedergang der römischen Welt* (Berlin: de Gruyter, 1993), 2.26.1, pp. 430-461; Joan E. Taylor, *The Immerser: John the Baptist within Second Temple Judaism* (Grand Rapids: Eerdmans, 1997); and for his baptism, Ernst Lohmeyer, *Das Urchristentum*, Vol. 1, *Johannes der Täufer* (Göttingen: Vandenhoeck & Ruprecht, 1932), pp. 145-156; Simon Légasse, *Naissance du baptême* (Paris: Cerf, 1993), esp. pp. 27-55, and pp. 107-109, 133-134 for his baptism as the direct antecedent of Christian baptism; Bruce Chilton, "John the Baptist: His Immersion and his Death," and Craig A. Evans, "The Baptism of John in a Typological Context," in Stanley E. Porter and Anthony R. Cross, *Dimensions of Baptism: Biblical and Theological Studies* (London: Sheffield Academic Press, 2002), pp. 25-44 and 45-71.

2. Albrecht Oepke, "βάπτω, βαπτίζω (et al.)," in Gerhard Kittel, ed., *Theological Dictionary of the New Testament*, tr. Geoffrey W. Bromiley (Grand Rapids: Eerdmans, 1964), Vol. 1, p. 545, states that since the New Testament coins or reserves for John's and Christian baptism a word (βάπτισμα) not used elsewhere that has no cultic connections and always uses it in the singular, it understands the Christian action as something new and unique.

3. E.g., Matt. 3:1; Mark 6:25; Luke 7:20.

4. Mark 6:14, 24. The use of this alternative form indicates that the name "the Baptist" was given from his practice of administering baptism and not from his being part of a previous baptizing group.

his baptism in Jewish purificatory washings, in a "baptist movement" within Judaism, in proselyte baptism, or in the washings at Qumran.

John in Relation to Jewish Immersions[5]

John's baptism shared with Jewish washings the theme of purification or cleansing. In continuity with the message of the prophets John linked purity with a call for moral transformation and spiritual cleansing.[6] Josephus describes John's preaching and baptism in these terms.

> [John called the Baptist (βαπτιστής)] was a good man and exhorted the Jews to lead righteous lives, practice justice towards one another and piety towards God, and so to participate in baptism [βαπτισμῷ].[7] In his view this was a necessary preliminary if baptism [βάπτισις, "dipping"] was to be acceptable to God. They must not use it to gain pardon for whatever sins they committed, but for the purity [ἁγνείᾳ] of the body, implying that the soul was already thoroughly cleansed [προεκκεκαθαρμένης] by right behavior.[8]

The Gospels present a different picture (discussed below). Josephus is correct in describing John's call for moral purity, but his denial of its connection with forgiveness of sins is contradicted by the Synoptic Gospels. That denial may show Josephus's awareness that others interpreted John's baptism as bringing pardon and may be his effort to put John's baptism in the common Jewish understanding of purity; but that very effort makes his report suspect, for why did John create such a stir if there was nothing special about what he was doing?[9]

---

5. Scobie, *John the Baptist*, pp. 90-116; Webb, *John the Baptiser and Prophet*, pp. 163-216; Robert L. Webb, "John the Baptist," *Encyclopedia of the Dead Sea Scrolls*, ed. L. H. Schiffman and J. C. VanderKam (Oxford: Oxford University Press, 2000), pp. 85-89; Taylor, *The Immerser*, pp. 49-100.

6. Isa. 1:15-17; Ezek. 36:22-33.

7. The phrase is literally "to come together in baptism." The verb may mean to form an identifiable group, and baptism in the dative case may mean "by means of baptism." More likely, however, is the meaning represented in the translation, "to come together for baptism." Note Josephus's use of the general word for "dipping," βαπτισμός, rather than the word used in the Gospels for John's baptism and in the rest of the New Testament for Christian baptism, βάπτισμα.

8. Josephus, *Antiquities* 18.116-117 (5.2).

9. Hermann Lichtenberger, "Baths and Baptism," in L. H. Schiffman and J. C. VanderKam, eds., *Encyclopedia of the Dead Sea Scrolls* (Oxford: Oxford University Press, 2000), pp. 85-89. Webb, *John the Baptiser and Prophet*, pp. 165-168, on limitations in Josephus's basically reliable account and 170-172 on the accuracy of the Synoptic Gospels on John's baptism as being "for the forgiveness of sins." Joseph Thomas, *Le mouvement baptiste en Palestine et Syrie (150 av. J.-C.-300 ap. J.-C.)* (Gembloux: J. Duculot, 1935), pp. 82-83, makes the points that Josephus's view would not account for the crowd's enthusiasm for John and they did not need such a baptism for purity of body. Taylor, *The Immerser*, pp. 83, 87-100, supports the accuracy of Josephus's description and argues that the Gospels, instead of reporting a repentance-baptism, should be interpreted as reflecting an underlying Aramaic that could mean re-

It might be argued that the Gospel writers have read the Christian understanding back into John's baptism, but they were nearer in time and in faith to John than was Josephus, who may have been describing John's baptism according to what he knew of other Jewish practices, notably by the Essenes,[10] or, alternatively, to have been explaining John's baptism in a way intended to make it more acceptable to his Gentile readers. Moreover, although there was a connection between Christian baptism and repentance (Acts 2:38), the phrase "baptism of repentance" is used only of John's baptism,[11] thus preserving a distinctive terminology for John's baptism. More significant for the limitations on Josephus's report is his omission of any reference to the strongly eschatological frame of reference in which John set his call to repentance,[12] an omission that accords with Josephus's minimizing of eschatological fervor except by fringe elements. In short, it may be said that baptism as an act of prophetic symbolism set John's practice apart from other Jewish washings.[13]

Another view argues that John's practice was not new, for he was part of a larger pre-Christian baptizing movement that continued in the early Christian centuries.[14] On this view John adopted a rite known and appreciated in his environment; his originality was in putting baptism in relation to the imminent coming of the kingdom of God and the Messiah. The evidence for this movement is slender (treated in chap. 4, "Baptismal Movements"). The principal supports are the Essenes, the only group with a certainly pre-Christian date but about whom we now know much more (see chap. 4 and below), and the *Sibylline Oracles* 4, dated after John's time. The

pentance brought forgiveness of sins (inner purity) that resulted in an immersion for outward purity (see my discussion below).

10. Cf. Josephus's description of John's baptism with the information in the Qumran *Community Rule* quoted in chap. 4. Gerhard Delling, *Die Taufe im Neuen Testament* (Berlin: Evangelische Verlagsanstalt, 1963), pp. 39-40, rejects Josephus's interpretation of John's baptism as *gut "Qumranisch"* — I had reached the conclusion that Josephus's description was influenced by his knowledge of the Essenes before I read Delling.

11. Mark 1:4; Luke 3:3; Acts 13:24; 19:4. For the meaning of repentance in John's, Christ's, and apostolic preaching see Aloys H. Dirksen, *The New Testament Concept of Metanoia* (Washington, DC: Catholic University of America, 1932), pp. 203-206 on John, 207-209 on Jesus, and 210-214 on the apostles. He finds the repentance of the New Testament to be the same as the *teshubah* of Judaism, a conversion from sin to God. This otherwise excellent collection of sources on Jewish (pp. 107-164), secular Greek (pp. 165-196), and early Christian (pp. 8-70) uses of the concept of *metanoia* is too insistent on taking the things that often accompany *metanoia* and the ways it was expressed — contrition, confession of sin, amendment of life, and works of penitence — as included in the meaning of *metanoia* and gratuitously takes the works of penitence as a "satisfaction" for sins.

12. Matt. 3:7-12; Luke 3:7-17.

13. A. D. Nock, "Hellenistic Mysteries and Christian Sacraments," *Mnemosyne*, Ser. 4.5 (1952): 177-213 (pp. 192-193) = Zeph Stewart, ed., *Arthur Darby Nock: Essays on Religion and the Ancient World* (Oxford: Oxford University Press, 1972), pp. 791-820 (p. 803); Johannes Leipoldt, *Die urchristliche Taufe im Lichte der Religionsgeschichte* (Leipzig: Dörffling & Franke, 1928), p. 26, but his claim that people were baptized in John's presence rather than by him leaves his name unexplained. For examples of symbolic actions by prophets see 1 Kings 22:11; Isa. 20:2; Jer. 27:2; Ezek. 4:1-8.

14. Thomas, *Le mouvement baptiste*, especially pp. 85-88.

other major representatives of the baptizing movement either had connections with Jewish Christianity (Elchasaites, Ebionites) or claimed connections with John that were later and secondary (Mandaeans, chap. 4). The association of baths with forgiveness of sins was made with certainty only by those groups that were later than John.[15] There does appear to have been a great interest in some circles in purification and more diligent observance of water rites to achieve it, but John's originality seems to have included his practice (a unique administered rite rather than repeated self-immersions) and the meaning he gave the rite (forgiveness and repentance) as well as the eschatological context in which he put it.

Many scholars have found in proselyte baptism the background to John's practice.[16] Both represented a one-time change in a person's life in contrast to the repeated immersions for purification in the ordinary life of observant Jews. Against this background John's baptism is understood as gaining its point as indicating that Israel needed to make the same change that Gentiles made in becoming Jews.[17] As attractive as the supposition is, this interpretation founders on the uncertain date of the origin for proselyte baptism (chap. 4). It must transport the later meaning of the rite back into the first exercise of a purificatory washing by a new convert at an earlier period than John, for which there is no evidence. Although the instruction of proselytes included punishment for violators of the commandments and reward for their fulfillment,[18] it lacked the eschatological urgency of John's message. The one-

---

15. Thomas, *Le mouvement baptiste*, p. 429, interprets Josephus, *Antiquities* 18.19 (1.5), about the Essenes as, "They do not offer sacrifices because they have more confidence in their ablutions" (he discusses the text with a more literal translation on p. 12). This translation depends on inserting a negative, which has poor textual support, and taking the "different purifications" (διαφορότητι ἁγνειῶν) as "ablutions" (which would have been included but more was involved) — see the notes in Louis H. Feldman's translation of Josephus for Loeb Classical Library (Cambridge: Harvard University Press, 1965), Vol. 9, pp. 16-17. At any rate, nothing is said about substituting these purifications for sacrifice as the means of forgiveness of sins. Thomas argues that the replacement of the temple and sacrifices with baths as the means of forgiveness of sins was part of the spiritualization of cult at this time (pp. 426-430), but a more likely occasion for Jews would have been the destruction of the temple in 70; for Jewish Christians the association of baptism with forgiveness of sins was already present but might have received a new emphasis (as in the Ebionites) after 70. Note Lupieri, "John the Baptist," p. 440, for the claim that remission of sins was offered by no known Jewish purifying act of John's day.

16. Leipoldt, *Die urchristliche Taufe*, pp. 25-28; H. H. Rowley, "Jewish Proselyte Baptism and the Baptism of John," *Hebrew Union College Annual* 15 (1940): 313-334; reprinted and updated in the notes in H. H. Rowley, *From Moses to Qumran* (New York: Association Press, 1963), pp. 211-235 (while acknowledging important differences, he finds the closest parallels to John's baptism in proselyte baptism); Carl H. Kraeling, *John the Baptist* (New York: Charles Scribner's Sons, 1951), pp. 99-100; an extensive listing of those taking this position is found in Joachim Gnilka, "Die essenischen Tauchbäder und die Johannestaufe," *Revue de Qumran* 3 (1961): 185-207 (185-186).

17. The report in Luke 3:14 that soldiers responded to his preaching might indicate that John baptized non-Jews, but Jewish soldiers who enforced the work of the tax collectors cannot be ruled out. Lohmeyer, *Das Urchristentum*, Vol. 1, pp. 151-152, points out that John's was a one-time baptism like proselyte baptism, but the difference was that John's gave no community (this might be a problematic claim) and proselyte baptism had no eschatological motif.

18. *b. Yebamoth* 47a, "The world to come was made only for the righteous."

time character of John's baptism derived not from proselyte baptism but his prophetic call announcing the messianic end times.

The discovery of the Dead Sea Scrolls brought considerable speculation of a link between John the Baptist and the people of the Scrolls.[19] The case for a connection is circumstantial but plausible. John came from a priestly family, and the Qumran community was led by priests; his parents were elderly at the time of his birth, and the Essenes reared orphan children; his activity was located in the wilderness near where Qumran was; his ministry was based on Isaiah 40:3, an important verse at Qumran; and he practiced immersion, a rite important to the Essenes. Josephus's accounts indicated that both the Essenes and John required a life change before baptism.[20] On the other hand, there are differences on the key points. The Qumran community, following the Hebrew text of Isaiah 40:3, construed "in the wilderness" with "prepare the way for the Lord" (and so justified their place of settlement); Christians, following the Greek text, construed "in the wilderness" with "the voice crying" (and so explained the location of John's preaching).[21] Although there was a strong eschatological orientation at Qumran, this feature is not connected with its washings.[22] These washings occurred daily, but John's baptism was nonrepeatable. Although a community resulted from John's preaching,[23] this may not have been paramount in his intentions; but if so, his baptism had a function that baptism did not have at Qumran, where an oath to observe the commandments was the central initiatory act[24] before one was admitted to the water and to the meals of the community.[25]

19. For the question in general, James H. Charlesworth and Raymond E. Brown, *John and the Dead Sea Scrolls* (New York: Crossroad, 1991).

20. *Jewish War* 2.138 (8.7); *Antiquities* 18.117 (5.2).

21. 1QS viii.13-14; Matt. 3:3.

22. 1QS iv.19-22 does use "purifying waters" as an image for the eschatological cleansing.

23. Luke 11:1; Acts 19:1-3. Webb, pp. 197-202, argues that John's baptism was initiatory; Bruce Chilton, *Jesus' Baptism and Jesus' Healing* (Harrisburg: Trinity Press International, 1998), pp. 25-26, and Légasse, *Naissance du baptême*, pp. 43-47, on the contrary, denied that his baptism was an initiation into a sect and that John founded a sect. The evidence for the continuation of a sect of "Johannites" is assembled and argued by Thomas, *Le mouvement baptiste*, pp. 89-139.

24. Daniel Vigne, *Le baptême de Jésus dans la tradition judéo-chrétienne* (Paris: J. Gabalda, 1992), pp. 295-298, discusses the practice of taking oaths beside a river, because rivers were considered the proper places for communication with the divine, but he does not include the Qumran community in his discussion. His material prompts the question of an association between the initiatory oath at Qumran and the initial bath on admission to the community.

25. See chap. 4. H. H. Rowley, "The Baptism of John and the Qumran Sect," in A. J. B. Higgins, ed., *New Testament Essays: Studies in Memory of T. W. Manson* (Manchester: Manchester University Press, 1959), pp. 218-229, early rejected John's relation to Qumran. Lichtenberger, "Baths and Baptism," p. 86, judges that "it cannot be proved John derived his baptism from Qumran rituals." Webb, "John the Baptist," p. 421, similarly concludes, "[There was] no direct link between John and the Qumran community." Leonard F. Badia, *The Qumran Baptism and John the Baptist's Baptism* (Lanham, MD: University Press of America, 1980), outlines the similarities and differences of the practices of John and those at Qumran — summarized on pp. 49-51. Hartmut Stegemann, *The Library of Qumran* (Grand Rapids: Eerdmans, 1998), pp. 221-222, has an extensive list of differences in their baptisms, as on other things (pp. 223-225); a shorter but pointed list is found in Légasse, *Naissance du baptême*, pp. 54-55.

One must reckon with another factor influencing John's practice. Passages in the Prophets and Psalms spoke of cleansing by water in moral and spiritual terms.[26] Using the language of one of the purifications by priests, Ezekiel said for God, "I will sprinkle clean water upon you, and you shall be clean from all your uncleannesses" (36:25). Isaiah quoted God, "Wash yourselves; make yourselves clean; . . . cease to do evil" (1:16) and, "I will pour water on the thirsty land, . . . I will pour my spirit upon your descendants" (44:3). Zechariah promised, "A fountain shall be opened . . . to cleanse them from sin and impurity" (13:1). The Psalmist prayed, "Purge me with hyssop, and I shall be clean; wash me, and I shall be whiter than snow. . . . Create in me a clean heart, O God, and put a new and right spirit within me" (Ps. 51:7, 10). The Gospels describe John's ministry in the light of Malachi 3:1–4:6.[27]

To summarize the relation of John's baptism to some of the Jewish washings, to proselyte baptism, and to the baths of the Essenes: Like all of these, John's baptism was an immersion.[28] Unlike all of them, it was an administered rite and not a self-immersion.[29] This practice provides the most plausible explanation for the description of John as "the Baptist": He was doing something different, or else the designation would not have distinguished him.

John's baptism, moreover, shared with all the Jewish practices the feature of purification or cleansing. It differed from them, however, in being an eschatological rather than a ceremonial or ritual purification. His call for repentance was to prepare the people against God's coming judgment.[30] The eschatological expectation agreed with the outlook of the Qumran community, but that viewpoint is not connected in the texts with their baths, although the imagery of cleansing by water was used to describe the eschatological cleansing. Moreover, their approach was separatist and not addressed to the whole nation. John's baptism had in common with later proselyte baptism being a one-time immersion and not a repeated rite.[31] It differed from proselyte baptism in being offered to Jews. They were the ones in need of repentance and

---

26. Scobie, *John the Baptist*, pp. 71-73, 113-114; Delling, *Die Taufe*, pp. 53-55, for the one-time cleansing of the end time spoken of by the prophets as the basis of John's baptism.

27. Lars Hartman, *'Into the Name of the Lord Jesus': Baptism in the New Testament* (Edinburgh: T&T Clark, 1997), p. 16.

28. John 3:23; Matt. 3:16; Mark 1:10.

29. Matt. 3:11; Mark 1:4, 5, 8; Luke 3:16; John 1:26. Codex D and several manuscripts of the Old Latin read at Luke 3:7 that the people were baptized "before" John, which would have been the practice in proselyte baptism. Codex D often reflects a knowledge of Jewish practices, but the indication of self-immersions here is contradicted by all the other references to John as doing the baptizing. Kurt Rudolph, *Antike Baptisten: Zu den Überlieferungen über frühjudische und -christliche Taufsekten*, Sitzungsberichte der Sachsischen Akademie der Wissenschaft zu Leipzig 121.4 (Berlin: Akademie, 1981), p. 10, is among those who understand John's practice as a self-baptism (a purification bath) with John as witness. To the contrary, Albrecht Oepke, "βάπτω, βαπτίζω (et al.)," in Gerhard Kittel, ed., *Theological Dictionary of the New Testament*, tr. Geoffrey W. Bromiley (Grand Rapids: Eerdmans, 1964), Vol. 1, p. 537, points out that after John Christianity used βαπτίζειν in the active and passive, whereas for Jews and Gentiles the middle is most common (in rites of washing).

30. Matt. 3:2, 7-12; Luke 3:16-17.

31. Cf. Matt. 3:7.

cleansing. Distinctive of John's baptism in relation to the comparable Jewish immersions was its explicit link with repentance and forgiveness of sins so that the people would be ready for the coming of the Lord.[32] His baptism was a conversion baptism but not a variation of proselyte baptism; its premise was repentance, and its purpose was the forgiveness of sins; it was not the basis of a new Israel or to join a new community (the goal was a renewal of Israel).[33]

To anticipate the subsequent material: John's baptism was like Christian baptism in its being a one-time administered immersion for the forgiveness of sins. It differed, however, in being accompanied by a confession of sins rather than a confession of faith.[34] Related to the latter is the connection of Christian baptism with the name of Jesus. New Testament writers made the distinction that instead of calling for faith in Jesus, John taught people to believe on the one to come.[35]

The major difference that was stressed, in addition to the connection with faith in Jesus as the Messiah who had come, was the offer of the Holy Spirit in Christian baptism.[36]

New Testament Texts about John's Baptism

Without judging the historical order of composition of the Gospels and their literary relationships, I will discuss the Synoptic Gospels in ascending order of the length of their treatment of John's baptism — Mark, Matthew, Luke — and then the Gospel of John. The baptism of Jesus by John will be discussed separately in the next chapter because of its importance for Christian baptism.

Mark's treatment of John the Baptist (Mark 1:1-8) is the briefest in the Gospels, but he makes their essential points: John was the voice crying in the wilderness to prepare for the coming of the Lord (1:2-3); he had an ascetic lifestyle (1:6); great numbers came out to be baptized by him (1:5); his baptism was associated with repentance, confession of sins, and their forgiveness (1:4); and he announced the coming of the Messiah, who would baptize in the Holy Spirit (1:7-8). For Mark the story of Jesus Christ, the gospel (1:1), begins with the ministry of John the Baptist.[37] The location at the Jordan River for John's baptizing is no doubt significant but not spelled out. The Mishnah judges the waters of the Jordan invalid for purifying baths because they were "mixed waters."[38] Did John choose the Jordan for the purely utili-

---

32. Mark 1:4, "a repentance baptism for the forgiveness of sins"; 1:5, "they were baptized by him in the Jordan River, confessing their sins."

33. Gnilka, "Die essenischen Tauchbäder und die Johannestaufe," pp. 203-204. "John's baptism stands between the cultic purification of the temple and Christian baptism" (p. 207).

34. Contrast Mark 1:5 and Acts 22:16.

35. Acts 19:4; cf. Mark 1:7.

36. Acts 19:2-3; Mark 1:8.

37. Cf. Acts 1:21-22; 10:37; 13:24.

38. *m. Parah* 8.10. Is this because its tributaries were "intermittent" streams or because they

tarian purpose of water for an immersion, in order to distinguish his baptism from ordinary Jewish purifications, or for some symbolic purpose, such as symbolizing a new exodus of salvation?[39] Mark does not include the note of eschatological purification in his account and omits "fire" from the description of the Mightier One's baptism. One may wonder if the "repentance baptism for the forgiveness of sins" meant a present forgiveness or only the promise of eschatological forgiveness, but the former is likely correct, since the baptism was submitted to individually.[40] That John's baptism brought forgiveness of sins carried with it an implicit criticism of the Jerusalem temple and its rituals. In Israel forgiveness of sins was obtained through the sacrifices at the temple; the offer of forgiveness of sins through repentance-baptism provided another means of obtaining what normally was thought to be obtained at the temple.[41] The implication of Jesus' words in Mark 11:27-33 (= Matt. 21:23-27; Luke 20:1-8) is that John's baptism had the authority of heaven behind it.

According to Matthew 3:1-12, John's message was repentance (3:2), made urgent by the imminent approach of the kingdom of heaven and the coming of wrath (3:2, 7). The people of Judaea were not to trust in being children of Abraham, for God's judgment would punish those without good fruit (3:9-10). Repentance required results, "fruit worthy of repentance" (3:8). His baptism was done with reference to repentance (3:11) and was accompanied by a confession of sins (3:6). The immersion took place in the Jordan River and was administered by John himself (3:6). This water baptism was preparatory to the coming of the Lord (3:3), one mightier than John who would bring a Holy Spirit and fire baptism (3:11). The baptism with fire was the eschatological fire that would destroy the wicked (3:12). All was not threat, however, for the righteous (the wheat — 3:12) would be gathered into God's granary, and the site of John's ministry — the wilderness — had connotations of the prophetic call to return to the wilderness for the new exodus of salvation (cf. Hos. 2:14-15 as well as Isa. 40:1-5).

The principal exegetical questions relevant to John's baptism according to Matthew occur in 3:11 — the meaning of the prepositions in the phrases "baptism εἰς repentance" and baptism ἐν ὕδατι and ἐν πνεύματι ἁγίῳ καὶ πυρί, and whether Holy Spirit and fire refer to two different baptisms or the same baptism under two images (3:11). The first phrase is discussed below under the meaning of John's baptism. As to the second pair of phrases, does the preposition ἐν mean "in" or "with" the elements

---

flowed through pagan lands? If this ruling was recognized in John's day, there is an immediate indication that his immersion had a different purpose from the ordinary purification baths.

39. Colin Brown, "What Was John the Baptist Doing?" *Bulletin for Biblical Research* 7 (1997): 37-50, answers that his baptisms were a new crossing of the Jordan, marking the boundary between impurity and the renewed Israel.

40. Hartman, *'Into the Name of the Lord Jesus,'* pp. 14-15.

41. Webb, *John the Baptiser and Prophet*, pp. 203-205; Chilton, *Jesus' Baptism and Jesus' Healing*, pp. 18-19, denies that an offer of remission of sins by another means was necessarily a challenge to the temple; F. Avemarie, "Ist die Johannestaufe ein Ausdruck von Tempelkritik? Skizze eines methodischen Problems," in B. Ego et al., eds., *Gemeinde ohne Tempel/Community without Temple* (Tübingen: Mohr/Siebeck, 1999), pp. 395-410.

mentioned? The meaning "in" (ἐν as locative, the place) would be more consistent with the practice of immersion; the meaning "with" (ἐν as instrumental, the means of the baptism) would call attention to the contrasting elements and, while allowing for another application of the elements, would not be inconsistent with an immersion. The meaning "in" is required in verse 6, "in the Jordan River," which defines the meaning of "in water" in verse 11. The basic meaning of an immersion, a submerging, is preserved in the imagery of a baptism in Holy Spirit and in fire. Whatever action is indicated by the baptism in water is indicated for the other(s).

Grammatically "in" or "with" "Holy Spirit and fire" could refer to a single action or event under two aspects (the coming of the Spirit is likened to tongues of fire in Acts 2:2-4).[42] Since fire refers to judgment and punishment in verses 10 and 12, presumably it does in verse 11 also.[43] Fire associated with judgment (Mal. 4:1) was also purifying (Mal. 3:1-6; cf. Isa. 42:2-5 for both ideas). To take fire, then, as the secondary element and make the phrase refer to one baptism whose primary element is the Holy Spirit goes against the immediate context. But to take the baptism in fire as primary would require the baptism in Holy Spirit to have a negative meaning contrary to its interpretation elsewhere in the New Testament. Hence, probability inclines toward separating the baptism in Holy Spirit from the baptism in fire. Even if grammatically the two baptisms are linked, they may be temporally distinct: possibly a baptism inaugurated in the Spirit and consummated in fire.

Luke 3:1-20 is similar to Matthew but with considerable expansion. The quotation from Isaiah 40 continues beyond verse 3 of Isaiah 40 to include verse 5 in the Old Greek, "And all flesh will see the salvation of God" (3:4-6). The major expansion is in the instructions John gave to the crowds, the tax collectors, and the soldiers concerning what repentance involved for each of them (3:10-14); the instructions spell out "the fruits worthy of repentance" (3:8) and show repentance necessarily to include a particular way of life. Luke lacks the description of John's clothing and diet. John is identified as "son of Zechariah" (3:2), although elsewhere Luke uses the designation "John the Baptist" (7:20, 33; 9:19). He directs the charge "offspring of vipers" to the crowds (3:7) and not just to the Pharisees and Sadducees as in Matthew. Luke puts John's declaration of unworthiness and the contrast of his baptism with that of the one coming after him in the context of the people's speculation whether he might be the Messiah (3:15).

Otherwise, many of Luke's words are identical, including the emphasis on repentance (3:8), the warning against trusting in descent from Abraham (3:8), the announcement of eschatological judgment (3:7, 17), and the contrast of baptism in (without the preposition ἐν) water with baptism in Holy Spirit and fire (3:16).[44] The

---

42. Cf. Isa. 4:4-5 for God washing away filth by a spirit of burning.

43. For fire associated with judgment see Dan. 7:9-10 and in Matt. see 13:30, 42; 25:41. The major study of the baptism of fire, E. M. Edsman, *Le baptême de feu* (Uppsala: Almqvist & Wiksell, 1940), discusses mainly the imagery in eschatology but also in worship (baptism, mystical experience) and finds that Dan. 7:10 and Matt. 3:11 played an important role. The multiple and varied nature of fire included that it deifies, vivifies, punishes, and destroys.

44. The words are recalled by the resurrected Jesus according to Acts 1:5 and 11:16.

summary characterization of John's baptism relates it not only to repentance but also to forgiveness of sins: "preaching a baptism of repentance [a repentance baptism] for the forgiveness of sins" (3:3; cf. Acts 13:24; 19:4), identical with Mark 1:4.[45] For Christians, as expressed by Luke, John the Baptist was the bridge between the old ("the Law and the Prophets") on one side and on the other side the new ("the good news of the kingdom of God") — Luke 16:16.

Luke enlarges on Jesus' commendation of John that "among those born of women no one is greater than John" (Luke 7:28; cf. Matt. 11:11) by adding a strong statement of the need for baptism and strong endorsement of the divine authority behind John's baptism:

> And all the people who heard, including the tax collectors, acknowledged the justice of God, being baptized [βαπτισθέντες] with John's baptism [βάπτισμα]. But the Pharisees and the lawyers, not being baptized [βαπτισθέντες] by him, rejected for themselves the will of God. (Luke 7:29-30)

This statement makes explicit the implication of the divine origin of John's baptism in Luke 20:4 (also Matt. 21:25 and Mark 11:30).

Luke in his Acts of the Apostles (19:1-7) records Paul's encounter with a group of disciples in Ephesus who, like Apollos at one time (Acts 18:25), knew only the baptism of John. They are usually taken to be evidence for the continuing presence and spread of disciples of John the Baptist, but it is possible that they were followers of Jesus with incomplete instruction. Since they said they had not heard of the Holy Spirit (19:2), some have questioned whether the saying attributed to John about the coming one baptizing with the Holy Spirit[46] could have been spoken by him. However, these were not personal disciples of John, having been taught his baptism only recently (18:24-26). Luke includes the episode in part to show the distinctiveness of Christian baptism — "in the name of the Lord Jesus" (i.e., on the faith that Jesus has come and not just would come, 19:4-5) and bestowing the Holy Spirit (19:2, 6) — and to make the point that after Jesus' death and resurrection baptism in his name superseded the baptism of John. The manifestation of the Spirit in the speaking in tongues occurs in Acts at each significant moment in the spread of the gospel — to Jews (Acts 2:1-45, 16), to Samaritans (8:15-18), to Gentiles (10:44-48), and to the disciples of John (19:1-7). Each incident was noteworthy as being exceptional and requiring an obvious manifestation of God's acceptance of the people involved.[47]

---

45. Βάπτισμα μετανοίας εἰς ἄφεσιν ἁμαρτιῶν. Luke 1:77 connects the forgiveness of sins with the ministry of John: his father prophesied that he would "give knowledge of salvation to his people in the forgiveness of their sins." The forgiveness of sins is a Lukan concern — Luke 24:47; Acts 2:38; 5:31; 10:43; 13:38; 26:18. The phrase "for the forgiveness of sins" occurs in Luke 3:3; 24:47; Acts 2:38; Matt. 26:28; and Mark 1:4. Other than in this full phrase, "forgiveness of sins" occurs only in Col. 1:14.

46. Found in all four Gospels: Matt. 3:11; Mark 1:8; Luke 3:16; John 1:33.

47. Anthony Ash, "John's Disciples: A Serious Problem," *Restoration Quarterly* 45 (2003): 85-93. And see chap. 10 on Acts.

The Gospel of John concentrates its account of the ministry of John the Baptist on his testimony to Jesus, which becomes more personal and more explicit than in the Synoptics (1:19-37). It puts on John the Baptist's lips the quotation of Isaiah 40:3 in order to indicate his identity (1:23). When asked why he was baptizing, the Baptist replied that he baptized in water, but there was one coming after him of whom he was not worthy who would baptize in (with) Holy Spirit (1:26-27, 33). Jesus was the Lamb of God who would truly take away the sins of the world (1:29). John's baptism may have had a temporal priority, but Jesus had an ontological priority over John (1:30). John's baptism was the occasion of revealing to Israel the Son of God (1:31, 34). John's function was to bear testimony to him (1:6-8, 19, 32, 34; 3:27-30). The Fourth Gospel locates John's baptizing on the east bank of the Jordan river (1:28; 3:26; 10:40), but not exclusively in the river, for he employed other abundant sources of water (3:23). The debate between the disciples of John and a Jew (or Jews) concerning purification (John 3:25) indicates that John's baptism had a different kind of purification in view from that in Jewish baptisms.

The Meaning of John's Baptism

From the primary sources for John's baptism as surveyed above — the Gospels and Josephus — one may draw up a composite list of the functions ascribed to or implicit in John's baptism.[48] (1) It expressed conversionary repentance, a turning to a new way of life. (2) It mediated divine forgiveness. (3) It purified from uncleanness, ritual and moral. (4) It foreshadowed the ministry of an expected figure (from the Christian perspective this made John the forerunner of Jesus Christ), so it had an eschatological dimension. (5) It was an initiation into the "true Israel" — not, however, a closed community like Qumran but the renewed people of God. (6) It was a protest against the temple establishment by offering an alternative means of forgiveness of sins. Most of these points would command a general agreement among students of John the Baptist, although points (5) and (6) are less commonly accepted or expressed.

The phrase "baptism of repentance for forgiveness of sins" (Mark 1:4; Luke 3:3; cf. Acts 13:24) has usually been interpreted in a straightforward way as referring to a forgiveness of sins (perhaps only realized eschatologically, but this is less likely) as the object or goal of the immersion. Because of the importance of this point in Christian baptism, note must be taken of an alternative interpretation.[49] The argument builds on the thought that Qumran made an advance on Old Testament practices with the idea that moral sin can ritually defile the flesh. The Dead Sea Scrolls appear to make a distinction between inner cleansing, effected by the spirit, and

---

48. I follow in this listing Robert L. Webb, "Jesus' Baptism: Its Historicity and Implications," *Bulletin for Biblical Research* 10.2 (2000): 261-309.

49. See Taylor in note 9.

outer cleansing effected by water.[50] Against this background at Qumran, and accepting Josephus's description of John's baptism as accurate, the argument proceeds to reinterpret the passages in the Gospels to agree with the Dead Sea Scrolls and Josephus. Thus the Gospels are understood to mean that repentance brought the forgiveness of sins and this led to baptism. The linguistic basis of the argument rests on a possible meaning of a possible underlying Aramaic. Although it is granted that some contemporary texts[51] do connect immersion with pleading for forgiveness, it is claimed that Josephus and the Synoptics (according to this new interpretation) present John's baptism as bodily cleansing that follows after people have made their heart right by repentance.[52] In support of this interpretation Matthew 3:7-10 and Luke 3:7-9 are understood as meaning that the people who came to John must bear fruits of repentance before their baptism and Matthew 23:25-26 as meaning that inner cleansing must precede outer cleansing.

A fundamental objection to the new interpretation pertains to its methodology. It would seem to be historically unsound to prefer the later source (Josephus), with his acknowledged biases and limitations (see above), over the earlier Synoptic Gospels, even with their Christian perspective. The Christians and the Gospels, with their freely admitted continuity with John's ministry, were in a better position to report his message. Hence, the crucial factor is the meaning of the Gospel texts themselves. The interpretation of these texts ultimately depends on whether for the authors of the Greek Gospels the "forgiveness of sins" is to be construed with baptism or with the repentance. The normal construction in Greek would be to construe the prepositional phrase with the main noun, not with the qualifying noun in the genitive case. Luke does have the construction "repentance for forgiveness of sins" (24:47 in the better manuscripts), but repentance in this statement is in the same grammatical position as baptism in the accounts of John's preaching. The uniform early Christian understanding was that baptism was "in order to," not "because of," the forgiveness of sins (Acts 2:38).[53] Matthew 3:11 has the exceptional construction "I baptize for [εἰς] repentance." If the normal meaning of εἰς, "in order to" or "in the direction of," is observed, then Matthew puts the sequence in the reverse of the interpretation being advanced. However, Matthew's statement is a variant of Mark and Luke's "baptism of repentance" and means "with reference to repentance."[54] Alter-

---

50. B. E. Thiering, "Inner and Outer Cleansing at Qumran as a Background to New Testament Baptism," *New Testament Studies* 26 (1979-80):266-277, pursued further in "Qumran Initiation and New Testament Baptism," 27 (1980-81):615-631.

51. *Testament of Levi* 2.3B; *Sibylline Oracles* 4.162-170; *Life of Adam and Eve* 6, cited in chap. 3.

52. Taylor, *The Immerser*, pp. 83, 87-88.

53. See discussion in chap. 10.

54. The use of εἰς for "with reference to" is found in Acts 2:25; Hermas, *Similitudes* 9.26.6 (103.6). If one keeps the usual force of εἰς, a possible meaning would be a baptism that calls for a repentant life, a reformation (of life), but that gives to "repentance" a force it does not normally have, inasmuch as the "fruits of repentance" (Matt. 3:8) are distinguished from the repentance itself. It is possible, however, that repentance does carry the meaning of its results here.

natively, but less likely, John's statement in Matthew means his general practice of baptism (not its reception in individual cases) was a call to people to repent. The new interpretation of John's baptism imposes an unjustified temporal sequence on Matthew 3:7-10 and Luke 3:7-9 and transfers Matthew 23:25-26 from a controversy about the ritual practices of the Pharisees to apply to John's teaching.

The Manner of John's Baptism

The possible Jewish antecedents to John's baptism — washings for purity, the washings at Qumran, and proselyte baptism — all involved a full bath, an immersion. Running water was necessary for the most severe cases of impurity.[55] The New Testament texts are supportive of John's baptism being an immersion but do not give much indication of the manner in which this may have been carried out.[56]

The use of the verb βαπτίζω indicates an immersion (chap. 2). Although the force of the preposition "in" (ἐν) cannot be pressed, it is to be noted that John's baptism was "in the Jordan river" (Mark 1:5). Mark 1:9, Jesus was baptized "into [εἰς] the Jordan by John," may not say more than 1:5, for the prepositions εἰς and ἐν could merge into one another in meaning (also in Mark), but the usage here is suggestive. Jesus then "came up out of the water" (Mark 1:10; Matt. 3:16). Although it is possible that the "coming up" refers to rising from an immersion, more likely it means stepping out of the water in which the baptism was performed. Nonetheless, the going to a river and actually being in its water imply an action requiring more water than a pouring or sprinkling. The Gospel of John reports that one of the places where John baptized was Aenon near Salim, "because there was much water there" (John 3:23). The phrase is literally "many waters" and suggests springs of water, but again the indication is that the site was appropriate for the kind of baptism because "water was abundant there" (NRSV).

The Jewish practice was self-immersion. Since the requirement was for no part of the body to be left untouched by the water, there was no place for an administrator or assistant to have a part in placing the body under the water. The person stood, sat, kneeled, or squatted in the water to the neck and dipped his or her head under the water and raised it up. If this action provided precedent for John's baptism, then his role as the "baptizer" was not to lay the body down in the water in the manner of baptism in modern churches that practice immersion. If he guided the head under the water but wanted to observe the Jewish practice of the water touching all parts, he may have removed his hand before the baptizand raised his or her head. Since John broke with precedent in administering the baptism, the antecedents may not have influenced his manner of baptizing. More significant than the exact manner

---

55. But one was not always immersed in it — Lev. 14:5-6, 50-52 (skin diseases and mold in a house), 15:13 (bodily discharge), Num. 19:17 (touching a corpse), and Deut. 21:4 (bloodguilt).
56. Webb, *John the Baptiser and Prophet*, pp. 179-183.

would have been the reason for the change in practice. Presumably there was a symbolic purpose in his action. This is not stated, but what suggests itself is the thought that one cannot effect one's own cleansing.[57]

---

57. Légasse, *Naissance du baptême*, pp. 42-43.

PART TWO

Baptism in the New Testament

6. Baptism of Jesus — I

New Testament Texts

The baptism of Jesus could, strictly speaking, be treated as an antecedent to Christian baptism. It is presented in the Gospels in many respects as a unique event. It may also be seen as the transition between the John's baptism and Christian baptism. Since the baptism of Jesus was later considered the foundation of Christian baptism, we treat it here in the unit on the beginning of Christian baptism, although it was properly *sui generis*.

The earliest accounts of the baptism of Jesus are found in the canonical Gospels. As a practical matter, we cannot go behind these texts to "what really happened." Moreover, these texts were what shaped later Christian thought, along with the practices that writers knew in their communities, practices that were themselves influenced by these texts when they came to be read as canonical authorities. So, our concern will be primarily with the texts as we have them and only secondarily with occasional matters of historicity. There is little indication that the texts were shaped by later Christian practice.

As recognized by nearly all scholars of the Gospels, the event of the baptism of Jesus by John the Baptizer is itself certainly historical. Since the lesser figure would have received baptism from the greater, a baptism of Jesus by John could only have been an embarrassment to later Christian faith; hence, the emphasis in the Gospel accounts on John's declaration that the one coming after him was greater than he and had a superior baptism to offer.[1] In view of the problem that some later had with a sinless Jesus coming to receive from John a "baptism of repentance for forgiveness of sins," reflected perhaps already in Matthew's account,[2] the event would not have been

---

1. Matt. 3:11; Mark 1:7-8: Luke 3:16; John 1:26-34. See chap. 5.
2. Mark 1:4; Matt. 3:13-15; cf. noncanonical accounts below. For the "embarrassment" of Jesus' baptism see M.-A. Chevallier, "L'apologie du baptême d'eau du premier siècle: Introduction

invented by Jesus' disciples nor accepted if invented by others. Furthermore, all layers of the Gospel traditions and early formulations of the apostolic kerygma (Acts 1:22; 10:37) include the baptism of John as part of the career of Jesus and the beginning of the Christian story. The early disciples knew the baptism to have occurred and accepted the event as preparatory and anticipatory of Jesus' ministry.

The event of the baptism is associated in the Synoptic Gospels with Jesus' recognition and acceptance of a special relationship with his God and Father that marked the beginning of his messianic ministry. Here in particular we cannot now penetrate beyond the texts to what Jesus' experience was — a psychological conviction given an imaginative literary coloring, a vision by Jesus, an objective occurrence hidden perhaps from others than Jesus and John.[3] Such interpretations are secondary for an understanding of the event as it relates to the development of Christian baptism. Whatever Jesus' experience, the importance of the event for the disciples was the meaning it had for their faith and later their practice of baptism. Although the New Testament never asserts that the baptism of Jesus was the foundation of Christian baptism or a prototype for it, and indeed in the nature of its importance for Christology it was a unique event, the declaration of Jesus' Sonship and the coming of the Holy Spirit on him at this time provide a parallel to the promises attached in a lesser sense to Christian baptism.

We discuss the accounts in the order Mark, Luke, Matthew, and John, but once more without indicating any view of the relationships of the Gospels.

Mark, as the other Gospels, uses the account of the baptizing ministry of John the Baptist to set the stage and moves swiftly from it to the baptism of Jesus (1:9-11). Jesus came from his home in Nazareth of Galilee to be baptized by John, so he made a conscious decision involving some effort to identify with and submit to John's ministry. Whereas in Mark 1:5 the others confessed sins at their baptism, Jesus in the otherwise parallel account in 1:9-10 did not. The baptism was administered by John "in [εἰς] the Jordan River." The Greek preposition means "into," but it was often used with the sense "in." It should not, therefore, be pressed to indicate in itself that the baptism was an immersion into the Jordan, but since every indication that John's baptism was an immersion like other Jewish washings, the literal meaning of the preposition would be consistent with that action, as indeed would be the meaning "in." The preposition εἰς is probably the correct reading in 1:10 also, where the Spirit comes down "to" or "into" Jesus.[4] The effect of the wording in the two passages, then, is to balance the act of Jesus descending (being dipped) into water with the Spirit subsequently descending into Jesus. Verse 10 has the explicit balance of Jesus

---

secondaire de l'étiologie dans les récits du baptême du Jesus," *New Testament Studies* 32 (1986): 528-543; other factors, however, influenced the Evangelists in their reports of the baptism of Jesus.

3. G. R. Beasley-Murray, *Baptism in the New Testament* (Grand Rapids: Eerdmans, 1973; first published 1962), pp. 55-62, for the view that the baptism, instead of being the start of Jesus' messianic consciousness, was his formal inauguration in that role.

4. Most manuscripts read ἐπί, "upon," but this may be a later harmonizing reading to agree with Matthew and Luke that would also seem to accord with the imagery of a dove descending.

"coming up out of" (ἀναβαίνων, "ascending from") the water and the "Spirit coming down" (καταβαῖνον, "descending") on or to Jesus. Whether the coming up out of the water refers to coming up from an immersion or walking out of the river is not clear, but certainly Jesus is pictured as having been in the river, something unnecessary for any action other than an immersion.

The Spirit descending "like a dove" has been thought to recall Genesis 1:2, where the Hebrew verb for the Spirit "hovering over" the waters is a word used for the hovering or fluttering of a bird.[5] There may also be an allusion to the dove sent out by Noah and returning to the ark (Gen. 8:8-11). Both texts were baptismal types in patristic interpretation. The coming of the Spirit was accompanied by a voice from heaven, "You are my beloved Son."[6] The words echo, if they do not directly allude to, Psalm 2:7, on which more below. This language for the king in Psalm 2 is applied to the Lord's Servant in Isaiah 42:1, where this description of the Servant is followed by the promise, "I will put my Spirit upon him." "Beloved" in the Greek Old Testament and even in secular Greek had the nuance of "only." The emotional force of "beloved son" is seen in Genesis 22:2. The combination of Psalm 2:7 with Isaiah 42:1 points to Jesus as both messianic King and Suffering Servant. Jesus at his baptism, therefore, received the Holy Spirit and acknowledgment of his Sonship. The same two ideas in a diminished sense were central to Christian baptism, the gift of the Holy Spirit and incorporation into (or adoption as) "the sons of God."

Jesus' description of his anticipated death as a baptism (Mark 10:38) is discussed in chapter 8.

Although giving the longest account among the Synoptic Gospels of the ministry of John the Baptizer, Luke is the briefest on Jesus' baptism (3:21-22). Luke passes quickly from Jesus' baptism to the divine acknowledgement, but he adds three details to the other accounts. Characteristic of his interest in prayer, Luke alone mentions that Jesus was praying at his baptism, but the prayer is noted after the baptism, so it was not the prayer of a penitent. The Holy Spirit came while Jesus was praying. Also characteristically, he identifies the Spirit as Holy Spirit. He further explains that the Spirit came "in bodily form like a dove," so that it was the appearance of the Spirit and not just his descent that was like a dove. Codex Beza has the reading εἰς, but all other manuscripts read ἐπί, "upon" him. Luke 4:16-21 quotes the language of anointing from Isaiah 61:1 in reference to the coming of the Spirit. The coming of the Holy Spirit on Jesus was his anointing as the Messiah ("anointed with the Holy Spirit" — Acts 10:38).

The designation of Jesus as "my beloved Son" picks up the earlier reference in Luke 1:35 to Jesus as "Son of God." Codex Beza and seven manuscripts of the Old Latin version enlarge the divine acknowledgment with the further words of Psalm 2:7, "Today I have begotten you." This fuller statement is attested in a number of early Christian texts that quote the heavenly voice in this fuller form of Psalm 2:7

---

5. So in Deut. 32:11.
6. Compare the prediction of "a new priest" in *Testament of Levi* 18.6-7, quoted below.

and so confirm the interpretation of the baptismal acknowledgment as a deliberate reference to the Psalm text, read messianically.[7]

Matthew's fuller treatment of Jesus' baptism by John contains the main points of Mark and Luke plus some distinctive concerns (3:13-17). Jesus came from Galilee to (ἐπί) the Jordan in order to be baptized by John. John protested that he needed to be baptized by Jesus. The inclusion of this exchange between John and Jesus is likely a response to the difficulty felt by some at Jesus being baptized by John. The difficulty was perhaps the thought that someone without sin did not need baptism or that baptism was administered by a superior to an inferior. Jesus answers that the baptism would "fulfill all righteousness." Righteousness was an important concept for Matthew. It often refers to God's saving activity, but here it likely means to obey God's plan.[8] In receiving baptism Jesus identified with the people of Israel to whom John addressed his message and started on a path that led to the cross (Matt. 16:21-23).[9] He also set an example of obedience for others.

As Jesus came up from the water, the heavens were opened and he saw the Spirit of God[10] descending like a dove.[11] Matthew alone has the voice from heaven use the third person, "This is," rather than the second person, "You are"; but there is no indication that others heard the declaration, and only Jesus (as also in Mark and Luke) is said to have seen God's Spirit descending.[12] Other than the difference between a third-person and a second-person declaration, the words are the same in the three Synoptic Gospels. Only Matthew makes further use of the full phrase, "This is my Son, the Beloved, with whom I am well pleased" — repeating the same words in the

---

7. Daniel Vigne, *Le baptême de Jésus dans las tradition judéo-chrétienne* (Paris: J. Gabalda, 1992), pp. 21-24, 120-130; he concludes that the authenticity of this reading "may be considered as established" — p. 107; pp. 22-23, notes 6 and 7, give references that cite the text in this form before the great Gospel rescensions of the fourth and fifth centuries. Some of these are Justin, *Dialogue with Trypho* 88.8 (the mention of the "form of a dove" indicates he is following Luke) and 103.6 (in a context that has been following Matthew but includes details from Luke); Clement of Alexandria, *Instructor* 1.6.25; cf. *Gospel of the Ebionites,* quoted below; Origen, *Commentary on John* 1.32; Lactantius, *Divine Institutes* 4.15. *Apostolic Constitutions* 2.32 quotes Psalm 2:7 as applying to all the baptized. Kilian McDonnell, *The Baptism of Jesus in the Jordan: The Trinitarian and Cosmic Order of Salvation* (Collegeville: Liturgical, 1996), pp. 90-93, argues that the passage is not necessarily Adoptionist, the meaning being that "to be known [as God's Son] is to be born" and that the event marked not the origin of the Son but his manifestation.

8. Cf. Matt. 5:6, 10; 6:33; 21:32, where John's ministry was part of "the way of righteousness."

9. Oscar Cullmann, *Baptism in the New Testament* (London: SCM, 1950), pp. 16-22. Note the corrective by Beasley-Murray, *Baptism in the New Testament*, pp. 49-55, that one can read the baptism as an act of solidarity with the people but not as an act of identification instead of the people.

10. Mark has "Spirit"; Luke "Holy Spirit." Matthew alone uses "Spirit of God" — 12:28; cf. 12:18.

11. The pagan critic Celsus considered the narrative about a dove alighting upon Jesus at his baptism by John to be "a fiction" and put in the mouth of a Jew the objection, "What credible witness beheld this appearance? Or who heard a voice from heaven declaring you to be the Son of God?" Origen thought Celsus took the account from Matthew and "perhaps also from the other Gospels" (*Against Celsus* 1.40-41; his response continues through 48).

12. Perhaps the third-person statement indicates a revelation to John (John 1:33), if not to others, and the second-person address serves as a confirmation to Jesus.

account of the Transfiguration of Jesus (17:5).[13] It may be that Matthew is picking up on the baptismal event in his Trinitarian formula at the close of his Gospel — the Father who spoke from heaven, the Son who was acknowledged, and the Holy Spirit who descended.

The Gospel of John contains no direct account of the baptism of Jesus but does allude to it. The author assumes the event is known, and he is content to recall and interpret it.[14] The purpose of John's baptizing was to reveal Jesus (1:31). John the Baptizer testified (1:32) that he had seen the Spirit descend as a dove from heaven and abide on him (a distinctively Johannine touch that the Spirit remained on him). The coming of the Holy Spirit as a dove is the only feature of the baptism of Jesus mentioned in all four Gospels. The event was no doubt significant for Jesus, for his self-consciousness and for the inauguration of his public life. It was early taken as his anointing and so indicative of his messianic role (Acts 10:38). The coming of the Holy Spirit was also significant for the the understanding of Christian baptism, which was associated with the coming of the Holy Spirit. The Fourth Gospel indicates that the coming of the Spirit, whatever its significance for Jesus' self-understanding, was the moment of revelation to John the Baptist too (1:31, 33, 34). The confession of Jesus as the "Son of God" is placed on John's lips (1:34).

Another matter related to the baptism of Jesus that occurs in all four Gospels is John the Baptist's testimony about the coming baptism "in the Holy Spirit," now expressly said to be administered by Jesus (1:33). John also identifies Jesus as the one who "takes away the sin of the world" (1:29). Thus his testimony ascribes to Jesus two basic characteristics of the Christian age, the removal of sin and the bestowal of the Holy Spirit.

Only the Fourth Gospel tells us that Jesus through his disciples was engaged in a baptizing ministry parallel with or in conjunction with John's (3:22-23, 26; 4:1-2). Since Jesus identified himself with John's baptism, and since his participating in John's ministry might have seemed to compromise his superiority to John, the account may be accepted as resting on early historical remembrance.[15] That Jesus was himself baptized and at least for a time along with his disciples practiced baptism would easily explain why the disciples in the postresurrection period implemented this practice.

---

13. "This is my Son" picks up Ps. 2:7, and "Beloved, with whom I am well pleased" picks up Isa. 42:1; Matthew also quotes Isa. 42:1 in 12:18. The statement occurs in reference to the Transfiguration also in 2 Pet. 1:17 with a slight change in wording (in some manuscripts conformed to the exact wording of Matthew).

14. Daniel Alain Bertrand, *Le baptême de Jésus: Histoire de l'exégèse aux deux premiers siècle* (Tübingen: Mohr, 1973), p. 17.

15. Beasley-Murray, *Baptism in the New Testament*, p. 69, defends the historicity of Jesus' baptizing, or authorizing his disciples to do so, during his ministry.

Early Noncanonical Accounts of the Baptism of Jesus

The early noncanonical references to the baptism of Jesus by John do not add significantly to the historical evidence about Jesus' baptism but do indicate early interpretations of the event and in some cases witness to independent traditions about it.[16]

The composition of the *Gospel of the Ebionites* belongs possibly to the early second century. The preserved fragments have the character of a harmony of the Synoptic Gospels.[17] They concern especially John the Baptist, with whose ministry this Gospel began, and the baptism of Jesus. These accounts are based on the Synoptic Gospels and have no independent historical value.

> It came to pass in the days of Herod the king of Judaea, when Caiaphas was high priest, that there came one, John by name, and baptized with the baptism of repentance in the river Jordan. . . .
>
> It came to pass that John was baptizing; and there went out to him Pharisees and were baptized, and all Jerusalem. . . .
>
> When the people were baptized, Jesus also came and was baptized by John. And as he came up from the water, the heavens were opened and he saw the Holy Spirit in the form of a dove that descended and entered into him. And a voice sounded from heaven that said: You are my beloved Son, in you I am well pleased. And again: I have this day begotten you. And immediately a great light shone round about the place. When John saw this, he says to him:
>
> Who are you, Lord? And again a voice from heaven rang out to him: This is my beloved Son in whom I am well pleased. And then, John fell down before him and said: I beseech you, Lord, baptize me. But he prevented him and said: Suffer it; for thus it is fitting that everything should be fulfilled.[18]

The new details are the appearance of a great light shining around the scene, of which more below, and the expansion of the words of the heavenly voice by additional words from Psalm 2:7, as occurred in some witnesses to the Gospel of Luke.

The *Gospel of the Nazarenes* likewise derives from the first half of the second

---

16. Bertrand, *Le baptême de Jésus*; Daniel Vigne, *Le baptême de Jésus dans las tradition judéochrétienne* (Paris: J. Gabalda, 1992), does find in the early Jewish-Christian sources authentic recollections as well as the earliest interpretations of the event. Oxyrhynchus Papyrus 840 is discussed in chap. 16.

17. A. F. J. Klijn, *Jewish-Christian Gospel Tradition* (Leiden: Brill, 1992), p. 42, "The Gospel according to the Ebionites is a representative of a widespread attempt in early Christianity to harmonise Gospel traditions on the basis of existing Gospels," a contention supported by detailed analysis of the texts in the remainder of the book.

18. Fragments 1-3, quoted by Epiphanius, *Panarion* 30.13.6, 4-5, 7-8. I follow the rearranged order and the translation (with modifications) in Wilhelm Schneemelcher, *New Testament Apocrypha*, Vol. 1, *Gospels and Related Writings* (Louisville: Westminster/John Knox, 1991), p. 169. For a commentary of the passage see Klijn, *Jewish-Christian Gospel Tradition*, pp. 70-73, showing that except for the appearance of the light (pp. 72-73) the passage is a composite of words and phrases from the Synoptic Gospels with the influence of Matthew predominant.

century. It is closely dependent on the Gospel of Matthew and has been compared to a "targum-like rendering of the canonical Matthew."[19] The notice about the baptism of Jesus is unique in early Christian literature:

> Behold, the mother of the Lord and his brothers said to him, "John baptizes for the remission of sins; let us go and be baptized by him." But he said to them, "What sin have I committed that I should go and be baptized by him? Unless, perhaps, the very words which I have said are only ignorance."[20]

This conversation reflects concern over why Jesus submitted to John's baptism, a concern apparently lying behind Matthew's account and to which the Matthean Jesus gives a more orthodox, or at least a more straightforward answer. The meaning may not be the implication of Jesus having sins of ignorance but of ignorance as to another reason for baptism besides forgiveness.[21] Or, the sense may be that he did not know if he was truly pure (although he was). Or by changing the punctuation, the second statement too may have been a question, "Do you believe I have said this in ignorance?" On this interpretation, there is a double question, the second of which reinforced the first; both questions had only one answer — Jesus had not sinned.[22] The statement that John baptized "for [or unto] the remission of sins," however, does not come from Matthew but is found in Mark 1:4 and Luke 3:3.

The *Gospel of the Hebrews* was sometimes confused with the *Gospel of the Nazaraeans* and like it originated in the first half of the second century but unlike it probably belonged to Egypt.[23] This Gospel contains semitic features like the Holy Spirit as female and as speaking in the manner of the divine wisdom in the Wisdom literature. Its reference to the baptism of Jesus focuses upon the coming of the Spirit:

> And it came to pass when the Lord was come up out of the water, the whole fount of the Holy Spirit descended upon him and rested on him [Isa. 11:2; 61:1]

---

19. Philipp Vielhauer, *Geschichte der urchristlichen Literatur* (Berlin: de Gruyter, 1975), p. 652, cited in Schneemelcher, *New Testament Apocrypha*, Vol. 1, p. 159 (cf. also 157). For the Nazarenes, see Petri Luomanen, "Nazarenes," in Antti Marjanen and Petri Luomanen, eds., *A Companion to Second-Century Christian "Heretics"* (Leiden: Brill, 2005), pp. 279-314, who finds that the name did not apply to a defined group with clear boundaries.

20. Jerome, *Against the Pelagians* 3.2. Jerome describes the work as "the Gospel according to the Hebrews, which is written in the Chaldee and Syrian [Aramaic] language but in Hebrew characters and is used by the Nazarenes to this day (I mean the Gospel according to the Apostles, or, as is generally maintained, the Gospel according to Matthew)."

21. McDonnell, *The Baptism of Jesus in the Jordan*, p. 21.

22. Vigne, *Le baptême de Jésus*, pp. 141-144.

23. Vigne, *Le baptême de Jésus*, pp. 25-32, argues the case for these two titles being the same work, coming at the latest from the end of the first century, and not having been regarded as heretical by its early orthodox users. I follow Philipp Vielhauer and Georg Strecker in distinguishing the works — Schneemelcher, *New Testament Apocrypha*, Vol. 1, pp. 134-178. Cf. Klijn, *Jewish-Christian Gospel Tradition*, who concludes from an examination of the statements of Christian authors about these Gospels that they belong to three separate Jewish-Christian groups (p. 30); "The presence of three Jewish Christian Gospels is an established fact" (p. 41).

and said to him: "My Son, in all the prophets was I waiting for you [Wis. 7:27] that you should come and I might rest in you [Sir. 24:7]. For you are my rest [Ps. 132:14]; you are my first-begotten Son [Ps. 2:7] that reigns for ever [Ps. 89:29; Luke 1:33]."[24]

Jesus was distinguished from the earlier prophets, wise men, and kings in that the "whole fount of the Holy Spirit" and not just a portion rested in him. Notably, the words "My Son" are spoken by the Holy Spirit, who is viewed as Jesus' "Mother," a development perhaps from "Spirit" being feminine in Semitic languages.[25] There is also a reference to the messianic anointing of Jesus to be found in the allusion to Psalm 2:7 and the statement of the Lord's everlasting reign, words indicating that the begetting did not occur at the baptism and that the Christology was orthodox.[26]

The late *Gospel of Nicodemus* is thought to have made use of early Jewish-Christian material, perhaps Ebionite. It includes the *Acts of Pilate*, derived from a Christian legend known in the second century, and an account of Christ's descent into Hades between his death and resurrection. The compiler of the present form of the work gives himself a date in the fifth century, but the contents provide evidence for a sixth-century date.[27] The prologue to the *Acts of Pilate* begins with "Ananias, an officer of the guard," professing to have come to know the "Lord Jesus Christ from the sacred scriptures." These he "approached with faith, and was accounted worthy of holy baptism."[28] The description "holy baptism" sounds like later language, but the description of the baptism of Jesus, if not a late summary, could rest on earlier sources. Thus, the *descensus* part of the document begins with the righteous dead raised in connection with the resurrection of Jesus (Matt. 27:52) bringing their testimony to some of the Jewish leaders. John the Baptist's identification of himself and his ministry included these words:

> [I] preached repentance to the people for the forgiveness of sins. And the Son of God came to me, and when I saw him afar off, I said to the people: "Behold, the Lamb of God, who takes away the sin of the world" [John 1:29]. And with my hand I baptized him in the river Jordan, and I saw the Holy Spirit like a dove coming

---

24. Jerome, *In Isaiah* 4 on Isa. 11:2. Translation in Schneemelcher, *New Testament Apocrypha*, Vol. 1, p. 177. Jerome introduces his quotation in a similar but less full way as he introduced our preceding quotation from the *Gospel of the Nazarenes:* "According to the Gospel written in the Hebrew speech, which the Nazareans read." He apparently thought the two works the same.

25. Aphrahat, *Demonstrations* 6.17, "Our Lord, who was born from the Spirit, was not tempted by Satan until in baptism he received the Spirit from on high."

26. Vigne, *La baptême de Jésus*, pp. 116-120; cf. 129-132 for the Nazaraeans and the great church regarding the begetting at the baptism as declarative and juridic in contrast to the Ebionites, for whom it was generative and ontological.

27. G. C. O'Ceallaigh, "Dating the Commentaries of Nicodemus," *Harvard Theological Review* 56 (1963): 21-58, argues that internal evidence demands a *terminus post quem* of 555; he adopts the title "Commentaries" as what the author entitled his work.

28. Felix Scheidweiler, "The Gospel of Nicodeumus," in Schneemelcher, *New Testament Apocrypha*, Vol. 1, pp. 501-536 (505).

upon him, and heard also the voice of God the Father speaking thus: "This is my beloved Son, in whom I am well pleased" [Matt. 3:16-17]. And for this reason he sent me to you, to preach that the only begotten Son of God comes here, in order that whoever believes in him should be saved, and whoever does not believe in him should be condemned. (18.2)[29]

This account lacks the distinctive features of the Jewish-Christian Gospels that would confirm a dependence on them. It seems to be derived from a conflation of the canonical Gospels with special dependence on John. The next section of the *descensus* (19) anticipates the postmortem baptism of the righteous (chap. 13).

Early Christian authors attributed both Judaizing (chiliasm) and Gnostic ideas to Cerinthus, active at the turn from the first to the second century.[30] He gave an early interpretation of the baptism of Jesus not as a revelation of his true nature and mission but as a change in his metaphysical state. According to Irenaeus, Cerinthus taught that "After Jesus' baptism the Christ who is from the Ruler of all things descended on him in the form of a dove, and then he preached the unknown Father and performed miracles."[31]

Cerinthus anticipated in a simpler way the more elaborate versions of the experience of Jesus at his baptism to be found in subsequent Gnostic systems. The myth of a group whom Irenaeus identified as "Others," Sethian (chap. 17) or perhaps Naassenes (Ophites), had the divine Christ "announce his advent through John, prepare the baptism of repentance, and adopt Jesus," so that when he descended he might have a pure vessel. When Christ descended on Jesus, he then began to work miracles and announce the unknown Father.[32]

In a general description of the Valentinians, Irenaeus attributes to some of them a similar view but formulated according to the developed system that he knew through Ptolemy. He refers to those who say "Christ passed through Mary as water flows through a pipe, and at his baptism [βαπτίσματος] there came down to him in the form of a dove that Savior from the Pleroma, who was formed out of all its components."[33] In reference specifically to the version of Valentinianism developed by Marcus, Irenaeus states that in his system the powers who emanated from the Aeons generated the Jesus who appeared on the earth. He was brought into being by dispensation through Mary, and, on his passing through the womb, the Father of all

---

29. F. Scheidweiler, in Schneemelcher, *New Testament Apocrypha*, Vol. 1, p. 522.

30. Charles E. Hill, "Cerinthus, Gnostic or Chiliast?" *Journal of Early Christian Studies* 8 (2000): 135-172 resolves the differences in favor of Cerinthus as a Gnostic, who, like Marcion later, drew the conclusion that the Jewish interpretation of their scriptures was correct. Matti Myllykoski, "Cerinthus," in Marjanen and Luomanen, *A Companion to Second-Century Christian "Heretics,"* pp. 213-246, concludes Cerinthus was not an early Gnostic but, whether a Jew, Jewish Christian, or neither, he was a Christian who drew heavily on Jewish traditions.

31. Irenaeus, *Against Heresies* 1.26.1. He continues by noting that the views of the Ebionites with respect to the Lord were similar to those of Cerinthus (1.16.2).

32. Irenaeus, *Against Heresies* 1.30.12-14.

33. Irenaeus, *Against Heresies* 1.7.2.

chose him for recognition of himself. "When he came to the water, there came down to him like a dove" the power that was the seed of the Father.[34]

Such views as Irenaeus attributed to the Gnostics (on which see further chap. 17) were contrary to those of the mainstream of the church. Competing views of the significance of the descent of the dove on Jesus at the Jordan will appear in subsequent teachers.

A Christian version of the *Testaments of the Twelve Patriarchs* describes the "new priest" raised up by the Lord:

> The heavens will be opened, and from the temple of glory sanctification will come upon him, with a fatherly voice, as from Abraham to Isaac. And the glory of the Most High shall burst forth upon him. And the spirit of understanding and sanctification shall rest upon him [in the water].[35]

Either the whole passage has been shaped by a Christian, or the description seemed so strikingly similar to the revelation of Jesus at the Jordan that a Christian hand made the association explicit by adding the bracketed words. There is a similar allusion to the baptism of Jesus: "The heavens will be opened upon him to pour out the spirit as a blessing of the Holy Father."[36] Sandwiched between two certainly Christian statements, another passage speaks of the Most High, who will visit the earth, "crushing the dragon's head in the water."[37]

A Christian insertion in the Jewish *Sibylline Oracles* 1, dated about 150,[38] in recounting the incarnation and life of Christ refers to John the Baptist, a "voice . . . through the desert land." It describes baptism in Christian terms: "That every human person be illumined by waters, so that, being born from above, they may no longer in any respect at all transgress justice."[39] The Christian *Sibylline Oracles* 6, a hymn to Christ (second or third century), refers to his baptism in this way:

> "Since he was raised up the second time according to the flesh, when he was washed [ἀπολουσάμενος] in the flowing waters of the Jordan River . . . Having escaped the fire, he will first see God coming as the sweet Spirit on the white wings of a dove.[40]

There may be an allusion to immersion in the reference to his being raised up. Syrian tradition maintained the appearance of fire on the water at Jesus' baptism. Another reference speaks of the event without reference to the fire and continues to use the

---

34. Irenaeus, *Against Heresies* 1.15.3.
35. *Testament of Levi* 18.6-7.
36. *Testament of Judah* 24.2.
37. *Testament of Asher* 7.3. See the similar imagery in the *Odes of Solomon* in chap. 7.
38. J. J. Collins in James H. Charlesworth, ed., *The Old Testament Pseudepigrapha* (Garden City: Doubleday, 1983), 1.332. His translation is used in the quotations from Book 1.
39. *Sibylline Oracles* 1.339-341. On baptismal illumination see n. 44.
40. *Sibylline Oracles* 6.3-7.

Hellenistic language of washing instead of the Christian word baptism: "Wretched one [Coele-Syria], you did not recognize your God, who once washed [ἔλουσεν] in the streams of Jordan, and the Spirit flew as a dove."[41] A few lines later there is an odd, if not confused, passage describing a ritual that does use the word "baptism" but seems unrelated to orthodox Christianity:

> You shall sprinkle [σπείσεις] water on pure fire while you cry out, "As the Father begat you the Word, yet I sent out a bird, a word for a swift dispatcher of words, sprinkling [ῥαίνων] with holy waters your baptism [βάπτισμα] through which you were revealed out of fire." . . . But taking the head of this man and sprinkling [ῥάνας] it with water, pray three times. . . .[42]

In another part of the collection occurs more conventional Christian thinking that relates the baptism of Christians to the baptism of Christ. "The wood among the faithful . . . illuminating [φωτίζον] the elect with waters in twelve springs."[43] Illumination was a common term for baptism,[44] and the twelve springs of Elim (Exod. 15:27) were a type of the preaching of the Twelve.[45] This illumination of the elect results from Christ coming as a man to the creation, "illuminating [φωτίζων] by water,"[46] working miracles, and undergoing the passion.

From the first or second decade of the second century, Ignatius, bishop of Antioch, repeats the explanation of Jesus' baptism from Matthew 3:15. As part of what sounds like an early confession of faith or summary of the kerygma, he says: "Having been truly born of the virgin, baptized [βεβαπτισμένον] by John in order that all righteousness might be fulfilled by him."[47] In another passage, also incorporating confessional elements, Ignatius is the first to allude to the idea that by his baptism Jesus sanctified water for baptism, but he does so by referring the purification to the passion: "For our God Jesus the Christ was conceived by Mary according to the dispensation of God — of the seed of David and of the Holy Spirit; he was born and was baptized [ἐβαπτίσθη] in order that by his passion [τῷ πάθει] he might purify the water."[48] The πάθος might be taken as the experience of baptism ("by this experience") except that the word in Ignatius always refers to Jesus' passion,[49] and it seems that Ignatius intends to connect the baptism with the passion. These two pas-

---

41. *Sibylline Oracles* 7.66-67.
42. *Sibylline Oracles* 7.81-84.
43. *Sibylline Oracles* 8.245-247.
44. Justin, *1 Apology*, 61.14.
45. The springs of water are given a baptismal intepretation in Justin, *Dialogue* 86, but the twelve springs are the teaching of the twelve apostles in Irenaeus, *Proof* 46; Gregory of Nyssa, *Life of Moses* 2.133-134.
46. *Sibylline Oracles* 8.271.
47. Ignatius, *Smyrnaeans* 1.1.
48. Ignatius, *Ephesians* 18.2. Cf. in the New Testament "pure water" (Heb. 10:22) and "purified by water" (Eph. 5:26).
49. William R. Schoedel, *Ignatius of Antioch*, Hermeneia (Philadelphia: Fortress, 1985), p. 85.

sages are usually taken as giving two different reasons for the baptism of Jesus, but it may be that both passages are saying the same thing. If we take the exegesis of Matthew 3:15 noted above that at his baptism Jesus in solidarity with his people assumed the role of the Suffering Messiah in order to accomplish all righteousness (fulfilled at his death) and further remember that Jesus called his death a baptism (Mark 10:38), then his baptism announced his passion and received its efficacy from the passion, both of which were "for the forgiveness of sins" (Mark 1:4; Matt. 26:28).

The most striking new feature in noncanonical accounts of the baptism of Jesus (*Gospel of the Ebionites* and perhaps *Sibylline Oracles*) is the appearance of light or fire on the water. This feature is found in two manuscripts of the Old Latin version of the Gospels (Vercellensis [fourth century] and Sangermanensis [eighth century]) inserted at the end of Matthew 3:15, reading with some variation: "When he was baptized, such a bright light shone round about the water that all who approached were fearful."

The earliest fairly securely dated reference to a manifestation of light, in this case in the form of fire, occurs in Justin Martyr's account of the baptism of Jesus:

> John, the herald of his coming, came before him and preceded him in the way of baptism [βαπτίσματος] . . . When Jesus went to the Jordan river, where John was baptizing [ἐβάπτιζε], and when he went down to the water, a fire was kindled in the Jordan. And when he came up from the water, as the apostles of this very Christ of ours wrote, the Holy Spirit alighted upon him like a dove. We know that he had no need to have gone to the river, to be baptized [βαπτισθῆναι], or for the Spirit to come in the form of a dove, even as he submitted to be born and to be crucified, not because he needed such things, but [he did so] on behalf of the human race that from Adam had fallen under the power of death and the deceit of the serpent, since each one had sinned by personal transgression.[50]

Justin's concern in the passage was that the gifts of the Spirit (Isa. 11:1-3) no longer rested with the Jewish people but with Jesus and those to whom he gave them. Jesus did not need the Spirit, which he had from his birth, but the Spirit came in order to signify the transfer of the Spirit to a new people.[51] Jesus himself likewise had no need of baptism, but he submitted to it for the sake of human beings. The phrase "went down to [κατελθόντος . . . ἐπί] the water" refers to Jesus' approach to the Jordan as the time the fire was kindled on the water, but the subsequent phrase, "came up from [ἀναδύντος . . . ἀπό] the water," could refer to the emerging from the immersion as well as to stepping out of the river as the time of the descent of the Spirit. Later in the passage Justin explains that before Jesus came to the Jordan he was con-

---

50. *Dialogue with Trypho* 88.2-4. The whole chapter is studied by E. Bammel, "Die Täufertraditionen bei Justin," *Studia Patristica* 8.2 (1966):53-61, who identifies the extracanonical details as coming from one strand of Jewish-Christian tradition, and Vigne, *Le baptême de Jésus*, pp. 72-75.

51. Justin makes much of the gift of the Spirit in connection with Jesus' baptism — see also *Dialogue with Trypho* 87.2; 88.8 in this context; and 52.4.

sidered to be a carpenter, but at that time he was revealed for who he was.[52] He provides an early attestation of the accommodation of the words of the heavenly voice to Psalm 2:7, by declaring that David "spoke in the person of Christ what the Father would say to him" and quoting simply its words instead of the words in the Gospels, "You are my Son; this day I have begotten you."[53]

Justin's reference to "fire" is not only the earliest reference to the phenomenon that can be dated with some confidence but is also distinct from the light tradition, for he puts the appearance of the fire at the time when Jesus entered the water, whereas the reports of light put the phenomenon either at the baptism or after it as with the other divine acknowledgments. Light was a common feature of a theophany, and its accompaniment of Jesus' baptism would be theologically significant in association with the heavenly voice and the descent of the Spirit as testimonies to Jesus' unique status. Indeed, the most widely expressed form of the tradition speaks of "light" (as in Tatian, below), and may be the earlier version (if we could date the *Gospel of the Ebionites* with some certainty, we could speak with more confidence). In that case, might fire be Justin's rationalizing explanation of the tradition of the appearance of light that was followed by some others (*Preaching of Paul* below)? Or, is the appearance of the fire an early gloss interpreting John's words that Jesus would baptize with "the Holy Spirit and fire," so that both the Holy Spirit and the fire appeared at his baptism? The prevalence of the terminology of light would have been due to its theological significance, but such an interpretation could have been early or could have been a secondary development.[54]

The account of the baptism of Jesus in the *Diatessaron* of Tatian apparently included the statement that a "strong light streamed out" on the water, and his influence may account for its currency in the Syriac world.[55] He would have known this idea in some form from his teacher Justin, but both may depend on an earlier tradition.

The anonymous treatise *On Rebaptism* from North Africa in the mid-third cen-

---

52. See further in chap. 7 on Jesus' baptism revealing who he was, especially on Origen's calling Jesus' baptism a second birth.

53. *Dialogue* 88.8; he cites the expanded form also in 103.6.

54. H. J. W. Drijvers and G. J. Reinink, "Taufe und Licht: Tatian, Ebionäerevangelium und Thomasakten," in T. Baarda et al., eds., *Text and Testimony: Essays on New Testament and Apocryphal Literature in Honour of A. F. J. Klijn* (Kampen: Kok, 1988), pp. 91-110, argue that Justin preserves the earliest form of the tradition, in which fire as purifying and as a danger from which Jesus escapes is close to the significance of fire in Matt. 3:10-12. They further contend that Tatian introduced the light motif, which was important to his theology that connected light with the Logos, in order to parallel the first manifestation of the Logos at the creation in Gen. 1:1-2 with his second manifestation at his baptism, at both of which there is water. Klijn himself, *Jewish-Christian Gospel Tradition*, pp. 72-73, accepts this sequence and the corollary that the *Gospel of the Ebionites* was one of the writings influenced by Tatian. On the other hand, Tatian may have known the *Gospel of the Ebionites* or the tradition on which it drew, and Justin may have been the innovator introducing fire as the source of the light.

55. William L. Petersen, *Tatian's Diatessaron: Its Creation, Dissemination, Sigificance, and History in Scholarship* (Leiden: Brill, 1994), pp. 14-18, collects the early evidence for a reading that included fire or light on the water at the baptism of Jesus. See pp. 18-20 for testimonies that this reading was part of the *Diatessaron*; also, Drijvers and Reinink, "Taufe und Licht," pp. 95-98.

tury refers to an apocryphal book named *The Preaching of Paul* in which Christ, to the horror of the author, confessed his own sin and was almost compelled by his mother to receive John's baptism. "When he was baptized, fire was seen to be upon the water, which," he adds, "is written in none of the Gospels."[56] The light or fire at the Jordan accompanying Jesus' baptism was particularly preserved in Syriac sources.[57]

Four motifs are prominent in the early interpretations of the baptism of Jesus (canonical and noncanonical): the descent of the Spirit (sometimes interpreted as the fulfillment of Isa. 11:2), the beginning of the messianic ministry of Jesus, the identification and revelation of Jesus (with many variations as to who he was), and the purification of the water (or of Jesus, who identified himself with humanity).[58]

---

56. *On Rebaptism* 16–17. The author of *On Rebaptism* takes fire as a reference to the Holy Spirit, citing Acts 2:3-4 and Ps. 104:4. The confession of sin and the intercession of Mary are similar to statements in the *Gospel of the Nazarenes* cited above and may be the orthodox writer's ascribing the most objectionable meaning possible to such words. For different possibilities in interpreting the passage see Vigne, *Le baptême de Jésus*, pp. 146-147.

57. Kilian McDonnell, "Jesus' Baptism in the Jordan," *Theological Studies* 56 (1995): 209-236 (231-235); idem, *The Baptism of Jesus*, pp. 105-110. Augusto Cosentino, "Il fuoco sul Gordano, il cero pasquale, la columna del battistero Laterano," in *L'edificio battesimale in Italia: Aspetti e problemi: Atti dell'VIII Congresso Nazionale di Archeologia Cristiana . . . 21-26 settembre 1998* (Bordighera: Istituto Internazionale di Studi Liguri, 2001), 521-540, finds an echo of the tradition in the Western practice of dipping the paschal candle in the water of the font (527).

58. The first two are identified as the oldest and most constant interpretations by Bertrand, *Le baptême de Jésus*, pp. 135-136; the last two are my additions.

7. Baptism of Jesus — II

Later Christian Interpretation of the Baptism of Jesus: Texts

The interpretation of the baptism of Jesus will figure in the interpretation of the baptism of Christians taken up in subsequent chapters. Hence, many of the later references in Christian literature to the baptism of Jesus will be better treated in the context of the thought of individual authors, but at this point we will sketch the principal motifs in a topical manner.[1] One author relates the baptism of Christ and the baptism of the Christian for the Fathers according to these characteristics: The baptism of Christ was more than an act of humility but was a consequence of the abasement of the incarnation in assuming a sinful human nature; the baptism of Jesus was the institution of Christian baptism; it symbolized the tomb and resurrection; his baptism was the model; it purified the water; the cross gives power to water; the fount of the Holy Spirit now reposed on Jesus; the declaration of Sonship was parallel to the adoption of Christians; the opening of heaven symbolized the opening of paradise.[2] I elaborate on these in a different order.

The thought adumbrated by Ignatius (chap. 6) that the baptism of Christ purified water is picked up in several writers. Tertullian states the idea succinctly when he speaks of "Christ's being baptized [*baptizato*], that is, on his sanctifying the waters in his baptism [*baptismate*]."[3] Finding a type of baptism in the bitter waters sweetened

---

1. Robert L. Wilken, "The Interpretation of the Baptism of Jesus in the Later Fathers," *Studia Patristica* 11 (1972): 268-277; Kilian McDonnell, "Jesus' Baptism in the Jordan," *Theological Studies* 56 (1995): 209-236 (231-235); Kilian McDonnell, *The Baptism of Jesus in the Jordan: The Trinitarian and Cosmic Order of Salvation* (Collegeville: Liturgical, 1996), who discusses some motifs that I do not, such as divinization and clothing with the robe of glory (pp. 128-155). An earlier treatment, which I have not seen, was by J. Bornemann, *Die Taufe Christi durch Johannes in der dogmatischen Theologen der vier ersten Jahrhunderts* (1896).

2. P. T. Camelot, *La spiritualité du baptême: Baptises dans l'eau et l'Esprit*, 2nd ed. (Paris: Cerf, 1993), pp. 245-266.

3. *Answer to the Jews* 8.14.

by the tree Moses threw into it (Exod. 15:23-25), he explains: "That tree was Christ, who from within himself heals the springs of that nature which was previously poisoned and embittered, converting them into exceedingly healthful water, that of baptism."[4] He continues by referring to the water that flowed from the rock, identified as Christ (Exod. 17:6; 1 Cor. 10:4). He then begins a list of occasions in Jesus' life associated with water, naming first his baptism in water.[5]

It was regularly noted that Jesus had no need of purification for himself but by his baptism he provided for our purification.[6] Typical is Gregory of Nazianzus: "Jesus submitted to be purified in the river Jordan for my purification, or rather, sanctifying the waters by his purification (for indeed he who takes away the sin of the world had no need of purification)."[7] He combined the thoughts of Jesus' identification with humanity, the sanctification of water, and human sanctification: Jesus came to John the Baptist "to bury the whole of the old Adam in the water; and before this and for the sake of this, to sanctify Jordan; for as he is Spirit and flesh, so he consecrates us by Spirit and water."[8] As this quotation indicates, our human nature was plunged in the water with Jesus.[9] Ephraem the Syrian said Jesus' divine nature did not need baptism, but the baptism was a testimony to his humanity.[10]

By submitting to baptism Jesus identified himself with humanity in every respect, including its sinfulness. Origen saw Jesus as stained by reason of his birth as a voluntary act of assuming a human body.[11] From another perspective, commenting on Matthew 3:13, Origen says, "He was washed for our sins [ἀπολουόμενος τὰ ἡμέτερα ἁμαρτήματα] in order that we might be sanctified in his bath [τῷ λουτρῷ αὐτοῦ]."[12] More than an act of humility, the baptism was a consequence of the abasement of the incarnation.[13] Jesus assumed sinful human nature, and his asking for baptism showed he was truly and fully human.[14] To the Manichaean suggestion that since Christ was baptized he had sinned, an orthodox spokesperson replied, "No, rather, he was made sin for us, taking on him our sins. For this reason he was

---

4. Tertullian, *On Baptism* 4.1, in context would seem to refer to the Holy Spirit but may allude to Jesus' baptism; later in the passage (4.4) the waters receive their sanctifying power from the invocation of the Holy Spirit. Quotations are from the translation by Ernest Evans, *Tertullian's Homily on Baptism* (London: SPCK, 1964); this one is on p. 11.

5. Tertullian, *On Baptism* 9.2-4 (Evans, p. 21). See my chap. 19 for Tertullian's other types of baptism in the Old Testament and events in Jesus' life involving water.

6. Daniel Vigne, *Le baptême de Jésus dans las tradition judéo-chrétienne* (Paris: J. Gabalda, 1992), pp. 159-161, cites a long list of Greek and eastern authors to this effect. See also Camelot, *La spiritualité du baptême*, pp. 247-250.

7. *Oration* 38.16; also 29.20. Cf. Ambrose, *On Luke* 2.83.

8. Gregory of Nazianzus, *Oration* 39.15.

9. Cf. Ambrose, *On Luke* 2.91.

10. Ephraem, *Commentary on Diatessaron* 4.1.

11. Origen, *Homilies on Luke* 14.4. See further in chap. 23.

12. *Commentary on Matthew* 16.6. Origen then modifies his thought by saying that our sanctification is rather by his martyrdom as the baptism that released our sins.

13. Cyril of Alexandria, *Commentary on Luke* 3:21.

14. *Opus imperfectum in Matthaeum* 4.13-15.

born of a woman, and for this reason also he approached the rite of baptism."[15] Christian writers routinely connected Jesus' baptism with his birth, circumcision, and other expressions of his humanity in order to counter the suggestion that he needed baptism because of his own sin.

The feast of Epiphany, January 6, which celebrated the baptism of Jesus, was especially the occasion for noting that Jesus sanctified water by his baptism and so established the basis of Christian baptism.[16] Gregory of Nazianzus introduces his treatment of the feast by exhorting, "Christ is baptized, let us descend with him that we may also ascend with him."[17] His namesake, Gregory of Nyssa, after citing Naaman's washing in the Jordan as a type of baptism, explains: "The Jordan alone of rivers, receiving in itself the firstfruit of sanctification and blessing, conveyed in water channels like from some fountain the grace of baptism to the whole world."[18] As John Chrysostom put it, "This is the day [feast of Epiphany] on which he was baptized and he sanctified the nature of the waters."[19] Proclus, a fifth-century bishop of Constantinople, declares that in the feast of Epiphany "the sea rejoices greatly . . . (because) through the Jordan it receives the blessings of sanctification."[20]

As these passages about the purification of water indicate, Jesus' baptism became the pattern and basis for Christian baptism, although no New Testament text relates the baptism of Jesus to Christian baptism.[21] Cyril of Jerusalem combines the ideas of purification of the water and example for Jesus' followers: "Jesus sanctified baptism by being himself baptized. If the Son of God was baptized, what godly man is he that despises baptism? . . . He was baptized that he might give to them that are baptized a divine and excellent grace."[22] Ambrose, in common with other Christian

---

15. Hegemonius, *Disputation of Archelaus with Manes* 50 (fourth century).
16. Wilken, "The Interpretation of the Baptism of Jesus," pp. 274-276.
17. Gregory of Nazianzus, *Oration* 39.15.
18. Gregory of Nyssa, *On the Day of Lights (On the Baptism of Christ)* (PG 592D = GNO 9.235, 9-12). On this work and John Chrysostom's work cited next see Everett Ferguson, "Preaching at Epiphany: Gregory of Nyssa and John Chrysostom on Baptism and the Church," *Church History* 66 (1997): 1-17.
19. John Chrysostom, *On the Baptism of Christ* 2 (PG 49.365-366).
20. Proclus, *Homily on the Holy Epiphany* (PG 65.757C-D).
21. The important passage in Clement of Alexandria, *Instructor* 1.6 will be discussed in chapter 19. Simon Légasse, *Naissance du baptême* (Paris: Cerf, 1993), pp. 57-69, 133-34, looking only at the earliest sources, does not find Christ's baptism to be the basis of Christian baptism; McDonnell, *The Baptism of Jesus*, pp. 171-200, 244-246, taking a broader look, supports this claim and is able to discern hints of it earlier than the explicit claims; so also but less extensively Camelot, *Spiritualité du baptême*, pp. 245-266; Wilken, "The Interpretation of the Baptism of Jesus," pp. 273-274. Lothar Heiser, *Die Taufe in der orthodoxen Kirche: Geschichte, Spendung, und Symbolik nach der Lehre der Väter* (Trier: Paulinus, 1987), pp. 62-82, has a large collection of texts from the Greek Fathers (principally fourth century) on the baptism of Jesus as the pattern for the baptism of Christians. Perhaps it is best, as G. R. Beasley-Murray, *Baptism in the New Testament*, p. 64, contends, "to view the foundation of Christian baptism as *the total redemptive action which the baptism of Jesus set in motion.*"
22. Cyril of Jerusalem, *Catechetical Lectures* 3.11. Cf. Augustine, *Sermon* 273.12 and Ps.-Hippolytus, *On the Holy Theophany* 5 (cited in chap. 20).

authors, explained that Christ did not need a washing away of his sins, but we do, "Therefore, if baptism is for our sake, a pattern has been established for us."[23] Theodore of Mopsuestia believed that the baptism of Jesus gave "an emblem to the grace of our baptism." His baptism not only performed "the economy of the gospel" (pointing to his death and resurrection that abolished death) but also gave a symbol to our own baptism.[24] Thus he drew a "figure of the grace of baptism." Jesus did not need baptism because he was free from sin, "but he was baptized in our own baptism the symbol of which he depicted in this way." We "are baptized in the same baptism as that in which [Christ] was baptized," and his baptism was "symbolically drawn to the pattern of ours."[25] John Chrysostom, however, offered a caution against pressing the parallel of Jesus' baptism with ours. Jesus in receiving baptism from John had a baptism that was neither like Jewish washings nor like our baptism. He was not baptized to remove sin, to cleanse the soul, nor as having need of the supply of the Spirit.[26]

The voice of the Father, the declaration of Sonship, and the appearance of the Holy Spirit as a dove made the baptismal scene an obvious passage for comment in the Trinitarian and Christological controversies.[27] The use made of the event by Gnostics and Adoptionists (below) also focused attention on the event. Because the Arians saw the baptism of Jesus as another biblical indication that the Son was not truly God, Athanasius repeated the earlier teaching that when Jesus was baptized and anointed, this was done for the sake of his people, who are the recipients: "When the Lord, as man, was washed in Jordan, it was we who were washed in him and by him." And he applied to this event a usual distinction that he made in response to other Arian interpretations: Jesus was sanctified by the Spirit not in his divine nature but because he had become a human being. "It is not the Word . . . who is anointed with the Spirit . . . , but the flesh assumed by him which is anointed in him and by him."[28] Cyril of Alexandria placed the giving of the Spirit at the baptism of Jesus in the framework of the divine economy of salvation. When humanity fell into sin, the Spirit departed; but the Spirit returned to human nature when the dove descended on Jesus at his baptism.[29]

A related motif to the Trinitarian dimension of the baptism was the interpretation of this event, as in John 1:31-34, as the time of Jesus' revelation as the Son of God. John Chrysostom explained the name of the feast of Epiphany as indicating the bap-

---

23. Ambrose, *On the Sacraments* 1.5.16.

24. Theodore of Mopsuestia, *Catechetical Homilies*, translation by A. Mingana, *Woodbrooke Studies* 5 (Cambridge: W. Heffer & Sons, 1932), pp. 63, 69; cf. 67, 70.

25. Theodore of Mopsuestia, *Catechetical Homilies* 14 (Mingana, Vol. 6, 1933), pp. 65-66.

26. John Chrysostom, *On the Baptism of Christ* 3 (PG 49.367).

27. Wilken, "The Baptism of Jesus in the Later Fathers," pp. 270-272, discusses Athanasius and Cyril of Alexandria on this theme.

28. Athanasius, *Discourse Against the Arians* 1.12.47. "When he is baptized, it is we who in him are baptized" — 1.12.48.

29. Cyril of Alexandria, *Commentary on John* 2:1 (on John 1:32-33). See further chap. 44.

tism, and not the birth, as the time when the previously unknown Jesus was revealed to human beings, including John the Baptist himself.[30] Since Jesus did not need repentance, forgiveness, and a supply of the Spirit, Chrysostom gave two purposes for Jesus' baptism. The second was taken from Matthew 3:15, "to fulfill all righteousness," which Chrysostom defined as yielding to God and fulfilling all the commandments (such as circumcision, offering sacrifice, keeping sabbath, and observing the feasts, including the command by the prophet John to be baptized).[31] The first reason that he developed is taken from John 1:31-34, so that Christ might be identified. It was too troublesome to go house to house proclaiming who the Son of God was; besides, because of John the Baptist's kinship to Jesus, his testimony might be suspect. Hence, the Holy Spirit came at the baptism, where many people were gathering, to make him known.[32]

Also related to the Trinitarian aspects of Jesus' baptism was the motif of his anointing with the Holy Spirit.[33] Irenaeus gave extensive treatment to this topic. Against Gnostic interpretations that the Christ or the superior Savior came on Jesus at his baptism, Irenaeus insists that Jesus Christ was the same person after as before the baptism; there was no change in his being or nature.[34] The baptism brought the Spirit to him in a special, manifest way, equipping him for his messianic ministry, and gave him (or confirmed) the title "Christ." The Spirit was now united to his body.[35] It was the same Spirit of God prophesied in Isaiah 11:2 and 61:1 that came on him. God gave this same Spirit that came on Jesus to the disciples (Matt. 10:20; Acts 2:1-13; John 16:7), the Holy Spirit having become accustomed through fellowship with Jesus to dwell with human beings.[36] Irenaeus, as others, connected the coming of the Spirit at Jesus' baptism with Christian baptism of water and the Spirit: We need both, for "our body receives unity by the washing which is for incorruption as also our souls by the Spirit."[37] He discerned that the name Christ implies "he that anoints, he that is anointed, and the unction itself with which he is anointed," respectively the Father, the Son, and the Spirit.[38]

---

30. John Chrysostom, *On the Baptism of Christ* 2 (PG 49.365). Cf Ps.-Eusebius of Alexandria, *On Baptism*, below, and Ps.-Hippolytus, *On the Holy Theophany* 7 (chap. 20).

31. John Chrysostom, *On the Baptism of Christ* 3-4 (PG 49.368-369).

32. John Chrysostom, *On the Baptism of Christ* 3 (PG 49.368).

33. Vigne, *Le Baptême de Jésus*, pp. 78-81, 185-204; McDonnell, *The Baptism of Jesus*, pp. 111-127.

34. Daniel A. Smith, "Irenaeus and the Baptism of Jesus," *Theological Studies* 58 (1997): 618-642. He opts for Jesus' reception of the Spirit and the deification of his human nature as progressive: from the incarnation through the baptism and culminating in the resurrection.

35. Irenaeus, *Demonstration* 41.

36. Irenaeus, *Against Heresies* 3.17.1-2. Cf. 3.9.3, "Therefore the Spirit of God descended upon him, the one promised by the prophets to be anointed by him, so that we, receiving from the abundance of his unction, might be saved." *Demonstration* 53 suggests two anointings of Christ, a pre-temporal anointing "because through him the Father anointed and arrayed all things" and the anointing "according to his coming as man."

37. *Against Heresies* 3.17.2; cf. *Demonstration* 41.

38. *Against Heresies* 3.18.3.

Tertullian related the anointing of Christians at baptism to the anointing of priests in the Old Testament.[39] This gave the Lord his title of "Christ," but his anointing was a spiritual anointing, not with oil but with the Holy Spirit. The Christians' unction is physical with a spiritual effect, just as their baptism is with water but has a spiritual effect. The anointing of Jesus at his baptism became the basis for literal anointings in Christian baptism. Cyril of Jerusalem drew the parallel expressly: Jesus washed in the Jordan, and the Holy Spirit in his fullness alighted on him. "And to you in like manner, after you had come up from the pool of the sacred streams, there was given an unction, the antitype of that with which Christ was anointed, and this is the Holy Spirit."[40] Cyril of Alexandria stated that Adam's sin brought a loss of the Spirit, but in our baptism the Spirit returns.[41]

Lactantius develops the coming of God's Spirit on Jesus as a bestowal of heavenly power that enabled him to begin performing great miracles.[42] He makes this point in response to the charge by Jews (and pagans) that Christ worked miracles by magic.

> He was baptized by the prophet John in the river Jordan, that he might abolish in the spiritual bath [*lavacro*] not his own sins, for it is evident that he had none, but those of the flesh that he bore; that as he saved the Jews by undergoing circumcision, so he might save the Gentiles also by baptism — that is, by the pouring forth [*perfusione*] of the purifying wave. Then a voice from heaven was heard: "Thou art my Son, today I have begotten you." This voice is found to have been foretold by David [Ps. 2:7]. And the Spirit of God descended upon him, formed after the appearance of a white dove. From that time he began to perform the greatest miracles, not by magical tricks, . . . but by heavenly strength and power.[43]

The passage contains several familiar themes: Jesus' lack of personal sin but the sinfulness of his humanity; his identification with people so that he might save them (but the explanation that this was accomplished for Jews by his circumcision and Gentiles by his baptism is new — see further chap. 27); the quotation of the heavenly voice in the words of Psalm 2:7. The reference to the "pouring forth" of water is

---

39. Tertullian, *On Baptism* 7. Bernard Botte, "Deux passages de Tertullian: *De Baptismo* 7,1 et 8,2," in J. Fontaine and C. Kannengiesser, eds., *Epektasis: Mélanges patristiques offerts au Cardinal Jean Daniélou* (Paris: Beauchesne, 1972), pp. 17-19, argues that the text should read *christi dicti*, priests were called "christs" because they were anointed.

40. Cyril of Jerusalem, *Lectures on the Mysteries* 3.1.

41. Cyril of Alexandria, *Commentary on John* 5:2.

42. Jean Doignon, "La scène évangélique du Baptême de Jesus commentée par Lactance (*Divinae institutiones* 4,15) et Hilaire de Poitiers (*In Matthaeum* 2,5-6)," in Fontaine and Kannengiesser, *Epektasis*, pp. 63-73 (63-67). Fragment 6, attributed to Melito of Sardis but probably belonging to the fourth century, suggested that Christ showed his divinity by the miracles he did after his baptism and showed his humanity by the thirty years before his baptism — Stuart George Hall, *Melito of Sardis:* On Pascha *and Fragments*, Oxford Early Christian Texts (Oxford: Clarendon Press, 1979), pp. xxx-xxxi, 68-71.

43. Lactantius, *Divine Institutes* 4.15.2. Cf. Cyril of Alexandria, *On the Trinity* 5.591 for sanctification touching only his flesh.

sometimes taken as an indication of aspersion in baptism, but the phrase may only refer to the providing of water for baptism. If it refers to the act of baptism, the phrase may refer to the water pouring over a person in an immersion and so emphasize the role of the water rather than the act of dipping.[44] The apologetic context of Lactantius's quotation is to relate Jesus' miracles to the coming of divine power on him, and this occurred at his baptism.

The heavenly voice declared Jesus to be God's Son. The interpretation of this event as the revelation of his Sonship (above) stood in contrast to views that understood the event as making Jesus God's son or in some way effecting a change in his status. Adoptionists took the heavenly words literally. Theodotus of Byzantium said that Jesus was a mere man, born of a virgin, who "at his baptism in Jordan received Christ, who came from above and descended upon him in form of a dove." He manifested miraculous powers only after this.[45] In the Valentinians cited in chapter 6 the Savior came on the Christ; in Theodotus, as in Cerinthus (chap. 6), the Christ came on Jesus, but in the latter teacher to reveal the unknown Father and in the former for the purpose of adopting him as God's.

Others, more orthodox, related the heavenly declaration either to Jesus' humanity or to the beginning of his messianic ministry, some expressly paralleling the eternal generation of the Son of God and the baptismal birth. Origen spoke of the baptism of Jesus as a "second birth" after his physical birth, for after his baptism he began his real life and work.[46] One wonders if the language of a second birth at the Jordan is a reflex of the doctrine of baptism as a rebirth for Christians (John 3:5). Methodius cites the words of the Father at the baptism of Jesus according to Psalm 2:7 and explains that he was "declared to be God's Son without limit and without regard to time, for he says, 'You are,' not 'You have become.'" The expression "signifies that he willed that he who existed before the ages in heaven should be begotten on the earth — that is, that he who was before unknown should be made known."[47]

Hilary of Poitier's commentary on Matthew's account of the baptism of Jesus highlights a double mystery in the baptism.[48] First, there is the mystery of the salvation of humanity by the purification of the flesh, of which the baptism of the Lord gave an example. He had no sin, so baptism was superfluous for Jesus, but he took a

---

44. C. Bigg, "Notes on the Didache," *Journal of Theological Studies* 5 (1904): 579-589 (p. 581), because of the usage in Virgil, *Georgics* 3.45, where *perfundo* is used of dipping sheep, thinks Lactantius's usage is more literary than descriptive.

45. Hippolytus, *Refutation of All Heresies* 7.35 (23).2; 10.23 (19).2. This view, as Hippolytus notes, was similar to the views of the Ebionites and Cerinthus (see preceding chapter).

46. Origen, *Homilies on Luke* 28.4. Origen quotes the "Western" variant of Luke 3:22 in *Commentary on John* 1.204 (29) and *Homilies on Ezekiel* 6.3 (explaining that "today" lasts forever), but he may have in mind Ps. 2:7; the standard text occurs in *Against Celsus* 2.72; *Homilies on Numbers* 18.4; *Homilies on Luke* 27.5 (with reference to the resurrection), but since Matt. 3:17 is identical except for the third person instead of Luke's second person, Origen may reflect Matthew. Ephraem the Syrian also spoke of Jesus' baptism as a "second birth" — *Commentary on the Diatessaron* 4.3.

47. Methodius, *Banquet* 8.9.192-193.

48. Doignon, "La scène évangélique du Baptême de Jesus," pp. 68-73.

body in order to accomplish our salvation. He sanctified humanity by his incarnation and his baptism.[49] The second mystery is the divine filiation expressed by the visible descent of the Spirit on Christ and the divine voice. Hilary quotes the voice in the words of Psalm 2:7, taken from the Western text of Luke 3:22. Christians too at baptism receive the glorious anointing and by the voice of God become by legal adoption the children of God.[50]

Gregory of Nyssa spoke of three births of Christ and also of Christians — physical birth, birth of water and Spirit, and the resurrection from the dead. The three births in this world were suggested by the use of "firstborn" for Christ four times in Scripture: "firstborn of creation" (Col. 1:15), "firstborn among many brethren" (Rom. 8:29), "firstborn from the dead" (Col. 1:18), and "he brings the firstborn into the world" (Heb. 1:6). Likewise, "there are in us three births." With reference to our theme, Christ became the "firstborn among many brethren" because:

> [P]urposing to change us from corruption to incorruption by the birth from above, the birth by water and the Spirit, he himself led the way in this birth, drawing down upon the water by his own baptism the Holy Spirit, so that in all things he became the firstborn of those who are spiritually born again and gave the name of brethren to those who partook in a birth like to his own by water and the Spirit.[51]

Ephraem the Syrian used the image of a womb to link the three mysteries of incarnation, Christ's baptism, and his descent into Sheol (Hades).[52] He extends the thought by speaking of four begettings of Christ, adding his eternal begetting by the Father (*Sermon on Our Lord* 1-2; 2.5 quoted in chap. 31, n. 30).

As indicated by the preceding quotations, the baptism of Jesus was connected not only backward with his birth from Mary but also forward with his death and resurrection. His baptism was interpreted as a struggle with Satan in which Jesus descended into a watery grave, image of Satan's underworld abode, and came up victorious in anticipation of his later descent into Hades and victorious emergence from death.[53] The correlation of the baptism with Jesus' descent into Hades at his death is

---

49. Hilary, *On Matthew* 2.5.
50. Hilary, *On Matthew* 2.6. Hilary refers to Jesus' baptism at the Jordan as a birth event in *On the Trinity* 8.25 and *On Psalms* 2.29-30.
51. Gregory of Nyssa, *Refutation of the Confession of Eunomius* 79-81 (*GNO* 2.344.20-346.5 [*PG* 45.501B-504A]); cf. *Against Eunomius* 3.2.45-54 (*GNO* 2.67.64-70.18 [*PG* 45.633B-637B]). Gregory of Nazianzus stated the thought succinctly: "The Word recognized three births for us, namely, the natural birth, that of baptism, and that of the resurrection" (*Oration* 40.2).
52. Ephraem, *Hymns on the Church* 36.3-6; cf. *Hymns on Faith* 10.17. McDonnell, *The Baptism of Jesus*, pp. 103-106. Vigne, *Le baptême de Jésus*, pp. 127-129, notes that Psalm 2 is applied to these three births of Jesus in the New Testament (Heb. 1:5 [but is this a pretemporal begetting?]; Acts 13:33; Heb. 5:5) and cites John of Nicaea for the curious detail that in the Lukan writings each "birth" is followed by a period of forty days (Luke 2:22; 4:2; Acts 1:3).
53. Per Lundberg, *La typologie baptismale dans l'ancienne église* (Uppsala: Lorentz, 1942), beginning with later liturgical texts, shows the early Christian interpretation of Jesus' baptism as a *descensus*

alluded to in the *Odes of Solomon*.[54] The collection speaks expressly of Christ overthrowing the devil ("the dragon with seven heads" — *Ode* 22.5) and shattering the realm of death (*Ode* 42.11). The allusion to his baptism in the line, "The dove fluttered over the head of our Lord Messiah" (*Ode* 24.1) connects that event with the Lord's escape from the powers of the underworld ("the chasms"): "The chasms were submerged in the submersion of the Lord, And they perished in that device with which they had remained from the beginning" (*Ode* 24.7).[55]

Cyril of Jerusalem, following his passage cited above about Jesus' being baptized sanctifying baptism for the sake of human beings, relates it to winning a victory over Satan and death:

> According to Job, there was in the waters the dragon that "draws up Jordan into his mouth" [Job 40:23, Gk.]. Since, therefore, it was necessary "to break the heads of the dragon in pieces" [Ps. 74:13], he went down and bound the strong one in the waters, that we might receive power to "tread upon serpents and scorpions" [Luke 10:19]. The Life encountered him, that the mouth of Death might henceforth be stopped and all we that are saved might say, "O death, where is your sting? O grave, where is your victory?" [1 Cor. 15:55]. The sting of death is drawn by baptism.[56]

A late work, *On Baptism*, from about the year 500, ascribed to the fictitious Eusebius of Alexandria, continues to express the motif of the baptismal victory of Christ over the devil but without direct association with the descent into Hades.[57] The work touches on several motifs common in the treatment of Jesus' baptism: Jesus had "no need of washing" (86.372D); his baptism "sanctified the nature of the waters" (86.372C); the baptism was the beginning of Jesus' manifestation to the

---

ad inferos in which he conquered and crushed Satan (pp. 10-17 and passim), to which other Old Testament types are related. The theme is treated more briefly in McDonnell, *The Baptism of Jesus*, pp. 156-170.

54. This earliest Christian hymnbook (more in chap. 13) survives in Syriac, presumably its original language, and has been dated as early as A.D. 100. See the summary of argumentation by James H. Charlesworth, "Odes of Solomon," in James H. Charlesworth, ed., *The Old Testament Pseudepigrapha* (Garden City: Doubleday, 1985), 2.726-727. Such an early date for an original Christian work in Syriac is notable but not impossible.

55. The passage is widely taken as a reference to Christ's *descensus* into Hades — see the note in James H. Charlesworth, *The Odes of Solomon* (Missoula: Scholars, 1977), pp. 99-100, whose translation I follow. More passages on this theme are quoted in chap. 13.

56. Cyril of Jerusalem, *Catechetical Lectures* 3.11. For the use of Ps. 74:13 in baptismal liturgies, see Lundberg, *La typologie baptismale*, p. 10. Another text influential on representations of the baptism of Jesus in the Jordan in art was Ps. 114:3.

57. Everett Ferguson, "[Ps]-Eusebius of Alexandria, 'On Baptism [of Christ]': A Contest between Christ and the Devil," *Studia Patristica* 42 (2006): 127-131. *On Baptism* [PG 86.372-380] is "Sermon" 11 in the collection ascribed to Pseudo-Eusebius. Hades is discussed in number 13, *On the Coming of John into Hades, and on the Devil,* and number 15, *On the Devil and Hades*. For the devil's reaction to Jesus' coming for baptism, cf. Ps.-Hippolytus, *On the Holy Theophany* 4, discussed in chap. 20.

world (86.372C); his baptism gave an example for others (86.372D); and it illustrated the mystery of the divinity hidden in the humanity of Jesus (86.373D-376A). The special emphasis of the author, however, is that Jesus "came to baptism to abolish the power of the Enemy" (86.373A). The baptism was a demonstration of victory over the devil. Jesus gave the example of baptism "in order that we might trample on the devil in the water; for if we keep baptism undefiled, we have power to trample on him," followed by quotation of Luke 10:49 (86.372D). The devil expected to lock Jesus up in Hades as also other human beings, but the thought that Jesus might be the Christ provoked the lamentation, "Woe is miserable me that my power is checked; my stings are despised; my strength is weakened" (86.376C) The author carries through the theme of the baptism as a contest between Christ and the devil by including an account of the temptations that followed Jesus' baptism (86.376D–377D).

The *descensus* theme of Christ's victory over the forces of evil obviously had cosmic consequences. These two motifs are brought together in the fragments of *On Baptism* ascribed to Melito of Sardis. He associated Christ's baptism with the descent into Hades: "King of heavens and creation's Captain, Sun of uprising who appeared both to the dead in Hades and to mortals in the world, he also alone arose a Sun out of heaven."[58] These words are preceded by a longer passage expressing the less common motif of cosmic parallels to Jesus' baptism. Melito cites many examples from nature of being bathed (λούεται) in rains and rivers and then refers to the ancient view that the sun at night passed through the cosmic Ocean before rising again the next day. The passage is quoted and studied in chapter 14. The point of Melito's elaborate comparison was that what happens to the heavenly bodies is a justification and explanation for the baptism of Jesus: "Now if the sun with the stars and moon is washed [λούεται] in the ocean, why is not Christ also washed [λούεται] in Jordan?"[59] There is a reference to the baptism of Christ in fragment 15 attributed to Melito.[60]

Gregory of Nazianzus expressed the cosmic dimension of baptism by a different image: When Jesus came up from the water, "with himself he carries up the world." He continued by finding in the opening of heaven an allusion to Paradise: Jesus saw "the heaven opened which Adam had shut against himself and all his posterity, as the gates of Paradise by the flaming sword."[61] Another result of the baptism of Jesus was opening the return to paradise, the gates of which had been shut since the sin of Adam.

The baptism of Jesus was connected with the fulfillment of the old covenant and its replacement by the new covenant. John Chrysostom says that the baptism of Jesus brought Jewish baptism to an end and was the beginning of Christian baptism:

---

58. Melito, Frg. 8b, *On Baptism*, in Hall, *Melito of Sardis*, p. 73.

59. Hall, *Melito of Sardis*, p. 73. The text is also given in Adolf von Harnack, *Marcion, das Evangelium vom fremden Gott*, Texte und Untersuchungen 45 (Leipzig, 1924), pp. 422*-423*, who suggests that the statement is anti-Marcionite.

60. Hall, *Melito of Sardis*, pp. xxxvii-xxxviii, 82-84, who allows that it is possibly authentic. Fragment 6 is referred to above at note 42.

61. Gregory of Nazianzus, *Oration* 39.16.

"Having brought Jewish baptism to its fulfillment, at the same time he opens the way for that of the church"; at the Jordan the Law ended and grace began.[62]

Later Christian Interpretation of the Baptism of Jesus: Art

The later literary interpretations of the baptism of Jesus were influenced by contemporary practices in the baptismal liturgy. The same is even more evident in the depictions of Jesus' baptism in Christian art, so this section will anticipate and introduce material treated further in later parts of this book. Most, indeed nearly all, depictions of baptism in early Christian art are arguably of the baptism of Jesus, so this will be the appropriate place to discuss the evidence that art contributes to the study of baptism in the early church.[63] Even if some of the scenes were not intended to represent Jesus' baptism, the Gospel accounts of his baptism have influenced the way the scene was shown.

The earliest paintings in the Roman catacombs are around 200 or the early third century. They contain twelve pictures of a baptism.[64] One of the earliest, if not the earliest, of Christian frescoes is in the crypt of Lucina in San Callisto (see Figure 1). It shows a nude, fully grown Jesus coming out of the water, which is sketched in brief strokes around his whole body to the neck, and being received by John the Baptist

---

62. John Chrysostom, *Homilies on Matthew* 12.3. But see above on the difference Chrysostom drew between Jesus' baptism and Christian baptism. Ephraem the Syrian, *Commentary on the Diatessaron* 4.1 — the baptism of Jesus brought John's baptism to an end, and Jesus baptized again all who received John's baptism.

63. H. Leclercq, "Baptême de Jésus," in *Dictionnaire d'archéologie chrétienne et de liturgie* (Paris: Letouzey et Ané, 1925), Vol. 2, cols. 346-380; Johannes Kollwitz, *Das Christusbild des dritten Jahrhunderts* (Münster, 1953), pp. 26-30 (interprets the baptismal scenes, especially in the catacomb of Callistus, in relation to pictures of the Shepherd [also, p. 10], Philosopher, and Fisherman in the same rooms — all expressing the fundamental theme of Christian art as salvation); L. deBruyne, "L'Initiation chrétienne et ses reflets dans l'art paléochrétien," *Revue des sciences religieuses* 36 (1962): 27-85; Günter Ristow, *Die Taufe Christi* (Recklinghausen: Aurel Bongers, 1965), Eng. trans. *The Baptism of Christ* (1967); Gertrud Schiller, *Iconography of Christian Art* (London: Lund Humphries, 1971), pp. 127-143; U. Mielke, "Taufe, Taufszenen," in *Lexikon der Christlichen Ikonographie* (Freiburg and Rome: Herder, 1972), vol. 4, pp. 244-247; A. M. Fausone, *Die Taufe in der frühchristlichen Sepulkralkunst* (Vatican City: Pontificio Istituto di Archeologia Cristiana, 1982); Robin M. Jensen, "Living Water: Images, Setting, and Symbols of Early Christian Baptism in the West," (Ph.D. diss., Columbia University, 1991); Ernst Dassmann, "Baptism II. Iconography," in Angelo Di Berardino, ed., *Encyclopedia of the Early Church* (New York: Oxford University Press, 1992), pp. 108-109; Fabrizio Bisconti, "L'iconografia dei battisteri paleocristiani in Italia," in *L'edificio battesimale in Italia: Aspetti e problemi: Atti dell'VIII Congresso Nazionale di Archeologia Cristiana . . . 21-26 settembre 1998* (Bordighera: Istituto Internazionale di Studi Liguri, 2001), 405-440 (includes much more than the baptismal scene); Everett Ferguson, "Baptism (Iconography)," in P. C. Finney, ed., *Encyclopedia of Early Christian Art and Archaeology* (Grand Rapids: Eerdmans, forthcoming).

64. Aldo Nestori, *Repertorio topografico delle pitture delle catacombe romane* (Vatican City: Pontificio istituto di archeologia cristiana, 1975), p. 187 (the location in Domitilla is omitted before the numbers 42 and 77).

(of about equal size to Jesus) standing on the shore. A dove descends toward the head of Jesus. This moment of emerging from the water (Matt. 3:16) occurs in only one other depiction of baptism (SS. Pietro e Marcellino, room 21). This representation of an immersion, focusing on a moment mentioned in the Gospel record and emphasizing the descent of the Holy Spirit, despite the deteriorated condition of the painting, is particularly effective, but it did not survive as the normative iconography for baptism.

Other early paintings in the catacombs show the features that became standard. The baptizand is a naked youth, about half the size of the baptizer.[65] Factors influencing this representation, which is symbolic and not realistic, include the convention that persons receiving a benefit are shown smaller than others (in Christian art those drinking the miraculous water from the rock, the blind and others healed by Jesus, and Isaac sacrificed by Abraham). It was artistically easier to show the administrator's hand on the head of the candidate if the latter was shorter, but this factor does not adequately account for how short the recipient often is. The size of the person being baptized is not an indication of infant or child baptism, for the person is too large for this circumstance to be the explanation. In ancient art the more important figure in a scene was shown larger than other figures. If this convention was observed in the baptismal pictures, then the emphasis was on the humility of Jesus in submitting to baptism, a frequent theme in the literary sources. Perhaps more important was the theological teaching that baptism was a new birth.[66] The same motif of new birth applies to the nudity. Moreover, baptism, as a bath and like some mystery initiations, was received naked. There were the further motifs of taking off like clothing the old way of life and being restored to the original condition of paradise.[67] Other nude figures in Christian art appear in paradise (Adam and Eve), in an instance of deliverance (Daniel), or in a combination of the two motifs (Jonah). The small, nude Christ may also be visualization of Christ's assuming a humiliated and abased condition of which the literary sources speak.

Some scenes attempt to show a large amount of water, as does the painting in the crypt of Lucina. Also in the San Callisto catacomb, in room 22 (A3 — "Chapel of the Sacraments," dated 220-230), a spray of water surrounds the body of the baptizand as well as being painted at the feet; this may represent the body covered

---

65. With reference to the size of the baptizand, the quantity of water shown, and the streams flowing from a dove toward the head of the baptizand, H. F. Stander makes the pertinent observation that early Christian art was not illustrative or narrative but symbolic and must be interpreted in context — "Baptism and the Interpretation of Early Christian Art," *Hervormde Teologiese Studies* 43 (1987): 316-324.

66. John 3:5; 1 Peter 1:23; new Christians as children in Clement of Alexandria, *Instructor* 1.6.25, 31-35. Whether the pagan representation of Persephone purifying a boy at Eleusis (chap. 2) represented a wide enough convention to be known by Christian artists is problematic; at any rate there is the difference that in the Christian scenes a deity does not perform the baptism. Cf. my comment on Ps.-Hippolytus, *On the Holy Theophany* 7 in chap. 20.

67. Col. 3:9-10 for taking off clothing; Gen. 2:25; Cyril of Jerusalem, *Lectures on the Mysteries* 2.2; John Chrysostom, *Baptismal Instructions* 11.28-29 for paradise.

with water in an immersion or show the completed act (as is done in some of the healings) with the water dripping off the body (see Figure 3; cf. Figure 2). The baptism is flanked by a fisherman and by the healing of the paralytic. Other scenes in the room all point to Christ and include a Good Shepherd[68] in the ceiling, the Samaritan woman at the well, Moses and the rock, Jonah (thrice), philosopher with scroll, orans, and eucharistic scenes. In SS. Pietro e Marcellino, room 78 (early fourth century) the water comes to the hips. Usually, however, the water is shown only to the feet or at the most to the knees. This accords with the art's allusive nature, which was designed only to show the presence of water. Since a picture can capture only one moment, a realistic depiction of immersion was not possible, and the representation of a quantity of water was artistically difficult (especially in the case of sculpture). Later representations, however, did succeed in showing the water to the waist or above.

One of the scenes often claimed as representing an aspersion is a much damaged painting from the fourth century in SS. Pietro e Marcellino, room 43 (see Figure 4). It shows eight rays descending from the large dove to the water and encompassing Jesus. The rays are so prominent that unless one looks carefully it is easy to overlook that the picture clearly has the hand of John, whose figure is no longer extant, resting on the head of Jesus and not pouring out anything. The rays coming from the dove have been interpreted as water, the oil of the Holy Spirit, the breathing out of the Spirit (John 20:22), or rays of light.[69] The last interpretation would emphasize the baptism as a theophany and so would accord with the significance of the feast of Epiphany in the fourth century, but the fact that Epiphany as a celebration of the baptism of Jesus was mainly an eastern feast in the fourth century diminishes the likelihood of this attractive interpretation.

Despite claims that the art represents a pouring or sprinkling, the hand of the administrator is never shown pouring water but uniformly rests on the head of the baptizand, a feature absent from the Gospel accounts, so drawn from liturgical practice. The hand on the head is commonly taken to refer to the postbaptismal imposition of the hand with prayer for bestowal of the Holy Spirit.[70] This interpretation

---

68. For the Good Shepherd in baptisteries see chap. 26 on Dura Europus.

69. Other scenes showing something coming from the beak of the dove down on the head of Jesus or the baptizand include a grave stone in Aquileia (chap. 41) and an ivory triptych now in Berlin depicting the baptism between pictures of the slaughter of the innocents and the miracle of turning the water into wine; in this latter what streams from the dove is distinct from the water that flows from a rock and surrounds Jesus and so likely represents chrism or myron (Lothar Heiser, *Die Taufe in der orthodoxen Kirche: Geschichte, Spendung, und Symbolik nach der Lehre der Väter* [Trier: Paulinus, 1987], p. 85 and plate II). *Dumbarton Oaks Papers* 8 (1954), illustration 13, shows a baptism of Christ in an eleventh-century manuscript in which lines come down from a dove while Christ stands naked, waist deep in water, with the hand of the administrator on his head; if there is a continuity of artistic convention, this would indicate that in the catacomb painting it is not water coming from the beak of the dove.

70. Cf. Tertullian, *On Baptism* 8.1. This is argued by L. deBruyne, "L'Imposition des mains dans l'art chrétien ancien," *Rivista di archeologia cristiana* 20 (1943): 113-278 (212-247), but in doing so he vi-

would make the gesture a duplicate for the significance of the dove, representing the coming of the Holy Spirit. Literary sources offer an alternative and more plausible interpretation. The baptizer placed his hand on the head of the candidate, who was standing in the water, when he asked for a confession of faith.[71] The gesture might not only refer to this moment of confession but could also be functional. The triple immersion accompanied the confession, and the administrator's hand, therefore, was in position to guide the candidate's head into the water. The hand on the head plunging it into the water would be a natural extension from the self-immersions of Judaism. One painting in fact shows the baptizand's body leaning forward, although the position may be the awkward result of the artist's lack of skill rather than being an intentional representation of a dipping (San Callisto, room 21, dated 220-230 — Figure 3). (Another unusual feature is that two "philosophers" or teachers [one in a gesture of speech and one holding a scroll] flank the baptism; several other pictures in the room have scenes involving water — Jonah, a ship, Moses and the rock, a fisherman, and a dolphin on a trident.)

Efforts to determine from iconography whether a scene is the baptism of Jesus or of a new Christian are not wholly successful. The principal considerations are the presence or absence of the dove and the clothing of the baptizer — *exomis* tunic or animal skin for John the Baptist and tunic with pallium for a bishop. But neither distinction holds consistently: the dove as a symbol of the Holy Spirit could appear in the baptism of a Christian, and artistic or spatial considerations could cause its omission from a baptism of Christ; accommodations of the biblical scene to contemporary practice or accommodations of a contemporary scene to the biblical origins of baptism could influence the clothing of the baptizer.

The latest representation of the baptism of Christ in the catacombs (sixth or seventh century) is a fresco in the catacomb of Pontianus in a room adapted as a baptistery.[72] The scene announces western medieval and Byzantine features. A full-

---

olates his own canon that the tendency of early Christian art was to simplification by giving two symbols — dove and hand — of the same thing (the gift of the Holy Spirit). A distinction between the baptismal grace of the Spirit and the separate sacrament of confirmation is anachronistic. See my critique in "Laying On of Hands: Its Significance in Ordination," *Journal of Theological Studies,* n.s. 26 (1975): 1-12 (3-4, 7-9); reprint in *Church, Ministry, and Organization in the Early Church Era,* Studies in Early Christianity 13 (New York: Garland, 1993), pp. 147-158 (149-150, 153-155). If the hand on the head of the baptizand in Christian art does relate to an invocation of the Holy Spirit, the scene testifies to the unity of water and the Spirit in Christian initiation.

71. Hippolytus (?), *Apostolic Tradition* 21.12-18.

72. The catacomb itself is third century, but such an early use of the room as a baptistery is doubtful. Monica Ricciardi, "Nuove ricerche sul battistero nella catacomba di Ponziano a Roma," in *L'edificio battesimale in Italia: Aspetti e problemi: Atti dell'VIII Congresso Nazionale di Archeologia Cristiana . . . 21-26 settembre 1998* (Bordighera: Istituto Internazionale di Studi Liguri, 2001), 957-974, suggests that in the first phase the basin was for the *fossores* in maintenance of the cemetery and in the performance of funerary rites and the sacramental use in the second phase coincides with the pictorial decoration when the catacomb was no longer used for burial. The basin, which measures about two meters by one meter, with a depth of about one meter, had dimensions suitable for baptism.

sized, bearded Christ stands in water to his waist, and John wears an animal skin exomis and holds a staff. Rays (of light?) descend from the dove to the head of Jesus. A deer drinks from the water (Ps. 42:1), a motif known from earlier baptisteries (as at Naples), and a tree is growing nearby. Both John and Jesus are nimbed, as is an angel attendant who holds Jesus' clothes (representing the garment of immortality?). In such cases where there is the presence of an additional person or persons various interpretations are offered: God, angel(s) (Tertullian, *On Baptism* 5–6), an apostle or other witness, human attendant(s) at the baptism, human sponsor(s) (Hippolytus, *Apostolic Tradition* 16.1-4).

The oldest identifiably Christian sarcophagi come also from the third century, but later than the earliest catacomb paintings. Among the oldest is one from the last third of the third century found in the Church of Sta. Maria Antica on the Roman forum (see Figure 6).[73] The scenes around this tub-shaped sarcophagus are Neptune pouring from a vessel the water that unites many of the scenes, a ship, a sea monster, Jonah at rest, female orans, seated male philosopher, Good Shepherd, baptism of Jesus, and two fishermen with net. Although the other scenes are borrowed from pagan art, the presence of the baptism and Jonah in comparable positions gives a Christian interpretation to them. The iconography of the baptism is esentially the same as that in the catacomb paintings. The dress of John is that of a Cynic philosopher; his hand is on the head of Jesus; the dove is proportionately quite large; the water covers only the feet of the small nude Jesus but is approximately the same height as that in which the sea monster is shown and on which the ship floats, so it is allusive.[74]

From near the same time is the sarcophagus from the Via della Lungara, now in the Museo Nazionale delle Terme in Rome (see Figure 7).[75] It has a male fisherman, female orans, and a male Good Shepherd on the front. On the left side is a baptism of a new Christian, if the absence of a dove is an indication. The baptizer dressed as a philosopher holds a scroll in his left hand; the water comes to the baptizand's knees. A leafing tree and a dead tree flank the baptism. Are the trees an allusion to John's preaching (Matt. 3:8-10), to Psalm 1:3-4 (cf. *Barn.* 11.6-8 for its baptismal usage), or to the convert's passing from death to life? The placing of a Good Shepherd and an orans together is fairly common on sarcophagi. Putting a baptism with them may allude to the instruction and confession accompanying a baptism, or the scenes may keep their usual connotations of philanthropy (Good Shepherd) and piety (orans), with the baptism a way of certifying that the deceased died a Christian.

Of the twenty western sarcophagi with a baptismal scene most are from the fourth century.[76] Although the standard features continue to be present, there was a considerable expansion of the repertoire of accompanying scenes. Among the new

73. F. W. Deichmann, ed., *Repertorium der christlich-antiken Sarkophage* (Wiesbaden, 1967), #747.
74. An immersion is even more difficult to depict in sculpture than in painting, but some later representations (below) do show the water as deeper.
75. Deichmann, *Repertorium der christlich-antiken Sarkophage*, #777.
76. Fausone, *Die Taufe in der frühchristlichen Sepulkralkunst*, 140-207.

scenes on sarcophagi are the crossing of the Red Sea (e.g., in Saint Trophimus, Arles, and in the Gallo-Roman Museum, Lyon), an event considered a type of baptism.[77]

A notable variation in the iconography that is found in some fourth-century sarcophagi alludes to the presence of water by showing a vertical column of water descending from a rock instead of having a horizontal stream at the feet of the baptizand (cf. Figure 8). This representation was taken over from depictions of Moses miraculously producing water from a rock (Exod. 17:6; Num. 20:11) that was also adapted to the apocryphal account of Peter producing water while in prison in order to baptize his guards. The vertical waterfall may also allude to the tradition that the Jordan rose up when Jesus was baptized, even as its waters piled up when Israel crossed into the promised land (Josh. 3:11, 16; cf. Ps. 114:3-8).[78] An erroneous restoration on a fourth-century sarcophagus in the Vatican's Museo Pio Cristiano #13 shows a pouring: John holds a shell in the column of water coming from the rock.[79]

The association of a baptism with other scenes (to many of which patristic and liturgical texts give a specifically baptismal interpretation) in the same chambers of the catacombs and on the same sarcophagus (from which we have given only a sampling) provides a conceptual context for the significance of baptism. These include depictions of a philosopher, a fisherman and fish,[80] Noah,[81] Abraham sacrificing Isaac, Moses striking the rock,[82] the Good Shepherd,[83] Jonah, Daniel and the lions, Jesus healing the paralytic,[84] the Samaritan woman at the well,[85] and Jesus raising Lazarus.[86] Such collocations associate baptism with teaching and faith[87] and identify the act with forgiveness of sins, salvation, deliverance from death, and hope of resurrection and eternal life — all dependent on relation to Christ.

A fourth-century inscribed grave stone from Aquileia with a unique representation of baptism (a girl and not Jesus) is discussed in chapter 41 (see Figure 5). If the vertical lines surrounding the baptizand are meant to represent water rather than

77. 1 Cor. 10:1-2; Tertullian, *On Baptism* 9.1; Origen, *Homilies on Exodus* 5.1-2.
78. Cf. Ps.-Hippolytus, *On the Holy Theophany* 2, discussed in chap. 20.
79. Deichmann, *Repertorium der christlich-antiken Sarkophage*, #183.
80. Clement of Alexandria, *Instructor* 3.11.59.2; Tertullian, *On Baptism* 1.3.
81. Justin, *Dialogue* 138, bringing together the water of the flood, the faith of Noah, the wood of the ark (the cross), and the number eight of persons in the ark (eight symbolizing the eighth day, the day of Jesus' resurrection) as effecting salvation for Noah and for the Christian.
82. Gregory of Elvira, *Tractate* 15.
83. Psalm 23 was used liturgically at baptism. See Johannes Quasten, "Das Bild des Guten Hirten in den altchristlichen Baptisterien und in den Taufliturgien des Ostens und Westens," in F. J. Dölger, ed., *Pisciculi, Ergänzungsband zu "Antike und Christentum"* (Münster: Aschendorff, 1939), pp. 220-244; Johannes Quasten, "The Painting of the Good Shepherd at Dura-Europos," *Medieval Studies* 9 (1947): 1-18; repr. in Paul Corby Finnedy, ed., *Art, Archaeology, and Architecture of Early Christianity*, in E. Ferguson, Studies in Early Christianity 18 (New York: Garland, 1993), pp. 273-294.
84. Mark 2:1-12 or John 5:2-16; the latter in Tertullian, *On Baptism* 5.5-6.
85. Irenaeus, *Against Heresies* 3.17.2.
86. Noah, Abraham and Isaac, Moses, Jonah, Daniel, and Lazarus were examples of deliverance.
87. DeBruyne, "L'Initiation chrétienne et ses reflets dans l'art Paléochrétien," 29-52, 81-85.

light, then the emphasis may be on flowing ("living") water, something important in the early representations of baptism.[88]

With the fifth and sixth centuries representations of baptism begin to appear apart from a sepulchral context, introduce new iconographical features, and occur in a variety of media other than painting and sculpture. The earliest (fifth century) of several ivory carvings to preserve a baptism is in the British Museum (EC 293 — see Figure 9).[89] It introduces a majestic bearded angel as witness. If the streams flowing down to the head of Jesus are water and not oil or grace, the nudity, the hand of the administrator on the head, and the lines around the body of Jesus may still indicate an immersion. A beautifully done ivory carving, also in the British Museum (EC 294), perhaps from Egypt in the sixth century, shows the hand of God, the dove with its beak in a bowl, John's hand on the head of Christ, who is standing in water to his thighs, a witness in the background, and at Christ's feet a cowering and retreating personification of the river god.[90] The ivory Werden Casket in the Victoria and Albert Museum (London) has been dated to the fifth, sixth, or even ninth century. A river god on the left watches the baptism of a small Jesus by John with a dove above. Water flows out of a jug to the ankles of Jesus.

From the fifth century come two spectacular mosaic depictions of baptism in Ravenna. Bishop Neon added the impressive mosaic decorations to the Baptistery of the Orthodox in Ravenna in the mid-fifth century (see Figure 11).[91] The central disc of the dome, directly above the baptismal font, represents the baptism of Jesus, who is full sized and stands in water to his waist, flanked to the left by John on the shore and to the right by a personification of the Jordan as a river god. Unfortunately a restoration in the nineteenth century introduced questionable elements, including the heads of John and Jesus, the top of John's staff, and the right hand of John holding a patera over the head of Jesus. In such cases the restorer was accustomed to an aspersion and no longer understood the significance of the hand on the head.[92] A possibly

---

88. *Didache* 7.1-2; Hippolytus (?), *Apostolic Tradition* 21.2.

89. Lieselotte Kötzsche-Breitenbruch, "Das Elfenbeinrelief mit Taufszene aus der Sammlung Maskell im British Museum," *Jahrbuch für Antike und Christentum* 22 (1979): 195-208.

90. A river deity is common in depictions of Jesus' baptism, especially from the fifth century forward. Robin Jensen, "What Are Pagan River Gods Doing in Scenes of Jesus' Baptism?" *Bible Review* 9 (1993): 34-41, 54-55, considers the aspects involved in such depictions: artistic borrowings of classical models, personification of natural objects, geographical marker (the Jordan River with its typological and allegorical importance), and waters as inhabited by demons. I would add the motif of the victory of Jesus over the devil.

91. Spiro K. Kostof, *The Orthodox Baptistery of Ravenna* (New Haven: Yale University Press, 1965). See further in chap. 49.

92. Clementina Rizzardi, "La decorazione musiva del battistero degli ortodossi e degli Ariani a Ravenna: Alcune considerazione," in *L'edificio battesimale in Italia: Aspetti e problemi: Atti dell'VIII Congresso Nazionale di Archeologia Cristiana . . . 21-26 settembre 1998* (Bordighera: Istituto Internazionale di Studi Liguri, 2001), 915-930, reproduces a drawing made in 1690 showing the same features as the restoration as evidence that the restorer was not mistaken and uses this to argue that both immersion and aspersion were early (915-924).

ancient representation of such a scene is a spoon from Aquileia of the fourth or fifth century. It is now lost, and all we have is a possibly unreliable drawing. This shows the baptizer holding a patera in the water (?) flowing from the dove just above the head of the nude baptizand in a small basin; there are two other figures.[93]

The mosaic in the dome of the Baptistery of the Arians from the late fifth century shows some features that would have been in the original of the Baptistery of the Orthodox, on which it was modeled (see Figure 12). Jesus with a nimbus is grown but beardless and stands in water to his waist. John, who is bearded and wears an exomis of animal skin, lays his right hand on Jesus' head, which is joined to the dove's beak by a cone of light (which could be relevant to some of the scenes discussed above, or should we think of the Spirit or anointing oil as coming from above?). The personified Jordan raises a hand in adoration, or is it in terror or astonishment as in some of the literary interpretations noted above? The personified Jordan has two lobster pincers on his head. (Is the identification of the river god with the devil how the devil acquired horns in later representations?) In both baptisteries the baptizand, on looking up, would have seen Jesus as a model of his/her own baptism.

The ivory throne of Bishop Maximian (sixth century) in the Archiepiscopal Museum in Ravenna shows on its back side a baptism along with the triumphal entry, healing a blind man, the Samaritan woman at the well, the multiplication of loaves and fish, and turning water to wine at Cana. Two angels are in attendance, and the personified Jordan makes a gesture of astonishment.[94] The technique of showing the water, which reaches to Jesus' waist, by ridges in the carving gives the effect of transparency.

A Christian gem of sard in the Ashmolean Museum (#71), Oxford, of uncertain date and questionable authenticity, contains a unique representation of baptism. Both baptizer and baptizand are clothed and stand in water below the knees; the dove on the head of the baptizand makes up the difference in height from the other figure; the baptizer extends both arms to the baptizand, who is shown in the orans posture (in the catacombs only in SS. Pietro e Marcellino, room 17; cf. Luke 3:21).

A miniature illustration in the sixth-century Syriac Rabbula Gospels (fol. 4b) has the Trinitarian feature (Matt. 28:19) of the hand of God extending from heaven with a finger pointing toward Jesus, and the dove directly above Jesus, who is waist-deep in the water (see Figure 10). Another element indicating a theophany is a flame of fire on the water, a motif noted in early noncanonical accounts of the baptism (preceding chapter).

---

93. C. F. Rogers, *Baptism and Christian Archaeology: Studia biblica et ecclesiastica*, Vol. 5 (1903), p. 267, fig. 22; G. C. Menis, "Il battesimo ad Aquileia nella prima metà del IV secolo," in *L'edificio battesimale in Italia: Aspetti e problemi: Atti dell'VIII Congresso Nazionale di Archeologia Cristiana . . . 21-26 settembre 1998* (Bordighera: Istituto Internazionale di Studi Liguri, 2001), 685-708, gives a reproduction (707); he understands the catechumen as being immersed, the figure with a dish as representing an unction, and the second figure on the left as inviting to the eucharist (an altar shown).

94. Ps. 114:3, 5; cf. Cyril of Jerusalem, *Catechetical Lectures* 12.15.

A picture on a wooden box from Palestine (dated sixth/seventh century) has the features that characterized the depiction of Jesus' baptism in Byzantine art.[95] Water covers the nude Christ to his shoulders. Rays in the midst of which is the dove of the Holy Spirit descend from the hand of the Father in the sky. The hand of John the Baptist, who is on the shore, is on Jesus' head. Two persons behind John witness the baptism. On the opposite shore two angels (filling the role of deacons in the baptismal liturgy) hold garments.

The art largely accords with what is found in the written texts concerning the baptism of Jesus. The scene's relative frequency presents the baptism of Christ as the model of Christian baptism. The usual presence of the dove associates baptism with the coming of the Holy Spirit. The hand of the baptizer on the baptizand's head emphasizes the moment of confession of faith in Christian baptism. The nudity emphasizes the motifs of new birth and deliverance to paradise. Some representations make more of an effort at a realistic depiction of the action of baptism as an immersion by showing a quantity of water; others only allude to the presence of water. The nudity and the administrator's hand on the head would suggest a full bath by means of a dipping.

---

95. The wooden box is now in the Biblioteca Apostolica Vaticana, Inv. no. 1883.

8. Other References to Baptism in the Gospels

Although the Gospels were written after the letters of Paul, it is better to keep the discussion of the other texts relevant to baptism in the Gospels together with the discussion of the baptism of Jesus. Since historical order is not important for this purpose, I follow the canonical order of the Gospels. This is appropriate, furthermore, because the other foundation for Christian baptism, in addition to the baptism of Jesus, is his commission to his disciples in Matthew 28:16-20.

Matthew

Apart from references to John the Baptist and his baptism, the only mention of baptism in Matthew after the account of Jesus' baptism is Matthew 28:19. This fact is in keeping with Matthew's emphasis on those aspects of the teachings of Jesus relevant for the continuing practice of the church[1] and thus his book's function as a teaching Gospel for the church. Matthew concludes his Gospel with Jesus' declaration, commission, and promise:

> "All authority in heaven and on earth has been given to me. Go therefore and make disciples of all nations, baptizing them in the name of the Father and of the Son and of the Holy Spirit, teaching them to obey everything I have commanded you. And remember, I am with you always to the end of the age." (Matt. 28:18-20)[2]

---

1. For instance, Matthew like Mark but in contrast to Luke shortens the account of the Last Supper to those details pertinent to the church's observance of the eucharist (Matt. 26:26-30).

2. Among the many studies of the passage note for a survey of issues Karl Kertelge, "Der sogenannte Taufbefehl Jesu (Mt 28,19)," in H. Auf Der Maur and B. Kleinheyer, eds., *Zeichen des Glaubens: Studien zu Taufe und Firmung: Balthasar Fischer zum 60 Geburtstag* (Freiburg: Herder, 1972), pp. 29-40. His exegetical notes include the ecclesiological dimension of baptism ("disciples") and its connection with the Gentile mission.

The historicity of this command is widely rejected in New Testament critical scholarship.[3] On the other hand, no more likely explanation of the general, if not indeed universal, adoption of the practice of baptism by Jesus' disciples after his resurrection has been advanced than that there was some authorization by Jesus himself.[4] Without some such directive from Jesus it is hard to account for the general acceptance of baptism in all parts of the church from its earliest days, and a postresurrection setting is most likely for such a directive. The absence of the command to baptize in the other Gospels is not such weighty evidence against the Matthaean account as might at first appear. The ending of Mark is a special case discussed below, but briefly two observations are in order: if the Gospel originally ended at 16:8, then there are no resurrection appearances at all and so no opportunity to record any postresurrection instructions; and even if Mark 16:9-20 are not original, they may rest on early independent tradition or if dependent on Matthew attest an early acceptance of his account as authentic. Without referring specifically to baptism, Luke and John perhaps allude to it in their accounts of Jesus' commissioning his disciples. Luke, who frames his account according to Old Testament prophecy, in which there would not be a specific reference to baptism, uses language that he elsewhere associates with baptism: repentance, forgiveness of sins, preaching in Jesus' name (Luke 24:47; cf. 3:3 and Acts 2:38). John 20:21-23 likewise connects the sending of the disciples with possession of the Holy Spirit and with bringing forgiveness of sins. The association between baptism and forgiveness of sins that will run through this study suggests that there is a parallel between the connection made in Matthew and the long ending of Mark of the commission with baptism and the parallel connection in Luke and John of the commission with the forgiveness of sins.[5]

The reluctance of the church in Jerusalem to embark on a mission to Gentiles is not inconsistent with the commission of Matthew 28:19. Peter's initial hesitancy and the issue between Paul and certain Jerusalem Christians was not whether Gentiles were to be accepted into God's reign but the nature of the mission to them, its timing, and the terms of their acceptance (discussed further in chap. 10).

A textual question involves the presence of the Trinitarian formula, "into the name of the Father, the Son, and the Holy Spirit." Eusebius cited the command in various forms, most often omitting the phrase about the Trinity. This led to the con-

---

3. Jack Dean Kingsbury, "The Composition and Christology of Matt. 28:16-20," *Journal of Biblical Literature* 93 (1974):573-584, argues that the whole is a Matthaean composition. B. J. Hubbard, *The Matthean Redaction of a Primitive Apostolic Commissioning* (Missoula: Scholars Press, 1974), contends that a proto-commission is behind Matthew, Luke, and John (and Ps.-Mark); John P. Meier, "Two Disputed Questions in Matt. 28:16-20," *Journal of Biblical Literature* 96 (1977):407-424, concludes that behind this heavily redacted pericope lies a pre-Matthaean tradition. P. Boyd Mather, "Christian Prophecy and Matthew 28:16-20: A Test Exegesis," *Society of Biblical Literature Seminar Papers 1977* (Missoula: Scholars Press), pp. 103-115, argues that the words are those of an early Christian prophet speaking for Jesus.

4. G. R. Beasley-Murray, *Baptism in the New Testament* (Grand Rapids: Eerdmans, 1973 reprint), pp. 77-92, answers the objections to the historicity of a command from Jesus to baptize.

5. James Denney, *The Death of Christ*, 4th ed. (New York: Hodder & Stoughton, 1903), p. 73.

clusion that he knew the text in a shortened form, "Go, make disciples of all the nations in my name."[6] Since all other textual witnesses give the full text, most textual critics have accepted it as original. An examination of Eusebius's references where the baptismal command was omitted shows that it was superfluous to the context (for in every case the emphasis was on the universality of Christ's teaching in contrast to previous religious and civil law), and consideration of Eusebius's method of citing Scripture (omitting phrases he counted irrelevant and blending phrases from other passages he counted pertinent) deprives the argument for a shorter text of any validity.[7] New arguments, however, from context and from the poetry-like structure of other passages in Matthew have been advanced in support of a shorter text as original in Matthew 28:19.[8] It seems more likely to me that Eusebius paraphrased when his interest was the apostles' mission or the Lord's ethical teaching and cited the full text when Trinitarian concerns were at the forefront. The early and general acceptance of baptism in the Trinitarian name and the presence of the long form of the verse in all manuscripts and all witnesses to the text (except for Eusebius, and

---

6. F. C. Conybeare, "The Eusebian Form of the Text Matt. 28.19," *Zeitschrift für die neutestamentliche Wissenschaft* 2 (1901): 275-288. The view is accepted by Huub van de Sandt and David Flusser, *The Didache: Its Jewish Sources and Its Place in Early Judaism and Christianity* (Minneapolis: Fortress, 2002), pp. 286-289, but evidence cited in support (a Jewish-Christian source, a Coptic text, and a Sibylline Oracle) has no obvious reference to the ending of Matthew. For response to Conybeare's article see F. H. Chase, "The Lord's Command to Baptize (St. Matt. xxviii 19)," *Journal of Theological Studies* 6 (1905): 481-512 (483-499), with the conclusion that Matt. 28:19 is genuine and not a later interpolation. If credence is to be given to the Syriac translation of Eusebius's *Theophania* as a witness to its Greek, then the full Trinitarian form of the passage is quoted in 4.8 (Samuel Lee, *Eusebius: Bishop of Caesarea on the Theophania* [Cambridge: Cambridge University Press, 1843], p. 223) and later the shorthand form "make disciples of all nations" is given. I have not seen E. Riggenbach, *Der Trinitarische Taufbefehl* (Gütersloh: C. Bertelsmann, 1903). Kertelge, "Die sogenannte Taufbefehl Jesus (Mt 28, 19)," pp. 29-40, denies that the words were spoken by Jesus but affirms that they were in Matthew's Gospel and were a practice of Matthew's community; the words were integral to the whole Gospel; the practice of baptism was based on the giving of the Spirit by the resurrected Jesus.

7. Bernard Henry Cuneo, *The Lord's Command to Baptise: An Historico-Critical Investigation with Special Reference to the Works of Eusebius of Caesarea* (Washington: Catholic University of America, 1923), pp. 70-110.

8. Hans Kosmala, "The Conclusion of Matthew," *Annual of the Swedish Theological Institute*, Vol. 4, pp. 132-147, argued for the originality of Eusebius's short text from its poetic structure and the importance of the name of Jesus in Matthew. David Flusser, "The Conclusion of Matthew in a New Jewish Christian Source," in the same journal, Vol. 5, pp. 110-120, supported Kosmala by referring to a Jewish Christian text that rejected Matt. 28:19 among the sayings falsely ascribed to Jesus (because the sect rejected the Trinity); the contention that another saying, "Instruct people in accordance with instructions I have given you, and be for them what I have been for you," shows a dependence on Eusebius's shorter text is tenuous. H. B. Green, "Matthew 28:19, Eusebius, and the *lex orandi*," in Rowan Williams, ed., *The Making of Orthodoxy: Essays in Honour of Henry Chadwick* (Cambridge: Cambridge University Press, 1989), pp. 124-141, expanded the literary argument. Eusebius quotes Matthew 28:19 in three forms: (i) a summary form, "Go . . . nations" (9 times); (ii) the short text, "Go . . . nations in my name" (16 times); and (iii) the canonical text (5 times) (p. 126). Since the short text is Eusebius's preferred way of citing the passage, Green argues that he knew manuscripts with this reading. He sets out Matt. 11:28-30; 5:3-10; and 1:20b-21 as representing a similar structure to this short text (pp. 126ff.).

even in some places by him) are difficult to account for on other grounds than that the words are original in Matthew (especially when one considers that Matthew was the most widely used Gospel in the second century). Some words were necessary at the baptism — spoken either by the administrator, the candidate, or both — to show its purpose and distinguish it from what others did.

There is a comparable absence of the command to baptize and of the Trinitarian formula in a passage in the *Ascension of Isaiah* from perhaps the end of the first century:

> [The] Beloved will come forth [on the third day] and send out his twelve disciples, and they will teach all nations and every tongue the resurrection of the Beloved, and those who believe in his cross will be saved, . . . and many who believe in him will speak through the Holy Spirit, and there will be many signs and miracles in those days. (3.17-20)

If there is any dependence on Matthew 28, the passage is a thorough rewriting, but more likely it reflects an independent tradition. The Trinitarian formula is found already in *Didache* 7.1 (see chap. 12), either dependent on Matthew's text or independently drawing on the same liturgical practice as represented in Matthew.

The baptismal practice in Acts (chap. 10) records baptism "in the name of Jesus Christ" and similar expressions. The phrases used in Acts may not, however, reflect alternative formulas in the administration of baptism or alternative understandings of the meaning of the act. In some cases the description in Acts may mean a baptism administered on a confession of Jesus as Lord and Christ (cf. Acts 22:16), or it may be a general characterization of the baptism as related to Jesus and not a formula pronounced at the baptism.[9] In the later history the only formula regularly attested as pronounced by the administrator includes the triune name, but in Matthew it too may be descriptive rather than formulaic. If Matthew 28:19 is not a formula, then there is no necessary contradiction to the description "in the name of the Lord" in Acts and Paul.[10]

The Greek phrase "into the name of" (εἰς τὸ ὄνομα) occurs mainly in commercial or legal documents and carries the idea of "into the ownership or possession" of someone. The Hebrew phrase "into the name of" (לְשֵׁם) carries the idea of "with reference to," defining the intention or purpose of the act, or even in some instances

---

9. Joseph Crehan, *Early Christian Baptism and the Creed* (London: Burns, Oates & Washbourne, 1950), pp. 76-78 and passim, for the distinction that Matthew 28 authorized disciples to use the Trinitarian formula while Acts refers to the part taken by the candidate in confessing faith in Jesus; p. 87, for the claim that there is no New Testament evidence and none in the tradition where the baptizer used the name of Christ; pp. 156-158, quoting Photius (ninth century) on the traditional distinction that "into the name of the Lord Jesus Christ" meant the faith imparted by Christ and the Trinitarian formula as what was spoken by the baptizer.

10. F. H. Chase, "The Lord's Command to Baptize," pp. 507-508. Both "into the name of the Father, the Son, and the Holy Spirit" and "into the name of the Lord" occur in reference to baptism in the *Didache* (7.1 and 9.5).

"in worship to."[11] A Hebrew background has greater probability with reference to Matthaean usage, but the practical results may not have been greatly different. Something done by a person as an act of worship toward another brought the first person into a relationship of belonging to the object of the act, and someone to whom a person belonged or was obligated received acts of homage from that person. The suggestion has some merit that in a Jewish context faith in God by a convert to Jesus was assumed and reference at the baptism needed only to be made to Jesus as Lord or Christ, whereas in the Gentile context the baptism had to be defined in a fuller way as including God the Father and this led to the expanded version that incorporated the Holy Spirit as well. The verbal expression of the purpose or meaning of baptism as relating the baptizand to Christ or to Father, Son, and Holy Spirit might have been made either by the one being baptized, the baptizer, or in different words by both. Since in the Hebrew sources cited as parallel[12] the worshipper speaks the formula, it was likely spoken by the convert.

"The name," singular and occurring only once, before all three persons would emphasize one baptism with reference to the three and so indicate the intention of the act and not the names per se. The loss of this sense of one name (as may be seen in Justin Martyr's elaboration on each of the three names — chap. 14) could have led to triple immersions. If "name" functions here as it often does in rabbinic literature as a substitute for the Tetragrammaton, the Divine Name, then the genitives could be expressing possession, "the name that is possessed by the Father, the Son, and the Holy Spirit."[13] This interpretation would be consistent with the constant appeal to the baptismal formula as scriptural proof of Trinitarian doctrine in the fourth-century controversies. It would be further consistent with the meaning of "an act of worship toward." On the other hand, the many ways in which "in the name of" was used makes this only a possible interpretation and perhaps puts too much of a burden on the phrase in this context.

On a grammatical note, the initial participle, "going" (πορυεθέντες), is to be construed not as a circumstantial participle ("as you go") but as coordinate with the main verb (the participle getting its force from the main verb), "make disciples" (μαθητεύσατε), so that both are imperatives, "Go and make disciples." This construction of the participle "going" with an imperative to express a double command to "go and do something" is common in Matthew (2:8; 9:13; 10:7; 11:4; 17:27; 28:7).

---

11. Lars Hartman, *'Into the Name of the Lord Jesus': Baptism in the New Testament* (Edinburgh: T&T Clark, 1997), pp. 37-50; Huub van de Sandt and David Flusser, *The Didache*, p. 285. F. H. Ely, "The Lord's Command to Baptize (St. Matt. xxviii 19)," *Journal of Theological Studies* 8 (1907): 161-184, defends "into the name" against J. Armitage Robinson's preference for "in the name" in the same journal 7 (1906): 186-202, and affirms the meaning "immerse into" (but he adds that "baptize into" and "baptize in" are strictly synonymous, with "into" stressing entrance into and "in" encompassed by). The different Greek forms of the formula will be discussed in chap. 10.

12. Lars Hartman, *'Into the Name of the Lord Jesus'*, pp. 40-43, 49 (n. 53).

13. Charles A. Gieschen, "The Divine Name in Ante-Nicene Christology," *Vigiliae Christianae* 57 (2003): 115-158 (144).

Less certainty among commentators attaches to how the subsequent participles, "baptizing" and "teaching," are to be construed with the main verb, "make disciples." Are they circumstantial, describing the manner or means of "making disciples"; or are they coordinate imperatives, "baptize and teach" as following on the activity of making disciples?[14] Baptizing and teaching would seem to be certainly involved in making disciples, but the teaching described here is "teaching to observe everything I commanded you" and so may be taken as the postbaptismal teaching of how to live after one has become a disciple of Jesus and not the teaching involved in making disciples.[15] Hence, the suggestion is made, regardless of the grammatical construction, that the baptizing goes with making disciples and the teaching all things as a subsequent activity is subordinate to making disciples by baptizing.[16] On this view the sequence is (1) going, (2) making disciples (which would involve the preaching of Jesus, to which one responds in faith), (3) baptizing, and (4) teaching the responsibilities of the Christian life. This interpretation may correspond to normal activity but departs from Matthew's style and goes beyond the grammar. Matthew elsewhere uses two or three imperatives, joined by conjunctions, when sequential acts are commanded (2:13, 20; 8:4; 9:6).[17] In Matthew 28:19-20, moreover, the two participles following the imperative are not joined by a conjunction. In this construction the second participle often defines the other,[18] and so would make the baptism a "taught" baptism. Teaching to observe what Jesus commanded was an accompaniment to the baptizing.

Therefore, my understanding of Matthew 28:19-20 is that, while all the participles derive an imperatival force from the main verb, the initial participle is coordinate with the main verb ("go and make disciples") and the two participles subsequent to the verb are circumstantial, describing the means of making disciples, with the "teaching" accompanying the "baptizing" ("make disciples by baptizing them and [at the same time] teaching them").

14. Bruce J. Malina, "The Literary Sructure and Form of Matt. XXVIII.16-20," *New Testament Studies* 17 (1970): 87-103, on the participles as imperatives (89-91). A third alternative is presented by the reading of manuscripts B and D. They have the aorist βαπτίσαντες instead of the present tense βαπτίζοντες. That might give the sense of baptizing first and then discipling by teaching, a reading that if deliberate could be relevant to the practice of infant baptism. Or, the aorist might simply refer to the singular action of one baptism in contrast to rebaptism. Ordinarily the combination of B and D is significant, but since the reading here lacks any other support, it is likely that two scribes either accidentally made the same mistake or independently offered the same interpretive reading.

15. Robert Harry Smith, "Matthew 28:16-20, Anticlimax or Key to the Gospel?" *Society of Biblical Literature Seminar Papers 1993* (Atlanta: Scholars Press, 1993), pp. 589-603, argues for a primarily ethical reading of the passage.

16. G. R. Beasley-Murray, *Baptism in the New Testament*, pp. 88-90.

17. Cf. Matt. 8:5-6 for two participles (joined by the conjunction "and") following an indicative rather than an imperative but with the same grammatical relationship, except that the two participles are more nearly equivalent; 4:23 = 9:35 for three participles (joined by "and") following an indicative, where separate activities are involved.

18. Herbert Weir Smyth, *Greek Grammar* (Cambridge: Harvard University Press, 1959), pp. 477-78, § 2147f-g; p. 458, § 2063 on the circumstantial participle of means.

The main thrust of Matthew 28:18-20 is on the authority of Jesus as Son of God. Jesus has *all* authority; he gives a commission to make disciples of *all* nations; his disciples are to keep *all* his commands; and he assures them that he will be with them *all* the days that remain. The one with all authority will continue to be with his followers as they proclaim his authority. Unlike the rabbis, his disciples do not make disciples of themselves or establish a succession of teachers in a chain going back to Jesus but rather bring converts into direct discipleship to Jesus. He remains the one Teacher (Matt. 23:9-10), and all his followers are his disciples, who have the task of following his instructions. Baptism is part of the process of following him and accepting the position of a disciple.

The account of Jesus' blessing the little children (Matt. 19:13-15; Mark 10:13-16; Luke 18:15-17) has sometimes been cited as warrant for infant baptism. Neither of the Synoptic accounts gives a baptismal setting to the episode, and it is striking that in the patristic period only two texts employ the pericope in connection with infant baptism.[19] The wording of Matthew 18:3, "to become as children," means that they were not children and so the passage is not a reference to infant baptism.[20]

Mark

In addition to his references to the baptism of John, Mark refers to Jewish purification rituals in 7:4, "[The Pharisees and all the Jews] do not eat anything from the marketplace unless they are immersed, and there are many other traditions that they observe — dipping [or immersing, βαπτισμούς] cups, pots, bronze vessels, and beds." The verse contains several textual variants. "Western" witnesses clarify, "When they come from the marketplace, they do not eat...." A few Egyptian witnesses read, "Unless they are sprinkled [ῥαντίσωνται]."[21] I understand the immersing (or the sprinkling) to refer to the people and not what might be brought from the marketplace; the washing of inanimate objects comes in the next clause. Some good manuscripts omit "beds" from the list of objects immersed (and so omitted from the NRSV's preferred reading), but it seems more likely that this item would have been omitted as problematic than that it would have been added in transmission of the

---

19. Tertullian, *On Baptism* 18.5 (in opposing the practice); *Apostolic Constitutions* 6.15.7 (as authorizing the practice). Hans Windisch, "Zum Problem der Kindertaufe im Urchristentum," *Zeitschrift für die neutestamentliche Wissenschaft* 28 (1929): 118-142, comments that Jesus' words, rather than sanctioning infant baptism, declare it superfluous (p. 130). David F. Wright, "Out, In, Out: Jesus' Blessing of the Children and Infant Baptism," in Stanley E. Porter and Anthony R. Cross, eds., *Dimensions of Baptism: Biblical and Theological Studies* (London: Sheffield Academic Press, 2002), pp. 188-206, canvasses the history of the use of this text and concludes that it belongs more fittingly in service of thanksgiving or dedication for a child (pp. 205-206).

20. Wilhelm Michaelis, "Lukas und die Anfänge der Kindertaufe," in W. Eltester, ed., *Apophoreta: Festschrift für Ernst Haenchen* (Berlin: Töpelmann, 1964), in a discussion of Luke 18:15-17 (pp. 187-191).

21. The origin of this reading is unclear: strict Jews would have immersed before eating (see chap. 3 on Essene practice).

text. Some have thought that the list of items mentioned as baptized speaks against the translation "immerse" and that the word must refer to a washing.[22] However, the preceding verse mentions a "washing" (νίψωνται) of hands,[23] and presumably Mark would have used the same word again if that was what he meant.[24] Mark uses βαπτισμός for the Jewish ritual dippings rather than βάπτισμα, the word for the baptism administered by John and Christians.

Mark 14:20 uses ἐμβάπτω, "to dip in(to)," as does Matthew 26:23, when Jesus said that one of the Twelve, the one who dipped in the bowl with him, would betray him.[25]

Mark 10:38-39 uses βαπτίζω and βάπτισμα in a metaphorical sense that may be significant for the understanding of baptism and certainly is for the meaning of the words.[26]

> Jesus said to them, . . . "Are you able to drink the cup that I drink, or be baptized [βαπτισθῆναι] with the baptism [βάπτισμα] that I am baptized [βαπτίζομαι] with?" They replied, "We are able." Then Jesus said to them, "The cup that I drink you will drink; and with the baptism [βάπτισμα] with which I am baptized [βαπτίζομαι], you will be baptized [βαπτισθήσεσθε]."

Some see in Jesus' use of baptism in reference to his death the idea that Jesus' death was a general baptism for the sins of the world and by extension the doctrine found in Paul (chap. 9) of baptism as a death and resurrection.[27] Christian writers consistently affirmed that the cross gave to baptism its distinctive efficacy.[28] However, the passage does not liken baptism to a death but death to a baptism. It is more likely that in the sayings about a cup and a baptism Old Testament imagery about suffering is in mind.[29] It may be significant, nonetheless, that Mark and the Lukan parallel

---

22. The Mishnah tractate *Mikwaoth* discusses the immersion of vessels (6.1-2, 5-6; 10.1, 5), including beds (7.7). Other references to Jewish purifications of vessels are collected in Hermann L. Strack and Paul Billerbeck, *Kommentar zum Neuen Testament aus Talmud und Midrasch* (Munich: C. H. Beck, 1926; repr. 1961), Vol. 1, pp. 934-936 on Matt. 23:25.

23. Cf. Matt. 15:2 for washing hands and 23:25 for cleansing cups and plates.

24. Mark 7:3 says the Jews washed their hands πυγμῇ (meaning unclear and variously translated — with the fist, to the fist, to the elbow, with a handful of water, diligently or thoroughly), a difficulty that led some witnesses to omit the word and others to substitute πυκνά ("often").

25. Codex D has ἐμβαπτίζω.

26. Gerhard Delling, "ΒΑΠΤΙΣΜΑ ΒΑΠΤΙΣΘΗΝΑΙ," *Novum Testamentum* 2 (1958): 92-115, studies the imagery of the cup for God's judgment in wrath in parallel to immersion as a metaphor for being overwhelmed (pp. 93-102). Unlike some who find in the various metaphorical uses of *baptizō* (chap. 2) indications of a meaning other than immersion, Delling reaffirms that "Lexical observations lead to the simple determination" that βάπτισμα "designates above all most probably a plunging" (p. 98), since in extrabiblical Greek βαπτίζεσθαι was used metaphorically for an overwhelming situation (p. 100).

27. For the former Oscar Cullmann, *Baptism in the New Testament* (London: SCM Press, 1950), 19-20; for the latter, Alan Richardson, *An Introduction to the Theology of the New Testament* (London: SCM Press, 1958), pp. 339-340.

28. Per Lundberg, *La typologie baptismale dans l'ancienne église* (Uppsala: Lorentz, 1942), p. 200.

29. G. R. Beasley-Murray, *Baptism in the New Testament*, pp. 72-77. Note Isa. 51:17, 21; Jer. 25:15, 27-

(12:50) use the word for Christian baptism and not the general word for dippings (βαπτισμός) in this metaphorical reference to immersion in sufferings. For the meaning of the words it is clear that "baptize" here draws on its usage for being drowned or overwhelmed. The metaphorical use in Mark 10:35-40 comes from the usage of βαπτίζω for drowning, death. Jesus was referring to his sufferings and death. He was not sprinkled or poured on with a small amount of suffering. He was submerged; he was completely overwhelmed in suffering and death.

Morton Smith gave a baptismal interpretation to passages in the *Secret Gospel of Mark* that expand on Mark 10.[30] Independently Robin Scroggs and Kent I. Groff found in the nakedness and white garment of the youth in Mark 14:51-52 and 16:5 a reference to the Christian initiate who by baptism was identified with the death and resurrection of Jesus.[31] As intriguing as these interpretations may be, instead of adding to our knowledge of early Christian baptism, in their suppositions they are dependent on what is known about baptism from other sources.

The baptism of Jesus and his own engagement in baptism at the beginning of his ministry and the designation of his death at the end as a baptism might be thought to have been a sufficient warrant from his person and ministry for the disciples to practice baptism even without a specific command, but these features at the same time make such an authorization plausible.

The long ending of Mark contains a parallel to Matthew's account of Jesus' commission for his followers to baptize: "Go into all the world and proclaim the good news to the whole creation. The one who believes and is baptized [βαπτισθείς] will be saved, but the one who does not believe will be condemned" (Mark 16:15-16). Most text critics conclude from the absence of Mark 16:9-20 in manuscripts ℵ and B and other early witnesses that these verses were not part of the original text of Mark, and others find linguistic and stylistic differences in the passage from the rest of Mark; but there are significant advocates of their genuineness.[32] The passage origi-

---

29; Ezek. 23:31-35; and Hab. 2:16 for drinking the cup of God's wrath, and Job 22:11; Pss. 18:4; 42:7; 69:2, 15; 88:6-7; Isa. 30:27-28 and 43:2 for a deluge or being swept away in an overflowing stream for being overcome by disaster.

30. Morton Smith, *The Secret Gospel: The Discovery and Interpretation of the Secret Gospel according to Mark* (New York: Harper & Row, 1973), passim, esp. pp. 97-114, is his popular presentation. The question of the authenticity of *Secret Mark* has generated much discussion: Stephen C. Carlson, *The Gospel Hoax: Morton Smith's Invention of Secret Mark* (Waco: Baylor University Press, 2005); Scott Brown, *Mark's Other Gospel: Rethinking Morton Smith's Controversial Discovery* (Toronto: Wilfrid Laurier University Press, 2005); Peter Jeffery, *The Secret Gospel of Mark Unveiled: Imagined Rituals of Sex, Death, and Madness in a Biblical Forgery* (New Haven: Yale University Press, 2007).

31. "Baptism in Mark: Dying and Rising with Christ," *Journal of Biblical Literature* 92 (1973):531-548.

32. Notably, but with reservations, William R. Farmer, *The Last Twelve Verses of Mark* (London: Cambridge University Press, 1974). On the other side, J. Lee Magness, *Sense and Absence: Structure and Suspense in the Ending of Mark's Gospel* (Atlanta: Society of Biblical Literature, 1986), argues that the author intended to conclude the Gospel at 16:8. The long ending has received a major treatment in its own right as a second-century composition by James A. Kelhofer, *Miracle and Mission* (Tübingen: Mohr/Siebeck, 2000); earlier by Joseph Hug, *La finale de l'évangile de Marc (Mc 16, 9-20)* (Paris, 1978)

nated no later than the latter part of the second century, for Irenaeus quotes Mark 16:19 as from "the conclusion of Mark's Gospel."[33] Either as original or a later addition to Mark, the passage gives a significant commentary on the meaning of Matthew 28:19-20. Even if not part of Mark's original text, the passage is notable for its testimony to the early Christian conviction of the importance of baptism as a condition of salvation and its connection with (as an expression of) faith.

Luke

Luke contains parallels to Mark's passages using the words "baptize" and "baptism" where Matthew does not use them. Whereas Mark and Matthew refer to the ceremonial washing of hands before eating, Luke refers to a complete purification bath. Luke says in 11:38 that a Pharisee who had invited Jesus to a meal "was amazed to see that he was not first baptized [ἐβαπτίσθη] before the mid-day meal." One early papyrus (P[45]) and an eleventh-century manuscript read ἐβαπτίσατο, "he baptized [not] himself." This would have been more accurate to the Jewish practice, but the overwhelming manuscript evidence is that Luke accommodated the wording to Christian practice (although conceivably the passive could be used of a self-baptism). The reference is to the total washing that Essenes and apparently some Pharisees observed before the mid-day meal.[34]

A direct verbal parallel to the metaphorical language of Mark 10:38 occurs in briefer form in Luke 12:50: "I have a baptism [βάπτισμα] with which to be baptized [βαπτισθῆναι]." The saying in Luke is less obviously a reference to Jesus' death than in Mark (note the preceding pericope in Mark 10:32-34), yet the context is equally eschatological but with more emphasis on judgment and punishment. The parallel of verse 49 with verse 50 suggests that Jesus takes the consuming punishment (under the imagery of fire and flood) on himself.[35]

Luke contains one of the three New Testament passages using βάπτω, "dip."[36] In Luke 16:24 the rich man in torment asked Abraham to send Lazarus and have him dip [βάψῃ] the tip of his finger in water and cool the rich man's tongue.

---

and Paul Allen Mirecki, "Mark 16:9-20: Composition, Tradition, and Redaction" (Ph.D. diss., Harvard University, 1986).

33. Irenaeus, *Against Heresies* 3.10.5.

34. Friedrich Avemarie, *Die Tauferzählungen der Apostelgeschichte: Theologie und Geschichte* (Tübingen: Mohr Siebeck, 2002), p. 23, with others, takes Luke 11:38 of Pharisaic hand washing and considers Essene baths improbable. On the other hand, the use of βάπτω in 16:24 for dipping a finger suggests that βαπτίζω in 11:38 is different.

35. Gerhard Delling, "ΒΑΠΤΙΣΜΑ ΒΑΠΤΙΣΘΗΝΑΙ," pp. 102-112.

36. The other passages are John 13:26 (twice — mentioned below) and Rev. 19:13 ("garment dipped [βεβαμμένον] in blood"), but with variant readings for "sprinkled" (ἐρραντισμένον and variant spellings). Carroll D. Osburn, "Alexander Campbell and the Text of Revelation 19:13," *Restoration Quarterly* 25 (1982): 129-138, after a thorough review of the textual evidence concludes that ἐρραντισμένον is the preferable reading in Rev. 19:13 and has the meaning "splattered."

Luke's main references to baptism occur in his second volume, the Acts of the Apostles (chap. 10).

John

John has the greatest number of usages of the verb βαπτίζω of any of the Gospels but no usage of the noun βάπτισμα, and all the occurrences of the verb are to John's baptizing and the early parallel, baptizing by Jesus and his disciples (chap. 5). Some scholars, however, have seen several symbolic references to baptism in the Fourth Gospel's frequent mention of water — for example, the "living water" (ὕδωρ ζῶν) that wells up for eternal life that is central to Jesus' conversation with the Samaritan woman at the well of Jacob (4:7-15),[37] the healing water in the pool in Jerusalem (5:1-7), the healing of the blind man at the pool of Siloam (9:1-17), the washing of the disciples' feet by Jesus (13:5-10), and the blood and water that came from the side of the crucified Jesus (19:34).[38] This interpretation was anticipated in the spiritual exegesis of the church fathers.[39] Water thus occurs in a variety of contexts in the Fourth Gospel, often as a symbol of the Spirit, but also of Jesus himself and especially in passages where there is a call for a decision to believe.[40] The emphasis on water in John (the greatest number of references in any New Testament book; second is Revelation) may have been a counter to tendencies to denigrate matter and substitute a spiritual understanding for the use of material elements (see chap. 15).

The most important text in John for Christian baptism is John 3:3 and 5, "Except one is begotten from above [or, again, ἄνωθεν], that person cannot see the kingdom of God.... Except one is begotten of water and Spirit [ἐξ ὕδατος καὶ πνεύματος], that person cannot enter the kingdom of God."[41] The usual translation is "born," probably

---

37. The "rivers of living water" flowing out of the bosom of believers in John 7:38-39 is the Holy Spirit.

38. Oscar Cullmann, *Early Christian Worship* (London: SCM Press, 1953), pp. 80-88, 102-110, 114-116. G. R. Beasley-Murray, *Baptism in the New Testament*, pp. 216-226, shows the exegetical weaknesses in Cullmann's interpretation.

39. Tertullian, *On Baptism* 16.1; *On Modesty* 22.

40. The conclusions of Larry Paul Jones, *The Symbol of Water in the Gospel of John* (Sheffield: Sheffield Academic Press, 1997), pp. 219-231.

41. Carroll D. Osburn, "Some Exegetical Observations on John 3:5-8," *Restoration Quarterly* 31 (1989): 129-138, sets John 3:5 in the context of the whole chapter. Adolf von Harnack, "Die Terminologie der Wiedergeburt und verwandter Erlebnisse in der ältesten Kirche," *Texte und Untersuchungen*, Dritte Reihe, XII.3 (XLVII.3) (Leipzig: J. C. Hinrichs, 1918), pp. 97-143, gives an overview more devoted to the related imagery, with only pp. 106-123 on new creation and new birth. He suggests three lines that led Christians to the conception of birth from God: Messiah is begotten of God; the teacher in Judaism was the begetter and father of his students; and Jesus brought his disciples to think of God as Father (p. 110). The idea was not derived from the Mystery religions (p. 112). "Regeneration" (ἀναγέννησις) did not become strictly speaking a technical term for baptism the way "enlightenment" (φωτισμός) did (p. 141). See J. Ysebaert, *Greek Baptismal Terminology* (Nijmegen: Dekker & Van de Vegt, 1962), pp. 107-119, for the metaphorical use of "birth" in pagan antiquity and pp. 141-143 on Johannine usage.

because of Nicodemus's misunderstanding in verse 4. But if we take the ambiguous ἄνωθεν as "from above" (its meaning in 3:31 and 19:11) and follow the emphasis on the Spirit in verses 6-12 (esp. v. 8), then Jesus' statements concern primarily the divine begetting, not the human rebirth, although the latter would be implicit even if not explicit.[42] God gives new life through the Spirit (6:63) in the water.[43] John 3:5 became the most cited baptismal text in the second century and continued to be important afterward. Despite the overwhelming historical and majority contemporary consensus, there have been insistent efforts to remove John 3:5 from the dossier of baptismal texts. I will take one of the better attempts for examination.[44]

The arguments against the water in John 3:5 referring to baptism are the following: (1) baptism could have had no relevance to Nicodemus; (2) the entire focus of John 3 is on the Spirit; (3) Jesus could not have expected Nicodemus to understand Christian baptism (3:10); (4) there is no mystery if the work of the Spirit (3:8) is tied to baptism; (5) other references in John depreciate water baptism (3:22, 25-26; 4:1-2; 1:26, 33). The alternative interpretation offered is that the water is figurative for Spirit. When water is used figuratively in the Old Testament it refers to renewal or cleansing, especially in conjunction with "spirit." Most important here is Ezekiel 36:25-27, where the reference is to eschatological cleansing of which water is the symbol. John 3:5 is parallel to 3:3. The preposition "of" governs both water and Spirit; the birth has a water-Spirit source, forming a conceptual unity. There is only one birth, not two.

The last point is certainly correct: water and Spirit are united in producing the new birth or birth from above. The question, then, is why are two elements mentioned if only one is meant? The other arguments do not succeed in dehydrating the new birth. (1) The baptism of John the Baptist was relevant to Nicodemus, and the text of John 3 continues with a description of John's baptism (3:22-23), a discussion between John's disciples and a Jew over purification (3:25-26), and the baptizing activity of Jesus and his disciples (3:22; 4:1-2). The context certainly suggests that the water of 3:5 is the same kind of water as in 3:23. (2) The focus of John 3 is indeed on the Spirit, but does that eliminate the possibility that the Spirit might work in and through water? A material means of healing (3:14) is compared to Jesus' lifting up (on the cross?). (3) John was writing from a postresurrection standpoint and shapes the conversation of Jesus with Nicodemus in terms of the Christian-Jewish debate of

---

42. The same emphasis on the divine begetting occurs in John 1:12-13, which states that those who believe in the name of Jesus receive power to become children of God (not that they become children of God by believing alone — 12:42-43) and they have been born (ἐγεννήθησαν) from God. Otherwise the Fourth Gospel uses the verb of ordinary human birth (9:2, 19, 20, 32, 34; 16:21), but the father's role is in view in 8:41 and Jesus' statement in 18:37 of himself may be taken either of his divine begetting or (more commonly) of his birth. The epistle of 1 John uses a form of γεννάω ten times, always as coming from God and so with reference to the divine begetting (chap. 9).

43. Gerhard Delling, *Die Taufe im Neuen Testament* (Berlin: Evangelische Verlagsanstalt, 1963), pp. 89-92: what God works in (water) baptism he works through the Holy Spirit (p. 92). Adolf von Harnack, "Die Terminologie der Wiedergeburt," pp. 113-116 on John 3, observes that John 19:34 and 1 John 5:6-7 make a removal of water from John 3:5 very daring.

44. Donald A. Carson, *The Gospel according to John* (Grand Rapids: Eerdmans, 1991), pp. 191-196.

his own time — note the plurals in 3:11 — "we know," "we speak," "we have seen," "we testify," but "you [plural] do not receive our testimony." The familiarity to be assumed that Nicodemus had with John's baptism gave sufficient basis for Jesus directing his attention to a rebirth involving the Spirit as well as water. (4) Reading John 3:5 as a reference to baptism does not "tie" or limit the work of the Spirit to the water. Is it seriously to be advocated that he may work through any means except water? (5) Other readers of John's Gospel who take 3:5 as a reference to water baptism have not seen the other verses cited as "depreciating" baptism. The Fourth Gospel does depreciate John's baptism in comparison to Jesus' baptism (1:33). The statements of John 1:31, 33 prepare for the declaration of 3:5 and support the baptismal interpretation of the latter. What made Jesus' baptism superior was that it was accompanied by the activity of the Spirit and conferred the Spirit, the very thing John 3:5 says of it.

As to the interpretation that the water in John 3:5 functions as a symbol for the Spirit, one might wonder, of what then is the Spirit a symbol? The Old Testament prophetic passages that speak of a future cleansing of the people were understood by the baptizing and renewal movements in Judaism, beginning with the Essenes and Pharisees, as involving a literal washing as well as spiritual renewal. In the context of the Judaism of the time water would certainly have been understood literally and in no contradiction to activity by the Spirit of God. When John wrote, a reference to baptism would have seemed self-evident.

The other major alternative to a baptismal reference in John 3:5 has even less to commend it than the equation of water with Spirit. Some have suggested that the birth of water is a reference to physical birth, either the male semen or the waters in the womb. But as noted above, this cannot be, for the grammar allows only one begetting or birth (not two). The verbal parallels equate the birth of water and the Spirit (3:5) with the birth from above (3:3) and contrast it with the natural birth that Nicodemus mentions (3:4). The one begetting is derived from two elements — water and Spirit. This is not to put the two elements on the same level of importance.[45] As the subsequent verses in John 3 show, the emphasis is on the activity of the Spirit, the element that distinguished the new birth from the baptism of John with which Nicodemus would have been familiar. Only the Spirit of God can give a new birth, that is, impart new spiritual life. But the occasion, according to the Gospel of John, is when one in faith receives the Word (1:12-13; cf. 3:36) and submits to baptism. John 3:5 requires water, but not in the same way as it requires the Spirit. The water is the means or the occasion, and the Spirit is the Mediator of the new birth. The Spirit is free to move as he will (3:8), but that freedom includes working in or through water.

A moderate or intermediate approach presents water and Spirit as identifiable but not inseparable components of the same experience.[46] It is argued that in John 3

---

45. It may be that "Spirit" in 3:5 is epexegetical, in which case we should translate, "begotten of water, that is, of the Spirit," meaning not that the water stands for Spirit but that what is important about the begetting from the water is the begetting from the Spirit.

46. Jones, *The Symbol of Water*, pp. 65-76, 85-88, 231-238.

water is the means of believing in the realities manifested by Jesus. The baptismal interpretation of 3:5 is plausible in view of 3:23–4:2, but to see a reference to baptism alone is an unnecessary restriction in the meaning that reduces the imperative of believing; the water symbolizes the separation of those who believe in Jesus from those who do not. To this contention it may be responded that John certainly gives priority to believing, even as he does to the role of the Spirit, but this emphasis is consistent with speaking more confidently of a baptismal reference in 3:5, an interpretation that contextual considerations, provided by the preceding testimony of John the Baptist at the baptism of Jesus and the subsequent account of baptizing activities, support.

A further observation is that the connection of the Holy Spirit in baptism with the forgiveness of sins to be found in other writers may be because of the connection of the Holy Spirit and forgiveness in John 20:22-23.

John 3:5 provides a combination of the ideas of baptism, sonship (new birth), and the presence of the Holy Spirit that we will find included in Paul's baptismal theology.

Before turning to that, I note the use of the verb βάπτω in John 13:26, a passage that, like Luke 16:24 above, illustrates the way the New Testament uses this word for a literal dipping in a secular context. "Jesus answered, 'It is the one for whom I will dip [βάψω] this piece of bread in the dish and give it to him.' When he dipped [βάψας] the piece of bread, he gave it to Judas." Variant readings in both instances give a form of ἐμβάπτω, the word used in Matthew and Mark's accounts (noted above).

9. Baptism in the Pauline Epistles

The apostle Paul is a central figure for the study of Christian baptism.[1] His own experience and the evidence of his letters show baptism to have been practiced from the earliest days of the church. He included himself with his readers as baptized (1 Cor. 12:13), and his conversion must be placed within a very few years of the crucifixion. He takes baptism for granted as common ground with his readers and refers to it in order to make an argument about something else. The frequent references to baptism in his writings offer a profound understanding of its significance.[2]

One study concluded that Paul took over from the earliest Palestinian Christianity the following aspects of baptism: Baptism presupposes preaching and faith, but preaching and faith do not replace baptism; baptism occurs in the name of Jesus;

---

1. Out of the large literature on baptism in the New Testament as a whole note W. F. Flemington, *The New Testament Doctrine of Baptism* (London: SPCK, 1948) — his views summarized in the entry "Baptism," in George A. Buttrick et al., eds., *The Interpreter's Dictionary of the Bible* (New York: Abingdon, 1962), Vol. 1, pp. 348-353; Oscar Cullmann, *Baptism in the New Testament* (London: SCM, 1950); D. M. Stanley, "The New Testament Doctrine of Baptism: An Essay in Biblical Theology," *Theological Studies* 18 (1957): 169-215; G. R. Beasley-Murray, *Baptism in the New Testament* (Grand Rapids: Eerdmans, 1962; repr. 1973), the best single work on the subject; J. Ysebaert, *Greek Baptismal Terminology* (Nijmegen: Dekker & Van de Vegt, 1962); Gerhard Delling, *Die Taufe im Neuen Testament* (Berlin: Evangelische Verlagsanstalt, 1963); A. M. George, et al., *Baptism in the New Testament: A Symposium* (Baltimore/Dublin: Helicon, 1964); O. S. Brooks, *The Drama of Decision: Baptism in the New Testament* (Peabody: Hendrickson, 1987); Ben Witherington III, *Troubled Waters: Rethinking the Theology of Baptism* (Waco: Baylor University Press, 2007), is a popular treatment.

2. Beasley-Murray, *Baptism in the New Testament*, pp. 127-216; Delling, *Die Taufe im Neuen Testament*, pp. 108-132; Rudolf Schnackenburg, *Baptism in the Thought of St. Paul: A Study in Pauline Theology* (Oxford: Basil Blackwell, 1964); A. J. M. Wedderburn, *Baptism and Resurrection: Studies in Pauline Theology against Its Greco-Roman Background* (Tübingen: Mohr Siebeck, 1987); H. D. Betz, "Paul's Interpretation of Baptism," in Troels Engberg-Pedersen, ed., *Paul in His Hellenistic Context* (Minneapolis: Fortress, 1994), pp. 84-118.

it mediates the eschatological gift of salvation (forgiveness and the Holy Spirit); baptism is by the leaders of the community and orders the community.[3]

Galatians

Some think Galatians to be the earliest surviving letter from the apostle Paul. We begin with it, however, not because of this claim but because its passage on baptism introduces us briefly to some of the key aspects of Paul's baptismal theology. The passage occurs at a crucial place in the argument of Galatians. Paul was making the case against Judaizers, who insisted that Gentile converts to Christ must be circumcised in order to become a part of God's people. He argued that the Law of Moses was not binding on Gentiles, who can enter into covenant with God on the same basis as Abraham did, that is, through the promise of God received by faith. Christ is the "seed" ("offspring") of Abraham, and through him the promise to Abraham is fulfilled. All who are in Christ share the inheritance promised through Abraham to all nations. The passage that refers to baptism explains how one comes to be "in Christ." It is not by fleshly birth confirmed by circumcision.

> For in Christ Jesus you are all children of God through faith. As many of you as were baptized into Christ [εἰς Χριστὸν ἐβαπτίσθητε] have clothed yourselves with Christ. There is no longer Jew or Greek, there is no longer slave or free, there is no longer male and female, for all of you are one in Christ Jesus. And if you belong to Christ, then you are Abraham's offspring, heirs according to the promise. (Gal. 3:26-29)

The declaration "no longer Jew or Greek, no longer slave or free" (without "male and female") occurs in a baptismal context also in 1 Corinthians 12:13 and Colossians 3:11 (cf. Acts 2:39) and so may represent an affirmation in the baptismal service.

The passage continues in chapter 4:1-7 by affirming that those in Christ have received adoption as God's children, and because they are children they have received the Spirit of the Son enabling them to address God as "Abba, Father" (4:6). Note that here the sequence is not that the Spirit comes to make persons children of God but that because they are children they receive the Spirit. They become children because they are in Christ, the Son. And they enter into Christ at baptism. Baptism did not make them children of God. Faith did this (3:26). Even as faith justified Abraham, so one now receives the blessing of Abraham by faith (2:16; 3:6-9, 11, 22). One is a descendant of Abraham by faith, not by flesh (3:7). Faith is the reason why, but when does that faith make one an heir of the promises to Abraham? Paul binds faith and baptism together as two aspects of entering into Christ. One now belongs to Christ on the basis of faith in him by being baptized into him. If a distinction is to be made between the relation of faith and baptism to the blessings described, one might say that baptism is the time at which and faith is the reason why.

---

3. Otto Kuss, "Zur paulinischen und nachpaulinischen Tauflehre im Neuen Testament," *Theologie und Glaube* 42 (1952): 401-425 (401-402).

The distinctive of Christian baptism is its relationship to Christ. The baptized believer is now "Christ's" (3:29), the genitive case indicating either possession or belonging to the group derived from Christ. "Baptized into Christ" may be an abbreviated version of the formula "into the name of Christ," in which case the idea is a baptism with reference to Christ or as an act of worship directed toward him.[4] The "name" stood for the person in Hebraic thought, and this identification would have facilitated an association of the phrases "into the name" with "into Christ." Whether the idea of "into" in εἰς is to be pressed, the preposition at least expresses that Christian baptism is directed toward Christ. But in view of the preceding statement, "in Christ Jesus," and the following statement, "you put on Christ" (aorist, as is "baptized," so referring to the same moment as the baptism), we should probably give εἰς its full force. Baptism places one into Christ, so that one is now clothed with Christ, having put him on as one puts on clothing.[5] This has the effect of bringing to one the benefits that are Christ's, making one what Christ is — true descendant of Abraham, heir of the promises, son of God, recipient of the Spirit.

A few have put forward the idea that "baptized into Christ" does not refer to water baptism but is a metaphorical expression that says a person by faith is spiritually immersed into the being of Christ.[6] Although the verb "baptize" can have a metaphorical use, the context usually gives a clear indication of this. Without such an indication, the ordinary use of the word at the time in Jewish and Christian circles for the religious immersion of a person in water should be assumed.[7] And, as we shall see, the association of baptism with water is explicit in several Pauline texts.

---

4. Lars Hartman, *'Into the Name of the Lord Jesus': Baptism in the New Testament* (Edinburgh: T&T Clark, 1997), p. 56, says that "into Christ" was "certainly derived from the baptismal formula." Beasley-Murray, *Baptism in the New Testament*, pp. 128-130, had earlier suggested this and added that baptism was not identical with putting on Christ, which is the effect of "baptism to Christ." For the meaning of the phrase "into the name of" see chaps. 8 and 10.

5. The same word is used of being clothed with power in Luke 24:49 (the Holy Spirit according to Acts 1:8); in both cases a baptism, in Paul of water and in Luke of the Holy Spirit. This verse was the biblical basis for the later practice of clothing the newly baptized in a white garment and so is the starting point for John E. Farrell's doctoral dissertation "The Garment of Immortality: A Concept and Symbol in Christian Baptism" (Washington, DC: Catholic University of America, 1974; Ann Arbor: University Microfilms). He includes a discussion of the imagery of exchanging clothes in the Christian writers of the second to fifth century, pp. 132-225.

6. James D. G. Dunn, *The Epistle to the Galatians* (London: A & C Black, 1993), pp. 202-204, who concurs that "into Christ" is not an abbreviation for "into the name of Christ," because it puts one "in Christ." He understands the metaphor as drawn from the ritual act and finds support for the metaphorical interpretation in the subsequent metaphor of clothing. The use of a metaphor to explain a metaphor seems rather much; it is better to take the metaphor of clothing as drawing out the meaning of the literal act of immersion in water and to prepare for the conclusion drawn in 3:28-29.

7. Cf. Albrecht Oepke, "βάπτω, βαπτίζω (et al.)," in Gerhard Kittel, ed., *Theological Dictionary of the New Testament*, tr. Geoffrey W. Bromiley (Grand Rapids: Eerdmans, 1964), Vol. 1, pp. 539-540, that βαπτίζειν meant technically "to baptize in water" so it was unnecessary to specify the medium. Cf. Gerard-Henry Baudry, *Le baptême et ses symboles: Aux sources du salut* (Paris: Beauchesne, 2001), p. 5, that "baptize in water" is a pleonasm.

1 and 2 Corinthians

The verb "baptize" occurs more often in 1 Corinthians than in any other Pauline letter. Paul brings in baptism immediately as he begins his corrections of the behavior of the Corinthians.

> Each of you says, "I belong to Paul," "I belong to Apollos," "I belong to Cephas," "I belong to Christ." Is Christ divided? Was Paul crucified for you? Were you baptized [ἐβαπτίσθητε] into the name of Paul [εἰς τὸ ὄνομα Παύλου]? I give thanks that I baptized [ἐβάπτισα] none of you except Carpus and Gaius, so that no one might say that your were baptized [ἐβαπτίσθητε] into my name. I baptized [ἐβάπτισα] also the household of Stephanas; I do not know if I baptized [ἐβάπτισα] any others. Christ did not send me to baptize [βαπτίζειν] but to preach the gospel. (1 Cor. 1:12-17)

Paul's three questions assert positively that Christ is undivided, Christ alone died for them, and they were baptized in the name of Christ and of no other.[8] There is no doubt that this passage refers to water baptism. This meaning at the very beginning of the letter should determine the meaning of "baptize" elsewhere in the letter unless there are obvious reasons for a different usage (made explicit in 10:1-2 but even there dependent on the literal meaning).

There is clear allusion to the baptismal formula "into the name of Christ" in Paul's paraphrase, "into the name of Paul" and "into my name." The force of the argument is that the nature of one's baptism determines one's identity — whose name one wears, with whom one is associated, and to whom one is a disciple. The common experience of baptism into the name of Christ meant that all belonged to Christ. This was the basis for unity and showed the fallacy of the divisions in the church at Corinth.

For Paul's theology of baptism it is notable how the crucifixion of Christ and baptism are paralleled. It is as unthinkable to be baptized in Paul's name as that Paul was crucified for them. Hence, the reference to baptism leads immediately into a discussion of the "message of the cross" (1:18-24). The association of baptism with the death of Christ is drawn out in Romans 6.

A depreciation of baptism, therefore, is not to be concluded from this passage, only a depreciation of the administrator of the baptism. The passage is a clear indication that Christian baptism is an administered act and is not self-baptism. Christ was the essential referent of baptism, not the person who did the teaching or the administering of the baptism. Baptism into the name of Christ was the expected result of preaching the gospel.

An obvious allusion to baptism occurs in 1 Corinthians 6:11. Paul has listed sins

---

8. Schnackenburg, *Baptism in the Thought of Paul,* pp. 18-19. Joseph Crehan, *Early Christian Baptism and the Creed* (London: Burns, Oates & Washbourne, 1950), p. 14, translates, "Were you baptized for the sake and worship of Paul?"

in which some of the Corinthians were previously involved (6:9-11a). Then he contrasts what has occurred at their conversion: "But you had yourselves thoroughly washed [ἀπελούσασθε], but you were sanctified, but you were justified in the name of the Lord Jesus Christ and in the Spirit of our God." The three verbs are in the aorist tense; each refers to a singular occurrence. And the three statements are to be understood as occurring simultaneously, or at least as part of the same complex of events. The passive voice indicates that God did the sanctifying and justifying to the convert; the middle voice probably, therefore, does not have the force of "washing yourselves" but of getting yourselves washed (or the middle may be functioning simply as a passive), so the cleansing too would be by God. These are three images of salvation. "Washing" picks up on the use of water in baptism and the association of water with cleansing (so also Eph. 5:26 below). The Greek verb ἀπολούω occurs in the New Testament only here and in Acts 22:16 (on which see chap. 10), a usage that confirms the baptismal reference of this verse. Unlike the later theological distinction between sanctification and justification, here being made holy and being declared just are united with the purifying water. The three verbs belong together and are not to be separated from baptism. Hence, baptism is connected with sanctification and justification.

The two prepositional phrases referring to the Lord Jesus Christ and God's Spirit modify all three verbs. Baptism is connected with "the name of the Lord," an allusion to the baptismal confession or possibly a baptismal formula, and with the activity of the Holy Spirit (either the Spirit's role of cleansing and sanctifying in the water or as the resultant gift).[9] Baptism according to this passage mediates the cleansing from sins, including the serious sins of which some in Corinth had been guilty, and so made possible an inheritance of (or entrance into) the kingdom of God. The linking of forgiveness of sins by washing in the name of the Lord with the sanctifying gift of the Holy Spirit provides a striking connection with the understanding of baptism presented in the book of Acts (notably 2:38).

A passage in which baptism does not occur must be considered because it has been brought into the debate concerning the practice of infant baptism in the apostolic age. 1 Corinthians 7:14 declares children "holy" if one of the parents is a believer.[10] Some in the church at Corinth thought that they should separate from an unbelieving spouse, apparently on the conviction that marital relations with an unbeliever brought impurity to the believer. Paul throughout the context argues for maintaining the marriage (1 Cor. 7:12-13 on the specific issue of a believer married

---

9. Crehan, *Early Christian Baptism and the Creed*, p. 15, sorts out the relationships this way: washing is unto the worship of Jesus, sanctification is in the Holy Spirit, and justification is before God.

10. In addition to the commentaries and the bibliography on infant baptism in chap. 23, note Albrecht Oepke, "Urchristentum und Kindertaufe," *Zeitschrift für die neutestamentliche Wissenschaft* 29 (1930): 81-111, who collects the patristic exegesis of 1 Cor. 7:14 with the observation that none speaks of baptism or original sin in connection with the verse (pp. 84-86), and David F. Wright, "1 Corinthians 7:14 in Fathers and Reformers," in David C. Steinmetz, ed., *Die Patristik in der Bibelexegese des 16. Jahrhunderts* (Wiesbaden: Harrassowitz, 1999), pp. 93-113.

to an unbeliever). (If the unbeliever departs, that is another matter — 7:15.) Rather than impurity flowing from the unbeliever to the believer, the influence is the reverse: sanctification flows from the believer to the unbeliever (7:14).

Paul brings in children to support his contention. Their condition of holiness (accepted by Paul's opponents) is not because of baptism, for the argument parallels the child with the unbelieving mate. Being sanctified applies as well to the unbeliever, who by definition is unbaptized. (If the child of one Christian parent was "holy," then a child of two Christian parents obviously was also "holy.") Nor does sanctification here imply a vicarious salvation, for verse 16 gives as a reason for not separating the possibility of saving the unbelieving partner. Paul, therefore, is not using "holy" in its Christian sense of sanctification in Christ. He probably takes up the word from the arguments of those whom he is correcting. The sense would be the Old Testament (and pagan) concept of ritual purity. The verse says nothing about child baptism, but its implications would be negative for that practice. If the child were already baptized, Paul's argument was meaningless, for then s/he was obviously "holy." The child, like the unbelieving spouse, became a subject of baptism on becoming a believer.

A figurative use of baptism occurs in 1 Corinthians 10:1-3. Paul is warning the Corinthians about the danger of idolatry involved in participating in religious meals in a pagan context that included sacrificial food. It seems that some in the church had an exaggerated view of the protection that baptism and the eucharist gave them. Paul appeals to the example of the Israelites of the Exodus generation, seeing their experiences as "types" (10:6) from which Christians could learn (10:11).[11] Transferring to them the spiritual counterparts in Christian experience, he says: "Our ancestors were all under the cloud, and all passed through the sea, and all were baptized into Moses [εἰς τὸν Μωυσῆν ἐβαπτίσθησαν] in the cloud and in the sea, and all ate the same spiritual food."[12] Their experience of deliverance, comparable to Christian baptism and eucharist, did not preserve them from falling into idolatry, immorality, and provocative and complaining behavior (10:7-10).

---

11. Karl-Heinrich Ostmeyer, *Taufe und Typos: Elemente und Theologie der Tauftypologien in 1 Korinther 10 und 1 Petrus 3* (Tübingen: Mohr/Siebeck, 2000), compares the two passages according to terminology, matter/medium (water), and purpose (new creation and new life — the different imagery and types of 1 Corinthians and 1 Peter describe the same reality); his special interests are the meaning of τύπος and the qualities of water in early Judaism and Christianity (saving, yet associated with judgment, chaos, and death): exegesis of 1 Cor. 10:1-13 on pp. 137-145. Per Lundberg, *La typologie baptismale dans l'ancienne église* (Uppsala: Lorentz, 1942), pp. 135-145 — baptism transports the baptized across death into the new aeon.

12. Papyrus 46 and codex B read ἐβαπτίσαντο, "they baptized themselves," a reading accepted by Schnackenburg, *Baptism in the Thought of St. Paul*, pp. 94-95, as agreeing with Jewish self-administered baptism and as an unlikely alteration, whereas a change of this verb to the usual passive in Christian usage is more likely. The word "all" occurs five times in the passage in order to refute a false sacramentalism, which understood baptism and the eucharist as automatically guaranteeing salvation, by underscoring the fact that participation in the saving events did not guarantee that all would escape sin and judgment.

The Israelites did not have a literal water baptism, but Paul saw their being surrounded by the sea on each side and the cloud overhead as comparable. Cloud in the Bible is often a sign of the presence of God. The Christian practice shapes his description of the experience of Israel, and that historical experience should not be made determinative for understanding Christian practice. Being baptized "ἐν the cloud and in the sea" at first sight suggests that the baptism is "in" these elements,[13] but further reflection suggests that perhaps "baptize in" might be instrumental rather than locative, "baptized by" these elements, that is, they together provided the means for what Paul compares to a baptism, since the Israelites were not literally "in" either the sea or the cloud (note Exod. 14:19-29). The crossing the Red Sea was the means of Israel's salvation, as baptism was for Christians. The result of this "baptism" brought Israel into a relationship with Moses comparable to what Christian baptism did to Christ. It might be reasoned that they were not "in Moses," but their baptism was with respect to Moses and brought them into allegiance to him.[14] Strictly speaking this would be correct, but it may be overdrawing the analogy. Paul may have applied the terminology of baptism into Christ to the Israelites in relation to Moses for the sake of his typology without intending its full force to apply in the case of Moses. At any rate, it seems safer to determine the meaning of the phrase "baptize into" in its other contexts rather than to let what would seem to be required by this passage, which can at the most be seen only as an accommodative usage, to determine the meaning elsewhere.

The Corinthians' overconfidence in the objective value of baptism and Paul's argument taken together indicate that Christian baptism was the crucial break with the pagan past, brought deliverance and salvation, and carried with it obligations in regard to conduct demonstrating these realities.

The most controversial baptismal passage in 1 Corinthians is 12:13, introducing Paul's discussion of the church as the body of Christ in order to plead for unity among the divided Corinthian Christians. "For by one Spirit we all were baptized [ἐβαπτίσθημεν] into one body — whether Jews or Greeks, slaves or free — and we all were watered with the one Spirit." In keeping with the theme that all are members of "one body" (12:12), the passage emphasizes oneness — one Spirit puts into one body the members, who receive the one Spirit.[15] Baptism is the act that introduces a person into the one body, the church. As in 1 Corinthians 1, baptism indicates unity.

---

13. Cf. the rabbinic *Mekhilta* on Exodus 13:19, 21; 14:16 for the Israelites surrounded by clouds and sea. Origen, *Homilies on Numbers* 22, took the cloud as representing the Holy Spirit and the sea the baptismal water, but Paul does not make such a distinction and sees the cloud and the sea together as constituting a "baptism."

14. Beasley-Murray, *Baptism in the New Testament*, p. 128, finds this verse a reason for not understanding baptism with reference to Christ as "into" Christ. Likewise, Schnackenburg, *Baptism in the Thought of St. Paul*, pp. 22-23, understands "baptism to Moses" to mean adherence to Moses, to belong to him; Delling, *Die Taufe*, pp. 111-113.

15. Schnackenburg, *Baptism in the Thought of St. Paul*, pp. 26-29 — not only is baptism "to Christ," but it is also "to one body" (p. 26).

Paul's use of the first-person plural "we" is significant from the historical standpoint as indicating the practice of baptism at the time of Paul's conversion, which must be dated within a few years of the beginning of the church.

Some scholars argue that "baptize" here is metaphorical and refers to the spiritual transformation by which the Spirit puts the believer in the one body which is Christ.[16]

In favor of the majority view that the reference is to water baptism are the following considerations: (1) 1 Corinthians 1:13 clearly employs water baptism as an argument for unity in the same way as 12:13 argues for unity; (2) in Ephesians 4:4-6 baptism is distinct from the Spirit as bases of unity; (3) the phrase "neither Jews nor Greeks, slaves nor free" elsewhere is in a literal baptismal context (Gal. 3:28; Col. 3:11).

Commentators are equally divided whether the preposition ἐν is locative ("in") or dative ("by"). Water baptism would be consistent with either translation: in the former case the Spirit provides the atmosphere or influence in which the baptism occurs; in the latter, the Spirit is the means by which baptism puts one into the body. The metaphorical interpretation of baptism as standing for conversion or spiritual transformation, however, requires the translation "in" the Spirit. In favor of this reading is the fact that the six other usages of "baptism in the Holy Spirit" seem to have the Spirit as the element.[17] These passages, however, are reporting only two sayings in a set phrase (always "Holy Spirit," not simply "Spirit"), and none is in Paul. If instead of looking at "baptism in" we look at "in the Spirit," we find that Paul's usage is normally instrumental.[18] If that meaning continues in this verse, then the interpretation of spiritual baptism falls. Paul says that by means of the one Spirit a person is introduced into the one body. The whole message about being members of one body requires that the preposition εἰς have its full force of "into" and not the weakened sense of "toward" or "with reference to."

The last phrase is also problematic. Although it has been referred to the eucharist or to confirmation, it probably continues the reference to baptism. The verb ποτίζω in the passive can mean "be given a drink" or "to be watered or irrigated." The latter is more common and is probably to be preferred here.[19] This would be a metaphorical description of receiving the Spirit as land receives water. The use of a metaphor here does not argue that "baptize" is a metaphor.[20] Contrary to the inter-

---

16. For the meaning "submerged in the Spirit," see James D. G. Dunn, *Baptism in the Holy Spirit* (Philadelphia: Westminster, 1970), pp. 127-131, and my detailed reply in the discussion of 1 Cor. 12:13 in *The Church of Christ: A Biblical Ecclesiology for Today* (Grand Rapids: Eerdmans, 1996), pp. 191-195 (esp. n. 45).

17. Matt. 3:11; Mark 1:8; Luke 3:16; John 1:33; Acts 1:5; 11:16.

18. In 1 Corinthians alone note 6:11; and in this chapter 12:3 (twice) and 9 (twice); possibly 14:16 (not all manuscripts have ἐν).

19. Schnackenburg, *Baptism in the Thought of St. Paul*, pp. 84-86, who paraphrases, "All have been drenched over and over (through the overflowing) of the one Spirit" (p. 85).

20. To the contrary, Dunn, *Baptism in the Holy Spirit*, 130-131, finds this phrase a confirmation that the whole verse is speaking of spiritual realities and relationships in metaphorical language; so too does Gordon D. Fee, *The First Epistle to the Corinthians*, New International Commentary on the New

pretation of this as another metaphor for a spiritual baptism, the image is suggested by water baptism. The usage would be parallel to Galatians 3:27, where literal baptism is followed by a metaphor descriptive of its effect. It is stretching the metaphor beyond what it says to see in the irrigation or watering a reflection of pouring as the action in baptism.[21] And, if the meaning is "made to drink" or "given a drink," that interpretation is not possible. The thought is that, not only is the Spirit active in baptism as the means of placing one in the body of Christ, but also the convert, depending on the meaning adopted, now either received (aorist, point action concurrent with the baptism) the Spirit into himself or herself[22] or is saturated by the influence of the Spirit. The verse thus expresses two aspects of the working of the Spirit in baptism.

The most problematic baptismal text in 1 Corinthians is 15:29 — "Otherwise, what will those people do who are being baptized [οἱ βαπτιζόμενοι] on behalf of the dead? If the dead are not raised at all, why are people baptized [βαπτίζονται] on their behalf?" The statements occur as part of Paul's argument on behalf of a bodily resurrection. A common interpretation is that some in Corinth, in their exaggerated confidence in the power of baptism, were practicing a vicarious baptism for the benefit of those who had died without receiving baptism.[23] It is suggested that Paul did not pause to correct the idea because his concern was with an *ad hominem* argument on behalf of the resurrection. However, presumably a vicarious baptism could have some benefit for a person's soul in the afterlife other than assuring a bodily resurrection,[24] but Paul's adducing the argument would show how intimately he connected baptism with resurrection. Alternative interpretations focus on possible meanings of the preposition "on behalf of." If it does not mean here "instead of" or "for the

---

Testament (Grand Rapids: Eerdmans, 1987), pp. 603-606, who affirms the two clauses are Semitic parallelism, but the parallelism he sets forth in English does not correspond to the Greek. (Fee correctly observes that this is not a second experience of the Holy Spirit — the whole argument is based on "their common reception of the Spirit.") Beasley-Murray, *Baptism in the New Testament*, pp. 169-170, accepts the figurative use of the latter clause, which he renders, "saturated in his outpouring" (pp. 170, 276) and the literal water baptism of the former.

21. G. J. Cuming, "ΕΠΟΤΙΣΘΗΜΕΝ (I Corinthians 12.13)," *New Testament Studies* 27 (1980-1981): 283-285. He translates "watered," or "we all had one Holy Spirit poured over us," as based on the liturgical action of pouring water over the candidate. The assumption that something in the ceremony was the basis of the imagery is unnecessary: the meaning ascribed to the event was sufficient to account for the imagery. The usual Greek word for the pouring out of the Holy Spirit is ἐκχέω, and nothing in the texts using this verb suggests that the word reflects the manner of contact with the water (see discussion of Acts 2:17-18, 33 in chap. 10 and Titus 3:5-6 below).

22. Cf. John 7:38-39 for the Spirit as rivers of living water in the believer.

23. Michael F. Hull, *Baptism on Account of the Dead (1 Cor. 15:29)* (Atlanta: Society of Biblical Literature, 2005), effectively removes any basis for a reference to a vicarious or anomalous baptism in the text. His own interpretation is "baptized on account of (resurrection) of the dead." This has more to commend it than his structuring the chapter so that the statement is part of its central section.

24. A new approach suggesting the rite was part of funerary rituals is taken by Richard E. DeMaris, "Corinthian Religion and Baptism for the Dead (1 Corinthians 15:29): Insights from Archaeology and Anthropology," *Journal of Biblical Literature* 114 (1995): 661-682.

benefit of," might it mean "because of," "out of regard for," or "with a view to" so that one is baptized to fulfill the request of someone now dead? Or, so as to be reunited with the dead in the resurrection?[25] Or, was the baptism for the sake of their own dead bodies? This is only a sampling of the interpretations that have been put forward. No explanation is fully satisfactory, but the verse says more about some of the Corinthians' thoughts on baptism and nothing certain about Paul's understanding beyond what is known from other texts.

Some see a baptismal allusion in 2 Corinthians 1:21-22, "God has anointed us and sealed us and given us the guarantee of the Spirit in our hearts." The verse does use language later associated with baptism, but since here God does the anointing, sealing, and making the down payment, it is better to understand these images as three figures of speech describing the significance of God's gift of the Spirit to Christians. This occurred at baptism, but the concern of Paul in this passage was not with baptism itself. The seal in early Christianity, as in this passage and in Ephesians below, is predominantly associated with the Holy Spirit. As will be observed in later chapters, the terminology of seal was then applied to baptism (apparently because the Holy Spirit was given in baptism) and then to the postbaptismal anointing (when the Holy Spirit was associated with the anointing).

Romans

The key, indeed distinctive, baptismal passage in Paul is Romans 6:1-11. The statements about baptism are to be read in the light of the preceding discussion of faith (3:21–5:21). The question, "Do you not know?" implies a common teaching in regard to baptism that Paul makes the basis of his further exposition. The connection of baptism with the death of Christ for human sins was part of the early Christian message, but Paul proceeds to deepen this association and carry it further by his distinctive thought of dying and rising with Christ.[26] Paul is responding to the charge (ei-

---

25. Maria Raeder, "Vikariatstaufe in 1 Cor. 15:29?" *Zeitschrift für die neutestamentliche Wissenschaft* 46 (1955): 258-260.

26. Schnackenburg, *Baptism in the Thought of St. Paul*, pp. 32-37. Paul's language is only a short move from Matthew 12:40. Kuss, "Zum paulinischen und nachpaulinischen Tauflehre," pp. 403-407 — Rom. 6:1-11, "the central passage" in Paul's doctrine of baptism. Günter Wagner, *Pauline Baptism and the Pagan Mysteries: The Problem of the Pauline Doctrine of Baptism in Romans VI.1-11 in the Light of Its Religio-Historical 'Parallels'* (Edinburgh: T&T Clark, 1967), and Wedderburn, *Baptism and Resurrection*, refute the idea that the Mysteries influenced Christians to think they shared in Christ's resurrection in baptism; for the latter Paul in Romans 6 was not correcting such a misunderstanding by putting Christians' resurrection in the future; Colossians and Ephesians developed Paul's thought in Romans 6 and were not a reversion to a pre-Pauline baptismal theology. More open to broader parallels is Hans Dieter Betz, "Transferring a Ritual: Paul's Interpretation of Baptism in Romans 6," in Troels Engberg-Pedersen, ed., *Paul in His Hellenistic Context* (Minneapolis: Fortress, 1994), pp. 84-118 (particularly 107-116 on Paul's interpretation of baptism as initiation). Primarily concerned with Pauline theology are Robert C. Tannehill, *Dying and Rising with Christ: A Study in Pauline Theology*

ther a real objection or one imagined so that Paul can make a clarification) that his gospel of grace leads to antinomianism. He answers by drawing out the moral implications of becoming a Christian. In doing so he offers a profound association of baptism with the death and resurrection of Christ. The baptismal participation in the death and resurrection of Christ results in a new life of righteousness. The verses on baptism are the following:

> Do you not know that all of us who have been baptized into Christ Jesus [ἐβαπτίσθημεν εἰς Χριστὸν Ἰησοῦν] were baptized [ἐβαπτίσθημεν] into his death? Therefore we have been buried with him in baptism [βαπτίσματος] into death, so that, just as Christ was raised from the dead by the glory of the Father, so we too might walk in newness of life. (Rom. 6:3-4)

Once more Paul uses the phrase "baptized into Christ," which may mean "to Christ" or "with reference to (with regard to) Christ." But here he further uses the same phrase "baptized into" followed by "his [Christ's] death." It seems to me that "baptism into the name" (being a formula) is not the same as baptism "into the death" and "into the one body" (1 Cor. 12:13), and thus possibly not the same as "into Christ." The phrase may not have to have the same force in each usage, but in close parallel here the natural conclusion is to construe them the same way. To understand baptism as "to" or "with regard to" his death does not do justice to the further statements.[27] That we "were buried with him through baptism" implies that our baptism was more than "with reference to his death" but was "into his death." Likewise verse 5, "we have been united with him in a death like his," says we have "become (his) kindred" or "(possessing) a like nature" by "the likeness [or form] of his death."[28] These strong statements suggest that baptism is more than something done with reference to his death but is an actual participation in it. Even if the meaning is "baptized in order to be united with Christ," that would include his death.

Dying with Christ meant a death to sin (6:2). The whole discussion in Romans 6 presupposes a connection of baptism with forgiveness of sins. Moreover, Paul especially wants to say that there is a new life. The burial with Christ was so that, even as Christ was raised, "we might walk in newness of life" (6:4). Paul does not expressly say that in baptism one is raised as Christ was raised; our resurrection is

---

(Berlin: A. Töpelmann, 1967); Robert Schlarb, *Wir sind mit Christus begraben* (Tübingen: J. C. B. Mohr, 1990); and Sorin Sabou, *Between Horror and Hope: Paul's Metaphorical Language of Death in Romans 6:1-11* (Carlisle: Paternoster, 2005).

27. Beasley-Murray, *Baptism in the New Testament*, pp. 129-130, does not draw back from his understanding of εἰς in this passage (also in Gal. 3:27), so he renders "with reference to his death." Similar reserve about "baptism into his death" is expressed by Schnackenburg, *Baptism in the Thought of St. Paul*, pp. 25-26.

28. Schnackenburg, *Baptism in the Thought of St. Paul*, pp. 44-53, discusses the thought, concluding that σύμφυτος does not mean "planted with" but "to grow together," "natural, inborn," and ὁμοίωμα means "copy" or "form" (which he favors) in a concrete sense: "united with the 'form' of Christ's death" (p. 53). More on this below.

stated to be future in 6:5.[29] However, so is "the living with him" (6:8), which is also to be in the present (6:11). The walking "in newness of life" implies a resurrection (note the words about Christ's death to sin and living to God — 6:9-10 — which is the pattern for believers). Likewise, the death and resurrection of Christ belonged together in the early Christian proclamation, so a resurrection for the baptized is implicit here. The association, even identification, of the believer with Christ is shown by the quite striking number of words compounded with the preposition "with" (σύν) — "buried with" (6:4), "united with" (6:5), "crucified with" (6:6), "died with and shall live with" (6:8). The believer is described as actually present with and involved with the unique experiences of Christ. The future resurrection requires a present resurrection in manner of life. The conclusion in verse 11, "So you also must consider yourselves dead to sin," reflects the association of baptism with forgiveness of sins. Even so, there is no participation in the death, burial, and resurrection of Christ without baptism.

The passage may have implications for the action of Christian baptism. The theology stated here can be advocated without a physical likeness in the action of baptism, and many believers have divorced the theology from their practice in the administration of baptism.[30] However, the description of baptism in terms of death, burial, and subsequent walking (after a rising) in a new life is certainly consistent with an immersion, and the likeness of the action to a burial may even have suggested the analogy. Even if one should not move from Pauline theology to the ritual of baptism, one might wonder if Paul moved from the ritual practice to his theology. Hence, Paul's use of the word "likeness" (or "form," ὁμοιώματι) in verse 5 may be understood accordingly.[31] The association of the word "baptize" in classical usage with a person drowning ("to cause to perish") or a vessel sinking (chap. 3) may also be in the background of Paul's association of baptism with death, but this interpretation may presume too much. One might rather look to the example of symbolic actions performed by the prophets, which (as we have seen) may have influenced John the Baptist's use of baptism. However, with John the action symbolized cleansing; with Paul the action represented the death and resurrection of Christ now experienced by the believer. Later interpreters in the church, as we shall see, made the connection between baptism as an immersion and a literal burial and resurrection. "[T]he fit-

---

29. His reservation about speaking of a baptismal resurrection may be due to wrong conclusions some at Corinth drew from this idea (1 Cor. 4:8; 15:12; cf. 2 Tim. 2:18); hence he does not speak of resurrected "with" Christ but of being raised "as" Christ was — Delling, *Die Taufe*, p. 130.

30. For example, Georg Kretschmar, *Die Geschichte des Taufgottesdienstes in der alter Kirche* in *Leiturgia*, Vol. 5, 31-35 (1964-1966), p. 17, says Paul was probably not thinking of immersion, and only in the fourth century did the church under the influence of mystery cults understand Paul in this way. (The motive assigned for this interpretation seems quite unlikely at that date.)

31. Betz, "Transferring a Ritual," pp. 115-116, although distinguishing a description of baptism from an explanation of its meaning, translates, "we have been united with the likeness of his death" and identifies the likeness as baptism. I find this to be indicative that the "similitude" has to do with the action of baptismal immersion so that Paul's words contain both a description and the meaning.

ness of baptism to be a means of response to the offer of the gospel is grounded in its fitness to be an embodiment of the gospel."[32]

The association of baptism with the death of Christ that brought forgiveness of sins is likely to have been an idea already current in the church that Paul deepened. In that case his special contribution in this passage was to draw out the moral implications of baptism into the death of Christ.

A similar reference to the resurrection as in 6:4 occurs in reference to the confession of faith in Romans 10:9-10. That the context of this confession was baptism is indicated by the language of "Lord Jesus" and "salvation," an interpretation strengthened by the "no distinction of Jew and Gentile" of verse 12, akin to the baptismal language noted above in Galatians 3:28 and 1 Corinthians 12:13. Other passages indicate a baptismal confession of faith (Heb. 10:22-23; possibly Rom. 13:11, a point in time when "we first came to faith"; 1 John 4:15; Acts 8:37). The standard designation of Christians later as "believers" is scarcely understandable without an express confession.[33]

Colossians

The Epistle to the Colossians opposed teaching that made Christ only one of the spiritual powers and supplemented faith in him with various rituals and a wisdom that Paul characterizes as "deceitful philosophy" (2:8). To counter this teaching Paul emphasized that the fullness of deity lived bodily in Jesus, all spiritual powers are subject to him, and in him Christians have all the fullness (2:9-10). The passage of concern to us is bracketed by the affirmation of Christ as "head of every ruler and authority" (2:10) and the declaration of his triumph over the "rulers and authorities" at the cross (2:15).[34]

Christ came to occupy his position of headship through his death and resurrection. By sharing in that experience of Christ, his followers enjoy the results of his triumph over the spiritual powers (2:15).

---

32. Beasley-Murray, *Baptism in the New Testament*, pp. 99-100.

33. Alois Stenzel, S.J., *Die Taufe: Eine Genetische Erklärung der Taufliturgie* (Innsbruck: Felizian Rauch, 1958), p. 30.

34. Otto Böcher, *Dämonenfurcht und Dämonenabwehr: Ein Beitrag zur Vorgeschichte der christlichen Taufe* (Stuttgart: W. Kohlhammer, 1970), collected the evidence for demonology in the Greek, Roman, and Jewish worlds and then in *Christus Exorcista: Dämonismus und Taufe im Neuen Testament* (ibid., 1972) summarized that material and examined the demonology of the New Testament. In spite of the title, there is little specifically on baptism, and Georg Kretschmar, "Recent Research on Christian Initiation," *Studia Liturgica* 12 (1977): 87-106 (pp. 98-99) is correct that he did not connect the general demonistic worldview with baptismal exorcism. Of the passages Böcher treated, Col. 2:11-14 and 1 Pet. 3:21-22 (see my chap. 11) are the ones for which the best case can be made for exorcistic baptism as participation in the victory of Christ over demons (pp. 170-175). More can be said for what he only hints at, that in the postapostolic development the rich expansion of baptismal rites was accompanied by an understanding of baptism as a highly exorcistic lustration (p. 175).

In Christ you were circumcised with a circumcision not made with hands in the stripping off of the body of flesh in the circumcision of Christ, when you were buried with him in baptism [βαπτισμῷ], in which you were also raised with him through faith in the working of God, who raised him from the dead. And when you were dead in your trespasses and uncircumcision of your flesh, God made you alive with him, having forgiven us all our trespasses. (Col. 2:11-13)

Between the "in whom (Christ)" of verse 11 and the "in which (or in whom)" of verse 12 there are three phrases with the preposition "in" that are not only formally parallel but also factually identical: stripping off the flesh, circumcision of Christ, and baptism.[35] The "circumcision of Christ" is not perfectly clear but seems to be an image for his death on the cross. Instead of cutting off a small part of the flesh as in literal circumcision, his death is viewed as stripping off all the flesh. The description of Christ's death as a circumcision may have been aided by Jewish ideas of death and a new life in connection with a proselyte's circumcision, if these rabbinic ideas were around as early as Paul. When one enters into Christ's death, that person receives a spiritual circumcision, a circumcision that is not done by a human hand. The baptism is not itself the spiritual circumcision, for baptism is performed by human hands. Rather, the circumcision is received in baptism. This passage has been the basis of the view that baptism is Christian circumcision; but if that was the equivalence intended here, there would have been a ready answer to Judaizers who insisted that Gentile converts be circumcised, for the reply was at hand that Gentiles already had the equivalent and so had no need of circumcision. Although not stated here, elsewhere the spiritual circumcision is the work of the Holy Spirit (Rom. 2:28-29; cf. Phil. 3:3).[36] It is likely that circumcision was one of the practices that the errorists in Colossae were promoting along with other features of the Jewish law (2:16). Christ's death has made it unnecessary for Gentiles (2:17). When dead in uncircumcision, they were made alive by God (through his Spirit). The forgiveness of transgressions made this possibile.

Baptism brings a person into this circumcision of Christ on the cross. The believer shares Christ's circumcision (death), burial, and resurrection. I have translated above, "baptism in which you were raised," construing the pronoun with the immediately antecedent noun. But the parallelism of the whole passage would be impressive if the pronoun is masculine, "in whom," so that we have circumcision in him, burial with him, and being raised in him.[37] This passage says explicitly what Romans 6:3-4 only implied, that in baptism one not only is buried with Christ but is also raised with him.

---

35. Delling, *Die Taufe*, p. 122.

36. As circumcision was the sign of the covenant for Jews (Rom. 4:11), the Holy Spirit was the sign or seal for Christians (2 Cor. 1:21; Eph. 1:13; 4:30). Schnackenburg, *Baptism in the Thought of St. Paul*, pp. 70-71, is among those who see in the words here a comparison of baptism to circumcision; he coins the expression "Christ-circumcision" (p. 111) for this aspect of baptism.

37. Schnackenburg, *Baptism in the Thought of St. Paul*, pp. 67-73 (67-68 on the structure of the passage).

Baptism is a confession of faith in the resurrection of Jesus by God. It is done in faith in the activity of God, who raised him from the dead. God is at work throughout the passage: the passive voices — were circumcised, were buried, were raised — are the "divine passives" for what God did. Not only did he raise Christ, but he also made the one baptized alive and forgave his/her sins. The "with Christ" emphasis is obvious: "buried with him," "raised with him" (2:12), and "made alive with him" (2:13).

On the relation of faith and baptism in Paul, Kuss concludes with reference to Galatians 3:26-27 and Colossians 2:12 that faith can never be excluded, but Paul gives no indication of a Christianity without baptism. Baptism had an initiatory character, for individual salvation introduces one to the body of Christ, but Paul warned against a magical view of baptism (1 Cor. 10:1-6).[38]

According to the preferred reading, the passage does not use for baptism the usual Christian word βάπτισμα, but the word used more generally for other baptisms or washings, βαπτισμός. Many manuscripts, including the later Byzantine texts, give the more familiar Christian word. All transcriptional probability favors that the more common Christian term was substituted for the other, since Christian baptism is obviously under consideration. Why would Paul use the more general word? My conjecture would be that he borrows the term from the language of the opponents, who were treating baptism as they did other ritual ordinances.[39] Hence, Paul fills it with its Christian content of association with the death and resurrection of Christ as the unique means of coming to fullness in Christ, having the bond of indebtedness erased, and sharing in his triumph over the spiritual forces.

The baptismal language continues in Colossians 2:20–3:17. "You died with Christ" (2:20; 3:3); "You have been raised with Christ" (3:1); therefore, "put to death what is earthly" (3:5); "remove" (3:8) and "strip off" (3:9) the old way of life; "put on as clothes" (3:10, 12) the new life.

In summary, Colossians makes explicit the connection of baptism with faith, specifically faith in the resurrection of Christ. Baptism accomplishes a forgiveness of sins (cf. 2:13-14 with 3:13) and so delivers one from the powers of this world into the kingdom of Christ (2:15; cf. 1:13-14). It places one in the church, the body derived from Christ, of which he is head by reason of his resurrection (1:18; 3:15). Colossians' use of burial and resurrection for baptism likely indicates immersion. One's life is now "hidden with Christ in God" (3:3), so there is a kind of life that is consistent with that reality as one waits for the coming glory (3:4).

---

38. Kuss, "Zum paulinischen und nachpaulinischen Tauflehre," pp. 415-417.

39. This would lend some support to the proposal by Harold W. Attridge, "On Becoming an Angel: Rival Baptismal Theologies at Colossae," in Lukas Bormann, Kelly Del Tredici, and Angela Standhartinger, eds., *Religious Propaganda and Missionary Competition in the New Testament World: Essays Honoring Dieter Georgi* (Leiden: Brill, 1994), pp. 481-498, that the opponents had an initiation ritual involving baptism that transformed one into an angelic state and brought revelatory experiences leading to an ascetical life, features to be found together later in the Nag Hammadi tractate *Zostrianos* (see chap. 17).

Ephesians

Without mentioning baptism, Ephesians 2:4-6 may have baptism in mind, in view of the verbal parallels with Colossians 2:12-13; 3:1.[40] Ephesians then declares the unity of Jew and Gentile because Christ made peace for them in one body (2:11-22). Chapter 4 then gives the exhortation to "maintain the unity of the Spirit in the bond of peace" (4:3). There follows a listing of the items that give the basis for this unity. Baptism appears among the seven foundation unities of Christianity: "There is one body and one Spirit, even as you were called in one hope of your calling, one Lord, one faith, one baptism [βάπτισμα], one God and Father of all, who is over all, and through all, and in all" (4:4-6). The list seems to be built up from three sets of three. "One Lord, one faith, and one baptism" may be the original grouping. There is a natural progression from the one Lord to the faith that is related to him (I take faith here to be objective, "the faith," rather than the subjective personal believing) to the baptism where faith in his lordship is confessed and expressed. "One body and one Spirit" is a natural pairing (1 Cor. 12:12-13), to which is added the calling to Jesus as Lord that produces the one hope (cf. 2 Thess. 2:14; 1 Thess. 2:12) in order to connect with the next triad. The statement is then climaxed with the one God, who is given a triple description — over, through, and in all. The inclusion of baptism in such an impressive list of the foundational verities of Christianity and basic principles of Christian unity testifies to its importance. The statement has been widely used to mean "no rebaptism," but such was not in the author's view. Having the same faith and the same baptism is a basis of unity. Baptism is related to unity elsewhere in Paul (Gal. 3:27-28; 1 Cor. 12:12-13).

There is very likely a reference to baptism in 5:26. Christ gave himself up for the church "in order that he might sanctify her, purifying her by the washing [τῷ λουτρῷ, bath] of water with the word [ἐν ῥήματι]." The context compares the relations of husbands and wives with the relations of Christ and the church. In view of this marriage context elements of a wedding ceremony that could be related to Christian practice are likely being drawn on. The bride took a bath before the wedding, hence the reference to a washing expressly said to be in water, which would parallel the baptism of Christ's "bride," the church, taking place in the conversion of each of its members. There was also a wedding contract, an exchange of vows, hence the reference to a "word." Baptism was not a ritual without words, but what words are meant is the subject of varying interpretations. The preposition ἐν can mean "by" or "together with," which seems the natural meaning here. The "word" may refer to the proclamation of the gospel, which is the basis of baptism.[41] It may refer to the formula pronounced by the administrator, identifying the nature of the bap-

---

40. Nils Dahl, "The Concept of Baptism in Ephesians," *Studies in Ephesians* (Tübingen: Mohr Siebeck, 2000), pp. 413-439, discusses, in addition to the explicit baptismal passages in 4:5 and 5:26, the presence of baptismal motifs in 1:3ff; 4:17-24; 2:11-22.

41. In general this interpretation finds no support in early Christian literature, but see Cyril of Jerusalem, *Cathechetical Lectures* 3.5, but only an implied reference to proclamation.

tism.⁴² It may refer to the candidate's confession of faith at baptism.⁴³ Or, in terms of the wedding context, it may be the Lord's promise as corresponding to the bridegroom's betrothal vows.⁴⁴ I think the wedding context favors either of the latter two interpretations, but since we have no confirmatory evidence for anything corresponding to the Lord's word of promise in the baptismal ritual, I favor the confession by the person being baptized (for which there is ample evidence) as the "word" accompanying the washing.⁴⁵

The formal opening passage of praise in Ephesians refers to conversion but does not mention baptism: "In him [Christ] you also, when you had heard the word of truth, the gospel of your salvation, and had believed in him, were marked with the seal of the promised Holy Spirit" (1:13). We might deduce from other passages that baptism was the time of the sealing with the Holy Spirit (cf. 4:30 for the imagery of a seal, which marked ownership), but Ephesians does not expressly say this.

Titus

Titus 3:5 offers formal similarities to John 3:5. The whole passage has been taken as a hymn, identified in 3:8 as a "faithful saying."

> When the goodness and loving kindness of God our Savior appeared,
> not by works of righteousness that we ourselves did
> but according to his mercy he saved us
> through the washing of regeneration [λουτροῦ παλιγγενεσίας] and
>   renewal [ἀνακαινώσεως] of the Holy Spirit,

---

42. John Chrysostom took it to refer to the triune divine name — *Homilies on Ephesians* 30 on 5:26. As a variation on this view Charles A. Gieschen, "The Divine Name in Ante-Nicene Christology," *Vigiliae Christianae* 57 (2003): 131, understands the "word" (singular) not as the words of the baptismal formula but the Divine Name invoked by the formula.

43. In commenting on John 15:3, Augustine in *Tractates* [or *Expositions*] *on John* 80.3 asks, Why not say cleansed by reason of baptism? "Take away the word, and what is the water except water? The word is added to the elemental substance, and it becomes a sacrament, also itself a visible word." He then identifies the word with the confession of Rom. 10:8-10 and cites Eph. 5:26. Augustine's passage, however, also gives support to the other interpretations, the words of the administrator or the Lord's word of promise: "The word of faith has so much power in the Church of God that, through the very one who believes, offers, blesses, immerses, it cleanses even the tiny infant, not yet having the capacity with its heart to believe to justice and with its mouth to make profession of faith to salvation. All this is done through the word of which the Lord says [John 15:3]." Translation by John W. Rettig, *The Tractates on Gospel of John: Tractates 55-111*, Fathers of the Church 90 (Washington: Catholic University of America, 1994), p. 117. A similar comment to the first statement in *Tractates on John* 15.4 on John 4, after quoting Ephesians 5:25-27, says that the baptism of Christ is a bath of water in the word. "Take away the water, there is no baptism. Take away the word, there is no baptism." (Ibid., Vol. 79 [1988], p. 80.)

44. Kretschmar, *Die Geschichte des Taufgottesdienstes*, p. 31, suggesting that, since Christ sanctifies, the word would be his word.

45. As does Crehan, *Early Christian Baptism and the Creed*, pp. 18-19.

whom he poured out [ἐξέχεεν] on us richly through Jesus Christ our Savior,
in order we might be justified by his grace
and become in hope heirs of eternal life.

(Titus 3:4-7)

The key phrase in Titus 3:5 might be translated as "the washing of a new beginning and the being made new by the Holy Spirit." The passage offers the rich theological context of baptism: salvation from God by grace (2:11) through Jesus Christ that justifies and gives hope of eternal life. Not only is the divine goodness, kindness, and mercy underscored, but the human response of faith is not neglected, for those who have experienced these favors are described in 3:8 as "those who have come to believe in God." The same verse says, as we have found in other passages, that the baptized are expected to "devote themselves to good works."

The word λουτρόν was first a bath or a place of bathing and then the water used for bathing or washing. Here and in Ephesians 5:26 above the word refers to the act rather than the place of washing. The washing is not figurative (such a usage would be unprecedented) for the work of the Holy Spirit; that interpretation might have been avoided if the translation "bath" were more common. The theological ideas of the passage are elsewhere associated with baptism, which is indicated here by the "washing." Baptism is not a human work, but is a work of God.

The word for "regeneration" is not the same as the word used in 1 Peter 1:3 and 23 (chap. 11). "Regeneration" [παλιγγενεσία] was used by Stoics for the starting over of the world after each periodic conflagration in their cycles of existence.[46] The word was used by Christians in relation to eschatological new beginnings that have their initiation through the work of Christ (cf. Matt. 19:28, the renewal of the world). The two phrases, "bath of regeneration" and "renewing of the Holy Spirit," are both dependent on the verb "saved." They have commonly been taken as parallel,[47] that is, expressing two means of salvation that worked simultaneously, as in John 3:5. (A separate outpouring of the Holy Spirit, therefore, is not in view.) Recently another interpretation has gained favor, according to which both the regeneration and renewal (admittedly virtually synonymous expressions) are construed with the "bath" and both are jointly effected by the Holy Spirit. So we could paraphrase, "the bath of regeneration and renewal that is effected by the Holy Spirit." Some manuscripts of the "Western" text seem to have taken this interpretation, for they insert the preposition "through" again before "Holy Spirit." This construction is especially favored by those who want to take the "washing" as equivalent to the work of the Holy Spirit, so they would render the thought as "the Holy Spirit effects a spiritual washing of regeneration and renewal." But this construction in no way requires the "washing" to

---

46. See Ysebaert, *Greek Baptismal Terminology*, pp. 90-107, on the non-Christian usage of the word; Delling, *Die Taufe*, pp. 96-100, for the meaning "new creation" or "new beginning."

47. Theodoret, *Commentary on Titus* 3:5, "The kind Master through his only Son set us free from our former evils through saving baptism, granting us forgiveness of sins, creating us anew and renewing us, counting us worthy of the gift of the Spirit, and showing us the way of righteousness."

be in anything other than with water.[48] The washing is the occasion of the regeneration and renewal by the Spirit, so we could paraphrase, "The Holy Spirit effected regeneration and renewal in the bath." Thus whether we understand two parallel but separate clauses or the whole statement combined in one clause does not greatly affect the meaning.

Those who want to eliminate water from the passage are right in one respect: the passage is a strong affirmation of the work of the Holy Spirit. The Spirit effects renewal, or regeneration and renewal. God pours the Spirit out richly in Christ on the convert. Thus the passage combines the work of God, Christ, and the Holy Spirit. Where some interpreters go wrong is in failing to see that this may be connected with and concentrated in baptism. The author of Titus expressly excludes understanding baptism as "works righteousness." God, Christ, and the Holy Spirit may work through human and material means to bring about the rich blessings described in these verses.

Titus 1:6 requires that the children of an elder/bishop be believers (cf. 1 Tim. 3:4). The requirement was superfluous if infant baptism was routine, for baptized children were by definition "believers," and so would say nothing about the man's leadership of his family.

Summary

What Luke expresses as forgiveness of sins and John and 1 Peter express as new birth, in Paul is the end of the old and the beginning of the new life. Contrary to the modern evangelical understanding that faith effects this new life and baptism is a subsequent human work, for Paul it is God who does everything and a person nothing in baptism and the new life that God gives to faith begins at baptism. The Christian's existence as a Christian does not occur without baptism.[49]

Paul's characteristic teaching relative to baptism is to connect it with the death and resurrection of Christ and draw out its moral consequences. The association of baptism with the death of Christ ties it to the means of forgiveness of sins, and the association with resurrection ties it to the new life of the Spirit consequent to baptism. Paul sets baptism in the context not only of the atoning death of Christ but also of the response of faith. Baptism was an immersion in water. Efforts to make "baptize" metaphorical in some passages are inconsistent with those texts where Paul certainly had water baptism in mind and with the prevailing usage of the word among Christians. According to Paul, the Holy Spirit is both active in baptism and an abiding presence in the life of the baptized believer. Baptism is the occasion of divine ac-

---

48. The question of interpretation may be stated as the regeneration that effects a "washing" or a washing that effects regeneration. If the former is thought to remove water from the statement, it is an unlikely interpretation; see Beasley-Murray, *Baptism in the New Testament*, pp. 209-216.

49. I have given my wording to thoughts expressed by Delling, *Die Taufe*, pp. 148-149.

tivity in bringing the benefits of the death of Christ to the believer and in introducing one into the community of salvation.

Baptism as a bath of cleansing, into the name of Jesus, and in unity with the work of the Spirit were ideas Paul shared with the early church in Jerusalem according to Acts (chap. 10). His distinctive features included relating baptism to the circumcision of Christ (his death), putting on Christ, and being buried with Christ. Baptism was a fundamental means of salvation, but always as related to the cross of Jesus and as an act of faith. Human cooperation (in faith) is presupposed, but the decisive action for Paul comes from God alone. Baptism into Christ was also baptism into the body of Christ, the church. Hence, it carried consequences for one's manner of life.[50]

---

50. In this paragraph I have summarized Schnackenburg, *Baptism in the Thought of St. Paul*, pp. 106-11, 121-127 (on faith and baptism belonging together); cf. his excellent recapitulation on Paul's teaching, pp. 204-207. He delineates the "sacramental" character of baptism on pp. 127-138. I have avoided the word "sacrament" and would understand Paul (and the New Testament) as saying that God acts through the symbol (in this case the water of baptism), in contrast to a separation of the symbol from the effect (as many Protestants make) and to an emphasis on the symbol effecting the blessing (as in some Roman Catholic theology). As to his question of the relation of the Spirit to baptism — is the Spirit first imparted and then followed by the salvation event in baptism, or is the baptized person drawn into the process of salvation and because of it receiving the Spirit, or is the receiving of the Spirit a parallel event to dying with Christ? (p. 164) — I would say the New Testament texts support, in different respects, all three: the Spirit through the word of God leads one to conversion, works in baptism in imparting the new life, and is received as an indwelling gift.

10. The Acts of the Apostles

Because it includes so many accounts of conversion, the book of Acts has the largest number of occurrences of "baptize" and "baptism" of any New Testament writing. My approach will be to examine each passage that speaks of baptism and then take an overview of some problems and offer some conclusions from the accounts of baptism. Luke worked with earlier material that he stamped with his own style. The extent of what was traditional and what was Luke's contribution is still a matter of discussion.[1] As best I can, I shall interpret Luke's accounts of baptism on his own terms.

Acts 1–2

After the prologue, Acts begins with the resurrected Jesus commanding the apostles to remain in Jerusalem to await the promise of the Father, "For John baptized with water [ὕδατι], but you will be baptized [βαπτισθήσεσθε] with [ἐν] the Holy Spirit not many days from now" (1:4-5). Thus Jesus picks up the words of John the Baptist recorded in Luke 3:16 but without the addition of "with fire." Acts 1:5 (and 11:15-16),

---

1. A comprehensive and detailed treatment is given by Friedrich Avemarie, *Die Tauferzählungen der Apostelgeschichte: Theologie und Geschichte* (Tübingen: Mohr Siebeck, 2002), whose main concerns are tradition and historicity, which are not mine. My observation would be that Luke was a singularly inept author or editor if he created whole cloth or incorporated only independent traditions of such seemingly incongruous narratives. Hence, I seek interpretations that give some consistency to the whole. Jean Jacques von Allmen, "Notizen zu den Taufberichten in der Apostelgeschichte," in Hansjörg Auf Der Maur and Bruno Kleinheyer, eds., *Zeichen des Glaubens: Studien zu Taufe und Firmung: Balthasar Fischer zum 60. Geburtstag* (Freiburg: Herder, 1972), pp. 41-60, has a pastoral emphasis. Gerhard Delling, *Die Taufe im Neuen Testament* (Berlin: Evangelische Verlagsanstalt, 1963), pp. 58-74, emphasizes that baptism is inseparable from salvation in Christ (p. 63) and that the normal pattern was for the Spirit to be given with baptism (p. 68).

like Luke 3:16, is not a contrast of a Christian baptism in water and a Christian baptism in the Spirit; rather, the contrast is with John's water baptism without the Spirit. In Jesus' further statement, "You will receive power when the Holy Spirit has come upon you, and you will be my witnesses" (Acts 1:8), there is a further connection with Jesus' commission in Luke 24:45-49 with the repetition of the idea of remaining in Jerusalem, of the words of promise and power for the coming of the Holy Spirit, and of their task as witnesses. While waiting in Jerusalem, the apostles and "brothers" (which included women — 1:14), totalling about 120, selected a successor to Judas in order to fill out the number of the Twelve, one of whose qualifications was that the person have been a follower of Jesus since "the baptism of John" (βαπτίσματος Ἰωάννου).

Luke clearly understood the promise of baptism (in, with, or by) the Holy Spirit as accomplished in the events of Acts 2:1-4.[2] The sound of a blast of wind filled the house (2:2), tongues as of fire rested on each (2:3), and all were filled with the Holy Spirit and spoke in other tongues (languages) (2:4). All the statements are descriptions of the effects of the coming of the Holy Spirit. Peter explained what had happened as a fulfillment of the prophecy of Joel 2:28-32 (Gk. 3:1-5). That prophecy gave the word of God as saying, "I will pour out [ἐκχεῶ] of my Spirit upon all flesh." God poured out the Spirit, but that pouring (a figure for God's action in sending the Spirit) was not itself the baptism of the Holy Spirit but made the baptism possible. The baptism was the result of the coming (the pouring out) of the Holy Spirit, who filled the house (surrounding each), rested upon each, and filled each. How a medium (in this case the Holy Spirit) comes to be in a container (in this case the room) is distinct from what is done to a person in the medium (the baptism).

The closing words of the quotation from Joel, "Everyone who calls on the name of the Lord shall be saved" (2:21), and the further words of Joel 2:32 not quoted, "those whom the Lord calls," are picked up in the account of the results of Peter's sermon. The theme of the sermon was that the resurrection of Jesus made him "Lord and Christ" (2:36).[3] The hearers asked what they must do, and Peter replied, "Repent, and be baptized [βαπτισθήτω], every one of you, in the name of Jesus Christ so that your sins may be forgiven, and you will receive the gift of the Holy Spirit" (2:38).[4] This promise, he assured his hearers, was for them, their children, and for those "far away" whom "the Lord our God shall call" (2:39). He exhorted them, "Save

---

2. The Lukan characteristics and possible pre-Lukan material in Acts 2 are discussed by Friedrich Avemarie, *Die Tauferzählungen,* pp. 177-213, with Acts 2:36-41 as a paradigm of Luke's baptismal theology — pp. 177-178; the call to baptism in 2:37-41 also on pp. 112-118.

3. Joseph Crehan, *Early Christian Baptism and the Creed* (London: Burns, Oates & Washbourne, 1950), p. 9, points to Acts 4:12 as a summary of what was developed in Acts 2:21, 36; salvation is by invoking the Name, which is done by confessing Jesus as Lord and Christ at baptism. He further adds that in Acts Christians were "those who invoke the Name" (9:14, 21; cf. 1 Cor. 1:2; 2 Tim. 2:22) — p. 12.

4. Delling, *Die Taufe,* p. 146, concludes that two lines in the baptismal understanding of the early church, not only in Acts but throughout the New Testament, are that baptism imparts forgiveness and the Holy Spirit. These two basic effects of baptism continued in later sources as well.

yourselves [be saved] from this corrupt generation." Those who received his message "were baptized" (ἐβαπτίσθησαν) — 2:40-41.

Acts 2:38's words about repentance, baptism, and forgiveness of sins connect with the commission in Luke 24:47 and the description of John's baptism in Luke 3:3. In the light of these verses the double command of Acts 2:38 seems straightforward enough that repentance and being baptized both have as their purpose the forgiveness of sins. Some, however, have sought to separate "repent" from "be baptized" and construe the "for forgiveness of sins" only with "repent" ("repentance for forgiveness of sins" occurs in Luke 24:47 according to the preferred text[5]). The grammatical basis for this exegetical move is that "repent" is a second-person plural second aorist imperative and "be baptized" is a third-person singular aorist passive imperative. However, the combination of a second-person plural imperative with a third-person singular imperative is common in the Septuagint and early Christian literature and serves to individualize and make emphatic the need for each individual to do what is commanded.[6] Another effort to break the connection between the forgiveness of sins and the command to be baptized appeals to the second-person plural pronoun "your" with sins, arguing that this does not agree with the third person singular "each one" be baptized.[7] However, the singular "each one" occasionally serves as the antecedent of a plural pronoun (as in Acts 3:26).[8] Yet another approach is to take the preposition "for" (εἰς, "into" or "in order to") as expressing cause ("because of") instead of purpose.[9] The claim for this usage has been thoroughly refuted.[10]

The distinctive nature of the baptism commanded is that it is "in the name [ἐπὶ τῷ ὀνόματι] of Jesus Christ." Since Acts employs three different prepositions to describe baptism in the name of Christ, a separate section below will discuss the variations in this formula. Here ἐπί might be employed to avoid a repetition of εἰς, which occurs in the following phrase, "for [unto] forgiveness of sins." Or, it may refer to the pronouncing of the name of Jesus Christ ("upon the name of Jesus Christ") in ac-

---

5. The majority of manuscripts read, "repentance and forgiveness of sins." "Repentance and forgiveness of sins" occurs in Acts 5:31. In view of Acts 2:38, both Luke 24:47 and Acts 5:31 may be Luke's shorthand including baptism; see comments on Acts 10:43 below.

6. Carroll Osburn, "The Third Person Imperative in Acts 2:38," *Restoration Quarterly* 26 (1983): 81-84, citing Exod. 16:29; Josh. 6:10; 2 Kings 10:19; Zech. 7:10; 1 Macc. 10:63; *Didache* 15.3; Ignatius, *Magnesians* 6.2.

7. Luther B. McIntyre Jr., "Baptism and Forgiveness in Acts 2:38," *Bibliotheca Sacra* 153 (1996): 54-59.

8. Ashby L. Camp, "Reexamining the Rule of Concord in Acts 2:38," *Restoration Quarterly* 39 (1997): 37-42, referring also to John 7:53 and Rev. 20:13, where "each" is used with a third-person plural verb.

9. J. R. Mantey, "The Causal Use of *eis* in the New Testament," *Journal of Biblical Literature* 70 (1951): 45-48, 309-311.

10. Ralph Marcus, "On Causal *eis*," *Journal of Biblical Literature* 70 (1951): 129-130 and 71 (1952): 43-44; M. J. Harris, "Prepositions and Theology in the Greek New Testament," in Colin Brown, ed., *Dictionary of New Testament Theology* (Grand Rapids: Zondervan, 1978), Vol. 3, pp. 1208-1210; J. C. Davis, "Another Look at the Relationship between Baptism and Forgiveness of Sins in Acts 2:38," *Restoration Quarterly* 24 (1981): 80-88.

knowledgment of the proclamation that Jesus is the Christ (2:36). As such, the ἐπὶ τῷ ὀνόματι may deliberately pick up the ἐπικαλέσηται τὸ ὄνομα ("shall call upon the name") of the Lord of 2:21 (= Joel 2:32). "Lord" in Joel is God; in Acts 2 "Lord" is Jesus.

The commands and statement of their purpose are followed by the promise (cf. 2:39) that "you shall receive the gift of the Holy Spirit" (2:38). Is the gift the Holy Spirit himself or something given by the Holy Spirit? "Gift of" may be a gift given by the person in the genitive case, for example, "gift of God" (John 4:10; Acts 8:20 with reference to the ability to confer the Holy Spirit by the laying on of hands — 8:19) and "gift of Christ" (Eph. 4:7). On the other hand, "gift of" may identify in the genitive case what the gift is, for example, "gift of righteousness" (Rom. 5:17) and "gift of grace" (Eph. 3:7). The phrase "receive the Holy Spirit" in Acts 8:15, 17, 19; 10:47; and 19:2 favors the interpretation "receive the gift of the Holy Spirit" in 2:38 as the Holy Spirit.[11] The phrase "receive the promise of the Holy Spirit" in Acts 2:33 is grammatically and conceptually parallel and in context is almost certainly the "promised Holy Spirit."[12] Acts 1:8's "receive power" occurs when the Holy Spirit comes. Most interpreters hold that Acts 5:32 is parallel to 2:38, "the Holy Spirit whom God gave to those who obey him," so that the Holy Spirit is the gift (cf. Heb. 6:4). Moreover, the same phrase, "gift of the Holy Spirit," occurs in 10:45 with apparent reference to the Holy Spirit (cf. Acts 11:17).

The use of this same phrase in Acts 10:45, taken with 11:17, identifying the pouring out of the Holy Spirit on Cornelius with the experience on Pentecost in Acts 2, raises the question, Does Peter offer to the converts in 2:38 the same experience he and others had in 2:1-4? Such may not be a safe inference. That experience, as we have seen, is described as a baptism in the Holy Spirit. In the present text (2:38) the baptism is "in the name of Jesus Christ" (a water baptism) and is distinguished from the promised gift of the Holy Spirit. It may be, therefore, that 10:45 is not an exact parallel to 2:38. In both cases the Holy Spirit is given, but in 10:45 the emphasis is on the manifest results of the coming of the Spirit, the "speaking in tongues" (10:46) comparable to 2:4, whereas in 2:38 the results are left unspecified (and many varied manifestations of the working of the Spirit were possible, as we know from Paul, e.g., 1 Cor. 12). If the gift of the Spirit promised to baptism in Acts 2:38 is different from the baptism in (or with) the Holy Spirit in 2:1-5 and 10:44-46, then several problems are avoided (see further below on Acts 10 and on the Holy Spirit and Baptism).

That the promise was to Peter's hearers and their children (2:39) is not an indication of infant baptism.[13] On this occasion, at any rate, those who were baptized were "those who received his word" (2:41) and could repent (2:38); in the larger context the "sons and daughters" (2:17) were old enough to prophesy.

The later church was somewhat exercised over the question of why there is no

---

11. Outside of Acts, "receive the Holy Spirit" occurs in John 20:22 and Gal. 3:2.
12. Cf. Luke 24:49; Acts 1:4. The "promise of the Holy Spirit" occurs also in Paul, Gal. 3:14.
13. Wilhelm Michaelis, "Lukas und die Anfänge der Kindertaufe," in W. Eltester, *Apophoreta: Festschrift für Ernst Haenchen* (Berlin: Töpelmann, 1964), p. 192.

record of the Twelve and other disciples gathered at Pentecost before the coming of the Holy Spirit receiving Christian baptism. Some of the explanations offered will be examined in later chapters, but the events discussed here may prompt a solution. Since the successor to Judas was to have been part of the apostolic company "from the baptism of John" (1:22), it seems a reasonable inference that they had all received John's baptism. If so, that water baptism was deemed sufficient[14] when it was completed by the baptism of the Holy Spirit that they received in Acts 2:1-2. As noted in chapter 5, a major difference between John's baptism and Christian baptism was that the latter brought the Holy Spirit. The baptism in the Holy Spirit in Acts 2 joined with the disciples' faith in Jesus completed the deficiency in John's baptism that they had received earlier.

Luke records that those baptized and added to the number of the disciples that day totaled about 3,000 persons (2:41).[15] In the past a common objection to Luke's narrative and/or to the practice of immersion has been that there were not sufficient facilities in Jerusalem to immerse that number without contaminating the available drinking supplies. That objection can no longer be made, because scores of immersion pools (*mikwaoth*) have been found on or around the temple mount. Their presence could have been assumed, because of the need to provide for the daily purifications by the priests and for worshippers who came to offer sacrifice and fulfill vows. We now have a fairly good idea of the extensive provisions for these ritual baths.[16]

Luke puts representative or programmatic material early in his narratives that are then treated more briefly in other occurrences. Thus, Acts 2:14-36 is a representative statement of preaching to Jews, and 2:42-47 a summary description of the life of the early community. Therefore, Acts 2:37-41 should be considered Luke's understanding of the normal pattern of response to Christian preaching. Luke has placed here his understanding of an exemplary account of what was involved in becoming a Christian. Those who receive the apostolic message (2:41), recognize Jesus as Lord and Messiah (2:36), repent, and are baptized in his name (2:38) receive forgiveness, the Holy Spirit, and salvation (2:38-39, 46), and then participate in the life of the community (2:41-47). Variations from this pattern would be noted for their special significance. We shall test this conclusion in the subsequent accounts of baptism recorded in Acts.

Acts 8:4-25

Philip, one of the seven leaders among the Hellenists in the church at Jerusalem (6:1-6) proclaimed the Christ to Samaria. This was an important stage in the spread of

---

14. This option was maintained along with other considerations by Tertullian, *On Baptism* 12.3-4.

15. The conjunction of "added" with "baptized" may imply baptism at the other notices by Luke of additions to the community — Acts 2:47; 5:14; 11:24 — so concluded by von Allmen, "Notizen zu den Taufberichten in der Apostelgeschichte," p. 41, n. 1.

16. See chap. 4, n. 27. William H. Jones, "Jewish Mikvah and Christian Baptism" (M.Th. thesis, McMaster Divinity College, Hamilton, Ontario, Canada).

the gospel from Jerusalem to Judea and Samaria (1:8). Many Samaritans "listened eagerly" to Philip's preaching and saw the signs he performed (8:6). Those who "believed Philip, who was preaching the good news concerning the kingdom of God and the name of Jesus Christ, were baptized [ἐβαπτίζοντο], both men and women" (but nothing said about children — 8:12[17]). The Samaritans had previously "listened eagerly" to Simon, who had amazed the people by his magic. Simon too "believed, and having been baptized [βαπτισθεὶς], he stayed constantly with Philip" (8:13 — the same things are said of him as are said of the other Samaritans), because now he was amazed at Philip's great miracles.

From Luke's perspective, there was an anomaly thus far about the conversion of the Samaritans. They had been "baptized [βεβαπτισμένοι] into the name [εἰς τὸ ὄνομα] of the Lord Jesus" (8:16), but as yet the Holy Spirit had fallen on none of them. The wording seems to indicate that the normal expectation was for the Holy Spirit to come in connection with baptism (even if not automatically so). Since the gift of the Holy Spirit was promised at baptism in 2:38, it may be that Luke's wording here implies that the Samaritans received the indwelling presence of the Spirit when they were baptized into the name of Jesus, but no special or external manifestations of the working of the Spirit were present (he had not "fallen" on any of them).[18] Baptism into the name of the Lord Jesus is thus clearly water baptism and not something done by the Holy Spirit. "When the apostles at Jerusalem heard that Samaria had received the word of God, they sent Peter and John to them" (8:14). By prayer and the laying on of hands Peter and John gave them the Holy Spirit (8:15, 17).[19] There was apparently some visible or auditory expression (such as speaking in tongues) that could be perceived by others, for Simon "saw" (or understood) that by the laying on of the apostles' hands the Spirit was given and wanted for himself the power to be able to do the same (8:18-19).[20]

It may be that the delay in God's giving special manifestations of the Spirit to the Samaritans until apostolic representatives arrived from Jerusalem was to emphasize the significance of the expansion of the gospel to Samaria and to confirm the unity of Jews and Samaritans in the church. In view of the centuries of animosity be-

---

17. Contrast the way children are specified in Matt. 14:21 and parallels.

18. This seems to me to be a better explanation of the episode than Avemarie, *Die Tauferzählungen*, pp. 221, 242, 254-255, 264-266, that Philip practiced a Christianized version of John's baptism that was related to the preaching of the kingdom of God and to the name of Jesus but did not give the Holy Spirit. Nikolaus Adler, *Taufe und Handauflegung: Eine exegetisch-theologische Untersuchung von Apg 8, 14-17* (Münster: Aschendorff, 1951), argues from this passage for the Roman Catholic understanding of a separate sacrament of confirmation.

19. Everett Ferguson, "Laying On of Hands: Its Significance in Ordination," *Journal of Theological Studies*, n.s. 26 (1975): 1-12, shows that in Christian usage the basic meaning of the laying on of hands was blessing. As such, it was always accompanied by prayer that spelled out the content of the blessing intended. In Acts 8:15-17 the blessing was the imparting of the Holy Spirit.

20. The "gift of God" (8:20) is not the Holy Spirit but the power possessed by apostles to impart the Spirit in some special way. Similarly, "this matter" in 8:21 is this gift of God he wanted to buy, not the Christian message or salvation.

tween Jews and Samaritans, incorporating Samaritans into the new people of God and their acceptance by Jewish believers was not something that could be taken for granted and needed a special show of divine favor related to the leadership of the Jerusalem church.

Acts 8:26-40

The conversion of Samaritans is followed by an account of the conversion of someone outside Jewish cultic purity, a eunuch.[21] Whether this Ethiopian court treasurer was a Jew or a proselyte is not stated,[22] but he was a devout person who had been to Jerusalem to worship and while riding in his chariot on his way home was reading the prophet Isaiah. The passage he was reading included Isaiah 53:7-8, from which, according to Luke's abbreviated account, Philip "preached to him Jesus" (8:32-35). Preaching Jesus must have included some mention of baptism, for "As . . . they came to a certain water, the eunuch said, 'Look, water, what prevents me from being baptized [βαπτισθῆναι]?" (8:36).

It has been argued that some statement about "What prevents?" was part of a primitive baptismal formula.[23] The appearances of the word "prevent" (or "hinder") in other baptismal texts each have a natural place in the respective narratives so that the theory of a formula seems gratuitous. Moreover, the word is spoken sometimes by the candidate, sometimes by the baptizer, and on the different occasions has a different referent for the hindrance. In the narrative setting of Acts 8:36 a more likely explanation of the wording is the eunuch's awareness of his anomalous condition relative to Judaism, which would prompt his query whether he was acceptable for membership among Jesus' followers.

An early reading, but not found in the major manuscripts, adds with some variation verse 37, "And Philip said to him, 'If you believe with all your heart, you may.' He answered and said, 'I believe that Jesus Christ is the Son of God.'" The reading is attested for the second century by Irenaeus.[24] It is more likely that in the transmission of the text the verse was added than that it was omitted. The eunuch's question called for a reply, and perhaps some could not feature a baptism without a confes-

---

21. Deut. 23:1. Isa. 56:3-5 announced to those eunuchs who kept the covenant a future place in the house of the Lord.

22. Avemarie, *Die Tauferzählungen*, pp. 54-67, discusses the question and concludes that Luke leaves his status unclear, perhaps because the report came to him unclear; p. 290 states that it is improbable that he was a Jew but that he was a sympathizer and perhaps a proselyte. Since his conversion did not lead to reception into the community, his baptism did not become a test case like Cornelius's.

23. Oscar Cullmann, *Baptism in the New Testament* (London: SCM, 1950), pp. 71-80, on the basis of the occurrence of the verb κωλύειν in this passage; Acts 10:47; 11:17; Matt. 3:13-14. Its further appearance in Mark 10:13-14 is used to give a baptismal interpretation to Jesus' blessing the children. Among the refutations of use of this formula in the baptismal ritual, note Avemarie, *Die Tauferzählungen*, pp. 87-92, 294.

24. *Against Heresies* 3.12.8.

sion of faith. The counterproposal that the verse was omitted when infant baptism became common founders on its omission in P[45] from the early third century. Even if not original, the verse must go back to an early edition of the Acts and retains importance as historical testimony to Christian practice at least as early as the second century. Baptism was preceded by a confession from the candidate that "Jesus Christ is the Son of God."

The description of the baptism suggests an immersion, for "both Philip and the eunuch went down into the water, and he baptized [ἐβάπτισεν] him" (8:38). Then they came up out of the water (8:39). A dipping administered by Philip is the most natural explanation for Philip entering the water with the eunuch. These details are to be understood as having occurred in other cases of baptism. Luke's own association with the Hellenists of the early church and Philip in particular[25] plus the detail in which the event is recorded supports the likelihood that the account was derived from Philip himself.

That the Spirit took Philip away after the baptism shows that his task was complete and nothing further was necessary for the conversion of the Ethiopian; baptism was the regular climax of Luke's conversion stories.[26] Codex Alexandrinus and some later manuscripts make an insertion so that 8:39 reads, "[T]he Holy Spirit fell upon the eunuch, and the angel of the Lord took Philip away." The words between "Spirit" and "Lord" could have fallen out of the sources of the other extant witnesses, but this seems unlikely, and we probably have a scribal insertion to add the coming of the Spirit on the Ethiopian in order to make clear there was no deficiency here comparable to that in the preceding case of the Samaritans.

Acts 9:1-19; 22:3-21

In the structure of Acts, the call of Saul (soon to be better known as Paul) as an apostle prepares for the inclusion in the church of Gentiles, of whom Cornelius's household was representative (10–11). The story of Saul's conversion occurs three times in Acts, in two of which his baptism is mentioned.[27] Conversion was involved, but the narratives would more properly be described as his call as an apostle to the Gentiles. Although some see Saul as saved when Jesus appeared to him, the text does not read

---

25. Acts 21:8, "we went into the house of Philip."
26. Avemarie, *Die Tauferzählungen*, p. 268. His further conclusion (p. 272) from the absence of a mention of the giving of the Spirit to the Ethiopian, that Philip's baptism was intermediate between John's and full Christian baptism and did not give the Spirit, makes too much of what the text does not say. As he recognizes (p. 270), when Luke reports a reception of the Spirit in connection with baptism there was a recognizable special occasion.
27. Avemarie, *Die Tauferzählungen*, pp. 295-336, affirms that all three versions have a Lukan stamp on their idiom but also contain a substantial number of expressions found only in Paul in the New Testament, so Luke had a verbally fixed and probably a written tradition as basis for his accounts of Paul's conversion.

that way. The supernatural aspects of the account, particularly the appearance of the resurrected Jesus, are not presented as typical of conversions but serve to provide Paul with the qualifications and commission from Jesus as an apostle.[28] Jesus instructed Saul to go into Damascus, where he would be told what he must do (9:6). He spent three days fasting and praying, not the immediate actions of a saved person (9:9, 11; contrast 8:40).

The Lord also appeared to the disciple Ananias with the instructions to go to Saul and lay hands on him so that he might recover the sight he lost as a result of the blinding light accompanying the revelation of Jesus (9:12).[29] Ananias went to Saul, and "laid his hands on him" (9:17). He explained that "the Lord Jesus, who appeared to you on your way here, sent me so that you may regain your sight and be filled with the Holy Spirit" (9:17). Saul's sight returned, and then "he got up and was baptized [ἐβαπτίσθη]" (9:18).

The two purposes of regaining sight and receiving the Holy Spirit were accompanied by two actions performed by Ananias and received by Saul: the imposition of hands and baptism. I would read the first action as accomplishing the first purpose and the second action the second purpose. Some assume that the imposition of the hands of Ananias was the means for the bestowal of both sight and the Holy Spirit,[30] but the earlier statement (9:12) connected the laying on of hands only with the restoration of Saul's sight, and that was the immediate result of the gesture (9:18). The next thing that happened was Saul's baptism. The statement that Paul "got up" (apparently from kneeling or prostration in prayer) suggests that he had to go elsewhere to be baptized (passive voice, so not self-administered). The other purpose, in addition to healing, for Ananias's coming was for Saul to receive the Holy Spirit (9:17). That gift would have been received in the baptism, presumably administered by Ananias.

The conversion/call of Paul in Acts 9 is narrated in the third person by Luke; in Acts 22 Luke quotes Paul's own account of the events. For the study of baptism we may limit ourselves to the meeting of Ananias with Paul (22:12-16). In Paul's account no mention is made of the laying on of hands. Instead he quotes Ananias's words, "Regain your sight" (22:13), and he places on Ananias's lips a statement of his apostolic commission to be Jesus' witness. The memorable moment was the baptism. Ananias said, "What are you waiting for? Get up [cf. 9:18], be baptized [βάπτισαι] and wash away [ἀπόλουσαι] your sins, calling on his name [ἐπικαλεσάμενος τὸ ὄνομα]."

Paul's account lays the emphasis on what he was expected to do. Once more, he had to "get up." "Be baptized" is actually middle voice. The middle voice expressed what one did to oneself, for oneself, or to involve oneself.[31] The latter two would ex-

---

28. Acts 1:22; 9:15; 22:14-15; 26:16-18.
29. The most frequent use of the gesture of laying on of hands was in healing — Mark 6:5; 7:32; 8:23, 25; 16:18; Luke 4:40; 13:13; 28:18.
30. This common view is held by Avemarie, *Die Tauferzählungen*, p. 323.
31. Stanley E. Porter, "Did Paul Baptize Himself? A Problem of the Greek Voice System," in Stanley E. Porter and Anthony R. Cross, *Dimensions of Baptism: Biblical and Theological Studies* (London: Sheffield Academic Press, 2002), pp. 91-109.

press the force of the middle voice here. In the Jewish context of ceremonial purification, one would translate, "Baptize yourself." In the Christian context of an administered baptism, however, the meaning of the middle voice would be brought out by the translation, "Get yourself baptized" or "Experience baptism." Such a translation keeps the emphasis on what Paul did but also brings out that the action was something done to him but in his interest.

That a water baptism is intended is underscored by the next verb, "wash away." This is the verb we found in Josephus and others to describe the baptisms of the Jews and of John. The use again of a middle imperative verb may mean "you wash away," or, to give it the same force as the verb for baptize, we could translate, "get your sins washed away." The washing away of sins is associated with the baptism.

Special interest attaches to this verse, not only because it associates baptism with forgiveness of sins, but also because of the further statement that the baptism was accompanied by a "calling on his name." Is this God or the Righteous One (22:14)? According to the flow of thought probably the latter, for the pronouns at the end of verse 14 and in verse 15 refer to him. The language picks up the quotation from Joel 2 that introduced Peter's sermon in Acts 2:21. In Joel the "name of the Lord" was God, but in Peter's application the reference was to Jesus Christ (2:38). The salvation that comes to those who called on the name of the Lord is associated here, as in Acts 2, with baptism. In Acts 22:16 the calling on the name is clearly done by the one being baptized, not by the baptizer. It may refer to a prayer (cf. Luke 3:21) or to a confession of faith (Acts 8:37 in the western text); as an invocation of the Name it may be considered an equivalent to "baptism in the name of Christ."[32] The wording here may give some indication that the formula "in the name" refers to what was spoken or affirmed by the baptizand rather than to something pronounced by the administrator.

The accounts of Paul's baptism include a calling on the name of Jesus, the removal of sins, being filled with the Holy Spirit, and reception into a local community — all characteristic of Luke's understanding of Christian conversion baptism. Paul's conversion occurred not long after the beginning of the church in Jerusalem; his baptism (supported by his own statements about baptism — chap. 9) at Damascus confirms that baptism was an established Christian custom quite early.

Acts 10:1–11:18

The events of Acts 10 have been described as "the Gentile Pentecost," because as the Holy Spirit came on Jews (represented by the disciples) in Acts 2, so he came on

---

32. Crehan, *Early Christian Baptism*, pp. 7-9. Delling, *Die Taufe*, p. 78, in support of the contention that there is in the New Testament no confession by the baptizand, gives as the meaning, "Let yourself be baptized and become a Christian," an interpretation that does not give adequate force to the biblical phrase ("to call on the name of the Lord") as an act of worship.

Gentiles (represented by the household of Cornelius) in Acts 10. The details and sequence of the events, however, are somewhat different.[33] Elaborate supernatural staging took place in order to bring the preacher (Peter) and the persons needing the message (Cornelius's household) together. An angel directed Cornelius to send for Peter, and Peter received a vision three times from God and a command from the Holy Spirit convincing him to go to Cornelius's house. The triple account of the story, once in narrative form by Luke (10:1-48) and twice in Peter's words (11:4-17; summarily in 15:7-11) — comparable to the triple account of Paul's conversion/call, shows its importance for Luke's purposes. Whether Cornelius and his household constituted the first case chronologically of Gentiles accepted into the church, their conversion became the test case for receiving uncircumcised Gentiles. The whole narrative shows that baptism functioned as the means of integration into the Christian community.

As in the other accounts where heavenly beings are involved — an angel and the Holy Spirit with the Ethiopian treasurer, the Lord himself with Saul — human messengers actually deliver the message of salvation, the normal means of spreading the gospel in Luke's own day. Even with the elaborate efforts to get Peter and Cornelius together, it was necessary that words be spoken "by which you will be saved" (11:14). Peter's sermon told the story of Jesus from "the baptism [βάπτισμα] which John preached" until his resurrection and appearances (10:36-42).[34] Jesus' baptism by John was the time when "God anointed him with the Holy Spirit and power" (10:38). Peter's concluding declaration was that "All the prophets testify that by Jesus everyone who believes in him receives forgiveness of sins through his name" (10:43). The similarity of the latter phrase to Acts 2:38 implies baptism, and the allusion is made explicit in 10:47.

The crucial passage for our study is as follows:

> While Peter was still speaking, the Holy Spirit fell on all who heard the word. The circumcised believers who had come with Peter were astounded that the gift of the Holy Spirit had been poured out [ἐκκέχυται] even upon the Gentiles, for they heard them speaking in tongues and extolling God. Then Peter said, "Can anyone forbid the water for baptizing [βαπτισθῆναι] these who have received the Holy Spirit just as we did?" And he commanded them to be baptized [βαπτισθῆναι] in the name [ἐν τῷ ὀνόματι] of Jesus Christ. (Acts 10:44-48)

The water baptism is distinguished from the pouring out of the Holy Spirit, which here precedes it. The pouring out of the Spirit is done by God; the result on the recipients was a baptism in the Holy Spirit. The Holy Spirit was given in order to convince Peter to baptize Gentiles. The event is identified with what happened to Jesus'

---

33. Avemarie, *Die Tauferzählungen*, pp. 340-398.

34. Cf. the qualifications for an apostle in 1:22; Peter's words constitute an outline of the Gospel of Mark. Another reference to John's proclaiming a "baptism of repentance" as a part of Christian preaching occurs in 13:24.

disciples in Acts 2: "these have received the Holy Spirit just as we have" (10:47); "The Holy Spirit fell on them just as upon us at the beginning" (11:15). And that coming of the Holy Spirit was described as "being baptized in the Holy Spirit" (1:5; and see discussion of 2:1-4 above). Peter linked this event with the Pentecost occurrence, both fulfilling Jesus' words, "John baptized with water, but you will be baptized with [βαπτισθήσεσθε ἐν] the Holy Spirit" (11:16). The coming of the Holy Spirit produced evidence available to the senses, the speaking in tongues — as at Pentecost — so that others knew it had happened. The coming of the Holy Spirit on Jews in Acts 2:1-5, 17-18 and on Gentiles in Acts 10:44-46 (11:15-17) is in both cases the premise for the offer of baptism and salvation (2:38; 10:47 and 11:14).

The purpose of this special occurrence of the coming of the Spirit is evident from the use made of it in 11:1-18. It justified to the other apostles and brothers in Jerusalem Peter's going to the uncircumcised and eating with them (11:1-3). The point of criticism was not that "Gentiles had accepted the word of God," but that they had been received while uncircumcised and had participated in table fellowship. The problem was the conditions under which they received the word and how they were to be treated by observant Jews. In the making of proselytes the decisive step was circumcision, and when proselyte baptism became normal it followed on circumcision. But Peter reasoned that to withhold baptism from these uncircumcised Gentiles would be to "hinder God" (11:17).

The elaborate divine efforts to bring about the offer of salvation to Gentiles and the extraordinary outpouring of the Holy Spirit accompanying Peter's message showed that God had declared Gentiles "clean" (10:14, 28; 11:9). As with the spread of the gospel to Samaria, so with its spread to Gentiles,[35] there was an unusual manifestation of the Holy Spirit accompanying the event and giving divine certification to the development. In Samaria the presence of the Spirit was withheld until representative Jerusalem apostles could certify the incorporation of a people previously separated from Israel into the church. Here in Acts 10 an even more significant step was taken in extending the gospel to Gentiles and receiving them in their uncircumcision on equal terms with circumcised believers. Only in this case and the similar occurrence for Jews in Acts 2 is the pouring out of the Spirit described as resulting in a baptism in the Holy Spirit.

The result of the aftermath of Peter's going to Cornelius showed further its purpose: the Jewish believers acknowledged, "Then God has given even to the Gentiles repentance that leads to life" (11:18). The baptism of the Holy Spirit in the case of Cornelius, instead of eliminating the need for water baptism, was the justification for administering it (10:47-48). That Peter commanded water baptism shows the norm: if these Gentiles received the Holy Spirit, then they have to be baptized in water. The implication of 11:17 is that God would have been hindered in giving salvation if they were denied baptism. The faith (10:43; cf. 11:17) and baptism (10:47) of

---

35. Note the same phrase about the apostles hearing that Samaria and the Gentiles received the word of God in 8:14 and 11:1.

Cornelius's household was characterized as repentance (11:18). The various statements about hearing (10:44) or accepting (11:1) the word that brings salvation (11:14), fearing God and doing righteousness (10:35), believing in the one raised from the dead (10:39-43), repenting (11:18), magnifying God (10:47), being baptized (10:48), being cleansed by God (10:15; 11:9) are summary statements referring to different aspects of the conversion experience. The response to Peter's message brought forgiveness of sins, and all was related to the name of Jesus Christ (10:43, 48). The baptism of the Holy Spirit was a special circumstance with a special purpose and not part of the usual pattern of conversion in Acts.

The conversion of Cornelius's household is the first of the cases of household baptism in Acts (with 11:14; cf. 16:15 16:31; 18:8; 1 Cor. 1:16).[36] Households in the ancient world commonly followed the religion of the head of the family. These cases of household conversion have been an argument on behalf of infant baptism in New Testament times.[37] It is true that the word for house (οἶκος, family or household) included any infants or children that might be present, but it did not necessarily mean there were infants in the family. The term included relatives, slaves, client freedmen, and other dependents. The presence of children must be determined in each instance.[38] The household in Cornelius's case "feared God" (10:2), heard Peter's message (10:33, 44; 11:14), believed (10:43; cf. 11:17), repented (11:18), received the Holy Spirit and spoke in tongues (10:44, 46), and magnified God (10:46) — descriptions hardly applicable to small children.

---

36. Joel B. Green, "'She and Her Household Were Baptized' (Acts 16:15): Household Baptism in the Acts of the Apostles," in Stanley E. Porter and Anthony R. Cross, *Dimensions of Baptism: Biblical and Theological Studies* (London: Sheffield Academic Press, 2002), pp. 72-90, discusses the function of the household baptisms in Acts apart from the question of infant baptism.

37. Joachim Jeremias, *Infant Baptism in the First Four Centuries* (London: SCM, 1960), pp. 19-40; idem, *The Origins of Infant Baptism* (Naperville: Allenson, 1963), pp. 12-32. Note the response by Kurt Aland, *Did the Early Church Baptize Infants?* (London: SCM, 1963), pp. 87-94. Michaelis, "Lukas und die Anfänge der Kindertaufe," pp. 191-193, after examining the references to the baptism of households concludes negatively against Jeremias that there is no indication that Luke was a witness for the practice of infant baptism, for children as such are not mentioned in any instance. Green, "'She and Her Household Were Baptized' (Acts 16:15)," pp. 72-90, shifts the focus from infant baptism to the sociological point that in Acts the household became the new culture center for the people of God and in particular a substitute for the temple.

38. They are specified by Ignatius, *Smyrnaeans* 13.1, "I greet the households of my brothers with the wives and children." Unless the statement is careless, he seems to distinguish the children from the households in *Polycarp* 8.2, "I greet all individually and the [widow] of Epitropus with all the household of her and her children." A quite late apocryphal work sometimes cited is the *Acts of Philip* (my chap. 13): in chap. 58 reference is made to sons, daughters, and slaves without use of *oikos*; then in chapter 63 there is the statement, "Having instructed them, he baptized all those of the house into the name of the Father, the Son, and the Holy Spirit" (*oikia* is used for the house itself in 51, 61, and 64).

Acts 16:12-15

As Acts 8 put together two accounts of baptism significant for the spread of the gospel to new people, Acts 16 puts together accounts of two baptisms in Philippi that are the first recorded on the continent of Europe. The first is the businesswoman Lydia, "a worshipper of God," either a Gentile proselyte or adherent to Judaism. The word for "place of prayer" was a term for "synagogue," that is, a recognized place of Jewish meeting, but it may not refer here to a special building. The location was "beside a river." Proximity to a body of water was often a consideration for the site of a synagogue in order to facilitate purifications. In this instance the location was convenient for Christian baptism.

"The Lord opened her heart to pay attention to the things spoken by Paul. When she was baptized [ἐβαπτίσθη], along with her household, she urged us" to stay with her (16:14-15). Few details are given. As in the other accounts, baptism follows a careful listening to spoken words (16:13-14). Lydia's immediate receptiveness is attributed to God's opening her heart (through the words spoken by Paul, the circumstances of her life, some direct preparation, or creating the disposition to believe?). Her faith in the Lord is alluded to in her words in 16:15, which perhaps imply by her insistence that something about her circumstances made acceptance of her hospitality a matter that she thought might make Paul's company hesitant. Her home remained a place of Christian meeting (16:40, but see 16:16). The composition of Lydia's household is not specified, perhaps consisting of women engaged in business with her or her slaves and freed clientele. Only women are specified as present, so if she had male slaves they were not present on this occasion. The presence of children is particularly problematic, but if present they were old enough to join Lydia in listening to Paul's words and to believe them.

Acts 16:16-34

Paul's expelling a "spirit of divination" from a slave girl exploited as a fortune-teller for monetary gain by her owners provoked them to bring charges before the magistrates against Paul and Silas. While the missionaries were imprisoned, an earthquake freed the prisoners from their chains. The jailer rushed in and brought Paul and Silas out. He asked,

> "Sirs, what must I do in order to be saved?" They said, "Believe on the Lord Jesus, and you and also your household will be saved." And they spoke the word of the Lord to him, along with all those in his house. And taking them in the same hour of the night, he washed their stripes, and he was baptized [ἐβαπτίσθη] immediately, as also all those who were his. . . . He and his entire household rejoiced, having believed in God. (16:30-34)

Luke's condensed version does not explain how the pagan jailer knew to ask for salvation or what content he put in the word. He may have meant deliverance from punishment if any of the prisoners escaped (deliverance from illness or danger was a common use of the word "saved"), but if so, Paul and Silas quickly moved the subject to a different level.

The command to believe on the Lord Jesus was followed immediately by Paul and Silas speaking the word of the Lord so that the jailer would know about him in whom he was told to believe and so to provide a basis for believing in him. Believing in the Lord Jesus also brought faith in God (16:34). By washing the prisoners' stripes, the jailer expressed his repentance. This account specifies what other accounts imply, namely that baptism followed immediately on acceptance of the Christian gospel. "The same hour of the night" contrasts with the later practice of delay of baptism for increasingly longer periods of time. We are not told where the baptism occurred, but it was outside the prison (16:30), not in the jailer's house (16:34), and where there was water for washing the prisoners' wounds (16:33).

The conversion of the Philippian jailer provides an explicit mention of household baptism (16:33). His household, "those who were his," are joined with him throughout the passage, as indeed they would have been expected to follow what he did. Accordingly, we may say that everyone involved was called on to believe in Jesus (16:31); the whole household is expressly said to have been addressed by Paul and Silas (16:32), to have joined the jailer in baptism (16:33), and to have rejoiced that he believed in God (16:34).

Acts 18:8

Acts 18:8 contains in succinct form a summary of what has been found frequently in the accounts of conversion in Acts: "Crispus, the ruler of the synagogue, believed in the Lord, with all his household. And many of the Corinthians, on hearing, were believing and were being baptized [ἐβαπτίζοντο]." Crispus (cf. 1 Cor. 1:14) provides another instance of household conversion: the text affirms that his "whole househod" believed. The next statement repeats the sequence characteristic of the Acts accounts: hearing, believing, and being baptized. I have translated the present tense of the participle for hearing and the imperfect tenses for believing and being baptized to bring out their progressive nature. This sequence was a continuing process at Corinth. In Acts faith comes from hearing the word of the Lord (14:1; 17:11-12) and results in baptism.

Acts 18:24–19:7

The story of Apollos and the twelve disciples (of John?) in Ephesus provides one of the more difficult baptismal texts in Acts.[39] Apollos had been "instructed in the Way

---

39. See further the discussion in chap. 5. Anthony Ash, "John's Disciples: A Serious Problem," *Res-*

of the Lord" and "he taught accurately the things concerning Jesus," but "he knew only the baptism [βάπτισμα] of John" (18:25) until Priscilla and Aquila taught him more accurately. When Paul came to Ephesus, "he found some disciples" (19:1). He asked them if they received the Holy Spirit when they believed, and they replied that they had not heard if there is a Holy Spirit (19:2). Paul went immediately to a second question, "Into what, then, were you baptized [ἐβαπτίσθητε]?" Paul assumes a connection between their believing and their being baptized. They go together. Also, he assumes a connection between baptism and the giving of the Holy Spirit; the ignorance of these disciples about the Holy Spirit raised a question about their baptism. They replied that they were baptized into the baptism [βάπτισμα] of John (19:3). The deficiency in their understanding was the same as Apollos's, but what their connection was if any with Apollos is not stated.

Paul proceeded to explain that "John baptized [ἐβάπτισεν] with a baptism [βάπτισμα] of repentance, saying for people to believe on the one coming after him, that is, on Jesus" (19:4). "When they heard this, they were baptized [ἐβαπτίσθησαν] into the name [εἰς τὸ ὄνομα] of the Lord Jesus" (19:5). Three distinguishing marks of Christian baptism come out in this passage: baptism is connected with faith in Jesus, hence the baptism is in his name, and baptism is associated with receiving the Holy Spirit. These were all points of capital importance for Paul (chap. 9). Baptism "into the name of the Lord Jesus" (19:5) is specifically contrasted with John's baptism and so marks the new baptism as Christian baptism.

"When Paul laid his hands on them, the Holy Spirit came upon them, and they spoke in tongues and prophesied" (19:6). As was true in Samaria in Acts 8, the laying on of an apostle's hands brought a special manifestation of the Holy Spirit. Here the auditory signs of the coming of the Holy Spirit are specified — speaking in tongues and prophesying. The special manifestation of the Spirit discernible by the senses that followed the baptism was presumably to dramatize the deficiency of John's baptism and the superiority of Christian baptism.

This narrative is the only example in the New Testament of a "re-baptism." Why did it occur here, when we do not read of others (such as Jesus' own disciples) being re-baptized. Would not simply giving the Holy Spirit by laying on of hands remedied any deficiency? We can only speculate from what is said in the text. Possibly there was an inadequacy in their faith about Jesus as well as in their knowledge about the Holy Spirit; even though they are called "disciples," they may not have known accurately, as Apollos did, the things concerning Jesus (which in turn may be a reason why nothing is said of Apollos being re-baptized). They may have known only that there was someone coming but not have known that he had come or that this one was Jesus. A variation of this view is to affirm that where Jesus was acknowledged as the Christ and the Spirit was possessed, no baptism beyond John's was necessary

---

toration Quarterly 45 (2003): 85-93. Avemarie, *Die Tauferzählungen,* pp. 413-440, surveys the views of major interpreters and concludes that this episode supports his view that in the earliest Christian times there was no uniform baptismal practice.

(this was the case with Apollos), but where both these elements were missing, baptism in the name of Jesus had to be administered.[40] Or perhaps the problem was a matter of timing: although John's baptism was valid for a time, these twelve, unlike the disciples of Jesus, may have received their baptism after Jesus' commission had replaced John's baptism.

Baptism in(to) the Name of Jesus

Luke in Acts uses three different prepositions for the formula "in the name of" with reference to baptism.[41] This variation of prepositions in the phrase is common in the rest of the New Testament. Most common in Luke and in the New Testament as a whole is "in the name of [ἐν τῷ ὀνόματι]."[42] More common in the context of baptism is "into the name of [εἰς τὸ ὄνομα]," never in Luke-Acts in a nonbaptismal context.[43] "Upon the name of [ἐπὶ τῷ ὀνόματι]" is frequent in Luke-Acts but only once in reference to baptism.[44]

For many of the New Testament occurrences there seems to be little if any distinction in meaning to be made. Insofar as shades of meaning can be discerned, "in the name of" often refers to acting in someone's name (mentioning their name) and so sometimes with the connotation "by the authority of." "Upon the name of" implied calling on someone's name, especially in invoking that person, and so could have the same connotation. "Into the name of" is now generally referred to a Semitic phrase (see chap. 8 on Matt. 28:19) for an act directed toward someone, particularly in worship. The meaning "with reference to" or "bearing [someone] in mind" covers all the cases. Hence, Hartman concludes that Luke in writing Acts thought there was hardly any difference in meaning of the formulas "into," "in," and "because of" the name.[45] Although the number of occurrences is too limited to speak with certainty,

---

40. Beasley-Murray, *Baptism in the New Testament*, pp. 111-112. The interpretation of Acts 18:25 as "fervent in the (Holy) Spirit" and so indicating full possession of the Holy Spirit (p. 110) overburdens the language.

41. Lars Hartman, *'Into the Name of the Lord Jesus': Baptism in the New Testament* (Edinburgh: T&T Clark, 1997), pp. 37-50; Avemarie, *Die Tauferzählungen*, pp. 26-43.

42. Acts 2:38 (variant reading in B and D); 10:48; and in a nonbaptismal context Luke 9:49; 10:17; 13:35 (quoting Ps. 118:26); Acts 3:6; 4:7, 10; 9:28. For other uses in the New Testament, Matt. 21:9 (only in this quotation from Ps. 118:26 in Matthew); Mark (who shifts back and forth between ἐν and ἐπί in the same context) 9:38, 41; 11:19; 16:17; John 5:43 (twice); 14:13, 14, 26; 16:23, 26; 17:11, 12; 20:31; 1 Cor. 5:4; 6:11 (baptismal); Eph. 5:20; Phil. 2:10; 2 Thess. 3:6; Jas. 5:10, 14; 1 Pet. 4:14, 16.

43. Acts 8:16; 19:5; elsewhere Matt. 28:19; 1 Cor. 1:13, 15. It does appear outside Luke and Paul where baptism is not in view — Matt. 10:41, 42; John 1:12; 2:23; 3:18 (who, however, prefers "in the name"); 1 John 5:13; Heb. 6:10.

44. Acts 2:38; in other contexts in 4:17, 18; 5:28, 40; Luke 1:59 (different meaning); 9:48; 21:8; 24:47 (but related to conversion). Other nonbaptismal uses in the New Testament are Matt. 18:5; 24:5; Mark 9:37, 39; 13:6. This phrase is strikingly absent from the rest of the New Testament, but Jas. 2:7 may be significant, even for baptism, "the good name which was called [ἐπικληθέν] upon you."

45. Hartman, *'Into the Name of the Lord Jesus'*, p. 37.

Luke's limitation of "into the name of" to baptism and its usage by Paul in the same context may suggest that this was the more common expression. Matthew 28:19 then would reflect a common terminology expanded to include the Father and the Holy Spirit. If shades of meaning in regard to baptism are to be distinguished between the phrases, "into the name" means bringing a person into a relationship with the person of Jesus Christ toward whom the act is directed; "in the name" means acknowledging Jesus as the one for whom and by whose authority the act is done; "upon (or because of) the name" may include an allusion to calling on Jesus' name in the act of baptism (cf. the discussion on Acts 2:38 above for the possibility that this phrase refers to a confession by the candidate, "calling on the name of Jesus" as Lord and Christ — as was done in 22:16). The importance of the phrases for the study of baptism is that they identify Christian baptism as done with reference to Christ — an expression of faith in him and in worship toward him. Baptism "in the name" signified the intention of the act and so distinguished it from other washings. There is a solidarity between the preaching of the name, the confession of the name, and baptism in the name.[46]

Hartman concluded from his study of the phrase "into the name of" that the Semitic origin of the expression points to its use in the earliest days of the still Aramaic-speaking church. Greek speakers then rendered it by different Greek prepositions with no great difference of meaning intended. The confession of Jesus as Lord in the baptismal formula has important Christological consequences for him as a heavenly authority.[47]

The Holy Spirit and Baptism

Much of the data concerning the relation of baptism to the Holy Spirit is found in the Acts of the Apostles.[48] The exposition of the relevant passages above permits some summary conclusions to be drawn.

---

46. T. Maertens, *Histoire et pastorale du rituel du catéchuménat et du baptême* (Bruges: Biblica, 1962), pp. 45-47.

47. Hartman, *'Into the Name of the Lord Jesus'*, pp. 43, 47-48. His earlier considerations of the Christological significance of the baptismal formula include "Baptism 'Into the Name of Jesus' and Early Christology," *Studia Theologica* 28 (1974): 21-48, highlighting the significance of the eschatological expectation and the remission of sins; and "Early Baptism — Early Eschatology," in A. J. Malherbe and W. Meeks, eds., *The Future of Christology: Essays in Honor of Leander E. Keck* (Minneapolis: Fortress, 1993), pp. 191-201.

48. M. Quesnel, *Baptisés dans l'Esprit: Baptême et Esprit Saint dans les Actes des Apôtres* (Paris: Cerf, 1985), argues from the differences in the descriptions that the Peter narratives in Acts 2 and 10 (e.g., the conferring of the Holy Spirit tied to the water rite) and the Philip and Paul narratives in Acts 8, 9, and 19 (Spirit not given by the water ritual but by a separate laying on of hands) come from two different sources and represent the different perspectives of Luke and the Palestinian Jewish Christianity in the Peter narratives and those from a Gentile Christian milieu in the Philip and Paul narratives. The problems with this analysis methodologically and in specifics are laid out by Avemarie, *Die*

Only two events are described as conferring a "baptism of the Holy Spirit" — the descent of the Spirit on Jewish disciples in Jerusalem (1:5) in Acts 2 and on the Gentile household of Cornelius in Caesarea (11:16) in Acts 10–11. Nothing is said about water baptism of those who received the Holy Spirit in the first case, but it is safe assumption and seems to be implied (1:22) that they had received John's baptism. The descent of the Spirit preceded the water baptism of Cornelius's household and indeed served to guarantee that it was proper to baptize them (10:47). Special observable manifestations of the working of the Spirit ("speaking in tongues" — 2:4, 6; 10:46) accompanied those occasions and two others — the twelve disciples of John in Ephesus ("speaking in tongues" again — 19:6) and the Samaritans (8:17-18). What the observable phenomenon was in the case of the Samaritans is not mentioned, but likely it was the same as in the other cases, "speaking in tongues." In both of the latter cases the imparting of the Holy Spirit came through the medium of the laying on of hands by apostles (8:17-18; 19:6). All four incidents represent important stages in the spread of the gospel of Christ: its first proclamation to Jews, its offer to Samaritans, its extension to Gentiles, and its replacement of the preparatory work of John the Baptist. This fact would indicate that observable manifestations of the Spirit served to provide divine authorization for the proclamation and spread of the gospel and of the incorporation of all peoples into the church of Christ. These were not ordinary experiences to be expected by all converts and were applicable only to key persons (the Jerusalem disciples) or representative persons (Samaritans, Cornelius's household, twelve disciples of John) in the unfolding of the Christian mission.

The Holy Spirit, however, was promised as a "gift" (2:38) to be received by all who identified with Christ through baptism in his name. This presence of the Spirit in the believers' lives as a result of baptism is suggested by other passages following the programmatic statement of Acts 2:38 — note 5:32; 8:16; 9:12, 17-18; 19:2-3. This sequence agrees with passages studied in other chapters — John 3:5, "born of water and the Spirit"; Titus 3:5, "washing of regeneration and renewal of the Holy Spirit"; Galatians 3:26-27 and 4:6, "because you are sons, God sent the Spirit"; 1 Corinthians 12:13, "by one Spirit baptized into one body and made to drink [or be irrigated with] one Spirit."

Summary on Baptism in Acts

The accounts of conversion in Acts ordinarily include mention of baptism.[49] The practice of Christian baptism involved the use of water as distinct from the baptism

---

Tauferzählungen, pp. 12-17. For the subject of the Spirit and baptism as a whole in Acts, see the latter, pp. 129-174, and Beasley-Murray, *Baptism in the New Testament*, pp. 104-122. Jon A. Weatherly, "The Writer's Versus the Reader's Purpose: Interpreting Acts Theologically," *Stone-Campbell Journal* 5 (2002): 93-112, says in regard to baptism and the Spirit that Luke narrates exceptions to the norm (8; 10; 19) in order to make other points. I rather think the special manifestations of the Spirit that appear to be "exceptions" are to mark the significant stages in the advance of the gospel.

49. For this concluding section compare von Allmen, "Notizen zu den Taufberichen," pp. 41-60.

of the Holy Spirit, and where any details are given an immersion is either implied or is consistent with what is said. The baptism was an administered act and not self-performed. It was done in the name of Jesus Christ, a characteristic that may include a confession of faith in him. The baptism was always preceded by a preaching of the gospel. That message called for faith in Jesus and repentance of sins.[50] All the accounts of conversion involve persons of a responsible age, with no certain indication of infants or children being included.[51] Baptism promised forgiveness[52] and the coming of the Holy Spirit to the person baptized. Baptism was viewed as both a human act and an act in which God was at work.[53]

Luke showed no interest in who performed the baptism (explicit only in Acts 8:38 and implicit in 8:12 and 9:18). Peter's command in Acts 10:48 was presumably carried out by the six Jewish brothers who accompanied him (10:23, 45; 11:12). In the cases of the Corinthian converts (Acts 18:8), according to 1 Corinthians (see my chap. 9) Paul would have baptized some of the first converts, who in turn would have baptized others. With the exception of the account of the baptism of the Ethiopian treasurer, the stories of conversion in Acts do not end with the baptism but continue with some notice of the community activity or involvement by the persons involved.

---

50. Avemarie, *Die Tauferzählungen*, pp. 82-87; von Allmen, "Notizen zu den Taufberichten," pp. 41-42.

51. Women are specified along with men in Acts 5:14 and 8:12, but children are never mentioned as being baptized (see on 2:39 above). The mention of children with women in 21:5 (also in the D text of 1:14) shows that when Luke meant to include children he did so specifically, so I would draw the opposite conclusion from von Allmen, "Notizen zu Taufberichten," p. 42, n. 5, that this verse indicates children were baptized with their parents. Avemarie, *Die Tauferzählungen*, pp. 100-103 (cf. 440), leaves infant baptism open on theological grounds; the historical and theological considerations are thoroughly canvassed in Beasley-Murray, *Baptism in the New Testament*, pp. 306-386.

52. Avemarie, *Die Tauferzählungen*, pp. 104-128. See further chap. 9, summary on the New Testament, for theological motifs found in Acts as well as in the rest of the New Testament.

53. Avemarie, *Die Tauferzählungen*, pp. 99-100. Cf. his summary of Luke's conception of what Christian baptism is supposed to be: a visible expression of individual conversion, what a person does on coming to faith and at the same time a gift of God that the church cannot deny, performed in the name of the Lord, bringing a consciousness that one receives forgiveness of sins and salvation, bound with outpouring of the Holy Spirit by the laying on of hands [?], reception into the community of all believers, and having consequences for daily life (p. 452).

11. Baptism in the Rest of the New Testament and Summary

Most of the passages relevant to baptism in the New Testament have been covered in the preceding chapters. Five documents remain to be examined: Hebrews, James, 1 Peter, 1 John, and Revelation. Only 1 Peter makes a truly significant contribution to our study.

Hebrews

The author of Hebrews identifies "baptisms" as among the foundation principles that he wants his readers to go beyond as they grow toward maturity. The items mentioned were presumably part of elementary instruction to new converts: "Repentance from dead works, faith in God, teaching of baptisms [βαπτισμῶν], laying on of hands, resurrection of the dead, and eternal judgment" (Heb. 6:1-2). These items could be interpreted as primarily belonging to the Jewish foundation of the church. But they also formed part of the "beginning (or chief) doctrine of Christ." By selection and arrangement Jewish teachings have been Christianized to an extent. Repentance and faith were central to Christian conversion and suggest that the listing pertains to items associated with initiation.

The word for "baptisms" is not the usual word for the baptism of John and for Christian baptism (βάπτισμα) but the word used for Jewish washings (also by immersion).[1] The use of the latter word in Hebrews 9:10 in reference to the ceremonial regulations connected with the sacrificial ritual of the first tabernacle confirms the usage for Jewish practices: "[F]ood and drink and various baptisms [βαπτισμοῖς],

---

1. For different interpretations that have been advanced, see Harold W. Attridge, *Epistle to the Hebrews* (Philadelphia: Fortress, 1989), p. 164, to which add Anthony R. Cross, "The Meanings of 'Baptisms' in Hebrews 6:2," in Stanley E. Porter and Anthony R. Cross, eds., *Dimensions of Baptism: Biblical and Theological Studies* (Sheffield: Sheffield Academic Press, 2002), pp. 163-186, who suggests that martyrdom be included in the "baptisms."

ordinances for the body imposed until the time of setting things right." This usage would indicate that the author in chapter 6 has taken items from the Jewish background as illustrative of the foundation principles with which they are not to rest content but are to build on as they move toward maturity or completeness in their Christian understanding. Elementary Christian instruction evidently included the difference between Christian baptism and ritual washings.

"Dead works" occurs also in Hebrews 9:14, where the contrast with "worship of the living God" suggests that the "dead works" have to do with the acts of pagan worship. This phrase, therefore, also points to the original Jewish context of the listing.

The six items in Hebrews 6:1-2 fall into three pairs, the first two being "repentance from dead works and faith toward God" (not Christ) and the last two being "resurrection of the dead and eternal judgment." These pairs would indicate that "baptisms and laying on of hands" also belong together. The laying on of hands was used in Judaism for blessing, healing, and appointment to certain functions,[2] but would hardly constitute a basic element in Jewish practice. The inclusion of baptisms and laying on of hands would have been dictated by Christian practice.

How the laying on of hands was thought to function, particularly in relation to baptism, is not self-evident from the passage in Hebrews. Many would identify it with the imparting of the Holy Spirit and the origins of the sacrament of confirmation (cf. Acts 8:17-18; 19:6; but both of these occasions were exceptional — chap. 10). It may be, however, that part of the baptismal ceremony was a laying on of hands and prayer (perhaps including a petition for the coming of the Holy Spirit), expressing the primary sense of the gesture in Christian usage as an act of blessing and therefore a sign of acceptance into fellowship. This would be in keeping with one strand of the Jewish background of the gesture and would account for its normal presence later in Christian baptism; its secondary association with the invocation of the Holy Spirit then became primary as different acts in the ceremony were assigned a significance according to the developed doctrinal meaning of baptism. But any determination of the meaning of the act in Hebrews must remain hypothetical.

The subsequent verses in Hebrews 6 include ideas with later baptismal associations: "those once enlightened [φωτισθέντας],[3] who have tasted the heavenly gift, have become partakers of the Holy Spirit, have tasted the good word of God and the powers of the age to come" (Heb. 6:4-6). But in Hebrews the association may be only with conversion and acceptance of Christ, of which baptism was a part, but not specifically with baptism.[4]

There is a more definite allusion to baptism later in the book: "Let us draw near with a true heart in full assurance of faith; having our hearts sprinkled [ῥεραν-

---

2. Everett Ferguson, "Laying On of Hands: Its Significance in Ordination," *Journal of Theological Studies*, n.s. 26 (1975): 1-12; repr. Everett Ferguson, ed., *Church, Ministry, and Organization in the Early Church Era*, Studies in Early Christianity 13 (New York: Garland, 1993), pp. 147-158.

3. "Enlightened" with apparent reference to conversion occurs also in Heb. 10:32.

4. The participles are all aorists, and so are associated with a one-time experience or event (or complex of events).

τισμένοι] from an evil conscience and our bodies washed [λελουσμένοι] with pure water, let us hold fast the confession of our hope without wavering" (10:22-23). If I continued the quotation through verse 24, we would find the sequence faith, hope, and love. For the study of baptism it is important to note the association here of faith and confession with the sprinkling (with blood) and the washing with water.

As elsewhere, the author of Hebrews connects Christian practices with Jewish antecedents. The basis of his language is the purifications that involved sprinkling with blood and washing with water.[5] That the sprinkling here does not refer to baptism is indicated by the fact that it is applied to the hearts; more likely it is a reference to the spiritual application of the blood of Jesus (referred to in v. 19).[6] It might be thought that if the inward application of the blood of Jesus that brings forgiveness is described as a sprinkling, then the outward baptism that appropriates that forgiveness should be administered in the same way. However, in the Old Testament background different words describing distinct acts were employed for the sprinkling of blood and the washing in water. The same is true here. As the washing or bathing prescribed in the Law was understood in New Testament times as an immersion, so should the washing here be understood. The cleansing in the Christian context is not from physical impurity but a cleansing of the conscience from sin (10:2, 10-12). Baptism thus replaces all ritual baths of purification. The cleansing power is in the death of Jesus. Christian baptism fits into this cleansing because it is related to Jesus the great high priest (10:21), who opened "the new and living way" by his blood (10:19-20). Baptism is further related to a true heart of faith that is confessed with hope (10:22-23).

James

Although the Epistle of James does not employ the words for baptism, it appears to make definite allusions to the act and its meaning.[7] "The good name which was called upon [or, invoked over] you" (Jas. 2:7) was the name of Jesus invoked in baptism. In the Old Testament the calling of God's name upon his people (Deut. 28:10; Jer. 14:9 — same word and construction) meant they belonged to him; in the same way those baptized in the name of Jesus became his community.

James 1:18, "He gave birth [ἀπεκύσεν] to us by the word of truth," although not employing the usual vocabulary of new birth, seems a clear allusion to this doctrine associated with baptism (see the discussion of John 3:5 and 1 Pet. 1:23). The "word of

---

5. Lev. 14:6-8, 15-16, quoted in my chapter 4. The consecration of the high priest included washing with water and sprinkling with blood (Lev. 8:6, 30). Ezek. 36:25 in contrast mentions sprinkling with clean water.

6. Cf. 1 Pet. 1:2 for "sprinkled with Christ's blood."

7. Franz Mussner, "Die Tauflehre des Jakobusbriefes," in Hansjörg Auf Der Maur and Bruno Kleinheyer, eds., *Zeichen des Glaubens: Studien zu Taufe und Firmung: Balthasar Fischer zum 60. Geburtstag* (Freiburg: Herder, 1972), pp. 61-67, whom I follow in this section.

truth" might be the baptismal confession or baptismal formula but more likely is the Christian message (cf. Eph. 1:13, where the "word of truth" is "the gospel of your salvation"), which is here presented as the means (instrumental dative) of producing a new birth by which people become the firstfruits of God's creatures.

The word of truth in 1:18 would be the same as "the implanted word that has the power to save your souls" in 1:21. This implanted word is the spoken word of the gospel that must be internalized. It is a corollary of a person's removing (taking off) the old life of wickedness. In a broader sense it may be associated with the moral teaching of the letter, which corresponds to the baptismal instruction paralleled in other New Testament letters.

1 Peter 3:21

The whole or most of 1 Peter has been thought to reflect a liturgy, homily, or treatise dealing with baptism.[8] Baptismal imagery is often reflected in the book. We shall discuss only the one explicit reference to baptism and the terminology of one of the images.[9]

First Peter 3:18-22 contains several exegetical knots, the principal one of which does not affect the teaching on baptism and the other two of which affect the nuances of the declaration about baptism but not its main points. Jesus' preaching to the spirits in prison has been the subject of major studies.[10] It functions in the context as an encouragement to Christians to be ready to give a defense of the Christian hope to everyone who might make an inquiry of them, probably in a formal legal inquiry (3:15). Christ himself suffered in the flesh, and he preached to the disobedient spirits.

The author connects that subject with baptism and the Christian hope of the resurrection by making reference to the flood in the days of Noah:

> The longsuffering of God waited in the days of Noah, while the ark was being built, in which a few (that is, eight persons) were saved by water. Baptism, the antitype of this, now saves you, not the putting off of the filth of the flesh but the pledge to God of a good conscience through the resurrection of Jesus Christ. (1 Pet. 3:20-21)

---

8. G. R. Beasley-Murray, *Baptism in the New Testament* (Grand Rapids: Eerdmans, 1973 reprint of 1962), pp. 251-258, discusses the various proposals, their weaknesses and their justification.

9. Karl-Heinrich Ostmeyer, *Taufe und Typos: Elemente und Theologie der Tauftypologien in 1 Korinther 10 und 1 Petrus 3* (Tübingen: Mohr/Siebeck, 2000), pp. 162-198, 206, finds in the use of the crossing of the Red Sea and the flood the same baptismal theology in 1 Corinthians 10 and 1 Peter 3. Exegesis of 1 Pet. 3:20-21 on pp. 145-161.

10. Bo Reicke, *The Disobedient Spirits and Christian Baptism* (Copenhagen: E. Munksgaard, 1946; New York: AMS, 1984); William Joseph Dalton, *Christ's Proclamation to the Spirits* (Rome: Pontifical Biblical Institute, 1965); Per Lundberg, *La typologie baptismale dans l'ancienne église* (Uppsala: Lorentz, 1942), pp. 101-116, discusses 1 Pet. 3:19ff. for the connection of baptism with the theme of Christ's *descensus* into the underworld.

The conceptual problem that we think of Noah's family being saved from the water, not by it, the difficulties of the grammar, and in some cases a reluctance to give too much emphasis to water as the means of salvation have led to proposals of alternative translations. These difficulties are complicated by the problematic meaning of two of the words. The difficulties are interrelated, but I shall deal with each separately, although that involves a certain repetitiveness.

As to the conceptual problem, the biblical perspective may be that the salvation was not from the water but from the wickedness that pervaded the earth in Noah's day,[11] and the water was the means for this deliverance.[12] Such an understanding would bring the reference into line with the comparison to Christian baptism. On the other hand, there is an attractive alternative translation of verse 20 that satisfies our natural expectations: "Into which ark a few (that is, eight persons)[13] were safely delivered through the water." This rendering gives full significance to the verb plus the preposition διά (with the meaning "through" rather than "by means of").[14] This proposal might seem to make the ark the means of salvation, but that understanding founders on the next verse, where the neuter relative pronoun ὅ would seem to refer to "water" and in any event cannot refer to "ark," which is feminine.

A way around the difficulty is to take the neuter pronoun of verse 21 as referring not to the water but to the whole preceding clause, that is, to the salvation of Noah's family or the passage through the water, which then becomes the symbol of baptism. To make this clear, it has been suggested that the ὅ be amended to ᾧ, "in which."[15]

If with some manuscripts the pronoun is omitted, the grammar is simplified, and verse 21 stands alone. I have preferred to follow the majority of manuscripts, retaining the neuter pronoun, and to take as its antecedent the preceding word, the neuter noun "water." This is surely simpler and the more obvious relationship of the words.

Moreover, I would construe the pronoun ὅ, referring to water, with "antitype," understood as a noun, and refer both to baptism. To give a more literal rendering than that above, "[W]ater, which antitype [the antitype of which], baptism, now saves also you," or "[W]ater, which in its antitype, baptism, now saves also you." The

---

11. Gen. 6:5, 11-13; 2 Pet. 2:5; cf. Acts 2:40.

12. Ostmeyer, *Taufe und Typos*, pp. 148-151, on the meaning of water (in general, water of life, new creation, and new birth) in 1 Peter.

13. The number "eight" was to have a great symbolic reference later in reference to baptism as related to salvation, the heavenly realm, and the afterlife, and it may be specified here because of already having such associations.

14. David Cook, "I Peter iii.20: An Unnecessary Problem," *Journal of Theological Studies*, n.s. 31 (1980): 72-78. Of the other passages cited from 1 Peter (2:8; 3:4; 4:4) for the resumption of a complex antecedent by a relative pronoun, only 2:8 really fits; and the Septuagint passages for "escape into" are not truly parallel to 1 Pet. 3:21, where the emphasis on escaping is not on getting into the ark but on deliverance with reference to the water.

15. Beasley-Murray, *Baptism in the New Testament*, p. 260, accepts this proposal from F. J. A. Hort. Reicke, *The Disobedient Spirits and Christian Baptism*, pp. 143-172, among others, also accepts the reference to the preceding action and not the water, but without resorting to the emendation.

former makes clearer that baptism saves, the latter puts more emphasis on the water in baptism as saving, but both renderings convey the idea that grammatically baptism, not the water of the flood, "saves you."[16]

"Antitype" is one of the two problematic words in verse 21.[17] "Antitype" may mean in general what corresponds to something else, or in particular a copy of the real (Heb. 9:24). The meaning of a pattern of which something else is a type or copy is rarer and mainly patristic. More important than the distinction between what is real and what is a copy is the distinction that in most occurrences the type precedes the antitype.[18] The meaning of "copy" is what leads many to see the water of the flood as the "antitype." Although the sense of the word order in 1 Peter 3:21 is difficult on any reading, it becomes quite difficult if the water is the antitype. Construing baptism with "antitype," on the other hand, has led to taking the meaning here in the unlikely sense of "pattern."[19] It is better to take baptism as the antitype all right, but the general meaning of "corresponding to" will cover the usage, and the fact that baptism is subsequent to the flood to which it corresponds sufficiently accounts for the choice of the word. The correspondence is that as the waters saved Noah's company, "baptism saves you." Hence, in Christian interpretation baptism became the fulfillment of that for which the water of the flood served as a type, but this was a theological meaning of the relationship not in the word "antitype" itself. Baptism is placed at the end of the clause in Greek in order to prepare for the subsequent clause describing the nature of baptism.

Whatever the correct explanation of the philological and grammatical difficulties in the passage, the point of the comparison is salvation in God's judgment. The salvation or deliverance through the water of baptism, comparable to that of Noah's flood, is from "the futile ways inherited from your ancestors" (1:18) and from "sins" (2:24). It has to do with "souls" (1:9) and so is ultimately eschatological (1:5; 2:2). Thus the author of 1 Peter distinguishes the baptism that "saves" souls from ordinary baths and ceremonial washings that "take off dirt from the flesh" (3:21), either physical dirt or ritual impurity or both.[20] This negative statement about what Christian

---

16. The latter is the view of Reicke, *Disobedient Spirits*, pp. 145-146, as part of his argument that the appositional antecedent (baptism) to the previous sentence was drawn into the relative clause. He translates, "Which 'antitypical' baptism [i.e., Noah's] now saves you." That result hardly commends the interpretation (so in stronger terms Beasley-Murray, *Baptism in the New Testament*, p. 260).

17. Ostmeyer, *Taufe und Typos*, examines the word on pp. 25-36, 39-49, and in 1 Pet. 3:20-21 on pp. 145-148.

18. The original meaning, which continued, was that τύπος is the blow and ἀντίτυπος is the resistant object, as in hammer and anvil, stamp and die, or blow and counterblow.

19. E. G. Selwyn, *The First Epistle of St. Peter* (London: Macmillan, 1946), pp. 203-205, following the logic of the word order, takes the "you" as the antitype of the eight who were saved: "And water now saves you too, who are the antitype of Noah and his company, namely the water of baptism." (So too does Ostmeyer, *Taufe und Typos*, p. 148.) On this rendering the neuter relative pronoun refers to the water. One could also construe it with "antitype," and render literally, "Which antitype, even you [corresponding to the eight saved through water], baptism now saves." Seeing the correspondence in the persons instead of the events is unlikely.

20. "Take off" or "put off" occurs also in 2:1 for putting off all evil.

baptism is not is balanced by a positive statement of its inner, spiritual significance as related to a "good conscience."

The other difficult word in 1 Peter 3:20-21 is what I have translated "pledge." The noun's basic meaning is "question," from which comes the meaning "request" and so the usual translation of "appeal to God for a good conscience." However, the word could be used for the "answer" to an inquiry. Accordingly, many prefer the translation "a pledge to God."[21] The papyri contain instances where the word is the equivalent of the Latin *stipulatio*, the demand (in question form) made by a prospective creditor of a debtor and then the contract resulting from a positive response.

Since the *stipulatio* was put forward by the creditor, it is argued that the reference here is to the divine promise received in baptism and not a vow made by the candidate.[22] This would accord with the general thrust of the passage emphasizing what God does in bringing salvation. On the other hand, with the phrase "not putting away the dirt of the flesh," there is a shift to the human response, which would seem to be carried forward in the next phrase. A decisive consideration is the prepositional phrase "toward God," placed with the word for "pledge" (or "appeal") and not with "good conscience." Whatever is indicated by the word under consideration, it is directed toward God, not received from him. Hence, I would opt for the secondary meaning of a *stipulatio*, the contract or pledge made in response to what is required. If this legal background is behind the usage in 1 Peter 3:21, then the translation "pledge" (or something comparable, such as "agreement" or "undertaking to be loyal") is established. The "good conscience" could be a subjective genitive, "from a good conscience," or an objective genitive, "for a good conscience." The translation "appeal" would permit either (but more naturally suggests an objective genitive), but the translation "pledge" (although possible with an objective genitive) would more naturally go with a subjective genitive. "Good conscience" (also in 3:16; cf. 2:19) carries the idea of a "good will," a "disposition," or a mental attitude of loyalty to God.[23] If we think of the "pledge" as a "contract," then "good conscience" might be the equivalent of "in good faith." On the interpretation adopted here, baptism is a pledge of loyalty to God; it proceeds from a motive of inner purity and is not an act of external cleansing.[24]

Peter further identifies the saving power of baptism to come "through the resurrection of Jesus Christ." The resurrection is important for the theme of hope in 1 Peter (1:3, 13, 21; 3:15). Baptism is set in the context of Christ's death for sins (3:18) and resurrection to heavenly authority (3:22). The subjection of all spiritual powers

---

21. E.g., Reicke, *Disobedient Spirits*, pp. 182-186; Selwyn, *The First Epistle of St. Peter*, pp. 205-206; Joseph Crehan, *Early Christian Baptism and the Creed* (London: Burns, Oates & Washbourne, 1950), pp. 10-12, 98-99, who takes ἐπερώτημα = *stipulatio* = pledge (as explained below).

22. Arnold Ehrhardt, "Christian Baptism and Roman Law," in *The Framework of the New Testament Stories* (Manchester: Manchester University Press, 1964), pp. 234-255.

23. Reicke, *Disobedient Spirits*, pp. 174-182.

24. Heb. 9:13-14 also contrasts Jewish purification with a purifying of the conscience by the blood of Christ.

to Christ (3:22) assures the readers that they have nothing to fear from the spiritual powers (3:18).

The phrase "through the resurrection of Jesus Christ" connects the passage on baptism with a word that became important in later baptismal theology, "to be begotten again" (ἀναγεννάω — appearing in the New Testament only in 1 Pet. 1:3 and 23). "God . . . begat us again [gave us a new birth] to a living hope through the resurrection of Jesus Christ" (1:3). Both the new begetting or new birth and the salvation in baptism are effected, according to Peter, by the resurrection of Jesus from the dead.

This begetting again came about also "through" the word of God, that is, the preaching of the crucified and resurrected Jesus. Unlike the first, physical begetting, this one came "not from corruptible seed but from incorruptible seed, through the living and abiding word of God" (1:23). That abiding word was the "good news preached to you" (1:25). That message was received in faith (1:5, 7, 9, 21), a faith that produced obedience, for purification of souls was effected not only by the blood of Jesus (1:18-19, "ransomed") but also "by obedience to the truth" (1:22; cf. 1:2). Those so purified, saved, and begotten again were as obedient children to live a holy life that accorded with their new spiritual birth (1:14-16, 22; 2:1-3; 4:2).

In this larger context of 1 Peter the reader is to understand the strong affirmation of the place of baptism in salvation declared in 3:21.

1 John

The first letter of John contains a probable reference to the baptism of Jesus and a possible allusion to part of the Christian baptismal ceremony. The reference to Jesus' baptism occurs in the following passage:

> Who is the person who overcomes the world except the one who believes that Jesus is the Son of God. This is he who came through water and blood, Jesus Christ, not with the water only but with the water and with the blood. The Spirit is the One who testifies, because the Spirit is the truth. There are three who testify: the Spirit, the water, and the blood, and the three are in agreement. (1 John 5:5-8)

The author of 1 John was opposing a teaching that denied or minimized the human nature of Christ (2:22-23; 4:2-3; cf. 2 John 7). Hence, I have begun the quotation with the affirmation that the "one who overcomes" is the one who believes that Jesus, the human person, is the Son of God. The reality of the incarnation that the Gospel of John had declared (John 1:14) is, therefore, the context in which this passage is to be understood.

Probably the majority of interpreters interpret the coming (aorist, so a singular coming) of Jesus with the water as his baptism. Some go further and see in this statement, and especially in the next statement about the water testifying (present tense, a continuing witness), a reference to the continuing practice of Christian baptism.[25] Some bring forward as support for a sacramental reading of this text the statement in John 19:34 that blood and water came out of the wounded side of Jesus, indicating that the sacraments of eucharist and baptism had their origin in the death of Christ. The theological affirmation may be true, but in both the Gospel and Letter of John the emphasis is surely on the real and complete human nature of Jesus, who is also the divine Christ and Son of God.

The erroneous teaching being opposed is perhaps that of Cerinthus, a contemporary of the writing of 1 John, or a similar teaching. Cerinthus's view, as reported by Irenaeus, was that the divine Christ came on the man Jesus after his baptism in the form of a dove and then departed from him before his crucifixion.[26] To a view that associated the divine Christ with baptism but separated him from the death on the cross, the author of 1 John is emphasizing that the same one who came with water came also with blood, referring to the reality of the human death. The blood of Jesus had special significance for the author (1:7; cf. 2:2).

An important alternative interpretation of the error being opposed is that those who had withdrawn from the Johannine community (2:19) accepted the incarnation but identified it as occurring with the baptism of Jesus. The author in opposing them does not refer to Jesus' baptism but by "water and blood" refers to the "blood and water" that came from Jesus' side (John 19:34) as both testifying to the reality of his death (cf. 19:30 for Jesus' giving up his Spirit), a death that had salvific significance. The Spirit gave his testimony through the Beloved Disciple (John 19:35) and is symbolized by water (John 7:38-39). If there is a reference to baptism and eucharist in the passage, it comes only in verse 8.[27] The change in order of blood and water will be variously assessed as to its significance. I have preferred the interpretation that applies water and blood separately to Jesus' baptism and death because of their external historical confirmation of a teaching that distinguishes their place in the scheme of redemption,[28]

---

25. T. W. Manson, "Entry into Membership of the Early Church," *Journal of Theological Studies* 48 (1947): 25-32 suggested that the order Spirit, water, and blood in verse 8 referred to the Syrian initiation ceremony of anointing, baptism, and eucharist. The proposal is more ingenious than compelling as an exegesis of this passage. Many others, without being so specific, have seen an allusion to the sacraments in John's statements.

26. *Against Heresies* 1.26.1. That John and Cerinthus were contemporaries, ibid. 3.3.4.

27. Raymond E. Brown, *The Epistles of John* (Garden City: Doubleday, 1982), pp. 572-585, 594-599. Brown (pp. 575-578) discusses the principal interpretations of "water and blood": sacraments of baptism and eucharist, the incarnation (birth of Jesus), baptism and death of Jesus (which I have preferred), and the death of Jesus (Brown's preference).

28. I grant that the correspondence of the view of Cerinthus with that implied in 1 John is not exact, but the existence of the views that deity came on Jesus at his baptism and that the divine Christ did not suffer but ascended without being crucified has other confirmation (Ptolemy, according to Irenaeus, *Against Heresies* 1.7.2; others unidentified in 1.30.13; for the latter view, Basilides, according to 1.24.4). I affirm only that a comparable teaching is in view in 1 John; of course Brown could say the same, except that there is no independent confirmation for the existence of exactly the view about Jesus' baptism that he attributes to the opponents.

whereas the alternative view connecting both water and blood with the death depends on an exegesis solely within the context of the Gospel and Letters of John.

The testimony of the Spirit confirms the witness of the water and the blood. The reference may be to the coming of the Spirit on Jesus after his baptism, or in the context of 1 John to his continuing presence in the apostolic preaching about Jesus Christ (2:20-24, 27; 4:2, 6). The united testimony of Spirit, water, and blood is to the apostolic teaching about the revelation of Jesus Christ, Son of the Father (1:1-4).

The testimony of the Spirit connects with 1 John 2:20, "You indeed have an anointing [χρῖσμα] from the Holy One, and you all know," and 2:27, "As for you, the anointing that you received from him abides in you, and so you have no need for anyone to teach you, but as his anointing teaches you about all things and is true and not a lie, just as it taught you, abide in it [or him]." Although some understand the "anointing" to be literal,[29] it is better to take it as a metaphorical reference to the Holy Spirit, referring to the effect of receiving of the Spirit, which in the verb form is described as an anointing (χρίω).[30] This explanation is to be preferred because the anointing is said to teach (2:27), and a result of it is for one to know (2:20). What is said in 1 John about the anointing is said in the Gospel of John (esp. 14:17, 26) about the Holy Spirit. Moreover, there is a parallel statement about abiding in 2:24, "As for you, abide in what you heard from the beginning." The anointing is closely connected with the message heard from the beginning (cf. 1:1, 5; 2:7; 3:11). The Spirit and the word belong together. The Spirit in 1 John functions primarily as source of apostolic teaching (cf. 4:1-6). "All" Christians (2:20) "received" (aorist, a single event — 2:27) an anointing with the Spirit in connection with their acceptance of the word about Jesus (probably at their baptism, but this is not said).

Another possible allusion to baptism occurs in 1 John 2:12, where forgiveness of sins is said to occur "on account of his name."

Without specific baptismal reference, 1 John picks up the usage of spiritual begetting or birth (γεννάω) from the Gospel of John. Since this is uniformly said to be "from" (ἐκ) God, the emphasis is on the divine begetting.[31] It is associated with believing (1 John 5:1), loving (4:7; 5:1), not sinning (3:9; 5:18), overcoming the world (5:4), and doing righteousness (2:9) — baptismal motifs.

---

29. See the discussion of different interpreters and various questions related to this passage in Brown, *The Epistles of John*, pp. 341-349, 359-361, 369-370, 374-376. Brown identifies the anointing with the Holy Spirit yet sees it as more likely physical than figurative (pp. 348, 369), but the arguments that he canvases seem to me to favor the figurative interpretation. Beasley-Murray, *Baptism in the New Testament*, pp. 233-236, argues from the parallel between 2:24 and 27 that "the chrism is the truth of the Gospel" (p. 235).

30. 2 Cor. 1:21; usually with reference to Jesus as the Christ — Luke 4:18; Acts 4:27; 10:38; Heb. 1:9. A noun ending in -μα ordinarily has a passive meaning, a thing (in this case "ointment"), rather than an active meaning, an action; but χρῖσμα was often used of the act of anointing. In this passage I think we may keep the passive sense of "a thing," but not as the unction or oil but as the effect of the action of anointing, a meaning -μα nouns may have.

31. 1 John 2:29; 3:9 (twice); 4:7; 5:1 (thrice); 5:4; 5:18 (twice).

Revelation

Revelation contains no passage on baptism, but many interpreters have seen in the language about writing the divine name on the forehead of Christians and their being sealed on their foreheads a reference to a component of the baptismal ceremony.[32] Some tracing (perhaps with oil) of a mark representing the divine name (Ezek. 9:4, probably the Hebrew letter *taw*) on the forehead of the baptizand marked that person as belonging to the Lord. The seal was a mark of ownership. This practice was part of the baptismal liturgy later and would account for the frequent use of "seal" to mean baptism in early second-century authors. The language in Revelation, however, could be figurative and later have been given literal application in keeping with the tendency of the liturgy to include visible symbolic acts to express the spiritual meaning of baptism.

Revelation has a possible usage of βάπτω ("dip") with variant readings for "sprinkle." Revelation 19:13 describes the messianic King of kings and Lord of lords as "clothed with a garment dipped [βεβαμμένον] in blood, and his name is called 'the Word of God.'" Other readings give different forms of the root verb for "sprinkle": ἐρραμμένον or ῥεραμμένον (alternative spellings of the perfect passive participle of ῥαίνω, "having been sprinkled"), ἐρραντισμένον or ῥεραντισμένον (alternative spellings of the perfect passive participle of ῥαντίζω, "having been sprinkled"), and περιρεραμμένον or περιρεραντισμένον (perfect passive participles of περιρραίνω and περιρραντίζω respectively, "having been besprinkled").[33] "Dipped" has better manuscript support, but "sprinkled" (in the second pair listed) has the earliest patristic attestation.[34] Use of Genesis 49:11 would favor "dipped," but Isaiah 63:3 would favor "sprinkle." Either verse could have influenced a scribal change. The prevalent association of "blood" with sprinkling in the Old and New Testaments may have suggested that reading. Although "sprinkle" has good support and is a reading that originated early, the variety of forms in which this reading is attested suggests to me independent accommodations (either to the text of Isaiah or to the idea of sprinkling blood) rather than variations on a common original reading.

Summary of New Testament Information on Baptism

The discussion by three scholars of baptism in the New Testament may serve to summarize its doctrinal meaning in the New Testament as a whole.

The earliest of these, working primarily with Paul and post-Pauline authors (he includes Hebrews and 1 Peter as influenced by Paul or developing his ideas), finds in

---

32. Rev. 3:2; 7:3; 14:1; 22:4. Charles A. Gieschen, "The Divine Name in Ante-Nicene Christology," *Vigiliae Christianae* 57 (2003): 132-134.

33. Carroll Osburn, "Alexander Campbell and the Text of Revelation 19:13," *Restoration Quarterly* 25 (1982): 129-138. Osburn argues for ἐρραντισμένον as the original reading with the meaning "splattered."

34. Beginning with Irenaeus, *Against Heresies* 4.20.11.

these authors the elements of a New Testament doctrine of baptism:[35] (1) Baptism is adult baptism, initiatory and unrepeatable. (2) It is connected to the eschatological baptism of John but has its specific character from the saving work of Christ. (3) It sets one in the eschatological community of salvation. (4) It effects salvation, forgiveness of sins, freedom from the rule of sin and death, purification, and washing; it gives the Holy Spirit and a part in the death and resurrection of Christ; it names Christ and is a rebirth. (5) It has an instrumental character. (6) It is a sacrament (not magical); faith cannot replace it, and it is not a confirmation of what occurs already by faith. (7) It is closely bound with paraenesis of daily life. (8) Infant baptism depends on theology.

Another begins by noting the association of baptism with the objective grace of God.[36] Many statements in the New Testament speak of what God does in baptism; it is the gracious action of God. Baptism, moreover, is often associated with faith, as an expression of one's belief in Christ. *"God's gracious giving to faith belongs to the context of baptism, even as God's gracious giving in baptism is to faith."*[37] Baptism, moreover, is related to the activity of the Holy Spirit. Baptism is the occasion when the Spirit brings new life, and baptism conveys the Spirit; but his work is not necessarily tied to baptism. Baptism introduces one into the church; one is in the church because of being in Christ. Baptism as a moral and religious act is closely connected with ethics. Most of the passages about baptism in the epistles are in the context of exhortations about Christian living. Paul's paraenesis is simply a repetition of what happened in baptism. Baptism also means hope; there is an eschatological reference in baptism. Baptism derives its importance from being an embodiment of the gospel of Christ's death for sin and resurrection to glory.

A more recent writer identified certain motifs of baptism that belonged to the viewpoint of the earliest disciples of Jesus, most derived from John's baptism but then Christianized, motifs that in different formulations remained notably constant throughout all layers of the New Testament.[38] These include an eschatological perspective, confession of the present lordship of the resurrected Jesus, a preaching of the gospel about Christ, the call to conversion (repentance) and faith, the offer of the forgiveness of sins, the entrance into the people of God, and the possession of the Holy Spirit. The similarity of these compilations, the first two from a more theological standpoint and the third from a more historical approach, is notable, a similarity resulting from a careful exegetical approach by the writers.

Not much detail is given in the New Testament concerning the administration of baptism. Some descriptions and imagery imply, if not require, an immersion, and

---

35. Otto Kuss, "Zum paulinischen und nachpaulinischen Tauflehre im Neuen Testament," *Theologie und Glaube* 42 (1952): 401-425 (pp. 424-425).

36. Beasley-Murray, *Baptism in the New Testament*, pp. 263-305.

37. Beasley-Murray, *Baptism in the New Testament*, p. 273 (italics his).

38. Lars Hartman, *'Into the Name of the Lord Jesus': Baptism in the New Testament* (Edinburgh: T&T Clark, 1997), pp. 50, 79-81, 99-102, 142-145. For Christian baptism as a "Christianised Johannine baptism" — p. 35.

nothing is inconsistent with immersion. The only act in addition to the water rite for which there is a definite reference is the laying on of hands, and that is mentioned only in exceptional cases. An anointing may be implied in some references, but these can all be accounted for as figurative descriptions of the gift of the Holy Spirit, even as Jesus' reception of the Spirit was described as an anointing. As suggested in the preceding paragraphs on theology, baptism was closely wrapped up with a human response of repentance and a confessed faith to the preaching of God's redemptive work in Christ. A reference to Christ (as part of or in addition to mention of the Father, Son, and Holy Spirit) was made, often in the form of a verbal confession by the candidate. Hence, no example of infant baptism occurs.

There is an impressive array of blessings attached to baptism,[39] centering in the ideas of forgiveness of sins and new life from the gift of the Holy Spirit. The New Testament texts provide the ideas that were foundational for the later developments of the theology of baptism.

---

39. See the list in Beasley-Murray, *Baptism in the New Testament*, p. 264.

PART THREE

The Second Century

12. Apostolic Fathers

For this unit on the second century we follow traditional groupings of the documents.[1] The so-called Apostolic Fathers brings together a disparate group of writings that belong to the earliest noncanonical works not regarded as heretical by the mainstream of the church.

Didache

The date and unity of the *Didache* ("The Teaching of the Lord through the Twelve Apostles to the Nations") are much controverted, and its chapter on baptism is intimately connected with these issues.[2] The Jewish affinities of the account agree with an early date,[3] perhaps end of the first century or beginning of the second, but the existing form of the text is suspect of interpolation.

---

1. For the period in general see Jack P. Lewis, "Baptismal Practices of the Second- and Third-Century Church," *Restoration Quarterly* 26 (1983): 1-17.

2. For studies of baptism in the *Didache*, note André Benoît, *Le baptême chrétien au second siècle* (Paris: Presses Universitaires de France, 1953), pp. 5-33; Willy Rordorf, "Le baptême selon la *Didachè*," in J. von Allmen et al., eds., *Mélanges liturgiques offerts au R. P. Dom Bernard Botte O.S.B. de l'Abbaye du Mont César* (Louvain, 1972), pp. 499-509; reprint in *Liturgie, foi et vie des premiers chrétiens: Études patristiques* (Paris: Beauchesne, 1986), pp. 175-185; English translation in Jonathan A. Draper, ed., *The Didache in Modern Research* (Leiden: Brill, 1996), pp. 212-222; Nathan Mitchell, "Baptism in the *Didache*," in Clayton N. Jefford, ed., *The Didache in Context: Essays on Its Text, History, and Transmission* (Leiden: Brill, 1995), pp. 226-255; Huub van de Sandt and David Flusser, *The Didache: Its Jewish Sources and Its Place in Early Judaism and Christianity* (Minneapolis: Fortress, 2002), pp. 273-291; Aaron Milavec, *The Didache: Faith, Hope, & Life of the Earliest Christian Communities, 50-70 C.E.* (New York: Newman, 2003), pp. 253-284 (text and translation of the whole, pp. 12-45).

3. Explored extensively in van de Sandt and Flusser, *The Didache*. Milavec, *The Didache*, places the document 50-70 but without a specifice section devoted to the date.

Chapter 7 offers the earliest surviving description of the administration of baptism, but does not say much about the meaning of the act.

(7.1) Concerning baptism [βαπτίσματος], baptize [βαπτίσατε] in this way: after speaking all these words, baptize [βαπτίσατε] into the name of the Father, the Son, and the Holy Spirit in living water. (2) If you do not have living water, baptize [βάπτισον] in other water; if you are not able in cold water, in warm. (3) If you do not have either, pour [ἔκχεον] water on the head three times into the name of the Father, Son, and Holy Spirit. (4) Before the baptism [βαπτίσματος], the one baptizing [βαπτίζων], the one being baptized [βαπτιζόμενος], and others if they are able are to observe a preliminary fast. Command the one being baptized [βαπτιξόμενον] to fast beforehand for one or two days.

The baptism followed a period of instruction in the "Two Ways" of life and death detailed in chapters 1–6, which was basically Jewish moral teaching supplemented by its interpretation in the sayings of Jesus.[4] Baptism carried with it a commitment to a certain manner of life. The event was prepared for by a brief time of fasting,[5] an expression of remorse and repentance. The baptism is clearly an administered rite with some witnesses present. Nothing is said about who the administrator was to be. Elsewhere the *Didache* refers to apostles (missionaries?), prophets, teachers, bishops, and deacons as leaders of the community, and one of these might have presided at the baptism.[6] The prayer for the "ointment" that is found in the Coptic version of the *Didache* 10.3-12.2 was not for oil in a baptismal anointing.[7]

---

4. Willy Rordorf, "Un chapitre d'éthique Judéo-chrétienne: Les Deux voies," *Recherches de sciences religieuses* 60 (1972): 109-128; reprint in *Liturgie, foi et vie*, pp. 155-174; English translation in Draper, *The Didache in Modern Research*, pp. 148-164; the "Two Ways" is discussed more fully in van de Sandt and Fluser, *The Didache*, pp. 55-270, and Milavec, *The Didache*, pp. 53-227.

5. Jonathan A. Draper, "Ritual Process and Ritual Symbol in *Didache* 7-10," *Vigiliae Christianae* 54 (2000): 121-158, interprets this section of the *Didache* in terms of ritual theory as an aggregation rite within the whole initiation process that included instruction, fasting, baptism, prayer, and eucharist (pp. 127-128); cf. Milavec, *The Didache*, pp. 253-258, on fasting and p. 270 on the ritual sequence.

6. Clayton N. Jefford, "Presbyters in the Community of the *Didache*," *Studia Patristica* 21 (1989): 122-128, suggests that the instructions in the *Didache* are addressed to presbyters. This seems unlikely, since presbyters are not mentioned, and the tenor of the document is instructions to the community. Milavec, *The Didache*, argues that the mentor, who has been responsible for the training of the candidate, administered the baptism (e.g., pp. 76, 268, 275).

7. Text, translation, and commentary of this Coptic papyrus by F. Stanley Jones and Paul A. Mirecki, "Considerations on the Coptic Papyrus of the *Didache* (British Library Oriental Manuscript 9271)," in Jefford, *The Didache in Context*, pp. 47-87. Stephen Gero, "The So-Called Ointment Prayer in the Coptic Version of the Didache: A Re-Evaluation," *Harvard Theological Review* 70 (1977): 67-84, understands the reference to be to incense, not ointment. Joseph Ysebaert, "The So-Called Coptic Ointment Prayer of Didache 10,8 Once More," *Vigiliae Christianae* 56 (2002): 1-10, points out that the Coptic word means "good smell" and so the prayer is a thanksgiving for the aroma of Christians to God because of Jesus. Milavec, *The Didache*, pp. 264-266, concurs that there was no baptismal anointing practiced in the community of the *Didache*. A. H. B. Logan, "Post-Baptismal Chrismation in Syria: The Evidence of Ignatius, the *Didache*, and the *Apostolic Constitutions*," *Journal of Theological Studies*,

The baptism was administered with a formula identical to the words of Matthew 28:19. There is another reference to baptism in the *Didache:* "No one is to eat or drink of your eucharist except those who have been baptized [βαπτισθέντες] into the name of the Lord" (9.5). The longer Trinitarian statement was spoken at the baptism, apparently by the administrator; the shorter expression is a summary statement of the character of the baptism, that is, Christian baptism.[8] As discussed in chapters 8 and 10, the words "into the name of" carried the idea of something done with reference to or out of regard for an object, especially as an act of worship toward deity. Although the presence of faith in the convert is not explicit, it is is implied in the submission to instruction and the reference to the divine names.[9]

Particular importance attached to the words spoken, for even if pouring was substituted for immersion, the threefold divine name was pronounced (only now without the definite article before each as is the case in the first statement). The triple pouring mentioned with the three names might imply a similar triple immersion, once for each of the names. This, however, is not stated and may not be implied.[10] The triple pouring may have been a compensation for the lack of sufficient water for an immersion and an effort to approximate the covering of the body with water as nearly as possible — three times and not another number perhaps suggested by the triple divine name. Nothing is said in the text of sprinkling. That a triple pouring is a reflex of triple immersion is likely if the section on pouring is a later interpolation (see below) after triple immersion was the norm, but if the section is original or early (even if an interpolation), then the sequence may be the reverse. If the pouring was done three times in order to douse the person in imitation of an immersion, then the development of a triple immersion may have been influenced by the triple action in the substitute procedure.

The later statement in 9.5 about sharing in the eucharist confirms what is implied by the presence of witnesses who share in the fast, namely that baptism was not only an adhesion to the Lord but also an admission to the community of his followers. Membership in the community of the Lord and a commitment to right conduct are the principal points of significance to baptism that can be deduced from what the *Didache* says.

The whole account in the *Didache* presupposes the baptism of persons of responsible age: those who received detailed instruction in the moral life, those who fasted, and those who joined in the communal eucharist (9–10). The earlier instructions to parents say nothing about their bringing their children for baptism (4.9),

---

n.s. 49 (1998): 92-108 (107), is among those who think the arguments for the genuineness of the prayer are more plausible.

8. Benoît, *Le baptême chrétien*, pp. 7-11. Milavec, *The Didache*, pp. 266-268, 270-272, contends that the Trinitarian statement too is a description of the rite and not a formula; the words spoken at the baptism were a recitation of the teaching in chapters 1–6.

9. Faith is also affirmed in *Didache* 16.2, 5.

10. Milavec, *The Didache*, p. 264, surmises that there was only one immersion, for thrice would have been stated if that was the practice, as it is mentioned in regard to the pouring.

and instructions for master and slaves indicate the latter were not required to follow the faith of their owners (4.10-11).[11]

Baptize has its normal meaning of "immerse."[12] This was to be done "in living (running or moving) water."[13] The valuation of different kinds of water is another indication of the Jewish environment of the *Didache*.[14] Running water was called "living" because it had motion.[15] Such water was the appropriate place for an act that imparted life (spiritual). "Living" or "life" is an important concept for the compiler of the work. Christians serve a living God (6.3) by walking in the way of life (1–4) and giving thanks for life and immortality (eternal life) made known through Jesus (9.3; 10.3).

If running water was not available, other water, that is, collected water, could be used. Apparently some question was raised in the community about the suitability of other kinds of water, and provision was made for accepting alternatives. Cold water was that gathered in a natural pond or lake;[16] warm water was stored in a man-

---

11. These and further considerations are urged by Milavec, *The Didache*, pp. 259-261, against the communities of the *Didache* baptizing infants.

12. "Baptism was normally a baptism by immersion; but if there was not a sufficient quantity of water to practice immersion, baptism *per infusionem* was also permitted" — Rordorf, "Baptism according to the Didache," p. 219. C. Bigg, "Notes on the Didache, I. On Baptism by Affusion," *Journal of Theological Studies* 5 (1904): 579-584, assembled the evidence that may be adduced for affusion (limited in extent and some of it even misinterpreted) along with some of the passages showing that baptism in the first five centuries was immersion.

13. Theodor Klauser, "Taufet in lebendigem Wasser! Zum religions- und kulturgeschichtlichen Verständnis von Didache 7,1-3," in Theodor Klauser and A. Rükker, eds., *Pisciculi: Studien zur Religion und Kultur des Altertums, F. J. Dölger zum 60. Geburtstage* (Münster: Aschendorff, 1974), pp. 157-164, collects references to the use of running water (p. 160), the original practice that gave the name *fons* to the baptismal font and prompted an effort to duplicate flowing water in baptisteries (pp. 162-63). His suggestion that in certain regions the baptism was performed by the person standing in water and water was poured over the head (more recent advocates of this practice in chap. 55) may have been an intermediate transition stage from *submersio* to *perfusio*, but the art work used in support of this view may have another interpretation (chap. 7). Oskar Skarsaune, *In the Shadow of the Temple: Jewish Influences on Early Christianity* (Downers Grove: InterVarsity Press, 2002), p. 365, n. 34, in discussing this passage and its Jewish affinities, would refine the definition of "living water" not so much as running water as water that "flows or has flown from a natural source" and "has come from this source through an unbroken stream" (including pipes as well as a river); drawn water is "water cut off from natural sources, as water in a bucket or rainwater in a pond when the rain has ceased." Renate Pillinger, "Die Taufe nach der Didache," *Wiener Studien*, n.s. 9 (1975): 152-162, similarly considers it doubtful that the *Didache* speaks of baptism in a spring or river; the water could be collected from such a source (pp. 152-55); hence a Christian cult room could be the location (p. 157 — that I consider doubtful at an early date).

14. Note the ranking of kinds of water in the Mishnah discussed in chap. 4, and for running water cf. Lev. 14:5, 6, 50, 51; Num. 5:17; 19:17 (LXX). The ranking of different kinds of water in the *Didache* does not correspond exactly to the Mishnah's list but reflects a similar concern, and in both "living water" is the best.

15. [Ps.] Plutarch, *Is Fire or Water More Useful?* 9 (= *Moralia* 957D).

16. Cf. Josephus, *Life* 11 (2), on the practice of Bannus bathing in cold water (cited in chap. 4). Cold water was probably thought to be closer to natural running water.

made place (as a cistern or a mikveh).[17] In the absence of a sufficient amount of water (whether from a flowing source or still) for covering the body,[18] water could be poured over the head, as representing the whole of the body, or since the person was likely standing, in order for it to run down over the rest of the body.[19] The apparently real possibility of a scarcity of water suggests a provenance such as rural western Syria.

Eduard Stommel, as part of his argument that baptism was a pouring while the candidate stood in the water, explains the passage as saying that the action of the baptizer was the same in each case (pouring water over the head), and the only difference was whether the candidate stood in running or still water or received the baptism while not standing in water.[20] However, "baptize" is expressed by one word and pouring by another, surely suggesting that a different action is indicated. The baptism, not where the candidate stood, was said to be "*in* living water," and this was not said of the kind of water poured on the head. The pouring was probably an effort to simulate running water. Why would the writer say, "pour water three times on the head," only after other options had been exhausted if that was what was to be done in any case? If the procedure had been as Stommel interpreted it, the natural way to word the passage would have been different. The same consideration applies to the interpretation that according to *Didache* 7.1-2 the whole body of the baptizand was to come in contact with the water, but if there was not sufficient water for that, then at least the head (7.3).[21] Why the change in verb from βαπτίσατε or βάπτισον to ἔκχεον if the same action was intended in both cases?

There is, moreover, a question as to when the statements of exceptions to the

---

17. Milavec, *The Didache*, p. 263, argues that the warm water was not artificially heated as for a sick person or for use in a cold climate, ideas foreign to the context.

18. Rordorf, "Baptism according to the Didache," p. 219, cites the Georgian version, "If, however, you do not have enough of either, then pour out some water three times over the head," which is a correct interpretive translation. Gregor Peradse, "Die 'Lehre der zwölf Apostel' in der georgischen Überlieferung," *Zeitschrift für die neutestamentliche Wissenschaft* 31 (1932): 111-116, reports on a manuscript copy from the nineteenth century of an earlier manuscript, the postscript of which says it was translated from the Greek by a person of a name known only from the fifth century. There are no great departures from the Greek text, which confirms it. The addition of "sufficient" in 7.3 is the only change from the Greek noted in the collation for chapter 7.

19. Van de Sandt and Flusser, *The Didache*, p. 283, cite *b. Berakah* 22a for the rabbis' permission when under constraint to pour nine portions of pure water for purification over a person who had a nocturnal pollution. Milavec, *The Didache*, p. 264, notes that the exception does not provide for a mere token quantity of water but the pouring of as much water as was available in order to obtain as complete a soaking as possible, a dousing (p. 262) instead of the usual dunking. He discounts the possibility suggested in my next sentence that the exception points to a place where water was necessarily scarce.

20. Eduard Stommel, "Christliche Taufriten und antike Badesitten," *Jahrbuch für Antike und Christentum* 2 (1959): 5-14 (*Didache* on p. 11). This interpretation imports into the text ideas that it does not contain. His arguments for pouring as the normal mode of baptism, and those of Klauser and Pillinger (note 13 above), will be further evaluated in chapter 55.

21. Renate Pillinger, "Die Taufe nach der Didache," p. 160, n. 35.

living water entered the text.[22] Since Jewish usage normally distinguished the actions of dipping, pouring, and sprinkling and the circumstances in which each was used (chap. 4), the allowance of pouring instead of immersion is an anomaly that can be accounted for, if not a later interpolation, only as a different method of covering the body with water or as a break with Jewish practice in accommodation to a Gentile setting. The change from the second person plural (7.1) to the second person singular (7.2-3) may mark an addition from another source or an addition by the compiler of the present form of the text; other such changes occur at seams that commentators see in the text of the *Didache*.[23] The fourth-century compiler of the *Apostolic Constitutions* used the *Didache* as the basis for his seventh book. The section on baptism (7.22) does not include the instructions on different kinds of water or on the possibility of pouring; he may have found them no longer relevant in a time of baptisteries, have objected to them, or perhaps not have found this section in his copy of the *Didache*. If the section with these alternatives was an interpolation, its date cannot be established. The only complete text is the Jerusalem manuscript 54 (Bryennios), dated 1056, and the Georgian version, possibly derived from the fifth century. The continued Jewish concern with the relative value of types of water indicates that the section, whether part of the redactional activity of the compiler of the *Didache* or a later insertion into his text, was still quite early, likely no later than the second century.

1 Clement

Baptism does not occur in the Greek text nor the Syriac and Coptic translations of *1 Clement*. However, the Latin version of 42.4, after the clause "(The apostles) preaching from region to region and city to city," adds the clause, "baptizing those who were obedient to the will of God" *(eos qui obaudiebant voluntati dei baptizantes)*. It is certainly more likely that such a clause would have been added

---

22. J. P. Audet, *La Didachè* (Paris, 1958), pp. 105-110, 365-367. That these concessions are redactional is supported by Kurt Niederwimmer, *The Didache: A Commentary* (Minneapolis: Fortress, 1998), pp. 125-130 (Niederwimmer, p. 128, n. 24, makes the mistake of identifying the art scenes as a pouring, when actually the hand of the administrator rests on the head of the baptizand); idem, "Der Didachist und seine Quellen," in Jefford, *The Didache in Context*, pp. 15-36 (29); Nathan Mitchell, "Baptism in the *Didache*," in the same, pp. 249-252. Redactional layers in the *Didache* are commonly accepted by scholars, but Aaron Milavec, "The Pastoral Genius of the Didache: An Analytical Translation and Commentary," in Jacob Neusner, et al., eds., *Religious Writings and Religious Systems*, Vol. 2: *Christianity* (Atlanta: Scholars, 1989), argues for the internal coherence and so one author for the document as a whole; now carried through comprehensively in his book *The Didache* (summarized, pp. 58-60).

23. Milavec, *The Didache*, pp. 244-246, argues that the change is not the sign of a clumsy interpolation but an intelligible change from instructions to the various mentors when several were immersed to instructions to a single administrator who did the actual pouring. However, this is not as plausible as he thinks, for a single individual did the immersing also.

than that it would have been omitted. On the other hand, an accidental omission cannot be ruled out. Since κηρύσσοντες ("preaching") and βαπτίζοντες ("baptizing") come at the end of their respective clauses and have the same last five letters, the eye of a copyist or translator could easily have skipped the intervening words and gone directly to the main clause, "they appointed their firstfruits." The reference to the apostles preaching and baptizing says nothing exceptional and would have been a traditional understanding by the time of the writing of 1 Clement.[24] The association of baptism with the will of God may reflect Luke 7:29-30.

There may be allusions to baptism elsewhere in the letter.[25] Noah (a preacher of repentance that brought salvation to those who obeyed[26] — 7.6 — and a preacher of regeneration of the world, παλιγγενεσία — 9.4), Jonah (who preached repentance that brought expiation of sins and salvation to the people of Nineveh — 7.7), and the Red Sea (with the destruction of Pharaoh and his army because of their hardness of heart — 51.5) provided Old Testament stories much exploited in connection with Christian baptism. So too was the theme of repentance, but in 1 Clement the call is to those already Christians to repent of their actions. The divine gifts of eternal life, righteousness, freedom, confidence, and holiness (35.1-2) that come from the light of knowledge in Jesus Christ, our salvation (36.1-2; 59.2), are motifs elsewhere associated with baptism. But we cannot affirm that the association was explicitly in the mind of Clement or of his readers.

2 Clement

Second Clement is a sermon of exhortation to repentance and moral living. By "doing the will of Christ we shall find rest" in the world to come (6.7). In that context there is the sermon's one use of the word "baptism": "With what confidence shall we enter into the royal house of God if we do not keep our baptism [βάπτισμα] pure and undefiled? Or who will be our advocate if we are not found to have holy and righteous works?" (6.9).[27]

The parallel wording in 8.6 identifies "seal" as a synonym for baptism in 2 Clement.[28] After quoting a word of the Lord "in the Gospel" similar to Luke 16:10-12, the

---

24. Matt. 28:19; Mark 16:16.
25. These are explored fully in Benoît, *Le baptême chrétien*, pp. 83-94.
26. Same association with obedience as in the Latin version of 42.4.
27. For baptism in 2 Clement see Benoît, *Le baptême chrétien*, pp. 95-114; Karl Paul Donfried, *The Setting of Second Clement in Early Christianity* (Leiden: Brill, 1974), pp. 124-128.
28. Σφραγίς is used in early Christian literature with the connotations of the result of preaching or faith, the mark of ownership (as a mark on a slave or beast), the protection God gives his property, the baptismal formula, Christ himself imprinted on the soul, the authentication of a document (and so God's confirmation) — according to Franz Dölger, Σφραγίς: *Studien zur Geschichte und Kultur des Altertums* V.3/4 (Paderborn, 1911), as summarized in Benoît, *Le baptême chrétien*, pp. 97ff. "Seal" was the most common designation of baptism in the second century and carried eschatological and juristic connotations according to Georg Kretschmar, *Die Geschichte des Taufgottesdienstes in der alter*

preacher explains: "He means this, keep your flesh pure and your seal [σφραγίδα] spotless in order that we may receive eternal life." The other use of "keep the seal" in 2 *Clement*, therefore, is also a reference to baptism: "For he says of those who did not keep the seal" that they will suffer eternal punishment (7.6). Depending on the date of 2 *Clement*, either this document or Hermas (below) offers the first application of "seal" (σφραγίς) to baptism. The word appears here as a technical term, meaning simply "baptism."

The further use in 2 *Clement* of "keep the flesh" as a receptacle of the Holy Spirit agrees with the baptismal use of "seal": "Keep the flesh in order that you may participate in the Spirit" (14.3). The author then identifies the flesh with the church and the Spirit with Christ (14.4). The participation in the Spirit may be spoken eschatologically,[29] for he then declares, "This flesh [literal or the church?] is so much able to participate in life and immortality, when the Holy Spirit is joined to it, and one is not able to express or say 'what things the Lord prepared for his elect'" (14.5). Nonetheless, the premise seems to be a present participation in the Spirit, for the "spiritual [preexistent] church" (14.1) is embodied in the present "living church" (14.2), its incarnation (as it were) as the "body of Christ" (14.3).[30] This language in 2 *Clement* about baptism, the seal, and the Spirit would agree with the New Testament usage of "being sealed" (in baptism) with the Holy Spirit.[31]

At a later time seal signified the separate rite that became confirmation, but that is not the usage in 2 *Clement* or Hermas. The progression of thought seems to be: (1) the seal referred to the Holy Spirit (in Paul); (2) since the Holy Spirit was given in baptism, seal was applied to baptism *(2 Clement);* (3) when the conferral of the Holy Spirit was associated with a separate postbaptismal act, seal was applied to it. The constant point of reference was the Holy Spirit.

In the context of exhortations to repentance, 2 *Clement* stresses the moral content of baptism. Thus Matthew 10:32 appears to be taken as referring to the confession of faith at baptism with the further call to continue confessing him by obeying his commands (3.1-4.1).[32]

The emphasis on repentance and keeping pure one's baptism, the seal, and the

---

Kirche, Leiturgia 5 (1964-66): 36-42. J. Ysebaert, *Greek Baptismal Terminology* (Nijmegen: Dekker & Van de Vegt, 1962), pp. 182-226, 245-253, 284-285, 390-426, studies the actions (touching, anointing, painting, tattooing, stamping, coining, and branding) associated with sealing in pagan antiquity and Judaism and its various applications in early Christianity, including for baptism.

29. So affirms Benoît, *Le baptême chrétien*, p. 105; cf. Donfried, *The Setting of 2 Clement*, pp. 126-128, 160-166.

30. Cf. 9.3 on the flesh as the temple of God. The present possession of the Spirit in the church would also be indicated if in the statement, "If any of us will keep her (church) in the flesh and not corrupt her, he will receive her in the Holy Spirit" (14.3), ἀπολήψεται has the force of "receive back" (and not just receive).

31. 2 Cor. 1:22; Eph. 1:13; 4:30.

32. Joseph Crehan, *Early Christian Baptism and the Creed* (London: Burns, Oates & Washbourne, 1950), p. 63, understands the quotation in 2 *Clement* as referring to the baptismal profession of faith.

flesh which received it shows the association of baptism with purification from sin, change of life, commitment to holy conduct, and receiving the Holy Spirit.

Ignatius

Ignatius's references to the baptism of Jesus were covered in chapter 6.[33] Ignatius, unlike the *Didache*, showed an interest in who performed baptism:

> It is not lawful apart from the bishop either to baptize [βαπτίζειν] or hold an agape. But whatever the bishop approves, this is pleasing to God, in order that everything you do may be safe and reliable. (*Smyrnaeans* 8.2)

Just before this statement Ignatius had said that nothing pertaining to the church was to be done apart from the bishop, and "Let that be considered a reliable eucharist which is done by the bishop or by whomever he permits" (*Smyrnaeans* 8.1). The word I have rendered "reliable" means something secure, firm, or steadfast. It could be translated "valid," except that such a translation suggests later ideas of sacramental validity that do not seem to be Ignatius's concern. The requirement that the baptism be performed by the bishop (or by someone whom he approved) is not motivated by concern for the "validity" of the act (as depending on the person performing it) but by concerns for unity and good order. Ignatius opposed assemblies not under the supervision of the bishop as providing opportunities for false teachings and as divisive.[34] In that situation he wanted all activities of the church to be under the supervision of the bishop, whether performed by him or not.

In Ignatius's letter *To the Ephesians*, he refers to the anointing received by Jesus (17.1, his wording perhaps indicating that anointing was important to his opponents), Jesus' baptism (18.2, quoted in chapter 6), and the eucharist (20.2, "breaking one bread"). There may be a liturgical significance to this sequence, for we shall see that Syriac sources gave prominence to a prebaptismal anointing.

In contrast to *2 Clement*'s exhortation to keep one's baptism pure, Ignatius saw baptism as part of the armor protecting Christians. With a similar moral concern, but now continuing his special interest in church unity (*Polycarp* 6.1), Ignatius used military imagery[35] in exhorting church members at Smyrna through their bishop Polycarp to faithfulness:

> Be pleasing to him in whose army you serve and from whom you receive your rations. May no one of you be found a deserter. Let your baptism remain as your

---

33. For his baptismal thought, see André Benoît, *Le baptême chrétien*, pp. 59-82.
34. *Ephesians* 5.2-3; 20.2; *Magnesians* 4; 6.1-7.2; *Trallians* 2.2-3.1; 7.2; *Philadelphians* 2.1; 4; 8.1; *Smyrnaeans* 6.2-7.2. For commentary on the whole passage, William R. Schoedel, *Ignatius of Antioch*, Hermeneia (Philadelphia: Fortress, 1985), pp. 238-244.
35. For the imagery but not its specific applications, cf. Eph. 6:10-17.

arms, your faith as your helmet, your love as your spear, your endurance as your armor. (*Polycarp* 6.2)

This indicates a realistic conception of the benefit imparted by baptism, comparable to Ignatius's realistic view of the blessings associated with the eucharist.[36] Baptism is related to the Christian qualities of faith, love, and endurance (the equivalent of hope).[37]

Taking these passages along with those referring to the baptism of Jesus, we may find in Ignatius's baptismal theology an interest in its purifying effect resulting from the righteous obedience of Jesus and his consequent passion, its connection with the church and the church's unity, and its continuing application to a faithful Christian life.

Epistle of Barnabas

The name Barnabas does not occur in the text but as a subscript to the *Epistle of Barnabas*. The work may be anonymous and wrongly ascribed in the manuscript tradition to Barnabas, a pseudonymous work (if the subscript is original), or a work by a Barnabas different from the New Testament companion of Paul (their identity is asserted in one manuscript and by Clement of Alexandria).[38] In his contrast of Jewish religious practices with Christian understandings, the author includes a description of Christian baptism.[39]

11.1 Let us inquire if the Lord was careful to give a revelation in advance concerning the water and the cross. It was written concerning the water with regard to Israel how they will not receive the baptism [βάπτισμα] that brings forgiveness of sins but will establish [another] for themselves.

2 For the prophet says, "Be astonished, Oh heaven, and let the earth shudder even

---

36. *Ephesians* 20.2; *Philadelphians* 4.1; *Smyrnaeans* 7.1.

37. For possible Pauline background, cf. 1 Thess. 1:3; 5:8; Titus 2:2. Schoedel, *Ignatius of Antioch*, p. 276.

38. For the document as a whole see Reidar Hvalvik, *The Struggle for Scripture and Covenant: The Purpose of the Epistle of Barnabas and Jewish-Christian Competition in the Second Century* (Tübingen: Mohr Siebeck, 1996), and Ferdinand R. Prostmeier, *Der Barnabasbrief* (Göttingen: Vandenhoeck & Ruprecht, 1999).

39. For baptism in *Barnabas* see Benoît, *Le baptême chrétien*, pp. 34-57; Everett Ferguson, "Christian and Jewish Baptism according to the *Epistle of Barnabas*," in Stanley E. Porter and Anthony R. Cross, eds., *Dimensions of Baptism: Biblical and Theological Studies* (London: Sheffield Academic Press, 2002), pp. 207-223. L. W. Barnard, "The Epistle of Barnabas — A Paschal Homily?" *Vigiliae Christianae* 15 (1961):8-22 (16-21), suggested a baptismal setting for the epistle. Contrasts by Christians of their baptism with Jewish baptismal washings are discussed in chap. 16. For the passage quoted below, Per Lundberg, *La typologie baptismale dans l'ancienne église* (Uppsala: Lorentz, 1942), pp. 178-184, emphasizing the connection between baptism and the cross of Christ.

more at this, because this people did two evil things. They abandoned me, the fountain of life, and they dug for themselves a cistern of death" [Jer. 2.12-13].

3 "Is my holy mount Sinai a barren rock? For you will be as young birds fluttering about when taken from the nest" [Isa. 16.1-2, Gk.].

4 Again, the prophet says, "I will go before you; I will level the mountains; and I will break the bronze gates and shatter iron bars; and I will give you treasures lying in darkness, hidden and invisible, in order that you may know that I the Lord am God" [Isa. 45.2-3; Ps. 106.16, Gk.].

5 And, "You will live in a high cave of a solid rock, and its water is dependable. You will see a glorious King, and your soul will cultivate the fear of the Lord" [Isa. 33.16-18].

6 And again he says in another prophet: "The one who does these things will be as a tree planted by streams of water, which will give its fruit in its season, and its leaf will not fall off, and everything he does will prosper.

7 "The wicked are not so, they are not so; rather they are like chaff, which the wind drives away from the face of the earth. Therefore, the wicked will not stand in the judgment, nor sinners in the counsel of the righteous; because the Lord knows the way of the righteous and the way of the wicked will perish" [Ps. 1.3-6].

8 Perceive how he defines the water and the cross together. For he says this: "Blessed" [Ps. 1.1] are those who with hope in the cross went down into the water, because he speaks of the reward "in its season" [Ps. 1.3]; at that time he says, "I will reward." For the present, what he says, "The leaves will not fall off" [Ps. 1.3], means this: Every word that proceeds out of your mouth in faith and love will be for conversion and hope to many.

9 And again another prophet says, "The land of Jacob was praised above every land" [? — the last phrase is in Ezek. 20.6, 15; Zeph. 3.19]. This means, he glorifies the vessel of his Spirit.

10 Next, what does he say? "A river was flowing along on the right, and beautiful trees come up out of it. Whoever eats of the trees will live forever" [based on Ezek. 47.1-12].

11 He means this: That we go down into the water full of sins and uncleanness, and we come up bearing as fruit in our heart reverence and having hope in Jesus in our spirit. And "whoever eats from these will live forever" [Ezek. 47.9; Gen. 3.22] means this: Whoever, he says, hears these when they speak and believes will live forever.

The author gives the heading "Concerning the water and the cross" to chapters 11 and 12, subdivided into "concerning the water" (11.1b) and "concerning the cross" (12.1). The water and the cross are linked by their relation to the forgiveness of sins. The negative statement about Jewish baptism not bringing forgiveness (11.1) implies that Christian baptism does, and this is made explicit at the end of the discussion: "we go down into the water full of sins and uncleanness," but we come up full of reverence and hope (11.11). "Forgiveness of sins" appears in 8.3 in the interpretation of those who sprinkled a mixture of ashes and water in Numbers 19 for purification as those who "preached to us the good news of forgiveness of sins and sanctification of the heart."[40] The phrase occurs again in 6.11 and 16.8, passages employing conversion motifs, for the means of "being made new." The efficacy of baptism in this regard is related to the cross; the water and the cross are brought together in 11.8. Moreover, "forgiveness of sins" occurs also in 5.1 as accomplished by the sprinkling of the Lord's blood (that is, at the cross).[41]

The quotations in 11.2-11 might seem to be an unlikely collection of proof-texts for baptism, but certain factors may have influenced the selection:[42] (1) anti-Judaism — ineffective (11.2-3) or unfruitful (11.7) waters versus dependable (11.5) waters and a negative judgment on Israel (11.2-3); (2) the distinction between the two peoples (11.6-8; cf. "us" and "them" in 11.4-5, 9-11); (3) the rock (11.3, 5), with perhaps allusion to the episode of water from a rock (Exod. 17:1-7; Num. 20:2-13; Ps. 78:15-17);[43] (4) the theme of life (11.2, 10-11). Psalm 1 was particularly appropriate for the author's purposes because of its association of wood and water, the judgment pronounced on the wicked, and the blessing of life. In his application of the Psalm, the tree is not only the cross but also the believer.

Barnabas uses "hope" the way other Christians use "faith." It is an important word for *Barnabas*,[44] and as such occurs once as a verb (11.8) and twice as a noun (11.8, 11) in this discussion of baptism. This hope comes from hearing words spoken in faith and love by those who have been baptized, words that produce in turn conversion and hope in others (11.8, 11).[45]

Two other passages in *Barnabas* (6.8-19; 16.7-10), without using the word "baptism," contain baptismal motifs, one anticipating aspects of chapter 11 and the other looking back to it. The two passages are linked with each other (as noted above) by the common reference to being made new again by the forgiveness of sins (6.11 and 16.8). This renewal is a new creation, having the soul of children, and having new hearts (6.11, 13, 14). The passages are further linked by the theme of this new heart as the temple in which the Lord dwells (6.15; 16.7-8).

The quotation in 11.9 about the land that is praised, interpreted as "the vessel of

---

40. Oskar Skarsaune, "Baptismal Typology in *Barnabas* 8 and the Jewish Background," *Studia Patristica* 18 (1989): 221-228. The association of the Old Testament practice with baptism comes from the water, not the sprinkling (see below on the different baptismal practice indicated by the author).

41. Cf. *Barnabas* 8.5 for "the kingdom of Jesus is on the wood [or tree]."

42. Everett Ferguson, "Christian and Jewish Baptism," pp. 214-220, discusses the quotations and the variant readings involved; Pierre Prigent, *Les testimonia dans le Christianisme primitif: L'Épitre de Barnabé I-XVI et ses sources* (Paris: Gabalda, 1961), pp. 90-99; Lundberg, *La typologie baptismale dans l'ancienne église*, pp. 178-184; Oskar Skarsaune, *The Proof from Prophecy: A Study of Justin Martyr's Proof-Text Tradition* (Leiden: Brill, 1987), pp. 378-379.

43. James N. Rhodes, *The Epistle of Barnabas and the Deuteronomic Tradition* (Tübingen: Mohr Siebeck, 2004), p. 63, identifies the "solid rock" as Jesus.

44. Hope appears as a verb in 1.3; 6.3, 9; 8.5; 12.2, 3, 7; 16.1, 8; 11.8; 17.1; 19.7 and as a noun in 1.4, 6; 4.8; 6.3; 11.8, 11; 16.2.

45. *Barnabas* 8.3 refers to the importance of the preaching of forgiveness of sins.

his Spirit" (is this the human body of Christ — cf. 7.3? the body of those who receive the Spirit in baptism? or those who speak the word of the Spirit?), is explained by the fuller treatment in 6.8-9, 13, 16-17. The "land" is first suffering humanity assumed by Christ in the incarnation, then Christians who through their connection with Christ are brought into the "good land," and finally the eschatological paradise, the fulfillment of hope. The "good land" flows with milk and honey, the food of children that those receive who live "by faith in the promise and by the word" (6.17) in anticipation of inheriting the covenant promises (6.19).[46]

Barnabas 16.7-10 looks back to chapter 11 in its reference to "When we received [aorist] forgiveness of sins" (16.8; cf. 11.1, 11) and to the "word of faith, his calling of promise" (16.9; cf. 11.8, 11) as the means of God's dwelling in human hearts. *Barnabas* 16.8 emphasizes the theme of newness associated with the individual believer and the church as God's holy temple (16.7-8, 9). "His word of faith" (16.9) is probably God's word, which must be spoken in order to produce faith and conversion (5.9; 8.3; 11.8, 11). A confession of faith may be alluded to in the phrase about God through his word "opening the door of the temple (which is the mouth)," which is followed by a statement of his "giving us repentance" (16.9).

These common links justify taking motifs from *Barnabas* 6 and 16 in connection with the discussion of baptism in chapter 11. Particularly notable is the way hope links the three passages: "Hope on Jesus" (6.9), "hope in the cross" (11.8) and "hope in Jesus" at baptism (11.11), "when we received forgiveness of sins and placed hope in the Lord's name" (16.8).

Whereas the *Didache* had spoken most about the administration of baptism and little about its meaning, *Barnabas* says little about the administration and much about the meaning of baptism. The action in baptism was an immersion. The description "we go down into the water" and "we come up" (11.8, 11) might refer to entering and exiting the water, but the importance *Barnabas* gives to these words as the decisive moment for the effects of baptism suggests that they refer for him to the action of baptism itself.[47] Moreover, if *Barnabas* 11.4 refers to Jesus' *descensus ad inferos* when he broke the gates of the hadean world and received "hidden treasures," there may be an allusion to going under the water as a parallel in baptism.[48] Since *Barna-*

---

46. For the theme of inheriting the covenant through Jesus note further 4.3; 13.1, 6; 14.5.

47. For the words καταβαίνω and ἀναβαίνω in reference to baptism, note Acts 8:38-39, where the reference is to entering and leaving the water as distinct from the baptism itself; Hermas, *Similitudes* 9.16.2, 4, 6 (= 93.2, 4, 6), and Cyril of Jerusalem, *Catechetical Lectures* 3.12, where the usage is not clear but may conform to *Barnabas*'s usage. The note in André Benoît and Charles Munier, *Le baptême dans l'église ancienne (Ier-IIIe siècles)*, Traditio Christiana 9 (Bern: Peter Lang, 1994), p. 19 n. 4, that "Les termes: descendre — remonter, n'impliquent pas obligatoirement un rite d'immersion" is correct if the reference is to entering and leaving the water but would be unnecessary for another act than immersion and is incorrect if the description is of the baptism itself.

48. Lundberg, *La typologie baptismale*, pp. 179-184. The *Odes of Solomon* 17.6-16 uses the same passage from Isa. 45:2-3 as does *Barnabas* to describe Christ's *descensus* and resurrection and the blessings of union with him.

bas's quotations involve "flowing" water, it is likely that the author presupposes running water, which was the *Didache*'s preference.[49]

The references to the "name of the Lord" in 16.8-9 in connection with forgiveness of sins and building the spiritual temple for the Lord's dwelling may suggest the administration of baptism in his name (ἐπί).[50] That would imply a confession of faith, which accords with the emphasis on hope (also faith and love — 11.8, 11). The baptism presupposes repentance (16.9). It was preceded by a preaching of the word of forgiveness that produced faith (8.3; 11.8, 11).

The distinctive feature of Christian baptism for *Barnabas* was its bringing forgiveness of sins (11.1, 11; 16.7-8). This forgiveness effects a new creation (6.14; 16.8-9), which is associated with a new birth (having a new soul — 6.11), entrance into the promised land (6.11, 13, 16-17), becoming the temple of God (6.15; 16.7-10), the expulsion of demons (16.7), and living forever (11.10-11).[51] The association of ideas, furthermore, connects baptism with entrance into the covenant with Jesus, "which was sealed in our heart" (4.8). Jewish circumcision was a seal (9.6), but *Barnabas*'s discussion of Jewish institutions and practices does not pair it with baptism. The consideration of circumcision occurs in chapter 9 and contrasts it with a spiritual circumcision. As seen above, the counterpoint in Judaism of Christian baptism is not circumcision but ritual washings. *Barnabas* thus seems to belong in the line of early Christian thought that associated the Christian equivalent to circumcision not with baptism but with God's work in the heart (by the Holy Spirit).[52]

As with the other writers, baptism for *Barnabas* leads to a moral life of obedience that glorifies God in the church (6.16; 11.6; 16.7; cf. the "way of light" in contrast to the "way of darkness" in 18–21).

Hermas

The *Shepherd* by Hermas comes from Rome in the first half of the second century. It is sometimes thought to be a composite of materials from multiple authors, but I will assume the unity of authorship (with possible later redactional work), for the incongruities in content seem to me to be adequately accounted for by a single au-

---

49. Prostmeier, *Der Barnabasbrief*, p. 430, with reference to 11.2, 5, 6, and 10.

50. Note Acts 2:38.

51. Although *Barnabas* does not say so, God's dwelling in the heart would imply the gift of the Holy Spirit in baptism.

52. Everett Ferguson, "Spiritual Circumcision in Early Christianity," *Scottish Journal of Theology* 41 (1988): 485-497 (487 and 493 on *Barnabas*); Benoît, *Le baptême chrétien*, pp. 46, 57; Hvalvik, *Struggle for Scripture and Covenant*, pp. 151, 153-154, 189-190. *Barnabas* 10.12 on circumcision is followed immediately by the discussion of baptism in 11; they are mentioned together in Justin Martyr, *Dialogue with Trypho* 19.2; 29.1. But neither draws a parallel between circumcision and baptism, and both offer other counterparts in Christianity to circumcision. For *Barnabas* that is the covenant sealed in the heart, or elsewhere God's circumcision of human ears and heart (9.1-9; 10.12).

thor writing over a period of perhaps decades and reflecting changing circumstances.[53] The statements about baptism reflect a uniform outlook.[54] This longest writing in the Apostolic Fathers contains the greatest number of references to baptism (but not the word itself) among the Apostolic Fathers; it also presents the strongest statements concerning the necessity of baptism for salvation in early Christian literature.

The imagery of the church as a tower occurs in what is probably the earliest part of the *Shepherd*.

> "The tower that you see being built is myself, the church." . . .
>
> I asked her, "Why, Lady, was the tower being built on the waters?" She said, . . . "Hear then why the tower was being built upon the waters. It is because your [plural] life was saved and will be saved through water. The tower has been founded by the spoken word of his almighty and glorious Name and is supported by the invisible power of the Master. . . .
>
> "Do you wish to know who are the other stones which fall near the waters and are not able to be rolled into the water? These are those who heard the word and wanted to be baptized [βαπτισθῆναι] into the name of the Lord, but when they remember the purity of the truth they change their minds and return again to their evil desires." (*Visions* 3.3.3, 5; 3.7.3 = 11.3, 5; 15.3)

Here is a strong affirmation of salvation by or through water, clearly a reference to baptism. The foundation of salvation, however, is in the Lord (Master). The "spoken word" may be the proclamation by the Lord: that understanding would parallel the next statement about "supported by the invisible power of the Master."[55] It is possible, however, that the reference is to the Name spoken at baptism, as in the continuation of the passage quoted. Baptism was the result of hearing the word and was administered "into the name of the Lord."[56] The presence of faith in those being built into the tower is referred to elsewhere in the interpretation of the tower.[57] Baptism meant not only individual salvation but also admission into the community of followers of the Lord. Baptism placed one in the church, as stones are laid in the building of a tower, and not to be baptized prevented one from entering the church.[58]

---

53. Carolyn Osiek, *Shepherd of Hermas: A Commentary*, Hermeneia (Minneapolis: Fortress, 1999), pp. 8-10.

54. Lage Pernveden, *The Concept of the Church in the Shepherd of Hermas* (Lund: CWK Gleerup, 1966), pp. 112-176 (esp. 162-176); Benoît, *Le baptême chrétien*, pp. 45-137; Lars Hartman, '*Into the Name of the Lord Jesus*': *Baptism in the New Testament* (Edinburgh: T&T Clark, 1997), pp. 177-186.

55. Osiek, *Shepherd of Hermas*, p. 69, understands the reference to be to God and sees three levels of meaning in the parable: creation, the church, and the life of the Christian in baptism as founded on the waters. The "Name" may be the substitution for the actual name of God according to Jewish usage.

56. Osiek, *Shepherd of Hermas*, p. 74, n. 49, considers the Lord here as Jesus on the basis of other passages in early Christian literature and statements in Hermas such as *Visions* 3.1.9 (= 9.9); 3.5.2 (= 13.2); and *Similitudes* 9.13.3 (= 90.3).

57. *Visions* 3.5.4 (=13.4); 3.6.1, 5 (= 14.1, 5).

58. Pernveden, *The Concept of the Church*, pp. 163 n. 2, 165.

I said, "Sir [or Lord, addressing the "Shepherd, the angel of repentance"],[59] I heard from some teachers that there is no other repentance except that one when we went down into the water and received the forgiveness of our former sins." He said to me, "You heard correctly, for it is so. The one who has received the forgiveness of sins ought no longer to continue in sin but to live in purity. Since you inquire carefully concerning all things, I will make clear also this to you, not in order to give an excuse to those who are going to believe or to those who now come to faith in the Lord. For those who now come to faith or who are going to believe do not have [a second] repentance for sins but have forgiveness of their former sins. Therefore, to those called before these days the Lord appointed a [second] repentance. . . . But I say to you," he said, "after that great and holy calling, if anyone should sin after being tempted by the devil, there is one repentance. But if one should sin and repent repeatedly, it is unprofitable to such a person, who shall scarcely live." (*Mandates* 4.3.1-4, 6 = 31.1-4, 6)

The certain teachers who advocated the singularity of repentance may have been making an application of Hebrews 6:4-6 (cf. 10:26-27). They restricted the forgiveness promised in baptism to previous sins ("former sins"), so that the benefits of baptism were not thought to flow forward as well as backward. Since baptism was not repeatable, this understanding involved the awkward position of not having a remedy for postbaptismal sin. Between these rigorists, who allowed for only one (baptismal) repentance, and those who thought of frequent repentance, Hermas took an intermediate position.[60] He received a revelation offering a repentance to Christians who had fallen into sin but warning those coming to faith in his day or in the future not to presume on this possibility as a justification for continuing in sin. As there was only one baptism, so there should be only one postbaptismal repentance, and even this offer (in view of the imminent coming of the Lord or the uncertainties of life?) should not be held out before people being baptized in his day.[61] The reference to "being tempted by the devil" (the part omitted from the quotation speaks of the "shrewdness of the devil") reminds us of the whole thrust of the *Shepherd* to deliver people from the power of sin, which is the devil's tool.

In expressing his main concerns, Hermas gives important information about his understanding of baptism. The action of baptism involved a going down or de-

---

59. *Vision* 5.3, 7 (= 25.3, 7).

60. Many passages in Hermas in fact reflect the idea of the Christian life as a life of penitence: *Visions* 1.1.3, 9 (= 1.3, 9); 2.1.2 (= 5.2); 2.2.3 (= 6.3); 3.1.5 (= 9.5); 4.1.3 (= 22.3); *Mandates* 2.7 (= 27.7); 3.3-5 (= 28.3-5); 4.1.10 (= 29.10); 5.1.7 (= 33.7); 9.4 (= 39.4); 12.3.2 (= 46.2); *Similitudes* 5.7.3-4 (= 60.3-4); 10.2.2-3 (= 112.2-3). But see *Visions* 2.2.4-5 (6.4-5) for the viewpoint expressed in *Mandates* 4.

61. Karl Rahner, *Theological Investigations,* Vol. 15: *Penance in the Early Church* (New York: Crossroad, 1982), pp. 57-113. He understands Hermas as saying that the possibility of penance is limited by the imminent end of the world, the principle of only one repentance (in baptism) is the ideal for the neophyte but does not preclude further penance after baptism (which, however, must not be a pretext for sin), and the newness in the revelation is of the impossibility of a later penance and the assurance of its effectiveness in the present cases (pp. 66-77).

scent into the water. The *Shepherd* agreed that baptism not only brought a forgiveness of sins but also the embarking on a life of sinlessness. It was preceded by repentance and so was a conversion-baptism; as baptism was a unique or one-time event, so in principle repentance should be. Most of Hermas's references to repentance are to repentance for postbaptismal sins, but repentance gets its meaning from its association with conversion from a sinful to a pure and holy life. Conversion also involved believing or coming to faith, and the object of believing was "the Lord."[62] The going down into the water and the believing are both said to bring the forgiveness of former sins. Elsewhere Hermas says that the Son of God "purified the sins of his people."[63] This faith was a response to the Lord's calling, probably expressed through the preached message.

Later in the *Shepherd* Hermas returned to the theme of the tower and the materials that went into its construction.

> I said, "Why, Sir, did the stones come up from the depth and were placed in the structure of the tower, after having borne these spirits?" "It was necessary," he said, "for them to come up through water in order that they might be made alive. They were not able otherwise to enter into the kingdom of God unless they put away the mortality of their former life. Therefore, even these who have fallen asleep [died] received the seal of the Son of God and entered into the kingdom of God. For," he said, "before a person bears the name of the Son of God he is dead, but whenever one receives the seal, that person puts away mortality and receives life. The seal then is the water. They went down into the water dead and they came up alive. The seal itself, then, was preached to them also, and they made use of it in order that they might enter into the kingdom of God. . . . These apostles and teachers who preached the name of the Son of God, when they fell asleep in the power and faith of the Son of God, preached also to those who had fallen asleep before them and gave to them the the seal of the preaching. They went down therefore with them into the water and came up again. The former went down alive and came up alive, but the latter who had fallen asleep previously went down dead but came up alive." (*Similitudes* 9.16.1-6 = 93.1-6)

This passage is an even stronger statement of the necessity of baptism for salvation than the preceding two. Even those (righteous) who had died before the Christian age had to be baptized in order to enter the kingdom of God.[64] The connection of baptism with entering the kingdom of God reminds one of John 3:5. In fact, the phrase

---

62. Hermas says that no one will enter into the kingdom of God without taking the name of the Son of God — *Similitudes* 9.12.4 = 89.4; 9.15.2 = 92.2.

63. *Similitudes* 5.6.2-3 (= 59.2-3). Thus, although Hermas seems to give greater prominence to the water in salvation than most early writers, he preserves an association of baptism with the saving work of Christ and faith in him.

64. Cf. *Sim.* 9.12.4 = 89.4, "No one shall enter into the kingdom of God without taking his holy name." In view of the passages at notes 55 and 56 and those below in the text on the name this is a clear baptismal allusion.

"to enter into the kingdom of God" is identical in John and in Hermas. John 3:5 is the most commonly used baptismal text in the second century. Whether a writer like Hermas in Rome in the early second century was already dependent on the Gospel of John might be considered unlikely,[65] yet if he shared only a common Christian terminology with the Gospel, that in itself is a strong indication that the language of "born of the water" was generally understood in the early church of baptism.

According to Hermas, when the apostles and teachers died, they continued their task of preaching and baptizing in the realm of the dead. This passage connects with the first one quoted above from Hermas about the place of hearing the word in receiving salvation. The connection of preaching with the response of baptism applied to those who had died as well as to the living. In this way the escape from death and the gift of life was made available. Baptism gave life, which was equivalent to entering the kingdom of God.

Hermas makes much of the practice of going down into and coming up out of the water. Since the apostles and teachers who did the baptizing did these things as well as the ones baptized, these words, like Acts 8:38-39, must refer to entering and leaving the water and not the baptismal action itself. The connection of baptism with the "name of the Son of God" is indicated by that as the topic of the preaching (*Sim.* 9.16.5 = 93.5), the declaration that before a person "bears the name of the Son of God" that one is dead (9.16.3 = 93.3),[66] and the description of believers as "called by the name of the Son of God" (9.17.4 = 94.4 quoted below) and those on whom "the name of the Lord was called" (8.6.4 = 72.4). The suggestion that the bath of Rhoda in the Tiber River witnessed by Hermas (*Vis.* 1.1.2 = 1.2) was her nude baptism and that Hermas was a minister (deacon) who functioned at the baptism in the absence of presbyters is hypothetical.[67]

Hermas, like 2 *Clement*, identifies the seal with baptism: "The seal is the water" (*Sim.* 9.16.4 = 93.4), which was "received" (9.16.3 = 93.3). Hermas's usage, however, is more varied than 2 *Clement*'s and is elaborated more. In a nonbaptismal context the seal is the mark received by martyrs and confessors.[68] The seal is "of the Son of God" and so is associated with the "name of the Son of God" (9.16.3 = 93.3).[69] The linking

---

65. Yet the Gospel of John was known in Egypt (Papyrus 52) by the time of Hermas, so it could have been known in Rome also.

66. On bearing the name cf. 9.13.2 = 90.2; 9.15.2 = 92.2; 9.17.4 = 94.4.

67. S. Giet, "Un témoignage possible sur l'administration du baptême dans les premières années du IIe siècle et sur le rôle ministériel d'Hermas," in *Atti del VI Congresso Internazionale di Archeologia Cristiana: Ravenna 23-30 Settembre 1962* (Rome: Pontificio Istituto di Archeologia Cristiana, 1965), pp. 191-197. Hermas as her slave would have assisted his mistress from the river on other occasions — Victor Saxer, *Les rites de l'initiation chrétienne du IIe au VIe siècle: Esquisse historique et signification d'après leur principaux témoins* (Spoleto: Centro italiano di studi sull'alto medioevo, 1988), p. 55.

68. *Sim.* 8.2.2-4 = 68.2-4 (cf. Rev. 9:4).

69. Benoît, *Le baptême chrétien*, p. 131, concludes that since the seal is the imprint on the baptized of the name of God's Son, it is the baptismal formula; but one cannot say that the seal does not include the gift of the Spirit (*Sim.* 8.6.3 = 72.3; 9.13.2 = 90.2; 9.17.4 = 94.4); on the seal as baptism, cf. also p. 121. Pernveden, *The Concept of the Church*, pp. 168-172, concludes that the seal is the "name of the Son of

of the seal with the name accords with the significance of a seal as denoting ownership and protection. The seal was preached (9.16.4 = 93.4) and so was called "the seal of the preaching" (9.16.5 = 93.5). In another passage the sequence of hearing, believing, and receiving the seal indicates the association of the seal with baptism and receiving the name of the Son of God:

> All the nations that dwell under heaven when they heard and believed were called by the name of the Son of God. When they received the seal, they had one way of thinking, one mind, and their faith became one and their love one, and they bore the spirits of the virgins along with the name. (*Sim.* 9.17.4 = 94.4)

Another passage offers the same sequence, but the statement further identifies the seal with the restoration of relationship with the Lord by repentance for postbaptismal sin:

> "... so that those who believed and received the seal yet have broken it and did not keep it whole[70] might recognize their own deeds and repent and receiving the seal from you [the Shepherd] might glorify the Lord, because he had mercy on them and sent you to renew their spirits." (*Sim.* 8.6.3 = 72.3)

The use of "seal" in relation to baptism, postbaptismal repentance, and martyrs is connected by the common element of a confession of the name of the Son of God.[71]

Although the gift of the Spirit at baptism is not explicitly stated, these references to bearing the spirits of the virgins and having persons' spirits renewed imply this idea. The virgins are identified as "holy spirits" and "powers of the Son of God," with which one is clothed when receiving the name of the Son of God (*Sim.* 9.13.2 = 90.2), something that occurred in baptism, and as Christian virtues (*Sim.* 9.15.2 = 92.2), which are gifts of the Spirit. Other passages speak of possession of the Spirit by Christians, and presumably this was received in baptism.[72] In repentance, the Spirit lost by reason of sin is recovered (*Sim.* 9.13.6-14.3). Hermas did not have a clearly developed individualized view of the Holy Spirit.[73]

Baptism in the *Shepherd* of Hermas, in summary, was associated with hearing

---

God, mediated through water and given in baptism" (p. 170). Saxer, *Les rites de l'initiation chrétienne*, p. 54, affirms that seven of Hermas's eight uses of "seal" are clearly equal to baptism and are never in relation to a chrism.

70. One thinks of the exhortation "to keep the seal" in 2 *Clement*.

71. Adalbert Hamman, "La signification de σφραγίς dans le Pasteur d'Hermas," *Studia Patristica* 4 (1961): 286-290. He concludes that one is marked by the name at baptism; martyrs continue to bear the name; but sinners and apostates lose it, and only return to this confession permits their access to the eschatological community (p. 290).

72. Benoît, *Le baptême chrétien*, pp. 127-131, cites *Mandates* 3.1 (= 28.1), which might be the human spirit; but in 5.1.2 (= 33.2) and 10.2.5 (= 41.5) specified as "the Holy Spirit that dwells in you." The Spirit replaces evil spirits in the human heart (*Mandates* 5.2.5-7 = 34.5-7; 3.2 = 28.2).

73. Pernveden, *The Concept of the Church*, pp. 172-175, who concludes that baptism for Hermas did not entail the imparting of the Spirit.

the word of the Lord, believing in the Lord, and repenting of sin. It was an immersion administered in the name of the Son of God and so was designated as a seal of his ownership and protection. Baptism brought forgiveness of sins, was necessary for eternal life and entering the kingdom of God, and perhaps was understood to confer the Holy Spirit.

13. Christian Pseudepigrapha and Apocrypha

References to baptism in early Christian pseudepigrapha and apocrypha do not add much to the understanding of the early Christian practice but by their novel stories and unusual features do reinforce the sense of baptism's importance for Christians. The *Acts of Thomas* will be discussed in chapter 26 on third-century Syria.

Some Pseudepigrapha

I begin with Christian reworkings of Jewish pseudepigraphal documents.

The book of *4 Baruch* ("The Things Omitted from Jeremiah the Prophet" or "The Rest of the Words of Baruch") is a Jewish work from the early second century redacted by a Christian some time later, perhaps mid-second century. A presumably Christian addition is the following: "And you will prove them with the water of the Jordan; whoever does not listen will become known; this is the sign of the great seal [σφραγῖδος]" (6.25).[1] No test by the water of the Jordan figures in the book's account of the return of the Babylonian exiles to Jerusalem. Is this an allusion to John's baptism or to baptism in general? "Seal," as seen in the last chapter, was used by early second-century authors for Christian baptism.

The *Apocalypse of Sedrach* originated as a Jewish work in the early Christian centuries. It received Christian additions at an unknown time and reached its final form much later in middle Byzantine times somewhere around 1000. In contrast to Hermas's heavy emphasis on the necessity of baptism for salvation but sharing his interest in repentance, *Sedrach* puts the emphasis in salvation on repentance. In re-

---

1. S. E. Johnson, "4 Baruch," in James H. Charlesworth, *The Old Testament Pseudepigrapha* (Garden City: Doubleday, 1985), 2.414-415; translation, p. 422. Greek text and translation also by Robert A. Kraft and Ann-Elizabeth Purintun, *Paraleipomena Jeremiou* (Missoula: Society of Biblical Literature, 1972).

sponse to Sedrach's request to be taught by what repentance a person may be saved, God said:

> By repentances, supplications, and liturgies, through draining tears and fervent groanings.... You know, Sedrach, that there are nations which have no law, yet fulfill the law; they are not baptized [ἀβάπτιστοι], but my divine spirit enters them and they are converted to my baptism [βάπτισμα], and I receive them with my righteous ones in the bosom of Abraham. And there are some baptized [βαπτισθέντες] with my baptism [βάπτισμα] and anointed with my divine myrrh, but they have become full of despair and they will not change their mind. (14.3, 5-6)[2]

The inclusion of anointing with myrrh alongside baptism puts this text at the earliest in the late second century and probably later. The concern for nations that have not received baptism and for those who have been baptized but do not change their mind suggests a post-Constantinian setting. Indeed, the whole atmosphere and language of the work belong to the Byzantine period.[3] On the other hand, some motifs could be quite early, such as the righteous in the bosom of Abraham. What is meant by "converted to my baptism"? Is this a conversion that is an equivalent to baptism, or as in Hermas the acceptance of a baptism administered posthumously? Although the passage indicates the possibility of salvation without baptism, it also shows the ordinary necessity of baptism by describing the means of salvation as an equivalent to baptism.

Odes of Solomon

The *Odes of Solomon* is a collection of Christian hymns surviving in Syriac, probably its original language, and variously dated from the beginning of the second century to some time in the third century.[4] There is no obvious reason from the text for the name of Solomon in the title, which may be secondary, so that the work is not properly pseudepigraphic. The odes do not speak expressly of baptism, but there are many baptismal allusions.[5]

---

2. S. Agourides, "Apocalypse of Sedrach," in Charlesworth, *The Old Testament Pseudepigrapha*, 1.605-607; translation, p. 613.

3. E.g., "temples" for churches and supplicating the saints in 11.8.

4. See chap. 7 for more on this work.

5. J. H. Bernard, *Odes of Solomon, Texts and Studies* 8.3 (Cambridge: Cambridge University Press, 1912), provides a commentary on the *Odes* in support of his interpretation of them as baptismal hymns; other students of the *Odes* accept baptismal allusions but not a baptismal context for the whole collection. Mark Pierce, "Themes in the 'Odes of Solomon' and Other Early Christian Writings and Their Baptismal Character," *Ephemerides Liturgicae* 98 (1984): 35-59. To the contrary, Susan E. Myers, "Initiation by Anointing in Early Syriac-Speaking Christianity," *Studia Liturgica* 31 (2001): 150-170 (pp. 158-166), argues that the references to water in the *Odes of Solomon* are sapiential rather than baptismal.

Ode 11 expresses the early Christian thought, "For the Most High circumcised me by his Holy Spirit," with which compare the *Epistle of Barnabas* 9 discussed in chapter 12, and then adds, "His circumcising became my salvation" (11.2, 3).[6] The ode is full of conversion language: "I received his knowledge" (11.4); I "turned towards the Most High" (11.9); "I . . . stripped off (folly) and cast it from me" (11.10); "I became like the land that blossoms and rejoices in its fruits" (11.12, with which compare *Barnabas* 11); and "My eyes were enlightened" (11.14). It contains possible baptismal allusions, such as the following:

> And speaking waters touched my lips
> From the fountain of the Lord generously.
> And so I drank and became intoxicated,
> From the living water that does not die.
>
> (11.6-7)[7]

"Living water" reminds one of the preferred water for baptism in *Didache* 7.

Ode 19.1 may allude to milk given to the newly baptized (cf. *Barnabas* 6.8-11, 17):

> A cup of milk was offered to me,
> And I drank it in sweetness of the Lord's kindness.[8]

The theme of Jesus' *descensus ad inferos* connected with his baptism was noted in chapter 7. Passages in the *Odes of Solomon* are relevant here and prepare for the more specific references in the following documents. Ode 39 combines the imagery of Israel crossing the Red Sea (or the Jordan under Joshua) with crossing the waters of death as an escape from destructive forces, a crossing in which believers follow the steps of the Lord Messiah:

> But those who cross [the raging rivers] in faith
> Shall not be disturbed.
> . . . .
> Because the sign on them is the Lord.
> And the sign is the Way for those who cross in the name of the Lord.
> Therefore, put on the name of the Most High and know him,
> And you shall cross without danger;
> Because rivers shall be obedient to you.
> The Lord has bridged them by his Word,
> And he walked and crossed them on foot.
> And his footsteps stand firm upon the waters, and were not destroyed;
> But they are like a beam of wood [cross] that is constructed on truth.

---

6. Quotations are from the translation of James H. Charlesworth, *The Odes of Solomon* (Missoula: Scholars, 1977), here p. 52.
7. Charlesworth, *The Odes of Solomon*, p. 52.
8. Charlesworth, *The Odes of Solomon*, p. 82.

And on this side and on that the waves were lifted up,
But the footsteps of our Lord Messiah stand firm.
. . . .
And the Way has been appointed for those who cross over after him,
And for those who adhere to the path of his faith.

(*Ode* 39.5-13)[9]

The allusive poetic language draws on two conceptions: voyage across the waters of death and imitation of the Savior who himself passed through the same waters. The sign of the Savior is the cross. The baptismal language of faith and the name of the Lord indicate that the experience of baptism is a crossing the sea of death with the Savior having led the way.

The *descensus* theme in relation to Christ's saving work being extended to those in Hades seems clear in the last ode in the collection. Ode 42 begins with a reference to the cross and resurrection and a bridal feast. Then come these lines:

I was not rejected although I was considered to be so,
And I did not perish although they thought it of me.
Sheol saw me and was shattered,
And Death ejected me and many with me.
. . . .
And I made a congregation of living among his dead;
And I spoke with them by living lips;
In order that my word may not be unprofitable.
And those who had died ran towards me;
And they cried out and said, Son of God, have pity on us.
And deal with us according to thy kindness,
And bring us out from the bonds of darkness.
. . . .
Then I heard their voice,
And placed their faith in my heart.
And I placed my name upon their head,
Because they are free and they are mine.

(42.10-11, 14-16, 19-20)[10]

The last lines about faith and placing the Lord's name on the head once more give a baptismal connection to this passage.

---

9. Charlesworth, *The Odes of Solomon*, p. 136. This Ode is studied by Per Lundberg, *La typologie baptismale dans l'ancienne église* (Uppsala: Lorentz, 1942), pp. 125-135, as based on Israel crossing the Red Sea and the baptism of Jesus seen as crossing the waters of death (the Red Sea a symbol of the Abyss or Hades).

10. Charlesworth, *The Odes of Solomon*, pp. 145-146.

Apocalypse of Peter

The *Apocalypse of Peter* comes probably from Egypt about A.D. 135. It survives entire only in an Ethiopic version, which preserves the content but not always the exact wording of the Greek original where this exists. The following passage, however, is available in Greek in a papyrus fragment.[11] The angels brought the elect and righteous to the Lord, and those in torment recognized the justice of their punishment.

> I will present to my called and chosen ones whomsoever they shall ask of me out of torment, and I will give them the fair [καλὸν] baptism [βάπτισμα] in salvation of the Acherusian lake, which they call in the Elysian field, a portion of righteousness with my holy ones. (14)[12]

The author shares with Hermas the view that the righteous who died before the coming of Christ must receive saving baptism before entering the heavenly kingdom. It was convenient for this purpose that pagan mythology included the Acherusian Lake in its geography of Hades.[13]

Epistle of the Apostles and Baptism of the Righteous Dead

The mid-second century *Epistle of the Apostles* survives in Ethiopic (only it is complete) and Coptic translations, which frequently diverge in wording. The setting of the work is a postresurrection revelation of Jesus to the apostles. The Coptic version contains these instructions from Jesus:

> For truly I say to you, whoever will hear you and believe in me, he will receive from you the light of the seal through me and baptism through me. . . .
> . . . And you will be called servants, for they will receive by my hand through you the baptism of life and the forgiveness of their sins. (41-42)[14]

---

11. M. R. James, "The Rainer Fragment of the Apocalypse of Peter," *Journal of Theological Studies* 32 (1931): 270-279, from which I translate (p. 271).

12. Cf. the translation of the Ethiopic by C. Detlef G. Müller, "Apocalypse of Peter," in Wilhelm Schneemelcher, *New Testament Apocrypha* (Louisville: Westminster/John Knox, 1992), Vol. 2, p. 633 (620-638). The passage later says, "I will cause the nations to enter into my eternal kingdom and show to them that eternal thing to which I have directed their hope."

13. Marinus de Jonge and L. Michael White, "The Washing of Adam in the Acherusian Lake (Greek *Life of Adam and Eve* 37.3) in the Context of Early Christian Notions of the Afterlife," in John T. Fitzgerald, et al., eds., *Early Christianity and Classical Culture: Comparative Studies in Honor of Abraham J. Malherbe* (Leiden: Brill, 2003), pp. 609-635 (616-617 on *Apocalypse of Peter*), with other later references in Christian literature. Erik Peterson, "Die 'Taufe' im Acherusischen See," *Vigiliae Christianae* 9 (1955): 1-20, argues for the Jewish origins of the motif of baptism in the Acherusian Lake — see our chap. 4 on the *Life of Adam and Eve* — and for a later reference see below on the *Revelation of Paul*.

14. Translation from C. Detlef G. Müller, "Epistula Apostolorum," in Schneemelcher, *New Testament Apocrypha*, Vol. 1, pp. 249-284 (p. 273). The Ethiopic reads, "the light of the seal that is in my hand" and "by my hand they will receive the baptism of life and forgiveness of sin."

The images of light and of a seal in connection with baptism are notable and conform to the language of the early second century. The reference to the hand in baptism perhaps alludes to the hand of the administrator resting on the head of the baptizand (chap. 7). The thought is expressed that it is actually the hand of Jesus that administers the baptism, but the Coptic makes clear that Jesus acts through the apostles. Hearing and faith precede the baptism, and the baptism brings life and forgiveness.

This passage makes clearer an earlier reference in the work, which provides another testimony to the belief that baptism was offered to the righteous dead. Only the Ethiopic is complete at this point. Jesus is speaking:

> I have descended and have spoken with Abraham and Isaac and Jacob, to your fathers the prophets, and have brought to them news that they may come from the rest which is below into heaven, and have given them the right hand of the baptism of life and forgiveness and pardon for all wickedness as to you, so from now on also to those who believe in me. (24)[15]

Here Jesus directly administers the baptism to the righteous of Old Testament times. It permits them to leave Hades and enter the heavenly rest. Baptism is again described as bringing life and forgiveness. It brought the same pardon to the righteous of earlier times as it did to the disciples of Jesus, and this pardon is offered to those in the future who would believe on Jesus.

The late *Gospel of Nicodemus*[16] in its account of Christ's *descensus ad inferos* includes the feature of Jesus conferring baptism on the righteous dead, a motif characteristic of the second century and so likely derived from an earlier source. When the righteous were raised in connection with the resurrection of Jesus (Matt. 27:52), an angel gave a message for Seth to deliver to Adam:

> [T]he only begotten Son of God shall become man and shall descend below the earth. And he shall anoint him [Adam] with that oil. And he shall arise and wash him and his descendants with water and the Holy Spirit. And then he shall be healed of every disease. (19)[17]

The washing with water and the Spirit alludes to John 3:5 and reflects the frequent use of the Gospel of John by the author. There is a fuller account of postmortem baptism at the close of the work but without an indication of who performed the baptism:

---

15. Müller, "Epistola Apostolorum," p. 265. The theme of postmortem baptism may be reflected in the *Martyrdom of Saints Perpetua and Felicitas* 7-8, where Perpetua's prayers for her seven-year old brother Dinocrates, who died of cancer, enabled him to drink from a pool of water and be refreshed; that this water-symbolism was some kind of baptism-substitute is suggested by David F. Wright, "At What Ages Were People Baptized in the Early Centuries?," *Studia Patristica* 30 (1997): 389-394 (p. 392).

16. See chap. 6 for information on its date.

17. Felix Scheidweiler, "The Gospel of Nicodemus," in Schneemelcher, *New Testament Apocrypha*, Vol. 1, pp. 501-536 (523).

[W]e two brothers[18] who also were sent by Michael the archangel and were appointed to preach the resurrection of the Lord, but first to go to the Jordan and be baptized. There also we went and were baptized with other dead who had risen again. Then we went to Jerusalem also and celebrated the passover of the resurrection. (27)

Taken together with the other passages about a postmortem baptism, this text would also reflect the belief that baptism was necessary for the righteous dead, when delivered from Hades, to enter Paradise. This was associated with the "Harrowing of Hell" by which Jesus at his death and resurrection delivered the "patriarchs, prophets, martyrs, and forefathers" (24.2) from Hades and did not reflect a "second chance" for those who died after his coming.

The work variously known as the *Revelation* or *Apocalypse* or *Vision of Paul* originated at least as early as the third century, but it underwent expansions, revisions, and abbreviations in its textual history, so that the best text available belongs to the late fourth or early fifth century.[19] In one passage not the righteous dead but repentant sinners receive a postmortem baptism, which is in the Acherusian Lake.

If there is anyone who is a fornicator and ungodly and who turns and repents and brings forth fruit worthy of repentance [Acts 26:20], first when he has come forth from the body he is brought and worships God and (he) is handed over from there at the command of God to the angel Michael and he baptizes him in Lake Acherusia. Thus he leads him into the city of Christ with those who have not sinned. (22)[20]

This provision accords with a spirit of leniency in the writing, for one of its features prominent in its medieval transmission was the granting of a respite from torment to the damned on Sundays.[21]

Another late work of the *descensus* literature, *The Questions of Bartholomew*, may go back to a third-century original of the *Gospel of Bartholomew*.[22] It contains a statement that recalls a theme often encountered in early texts: "Jesus answered [Bartholomew]: 'It is good if he who is baptized preserves his baptism without blame'" (5.8).[23] Another redaction of the primitive *Gospel of Bartholomew* is the

---

18. Sons of Simeon (Luke 2:25-28), who had recently died and came out of their graves when Jesus was raised — 17.1.

19. I have surveyed the secondary literature and arguments on the dating in "Psalm-Singing at the Eucharist: A Liturgical Controversy in the Fourth Century," *Austin Seminary Bulletin* 98 (1983): 52-77 (56-61).

20. Translation from Hugo Duensing/Aurelio de Santos Otero, in Schneemelcher, *New Testament Apocrypha*, Vol. 2, pp. 726-727.

21. Theodore Silverstein, *Visio Sancti Pauli*, Studies and Documents 4 (London, 1935), p. 12.

22. Felix Scheidweiler, "The Questions of Bartholomew," in Schneemelcher, *New Testament Apocrypha*, Vol. 1, pp. 537-553 (540).

23. Scheidweiler, "The Questions of Bartholomew," p. 551.

228 | THE SECOND CENTURY

Coptic *Book of the Resurrection of Jesus Christ* from the fifth or sixth century.[24] It records the apostles saying to Thomas, "You have resurrected a multitude of people of the town by baptism and the seal of Father, Son, and Holy Spirit" (23.2).[25] In accord with other apocalypses, the *Book of the Resurrection of Jesus Christ* relates a story that the son of Thomas told on his experience after his death and before he was restored to life. He said that when the time came to separate his soul from his body, the angel Michael signed his mouth in the name of Father, Son, and Holy Spirit. He carried his soul to heaven accompanied by the chanting of hymns. They crossed the river of fire, and Michael led him to the Acherusian lake and plunged him in it three times (21.4-6). There seems to be a deliberate allusion to the baptismal practice of the church.

Acts of Peter

The *Acts of Peter* dates from the latter half of the second century. The work is incompletely preserved. The major part survives in a Latin version made in the fourth century; it is supplemented by Greek texts of the martyrdom of Peter at the end and Coptic and other witnesses to episodes at the beginning of the work.

On Peter's journey by ship from Caesarea to Rome he spoke the words of God to Theon, the captain of the ship. When the ship met with a calm in the Adriatic, Theon said to Peter, "If you will count me worthy to be baptized with the sign of the Lord [*intingas in signo domini*], you have the opportunity." The narrative continues:

> And Peter went down by a rope and baptized [*baptizavit*] Theon in the name of the Father and of the Son and of the Holy Spirit. And he came up out of the water rejoicing with great joy, and Peter also was more cheerful because God had accounted Theon worthy of his name. And it came to pass that at the same place where Theon was baptized [*baptizatus est*], there appeared a young man shining with splendor, saying to them, "Peace be with you."

They went up and returned to the cabin.

> Peter took bread and gave thanks to the Lord. . . . "Most excellent, the only holy one, it is you who have appeared to us, you God Jesus Christ; in your name has this man been washed [*lotus*][26] and signed with your holy sign [*signatus est sancto tuo signo*]. Therefore in your name I impart to him your eucharist." (5)[27]

---

24. Introduction and French translation by Jean-Daniel Kaetli and Pierre Cherix, *L'évangile de Barthélemy d'après deux écrits apocryphes*, Vol. 1. *Questions de Barthélemy; II. Livre de la Résurrection de Jésus-Christ par l'apôtre Barthélemy* (Turnhout: Brepols, 1993).
25. Earlier it is said that "The apostle [Thomas] blessed and baptized 2,000 persons" (22.10).
26. The manuscript reads *locutus,* which does not make sense.
27. Translation from Wilhelm Schneemelcher, in Schneemelcher, *New Testament Apocrypha*, Vol. 2, pp. 291-292.

Several things are notable about this unusual account. The Latin verb *ting(u)o*, "dip" or "wet by plunging," was often used for the action in Christian baptism, but the transliterated Greek verb *baptizō* came to prevail over it. βαπτίζω certainly stood behind *baptizō* in the Greek original, but whether it or another word was translated by *tingo* cannot be determined. An immersion might seem unlikely, or at best difficult, under the circumstances. But both Peter and Theon went down to the water and went up from it, and Theon "came up out of the water rejoicing with great joy" (cf. Acts 8:39). Theon now lived up to his name, the Greek word for "god." The baptism was administered with the full Trinitarian formula. The author, however, seems to reflect a modalistic monarchianism in his identification of God and Jesus Christ, but we should not read too much into this, for theology was not his strong suit. Liturgical practices seem to be reflected in the greeting of peace. Whether the signing was the baptism itself, a prayer accompanied by making the sign of the cross on Theon, or an anointing with oil (also by the sign of the cross) is not obvious, but by the time of the Latin translation the last option would have been understood. If this was also true for the Greek original, we have the initiatory sequence of baptism, anointing, and eucharist.

Acts of Paul

The date and provenance of the *Acts of Paul* are late second century in Asia Minor.[28] It is a composite work, not all of whose parts survive, worked up from earlier traditions. Some parts circulated independently, but which of those parts were earlier than the composition or which were later separated from it is not clear. The *Acts of Paul* followed the *Acts of Peter*, for the former refers to the ship captain, "who had been baptized by Peter," except his name is given as Artemon.[29]

One of the independent pieces in the work and perhaps one of its earlier parts is the *Acts of Paul and Thecla* (or *Acts of Thecla*). A sermon of Paul, summarized in a series of blessings, contains the exhortation: "Blessed are they who have kept their baptism [βάπτισμα] secure, for they shall rest with the Father and the Son" (6).[30] This statement matches the concern in the early second century for maintaining the manner of life associated with baptism. And the identification of baptism with a seal occurs also in this section. Thecla said to Paul, "Only give me the seal [σφραγῖδα] in Christ, and temptation shall not touch me." And Paul said, "Have patience, Thecla, and you shall receive the water" (25).

---

28. The work is first attested by Tertullian, *On Baptism* 17, about 200.

29. Episode 10 in the Hamburg Papyrus, p. 7. I follow the translation by Wilhelm Schneemelcher in Schneemelcher, *New Testament Apocrypha*, Vol. 2, p. 258.

30. The passage is quoted by the fifth-century (?) *Epistle of Titus*, "Blessed are those who have kept the baptism of salvation, for they will enjoy eternal delight" — Aurelio de Santos Otero, "The Pseudo-Titus Epistle," in Schneemelcher, *New Testament Apocrypha*, Vol. 2, p. 70. In the context of this pseudepigraphon, keeping baptism probably meant maintaining celibacy.

Perhaps the best-known episode in the story of Thecla is her receiving the seal of the water by a self-baptism while wild beasts were turned loose on her in the stadium:

> Then they sent in many beasts, while she stood and stretched out her hands and prayed. And when she had finished her prayer, she turned and saw a great pit full of water and said: 'Now is the time for me to wash [λούσασθαι].' And she threw herself in, saying, 'In the name of Jesus Christ I baptize myself [βαπτίζομαι] on [for] the last day!' (34)

The people wept out of concern for her, and the governor feared she would be eaten by the seals in the water.

> So, then, she threw herself into the water in the name of Jesus Christ; but the seals, seeing the light of a lightning-flash, floated dead on the surface. And there was about her a cloud of fire, so that neither could the beasts touch her nor could she be seen naked. (34)

Thecla later reported the event to Paul: "I have taken the bath [λουτρόν], Paul; for he who worked with you for the gospel has also worked with me for my baptism [λούσασθαι, 'to be washed'[31]]" (40). The account is unusual in early Christian literature for the self-baptism, and its use by some to justify the right of women to administer baptism was part of Tertullian's objections to the *Acts of Paul*.[32] Otherwise, Thecla imitated church practice: a nude immersion (at least implied), baptizing "in the name of Jesus Christ," and describing the baptism with the words "wash" and "bath." The lightning-flash and cloud of fire may suggest the motif of illumination or may allude to the phenomenon of light that accompanied the baptism of Jesus (chap. 6).

The section about Paul in Ephesus describes his baptizing a woman, Artemilla.

> [Paul is speaking:] "And now, Artemilla, hope in God and he will deliver you, hope in Christ and he will give you forgiveness of sins and will bestow on you a crown of freedom, that you may no longer serve idols and steam of sacrifice but the living God and Father of Christ, whose is the glory for ever and ever. Amen" And when Artemilla heard this she with Eubula besought Paul that he would baptize her in God.[33]

The fragmentary subsequent part refers to Paul praying, laying his hand on Artemilla, and baptizing her in the name of Christ Jesus in the sea, and to a subsequent eucharist of bread and water.[34] The ascetic thrust of the *Acts of Paul,* as the

---

31. There is manuscript support for the alternate reading ἅγιον βάπτισμα.
32. Tertullian, *On Baptism* 17.4-5. See chap. 21.
33. The passage and the comments to follow are in the Hamburg Papyrus, pp. 2-4.
34. Carl Schmidt, Πράξεις Παύλου, *Acta Pauli nach dem Papyrus der Hamburger Staats- und Universitäts-bibliothek* (1936), p. 34 (manuscript p. 7, lines 31ff.).

other apocryphal acts, is indicated not only by the emphasis on celibacy but also by the use of water for wine in the eucharist. Paul offered to Artemilla forgiveness of sins and a crown of freedom; he called on her to have hope in God and Christ (similar to the usage in *Barnabas*), but a little earlier in another setting he had said that he preached so that people may "repent and believe."[35]

Shortly thereafter occurs an allusion to another famous episode in the *Acts of Paul*, the baptized lion, which was recounted earlier in a missing part of the work.

> The lion looked at Paul and Paul at the lion. Then Paul recognized that this was the lion which had come and been baptized. And borne along by faith Paul said: "Lion, was it you whom I baptized?" And the lion in answer said to Paul, "Yes."[36]

The story of the original event is supplied by a Coptic papyrus. Paul recounted the episode:

> There came a great and terrible lion out of the valley.... When I finished praying, the beast had cast himself at my feet. I was filled with the Spirit and looked upon him, and said to him: "Lion, what do you want?" But he said: "I wish to be baptized." I glorified God, who had given speech to the beast and salvation to his servants. Now there was a great river in that place; I went down into it and he followed me.... But I stood on the bank... and cried out.... When I had prayed thus, I took the lion by his mane and in the name of Jesus Christ immersed him three times. But when he came up out of the water he shook out his mane and said to me: "Grace be with you!" And I said to him: "And likewise with you."[37]

If the Coptic version faithfully represents the original Greek at this point, this passage would be the earliest explicit testimony to triple immersion in Christian baptism. The baptism, as in Thecla's self-immersion, was "in the name of Jesus Christ." The author of the *Acts of Paul* took the story of Androcles and a lion from pagan literature[38] and Christianized it with the baptism. The story employs the motif that animals could recognize power, wisdom, justice, and the divinity of emperors and applies it to the apostle. The story is important as showing the belief that the only way to attain eternal life is by baptism.[39]

---

35. Hamburg Papyrus, p. 1.

36. Hamburg Papyrus, pp. 4-5. For the story's popularity, see Bruce M. Metzger, "St. Paul and the Baptized Lion," *Princeton Seminary Bulletin* 39 (1945): 11-21. The setting in the *Acts of Paul* is Paul fighting wild beasts in the stadium at Ephesus. For Paul's language in 1 Cor. 15:32 as metaphorical, see Abraham J. Malherbe, "The Beasts at Ephesus," *Journal of Biblical Literature* 87 (1968): 71-80.

37. Translation slightly modified from R. Kasser in Schneemelcher, *New Testament Apocrypha*, Vol. 2, p. 262.

38. Aulius Gellius, *Attic Nights* 5.14.5-30.

39. Tomas Adamik, "The Baptized Lion in the Acts of Paul," in Jan D. Bremmer, ed., *The Apocryphal Acts of Paul and Thecla* (Kampen: Kok Pharos, 1996), pp. 60-74 with earlier bibliography.

The Coptic papyrus continues with the record of a great crowd "added to the faith" in Ephesus. Among them was a woman by the name of Procla known for her good works. "[Paul] baptized her with all her household."[40]

The concluding section of the *Acts of Paul*, the *Martyrdom of the Holy Apostle Paul*, quotes Paul as calling on his executioners, "Believe in the living God, who raises up from the dead both me and all who believe in him!" When they questioned him about salvation, he said to them, "Come quickly here to my grave at dawn, and you will find two men praying, Titus and Luke. They will give you the seal [σφραγῖδα] in the Lord" (5). "Seal" is evidently baptism, according to the usage in the story of Thecla above.

Acts of John

The *Acts of John* are usually dated in the second half of the second century; they are further removed from mainstream orthodoxy than the *Acts of Peter* and the *Acts of Paul*. One passage in the extant text, when compared with the rest of the work, is probably a secondary insertion: "After instructing them in the things concerning the Father and the Son and the Holy Spirit, he [John] baptized them" (57).[41] Another passage gives a more likely reference to baptism in the original text. John denounced a certain Fortunatus:

> Be removed, then, from those who hope in the Lord . . . from their resurrection to God, from their fragrance in which you can have no share, from their fasting, from their prayers, from their holy bath [λουτροῦ ἁγίου], from their eucharist, from the nourishment of their flesh, from their drink, from their clothing, from their love-feast, from their care of the dead, from their continence. . . . (84)[42]

This description of general Christian activities may reflect in part a liturgical sequence, if the "bath" is indeed a reference to baptism — fragrance (anointing?), fasting, prayer, bath, eucharist, love-feast. This book will illustrate the frequent use of "bath" for baptism.

Acts of Andrew

The *Acts of Andrew* derives probably from the late second century, about the time of the *Acts of John*, with which it shares a similar ideology and literary motifs. As in the other apocryphal Acts, there is a strong emphasis on the necessity of celibacy. The

---

40. Adamik, "The Baptized Lion," p. 265.
41. Knut Schäferdiek, "The Acts of John," in Schneemelcher, *New Testament Apocrypha*, Vol. 2, pp. 152-209 (p. 192). Schäferdiek dates the work to the third century — pp. 166-167.
42. Schäferdiek, "The Acts of John," p. 200.

work does not survive in its entirety, and reconstructing the order of the contents from witnesses to it is difficult.[43]

The Acts of Andrew and Matthias, which may represent the original beginning of the *Acts of Andrew*,[44] comes from the fifth century. Such a later date is reflected in some of the wording in the conclusion of Andrew's ministry in the city of the cannibals:

> Later he [Andrew] drew up plans for a church and had the church built on the spot where the pillar in the prison had stood. After baptizing [βαπτίσας] them, he handed on to them the commands of our Lord Jesus Christ. (32)[45]

Earlier in the work the demons explained that they were unable to kill Andrew because, "We saw the seal [σφραγῖδα] on his forehead and were afraid of him." The Latin translation has *crucem*, "cross," for "seal." What made this visible to the demons is not explained.

In the epitome of the *Acts of Andrew* made in the sixth century by Gregory of Tours *(Liber de virtutibus sancti Andreae apostoli)* the "blessed apostle" Andrew stopped an earthquake and storm of lightning and thunder by prayer. As a result, "The proconsul received the word of God, believed in the Lord with his whole house, and they were baptized *(baptizati sunt)* by the apostle of God" (4).[46] This is a sequence and wording that seems to be drawn from the canonical Acts of the Apostles: is it faithful to the original or due to Gregory's paraphrasing? Two accounts of conversion according to Gregory's epitome mention only the converts' believing (10 and 22).[47]

In the separately transmitted *Passion of Andrew* there is frequent mention of the seal (σφραγίς). Stratocles, the brother of the proconsul in Patras, was brought to faith by the miracles and teaching of Andrew. Stratocles and many others "were deemed worthy of the Lord's seal" (10). Andrew said to them, "If you keep this seal's impression unconfused with other seals that imprint different designs, God will commend you and receive you to his domain." Because of this the demons are put to flight, "since they have nothing to do with the symbol of the seal since it is kindred to light" (11). However, "if you pollute the brilliance of the grace given you, . . . it will do you no good to call on the God of your seal which you defiled by apostasizing from him" (11).[48] Although the theological setting is different from the emerging ortho-

---

43. Dennis MacDonald, *The Acts of Andrew and the Acts of Andrew and Matthias in the City of the Cannibals* (Atlanta: Scholars Press, 1990), pp. 1-59 (55-59), on date and place of composition; I follow his text and translation in what follows. The textual evidence is presented more completely in Jean-Marc Prieur, *Acta Andreae*, Corpus Christianorum, Series Apocryphorum 5 and 6 (Turnhout: Brepols, 1989).

44. So argued by MacDonald, *The Acts of Andrew*, pp. 3-47.

45. MacDonald, *The Acts of Andrew*, pp. 162-165.

46. MacDonald, *The Acts of Andrew*, pp. 194-195.

47. MacDonald, *The Acts of Andrew*, pp. 218-219, 280-281; in the latter there is a Greek witness to the text.

48. MacDonald, *The Acts of Andrew*, pp. 336-339.

doxy of the great church, these references to the seal are quite in keeping with the language of mainline Christian writers: seal apparently referring to baptism given to those who believed and were deemed worthy, the exhortation to guard the seal, its power to dispel demons, and its association with light.

Other Later Apocryphal Acts

Treating together the *Acts of Philip, Acts and Martyrdom of Matthew, Acts of Barnabas,* and *Acts of Thaddaeus* is a matter of convenience, but some of them may come from the same circles. Much uncertainty surrounds the date and provenance of these generally little-studied works. There is a certain common pattern about what is said in regard to baptism, whether the authors employ older traditions, reflect contemporary practice, imagine how things might have been done at an earlier time, or represent some combination of these factors.

The *Acts of Philip* may come from Encratite circles in Asia Minor in the fourth century.[49] Its accounts of conversion follow the pattern of teaching, the people believing, and baptism "into the name of Father, Son, and Holy Spirit" (36.7 = III.19).[50] Philip "taught the people concerning faith and the Son of God" and "baptized all the household into the name of Father, Son, and Holy Spirit" (63.19 = V.25).[51] Sometimes "seal" is used for the baptism: a multitude of men, women, and virgins believed in the Lord and were "sealed with the seal of Christ" (134.28 = *Martyrdom* 28).[52] The imagery is enlarged in another request, "Clothe me with your glorious garment and your brilliant seal that always shines" (144 = *Martyrdom* 38).[53]

For the *Acts of Philip* baptized persons are "enlightened in the Lord" (140 = *Martyrdom* 34). Christ through baptism sets free from the slavery of death (117.3 = *Martyrdom* 11).

The same usage of "seal" occurs in the *Acts and Martyrdom of Matthew,* "to give

---

49. The *Acts of Philip* have received the attention of François Bovon, "Les Actes de Philippe," *Aufstieg und Niedergang der römischen Welt* (Berlin: de Gruyter, 1988), Vol. 2.25.6, pp. 4431-4527; critical text by François Bovon, Bertrand Bouvier, and Frédéric Amsler, *Acta Philippi: Textus,* Corpus Christianorum: Series Apocryphorum 11 (Turnhout: Brepols, 1999).

50. I give first the traditional numbering of divisions in the text followed by the new numbering in Bovon et al. (n. 49). My text cites the reading of the Vatican manuscript (*Graecus* 824 — eleventh century). The Athos manuscript (*Xenophontos* 32 — fourteenth century) reads, "baptizing in the grace of Christ," which may preserve an earlier reading.

51. Other instances: a whole city believed in the name of Jesus, and Bartholomew commanded Stachys to baptize the believers into the name of Father, Son, and Holy Spirit (147 = *Martyrdom* 41); a variation in the formula — all believed in the Lord Jesus Christ, and Philip instructed and baptized them "in the name of the holy and consubstantial Trinity" (86.23 = VI.22), absent from the Athos manuscript.

52. The Athos manuscript reads, "They were washed and received the word of God his seal."

53. Other uses of seal: "he gave them the seal in Christ" (29.24 = II.24); "they believed and were counted worthy of the seal in Christ" (44.8 = IV.6).

them the seal in Christ" (8). The same chapter continues with the bishop Plato going out and baptizing people "in the water of the spring beside the tree [that had grown up miraculously from a rod planted by Matthew] into the name of the Father, the Son, and the Holy Spirit." Going into the church, they had communion of the eucharist and all were singing in the church all night praising God.

A fuller account of baptism occurs in the *Acts and Martyrdom of Matthew* 26. The marvels accompanying the arrival of the coffin containing the body of Matthew prompts a king to declare, "I truly believe in the true God Christ Jesus." He requests, "Give me the seal in Christ." The king had the coffin set up on the bed in the great room of the palace and requested to be baptized in it (?) and to share in the eucharist of Christ. The bishop [Plato] having prayed and ordered him to unclothe and having questioned him extensively, while the king confessed and wept over the things he had done, sealed [κατασφραγίσας] him, anointed him with oil, and "lowered him down [καθῆκεν] into the sea in the name of the Father, Son, and Holy Spirit." When he came up from the water, he was clothed with garments. The bishop blessed and thanked the holy bread and mixed cup. There are some puzzling things about the text (which has come down to us in variant forms). How does the first reference to baptism relate to the account of the immersion in the sea? What is the "seal" requested by the king (baptism?), and how does it relate to the sealing (sign of the cross?) done by the bishop in connection with the anointing that precedes the immersion? We seem to have here the "Syrian" order of anointing, water baptism, and eucharist (discussed in chap. 26 and later).

The *Acts of Barnabas* (fifth century?) reflects the same pattern as the *Acts of Philip*. Christians are defined at the beginning of the work as those "who teach holily the hope and were sealed" (1). The fullest statement is in chapter 26 concerning Mark: "Teaching the word of the Lord, enlightening them, and proclaiming the good news of the things I was taught by the apostles of Christ, who baptized me into the name of the Father, Son, and Holy Spirit, who also gave me the new name Mark in the water of baptism."[54] This would be an early reference to the practice of taking a new name at baptism. The work also refers to one "to whom was given the Holy Spirit at baptism" (17).

The *Acts of Thaddaeus*, which some would date as late as the sixth century, gives similar accounts. It begins with Thaddaeus saying he was baptized by John the Baptist (1). It relates Thaddaeus baptizing King Abgar and all his house; he taught a great multitude and baptized them into the name of Father, Son, and Holy Spirit. He anointed them with holy perfume and communicated to them the mysteries of the body and blood of Jesus (4). Thaddaeus recounts that Christ sent the apostles to preach repentance and forgiveness of sins in his name to all nations, baptizing them and promising the kingdom of heaven (a conflation of Luke 24:47; Matt. 28:19; and

---

54. A briefer statement in chapter 13: leading them down to the spring, he baptized them into the name of Father, Son, and Holy Spirit.

perhaps John 3:5). Agreeing with the other apocryphal acts and echoing Mark 1:5, the account says that many, hearing his teaching, believed and were baptized, confessing their sins (7).

Related to Thaddaeus is the *Letter of Abgar*, which contains the statement that Thaddaeus spoke to Abgar the word of the Lord and, after instructing him, he went down to the spring called Kerassa and baptized him with all his house (8).

Physiologus

The *Physiologus* went through stages of development, and its original Christian form has been dated from the late second to the late fourth century.[55] The work draws moral lessons from the phenomena of nature, especially of animals. It does not fit easily in any of the conventional classifications of Christian literature or my program of presentation, so I include it here as something of an appendix to Christian Pseudepigrapha and Apocrypha.

Physiologus 6 on the eagle refers to trine immersion. Chapter 11 on the snake makes the connection of the moral life with baptism.

---

55. An accessible English translation is M. J. Curley, *Physiologus* (Austin: University of Texas Press, 1979).

14. Apologists

With the exception of Justin Martyr the Greek apologists of the second century do not use the βαπτίζω/βάπτισμα family of words in their apologetic writings, and he does so only in the *Dialogue with Trypho*. Nevertheless, in the person of Justin Martyr they provide an important description of the baptismal ceremony, and some of them along with Justin also provide important information on the doctrinal meaning ascribed to baptism.

Justin Martyr

Justin Martyr was a Gentile from Samaria, was converted in Asia, and spent his later years teaching in Rome. He was martyred about 165. His *1 Apology*, written around 150, contains an account of Christian baptism. As an apologist Justin had every reason to present Christianity in the most favorable way; by the same token he had every need to be as accurate as his information allowed him to be. He was in a position to know general Christian practice and may be taken as representative of Christian baptism at the mid-second century, especially at Rome.[1] His outline of the ceremony of conversion closely approximates what is indicated in the *Didache*, a document with which he may have been familiar.[2]

> (61.1) We shall explain in what way we dedicated ourselves to God and were made new through Christ, lest by omitting this we may seem to act deceptively in our

---

1. André Benoît, *Le baptême chrétien au second siècle* (Paris: Presses Universitaires de France, 1953), pp. 138-185; George H. Williams, "Baptismal Theology and Practice in Rome as Reflected in Justin Martyr," in Andrew Blane, ed., *The Ecumenical World of Orthodox Civilization, Russia and Orthodoxy: Essays in Honor of George Florovsky*, Vol. 3 (Hague: Mouton, 1973), pp. 9-34.
2. M. A. Smith, "Did Justin Know the Didache?" *Studia Patristica* 7 (1966): 287-290, argues from the liturgical parallels that he did, but much of the similarity may come from common Christian practice and so be of limited probative value.

explanation. (2) As many as are persuaded and believe that the things said and taught by us are true and promise to be able to live accordingly are taught while fasting to pray and ask God for the forgiveness of past sins, while we pray and fast together with them. (3) Then they are led by us to where there is water, and in the manner of the regeneration [ἀναγεννήσεως] by which we ourselves were regenerated [ἀνεγεννήθημεν] they are regenerated [ἀναγεννῶνται]. For at that time they are washed [λουτρὸν ποιοῦνται] in the water in the name of God the Master and Father of all, and of our Savior Jesus Christ, and of the Holy Spirit. (4) For Christ also said, "Unless you are regenerated [ἀναγεννηθῆτε] you cannot enter into the kingdom of heaven.". . .

(9) And we have learned from the apostles the reason for this practice. (10) Since at our first birth we have been born without our knowledge or choice from the moist seed at the union of our parents with each other and have existed in bad habits and evil conduct, in order that we might not remain children of ignorance and necessity but become children of choice and knowledge and might obtain the forgiveness of sins committed in the past, there is called in the water upon the one who chooses to be regenerated [ἀναγεννηθῆναι] and who repents of sins the name of God the Master and Father of all. The one leading the person being washed [λουσόμενον] to the bath [λουτρόν] speaks only this name . . .

(12) This bath [λουτρὸν] is called illumination [φωτισμός], since those who learn these things are illuminated in their understanding. (13) And the person who is illuminated [φωτιζόμενος] is washed [λούεται] in the name of Jesus Christ, who was crucified under Pontius Pilate, and in the name of the Holy Spirit, who through the prophets foretold all the things about Jesus. . . .

(65.1) After we thus wash [λοῦσαι] the person who has been persuaded and who has given consent, we lead this one to where those called brothers and sisters have gathered together to make fervent prayers in common on behalf of themselves and of the one who has been illuminated [φωτισθέντος] and of all others everywhere. We pray that having learned the truth we may be accounted worthy and through our deeds be found good citizens and guardians of what is commanded in order that we may be saved with eternal salvation. (*1 Apology* 61.1-13; 65.1)

Without using the word "baptism" (Justin, in writing to pagans, instead of this "Christian" word uses "bath" and "wash"), Justin gives the fullest account of baptismal practice that we have from the second century. He claims the explanation for the practice comes from the apostles, and so was already traditional in his time.

Baptism was for those who were persuaded about Christian teaching and placed their trust in it and who promised to live the Christian life (61.2), those who chose to be regenerated and repented of their sins (61.10).[3] The phrase about those persuaded who gave consent (65.1) may allude to a confession of faith made in response to

---

3. Benoit, *Le baptême chrétien*, pp. 148ff., notes the passages in Justin where forgiveness of sins describes the result of repentance; he suggests that "to receive forgiveness of sins" may have been a technical term for baptism. For further discussion of repentance, see pp. 154-162.

questions (an interrogatory confession), but the wording of 61.3 and 10 sounds more like words pronounced by the baptizer over the candidate. The promise to live according to Christian teachings, repentance, involved a rejection of idols (49.5) and a change in moral life (14.2-4). The account, therefore, places a strong emphasis on the voluntary acceptance of baptism and the exercise of free will by the candidate.[4] The account clearly describes baptism of persons of responsible age. A period of listening to the word and instruction preceded the baptism.[5]

The immediate preliminaries to baptism included a period of prayer and fasting, describing a time of repentance, and focusing upon the significance of the coming event as a time of forgiveness of sins. The candidates were joined by others but not the whole congregation in the prayer and fasting.

At the time for the baptism itself the candidate was taken to where there was water, probably an outside natural source of water. When Justin refers to the administrator of the baptism in the singular, the one leading the candidate to the the place of washing (61.10), he may be thinking of himself as a teacher who has instructed the one preparing for baptism and as the one then performing the act.[6] The baptism was administered in the name of the three divine persons. In an explanatory comment not quoted above (61.11) Justin stated that no one could give a name to the ineffable God, so "Father" and "Master" are attributes and not names proper. The explanations of Jesus as "Savior," who was "crucified under Pontius Pilate," and of the Holy Spirit as the one who spoke through the prophets about Jesus (61.3, 13) contain elements found in early summaries of the rule of faith.[7] The words may reflect an elementary baptismal confession by the candidate or an expansion of the Trinitarian formula spoken by the administrator. Or, since Justin's eucharistic prayer praises Father, Son, and Holy Spirit (*1 Apol.* 65), so his description of the words at baptism may be more a prayer of the administrator than a "formula."

After the baptism, the participants returned to the place where the other Chris-

---

4. Free will is an important aspect of Justin's thought — see Eric F. Osborn, *Justin Martyr* (Tübingen: Mohr Siebeck, 1973), chapter 11.

5. Everett Ferguson, "Catechesis and Initiation," in Alan Kreider, ed., *The Origins of Christendom in the West* (Edinburgh: T&T Clark, 2001), pp. 229-268 (233-236 on Justin), for indications in Justin's *1 Apology* of the doctrinal and moral content included in this prebaptismal teaching.

6. In the *Acts of Justin and His Companions* 4 the magistrate evidently thought Justin had converted his associates, but in the cases recorded they claimed to have been Christians before studying with Justin.

7. Everett Ferguson, *Early Christians Speak*, 3rd ed. (Abilene: ACU Press, 1999), pp. 19-28. The description of Jesus as "crucified under Pontius Pilate" occurs most often in Justin as a formula in exorcism — *2 Apology* 6.6; *Dialogue* 30.3; 76.6; 85.2 — but he gives no indication that an exorcism was part of the baptismal preparation. Williams, "Baptismal Theology," p. 27, places some of the exorcism passages in a baptismal context. Cf. Benoit, *Le baptême chrétien*, p. 182, on demons in Justin, with reference to *Dialogue* 116.1-2 for a connection between becoming a Christian and deliverance from the power of the devil and demons. Paul F. Bradshaw, "The Profession of Faith in Early Christian Baptism," *Evangelical Quarterly* 78 (2006): 101-115, suggests that the "Trinitarian" words may not be a liturgical formula recited at baptism but part of the catechetical instruction (pp. 101-102).

tians were assembled and have been praying. There was an exchange of a kiss in greeting followed by the eucharist, representing the person's acceptance into the fellowship of the church. The association of the eucharist with baptism probably came about because baptism was often administered on the first day of the week (see later for baptism on the Sunday of Pasch or Pentecost), the day of the Christian assembly centered on the eucharist. In keeping with his apologetic purpose, Justin repeatedly emphasizes the good life expected of Christians (65).

Baptism was associated with the forgiveness of sins. This is implied in the preparatory prayers (61.2), and it is later stated explicitly that forgiveness is attained when in the water the divine name is called on the person (61.10; cf. 66.1 quoted below).[8]

Justin identifies the conversion baptism as the time when one is made new (61.1).[9] His preferred way of describing this experience of newness is shown by the repeated use of the words "regeneration" (rebirth) and "be regenerated" (born again). He draws the comparison of this new generation with physical generation inasmuch as both involve moisture (water of baptism and the moist seed of sexual union), but he was mainly interested in the contrast of the two generations and subsequent births. Natural birth is involuntary on the part of the child and results in sinful conduct. The new birth, on the other hand, is a matter of choice and knowledge and is associated with repentance and forgiveness of sins. Justin cites a saying of Christ in justification for the practice of baptism and its description as a new birth. The quotation expresses the idea of John 3:3, but with differences. Instead of "generated again" (or "from above") in the Gospel, Justin uses the compound verb found in 1 Peter 1:3, 23 (where there is a similar contrast between corruptible seed of natural birth and the incorruptible word of God), and instead of "kingdom of God" Justin uses "kingdom of heaven." Instead of "see" in John 3:3, Justin uses "enter" from John 3:5 (cf. Matt. 18:3). Justin may be quoting loosely, may be making a composite quotation, or may be drawing a statement from the continuing oral tradition of the words of Jesus. In favor of his knowledge of the Gospel of John is the fact that, following the quotation from Christ (not included in my translation above), Justin repeats Nicodemus's difficulty (John 3:4) about entering again into the mother's womb (61.5). In any event, it is evi-

---

8. Craig D. Allert, *Revelation, Truth, Canon and Interpretation: Studies in Justin Martyr's Dialogue with Trypho* (Leiden: Brill, 2002), pp. 240-251, by a creative reading that associates repentance and illumination with an inward washing, concludes that Justin knows two washings, the first and inward washing saves, so salvation comes before water baptism (pp. 243-44). This interpretation defies Justin's repeated use of "water" and "bath" for baptism, his relating washing to the Trinitarian name (so the literal baptism), and the passages where he explicitly puts forgiveness and salvation after baptism (1 *Apol.* 65.1; 66.1; *Dial.* 138). The interpretation of λουτρὸν ποιοῦνται (1 *Apol.* 61.3) as middle, "wash themselves" (p. 244), is incorrect; that it should be understood as passive is evident from the words about an administrator (1 *Apol.* 61.10) and "we wash them" (1 *Apol.* 65.1). Allert (p. 244) seems to think that repentance is the time of salvation for Justin (although none of the passages cited says so), but Justin rather puts regeneration after faith and repentance (1 *Apol.* 61.2-3) and separates repentance from salvation (*Dial.* 138.3).

9. For the motif in general, J. Ysebaert, *Greek Baptismal Terminology: Its Origins and Early Development* (Nijmegen: Dekker & Van de Vegt, 1962), pp. 87-154 ("Renewal, Re-creation, and Rebirth").

dent from Justin, Hermas, and others that John 3:3-5 reflected language in widespread use in the early decades of the church as referring to baptism.

Justin provides the first use of "illumination" (or "enlightenment") as a technical term for baptism, but it appears as already a traditional name.[10] This usage has a background in Hebrews 6:4 and the general use of the imagery of "light" for spiritual knowledge and proper conduct.[11] Enlightenment for Justin involved instruction, and his adoption of the word agrees with the intellectual and moral content he gives to the instruction associated with baptism and with the proper understanding of divinity (the nature of the divine persons) connected with the baptismal rite itself. We may see in this term the idea of the light of God which now fills the believer's life. Is the name also related to the fire Justin described as kindled on the Jordan at the baptism of Jesus (chap. 6)? Justin used the same phrase, "a fire was kindled," for the baptism of Jesus and for his own experience on hearing Christian instruction.[12] He elsewhere says that converts are "illumined [φωτιζόμενοι] by the name of Christ" and "are illumined by Christ [ἐφώτισεν]."[13] In the latter passage Justin contrasts the illumination that comes from Christ with illumination by the Jewish Law.[14] Justin uses illumination as a recognized term among Christians, and it became common as simply meaning baptism without further explanation.

In keeping with Justin's apologetic thrust of relating Christian teaching and practices to aspects of his pagan environment and with his great concern with demons, in the chapters (62, 64) between the quotations cited above he refers to demonic imitations of the Christian washing [λουτρόν].[15] The demons learned of this from Isaiah 1:16-20, quoted by Justin as a prophetic announcement foretelling baptism (61.6-8).[16] Justin mentions sprinklings [ῥαντίζειν] and complete washings [λούεσθαι] required as a preliminary to entering temples and offering sacrifices

---

10. Ysebaert, *Greek Baptismal Terminology*, pp. 157-178. An important conclusion is that there is no certainty that φωτίζειν ever formed part of the vocabulary of the mysteries (159-163). Benoit, *Le baptême chrétien*, pp. 165-169, notes that illumination is related to receiving the gifts of the Spirit in *Dialogue* 39.2, with the observation that intellectual illumination and the gift of the Spirit are not exclusive of each other. Gerard-Henry Baudry, *Le baptême et ses symboles: Aux sources du salut* (Paris: Beauchesne, 2001), pp. 61-71, on baptism as "the sacrament of light."

11. E.g., John 8:12; 1 John 1:5-7; *Barnabas* 18-19.

12. *Dial.* 88.3; 8.1. Williams, "Baptismal Theology," stresses the themes of light and fire in Justin's baptismal theology.

13. *Dial.* 39.2; 122.5.

14. Oskar Skarsaune, *In the Shadow of the Temple: Jewish Influences on Early Christianity* (Downers Grove: InterVarsity Press, 2002), pp. 358-359, with references suggesting that "illumined ones" was "a stock Jewish name for proselytes."

15. Cullen I. K. Story, "Justin's Apology I.62-64: Its Importance for the Author's Treatment of Christian Baptism," *Vigiliae Christianae* 16 (1962): 172-178, argues that these chapters are not a digression but fit the argument of chapter 61 that bases baptism on the authority of the triune God and brings illumination. The demons substitute their own authority and pervert the knowledge of God.

16. Isa. 1:16-20 is also quoted in *1 Apol.* 44.3-4 and alluded to in *Dial.* 18.2; 13.1. The phrase "wash your souls" in *Dial.* 18.2 (cf. "baptize your souls" in 14.2) is not inconsistent with or different from water baptism for Justin (*contra* Allert, *Revelation, Truth, Canon*, p. 245).

(62.1).[17] The demons also arranged, in imitation of the Spirit of God moving over the waters at creation (Gen. 1:2), for the image of Kore, daughter of Zeus, to be set up over springs of waters (at Eleusis) (64.1-4). Isaiah 1:16 and the combination of the Spirit and water at creation in Genesis 1:2 would often be invoked in later discussions of baptism. Other apologists such as Tertullian (chap. 21) would also follow Justin's lead in seeing in pagan rites demonic imitations of Christian practices.

Justin's introduction to his discussion of the eucharist summarizes his understanding of the meaning of baptism:

> This food is called by us eucharist, of which no one is allowed to partake except the one who believes the things taught by us to be true, was washed [λουσαμένῳ] in the bath [λουτρόν] for forgiveness of sins and regeneration [ἀναγέννησιν], and who lives in the manner Christ taught. (1 Apol. 66.1)

Faith, baptism for the forgiveness of sins, and the new life are what constitutes the Christian. These ideas were found in the account of baptism cited above. It is to be noted that here faith is not in the person of Jesus but in Christian teachings. The baptism is related to forgiveness involved in regeneration, and it is meant to result in living according to the teachings of Christ.

Justin makes explicit and frequent use of the βαπτ- family of words in the *Dialogue with Trypho,* where he addresses differences between Jews and Christians. The contrast Justin makes between Jewish washings and Christian baptism will be reserved for chapter 16.

Justin describes the message of John the Baptist in words almost exactly quoting Matthew 3:11-12 and Jesus' identification of John the Baptist (βαπτιστοῦ) with Elijah according to Matthew 17:11-13.[18] He further describes the ministry of John the Baptist (βαπτιστής) as foretold by Isaiah, quoting Isaiah 40:1-17, and continues by affirming that "there were no more prophets in your [Trypho's] nation after John," because Christ "put an end to his prophesying and baptizing [βαπτίζειν]," a claim supported by quoting words of Christ that are a conflation of Matthew 11:12-15 and Luke 16:16.[19] Following his discussion of the baptism of Jesus, Justin noted that "when John was seated by the Jordan and preaching a baptism of repentance [βάπτισμα μετανοίας]," in response to speculation that he might be the Christ he declared that he was not the Christ but that One Stronger was coming.[20] Justin's account of the baptism of Jesus was quoted in chapter 6.

---

17. His reference in this context to Moses removing his sandals at the burning bush may allude to the removal of clothes before entering the baptismal waters (62.3) — Williams, "Baptismal Theology," pp. 26-27.

18. *Dial.* 49.3, 5.

19. *Dial.* 50.2-51.3 (51.2 for Christ putting an end to John's baptizing); 52.3. There is a further reference to John the Baptist in 84.4, where in support of the virgin birth of Jesus "Elizabeth who bore John the Baptist" is cited as an instance of God's power to enable a barren woman to bear a child.

20. *Dial.* 88.7. The denial, "I am not the Christ," is stronger and more explicit than the Baptist's reply in John 1:25-31 — E. Bammel, "Die Täufertraditionen bei Justin," *Studia Patristica* 8.2 (1966): 53-61 (p. 58).

The *Dialogue with Trypho* adds further aspects to Justin's baptismal theology.[21] As part of the contrast of Christianity with Judaism Justin affirms that Christians have a spiritual circumcision.

> We who have approached God through him [Christ the Son of God] received the spiritual circumcision, not that according to the flesh . . . We received it through baptism [βαπτίσματος], since we were sinners, through God's mercy, and it is possible for all likewise to receive it. (*Dial.* 43.2)

The same preposition affirms that the spiritual circumcision is *through* baptism and *through* God's mercy. It should be noted that baptism is not the spiritual circumcision, any more than it is God's mercy, but the means or agency by which it is obtained. This passage explains the statement found earlier in the *Dialogue* interpreting Isaiah 1:16 as meaning, "God commands you to be washed [λούσασθαι] in this bath [λουτρὸν] and to be circumcised with the true circumcision."[22] The washing (baptism) and the being circumcised are not identical. "Washed" is repeated from the Greek translation of Isaiah 1:16, and the "be made clean and put away evil" of that verse is interpreted by Justin as the true circumcision. The means by which this true, spiritual circumcision associated with baptism or washing is accomplished is the Holy Spirit.[23]

In a passage appealing to Old Testament references to wood as figures of the cross of Christ — the rod of Moses at the Red Sea and with which he struck the rock, the tree that sweetened the waters at Marah, Jacob's rods that influenced the conception of sheep and his vision of the ladder to heaven, Aaron's rod that blossomed, the oak of Mamre, the stick that Elisha cast in the water — Justin connected the cross with the waters of baptism:

> Our Christ, by being crucified on the tree and giving purification through water, ransomed us who had been plunged [βεβαπτισμένους] in the most grievous sins which we committed. (*Dial.* 86.6)

The word for "baptized" is used here, as in classical sources, in its general (but metaphorical) sense of submerged or overwhelmed, not for the Christian rite, but is no doubt a wordplay suggested by the rite: those plunged in sins are now plunged in the water that purifies from sins. The usage here makes clear Justin's meaning of the word "baptize." He envisions people as completely, not partially, covered by sins. His

---

21. Williams, "Baptismal Theology," concentrates on this work instead of on *1 Apology* and speculates on possible liturgical expressions of aspects of the theology.
22. *Dial.* 18.2. Isa. 1:16 was an important verse on baptism for Justin (see further in chap. 16): "There is no other way through which forgiveness of sins will come to you and inheritance of the good things that have been promised except knowing this Christ and being washed [λουσάμενοι] in the bath [λουτρόν] for the forgiveness of sins that was proclaimed by Isaiah and then living without sin" (*Dial.* 44.4). Jews need a "second circumcision" (*Dial.* 12.3).
23. *Dial.* 29.1, quoted and commented on in chap. 16.

main point is the linking of water and wood, the sanctifying effect of water as a result of the crucifixion of Jesus on the tree.

That thought is developed further in a passage that gives the fullest statement of Justin's theology of baptism. He draws on a typology not mentioned in the earlier passage, the ark of Noah that saved from the flood:

> The mystery of saved people occurred at the flood. For righteous Noah with the others at the flood — that is, his wife, his three sons, and their wives — who in number were eight, were a symbol of the eighth day, on which our Christ appeared resurrected from the dead, being always the first in power. For Christ, the firstborn of all creation, became also the beginning again of a new race begotten again [regenerated, ἀναγεννηθέντος] by him through water, faith, and wood — the mystery of the cross — in the same manner as also Noah was saved by wood when he with his family was borne over the waters. . . . I mean that by water, faith, and wood those who have prepared themselves and repent of their sins shall escape the judgment of God that is coming. (*Dial.* 138.1-3)

An elaborate typology underlies the passage: Noah is a figure of Christ; his family are the saved; the number "eight" refers to the eighth day (or first day of the week) on which Christ was raised from the dead;[24] from Noah after the flood and from Christ after his resurrection came a new race (begotten or born again);[25] the saved in Noah's day and in the present are united by their faith;[26] water is baptism; and the ark is the cross. This passage ties together thoughts in the account of baptism in the *1 Apology* and the *Dialogue*. The effective means of redemption is the crucifixion of Christ (the wood typologies of *Dialogue* 86) and his resurrection. It is received by those who have been instructed in Christian teaching ("those previously prepared"), who have faith, and who repent of their sins — here Justin introduces emphases found in *1 Apology* 61. Justin through the Noah typology offers a balanced way of integrating his (and much of early Christian) thought on the process of salvation and the place of water baptism in it.

Justin's baptismal ceremony was somewhat more developed than can be ascertained from the New Testament but was still rather simple and similar to that described in the *Didache* without the latter's allowance for an alternative to immersion. A period of instruction, prayer, and fasting preceded the baptism. It required faith, repentance, and a commitment to live according to the teachings of Jesus. Baptism was administered in the triune name. It brought one into the fellowship of the Christian community, expressed in the sharing in common prayer and the eucharist. Baptism meant especially a forgiveness of sins, a regeneration, and an enlightenment. Other themes were deliverance from a former manner of life dominated by demonic influences and the sharing in the gifts of the Holy Spirit.

---

24. Cf. *Barnabas* 15.8-9.
25. 1 Pet. 1:3, 21; cf. 3:20-21.
26. Heb. 11:7.

Melito of Sardis

Melito wrote an apology, of which little survives, so he is better known for his only surviving complete work, *On Pascha*. He wrote the first known treatise *On Baptism* (Περὶ λουτροῦ, c. 170-180).[27] Only a fragment ascribed to this work survives, and its authenticity is questioned.[28]

> What sort of gold, silver, bronze, or iron, after being fired, is not baptized in water [βαπτίζεται ὕδατι], one in order that it may be brightened in appearance, another in order that it may be strengthened by the dipping [βαφῆς]? The whole earth is washed [λούεται] by rains and rivers. . . . [The passage continues with illustrations of baptism from nature, using λούω, including the heavenly bodies:] If you wish to observe the heavenly bodies being baptized [βαπτιζόμενα], hurry now to the ocean, and there I will show you a novel sight: the open sea spread out, the sea without limit, the depth unexplored, the ocean unmeasured, the water pure; the swimming pool [βαπτιστήριον, "baptistery"] of the sun, the place for the brightening of the stars, the bath [λουτρόν] of the moon. And how they are symbolically washed [λούονται μυστικῶς] learn faithfully from me.

The author then recounts the ancient mythology that the chariot of the sun, after traversing the sky above the earth, descends into the ocean, then rises again. Part of the description of that suboceanic journey is this:

> [T]he sun, inflamed like lightning, wholly undying, is washed [λούεται] in cold water but keeps his fire unsleeping. When he has bathed [λουσάμενος] in symbolic baptism [βαπτίσματι μυστικῷ], he rejoices greatly. . . . Although one and the same, the sun rises as new to human beings, strengthened from the deep, purified from the bath [λουτροῦ]. . . . [The stars and the moon] are washed [λούονται] in the sun's swimming-pool [βαπτιστήριον] like good disciples.

The conclusion from these heavenly examples about the suitability of Christ receiving baptism in the Jordan was quoted in chapter 7. The author's description of the sun's daily baptismal bath reflects Christian terminology and practice: pure water that purifies, cold water, baptistery, rising new, the comparison to disciples. According to the mythology the sun was submerged completely in the ocean and arose from it. That the author has a similar understanding of the action of Christian baptism is evident from his juxtaposition at the beginning of the quotation above of "being baptized" (βαπτίζεται) and "dipping" (βαφῆς, used of tempering and dyeing [chap. 3], from βάπτω). An immersion and a swimming pool can be expressed also as a washing and a bath.

---

27. Eusebius, *Church History* 4.26.2.
28. Stuart G. Hall, *Melito of Sardis: On* Pascha *and Fragments,* Oxford Early Christian Texts (Oxford: Clarendon, 1979), p. xxxii. I use his text (pp. 70-73) but offer my own translation. Robert M. Grant, "Melito of Sardis on Baptism," *Vigiliae Christianae* 4 (1950): 33-36, gives references to the Stoic affinities of the passage and concludes that the author used Stoic exegesis of Homer.

Some scholars find allusions to baptism in *On Pascha:* Israel "anointed the front doors" of their houses (14); Moses "sealed the doors of the houses" (15), Israel "was sealed" (16), and Christ "sealed our souls with his own Spirit" (67); Christ invites, "Receive forgiveness of sins, for I am your forgiveness" (103). There is manuscript support to read one of the subsequent phrases, "I am your washing [λουτρόν]," but the preferred reading is, "I am your ransom [λυτρόν]." No word for baptism occurs in the text, and these statements are not necessarily references to the ceremony of baptism.[29]

Fragment 12 attributed to Melito mentions foreshadowings in the Old Testament of the cross and baptism (for the latter, "Ezekiel called 'the water of forgiveness' the foreshadowing of holy baptism") and names two provisions for the forgiveness of sins: "suffering for Christ [martyrdom] and baptism [βάπτισμα]." The fragment, however, probably derives from the fourth century.[30]

Tatian

Tatian, Justin's not very slavish student, in his *Diatessaron* repeated the Gospel accounts of the baptism of Jesus with the addition of a manifestation of light (noted in chap. 6). His apologetic *Oration* does not discuss baptism but does contain an allusion to it. In discussing the begetting of the Logos at the beginning of the universe, Tatian compares human speech:

> Just as the Word begotten [γεννηθείς] in the beginning in turn begot [ἀντεγέννησε] our creation by fabricating matter for himself, so I too, in imitation of the Word, having been begotten again [ἀναγεννηθείς] and obtained understanding of the truth, am bringing to order the confusion in kindred matter.[31]

The association of baptism with begetting again (rebirth) and understanding the truth are themes characteristic of Justin; the paralleling of baptism with the first creation is a motif found in other Christian writers.

Theophilus of Antioch

Theophilus, bishop of Antioch, wrote his apology *To Autolycus* about 180. As part of a spiritual interpretation of the creation week in Genesis 1 Theophilus offers this explanation of the creation of animals on the fifth day:

---

29. Gerald F. Hawthorne, "Christian Baptism and the Contribution of Melito of Sardis Reconsidered," in David Aune, ed., *Studies in the New Testament and Early Christian Literature* (Leiden: Brill, 1972), pp. 241-251, argues against any baptismal allusion in the work.

30. Hall, *Melito of Sardis*, pp. xxxiii-xxxiv.

31. *Oration* 5 — text and translation of Molly Whittaker, *Tatian: Oratio ad Graecos and Fragments,* Oxford Early Christian Texts (Oxford: Clarendon, 1982), pp. 10-11.

On the fifth day came into existence the living creatures from the waters, through which the "manifold wisdom of God" [Eph. 3:10] is made plain. For who would be able to count their multitude and variety? Moreover, the things that come from the waters were blessed by God, in order that this might be a sign that people were going to receive repentance and forgiveness of sins through water and the "bath of regeneration [παλιγγενεσίας]" [Titus 3:5], namely all those who come to the truth and are born again [ἀναγεννωμένους] and receive a blessing from God. (*To Autolycus* 2.16)

Theophilus employs both the words for eschatological "regeneration" (Titus 3:5) and for moral/spiritual "begetting again" (1 Pet. 1:3, 23), apparently without difference in significance. He makes the familiar connection of "repentance and forgiveness of sins" with baptism. Although he does not use the latter word, that would clearly be the meaning with reference to those who receive forgiveness "through water," likened to the animals that "come from the waters." Both are blessed by God. In good apologetic fashion, Theophilus makes the point that regeneration and new birth are for those "who come to the truth." In another context Theophilus affirms that "faith leads the way in all matters" (*To Autolycus* 1.8). Although a limited statement, what Theophilus does say is parallel as far as it goes with what Justin Martyr said.

Theophilus makes another statement that has been brought into discussions of the baptismal ceremony. In defending the name "Christian," he appeals to anointing as "sweet and useful" (a pun on χριστός, anointed, and χρηστός, useful). "Wherefore we are called Christians on this account, because we are anointed with the oil of God" (*To Autolycus* 1.12). If Theophilus uses "oil" literally here, he is the first orthodox writer to refer to a literal anointing when one became a Christian.[32] Even if his statement is literal and not figurative, he was more interested in anointing as a metaphor than as a practice. Otherwise, Gnostic sources provide the earliest attestation of anointing in connection with baptism (chap. 17). The practice probably developed in the second half of the second century in both orthodox and unorthodox circles. Much of the development of liturgical actions in connection with baptism gave expression in literal acts to theological ideas associated with baptism, and it was natural to bring out the association of Christians with Christ ("the Anointed One") and the idea of being anointed with the Holy Spirit by anointing the baptized with that which symbolized the Holy Spirit, with whom Christ was anointed. Theophilus's words in praise of oil in the same section may hint at other considerations that encouraged the practice: "What person on entering into this life or being an athlete is not anointed with oil?" The anointing of a newborn child after its first bath would have suggested an anointing of the one who received the new birth in baptism, and the anointing of an athlete for the contests would have suggested the same for those who undertook the life of God's athlete.

---

32. The earliest manuscript of the work reads "mercy" (ἔλεος) instead of "oil" (ἔλαιον), but a corrector wrote "oil," in agreement with the other two manuscripts.

15. The Pseudo-Clementines and Jewish Christianity

Jewish-Christian accounts of the baptism of Jesus were included in chapter 6. In this chapter we are concerned primarily with Jewish-Christian sources included in the Pseudo-Clementine literature and secondarily with reports in Epiphanius. Of the Jewish groups that accepted Jesus as Messiah, those known as Ebionites received the most notice in Gentile-Christian sources.[1] Even they remain imperfectly known, but lustrations and baptism figure prominently in what is said about the Ebionites.[2]

Clement of Rome's name was adopted by two fourth-century works produced in Syria, the *Homilies* (in Greek) and the *Recognitions* (preserved in a Latin translation by Rufinus), both partially preserved in a Syriac translation. The extensive common material in these two works is widely accepted to come from a basic document *(Grundschrift)* of the first half of the third century. Jewish-Christian material probably from Jewish-Christian writings was incorporated in this basic document, or in some cases perhaps appropriated directly by the fourth-century works. The putative Jewish-Christian sources are from around 200 or earlier in the second century, and this possible dating accounts for the placement of the material in this unit, although the form in which it has come down to us is later in date.

---

1. For varying perspectives in the study of Jewish Christianity, see the Introduction and first seven articles collected in Everett Ferguson, ed., *Early Christianity and Judaism*, Studies in Early Christianity 6 (New York: Garland, 1993); among the major scholarly studies I have learned much from Hans Joachim Schoeps, *Theologie und Geschichte des Judenchristentums* (Tübingen: Mohr, 1949) (baptismal practices, pp. 202-211), whose conclusions are more popularly presented in his *Jewish Christianity* (Philadelphia: Fortress, 1969). See now Sakari Häkkinen, "Ebionites," in Antti Marjanen and Petri Luomanen, eds., *A Companion to Second-Century Christian "Heretics"* (Leiden: Brill, 2005), pp. 247-278.

2. Joseph Thomas, "Les ébionites baptistes," *Revue d'histoire ecclésiastique* 30 (1934): 257-296. He identifies stages in their evolution: influenced by Cerinthus in Christology, by Essenes in daily baths of purification, by Elkasaites (aversion to animal sacrifices, reverence for water, therapeutic power of running water — but may the influence have run the other way?), and the emergence of a distinct baptizing sect among the Ebionites, to which the Pseudo-Clementines testify.

Even this broad framework is disputed by some scholars, and where it is accepted, the agreement quickly disappears in the assignment of details to sources. Since there are so many divergent views,[3] instead of adopting a particular source theory, I will present the references to baptism *in toto* in systematic arrangement with observations about what seems to derive from Jewish-Christian source documents, especially what reflects some of Jewish Christianity's distinctive concerns. Most of the accounts of baptism were clearly in the basic writing, but were they yet earlier? Do the distinctive motifs come from a particularly Jewish-Christian source or from yet another strand of Christianity? What we have in the Pseudo Clementines has passed through a catholic filter but one with rather large holes; much of the Jewish content was found agreeable to the larger church's understanding.

A section at the end of this chapter on Epiphanius's parallels will confirm the Jewish-Christian origin of some of the material, if not the dates and specific source documents.

Washings for Purification

A particular strand of Jewish Christianity — influenced by the Essenes, kin to other baptizing groups, and to be identified with the Ebionites — is indicated for some of the material by the frequent reference to daily baths.[4] Thus Peter began successive days with a bath and prayer and bathed before taking food.[5] These baths seemingly

---

3. F. Stanley Jones, "The Pseudo-Clementines: A History of Research, Part I and Part II," *The Second Century* 2(1982): 1-33, 63-96; repr. in Everett Ferguson, ed., *The Literature of the Early Church*, Studies in Early Christianity 2 (New York: Garland, 1993), pp. 195-262. The extensive treatments on which I am most dependent are F. Stanley Jones, *An Ancient Jewish Christian Source on the History of Christianity: Pseudo-Clementine Recognitions 1.27-71* (Atlanta: Scholars, 1995); F. Stanley Jones, "Eros and Astrology in the Περίοδοι Πέτρου: The Sense of the Pseudo-Clementine Novel," *Apocrypha* 12 (2001): 53-78, who gives an outline of the basic writing ("Travels of Peter" — 58-61) and affirms that "astrological beliefs lie at the heart of this Christian novel" (53); F. Stanley Jones, "Jewish Christianity of the *Pseudo-Clementines*," in Marjanen and Luomanen, *A Companion to Second-Century Christian "Heretics,"* pp. 315-334, also on the "Travels (Circuits) of Peter"; and Georg Strecker, *Das Judenchristentum in den Pseudoklementinen,* Texte und Untersuchungen 70, 2nd ed. (Berlin, 1981), especially pp. 196-209 for baptism in the *Kerygmata Petrou* (*Preachings of Peter*, to be distinguished from *Preaching of Peter*, an apologetic work known through quotations by Clement of Alexandria), which he concludes derived from a Gnosticizing Jewish Christian c. 200 (pp. 209, 219).

4. Hence, identified as part of the Jewish-Christian baptist movement by Joseph Thomas, *Le mouvement baptiste en Palestine et Syrie (150 av. J.-C.-300 ap. J.-C.)* (Gembloux: J. Duculot, 1935), pp. 174-177. Strecker, *Das Judenchristentum*, pp. 208-209, however, questions this and says no direct line between the *Kerygmata Petrou* in particular and the baptizing sects (especially Elkesaites) is required. He asserts that the baths are simply the Jewish purification baths and notes that the baths of Peter are not expressly said to have been daily. A purely secular bath is referred to in *Homily* 5.30 (λελουμένον) as engaged in by Apion, the opponent of the Jews.

5. *Hom.* 10.1 and 11.1 — morning; 9.23 and 10.26 — before the evening meal meal that preceded going to bed; for the former compare *Recog.* 8.1 (note 7) and for the latter *Recog.* 4.3. Λουσάμενος is

were not obligatory, for "Peter bathed there in the reservoir with those who wished."[6] They occurred in a reservoir into which a stream of water flowed, but Peter and others also bathed in the sea.[7]

Other occasions for washing were related to sexual activity. A man should not have intercourse with his wife during her period but only after she was "purified and baptized [βαπτισθείση]," and "It is necessary to be baptized [βαπτίζεσθαι] after intercourse."[8] Maintaining these purity regulations was part of the instructions given to converts for their conduct after their initiatory baptism (see below).

In general the Pseudo-Clementines use words from the λούω family for the baths of purity and words from the βαπτίζω family for the Christian baptism of initiation.[9] Accordingly, Peter's exhortation, "Purify your heart from evil by [or in] heavenly reasoning and wash [πλύνετε] your body in the bath [λουτρῷ],"[10] is to be understood as referring to the bath of purification and not baptism; the context favors this view, for the discussion pertains to purification (inner and outer), specifically not approaching one's wife during her period. The use of λούω for the daily baths and βαπτίζω for the baths of purification associated with sexuality as well as for initiatory baptism does not appear to be significant for a difference in meaning or in method of bathing, but it may indicate that in one source of the Pseudo-Clementines a close association was made between purity from activity associated with sexuality and the cleansing from sins in Christian baptism.

Daily baths were practiced by the Essenes and other Jewish groups (chap. 4), and bathing by men after intercourse and by women after menstruation was derived from the Law of Moses (Lev. 15:16, 19-24, 32-33), so the Jewish origins of these practices and their early date seem assured. Different from the ablutions for physical purity was the conversion baptism that the Pseudo-Clementines describe as administered by Peter and his associates to new converts. Both the repeated washings and the one-time baptism were apparently by immersion, but the former were self-

---

used in each case in the Greek. For daily baths by the Ebionites see Epiphanius, *Panarion* 30.15.3; that they bathed continually, *Ancoratus* 2.30.4.

6. *Hom.* 10.26; *Recog.* 5.36. See Einar Molland, "La circoncision, le baptême et l'autorité du décret apostolique (Actes XV, 28sq.) dans les milieux judéo-chrétien des Pseudo-Clémentines," *Studia Theologica* 9 (1955): 1-39 = *Opuscula Patristica* (Oslo: Universitetsforlaget, 1970), pp. 25-59 (which I cite; here p. 52).

7. For a reservoir, references in note 5; for the sea: *Hom.* 8.2 (λουσάμενος) — before a meal; 14.1 (λουσάμενοι), 3 (λελουμένους) — others aside from Peter; *Recog.* 8.1 *(mari lavaremus)* — morning bath.

8. *Hom.* 11.30. Also 11.33, the necessity of "being baptized [βαπτίζεσθαι] after intercourse" (literally, "from [the impurity] of intercourse").

9. Molland, "La circoncision, le baptême," p. 27, nuancing Thomas, "Les ébionites baptistes," p. 290. Schoeps, *Theologie und Geschichte*, p. 209, distinguishes between λούεσθαι for baths and βαπτίζειν for baptism, but the references in the preceding paragraph concerning purification for sexual activity show that the distinction does not hold and at least must be modified. Schoeps, p. 208, further says that the Ebionites distinguished τὸ βάπτισμα from the daily οἱ βαπτισμοί.

10. *Hom.* 11.28.

administered. The presence of both daily baths and one-time conversion baptism among the Ebionites shows these were different rites and not contradictory to each other.

Initiatory Baptism

In narrating Peter's travels and preaching, the Pseudo-Clementines often note that people responded by being baptized. For example, in Tyre, "After they had been taught [κατηχηθέντες] these things for a few days by Peter and been healed, they were baptized [ἐβαπτίσθησαν]" (*Hom.* 7.5). Similarly, in Beirut after teaching and healing, he baptized [βαπτίσας] many and appointed a bishop over them (*Hom.* 7.12). Peter based his (and the other apostles') activities, according to the Pseudo-Clementines, on the command of Jesus in Matthew 28:19-20: "He sent us to the untaught Gentiles to baptize them for forgiveness of sins, and he commanded us first to teach them" (*Hom.* 17.7). The *Recognitions* includes a note that on a (unspecified) festival day the highly unlikely number of "about ten thousand were baptized" (3.72).[11] On another occasion in Laodicea a summary statement says that Peter "baptized multitudes."[12]

Several passages reflect a regular sequence in conversion and the activities surrounding baptism. The fullest account is the following invitation to baptism issued by Peter:

> Since I have resolved to stay three months with you, if any one desires it, let him be baptized; that, stripped of his former evils, he may for the future, in consequence of his own conduct, become heir of heavenly blessings, as a reward for his good actions. Whosoever will, then, let him come to Zacchaeus and give his name to him, and let him hear from him the mysteries of the kingdom of heaven. Let him attend to frequent fastings, and approve himself in all things, that at the end of these three months he may be baptized on the day of the festival [Passover?]. But everyone of you shall be baptized in ever flowing waters, the name of the Trine Beatitude being invoked over him; he being first anointed with oil sanctified by prayer, that so at length, being consecrated by these things, he may attain a perception of holy things.
>
> And when he had spoken at length on the subject of baptism, he dismissed the crowd. (*Recog.* 3.67-68)

As the subsequent quotations will show, some of this account reflects characteristic (but not exclusively) Jewish-Christian emphases — the need for good conduct, fasting,[13] baptism in running water — and language characteristic of the Pseudo-

---

11. So also *Recog.* 10.71.
12. *Recog.* 10.68 = *Hom.* 20.23 without the word "multitudes."
13. In *Hom.* 9.9-10 fasting is a means of expelling demons, but this is not a baptismal context. On

Clementines, such as invocation of the thrice-blessed name. Some other features correspond to the baptismal practices of the great church — turning one's name in for baptism, baptism at Passover (if that is the festival intended), and pre-baptismal anointing (especially in Syria).

Another account gives a similar sequence more briefly. In Tripoli of Phoenicia, Peter led the multitudes, "who fully received the faith of the Lord" (also described as "converted to the faith"), to "the fountains near the sea," baptized them, and celebrated with them the eucharist (literally, "breaking the eucharist") — *Recognitions* 6.15.[14] Embedded in the account is reference to the baptism of Clement, which is told more fully in the *Homilies* but in the events surrounding the baptism is almost identical:

> [Peter] ordered me [Clement] to fast for some days, and leading me to the springs near the sea, he baptized [ἐβάπτισεν] me as in ever-flowing water. Thus our brothers rejoiced at my God-given regeneration [ἀναγεννήσει]. (*Hom.* 11.35)

Other details occur in the account of the baptism of Clement's mother, Mattidia. Peter instructed her concerning the worship of God:

> We worship the one God, who made the world that you see, and we keep his law. . . . We do not share the table of Gentiles, since we cannot eat with them because they live impurely. When we have persuaded them to think and act according to the truth and have baptized them with the thrice-blessed invocation, then we live with them.[15]

When she learned that baptism was necessary for table fellowship with her family who had become Christians, she begged for baptism immediately, asking, "What hinders my being baptized today?"[16] and declaring her rejection of idolatry and her chaste life. Peter replied:

> She must fast at least one day first, and so be baptized; and this because I have heard from her a certain declaration, by which her faith has been made manifest

---

fasting as initially being penitential and a preparation for receiving the Spirit but exorcistic in later baptismal practice see Franz Josef Dölger, *Der Exorzismus im altchristlichen Taufritual* (Paderborn: Ferdinand Schöningh, 1909), pp. 80-86.

14. Cf. the parallel in *Hom.* 11.36: When a great crowd was persuaded, Peter "baptized [βαπτίσας] them in the springs near the sea and celebrated [κλάσας, "broke"] eucharist."

15. *Hom.* 13.4; almost identically in *Recog.* 7.29, where the wording of the last sentence is, "When Gentiles believe, and on the reception of the truth are baptized, and consecrated by a certain threefold invocation of the blessed name, and then we eat with them."

16. *Hom.* 13.5 = *Recog.* 7.30; cf. 7.36. Einar Molland, "A Lost Scrutiny in the Early Baptismal Rite," *Studia Patristica* 5 (1962): 104-108 = *Opuscula Patristica* (Oslo: Universitetsforlaget, 1970), pp. 231-234, accepts Oscar Cullmann's argument for such a question as part of the early baptismal rite and adduces these passages in the Pseudo-Clementines as additional support. See chapter 10 at n. 23 for the references and a rejection of this contention. Molland suggests that the early scutiny disappeared from the baptismal rite and was incorporated into the catechumenate because the catechumenate offered a better guarantee of a person's readiness for baptism (p. 234).

to me, and which has given evidence of her belief; otherwise she must have been instructed and taught many days before she could have been baptized.[17]

Mattidia protested that for two days she had only had some water to drink, but Peter insisted that her abstinence from food did not count unless it was a fast on account of the baptism (*Hom.* 13.11), adding for some unexplained reason that "this hour of day is not suitable for baptism" (*Hom.* 13.12).

The account of Mattidia's baptism the next morning implies a nude baptism. Peter took her and her household to the sea at a sheltered place "to baptize [βαπτίσαι] her unobserved." The baptism took place in the sea between two rocks. Meanwhile, Clement and the brothers "withdrew on account of the women and bathed [λουσάμνοι]." (The water suitable for baptism is elsewhere expressed as "the water of the fountain, river, or even sea."[18]) Later in the day Peter broke bread for the eucharist.[19]

The *Recognitions* concludes with Peter's teaching large numbers who "with one voice confessed the Lord" and "believing in God were baptized"; and "the whole multitude assembled daily to hear the word and believed in the healthful doctrine." Clement's father too decided to convert. Peter "proclaimed a fast to all the people, and on the next Lord's day he baptized him."[20]

A summary of the concerns in regard to conversion characteristic of the Pseudo-Clementines occurs in Peter's preaching in Tripoli:

> Choosing to worship the one God, avoiding the table of demons, accepting self-control with love for humanity and righteousness, being baptized [βαπτισάμενοι] with the thrice-blessed invocation for the forgiveness of sins, and devoting yourselves as much as you are able to perfect purity, you can be delivered from eternal punishment and be designated heirs of eternal blessings.[21]

Baptism here, as in other accounts in the Pseudo-Clementines, is in the context of a choice to worship God, to turn away from demons (idolatry), and to undertake a life of (especially sexual) purity.[22] It is accompanied by the invocation of the divine name(s) and brings forgiveness of sins (more in the next section below) and the hope of good things in eternity.

The preparation for baptism, according to one passage in the Pseudo-Clementines, included, in addition to fasting, receiving the imposition of hands.

---

17. *Recog.* 7.34; cf. *Hom.* 13.9 for the insistence on at least a one-day fast before baptism.
18. *Recog.* 4.32, cited more fully below. This statement and the "ever flowing water" of *Hom.* 11.35 above and *Recog.* 3.67 represent the Jewish preference for "living water" (*Hom.* 11.26).
19. *Hom.* 14.1; *Recog.* 7.38 records only that "she was baptized in the sea."
20. *Recog.* 10.71-72.
21. *Hom.* 9.23. Molland, "La circoncision, le baptême," p. 37, designates these as five conditions for inheriting eternal blessings.
22. Cf. *Recog.* 2.71 for the need of the purification by baptism in order to be rid of the unclean spirit.

Whether this was in blessing or in exorcism is not stated, but the word is commonly used for the gesture in blessing: "Whoever of you wish to be baptized [βαπτισθῆναι], begin tomorrow to fast and daily have hands laid on you [χειροθετεῖσθε], and inquire concerning whatever you wish."[23] Catechists were recognized as part of the clergy. The duties of catechists are mentioned after instruction on the duties of the bishop, presbyters, and deacons;[24] and another passage says honor is to be given to elders, catechists, deacons, widows, and orphans.[25]

The phrase about being baptized "at the thrice-blessed invocation" is characteristic of the Pseudo-Clementines and points to a special source.[26] The Trinitarian name immediately comes to mind as the reference of this phrase, and even if not the original reference probably is intended in the present form of the Pseudo-Clementines; but there is the possibility that the name of Jesus is meant as the "thrice blessed" name. There are also references to baptism "in the name of Jesus," "in his [Jesus'] name," and "on the invocation of his name."[27] Such a formula would agree with the description of baptism as "the baptism of Christ" (Syriac; Latin — "the faith of Christ and baptism"), "the baptism of our Jesus," "the baptism of Jesus" (both the latter in the Latin).[28]

A formal promise not to sin may also have been part of the baptismal ceremony among some Jewish Christians. This is indicated by the *Contestatio* 1 (= *Epistle of Peter to James* 4.1), certainly an early Jewish-Christian source that now prefaces the *Homilies*. It refers to two rites, ordination and baptism. In order to be appointed a teacher, a man must be circumcised, faithful, and proved for six years. Then he was to be brought "to a river or spring, which is living water, where the regeneration [ἀναγέννησις] of the righteous takes place." Since it was not lawful for him to swear an oath (cf. Matt. 5:34), he was commanded "to stand by the water and call to witness, as also we were commanded to do when we were regenerated [ἀναγεννώμενοι], for the sake of not sinning."

It was a Jewish concern not to eat with non-Jews. The Pseudo-Clementines make much of baptism as admitting one to table fellowship. The point was made early in the present form of the *Recognitions* and *Homilies*. Peter took food in private (apparently an ordinary meal and not an agape or eucharist) and ordered the at-the-time unbaptized Clement to eat by himself, explaining: "May God grant to you to be

---

23. *Hom.* 3.73. The chapter continues with two further references to Peter baptizing. The laying on of hands here has been interpreted as exorcistic (see Dölger, *Der Exorzismus in altchristlichen Taufritual*, p. 31), but I think it more likely to be a blessing.

24. *Epistle of Clement to James* 13; cf. also the listings in 14 and 15.

25. *Hom.* 3.71.

26. *Hom.* 9.19 and 23; 11.26; 13.4; *Recog.* 1.63 and 69; 3.67; 4.32; 6.9 ("threefold sacrament"?); 7.29.

27. *Recog.* 1.73; last two in 1.39. Jones, *An Ancient Jewish Christian Source*, pp. 161-162, notes the absence of these phrases from the Syriac but considers the Latin to have preserved the original. Strecker, *Das Judenchristentum*, p. 201, n. 1, considers that the "thrice blessed name" can scarcely mean any thing other than the church's triadic formula.

28. *Recog.* 1.54, 55; Jones, *An Ancient Jewish Christian Source*, pp. 87-89.

made like me in all things and, receiving baptism [βαπτισθέντα], to share the same table with me" (*Hom.* 1.22).[29]

Omitting the items mentioned only once or rarely, we arrive at a sequence in the Pseudo-Clementines involving instruction, fasting, baptism (in living water with the invocation of the triune [?] name), and eucharist. This sequence corresponds to the procedures described in the *Didache* and Justin Martyr and indicates a common practice in the second century among Jewish and Gentile churches. The content of the instruction, especially on the life expected of those baptized, will be touched on in the next section.

Baptismal Doctrine

Baptism in the Pseudo-Clementines is exalted as a "great gift" (*Hom.* 13.10), with which one may compare "the grace of baptism" (*Recog.* 7.38). Its greatness is expressed in the several invitations to baptism. In answering the question, "Why be baptized?" these invitations describe the benefits of baptism. One of the fullest occurs in Peter's teaching leading up to the baptism of "Clement":

> Someone will perhaps say, "What does being baptized [βαπτισθῆναι] in water contribute to piety?" First, that you act for the glory of God. Second, by being regenerated [ἀναγεννηθείς] from the water to God, on account of fear, you change your first generation which occurred from desire and thus you can attain salvation. Otherwise it is impossible. For thus the Prophet swore to us, saying: "Truly I say to you, unless you are regenerated [ἀναγεννηθῆτε] in living water into the name of Father, Son, and Holy Spirit, you cannot enter into the kingdom of heaven." Therefore, come. For there is something merciful there from the beginning, borne on the water, and it rescues from the coming punishment those baptized [βαπτιζομένους] at the thrice-blessed invocation. It offers as gifts to God whatever good deeds are done after baptism [βαπτίσματος] by those who have been baptized [βαπτισθέντων]. Therefore, flee to the water, for this alone can quench fiery desire. The person who will not approach it still carries the spirit of strife, on account of which he does not want to approach the living water for his salvation.
>
> Come, then, whether you are righteous or unrighteous. If you are righteous, being baptized [βαπτισθῆναι] is the only thing lacking for salvation; if unrighteous, to be baptized [βαπτισθῆναι] for the forgiveness of those things previously

---

29. *Recog.* 1.19 is almost identical except for the plural, because Peter's friends are included. Molland, "La circoncision, le baptême," pp. 41-43, uses the requirement of baptism before eating together as an argument that baptism was substituted for circumcision by the Pseudo-Clementine community (more on this topic below). He cites further *Recog.* 2.70-72; 4.37; *Hom.* 3.29 (the unbaptized Clement had to pray separately); and the accounts of the conversion of Clement's mother and father quoted above.

done in ignorance.... Delay brings danger because the appointed time of death is unknown. Show by doing good your likeness to the Father who begets you from water.[30]

This passage, as is common in the Pseudo-Clementines, identifies baptism with regeneration. The author quotes John 3:5 as the words of the Prophet (Jesus) with two additions: the water is "living water," and the three divine names are introduced, thus combining two of the main baptismal texts for the early church (John 3:5 and Matt. 28:19). There is one omission from John 3:5 — birth from the Spirit. That may be alluded to in the phrase "something merciful there [in the water] from the beginning, borne upon the water." The reference seems to be to the water and the Spirit of Genesis 1:1-2, which were often given a baptismal interpretation in the early church.[31] Grammatically, however, it is the word "mercy" that is borne upon the water and rescues from punishment; but mercy likely stands for the divine Spirit.[32]

Fear is a positive motivation for the second generation.[33] This regeneration, as life giving, is connected with "living water." It changes the results of the first generation. One's first birth came about as a result of sexual desire. There is no thought here of the transmission of Adam's sin, only of the drive to reproduction.[34] The good deeds following baptism were, for the author, especially a life of purity in sexual matters.[35] Baptism extinguished the fire of lust.

The parallel in *Recognitions* 6.9 is very close in content and wording. Modifications include the omission of "living" from water and of the triple divine name from

---

30. *Hom.* 11.26-27. The passage is studied by L. Cirillo, "Le baptême, remède à la concupiscence, selon la catéchèse ps.-clémentine de Pierre: *Hom.* XI 26 (*Réc* VI 9; IX 7)," in T. Baarda et al., eds., *Text and Testimony: Essays on New Testament and Apocryphal Literature in Honour of A. F. J. Klijn* (Kampen: Kok, 1988), pp. 79-90. He places the passage in the context of *Hom.* 11, in which the religion of God has three steps: recognize one's origin, be reborn of water, and observe the laws of purity. Strecker, *Das Judenchristentum*, pp. 196-209, gives a commentary on the whole context, *Hom.* 11.21-33 = *Recog.* 6.6-14, which he identifies as coming from the *Kerygmata Petrou*. He finds the baptismal terminology to be Gnostic (I would question this) but the interpretation of baptism and the ethical instruction to be bound to Jewish and Christian motifs. Holger Hammerich, "Taufe und Askese: Der Taufaufschub in vorkonstantinischer Zeit" (Diss., University of Hamburg, 1994), p. 85, notes that the word for "delay" (ἀναβολή) at the end of the passage is already the technical term used in the fourth century for the postponement of baptism.

31. Clement of Alexandria, *Prophetic Eclogues* 7.1; Tertullian, *Baptism* 4. The association of water and spirit, based on Gen. 1:2, is found in *Hom.* 11.22 = *Recog.* 6.7.

32. Strecker, *Das Judenchristentum*, p. 201, notes that the Targum names the Spirit of Gen. 1:2 the "spirit of mercy."

33. For fear in the *Kerygmata Petrou*, see Strecker, *Das Judenchristentum*, pp. 200-201. In the Pseudo-Clementines it is a sign of believing.

34. Strecker, *Das Judenchristentum*, p. 199; Cirillo, "Le baptême," p. 87. Note their studies of ἐπιθυμία in the Pseudo-Clementines — Strecker, pp. 199-201; Cirillo, pp. 79-90; cf. Molland, "La circoncision, le baptême," pp. 40-41.

35. Strecker, *Das Judenchristentum*, pp. 203-207, noting the virtual absence of the Holy Spirit from the baptismal doctrine of the *Kerygmata Petrou*, comments that baptism is understood fundamentally as not pneumatic but moralistic (p. 203).

the quotation of John 3:5, bringing it more nearly in line with the Gospel text. The regeneration is to be born again "of water and of God." Other differences include additions: "weakness" of the first birth and "power of" mercy (a clearer allusion to the Spirit that is probably a secondary insertion). A change is that the waters "quench the future fire." The righteous should be baptized "so that perfection may be accomplished in him and he may be born again to God," and the unrighteous so that "pardon may be granted to him for his sins." Other notable expressions are "souls consecrated by baptism" and the continuation at the beginning of the next chapter, "When you have been regenerated by water, show by good works the likeness in you of the Father who begat you" (6.10). The passage proceeds to enjoin abstinence from relations with a woman in her period and to expound on the goodness of washing the body with water for purity (6.10-11).

Recognitions 9.7 picks up the theme of two generations. Our first birth descended from the fire of concupiscence, but the second birth by water ("being regenerate in water") extinguishes this fire. This quenching of the fire of desire is related to "good works" and to being "enlightened by the heavenly Spirit." The author of the basic writing allows that astrological fate rules over the first birth of human beings, but regeneration by baptism delivers one from the control of fate.[36] That regeneration provides an escape from fate is a distinctive application of this aspect of baptism.

The chapter that precedes *Recognitions* 6.9 speaks strongly of the necessity of baptism, exalting water as the original element of creation that God ordered for the rebirth of human beings.

> You see that all things are produced from waters. But water was made at first by the Only-begotten. . . . When you have come to the Father, you will learn that this is his will, that you be born anew by means of waters, which were first created. For he who is regenerated by water, having filled up the measure of good works, is made heir of him by whom he has been regenerated in incorruption. Therefore, with prepared minds, approach as sons to a father, that your sins may be washed away. . . . And do you suppose that you can have hope towards God, even if you cultivate all piety and all righteousness, but do not receive baptism? . . . For merit accrues to men from good works, but only if they be done as God commands. Now God has ordered every one who worships him to be sealed by baptism. (*Recog.* 6.8)

The passage reflects the exaltation of water found in the Jewish baptismal movement (chap. 4). It brings together two of the characteristic ideas of the Pseudo-Clementines in reference to baptism — its association with forgiveness of sins and with regeneration.[37] The Pseudo-Clementines place a great emphasis on good

---

36. Jones, "Eros and Astrology," pp. 76-77. Cf. parallels in *Recog.* 9.31; *Hom.* 19.23, "We can show you how by being regenerated [ἀναγεννηθεὶς], changing your [first] birth, and living according to law you will attain eternal salvation."

37. In addition to passages cited in the body of our discussion, note on the forgiveness of sins

works; here they are meritorious only as related to the commands of God. One of his commands is to be baptized. Here, as in other early Christian writings, baptism is a seal.

A comparable passage in the *Homilies* brings the forgiveness of sins and regeneration even closer together.

> This is the worship God has appointed: to reverence only him, to trust in the Prophet of truth alone, and to be baptized [βαπτισθῆναι] for the forgiveness of sins and thus through this most pure dipping [βαφῆς] to be regenerated [ἀναγεννηθῆναι] to God through the saving water. (*Hom.* 7.8)

This strong affirmation about the place of baptism in the true worship of God is related to believing in the Prophet (Jesus) and makes certain (if there could be any doubt in a Jewish context) that baptism was a dipping. The passage continues with the kind of conduct expected: a restatement of the apostolic decree of Acts 15:20, 29.[38] It is further noted that as a result of Peter's exhortation, "Many repented, believed, and were healed."

A qualification on the present effectiveness of baptism by seemingly placing the forgiveness in the future occurs in a statement on the necessity of not sinning after baptism: "He has bestowed on people holy baptism, to which, if any one makes haste to come, and for the future remains without stain, all his sins are thenceforth blotted out, which were committed in the time of his ignorance" (*Recog.* 10.49).

The strong emphasis on chastity in the Pseudo-Clementines[39] introduces a possible exception to the necessity of baptism in Peter's words of consolation to Clement's mother. She had nearly died in a shipwreck in her search for her son.

> You were in danger in the deep, yet you did not die. If you had died, the deep itself would have become for you a baptism [βάπτισμα] for the salvation of your soul on account of your self-control. (*Hom.* 13.20)

Recog. 2.19 ("Clement" describes himself as at a given time "not yet washed from the sins that I had committed in ignorance"); on regeneration *Recog* 3.75 (a contrast of carnal birth with "the generation that is by baptism"); *Hom.* 19.23 ("By being regenerated [ἀναγεννηθείς], changing your first birth, and living according to the law, you may attain eternal salvation"); and 11.24 ("Having been regenerated [ἀναγεννηθείς] by [or in] the firstborn water" — an exaltation of water paralleling the description in the passage quoted in the text of water as "first created"). I note that Justin, *1 Apology* 61 also combines the ideas of forgiveness and regeneration. Strecker, *Das Judenchristentum*, pp. 199-200, notes other points of contact between the *Kerygmata Petrou* and Justin's doctrine of baptism.

38. This is one of the passages cited by Molland, "La circoncision, le baptême," pp. 45-52, for the acceptance of the authority of this decree as applied to Gentile converts by the Jewish Christians of the *Preachings of Peter* and for their interpretation of it. This passage is cited (p. 49) for its list of eight elements of true religion, only the first part of which I have quoted in the text. Other passages cited are *Recog.* 4.36; 6.10; *Hom.* 7.4; 8.23; 11:27-30. The prohibition of formication was understood to include the requirement of washing after intercourse and menstruation (p. 50).

39. Jones, "Eros and Astrology," p. 76, with reference to *Recog.* 7.38 and *Hom.* 13.13, cited below, n. 43.

The recollection in this context of drowning as one meaning of baptism reinforces the understanding of immersion as the practice in baptism. The attractiveness of the possibility of salvation by reason of chastity reappears in the following chapter, where it is suggested that "erring Gentiles might have been saved on account of chastity alone." This possibility, however, is cancelled by a divine law to the contrary.[40]

A distinctive interpretation connected with baptism as bringing forgiveness of sins concerns the parable of the wedding banquet (Matt. 22:1-14).

> The Father has ordered us through the Prophet of the truth . . . to clothe you with a clean wedding garment, which is baptism [βάπτισμα] that brings forgiveness of the bad things done by you, and to lead good persons by their repentance to the banquet of God.[41]

There follows the instruction to take off one's foul garment, "You cannot remove this garment otherwise than first being baptized [βαπτισθῆτε] for [ἐπὶ] good works," and become the garment of the divine Spirit.[42]

Another description by "Peter" of the benefits of baptism speaks, instead of extinguishing desire, of driving out evil spirits.

> In the present life, when you have been washed [ἀπολουσάμενοι] in an ever-flowing [ἀενάῳ] river, spring, or indeed even in the sea at the thrice-blessed invocation, you are able not only to drive out the spirits lurking in you but also (if you no longer practice sin and believe in God unwaveringly) you will drive out from other persons the evil spirits and cruel demons with their terrible sufferings. (*Hom.* 9.19)

Note the strengthened form of the verb for "washing" and the alternative "ever-flowing" for "living" water. Baptism makes it possible for one to banish the evil spirits from his life and in addition, if continuing in faith and avoidance of sin, to expel them from others. The comparable invitation to baptism in *Recognitions* 4.32 also mentions the three sources of suitable water and the "threefold name of blessedness," but further specifies that the washing removes sins and that the sufferings from the demons include sicknesses.

As noted, there is a great concern in the Pseudo-Clementines with a life of purity and good works to follow after baptism. The association of chastity with righteous living is often made: "Salvation in the other world is granted only to those who are baptized [βαπτισθεῖσι] on account of hope in him and practice righteousness with chastity."[43] Notable also is the basis of baptism in trust in God — expressed

---

40. See n. 54 for the quotation of this law and other references on the necessity of baptism for salvation applying to all.
41. *Hom.* 8.22. Cf. *Recog.* 4.35, "That we should give you wedding garments, that is the grace of baptism."
42. *Hom.* 8.23.
43. *Hom.* 13.13 = *Recog.* 7.38.

here as it was in *Barnabas* and other sources influenced by Jews with the word "hope." The importance of the emphasis on good works comes out in the way Peter includes it in an exhortation on the importance of baptism:

> I condemn the many who, when they have been baptized [βαπτισθέντες] and say that they believe, do nothing worthy of faith, nor do they urge those whom they love ... to be baptized. For if they believed that God grants eternal life with good works to baptism [βαπτίσματι], they would urge those whom they love to be baptized [βαπτισθῆναι] without delay.[44]

The connection of baptism with believing is common, but here the believing is more the content of the teaching than personal faith in God and Christ.

A characteristic of Ebionite teaching was that the Prophet[45] came to abolish the temple sacrifices and instituted water baptism to replace them as the means of forgiveness of sins. This view is affirmed several times in *Recognitions* 1.27-71 (notably 1.39; 1.55.3-4; 1.69.4), a section that with a few redactional elements incorporates an early Jewish-Christian source.[46]

> [T]he time came when it was fitting for the prophet to appear who was proclaimed earlier by Moses. At his coming, by the mercy of God, he would admonish them first to stop and cease with their sacrificing. In order that they not think that they were being deprived of the forgiveness of sins that accrued through sacrifices and in order that this might not be a hindrance with the result that they would not believe, baptism through water for the forgiveness of sins was instituted. What in truth gives forgiveness of sins was manifested to them. It is able to preserve in eternal life those who are perfect so that they will not die.[47]

The practice of vegetarianism by the Ebionites is likely related to their rejection of animal sacrifice.[48]

A few chapters later the viewpoint is elaborated:

44. *Hom.* 13.10. Almost identical words occur in *Recog.* 7.35.

45. The Prophet announced by Moses (Deut. 18:15-20) is a regular description of the role of Jesus in the Pseudo-Clementines. The command to listen to that Prophet is developed in *Recog.* 2.33, where Peter says that he (also called Master and Lord) sent the apostles to teach all nations the things he committed to them and that they could speak nothing different.

46. Jones, *An Ancient Jewish Christian Source.* He translates the Latin (by Rufinus) and Syriac texts of the passage and concludes that it was written about 200 by a Jew, perhaps in Jerusalem, who accepted Christianity as the religion intended by Moses (Jesus is the Prophet proclaimed by Moses and is the Christ who will come again) and with it the Gentile mission and who stood in genetic relationship to the earliest Jewish Christianity (pp. 159-167).

47. *Recog.* 1.39. I quote the translation of Jones, *An Ancient Jewish Christian Source,* p. 69, from the Syriac, which is somewhat fuller, except that the Latin adds that the baptism which absolves from all sins is "through the invocation of his [the prophet's] name" (see above, nn. 27 and 28) and at the point where the quotation closes adds, "purified not through the blood of animals but through the purification of God's wisdom." The mission of the Prophet to abolish sacrifice is developed more fully in 1.37.

48. Schoeps, *Jewish Christianity,* pp. 99-101. *Hom.* 8.15; 12.6.

I am speaking not of Moses but of the one who was called Son by God in the baptismal water. For Jesus is the one who by the grace of baptism extinguished the fire that the high priest had lit for sins. For when he appeared, the chrism ceased through which the office of high priest, prophet, or king was conferred.[49]

The writer alludes to the designation of Jesus as Son of God at his baptism (Matt. 3:17). With the coming of Jesus there ceased the anointing to the offices of high priest (especially), but also prophet and king. Does this indicate that a baptismal anointing was absent for this community? The author's main interest was that the water of baptism extinguished the fire of sacrifice. The water of baptism is said in the Pseudo-Clementines to have extinguished five kinds of fire: the fire of sacrifice, the fire of idols' origin, the fire of concupiscence that is the source of our first birth, the fire of sin, and the fire of punishment in the world to come.[50]

"When the coming of Christ was at hand for the abolition of sacrifices and for the bestowal of the grace of baptism," "the enemy" produced schisms among the people — Sadducees, Samaritans, scribes and Pharisees.[51] Another schism was produced by the disciples of John who "proclaimed their own master as the Christ."[52] The enemy arranged these schisms "so that the faith of Christ and baptism might be hindered by them."

In controversy with the high priest over sacrifices and the baptism introduced by Jesus, Matthew, representing the Twelve, declared:

"One who is not baptized not only is rejected from the kingdom of heaven but also is in danger at the resurrection of the dead and, even though he is good in his manner of life and righteous in his mind, will fall short of eternal life."[53]

The words attributed to Matthew state the viewpoint we find elsewhere in the Pseudo-Clementines that a good life is not sufficient for salvation if one is not baptized.[54] The wording here, as elsewhere, reflects John 3:5 about entering "the kingdom of heaven."

"Peter" summarized his appeal to the Jews:

---

49. *Recog.* 1.48, quoting the translation of the Latin by Jones, *An Ancient Jewish Christian Source*, p. 80. The Latin has clarified the sense somewhat.

50. Molland, "La circoncision, le baptême," p. 41.

51. *Recog.* 1.54.

52. *Recog.* 1.60 repeats the assertion of "one of John's disciples" that John was the Christ.

53. *Recog.* 1.55, quoting the Syriac in Jones, *An Ancient Jewish Christian Source*, p. 89. Strecker, *Das Judenchristentum*, p. 198, notes that the Pseudo-Clementines give two bases for the necessity of baptism: God so ordered it, and those reborn from water exchange the first birth by passion (*Hom.* 11.26 = *Recog.* 6.9).

54. Note *Hom.* 11.27 quoted above and also *Hom.* 11.25: "Do not think that, even if you are more pious than all the pious people but are unbaptized [ἀβάπτιστος], you can have any hope. . . . If you do not want to be baptized [βαπτισθῆναι] as God desires, you serve your own will and oppose his will." *Hom.* 13.21 refers to a law that "not even a righteous person who is unbaptized [ἀβάπτιστον] enters into the kingdom of God," probably with reference to John 3:5.

> I showed them that in no other way could they be saved, unless through the grace of the Holy Spirit they hastened to be washed with the baptism of threefold invocation and received the eucharist of Christ the Lord, whom alone they ought to believe concerning those things which he taught.[55]

Since the Syriac omits reference to the eucharist, doubt is raised about whether it was regularly part of the baptismal sequence in the early sources of the Pseudo-Clementines, but the Syriac does support the understanding of the "threefold invocation" as a reference to the names in the Trinity. However, both the Syriac and the Latin minimize the role of the Holy Spirit as a person: for the Syriac, receiving the "holy spirit" is a reference to receiving the truth, and for the Latin, it is not the Spirit but the Spirit's grace that is operative. Such a treatment accords with the omission of "and the Spirit" from references to John 3:5.

The final passage in the source behind *Recognitions* 1 to be noted is in a speech attributed to James.

> [He demonstrated] that unless one wash in the name of the glorious Trinity in the waters whose flow is living, just as the prophet of truth showed, there will be no forgiveness of sins for him and he will also not enter into the kingdom of God.[56]

Here the forgiveness of sins is paired with entering the kingdom instead of with regeneration, but the thought may not be so different, because entering the kingdom may also be derived from the saying found in John 3:5. The passage concludes with James speaking much concerning the Paraclete (giving an attention to the Holy Spirit not prominent in the other baptismal texts) and baptism over the course of seven days and persuading the people to make haste to receive baptism.

The Pseudo-Clementines never say expressly that baptism replaces circumcision, but it has been argued that the extensive passages about baptism in conversion with no reference to circumcision, which was the key act in making a proselyte, indicate that this was part of the understanding of the community behind the Pseudo-Clementines and distinguished it from the (other?) Ebionites for whom circumcision was a requirement.[57] Although the absence of a requirement for Gentiles to be circumcised distinguishes the Pseudo-Clementines from the reports of the heresiologists about the Ebionites, nonetheless, since Jews expected to con-

---

55. *Recog.* 1.63. I render the Latin here. The Syriac has simply, "You will be able to receive the holy spirit, which is truth, through baptism of the name of the glorious Trinity." It continues, "You will make confession, you will believe only in God regarding the things that he has taught, and thus you will receive redemption and eternal life" — Jones, *An Ancient Jewish Christian Source*, p. 98.

56. *Recog.* 1.69, quoting the Syriac in Jones, *An Ancient Jewish Christian Source*, p. 105. The Latin uses "baptized" instead of "washed" and "threefold blessedness" instead of "Trinity," and it lacks the description of the water as "whose flow is living."

57. Molland, "La circoncision, le baptême," pp. 31-45.

tinue circumcision for themselves,[58] it would not be exactly correct to say baptism replaced circumcision (even if it assumed some of the same significance in conversion for Gentiles). It is possible also that the later redactors removed any reference to circumcision.

There may be a reference to Jewish baptism in a section of contrasts: pious with impious persons, prophets and false prophets, philosophers and false philosophers, Arabs and other who have imitated the circumcision of the Jews, worship of demons and divine worship, "baptism to baptism," laws to the law, false apostles to apostles, and false teachers to teachers.[59] In the middle of the sequence the author reverses the order in which the true and the false are mentioned. Out of these contrasts only the two baptisms are given no description, but the proximity to circumcision suggests the possibility of a contrast of Jewish and Christian baptism. Another possibility is that the contrast of false and true worship is meant to indicate demonic imitations in pagan washings in distinction to Christian baptism.

We may summarize the meaning of baptism according to the Pseudo-Clementines in the words of H. J. Schoeps. He identified a threefold meaning for baptism as held by the Ebionites: it was an initiation rite and as such a rebirth; it frees from appetite and thus the power of demons and also takes away sins; and most important it substituted for the sacrificial fire kindled by the high priest for atonement of sins.[60] We would add that baptism was a conscious choice based on believing in the one God and accepting the teachings of his Prophet, Jesus. It carried with it an obligation to live a life of purity (chastity) and righteousness.

Epiphanius on the Ebionites

Earlier heresiologists were mainly interested in Ebionite Christology and the Jewish way of life. Epiphanius, *Panarion* 30, gives a fuller treatment to the Ebionites and is the source of our quotation on the baptism of Jesus in the *Gospel of the Ebionites* (chap. 6). Some of his information came from oral reports, but he apparently knew and had read some Ebionite writings. He refers specifically to Clement's so-called *Peregrinations of Peter* (*Panarion* 2.30.15.1) and the *Degrees* [or *Ascents*] *of James* (*Panarion* 2.30.16.7), names given by modern scholars to some of the source material in the Pseudo-Clementines. Epiphanius's tone is very prejudicial, but he seems to have had access to some accurate information.[61]

Some of Epiphanius's information on the Ebionites directly agrees with points noted in the discussion of the Pseudo-Clementine literature above: Ebionites abstained from meat (*Panarion* 2.30.15.3), and Christ came to abolish sacrifice

---

58. Note *Contestatio* 1 (*Epistle of Peter to James* 4.1) for the requirement that teachers be circumcised.
59. *Recog.* 8.53.
60. Schoeps, *Theologie und Geschichte des Judenchristentums*, pp. 209-210 (with full listing of references); idem, *Jewish Christianity*, pp. 104-105.
61. Thomas, "Les ébionites baptistes," pp. 262-275.

(*Panarion* 2.30.16.4-5). Otherwise, Epiphanius spends much time on the importance of circumcision to Ebionites,[62] a topic on which the Pseudo-Clementines have little to say. He holds that their Sabbath observance, circumcision, and daily baths stand together as discredited Jewish practices (*Panarion* 2.30.32.1).

Epiphanius refers to the claim by the Ebionites that Peter bathed daily and that that they have purification through these daily immersions (baptisms).[63] He also refers to the Ebionite practice of immersing (often with clothes on) after touching a Gentile and after sexual intercourse.[64] We find in the Pseudo-Clementines insistence on the latter practice; the former practice has a parallel in the avoidance of eating with the non-baptized.

In view of Epiphanius's negative attitude toward the Ebionites and extended refutation of some of their practices, his note on their practice of initiatory baptism and of the eucharist is significantly brief:

> They also receive baptism [βάπτισμα], apart from being baptized [βαπτίζονται] daily. And they celebrate mysteries year after year, if you please, in imitation of the sacred mysteries of the church, using unleavened bread — and the other part of the mystery with water only.[65]

Epiphanius notes the bread and water eucharist ("mystery" was by his time a word regularly used for the eucharist). Absence of comment about their one-time or initiatory baptism indicates either a lack of information on his part or perhaps the absence of significant differences. Our discussion above showed many of the same ideas in common between the Pseudo-Clementines and the great church of which Epiphanius was a part, but with some significantly different emphases (of which Epiphanius may not have been aware or chose to overlook).

Observations

If those students of the Pseudo-Clementines who say that at least some of the baptismal teaching and practice recorded in the Pseudo-Clementines go back to Jewish-Christian components (and are not simply a reflection of catholic redaction in the third century) are right, then some significant conclusions follow. The agreements

---

62. *Panarion* 2.30.26.1-2; 28.1-9; 33.1-2; 34.2.

63. *Panarion* 2.30.15.3; 30.21.1-2; cf. *Anacephalaeosis* 2.30.4, "They continually immerse themselves [βαπτίζονται] in water, summer and winter, for purification."

64. *Panarion* 2.30.2.3-5. They are baptized (βαπτίζεσθαι) in the sea or other water after intercourse. If one meets another after his plunge (καταδύσεως) and baptism (βαπτισμοῦ — note the general word for dippings for purification and not the Christian word for baptism, which occurs in my next quotation for their initiatory baptism), he runs to be baptized again with clothes on. The baptism is a "plunge," not two separate acts.

65. *Panarion* 2.30.16.1. I use, but modify, the translation of Frank Williams, *The Panarion of Epiphanius of Salamis, Book I (Sects 1-46)* (Leiden: Brill, 1987), pp. 131-132.

(or substantially so) with baptism in the Gentile church of the second century is a confirmation that these common elements go back to the first-century church.

The realistic doctrine of baptismal blessings in the Pseudo-Clementines stands in contrast to some views expressed by those on the opposite end of the spectrum of early Christianity (chap. 17).

16. Jewish and Christian Baptisms

The Jewish Christians of the Pseudo-Clementines (and Gentiles influenced by them) observed Jewish baths of purification and the one-time conversion baptism. Gentile Christians (and Jewish converts who identified with their practice) generally rejected the frequent religious baths and made a contrast between the two baptismal practices. The reader must recognize the polemical context in which Christians made the contrast of their baptism with Jewish washings and remember that there were metaphorical and spiritualizing applications of the idea of purification by washing made by Jews.[1]

The *Epistle of Barnabas* 11 (chap. 12) made the contrast between Jewish baptism with Christian baptism on the basis that the former did not bring forgiveness of sins but the latter did. This distinction continued to be reiterated in later Christian comments on the difference between Christian and Jewish practice. It seems to be correct for Jewish washings, where the concern was with ceremonial purity (chap. 4). Some later Jewish baptismal movements may have moved to associate their baptismal practice with forgiveness of sins, but there is a question about how early this occurred. The likelihood is that any groups under Jewish influence making this association (e.g., Elkasaites) were dependent in some way on the practice of John the Baptist and his followers.

A striking feature of Christians' comments on Jewish practice is that they seem oblivious to proselyte baptism. Their comments have to do with Jewish ritual washings for purification. Perhaps the tradition making the contrast of the two rites in terms of forgiveness of sins was established before proselyte baptism became current.[2] Or, it may be that the church writers saw proselyte baptism as only another ex-

---

1. Jonathan D. Lawrence, *Washing in Water: Trajectories of Ritual Bathing in the Hebrew Bible and Second Temple Literature* (Atlanta: Scholars Press, 2006), p. 201.

2. See chap. 4 for the problem of dating the origin of baptism as part of the ritual of conversion to Judaism.

pression of the basic idea of ceremonial purity associated with the other occasions for the act among Jews, an interpretation that may have been behind the practice initially before it was enriched with deeper moral and religious significance.

Justin Martyr

Most of Justin's comments on Christian baptism were discussed in chapter 14, but we have reserved for here the contrast he made between Jewish and Christian practice in this regard. This distinction is part of his argument with the Jew Trypho *(Dialogue with Trypho)* wherein he spiritualizes other differences between Jews and Christians — circumcision, Sabbath, sacrifices, priesthood. His approach on these matters is quite similar to that of the *Epistle to Barnabas*, with the significant exception that he did think these institutions were given to the Jews to be kept literally by them (imposed because of their hardness of heart, he says) until the Christ came.

Justin refers in one passage explicitly to the purification baths of the Jews. He has Trypho acknowledge that Jews after the destruction of the temple could no longer observe the sacrifices there, but some things they could observe: "keeping Sabbath, being circumcised, observing the new moon, and being baptized [βαπτί- ζεσθαι] after touching anything forbidden by Moses or after sexual intercourse" *(Dial.* 46.2). He employs the Christians' preferred word, *baptisma*, for Jewish baptism as well, perhaps to highlight his understanding that the difference was not in the act but in the significance of the act. He will similarly use the same word "circumcision" for the Jewish physical act and the Christian meaning given to this word, but in this case there was no physical correspondence in the actions.

Early in the *Dialogue* Justin has a point of contact with the tradition of exegesis in *Barnabas*. He gives a Christological and baptismal interpretation of Isaiah 52:10-54:6 in *Dialogue* 12-14.[3] The discussion is sandwiched between two quotations of the promise of an "everlasting covenant" through a "ruler given to the nations" (Isa. 55:3-5 — *Dial.* 12.1 and 14.4). The sins of the people required a "second circumcision," but the Jews were making much of their flesh *(Dial.* 12.3). The same is true of other ordinances, including, "If any one does not have clean hands, let him wash [λουσάσθω], and he is clean" (12.3). A spiritual washing is apparently intended, for Justin continues:

> For Isaiah [alluding to Isa. 1:16] indeed did not send you to a bath [βαλανεῖον] to wash away [ἀπολουσομένους] there murder and other sins, which not even all the water of the sea is sufficient to purify, but it is likely that even of old this very thing that he said referred to the saving bath [λουτρὸν] for those who change their mind and no longer "purify themselves with the blood of goats and sheep or the ashes of a heifer or offerings of fine flour, but by faith through the blood of Christ" [cf. Heb. 9:13-14] and his death. *(Dial.* 13.1)

---

3. D. Jeffrey Bingham, "Justin and Isaiah 53," *Vigiliae Christianae* 54 (2000): 248-261.

There follows as the justification for his death the quotation of Isaiah 52:10–54:6. The blood and death of Jesus bring a cleansing that is received through baptism associated with repentance and faith.

Justin makes the same contrast as *Barnabas,* including the citation of Jeremiah 2:13 with its contrast of the water of life with broken cisterns:

> By the bath [λουτροῦ] of repentance and of the knowledge of God, which is for the transgression of the peoples of God, as Isaiah cried out, we have believed and make known that this very thing that was prophesied, namely baptism [βάπτισμα], is alone able to purify those who repent and is the water of life. But "the cisterns that you have dug for yourselves are broken" and unprofitable. For what is the benefit of that baptism [βαπτίσματος] which cleanses only the body and flesh? Baptize [βαπτίσθητε] your soul from wrath, covetousness, envy, hatred — and behold the body is pure! (*Dial.* 14.1-2)

Although Justin uses different words for the secular bath *(balaneion)* and the religious bath *(loutron),* he employs the Christians' preferred word, *baptisma,* for the Jewish baptism as well. He contrasts the two baptisms, saying the Jewish bath washed only the body whereas the Christians' washed the soul from sins. "Baptize your soul" may be metaphorical, but, if so, is suggested by Christian water baptism. The latter had its effect because of Christ's atoning death for human sins; this effect was dependent on faith and repentance.

Justin repeats his contrast of the two baptisms in much the same terms a few chapters later in the *Dialogue.* He argues that fleshly circumcision was not necessary for all men but was for Jews alone. Nor do Christians practice the Jewish washings. After quoting Isaiah 1:16, he comments: "God commands you to be washed [λούσασθαι] in this bath [λουτρὸν] and to be circumcised with the true circumcision."[4] He continues:

> We do not accept that useless baptism [βάπτισμα] in cisterns, for it has nothing to do with the baptism [βάπτισμα] of life. [There follows a quotation of Jer. 2:13.] You who are circumcised in the flesh have need of our circumcision, but we who have ours [spiritual circumcision] do not need yours. (*Dial.* 19.2-3)

The discussion of baptism and circumcision together may make one think of proselyte baptism, but the order (baptism and then circumcision) is the reverse of Jewish practice. The thought is probably due to the Christian association of baptism with receiving the Holy Spirit, who effects the true spiritual circumcision. If so, there is no reason to think that Justin has in mind any other Jewish practice than the ceremonial washings.

Baptism and circumcision are treated as separate rites with separate meanings. That usage offers a clarification of another passage in which the difference of Chris-

---

4. *Dial.* 18.2, discussed in chap. 14.

tian baptism is expressed not in terms of forgiveness of sins but in terms of its relation to the Holy Spirit.

> What reason for circumcision then do I have who have been testified to by God? What need of that other [Jewish] baptism [βαπτίσματος] do I have who have been baptized [βεβαπτισμένῳ] with [or, in — dative case] the Holy Spirit? (*Dial.* 29.1)

Justin does not speak of "baptism with the Holy Spirit" in the way the New Testament does in contrast to water baptism, but he refers to water baptism in which the Holy Spirit is at work.[5] The true spiritual circumcision administered by the Holy Spirit comes "through baptism," but is not baptism itself.[6] This accords with the way in which the gift of the Holy Spirit is treated in other passages in early Christian literature as the Christian counterpart of fleshly circumcision in Judaism.[7]

Oxyrhynchus Papyrus 840

A fragment of an apocryphal Gospel is found in a papyrus from the fourth century, but the editors assign the original to the late second century.[8] It records an episode in which Jesus and his disciples enter the court of the Israelites of the temple in Jerusalem. A "Pharisaic chief priest" named Levi criticized them for not having bathed before entering the sacred area.[9] The author knew the Jewish preference for running water in purifications, the typical design being a *mikveh*. However, he did not have a high regard for the purity of the water and made uncomplimentary, indeed unfair, comparisons. The following is part of the critic's charge with Jesus' reply:

---

5. See G. W. H. Lampe, *The Seal of the Spirit*, 2nd ed. (London: SPCK, 1967), pp. 84-85.
6. *Dial.* 43.2, quoted in chap. 14.
7. Everett Ferguson, "Spiritual Circumcision in Early Christianity," *Scottish Journal of Theology* 41 (1988): 485-497 (493-494 on Justin). See also André Benoît, *Le baptême chrétien au second siècle* (Paris: Presses Universitaires de France, 1953), pp. 170-177, but he makes a more direct association of baptism with circumcision than my interpretation warrants.
8. B. P. Grenfell and A. S. Hunt, *The Oxyrhynchyus Papyri* (London: Egyptian Exploration Fund, 1908), Vol. 5, pp. 1-10. The translation below modifies theirs (restored text, pp. 6-7; translation, pp. 7-8). There are no firm indications of the date in the preserved text; the editors argue for a date before 200 (p. 4). See Joachim Jeremias and Wilhelm Schneemelcher in Wilhelm Schneemelcher, *New Testament Apocrypha* (Louisville: Westminster, 1991), Vol. 1, pp. 94-95, for bibliography and alternative translation. There is now a major study by Michael J. Kruger, *The Gospel of the Saviour: P.OXY 840 and Its Place in the Gospel Traditions of Early Christianity* (Leiden: Brill, 2005).
9. François Bovon, "Fragment Oxyrhynchus 840: Fragment of a Lost Gospel, Witness of an Early Christian Controversy over Purity," *Journal of Biblical Literature* 119 (2000): 705-728, offers a different interpretation from the straightforward reading I follow: the fragment belongs either to second-century "Gnostic opposition to a Jewish Christian baptist movement or to the mainstream church" or to third-century "Manichaean polemic against the Elkesaites" (p. 728). Apart from the problematic thesis itself there are details that do not fit the proposals: recently discovered *mikvaoth* have the two sets of steps for entering and exiting the Jewish baptismal pools (p. 717); and the orthodox practices in regard to baptism and sacred vessels which are cited are much later than the second-third centuries assigned to the fragment (pp. 719, 720-721).

"Who gave you permission to walk in this place of purification and to see these holy vessels, when you are not washed [λουσαμένῳ] and the feet of your disciples have not been baptized [or bathed, βαπτισθέντων]? . . . No one walks here unless he has washed himself [λουσάμενος] and changed his clothes."

The Savior answered him, "Are you, then, being in the temple, clean?"

He said, "I am clean, for I washed [ἐλουσάμην] in the pool of David, having descended by one set of stairs and ascended by another. . . ."

The Savior answered, ". . . [Y]ou have washed [ἐλούσω] in these running waters wherein dogs and swine have been cast night and day, and you have cleansed [νιψάμενος] and wiped the outside skin which also the harlots and girls who play the pipe anoint, wash [λούουσιν], wipe, and beautify for the lust of men, but within they are full of scorpions and all wickedness. But I and my disciples, who you say were not baptized [βεβαπτίσθαι] [for ceremonial purification], have been dipped [βεβάμμεθα] in the waters of eternal life.

The reference to dogs and swine is a particularly biting anti-Jewish remark, and the cleansing of the outward body is exceedingly denigrated by the comparison to prostitutes beautifying their bodies. The author knows the Jewish practice of building *mikvaoth* with two sets of stairs, one for entering and the other for exiting the pool (lines 24-27), and refers to putting on white clothes (lines 27-28).

Of more importance for this study is the word usage. Λούω seems to be equivalent to βαπτίζω (lines 14-16), and the text can be read to distinguish λούω (bathe) from νίπτω (wash a part — lines 34-35). The word βαπτίζω occurs twice for Jewish rites (first for the feet, lines 15-16, and the second time for the body, lines 42-43 as restored) and βάπτω (line 43) for the baptism of Jesus and his disciples. It is notable that the verb normally used for the Christian rite is used for the Jewish practice, a usage that would indicate a continuity as far as the action is concerned.[10] The verb normally used for a secular or nonreligious "dipping" is used here for the Christian practice. The meaning as far as the action is concerned is the same, and the usage indeed makes explicit that the Christian rite was a dipping in water. The implied contrast in significance is the same as one of Justin's points, namely that the Jewish practice was only external and did not touch the inner person, whereas the Christian ceremony brought eternal life. In the description of the baptism of Jesus and his disciples, the author writes from the standpoint of the church of his time and not of the ministry of Jesus.

---

10. A distinction was often made in the nouns employed: βάπτισμα for John's and Christian baptism; βαπτισμός for Jewish and other washings — see chap. 11 at n. 1. Justin, however, as noted above, used the Christian terminology in both verb and noun for the Jewish practice. Although the question about "baptizing" the feet is put in the mouth of the Jew, could the wording reflect an early baptismal interpretation of the foot washing in John 13?

Pseudo-Cyprian, *Against the Jews*

A Latin sermon preserved in the works of Cyprian has been dated to the end of the second century.[11] A theme running through the sermon is the old and new covenants. Israel abdicated her inheritance, so a new covenant has been given to Gentiles (*Against the Jews* 3), but individual Jews can be restored on repentance. Remission of sins is now appointed for all (6). The kingdom is "in us," not in Jerusalem (7). The invitation is offered to "receive salvation," and the author quotes Isaiah 1:15-16 (8) and 2:3-4 (9). There is now a reversal of roles between Jews and Gentiles.

> It follows, therefore, that Israel is rebuked by the hand laid on at the baptismal bath [*lavacrum*], and there it is witnessed what he believed. And after the reception of the seal [*signo*], purified by the Spirit, he prays to receive life through the food of thanksgiving, namely of the bread which comes from benediction. . . . Those learn who one time taught; they keep commandments who once commanded; are dipped [*intinguntur*] who used to "baptize" [*baptizabant*] and are circumcised who used to circumcise. Thus the Lord wanted the Gentiles to flourish. You see to what extent Christ has loved you. (*Against the Jews* 10.79-82)

Authors in Latin sometimes gave the literal translation *intinguo* of the Greek βαπτίζω and sometimes gave a transliteration (as was often done with technical religious words), *baptizō*. It is interesting that this author employed the literal translation *intinguo* (equivalent to βάπτω) for the Christian act and (as did the author of the uncanonical Gospel in *Oxyrhynchus Papyrus* 840) *baptizo* for the Jewish practices. Baptism is the occasion of receiving the seal. There seems to be allusion to the sequence of the baptismal ceremony: the imposition of the hand of the administrator at the time of the baptismal confession of faith, being purified by the Spirit, joining in prayer, and receiving the eucharist.

The author makes a contrast between what Jewish leaders formerly did and do now: teach, baptize, and circumcise. Is this a reference to proselyte baptism or is it simply the usual contrast between selected Jewish religious activities and their Christian counterpart? The order, even as in Justin once (above), is baptism and then circumcision. Is the order accidental, or does the author not know the sequence in the Jewish conversion ceremony, or does he deliberately make the order correspond to the Christian understanding of baptism resulting in circumcision by the Spirit? Once more, baptism and circumcision are not paired as opposites, as they might be, since both were considered the seal of their respective covenants. Rather, Jewish baptism(s) is (are) contrasted with Christian dipping (as in the *Oxyrhynchus Papyrus* above), and (I would paraphrase according to the usual polemic) fleshly circumcision is contrasted with spiritual circumcision. That the church flourishes and that some Jews accept Christ show God's love for Gentiles.

---

11. Dirk Van Damme, *Pseudo-Cyprian Adversus Iudaeos* (Freiburg, 1969). My translation below has benefitted from his German translation.

Tertullian, *An Answer to the Jews*

Tertullian's baptismal theology will be discussed in chapter 21. His *Answer to the Jews* does not mention Jewish or Christian baptism: the Jewish practices he treats as superseded in Christianity are circumcision, Sabbath, and sacrifices. What he says and does not say about circumcision correspond to the other second- and third-century sources included in this chapter. Adam, Noah, Enoch, Melchisedek, Lot, and Abraham pleased God without (or, in Abraham's case, before) circumcision. God gave it to Israel as "a sign [but] not for salvation" (*Answer to the Jews* 3). Carnal circumcision was temporary, but "the spiritual circumcision has been given for salvation to an obedient people," with Jeremiah 4:3-4; 31:31-32 and other passages quoted in support (3; cf. 9). Christ came as the "giver of the new law, observer of the spiritual sabbath, priest of the eternal sacrifices, eternal ruler of the eternal kingdom," who "suppressed the old circumcision" (6). Nothing is said about baptism replacing circumcision or having the same function; the spiritual circumcision is again that of the heart.

Where Tertullian in this treatise may allude to baptism is in connection with the ministry of Jesus and the forgiveness of sins: "Sins were remitted, which, through faith in the name of Christ, are washed away [according to an emendation] for all who believe on him" (8). An explicit reference is then made to Christ's baptism and its effect of sanctifying the waters[12] and so bringing all previous spiritual grace-gifts to completion (8).

Cyprian, *Testimonies against the Jews*

From the mid-third century we have preserved an example of a *testimonia* book, a collection of scripture quotations on certain topics. This type of work is widely considered to have been current from the beginnings of the church, a hypothesis given some confirmation by the discovery of such collections among the Dead Sea Scrolls. Books 1 and 2 of Cyprian's *Testimonies* are directed against the Jews, the first on the replacement of features of the old covenant in the new covenant and the second on prophecies fulfilled in Christ.

One of the headings in book 1 of Cyprian's *Testimonies* is "That the old baptism should cease, and a new one should begin" (1.12). The passages quoted under this heading are Isaiah 43:18-21; 48:21; Matthew 3:11; and John 3:5-6. Since the *Testimonies* are simply collections of scriptures, Cyprian does not explain what he meant by the "old baptism," but presumably he as other Christian authors referred to the ceremonial washings and not particularly to proselyte baptism. The New Testament passages chosen for comment are notable, since both connect baptism with the Holy Spirit. Matthew 3:11 is apparently understood in the same way as Justin understood Christian water baptism: instead of being contrasted with the baptism of the Holy Spirit,

---

12. Quoted in chap. 7 at n. 3.

the water baptism derived from Christ involved the working of the Holy Spirit. The importance of John 3:5 as a baptismal text for Cyprian, as for other early Christians, is shown in book 3, which deals mostly with moral duties of Christians: one of its headings is "That unless a man have been baptized and born again, he cannot attain to the kingdom of God," followed by the quotation of John 3:5-6 and 6:53 (3.25).

The special feature of Christian baptism for Jews, according to Cyprian, is "That by this alone the Jews can receive pardon of their sins, if they wash away the blood of Christ slain, in his baptism, and, passing over into his church, obey his precepts" (1.24). The passage quoted is Isaiah 1:15-20, an important Old Testament testimony to baptism for early Christians, especially in controversy with Jews. The connection of baptism with forgiveness of sins, which was regarded as distinguishing Christian from Jewish baptism, is evident in other headings. A heading in book 3 is "That all sins are put away in baptism," with a quotation of 1 Corinthians 6:9-11 (3.65); another is "That God is more loved by him who has had many sins forgiven in baptism," quoting Luke 7:47 (3.116).

Physical circumcision was among the items treated as replaced in the "new covenant" (1.11): "That the first circumcision of the flesh is made void, and the second circumcision of the spirit is promised instead" (1.8). The passages quoted are Jeremiah 4:3-4; Deuteronomy 30:6; Joshua 5:2; and Colossians 2:11. Here Cyprian makes one of his rare elaborations on the scriptures quoted, making the point that Justin and Tertullian before him had asserted that Adam, Enoch, Noah, and Melchizedek pleased God without being circumcised. Moreover, this sign did not pertain to women, but now "all are sealed by the sign of the Lord." Unless this latter statement is an allusion to baptism, Cyprian like his predecessors we have cited does not correlate circumcision with baptism but with the inner working of God's Spirit through Christ. Indeed, he, as they, treat circumcision and Jewish baptism as separate institutions with separate fulfillments in Christianity.

Didascalia

The Syriac *Didascalia* from the third century continues the polemic against Jewish ceremonial washings in contrast to the one baptism of Christians (for the document's positive information on Christian baptism, see chap. 26). The author was addressing those who were following Jewish practices or were being influenced by them. Hence, he frequently protests against the "Second Legislation," the ceremonial part of the Law of Moses instituted after Israel's fall into idolatry in the episode of the golden calf (Exod. 32) when Moses was receiving the "Ten Words." Among the many requirements imposed "from that time" were "taboos, and purifications, and baptisms, and sprinklings."[13] After being converted from "the People [the Jews] to

---

13. *Didas.* 26. I cite the translation of Sebastian Brock, *The Liturgical Portions of the Didascalia*, Grove Liturgical Study 29 (Bramcote: Grove, 1982), here p. 31.

believe in God our Saviour Jesus Christ," one should not "keep vain obligations, purifications and sprinklings and baptisms and distinction of meats."[14]

The washings that the *Didascalia* comments on had to do with sexual activity: the woman in the seven days of her flux and the man after marital intercourse. The author indicates that one will be baptizing himself and washing his clothes and his couch so often as to be able to do nothing else. If one baptizes after these activities, he should baptize after the other occasions of impurity stipulated in the Law, like touching a bone or entering a tomb. But observing these requirements of the "Second Legislation" is to "undo the baptism of God."[15] Christians can observe the eucharist in cemeteries, and husbands and wives after intercourse can assemble in church "without ritual bathing, for they are clean." "But if a man should corrupt and defile another man's wife after baptism, or be polluted with a prostitute, and rising up from her should bathe in all the seas and oceans and be baptized in all the rivers, he cannot be made clean."[16]

The author uses the same word, "baptism," for the Jewish washings and the Christian rite. Observing the Jewish baptisms is to "undo the perfect baptism of God which wholly forgave thee thy sins."[17]

Christian baptism is singular. In the sufficiency of a single event Christian baptism was like circumcision. The document makes the by now familiar contrast between the circumcision of the heart and fleshly circumcision (quoting Jer. 4:3-4 and Joel 2:13): "For the faithful, the spiritual circumcision of the heart is sufficient."[18] The passage continues in reference to baptism, yet not as a counterpart to circumcision but as a different activity. The point of comparison, indicated by the word "too" or "also," is the sufficiency of a single occurrence: "And with regard to baptism, too, a single one is sufficient for you, in that it has perfectly forgiven you your sins."[19] The *Didascalia* shares with earlier writings a double emphasis: the Christian equivalent to circumcision is not baptism but spiritual heart surgery, and the multiple Jewish washings for ceremonial purity are distinguished from the single Christian baptism for forgiveness of sins.

Epiphanius on the Samaritans and Others

Epiphanius is cited at various points on baptismal practices of Jewish sects (chap. 4) and Christian heretics (chap. 17). He extends the polemic against Jewish baptisms to include the Samaritans. The Samaritans' adherence to the Law of Moses would have,

14. *Didas.* 26. The translation here is from R. Hugh Connolly, *Didascalia Apostolorum* (Oxford: Clarendon, 1929), p. 216.
15. *Didas.* 26 (Connolly, pp. 248, 250).
16. *Didas.* 26 (Brock, p. 33).
17. *Didas.* 26 (Connolly, p. 248).
18. *Didas.* 24 (Brock, p. 30).
19. *Didas.* 24 (Brock, p. 30).

of course, included observance of the purification rituals. Most Christian writers would have had little or no contact with Samaritans, and Epiphanius may have had only limited knowledge. He treats them first in his discussion of seven sects from among the Jews.

Epiphanius mentions among the customs of the Samaritans that "Whenever they touch someone who is a Gentile, they immerse themselves [βαπτιζόμενοι] in water with their clothes on."[20] Touching a corpse also made one unclean and required purification. Epiphanius argues, implausibly, that the Law's requirement about touching a corpse really referred to laying hands on Christ to crucify him. The Law's requirement of washing clothes and being impure until evening (Lev. 11:24-25; cf. Num. 19:19) is given a Christian meaning by Epiphanius: Those who crucified Christ were impure until their sun should set and "another light dawn on them through the baptism [βαπτίσματος] of water, the 'laver of regeneration' [Tit. 3:5]." Then he quotes Acts 2:38 for the need of Christian baptism.

In his discussion of the Hemerobaptists (chap. 4) and their daily baths for cleansing of sin, Epiphanius asserts:

> Not ocean, not all the rivers and seas, the perennial streams and brooks, and all the water in the world together, can wash away sin — this is not reasonable and is not God's ordinance. Repentance cleanses, and the one baptism, through the name in the mysteries.[21]

The Jewish baptizing sects would have agreed on the need for repentance. Nonetheless, Epiphanius was stating the common Christian position on the one baptism, accompanied by repentance, and given through the three divine names.

Conclusion

By the third century the main lines of Christian polemic against Jewish (Old Testament) ritual practices were well established. The same motifs found in this chapter in regard to Jewish and Christian baptisms were repeated by later Christian authors, but enough has been quoted to show the line of argument. Some of the later statements will be included in the treatment of the teachings about baptism by individual authors. Notice the graphic fourth-century statement by Pseudo-Macarius, *Homilies* 47.1, quoted in chapter 47, which contrasts a baptism that purifies the body with a baptism that includes a purifying of the soul by the Spirit.

---

20. Epiphanius, *Panarion* 1.9.3.6; cf. 2.30.2.5 for Ebionites, and Hippolytus, *Refutation of All Heresies* 9.15.3-6, for Elchasaites baptizing fully clothed.
21. *Panarion* 1.17.2.4.

17. Marcionites, Those Called Gnostics, and Related Groups

Writers in the mainstream of the church occasionally referred to the baptismal practices and ideas of those whom they considered to have deviated from catholic orthodoxy. What caught their attention was often practices that they thought peculiar or at least different from what they were familiar with. That means that there may often have been more similarities than differences, in spite of the impression left by some antiheretical statements. Nevertheless, there are in some sources for "heretical" groups express antibaptismal passages.[1] For Valentinians and Sethians we have preserved from the Nag Hammadi library of Coptic writings some of their own writings. These do not give systematic treatment to baptism, but they offer fairly frequent reference to baptism and offer some control on what their catholic opponents had to say about them. We organize this chapter according to the Marcionites, Valentinians, Sethians, and miscellaneous other groups.

Marcionites

The Marcionites were not properly Gnostics, but they were considered by their orthodox opponents a prime example of heretical views on God, the world, scripture, and salvation. We know them almost exclusively through what is preserved in their opponents' writings with all the limitation that fact imposes. However, the agreement of a number of their critics gives some assurance of the main outline of Marcion's teachings. References to their teaching and practice in regard to baptism, however, are not so numerous. The indications are that in this regard they did not deviate that much from the church which excluded them.[2]

---

1. A good list of antibaptismal texts, given a maximalist interpretation, is found in François Bovon, "*Fragment Oxyrhynchus 840*, Fragment of a Lost Gospel Witness of an Early Christian Controversy over Purity," *Journal of Biblical Literature* 119 (2000): 705-728 (723-726). See also Augusto Cosentino, *Il battesimo gnostico: Dottrine, simbole e riti iniziatici nello gnosticismo* (Cosenza: Lionello Giordino, 2007).

2. Adolf von Harnack, *Marcion: Das Evangelium vom Fremden Gott*, 2nd ed. (Leipzig: J. C. Hin-

Tertullian is our principal source for Marcion's scriptures and ideas. Marcion ascribed the creation of the world to the inferior God of the Old Testament, different from the supreme Father of Jesus Christ. Tertullian saw this negative attitude toward creation as inconsistent with Marcionite religious practices:

> Indeed, up to now, he [the "better God"] has not rejected the Creator's water in which he washes his own people; nor the oil with which he anoints them; nor that combination of honey and milk with which he gives them the nourishment of children; nor the bread by which he represents his own body. Thus in his own sacraments he uses the elements borrowed from the Creator. (*Against Marcion* 1.14.3).

The implications are that the initiation ceremony practiced by Marcionites in Tertullian's day was the same as what Tertullian knew (see chapter 21): baptism in water, anointing with oil, tasting milk and honey, and partaking of the eucharist (except that for the ascetic Marcionites wine is significantly absent). Although Tertullian saw the practices as inconsistent with the doctrine, Marcion's view, it seems, would have been that use of the Creator's water (and the principle would apply to other elements) subverts the material element by making it the means of transition from the Creator's power to the Father's.[3]

One fundamental difference in Marcionite practice from that of the great church was his administering of baptism only to the sexually continent. Tertullian notes this policy in contrasting Marcion's requirement of celibacy with the church's recommendation of it:

> The flesh is not, according to Marcion, immersed [*tinguitur*] unless it be in virginity, widowhood, or celibacy, or has purchased baptism by divorce. (*Against Marcion* 1.29.1)

The practice of the catholic church and the Marcionite church was immersion; the difference was in the persons eligible to receive it.

Tertullian twice in an antiheretical context comments on 1 Corinthians 15:29, "baptism for the dead."[4] Later writers say the Marcionites practiced baptism on behalf of the dead.[5] It was also said that they permitted women to administer bap-

---

richs, 1924), pp. 144-145, with reference to Cyprian, *Letters* 73.4; 74.7; Augustine, *On Baptism against the Donatists* 3.15; Tertullian, *Against Marcion* 1.14; 1.23; 3.22, tr. John E. Steely and Lyle D. Bierma: Adolf von Harnack, *Marcion: The Gospel of the Alien God* (Durham: Labyrinth, 1990), pp. 93-94. A recent introduction is by Heikki Räisänen, "Marcion," in Antti Marjanen and Petri Luomanen, eds., *A Companion to Second-Century Christian "Heretics"* (Leiden: Brill, 2005), pp. 100-124.

3. R. Joseph Hoffmann, *Marcion: On the Restitution of Christianity* (Chico: Scholars, 1984), pp. 21-25, but I find his use of parallels in Mithraism to be a misunderstanding. Is the reference to anointing by Marcionites a confirmation that the practice was as early as Marcion in the great church, or did Marcionites adopt the practice later?

4. *Against Marcion* 5.10; *On the Resurrection of the Flesh* 48. Tertullian's own interpretation is that "the dead" means "dead bodies," so the meaning is that baptism benefits bodies that are going to die.

5. Epiphanius, *Anacephalaeosis* 3.42.3 (performed for catechumens who died before receiving baptism); John Chrysostom, *Homilies on 1 Corinthians* at 15:29; Eznik, *De sectis* 4.

tism,⁶ something to which Tertullian took strong exception but without mention of Marcionites.⁷ Cyprian mentions Marcionites "baptized in the name of Jesus Christ" (*Letters* 73 [72].4.1), but this may not have been in contrast to use of the triple name.⁸ Epiphanius reported that Marcionite baptism could be given three times, so that if one sinned after baptism that person could be baptized again for the remission of sins.⁹

Valentinians

Of the so-called Gnostic groups, the Valentinians were the closest to the orthodox, so we take them up first, although the Sethian systems probably preceded them. Our approach will be to consider first the testimonies by antiheretical writers and then information from the Nag Hammadi tractates. Finally, a cautious synthesis from these sources will be offered about the baptismal ceremony of Valentinians, for it must not be assumed that the branches of the followers of Valentinus were uniform in their practices and ideas.¹⁰

Views held by Valentinians on the baptism of Christ were treated in chapter 6. These were variations according to their mythical world of interpretations found in Cerinthus and Theodotus of Byzantium (also in chap. 6).

After an extended treatment of the followers of Marcus, another Valentinian, Irenaeus, discusses various ideas held by Gnostics about baptism. Presumably he is still discussing the Marcosians, but it seems that he brings in the views of others. Irenaeus says that by their tradition in regard to redemption (ἀπολυτρώσις) some

---

6. Epiphanius, *Panarion* 1.42.4.5 ("to give βάπτισμα)"; Eznik, *De sectis* 4.

7. *On Baptism* 17.

8. Hoffmann, *Marcion*, p. 23, n. 97, with reference to Augustine, *On Baptism* 3.15.20, on their use of the threefold formula, and see further in chapters 22 and 24 on Cyprian's usage.

9. *Panarion* 3.42.3.6-10. The support for more than one baptism was found in Luke 12:50 and Mark 10:38, where Jesus after his baptism by John says, "I have a baptism to be baptized with." Most of the time, other than in the biblical quotations, Epiphanius uses λουτρόν, but once he says it is lawful to give three λουτρῶνς, that is, three βαπτισμῶνς for forgiveness of sins (3.8). He summed up his objections to Marcion's practices in regard to baptism as three: he administered two or three baptisms after lapses into sin; other Marcionites were baptized for catechumens who died; and he allowed women to baptize — *Anacephalaeosis* 3.42.3 (using βάπτισμα for the multiple baptisms and the baptism for the dead, but λουτρόν for baptism by women). Harnack, *Marcion*, pp. 175-176 (Eng., p. 112), rejects Epiphanius's report as only hearsay on the grounds that multiple baptisms would have been impossible for the biblicist Marcion and the report was due to a misunderstanding of repentance described as a baptism. The prohibition against rebaptism in the Theodosian Code 16.6.1-7 is directed against Donatism, not Marcion (p. 367*).

10. For a recent introduction on the Valentinaians, see Ismo Dunderberg, "The School of Valentinus," in Marjanen and Luomanen, *A Companion to Second-Century Christian "Heretics,"* pp. 64-99. A collection and synthesis of sources on "Valentinian Initiation" is prepared by Einar Thomassen in *The Spiritual Seed: The Church of the Valentinians* (Leiden: Brill, 2006), pp. 333-414, which has aided me greatly.

have been instigated by Satan "to a denial of the baptism [βαπτίσματος] of regeneration [ἀναγεννήσεως] to God and a rejection of the whole faith" (*Against Heresies* 1.21.1). They say that it is necessary to receive perfect *gnosis* in order to be regenerated [ἀναγεννημένοι] and enter into the Pleroma. Their "redemption" baptism is distinguished from that of the visible Jesus and of John.

> The baptism [βάπτισμα] of the visible Jesus is for the forgiveness of sins, but the redemption of the Christ who descended on him is for perfection.[11] They hold the former pertains to the animal life but the latter to the spiritual. The baptism by John was proclaimed for repentance, but the redemption by the Christ brings about perfection. He spoke concerning this when he said, "I have another baptism with which to be baptized, and I hasten eagerly to it" [Luke 12:50 modified; they also quoted Mark 10:38 of this spiritual baptism]. . . .
>
> Some of them prepare for those being initiated a nuptial chamber and perform a mystical rite with certain verbal expressions. They assert this to be a spiritual marriage that is done by them according to the likeness of the pairs above. Others lead [the converts] to water and baptize them, pronouncing over them, "Into the name of the unknown Father of all, into Truth, the mother of all, into the One who came down on Jesus, into unity, redemption, and fellowship of the powers." . . . Next they anoint the initiate with balsam. . . .
>
> Some of them assert that it is superfluous to lead them to the water, but mixing oil and water together, they place it on the head of the initiates with expressions like those previously mentioned. This they claim to be the redemption. . . . Others renounce all these practices and assert the mystery of the inexpressible and invisible power ought not to be performed with visible and corruptible elements. . . . They hold the knowledge itself of the inexpressible Greatness is the perfect redemption.[12]

We cannot be sure whether Irenaeus reflects different views held by different groups or has distinguished ideas that might have been synthesized but with different aspects emphasized in different contexts. The impression is that many Gnostics practiced a water baptism followed by an anointing similar to what was done by Irenaeus's church, but with a different baptismal formula. For some an anointing was more important than baptism and could replace it.[13] The use of a mixture of oil

---

11. Hippolytus interprets these as two separate baptisms, but he seems to distort Irenaeus's report: "After baptism [βάπτισμα] they promise another, which they call redemption [ἀπολύτρωσιν]. By this they wickedly turn aside those who remain with them in hope for redemption, as if they could after once having been baptized [βαπτισθῆναι] obtain again forgiveness" (*Refutation of All Heresies* 6.41.2 [6.36] — in references from this work the first set of numbers is that of the critical edition by Miroslav Marcovich, *Hippolytus Refutatio omnium haeresium*, Patristische Texte und Studien 25 (Berlin: Walter de Gruyter, 1986); the latter is that in *Ante-Nicene Fathers*, Vol. 5.

12. Irenaeus, *Against Heresies* 1.21.2, 3, and 4. Epiphanius, *Panarion* 34.19.4-6 follows Irenaeus on the Marcosians.

13. A. H. B. Logan, *Gnostic Truth and Christian Heresy* (Peabody: Hendrickson, 1996), argues that

and water may have been part of a ritual in preparation for death.[14] Irenaeus considers the application of water (mixed with oil) to the head to be distinct from baptism. The emphasis of all these groups that Irenaeus discusses, however, was on the spiritual significance of knowledge of God and its resulting redemption.[15] In comparison with this spiritual recognition the water rite was depreciated, and for some at least this experience meant that acts involving material objects could be dispensed with. The nuptial couch will be considered below in connection with the *Gospel of Philip*.

Origen reported that Valentinians gave two baptisms, a practice he found refuted by Ephesians 4:5.[16] Has Origen confused the Valentinians with another group (Elkasaites? — chap. 4), misunderstood the language of baptism applied to two different things (in addition to water baptism a rite to prepare one for death, a baptism in the realm of the aeons, or an inner spiritual experience — see below), received mistaken information, or recorded something not otherwise attested?

As Irenaeus preserves material about the western branch of Valentinianism (Ptolemy and Marcus), Clement of Alexandria preserves material from its eastern branch (Theodotus) in his *Excerpts from Theodotus*.[17] The first reference to baptism in Clement's selections is a discussion of Paul's allusion to baptism for the dead in 1 Corinthians 15:29 (22.1-7). Theodotus's explanation is that "the dead" refer to human beings who are now dead in their present existence. "Those who are baptized [βαπτιζόμενοι]" are the angels of whom humans are a part and who are baptized for us. Here we have the Valentinian idea of each person having a heavenly counterpart (an angel, or in other sources a "twin"). In order for humans to enter the divine realm, their angel counterpart must enter also. The angels' "baptism" (metaphorical?) has a benefit for humans and in a way corresponds to human baptism:

> [The angels are baptized for us] in order that when we too have the Name we may not be hindered and held back from entering the Pleroma by the Limit and the

---

the Gnostics made postbaptismal unction central to Christian initiation. That could account for an action without explicit apostolic authorization in the New Testament, assuming the importance that it did in the church. Our first attestations of an anointing in connection with baptism pertain to the Gnostics; the great church could have borrowed it from the Gnostics, or the practice may have arisen before there was a clear separation between the Gnostics and the catholic church and then had a separate development in each.

14. Epiphanius, *Panarion* 36.2.5, says the followers of Heracleon, in imitation of Marcus, mixed oil with water and applied this mixture to the head of the dying.

15. It may be that the order of an initiation rite is reflected in the features of the Valentinian myth concerning the activities in the Pleroma of the aeons named Christ and the Holy Spirit reported by Irenaeus, *Against Heresies* 1.2.5-6: instruction by Christ regarding the nature of the aeons, proclamation of the knowledge of the Father, teaching by the Holy Spirit for the aeons to give thanks, and the giving of the seal by the Father.

16. Origen, *Commentary on Ephesians* 4:5.

17. I translate from the text in Robert Pierce Casey, *The Excerpta ex Theodoto of Clement of Alexandria*, Studies and Documents 1 (London: Christophers, 1934). For the baptismal ritual in this work, Victor Saxer, *Les rites de l'initiation chrétienne du IIe au VIe siècle: Esquisse historique et signification d'après leur principaux témoins* (Spoleto: Centro italiano di studi sull'alto medioevo, 1988), pp. 65-71.

Cross. Therefore at the imposition of hands they [Valentinians?] say at the end, "Into the angelic redemption," that is, the redemption which also angels have, so that the person who has received the redemption may be baptized [ἢ βεβαπτισμένος] in the name of him in whom also his angel had been previously baptized [προβεβάπτισται]. The angels were baptized [ἐβαπτίσαντο] in the beginning in the redemption of the Name that came down upon Jesus in the dove and redeemed him. (22.4-6)

Theodotus did not draw back from the conclusion that Jesus himself needed redemption (22.7). Since one of Irenaeus's sources identifies the redemption with anointing, the imposition of hands in this quotation is probably for the purpose of anointing and not a laying on of hands for exorcism or for blessing.[18] The Name in which one is baptized is the divine power that came on Jesus at his baptism (the Savior according to Ptolemy, as cited above from Irenaeus); a later selection (cited below) indicates baptism in the triple divine Name. Receiving the Name was an important concept for Gnostics.

While recording selections mainly on theological ideas, Clement includes much, although not in an organized way, about baptismal practice. Baptism was accompanied by a period of instruction:

It is not only the washing [λουτρὸν] that gives freedom, but also the knowledge of who we were, what we became, where we were or where we were thrown, where we are hastening, and from what we were redeemed, what birth is, and what is begetting again [or rebirth — ἀναγέννησις]. (78.2)

Preliminary to baptism there were "fastings, petitions, prayers, [lifting] hands, kneelings" in order to ward off unclean spirits, so that one may "go down pure" to the water. (The action with the "hands" is not specified and might be an imposition of hands by another, but the surrounding words are associated with prayer, so more likely the reference is to the gesture of prayer.[19]) These things were fitting, for "a soul is being saved out of the world" (83-84). The attention given to unclean spirits (below) implies some renunciation of them as part of the ceremony. And there is reference to an exorcizing of the water: "Water, both in being exorcized and used in baptism, not only separates from evil but also brings sanctification" (82.2).[20]

The baptism involved a going down (συγκαταβαίνει and κατέλθῃ — 83) and a

---

18. Hippolytus, *Refutation of All Heresies* 6.41.4 (6.36), says the followers of the Valentinian Marcus laid hands on the one receiving the redemption (a second baptism).

19. An imposition of hands in the baptismal rite is referred to in 22.5, discussed above.

20. Franz Josef Dölger, *Der Exorzismus in altchristlichen Taufritual: Eine religionsgeschichtliche Studie* (Paderborn: Ferdinand Schöningh, 1909), p. 11, with reference to the *Excerpts from Theodotus* and other works, sees in Gnosticism the promotion of initiation as exorcism. If correct, exorcism in the baptismal ritual would be another practice along with anointing with oil where Gnostic practice preceded and influenced orthodox practice. Pp. 160-167 discusses exorcism in the consecration of the baptismal water.

coming up (ἀναβαίνει — 77.2; ἀνελθεῖν — 77.3). The baptism was done "in the name of the Father, and of the Son, and of the Holy Spirit" (76.3; cf. "sealed by Father, Son, and Holy Spirit" — 80.3). An anointing and a sharing in the eucharist apparently followed, for in the discussion of the spiritual benefits of baptism the statement is made that "The bread and the oil are sanctified by the power of the Name and are not the same as they appeared to be when they were received, but by power have been changed into a spiritual power" (82.1). Over the bread and the oil, as well as the water, there was an invocation. Unless there is a physical rite behind the figurative language of the New Testament, a baptismal anointing is first attested among Gnostics, and the importance they gave to the rite may have encouraged acceptance of the practice by others; alternatively, the Gnostics may have adopted the rite from the church and given it their own meaning.

The special concern of the *Excerpts from Theodotus* is deliverance from "fate" and the "demons (angels of evil)" who administered it (72-75). The Lord came "in order to transfer those who believe in Christ from fate to his providence" (74.2). Before baptism fate rules over "others," but after it astrologers no longer speak the truth about a person, for that person is now liberated (75.1; 78.1). In the midst of these excerpts about deliverance from the rule of fate occurs a significant selection about baptism:

> As, therefore, the birth of the Savior released us from "becoming" and from fate, so also his baptism delivered us from fire and his passion delivered us from passion, in order that we might follow him in all things. For the one who has been baptized [βαπτισθείς] approached God and received "power to walk upon scorpions and snakes" [Luke 10:19], that is, the evil powers. And he commands his apostles, "Go, preach, and baptize into the name of the Father, the Son, and the Holy Spirit those who believe," into whom we are begotten again and become superior to all other powers.
>
> By reason of this, baptism is called death and the end of the old life, when we separate ourselves from the evil rulers, and life according to Christ, of which life he is the sole Lord. The power of transformation of the one who has been baptized [βαπτισθέντος] concerns not the body (for the same body comes up) but the soul. From the moment of coming up from baptism [βαπτίσματος] this person is called a servant of God even by the unclean spirits. (76.1–77.3)

The main thrust is still the deliverance from fate and the evil powers, but a bundle of other early Christian conceptions is also expressed here. There is deliverance also from passion (suffering), a begetting again (John 3:5), and death to the old life of sin (Rom. 6:3-5). The change affects the soul, not the body (cf. 1 Pet. 3:21). One has a new master now. Also notable is the paraphrase of the apostolic commission in Matthew 28:19 so that "make disciples" refers to "those who believe."

The concept of regeneration is elaborated later:

> Whom the mother generates [γεννᾷ] is led into death and into the world, but whom Christ regenerates [ἀναγεννᾷ] is transferred into life, into the Ogdoad.

> They die to the world but live to God, in order that death may be destroyed by death and corruption by resurrection. (80.1-2)

We meet here the Gnostic emphasis on baptismal resurrection and the designation of the divine Pleroma as the Ogdoad. The next selection makes the Gnostic contrast between material and spiritual results. Although material fire burns material things, the heavenly fire works on both mind and senses. Then the comparison is made with baptismal water:

> By analogy baptism [βάπτισμα] also is double in its effects: water affects that which belongs to the senses, quenching the fire felt by the senses; but the Spirit affects that which belongs to the intellect, extinguishing the fire that pertains to the intellect.... The Spirit given us from above has power not only over the bodiless elements but also over powers and evil rulers. (81.2-3)

The belief that baptism confers the Holy Spirit is given a Valentinian explanation but not one outside the bounds of orthodoxy. The interpretation does have a kinship with the association that Jewish Christians (chap. 15) made between baptism and extinguishing the fires of passion.

The close of the selections picks up again the imagery of a seal, this time to explain the significance of being a believer, who is now under new ownership. As a coin has an image and superscription (Matt. 22:20-21) to indicate ownership, so it is with the believer:

> He has through Christ as a superscription the name of God, and as an image the Spirit. Dumb animals also show to whom each belongs by a seal [brand] and are claimed by it. Even so, the faithful soul receives the seal of truth and bears "the marks of Christ" [Gal. 6:17]. (86.2)

The (baptized) believer now wears the name of God and possesses the Spirit, who gives the image to the person. With characteristic Valentinian emphasis, but by no means foreign to orthodox thinking, the seal is associated with truth.

Among the Nag Hammadi Codices are the fragmentarily preserved Valentinian pieces *On the Anointing, On Baptism A-B* (XI 40, 30-41, 38; 42, 1-43, 19), and *On the Eucharist A-B*. *On Baptism A* refers to the "first baptism for the forgiveness of sins" (XI 41, 11, 21-22)[21] and proceeds to speak of our exodus from the world into the Aeon (the "second baptism"? — 41, 36-38); *On Baptism B* speaks of souls becoming perfect spirits (XI 42, 36-37). These statements presumably are to be connected with the contrast Irenaeus (above) makes between physical baptism for the forgiveness of sins and the redemption of Christ for perfection.[22]

---

21. Jacques Ménard, *L'Exposé Valentinién: Les Fragments sur le baptême et sur l'Eucharistie (NH XI, 2)* (Québec: L'Université Laval, 1985), p. 59, translates (French) both times, "The first baptism is the rejection of sins." The "first baptism" occurs also in XI 40, 38 and in 42, 38-39.

22. Kurt Rudolph, *Gnosis: The Nature and History of Gnosticism* (San Francisco: Harper & Row,

The *Tripartite Tractate* has a section on baptism:

> As for the baptism which exists in the fullest sense, into which the Totalities [Pleroma] will descend and in which they will be, there is no other baptism apart from this one alone, which is the redemption into God, Father, Son and Holy Spirit, when confession is made through faith in those names. (I 5, 127, 25-34)[23]

The further statement that "they have come to believe what has been said to them" (128, 1) indicates a previous period of instruction.[24] The characteristics and benefits ascribed to baptism sound very much like orthodox statements: the necessity of faith with hope and its confession (128, 1, 5, 9, 11-12, 17-18), the use of the triple divine name (also in 128, 5), salvation (128, 4), perfection (128, 13), and redemption (128, 24). Is the baptism itself redemption, or is the point to contrast Valentinian baptism to a former baptism? An impressive list of names is given to baptism: "garment" (128, 21-24), "confirmation of the truth" (128, 25-26), "silence" (128, 31-32), "bridal chamber" (128, 33),[25] "light" that is worn (129, 1-4), "the eternal life," which is immortality (129, 7-8), "what is pleasing" (129, 9-14), even "God," since it is the "Totalities" (129, 15). These qualities are for "those who know they have known him" (128, 35-36) and "know . . . who is the one to whom they gave glory" (129, 32-34).

The main emphasis, as in other Gnostic texts, is on what are perceived to be spiritual realities, but this fact does not argue against the practice of an actual water baptism. Nonetheless, one does wonder in such a text as this how much is simply metaphor, drawn indeed from church practice but put to use for something else.

The fullest statement of Gnostic sacramental practice is found in the *Gospel of Philip*.[26] The text is late (perhaps late third century) and may reflect development

---

1983), p. 227, concludes that immortality and not the blotting out of sins was the characteristic Gnostic interpretation of baptism.

23. Translation by Harold W. Attridge and Dieter Mueller in James M. Robinson, ed., *The Nag Hammadi Library* (San Francisco: Harper & Row, 1988), p. 99.

24. Tertullian, *Against Valentinians* 1, indicates five years of instruction for "their perfect disciples" (so perhaps not for all?).

25. See also I 5, 122, 13-35 on the bridal chamber as representing union.

26. Einar Thomassen, "How Valentinian Is the *Gospel of Philip?*" in John D. Turner and Anne McGuire, eds., *The Nag Hammadi Library after Fifty Years* (Leiden: Brill, 1997), pp. 251-279, vindicates the work as presenting a coherent system of thought conforming to eastern Valentinian teaching, although it draws on older materials. In the same volume, Elaine Pagels, "Ritual in the *Gospel of Philip*," pp. 280-294, corrects some of her earlier writing ("A Valentinian Interpretation of Heracleon's Understanding of Baptism and Eucharist and Its Critique of 'Orthodox' Sacramental Theology and Practice," *Harvard Theological Review* 65 [1972]:153-169) and presents the current status of research on ritual practices in the work. Among earlier treatments, note E. Segelberg, "The Coptic-Gnostic Gospel according to Philip and its Sacramental System," *Numen* 7 (1960): 189-200; E. Segelberg, "The Baptismal Rite according to Some of the Coptic-Gnostic Texts of Nag-Hammadi," *Studia Patristica* 5 (1962): 117-128, principally on the *Gospel of Truth* and the *Gospel of Philip*; D. H. Tripp, "The 'Sacramental System' of the Gospel of Philip," *Studia Patristica* 17.1 (1982): 251-260, who characterizes the work as a homily or sermon notes, not as a collection of extracts, on the theme of Life and its transmission, in which sacramental initiation is a model for the possibility of growth in spiritual life.

within the Valentinian school, or at least a bringing together of earlier traditions into a synthesis. "The Lord did all things by means of a mystery: baptism, chrism, eucharist, ransom [redemption], and bridal chamber" (60; II 3, 67, 27-30).[27] The first three of these items may be taken as steps in the conversion/initiation process; the last two seem to be interpretations of its meaning.[28] The author uses the term "mystery," which became the technical term in the Greek church for what the western church called sacraments.

The *Gospel of Philip* associates fire and water, perhaps in interpretation of the Gospels' language of baptism with water and baptism with fire. They bring sanctification: the water (apparently baptismal) of visible elements and fire (contained in the chrism) of the hidden elements (22; II 57, 23-28). "Soul and spirit are constituted of water and fire; a bridegroom's attendant is constituted of water, fire, and light. Fire is chrism; light is fire" (58; II 67, 3-6). The basis of the latter statement may be the baptism of Jesus and the role of John the Baptist. The following passage, which speaks of rebirth, resurrection, restoration, and the bridal chamber, refers to producing the name of "father, son, and holy spirit" (59; II 67, 19-22). The statements about fire and water express the superiority of chrism to water, made explicit in another saying: "Chrism has more authority than baptism. For because of chrism we are called Christians, not because of baptism" (83; II 74, 12-15).[29] The thought seems to be, in addition to the etymological association of baptism and Christian, that baptism gives the name, but anointing gives the reality. The passage continues with the explanation that Christ was named for chrism, "for the father anointed the son; and the son anointed the apostles, and the apostles anointed us." This superiority of the chrism is further affirmed by the declaration, "Whoever has been anointed has everything: resurrection, light,[30] cross, holy spirit." The father gave the anointing in

---

27. I use the translation of Bentley Layton, *The Gnostic Scriptures* (Garden City: Doubleday, 1987), and his numbering system of the sayings (here p. 341) followed by the codex, page, and line number.

28. April D. DeConick, "The True Mysteries: Sacramentalism in the *Gospel of Philip*," *Vigiliae Christianae* 55 (2001): 225-261 (231-239 on baptism and chrism as parallel to the washing, anointing, and clothing of a Jewish priest). She interprets the sacramental theology of the *Gospel of Philip* as reflective of similar traditions developing simultaneously in early Jewish mystical circles. D. H. Tripp, "The 'Sacramental System,'" sees a mystery in three phases (baptism, chrism, eucharist), with baptism and chrism described as redemption and eucharist as the bridal chamber. The overlapping of these five items in the *Gospel of Philip* may illustrate the tendency of motifs connected with baptism to become distinct rituals — Wayne Meeks, "The Image of the Androgyne: Some Uses of a Symbol in Earliest Christianity," *History of Religions* 13 (1974): 165-211 (190-191).

29. The *Gospel of Truth* declares that "Those whom he [the Father] anointed are the ones who have become perfect" (I 3, 36, 13-31 [this quotation, 19-20] — Harold W. Attridge and George W. MacRae, trans., in James Robinson, ed., *The Nag Hammadi Library* (San Francisco: Harper & Row, 1988), p. 48. E. Segelberg, "The Baptismal Rite," pp. 120-124, in trying to piece together the initiation ritual reflected in the *Gospel of Truth*, notes that the Spirit-chrism is central and nothing is said about baptism.

30. An allusion to the appearance of light at the baptism of Jesus? — D. H. Tripp, "The 'Sacramental System,'" pp. 254-55.

the bridal chamber (II 74, 16-22). Such passages may be a critique of those (orthodox) Christians who used water only and not oil in their initiation.[31]

The experience of Jesus was the pattern for his followers:

> Jesus appeared . . . Jordan, the fullness of the kingdom of heavens. The person who was born [begotten] before all things was reborn [begotten again]; the one anointed in the beginning was reanointed; the one who had been ransomed ransomed others in turn. (72; II 70, 34-71, 3)[32]

The following passage says he revealed the great bridal chamber (73; II 71, 7), on which see below. Baptism, chrism, and eucharist (identified with the bridal chamber) convey rebirth, resurrection, and reunion, reenacting Jesus' divine birth, resurrection, and reunion with his *syzygos* in the Pleroma.[33]

There are some indications of the baptismal ritual. The author describes God as a dyer. "Those whom god dips, he dips [or baptizes] in water" (37; II 61, 12-20). The description of a dyer is given also to the son of man in 47 (II 63, 25-30), and all the dyes placed in the caldron come out white. Another passage that mentions the bread, cup, and oil says the person goes "down into the water" (84; II 74, 29-75, 1). Shortly thereafter the author says the eucharistic cup contains wine and water, refers to "living water," and states "accordingly, when one is about to descend into the water, one strips naked in order to put on" Christ ("the living man") (86; II 75, 14-24).[34] Total immersion would seem to be indicated. The use in some way of the names "father, son, and holy spirit" is also indicated (59; II 67, 19-22). Anointing followed and did not precede the immersion. This order would argue against a Syrian provenance for the *Gospel of Philip* (chap. 26).

More is said in the *Gospel of Philip* about the meaning of baptism. Some of this accords with usual Christian thinking. Thus one receives the Holy Spirit and the name Christian in baptism:

> Anyone who goes down into the water and comes up without having received anything and says, "I am a Christian," has borrowed the name. But one who receives the holy spirit has the gift of the name. Anyone who has received a gift will not have it taken away. But one who has borrowed something will have it taken back. So it is with us, if something comes to pass through a mystery. (51; II 64, 22-31)[35]

---

31. So D. H. Tripp, "The 'Sacramental System,'" p. 254. The oil was olive oil — 80; II 73, 17.

32. Elaine Pagels, "Irenaeus, the 'Canon of Truth,' and the *Gospel of John:* 'Making a Difference' through Hermeneutics and Ritual," *Vigiliae Christianae* 56 (2002): 339-371, notes that for the *Gospel of Philip* Jesus' birth and resurrection are paradigms for the experience of everyone who is baptized and receives the Holy Spirit; like Christ they become children of the Father and the Holy Spirit (p. 357). The main thesis of her article, however — that Irenaeus identified heretics not so much by their beliefs as by their different practices and objected to their initiation ritual as divisive (which he did) — is not so persuasive.

33. Elaine Pagels, "Ritual in the *Gospel of Philip,*" p. 286.

34. Another reference to undressing is 55 (II 66, 16-19), "when we put off the flesh."

35. A comparable passage in *The Testimony of Truth* says that those who confess "We are Chris-

This passage is not a contradiction to the earlier quoted statement that the name Christian itself derives from anointing and not from baptism. Moreover, "We are reborn [begotten again] by the holy spirit," and that through Christ, and we are anointed by the spirit. Baptism requires two things, light and water, and the light is the chrism (67; II 69, 4-14). The idea that Jesus "perfected the water of baptism" was found in orthodox writers, but in the following statement there is a Gnostic rephrasing that contradicts Paul's association of baptism with death (Rom. 6:3-4), for Jesus emptied the water of death so that "we go down into the water but not into death" (92; II 77, 7-11).

The *Gospel of Philip* further reflects characteristic Valentinian emphases about baptism. One of these is that baptism gives the Name (59; II 67, 19-20).[36] Another characteristic feature is the association of baptism with ransom or redemption. A fragmentary saying appears to use "go down into the water" in connection with ransom followed by a quotation of Matthew 3:15 (78; II 72, 29-73, 1). The following section affirms the characteristic doctrine that resurrection comes now through baptism:

> People who say they will first die and then arise are mistaken. If they do not first receive resurrection while they are alive, once they have died they will receive nothing. Just so it is said of baptism, "Great is baptism!" For if one receives it, one will live. (79; II 73, 1-8)

The statements about what is accomplished in baptism and those that disparage baptism may be reconciled in the thought that spiritual realities come through images of the real thing (cf. 59; II 67, 9-27), but the latter is what is really important.

Some of these ideas are brought together in an interpretation of the temple in Jerusalem:

> The holy building is baptism, the holy of holy is ransom, the holy of holies is the bridal chamber. Baptism possesses resurrection and ransom; ransom is in the bridal chamber. (68; II 69, 23-27)

The bridal chamber is often mentioned[37] and understandably has caught much scholarly attention. Some thought there might be reference to a literal bodily union as the climax of the initiation,[38] but in a movement better known for its ascetic em-

---

tians" in word only and not with power are foolish and give themselves over to ignorance and a human death, "thinking they will live when they are really in error" (NHC IX 3, 31, 22-32, 3) — perhaps a polemic against martyrdom, for a little later the author speaks against those who, "when they are 'perfected' with a martyr's death," think within themselves, "If we deliver ourselves over to death for the sake of the Name we will be saved."

36. The theology of the Name is more fully expressed in *Gospel of Truth* (I 3, 38, 7-39, 28). Note the name of the Father resting on their heads (38, 36-37).

37. Nos. 53 (II 65, 11), 59 (67, 16), 60 (67, 30), 68 (69, 24-37), 70 (70, 18-21), 71 (70, 33), 73 (71, 7-9), 83 (74, 22), 102 (82, 17, 23 — literal here in reference to marriage), 105 (85, 21 — in a fuller interpretation of the temple parallel to the passage quoted in the text), 107 (85, 33).

38. Irenaeus, *Against Heresies* 1.21.3 (quoted above) misunderstood the "nuptial couch" as refer-

phasis this interpretation seems unlikely.[39] More likely is the spiritual experience of reunion with one's angel, or heavenly self. This may be both present and eschatological.[40] Where the bridal chamber is used in reference to human marriage, the union was a reflection of the conjunctions of the aeons.[41]

The *Gospel of Philip* takes a realistic view of the sacraments. Although these types and images are "contemptible," they convey divine reality. No one will receive the perfect light who has not already received it here through these symbols (107; II 86, 6-7). The ritual performance of baptism, however, does not always accomplish the desired results. How the initiate understands Jesus' birth and resurrection interprets what happens to that one in baptism.[42] The *Gospel of Philip* reflects a sacramental ritual of baptism, chrism, and eucharist like that practiced by its orthodox opponents; the difference between the two groups was not so much in the actions as in the conceptual world that gave these actions their meaning.

On the Origin of the World (NHC II 5 and XIII 2 — also known as *Writing without Title*) is a possibly Valentinian work from Egypt dated either from the late second or to the early fourth century. According to the Valentinian classification of three groups of human beings — spirit-endowed, soul-endowed, and earthly — it distinguishes three baptisms: "The first is the spiritual, the second is by fire, the third is by water."[43] Spiritual baptism is probably to be understood as an experience more than a baptism in the Spirit, and baptism by fire is probably purifying rather than destructive. The association of water baptism with earthly people would depreciate it.

The Testimony of Truth may come from an offshoot of the Valentinians; it approximates the polemic against baptism to be found in some Sethian documents (below). The author refers to the baptism of the "Son of Man":

---

ring to a separate ritual, about which he is vague, but he may have taken the expression literally. The words used refer to the room for the marriage feast, not the marriage bed.

39. Jean-Marie Sevrin, "Les noces spirituelles dans l'Évangile selon Philippe," *Le Muséon* 87 (1974): 143-193, establishes that the bridal chamber was not a separate rite. Against the idea of it standing for some separate ritual act are the statements elsewhere that the anointing is given in the bridal chamber (83; II 74, 21, referred to above) and here that ransom is in the bridal chamber (68; II 69, 27); in the *Tripartite Tractate* baptism is called the bridal chamber (I 5, 128, 33-35).

40. For the present — Clement, *Excerpts from Theodotus* 21-22; 35-36; for the future — *Excerpts from Theodotus* 64-65; Irenaeus, *Against Heresies* 1.7.1. Turner, "Ritual in Gnosticism," in E. H. Lovering Jr., ed., *SBL 1994 Seminar Papers* (Atlanta: Scholars, 1994), p. 149, suggests the bridal chamber is a proleptic enactment of entrance into the Pleroma, symbolized by a kiss (the suggestion goes back to H.-M. Schenke, accepted by Segelberg, "The Coptic-Gnostic Gospel," p. 198). The *Acts of Thomas* presents the bridal chamber as continence (124) and the eschatological reward for continence (12).

41. April D. DeConick, "The Great Mystery of Marriage: Sex and Conception in Ancient Valentinian Traditions," *Vigiliae Christianae* 57 (2003): 307-342. She concludes that for physical intercourse to imitate the marriages of the aeons sexual relations were supposed to be a matter of the will for the purpose of procreation and not be driven by passion.

42. Elaine Pagels, "Ritual in the *Gospel of Philip*," pp. 283, 285, 288-89, 291.

43. NHC II 5, 122, 13-16. Trans. by Hans-Gebhard Bethge and Bentley Layton in Robinson, *The Nag Hammadi Library*, p. 186.

He came [to the] world by the Jordan River, and immediately the Jordan [turned] back. And John bore witness to the [descent] of Jesus. For it is he who saw the [power] which came down upon the Jordan River. (NHC IX 3, 30, 20-29)[44]

He shows a familiarity with traditions about the baptism of Jesus, but he proceeds to give an allegorical interpretation of the event: the water of the Jordan is the desire for sexual intercourse, John is the archon of the womb, and the dominion of carnal procreation came to an end. Another reference to Jesus' baptism when the Holy Spirit came down as a dove leads to an interpretation of the virgin birth[45] as Gnostics being virgins reborn by the word (39, 23-40, 7).

The attitude of the author of *The Testimony of Truth* is expressed in the statement that some do not know what salvation is, but they enter into death in the waters. "This [is] the baptism of death which they observe" (IX 55, 4-15). Then he draws a sharp contrast:

> There are some who, upon entering the faith, receive a baptism on the ground that they have [it] as a hope of salvation, which they call "the [seal,"] not [knowing] that the [fathers of] the world are manifest that [place. But] he himself [knows that] he is sealed. For [the Son] of [Man] did not baptize any of his disciples. But [... if those who] are baptized were headed for life, the world would become empty. And the fathers of baptism were defiled.
>
> But the baptism of truth is something else; it is by renunciation of [the] world that it is found. [But those who] say [only] with the tongue [that they] are renouncing it [are lying]. (IX 69, 7-26)

The author reasons from Jesus not administering baptism against the practice. Ordinary baptism placed one under the powers (fathers) of the world. The true seal and the true baptism are the renunciation of the world. The renunciation made by the author's opponents did not go far enough in a separation from the world.

A synthesis of the sources for Valentinian initiation gives the following sequence: a (lengthy) period of preliminary instruction; preparatory disciplines of fasting, prayers, and confession (?); undressing; renunciation of evil spirits; (trine) immersion with the invocation of Father, Son, and Spirit; a profession of faith; anointing with oil; imposition of hands; a peace greeting and kiss; a procession with lamps.[46] The procedure did not differ significantly from that in the great church, and the Valentinian texts provide the earliest evidence for some of the practices.

Although these texts reveal something about the baptismal ritual, their main concern was with spiritual experience. That the spiritual meaning of baptism had priority over the outward, physical act could also be said about the orthodox view of

---

44. Translation by Søren Giversen and Birger Pearson in Robinson, *The Nag Hammadi Library*, p. 450 and subsequently.

45. Cf. IX 3, 45, 14-18 for Christ passing through the womb of a virgin, who was found to be a virgin again after giving birth.

46. Einar Thomassen, *The Spiritual Seed*, 333-334.

baptism. The statements in the two systems, however, are placed in different worldviews and different plans of salvation. The orthodox writers saw that clearly.

Sethians

Sethian documents presuppose the descent of a savior figure in the form of Seth (or Christ) into the world comparable to the descent of the initiate into the water. Spiritual enlightenment brings an ecstatic vision and provides an ascent from the world of earthly water into the realm of light. Hence, these writings make frequent reference to baptism. Many of the references seem to be metaphorical, but that usage does not preclude a literal rite and indeed there seem to be many allusions to some sort of ritual activity involving water baptism.[47]

The *Apocalypse of Adam* contains a polemic against those who say the Illuminator was born of a virgin and came to the water (baptism) of the created world which is defiled (V 78, 18-79, 18; 84, 19).[48] The "holy baptism" of "living water" has been drawn into the will of the powers who rule the world (V 84, 5-20). The Illuminator's true seed, however, "receive his name upon the water" (V 83, 4-6).[49] Gnosis (the hidden eternal knowledge) is the holy baptism:

> This is the hidden knowledge of Adam, which he gave to Seth, which is the holy baptism of those who know the eternal knowledge through those born of the word and the imperishable illuminators, who came from the holy seed. (V 85, 19-31).[50]

---

47. For a recent introduction to Sethianism, including their baptismal practice, see Michael A. Williams, "Sethianism," in Marjanen and Luomanen, *A Companion to Second-Century Christian "Heretics"*, pp. 32-63. For their initiation rituals, Jean-Marie Sevrin, *Le dossier baptismal Séthien; Études sur la sacramentaire gnostique* (Québec: Université Laval, 1986); Turner, "Ritual in Gnosticism," pp. 136-181 (139-155 on baptism); John D. Turner, "The Sethian Baptismal Rite," in P.-H. Poirier, ed., *Coptica, Gnostica, Manichaica: Mélanges offerts à Wolf-Peter Funk à l'occasion de son soixantième anniversaire* (Québec: Université Laval; Louvain: Peeters, 2006). To their work I am much indebted for making sense of the Sethian texts.

48. Jean-Marie Sevrin, *Le dosier baptismal*, pp. 171-172, 180-181, concludes that this is not a polemic against baptism, which the document connects with *gnosis* and purity, but against those who soil it by their conduct, which was contrary to the Sethian ethic of abstention.

49. Translation by George W. MacRae, in Robinson, *The Nag Hammadi Library*, p. 285. *Melchizedek* seems to make a contrast between receiving the baptism of the waters which are above and baptism in other water (the text is fragmentary — NHC IX 1, 7, 27-8, 9). The name of the Illuminator or Savior is probably Seth.

50. MacRae, in Robinson, *The Nag Hammadi Library*, p. 286. Francoise Morard, *L'Apocalypse d'Adam (NH V,5)* (Québec: L'Universite Laval, 1978), text and translation, pp. 60-61, and commentary, p. 124, attributes the passage to a redactor and declares the postion as clearly spiritualizing (referring to *Gospel of the Egyptians* (III, 63, 9-19, cited below). Sevrin, *Le dossier baptismal*, pp. 164, 180, states that the author does not interpret a ritual event in a spiritual sense but gives the name of baptism to a transcendent reality (salvation is identified as a baptism), but says that this usage constitutes a presumption that there was an actual practice of baptism.

The orthodox would have reversed this equation.

The polemic against Jesus' baptism and Christian baptism is explicit in the *Paraphrase of Shem.* "The demon will also appear upon the river to baptize with an imperfect baptism, and to trouble the world with a bondage of water."[51] "Many who wear erring flesh will go down to the harmful waters through the winds and the demons." Water is "frightful," "insignificant," and a source of bondage, not of release.

> O Shem, they are deceived by manifold demons, thinking that through baptism with the uncleanness of water, that which is dark, feeble, idle, and disturbing, he will take away the sins. And they do not know that from the water to the water there is bondage.... For I foretell it to those who have a heart. They will refrain from the impure baptism. And those who take heart from the light of the Spirit will not have dealings with the impure practice.... For if they mix with the evil ones, they become empty in the dark water. For where the water has been mentioned, there is Nature, and the oath, and the lie, and the loss. For only in the unbegotten Spirit, where the exalted Light rested, has the water not been mentioned, nor can it be mentioned.[52]

Water was thus associated with the created order, with darkness and impurity, and cannot take away sins. To think otherwise is a demonic deception. Accordingly, near the close of *Zostrianos,* there is the warning, "do not baptize yourselves with death."[53]

Sethians, however, had their own ritual practices, apparently including a water rite. There are traces of a ritual structure in the *Trimorphic Protennoia.* Reference is made to the "water of life" with the further explication that the divine Christ descended for the sake of the spirit (or highest self) "which has come to exist out of the water of life and out of the baptism [or bath] of the mysteries."[54] An invitation is given to those "who have become worthy of the mystery" to enter the perfect light; they will be glorified, enthroned, given robes, and "the baptists [baptizers] will baptize you."[55] The same items are mentioned but in a different order three pages later.

---

51. NHC VII 1, 30, 22-27. Frederik Wisse, trans., in Robinson, *The Nag Hammadi Library,* p. 354. Turner, "Ritual in Gnosticism," p. 147, describes the "negative connotation" immersion in water could have for Gnostics as an immersion in materiality.

52. VII 36, 25-38, 27. Robinson, *The Nag Hammadi Library,* pp. 356-57. Cf. "You baptized our souls in the water of darkness!" (*The Book of Thomas the Contender* — NHC II 7, 144, 1; trans. by John D. Turner in Robinson, *The Nag Hammadi Library,* p. 206). If not figurative, this too would be the same kind of polemic against orthodox baptism.

53. NHC VIII 1, 131, 2; trans. by John N. Sieber in Robinson, *The Nag Hammadi Library,* p. 430.

54. NHC XIII 1, 37, 2; 41, 20-24. "Water of life" again in the quotation below. I use the translation of Layton, *The Gnostic Scriptures,* pp. 91, 94. Sevrin, *Le dossier baptismal,* p. 62 understands the "bath of the mystery" as the revelation of the mystery and denies an allusion to a rite; the attention is on the communication of revelation and on *gnosis.* He further (pp. 77-79) observes that the spiritualization of baptism to designate *gnosis* and illumination does not mean the rite of baptism was not practiced in reality.

55. XIII 44, 32; 45, 12-20.

After fragmentary lines that mention water and stripping from a person the thoughts associated with chaos and darkness, the text continues with the person clothed in shining light and delivered to those who bestow a robe. "I delivered that person unto the baptists . . . to be baptized; and they washed that person in the wellspring of the water of life."[56] The person is next delivered to the enthroners and the glorifiers and then taken into the luminous place, and mention is made of the "five seals." The person who has received the five seals represents those who have "taken off the robes of ignorance and put on shining light."[57] The theme of enlightenment is the point of the passage; the theme is similar to that in Justin Martyr and other orthodox writers, and like them it is connected with imparting doctrine (although with a different content), but with a stronger experiential significance. The steps of investiture, baptism, enthronement, glorification, and rapture into the realm of light may be the five seals (but see on the *Gospel of the Egyptians* below). This sequence is close to that in Mandaean baptism. The five seals are identified with *gnosis:* they destroy ignorance and deliver from the power of the world rulers. This text also provides the basis for interpreting the five seals as sacred names of five higher beings.[58]

The *Gospel of the Egyptians* (second or third century) says more about baptism in a section that may reflect a liturgical structure. It begins by reciting that the "great Seth," at the third of his appearances (identified as the flood, the conflagration, and the judgment of the rulers), for the purpose of saving the race that went astray, instituted "baptism through a Logos-begotten body . . . in order that the saints may be begotten by the holy Spirit, . . . the holy baptism that surpasses the heaven."[59] Baptism is a transcendent reality instituted by the historical Jesus (Seth) that reflects an actual ritual. It effects regeneration by the Holy Spirit, *gnosis* (deliverance from the world), and reconciliation of the world with itself.[60]

There follows the invocation of the Powers that preside over baptism (III 2, 64, 9-65, 26)[61] — including those that preside over "the spring of truth," "over the baptism of the living, and the purifiers," and "over the gates of the waters." At the end of the section mention is made of "Yoel, who presides over the name of him to whom it will be granted to baptize with the holy baptism that surpasses the heaven" (III 2, 65, 23-25). Next comes a renunciation:

---

56. Yvonne Janssens, *La Protennoia Trimorphe (NH XIII,1)* (Québec: L'Université Laval, 1978), p. 45, ll. 18-19, translates (French), "they were plunged in the source of the water of life."

57. XIII 47, 35-48, 21; 48, 21-35; 49, 30-31. The "five ineffable seals" are mentioned again in 50, 9-11 as proclaimed, "so that I [Savior or Word] might dwell in them and they too might dwell in me."

58. Sevrin, *Le dossier baptismal*, pp. 71-75.

59. NHC III 2, 62, 24-64, 9. I use the translation of Alexander Böhlig and Frederik Wisse in Robinson, *The Nag Hammadi Library*, here p. 216 (63, 10, 14, 24-25) and subsequent translations through p. 218, and I follow the outline of Turner, "The Sethian Baptismal Rite." Cf. the treatment of the *Gospel of the Egyptians* in Sevrin, *Le dossier baptismal*, pp. 80-144.

60. Sevrin, *Le dossier baptismal*, pp. 91-94.

61. Three of these — Micheus, Michar, and Mnesinous — are said to be over "holy baptism and the living water" in *Apocalypse of Adam* (V 5, 84, 5-7 — referred to above).

They who are worthy of (the) invocation [*epiclesis*], the renunciations of the five seals in the spring-baptism, these will know their receivers as they are instructed about them, and they will know them (or: be known by them). These will by no means taste death. (III 2, 66, 2-8)

This is an important statement of the effects of Sethian baptism: to know (and be known?) and to escape death. "They who are worthy" may be the Sethians.[62] The invocation was to place the initiate under the protection of the Powers. The renunciations would have been a ritual rejection of the world. Baptism was the place, time at which, or means of receiving the five seals. The text of the *Gospel of the Egyptians* in codex IV 2 (78, 1-10) mentions only the baths (the plural may indicate multiple immersions as part of the initiation) by which one makes renunciation and the seals conferred by the baths, so the only ritual action is the baptism itself.[63] More is said on the five seals below.

At this point presumably occurred the actual baptism, accompanied by prayer or a hymn to Yesseus, Mazareus, or Yessedekeus,[64] addressed as "O living water" with the fivefold ascription, "Really truly," and the pronunciation of various vowel sounds (III 2, 66, 8-22).[65] Then there is the postbaptismal profession that "This great name of thine is upon me, O self-begotten [*Autogenes*] Perfect one" (III 2, 66, 22-67, 4).[66] The concluding words of praise (III 2, 67, 4-68,1) may allude to an embrace or joining hands to form a circle ("I have stretched out my hands while they were folded. I was shaped in the circle of the riches of the light" — 67, 6-9)[67] and an anointing ("the incense of life is in me," which is said to be mixed with water [cf. the oil and water of the Valentinians above], perhaps to purify it? — 67, 22-23).

The heart of the *Gospel of the Egyptians,* the section that precedes this initiatory ritual, is structured around five doxologies to the Pentad (IV 2, 59, 13-29; III 2, 49, 23-50, 9; 53, 16-54, 6; 55, 19-56, 3; 61, 24-62, 11) and may have been recited in turn after each of the five phases of the initiation ritual reflected in the *Trimorphic Protennoia.*[68] The components of the initiation ceremony in the *Gospel of the Egyptians* are summarized at the end of this section on Sethian Gnosticism.

Important to the Sethians were the five seals, to which frequent reference is made in the *Gospel of the Egyptians.*[69] These texts do not explain what the five seals were, something the author and the readers knew. The long recension of the *Apocryphon of*

---

62. Sevrin, *Le dossier baptismal,* p. 112, proposes to read instead of "worthy" the "dignitaries" who preside at the ritual, but III 55, 12-16 makes this unlikely.

63. Sevrin, *Le dossier baptismal,* pp. 110-117.

64. The same names, also identified with the living water, are found at the conclusion of the *Apocalypse of Adam* (V 5, 85, 30).

65. Sevrin, *Le dossier baptismal,* p. 126, suggests that the quintuple refrain underlines five invocations that accompany a quintuple immersion.

66. See below on *Melchizedek* (NHC IX, 1, 16, 12-15).

67. This is unique in our sources, but a circle did represent perfection.

68. Turner, "Ritual in Gnosticism," p. 144; also "The Sethian Baptismal Ritual."

69. NHC IV 2, 58, 6; 59, 1, 27; III 2, 55, 12; 63, 3; 66, 3.

John contains a hymnic passage at its conclusion in which Pronoia declares, "I raised him up and sealed him in the light of the water with five seals, in order that death might not have power over him from this time on."[70] Possible explanations include the five elements of initiation in the *Trimorphic Protennoia* (above), five immersions (cf. orthodox use of "seal" for baptism), the transcendental pentad of names (only in the *Trimorphic Protennoia*), and/or a fivefold renunciation or profession (hinted at in III 2, 3-4) made in connection with baptism, five signings, or five anointings.[71]

The much damaged tractate *Melchizedek*, from about the year 200, mentions that Jesus Christ will receive water baptism (NHC IX 1, 7, 28). The efficacy of this baptism seems connected to its rapport with the waters above (8, 1-2). Melchizedek (the recipient of the heavenly revelation) must also receive a water baptism (8, 3-4).[72] Melchizedek celebrates a liturgy that occupies the central part of the tractate (14, 15-18, 24).[73] The preface explains to the future baptizand the effects of Gnosis, which will be acquired by baptism in the receiving of the name. A key statement says, "According to the [perfect] laws I shall pronounce my name as I receive baptism [now] (and) for ever, (as a name) among the living (and) holy [names], and (now) in the [waters]" (16, 12-15).[74] Receiving the Name is important here, as in some other Gnostic documents. It seems that the celebrant, speaking in the place of the one being baptized, pronounced the proper name that is conferred by baptism, and then the baptizand himself spoke the name.[75] In contrast to some other Gnostics, the author does not consider the waters (always plural, indicating a mass of water?) defiled,

---

70. II 1, 31, 22-25. Trans. by Frederik Wisse in Robinson, *The Nag Hammadi Library*, p. 122.

71. Alastair H. B. Logan, "The Mystery of the Five Seals: Gnostic Initiation Reconsidered," *Vigiliae Christianae* 51 (1997): 188-206, refers to the various interpretations; he suggests that the five seals referred to an anointing with an ointment of some kind the organs for which souls can be assumed to possess equivalents: two eyes, two ears, and a mouth. Sevrin, *Le dossier baptismal*, pp. 31-37, understands the passage as mythical but corresponding to the initiatory rite of the group; he favors a fivefold baptism over a fivefold signing (I would note, however, that light is associated with oil in the Valentinian texts above); on pp. 256-257 he more strongly excludes the possibility of an unction and argues for a quintuple immersion. He further understands the anointing of the Unbegotten Son by the Spirit (III 9, 24-10,9; II 6, 23-33) as the water rite interpreted as an unction, since the work shows no interest in oil (pp. 38-46).

72. I follow the interpretation and translation of Wolf-Peter Funk, Jean-Pierre Mahé, and Claudio Gianotto, *Melchisédek (NH IX, 1): Oblation, baptême et vision dans la gnose Séthienne* (Québec: Université Laval; Louvain: Peeters, 2001), here from the commentary by Claudio Gianotto, pp. 140-141; subsequent comments from the introduction and translation by Mahé. English translation by Søren Giversen and Birger A. Pearson in Robinson, *The Nag Hammadi Library*, pp. 440-444.

73. Mahé, *Melchisédek*, outlines it: a preface (14, 23-16, 11); a performative statement implying a ritual act and the occurrence of a baptism in water (16, 12-16); hymn of acclamation (16, 16-18, 7); a hortatory blessing (18, 7-23) — pp. 43-50. He understands this ritual as a real practice, although in a mythical setting; its purpose was to strengthen Sethians in their competition with the rites of contemporary Christian assemblies (p. 44).

74. English translation by Søren Giversen and Birger A. Pearson in Robinson, *The Nag Hammadi Library*, pp. 442-443.

75. The name pronounced was perhaps that of Melchizedek, and the initiate was thereby identified with Melchizedek — Sevrin, *Le dossier baptismal*, pp. 235-238.

perhaps because Christ purified them (8, 5).[76] The baptism was administered once for all time (16, 13-14). Full illumination was possible only after baptism.

Zostrianos (probably mid-third century), another fragmentarily preserved treatise, mentions being sealed in connection with baptism, but the sealing, like the baptisms, is given a celestial rather than an earthly setting.[77] Francoise Morard summarized the contents of *Zostrianos* in relation to baptism: The Perfect Man holds a discourse in which he explains to Zostrianos that the water of baptism that he has received in the course of his transmigration (6, 7-7, 21) is the water of life that baptizes in Autogenes, the water of beatitude that pertains to the knowledge of divinity (15, 4-12); that the first perfect water of Autogenes is the life of the perfect souls and perfect Word of God (17, 4-16). He explains that the passage to Autogenes, in which he has been baptized, is knowledge of the All (25, 11-16). Only the superior baptism, that of perfect water, that is, perfect knowledge of truth, permits the rebirth of the holy seed of children of Seth.[78]

Looking more particularly at passages mentioning baptism, we find that many baptisms occur. Some, if not all, of this baptismal language appears to become metaphorical for stages of visionary ascent, for the voyage of the soul is described as a progression of baptisms in the waters:[79]

> Then I knew that the power in me was set over the darkness because it contained the whole light. I was baptized there, and I received the image of the glories there. . . .
>
> [A]fter washing there seven times [in] living [water], once for each [of the] aeons. I did not cease until [I saw] all the waters. . . .
>
> I was baptized . . .
>
> I ascended to the Repentance which really exists [and was] baptized there four times. . . .
>
> I was baptized in the [name of] the divine Autogenes [Self-begotten] by those powers which are [upon] living waters, Michar and Micheus. . . .
>
> I was [baptized] for the second time in the name of the divine Autogenes by these same powers. . . .
>
> I was baptized for the third time in the name of the divine Autogenes by each of these powers. . . .
>
> I was baptized for the fourth time by [each of] these powers. . . .[80]

Baptism consists in knowledge itself of each of the Aeons.[81]

---

76. Mahé, *Melchisédek*, pp. 47, 48.
77. NHC VIII 1, 6, 14; 57, 11, 20, 24; 58, 13, 25; 129, 14. Turner, "Ritual in Gnosticism," p. 144.
78. Morard, *L'Apocalypse d'Adam*, p. 126, suggests that the opposition of a baptism of material water to a baptism of knowledge may be due to the third-century interpolator working on an earlier text.
79. Turner, "Ritual in Gnosticism," pp. 146-47; Layton, *The Gnostic Scriptures*, p. 121.
80. NHC VIII 1, 5, 14-7, 21. Translation by John N. Sieber (here and subsequently) in Robinson, *The Nag Hammadi Library*, p. 405.
81. Sevrin, *Le dossier baptismal*, p. 193, with reference to VIII 1, 23, 2-20.

Another passage says that Yoel "baptized me," followed by mention of receiving "a holy spirit." Later "[Yoel] baptized me again." Yoel then explained, "You have [received] all the [baptisms] in which it is fitting to [be] baptized, and you have become [perfect]."[82] *Zostrianos*'s closing exhortation is:

> Do not baptize yourselves with death nor entrust yourselves to those who are inferior to you.... Flee from the madness and the bondage of femaleness and choose for yourselves the salvation of maleness. You have not come to suffer; rather, you have come to escape your bondage.[83]

One baptizes oneself in death by living for inferior realities.[84]

Zostrianos, and perhaps the other Sethian texts, "conceive the baptismal rite as a series of visionary experiences resulting in complete enlightenment and therefore total salvation."[85] Thus in these texts the water is of a heavenly nature, Living Water in a spiritual sense, and associated with light or enlightenment. The references, however, to an investiture consisting of inscription in glory, a seal, and a crown projected into a mythical universe indicate that the metaphorical usage may have been compatible with a ritual practice.[86]

The *Pistis Sophia* and the two *Books of Jeu* represent a late form of Sethian Gnosticism from the third century. They have a lot to say about baptism but for the most part represent ideas already encountered. In order to keep the baptismal focus I will lift the statements out of their mythological context.

In the *Pistis Sophia* Jesus after his resurrection revealed to his disciples that before Elizabeth conceived John the Baptist he had placed in her a power by which John "should be able to preach before me, and prepare my water and baptize with water of forgiveness" (1.7 [12]).[87] Mercy is the Spirit that came down on Jesus when he received baptism from John (1.62 [123, 125]).[88] The document quotes Jesus' words in Luke 12:49-52 about Jesus' baptism that purifies souls (3.116-117 [299-301]).

The connection of baptism and forgiveness of sins is often made: Pistis Sophia repents, saying, "Give me the baptism and forgive my sins" (1.57 [111]); peace "baptized the race of mankind until they became strangers to sin" (1.61 [122]); the myster-

---

82. NHC VIII 1, 60, 23; 61, 13, 23; 62, 13-15 (pp. 418-419).

83. VIII 1, 131, 2-10 (p. 430). For salvation as escape from the weakness and subjection to cosmic forces of femaleness into maleness, cf. *Excerpts from Theodotus* 79-80.1.

84. This is the interpretation of Sevrin, *Le dossier baptismal*, p. 201.

85. Turner, "Ritual in Gnosticism," p. 141.

86. Inscription (VIII 6, 13; 129, 13-14); seal (6, 14; 129, 14); crown (129, 15); investiture (129, 6-16). Sevrin, *Le dossier baptismal*, pp. 201-202, argues for a ritual behind *Zostrianos*. He suggests that 24, 17-25, 20 seems to describe an initiation and that the repeated baptisms marked the steps of a progressive initiation (pp. 194, 203).

87. I use the translation of Violet MacDermot, *Pistis Sophia*, Nag Hammadi Studies 9 (Leiden: Brill, 1978), with her references and the page number in brackets.

88. Cf. 4.141 (368) for the Father sending the Holy Spirit as a dove on Jesus; 3.133 (347-348) for John's prophecy that in contrast to his baptism of water Jesus would purify by fire.

ies of baptisms forgive sins (3.115 [296-299]); the first baptism is "the true mystery of those whose sins will be forgiven" (4.142 [372]). Jesus brought into the world fire, water, wine, and blood; the first three were mysteries that purify all the sins of the world and make one worthy of the kingdom, but the blood was a sign concerning the body of mankind (4.141 [367-369]).[89]

Possible ritual references in the *Pistis Sophia* include Jesus' statement that he had baptized a woman three times but she had not done what was worthy of the baptisms (3.122 [310]). Particularly important to the document is the association of the words "mystery," "baptism," "anointing," and "sealing." The archons who repent come to "the place of those of the Midst [μέσος]," who "will baptize them, and they will give them the spiritual inunction, and they will seal them with the seals of their mysteries" (2.86 [197]).[90] "The seven virgins of the light examine [the] soul and baptize it with their baptisms, and give it the spiritual inunction" (3.128 [325]).[91]

There are enigmatic statements, like "Thou didst baptize the power of Sabaoth the Good" (2.63 [128]). Such and the frequent reference to "mysteries" raise the question how much of the baptismal language is figurative. In keeping with other Gnostic sources the "seals" and anointing are quite prominent.

The *Books of Jeu* have much in common with the *Pistis Sophia* and seem to give more specificity to some of its statements. Jesus says to his disciples:

> I will give to you the three baptisms: the water baptism, the baptism of fire and the baptism of the Holy Spirit. . . . And after these things I will give to you the mystery of the spiritual inunction. (2.43 [102])[92]

These things would make them "sons of the Pleroma" (2.44 [105]). Jesus caused his disciples to be clothed with linen garments and amidst ritual actions sealed them with the seal (2.45 [106-107]). Wine in pitchers became water, and Jesus baptized the disciples, gave them from the offering, and sealed them.

> And the disciples rejoiced . . . because their sins were forgiven . . . and they were numbered among the inheritance of the Kingdom of Light, and because they were baptized with the water of life of the seven virgins of the light, and they had received the holy seal. (2.45 [108]).

Then comes the ritual of the baptism with fire. Jesus offered incense, caused the disciples to be clothed in linen, performed other ritual actions, including the setting

---

89. Cf. 4.143 (372-374) for the one baptism of fire, the baptism of the Holy Spirit of the light, and a spiritual inunction.

90. The "mystery knows why sin came into existence, and why the baptisms and the mysteries of the light" and the fire of punishment and the seals of the light and other things — 2.91 (209).

91. A fuller parallel statement in 3.112 (290); cf. 3.128 (324) — the virgins of light are in charge of baptism, and they baptize the soul and seal it with the sign of the kingdom.

92. Quotations are from the translation of Violet MacDermot, *The Books of Jeu and the Untitled Text in the Bruce Codex*, Nag Hammadi Studies 13 (Leiden: Brill, 1978), with her references and the page number in brackets.

forth of a cup of wine and loaves of bread, and prayed for them to receive the baptism of fire. One petition was: "[B]ring the water of the baptism of fire of the Virgin of the Light, that I may baptize my disciples in it" (2.46 [111]). A sign happened in the fire of the incense. And

> Jesus baptized his disciples. And he gave them of the offering, and he sealed them on their foreheads with the seal of the Virgin of the Light which would make them to be numbered within the Kingdom of the Light.
>
> And the disciples rejoiced becuse they had received the baptism of fire, and the seal which forgives sins, and because they were numbered within the inheritance of the Kingdom of the Light. (2.46 [111-112])

It was now time to receive the baptism of the Holy Spirit. A similar ritual was repeated, and Jesus "sealed the disciples" and prayed. A sign occurred in the offering. Then,

> [Jesus] baptized all his disciples with the baptism of the Holy Spirit. And he gave to them from the offering. He sealed their foreheads with the seal of the seven virgins of light. . . . And the disciples rejoiced . . . because they had received the baptism of the Holy Spirit, and the seal which forgave sins. (2.47 [113-114])

This was done while the disciples were clothed in linen garments and crowned with myrtle. There is a further sealing ceremony in 2.48, which is presumably the promised "mystery of the spiritual inunction" (2.43 [102] above). A summary statement in 2.49 refers to the baptisms, offerings, and seals.

The specificity certainly indicates a literal ritual, but we are not told how the baptism was performed nor informed about the content of the sealing. It is notable that the sealing is identified with the forgiveness of sins.

The Sethian baptismal rite as reconstructed mainly from the *Gospel of the Egyptians*, into which the other evidence may be fitted, would have included the following elements:[93] recitation of a long list of entities (a prebaptismal profession of *gnosis*); an invocation; a renunciation of the world (basis for including this as a separate item is slender); the baptism proper (a formula used, performed by a mystagogue, included multiple immersions — perhaps five, for conferring the five seals — perfume mixed with the water, and unrepeatable); hymns accompanying and following the baptism; joining of hands in a circle. The spiritual significance of baptism focused on the following aspects: *gnosis* or salvation;[94] separation from the world and liberation from the powers that rule it (but water was viewed more as vivifying and fruitful than as purifying); illumination and union. Those texts that speak nega-

---

93. I follow here Sevrin, *Le dossier baptismal*, pp. 140-141, 253-258, and the similar list in Turner, "The Sethian Baptismal Rite." For the following description of the doctrine of baptism — Sevrin, pp. 269-275.

94. Passages connecting baptism with knowledge include *Trimorphic Protennoia*, NHC XIII, 36, 4-27; *Gospel of the Egyptians* III, 65, 26-66,8; 66, 22-68, 1; *Zostrianos* VIII, 22, 4-15; 23, 2-20; 24, 17-25, 20.

tively of baptism have in mind rival systems that are opposed not because of the rite but the meaning given to it. Nonetheless, the Sethian texts do spiritualize baptism by projecting it spatially into the Pleroma and temporally into the story of myth. They do not correlate the spiritualized meaning of baptism with the physical rite, but certainly the former had the priority in importance without making the latter superfluous or eliminating it altogether.

Sethian baptism, whether metaphorical or ritual or both, shows few points of contact with Christian baptism, and these superficial and reinterpreted. This feature leaves open the possibility of its non-Christian origin, perhaps in a Jewish baptizing sect, whose practice was then placed in a Gnostic framework, given a new meaning, and subsequently lightly Christianized.[95]

Others

Irenaeus places Menander next to Simon of Samaria in his succession of heretics leading to the developed Gnostic systems of the second century with which he was especially concerned. His brief notice says Menander gave a knowledge by which one could overcome the angels who made the world and concludes with this claim: "By the baptism [*baptisma*] into him his disciples receive resurrection and are unable to die any more but continue immortal without growing old" (*Against Heresies* 1.23.5; summarized also in Eusebius, *Church History* 3.26.2). If this promise was meant literally, one can understand why we do not hear about Menander's disciples later. These words, however, may be a garbled version of the common claim that baptism brings resurrection and immortality, over which physical death has no power.

Cerinthus's interpretation of the baptism of Jesus was considered in chapter 6. Epiphanius has an extended discussion of him and his followers, of uncertain value. It includes the information that among the Cerinthians, like the Marcionites noted above, when some of their adherents died without having received baptism, others would be baptized in their names so that they would not be punished at the general resurrection. Some reported that this was the practice to which 1 Corinthians 15:29 referred.[96] Epiphanius adds that others (apparently orthodox rather than other Cerinthians) explain the text, and he seems to approve this interpretation as referring to catechumens who are dying (deathbed baptism), so that they may die in hope, having received the baptismal forgiveness of sins.

Basilides, active in Egypt early in the second century, may not have been so much a Gnostic himself as a precursor, a Gnostic in seed.[97] Clement of Alexandria

---

95. This is the conclusion of Sevrin, *Le dossier baptismal*, pp. 284-294. He considers the Sethian baptismal practices, nonetheless, to be post-Christian.

96. Epiphanius, *Panarion* 2.28.6.4-5.

97. Daniel Vigne, "Enquête sur Basilide," in André Dupleix, ed., *Recherches et tradition: Mélanges patristiques offerts à Henri Crouzel, SJ* (Paris: Beauchesne, 1992), pp. 285-313 (300). On the other hand, Birger A. Pearson, "Basilides the Gnostic," in Marjanen and Luomanen, *A Companion to Second-*

reports that the followers of Basilides were among those who sought to establish a chronology of the life of Christ. They seem to have had the first Christian liturgical calendar.[98] They not only calculated the date of Jesus' baptism, but they also celebrated it annually:

> Those who followed Basilides also observe as a festival the day of Christ's baptism and pass the night before in readings. They say it occurred in the fifteenth year of Tiberius (A.D. 29) on the fifteenth day of the month Tubi (January 10), but some say on the eleventh of the same month (January 6).[99]

The "some" are not identified — other Basilideans or another group in the (Alexandrian) church? But their calculation became the established date for the observance of the baptism of Jesus in the eastern churches and not the date advanced by most Basilideans. The number 365 was important in the cosmology of Basilides, and the doctrine of Basilides was tied to an annual calendar. The baptism of Jesus was the beginning of the redemptive mission of the Savior, the likely time at which he was enlightened and received the Spirit and Sonship.[100] The baptism was so important to the Basilideans that it was celebrated each year.

The Naasenes, or Ophites, were an early group that styled themselves Gnostics.[101] They offered enlightenment to men who were blinded from birth but presented themselves as spiritual. They talked of water in a figurative way and apparently gave primacy to an anointing: "And of all people, we Christians alone are those who in the third gate celebrate the mystery, and are anointed there with the unspeakable chrism from a horn, as David was anointed, not from an earthen vessel."[102]

Hippolytus's report on Justin the Gnostic, author of a book entitled *Baruch*, offers information that provides a framework for understanding Sethian texts that seemingly refer to a heavenly and an earthly baptism. When one has sworn the initiatory oath to keep secret the mysteries he has learned,

> He drinks from the living water, which is to them a bath [λουτρὸν], as they suppose, a fountain of living water springing up. For there has been a separation, [Justin] says, between water and water. There is a water that is below the firmament of the evil creation in which earthly and animal persons are washed [λούονται], and there is a living water above the firmament of the Good in which

---

Century Christian "Heretics," pp. 1-31, affirms he was a Gnostic and more importantly a Christian (p. 28).

98. Vigne, "Enquête sur Basilide," pp. 311-312.

99. Clement of Alexandria, *Miscellanies* 1.21.145-146.

100. Hippolytus, *Refutation of All Heresies* 7.20-27 (7.8-15); 10.14 (10.10), for the system of Basilides, in which the concept of Sonship was important. Vigne, "Enquête sur Basilide," pp. 300-313.

101. Hippolytus, *Refutation of All Heresies* 5.6-11 (5.1-6), places them first in his treatment of Gnostic groups.

102. Hippolytus, *Refutation of All Heresies* 5.9.22 (5.4). Cf. Origen, *Against Celsus* 6.27, where Celsus quotes an Ophite (?), "I have been anointed with white chrism from the tree of life."

living spiritual persons are washed [λούονται], in which Elohim also was washed [λουσάμενος] and did not repent.[103]

Here we meet the Valentinian division of humanity into three classes, characterized respectively by matter, soul, or spirit. The earthly water pertains to the first two; the heavenly to the last. Striking is the claim that Elohim (God) too washed in the heavenly water. It is living water, and the initiate drank of this water. Since λουτρόν was a regular word in the church for baptism, presumably there was a washing as well as a drinking of water (unless the drinking was understood as a symbolical washing); and, as in the Sethian texts above, the emphasis on the heavenly washing (this was metaphorical, I assume) may not preclude a literal rite that had a significance for the spirituals it did not have for others.

The Archontics discussed by Epiphanius represent a late form of Gnosticism centered on the figure of Seth. They rejected the baptism of the church, although some may have been baptized earlier, and denied any value to participating in the mysteries, which were instituted in the name of Sabaoth, identified with the God of the Jews, who gave the law, and so not coming from the supreme deity. "Mysteries" would include the eucharist, but Epiphanius here specifies baptism and apparently anointing: The Archontics "spoil the aromatic oil of sweetness — God's holy mysteries granted to us in the bath [λουτρὸν] for the forgiveness of sins."[104]

The occasion for Tertullian's treatise *On Baptism* (chap. 21) was the success of a woman who was a member of the Cainite sect in persuading some in Carthage that water baptism was of no value.[105] "A female viper from the Cainite sect, who recently lived in this place, carried off a good number by her most venomous doctrine, more than anything else refuting baptism." This was in keeping with her nature, since vipers generally frequent dry and waterless places. Christians, on the other hand, as "little fishes," "are kept safe only by abiding in the water." "That most monstrous woman, who had no right to teach even sound doctrine [1 Tim. 2:12], knew full well how to kill the little fishes by taking them away from the water."[106] Her doctrine apparently disparaged water as a material element without efficacy for salvation, for Tertullian proceeds to praise water and its exalted place from creation, so much so

---

103. Hippolytus, *Refutation of All Heresies* 5.27 (5.22).
104. Epiphanius, *Panarion* 1.40.2.6, 9. In 2.6, he says, "they anathematize the bath [λουτρόν]," although "some had previously been baptized [βεβαπτισμένοι]"; in 2.9, "they anathematize baptism [βάπτισμα]"; and in 2.8, "they flee the baptism [βάπτισμα] of the church." Epiphanius evidently uses βάπτισμα and λουτρόν interchangeably, and this seems to be his usual practice.
105. The newly published *Gospel of Judas*, pp. 55-56, speaks of those baptized in Jesus' name, but the subsequent text is missing, so what attitude the document takes toward baptism is unknown (Rodolphe Kasser, Marvin Meyer, and Gregor Wurst, *The Gospel of Judas* [Washington, D.C.: National Geographic, 2006], pp. 42-43). Irenaeus, *Against Heresies* 1.31.1, refers to the *Gospel of Judas* in connection with speculation about Cain by "others" (among the Sethians).
106. Tertullian, *On Baptism* 1.2-3. The Cainites opposed the God of the Old Testament as a malevolent deity and inferior to the higher deity Sophia. They honored those like Cain who were enemies of the Old Testament God.

that he apologizes, "I fear lest I seem to have collected the praises of water more than the reasons for baptism" (*On Baptism* 3.6).

The Mandaeans, the only surviving Gnostic community, were discussed in chapter 4 because of their connection with Jewish baptizing sects.

18. Irenaeus

Irenaeus was the first major literary opponent of the Gnostics whose work survives. His material on their views about baptism was presented in chapter 17, and his treatment of the baptism of Jesus was considered in chapter 6. His two major works, both surviving in translation, are *Against Heresies* and *Demonstration* (or *Proof*) *of the Apostolic Preaching*. Irenaeus's brief statements about baptism summarize the "orthodox" practice and understanding of baptism in contrast to the views surveyed in the preceding chapter.[1]

Because of the polemical concerns of his *Against Heresies* and the instructional purposes of his *Demonstration of the Apostolic Preaching*, Irenaeus has little about the ceremony of baptism. He assumes a period of preparation for baptism and so must explain the accounts of immediate baptism in the Acts of the Apostles. Peter would not have given baptism so readily to the household of Cornelius (Acts 10) if he had not heard them prophesying when the Holy Spirit came on them; and if the Holy Spirit had not rested on them, someone could have raised objection to the baptism of Gentiles.[2] Similarly Philip baptized the Ethiopian treasurer because only baptism was lacking to one who, from his reading of scripture, "was previously instructed [*praecatechisatus*] by the prophets."[3] Paul had to labor (1 Cor. 15:10) in teaching Gentiles, but instruction *(catechisatio)* of Jews was relatively easy because of their knowledge of the scriptures.[4] It is not clear whether Irenaeus is dealing with a question raised about a long preparation that prompts a defense of catechesis or he is merely explaining why there were immediate baptisms in scripture.

---

1. André Benoit, *Le baptême chrétien au second siècle* (Paris: Presses Universitaires de France, 1953), pp. 186-218; A. Houssiau, "Le baptême selon Irénée de Lyon," *Ephemerides theologicae lovanienses* 60 (1984): 45-59. David N. Power, *Iranaeus of Lyons on Baptism and Eucharist* (Nottingham, 1991).

2. *Against Heresies* 3.12.15.

3. *Against Heresies* 4.23.2.

4. *Against Heresies* 4.24.1-2.

One passage brings together three of Irenaeus's main views in regard to baptism: "'You were washed' [1 Cor. 6:11], believing in the name of the Lord and receiving his Spirit."[5] On the human side, Irenaeus strongly asserted the necessity of faith for salvation. Faith was central to baptism, for "It is faith that maintains our salvation."[6] "Human beings can be saved in no other way . . . except by believing" in him who was crucified and gives life to the dead.[7] Irenaeus also spoke of conversion and repentance and of obedience in relation to salvation,[8] but he gives no indication that these ideas received the liturgical expression that faith did.

Irenaeus implies a confession at baptism of the faith that had been taught. He refers to "the one who in himself holds unwaveringly the rule [κανόνα] of truth that he received through baptism [διὰ τοῦ βαπτίσματος]" and so is able to recognize the true content of the scriptures in contrast to the use made of them by false teachers.[9] The summary of this rule of truth that follows (*Against Heresies* 1.10.1) is structured according to the three divine persons.[10]

The baptism was administered with the Trinitarian formula. Concerning the faith handed down by the disciples of the apostles, he says:

> First of all, [it] admonishes us to remember that we have received baptism for remission of sins in the name of God the Father, and in the name of Jesus Christ, the Son of God, who became incarnate and died and was raised, and in the Holy Spirit of God.[11]

Baptism is again connected with the Trinity in a passage that follows shortly after: "Therefore the baptism of our rebirth comes through these three articles, granting us rebirth unto God the Father, through His Son, by the Holy Spirit."[12] The "three articles" perhaps, but not necessarily, allude to a triple immersion.[13]

---

5. *Against Heresies* 5.11.2.
6. *Demonstration* 3. My quotations of the *Demonstration* are taken from the translation by Joseph P. Smith, *St. Irenaeus: Proof of the Apostolic Preaching*, Ancient Christian Writers 16 (New York: Newman [Paulist], 1952), here p. 49. See more on faith below.
7. *Against Heresies* 4.2.7. On salvation by faith cf. *Demonstration* 3; 35; 52-53. This faith is produced by the truth — 7.
8. *Against Heresies* 4.41.3 and 1.10.1 on repentance (the necessity of repentance in general in 3.23.3; 4.40.1); 5.16.2 on obedience.
9. *Against Heresies* 1.9.4. *Demonstration* 3; 6-7 on the three articles of faith implies instruction and profession of faith.
10. Cf. the summary in *Against Heresies* 3.4.2 of the tradition of the apostles written by the Spirit in the hearts of barbarians who do not have the scriptures.
11. *Demonstration* 3 (Smith, p. 49).
12. *Demonstration* 7 (Smith, p. 51); cf. the next note and *Against Heresies* 3.17.1, where Matt. 28:19 is quoted (Irenaeus's passage is quoted at n. 32).
13. Cf. the "three articles of our seal" in *Demonstration* 100 (Smith, p. 109), explained as Father, Son, and Spirit. Houssiau, "Le baptême," pp. 58-59, discusses the word "seal" in Irenaeus; he concludes on this passage that "'Seal' probably designates baptism itself, in the course of which the three articles were professed" (p. 58).

That the baptism was indeed by immersion seems to be confirmed by the use of the story of Naaman (2 Kings 5:14) in a fragment that is probably genuine.[14]

> [Scripture] says, "And he [Naaman] baptized himself in the Jordan seven times." It was not in vain that Naaman the leper of old, when he was baptized [βαπτισθεὶς], was cleansed, but it was a sign to us. We who are lepers in our sins are cleansed from our old transgressions through the holy water and the invocation of the Lord.[15]

The use of *baptizō* in the Greek version provided the basis for taking the story of Naaman as a type of Christian baptism (chap. 4). Its usage there, in keeping with the Hebrew original, clearly meant "dipped." The cleansing in Christian baptism, however, involves not just the water of the Old Testament story but also the invocation of the Lord. The invocation (ἐπίκλησις) likely refers to the baptismal formula as a calling on the Lord, for there is no indication in Irenaeus of an invocation of the Holy Spirit to come on the water that we will encounter in Tertullian and the *Apostolic Tradition*.[16]

There is nothing in what survives from Irenaeus about an anointing, a laying on of hands, or a signing in connection with baptism.[17] It would be precarious to argue from silence against any of these items being performed, for mentioning them might not have fit Irenaeus's purposes. Nevertheless, when the language of anointing is employed, it is used figuratively for the gift of the Spirit and not for a literal application of oil.[18]

Irenaeus offers a much richer doctrinal fare in regard to baptism. As the quotations above indicate baptism brought a forgiveness, a cleansing, of sins. Taking up the words of Peter's sermon to the household of Cornelius (Acts 10:43),[19] Irenaeus says, "He [Peter] commanded them to be baptized [*baptizari*] into him [Christ] for the remission of sins," words not in the text commented on, so reflecting Irenaeus's understanding of baptism.[20] Remission of sins is also said to have been received by those who believed in Jesus.[21]

---

14. D. Bruno Reynders, *Vocabulaire de la "Demonstration" et des fragments de Saint Irénée* (Louvain, 1958), p. 74.

15. Irenaeus, Fragment 34 (W. W. Harvey, *Sancti Irenaei Libros quinque adversus haereses* [Cambridge, 1857; repr. Ridgewood, NJ: Gregg, 1965], #33).

16. The invocation of the Lord, alternatively to the administrator's words, might be the candidate's profession of faith.

17. *Against Heresies* 4.38.2 mentions Paul's laying on of hands to give the Holy Spirit, but the context is not baptismal.

18. Houssiau, "Le baptême," p. 49, with reference to *Against Heresies* 3.9.3 and *Demonstration* 47 concerning the anointing of Jesus with the Spirit.

19. "All the prophets testify about [Jesus Christ] that everyone who believes in him receives forgiveness of sins through his name."

20. *Against Heresies* 3.12.7; 3.12.2 quotes Acts 2:38 but does not develop it in regard to baptism; 4.22.1 cites Isaiah 4:4 and John 13:5 for the disciples having been "cleansed and washed."

21. *Against Heresies* 4.27.2. The context is Jesus' descent into the underworld in order to preach to the righteous there, "to whom he forgave sins in the same way as he did us," for which other texts are cited in chapters 12 and 13.

For Irenaeus the Holy Spirit is given in baptism.[22] This is stated expressly: "When there abides constantly in them the Holy Spirit, who is given by Him in baptism."[23] Commenting on 1 Corinthians, Irenaeus asked, "When do we bear 'the image of the heavenly man'? [1 Cor. 15:49]" and answers, with the quotation at note 5 above.[24] The passage continues by affirming that we have washed away our former manner of life and now do the works of the Spirit. The gift of the Spirit in baptism is perhaps related to the description of baptism as "the seal of eternal life."[25] A belief that the Spirit was given in baptism did not in itself rule out a separate act associated with or symbolizing the giving of the Spirit, but it is notable that Irenaeus speaks only of the coming of the Spirit in baptism itself and not in a separate postbaptismal act.[26]

Irenaeus describes baptism as an act in which both the water and the Spirit are at work. The water washes the body and the Spirit cleanses the soul. Thus he declares that we cannot be made one in Christ Jesus without the "water from Heaven," by which he means the Holy Spirit. "For our bodies receive unity through that bath [*lavacrum* — Titus 3:5] which is for incorruption and our souls by the Spirit. Wherefore both are necessary."[27] When Christ was baptized, the Spirit of God united with his body. Similarly, after Christ sent out the apostles in the power of the Holy Spirit, they showed the way of life to the Gentiles, "purifying their souls and their bodies through the baptism of water and of the Holy Spirit."[28] The washing of the body and the purifying of the soul might be distinguishable in principle but were not separable in fact. The water and the Spirit worked together in the one baptismal event.

Like the writers cited in chapter 16, Irenaeus paralleled the Jewish circumcision of the flesh and the Christian circumcision by the Spirit. Circumcision was given as a sign to identify the race of Abraham. "Circumcision according to the flesh typified the spiritual circumcision." Irenaeus then quoted Colossians 2:11 about a circumcision not made with hands and Deuteronomy 10:16 about circumcising the heart.[29] He did not use circumcision as an analogy to baptism.

---

22. Houssiau, "Le baptême," p. 55.

23. *Demonstration* 42 (Smith, p. 74). Cf. *Against Heresies* 5.18.2 for the Spirit as "living water" (John 7:39), whom the Lord gives to those who correctly believe.

24. *Against Heresies* 5.11.2. See Benoit, *Le baptême,* pp. 208-211, for what the Spirit does for people according to Irenaeus.

25. *Demonstration* 3 (Smith, p. 49); cf. *Against Heresies* 3.17.3. André Benoit, *Le baptême,* p. 212, sees an allusion to the baptismal formula. See n. 13 above.

26. Special gifts of the Spirit were imparted separately. In *Demonstration* 7 the mutual working of the three divine persons in baptism is asserted, but with the understanding that according to the Father's good pleasure the Son administers the Spirit to those whom he will — a reference to special spiritual gifts (Smith, p. 52; see his note on pp. 144-145); similarly *Demonstration* 41, after referring to the working of the water and the Spirit in baptism (quoted below), refers to the apostles dispensing the Holy Spirit to the faithful. The promise by the prophets of the pouring out of the Spirit is mentioned in *Demonstration* 89 without reference to the means of his coming.

27. *Against Heresies* 3.17.2.

28. *Demonstration* 41 (Smith, p. 74).

29. *Against Heresies* 4.16.1; cf. *Demonstration* 24.

What Irenaeus says in contrasting orthodox with heretical baptism indicates his central conception: The teachings of heretics were a denial of "the baptism [βαπτίσματος] of regeneration [ἀναγεννήσεως] to God."[30] As cited above, baptism is "rebirth to God" by which we become his children (*Demonstration* 3) and is characterized as a "baptism of rebirth" and "gives rebirth to God" (*Demonstration* 7).[31] Regeneration is Irenaeus's most frequently recurring motif in regard to baptism. Christ in Matthew 28:19 gave to his disciples "the power of regeneration [*regenerationis*] into God."[32] Because of sin humanity "was in need of the bath of regeneration [*lavacro regenerationis* — Titus 3:5]," and the healing of the blind man in John 9:7 gave him "the regeneration that is by the bath [*lavacrum regenerationem*]."[33] The treatment of Naaman's sevenfold bath in the Jordan[34] concludes, "Being regenerated [ἀναγεννώμενοι] spiritually, as the Lord said, 'One who is not regenerated [ἀναγεννηθῇ] by water and the Spirit cannot enter into the kingdom of heaven.'"[35]

Regeneration was a broader category for Irenaeus than the baptism that was related to it. Jesus' virgin birth "regenerates [*regenerat*] people to God."[36] They escape the generation that produces death by "the regeneration [*regenerationem*] which is from the virgin by faith."[37] Regeneration was also connected to the resurrection of Jesus, but in this passage with reference to those who lived before Jesus.

> For the Lord, being born, was "firstborn from the dead" [Rev. 1:5], and receiving the earliest fathers into his bosom, he regenerated them into the life of God. He himself was made the beginning of those who live, as Adam was made the beginning of those who die. Therefore Luke, when he began the genealogy of the Lord, carried it back to Adam [Luke 3:23-38], indicating that he regenerated [*regeneravit*] them into the gospel of life and they did not regenerate him.[38]

The final resurrection of the righteous is a salvation and regeneration of the flesh.[39]

---

30. *Against Heresies* 1.21.1, cited in chapter 17. For the use of "regeneration" by Marcus, see 1.14.6. Houssiau, "Le baptême," p. 53, notes that for Irenaeus the expression is never "birth from [ἐκ] God," but "birth to [εἰς] God."

31. J. Armitage Robinson, *St. Irenaeus: The Demonstration of the Apostolic Preaching* (London: SPCK, 1920), in both chapters renders the Armenian "regeneration." L. M. Froidevaux, *Irénée de Lyon: Démonstration de la prédication apostolique*, Sources chrétienne 62 (Paris: Cerf, 1959), refers to the underlying Greek as ἀναγέννησις, which he renders "nouvelle naissance," keeping "regeneration" for παλιγγενεσία.

32. *Against Heresies* 3.17.1.

33. *Against Heresies* 5.15.3.

34. Fragment 34 (Harvey 33), referred to above.

35. John 3:5 is quoted with the change of the verb from γεννηθῇ and of "kingdom of God" to "kingdom of heaven," both of which readings have some early support.

36. *Against Heresies* 4.33.11.

37. *Against Heresies* 4.33.4. The reference to the virgin is presumably to Mary and the virgin birth of Jesus, but possibly the church.

38. *Against Heresies* 3.22.4.

39. *Against Heresies* 5.2.2; cf. 5.15.1, "a second generation."

Since regeneration clearly refers to baptism in some passages,[40] Irenaeus has been adduced as a witness to the practice of infant baptism:

> He sanctified every age of life by having the like age in himself. For he came to save all by means of himself, all (I say) who by him are born again [*renascuntur*] to God — infants, children, boys, youths, and the old. He therefore lived through every age, made an infant for infants and sanctifying infants; a child for children, sanctifying these by having this age and accomplishing for them at the same time an example of piety, righteousness, and submission; a youth for youths, becoming an example for youths and sanctifying them to the Lord. So, also, an older person for those who are older so that he might be a perfect teacher for all. . . .[41]

This may be the earliest reference to infant baptism.[42] Before rushing to accept a reference to infant baptism here, we should be cautious. For one thing, the verb used, *renascor* ("reborn"), is different from *regenero* ("to regenerate"), the verb related to *regeneratio* in the passages on baptism.[43] But if we accept the two words as conceptually the same, there is another consideration. Besides its reference to baptism, regeneration is used by Irenaeus for Jesus' work of renewal and rejuvenation effected by his birth and resurrection without any reference to baptism. That could be the case here. And such a reference better fits the context of recapitulation in which this passage occurs.[44] The coming of Jesus brought a second beginning to the whole human race. He sanctified every age of life. Accepting his renovation by being baptized is another matter and falls outside the purview of this passage.

Problematic for some advocates of infant baptism is Irenaeus's affirmation of the innocence of children. Those who are saved are "those who believed in God and continued in his love . . . and innocent children, who have had no sense of evil." "Who are they that are saved now and receive eternal life? Are they not those who loved God, believed his promises, and have become 'in malice as little children' [1 Cor. 14:20]."[45]

---

40. E.g., *Against Heresies* 1.21.1; 3.17.1.

41. *Against Heresies* 2.22.4.

42. Chapter 23 considers other passages claimed for this distinction and discusses the origin and development of infant baptism. Another possibility in Irenaeus is *Adversus haereses* 1.10.1, where he refers to "those who have kept God's commands and persevered in love, either from the beginning or from their repentance." Is the "beginning" the beginning of life or beginning of the Christian life? If the latter, the repentance may be from postbaptismal sin; but since repentance is more likely conversion repentance, then either the beginning of life or the age of conversion is indicated. For one raised in a Christian home, keeping the commandments and persevering in love might still apply to the beginning of life without implying infant baptism.

43. Where we have the Greek, *regeneratio* translates ἀναγέννησις — *Against Heresies* 1.14.6; 1.21.1-2; Frg. 34 (Harvey 33).

44. Cf. *Against Heresies* 4.38.2. Benoit, *Le baptême*, pp. 216-218, concludes that since infants, like Adam, are not capable of receiving the Holy Spirit, the theology of Irenaeus was not favorable to the initiation of infants.

45. *Against Heresies* 4.28.3.

19. Clement of Alexandria

Terminology and the Meaning of Baptism

As a well-educated convert to Christianity, Clement of Alexandria sometimes employed βαπτίζω according to its secular usages (chap. 3). He applies it to a "sinking [βαπτιζομένη] ship."[1] He uses it figuratively of drunkenness — "steeped [or overwhelmed, βαπτιζόμενος] by drunkenness into sleep"[2] — and of being "overwhelmed [βεβαπτισμένος] in ignorance."[3] Clement speaks ironically of the different purpose of baptism for those who gave a libertine interpretation of Christianity: in contrast to 1 Corinthians 6:9-11, "they have a washing [ἀπολούοντες] with a view to licentiousness and are baptized [βαπτίζουσι] from self-control into fornication."[4] If there is a figurative sense of change of state or condition here, it is closely tied to water baptism by the parallel use of "washing." Clement uses, in addition to βάπτισμα, λουτρόν and other terms for Christian baptism.

Clement of Alexandria exhorted his pagan readers in these words: "The Lord invites to the bath [λουτρόν], to salvation, to enlightenment."[5] These were key terms for Clement, not only in addressing pagans but in his instruction for Christians. In a particularly important passage for his understanding of baptism Clement of Alexandria speaks of our being "regenerated" (ἀναγεννηθέντες) based on the example of Jesus' baptism. He then summarizes: "This work is variously called a grace gift [χάρισμα], illumination [φώτισμα], perfection [τέλειον], and bath [λουτρόν]."[6]

---

1. *Who Is the Rich Man That Is Saved?* 34.
2. *Instructor* 2.2.
3. *Exhortation* 1.3.
4. *Miscellanies* 3.18.109.
5. *Exhortation* 10.94.2.
6. *Instructor* 1.6.26.2. Clement's names for baptism are studied in the dissertation by Harry A. Echle, "The Terminology of the Sacrament of Regeneration According to Clement of Alexandria" (Catholic University of America, 1949). The subsequent parts of Clement's passage are studied by

The terminology of regeneration is Clement's favorite imagery for baptism.[7] Thus he says God made human beings from dirt but gives them regeneration (ἀναγεννῆσαι) in water, growth in spirit, and education in word.[8] Similarly Clement has the Savior say, "I gave regeneration [ἀνεγέννησα] to you who were generated [γεγεννημένον] by the world to death."[9] He interprets Matthew 18:3 ("Unless you are converted and become as little children") to refer to the Lord's will for us to be as pure in body and holy in soul as he generated (γεγέννηκεν) us "from water, our mother."[10] He further connects the Spirit with the water because baptism cleanses soul and body: "Regeneration [ἀναγέννησις] is of water and Spirit [John 3:5], as was all generation [γένεσις — creation, or origination]," with a citation of Genesis 1:2. He continues, "Baptism occurs through 'water and Spirit,'" and interpreting the waters above the heaven in Genesis 1:7 as allegorically the Holy Spirit, he affirms that earthly water cleanses the body but the heavenly water (the purifying Spirit) cleanses the human spirit.[11] In this context Clement can speak of baptism as the sign (σημεῖον), apparently in a realistic sense, of regeneration (ἀναγεννήσεως).[12] Clement

---

A. Orbe, "Teologia bautismal de Clemente Alejandrino según Paed. I, 26,3-27,2," *Gregorianum* 36 (1955): 410-448, who interprets the passage as anti-Valentinian.

7. I have opted for the translation "regeneration" over "new birth" or "being born again" because the emphasis is on the divine function of imparting new life and better represents the linguistic contrast between physical generation and spiritual regeneration. Those who render "new birth" probably have the same idea in mind, but unless the passage indicates an emphasis on "female" imagery, it seems better to use a term reflecting the "male" role. The advantage of "new birth" terminology would be to distinguish ἀναγέννησις from παλιγγενεσία, which usually had a different conceptual significance, but I will try to show those conceptual differences in other ways.

8. *Instructor* 1.12.98.2. See A. von Harnack, "Die Terminologie der Wiedergeburt und verwandter Erlebnisse in der ältesten Kirche," *Texte und Untersuchungen* 42 (1918): 97-143. The discussion of rebirth in J. Ysebaert, *Greek Baptismal Terminology: Its Origins and Early Development*, Graecitas christianorum primaeva 1 (Nijmegen: Dekker & Van de Vegt, 1962), pp. 89-154, mainly treats παλιγγενεσία.

9. *Who Is the Rich Man?* 23.2. Cf. the contrast of regeneration [ἀναγέννησις] with "fleshly birth" (*Miscellanies* 3.12.83), and the statement: "He wishes us to be converted and become as little children, knowing the true Father, being regenerated [ἀναγεννηθέντας] through the water, since this seed is different from that in the created world" — *Miscellanies* 3.12.88.1.

10. *Miscellanies* 4.25.160.2. *Exhortation* 9.82.4 similarly combines Matt. 18:3 and John 3:5, "'Unless you become as little children and are regenerated [ἀναγεννηθῆτε],' as scripture says, you will not receive the One who is truly Father 'nor enter into the kingdom of heaven.'" Cf. "the children drawn out of the water" (*Instructor* 3.11.59.2) in allusion to Christian salvation, not a reference to literal children.

11. *Prophetic Eclogues* 7-8. The *Excerpts from Theodotus* 81 quotes, apparently approvingly, concerning the dual nature of baptism: Water extinguishes the fire of the senses in our nature, and the Spirit extinguishes the immaterial fire of demons, evil spirits, and the devil. Cf. the similar thought in Tertullian, *On Baptism* 7-8, except that Tertullian associates the Spirit with the subsequent anointing and laying on of hands. Franz Josef Dölger, *Der Exorzismus in altchristlichen Taufritual* (Paderborn: Ferdinand Schöningh, 1909), pp. 4-7, says *Prophetic Eclogues* 7 reflected a Gnostic view, but it does not necessarily contradict Clement's denial of the Valentinian view that unclean spirits dwell in the soul of the unbeliever (*Miscellanies* 2.20.114.3-6) and affirmation that not demons but what they sow in the sinner's soul is driven out.

12. *Prophetic Eclogues* 5. Carlo Nardi's commentary, *Il battesimo in Clemente Alessandrino: Interpretazione di* Eclogae propheticae *1-26*, Studia Ephemeridis "Augustinianum" 19 (Rome: Institutum

emphasizes the divine life, immortality, that results from regeneration.[13] This regeneration has moral consequences: "We who have put off the old person, removed the old garment of evil, and put on the incorruption of Christ in order that we may become new, a holy people, having been regenerated [ἀναγεννηθέντες], we keep the [new] person undefiled and are innocent as a baby of God, having been cleansed from fornication and wickedness."[14]

This regeneration is God's gracious gift. Clement explains in our text passage that regeneration is called a *charisma* because "in it the penalties belonging to our sins are removed."[15] "Being a perfect God, he surely gives perfect gifts."[16]

Illumination is another concept important for Clement, and it is quite prominent in this context. He defines illumination as "to know God."[17] "When we are baptized, we are illuminated [φωτιζόμεθα]; and when we are illuminated, we are adopted; and when we are adopted, we are perfected; and when we are perfected, we are made immortal."[18] Baptism is called an illumination, because by its holy, saving light we attain a clear vision of the divine.[19] The one who has been regenerated and illuminated is immediately delivered from darkness and instantly receives the light.[20] Baptism "rubs out the sins that obscure the divine Spirit" so that the "spiri-

---

Patristicum "Augustinianum," 1984), 64-66, discusses water as well as Spirit as the instrumental cause (διά) of regeneration in Clement and in the Christian tradition before and after him. Regeneration (ἀναγέννησις) is baptism in *Miscellanies* 3.12.83.1.

13. This is stressed by Orbe, "Teologia bautismal," pp. 410, 441-446. Note p. 444, "There descends on the Christian the same divine life that descended fully on Jesus. . . . The one difference resides in the quantity: On Jesus descended *omnis fons Spiritus Sancti;* on the neophyte a participation in it. But it is always the same Spirit, the perfect Life of God."

14. *Instructor* 1.6.32.1, 4.
15. *Instructor* 1.6.26.2.
16. *Instructor* 1.6.26.3.
17. *Instructor* 1.6.25.1. Elsewhere Clement says, "The instruction that reveals hidden things is called illumination" (*Miscellanies* 5.10.64.4). Illumination or enlightenment as a name for baptism is studied in J. Ysebaert (n. 8), pp. 158-178. Arkadi Choufrine, *Gnosis, Theophany, Theosis: Studies in Clement of Alexandria's Appropriation of His Background* (New York: Peter Lang, 2002), pp. 41-45, 69-76, considers baptismal illumination in Clement in relation to its background in Basilideans and Valentinians, especially the *Gospel of Truth*, and the theme of illumination in general in his chapter 2, pp. 77-158. Fabrizio Tiddia, "Terminologia della luce e battisimo nelle iscrizioni greche cristiane," *Vetera Christianorum* 38 (2001): 103-124, finds the preponderance of inscriptions referring to light to be of eastern origin. He classifies them according to use of νεοφώτιστος for the baptized; νεοφωτιστήριον for the baptistery; the general terms φῶς or φωτίζω; and those that cite biblical passages. Possible explanations of the connection of light and baptism, especially in the East, are light's symbolic value in pagan antiquity as associated with divinity and salvation, the spiritual meaning of light in the Old Testament, and the connection of the appearance of light at the baptism of Jesus in Syrian writers (cf. my chap. 6).
18. *Instructor* 1.6.26.1.
19. *Instructor* 1.6.26.2.
20. *Instructor* 1.6.27.2-3. Choufrine, *Gnosis*, pp. 41-42, cites 1.6.28.1 for an immediate and sudden inner awakening comparable to that in Basilideans and Valentinians. But for Clement the illumination is related also to instruction, as subsequent citations show.

tual eye becomes full of light" and able "to see the divine, as the Holy Spirit flows down upon us from heaven." One becomes "light in the Lord" (Eph. 5:8).[21] "Knowledge is illumination," but this is a moral knowledge, for "the one grace of illumination is to be no longer the same as before one's washing."[22]

Regeneration is also perfection or completion. "When we were regenerated [ἀναγεννηθέντες], we immediately received the perfection [τὸ τέλειον] which we sought." As Clement proceeds to explain, "The one who knows the Perfect [i.e., God] is not incomplete."[23] And he adds, "We say that what is in need of nothing is perfect. And what is yet lacking to the person who knows God?"[24] To be regenerated [ἀναγεννηθῆναι] is perfection.[25]

Clement's fifth name for baptism in this listing is "bath" or "washing" (λουτρόν). It is a bath because "through it we thoroughly cleanse ourselves of sins."[26] "Transgressions are forgiven . . . by the baptism that pertains to the Word [λογικῷ βαπτίσματι]. We thoroughly wash all sins away from ourselves [ἀπολουόμεθα] and at once are no longer evil."[27] Another passage that speaks of the communion of the Word [ὁ λόγος] with baptism says "baptism [βάπτισμα] is for [ἐπὶ] the forgiveness of sins."[28]

Another term used by Clement for baptism but not included in the list in *Instructor* 1.6.26 is "seal" (σφραγίς).[29] A seal identified ownership, and in early Christian literature the word's religious usage was almost exclusively a reference to baptism.[30] Baptism is clearly the seal in several passages in Clement, one of which calls

21. *Instructor* 1.6.28.2.
22. *Instructor* 1.6.29-30.
23. *Instructor* 1.6.25.1. Orbe, "Teologia bautismal," finds Clement's emphasis on illumination and especially on perfection as a refutation of the Valentinian contrast between (imperfect) ecclesiastical baptism (in water) that only brings forgiveness of sins, whereas the Gnostic baptism of the Spirit brings light and perfection. In contrast, Clement emphasizes that there is only one baptism that brings all these things.
24. *Instructor* 1.6.26.2-3.
25. *Instructor* 1.6.27.2, quoted below at n. 40.
26. *Instructor* 1.6.26.2. Discussed by Ysebaert (n. 8), pp. 13-83.
27. *Instructor* 1.6.29-30.1.
28. *Instructor* 1.6.50.4.
29. This is the chapter of Echle's dissertation, "The Terminology of the Sacrament," published in Studies in Sacred Theology (Second Series), No. 30 (Washington, D.C.: The Catholic University of America Press, 1949). For the seal in Clement as a "character" imprinted on a person at baptism, and not some additional rite of confirmation, see G. W. H. Lampe, *The Seal of the Spirit,* 2nd ed. (London: SPCK, 1967), pp. 115, 153-157.
30. Clement's *Excerpts from Theodotus* 86 notes some of the secular usages of the word, and its reference to "the seal of truth" refers to baptism, which is the clear meaning of the seal in 80.3 and 83. *Prophetic Eclogues* 25.1 cites Heracleon for a unique practice by an unidentified "some" who "marked with fire the ears of those who are sealed." Contemporary with Clement, but from Asia Minor, the *Epitaph of Abercius* says, "I saw a people there [Rome] who bore a shining seal." In keeping with the inscription's figurative language, the allusion is probably to baptism. H. Leclercq, "Abercius," *Dictionnaire d'archéologie chrétienne et de liturgie,* Vol. 1 (Paris, 1924), col. 74, for text and discussion.

baptism, as "a seal of the Lord," a "perfect protection."[31] The terminology of "the seal of knowledge" relates the idea also to illumination.[32] So too does the declaration that this seal is a manifest "light" united with the soul in a passage that connects the seal with the subsequent life, for it is a "seal of righteousness" that results in one becoming "perfect."[33] One passage in particular seems to distinguish baptism and the seal: For those who consider faith a product of nature "baptism is no longer reasonable, nor the blessed seal, nor the Son, nor the Father."[34] I would suggest that Clement is either borrowing the terminology of the opponents to whom he refers or is applying "seal" to the Holy Spirit given in baptism, not to a postbaptismal anointing.

Jesus' Baptism

The passage on which we have based our discussion of Clement's terminology for baptism begins with a discussion of the Lord's baptism, quoting Matthew 3:17 and adding the phrase, "Today I have begotten you."[35] In view of the things said about baptism, the baptism of Christ was a problem, intensified by the conclusions drawn by those with whom Clement disagreed, but Clement turns the baptism of Jesus to the support of the church's understanding of baptism. The names he gives for baptism are based on the account of Jesus' baptism. He asks,

> Will they not confess, though unwillingly, that the Word, perfect offspring of the perfect Father, was regenerated [ἀναγεννηθῆναι] perfectly in order to give a prefiguration according to the plan of God? And if he was perfect, why was the perfect one baptized [ἐβατίζετο]? They say, "It was necessary to fulfill the promise concerning humanity." Most excellent, for I say, "Did he become perfect when he was baptized [βαπτίζεσθαι] by John?" Evidently so. "Did he then not learn anything more from him?" No indeed. "Is he perfected in the bath [λουτρῷ] alone, and is he sanctified by the descent of the Spirit?" Such is the case. The same is true for us, of whom the Lord became the pattern.[36]

Jesus' baptism by John perfected him according to his humanity, not with reference to his deity, and the same perfection and sanctification that came to his humanity comes also to human beings by baptism. The parallels are carried further: The Lord's

---

31. *Who Is the Rich Man?* 42.4; also 39.1; *Miscellanies* 2.9.43.5; *Prophetic Eclogues* 12.9. See discussion in Echle, "The Terminology of the Sacrament," pp. 24-30, and Nardi, *Il battesimo,* pp. 115-116, for the seal in Clement as baptism in water.

32. *Miscellanies* 1.5.31.5.

33. *Miscellanies* 6.12.104.1. Cf. 4.18.116.2 for "the impress of righteousness full of light."

34. *Miscellanies* 2.3.11.2. The various interpretations of the seal are considered by Echle, "The Terminology of the Sacrament," pp. 22-24.

35. The addition is discussed by Orbe, "Teologia bautismal," pp. 434-441. It is consistent with Clement's frequent use of (re)generation imagery, here related to the baptism of Jesus.

36. *Instructor* 1.6.25.3-26.1. Choufrine, *Gnosis,* pp. 54-65.

temptations after his baptism are a type of our temptations.[37] Jesus' baptism not only served as a pattern but also purified water: "The Savior was baptized, although he did not need to be, in order that he might sanctify all water for those who are being regenerated [ἀναγεννωμένοις]."[38] His baptism "delivered us from fire," and he has commanded his apostles to baptize.[39]

Faith and Repentance

This basic text for Clement's baptismal views furthermore associates baptism with faith and repentance. Following one of his statements of baptismal illumination, Clement says, "Instruction [κατήχησις] leads to faith, and faith together with baptism is trained [παιδεύεται] by the Holy Spirit, since faith is the one universal salvation of humanity."[40] Clement finds this sequence of hearing the teaching, believing, and being baptized in Galatians 3:23-28 and 1 Corinthians 12:13.

Subsequent to those quotations, he proceeds to say:

> There follows of necessity to the one who has been reminded of better things repentance for the worse things. . . . In the same manner we ourselves, having repented of our sins, having renounced our faults, and being purified in baptism run back to the eternal light, children to their Father.[41]

Elsewhere Clement in a passage that later refers to baptism says that "the sins committed before coming to faith are forgiven before the Lord in order that they may be as if they had not been done."[42] In response to the view of Basilides and Valentinus that he felt made faith a product of nature Clement asks, "Where then is the repentance by the former unbeliever, through which comes the forgiveness of sins?"[43] In

---

37. Cf. *Excerpts from Theodotus* 85.1.

38. *Prophetic Eclogues* 7.2. The presence of the Spirit at creation (7.1) and at the baptism of Jesus sanctified all water. This correlation is important for Nardi's analysis of *Prophetic Eclogues* 1-26 (*Il battesimo*, pp. 49-86 on the water and the Spirit in baptism). For other passages in Christian literature on this theme, see chapter 7.

39. *Excerpts from Theodotus* 76.1-3. The declaration bracketed by these two statements, "The one baptized with reference to God advanced to God and received 'power to walk upon scorpions and snakes,' that is the evil powers," is ambiguous, but probably refers to Jesus, but the same power is affirmed at the end of the passage for all those born again by baptism. Nardi with reference to *Prophetic Eclogues* 25-26 relates baptism to eschatological fire (*Il battesimo*, pp. 217-239).

40. *Instructor* 1.6.30.2. "Believing alone and being regenerated [ἀναγεννηθῆναι] is perfection in life" — *Instructor* 1.6.27.2. "Nothing is lacking to faith, which is complete in itself" — *Instructor* 1.6.29.2. See the passage cited at n. 61. Clement evidently saw no contradiction between affirming "faith alone" and affirming baptism as the occasion of initiation into essential spiritual blessings. Faith for him included baptism.

41. *Instructor* 1.6.32.1.

42. *Miscellanies* 4.24.153.3. The reference to baptism (λουτρόν) is in 154.3 on sins committed before and after baptism.

43. *Miscellanies* 2.3.11.2.

discussing purification by water, he says, "An adequate cleansing for a person is genuine and sure repentance."[44]

The necessity of faith and repentance implies that Clement has in mind those of sufficient age to believe and repent. Although he often refers to new Christians as "babies," he has no reference to infant baptism. The one occasion where there is clear indication of the age of a person baptized is in the story of the apostle John leaving a young man in the care of a bishop. "The presbyter took home the youth delivered to him, raised, took care of, cherished, and finally baptized [ἐφώτισε, "illuminated"] him."[45]

Ceremony of Baptism

In contrast to the rather full baptismal theology expressed in these passages Clement gives no explicit description of the baptismal ceremony. In addition to the statement already cited that "Catechesis leads to faith," there are other indications that baptism was preceded by a period of instruction. "For it is impossible to believe without instruction [κατηχήσεως]."[46] With reference to 1 Corinthians 3:1-3, Clement refers to the interpretation that "milk" is the proclamation of the gospel and "meat" is faith given substance by instruction (κατήχησις).[47] He once identifies the "fleshly" as those "recently instructed [recent catechumens — νεωστὶ κατηχουμένους] and still babes in Christ." But then he continues in a way that identifies the "fleshly" as those not yet baptized: The "spiritual" have believed in contrast to the "fleshly," who are "the newly instructed [or new catechumens — νεοκατηχήτους] but not yet purified."[48] Elsewhere he says that the "new catechumen" [νεοκατηχήτῳ] receives teaching in wisdom.[49] Again, he observes that milk is catechetical instruction (κατήχησις), "as it were the first food of the soul."[50] These apparently inconsistent statements are probably to be explained, in spite of my sometimes literal rendering of the underlying Greek, by the circumstance that *catechesis* was not yet a technical

---

44. *Miscellanies* 4.22.143.1.
45. *Who Is the Rich Man?* 42.4.
46. *Prophetic Eclogues* 28.3 — Nardi, *Il battesimo*, pp. 143-176, for the content of the baptismal catechesis in Clement. Clement's interpretation of Lev. 19:23 about not eating the fruit of trees for three years to indicate the need of time in order to be "solidly catechized" (*Miscellanies* 2.18) may indicate a three-year catechumenate as in the *Apostolic Tradition* (chap. 20), but this may not be a literal period of time, for Clement is mainly interested in the fourth year (four virtues) and the Leviticus passage says eat the fruit only in the fifth year (19:25). For Clement's information on catechesis and rites associated with baptism, see Victor Saxer, *Les rites de l'initiation chrétienne du IIe au VIe siècle: Esquisse historique et signification d'après leur principaux témoins* (Spoleto: Centro italiano di studi sull'alto medioevo, 1988), pp. 65-99.
47. *Instructor* 1.6.38.1.
48. *Instructor* 1.6.36.2-4.
49. *Miscellanies* 6.15.120.1. The same word is found in *Instructor* 1.6.36.3.
50. *Miscellanies* 5.10.66.2.

term and so could be applied to instruction at various stages of a person's being brought to faith and conversion.

Nardi's analysis of the *Prophetic Eclogues* finds in its chapters 14–16 reference to the prebaptismal preparatory practices of fasting, praying, and doing good works.[51]

There are, moreover, several allusions to the baptismal practice known to Clement. Is baptismal immersion in mind when he exhorts (with reference to Eph. 6:14-17), "Let us extinguish the Evil One's fiery darts whose points are watery and pliant because of having been dipped [βεβαμμέναις] by the Logos"?[52]

More definite are the indications of the use of the names of the Trinity in baptism. I suggested above that the reference to the seal, the Son, and the Father may be such an indication.[53] Also to be considered is the statement made in commenting on the story of Abraham (Gen. 22:3-4, 12, 18), "The three days may be the mystery of the seal, through which God is truly believed."[54] The seal is a designation of baptism, and the association of "three" with truly believing would be suggested by the use of the threefold divine name in baptism. The *Excerpts from Theodotus* 76.3 quotes the command of Matthew 28:19 to baptize "'into the name of the Father, Son, and Holy Spirit,' in whom we are regenerated [ἀναγεννώμεθα]." Explicit is the following statement: "The one to whom Christ gives regeneration [ἀναγεννᾷ] . . . [this one who] has been sealed [σφραγισθείς] by the Father, Son, and Holy Spirit is delivered from every other power and has been released by the three names from all corruption."[55]

The extensive development of the imagery of regeneration in *Instructor* 1.6 with Christians as infants nourished on milk and the correlation of milk with blood make it possible that Clement knew a baptismal eucharist that included milk (and honey) with the bread and wine.[56]

Clement's *Exhortation to Endurance, To the Newly* [νεωστί] *Baptized* says nothing about baptism, but if the title is accurate there is implied postbaptismal moral instruction.[57]

The quotation of Ephesians 5:14, "Awake, you sleeper, and arise from the dead, and Christ the Lord will shine on you," in a context of exhortation to "become little

---

51. Nardi, *Il battesimo,* pp. 121-142.

52. *Exhortation* 11.116.4. Note the description of the one baptized (βαπτισθέντος) as one who "comes up" [ἀναβαίνει] in *Excerpts from Theodotus* 77.2.

53. *Miscellanies* 2.3.11.2. See at n. 34. Cf. the characteristically figurative language, "We are protected by the power of God the Father and the blood of God the Son and the dew [δρόσῳ] of the Holy Spirit" (*Who Is the Rich Man?* 34) — the association of the Holy Spirit with water is to be noted.

54. *Miscellanies* 5.11.73.2.

55. *Excerpts from Theodotus* 80.2-3. Again, I am assuming Clement cites these excerpts with approval, unless he stipulates a correction.

56. Relevant passages include *Instructor* 1.6.38.1-3, 39-40, 42.3-43.3, 46.1, 47.1-3, 49.4, 50 (express reference to baptism), and 51.1. The last two passages speak of milk's capacity of mixing with water, with honey, and with wine; whether one can go from these statements to the presence of separate cups for these items in the baptismal eucharist remains conjectural.

57. A. Guida, "Un nuovo testo di Gregorio Nazianzeno," *Prometheus* 2 (1976): 193-226, attributes the work to Gregory of Nazianzus.

children and be *regenerated* [ἀναγεννηθῆτε],"⁵⁸ lends support to the suggestion that this passage in Ephesians quotes from a baptismal hymn.

Clement accepted the view of Hermas that the righteous (Gentiles and Jews, according to Clement) who lived before Christ needed baptism. He quotes from Hermas about the apostles and teachers after their death preaching to the righteous dead, giving them "the seal of the preaching [τὴν σφραγῖδα τοῦ κηρύγματος]"; "they descended with them into the water and they ascended with them [κατέβησαν οὖν μετ' αὐτῶν εἰς τὸ ὕδωρ καὶ πάλιν ἀνέβησαν]" so that they might be made alive.⁵⁹

Jewish and Pagan Antecedents

The preceding quotation occurs at the conclusion of an anti-Judaic passage. Clement elsewhere contrasts the one-time Christian baptism with the many washings of the Law of Moses. The Lord washes clean by one baptism (ἑνὸς βαπτίσματος), encompassing in one baptism the many washings of Moses.⁶⁰ A positive image from the Old Testament is drawn from the instructions for the high priest to wash his body, put on his robe, and offer sacrifice (Lev. 16:23-24). This exhibits the true "Levite and Gnostic, the chief of the other priests, those who are washed in water, clothed with faith alone, and expecting their own individual abode."⁶¹ True to his usual spiritualizing, Clement proceeds to describe the Lord after his incarnation hastening to the world of ideas, washing himself from the things of this world, not in water but purified by the Gnostic Word.

Clement drew anticipations of Christian baptism from pagan as well as Jewish practices. He understands the purificatory washings of Greeks and Jews as an image (εἰκών) of Christian baptism, citing Homer as dependent on Moses for purification by water.⁶² He has such purification rites in mind as he issues the call to his readers, "Receive then the water of the Logos, you who are polluted wash yourselves, purify yourselves from custom with the drops of truth."⁶³

Quite significant for future developments was Clement's occasional adoption of terminology from initiation into the pagan Mystery Religions in order to interpret the significance of Christian baptism. The extent to which Clement was influenced by the Mystery Religions can easily be exaggerated, and it seems that he uses the ter-

---

58. *Exhortation* 9.84.2.
59. *Miscellanies* 2.9.44.1-3, quoting Hermas, *Similitudes* 9.16.5-7 (= 93.5-7); also, *Miscellanies* 6.6.45.4 and 46.1-2, 5. Choufrine, *Gnosis*, pp. 102-111, accepting *Excerpts from Theodotus* 18 as from Clement himself, argues that Christ as well as the apostles baptized and preached in Hades: "The 'Savior' who 'descended' into Hades thus is the same Light that descends as 'the holy spirit' both in Christian baptism and, by implication, in the baptism of Jesus" (p. 119).
60. *Miscellanies* 3.12.82.6. See chapter 16 for this common theme.
61. *Miscellanies* 5.6.39.3-4.
62. *Miscellanies* 4.22.141.4-142.3, quoting *Odyssey* 4.750 (cf. 4.760; 17.48, 58) and 2.261.
63. *Exhortation* 10.99.3.

minology as illustrative in order to communicate with pagan readers rather than his thought being shaped by mystery conceptions. Even so, mystery terminology is rare in reference to the sacraments.[64] One passage that may have baptism in mind draws on the language of Dionysiac ceremonies, but Clement gives the description a Christian content:

> O truly sacred mysteries! O light without stain! I am led by torches to contemplate the heavens and God. I am initiated and become holy. The Lord is the hierophant. He brings to the light and seals [σφραγίζεται] the initiate. He presents to the Father the believer whom he keeps safe forever. These are the Bacchic revelries of my mysteries. If you wish, be initiated yourself, and you will join the chorus together with the angels.[65]

Although the invitation to initiation is present, and the invitation in some sense begins in the present, Clement thinks primarily of the entrance into heaven as the Christian initiation. Shortly before the passage quoted, he said,

> The Word of God will be your Pilot, and the Holy Spirit will bring you to anchor on the shores of heaven; then you will contemplate God, will be initiated in those holy mysteries, and will enjoy those things stored up in heaven.[66]

The passage quoted above (n. 54) about the "mystery of the seal" may designate baptism a mystery but could as well be a reference to the hidden meaning of the "three days" as referring to the triune divine names.

Clement and Those Called Gnostics

Clement's *Excerpts from Theodotus* have already been drawn on (chap. 17) to describe Valentinian baptism, and I have not hesitated sometimes to cite the work in this chapter in filling out the picture found in Clement's other writings. The similarities between Theodotus and Clement include preparatory rites of fasting, prayer, and exorcism (85; 82.2), catechetical instruction (cf. 78), the use of water with the Trinitarian names (80.3; 82.2; 83), the use of bread and oil (82.1), the laying on of hands (22.5), and the interpretation of baptism as a seal (86).[67] I consider it likely that there

---

64. H. G. Marsh, "The Use of ΜΥΣΤΗΡΙΟΝ in the Writings of Clement of Alexandria with Special Reference to His Sacramental Doctrine," *Journal of Theological Studies* 37 (1936): 64-80; Harry A. Echle, "Sacramental Initiation as a Christian Mystery Initiation according to Clement of Alexandria," in A. Mayer et al., eds., *Vom Christliche Mysterium* (Düsseldorf, 1951), pp. 54-65.

65. *Exhortation* 12.120.1-2.

66. *Exhortation* 12.118.4.

67. François Sagnard, *Clément d'Alexandrie: Extraits de Théodote,* Sources chrétiennes 23 (Paris: Cerf, 1970), pp. 229-239. Thomas M. Finn, *Early Christian Baptism and the Catechumenate: Italy, North Africa, and Egypt,* Message of the Fathers of the Church 6 (Collegeville: Liturgical, 1992), pp. 174-191, includes a comparison of Theodotus and Clement (esp. 177-178).

was an anointing with oil as part of the baptismal initiation at Alexandria at this time, but *Instructor* 2.2.19.4, "We have been anointed with the spiritual blood of the Lord," is not likely to be an allusion to this practice. The same is true for a laying on of hands, again not expressly mentioned by Clement in connection with baptism (*Instructor* 3.11.63.1 is not baptismal). Differences from Theodotus would mainly have come in the interpretation of baptism, but even here the use of the baptism of Jesus as a model (76; 85), the teaching that baptism brings deliverance from the powers of evil and incorporation into Christ and his life (76-77), the interpretation of the dual cleansing of body and soul by the water and the Spirit (81, but contrast 77.2), and the understanding of baptism as regeneration (80.2) agree with Clement's theology. Without parallel in Clement but not objectionable to him was the baptism of Jesus releasing us from fire (76.1) and the claim as part of Theodotus's emphasis on the Name that the Name gives water the power to sanctify (82).[68] The teaching that fate is real before baptism but that after baptism the astrologers are no longer right (77-78) would not have been Clement's view, although he would have shared the conviction that baptism delivers from unclean spirits. More distinctively Valentinian, without parallel in Clement, is the interpretation of 1 Corinthians 15:29 as the angels baptized for us who are "dead" spiritually so that we may enter the Pleroma (22) and the understanding of the baptism of Jesus as uniting us with the beings in the Pleroma (36.2).

Clement concludes that the views of Basilides and Valentinus mean that "The minister, preaching, and baptism are superfluous."[69] He mocks the baptism of those who follow the "knowledge falsely so-called" (libertine Gnostics) as a "washing" in order to commit licentiousness instead of being the baptism that purifies from it (1 Cor. 6:9-11). It is no surprise then that, prompted by Proverbs 9:17, he considers "heretical baptism" to be "no proper and genuine water."[70]

The baptismal interpretation of Clement's quotations from *Secret Mark*[71] depends too much on inference rather than on what is explicit in the text itself.

The Baptism of the Apostles

In view of the importance attached to baptism, the failure of the scriptures to relate a baptism of the apostles presented a problem. A late quotation from Clement's *Hypotyposes* indicated that he gave an answer to the question.

---

68. I have concluded (chap. 17) that this was a reference to the triple divine names invoked at baptism (with which Clement would have concurred), not an invocation on the water (known shortly afterwards from other sources).

69. *Miscellanies* 2.8.38.1.

70. *Miscellanies* 1.19.96.3-4.

71. Morton Smith, *Clement of Alexandria and a Secret Gospel of Mark* (Cambridge: Harvard University Press, 1973), pp. 167-188.

Yes, truly [the apostles] were baptized, as Clement the Stromatist mentions in the fifth book of his *Hypotyposes*. For in interpreting the apostolic saying, "I am thankful that I baptized no one of you" [1 Cor. 1:14], he says, "Christ is said to have baptized only Peter, and Peter Andrew, and Andrew James and John, and they the others."[72]

Postbaptismal Sin

Since baptism brought a forgiveness of sins, consideration had to be given to postbaptismal sins. Clement, in alluding to the penitential discipline imposed on Christians who sinned, made a distinction in the basis of the forgiveness in each case: "Let it be known, then, that those who fall into sins after the bath [λουτρόν] are disciplined; for the deeds done before are forgiven, but those that are done afterward are purged."[73] Some of what might be involved in this purging (or purifying) is included in the account of the restoration of the young Christian who had become captain of a band of robbers. "Baptized [βαπτιζόμενος] a second time with tears," he was "purged by repentance, brought back to the church," and became a "great example of regeneration [παλιγγενεσία]."[74] Again, Clement says, "God gives forgiveness of past sins, but of later sins each one gives to himself." It seems impossible to overcome ingrained sins, but "By the power of God, human intercession, the help of brothers and sisters, sincere repentance, and constant care they are corrected."[75] Clement expected that the one who had come to faith and had obtained forgiveness from the Lord, "By attaining knowledge (γνῶσις) and so no longer sinning, provides forgiveness from himself of the rest of his sins."[76]

Concluding Comments

In addition to the biblical passages already referred to — Matthew 3:16-17; 18:3; Galatians 3:26-27; 1 Corinthians 12:13; John 3:3, 5 and/or 1 Peter 1:23 (regeneration);

---

72. John Moschus, *Spiritual Meadow* 5.176 (Migne, PG 87.3045CD). Harry A. Echle, "The Baptism of the Apostles: A Fragment of Clement of Alexandria's Lost Work Ὑποτυπώσεις in the Pratum Spirituale of John Moschus," *Traditio* 3 (1945): 365-368, notes other explanations of the baptism of the apostles (see chap. 21 on Tertullian's discussion) and later testimonies to the same tradition assigned by John Moschus to Clement. Simon Legasse, *Naissance du baptême* (Paris: Cerf, 1993), has an appendix, "Were the First Disciples of Jesus Baptized?" (pp. 135-148), based on his article in the *Bulletin de littérature ecclésiastique* 79 (1978): 3-18.

73. *Miscellanies* 4.24.154.3.

74. *Who Is the Rich Man?* 42.14-15. Cf. the reference to "repentance for sins after baptism" — *Miscellanies* 6.14.109.3. The reference to a second baptism with tears is a comparison of penitence to baptism and not an indication of baptism by infusion — Victor Saxer, *Les rites de l'initiation*, p. 85. Is it significant that Clement uses here παλιγγενεσία instead of his usual ἀναγέννησις?

75. *Who Is the Rich Man?* 40.1, 6.

76. *Prophetic Eclogues* 15.2 (discussed by Nardi, *Il battesimo*, p. 134).

Titus 3:5 (bath); Leviticus 16:23-24 (priest's bath) — Clement associated other passages with baptism: Isaiah 55:1 ("Come to the water");[77] 1 Corinthians 6:11 ("'You were washed,' not simply as others, but you cleansed thoroughly the passions of the soul with knowledge");[78] 1 John 3:9 (the seed is "God's word in him who is regenerated through faith");[79] and 5:8 ("the Spirit is life, the water is regeneration and faith [*regeneratio ac fides*], and the blood is knowledge [*cognitio*]").[80]

Clement of Alexandria combined an immaterial spirituality with a material sacramentality — an emphasis on faith, regeneration by the Spirit, and divine illumination with a high view of water baptism. This combination of a sense of mystery with material elements continued in the Greek Orthodox tradition.

---

77. *Exhortation* 10.94.1-2.
78. *Miscellanies* 7.14.86.4-5.
79. *Hypotyposeis* on 1 John 3:9. Cassidorus's Latin both here and in the next quotation is *regeneratio*. Note the association of faith with regeneration and, made explicit in the next quotation, with water.
80. *Hypotyposeis* on 1 John 5:8.

PART FOUR

The Third Century to Nicaea (325)

20. Writings Attributed to Hippolytus

Major challenges to the unity of authorship of the writings attributed to Hippolytus have resulted in assigning the major works belonging to the third century to two or possibly three authors.[1] Treating works in the Hippolytan corpus relevant to the study of baptism together in this chapter is a matter of convenience for organizational purposes and not an affirmation that I accept common authorship. I treat them in the order of their relationship with a historical figure named Hippolytus. The *Commentary on Daniel* belongs to someone named Hippolytus;[2] it is associated with the treatise *On Christ and Antichrist*; the *Against Noetus* is probably authentic; the *Apostolic Tradition* is a composite community document, perhaps originating with the "Hippolytan" community in Rome but expanded and modified later;[3] and *On the Holy Theophany* I judge to have no connection with Hippolytus or the third century but ascribed to him as part of a later tendency to use his name as a way of

---

1. Allen Brent, *Hippolytus and the Roman Church in the Third Century: Communities in Tension before the Emergence of a Monarch-Bishop* (Leiden: Brill, 1995), chapters 4 and 5, reviews and evaluates the arguments by various scholars for two separate authors. He identifies the reconstructed statue of Hippolytus now at the entrance to the Vatican Library as originally a female figure that was accepted by the "Hippolytan" church-school community in Rome as a personification of wisdom (chaps. 1–2). The list of works on the plinth of the statue were community works and not one person's writings. Of two works not listed on the statue, the *Refutation of All Heresies* (and writings associated with it) came from an early presbyter-bishop of the community antagonistic to the community led by Zephyrinus and Callistus, and *Against Noetus* (and writings associated with it) came from his successor (named Hippolytus) who effected reconciliation with the rival (majority) group (chapter 3). I find the case for different authorship more successful than the argument that the monarch bishop was not established in Rome until 235 (chaps. 6–7), although my disagreement is not so much about the situation described as the definition given to a monarch bishop. J. A. Cerrato, *Hippolytus between East and West: The Commentaries and the Provenance of the Corpus* (New York: Oxford University Press, 2002), favors an eastern origin for the commentaries ascribed to Hippolytus.

2. Different from the author of the *Refutation of All Heresies* — Brent, *Hippolytus and the Roman Church*, pp. 273-276, 280-284.

3. Brent, *Hippolytus and the Roman Church*, pp. 184-203, 301-306, 458-475.

identifying works that were not apostolic with someone believed to be close to the apostolic age and to transmit its teachings.[4]

Commentary on Daniel

Jerome ascribed a commentary on Daniel to Hippolytus,[5] and considerable parts are preserved in Greek. The comments on the story of Susanna in the Greek version of Daniel include a Christian interpretation dependent on baptismal practice.

The "opportune day" of Susanna 15 (Theodotion's text) is identified as the Pasch, "at which the bath [λουτρόν] is prepared," and "Susanna washes herself [ἀπολουομένη] and is presented as a pure bride to God."[6] The two maidens accompanying her are the "faith in Christ and love for God" that, as custom required, the church confesses when receiving the bath (λουτρόν).

Susanna's request for "olive oil and unguents" (17) is explained: "For faith and love prepare oil and unguents for those being washed [λουομένοις]." The unguents are the commandments of the holy Word. "The olive oil is the power of the Holy Spirit; with these believers are anointed as with ointment [ὡς μύρου χρίονται] after the washing [λουτρόν]."

This information is consistent with what we know of general Christian baptismal practice and specifically of western practice at the beginning of the third century according to Tertullian (chap. 21).[7] Baptism was commonly administered at Passover. The word for "bath" ("laver" or "washing") was often used for baptism. Faith and its confession were required as part of the baptismal rite. The washing was followed by an anointing with olive oil. The association of olive oil with the Holy Spirit was common, and Tertullian identified the postbaptismal anointing with a spiritual anointing.

On Christ and Antichrist

In the description of the church as a ship Hippolytus says that the church possesses the "laver of regeneration [Titus 3:5] that renews believers" (59).

Against Noetus

The work *Against Noetus* is an early example of a long tradition of quoting Matthew 28:19 in support of the doctrine of the Trinity. By this command Christ showed that anyone who omitted one of these failed to glorify God perfectly (*Against Noetus* 14).

---

4. Cf. Brent, *Hippolytus and the Roman Church*, pp. 178, 195-196.
5. *Lives of Illustrious Men* 61.
6. Cf. Eph. 5:26-27.
7. See note 19.

Apostolic Tradition

For the subject of baptism the most important of the writings associated with the name Hippolytus is the so-called *Apostolic Tradition*. The identification of the *Egyptian Church Order* with the *Apostolic Tradition* listed on the statue that was restored in the Renaissance as belonging to the early third-century Hippolytus of Rome was the work of Eduard Schwartz[8] and especially R. H. Connolly.[9] The identification was disputed but came to prevail and was the basis for the influential attempts at restoration of the document by Gregory Dix[10] and Bernard Botte.[11] The *Apostolic Tradition* has had a huge modern influence, but there is now some drawing back from attachment to the document.

Jean Michel Hanssens distinguished between various persons named Hippolytus in the early church. He argued that the *Apostolic Tradition* offered an "ideal" liturgy but presented evidence that the affinities of the liturgical material were more with Alexandria and Egypt than with Rome.[12] But if Hippolytus was Greek and perhaps came from Egypt, this would not militate against his producing the *Apostolic Tradition* in Rome.[13]

More recently the argument has gained favor for the separation of the church order from the writings of Hippolytus and for the description of it as "living literature," a composite work collecting community rules from different places and times.[14] Paul Bradshaw, Maxwell E. Johnson, and L. Edward Phillips, in the work from which I take the quotations below, carry this approach further in describing the work as "an aggregation of material from different sources, quite possibly arising from different geographical regions and probably from different historical periods, from perhaps as early as the mid–second century to as late as the mid–fourth century."[15]

Accepting the description of the *Apostolic Tradition* as church-use literature or

---

8. *Über die pseudoapostolischen Kirchenordnungen* (Strasbourg: Trubner, 1910).

9. *The So-called Egyptian Church Order and Derived Documents*, Texts and Studies 8.4 (Cambridge: Cambridge University Press, 1916).

10. *Apostolic Paradosis: The Treatise on the Apostolic Tradition of St. Hippolytus of Rome* (New York: Macmillan, 1937; 2nd ed., London: SPCK, 1968).

11. *La tradition apostolique de saint Hippolyte: Essai de reconstitution* (Münster: Aschendorff, 1963; 5th ed. 1989).

12. *La liturgie d'Hippolyte: Ses documents, son titulaire, ses origines et son charactère*, Orientalia Christiana Analecta 155 (Rome: Pontificium Institutum Orientalium Studiorum, 1959; 2nd ed. 1965). But it might be countered that Hanssens does not so much establish an Alexandrian origin for the liturgical material as that this was where its influence was the greatest.

13. As Brent, *Hippolytus and the Roman Church*, p. 353, observes, cultural space is not the same as geographical space, especially since communities from many different regions assembled in Rome.

14. This has been especially argued by Marcel Metzger, "Nouvelles perspective pour le prétendue *Tradition apostolique*," *Ecclesia Orans* 5 (1988): 241-259; "Enquêtes autour de la prétendue *Tradition apostolique*," *Ecclesia Orans* 9 (1992): 7-36; "A propos des règlements écclesiastique et de la prétendue *Tradition apostolique*," *Revue des science religieuses* 66 (1992): 249-261. The position is accepted by Brent, *Hippolytus and the Roman Church*, pp. 195-196 (noted above).

15. *The Apostolic Tradition: A Commentary*, Hermeneia (Minneapolis: Fortress, 2002), p. 14.

"living literature" so that it does not have a single author, Christoph Markschies observes that the name of Hippolytus entered the transmission of the church order material relatively late, at the end of the fourth century.[16] Although accepting the titles on the statue as coming from a Roman author named Hippolytus, he claims that there is no certain argument that the *Grundschrift* of the church order now called the *Apostolic Tradition* or that its preserved translations bore that title.[17]

Alaistair Stewart-Sykes has carried further the interpretation by Allen Brent and identifies two members of the same school in Rome whose different viewpoints are both reflected in their successive redactions of the *Apostolic Tradition*. Although scholars have to try to recover the original work from its derivative documents, there was at one time a finished product by the community in Rome responsible for it. This holds true whatever the earlier material incorporated and whatever modifications the derivative documents introduced.[18]

My approach to the material on baptism will be to follow the earliest available witnesses to the text without trying to sort out redactional layers (except in obvious cases). Although the connection with Hippolytus is problematic, and there certainly are layers from different periods and places in the work, the different sources from widely scattered geographical areas (represented by different languages — Latin, Greek, Syriac, Coptic, and others) from the fourth and fifth centuries argue for a third-century original of the base document; and this wide acceptance of the work suggests an influential center such as Rome. I will refer to this church order as the *Apostolic Tradition* according to well-established convention without committing to its identification with the work of that name on the statue at the Vatican Library.

The material on baptism in the *Apostolic Tradition* has many points of contact with information in Tertullian (chap. 21), and that suggests a western origin in the early third century for the ceremonies described.[19] These would be based on second-century practices, but the witnesses to the text of the *Apostolic Tradition* incorporate later (third- and fourth-century) elements, only some of which will I attempt to identify. Points of contact with Jewish practices are often commented upon.[20] Un-

---

16. "Wer schrieb die sogennante *Traditio Apostolica*?" in Wolfram Kinzig, Christoph Markschies, and Markus Vinzent, *Tauffragen und Bekenntnis* (Berlin: de Gruyter, 1999), pp. 1-74 (20, 39-44).

17. Markschies, "Wer schrieb," pp. 21-38.

18. Alaistair Stewart-Sykes, *Hippolytus on the Apostolic Tradition* (Crestwood: St. Vladimir's Seminary Press, 2001), pp. 22-32.

19. The similarities of the rites in Tertullian and in the *Apostolic Tradition* are conveniently charted in Georg Kretschmar, *Die Geschichte des Taufgottesdienstes in der alter Kirche*, in *Leiturgia*, Vol. 5 (1964-1966), pp. 86-114 (89-91), and Frank C. Quinn, "Confirmation Reconsidered," in Maxwell Johnson, ed., *Living Water, Sealing Spirit* (Collegeville: Liturgical, 1995), p. 223; see also Everett Ferguson, *Early Christians Speak*, 3rd ed. (Abilene: ACU Press, 1999), pp. 35-37.

20. For the Jewish associations of the baptismal rite, see Reuben J. Zwi Werblowsky, "On the Baptismal Rite according to St. Hippolytus," *Studia Patristica* 2 (1957): 93-105. He points out that to defer baptism of menstruous women (20.6) has nothing comparable in rabbinic literature on the admission of female proselytes; nudity (21.3) was normal in Greco-Roman baths as well as in Jewish lustrations; the preference for flowing water (21.2) would go back to Jewish practice; and the closest indication of a

fortunately, the Latin is lacking the prebaptismal sections and picks up only in the midst of the account of the immersions.

Newcomers to the faith were brought to teachers by Christians who testified to their readiness to be instructed, and they were examined as to their motives for coming, their social and marital status, and whether they had a demon (15). A person involved in certain occupations had to cease from these or be rejected from catechetical instruction (16). The witnesses to the text vary in the contents, but the prohibited activities objected to also by Tertullian (*On Idolatry* and *On the Shows*) include: brothel keepers, makers of idols, actors, teachers, charioteers, gladiators, soldiers, magistrates, prostitutes, and magicians.

The catechumens were to hear the word for three years, but the provision is made that character and not time is judged in determining one's readiness (17) for baptism. This three-year period of instruction is rare in early Christian literature. After the teacher finished each lesson, the catechumens prayed by themselves, separate from the faithful, and they did not exchange the kiss of peace, which was given only among the faithful (18). After a time of prayer, the teacher (who might be a layman) dismissed the catechumens with the blessing of prayer and the laying on of hands (19.1). Assurance is given that if a catechumen becomes a martyr, "he will be justified, for he received baptism in his own blood" (19.2).

When it was time for the catechumens to receive baptism, they were examined again as to whether they had lived virtuously and engaged in good works, and their sponsors testified on their behalf (20.1-2).[21] Then began a period of daily imposition of hands and of exorcism (20.3-4).[22] The frequent exorcisms show that the catechumens were not clean but still part of the world.

The immediate preparation for baptism involved bathing on the fifth day of the week (Thursday) (20.5-6). Preparation day (Friday) was to be spent in fasting. On the Sabbath (Saturday) the candidates for baptism prayed on bended knees, and the bishop laid his hand on them and exorcised them (20.7-8). They spent the whole night being read to and instructed (20.9).[23] The practices are usually interpreted in terms of baptism at the Pasch (Easter), for which compare Tertullian, but the text does not specify this season, only that it was done on Sunday, and the instructions may apply to whenever the baptism was to be performed.

Jewish ancestry for the baptismal rite would be the loose hair and removal of jewelry. The major difference is that a context of demonism and exorcism is totally absent from rabbinic speculation on the meaning of lustration but was central to Hippolytus.

21. The "sponsors" (first mentioned by Tertullian — next chapter) likely functioned originally to guarantee the readiness of adults for baptism, not to answer on behalf of infants, as came to be true later (and already in Tertullian).

22. Henry Ansgar Kelly, *The Devil at Baptism: Ritual, Theology, and Drama* (Ithaca: Cornell University Press, 1985), pp. 81-93.

23. Hanssens, *La liturgie d'Hippolyte,* pp. 448-451, argues that in view of the Jewish terminology employed this vigil was on our Friday night to Saturday morning, as is known in the Alexandrian liturgical practice, but most take the reference according to later Roman practice to be a Saturday night vigil.

The chapter dealing with the actual administration of baptism (21) is unfortunately full of textual uncertainties, giving rise to the theory that this chapter and the preceding one incorporate at least three strata of material.[24] At cockcrow prayer was said over the water (21.1). The instructions for the water to be flowing (21.2) into the baptismal pool (κολυμβήθρα) may reflect earlier practice of baptism in running water (*Didache* 7). If both the directions for prayer over the water and the use of flowing water are original to the *Apostolic Tradition*, a question is raised about the theory that invocation of the Holy Spirit on the water was introduced when a change was made from natural sources of water to use of manmade structures;[25] but we may have directions from different stages of baptismal practice included. The Arabic and Ethiopic versions state that in the absence of water to flow into the place of baptism, any water that can be found is to be poured into the font.

One received baptism naked (21.3, 11).[26] Factors possibly influencing this custom were nudity in Jewish washings and proselyte baptism, initiations to some of the mystery religions,[27] and bathing customs. It is usually assumed that this meant complete nudity, but since the words γυμνός and *nudus* could mean lightly clothed in one's undergarment, the *Apostolic Tradition* may not necessarily require total nakedness.[28] The direction to baptize small children first, then men, and finally women (21.4-5) is notable for the inclusion of children and is discussed in chapter 23. (Women were last perhaps for the sake of decency so that they would not be seen by the men.) The women were to have their hair loose[29] and to lay aside any jewelry and other foreign objects (amulets?) before entering the water.

24. Bradshaw et al., *The Apostolic Tradition*, pp. 108, 124-129.

25. Georg Kretschmar, *Die Geschichte des Taufgottesdienstes*, in *Leiturgia* Vol. 5, nos. 31-35 (1964-1966), p. 92, understands the prayer not as consecration in the sense of the later liturgies but according to Jewish thought as a thanksgiving and petition for God to act. Leonel L. Mitchell, "The Thanksgiving over the Water in the Baptismal Rite of the Western Church," in Bryan D. Spinks, ed., *The Sacrifice of Praise* (Rome: Edizione Liturgiche, 1981), pp. 229-244, starts with this text but mainly surveys the later history of the practice.

26. John E. Farrell, "The Garment of Immortality: A Concept and Symbol in Christian Baptism" (Washington, DC: Catholic University of America dissertation, 1974; Ann Arbor: University Microfilms), pp. 60-127, discusses the theology of nudity in relation to baptism in writings of the first five centuries.

27. As shown in pictures of initiation into Mithraism and in the worship of Dionysus (if the scenes in the Villa Item at Pompeii are indeed a Dionysiac initiation). J. Gwyn Griffiths, *Apuleius of Madauros, The Isis-Book (Metamorphoses, Book XI): Introduction, Translation and Commentary*, Études préliminaires aux religions orientales dans l'empire romaine 39 (Leiden: Brill, 1975), pp. 192, 239, 293. Plotinus likens the soul in its ascent to the Good taking off what it put on in its descent to the fact that "for those who go up to most sacred rites there are purifications and taking off clothes to go up naked" (*Enneads* 1.6.7).

28. Laurie Guy, "'Naked' Baptism in the Early Church: The Rhetoric and the Reality," *Journal of Religious History* 27 (2003): 133-142, argues the possibility that the practice was for one to be lightly clothed and that the rhetoric of nudity matched the dramatic ritual of baptism and expressed the radicalness of the change it depicted.

29. W. C. van Unnik, "Les chevaux defaits des femmes baptisées: Un rite de baptême dans l'Ordre Ecclésiastique d'Hippolyte," *Vigiliae Christianae* 1 (1947): 77-100.

The directions for the bishop to prepare oil of thanksgiving and oil of exorcism and the position taken by a deacon and a presbyter (21.6-9) break into the account and are suspect of being a later interpolation. The candidate is commanded to say, "I renounce [ἀποτάσσεσθαι] you, Satan, with all your service and all your works" (21.9 — Sahidic).[30] The person was then anointed (by the deacon?) with the oil of exorcism (21.10-11). The position of this anointing suggests its association with the preceding renunciation, and the name indicates its purificatory and exorcistic character. The deacon then went down into the water with the baptizand and enjoined him to make a positive declaration of faith in the fashion of later Trinitarian confessions (21.12). Since the wording includes formulae from the fourth-century controversies (e.g, ὁμοούσιος in the Sahidic), this version of how the candidate declared adherence to God is certainly later than Hippolytus.

The Latin version survives from the middle of 21.14 with the words, ". . . having [his] hand laid on his head, let him baptize [him] once." Some of the versions have an awkward joining of the declaratory confession with an interrogatory confession, but there is an agreement among the sources of a triple immersion. Taking the witness of the Latin version, the *Canons of Hippolytus,* and the *Testament of the Lord* together with other indications of third-century practice leads to the conclusion that the administrator with his hand on the head of the baptizand asked three questions (concerning faith in God, then Christ, and then the Holy Spirit) and at each affirmative response dipped the person's head under the water (21.15-18).[31] The baptismal questions and affirmative replies inseparably bound faith and baptism together.[32] As the versions of the *Apostolic Tradition* make clear, the hand on the head was functional in the immersions, but the normal presence of this gesture in artistic depictions of baptism had the further purpose of alluding to the confession of faith that was linked with baptism.[33] Some of the

---

30. Kretschmar, *Die Geschichte des Taufgottesdienstes,* p. 97, cites various forms of the renunciation. Usually the renunciation is threefold with Satan always at the head of the list but the other items varying.

31. For the connection of the interrogatory confession and baptismal formula see E. C. Whitaker, "The History of the Baptismal Formula," *Journal of Ecclesiastical History* 16 (1965): 1-12; repr. in Everett Ferguson, *Conversion, Catechumenate, and Baptism in the Early Church,* Studies in Early Christianity 11 (New York: Garland, 1993), pp. 379-390.

32. Paul F. Bradshaw, "The Profession of Faith in Early Christian Baptism," *Evangelical Quarterly* 78 (2006): 101-115, accepts the view that the interrogations and responses (according to Roman law) originally meant a contract rather than commitment to a creedal position, as they became later. The questions articulated a transfer of allegiance but came to be changed from personal commitment to the content of the faith (see chap. 21). In the case of infants the profession was made by someone else (cf. Tertullian's "sponsors" — chap. 21), and in the fourth century this was done for those too sick to make their own profession (chap. 39) — pp. 109, 112-113.

33. The basic meaning of the gesture was bestowal of a blessing, and that meaning may apply in baptism as well, in which case the blessings are adoption by God and bestowal of the Holy Spirit — Everett Ferguson, "Laying On of Hands: Its Significance in Ordination," *Journal of Theological Studies,* n.s. 26 (1975): 1-12; repr. in Everett Ferguson, ed., *Church, Ministry, and Organization in the Early Church Era.* Studies in Early Christianity 13 (New York: Garland, 1993), pp. 147-158. This laying on of hands at the immersions is to be distinguished from postbaptismal actions, although it is possible that the artistic representations of baptism conflate the two.

versions include expansion of the facts about Christ, and there is considerable variation in the wording of what is included in the confession about the Holy Spirit (the holy church is best attested, and after it the resurrection).[34]

The close parallels of the Latin version (in interrogatory form) with the Old Roman Symbol attested in declaratory form in the fourth century has led many scholars to conclude that the fourth-century declaratory Roman baptismal creed originated in the interrogatory confessions of the *Apostolic Tradition*.[35] This view has been challenged with the counterargument that the agreements are due to the Latin translation's accommodating the wording of the *Apostolic Tradition* to the form of confession in use in the fourth century and that the Roman Symbol was not adopted until the fourth century.[36] However, a good case can be made that, although the baptismal questions are older than the declaratory formulae, an early form of the Roman Symbol belongs to the first half of the third century.[37]

After the third immersion a presbyter anointed the baptizand with the oil of thanksgiving (21.19 — Bohairic and Arabic).[38] After drying off, the newly baptized dressed and entered the church (21.20).[39] "The bishop, laying [his] hand on them," invoked God to send grace on them (21.21 — Latin; the eastern versions add in addition that they be made worthy to be filled with the Holy Spirit), then anointed the

---

34. Kretschmar, *Die Geschichte des Taufgottesdienstes*, p. 96, suggests that in Hippolytus there was an original five-member formula of catechetical origin which mentioned God, Christ, Holy Spirit, church, and resurrection that was then made triadic and understood in a Trinitarian way. The *Epistle of the Apostles* 5 has a five-member confession, except including the forgiveness of sins instead of the resurrection.

35. Rufinus, *Commentary on the Apostles' Creed*; Marcellus of Ancyra in Epiphanius, *Panarion* 72.3. J. N. D. Kelly, *Early Christian Creeds*, 2nd ed. (London: Longmans, 1960), pp. 30-61, 104, 113-119, 126-130.

36. Wolfram Kinzig, "'... natum et passum etc.' Zur Geschichte der Tauffragen in der lateinischen Kirche zu Luther," and Markus Vinzent, "Die Entstehung des 'Römischen Glaubensbekenntnisses,'" in Kinzig et al., *Tauffragen*, pp. 93-94, 189-196. Kinzig assembles a large collection of sources for the development of an interrogatory confession of faith — "'natum et passum,'" pp. 116-140.

37. Liuwe H. Westra, *The Apostles' Creed: Origin, History, and Some Early Commentaries* (Turnhout: Brepols, 2002), pp. 30-68. Maxwell Johnson, "The Problem of Creedal Formulae in *Traditio Apostolica* 21:12-18," *Ecclesia Orans* 22 (2005): 159-175, reviews the debate and, although allowing for an earlier form of the Roman Symbol, maintains the position of Bradshaw et al., *The Apostolic Tradition*, that the creedal statements of the Latin version of the *Apostolic Tradition* reflected the fourth-century state of the text.

38. Kretschmar, *Die Geschichte des Taufgottesdienstes*, pp. 95-96, suggests that anointing the whole body after baptism may have derived from secular bathing practice but was now theologically grounded and performed by a presbyter rather than by oneself; he identifies the unction on the forehead (below) with the imparting of the Holy Spirit. For the anointings in the baptismal ceremony, Ch. Munier, "Initiation chrétienne et rites d'onction (IIe-IIIe s.)," and "Rites d'onction, baptême et baptême de Jésus," *Revue des sciences religieuses* 64 (1990): 115-125, 217-234.

39. That nothing is said of a special garment, not even in the later witnesses to the text of the *Apostolic Tradition*, argues against the hypothesis of Farrell, "The Garment of Immortality," pp. 265-275, that the custom of clothing the newly baptized with a white linen garment was introduced toward the middle of the second century.

head (21.22), signed the forehead,[40] and offered a kiss to each one (21.23-24). Two postbaptismal anointings are without parallel in the early sources, and their presence raises suspicion of two practices being blended, one of which exalted the role of the bishop in the baptismal rite, perhaps by completing the baptismal rite performed by presbyters associated with the house churches of Rome.

In the church the newly baptized now joined the faithful in prayer and the exchange of the kiss of peace (21.25-26). The description of the baptismal eucharist (21.27-37) includes the bringing of the elements by the deacons to the bishop for him to give thanks over them (21.27) and the breaking and distribution of the bread, received with an "Amen" (21.31). It also contains some unusual features: There was a cup of water (as a sign of washing — 21.29, 33) and a cup of milk and honey (fulfilling the promise of "the land of milk and honey" and representing nourishment of children — 21.28, 33) in addition to the usual cup of wine (mixed with water) for the blood of Christ (21.27, 33). The bishop was to give an explanation of these things (21.30), but only to the baptized (21.39-40). "When these things have been done, let each one hasten to do good work" (21.38).

Not much is said in regard to the theology of baptism. The bishop's prayer at the postbaptismal imposition of hands (21.21) speaks of the baptized having received "forgiveness of sins through the laver of regeneration of the Holy Spirit" (Latin). This statement puts the activity of the Holy Spirit in the baptism, whatever postbaptismal gift may be assumed. The grace for which this prayer asks was to enable the person to "serve according to your will." The directions about the water and instructions about women removing anything that would prevent the water from touching the whole body imply the notion of purification. The Trinitarian connections of baptism are perhaps to be seen in the correlation of three renunciations, three immersions, and three cups.[41]

On the Holy Theophany

Although the conservative listing by B. R. Suchla in the *Dictionary of Early Christian Literature* places *On the Holy Theophany* among the "Uncertain Works,"[42] I doubt that it belongs in the third century. From the fourth century we have several sermons preached at the feast of the baptism of Jesus (his "theophany" or "epiphany") and exhortations to enroll to receive baptism preached near that time; and the content of this work relates it to these categories of sermons, for it is a sermon on the baptism of Christ concluded with an invitation to baptism.[43]

40. Cf. *On the Antichrist* 6 for Christ giving a seal to his people.
41. Kretschmar, *Die Geschichte des Taufgottesdienstes*, p. 114.
42. Siegmar Döpp and Wilhelm Geerlings, eds., *Dictionary of Early Christian Literature* (New York: Crossroad, 2000), p. 287.
43. S. J. Voicu, "Pseudoippolito in Sancta Theophania e Leonzio di Constantinopoli," *Studia Ephemeridis Augustinianum* 30 (1989): 137-146, assigns the sermon to Leontius of Constantinople, but

Chapter one is a praise of water:[44] "For with water all things are washed and nourished, and cleansed and bedewed."[45]

Chapter two takes up the baptism of Christ as a further proof of the dignity of water. The author, who delights in rhetorical paradoxes, declares the marvel that Jesus, identified with the "River of God" in Psalm 46:4, was "dipped in a little water." Another indication of Jesus' immersion is the statement that he was "covered" with the waters. The sermon appeals to Psalms 77:16 and 114:5 for the waters of the Jordan retreating in fear at the presence of the Lord, a motif represented in Christian art depicting the baptism.[46] Chapter three continues the paradoxes in describing the testimony of John the Baptist.

In chapter four the author presents the devil as confounded by Jesus coming to baptism in humility without royal retinue.[47] A further note about the manner of baptism occurs in the phrase "he bent his head to be baptized by John." The author elaborates the protest by John against baptizing Jesus. In chapter five Jesus responds, "Baptize me, John, in order that no one may despise baptism." Hence, no one should scorn to be baptized "by the hand of a poor priest."

Chapter six takes up the blessings that come from Jesus' baptism. In this regard notice is especially given to the opening of the heavens. According to chapter seven, the baptism was the time at which the Son of God was revealed.[48] The author's observation that in appearance the baptizer is superior to the baptized is probably the reason that in art the baptizer is larger than the baptizand.

Chapter eight contains a high doctrine of baptism. It is the fountain of life. The Father sent his Son into the world for him to wash humanity with "water and the Spirit." By this means he begets "us again to incorruption of soul and body" so that a person becomes "immortal" (which is equal to being "God"). "If one is made God by water and the Holy Spirit after the regeneration of the pool [κολυμβήθρας], he is found to be also joint-heir with Christ after the resurrection from the dead." Therefore, the author invites, "Come . . . to the immortality of the baptism." The baptized is "begotten again and endued with life." Throughout the passage there is the association of water and Spirit. Chapter nine then elaborates on the work of the Spirit from creation to his coming as the Comforter.

Chapter ten interprets Isaiah 1:16-19 as a foretelling of the cleansing by holy baptism. The author then concludes the sermon with the invitation to baptism, "Be begotten again [ἀναγεννήθητι] into adoption," and the call to cease from sin. Something of baptismal theology and some details of the baptismal ceremony are alluded to:

---

even if it is sixth century (and so beyond the boundaries of this study), it contains earlier motifs so as to justify a full treatment.

44. For this compare from the third century Tertullian, *On Baptism* 3-5.

45. Quotations are from the translation by S. D. F. Salmond in Alexander Roberts and James Donaldson, eds., *Ante-Nicene Fathers* (repr. Peabody: Hendrickson, 1994), Vol. 5, pp. 234-237.

46. See chap. 7.

47. Cf. the sermon of Ps.-Eusebius of Alexandria, *On Baptism*, discussed in chap. 7.

48. See chap. 7 for other statements of this theme.

> The one who with faith goes down to the bath [λουτρόν] of regeneration [ἀναγεννήσεως], separates from the Evil One and associates himself with Christ, renounces the Enemy and confesses that Christ is God, puts off the bondage and puts on the adoption, comes up from baptism bright as the sun . . . , a son of God and joint-heir with Christ. (10)

The author refers to a verbal renunciation of Satan *(apotaxis)*, the association with Christ *(syntaxis)*, and the baptismal confession of faith. The candidate goes down into the bath and comes up from it. The more common word ἀναγέννησις is substituted for παλιγγενεσία in the allusion to Titus 3:5. Baptism changes the condition of one from bondage to adopted sonship. The imagery of shining like the sun perhaps alludes to the language of enlightenment for baptism.

21. Carthage: Tertullian

Tertullian wrote the first surviving treatise on baptism,[1] and that will provide the main source for our treatment, supplemented by his other fairly frequent comments. Tertullian's *On Baptism* may have originated in instruction given to those preparing for baptism or recently baptized,[2] but since it contains an antiheretical thrust[3] and other material dealing more broadly with baptism, its present form may be seen as a general treatment of the subject.

Antecedents to Christian Baptism

Tertullian noted antecedents to baptism in the use of water in religious ceremonies by pagans (*Baptism* 5.1-3).[4] He describes these pagan rituals in Christian terms, asserting they were demonic imitations. Their waters are "barren," in contrast to the waters where God's angel imparts power to them (5.1, 4-7).

Tertullian, furthermore, contrasted Christian with Jewish practice. "Jewish Israel washes [*lavat*] every day, because every day it is defiled. That this might not become the practice among us is the reason why the rule was laid down about a single washing [*lavacro*]."[5] Tertullian is once more reading someone else's practice in Christian terms, for he has in mind moral sin and not ritual purification.

---

1. Ernest Evans, ed. and trans., *Tertullian's Homily on Baptism* (London: SPCK, 1965). See his introduction, pp. xii-xxxiii, for the contents of the treatise, the baptismal service known to Tertullian, and Tertullian's doctrine of baptism. See also Jean Razette, "La condition du chrétien d'après le *De Baptismo* de Tertullien," *Antonianum* 49 (1974): 14-46. I use Evans's translation with occasional modifications.

2. *Baptism* 1.1 indicates that Tertullian has in view both "those at present under instruction" and those who have simply believed but "have not examined the reasons for what has been conferred upon them"; but 20.5 addresses those whom "the grace of God is waiting."

3. It begins by referring to a woman of the Cainites who denied baptism — see chap. 17.

4. Discussed in chapter 2.

5. *Baptism* 15.3; he had earlier (15.1) appealed to the Lord's Gospel (probably a reference to John 13:10, cited in 12.3) and the apostle's letter (Eph. 4:5) for Christians having a single baptism.

Biblical events provided Tertullian with the proper antecedents to Christian baptism. He appealed to the following: creation (Gen. 1:1-2) — there was the junction of Spirit and water, and the first life came from the waters (*Baptism* 3); the flood in the days of Noah (Gen. 6–8) — the waters cleansed the earth, and the dove symbolized the Holy Spirit (*Baptism* 8); Israel's crossing the Red Sea at the exodus from Egypt (Exod. 14:26-31) — the escape from bondage and the destruction of the enemy in the water (*Baptism* 9.1; cf. 20.4); Moses throwing a tree into the bitter waters to sweeten them (Exod. 15:22-26) — Christ converting the springs of nature into healthful water (*Baptism* 9.2; cf. *Answer to the Jews* 13); the water that flowed from the rock to quench Israel's thirst (Exod. 17:6; Num. 20:7-11; 1 Cor. 10:4) — Christ gives baptism (*Baptism* 9.3).[6] Elsewhere Tertullian contrasts Naaman's sevenfold washing (2 Kings 5:10) with the single washing by Christ (*Against Marcion* 4.9). From the New Testament Tertullian spent much time on John 5:2-9, where he provides an early attestation for the insertion of verse 4 about an angel coming down to stir the water in the pool and effecting a cure of the first person to enter the pool (*Baptism* 5.5-6; 6.1).

The baptism of John the Baptist occasioned the question whether it was from heaven or the earth (Matt. 21:25). Tertullian replied that it was divine in commission but not in its own power (*Baptism* 10.2); it was earthly because repentance is a human act (10.3).[7] To be truly heavenly it would have had to forgive sins and impart the Holy Spirit, gifts granted by God alone (10.3). John's baptism "for forgiveness of sins," therefore, was only a promise for the future forgiveness that Christ would give (10.5-7). Although correct according to the biblical text in regard to the gift of the Holy Spirit, the point about forgiveness of sins is gratuitously depreciating of John's baptism. Tertullian understood the Baptist's words about the coming One's baptizing "in the Spirit and in fire" (Matt. 3:11) to mean, "A true and steadfast faith is baptized [*tinguitur*] with the Spirit[8] unto salvation, but a feigned and feeble faith is baptized [*tinguitur*] with fire unto judgment" (10.7).

Tertullian defends baptism by appealing to the example of Christ. The Spirit came down on Christ in the form of a dove, showing the affinity of the Spirit with water (*Baptism* 8.3). "Baptism is made blessed in Christ by water" (9.3).[9] In response to the objection that Jesus himself did not baptize (John 4:2), so baptism must not be necessary, Tertullian responded that what one's agents do that person does (11.1-3).

Tertullian also dealt with the problem that the record says nothing about the apostles receiving baptism. The requirement that baptism was necessary for salvation (he quotes John 3:5) combined with the unbaptized condition of the apostles meant either that the salvation of the apostles (except for Paul) was in doubt or the

---

6. Razette, "La condition du chrétien," p. 29, considers the creation and exodus to be the major types, for baptism is the sacrament of life and of liberation (p. 32).

7. See *On Repentance* 2 for John's "baptism of repentance" preparing the way.

8. Evans, *Tertullian's Homily on Baptism*, pp. 24-25, proposes this reading to fit the context, but the manuscripts read "water."

9. Cf. *Answer to the Jews* 8.14 in chap. 7 with further references and discussion.

rule was invalid (*Baptism* 12.1-2). Tertullian considers several possibilities. One consideration is that they had received John's baptism, implied in John 13:10 (12.3-5). Other persons suggested that the apostles received a substitute baptism *(baptismi vicem)* when in the boat they were engulfed *(mergerentur)* in the waves (Matt. 8:24) and that Peter was sufficiently dipped *(mersum)* when he walked on the sea (Matt. 14:29-30) — *Baptism* 12.6. Tertullian scoffed at the explanation: "It is one thing, I imagine, to be aspersed *(aspergi)*, or to be cut off by the violence of the sea, and quite another to be baptized *(tingui)* by the rule of religion" (12.6).[10] Ultimately, Tertullian dismisses the question of whether or when the apostles were baptized. Their calling by the Lord superseded the necessity of baptism, and the Lord could pronounce one forgiven without baptism (Matt. 9:2, 22) — 12.8-9. Their circumstances do not apply to us, for whom the necessity of baptism holds (see further below).[11]

Faith and Repentance

Baptism presupposed faith and repentance. The discussion of John's baptism (a baptism of repentance) includes the statement, "Repentance comes first, and remission follows" (*Baptism* 10.6), and the words quoted above that baptism with the Spirit accompanies a true faith (10.7). Sins are cancelled "in response to faith signed and sealed [*obsignata*] in the Father and the Son and the Holy Spirit" (6.1). Elsewhere Tertullian says of the church at Rome that "She seals her faith with water."[12] Or, again, "Sins were remitted, which, through faith in the name of Christ, are washed away for all who believe on him."[13] Tertullian devoted another treatise to the subject of repentance, in which he first discussed the repentance that must precede baptism (*On Repentance* 4–6) before turning to repentance for postbaptismal sin (7–12). He affirmed that repentance required that a person cease sinning:

> Baptismal washing [*lavacrum*] is a sealing [*obsignatio*] of faith, which faith is begun and commended by the faith of repentance. We are not washed in order that we may cease sinning, but because we have ceased, since in heart we have been bathed [*loti*] already. . . .

---

10. The proponent(s) of this interpretation used the word *mergo* — to plunge, immerse, overwhelm — perhaps to make what happened to the apostles as much like Christian baptism as possible; but Tertullian describes the event as a sprinkling. They were closer to the Gospel text than Tertullian, for it says the boat was "hidden" (καλύπτεσθαι — Matt. 8:24) by the waves. It is not clear whether Tertullian is contrasting the "sprinkling" of the apostles in the boat (and Peter's beginning to drown) and the "immersing" in the church or the nonreligious experience of the apostles with the total ceremony of the church.

11. For other explanations of the problem that there was no record of the baptism of the twelve apostles see chap. 19, n. 72.

12. *Prescription against Heretics* 36.

13. *Answer to the Jews* 8.

And so it is becoming that learners desire baptism [*intinctionem*], but do not hastily receive it.[14]

The association of repentance with baptism and salvation is clear in the language of "second repentance" for postbaptismal sin.[15]

Although faith was essential, faith alone did not suffice for salvation. Tertullian dealt with the argument of some "most villainous" persons (perhaps the Cainites of his chap. 1) that since Abraham pleased God "with no sacrament of water," faith alone was sufficient (*Baptism* 13.1). He replies that before the Lord's passion and resurrection this might have been true, but now "the sacrament has been expanded and the seal of baptism added, in some sense a clothing for the faith which was previously unattired" (13.2).[16] Faith is not able to save apart from its own law, and by that law (Matt. 28:19 and John 3:5 are quoted) "faith was put under obligation to the necessity of baptism [*baptismi*]" (13.3). After the commands given by the Lord, all believers were baptized (*tinguebantur*). As an example, "When Paul had believed he was then baptized [*tinctus*]" (Acts 9:6 is quoted; cf. 9:18 — *Baptism* 13.4).[17]

The requirement of faith and repentance meant that preaching preceded baptism. In answering the argument that Paul's statement, "Christ sent me not to bap-

---

14. Tertullian, *On Repentance* 6.16-17, 20. The chapter says that baptism without right preparation is built on sand. Holger Hammerich, "Taufe und Askese: Der Taufaufschub in vorkonstantinischer Zeit" (Diss., University of Hamburg, 1994), pp. 102-107, studies the passage and notes the inseparable relation of repentance and baptism for Tertullian (p. 105). Cf. *On Modesty* 10, "Even if pardon is the 'fruit of repentance,' even pardon cannot co-exist without the cessation from sin." Preliminary to this ceasing from sin is that repentance (*poenitentia*) is a confession of fault — *On the Flesh of Christ* 8. For Tertullian's concept of repentance see Aloys H. Dirksen, *The New Testament Concept of Metanoia* (Washington, DC: Catholic University of America, 1932), pp. 52-57.

15. *Repentance* 7; Tertullian also speaks of "two planks [baptism and *exomologesis* = confession of sin] of human salvation" — *Repentance* 12.

16. Luis Abramowski, "Tertullian: Ampliat(i)o, fides integra, metus integer," *Vigiliae Christianae* 31 (1977): 191-195, clarifies the grammar of the passage and concludes that *sacramentum* here is a synonym for the "increased" or enlarged "faith" and, as often in Tertullian, has for its content *doctrina, traditio, fides (regula fidei)*. This "increased faith" is contrasted with the bare (*nuda*) faith that was sufficient for Abraham. I note that faith seems to stand for baptism in *Prescription against Heretics* 23, "Men who had put on faith from the apostles' hands," i.e., men who had received baptism from the hands of the apostles (an indication of their administration of baptism).

17. Tertullian's words later, "Faith unimpaired has no doubt of its salvation" (*Baptism* 18.6), in the context of a warning against too hasty reception of baptism, do not mean that faith will save without baptism but rather refer to a faith that is secure from an easy susceptibility to temptation. Only this kind of faith is certain of salvation; baptism is too weighty a matter to be rushed into, and a person who accepts it too quickly may not persevere. Evans, *Tertullian's Homily on Baptism*, p. 106, takes the words to mean that a person whose faith is complete can be sure that God will not let him die unbaptized. That explanation might fit Tertullian's advice to delay baptism but seems too simplistic for Tertullian's profound regard for faith and the gravity of the baptismal commitment. A better account of the context of this statement and more nearly approximating my interpretation is given by Abramowski, "Tertullian: Sacramento ampliat(i)o," p. 195 — Tertullian is not giving a consolation but a warning, and he speaks of faith after baptism (not before or without baptism), that is, an endurance in faith after baptism.

tize" (1 Cor. 1:17), did away with the need for baptism, Tertullian explained, "Preaching comes first, baptizing [*tinguere*] later, when preaching has preceded" (*Baptism* 14.2). Hence, *On Baptism* begins by addressing those under instruction (1.1). A major consideration in Tertullian's opposition to baptizing children (chap. 23) was that they should come, "when they are learning, when they are being taught what they are coming to: let them be made Christians when they have become competent to know Christ" (*Baptism* 18.5). In this context of the necessity of teaching is to be placed Tertullian's declaration, "Christians are made, not born."[18]

Ceremony of Baptism

Although Tertullian does not give a systematic description of the ceremony of Christian initiation, what he refers to closely corresponds to the ceremony outlined in the *Apostolic Tradition*, indicating that the activities described there were rather widespread in the Christian world.

The preliminary preparations for "those who are at the point of entering upon baptism [*baptismum*]" included "prayers, fastings,[19] bending of the knee, and all night vigils, along with the confession of all their former sins" (*Baptism* 20.1). Tertullian mentions sponsors in connection with children brought to baptism (18.4), and sponsors may have vouched for others as well.

Tertullian began his list of customs practiced in the church for which there was no mention in scripture that "When we are going to enter the water, but a little earlier, in the presence of the church under the hand of the bishop, we solemnly affirm that we renounce the devil and his pomp and his angels" (*On the Crown* 3). (Note that the laying on of a hand occurs here at the renunciation.) Another passage puts the renunciation in closer connection with entering the water: "When entering the water, . . . we bear testimony with our mouth that we have renounced the devil, his pomp, and his angels" (*On the Shows* 4).[20]

The fact that Christ's baptism sanctified water did not make unnecessary a prayer for God to send his Spirit upon the water. Tertullian said, "The nature of the waters, having received holiness from the Holy One, itself conceived power to make holy."[21]

---

18. *Apology* 18.4; similarly, "One becomes a Christian, is not born one" — *Testimony of the Soul* 1.

19. For fasting in connection with baptism see *On Fasting* 8.

20. Evans, *Tertullian's Homily on Baptism*, p. xxiii, translates *On the Crown* 3 in such a way as to suggest the renunciation was made twice, once in the church and again on entering the water. The same wording for the renunciation occurs in *On the Soul* 35.3. See for the renunciation Henry Ansgar Kelly, *The Devil at Baptism: Ritual, Theology, and Drama* (Ithaca: Cornell University Press, 1985), pp. 94-105, and Hans Kirsten, *Die Taufabsage: Eine Untersuchung zu Gestalt und Geschichte der Taufe nach den altkirchlichen Taufliturgien* (Berlin: Evangelische Verlagsanstalt, 1960); for the devil's pomp, J. H. Waszink, "Pompa Diaboli," *Vigiliae Christianae* 1 (1947): 13-41.

21. *Baptism* 4.1, which may allude to Jesus' baptism, but in context would seem to refer to the Holy Spirit.

Consequently, it makes no difference "whether one is washed [*diluatur*] in the sea or in a pond, a river or a fountain, a lake [reservoir] or a tub."[22]

> All waters, when God is invoked, acquire the sacred significance of conveying sanctity: for at once the Spirit comes down from heaven and stays upon the waters, sanctifying them from within himself, and when thus sanctified they absorb the power of sanctifying. (*Baptism* 4.4)

Tertullian is perhaps justifying the use of water other than what comes from a moving source ("living water") such as the *Didache* had required.

Tertullian's frequent use of *tingo* (to dip, to dye) and occasionally *mergo* (to immerse, to plunge) as interchangeable with the transliterated *baptizo* implies an immersion (see on the baptism of the apostles above).[23] So too do his words, "After we come up from the washing [*lavacro*]" (*Baptism* 7.1).[24] Tertullian's favorite word for baptism was *lavacrum* ("bath"), and he understood the word as referring to the whole body and so refers to baptism as a washing of the whole body in Christ (*On Prayer* 13).

Indeed, there was a triple immersion. Tertullian provides perhaps the earliest certain reference to this custom (but cf. discussion of *Didache* 6 in chap. 12): "We are immersed [*mergitamur*] three times, making a somewhat ampler pledge than the Lord has appointed in the Gospel" (*On the Crown* 3). An alternative translation would be, "We are thrice immersed, while we answer interrogations rather more extensive than our Lord has prescribed in the gospel."[25] What is "ampler" or "more extensive" — the three immersions instead of one or the threefold confession of faith accompanying baptism? I favor the former interpretation, but the two are interrelated. Tertullian mentions this custom among other traditional practices that had no express scriptural warrant. If we may accept Tertullian's evidence that the practice was already traditional in his time but lacked express apostolic authorization, we may inquire of reasons for its origin. Those who look to the influence of classical bathing

---

22. *Baptism* 4.3. Evans translates "cistern" instead of "lake," and *lacus* can have this meaning, but I rather think Tertullian is contrasting in each pair a larger with a smaller body of water and perhaps a moving body of water with still water, so I prefer the original meaning of "lake." Walter J. Conway, *The Time and Place of Baptism: A Historical Synopsis and a Commentary*, The Catholic University of America Canon Law Series 324 (Washington: Catholic University of America Press, 1954), pp. 32-43, cites statements from church fathers, popes, and councils on "The Place of Baptism from the Apostolic Age to the Council of Trent."

23. *On Repentance* 6, "For who will grant you, a person of so faithless repentance, one single sprinkling [*asperginem*] of any water whatever?" does not refer to usual practice, but means "If you do not genuinely repent, no one will give you even a sprinkling, much less an immersion."

24. See *Against Marcion* 1.28.3, quoted below on the doctrine of baptism.

25. Evans, *Tertullian's Homily on Baptism*, p. xxiii. Paul F. Bradshaw, "The Profession of Faith in Early Christian Baptism," *Evangelical Quarterly* 78 (2006): 101-115, also takes Tertullian's "fuller" to refer to expansions in the formulae and not to triple immersion (pp. 110-111). On the other hand, it may be noted that Jerome apparently read Tertullian as referring to the triple immersion — chap. 43 at n. 23.

customs on Christian baptism might suggest that it derives from the practice of three plunges at the baths (warm, hot, and cold). Another possible factor is that in the ancient world to say or do something three times indicated that one really meant it, one was really serious. More likely influences on adoption of the practice are an effort to contrast Christian baptism with Jewish proselyte baptism, or the Trinitarian controversies of the second century, or the triune formula in Matthew 28:19, "baptizing them in the name of the Father, of the Son, and of the Holy Spirit." If the Trinitarian formula was not the occasion for trine immersion, there was certainly a close association between the practice of triple immersion and the Trinitarian confession. For Tertullian says at another place: "Christ commanded that his disciples immerse [*tinguerent*] into the Father, Son, and Holy Spirit [Matt. 28:19], not into one; and indeed it is not once only, but three times, that we are immersed [*tinguimur*] into each individual person at each individual name" (*Against Praxeas* 26).

Some profession of faith was involved in the baptism. The passage in *On the Shows* 4, partially quoted above on the renunciation of the devil, associates "our seal [*signaculum*]" with baptism: "When we enter the water and profess the Christian faith in the words of its law."[26] This profession may have been a positive confession of faith by the candidate, but more likely it took the form of answering questions (as in the interrogatory confession of faith of the *Apostolic Tradition* and according to a possible translation of *On the Crown* 3 above).[27]

In addition, there may have been some formulaic words spoken by the administrator of baptism. A person "is sent down into the water, is washed [*tinctus*] to the accompaniment of very few words and comes up [outwardly] little or no cleaner than he was" (*Baptism* 2.1).

Whatever form these words spoken at the baptism took — whether spoken by the administrator, the candidate, or both — they expressed, as the statements above indicate, a Trinitarian statement: "Father, Son, and Holy Spirit" (*Baptism* 6.1). The passage later says that with mention of the Three a "profession of faith and promise of salvation are in pledge." To them there is necessarily added mention of the church, "because where there are the three, the Father and the Son and the Holy Spirit, there is the church, which is a body of three [Matt. 18:20]" (6.2). This statement is perhaps a confirmation that Tertullian knew a reference to the church included with the Holy Spirit in the baptismal confession, as we find it in the *Apostolic Tradition* 21.17. Tertullian, furthermore, quoted Matthew 28:19, "baptizing them in the Name of the Father and the Son and the Holy Spirit," as both imposing the law of baptism and

---

26. Cf. *On the Shows* 24, we renounce the pomp of the devil "when we receive the seal [*signaculo*] of faith."

27. In favor of an interrogatory rather than a declaratory confession in Carthage is Tertullian's allusion to 1 Pet. 3:21 — he argues that unless there is a bodily resurrection no pledge is secured by a bodily baptism *(baptismate)*, "for it is not the soul that is sanctified by the baptismal bath [*lavatione*]; its sanctification comes from the 'answer' [*responsione*]" (*On the Resurrection of the Flesh* 48.11). So also the statement that one receives the "ring" (previously interpreted as the seal of baptism) after being interrogated and thereby publicly seals the agreement of faith (*On Modesty* 9).

prescribing its form (13.3). Since the words spoken were a seal of faith, whether verbalized by both the candidate and the administrator or by only one, the baptism was administered in the context of a Trinitarian faith.

There was a person who administered the baptism; it was not a self-baptism. Tertullian assigns that role primarily to the bishop, whom he designates the "chief priest" (*Baptism* 17.1).[28] After him, the privilege of baptizing belongs to presbyters and deacons on the authority of the bishop. This limitation was to preserve the honor of the church and especially to prevent schisms (17.2). In cases of emergency any layman has the right to baptize (17.2-3). However, Tertullian would not countenance a woman baptizing. He evidently viewed presiding at baptism as a leadership role equivalent to teaching, which he quotes Paul in 1 Corinthians 14:35 as denying to a woman. Against those who appealed to the example of Thecla in the *Acts of Paul* (chap. 13) for a woman's right to teach and baptize (hers was a self-baptism), Tertullian rejected the work's authority and said the presbyter who composed it was removed from office (17.4-5).[29]

Tertullian and the *Apostolic Tradition* are early witnesses to actions added to the baptismal ceremony that would illustrate aspects of its meaning. Some of the motifs associated with baptism in earlier writers are for the first time confirmed as now expressed in symbolic acts.[30] Tertullian offers an express theological interpretation of some of these gestures.[31]

Tertullian's interpretation of the postbaptismal anointing and imposition of hands prepared for the development of confirmation as a separate liturgical rite and separate sacrament in the western church (in contrast to the eastern church, which kept the anointing as a part of the baptismal rite). He says that after we come up from the washing *(lavacro)*, we "are anointed with the blessed unction" (*Baptism* 7.1). Precedent for the unction *(unctione)* is found in the anointing of priests in the Old Testament (Exod. 30:30; Lev. 4:3, 5),[32] an act that also gave the Lord the title

28. Maurice Bévenot, "Tertullian's Thoughts about the Christian 'Priesthood,'" in *Corona Garatiarum: Miscellanea patristica, historica et liturgica Eligio Dekkers O.S.B. XII lustra complenti oblata* (Brugge: Sint Pietersabdij, 1975), pp. 125-137, translates, "the chief priest, if he may be so called, that is, the bishop" (p. 129), and argues that the phrase "even laymen have the right" is sarcastic, "if the bishop's authority is ignored, you'll be letting even laymen exercise the right!" (pp. 129-130).

29. Ellen Juhl Christiansen, "Women and Baptism," *Studia Theologica* 35 (1981): 1-8, argues from the practice of nude baptism that it is very likely that from the time of the New Testament women gave baptism to women. Protests from Tertullian and later from others would indicate that this was being done, but I would conclude that she goes beyond the evidence to find the practice common.

30. E.g., the association of baptism with the milk and honey that is the food of infants and that characterized the Holy Land in *Barnabas* 6.17 finds concrete expression now in the giving of milk and honey to the newly baptized in order to symbolize the new birth and entrance into the promised land.

31. Thus Evans, *Tertullian's Homily on Baptism*, p. xxix, refers to "subsidiary ceremonies [that] may have been (in their origin) illustrative tokens rather than effective signs."

32. Bernard Botte, "Deux passages de Tertullien: *De baptismo* 7,1 et 8,2," in J. Fontaine and C. Kannengiesser, eds., *Epektasis: Mélanges patristiques offerts au Cardinal Jean Daniélou* (Paris: Beauchesne, 1972), pp. 17-22 (here 17-19), emends *christus dicitur* to *christi dicti*, so that the reference is not to the high priest alone but to the priests, who were called "christs" because they were anointed.

"Christ" from his spiritual anointing with the Holy Spirit (Acts 4:27 quoted). The unction flows over the flesh but benefits the person spiritually in the same way that the fleshly act of baptism in water has a spiritual effect (7.2). That spiritual benefit is not spelled out, and it is not concluded that the anointing made the Christian people a spiritual priesthood. The meaning for Tertullian may be related to the next action.

In *On Baptism*, Tertullian separates the coming of the Spirit from baptism: "Not that the Holy Spirit is given to us in the water, but that in the water we are made clean by the action of the angel [he is commenting on John 5:4-9] and made ready for the Holy Spirit" (*Baptism* 6.1). "Next [after the unction] follows the imposition of the hand in benediction, inviting and welcoming the Holy Spirit" (*Baptism* 8.1). The Old Testament prefigurement of the imposition of hands was Jacob's blessing of Joseph's sons, Ephraim and Manasseh (Gen. 48:14 — *Baptism* 8.2). Jacob crossed his arms as he extended them, so that the younger son received the blessing of the right hand.[33] "At this point that most holy Spirit willingly comes down from the Father upon bodies cleansed and blessed, and comes to rest upon the waters of baptism as though revisiting his primal dwelling-place [an allusion to Gen. 1:2]" (8.3). Apparently the candidate was still standing in the baptismal water when the anointing and imposition of hands in benediction occurred, so the temporal difference was not great in the ceremony to which Tertullian gives this interpretation.[34]

Tertullian, in a fuller listing of events in Christian initiation also mentions making the sign of the cross:

> The flesh, indeed, is washed, in order that the soul may be cleansed; the flesh is anointed, that the soul may be consecrated; the flesh is signed (with the cross), that the soul too may be fortified; the flesh is shadowed with the imposition of hands, that the soul also may be illuminated by the Spirit; the flesh feeds on the body and blood of Christ, that the soul likewise may fatten on its God. (*On the Resurrection of the Flesh* 8)

Making a sign (presumably of a cross) is listed as a separate item but may have been part of the anointing, so that the sign of the cross was traced with the oil.

Tertullian concludes *On Baptism* with reference to those coming up from the most sacred washing of rebirth extending their hands in prayer in church and petitioning for grace and spiritual gifts (content unspecified — 20).[35] As the last quota-

---

33. Botte, "Deux passages," pp. 19-20, suggests that the text written by Tertullian was "X *deformantes*," that is, Jacob made his arms like a Greek cross, but the cross shape was read as an abbreviation and became *Xm = Christum*, that is, Jacob made the shape of Christ.

34. Tertullian elsewhere seems to associate the Spirit with baptism — *On the Soul* 1.4, "By whom has the Holy Spirit ever been attained without the sacrament [*sacramento*] of faith?" — and *On Modesty* 9.9, where the interpretation of the parable of the prodigal son identifies the robe as the Holy Spirit and the ring as the seal of baptism (cf. note 26) — but in both cases Tertullian may be thinking of the whole rite and not specifically of the water.

35. Kilian McDonnell and George T. Montague, *Initiation and Baptism in the Holy Spirit: Evidence*

tion above indicates, the eucharist followed the acts accompanying the baptism. That first communion of the new initiate included milk and honey. Tertullian's list of activities that had no express scriptural support but were traditional by his time says that after baptism the new converts are accepted and partake of a mixture of milk and honey (*On the Crown* 3).

As quoted in chapter 17, Tertullian says that initiation in Marcionite churches involved the use of water, oil, milk and honey, and bread (*Against Marcion* 1.14.3). If this statement applies to Marcion's own time, there would be presumptive evidence of the use of anointing with oil and taking milk and honey in the baptismal eucharist in catholic churches earlier in the second century than they are otherwise attested, but Tertullian (if not ascribing to Marcionites the usages of his own churches in the same way that he interpreted pagan usage of water in Christian terms) probably is referring to later Marcionites contemporary with himself. One may compare the sequence Tertullian sets forth: the church drinks in her faith from the scriptures, seals *(signat)* it with the water, clothes with the Holy Spirit, feeds with the eucharist, and exhorts to martyrdom (*Prescription against Heretics* 36.5).[36]

The most solemn time for baptism was the Pasch, for we are baptized into the Lord's passion (*Baptism* 19.1). Next in appropriateness was Pentecost, for it was during this period that the resurrected Lord appeared to the disciples, ascended to heaven, and gave the grace of the Holy Spirit (19.2). Nevertheless, "every day is a Lord's day: any hour, any season, is suitable." There may be "a difference of solemnity" but there is "no difference in the grace" (19.3).[37]

Tertullian's reference to the baptism of infants and others considered unfit for baptism will be discussed in chapter 23.

---

from the First Eight Centuries (Collegeville: Liturgical, 1991), pp. 100-104, understand the *charismatum* of this text gratuitously as observable experiential phenomena (p. 104).

36. Cf. *Prescription against Heretics* 40 for the devilish imitations of Christian rites in Mithraism: the devil immerses *(tingit)*, puts away sins in a laver *(lavacro)*, signs *(signat)* the forehead, and celebrates an oblation of bread.

37. Conway, *The Time and Place of Baptism*, pp. 2-31, cites quotations (beginning with Tertullian) from church fathers, popes, and councils on "The Time of Baptism from the Apostolic Age to the Council of Trent"; he notes the particular insistence of Rome on the Pasch and Pentecost as the only appropriate times except in cases of emergency, but the prevalence of infant baptism meant that the custom had largely ceased by the eleventh century (pp. 8-13). Paul F. Bradshaw, "'Diem baptismo sollemniorem': Initiation and Easter in Christian Antiquity," in E. Carr et al., eds., *ΕΥΛΟΓΗΜΑ: Studies in Honor of Robert Taft, S.J.* (Rome, 1993), 41-51; repr. in Maxwell E. Johnson, ed., *Living Water, Sealing Spirit: Readings on Christian Initiation* (Collegeville: Liturgical Press, 1995), 137-147, points out that apart from Rome and North Africa there is no trace of Paschal baptism before the fourth century and contends that even then, whatever the theory, it was never the normative *practice* in Christian antiquity. Maxwell E. Johnson, "Tertullian's 'Diem baptismo sollemniorem' Revisited: A Tentative Hypothesis on Baptism at Pentecost," in M. E. Johnson and L. E. Phillips, eds., *Studia Liturgica Diversa: Essays in Honor of Paul F. Bradshaw* (Portland: The Pastoral Press, 2004), pp. 31-44, suggests that in keeping with the precedent of Acts 2 Pentecost may have had priority as the time of baptism before the Pasch pushed it into a secondary position.

Doctrine of Baptism

The reference to the Pasch and Pentecost points to the connection of baptism with the death and resurrection of Christ. Christian baptism was not commanded earlier, because its benefits derive from Christ's death and resurrection. "The efficacy of the washing [*lavacri*]" was "ensured by his passion and resurrection: for neither could our death be annulled except by our Lord's passion, nor our life restored apart from his resurrection" (*Baptism* 11.4). With reference to Exodus 15:25, Tertullian says that human beings, who were perishing with thirst, "are revived by drinking the baptismal water of the tree of the suffering of Christ through the faith that is in him" and with reference to 2 Kings 6:4-7 that the world is freed from error "in baptism by the 'wood' of Christ, that is, by his suffering" (*Answer to the Jews* 13.12 and 19). This relationship to the death and resurrection of Christ accounts for Tertullian's statements about the doctrinal meaning of baptism.

Tertullian summarizes the doctrine of baptism in listing the items that he found inexplicable if one accepted Marcion's teachings: remission of sins, deliverance from death, regeneration *(regeneratio)*, and bestowal of the Holy Spirit (*Against Marcion* 1.28.2-3).[38]

> [Marcion] seals a person who according to him was never unsealed, washes [*lavat*] a person who according to him was never defiled, and into this sacrament of salvation he plunges [*mergit*] the flesh that has no share in salvation. (*Against Marcion* 1.28.3)

In discussing why Jesus did not baptize (*Baptism* 11.3-4), Tertullian indicates some of the components of baptism: repentance, forgiveness of sins, relationship with himself (Christ), the Holy Spirit, the church, and his passion and resurrection. Again, without a listing, *On the Soul* 39–41 refers to liberation from the power of the devil, regeneration, illumination, and the marriage of the soul to the Holy Spirit.

Tertullian most often expresses the significance of baptism in terms of forgiveness or cleansing from sins. Thus *On Baptism* begins by reference to the first two benefits listed in *Against Marcion:* "The sacrament of our water by which the sins of our former blindness are washed away [*ablutis*] and we are set at liberty unto life eternal" (1.1). Water embued with the Holy Spirit has the power to make holy or sanctify (4.1, 4), to save (4.3), and to cleanse spiritually (4.5 — a person's "spirit is in the waters corporally washed, and the flesh is spiritually cleansed"). Its particular characteristic is cleansing (5.2), so the devil inspired pagan rites, pretending to "wash away the sins he himself inspires" (5.3). God uses water every day to "save nations, destroying death by the washing away of sins" (5.6); the two ideas are connected, be-

---

38. This section of my treatment develops Evans, *Tertullian's Homily on Baptism*, pp. xxix-xxxiii. Cf. *On Baptism* 10.3, which states that only God forgives sins and grants the Holy Spirit. Razette, "La condition du chrétien," p. 23, finds the vocabulary and themes of *On Baptism* oriented to four centers of reflection: new birth, eternal life, divine image and likeness, and Holy Spirit.

cause "as the guilt is removed the penalty also is taken away" (5.6), for by baptism "death is washed away" (2.2). The canceling of sins in the water granted as a response to faith prepares for the coming of the Holy Spirit (6.1). In baptism, "we are immersed [*mergimur*] in water," but the fleshly act has "a spiritual effect, that we are set free from sins" (7.2). The flood (Gen. 6–8) was a kind of baptism *(baptismum)* by which "the ancient iniquity was cleansed away"; in the same way our flesh comes up from the washing *(lavacro)* that removes our old sins (8.4). "We enter into the bath *(lavacrum)* once only, once only are our sins washed away *(abluuntur)*"; "Happy is that water that cleanses *(abluit)* once for all" (15.3).

This association of baptism with forgiveness that is so prominent in *On Baptism* is present elsewhere in Tertullian. It is the premise of the argument in *On Repentance* (e.g., 6–7). The same is true for *On Modesty*. As instances, note: Tertullian understands the washing in 1 Corinthians 6:9-10 as referring to canceling sins committed before baptism (*lavacrum* — *Modesty* 16.5); sins before baptism *(baptisma)* "once for all washed [*diluendi*] through the grace of Christ, who once for all has suffered death for our sins" (18.15); "purged through the baptism [*baptisma*] of truth" (19.5). According to *On the Soul* 40, the soul is unclean until it receives regeneration.

As some quotations above indicate (*Baptism* 1; 5), forgiveness of sins meant also deliverance from the power of death. "By bathing *(lavacro)* death is washed away" (2.2). With reference to Peter's sermon in Acts 2 (that offered forgiveness of sins — v. 38), Tertullian explains that this was the exercise of the power of the keys of the kingdom promised to Peter in Matthew 16:19 — "Peter was the first to unbar, in Christ's baptism [*baptismo*], the entrance to the heavenly kingdom" (*Modesty* 21.12). This overcoming of death was a victory over the devil: The works of the devil were undone when the Son of God "set people free through baptism [*lavacrum*]," canceling the "handwriting of death" (cf. Col. 2:13-14) (*Modesty* 19.20). "The gentiles are set free from this present world by means of water, and leave behind, drowned in the water, their ancient tyrant the devil" (*Baptism* 9.1).

Tertullian further associated baptism with regeneration and new birth.[39] The first chapter of *On Baptism* describes Christians as "little fishes" (as Jesus Christ is the ΙΧΘΥΣ, Fish) "born [*nascimur*] in water" (1.10), and the last chapter speaks of "when you come up from that most sacred washing (*lavacro* — Titus 3:5) of the new birth *(novi natalis)*" (20.5). Christ's birth from a virgin was necessary because he "was going to consecrate a new order of birth" (*On the Flesh of Christ* 17). The removal of the guilt and penalty of sin restores a human being to the divine likeness (*Baptism* 5.7). No soul is without sin, but "when the soul embraces faith, being renewed [*reformata*] by its second birth [*navitatem*] of water and the power from above [cf. John 3:5], . . . it is also taken up by the Holy Spirit." It is now "wedded to the Spirit" (*On the Soul* 41).

As the preceding passage indicates, the new birth is associated with the Holy

---

39. Razette, "La condition du chrétien," pp. 18-20 — new birth produces a life for heaven, is a recreation, restores the likeness to God, and is the work of the Spirit.

Spirit. And the passage referred to before it continues by saying that the person receives the Spirit of God that was given when God first breathed in him (Gen. 2:7) but that was lost through sin (*Baptism* 5.7). Although Tertullian locates the coming of the Spirit at the postbaptismal imposition of hands (6; 8), he sometimes does not make this technical distinction and seems to imply the presence of the Spirit in baptism.[40] This is the impression left by the way water and Spirit are put together in *On Baptism* 3–5. The distinction in *On Baptism* 6 seems to be Tertullian's own effort to rationalize the postbaptismal ceremonies.

Not in the list in *Against Marcion* 1.28 but nonetheless an important result of baptism for Tertullian was that it gives admission to the church. Thus *On Baptism* closes with a description of those who come up from baptism spreading out their hands with their brethren in their mother's house (the church) — 20.5. The person purged from sin is admitted to the church (*Modesty* 19.5).

As part of Tertullian's emphasis on the meaning of baptism he gave much attention to the kind of life to which one was committed by baptism. That is behind his counsel against the hasty administration of baptism (*Baptism* 18.1, 6), although his recognition of the speedy baptisms in scripture would temper his words about the postponement of baptism. *On Repentance* is a strong message about living above sin after baptism. The thought is advocated with reference to Romans 6 ("walk in newness of life" — v. 4), for baptism of the flesh inaugurates its regeneration with a view to its salvation (*On the Resurrection of the Flesh* 47).

Some passages quoted above use the imagery of a "seal" in connection with baptism.[41] This language seems especially associated with the Trinitarian faith professed in baptism (in parallel to the renunciation of the devil) but may refer to the baptism itself or the whole ceremony. Tertullian interpreted the ring given by the father in the parable of the prodigal son (Luke 15:22) as the "sign of baptism" (*signaculum lavacri* — *Modesty* 9.11). Seal is not for Tertullian the sacramental sign of the bestowal of the Holy Spirit.[42] It is particularly associated by him with contractual language.[43]

Much more frequent in Tertullian is use of "sacrament" (*sacramentum*).[44] The word has a variety of meanings in Tertullian, reflecting its range of meanings in general Latin usage: a legal oath, a military oath of allegiance, a solemn engagement or

---

40. G. W. H. Lampe, *The Seal of the Spirit*, 2nd ed. (London: SPCK, 1967), pp. 157-162, for the inconsistency in Tertullian's presentation; cf. Razette, "La condition du chrétien," pp. 42-44.

41. *Baptism* 6.1; *Repentance* 6; *On Shows* 4 and 24; *Prescription against Heretics* 36.

42. Lampe, *The Seal of the Spirit*, p. 159.

43. Razette, "La condition du chrétien," pp. 36-37, with reference to *Baptism* 12.1; 17.6; 13.3; Joseph Crehan, *Early Christian Baptism and the Creed* (London: Burns, Oates & Washbourne, 1950), pp. 96-98, 100-102, on contractual language in Tertullian.

44. Comprehensively studied in D. Michaélides, *Sacramentum chez Tertullien* (Paris: Études augustiniennes, 1970); briefly, with reference to baptism as military oath by Crehan, *Early Christian Baptism and the Creed*, pp. 102-103; Evans, *Tertullian's Homily on Baptism*, pp. xxxviii-xl, who concludes that besides the general usage Tertullian means by *sacramentum* an act with a sacred meaning and also the sacred or secret significance of an act and sometimes not merely the token of grace but the effective means of conveying or receiving grace.

obligation, an initiation. But Tertullian also uses it for the essential content of the Christian faith or religion and occasionally prepares for its later techinical usage as a sign of a sacred action. Sacrament, evidently keeping the meaning of a pledge, refers sometimes to the renunciation of the devil (*Shows* 4; *Idolatry* 6). It sometimes refers to baptism (*Baptism* 1.1; *Against Marcion* 1.28.3). The "sacramental words" of *To the Martyrs* 3 in the context of military imagery is in keeping with the usage of the word "sacrament" for a military oath, here a vow, perhaps the renunciation of the devil or the confession of faith.[45]

These benefits attributed to baptism underscore its necessity. Tertullian declares that "It is prescribed that without baptism no person can obtain salvation" (*Baptism* 12.1). This standing rule derives from the Lord's pronouncement in John 3:5, "Except one be born of water he cannot have life." Shortly thereafter Tertullian quotes both Matthew 28:19 and John 3:5 (this time more fully and more accurately) in support of the necessity of baptism (13.3). With this understanding one can appreciate the vehemence of Tertullian's response to the woman from the Cainites who sought to destroy baptism (1.2-3).

In Tertullian's exposition of 1 Corinthians 15 in defense of the resurrection of the flesh he makes brief comment on verse 29, "baptism for the dead." He understands some in the Corinthian church as practicing a vicarious baptism for the benefit of the flesh of other persons in anticipation of the resurrection. Unless there were a bodily resurrection, there would be no benefit in a bodily baptism (*On the Resurrection of the Flesh* 48).

The benefits of baptism, however, do not accrue to those who receive baptism from heretics. The "one baptism" (Eph. 4:5) is that given in the church. Since heretics (he would have had Marcionites and Gnostics in mind) do not have the same God and the same Christ as the church did, they do not have the same baptism (*Baptism* 15.1-2).

An important modification to the normal necessity of water baptism applied to the times of persecution. Using Christ's comparison of his death with a baptism (Luke 12:50), Tertullian says, "We have a second washing *(lavacrum)*, it too a single one, that of blood" (*Baptism* 16.1). Appealing to 1 John 5:6 and the water and the blood that came from Jesus' side (John 19:34), he adds: "[The Lord] sent forth these two baptisms from out of the wound of his pierced side," one a washing in water and the other in blood. Blood shed in martyrdom "makes actual a washing which has not been received, and gives back again one that has been lost" by postbaptismal sin (16.1-2).[46]

---

45. Cf. the "baptismal sacraments" in *Veiling of Virgins* 2. J. Albert Harrill, "The Influence of Roman Contract Law on Early Baptismal Formulae (Tertullian, *Ad Martyras* 3)," *Studia Patristica* 35 (2001): 275-282, studies the passage in terms of the *stipulatio* in Roman law, showing that the confession of faith was decisive for the validity of baptism.

46. *Modesty* 22 also describes martyrdom as "another baptism," to which Jesus referred in Luke 12:50, and interprets the water and the blood from Jesus' side as the materials of the two baptisms. *Scorpiace* 12.10 says, "Baptism washes away filth, but martyrdom makes stains truly white."

Those catechumens caught up in persecution before receiving baptism could be assured of their salvation. Such persons may have been in mind in the following statement: The martyr, partaking of the fullness of God's grace, "settles every debt of sin by the compensation of his own blood; for all sins are forgiven by such a deed as this" (*Apology* 50.15). Similarly, the martyr, since martyrdom is "another baptism [*baptisma*]," is said "to have purged his own sins" (*Modesty* 22.4, 9-10). Tertullian in one place speaks expressly of God appointing for those who have lost their salvation after baptism a second means of comfort: "the fight of martyrdom and the baptism — thereafter free from danger — of blood" (*Scorpiace* 6). This "baptism" in which one lays down his life is described in terms of the first (water) baptism as procuring a "sure salvation," "a second new birth" (*Scorpiace* 6).

22. Carthage: Cyprian

Cyprian, bishop of Carthage (c. 248-c. 258), was a major participant in three controversies in the third century related to baptismal practices: infant baptism, baptism administered by heretics or schismatics, and clinical or sickbed baptism. His position on the first two of these controversies will receive separate treatment in the two subsequent chapters. For this section we extract statements made in these controversies and elsewhere in his writings for the practice and doctrine of baptism at Carthage in the mid–third century. Cyprian's information is consistent with that provided by Tertullian at the beginning of the century.[1]

Ceremony of Baptism

A catechumenate was in effect. Letters in the Cyprianic corpus make frequent reference to *catecumini* or *audientes* (hearers)[2] and also refer to a teacher of catechumens[3] and exorcists.[4]

Among the preliminaries to baptism there was a prayer or exorcism over the water. "If it is to be possible for water to clean away by its baptismal washing the sins of a person who is being baptized, then it is essential that the water should first be cleansed and sanctified by a bishop."[5] There was a prebaptismal renunciation of the

---

1. For the practices related to baptism see Victor Saxer, *Vie liturgique et quotidienne a Carthage vers le milieu du IIIe siècle* (Vatican: Pontificio istituto di archeologia cristiana, 1969), pp. 106-144.

2. Cyprian, *Letters* 8 (2).3.1 (from the Roman clergy to the Carthaginian clergy); 18 (12).2.2; 29 (23); 73 (72).22.1-2.

3. *Letters* 29 (23); 73 (72).3.2 *(doctor)*.

4. *Letters* 69 (75).15.2. There are general references to exorcism in *To Donatus* (*Letter* 1) 5; *To Demetrianus* 15; *Judgments of 87 Bishops* 8 (Crescens — "first exorcized" and then baptized); 37 (Vincent — a laying on of hands in exorcism).

5. Cyprian, *Letters* 70 (69).1.3, a letter from a council of thirty-two North African bishops, of

351

devil and the world. Cyprian makes frequent allusion to such but without making a formal renunciation explicit or giving an exact verbal formula, as when he says, "We renounced the world when we were baptized."[6]

The baptismal confession of faith took the form of response to a set of questions. Cyprian says that Novatian, schismatic bishop of Rome, used the same baptismal interrogation as the catholic church, acknowledging the same Father, Son, and Holy Spirit. He describes this as baptizing *(baptizare)* with the same symbol *(symbolo)* as we do.[7] The question about believing in the Holy Spirit apparently included an expansion, for the passage continues that "when they say, 'Do you believe in the forgiveness of sins and life everlasting through the holy church?' they are being fraudulent, since they have no such church."[8] In discussing the baptism of various groups he considered heretical, Cyprian speaks of confessing "the same Father with us, the same Son, the same Holy Spirit, and the same church."[9]

---

whom Cyprian signs first, so I treat the letter as representing him (as well as others). I use the translation of G. W. Clarke, *The Letters of St. Cyprian of Carthage,* Ancient Christian Writers 43, 44, 46, 47 (New York: Newman, 1984-1989) except as modified to give consistency in my presentations. A similar reference is found in *Judgments of the 87 Bishops* 18 (Sedatus). Exorcisms of the candidates for baptism may be included in *Letters* 69.15, "the devil . . . tortured by exorcists, by the human voice, and by divine power," but the reference may be more general.

6. *Letters* 13 (6).5.3. For renouncing the world cf. 11 (7).1.2; 57 (53).3.1; *Testimonies* 3.11; *Mortality* 26; *Lord's Prayer* 13; 19 (world, its riches and pomps); *Dress of Virgins* 7 (world "whose pomps and delights we renounced"); *Lapsed* 2. For renouncing the devil cf. *Lapsed* 8 ("renounced the devil and the world"); *Advantage of Patience* 12 (same phrase); *To Fortunatus* 7 (devil and the world); *Jealousy and Envy* 11 (renounced the devil). Saxer, *Vie liturgique,* p. 122, puts these together as a threefold renunciation — the devil, his pomps, and the world — but says the formula likely was not uniform. He further notes that Cyprian uses the plural, "pomps," but Tertullian the singular.

7. *Letters* 69 (75).7.1; cf. 70 (69).2.1. This is the first use of *symbolum* ("pledge") for the baptismal confession of faith, and may be the first time that a liturgical formula was used as a *locus theologicus.* So Eligius Dekkers, "'Symbolo Baptizare,'" in H. J. Auf der Maur et al., eds., *Fides Sacramenti, Sacramentum Fidei* (Assen: Van Gorcum, 1981), pp. 107-112. (For the meaning of *symbolum* as act, token, or pledge which seals the pact — Joseph Crehan, *Early Christian Baptism and the Creed* [London: Burns, Oates & Washbourne, 1950], p. 107.) Cyprian's statement is confirmed by Novatian, *Trinity* 1; 9; 29. A further indication of the use of an interrogatory confession in Cyprian's North Africa is provided by *Judgements of the 87 Bishops* 1 (Caecilius) — "sacramental interrogation" *(sacramentum interrogat); Rebaptism* 10 — "asking, and having heard from those who answered." Firmilian, writing to Cyprian, referred to the "baptismal interrogations" — Cyprian, *Letters* 75 [74].10.5-11.1.

8. *Letters* 69 (75).7.2. The same question, worded in a different order, "Do you believe in everlasting life and the forgiveness of sins through the holy church?" is cited as a baptismal interrogation in the letter of the thirty-two bishops headed by Cyprian — *Letters* 70 (69).2.1. Saxer, *Vie liturgique,* p. 125, proposes a text like this: "Do you believe in God the Father? Do you believe in the Son, Christ? Do you believe in the Holy Spirit, remission of sins, eternal life through the holy church?" To each of the three questions the candidate responded, "I believe." He concludes that the interrogatory confession left no place for a sacramental formula in the first person pronounced by the celebrant (p. 126) and excluded a declaratory Trinitarian formula by the candidate (p. 127).

9. *Letters* 73 (72).4.2. Cf. *Judgements of the 87 Bishops* 1 (Caecilius); 7 (Lucius), "the sound confession of the sacrament" with reference to Matthew 28:19.

In the same context as the preceding quotation Cyprian speaks of Marcionites being baptized "in the name of Jesus Christ."[10] His description of the faithful includes the statement, "That religious voice has named the name of Christ, in whom it has once confessed that it believed."[11] He elsewhere characterizes his baptism and that of others as being "in the name of Christ," but in proceeding to comment on Acts 2:38 he explains that "in the name of Jesus Christ" did not mean that the Father should be omitted but that the Son should be added to the Father.[12] Cyprian was responding to claims by those who said it was unnecessary to baptize those coming to the church from heretical bodies since the power of the name of Christ made the baptism effective no matter who administered it; he apparently was not referring to the "name of Christ" as constituting an alternative baptismal formula but a general description of baptism by all who claimed to be Christians.

By "baptism" Cyprian referred to the dipping in water. "Every time that water is named by itself in the Holy Scriptures, there is a prophetic allusion to baptism."[13] Cyprian identified the *lavacrum* (Eph. 5:26; Titus 3:5) — washing, or bath — with baptism.[14] He refers to "those dipped [*tincti*] beyond and outside the church."[15] We may infer a triple immersion from the triple interrogatory confession.[16]

Cyprian does not give a sequence of the initiatory actions as Tertullian does, but his postbaptismal actions apparently included an unction, imposition of hands, and signing.[17] An unction was a necessary consequence of baptism. "A person who is baptized has also to be anointed so that by receiving the chrism *(chrisma)*, or anointing *(unctio)*, he may become the anointed of God and receive within him the grace of Christ."[18] The subsequent statement indicates that "the oil with which the bap-

---

10. *Letters* 73 (72).4.1. See chap. 17 and chap. 24, where evidence is given that Marcion did not use a different baptismal formula.

11. *Lapsed* 2.

12. *Letters* 73 (72).16.1 and 17.2.

13. *Letters* 63 (62).8.1. This principle explains some of the extravagant interpretations in early Christian literature, but its context should be noted: Cyprian is responding to those who used water without wine in the eucharist, and he is robbing them of some of their proof texts. Here he cites Isa. 43:18-21; 48:21; and John 7:37-39. An example of Cyprian's appeal to water (possible allusions to Gen. 2:10; Ps. 1:3; Ezek. 47:12; Rev. 22:1-2) occurs in *Letters* 73 (72).10.3: the church is a paradise that waters fruit-bearing trees with the four Gospels and "spreads in a saving and heavenly flood the graces of baptism."

14. *Letters* 74 (73).6.1-2.

15. *Letters* 72 (71).1.1; cf. 70 (69).2.3; 73 (72).21.2. Contrary to the usage of Tertullian, Cyprian (except in reference to biblical texts) reserves *tinguo* and *tinctio* for heretical baptism — Clarke, *The Letters of St. Cyprian*, Vol. 47, p. 204, n. 15.

16. Saxer, *Vie liturgique*, p. 126. For nude baptism Pseudo-Cyprian, *De singularitate clericorum* 1.4, is cited.

17. I am not so confident as Saxer, *Vie liturgique*, pp. 129-130, that this is the sequence and that each was considered a separate act. He points out that according to Tertullian the order is unction, signation, and imposition of hands; in the *Apostolic Tradition* 21.21-23 it is imposition of hands, unction, and signation; Augustine later mentions only unction and imposition of hands (pp. 138-139).

18. *Letters* 70 (69).2.2. *Chrisma* and *unctio* are synonymous.

tized are anointed" was sanctified through a thanksgiving prayer on the altar, in the same way as the eucharistic elements.[19]

Because of the importance of imposition of hands[20] in the rebaptism controversy (chap. 24), Cyprian has more to say about it than about other postbaptismal rites. He links the power of the name of Christ in baptism with the laying on of hands for reception of the Holy Spirit.

> Now if they attribute the efficacy of baptism to the power of the Name, ... and if hands are there laid in the Name of the same Christ upon the person baptized so that he may receive the Holy Spirit . . .[21]

Cyprian here evidently follows Tertullian in attributing the gift of the Holy Spirit to the postbaptismal imposition of hands. He could also say, however, that "It is through baptism [*baptisma*] that we receive the Spirit," so it is only after being baptized and receiving the Spirit that one proceeds to drink the cup of the Lord.[22] Although he could acknowledge a distribution of the baptismal blessings among the several acts of the ceremony, he argued strenuously in the rebaptism controversy against a separation of baptism from the imparting of the Holy Spirit by the laying on of hands. He wanted to keep all the acts together as one unified ceremony.[23]

Cyprian is imprecise whether the marking with a sign was included with the anointing or with the imposition of hands, or was a separate act. He connects being sealed with the laying on of hands, but in some passages it is not clear whether this gesture was itself the sealing or the sealing was done in connection with it. He argues

---

19. The meaning of the passage and its difficult wording are discussed by Clarke, *The Letters of St. Cyprian*, vol. 47, pp. 201-203.

20. Saxer, *Vie liturgique*, pp. 133-135, discusses whether one or two hands were employed and decides in favor of one.

21. *Letters* 74 (73).5.1. For the giving of the Holy Spirit by the imposition of hands on heretics who came over to the catholic church, see 69 (75).11.3; 72 (71).1.1; 73 (72).6.2; *Judgments of the 87 Bishops* 5 (Nemesianus). I have quoted according to the emendation given by Clarke, *The Letters of St. Cyprian*, Vol. 47, p. 241, n. 17. His text in the body of the translation (p. 72) reads, "Why then, among heretics, are not hands laid, in the name of the same Christ, upon the person baptized so that he may receive the Holy Spirit?" Clarke's concern with this text in which Cyprian implies (incorrectly) that heretics do not attempt to impart the Holy Spirit is overcome if Cyprian is not attributing this position to heretics but to his opponents who wanted to accept their baptism: they apparently were recognizing the baptism of heretics but laid hands on them for reception of the Holy Spirit on their coming to the catholic church. This was the position of the author of *On Rebaptism* (chap. 24).

22. *Letters* 63 (62).8.3. From his quotation and interpretation of John 7:38 it is clear that he is thinking of the water act and not using "baptism" to stand for the ceremony as a whole. For the work of the Spirit in the water, see *Letters* 74 (73).5.4 (quoted below) on regeneration.

23. G. W. H. Lampe, *The Seal of the Spirit* (London: SPCK, 1967), pp. 170-178; Pierre Gaudette, "Baptême et vie chrétienne chez saint Cyprien de Carthage," *Laval théologique et philosophique* 27 (1971): 163-190, 251-279 (182-184). Cf. Cyprian's argument in *Letters* 74 (73).7.1-2 that one is born by baptism, not by the laying on of hands; the latter gives the Holy Spirit, but the two acts belong together, since there must be a person to receive the Spirit. His analogy is Adam, first created by God and then receiving the breath of life from God.

that, if someone can receive baptism and forgiveness of sins with a "perverted faith," then he could receive the Holy Spirit too by the same faith and "there is no need for hands to be laid upon him so that he may receive the Spirit and be sealed [*signetur*]."[24] And he continues, "By our [priestly] prayers and by the imposition of hands those who are baptized in the church obtain the Holy Spirit and are perfected with the Lord's seal."[25] With reference to Ezekiel 9:4-5 (mark on the foreheads), Cyprian does say, "For those only can escape who have been newborn and signed with the sign of Christ." He explains that "the sign pertains to the passion and blood of Christ," so the sign made was the cross.[26]

Sickbed Baptism

Cyprian defended affusion, in contrast to normal usage in the church, in cases of sickbed or clinical baptism. Others took a depreciatory view of the practice, whether in disparagement of the delay of baptism until one was on his deathbed or with reservations about a procedure other than immersion or perhaps both.

An otherwise unknown bishop by the name of Magnus had written Cyprian about the validity of baptisms administered by followers of Novatian (see further in chap. 24 on Novatian and sickbed baptism) and of baptisms by aspersion given on a sickbed. Cyprian's reply to the latter question may be given fairly extensively, for it is largely self-explanatory.

> You have asked also, what I thought concerning those who obtain God's grace in sickness and weakness, whether they are to be accounted legitimate Christians, because they are not washed [*loti*] with the water of salvation but have it poured [*perfusi*] on them. . . . [Each should judge what he thinks is right and act accordingly. My judgment is this:] The divine blessings can in no way be mutilated and weakened. . . . [Washing away the stains of sin is different from the washing of an ordinary bath.] In the sacrament of salvation, when necessity compels and God bestows his mercy, the divine abridgements [*compendia*] confer the whole benefit on believers. Nor should anyone be troubled that sick persons seem to be sprinkled [*aspargi*] or poured upon [*perfundi*] when they obtain the Lord's grace. . . . [Ezek. 36:25-26; Num. 19:8, 12, 13; 8:5-7; 19:9 quoted.] Whence it appears that the sprinkling of water also holds equally with the washing [*lavacri*] of salvation. When this is done in the church, where the faith both of the receiver and giver is sound, all things may stand firm and be consummated and perfected by the majesty of the Lord and the truth of the faith. (*Letters* 69 [75].12.1-3)[27]

---

24. *Letters* 73 (72).6.2; cf. 69 (75).2.2, "sealed [*consignari*]" at the fountain.
25. *Letters* 73 (72).9.2.
26. *To Demetrianus* 22; cf. *Testimonies* 2.22 on the sign of salvation marked on foreheads with reference to Ezek. 9:4-6; Exod. 12:13; Rev. 14:1.
27. I have provided my own translation of this passage.

Cyprian treats the manner of the administration of baptism to those seriously ill as a matter of opinion,[28] so he is not dogmatic, but he asserts his position in favor of the practice vigorously, perhaps because of the doubts expressed about it. It was evidently a fairly recent development without an established tradition behind it and so subject to conflicting viewpoints.

The objectors to sickbed baptism addressed in this passage based their concerns on its being administered by pouring (or sprinkling) rather than being a complete washing.[29] Hence, Cyprian assembles a number of Old Testament references to sprinkling in order to bolster his case for divine approval of the practice. The critics called those "who obtained the peace of Christ by the saving water and legitimate faith, not Christians, but Clinics [*clinici*]." They considered that "those who have only been sprinkled with the saving water" to be "still empty and void," so if they recovered from their illness, they should be baptized.[30] To this, Cyprian replies that the Holy Spirit is not given by measure (John 3:34) but is poured out completely on the believer.[31]

Cyprian's word usage shows washing *(lotus)* was distinct from sprinkling or pouring, which were not the normal practice.[32] *Perfundo* meant to pour a large amount of a liquid, to wet or drench, and so would perhaps have been intended to imitate an immersion by overspreading the body with water as was done in a bath. *Aspergo* was to sprinkle and so referred to scattering a smaller amount of something, although it too could mean to splash or bedew. Cyprian grants that the practice is an abridgement or an abbreviation. This could refer to a shortened ceremony,[33] but since the objection to the practice has to do with the manner of the application of the water, I rather think the reference is to the changed procedure, a lessened amount of water. Since the procedure is different from normal, Cyprian insists that everything else must be the same: it is to be done "in the church,"[34] where the faith of both the giver and the receiver must be sound (not heretical) — stated twice in the passage (12.2 and 3).

---

28. *Letters* 69 (75).12.1; 13.3.

29. Augustine, *On Baptism against the Donatists* 6.7.10, understands the matter this way: Cyprian was asked whether there was any difference in efficacy of baptism by sprinkling or immersion; Cyprian made it a matter of judgment, but Augustine affirms the identity of all baptisms on the basis of the custom of the universal church confirmed by general councils.

30. *Letters* 69 (75)13.1, 3. Clarke translates the latter statement as Cyprian's inference from the objectors' position rather than their own statement.

31. *Letters* 69 (75).14.1.

32. Clarke, *The Letters of St. Cyprian*, Vol. 47, pp. 186-187, nn. 38 and 40, favors the normal practice as the candidate standing in water to the waist while water was poured over him. The evidence of baptisteries will be treated later in this book, but Clarke is wrong on the pictorial evidence representing the procedure he suggests (see chap. 7). Moreover, there would seem to be no grounds for the objection to the mode of sickbed baptism if pouring was the normal practice. Nor would Cyprian feel called upon to distinguish Christian practice from secular bathing practices nor use a separate vocabulary.

33. So Clarke, *The Letters of St. Cyprian*, Vol. 43, p. 147, n. 41.

34. I take the phrase to mean "not by heretics," certainly not in this context "the meeting place of the church," but possibly "with the presence of some of the church."

The giving of baptism in an abridged form to those seriously ill is a testimony to the importance attached to baptism. Only if an objective value was attached to baptism can we understand the debate and the future development. Because there was a value in baptism, that value in itself was considered paramount over accompanying features. There is also implicit in Cyprian's argument the view that if water worked the cleansing, could the amount of water or manner of application be essential? Receipt of baptism was considered so necessary for salvation that it was better to give a substitute version than not to give it at all. And this accords with what Cyprian says about the benefits and the theological meaning attached to baptism.[35] Perhaps the martyrs' "baptism of blood" prepared for the concept of a less than total immersion. Emergency or deathbed baptisms became increasingly common, especially in the fourth century (chap. 39). Acknowledgment of the efficacy of sprinkling or pouring in such cases is the reason, I suspect, for the later spread in the West of these substitutes for immersion in other circumstances.

Doctrine of Baptism

Christian baptism was superior to Jewish baptism. One of Cyprian's points about the many changes from the Mosaic dispensation to the Christian was "That the old baptism *(baptisma)* should cease, and a new one should begin." Passages cited are Isaiah 43:18-20; 48:21; Matthew 3:11; John 3:5-6.[36] Hence, "By this alone the Jews can receive pardon of their sins, . . . in his [Christ's] baptism," that is, the baptism instituted by Christ.[37]

A summary of what baptism does for one is found in the earliest of Cyprian's writings, an apology *To Donatus* (sometimes accounted as letter 1):

> By the help of the water of new birth, the stain of former years was washed away, and a light from above, serene and pure, was infused into my reconciled heart; after that, by the means of the Spirit breathed from heaven, a second birth *(nativitas secunda)* restored me to a new person. . . . So that now to be able not to sin is the beginning of the work of faith. (4)

Another extended statement, but dispersed and not listed, occurs in a letter to Pompey in response to Stephen of Rome on the baptism of heretics (*Letter* 74 [73]): renewed and sanctified (74.5.1), sins cast off and formed spiritually into a new person (74.5.2), put on Christ (74.5.3), regeneration and second birth (74.5.4; 6.2), the

---

35. Gaudette, "Baptême et vie chrétienne," pp. 163-190, 251-279.
36. *Testimonies against the Jews* 1.12. The Isaiah references are also in *Letters* 63 (62).8, noted above. Circumcision is treated separately in *Testimonies* 1.8, where the usual contrast is made between the circumcision of the flesh and the circumcision of the spirit, with the added note (according to one reading) that the sign of circumcision did not apply to women, but "all are sealed with the sign of the Lord."
37. *Testimonies* 1.24. Cf. *Letters* 73 (72).17.2 — The Jews "received the most ancient baptism of the law and of Moses; they needed, therefore, to be baptized, in addition, in the name of Jesus Christ."

dying of the old self so that the new may be born (74.6.1), cleansing of sins (74.5.4; 6.2), salvation (74.11.3; cf. 63 [62].8.4 — "saving waters of baptism"), and identification with the church (74.7.2; 11.3 and passim). All of these benefits were the result of the grace of God.

Cyprian often connected the forgiveness of sins with baptism.[38] His characteristic way of expressing this relationship is that God (or Christ) forgives in baptism (only secondarily and loosely could it be said, as he does in various passages, that the water or the administrator of baptism effected forgiveness). "Christ puts away sins in baptism."[39] Forgiveness of sins "is given in baptism."[40] One of the headings of Cyprian's *Testimonies* was "That all sins are put away in baptism," with quotation of 1 Corinthians 6:9-11 (3.65; cf. 3.116). The cleansing or purifying effect of baptism was not like the bodily washing away of filth, but the contagion of sin was washed away and the mind was purified by the merit of faith.[41]

The forgiveness of sins in baptism is sometimes stated in association with the work of the Holy Spirit. In his argument against accepting the baptism administered by those outside the church Cyprian says, "Now in baptism we are each forgiven our sins; and the Lord asserts clearly in his Gospel [citing John 20:21-22] that sins can be forgiven only through those who possess the Holy Spirit." The passage continues with the affirmation that only those baptized with the baptism of the church are able "to receive the forgiveness of sins, to be sanctified, and to become temples of God."[42] The view of Cyprian's opponents in the rebaptism controversy that one could be baptized outside the church and obtain forgiveness meant for Cyprian that the person could obtain the Holy Spirit also.[43]

The sanctification and purification of baptism constituted a new birth:

> All who arrive at the divine bath [*lavacrum*] by the sanctification of baptism [*baptismi*], put off the old self by the grace of the saving laver, and, renewed by the Holy Spirit from the filth of the old contagion, are purged by a second birth.[44]

Here are brought together the divine gift and grace, the sanctifying effect of the water of baptism, the renewal by the Holy Spirit, and the new birth that replaces the old person. Similarly, "Those who believe — those sanctified by him and restored by the

---

38. Gaudette, "Baptême et vie," pp. 175-178.

39. *Letters* 73 (72).19.1.

40. *Letters* 73 (72).7.1; 11.2 (saving water); and 18.2-3 ("the forgiveness of sins and sanctification of baptism"); *Works and Alms* 2 ("in baptism forgiveness of sins is granted once for all"); cf. *Letters* 70 (69).1.3 — one who administers baptism gives forgiveness of sins.

41. *Letters* 69 (75).12.

42. *Letters* 69 (75).11.1, 3; cf. 70 (69).1.3 — one who does not have the Holy Spirit cannot sanctify the water. The temple of God is where the Holy Spirit lives — *To Donatus* 15. Cf. *Letters* 74 (73).5.2 for the one reborn becoming a temple of God so that one who has "cast off his sins in baptism, has been sanctified and formed spiritually into a new man has certainly been made fit for receiving the Holy Spirit."

43. *Letters* 73 (72).6.2-7.1; also 73.12.2 and 17.1.

44. *Dress of Virgins* 23; cf. 2 — "when purged from all the filth of the old contagion by the sanctification of the laver [*lavacri*] of life."

nativity of spiritual grace *(gratiae spiritalis nativitate reparati)*, have begun to be children of God"; "the name of children is attributed to those to whom forgiveness of sins is granted."[45] Cyprian combined Pauline and Johannine ideas when he says, "It is in baptism that the old man dies and the new man is born."[46]

Cyprian fairly often draws on the language of regeneration and rebirth.[47] His conversion was a "being born again," so that he was "quickened to a new life in the laver of saving water."[48] The same is true for others: "They who as yet are by their first birth of earth, may, being born of water and of the Spirit, begin to be of heaven."[49] The Spirit was active in the water, apart from the question whether the Spirit was given by the water or by the imposition of hands (discussed above). Both water and the Spirit are necessary for the spiritual birth.

> We are born in Christ through the waters of regeneration.... Water by itself cannot cleanse sins and sanctify a person unless it possesses the Holy Spirit as well. Thus either they [who accept heretical baptism] have to allow that the Spirit is also to be found where they argue there is baptism, or there is no baptism where there is no Spirit, for there cannot be baptism without the Spirit. (*Letters* 74 [73].5.4)[50]

Baptism drives out the devil: "In baptism the devil is driven out by the faith of the believer, and he comes back again if that faith should falter."[51] Cyprian appeals to Israel's escape from Pharaoh at the Red Sea ("that sea was a sacrament of baptism [*sacramentum baptismi*]") — on the basis of 1 Corinthians 10:1-2, 6 — to illustrate that the power of the devil stops at the "saving water." When human beings "come to the water of salvation and to the sanctification of baptism, . . . there the devil is beaten down." The wicked spirits can no longer remain in the body of a person "baptized and sanctified, in whom the Holy Spirit is beginning to dwell."[52] Baptism,

---

45. *Lord's Prayer* 10.
46. *Letters* 74 (73).6.1. Cf. his description of Christians as those "who in baptism have both died and been buried in respect to the fleshly sins of the old person, who have risen again with Christ in the heavenly regeneration" — *Jealousy and Envy* 14.
47. Gaudette, "Baptême et vie," pp. 178-181, noting the connection of the new birth with the bringing of light and power.
48. *To Donatus* 3; cf. *Letters* 73 (72).12.1 — baptism gives life.
49. *Lord's Prayer* 17; cf. 9, "The new person, born again and restored to his God by his grace" and 10, "the nativity of spiritual grace"; *Jealousy and Envy* 13, "one who has already become filled with the Holy Spirit and a child of God by heavenly birth"; *Dress of Virgins* 23, cited at n. 44; *Judgments of 87 Bishops* 10 (Munnulus), after quoting Matt. 28:19, says, "truly to be born again and to be baptized" (*renasci et baptizari*); *Testimonies* 3.25 cites John 3:5-6 on the necessity of being "baptized and born again" in order to attain the kingdom of God.
50. Cf. the assertion in *Judgments of the 87 Bishops* 5 (Nemesianus) with reference to John 3:5, "Neither can the Spirit operate without the water, nor the water without the Spirit," but there is a further reference to the imposition of the hand.
51. *Letters* 69 (75).16.1.
52. *Letters* 69 (75).15. The exodus as prefiguring Christian experience is also in *To Fortunatus* 7.

because in it forgiveness of sins is granted, extinguishes the fire of Gehenna and delivers from death.[53]

Cyprian maintained a varied usage of the word *sacramentum:* the confession of faith as an oath binding one to Christ,[54] the whole of the divine mystery,[55] and the rites that signify this mystery.[56]

Cyprian was bishop during a time of persecution and became himself a martyr, so we expect him to honor the "baptism of blood." Yet not even confessing Christ and being put to death benefits the heretic, who is outside the church.[57] But catechumens who "hold the faith and truth of the church complete" and are martyred "are not in fact deprived of the sacrament of baptism, inasmuch as they are baptized with the greatest and most glorious baptism of all, that of blood." With reference to Luke 23:43 Cyprian understood the Lord to have promised "that those baptized in their own blood and sanctified with a martyr's suffering are made perfect and obtain the grace that God has promised."[58] Obviously this was not a literal immersion in blood, but the usage took its rise from Jesus' metaphorical language in Luke 12:50, to which Cyprian alludes. Martyrdom was a "baptism" in procuring the same effects as water baptism.

Indeed, martyrdom was even greater than baptism. In a pastoral rather than a polemical context Cyprian gives this praise to martyrdom:

> We give to believers a first baptism when God permits. We also prepare each one for the second; urging and teaching that this is a baptism *(baptisma)* greater in grace, more sublime in power, superior in honor — a baptism in which angels baptize *(baptizant)* — a baptism in which God and his Christ exult — a baptism after which no one sins any more — a baptism in which the increase of our faith is consummated — a baptism which, as we withdraw from the world, immediately associates us with God. In the baptism *(baptismo)* of water is received the remission of sins, in the baptism of blood the crown of virtues. (*To Fortunatus,* pref. 4)

Here is an exception not only to the usual insistence on the necessity of baptism for salvation but also to the insistence that there is only one baptism (chap. 24). The latter exception may be reconciled by the "one baptism" applying to water baptism.

Not only Cyprian's theology of martyrdom but also his teachings in the areas of moral and pastoral theology, in which he is best known, are rooted in his baptismal theology.[59] He stated the principle of the Christian life as becoming what one has

---

53. *Works and Alms* 2, cited below; *Letters* 55 (51).22.
54. *Letters* 30 (30).3.1.
55. *Lord's Prayer* 28.
56. *Letters* 72 (71).1.2. The different usages are those noted by Saxer, *Vie liturgique,* p. 109.
57. *Letters* 73 (72).21.1-2.
58. *Letters* 73 (72).22.2. With reference to this passage, Saxer, *Vie liturgique,* p. 108, notes that catechumens who were martyred had fulfilled the conditions of salvation: a personal faith, the liturgical requirement of confession, and sharing in the death of Christ (so that he substituted for their baptism). Cf. Ps.-Cyprian, *On the Glory of Martyrdom* 30, for martyrdom bringing forgiveness of sins.
59. Gaudette, "Baptême et vie," pp. 251-279.

begun to be. "We pray that we who were sanctified in baptism may be able to persevere in that which we have begun to be."[60] This perseverance required faithfulness to what one had received from God. In the context of the great pressures that persecution brought to bear on Christians, Cyprian could even say that to attain faith and virtue was a small matter in comparison to being able to preserve them and bring them to perfection.[61]

In one of his moral treatises, Cyprian goes so far as to present almsgiving and works of righteousness as another way of bringing forgiveness of postbaptismal sins. Citing Sirach 3:30, he comments:

> As in the laver of saving water the fire of Gehenna is extinguished, so by almsgiving and works of righteousness the flame of sins is subdued. And because in baptism remission of sins is granted once for all, constant and ceaseless labor, following the likeness of baptism, once again bestows the mercy of God. . . . Those who, after the grace of baptism, have become foul, may once more be cleansed.[62]

The forgiveness of sins is the common element that permits this language. It is notable that Cyprian brings this exhortation to almsgiving into express relation to baptism, yet preserving its unique significance.

Having become children of God, Christians must act accordingly.[63] Their goal is to reach the new world that is to come, which provides the norm for living as a Christian.[64]

The necessity of baptism for salvation was a driving force for Cyprian, not only in his defense of sickbed baptism but also in his defense of infant baptism and his concerns about heretical baptism, subjects to which we now turn.

---

60. *Lord's Prayer* 12; cf. *To Donatus* 5 ("what we have already begun to be") and 14 (the soul "begins to be what it believes itself to be").
61. *Letters* 13 (6).2.
62. *Works and Alms* 2.
63. *Lord's Prayer* 10-11.
64. Gaudette, "Baptême et vie," pp. 264-271.

23. Origin and Early Development of Infant Baptism

Tertullian provides the first certain literary reference to infant baptism, and that because he opposed the practice (chap. 21).[1] Efforts to find the practice in the New Tes-

---

1. Older scholarship was represented by Jules Corblett, *Histoire dogmatique, liturgique, et archéologique du sacrement de baptême*, 2 vols. (Paris, 1881), Book VII. The twentieth-century discussion featured Joachim Jeremias, *Die Kindertaufe in den ersten vier Jahrhunderten* (Göttingen: Vandenhoeck & Ruprecht, 1958) = *Infant Baptism in the First Four Centuries* (London: SCM, 1960), who made the strongest case for the practice originating in apostolic times; Kurt Aland, *Die Säulingstaufe im Neuen Testament und in der Alten Kirche* (München: C. Kaiser, 1961) = *Did the Early Church Baptize Infants?* (Philadelphia: Westminster, 1963), who refuted Jeremias's historical arguments but supported the practice on theological grounds; Joachim Jeremias, *Nochmals: Die Anfänge der Kindertaufe* (München: C. Kaiser, 1962) = *The Origins of Infant Baptism* (Naperville: Allenson, 1963), which grants that there is no direct provable evidence before Tertullian but responds to Aland's criticisms; Kurt Aland, *Die Stellung der Kinder in den frühen christlichen Gemeinden — und ihre Taufe* (München: C. Kaiser, 1967); idem, *Taufe und Kindertaufe* (Gütersloh: Gütersloher Verlagshaus, 1971). Michael Gärtner, *Die Familienerziehung in der Alten Kirche* (Cologne: Böhlau, 1985), pp. 64-86; a recent survey with an ecumenical interest is A. S. Yates, *Why Baptize Infants? A Study of the Biblical, Traditional and Theological Evidence* (Norwich: Canterbury Press, 1993); Anthony N. S. Lane, "Did the Apostolic Church Baptise Babies? A Seismological Approach," *Tyndale Bulletin* 55 (2004): 109-130, who argues that infant baptism and believers' baptism co-existed in the early centuries. Significant contributions to the study of infant baptism in the early church by David F. Wright include: "The Origins of Infant Baptism — Child Believers' Baptism?" *Scottish Journal of Theology* 39 (1987): 1-23; "How Controversial Was the Development of Infant Baptism in the Early Church?" in James E. Bradley and Richard A. Muller, eds., *Church, Word and Spirit: Historical and Theological Essays in Honor of Geoffrey W. Bromiley* (Grand Rapids: Eerdmans, 1987), pp. 45-63 (apart from Tertullian it was not controversial, and Tertullian never states that he is opposing a novel practice); "At What Ages Were People Baptized in the Early Centuries?" *Studia Patristica* 30 (1997): 389-394; "Infant Dedication in the Early Church," in Stanley E. Porter and Anthony R. Cross, eds., *Baptism, the New Testament and the Church* (Sheffield: Sheffield Academic Press, 1999), pp. 352-378; "The Apostolic Fathers and Infant Baptism: Any Advance on the Obscurity of the New Testament?" in Andrew Gregory and Christopher Tuckett, eds., *Trajectories through the New Testament and the Apostolic Fathers* (Oxford: Oxford University Press, 2005), pp. 123-133, returns a negative answer; *What Has Infant Baptism Done to Baptism? An Enquiry at the End of*

tament (from the use of the verb "hinder" in Jesus' blessing of the children and from household conversions) were discussed earlier (chap. 10). Some second-century passages have been thought to imply infant or child baptism. Justin Martyr says he knew of "many men and women of the age of sixty and seventy years who were disciples of Christ from childhood and remain celibate" (*1 Apology* 15.6). His emphasis in context is on their sexual purity; being "disciples from childhood" says nothing about the age of their baptism, for someone raised in a Christian home could be spoken of in the same way. Similarly, Polycarp's declaration, "Eighty-six years I have served my King and Savior" (*Martyrdom of Polycarp* 9.3), even if giving his age at the time, could have been spoken without dating his baptism.[2] Nor does the *Acts of Justin* 4, which records the confession of two of Justin's students that they received Christian instruction from their parents, say anything about the age of their baptism. Clement of Alexandria makes frequent use of the language of childhood in reference to Christians, but he apparently says nothing about baptism of actual children.[3] The Pseudo-Clementines contain a Jewish-Christian teaching against eating with Gentiles before their baptism, even if "father, wife, child [τέκνον], or brother" (*Homilies* 13.4 = *Recognitions* 7.29), but in the same context (*Homilies* 15.1-2 = *Recognitions* 10.1-4) the "children" (τέκνοις) are grown children (referring to the children of *Homilies* 12). A more likely reference to infant baptism comes from Irenaeus (*Against Heresies* 2.22.4), written about the time the practice apparently began, but in context it too probably does not have such in view (discussed in chap. 18).

Tertullian

That brings us to Tertullian. He refers to the baptism of small children as something already being done and for which a practical and scriptural rationale was advanced (themselves indications of a new practice that needed justification), but in view of Tertullian's respect for tradition at this period of his life[4] evidently not a practice of

---

Christendom (Carlisle: Paternoster, 2005); his articles on the subject are now collected in David F. Wright, *Infant Baptism in Historical Perspective: Collected Studies* (Carlisle: Paternoster, 2007). Collections of texts are in J. C. Didier, *Le baptême des enfants dans la tradition de l'église* (Tournai: Desclée, 1959) (cf. also his *Faut -il baptiser les enfants? La réponse de la tradition* [Paris, 1967]) and H. Kraft, *Texte zur Geschichte der Taufe, besonders der Kindertaufe in der alten Kirche*, 2nd edn. (Berlin: de Gruyter, 1960); I translate and discuss the principal passages in *Early Christians Speak*, Vol. 1, 3rd ed. (Abilene: ACU Press, 1999), pp. 53-64.

2. The *Life of Polycarp* is probably legendary on the matter, but its account of Polycarp being purchased as a slave boy by a Christian woman who raised him is inconsistent with his being baptized as an infant. What is said about Polycarp's teaching, furthermore, is contrary to infant baptism: "He said they could not otherwise receive the impression of the seal which is given by baptism" until their hearts were softened by hearing Scripture and its interpretation (*Life of Polycarp* 19) — J. B. Lightfoot, *The Apostolic Fathers*, Part 2, Vol. 3 (London: Macmillan, 1885), pp. 1015-1047 (Greek), 1068-1086 (English).

3. E.g. *Instructor* 1.5-7; 3.11.59.2; *Miscellanies* 4.25.160.1-2.

4. *On the Crown* 3, written a few years later, defends traditional customs lacking scriptural authority. Lane, "Did the Apostolic Church Baptise Babies?" p. 114, reasons that Tertullian "would hardly

long standing. Just as he would scarcely have made reference to an unknown practice, nor would he have rejected a generally accepted one. His full statement, partially cited in chapter 21, is in the context of a warning against giving baptism too hastily:

> According to the circumstances and nature, and also age, of each person, the delay of baptism is more suitable, especially in the case of small children. What is the necessity, if there is no such necessity, for the sponsors as well to be brought into danger, since they may fail to keep their promises by reason of death or be deceived by an evil disposition which grows up in the child? The Lord indeed says, "Do not forbid them to come to me." Let them "come" then while they are growing up, while they are learning, while they are instructed why they are coming. Let them become Christians when they are able to know Christ. In what respect does the innocent period of life hasten to the remission of sins? Should we act more cautiously in worldly matters, so that divine things are given to those to whom earthly property is not given? Let them learn to ask for salvation so that you may be seen to have given "to him who asks." (*On Baptism* 18)[5]

This statement is preceded by explanations of the speedy baptisms in Acts and followed by specifying that the baptism of the unmarried and widows also ought to be delayed until they are married or until they are firmly established in continence. The connection seems to be that baptism should be given only to those prepared to accept its responsibilities and live by them. Tertullian reasons that the disposition of earthly property is not given to minors; with even less reason should heavenly affairs be entrusted to them.

Tertullian refers to the practical consideration of "necessity" or "emergency baptisms." I take these to be cases of children whose illness threatened death, about which more below (under Inscriptions). Tertullian seemingly does not argue against baptism in these cases but in ordinary circumstances. Tertullian further attests to the accommodation made in the baptismal ceremony by the presence of "sponsors" who make promises on behalf of the child; this practice too will be discussed further below. Their function shows that the church baptized children only if there was a sufficient guarantee that they would be brought up in the faith.[6]

---

have neglected to use" the argument from novelty against infant baptism "if he could"; but a polemicist need not use every argument in his arsenal, and this consideration loses its force if Tertullian was willing to make a concession in cases of emergency baptism.

5. Studied by Holger Hammerich, "Taufe und Askese: Der Taufaufschub in vorkonstantinischer Zeit" (Diss., University of Hamburg, 1994), pp. 96-102, as a key passage in his examination of the antecedents to the delay of baptism common after Constantine's time. *On Repentance* 6 shows that already in Tertullian's time the fear of postbaptismal sin was an excuse for delaying baptism; Tertullian balances his warning against hasty baptism with a warning against unnecessary delay.

6. Evidence for sponsors is collected by T. Maertens, *Histoire et pastorale du rituel du catéchuménat et du baptême* (Bruges, 1962), pp. 71-77; cf. also 97-101 on the *Apostolic Tradition* and pp. 137-145 on later evidence with its move from the idea of guarantee to that of spiritual paternity. R. F. G. Burnish, "The Role of the Godfather in the East in the Fourth Century," *Studia Patristica* 17.2 (1982): 558-564, finds them responsible for encouragement, counsel, and correction of those new in the faith. Although rec-

Tertullian confronts an already definite scriptural argument for baptizing children, namely Jesus' words in Matthew 19:14. Tertullian's response underscores the importance for him of teaching, learning, and personal knowledge of and commitment to Christ — the reasons for his advocacy of a delay of baptism until these conditions had been fully satisfied. He joins a host of earlier Christian writers in the affirmation of the innocence of children,[7] a condition making infant baptism inconsistent in his view with the generally recognized meaning of baptism as bringing the forgiveness of sins.

Tertullian did recognize a "corruption" of the soul that proceeded from the sin of Adam and has some strong words to say about its natural evil, but he did not equate that with guilt or loss of the image of God and free will.[8] Unlike Cyprian, Tertullian did not connect the inclination to sin that he saw in inherited human nature with a need to baptize babies. Baptism must await the person's recognition of sin and so the need of seeking salvation. The importance of a clear personal decision before baptism for Tertullian (chap. 21) made the baptism of small children appear irresponsible; someone who could not repent must be dissuaded from baptism. Moreover, the understanding of baptism as a legal contract (cf. the legal language at the end of the quotation above) was inconsistent with this practice.[9]

---

ognizing as plausible the origin of godparents at baptism as a development from the guarantors of the candidates, Hammerich, "Taufe und Askese," pp. 181-184, suggests the hypothesis that the sequence is the reverse since the earliest mention (Tertullian) is in connection with infant baptism.

7. Hermas, *Similitudes* 9.29.1-3 (= 106.1-3); 9.31.3 (= 108.3); *Mandates* 2.1 (= 27.1); *Barnabas* 6.11; Papias, Fragment 8 ("They used to call those who practiced a godly guilelessness 'children,'" quoted by Maximus the Confessor in a scholion on Dionysius the Areopagite); Aristides, *Apology* 15.11; Athenagoras, *On the Resurrection* 14; Clement of Alexandria, *Instructor* 1.7.53.1; *Miscellanies* 4.25.160.1-2; Irenaeus, *Against Heresies* 4.28.3 — all quoted in my *Early Christians Speak*, vol. 1, pp. 53-54; to which add Minucius Felix, *Octavius* 2.1. This view continued to be expressed in the fourth century, especially in the East: Gregory of Nazianzus, *Oration* 11.23; Gregory of Nyssa, *On Infants Who Die Prematurely* (PG 46.177D, "innocent babe"); John Chrysostom, *Matthew* 28.3; Theodore of Mopsuestia, *On Psalms* 50.7; in the West by Ambrose, *Paradise* 31; Ambrosiaster, *Questions* 80.2. Hans Windisch, "Zum Problem der Kindertaufe im Urchristentum," *Zeitschrift für die neutestamentliche Wissenschaft* 28 (1929): 118-142, comments on the passages about the innocence of children that their baptism could give nothing they do not already possess (p. 131). For the philosophical background and study of the meaning of the description, see Hans Herter, "Das unschuldige Kind," *Jahrbuch für Antike und Christentum* 4 (1961): 146-162.

8. *On the Soul* 16 and especially 40-41; J. H. Waszink, *Q. S. F. Tertulliani, De Anima* (Amsterdam: J. M. Meulenhoff, 1947), p. 446. *Testimony of the Soul* 3.2 refers to the condemnation of death transmitted from Adam, not eternal condemnation; *On the Soul* 11 declares that the spirit neither of God nor of the devil is naturally planted in a soul at birth, a declaration inconsistent with original sin; similarly chapter 41 says that just as no soul is without sin, so neither is any soul without seeds of good. There is no contradiction between *On the Soul* 39-41 and *Baptism* 18 if guilt is not imputed for the corruption in human nature. Eduard Nagel, *Kindertaufe und Taufaufschub: Die Praxis vom 3.-5. Jahrhundert in Nordafrika und ihre theologische Einordnung bei Tertullian, Cyprian und Augustinus* (Frankfurt am Main: Peter D. Lang, 1980), pp. 35-49, in a generally good discussion goes too far in interpreting Tertullian as positing a "guilt inherited from Adam" (p. 46).

9. Nagel, *Kindertaufe und Taufaufschub*, pp. 55-76. Some other statements in *On Baptism* 18 are commented on in chap. 21.

Tertullian is evidence for the practice of infant baptism in the late second century in North Africa, a region where major theological support for the practice was later to be found. His opposition is an indication that the practice was neither long established nor generally accepted. Tertullian, however, never states that he is opposing a novel practice; rather, it was unnecessary (the innocence of children) and carried risks of the child later developing an evil disposition (an argument that shows Tertullian accepted baby baptism as real baptism, even if needless and unwise, for if not, baptism could be repeated for forgiveness later).[10] Evidence for infant baptism soon appears in other regions.

The *Apostolic Tradition*

If the *Apostolic Tradition* ascribed to Hippolytus can indeed be dated to early third-century Rome, then the evidence of Tertullian can be fleshed out and extended in its geographical scope. On the other hand, if the document is separated from Hippolytus and Rome, its testimony to infant baptism, as reflecting a later practice, loses some significance.

The relevant passage is unfortunately part of the text absent from the Latin version. All the other principal witnesses to the text, except the *Apostolic Constitutions*, contain a reference to baptizing children first, then men, and finally women. Both infants and older children are in view. The Sahidic version seems best to preserve the original:

> And first baptize (βαπτίζειν) the small children. And (δέ) each one who is able to speak for themselves [sic], let them speak. But (δέ), those not able to speak for themselves, let their parents or (ἤ) another one belonging to their family (γένος) speak for them.
>
> Afterward, baptize (βαπτίζειν) the grown men, and (δέ), finally, the women ... (*Apostolic Tradition* 21.4-5)[11]

The baptismal renunciation of Satan and Trinitarian confession of faith were considered so important to the ceremony that provision was made for parents or other family members to speak the words on behalf of children who could not do so or could not responsibly do so. Earlier in the document the *Apostolic Tradition* required sponsors who attested to the manner of life of catechumens now presented for baptism (20.1-2).[12] Now it is parents or family members who speak for the children. The

---

10. Wright, "How Controversial Was the Development of Infant Baptism in the Early Church?" pp. 47-48.

11. The translation is from Paul E. Bradshaw, Maxwell E. Johnson, and L. Edward Phillips, *The Apostolic Tradition: A Commentary,* Hermeneia (Minneapolis: Fortress, 2002), p. 112. See their comments on p. 130 for the possibility that children up to the age of seven might be included in the word for "small children."

12. Their function, therefore, was different from the witnesses in Jewish proselyte baptism, who

latter provision is an indication that the baptismal ceremony as originally developed was designed for those of sufficient age to make a meaningful confession of faith on their own. The accommodation to small children is clearly a secondary development.[13] In Roman law when a mute or deaf person or a small child could not make the *stipulatio* (see chaps. 11, 21) in entering into a contract, a *sponsor* could make the verbal declarations for them; this practice makes more understandable the readiness with which the church accepted the role of parents or guardians in speaking for infants in making the baptismal commitments.[14]

Nonetheless, the baptismal ritual would have looked quite different if as originally conceived it had children in view.

Origen

Origen's baptismal teaching as a whole will be presented in chapter 25. He refers to infant baptism in three interrelated passages. All three respond to questions asking for a justification of baptizing infants for the forgiveness of sins and offer a defense in terms of a stain attached to birth, citing the same Old Testament passages. The *Homilies on Luke* were preached in Caesarea between 231 and 244.

> Christian brethren often ask a question. The passage from Scripture read today encourages me to treat it again. Little children are baptized "for the remission of sins." Whose sins are they? When did they sin? Or how can this explanation of the baptismal washing be maintained in the case of small children, except according to the interpretation we spoke of a little earlier? "No man is clean of stain, not even if his life upon the earth had lasted but a single day" [Job 14:4-5]. Through the mystery of baptism, the stains of birth are put aside. For this reason, even small children are baptized. For "Unless born of water and the Spirit one cannot enter the kingdom of heaven." (*Homilies on Luke* 14.5 on Luke 2:22)[15]

---

testified to the legal validity of the act, not to the worthiness of the candidate — Georg Kretschmar, *Die Geschichte des Taufgottesdienstes in der alter Kirche*, in *Leiturgia*, Vol. 5 (1964-66), pp. 69-70.

13. The liturgical evidence for the temporal priority of adult baptism is recognized by those favorable to infant baptism: Maertens, *Histoire et pastorale du rituel du catéchuménat et du baptême*, pp. 185-203, 226-230, 232-247, 298-311; J.-C. Didier, "Une adaptation de la liturgie baptismale au baptême des enfants dans l'église ancienne," *Mélanges de science religieuse* 22 (1965): 79-90; repr. in Everett Ferguson, ed., *Conversion, Catechumenate, and Baptism in the Early Church*, Studies in Early Christianity 11 (New York: Garland, 1993), pp. 401-412. Otherwise, Kretschmar, *Die Geschichte des Taufgottesdienstes*, 99-100, understands the fact that others make answers for infants to mean that the confession is not a vow of individuals but the confession and pledge of the church.

14. Paul F. Bradshaw, "The Profession of Faith in Early Christian Baptism," *Evangelical Quarterly* 78 (2002): 101-115 (p. 113).

15. I quote the translation of Jerome's Latin version by Joseph T. Lienhard, *Origen: Homilies on Luke, Fragments on Luke*, Fathers of the Church 94 (Washington: Catholic University of America Press, 1996), here pp. 58-59. A shortened version survives in the Greek catena, but the Greek contains the main points (translated in my *Early Christians Speak*, Vol. 1, p. 55).

The *Homilies on Leviticus* were preached in Caesarea between 238 and 244; they survive in a Latin translation by Rufinus.

> [After quotation of Ps. 51:5 and Job 14:4:] These verses may be adduced when it is asked why, since the baptism of the church is given for the remission of sins, baptism according to the practice of the church is given even to infants; since indeed if there is in infants nothing which ought to pertain to forgiveness and mercy, the grace of baptism would be superfluous. (*Homily on Leviticus* 8.3.5 on Lev. 12:2-7)

The *Commentary on Romans* belongs to Origen's mature works in Caesarea, about 246; it is preserved in the Latin translation of Rufinus.

> [After reference to Lev. 12:8:] For which sin is this one dove offered? Was a newborn child able to sin? And yet it has a sin for which sacrifices are commanded to be offered, and from which it is denied that anyone is pure, even if his life should be one day long [Job 14:4-5]. It has to be believed, therefore, that concerning this David also said what we quoted above, "in sins my mother conceived me" [Ps. 51:5]. According to the historical narrative no sin of his mother is revealed. On this account also the church had a tradition from the apostles to give baptism even to infants. For they to whom the secrets of the divine mysteries were given knew that there are in all persons the natural stains of sin which must be washed away by the water and the Spirit. On account of these stains the body itself is called the "body of sin." (*Commentary on Romans* 5.9.11 on Rom. 6:5-6, the "body of sin")[16]

Origen reaffirms the usual Christian understanding of baptism as for the forgiveness of sins, and that understanding presented a problem for the practice of baptizing infants. Origen witnesses to questions about the practice of infant baptism and the argument that was urged against it, namely that infants had no sins to be forgiven by baptism. The subject of discussion may have been more a matter of *why* baptize infants than *whether* to do so. In response, Origen offers a modification of the earlier affirmations of the innocence of children. Before the reader jumps to the conclusion that Origen is an early witness to the doctrine of original sin (inheritance of the guilt of Adam's transgression), note should be taken of the larger context of the passage in the *Homilies on Luke*. Earlier in the same homily Origen contrasts sin (of which Jesus had none) and stain and explains that Jesus needed the purification recorded in Luke 2:22 because of the stain involved in his taking a human body for human salvation (*Homilies on Luke* 14.3). "Every soul that has been clothed with a human body has its own 'stain'" (14.4). Origen, therefore, is working with the category of ceremonial, bodily defilement from the Old Testament ritual law.[17] The same

---

16. I have slightly modified the translation of Thomas P. Scheck, *Origen: Commentary on the Epistle to the Romans Books 1-5*, Fathers of the Church 103 (Washington: Catholic University of America Press, 2001), p. 367.

17. Jean Laporte, "Models from Philo in Origen's Teaching on Original Sin," in M. E. Johnson, ed., *Living Water, Sealing Spirit: Readings on Christian Initiation* (Collegeville: Liturgical, 1995), pp. 101-117

impurity that attached to Jesus' birth applies to all human beings.[18] The *Commentary on Romans* makes clear that Origen is applying the same understanding of "sin" as a physical "stain" in all three of the Old Testament passages to which he refers. Origen's innovation is to extend the baptismal forgiveness of sins to ceremonial impurity, particularly that associated with childbirth. It remained for a later age to extend the concept to inherited sin (chap. 52).

That the interpretation advanced in the preceding paragraph is correct is evident from Origen's commentary on Matthew 18:2-4. There he elaborates on the condition of the child as not having tasted sensual pleasures; not having fully attained reason so not knowing anger, grief, pleasure of passions, or fear; being forgetful of evils; being humble. In these respects, being converted means an adult attains the condition of the child (*Commentary on Matthew* 13.16).

Origen's statements indicate that infant baptism preceded this justification for the practice. As has often been true in Christian history, the practice preceded its doctrinal defense.[19]

Origen's further defense of infant baptism appealed to a "tradition from the apostles." He offers no further evidence for this claim. His citation of John 3:5 in the first passage quoted above and allusion to it in the third passage may mean that the understanding of this passage as excluding from the kingdom anyone (infants as well) who had not received the new birth was the basis of his statement. John 3:5 was a common baptismal text of the second century (chaps. 8, 12, 14, 15, 16, 18). The idea of apostolic origin may also be based on the baptismal interpretation of Matthew 19:14 that Tertullian sought to counter. Origen's *Commentary on John* does not survive for John 3:5,[20] and his *Commentary on Matthew* 15.6-9 (on Matt. 19:13-15) does

---

— infant baptism for Origen removes the defilement resulting from birth, not Augustine's "inherited sin." Distinguishing Origen's view from Augustine's, Wright, "How Controversial Was the Development of Infant Baptism in the Early Church?" pp. 45-63, understands Origen to refer to forgiveness of the precosmic fall of souls.

18. Origen, *Homilies on Jeremiah* 5.14, interprets the circumcision of the heart in Jer. 4:4 as meaning that everyone is born uncircumcised and so with the stain of Job 14:4-5, a passage cited in the justification for infant baptism.

19. Contrary to Aland's view that a change in understanding about the condition of an infant occasioned the introduction of infant baptism in the late second century — *Die Säulingstaufe im Neuen Testament and in der Alten Kirche*, p. 75 (= *Did the Early Church Baptize Infants?* pp. 103-104) — the reverse relationship was recognized by Jeremias, *Nochmals*, p. 62 (= *Origins of Infant Baptism*, pp. 73-74), and earlier by N. P. Williams, *The Ideas of the Fall and of Original Sin* (London, 1972), pp. 220-226; J. C. Didier, "Un cas typique de développement du dogme à propos du baptême des enfants," *Mélanges de science religieuse* 9 (1952): 191-213 (194-200); Jaroslav Pelikan, *Development of Christian Doctrine: Some Historical Prolegomena* (New Haven: Yale University Press, 1969), pp. 73-94 (87); G. M. Lukken, *Original Sin in the Roman Liturgy* (Leiden: Brill, 1973), pp. 190-200. Mark Searle, "Infant Baptism Reconsidered," in M. E. Johnson, ed., *Living Water, Sealing Spirit: Readings on Christian Initiation* Collegeville: Liturgical, 1995), pp. 365-409, observes that where sacraments are concerned, practice preceded theology (p. 366).

20. Frg. 36 from the catena is on John 3:5, but see chap. 25 for doubts as to its authenticity. In any case, the fragment does not apply John 3:5 to infant baptism.

not bring in baptism. Or, the claim of apostolic tradition may rest on some teaching not dependent on scriptural interpretation.

The *Commentary on Matthew* 15.36 (on Matt. 20:1-16) refers to those "called from childhood" and "faithful from childhood," but, as in the passages cited at the beginning of this chapter, these expressions say nothing about the age of baptism. Origen's *Homilies on Joshua* 9.4 (on Josh. 8:32) has been cited in support of infant baptism, but Origen addresses adults here.

Cyprian

Cyprian and his fellow bishops, totaling sixty-six, in council at Carthage (perhaps in 252) responded to a question from the bishop Fidus concerning the day of baptizing an infant (Cyprian, *Letters* 64 [58].2-6). Fidus reasoned that the newborn should not be baptized before the eighth day after birth, arguing that the law of circumcision, which was taken as a figure of baptism and was given on the eighth day (Lev. 12:3), was to be observed.[21] A practical consideration urged by Fidus was that the newborn child was too repulsive to be given the kiss of peace on the foot that accompanied the North African baptismal ceremony.[22] Cyprian and his colleagues unanimously rejected Fidus's reasoning and allowed for baptism immediately after birth. That all the bishops rejected Fidus's argument shows that there was no direct connection between circumcision and baptism in the theological reflection of the time,[23] or if there was, the law regarding circumcision could not be applied to the administration of baptism. The provision for baptism before the eighth day seems to indicate that the concern was with emergency baptisms.

Cyprian's letter to Fidus conveying the decision of the council argues that an infant and an older person are equal before God and there is an equality in the divine gift (*Letters* 64 [58].3).[24] A bishop, "in giving grace and making peace," should not be repelled at the thought of kissing a newborn but should consider the baby as recently coming from the hands of God who made it (64 [58].4). Cyprian repeats earlier Christian thought on the eighth day by identifying it with the day of Jesus' resurrection (the first day after the Sabbath) and with his giving "spiritual circumcision [*circumcisionem nobis spiritalem*]" so that the physical circumcision was a figure that had ceased (64 [58].4). Cyprian does not correlate circumcision with baptism but contrasts it with spiritual circumcision.

---

21. In Jewish practice male children of proselytes born before the baptism of the mother were circumcised immediately, but those born after the baptism of the mother were circumcised on the eighth day. Would this have had a bearing on Fidus's reasoning?

22. G. W. Clarke, "Cyprian's Epistle 64 and the Kissing of Feet in Baptism," *Harvard Theological Review* 66 (1973): 147-152.

23. Nagel, *Kindertaufe und Taufaufschub*, p. 93.

24. For Cyprian's practice and grounding of infant baptism see Nagel, *Kindertaufe und Taufaufschub*, pp. 90-96.

The ruling of the council is stated in the following words:

> For this reason we think that no one is to be hindered from obtaining grace by that law which was previously established, and that spiritual circumcision ought not to be hindered by fleshly circumcision, but that absolutely everyone is to be admitted to the grace of Christ. . . . If, when they afterwards come to believe, forgiveness of sins is granted even to the worst transgressors and to those who have previously sinned much against God, and if no one is held back from baptism and grace; how much less ought an infant to be held back, who having been born recently has not sinned, except in that being born physically according to Adam, the infant has contracted the contagion of the ancient death by its first birth. The infant approaches that much more easily to the reception of the forgiveness of sins because the sins remitted to it are not its own but those of another. (*Letters* 64 [58].5)

Cyprian, like Origen, associates infant baptism with infant sin,[25] only he does not directly connect it with the stain of childbirth. Such may nonetheless be in the background of the argument, for the verse specifying the eighth day (Lev. 12:3) occurs in the passage about purification that formed part of the basis of Origen's reasoning.[26] Rather, Cyprian refers expressly to the sin of Adam that brought the inheritance of physical death to his descendants, so one should be cautious about concluding too much of a doctrine of original sin in Cyprian's reference to the sins (note the plural) of another.[27] After fifty years, the opposition to infant baptism voiced by Tertullian is no longer heard in North Africa; his premise of the innocence of children does not enter into the discussion. Eastern theologians in the fourth century, as we shall see, defended the baptism of small children on the basis of other benefits conferred and continued to accept the sinlessness of infants.

That baptism brings forgiveness of sins is once more central to the argumentation. Baptism brings grace even to hardened sinners who have come to faith; how much more readily is it effective to an infant who has not committed a sin. The practice of baptizing infants is the premise of the speculation about the condition of the newborn. As we shall see in chapter 52, even in Augustine the argument is from infant baptism to original sin.[28]

Cyprian elsewhere attests the practice of infant baptism. Referring to Christians who yielded to pressure and participated in pagan sacrifice during the Decian perse-

---

25. Augustine, *Against Julian* 1.3, saw this text as teaching original sin.
26. Commodian, *Instructions* 46 [?], variously dated from the third to the fifth century, "In baptism the coarse dress of your birth is washed"; 51 on infants does not speak of their baptism but exhorts adults to "be born again."
27. Nagel, *Kindertaufe und Taufaufschub*, pp. 93-96, for Cyprian's two arguments against Fidus as sameness of all of every age before God and the taint on humanity by the sin of Adam. The "contagion of the ancient death" is what is inherited, not original sin as such, but there may be the beginning of a theology of original sin.
28. After his time, the procedure is the reverse (chap. 39).

cution, Cyprian says that "infants in the arms of their parents, either carried or conducted, lost while yet little ones what in the very first beginning of their nativity they had gained" (*Lapsed* 9). Without expressly mentioning baptism, Cyprian seems clearly to allude to it. These children, he continues, will at the judgment be able to say that their parents involved them in idolatry.

Later in the treatise *Lapsed* Cyprian tells a story involving the presence of a small girl in the church's eucharist. Left by her fleeing parents with a wet-nurse, the child had been given bread soaked in wine that had been used in a pagan sacrifice. When her mother returned and took her to church, the child, although not able to talk, refused the eucharistic wine offered her by the deacon. Forced by the deacon to take some of it, she began sobbing and vomited (*Lapsed* 25). Cyprian told the story to illustrate the serious consequences of idolatry and its incompatibility with Christian profession, but it testifies to the practice of infant communion. In accepting infant communion as well as infant baptism, Cyprian showed a consistency not always observed by advocates of the latter practice.

Fidus's inquiry did not question infant baptism itself, only the appropriateness of giving it to a baby two or three days old. A verdict accepted by sixty-six bishops indicates a well-established and accepted practice. The information still does not say how often or under what circumstances the baptism of small children occurred. It is easy to read Cyprian and Origen in the light of a later custom of routine and near universal practice of infant baptism and assume that is what they were talking about. A broader look at the evidence, however, will considerably modify that conclusion.

Inscriptions

The earliest surviving Christian inscriptions come from the end of the second or beginning of the third century. They are overwhelmingly burial inscriptions. The thought of the innocence of children continued to be expressed with no reference to baptism: "Eusebius, an infant without sin by reason of his age, going to the place of the saints, rests in peace" (*ILCV* 2155).[29]

Many inscriptions mention the age of the deceased and/or the date of death. Some mention the date of the person's baptism. Where both items of information occur, there is a close correlation between the time of the baptism and the time of death.[30] The word "baptism" is rare in the inscriptions, but the fact of baptism is in-

---

29. I translate and cite the numbers of the Latin inscriptions from E. Diehle, *Inscriptiones latinae christianae veteres*, 2nd edn. (Berlin, 1961). This inscription may refer to burial among the martyrs rather than to the soul going to the heavenly church.

30. Everett Ferguson, "Inscriptions and the Origin of Infant Baptism," *Journal of Theological Studies*, n.s. 30 (1979): 37-46; repr. in Everett Ferguson, ed., *Conversion, Catechumenate, and Baptism in the Early Church*, Studies in Early Christianity 11 (New York: Garland, 1993), pp. 391-400, translates more of these inscriptions than are given below. Hammerich, "Taufe und Askese," pp. 157-180, studies the inscriptions relevant to children and infant baptism, noting that in no case of the express mention

Origin and Early Development of Infant Baptism | 373

dicated by "believer," "received (grace)," and "neophyte" (= newly baptized). The phrase "in peace" does not necessarily indicate that a person was baptized.[31] Some representative and some particularly revealing inscriptions may be cited from the third and fourth centuries.

One of the earliest dated inscriptions (A.D. 268) to refer to baptism comes from the catacomb of Callistus:

> Pastor, Titiana, Marciana, and Chreste made this for Marcianus, a well-deserving son in Christ the Lord. He lived twelve years, two months, and . . . days. He received grace [*crat(ium)* (*sic* — read *grat*) *accepit*] on September 20 when the consuls were Marinianus and Paternus the second time. He gave up (his soul) on September 21. May you live among the saints in eternity. (*ILCV* 3315)

Pastor and Titiana are presumably the parents, and Marciana and Chreste the boy's sisters or other members of the family. The words "Christ the Lord" and "live among the saints" identify the family as Christians, but the boy was not baptized until the age of twelve and only then, it seems, because of the onset of death (on the next day).[32]

Two third-century inscriptions from the catacomb of Priscilla do refer to small children and similarly seem to be cases of emergency or deathbed baptism:

> Sweet Tyche lived one year, ten months, fifteen days. Received (grace) on the eighth day before the Kalends. . . . Gave up (her soul) on the same day. (*ILCV* 1531)
>
> Irene, who lived with her parents eleven months and six days, received (grace) on April 7 and gave up (her soul) on April 13. (*ILCV* 1532)

Particularly telling in regard to the motivations behind these baptisms is the following:

> Sacred to the divine dead. Florentius made this monument for his well-deserving son Appronianus, who lived one year, nine months, and five days. Since he was dearly loved by his grandmother, and she saw that he was going to die, she asked from the church that he might depart from the world a believer. (*ILCV* 1343)

---

of baptism does it occur immediately after birth (pp. 173-174), but working with the improper rubric of the "delay of baptism" (which assumes that baptism at the earliest possible moment is the norm), he does not push on to the full implications of the definite cases of emergency baptism to this circumstance accounting for the other cases as well.

31. E.g., "Boniface, a hearer in peace, who lived one year and four months" (*ILCV* 1509B), a child who had been enrolled as a catechumen but died unbaptized yet "in peace."

32. Jeremias, *Infant Baptism*, p. 8, and *Origins of Infant Baptism*, pp. 49-54, understands this and other cases of emergency baptism in third-century inscriptions as the baptism of children of non-Christians or of catechumens. That interpretation does not accord with the wording of this inscription, and if this was a "missionary baptism" of the conversion of the family, the coincidence with the fatal illness of the boy is remarkably fortuitous. It seems more natural to understand the family (or at least the parents) as already Christians and not make the inscription fit a theory of the routine baptism of the children of Christian parents.

The assumption might be that Florentius was not a Christian, but since the grandmother was, this was not an ordinary "missionary baptism." We do not know the religious condition of the father: he might have been a Christian who did not see the necessity of baptizing his small boy but conceded to the urging of the grandmother. Notice that the initiative came from a family member and not from the church. To be baptized was equivalent to being made a believer, and the grandmother felt it important for the child to die in this condition.

The non-Christian status of a child at birth is stated in one inscription:[33]

> Her parents set this up for Julia Florentina, their dearest and most innocent infant who was made a believer. She was born a pagan on the day before the nones of March before dawn when Zoilus was a censor of the province. She lived eighteen months and twenty-two days and was made a believer in the eighth hour of the night, almost drawing her last breath. She survived four more hours so that she entered again on the customary things [eucharist placed in her mouth?]. She died at Hybla in the first hour of the day on September 25. . . . (*ILCV* 1549, dated A.D. 314)

When the parents became Christians is unknown. The daughter's baptism, which made her a "believer," was clearly prompted by the onset of death.

A few Latin inscriptions from various sites and referring to persons of various ages may be quoted for their indication of the proximity of baptism to the time of death.

> Postumius Eutenion, a believer, who obtained holy grace the day before his birthday at a very late hour and died. He lived six years and was buried on the eleventh of July on the day of Jupiter on which he was born. His soul is with the saints in peace. Felicissimus, Eutheria, and Gesta his grandmother, for their worthy son Postumius. (*ILCV* 1524, Rome, early fourth century)
>
> In the consulship of Ursus and Polemius the girl named Felite, more or less thirty years old, obtained (grace) on March 26 and died in peace after April 29 on the day of Mercury at the ninth hour. (*ILCV* 1539, Catacomb of Domitilla, Rome, A.D. 338)
>
> Here is laid Fortunia, who lived more or less four years. The parents set this up for their dearest daughter. She obtained (grace) on July 27 . . . and died on July 25 [*sic* — the workman perhaps exchanged the dates]. Gratian for the second time and Probus were the consuls. (*ILCV* 1525, Capua, A.D. 371)
>
> For the well-deserving Antonia Cyriaceti, who lived nineteen years, two months, twenty-six days. Received (the grace) of God and died a virgin on the fourth day. Julius Benedictus her father set this up for his sweet and incomparable daughter. November 20. (*ILCV* 1529, Rome)
>
> For Flavia, dearest infant, who with sound mind obtained the grace [*gratiam*

---

33. Christine Mohrmann, "Encore une fois: *paganus*," *Vigiliae Christianae* 6 (1952): 113-114.

consecuta] of the glorious font on Easter day and survived after holy baptism five months. She lived three years, ten months, seven days. The parents, Flavian and Archelaius, for their pious daughter. Burial on the eighteenth of August. (*ILCV* 1533, Salona, late fourth century)

In the late fourth century the word "neophyte" appears several times in Latin inscriptions. Where ages are given they are mostly young, but neophytes could be any age, as a few examples show.

Flavius Aurelius, son of Leo, marvellously endowed with the innocence of generous goodness and industry, who lived six years, eight months, eleven days. A neophyte, he rested (in peace) on July 2 in the consulship of Julius Philip and Sallias. . . . (*ILCV* 1477, St Agnes Outside the Walls, Rome, A.D. 348)
    For the well-deserving Perpetuus in peace, who lived more or less thirty years. . . . Buried April 13, died a neophyte. . . . (*ILCV* 1478, Rome, A.D. 370)
    For Proiectus, an infant neophyte, who lived two years, seven months. (*ILCV* 1484C, Ravenna)
    For the well-deserving Eugenia of happy memory who lived not nineteen years, a neophyte. (*ILCV* 1488B, Naples)

The word "neophyte" by itself indicates that the baptism was recent even when the date of the baptism is not given. As in the other cases cited above, it seemed important to specify that the person had indeed been baptized before dying.

A metrical inscription from Hippo, North Africa, in the late fourth or early fifth century, the time and place of Augustine, reflects the thinking in that period:

Here lies the body of a boy to be named.
O blessed boy, the earth held you for a few days,
An infant, and sent you back to the heavenly kingdom.
You were born only so that you might attain to rebirth.[34]

The last line evidently refers to baptismal regeneration and its efficacy in securing entrance into the kingdom of heaven. Nothing explicitly alludes to original sin, so we do not know if this inscription witnesses to a routine baptism of the newborn or is another case of emergency baptism.

Only beginnings have been made toward collecting the Greek Christian inscriptions. A few that have been brought into the discussion of infant baptism may be cited here. Their information is in accord with the Latin inscriptions.

Some Greek inscriptions actually give no indication of the time of the person's baptism. An inscription on the lid of a marble sarcophagus from a suburb of Rome, dated 238, identifies "the most God-beloved Heraclitus" as eight years old and ill before his death, information which suggests his illness was the reason for his bap-

---

34. J. Gagé, "Une épitaphe chrétienne d'Afrique," *Revue d'histoire et de philosophie religieuses* 9 (1929): 377-381. My thanks to Dorothy Pikhaus for calling this inscription to my attention.

376 | THE THIRD CENTURY TO NICAEA (325)

tism (*CIG* III.6408).³⁵ Another early inscription from Rome is often brought into the discussion:

> A believer from believers, Zosimus lies here. He lived two years, one month, twenty-five days. (*CIG* IV.9817)³⁶

The parents were Christians, but when Zosimus was baptized cannot be determined. We may have here another case of emergency baptism. Another offers a problem in meaning and so in translation:

> Tomb of the two Alcinous and of Alexander, comrades [reading συνήμων for συνέμων]. Three twelve-year old boys, believers (from their birth [γενετῇ], I escorted on their last journey) (I escorted on their last journey to their f(F)ather [γενέτῃ]). (*CIG* IV.9715)³⁷

The former reading would offer unambiguous evidence of infant baptism of the children in two (Christian) families. The latter reading says nothing about the time they became "believers." Apparently they died in the same circumstances and so were buried together; the author of the inscription accompanied their corpses to their grave. I consider the latter reading more likely.

Other Greek inscriptions attest baptism shortly before death:

> Achillia, a neophyte [νεοφώτιστος], fell asleep in her first year, fifth month, on February 24. (*CIG* IV.9810)
>
> Here lies Macaria, daughter of John of the village Nikeratos. She lived three years, three months, sixteen days. She died a believer [πιστή] on the twenty-fourth of the month Sandikou in the eleventh consulship of Honorius Augustus and the second of Constantius. (*CIG* IV.9855)

A three-year-old girl is the subject of an epitaph from Macedonia. The parents' grief is comforted through Christ, who gave her from an eternal spring (πηγῆς) the life of heavenly beings.³⁸ The spring is the fount (font) of baptism that brings salvation. Another inscription, possibly third century, is less explicit about the baptismal status of the child:

> Here lies an infant bereft of an ordinary life, the father's pleasantness and the mother's comeliness, their firstborn, two years old, an object of God's care, pleas-

---

35. I translate the Greek inscriptions from A. Boeckh, *Corpus Inscriptionum Graecarum* (Berlin, 1828-1877).

36. Jeremias, *Infant Baptism*, pp. 55-56, dates it late third century.

37. The first translation follows the reading adopted by Jeremias, *Origins of Infant Baptism*, pp. 53-54; the latter that of Aland, *Did the Early Church Baptize Infants?* p. 76.

38. S. R. Llewelyn, "Baptism and Salvation," in S. R. Llewelyn, ed., *New Documents Illustrating Early Christianity* (Macquarie University: Ancient History Documentary Research Centre, 1998), Vol. 8, pp. 176-179 (p. 177), with reference to D. Feissel, *Recueil des inscriptions chrétiennes de Macédoine 5* (Paris, 1983), #265, lines 17-19.

ant child of sunshine. Grieving, you gave birth to the sweet and gentle. Child of God. (*CIG* IV.9727)

Reading the inscriptions pertaining to baptism leaves certain definite impressions: (1) there was no common age at which baptism was administered; (2) there is no evidence that infants were routinely baptized shortly after birth, and indeed the evidence shows the opposite; and (3) the correlation between the time of baptism and the time of death, where these can be determined from the inscriptions, shows the prevalence of emergency baptism, and from the available inscriptional evidence only that practice can be demonstrated in regard to children.[39]

Jeremias offers two explanations in addition to emergency baptism for the various ages at which, according to the inscriptions, children were baptized: in the third century missionary baptism and in the fourth century the phenomenon of the delay of baptism.[40] The explanation that the children of various ages who were baptized were children of catechumens is a hypothesis not arising from the texts themselves[41] and an unnecessary one in view of the correlation of the baptism with imminent death.[42] It might be countered that the baptism of children born to Christian parents was taken for granted and so did not need to be mentioned in the epitaphs and was noted only in cases where the status of the child might be in doubt. But that is precisely the issue to be proved and cannot be assumed. If baptism was important for the child's condition in the afterlife, it would surely be mentioned some of the time if the practice was normal. The deliberate delay of baptism is attested only in the fourth century and so does not apply to third-century inscriptions.

What Was the Origin of Infant Baptism?

Various proposals have been advanced to account for the origin of infant baptism. (1) Jewish proselyte baptism and the solidarity of the family in ancient societies. This position, taken by Joachim Jeremias,[43] suffers from the uncertainty about the begin-

---

39. Lane, "Did the Apostolic Church Baptise Babies?" p. 119, notes, "That the inscriptions only record baptismal dates in the case of emergency/deathbed baptism in no way proves that all baptisms were such, either for adults or for children." The difference, however, is that other evidence shows the normal practice of baptism of believers at other ages of life; whereas, although there is evidence for baptism of babies in nonemergency situations, there is none for it as a normal or routine practice until the late fourth or fifth centuries. I introduce the inscriptional evidence not to argue that infant baptism obtained only in emergency situations but to offer an explanation of its origin.

40. Jeremias, *Infant Baptism*, pp. 80, 90.

41. Only in the case of the Appronianus inscription (*ILCV* 1343 quoted above) is there the possibility that the father was not a Christian, but the grandmother was.

42. Indeed, where the person was a catechumen, this might be expressly mentioned, so presumably this one had not received baptism: *ILCV* 1508 (dated A.D. 397, a sixty-year-old); 1509A (a nine-year-old); 1509B (quoted in note 31 above).

43. *Infant Baptism*, pp. 19-58; *The Origins of Infant Baptism*, pp. 12-32.

ning of proselyte baptism itself, and its biblical basis in the household and other New Testament texts was examined in the relevant chapters.

(2) A change in attitude toward children and the acceptance of a doctrine of original sin. Kurt Aland proposed this instead of Jeremias's view as the occasion for the introduction of infant baptism.[44] We have nuanced the interpretation of the texts in Origen and Cyprian to show that the idea of a stain associated with birth (derived from Jewish purity regulations) preceded the association of this with the sin of Adam. This view is attested only after the practice of infant baptism began, and after this view was advanced theologians (especially in the eastern churches) defended infant baptism on other grounds than this.

(3) The initiation of children in the mystery religions.[45] Most of the evidence adduced concerns children but not the newborn. It is dubious that the practices of mystery religions were influencing Christian activities in the earliest period.

(4) The old Punic practice of child sacrifice.[46] Since infant baptism is first attested in North Africa and found its strongest support there, some suggest that this practice left a residue in the thinking of people that their children must be dedicated to the deity. This supposition lacks any support in the sources, and if it had any validity it would apply only to the firstborn.

(5) The extension of children's baptism to baby baptism. David Wright proposed that a believers' baptism of children was extended to younger and younger ages.[47] This hypothesis would account for the continued coexistence of both adult and children's (including infant) baptism in the early centuries, the emergence of infant baptism at different times in different places, and the provision for sponsors to answer for children who could not speak for themselves. It fails to account for the difference felt between persons who could speak for themselves and those who could not and for what motivated the move to those at the beginning of life.

(6) The evidence of the inscriptions surveyed above prompts me to offer an alternative explanation for the origins of infant baptism.[48] John 3:5 had left a strong impression on the second-century church as requiring the necessity of baptism for entrance into heaven.[49] When a child of Christian parents (or of catechumens) be-

---

44. *Did the Early Church Baptize Infants?* pp. 100-111.

45. Johannes Leipoldt, *Die urchristliche Taufe im Lichte der Religionsgeschichte* (Leipzig: Dörffling & Franks), pp. 73-78, includes proselyte baptism along with the practices of the mysteries as making probable that the first Christians practiced infant baptism. A. Oepke, "Zur Frage nach dem Ursprung der Kindertaufe," in R. Jelke, ed., *Historische-kritische und theologische Schriftauslegung: L. Ihmels-Festschrift* (Leipzig: Dorffling, 1928), pp. 84-100 (92-94), collected the evidence for children dedicated in the mystery religions.

46. Joseph R. Moore Jr., "A Case for the Punic Origin of Infant Baptism in Christian Churches: A Research Report Based on Historical, Linguistic and Archeological Sources" (Charlotte, NC, 1987), to my knowledge unpublished.

47. Wright, "The Origins of Infant Baptism — Child Believers' Baptism?" pp. 1-23.

48. Advanced already in my "Inscriptions and the Origin of Infant Baptism," pp. 44-46.

49. Hermas, *Similitudes* 9.16.3 (= 93.3); Justin, *1 Apology* 61; Theophilus, *To Autolycus* 2.16; Irenaeus, *Against Heresies* 3.17.1-2; Clement of Alexandria, *Miscellanies* 4.25; Tertullian, *On Baptism* 12.

came seriously ill, there was the natural human concern about the welfare of the child's soul and a desire to make every preparation for the afterlife. Request from parents or family members for the baptism of a gravely sick child would have been hard to refuse. The inscriptions, I propose, are the key to understanding the origin of infant baptism. The practice of such "baptisms of necessity" was recognized already by Tertullian, our first attestation (literary or of any kind) of infant baptism. When we recall the high infant mortality rate of the ancient world, it is easy to understand how an emergency practice eventually became a normal practice.[50] The early acquiescence in the emergency baptism of infants would account for the lack of controversy in the early church over the acceptable age for baptism.[51]

Conclusion

The fact is that "we cannot give the name of anyone before the fourth century not in an emergency situation who was baptized as an infant."[52] For example, Perpetua's infant seemingly did not receive baptism with her in prison (*Martyrdom of Perpetua* 3). Tertullian, Cyprian, and Augustine have had more importance in the discussion of infant baptism than necessary because so many modern scholars approach the subject with only two alternatives in mind: the baptism of infants or the delay of baptism. Chapter 39 will discuss these options as well as another alternative.

The liturgy and theology of baptism, as well as the practice of leading Christian families, show that in the fourth century (chap. 39) infant baptism was not yet the norm. That situation began to change late in the fourth century.

---

50. Searle, "Infant Baptism Reconsidered," p. 367, comments that too little consideration has been given to the relationship between infant baptism and clinical or deathbed baptism, and p. 369 observes that the Gelasian *Order for the Making of a Catechumen or for Baptizing* was nothing other than a rite for baptizing the dying.

51. Wright, "How Controversial Was the Development of Infant Baptism in the Early Church?" pp. 45-63, and other articles cited in the notes.

52. Wright, "At What Ages Were People Baptized in the Early Centuries?" pp. 389-394, on which this paragraph is based.

24. The Controversy over "Rebaptism" in the Third Century

A sharp controversy erupted in the mid–third century over whether the church should accept baptisms administered by heretics and schismatics. The principals in that controversy were Stephen, bishop of Rome (254-257), and Cyprian, bishop of Carthage (248-258), but behind them was a period of time in which different practices had developed.

Early Statements

Clement of Alexandria had declared "heretical baptism" to be "no proper and genuine water."[1] Tertullian said that what heretics "do not have in the right form [*rite*], without doubt they do not have it [baptism] at all."[2] Since theirs was not the "one baptism," presumably converts from a heretical body would have been baptized according to the ceremony of the church. Although Tertullian does not say this expressly here, it is strongly implied and may have been stated in what he says he had written in Greek (not preserved).

Hippolytus reports among his charges against Callistus that "Under him, a second baptism [βάπτισμα] was for the first time presumptuously attempted by them."[3] This is a puzzling statement, for the tradition of the Roman church not many years later (see below) opposed a second baptism or rebaptism of converts from heretical and schismatic bodies. It may be that Hippolytus is speaking metaphorically of Callistus's policy of granting forgiveness and reconciliation to those guilty of serious sin, a policy that Hippolytus disapproved. In the next section of the *Refutation of All Heresies* Hippolytus takes up the Elchasaites, who did practice a second baptism

---

1. *Miscellanies* 1.19.96.3-4.
2. *On Baptism* 15.2.
3. *Refutation of All Heresies* 9.12 (7).25.

(and more) to their members for the forgiveness of sins (chap. 4); the author may be preparing for that discussion by finding in common between Elchasai and Callistus a forgiveness for postbaptismal sins, one by an actual repeated baptism and the other by a rite of reconciliation that had the same promised effect.

Bishop Agrippinus of Carthage in a council about 220 legislated the logical conclusion from a rejection of the validity of baptism administered by heretics by requiring converts from those bodies to receive the "one baptism" in the church.[4] The question of what to do with those converted to the catholic church from a heretical or schismatic body was evidently being discussed from early in the third century, if not earlier. Those who advocated a new baptism for them appeared as innovators.[5]

Novatian

In the background of the dispute between Stephen and Cyprian was the schism caused by Novatian's "church of the pure." Novatian had been a presbyter in the church of Rome during the persecution under Decius, and when Cornelius was elected its bishop (251), he had three Italian bishops ordain him as a counter-bishop. Novatian rebaptized those who came to his church from the communion of Cornelius. Cyprian cites a letter from Bishop Iubianus: "You pointed out that followers of Novatian rebaptize those whom they entice away from us."[6] Others who practiced a new baptism did so on the grounds either of doctrinal error by heretics or the baptism being administered outside the one church (Cyprian urged both reasons); Novatian, it seems, anticipated the later Donatist position (chap. 52) of rejecting baptism on the grounds of the moral character of the administrator and compromise with those who lapsed in persecution.

Novatian's own baptism was under a cloud. Because of his later schism, his became the most famous case of sickbed or emergency baptism (chap. 22) in the early church. His rival Cornelius, as part of his efforts to discredit Novatian, passed on the report:

> While being treated by the exorcists, he fell into a serious illness and was thought to be about to die. On the very bed on which he lay, he received [grace, baptism][7] by [water] being poured over him [περιχυθεὶς], if indeed it may be said that such a

---

4. Cyprian, *Letters* 71 (70).4.1; 73 (72).3.1; cf. 70 (69).1.2. The council and Agrippinus were later referred to by Augustine, *On the One Baptism* 13.22; *Against Crescens* 3.3.3; *On Baptism against the Donatists* 1.3.12; 4.6.

5. G. W. Clarke, *The Letters of St. Cyprian of Carthage*, Vol. 4, Ancient Christian Writers 47 (New York: Newman, 1984-1989), pp. 196-198, discusses Agrippinus's council and the indications that the North Africans changed the earlier practice.

6. Cyprian, *Letters* 73 (72).2.1. Dionysius of Alexandria, in Eusebius, *Church History* 7.8, apparently has the same practice in mind, when he says of Novatian, "He rejects the holy baptism [λουτόν]," that is, the baptism administered by the church from which he had withdrawn, not the practice itself.

7. An example of this common shortened Christian expression with the object unexpressed.

one received it. Nor when he recovered did he receive the other things which must be received according to the rule of the church, and he was not sealed [σφραγισθῆναι] by the bishop. Since he did not obtain these things, how could he obtain the Holy Spirit?[8]

When later the bishop wanted to ordain him as a presbyter, there was opposition from the clergy and many laypersons on the grounds that it was not lawful for someone "who received pouring [περιχυθέντα] on his bed because of illness to become a clergyman," but an exception was made in this case.[9] The verb "pouring around" suggests soaking with water the body on the bed, hence covering it in imitation of an immersion. The basis of the objection by the clergy and many people in Novatian's case is not made explicit. If it was to the substitution of pouring, the lack of agreement betrays the absence of a fixed procedure and shows the lateness of the innovation. The problem in Cornelius's eyes, however, seems not to be so much the abridged action (contrast the discussion in Cyprian, chap. 22) but the delay of baptism until death threatened called into question the fullness of devotion and because the failure to receive the full initiatory ceremony, particularly the sealing by the bishop, left the ceremony in doubt.[10] Sealing is here the signing with chrism and/or imposition of hands.

Novatian held to the same Trinitarian faith as the majority in the Roman church did, and he used the same baptismal symbol (questions).[11] He also refers to the baptismal renunciation of the devil (*Public Shows* 4). His baptismal doctrine also was the same. In baptism and in the resurrection the flesh is raised up to salvation by being restored to innocence when the mortality of guilt is removed (*Trinity* 10). The Holy Spirit along with water effects the second birth, being the seed of a divine generation

---

8. Cornelius, letter to Fabius of Antioch, in Eusebius, *Church History* 6.43.14-15. The "clinical baptism" of Novatian is studied by Holger Hammerich, "Taufe und Askese: Der Taufaufschub in vorkonstantinischer Zeit" (Diss., University of Hamburg, 1994), pp. 143-155: Novatian did not delay his baptism out of fear of sin after baptism; the philosophy to which he dedicated himself was asceticism, and his high evaluation of asceticism is the key to his late baptism; he understood baptism as a vow of asceticism; he put off baptism, but his illness forced the decision.

9. Still from Cornelius's letter, Eusebius, *Church History* 6.43.17. The Council of Neocaesarea (in the early fourth century), canon 12, preserves a prohibition against ordaining to the presbyterate a person baptized in sickness. See the contemporary discussion of the validity of the practice of sickbed baptism in Cyprian, *Letters* 69 (75).12.1-3 (chap. 22).

10. Cf. *On Rebaptism* 4 (quoted below) for one baptized who died before receiving imposition of the bishop's hands. The Spanish council of Elvira in the opening decade of the fourth century, canon 38, required that a baptism performed in cases of necessity by a layman be completed by the imposition of a bishop's hand. G. W. H. Lampe, *The Seal of the Spirit*, 2nd ed. (London: SPCK, 1967), pp. 178-180, understands the sealing as consignation with chrism. For sickbed baptism in the dispute between Cornelius and Novatian, see Clarke, *The Letters of St. Cyprian*, Vol. 47, pp. 176-177. Georg Kretschmar, *Die Geschichte des Taufgottesdienstes in der alter Kirche* in *Leiturgia*, Vol. 5, 31-35 (1964-1966), pp. 141-142, explains the doubts about Novatian's baptism as due to the absence of exorcisms (Cornelius mentions the "other things" connected with baptism that he did not receive), so demons may have been baptized with him.

11. Cyprian, *Letters* 69 (75).7.1 (cited in chap. 22); Novatian's own treatise, *On the Trinity*, especially 1; 5; 29.

and pledge of a promised inheritance who also makes us God's temple (*Trinity* 29). One is "born again of water" (*Chastity* 2). By baptism one has died to the elementary principles and physical regulations (Col. 2:18-23 quoted) of the world (*Jewish Meats* 5).

Stephen of Rome

Stephen of Rome and Cyprian of Carthage represented the two viewpoints on heretical baptism.[12] Stephen's position, unfortunately, is known only from some brief citations by others. He took his stand on the traditional practices of the Roman church and buttressed their correctness by appeal to the status of its bishops as successors of Peter.

Cyprian's *Letter* 74 (73) was addressed to Pompey, who had requested a copy of a letter from Stephen to Cyprian, now regrettably lost. Cyprian sent it along with this letter as a refutation. It contains the following quotation from Stephen's letter:

> "And so, in the case of those who may come to you from any heresy whatsoever, let there be no innovation beyond what has been handed down: hands are to be laid on them in penitence, since among heretics themselves they do not use their own rite of baptism on other heretics when they come to them, but they simply admit them to communion." (74 [73].1.2)[13]

Stephen's practice, therefore, was not limited to schismatics, such as Novatian, whose theology agreed with his and who used the same baptismal formula.[14]

---

12. J. Jayakiran Sebastian, "... Baptisma unum in sancta ecclesia ...," in *A Theological Appraisal of the Baptismal Controversy in the Work and Writings of Cyprian of Carthage* (Ammersbek bei Hamburg: Lottbek [Peter Jensen], 1997), pp. 71-144, analyzes the sources for study of the conflict in the letters of Cyprian and elsewhere. Hubert Kirchner, "Der Ketzertaufstreit zwischen Karthago und Rom und seine Konsequenzen für die Frage nach den Grenzen der Kirche," *Zeitschrift für Kirchengeschichte* 81 (1970): 290-307; repr. in Everett Ferguson, ed., *Conversion, Catechumenate, and Baptism in the Early Church*, Studies in Early Christianity 11 (New York: Garland, 1993), pp. 414-431; Kretschmar, *Die Geschichte des Taufgottesdienstes*, pp. 107-109. J. P. Burns, "Social Context in the Controversy between Cyprian and Stephen," *Studia Patristica* 24 (1993): 38-44, points out that Cyprian and Stephen differed on the boundary between the church and the world. A schismatic Christian was in some sense in the kingdom of Christ, but communion with the church was necessary for salvation. In Carthage the church was small enough for the bishop to have face-to-face contact with its members and there was a greater sense of separation from society than was true of the larger Roman church. The Roman position was not so much a concession to schismatics as an assertion of episcopal authority; its bishops treated Novatianists as they did other regional assemblies in Rome, the initiation of whose converts (baptized by presbyters) was completed by the imposition of the bishop's hands.

13. I continue to quote from the translation by Clarke, *The Letters of Cyprian of Carthage*.

14. S. G. Hall, "Stephen I of Rome and the One Baptism," *Studia Patristica* 17.2 (1982): 796-798; S. G. Hall, "Stephen I of Rome and the Baptismal Controversy of 256," *Miscellanea historiae ecclesiasticae* 8 (1987): 78-82, where he argues that Stephen was reacting to the practice of Novatianists' baptizing those who came to them from other Christian groups, an innovation in regard to Roman practice, and was angry at Cyprian and Firmilian for the support that their viewpoint gave to his local rival.

Cyprian concluded that "any heresy whatsoever" included Marcion, Valentinus, and Apelles.[15]

Stephen considered the practice of what was in his eyes "rebaptism" to be an innovation. The appeal to established custom occurs frequently in the discussion.[16] Cyprian was sensitive on this score and often claimed he was following the practice of his predecessors.[17] But ultimately he appealed to a higher standard: "A custom without truth is but error grown old."[18]

Stephen may also have made a theological argument from the power of the name of Jesus; or if not he, some of his supporters did.[19] Cyprian comments:

> Now if they attribute the efficacy of baptism to the power of the Name, so that he who is baptized in the Name of Jesus Christ, no matter where nor in what manner, is judged renewed and sanctified, and if hands are there laid in the Name of the same Christ upon the person baptized so that he may receive the Holy Spirit, why does the same power of the same Name, which they maintain had efficacy in the sanctification of baptism, have no efficacy in the laying-on of hands? (74 [73].5.1)[20]

Cyprian detects an inconsistency in attributing power to the name of Christ in baptism that is not acknowledged in the case of the postbaptismal imposition of hands. However, the inconsistency exists only in Cyprian's understanding of the two ceremonies. For Stephen the laying on of hands when the heretic joined the catholic church was the same action used in reconciling penitents (74 [73].1.2 quoted above). This could have been considered a renewing of the Holy Spirit, but it had nothing to do with whether a person had received the Holy Spirit in connection with baptism. (The author of *On Rebaptism,* discussed below, did make the argument Cyprian responds to here.) Baptism "in the name of Christ" is probably not meant to indicate a different baptismal formula from that involving the Trinitarian names but rather a description of the ceremony and its basis in faith in Jesus Christ.[21]

---

15. *Letters* 74 (73).7.3. The phrase "any heresy whatsoever" was picked up from Stephen's letter also by Dionysius of Alexandria, as referred to by Eusebius, *Church History* 7.2.

16. On the argument from custom in defense of not rebaptizing, cf. 71 (70).2.1; 3.1; 73 (72).13.1 (some defeated by reason of appeal to custom, "as if custom were superior to truth"), 3; 74 (73).3.1 (presumption puts human tradition before divine ordinance); 75 (Firmilian) (74).19.1-2; Eusebius, *Church History* 7.2-3.

17. See references in n. 4; in the present context (74 [73].2.2ff.) Cyprian tries to turn the charge of innovation against Stephen by appealing to scriptural and apostolic teaching.

18. *Letters* 74 (73).9.2.

19. Firmilian in Cyprian, *Letters* 75 (74).18.1, attributes the argument to Stephen, but see the comments below at nn. 25, 26, 54.

20. I follow the reading suggested by Clarke, *The Letters of St. Cyprian,* Vol. 47, p. 241, n. 17. The argument from the power of the name of Jesus receives frequent attention in *Letters* 73 (72).14.3; 16.1-2; 17.1; 18.1.

21. Cyprian, *Letters* 73 (72).5.2, implies that Marcion used the three names in his baptisms, for Cyprian argues that Marcion did not believe in the same Trinity, the same God the Father, and the

Cyprian's *Letter 74* (73) makes frequent mention of the "one baptism" (Eph. 4:5) as belonging to the church and not to heretics (74 [73].2.2; 3.1; 11.3), once as part of a rearranged listing of six of the seven "ones" in Ephesians 4:4-6 (74 [73].11.1). This emphasis is likely in response to another theological argument made by Stephen or his supporters, namely that "the one baptism" of scripture precluded the practice of rebaptism. "Some of our colleagues think that there is no need for those who have been bathed [*tincti sunt*] among heretics to receive baptism when they come over to us — on the grounds that, so they contend, there is only one baptism" (*Letter 71* [70].1.2). Cyprian agreed that there is only one baptism, but it is given only in the church. He strongly maintained that what the heretics gave was not true baptism (see below); therefore, what he administered to converted heretics was not "rebaptism": "Those who come from heresy are not being rebaptized with us, they are being baptized" (71 [70].1.3).[22] So, his opponents, who refused "to baptize those who come to them, asserting the oneness of baptism," were in effect those who created two baptisms, by acknowledging one baptism among heretics and one baptism in the church (71 [70].1.3). Which side possessed the one baptism depended on whose definition of baptism was accepted.

Stephen noted that the heretics themselves did not require a new baptism of those who came to them from among the various Christian groups in Rome. He probably intended this as a support for the antiquity of the practice of receiving converts from other Christian groups without baptizing them: the heretics were following the practice of the catholic church. Cyprian, however, saw the argument in reverse and took exception to the idea of the church following the example of heretics (74 [73].4.1).

Particularly disturbing to Cyprian was the threat of a break in communion from Stephen: "Does he give honor to God who . . . considers that those priests of God who seek to protect the truth of Christ and the unity of the church deserve to be excommunicated?" (74 [73].8.2).[23] Although Cyprian argued his case vigorously and sought to gain support for it, he was committed to unity and did not want the issue to cause a break in communion.

Anonymous, *On Rebaptism*

The fullest surviving argument against "rebaptism," if not the best statement of the case, is an anonymous tract, *On Rebaptism*, probably coming from a bishop who was

---

same Christ as catholics did; the same letter, 18.1, might suggest that some used the name of Jesus Christ in contrast to the Trinitarian formula.

22. Cf. the similar statement in *Letters* 73 (72).1.2, "By this [one] baptism we do not rebaptize but rather *baptize* all those who, coming as they do from spurious and unhallowed waters, need to be washed clean and sanctified in the genuine water of salvation."

23. Clarke, *The Letters of Cyprian*, Vol. 47, pp. 243-244, n. 29, gives the information on what prompted Cyprian's words.

one of Cyprian's opponents in North Africa.[24] The author states the issue at the beginning of the tract:

> Whether according to the most ancient custom and ecclesiastical tradition it would suffice, after that baptism which they have received outside [the church] indeed, but still in the name of Jesus Christ our Lord, that only hands should be laid upon them by the bishop for their reception of the Holy Spirit, and this imposition of hands would afford them the renewed and perfected seal of faith; or whether, indeed, a repetition of baptism would be necessary for them, as if they should receive nothing if they had not obtained baptism afresh, just as if they were never baptized in the name of Jesus Christ.[25]

He makes no distinction between the baptism of heretics and schismatics.

The anonymous author repeats the argument that the power of the name of Jesus provides theological reason for rejecting "rebaptism." The "one baptism" is that where the name of Jesus is invoked, and when "once invoked, it cannot be taken away by anyone" (10). To invoke the name of Jesus has great power that is not to be disdained.

> The power of the name of Jesus invoked upon any person by baptism affords to him who is baptized no slight advantage for the attainment of salvation. . . . The person on whom, when being baptized, invocation should be made in the name of Jesus, although he might obtain baptism under some error, still would not be hindered from knowing the truth at some other time, and correcting the error and coming to the church and to the bishop, and sincerely confessing our Jesus publicly, so that then, when hands are imposed by the bishop, this person might also receive the Holy Spirit and would not lose that former invocation of the name of Jesus. (6)[26]

Or, again:

> It behooves us to consider that invocation of the name of Jesus ought not to be thought futile by us on account of the veneration and power of that very name, in which name all kinds of power are accustomed to be exercised, and occasionally some even by people outside the church. [Quotation of Matt. 7:22-23.] . . . This invocation of the name of Jesus ought to be received as a certain beginning of the mystery of the Lord common to us and to all others, which may afterwards be filled up with the remaining things. (7)

---

24. Paul Mattei, "'Extra ecclesiam nulla salus' et puissance du nom de Jésus: Tensions et fractures dans la théologie du *De rebaptismate*," *Studia Patristica* 24 (1993): 300-305.

25. *Rebaptism* 1. The "perfect seal of faith" is applied to reception of the Spirit by imposition of hands in 10. Cf. "Heretics who are already baptized in water in the name of Jesus Christ must only be baptized with the Holy Spirit" (12). I use but modify the translation by Ernest Wallis in A. C. Coxe, *Ante-Nicene Fathers*, Vol. 5 (repr. Peabody, MA: Hendrickson, 1994), pp. 667-678.

26. *Rebaptism* 6; also 10. A. C. Coxe, *Ante-Nicene Fathers*, Vol. 5, pp. 667-678.

The Controversy over "Rebaptism" in the Third Century | 387

By baptism "in the name of Jesus Christ" the author almost seems to be referring to a different baptismal formula, for he quotes Matthew 28:19 as what ought to be observed in the church (7). However, by that statement, in the context of his argument, he seems to mean a baptism in the Holy Spirit as well as in water. On this reading he was not referring to an alternative baptismal formula but by "the name of Jesus" was referring to baptism as ordained by Christ.[27]

The author of the tract on *Rebaptism* had the same ecclesiology (church is our mother — 1) as Cyprian and the same view that the Holy Spirit does not work outside the church.[28] From these premises he tried to turn the flank of Cyprian's position on baptism by exploiting a feature of the baptismal theology of North Africa since Tertullian that was accepted by Cyprian, namely the identification of the imparting of the Holy Spirit with the postbaptismal imposition of hands. Assembling the scriptural examples, principally in Acts 8 and 10, where the gift of the Spirit was separate in time from baptism, the author argued that baptism by heretics could be effective but the Spirit be given later at the time of a person's coming to the catholic church. For instance, even the apostles had previously received the same baptism as the Lord's (by John?) but received the Holy Spirit on the day of Pentecost (6). The author makes much of the deficiencies of faith and failings of the apostles and others who had been baptized and then come to a more accurate faith or repentance.

Rebaptism emphasizes the difference between the baptism of water and the baptism of the Holy Spirit (he means by this the work of the Spirit associated with baptism, not the miraculous outpourings described in the Acts of the Apostles — see *Rebaptism* 2; 4). The bath is only the exterior beginning. The baptism of water "is of less account provided that afterwards a sincere faith in the truth is evident in the baptism of the Spirit, which undoubtedly is of greater account" (6; also 2). Those who received baptism while holding heretical ideas of God or Christ will be condemned to eternal punishment, "because they did not believe in him although they were washed in his name" (13). Ideally the bath and the Holy Spirit were together, but not necessarily so. In defense of accepting baptism by heretics, the author makes *ad hominem* arguments: if a person is baptized by a bishop in the church but dies before the imposition of hands, "would you not judge him to have received salvation?" (4). And he asks, What about those baptized by bishops of bad character who may later be deprived of office or even of communion? Or by those bishops of unsound opinions or who are ignorant? Ignorantly or inadvertently asking or answering with the wrong words in the baptismal interrogations does not greatly injure the true faith (10). Then he makes the distinction between giving the water and giving the Spirit:

> As our salvation is founded in the baptism of the Spirit, which for the most part is associated with the baptism of water, . . . let it be conferred in its integrity and with solemnity. . . . Or, if by the necessity of the case it [baptism] should be ad-

---

27. So Mattei, "'Extra ecclesiam . . . ,'" p. 301.
28. That the Holy Spirit was not given in heretical baptism would also have been Stephen's view, according to Cyprian's argument in *Letters* 73 (72).6.2 and especially 74 (73).5.4.

ministered by lower clergy, let us wait for the result, that it [the Holy Spirit] may either be supplied by us [bishops], or reserved to be supplied by the Lord. If, however, it should have been administered by strangers, let this matter be amended as it can and as it allows. Because outside the church there is no Holy Spirit, sound faith moreover cannot exist, not alone among heretics, but even among those who are established in schism. And for that reason, they who repent and are amended by the doctrine of the truth, and by their own faith, which subsequently has been improved by the purification of their heart, ought to be aided only by spiritual baptism, that is, by the imposition of the bishop's hands and by the ministration of the Holy Spirit. Moreover, the perfect seal of faith has been rightly accustomed to be given in this manner and on this principle in the church. (10)

The imposition of hands on those formerly baptized in a group outside the communion of the church thus served both to complete their baptism and to reconcile them to the church.

The real basis of human salvation according to *Rebaptism* is faith in the heart and the sanctifying work of the Holy Spirit. The hearts of the household of Cornelius in Acts 10 were purified in virtue of their faith and were baptized by the Holy Spirit, receiving forgiveness of sins, and subsequently were baptized so as to receive the invocation of the name of Christ (5). Calling attention to this reversal of the usual sequence taught in the early church concerning the order of salvation was apparently prompted by the polemical situation. The author says elsewhere: "Hearts are purified by faith, but souls are washed by the Spirit; bodies are washed by water" (18).[29] The salvation of the confessor who becomes a martyr without having received baptism in water shows the effectiveness of faith and the name of Christ (11).[30] Yet, it is explained that martyrdom was not a "second baptism" as if there were "two baptisms" but was "a baptism of another kind" that effected the "same salvation," so there are "different kinds of one and the same baptism" (14). Thus "spiritual baptism" is threefold: the Spirit may be conferred by water in a proper baptism, by the blood of one's martyrdom, or by the Spirit himself directly (15).

Cyprian

Cyprian's general teaching on baptism has been covered in chapter 22. In this section we consider his arguments made in the context of the controversy over what those who disagreed with him called rebaptism. Cyprian responded to some practical arguments raised by those whose practice differed from his. They asked if the catechu-

---

29. Burkhard Neunheuser, *Baptism and Confirmation* (New York: Herder & Herder, 1964), p. 105, incorrectly finds in the "hearts purified by faith" a reference to a baptism of desire.

30. Notable are the use in the passage of "one who hears the word" for a catechumen and the pairing of "the hearer of the word" for the catechumen and "believer" for the one baptized. This latter reflects the normal usage that "believer" meant one baptized.

men put to death for confession of the name lost hope of salvation because of not yet having been baptized. Their point would have been that if Cyprian allows the salvation of some without baptism in the church, then he has no argument against allowing the admission to the church of those who indeed have been baptized even if in a heretical group. Cyprian's reply is that the martyred catechumen confessed a true faith, unlike the heretic, and indeed had a baptism, the glorious baptism of blood (*Letters* 73 [72].22.2).[31]

Another practical consideration concerned those who in the past had been received into the church without another baptism and had died in the meantime. Cyprian replied that the Lord in his mercy has power to pardon those who in innocence had been admitted to the church, but that did not mean that because error had been committed previously, one should go on committing error (*Letters* 73 [72].23.1). Those who had been baptized in the church, then fell away, and returned to the church were in a different situation; they were to be reconciled in the usual way of reconciling penitents by the laying on of hands (*Letters* 71 [70].2.1-2; 74 [73].12).

Some argued that the requirement of baptism (again) would discourage potential converts from heresies. Cyprian's response was that his experience was the opposite: when these persons were convinced about baptism in the true church, they eagerly accepted it (*Letters* 73 [72].24.1-3). There should be no concern that it was unlawful to baptize those already baptized among "God's enemies," for those who had received John's baptism (Acts 19:1-7) had submitted to the Lord's baptism (*Letters* 73 [72].25.1).

We may now highlight his main theological arguments against the acceptance of baptisms performed by heretics and schismatics. They may be found in the first half of his *Letter* 69 (75), to Magnus, who inquired if those who came to the church from the followers of Novatian should be treated in the same way as heretics and given baptism.[32] Cyprian says Novatianists should be treated in the same way as heretics; since they have withdrawn from the church, they are outside the church and must be baptized with "the one, true, and lawful baptism, that is to say, that of the church" (*Letters* 69 [75].1.1-3).[33]

Cyprian's arguments derive from the relation baptism has to his doctrines of the church, ministry, and the Holy Spirit. Fundamental is his doctrine of the unity of the church, whose ministers bestow baptism and related rites and within which is to be found the Holy Spirit. Drawing on themes in his treatise *Unity of the Church*, Cyprian often affirms the oneness of the church. One such statement, as part of the argument that the one baptism is only in the holy church, combines these themes: "There is but one baptism, and one Holy Spirit, and one Church founded by Christ

---

31. Cyprian denied that martyrdom was effective for a heretic's salvation — *Letters* 73 (72).21.1-2 (see chap. 22).

32. Clarke, *The Letters of Cyprian*, Vol. 47, pp. 173-174, considers it to be the first of Cyprian's letters dealing with the question of "rebaptism" and to belong to the early stage of discussion; Sebastian, ". . . baptisma unum . . . ," pp. 73-85, puts it in the middle of the controversy.

33. The same language is used in *Letters* 73 (72).21.3, quoted toward the end of this section.

our Lord upon Peter to be the source and ground of its oneness" (*Letters* 70 [69].3.1). In *Letter* 69 (75) the theme of the one church is the premise of the argument, "If there is only the one church" (69 [75].2.3), and is often repeated.[34] This unity of the church is intimately related to Cyprian's claim that "outside the church there is no salvation" (*Letters* 73 [72].21.2).[35] To the same effect is the assertion, "If one is to have God for Father, he must first have the church for mother" (*Letters* 74 [73].7.2).[36]

In addressing the question of heretical baptism, Cyprian asserts that this one church possesses and administers the one baptism. Valid and lawful baptism is only in the church. Early in *Letter* 69 (75) Cyprian identifies the church as "the enclosed garden," "the sealed fountain, a well of living water" of Song of Songs 4:12, 15. Only those who are inside the garden are allowed to drink of the fountain (69 [75].2.1).[37] He continues with the illustration of the ark of Noah (1 Pet. 3:20-21): only those in the ark were saved, and "to the church alone has the power to baptize been granted" (69 [75].2.2).[38] The church is one and cannot be both "inside and outside": "It follows, therefore, that . . . the church alone possesses the life-giving water and she alone has the power to baptize and cleanse" (69 [75].3.1). The "graces of the church's one and only baptism" are available only in the unity of the church and not in a division such as Novatian's (69 [75].5.2). The Novatianists have a different church, so when they ask the candidate for baptism, "Do you believe in the forgiveness of sins and life everlasting through the holy church?" they are acting fraudulently, for they are not that church (*Letters* 69 [75].7.2). Correct belief is necessary as well as the correct form in administering baptism, for false belief cannot receive the true baptism (*Letters* 73 [72].5.3).[39] The one

---

34. *Letters* 69 (75).4.2 ("one house only," i.e., the church); 5.1 (the one flock, whose oneness is related to the oneness of the Lord and the Father); cf. 73 (72).2.2, "We in fact hold in *our* possession the one church in all its entirety."

35. Cf. *Letters* 71 (70).3.2, "Forgiveness of sins can be granted only in the church"; 73 (72).24.3, "There can be no baptism outside the church nor can there be forgiveness of sins granted outside." Maurice Bévenot, "'Salus extra ecclesiam non est' (St. Cyprian)," in H. J. Auf der Maur et al., eds., *Fides Sacramenti, Sacramentum Fidei* (Assen: Van Gorcum, 1981), pp. 97-105, cites instances where Cyprian was not such a hardliner as the dictum might suggest. *Salus* for him was the condition of being a good Christian, enjoying the blessings made available by God through the church. Outside the church one is cut off from the helps without which one will not get to heaven — baptism, eucharist, preaching, exhortation, and the help of the community.

36. Similarly, "One can no longer have God for his Father who has not the church for his mother" — *Unity of the Church* 6.

37. Note the comparison of the church to paradise, in which are enclosed the fruit-bearing trees that the church waters by means of the four rivers (the four Gospels); outside paradise (the church) one is dry and parched — *Letters* 73 (72).10.3.

38. The same argument from the ark is used in *Letters* 74 (73).11.3 ("We cannot be saved except through the one and only baptism of this one church").

39. Cf. *Letters* 73 (72).4.2 — "If we and heretics have one and the same faith, then we can also have one and the same grace. If they confess the same Father with us, the same Son, the same Holy Spirit, and the same church — whether they be Patripassians, Anthropians, Valentinians, Apelletians, Ophites, Marcionites . . . — then they may also have the one baptism, seeing that they have the one faith as well."

baptism is to be found only within the one church (*Letters* 73 [72].13.3).⁴⁰ "No one can be baptized outside and away from the church," for the one baptism has been appointed to the holy church (*Letters* 70 [69].1.2), and the church and baptism cannot be separated from each other (*Letters* 73 [72].25.2).⁴¹

The church acted through its ministers, primarily the bishop, in the administration of baptism. Here Cyprian used language that others later found problematic in his position. He speaks as if the administrator of baptism actually gives the gifts associated with baptism. Part of his basic argument against accepting heretical baptism was this:

> They cannot possibly baptize who do not possess the Holy Spirit.
>
> Now in baptism we are each forgiven our sins; and the Lord asserts clearly in his gospel [John 20:21-23] that sins can be forgiven only through those who possess the Holy Spirit. (*Letters* 69 [75].10.2-11.1)

In the letter of the thirty-two bishops, headed by Cyprian, the question is asked, Can a person "give what he does not have himself?" (*Letters* 70 [69].2.3).⁴²

> How can a man possibly cleanse and sanctify water when he is himself unclean and when the Holy Spirit is not within him? . . . And how can a man who administers baptism possibly grant forgiveness of sins to another when he is himself unable to put aside his own sins, being outside the church?" (*Letters* 70 [69].1.3).

The dead cannot give life (*Letters* 71 [70].1.3).

> Only those leaders who are set in authority within the church and have been established in accordance with the law of the gospel and the institution of the Lord have the lawful power to baptize and to grant forgiveness of sins. (*Letters* 73 [72].7.2)

The church generally in the third century and later (see Augustine on the Donatists — chap. 52) came to reject the implications of Cyprian's idea that the administrator actually gave forgiveness and the Holy Spirit. Cyprian's fundamental thought, however, was that these gifts are found in the church and the minister is to be understood as the agent of the church. His statements about ministers not being able to give what they do not have are shorthand for this central claim.⁴³

---

40. So also *Letters* 73 (72).8.2 (baptism lawful for the church alone); and 10.1 (baptism given to the one church and her alone); 72 (71).1.1 (must be baptized in the church); 71 (70).2.3 (one water that can make sheep and it is found in the oneness of the holy church — cf. the "one flock" of 69 [75].5.1).

41. "Baptism can be separated neither from the church nor from the Holy Spirit" — *Letters* 74 (73).4.2.

42. On the council of these bishops in 255 reported in this letter see Joseph A Fischer, "Das Konzil zu Karthago im Jahr 255," *Annuarium historiae conciliorum* 14 (1982): 227-240.

43. Eligius Dekkers, "'Symbolo Baptizare,'" in H. J. Auf der Maur et al., eds., *Fides Sacramenti, Sacramentum Fidei* (Assen: Van Gorcum, 1981), pp. 107-112, affirms that Cyprian's opposition to hereti-

Apparently common ground between Cyprian and his opponents in the rebaptism controversy was the belief that the Holy Spirit was only in the church, for the opponents of baptizing converted heretics laid hands on these in order to impart the Spirit. Hence, the Holy Spirit figures prominently in Cyprian's argument. He poses a dilemma to his adversaries: If those "baptized" among those outside the church possess the Spirit, why are hands laid on them for receiving the Spirit when they come over to the church? If the heretic or schismatic does not have the Holy Spirit, then that person does not have forgiveness of sins either (*Letters* 69 [75].11.3). The gifts of the Spirit belong together and cannot be separated: "The Holy Spirit is not given by measure but is poured out completely on the believer" (*Letters* 69 [75].14.1). Cyprian's episcopal colleagues agreed:

> If a man has power to baptize, he also has the power to confer the Holy Spirit; conversely, if he cannot confer the Holy Spirit (being outside the church and therefore not with the Holy Spirit), neither can he baptize. (*Letters* 70 [69].3.1)

Cyprian's position in short was "Either he can obtain both [forgiveness and the Holy Spirit] through his faith, or being outside, he receives neither" (*Letters* 73 [72].6.2).

The Spirit and the water belong together in baptism. The second birth is a "spiritual birth . . . through the waters of regeneration." So Cyprian's adversaries, he asserts, are absurd to argue that one can be born spiritually among heretics while denying that the Spirit is with them.

> Water by itself cannot cleanse sins and sanctify man unless it possesses the Holy Spirit as well. Thus either they have to allow that the Spirit is also to be found where they argue there is baptism, or there is no baptism where there is no Spirit, for there cannot be baptism without the Spirit. (*Letters* 74 [73].5.4)

Baptism, Cyprian concludes, cannot be held in common between heretics and the church, for "we have in common with them neither God the Father nor Christ the Son nor the Holy Spirit nor faith nor church itself." Therefore, when they come from heresy to the church they must be baptized "in the one, genuine, and lawful baptism of the holy church, they must be born of both" water and the Spirit [John 3:5] (*Letters* 73.21.3).

Judgements of the Eighty-seven Bishops

The judgments concerning the baptism of heretics by the bishops who participated in a council at Carthage in 256 under the leadership of Cyprian have been preserved. We

---

cal baptism was based on the baptismal rite itself; even if heretics pronounced the same words, they did not have the same sense as in the church's teaching (see above and chap. 22). Although Cyprian seems to say that the administrator gives forgiveness and the Holy Spirit, this basic connection between baptism and the faith confessed means that it is anachronistic to attribute to Cyprian the idea of *opus operantis*.

select some of their statements that are representative of baptismal theology in North Africa and how it was applied to the question of heretical baptism.[44] Many of the statements closely parallel Cyprian's teachings and arguments but are not slavishly dependent on him. The most frequent aspect of baptism that is mentioned is its conferral of the forgiveness of sins. For instance, Nicomedes said, "Heretics coming to the church should be baptized, for the reason that among sinners without [the church] they can obtain no remission of sins" (#9).[45] If they had forgiveness, there would be no reason for heretics to come to the church.[46] Remission of sins and divine grace are mentioned together by Secundianus of Thambei (#80), and Theogenes (#14) speaks of the "sacrament of heavenly grace."[47] Saturninus makes the point that "If Antichrist can give to any one the grace of Christ, heretics also are able to baptize" (#64). "All heretics who come to the bosom of mother church should be baptized that . . . [they may be] purged by the sanctification of the laver" (#26 [Felix of Uthina]).

Other theological interpretations of baptism include the theme of new birth: "[Heretics] ought, when they come to the church our mother, truly to be born again and to be baptized" (#10 [Munnulus]). Vincentius speaks of the "regeneration of baptism" (#37 [Vincentius]). Heretics are spiritually "dead," so they "must be baptized and made alive" (#12 [Felix of Bagai]). Having said that "Since there cannot be two baptisms, he who yields baptism to the heretics takes it away from himself," Cassius describes baptism in the church as being "washed by the sacred and divine washing, and illuminated by the light of life" (#22 [Cassius]). Novatus says that those who "have been falsely baptized ought to be baptized in the everlasting fountain" (#4 [Novatus]).

Understandably, the Holy Spirit figures in the reasoning. In one of the longest interventions at the council, Nemesianus, in speaking of "being born again in the catholic church," affirms, "Neither can the Spirit operate without the water, nor the water without the Spirit," for the new birth requires "both sacraments [signs, mysteries]" (#5). He concludes that unless heretics receive "saving baptism" in the one catholic church, "they cannot be saved." Successus makes the Cyprianic argument, "If [heretics] can baptize, they can also bestow the Holy Spirit. But if they cannot give the Holy Spirit, because they have not the Holy Spirit, neither can they spiritually baptize" (#16).

The bishops at the council of Carthage in 256 refer to some items of the baptismal ritual: exorcism (#8 [Crescens];[48] #37 — imposition of hands in exorcism [Vin-

---

44. The translations are by Ernest Wallis in A. C. Coxe, ed., *Ante-Nicene Fathers*, Vol. 5 (repr. Peabody: Hendrickson, 1994), pp. 565-572. Introduction to the record of the bishops' judgments in Sebastian, "baptisma unum . . . ," pp. 120-131.

45. Also # 15 (Dativius); #25 (Victoricus); #40 (Victor of God); #41 (Aurelius); #48 (Pomponius); #53 (Marcellus); #80 (Secundianus of Thambei).

46. # 27 (Quietus); #39 (Sattius).

47. Cf. "The grace of saving baptism" (#11 [Secundinus of Cedias]).

48. Also # 1 (Caecilius of Bilta), # 31 (Lucius of Thebeste). Leaving aside the *Apostolic Tradition*, these are the first express mention of baptismal exorcism in the western church — Franz Josef Dölger, *Der Exorzismus in altchristlichen Taufritual* (Paderborn: Ferdinand Schöningh, 1909), pp. 12-13.

centius]), the sanctification of the water (#18 — "water sanctified in the church by the prayer of the priest washes away sins" [Sedatus]), "sacramental interrogation" (#1 [Caecilius]), likely the same as baptism in the Trinity (#10 [Munnulus]), giving the Holy Spirit by the imposition of hands (#24 [Secundinus of Carpi]).[49] The "one baptism in the catholic church" is a dipping (#72 [Peter of Hippo Diarrhytus]).

There are many statements about the faith to accompany baptism. For example, Clarus spoke of "baptizing the faith of believers" (#79). The theme of oneness is summarized by Felix of Marazana, "There is one faith, one baptism, but of the catholic church, which alone has the right to baptize" (#46).[50] The one baptism is that of the holy church (#14 [Theogenes of Hippo Regius]).[51] The Cyprianic theme of preferring reason and truth to custom is voiced by Libosus ("The Lord says, 'I am truth,' not 'I am the custom'" — #30) and Felix of Bussacene ("let no one prefer custom to reason and truth" — #63). All of the arguments are to make the point that heretics are to receive baptism in the catholic church, and this is not a rebaptism: "Certain persons without reason impugn the truth by false and envious words, in saying that we rebaptize, when the church does not rebaptize heretics, but baptizes them" (#35 [Adelphinus]).

Firmilian

Firmilian, distinguished bishop of Caesarea in Cappadocia, wrote to Cyprian in the autumn of 256. In this letter, in response to a letter from Cyprian, he covers much the same ground as the sources cited above, but he is useful as giving a third party perspective from the Greek East on the controversy between Stephen and Cyprian. Firmilian supported Cyprian's position, so his letter is appropriately preserved (in a Latin translation) in the corpus of Cyprian's *Letters* (75 [74]), and is indeed more negative about Stephen than what we find in Cyprian.[52]

Firmilian reports that for Stephen an important consideration was his position as bishop of Rome and successor of Peter: "He [Stephen] finds the location of his bishopric such a source of pride, who keeps insisting that he occupies the succession to Peter" (17.1); "Stephen vaunts that he has succeeded to the occupancy of the chair of Peter" (17.2).[53] Firmilian considered Stephen's defense of heretical baptism a misuse of his authority. Stephen had broken peace with Cyprian (6.2); his threat to excommunicate "everyone else" succeeded in excommunicating himself alone from everyone else (24.2).

---

49. The separation of the receiving of the Holy Spirit by the imposition of hands from baptism, according to the position of those who opposed "rebaptism," is rejected by Nemesianus (#5).

50. Nemesianus quotes Eph. 4:4-6 (#5).

51. Many statements relate baptism to the church: e.g., Caecilius, "I know only one baptism in the church, and none out of the church" (#1); Nemesianus, "receive saving baptism in the catholic church" (#5).

52. Clarke, *The Letters of St. Cyprian*, Vol. 47, p. 248.

53. There may be an allusion to such claims in Cyprian, *Letters* 71 (70).3.1, "[Peter] did not assert that he had the rights of seniority [*primatum*]."

Firmilian characterized the view of Stephen and his adherents this way: "Heretical baptism can produce remission of sins and the second birth, even though they admit themselves that heretics do not have the Holy Spirit" (*Letters* 75 [74].8.1). For Firmilian, however, the baptism administered by heretics, is an "unlawful and unholy immersion [*tinctionem*]" (8.2).

He rejected Stephen's claim to be following an apostolic custom in not baptizing converted heretics, because the heresies challenging the church (Marcion, Valentinus, Basilides) arose later than the apostles (5.2). Rome did not always follow ancient custom, having adopted a different practice in dating the Pasch from the Jerusalem church (6.1). Firmilian repeats Cyprian's protest against Stephen's preference for "custom in opposition to truth" (19.1).

Firmilian suggests that the North Africans had rejected error when they discovered truth on this matter but claims that in his region the custom had always been the true practice of not acknowledging heretical baptisms (19.3). He refers to a council at Iconium that considered whether the baptisms by Cataphrygians (Montanists) fell in the category of heretical baptisms and decided that they did (7.4; 19.4). He worded his argument against Montanist baptisms as a variation of Cyprian's argument against Marcion's baptism: the Cataphrygians did not have the Holy Spirit (i.e., their view of the working of the Spirit was different from that of catholics), and one who does not have the Spirit cannot have the Father and the Son either (7.3).

Stephen's claim that "the name of Christ has great efficacy" and so obviates the necessity of another baptism is countered by the conclusion that such a position means that all other acts of heretics were also effective.[54] The proper view, according to Firmilian, is that the name is effective only in the church (18.1-2). There is clarification that the appeal to the power of Christ's name was not an alternative baptismal formula in Firmilian's explicit statement:

> They consider there is no need to inquire who it is who has administered baptism, arguing that the person baptized can have obtained grace merely by the invocation of the Trinity, of the names of the Father and of the Son and of the Holy Spirit. (9.1)

To this contention Firmilian replies that the person invoking the Trinity must himself have the Holy Spirit and the baptism be performed with the Spirit (the sanctification of the baptismal waters). This was a more carefully worded statement than Cyprian's claims about the minister being able to give only what he possessed.

Advocates of accepting baptism by heretics contended that one might obtain the grace of baptism outside the church "by virtue of personal faith and disposition" (9.2).[55] Firmilian replies that among heretics there is a corrupt disposition and a false faith. This leads him to reflect on baptisms performed in the correct manner

---

54. Is this an independent confirmation that Stephen himself made the argument, or is this merely a deduction from Cyprian's general response to the position of his opponents?

55. This argument is referred to in *Letters* 73 (72).4.1-2.

but (on his view) under demonic inspiration. This occurs in a new piece of information he provides: an account of a woman who presented herself as a prophetess but who he claimed was possessed by demons. She performed liturgical functions in celebrating the eucharist and performing baptisms. In this account Firmilian refers to her "adopting the customary and legitimate wording of the baptismal interrogation" (10.2-5). Would Stephen extend his approval even to this baptism? he asks. His argument is that the correct Trinitarian creedal formula *(symbolum trinitatis)* and legitimate baptismal interrogation (11.1) are not enough for a valid baptism.

One of Firmilian's counterarguments is to ask those who defend heretical baptism whether it is of the flesh or of the spirit. "If they say the flesh [implied by those who accepted the baptism but imparted the Holy Spirit to those received into the church], then their baptism is no different from that of the Jews," comparable to an ordinary bath. "But if they say the spirit, then we must ask how it is possible for them to have spiritual baptism when they do not have the Holy Spirit" (13.1). Here we recognize Cyprian's argument, which did not acknowledge that there might be two workings of the Spirit in connection with baptism — one in cleansing from sin and another as an abiding gift.

Similarly, Firmilian contended that whoever puts on Christ (Gal. 3:27) could have received the Holy Spirit as well, unless one "separates the Spirit from Christ, so that Christ may indeed be with heretics but not the Holy Spirit" (12.1).

In addition to the above-mentioned points, other aspects of Firmilian's understanding of baptism emerge from his letter. Baptism is "saving laver" (4), granting forgiveness of sins (16). It effects regeneration: "The second birth, which is baptism, gives birth to sons of God" (14.1). What baptism does is stated in Firmilian's description of what Stephen conceded baptism among heretics did: it confers grace, washes away the filth of the old person, pardons ancient and deadly sins (past sins or Adam's sin?), generates sons of God, and revivifies for eternal life (17.2).

In view of these benefits of baptism, Firmilian found it important to affirm with Cyprian that the power to baptize belongs to the one church alone (6.2). The "one, true baptism of the catholic church" gives "the rebirth of the life-giving waters" (22.1.).[56] The presbyters of the church "possess the power of baptizing, of imposition of hands, and of ordaining" (7). Those who are baptized make up the membership of the church (17.2). Firmilian adopts the same images for the church as Cyprian had employed: "an enclosed garden, a sealed fountain, a paradise of fruit-laden trees," "the ark of Noah," outside of which all perish (15.1-2).

Dionysius of Alexandria

Dionysius, bishop of Alexandria (247/248-264/265), although he held to the necessity of baptizing heretics who came over to the church, tried to mediate in the contro-

---

56. Cf. the "one and only, the saving waters of the church" (15.2).

versy. He upheld Cyprian's view that each bishop must decide for himself and maintain unity with those of a different view against Stephen's threats of excommunication of those who differed from him.[57] We know his stance mainly from excerpts of his writings preserved by Eusebius of Caesarea's *Church History*, in which reference is made to six letters by Dionysius on the subject of rebaptism and from which he gives brief quotations.

In a letter to Sixtus (Xystus) II, successor of Stephen as bishop of Rome, Dionysius refers to a letter by Stephen that refused communion with churches that rebaptized (ἀναβαπτίζουσιν) heretics. Dionysius countered by appeal to synods of bishops in the East[58] that decreed for those coming over from heresies that they should be first instructed and then "washed [ἀπολούεσθαι] and thoroughly cleansed from the filth of the old and impure leaven" (*Church History* 7.5.5).

Dionysius wrote to an otherwise unknown Roman presbyter named Philemon a letter in which he affirmed that the practice of the North African bishops was not an innovation, for it had been practiced for a long time by the large churches known to him (*Church History* 7.7.5). He stated that the policy of rebaptism did not apply to those who had once received the church's baptism. He had learned from his predecessor Heraclas that those who had received holy baptism, went over to a heretical group, and then returned to the church he did not require to receive a "second baptism [ἑτέρου βαπτίσματος]" (7.7.5).

Dionysius did not accept the position of Novatian that refused reconciliation to those guilty of serious sins. In a letter to his namesake, Dionysius, in Rome he listed Novatian's faults as including making "the holy washing [τὸ λουτρὸν τὸ ἅγιον] ineffectual and overturning the faith and confession that precede it" (7.8). I think in view of the context that this is not a reference to Novatian's rebaptizing those who came to him from the catholic church but either to his not considering (from Dionysius's point of view) baptism as covering postbaptismal sins or (more likely) his not confessing the power of the church to forgive sins (i.e., the clause in the third article "I believe . . . in the forgiveness of sins"). We note again the importance placed on a confession of faith associated with baptism.

The second of Dionysius's three letters to Sixtus II, however, presented a variation on this matter, for a question of conscience had been presented to him that he sought advice about. A person who had long been accepted as a believer was present and heard the questions and answers of those being baptized.[59] He came in tears to Dionysius, acknowledging that his baptism among heretics had nothing in common

---

57. L. Edward Phillips, "The Proof Is in the Eating: Dionysius of Alexandria and the Rebaptism Controversy," in Maxwell E. Johnson and L. Edward Phillips, eds., *Studia Liturgica Diversa: Essays in Honor of Paul F. Bradshaw* (Portland: Pastoral Press, 2004), 53-63, stresses Dionysius's concern for unity.

58. He specifies synods in Iconium (see on Firmilian above), Synnada, and many others in Eusebius, *Church History* 7.7.5.

59. Eusebius, *Church History* 7.9.2. Hence the preceding passage (7.8) had in view a confession made in response to questions.

with this baptism and asking to receive this "purest cleansing, reception, and grace." Dionysius did not dare to do this to one who had been long in communion, had heard the thanksgivings (eucharist), and said the Amen, so he encouraged the person to continue to participate in the body and blood with firm faith and good hope. But this person was still reluctant to approach the table of the Lord (*Church History* 7.9.1-5).[60] We do not know what advice Sixtus II gave, but presumably, agreeing with Stephen, he would have endorsed Dionysius's policy, only with the reservation that hands should be imposed for reception of the Holy Spirit in reconciliation to the church. Dionysius's treatment of the case showed his policy was more moderate than what could have been expected from Cyprian (and see below for another instance where his policy more accorded with that of Stephen).

An Armenian translation of a work by Timothy Aelurus of Alexandria (c. 460 and translated between 506 and 544) quotes from three of Dionysius's letters.[61] A letter to Stephen of Rome asks the question that challenged Stephen's policy, How can the orthodox and heretics have in common any custom?[62] Dionysius's first letter to Sixtus appears more agreeable to the Roman practice. Sixtus had said to receive by the laying on of hands those who made profession in baptism of God Almighty, Christ, and the Holy Spirit; but those over whom there had not been invoked the name either of Father, Son, or Holy Spirit, these must be baptized but not rebaptized. Dionysius accepted this as sure and immovable teaching and tradition, citing Matthew 28:19.[63] His third letter to Sixtus specifies the heresies to which no concession was to be made — those who condemned the one God, Creator, and made him a lesser God [Gnostics] and those who did not believe that the Savior is God or that there was a real incarnation [Adoptionists and Docetists].[64]

Later Developments

The deaths of Stephen and Cyprian, the persecution under Valerian, and other concerns removed the rebaptism controversy from prominence (at least as far as surviving records go). The policy advocated by Stephen seems to have steadily gained ground in the subsequent decades, but not in its sweeping generalization. The issues were raised again, however, in the West in the fourth century by the Donatist movement in North Africa, to be considered later. At the beginning of that controversy the

---

60. The mention of questions and answers at baptism (*Church History* 7.9.2) is matched by the reference above (7.8) to faith and confession before baptism. This latter reference may have been to an adhesion to Christ following the renunciation, or both a declaratory creed and the baptismal questions and answers may have been employed at Alexandria.

61. F. C. Conybeare, "Newly Discovered Letters of Dionysius of Alexandria to the Popes Stephen and Xystus," *English Historical Review* 25 (1910): 111-114, with an English translation.

62. Conybeare, "Newly Discovered Letters," pp. 112-113.

63. Conybeare, "Newly Discovered Letters," p. 113.

64. Conybeare, "Newly Discovered Letters," p. 114.

Council of Arles (can. 9 [8]) decreed in regard to the practice of those in Africa (Donatists) who rebaptized *(rebaptizent)* that a heretic coming to the church should be questioned concerning the creed, and if he was baptized in the Father, Son, and Holy Spirit, hands were to be imposed and no more required, but if he did not give the Trinity as his faith, he was to be baptized *(baptizetur)*. That clarification in Stephen's position came to prevail in churches of the West and East.

The Council of Nicaea (325) in its canon 19 ruled in regard to the followers of Paul of Samosata that when they came to the catholic church they must be rebaptized (ἀναβαπτίζεσθαι). Athanasius later explained that, although the the disciples of the Samosatene used the proper formula of "Father, Son, and Holy Spirit," they used these names in a heretical sense and therefore their baptism was unprofitable.[65]

For the outcome of the controversy in the East, we may refer to the canonical legislation of Basil of Caesarea in Cappadocia, written about 374.[66] He reported with regard to the followers of Novatian that "It is right to follow the custom obtaining in each region," because different opinions were held concerning their baptism. The case of the Montanists, however, was different, for their baptism "seems to me to have no authority." He was astonished that Dionysius of Alexandria did not agree, apparently accepting Montanist baptism as orthodox. Basil continued, "The old authorities decided to accept that baptism which does not err from the faith." Making the distinction between heretics in regard to the faith and schismatics over ecclesiastical differences, Basil reported that the ancient authorities rejected the baptism of heretics altogether but admitted the baptism of schismatics on the ground that they still belonged to the church. Contrary to Dionysius's attitude, Basil declared the Montanists plainly heretical. He referred to the arguments of Cyprian and Firmilian in rejecting the baptism of the Novatianists, but he agreed to follow those in Asia who accepted their baptism.

---

65. Athanasius, *Discourses against the Arians* 2.18.43.
66. The remainder of the paragraph is taken from Basil, *Letters* 188 (First Canonical Letter), canon 1.

25. Origen

There is no single major discussion of baptism in Origen, but his voluminous writings contain abundant references to the subject.[1] Origen sets the early Christian theology of baptism in his own distinctive theological system, and he makes occasional reference to the baptismal liturgy. Origen placed baptism, "like the other sacraments, in a series of symbolisms, corresponding to the triple distinction of the Old Testament as shadow, the temporal Gospel as image, and the eternal Gospel as reality."[2] With reference to Origen's language of baptism itself, the baptism of John belonged with the Old Testament symbols as a shadow, baptism in the church is the image, and the eschatological baptism of fire and the final conforming to the resurrection of Christ are mystery.[3] Putting these distinctions together, we may speak of a fourfold use of baptismal language by Origen: the shadows or types in the Old Testament (including the baptism of John), Christian baptism in water, the spiritual baptism by the Holy Spirit, and the eschatological

---

1. This chapter is based on my "Baptism according to Origen," *Evangelical Quarterly* 78 (2006): 117-135. See also Hans Jörg Auf der Maur and Joop Waldram, "*Illuminatio Verbi Divini — Confessio Fidei — Gratia Baptismi:* Wort, Glaube und Sakrament in Katechumenat und Taufliturgie bei Origenes," in H. J. Auf der Maur et al., eds., *Fides Sacramenti Sacramentum Fidei* (Assen: Van Gorcum, 1981), pp. 41-95, rich in bibliographical references and references in Origen; Cécile Blanc, "Le baptême d'après Origène," *Studia Patristica* 11 (1972): 113-124; Henri Crouzel, "Origène et la structure du sacrement," *Bulletin de littérature ecclésiastique* 63 (1962): 81-104 (83-92 on baptism); Victor Saxer, *Les rites de l'initiation chrétienne du IIe au VIe siècle: Esquisse historique et signification d'après leur principaux témoins* (Spoleto: Centro italiano di studi sull'alto medioevo, 1988), pp. 145-194.

2. Henri Crouzel, *Origen* (San Francisco: Harper & Row, 1989), p. 223.

3. Crouzel, *Origen,* p. 225; Jean Daniélou, *Origène* (Paris: LaTable Ronde, 1948), pp. 71-72, for the purely figurative baptisms of the Old Testament and John, Christian baptism as the reality signified by the Old Testament figures and itself a figure of the reality to come, and baptism with fire by which Christians are purified before they enter glory. Crouzel, "Origène et la Structure," pp. 82-83, points out that μυστήριον for Origen refers to the spiritual, celestial, eschatological reality, and σύμβολον refers to the sensible image of that reality, a distinction not observed in Rufinus's Latin translation.

baptism of fire. Origen added another baptism in the experience of some Christians, the blood of martyrdom.

Origen could be quite flexible in his interpretations, at one time giving one explanation and at another time a different one. He may have been considering in his mind at various times different possible meanings, or given his advocacy of multiple meanings of Scripture, he may have considered all the possibilities as correct (provided, of course, that they contributed to edification and spiritual progress). I would, therefore, be cautious about committing too rigidly to any scheme of synthesizing his comments on baptism, but Crouzel's and Daniélou's classifications may provide a framework for looking at Origen's texts. With this introductory overview we will note the Old Testament passages in which he found baptismal teaching, look at the relation of water and Spirit baptism through the contrast of John's and Jesus' baptisms, adding a consideration of the eschatological baptism of fire, move to descriptions of the meaning of baptism, with a separate section on martyrdom as a baptism of blood, and conclude with his statements relative to the catechumenate and the ritual of baptism. We begin with the use of Old Testament passages to teach lessons about Christian baptism.

Old Testament Foreshadowings of Baptism

The *Commentary on John* devotes a section to the Old Testament shadows (or types), which in Origen's allegorical exegesis become identified with Christian baptism (6.43 [26].226–48 [29].249). Origen begins the discussion by invoking 1 Corinthians 10:1-4 about crossing the Red Sea as justification for a spiritual interpretation of Old Testament references to water, especially the Jordan River (6.43 [26].227).

Origen's fullest treatment of Israel's crossing the Red Sea occurs in the *Homilies on Exodus*.[4] Once more he quotes 1 Corintians 10:1-4 as the basis for his interpretation. "What the Jews supposed to be a crossing of the sea, Paul calls a baptism; what they supposed to be a cloud, Paul asserts is the Holy Spirit" (5.1).[5] This conjunction of water and Holy Spirit, Origen says, Paul wanted to be understood in a similar manner to what the Lord taught in John 3:5, which he also quotes. The understanding of John 3:5 as the literal water of baptism was already standard by Origen's time, but in view of his usual spiritualizing exegesis is to be noted. In the detailed treatment of the narrative, Origen finds in the journey of "three days" into the wilderness (Exod. 5:3) a reference to the death, burial, and resurrection of Jesus and connects

---

4. Jean Daniélou, *From Shadows to Reality: Studies in the Typology of the Fathers* (London: Burns & Oates, 1960), pp. 175-201, on "The Departure from Egypt and Christian Initiation" in early Christian literature (pp. 185-187 on Origen's use of the motif).

5. Translation by Ronald E. Heine, *Origen: Homilies on Genesis and Exodus,* Fathers of the Church 71 (Washington: Catholic University of America Press, 1982), p. 276. Elsewhere Origen identifies the Sea as baptism, the cloud as the Holy Spirit, the manna as the Word of God, the lamb as the Pascha, and the blood as his passion (*Commentary on the Song of Songs* 2.8 on Song of Songs 1:11).

this with baptism by a quotation of Romans 6:3-4 (5.2; see more below on dying and rising with Christ and on liturgy). He further notes that the waters which the Israelites feared, when struck with Moses' rod, became protective and not destructive. The crossing of the Red Sea on dry land by Israel is a lesson for Christians: "That you also who are baptized in Christ, in water and the Holy Spirit, might know that the Egyptians [spiritual evils] are following you and wish to recall you to their service" (5.5).[6]

> These attempt to follow, but you descend into the water and come out unimpaired, the filth of sins having been washed away. You ascend "a new man" [Eph. 2:15; 4:24] prepared to "sing a new song" [Isa. 42:10]. But the Egyptians who follow you are drowned in the abyss. (5.5)[7]

The description of descending into the water and ascending is drawn from Christian baptismal practice and not from the narrative, for Israel did not actually enter the water, and would seem to reflect the practice of immersion. Baptism washes away sins so that one becomes a new person, and demonic forces are drowned in the waters (Origen alludes to Luke 8:31).

The baptismal interpretation of the cloud and sea at the exodus, with the quotation of 1 Corinthians 10:1-4, occurs again in the *Homilies on Numbers* 7.2. The passage also refers to the regeneration (Titus 3:5) effected in the water and in the Holy Spirit.

The contemporary application of the exodus occurs elsewhere in Origen:

> Thus it is fitting, after the parting of the Red Sea, that is, after the grace of baptism, for the carnal vices of our old habits to be removed from us by means of our Lord Jesus, so that we can be free from the Egyptian reproaches [Josh. 5.9].[8]

Origen's special interest in the *Commentary on John* is Israel's crossing the Jordan (Joshua 3) as an equivalent to baptism.[9] He paraphrases Paul's words about crossing the Red Sea as applicable to crossing the Jordan: "'I do not want you to be ignorant, brothers, that our fathers all passed through the Jordan, and all were baptized [ἐβαπτίσαντο] into Jesus in the Spirit and in the river'" (6.44 [26].228). This interpretation was facilitated by the equivalence in Greek of the names Jesus and Joshua. "The Jesus who succeeded Moses was a type of Jesus the Christ who succeeded the dispensation through the law with the gospel proclamation" (6.44

---

6. Heine, *Origen: Homilies on Genesis and Exodus*, p. 283.
7. Heine, *Origen: Homilies on Genesis and Exodus*, pp. 283-284.
8. Translation by Barbara J. Bruce, *Origen: Homilies on Joshua*, Fathers of the Church 105 (Washington: Catholic University of America Press, 2002), p. 216.
9. Daniélou, *From Shadows to Reality*, pp. 261-275, on the crossing of the Jordan as a type of baptism (Origen is the principal representative of this interpretation — pp. 262-270); Per Lundberg, *La typologie baptismale dans l'ancienne église* (Uppsala: Lorentz, 1942), pp. 146-166. For the Jordan in Origen's thought, see Kilian McDonnell, *The Baptism of Jesus in the Jordan* (Collegeville: Liturgical, 1996), pp. 203-206.

[26].229). The contrast of the Law and the gospel is indicated by Israel's baptism being in the salty and bitter Red Sea, but the baptism of Jesus is superior, being in a river whose waters were sweet and drinkable (6.44 [26].229-230).

Origen develops the baptismal interpretation of Israel crossing the Jordan especially in his *Homilies on Joshua*. He connected the exodus from Egypt with the crossing of the Jordan by likening the former to entering the catechumenate and the latter to baptism that introduces one into the promised land (4.1). In this passage the Latin translation of Rufinus speaks of the "sacrament *(sacramentum)* of baptism" and the "mystic *(mysticum)* font of baptism." *Sacramentum* and *mysticum* probably represent the Greek word for mystery (μυστήριον) that since Clement of Alexandria was coming into use and became the technical word in the Greek church for what the Latins came to call the sacraments.[10] Baptism is described not only as a mystery but also as holy, bringing "heavenly grace" and the "gift of God" (4.2).

Elsewhere Origen makes a similar interpretation of the exodus from Egypt as entering the catechumenate (without using the word) and crossing the Jordan into the promised land as baptism. He speaks of one converted from an earthly life to the beginning of a spiritual life as departing from Egypt and in the desert being trained in the divine laws and impregnated with the divine oracles. Crossing the Jordan and entering the promised land is "by the grace of baptism" to arrive "at the Gospel precepts" (*Homilies on Numbers* 26.4). This is not the end of the story, for Origen goes on to speak of the soul's journey from this world to another, that is, the bosom of Abraham (Paradise) and the "river which rejoices the city of God" (Ps. 46.4).

Origen's *Homilies on Joshua* also could simply correlate the passing through the Red Sea and the passing through the Jordan as both baptisms (5.1). Those "who come to baptism for salvation and receive the sacraments of the word of God" should not do it "idly or negligently" (5.1).[11] Christians are the army of Christ; here "sacrament" is used of the soldiers' oath, implicitly compared to baptismal vows (see more below), and Origen warns of the battles that await after baptism (5.2). The exaltation of Joshua (Josh. 4:14) is likened to the revelation of Jesus' lofty divinity when one crosses the Jordan (5.3), probably an allusion to the instruction about the nature of Christ given in connection with baptism.[12]

The survey of events associated with the River Jordan in the *Commentary on John* next mentions Elijah and Elisha crossing the Jordan (2 Kings 2:8, 14). Although the crossing was on dry ground, Origen calls this event too, on the basis of 1 Corinthians 10:2, a baptism. "Having been baptized [βαπτισάμενος], Elijah had become better prepared for his assumption" into heaven (6.46 [27].238); and perhaps because Elisha crossed the Jordan twice, he received the gift he desired, a double portion of the spirit of Elijah (6.46 [27].239).

Next, Origen relates the story of Naaman, the Syrian general with leprosy

---

10. See chap. 19, n. 64.
11. Bruce, *Origen: Homiles on Joshua*, p. 59.
12. So Bruce, *Origen: Homilies on Joshua*, p. 62, n. 21.

(2 Kings 5), who was commanded by the prophet Elisha to wash (λοῦσαι) seven times in the Jordan (6.47 [28].242-245). Origen notes that Naaman was reluctant, because "He did not understand that our Jordan washes away the impurity of those with leprosy and heals them." Origen makes more explicit the baptismal interpretation of the event in his *Homilies on Luke*. Giving a spiritual interpretation of leprosy, Origen says:

> Men covered with the filth of leprosy are cleansed in the mystery of baptism by the spiritual Elijah, our Lord and Savior. To you he says, 'Get up and go into the Jordan and wash, and your flesh will be restored to you' [2 Kings 5:10]. . . . When [Naaman] washed, he fulfilled the mystery of baptism, 'and his flesh became like the flesh of a child.' Which child? The one that is born 'in the washing of rebirth' [regeneration — Tit. 3:5] in Christ Jesus. (33.5)[13]

Origen concluded his survey of Old Testament references to the Jordan (and other rivers) with this summary of the benefits of baptism based on these passages:

> Those who come to be washed [λούσασθαι] in the Son put away the reproach of Egypt [Josh. 5:9], become prepared for assumption (2 Kings 2:12), are purified from the foulest leprosy (2 Kings 5:9), receive a double share of grace gifts (2 Kings 2:9), and are made ready for the reception of the Holy Spirit, since the spiritual dove does not fly over any other river. (6.48 [29].250)

Elsewhere Origen repeats other common Old Testament passages used in connection with baptism. We quote below an allusion to Genesis 1:2, a text often invoked for the association of the Spirit and the water in baptism (*Commentary on John* 6.33 [17].169). A common type of baptism was the flood in Noah's day (Genesis 6–9).[14] Origen cites Genesis 6:14 as spoken not only concerning the time of the flood but also "concerning the mystery of baptism. For as the apostle Peter says, just as at that time Noah was saved out of the flood, so also now by means of a similar figure those who believe shall be saved through baptism" (1 Pet. 3:20-21).[15] The passage in 1 Peter assured the baptismal interpretation of the flood in the church. We note again the term "mystery" as applied to baptism. The strong assertion of salvation through baptism is related to Noah's being saved out of the waters of the flood.

Origen could also give a baptismal interpretation to passages that were not a part of the church's usual baptismal typology. Origen understood the command to

---

13. Translation by Joseph T. Lienhard, *Origen: Homilies on Luke, Fragments on Luke*, Fathers of the Church 94 (Washington: Catholic University of America Press, 1996), p. 136.

14. Daniélou, *From Shadows to Reality*, pp. 85-102, who does not cite the passage we quote on this theme, perhaps because of its brevity, but does develop Origen's historical, mystical, and moral interpretation of the ark in his *Homilies on Genesis* — pp. 104-110.

15. *Commentary on Romans* 3.1.11. Translation by Thomas P. Scheck, *Origen: Commentary on the Epistle to the Romans Books 1-5*, Fathers of the Church 103 (Washington: Catholic University of America Press, 2001), p. 184.

wash with water the entrails and feet of the animal for the burnt offering (Lev. 1:9) as "announcing the sacrament of baptism by a figurative prophecy" (*Homilies on Leviticus* 1.4.6).[16] He explains, "For he who cleanses his conscience washes 'the inward parts'; he washes his feet who receives the fullness of the sacrament."[17] The connection of water baptism with cleansing the conscience is to be noted (cf. Heb. 10:22; 1 Pet. 3:21). Origen relates the latter phrase to Jesus' washing his disciples' feet (John 13:8, 10); I take his words as meaning the complete effectiveness of the washing in reaching even the extremities.

Origen found a reference to the baptismal ritual in Song of Solomon 1:11-12 (*Commentary on the Song of Songs* 2.8).

The Baptisms of John the Baptist and Jesus

Origen's *Commentary on Romans* contains an extended excursus on circumcision (2.13.8-33). Circumcision was a command given only to the descendants of Abraham and not to Gentiles. The discussion of spiritual circumcision makes no reference to baptism, but baptism and circumcision are mentioned among the examples of the multiple Old Testament practices now superseded by the one act of Christ.

> Finally it ought to be said that just as many baptisms were necessary before the baptism of Christ, and many purifications were carried out before the purification through the Holy Spirit, and many sacrifices before the one sacrifice, the spotless lamb, Christ, offered himself to the Father as a sacrifice, so also there was need of many circumcisions until the one circumcision in Christ was imparted to all. (2.13.32)[18]

Origen may have had in mind the literal circumcision of Christ, to which he made reference earlier (2.13.29), or the spiritual circumcision effected by Jesus' death (Col. 2:11). For our purposes now, the important part of the statement is the contrast of the many baptisms previously performed with the baptism of Christ.[19]

Origen placed the baptism performed by John in the category of Old Testament washings and frequently contrasted it with the baptism administered by Jesus.[20]

---

16. Translation by Gary Wayne Barkley, *Origen: Homilies on Leviticus 1–16*, Fathers of the Church 83 (Washington: Catholic University of America Press, 1990), p. 36. Without mentioning baptism, Origen seems to allude to it in his comments on Num. 31:21-24 (purifying booty with water and washing clothes), quoting Job 14:4 about no one is pure — *Homilies on Numbers* 25.6.

17. Barkley, *Origen: Homilies on Leviticus*, p. 36.

18. Scheck, *Origen: Commentary on the Epistle to the Romans*, pp. 162-163.

19. The relation of baptism to circumcision will be discussed below under Origen's theology of baptism.

20. Blanc, "Le baptême," p. 116, for references on John's baptism as corporeal, having to do with the senses, and visible, and Jesus' baptism as incorporeal, having to do with the intellect, and invisible.

Thus, according to the *Commentary on Romans*, Jesus received John's baptism, not "the baptism which is in Christ but . . . the one which is in the law."[21] Origen understands this to be the meaning of Jesus' words in Matthew 3:15 about being baptized in order to fulfill all righteousness. "In that passage he is making known that John's baptism was a fulfillment of the old [law], not a beginning of the new [law]."[22] That is why in Acts 19:3-5 those baptized with John's baptism were rebaptized in the name of Jesus.

Origen paraphrases the words of John the Baptist in Matthew 3:11:

> He will deluge you bountifully with the gifts of the Spirit, since my baptism does not give any spiritual grace (well, yes, the "forgiveness of sins"). But he will forgive you and will give you the Spirit abundantly. (*Commentary on Matthew*, frg. 49)

At his baptism Jesus received the Spirit. Quoting John 1:33, Origen comments that at his baptism Jesus "received the Holy Spirit who remained on him so that he could baptize those coming to him in that very same abiding Spirit."[23] In spite of the contrasts he made between John's and Jesus' baptism, Origen had a positive appreciation of John's baptism. He stated that the Savior sanctified John's baptism.[24]

Origen's comments on baptism in the *Commentary on John* introduce themes to be explored further in our study, but for now we focus on the contrast he makes between John's baptism and Christ's. The *Commentary on John* contains a comparison of the accounts in all four Gospels of the events leading up to Jesus' encounter with John the Baptist and then their meeting (6.22 [13].120 — 36 [20].183; 50 [31].260-263). Expanding on the testimony of John (John 1:24-27) from the Synoptic Gospels (Matt. 3:11; Mark 1:8; Luke 3:16) and noting John 4:2 (that Jesus did not baptize but his disciples did), Origen emphasizes the contrast between John's and Christ's baptism: "Christ does not baptize in water, but his disciples. He reserves for himself to baptize in the Holy Spirit and fire" (6.23 [13].125).

Origen interprets John the Baptist's testimony to Jesus (according to Matt. 3:11) to include a further contrast of the Baptist's baptism as preparatory (improving people by repentance) with Jesus' baptism:

> [Jesus'] baptism is not bodily, since the Holy Spirit fills the one who repents and a more divine fire obliterates everything material and utterly destroys everything earthly, not only from the one possessing it but also from the one who hears those who have it. (6.32 [17].162)

---

21. *Commentary on Romans* 5.8.6. Scheck, *Origen: Commentary on the Epistle to the Romans*, p. 356.

22. Scheck, *Origen: Commentary on the Epistle to the Romans*, p. 356, with my addition of law; alternatively the contrast of old and new could refer to baptisms.

23. *Commentary on John* 6.42 (25).220. According to *Homilies in Joshua* 4.2, the exaltation of Jesus began at his baptism and occurs also at the baptism of the believer.

24. *Homilies on Luke* 7.1.

The Holy Spirit and fire here appear to be two aspects of one experience in the present.[25]

Shortly thereafter, still discussing the words of the Baptist in Matthew, Origen comments on the distinction and correlation of water and Spirit. The passage sets forth themes characteristic of Origen's baptismal thought: water, Spirit, invocation of the Trinity, the characteristics required of the one baptized, and the grace given in baptism.[26] The passage begins with reference to the miracles of healing by the Savior, which had the spiritual benefit of summoning people to faith:

> In the same way the bath [λουτρόν] through water is a symbol of the purification of the soul, which is washed clean from all filth of evil, and is in itself the beginning and source of divine gifts to the one who surrenders to the divine power at the invocations of the worshipful Trinity.
> ... [According to the Acts of the Apostles] the Spirit resided so manifestly in those being baptized, since the water prepared the way for the Spirit to those who sincerely approached. (6.33 [17].166-167)

The baptismal bath of water is presented here as an effective symbol. The washing of the body is a symbol of the cleansing of the soul, but it also effects what it symbolizes, being "in itself" the origin of divine gifts. The water, however, is effective only to the one who comes in faith, yielding to the divine power, and in conjunction with the invocation of the divine names. The water thus prepared for the indwelling of the Spirit. Near the beginning of this commentary Origen expressed a recognition that one could receive outward baptism without an inward effect: "Just as one is a Jew outwardly and circumcised, there being both an outward and inward circumcision, so it is with the Christian and baptism."[27]

The continuation of the passage introduces other themes to be treated later but may be quoted here to show that Origen did not divorce the water from the work of the Spirit, while clearly distinguishing them. Origen notes that John's baptism was inferior to Jesus' baptism on the basis of Acts 19:2-5 (6.33 [17].168).

> The bath of regeneration [ἀναγεννήσεως] did not come with John but with Jesus through his disciples. It is called the "bath of regeneration [παλιγγενεσίας λουτρόν]" which takes place with "renewal of the Holy Spirit" [Tit. 3:5], which Spirit is even now "borne above the water" [Gen. 1:2], since it is from God but does not intervene in everyone after the water. (6.33 [17].169)

A distinction between the Holy Spirit effecting regeneration (the two Greek words taken as equivalent) in water baptism and his being later imparted is made in

---

25. One of Origen's interpretations of Luke 3:15-16, noted below, combines them eschatologically.

26. Blanc, "Le baptême," p. 116; she notes on p. 117 that along with the accent placed by Origen on the spiritual reality there is the visible water in which baptism occurs.

27. *Commentary on John* 1.7 (9).40; Ronald E. Heine, *Origen: Commentary on the Gospel according to John Books 1-10*, Fathers of the Church 80 (Washington: Catholic University of America Press, 1989), p. 42, with a note about the textual uncertainties in the passage.

Origen's *Commentary on 1 Corinthians* 1:17: with reference to Acts 8:12-16, he says, "Philip baptized in water those being regenerated from water and the Holy Spirit, but Peter (baptized) in the Holy Spirit."

Sometimes Origen understands being baptized in the Spirit as occurring in Christian water baptism.

> The one who has died to sin and is truly baptized into the death of Christ, and is buried with him through baptism into death [Rom. 6:3-4], he is the one who is truly baptized in the Holy Spirit and with the water from above [John 3:5].[28]

At other times the Spirit is given after baptism (see on laying on of hands under liturgy below).

Joseph Trigg highlights the difference for Origen between water baptism and Spirit baptism.[29] He understands Origen to analyze baptism in the present age of the church according to a material and a spiritual experience: water baptism for the simple believer is the beginning of the process of sanctification, and the baptism of the Holy Spirit is the higher spiritual baptism that distinguishes the spiritual Christian. I can go with him thus far, but when he describes water baptism and the later baptism of the Holy Spirit in Origen as two rites of initiation,[30] this terminology is to be questioned.[31] Hence, although Origen recognized a distinction between water baptism and Spirit baptism (and gifts of the Spirit), I have called attention to those passages where he also links the working of the Spirit with baptism (see further below).

The Eschatological Baptism of Fire

It is not my intention here to cover all of Origen's (controversial) discussions of eschatological fire, only to mention how he brought baptismal language to bear on its purifying effect.[32] In the *Commentary on John* Origen says that as Jesus is a drink — to some water, to others wine, and to others blood — so he is "a baptism of water and Spirit, and fire, and to some even of blood" (6.43 [26].223).[33]

---

28. *Commentary on Romans* 5.8.3; Scheck, *Origen: Commentary on the Epistle to the Romans*, p. 355.

29. J. W. Trigg, "A Fresh Look at Origen's Understanding of Baptism," *Studia Patristica* 17.2 (1982): 959-965. The main thrust of Trigg's article is to distinguish two strands in Origen's thought: the perfectionist, according to which baptism carries an obligation not to sin, and the pastoral, in which baptism is the beginning and source of divine gifts but not their fulfillment.

30. Trigg, "A Fresh Look," p. 963.

31. Cf. Origen's words in his *Commentary on Ephesians* 4:5 critical of the Valentinians for giving two baptisms.

32. On the debt of sin for which even the righteous need purification after this life, see *Homilies on Leviticus* 15.3; *Against Celsus* 4.13; 5.15; *On First Principles* 2.10.4; cf. *Commentary on Matthew* 15.23 cited below. Carl-Martin Edsman, *Le baptême du feu* (Uppsala: Lundequistka, 1940), discusses the topic.

33. In the next paragraph he cites in support of the baptismal interpretation of martyrdom Luke

Origen distinguishes the baptism in the Holy Spirit and the baptism in fire in his *Homilies on Jeremiah*. Commenting on Luke 3:16, he says that they are not the same: "The holy person is baptized in the Holy Spirit, but the person who after believing and being counted worthy of the Holy Spirit sins again is washed [λούει] in 'fire.'" "Blessed is the one who is baptized in the Holy Spirit and has no need of the baptism that comes from fire. Triply to be pitied is the one who has need of being baptized in fire" (2.3.1-2).[34] Similarly, "Those who are not treated in the baptism of the Holy Spirit are baptized with fire, because they are not able to be purged with the purification of the Holy Spirit" (*Homilies on Ezekiel* 5.1).

In the *Homilies on Luke* Origen expresses the view that even the righteous will need a "sacrament to wash and cleanse us even after resurrection from the dead" (14.6).[35] He sets forth the three baptisms in water, Spirit, and fire in his comments on Luke 3:15-16, with primary attention to the baptism in fire:

> If anyone desires to pass over to paradise after departing this life, and needs cleansing, Christ will baptize him in this river [of fire] and send him across to the place he longs for. But whoever does not have the sign of earlier baptisms, him Christ will not baptize in the fiery bath. For, it is fitting that one should be baptized first in "water and the Spirit." Then, when he comes to the fiery river, he can show that he preserved the bathing in water and the Spirit. (*Homilies on Luke* 24.2)[36]

Later, recalling this earlier interpretation, he offers an alternative view in which the fire is judgment and not purification:

> If you are holy, you will be baptized with the Holy Spirit. If you are a sinner, you will be plunged into fire. One and the same baptism will be turned into condemnation and fire for the unworthy and for sinners; but to those who are holy and

---

12:50 and 1 John 5:8 ("Spirit, water, and blood") — 6.43 (26).224. See further my treatment of martyrdom as a baptism below.

34. Origen appears to think of Christian water baptism as baptism in the Holy Spirit. Another passage seems to to offer a different perspective from the comments on Jeremiah but may not have a baptismal reference: "Everything which passes through fire is changed through the fire and is made clean, but is purified in the water of purification; everything which does not pass through fire passes through water" (*Homilies on Numbers* 25.6).

35. Translation of Jerome's Latin by Lienhard, *Origen: Homilies on Luke*, p. 59. In view of this statement, the subsequent words about the "rebirth of baptism" and "purified by spiritual rebirth" may apply the language of rebirth to the eschatological baptism.

36. Lienhard, *Origen: Homilies on Luke*, pp. 103-104. Origen's *Commentary on Matthew* 15.23 appears to give another interpretation, placing the baptism of the Holy Spirit and fire at the water baptism. After citing the equivalent Matthaean text (Matt. 3:11), Origen continues: "In the regeneration through the bath [Titus 3:5] we were buried with Christ, for according to the apostle, 'We were buried with him through baptism' [Rom. 6:4]. In the regeneration of the bath through fire and Spirit we become conformed 'to the body of his glory' [Phil. 3:21] when Christ 'sits upon the throne of his glory' [Matt. 19:28]."

have been turned to the Lord in total faith, the grace of the Holy Spirit, and salvation, will be given. (*Homilies on Luke* 26.3)[37]

Baptism with the Holy Spirit and fire is here the same baptism, but with opposite effects depending on the character of the person receiving it.

Theology of Baptism

Origen's treatment of the baptism of Jesus in his *Homilies on Luke* sets forth the basic gifts of Christian baptism — forgiveness of sins and the abiding of the Holy Spirit.

> The Lord was baptized. The heavens were opened and "the Holy Spirit came down upon him" [Luke 3:22]. A voice from the heavens thundered and said, "This is my beloved Son, in whom I am pleased" [Luke 3:22]. We should say that heaven was opened at the baptism of Jesus and for the plan of forgiving sins. These are not the sins of him "who had committed no sin, nor was deceit found in his mouth" [1 Pet. 2:22]. The heavens were opened and the Holy Spirit came down for the forgiveness of the whole world's sins. After the Lord "ascended on high, leading captivity captive" [Eph. 4:8], he gave us the Spirit. The Spirit had come to him, and he gave the Spirit at the time of his resurrection when he said, "Receive the Holy Spirit. If you forgive anyone's sins, they will be forgiven" [John 20:22-23]. (27.5)[38]

By Origen's time the association of baptism with the forgiveness of sins was well established, and Origen often repeats this purpose for baptism. Earlier in his *Homilies on Luke* he applied the description of John's baptism in Luke 3:3 to Christian baptism. He begins with his etymology of "Jordan" and proceeds to a ringing invitation to catechumens to repent:

> "Jordan" means "descending." But the "descending" river of God, one running with a vigorous force, is the Lord our Savior. Into him we are baptized with true water, saving water. Baptism is also preached "for the remission of sins." Come, catechumens! Repent, so that baptism for the remission of sins will follow. He who stops sinning receives baptism "for the remission of sins." For, if anyone comes sinning to the washing, he does not receive forgiveness of sins. . . . Spend some time in good living. Keep yourselves clean of all stains and vices. Your sins will be forgiven when you yourselves begin to despise your own sins. (21.4)[39]

More will be said below on Origen's insistence on repentance as a prerequisite for baptism, but the premise of Origen's exhortation to catechumens to cease sinning is

---

37. Lienhard, *Origen: Homilies on Luke*, p. 110.
38. Lienhard, *Origen: Homilies on Luke*, p. 114.
39. Lienhard, *Origen: Homilies on Luke*, pp. 89-90, which translates the Latin, except that I have substituted "repent" based on the shorter Greek [μετανοεῖν] text.

the association of baptism with forgiveness. He states succinctly the purpose of baptism: "You have come to Jesus and through the grace of baptism have attained the remission of sins."[40] The debt of sin is "blotted out in the fountain of baptism."[41]

With the forgiveness of sins is associated the idea of cleansing. The command to Israel to wash their garments before receiving the law at Mt. Sinai (Exod. 19:10-11) means that "Your garments were washed once when you came to the grace of baptism; you were purified in body; you were cleansed from all filth of flesh and spirit."[42] Or, again, "Through the grace of baptism you have become a clean animal."[43] Another imagery is that of the redemption of humanity through the waters of baptism.[44]

The words "grace of baptism" in these quotations appear to have been a set phrase with Origen, appearing with great frequency. For example, to come to the "grace of baptism" is to be baptized into Christ's death (Rom. 6:3).[45]

Receiving the Holy Spirit also was closely linked with baptism. "You who desire to receive holy baptism and to obtain the grace of the Spirit."[46] The fact that the "sons of God" are led by the Spirit of God (Rom. 8:14) makes it fitting that the Savior, "Son of God in the proper sense," after his baptism was full of the Holy Spirit and led by the Spirit (Luke 4:1).[47] The way in which Origen speaks, bringing the possession of the Spirit into his references to baptism even when his main concern is another subject, shows how natural the connection was in his mind. Nevertheless, the connection was not automatic. In addressing both catechumens and the faithful, Origen observed that there were those washed in water but not at the same time in the Holy Spirit and catechumens who were not strangers to the Holy Spirit. He cited as scriptural examples Cornelius, who before descending into the water received the Holy Spirit (Acts 10:44), and Simon, who received baptism but who approached grace with hypocrisy and was deprived of the gift of the Holy Spirit (Acts 8:13-19).[48] In commenting of Ezekiel 16:4, Origen said, "We who receive the grace of baptism in the name of Christ are 'washed,' but I do not know who 'is washed in salvation.'" He cites the case of Simon, baptized by Philip in Acts 8, and appeals to catechumens lest they receive water but not the Holy Spirit (*Homilies on Ezekiel* 6.5), and further warns against sinning after the "washing of regeneration" (6.7)

Origen, moreover, frequently drew on the language of being begotten again, or born anew, based on John 3:3, 5. This experience derives from Jesus himself. By his

40. *Homilies on Joshua* 15.7; Bruce, *Origen: Homilies on Joshua*, p. 150.
41. *Homilies on Genesis* 13; Heine, *Origen: Homilies on Genesis and Exodus*, p. 194.
42. *Homilies on Exodus* 11.7; Heine, *Origen: Homilies on Genesis and Exodus*, p. 365. See the quotation of *Commentary on John* 6.33 (17).166 above on the water purifying the soul.
43. *Homilies on Leviticus* 9.4.4; Barkley, *Origen: Homilies on Leviticus*, p. 183. Cf. 8.3.5 on infant baptism — chap. 23.
44. *Commentary on the Song of Songs* 2.10 on Song of Songs 1:13.
45. *Homilies on Leviticus* 2.4.6; some other passages are *On First Principles* 1.3.2; *Homilies on Exodus* 8.4 and 5; 10.4; *Commentary on Romans* 3.1.12.
46. *Homilies on Leviticus* 6.2.5; Barkley, *Origen: Homilies on Leviticus*, p. 118.
47. *Homilies on Luke* 29.2; Lienhard, *Origen: Homilies on Luke*, p. 119.
48. *Homilies on Numbers* 3.1.

baptism Jesus took on "the mystery of the second birth. . . . He did this so that you too could wipe away your former birth and be born in a second rebirth."[49] Through a second birth the Lord Jesus Christ "wiped away the blemish of the first birth." Since it was instruction as well as birth that brought the dominion of death on human beings, Christ commanded his disciples to teach and to baptize (Matt. 28:19), "so that even our mortal birth would be changed by the rebirth of baptism, and the teaching of godliness might shut out the teaching of godlessness."[50] Origen interprets John 3:3, 5 and Romans 6:3-4 as equivalent. The first earthly birth is not repeated, but a new birth from above is received.

> The one who has died to sin and is truly baptized into the death of Christ and is buried with him through baptism into death, he is the one who is truly baptized in the Holy Spirit and with the water from above.[51]

Hence, a person becomes an infant in baptism.[52]

Origen treated the new birth of 1 Peter 1:23 (ἀναγέννησις) and John 3:5 as equivalent to the regeneration (παλιγγενεσία) of Titus 3:5.[53]

> The sacrament [σύμβολον] through water given those who have hoped in Christ, which is called the "washing of regeneration." For what does rebirth signify if not the beginning of another birth?[54]

In commenting on Matthew 18:10 he says that "through the 'bath of regeneration' [παλιγγενεσίας] — Titus 3:5] in which they were born [ἐγεννήθησαν] they desire 'as newborn [ἀρτιγέννητα] babes the pure spiritual milk' [1 Pet. 2:2]."[55] Again, in commenting on Matthew 19:28, the other passage where παλιγγενεσία occurs in the New Testament, he cites John 3:5 [ὁ γεννηθεὶς ἄνωθεν ἐξ ὕδατος καὶ πνεύματος] as a figure of the "other regeneration [παλιγγενεσίαν]" when the Son of Man sits on his throne of glory. Here Origen brings in again his view of the eschatological baptism of fire and Spirit. Everyone who attains the regeneration in Christ through the bath of regeneration attains the eschatological regeneration, which is the baptism in the Holy Spirit and fire of Matthew 3:11. In the regeneration of the bath "we were buried with Christ through baptism" (Rom. 6:4), but in the "regeneration of the bath through fire and Spirit we become conformed to the body of the glory [Phil. 3:21] of Christ."[56]

---

49. *Homilies on Luke* 28.4; Lienhard, *Origen: Homilies on Luke*, pp. 116-117, with the note that the redundancy is in the Latin.

50. *Commentary on Romans* 5.2.11; Scheck, *Origen: Commentary on the Epistle to the Romans*, p. 333.

51. *Commentary on Romans* 8.5.3; Scheck, *Commentary on the Epistle to the Romans*, p. 355.

52. *Homilies on Joshua* 9.4; *Homilies on Exodus* 10.4.

53. See *Commentary on John* 6.33 (17).169 quoted above.

54. *On the Pasch* 4.29-36; translation by Robert Daly, *Origen: Treatise on the Passover and Dialogue with Heraclides*, Ancient Christian Writers 54 (New York: Paulist, 1992), p. 29.

55. *Commentary on Matthew* 13.27.

56. *Commentary on Matthew* 15.23. Note the association of Rom. 6:4 with Titus 3:5. The passage

Indeed, the "bath [or washing] of regeneration" was Origen's favorite phrase for baptism, not only in passages commenting on παλιγγενεσία. In discussing postbaptismal sins, Origen sets in parallel the phrases "the one who sins after believing and receiving the forgiveness of sins" and "the forgiveness of sins and the dispensation of the bath of regeneration," indicating that the latter was a set phrase with him for baptism.[57] A catena fragment of Origen on Jeremiah interprets "water" not with the word "baptism," as might be expected, but as "the bath of regeneration."[58]

The catena fragments ascribed to Origen's *Commentary on John* contain a long passage on John 3:5 (Frg. 36). Ronald Heine has justly warned against the reliability of the fragments in general and, without discussing Fragment 36, concluded that Fragments 6-55 are not likely to have come from the lost books of this commentary.[59] Without disputing the doubts about the passage coming from the *Commentary on John*, we quote it extensively here because the passage has an interest that makes it worth including in our survey, even if it should not be the authentic voice of Origen. It does represent the kind of spiritualizing exegesis associated with Origen.

> The Savior interprets the manner of "being begotten from above." Since the subject is entering the kingdom of God, and it is impossible to attain this without being begotten of water and the Spirit, to be begotten [γεννηθῆναι] from above accompanies being begotten of water and Spirit. The one doing thus is begotten of the Spirit and becomes holy and spiritual from the Spirit. Since the one entering the kingdom of God is begotten not only from the Spirit but also from the water, one must consequently seek something from the Scripture concerning the water. Observe that it has a difference from the Spirit in thought [ἐπίνοια][60] only but not of purpose.... [Quotes John 7:38-39.] For if the Spirit is said to flow from the believer like rivers of living water, the water will differ from the Spirit in thought only. If then someone begotten from the Savior is wise from his wisdom, so also one begotten from the Spirit is holy and spiritual. And one purified by the water and irrigated for fruit bearing is begotten of water and the Spirit. Someone else will say the water here is spoken of the teaching that purifies the soul, which also accomplishes the being begotten from above....
>
> Since not only the soul is called to salvation but also the body itself, the instrument used for the soul's activities, it is fitting that the body also be sanctified

---

also introduces the Old Testament verses (Job 14:4-5; Ps. 51:5) used in support of the infant stain that justified baptizing infants (chap. 23).

57. *Homilies on Jeremiah* 16.5.2. Origen the realist recognized that those who received the "heavenly grace" in baptism might nonetheless turn back to the bitterness of sin — *Homilies on Joshua* 4.2 — or fall into the servitude of sin — *Homilies on Joshua* 10.3.

58. *Jeremiah*, catena 26.

59. Ronald E. Heine, "Can the Catena Fragments of Origen's Commentary on John Be Trusted?" *Vigiliae Christianae* 40 (1986): 118-134 (131). My impression of the style and contents of Fragment 36 is against its authenticity, but Crouzel, "Origène et la Structure," pp. 85, 90-91, treats the passage as authentic.

60. According to Crouzel, "Origène et la Structure," p. 85, "the human way of seeing things."

> by what the divine teaching calls the "bath of regeneration" [Tit. 3:5], also called divine baptism, no longer mere water. For it is sanctified by a mystic [μυστικῇ] invocation. Observe and understand its greatness and power in the mystagogy delivered by the Savior to his disciples.... [Quotes Matt. 28:19.] For if it is necessary first to be made a disciple by receiving the dogmas of truth and then to keep those things he commanded them concerning the ethical virtues, and so to be baptized into the name of the Father, Son, and Holy Spirit, how can the water that is received together with these words be still mere water, since it shares in some manner the power of the holy Trinity and is yoked together with ethical and intellectual virtue? Consider and understand the greatness of that for which it is received. For if this is on account of entering the kingdom of God, which surpasses in excellence, how great is the cause of entering it?

The author interprets the water in terms of the Spirit, for the water is the visible symbol of the substance of the Spirit. Yet he clearly emphasizes the importance of the water. The water was consecrated by the invocation of the divine Trinity, and this gave it its power. The calling on the Trinity sanctifies the water and the believer but is not an invocation on the water, as in *Apostolic Tradition* 21.1.[61] The use of Titus 3:5 and Matthew 28:19 to interpret John 3:5 removes any doubt about the understanding of the Johannine passage as baptism. The combination of these three verses is true to Origen's usage.

Origen also used the idea of dying and rising with Christ from Romans 6:3-4 to interpret the meaning of baptism.

> (T)eaching through these things that if someone has first died to sin, he has necessarily been buried with Christ in baptism. But if the person does not die to sin beforehand, he cannot be buried with Christ. For no one who is still alive is ever buried. But if one is not buried with Christ, he is not validly baptized....
>
> Therefore those who are hastening to baptism ought to take care as a matter of first importance that they should first die to sin....
>
> Now the newness of life is when we lay aside "the old man with his deeds" and "put on the new, who has been created according to God" [Eph. 4:22, 24; Col. 3:9-10].
>
> For you must not imagine that the renewing of the life, which is said to have been done once, suffices. On the contrary at all times and daily, this newness must, if it can be said, be renewed.[62]

The moral significance of baptism which Origen gives to dying with Christ as a dying to sin and to walking in newness of life is in keeping with Paul's own point in the

---

61. Auf der Maur, "*Illuminatio*," pp. 79-82.

62. *Commentary on Romans* 5.8.2, 10, 12, 13; Scheck, *Origen: Commentary on the Epistle to the Romans*, pp. 354, 358, 359. For the use of Romans 6:3-4, see also *Commentary on John* 1.182; 10.231-232, 243; *Commentary on Matthew* 15.23 (referred to above); *Homilies on Numbers* 15.4; *Homilies on Judges* 7.2. For other references, McDonnell, *The Baptism of Jesus in the Jordan*, pp. 201-202.

passage.⁶³ Death to sin must precede baptism. As will be seen below, death to sin was the meaning of repentance for Origen.

In the *Homilies on Joshua* the "mystery of baptism" includes being "baptized into his death" (Rom. 6:3) and means for the faithful to arrive at the exaltation of the cross (4.2). In the *Homilies on Exodus,* the "three days" of Exodus 5:3 are related to Christ: he died on day one, descended into Hades on day two, and arose on day three. These words contain the "mysteries of baptism," and Origen quotes Romans 6:3-4, paraphrasing the end of the passage as "arise from the dead with him" (5.2). Origen sees in baptism a foreshadowing in each person of the resurrection of the dead; he quotes Romans 6:4, "we were buried with Christ through baptism," as parallel with (what Paul does not say explicitly) "we arose with him" (*Homilies on Jeremiah* 1.16.2).⁶⁴ Baptism gives the Holy Spirit as a pledge, but we receive him fully when we come to perfection; in the same way baptism is a resurrection and a pledge of the perfect resurrection.⁶⁵

Origen expresses the eschatological significance of baptism without explicit reference to rising with Christ.

> Through the grace of baptism those who believe would be understood to be changed from men into a higher order, when the day of the resurrection arrives, when each of the saints shall be like the angels of God [cf. Matt. 22:30].⁶⁶

As indicated in the exodus typology above, baptism was a deliverance from the devil and evil spirits.⁶⁷ Commenting of Exodus 14:19-20, Origen says, "If you should depart from the Egyptians and flee the power of demons, see what great helps are prepared for you from heaven."⁶⁸ He interprets the Egyptians who pursued Israel as the "rulers of this world" and the "spiritual evils" (Eph. 6:12), and applies the words to his hearers by saying, "which you previously served."⁶⁹ Those who are baptized have nothing more to fear from demons.⁷⁰

After describing the influence of evil spirits as the soul being "prostituted to de-

---

63. Cf. *Commentary on Romans* 5.9.2; Scheck, *Origen: Commentary on the Epistle to the Romans,* p. 361, for baptism into Christ's death as a crucifixion of the old life of sin so that we might have hope of the likeness of his resurrection.

64. Henri Crouzel, "La 'première' et la 'seconde' résurrection des hommes d'après Origène," *Didaskalia* 3 (1973): 3-19, on baptism as a first resurrection.

65. *Homilies on Ezekiel* 2.5.

66. *Commentary on Romans* 3.1.12; Scheck, *Origen: Commentary on the Epistle to the Romans,* p. 184.

67. For Origen's vivid awareness of demonic forces and their efforts to entrap human beings, see Everett Ferguson, "Origen's Demonology," in James E. Priest, ed., *Johannine Studies: Essays in Honor of Frank Pack* (Malibu: Pepperdine University Press, 1989), pp. 54-66 and Henri Crouzel, "Diable et démons dans les homélies d'Origène," *Bulletin littérature ecclésiastique* 94 (1994): 303-331.

68. *Homilies on Exodus* 5.4; Heine, *Origen: Homilies on Genesis and Exodus,* p. 281.

69. *Homilies on Exodus* 5.5; Heine, *Origen: Homilies on Genesis and Exodus,* p. 283.

70. *Homilies on Judges* 7.2.

mons," Origen speaks of the soul united with Christ as its lawful husband. Baptism is the marriage to Christ.

> [God] does not wish us to sin further after recognition of himself, after the illumination of the divine word, after the grace of baptism, after the confession of faith and after the marriage has been confirmed with such great sacraments. He does not permit the soul whose bridegroom or husband he himself is called to play with demons, to fornicate with unclean spirits.[71]

After surveying the occasions in scripture where spouses were met at wells, Origen finds the Old and New Testaments to be in agreement: "There one comes to the wells and the waters that brides may be found; and the church is united to Christ in the bath of water."[72]

Origen often brings baptism into association with circumcision. Hence, Daniélou, for example, asserts that "Origen compares baptism to circumcision" and "It is the sacrament itself of baptism for which circumcision is the figure."[73] Or, one could nuance the interpretation and understand the gift of the Spirit in baptism as the spiritual counterpart to physical circumcision.[74] Daniélou cites for his view Origen's *Commentary on Romans*:

> If anyone in the church who is circumcised by means of the grace of baptism should afterwards become a transgressor of Christ's law, his baptismal circumcision shall be reckoned to him as the uncircumcision of unbelief....
>
> We might say that the catechumens are the ones who are still uncircumcised, or even Gentiles, and those who are believers by means of the grace of baptism are the circumcised. (2.12.4; 2.13.2)[75]

There are other passages to the same import. Origen interprets the second circumcision by Joshua (Josh. 5:2) as the circumcision through Christ, the Rock. "Christ came and gave to us the second circumcision through 'the baptism of regeneration' and purified our souls."[76] This would be a more precise statement: the spiritual circumcision is not baptism but is through baptism.

As an alternative, Origen could understand the second circumcision without reference to baptism as Jesus removing the vices and cutting off every defect (*Homilies on Joshua* 1.7), or, in other words, his cutting off the pollution of the flesh and

---

71. *Homilies on Exodus* 8.5; Heine, *Origen: Homilies on Genesis and Exodus*, pp. 326-327.

72. *Homilies on Genesis* 10.5; Heine, *Origen: Homilies on Genesis and Exodus*, p. 167.

73. Jean Daniélou, "Circoncision et baptême," in Johann Auer and Hermann Volk, eds., *Theologie in Geschichte und Gegenwart: Michael Schmaus zum sechzigsten Geburtstag* (Munich: K. Zink, 1957), pp. 755-776 (p. 773).

74. Everett Ferguson, "Spiritual Circumcision in Early Christianity," *Scottish Journal of Theology* 41 (1988): 485-497, but with minimal use of Origen.

75. Scheck, *Origen: Commentary on the Epistle to the Romans*, p. 143.

76. *Homilies on Joshua* 5.5-6; Bruce, *Origen: Homilies on Joshua*, pp. 63-64. A few paragraphs later Origen speaks more briefly of "the second circumcision of baptism" (p. 66).

purging the filth of sins from the heart (6.1). This spiritual circumcision would no doubt have been thought of as occurring in baptism, but the point is that it is not identical for Origen with baptism. This interpretation differs from seeing the baptismal circumcision as the giving of the Holy Spirit as a seal, but it accords with Origen's moral emphasis in regard to baptism as meaning that one should no longer live a life of sin.

Origen, in his *Homilies on Luke,* offers another interpretation of the circumcision of Christ that might be more nearly what Paul meant in Colossians 2:9-12, quoted by him in the passage. "When [Christ] died, we died with him and when he rose, we rose with him. So too we were circumcised along with him" (14.1).[77] Hence, we do not need circumcision of the flesh, for his death, resurrection, and circumcision "took place for our sake."

Baptism added one to the church. Origen interpreted Genesis 2:15 in this way: "Those who are being begotten again [ἀναγεννώμενοι] through divine baptism are placed in Paradise, that is, in the church."[78]

One of Origen's pregnant thoughts, but one that he uncharacteristically does not develop, is that "By being baptized into Jesus we will know that the living God is in us" (*Commentary on John* 6.44 [26].232).

Martyrdom

Eusebius cites Origen as somewhere (source unknown) calling martyrdom "the baptism [τὸ βάπτισμα] by fire" (*Church History* 6.4.3). The statement occurs in regard to Herais, a female student of Origen who while still a catechumen was killed for her faith, a death that took the place of ordinary water baptism for her. Eusebius may be mistaken, for Origen's usual phrase is a baptism of blood, and the baptism of fire is eschatological, but he could very well have used the latter phrase for martyrdom as accomplishing the final purification that he assigned to fire.

Jesus' passion was a martyrdom and was the greatest and the perfect baptism (*Commentary on John* 6.56 [37].290-291). His words comparing his approaching death to a baptism (Luke 12:50, quoted by Origen in this context, and Mark 10:38) provided the basis for applying baptismal concepts to martyrdom. Origen was a leading figure in defining the theology of martyrdom,[79] and that included martyrdom as a baptism.

Martyrdom brought a forgiveness of sins to the believer who had not yet received baptism and a forgiveness of any postbaptismal sins to the one who had been

---

77. Lienhard, *Origen: Homilies on Luke,* p. 56.
78. *Commentary on Genesis,* Book 3, on Gen. 2:15.
79. Pamela Bright, "Origenian Understanding of Martryrdom and Its Biblical Framework," in Charles Kannengiesser and William L. Petersen, eds., *Origen of Alexandria: His World and His Legacy* (Notre Dame: University of Notre Dame Press, 1988), pp. 180-199.

baptized. Origen, in interpreting Mark 10:38, explains the relationship of martyrdom to baptism:

> Inasmuch as the one who endures [martyrdom] receives forgiveness of sins, it is a baptism. For if baptism promises forgiveness of sins, even as we have received forgiveness with reference to the baptism in water and Spirit, and if the one who endured the baptism of martyrdom receives forgiveness of sins, martyrdom would with good reason be called a baptism. (*Commentary on Matthew* 16.6)

He continues with a proof text for martyrdom assuring one of salvation. That forgiveness of sins comes to one who endures martyrdom is evident from Matthew 10:32, because confession before people means that Jesus will confess that person before the Father.

The key work on the subject is Origen's *Exhortation to Martyrdom*. One of the bases of Origen's appeal is that when persons undertake to live the Christian life they enter into certain agreements with God (12). These agreements include the rejection of idolatry that was part of the renunciation of Satan made at baptism (17; see below under liturgy).

The principal passage is this:

> Let us be mindful of our sins, because there is no forgiveness of sins without receiving baptism, and that according to the laws of the gospel it is impossible to be baptized again with water and the Spirit for forgiveness of sins, and that a baptism of martyrdom has been given us. Martyrdom is named a baptism, as is evident from [Mark 10:38 and Luke 12:50 are quoted]. Consider the baptism of martyrdom, that even as the Savior's [martyrdom] brought purification to the world, martyrdom becomes a healing of the many who are being purified. (30)

It seems ironic that Origen's strongest statement on the necessity of baptism in order to receive forgiveness of sins occurs in the context of an "exception to the rule." Only Origen would not have considered the forgiveness granted in martyrdom an exception but as an extension of the Savior's death and of baptism as related to it.[80] So, he can say of the martyrs, "Being baptized in their own blood and washing away [ἀπολουσάμενοι] every sin at the altar in heaven" (39).

Another extended treatment occurs in the *Homilies on Judges*. Here the superiority of blood baptism is asserted, but its value is developed not in terms of the forgiveness of past sins but of preventing future sins, because few live above sin after water baptism.

> The baptism of blood alone is what makes us purer than the baptism of water did.... This baptism would be superior to that baptism which is given by water. For concerning the latter I admit that exceedingly few are those so blessed as to be able to maintain it unstained up to the end of life. The person who should be bap-

---

80. Crouzel, *Origen*, p. 224.

tized with the former baptism is now not able to sin any more. . . . By baptism in water past sins are purged; by baptism in blood indeed future sins are prevented. In the one case sins are dismissed; in this other case they are excluded. (*Homilies on Judges* 7.2)

The atoning value of martyrdom is not forgotten, however, for the passage continues by saying that the martyrs' blood reaches to the heavenly altar.

One passage seems to extend the redemptive effect of the martyrs' blood beyond themselves to others: "Perhaps also as we were purchased by the 'precious blood' (1 Pet. 1:9) of Jesus, . . . so some are purchased by the precious blood of the martyrs" (*Exhortation to Martyrdom* 50). Instead of a literal parallel, Origen may be thinking of the influence of the martyrs' deaths in bringing others to faith, but this seems unlikely in view of other passages where Origen wrestles with the meaning of various scriptures in attempting to understand ways in which the sacrificial death of martyrs benefitted others.[81]

Origen included martyrdom as one of the seven means of obtaining forgiveness in the Christian age: baptism, martyrdom, almsgiving, forgiving others, converting a sinner, abundant love, and repentance (*Homilies on Leviticus* 2.4.4-5). His *Commentary on Romans* 2.1.2 repeats three of these: the grace of baptism, repentance, and the glory of martyrdom.

Catechumenate and Prerequisites for Baptism

Against the charge by Celsus that Christians attempted to convert only those who were foolish and from the lower classes of society (*Against Celsus* 3.49), Origen responded with a description of the process of admitting converts in which he distinguished two stages of the catechumenate.

> The Christians, so far as they are able, test beforehand the souls of those who wish to become hearers and give a preliminary warning to them privately, before introducing them to the community, when they seem to devote themselves sufficiently to the intention of living a good life. At this time they introduce them. Privately they form one class of those who are taking the lead and are receiving admission but have not yet received the symbol [σύμβολον] of complete purification. They form another class of those who according to their ability are presenting themselves with the purpose of wanting nothing other than the things approved by Christians. For these some are appointed to make inquiry into the lives and activities of those who are being admitted in order that they might exclude those doing infamous deeds. (*Against Celsus* 3.51)

Origen, for his apologetic defense, underscores the testing of those who wished to become "hearers" (Cyprian used the same word for catechumens). The preliminary

---

81. *Commentary on John* 6.54 (36); *Homilies on Numbers* 10.2.

testing was followed by continued inquiry into the candidates' behavior. The *Apostolic Tradition* also attested these inquiries into conduct in order to exclude sinners.[82] Origen distinguishes those being instructed (κατηχούμενοι) and the faithful (πιστοί, which for him means the baptized).[83]

Moses and the prophets were the introduction to Christianity.[84] There was instruction both in private and in community.[85] The earlier stage of instruction concentrated on moral matters and simple faith as opposed to idolatry; more advanced instruction had to do with the deeper things of doctrine and the sacraments.[86]

> When you are reckoned among the number of catechumens and have undertaken to submit to the precepts of the church, . . . you daily devote yourself to hearing the law of God. . . . But if you also have entered the mystic font of baptism and in the presence of the priestly and Levitical order have been instructed by those venerable and magnificent sacraments, which are known to those who are permitted to know those things, then . . . you will enter the land of promise. . . . In this land, Jesus receives you after Moses, and becomes for you the leader of a new way.[87]

The catechumen was daily devoted to hearing the Law of God, but then as one came nearer the time of baptism, there was revealed the wisdom of divine things, especially the divinity of Christ.

> When, therefore, is his lofty divinity revealed to me? At that time, assuredly, when I crossed over the Jordan [baptism in this context] and was equipped with the various defenses of the sacraments for the future battle.[88]

The initial hearing of the Law was to restrain sin. By repentance and doing its works, one was prepared to receive the Holy Spirit.

> [You] who desire to receive holy baptism and to obtain the grace of the Spirit, first you ought to be cleansed by the law. First, having heard the word of God, you ought to restrain your natural vices and to set right your barbarous and wild habits that, having taken on gentleness and humility, you can receive also the grace of the Holy Spirit.[89]

---

82. *Against Celsus* 3.59-60, 69 continues the response to Celsus, emphasizing Christianity's moral purpose of improvement. Auf der Maur, "*Illuminatio*," pp. 45-52.

83. *Commentary on 1 Corinthians* frg. 63 on 1 Cor. 14:18-19; *Homilies on Numbers* 3.1. For the catechumenate under Origen see Saxer, *Les rites de l'initiation*, pp. 150-175.

84. *Against Celsus* 2.4.

85. *Commentary on John* 6.28.144 may possibly indicate that the first phase of instruction lasted three years.

86. *Homilies on Judges* 5.6. Cf. the passages cited above in regard to the exodus and Jordan typologies on the period before baptism as a time of instruction in the divine Law.

87. *Homilies on Joshua* 4.1; Bruce, *Origen: Homilies on Joshua*, pp. 54-55. The priestly and Levitical order would have been taken by Origen as the priests and deacons of the church.

88. *Homilies on Joshua* 5.3; Bruce, *Origen: Homilies on Joshua*, p. 62.

89. *Homilies on Leviticus* 6.2.5; cf. 6.5.2, "The word of the law has washed you and made you clean,

The catechumens were to quit a life of sin and so make themselves a fit dwelling place for the Holy Spirit.

The second phase of instruction included the Trinity and the resurrection. "If someone makes a pure and sincere statement about the Father, about his only begotten, and Holy Spirit, with a mystery worthy of the Deity, . . . but he does not likewise affirm the resurrection of the flesh," he is unclean and unfaithful.[90]

The later instruction also included teaching on the meaning of the sacraments. Origen finds evidence that the practice in his day of accompanying baptism with instruction as to its meaning was observed in apostolic times.

> The apostle . . . is showing by this question [Rom. 6:1, "Do you not know?"] that back then, i.e., in the age of the apostles, not only was the form of the mysteries given to those who were baptized, as we see happening in the present time, but also their effective power and meaning were imparted, as if to those who knew and had been instructed that those who are baptized are baptized into the death of Christ. . . .[91]

In commenting on Exodus 21:22-25 Origen describes a catechumen who falls into sin as "an infant yet unformed" (Gal. 4:19). "The 'infant which is formed' can be seen as the word of God in the heart of that soul which has followed the grace of baptism or which has manifestly and clearly conceived the word of faith."[92]

Auf der Maur and Waldram have emphasized the importance for Origen of the word in the preparation for baptism.[93] Origen makes many references to the *regula fidei*, "the tradition of the church and the apostles." He sets forth its essential contents pertaining to God, Christ Jesus, the Holy Spirit, the nature of the soul, free will, the devil and his angels, the creation of the world, and the scriptures.[94] Other passages provide similar summaries of essential Christian beliefs.[95] Such summaries

---

and the anointing and grace of your baptism remained uncontaminated"; Barkley, *Origen: Homilies on Leviticus*, pp. 118-119, 125. The former quotation is preceded by an important statement of the priority of the divine Word in salvation: "He cannot be a priest . . . whom the Law has not washed and the Word of God has not made pure and the divine Word has not cleansed" (6.2.4).

90. *Homilies on Leviticus* 5.10.3; Barkley, *Origen: Homilies on Leviticus*, p. 108.

91. *Commentary on Romans* 5.8.8; Scheck, *Origen: Commentary on the Epistle to the Romans*, p. 357.

92. *Homilies on Exodus* 10.4; Heine, *Origen: Homilies on Genesis and Exodus*, p. 352.

93. Auf der Maur, "Illuminatio," pp. 52-67, 89-95.

94. *On First Principles* 1.pref.4-8. Albert C. Outler, "Origen and the *Regulae fidei*," *Church History* 8 (1939): 212-221.

95. Origen declares that the Christian *kerygma* of Christ, which he summarizes, was well known among non-Christians (*Against Celsus* 1.7; cf. 3.15 on the rejection of idolatry). He lists the seeds of teaching as concerning the Trinity, eschatology, and the scriptures: the Father, the Son, the Holy Spirit, the resurrection, punishment, refreshment, law, prophets, and in general each of the scriptures (*Homilies on Jeremiah* 5.13). The *Commentary on John* discusses God, Christ, the Holy Spirit, free will, rewards, and punishments (32 [15-16].187-193). The *Matt. comm. ser.* 33 (852) presents the one God in the Law and the gospel; Christ the firstborn of all creatures and incarnate by birth from the virgin, his

would have been part of baptismal catechesis. The *regula* was not set over against scripture but was a guide to its interpretation: "It is certain that [the] union of the soul with the word cannot come about otherwise than through instruction in the divine books."[96]

The emphasis on the word and teaching had as a corollary the importance of faith. Passages already cited relate faith to baptism, and more will be said on that connection in the treatment of confession under liturgy. Origen's comments on Romans 6:8-10, given a baptismal interpretation, include the declaration that Christ by his death "freely bestowed his death of sin as if a certain reward of faith to every believer, namely to those who believe that they have died with him and have been crucified and buried together with him."[97]

Origen's emphasis on the need for repentance — to cease from sin and to reform one's life — has also appeared in passages introduced above and will appear again in the baptismal liturgy in the renunciation of Satan. Origen considered the efficacy of baptism to depend on repentance, on one's own choice of manner of life. In commenting on Matthew 3:11, that John's baptism was "for repentance," Origen offers this explanation:

> By the addition of this phrase Matthew teaches that baptism has its benefit from the intentional choice of the one being baptized. This benefit comes to the one who repents, but to one who does not approach baptism with repentance the result will be more serious judgment. (*Commentary on John* 6.33 [17].165)

Origen's homily on Luke 3:1-4 with reference John's baptism says, "If anyone wanted to repent, there was immediately a ready supply of water at the river" (*Homilies on Luke* 21.3 — see the continuation of the passage quoted on page 410 on the forgiveness of sins in baptism). He repeated his call for catechumens to repent, based on Luke 3:7-8:

> One who remains in his original state and does not leave behind his habits and his customs does not come to baptism properly. . . .
>
> So, whatever [John] says to them, he also says to you, men and women, catechumens! You are arranging to come to baptism. . . . Unless you expel wickedness and the serpent's venom from your hearts, [you are in danger of the wrath to come.]
>
> To you who are coming to baptism, Scripture says, "Produce fruit worthy of repentance."[98]

---

death on the cross, and his resurrection from the dead; the Holy Spirit in the patriarchs and prophets, given in the apostles; and the resurrection of the dead. The *Dialogue with Heraclides* begins with Heraclides' confession of his faith, and Origen then inquires of its details.

96. *Homilies on Genesis* 10.5; Heine, *Origen: Homilies on Genesis and Exodus*, p. 166.

97. *Commentary on Romans* 5.10.2; Scheck, *Origen: Commentary on the Epistle to the Romans*, p. 368.

98. *Homilies on Luke* 22.5, 6, 8; Lienhard, *Origen: Homilies on Luke*, pp. 94-95.

All this about the word, faith, and repentance might seem inconsistent with infant baptism. Origen's justification of the practice was discussed in chapter 23. If Origen ever felt a tension in his thought over the question, nothing survives, but the overwhelming tenor of his remarks shows what an anomaly infant baptism was in the thought and practice of the ancient church.

Liturgy

Origen could use the word "baptism" for the whole ceremony of initiation as well as for the actual water rite. Thus he refers to "the rites of the administration of baptism with its formulas, its gestures, its ceremonies, its questions and responses [*interrogationum ac responsionum*]" (*Homilies on Numbers* 5.1).[99] His vagueness on details might be explained if the *disciplina arcani* was observed in his time. He refers to the "sacraments of the faithful which they who have been initiated know,"[100] but the statement does not necessarily mean a conscious effort to keep some things secret from the uninitiated. Origen nowhere outlines the ceremony of baptism, but from occasional apparently sequential statements and what is known from other sources we will arrange items in their probable sequence.

Origen makes frequent reference to the renunciations of the world involved in baptism as part of his appeal for proper Christian conduct by his hearers (see above on martyrdom). "What does it help us to have renounced this age in baptism but to retain the former filth of our behavior and the impurities of our carnal vices?"[101] This was presumably a verbalized renunciation. Although Origen does not give an exact wording, he does indicate its contents in his comments on Numbers 21:22:

> We come to that moment we made these promises, this declaration to the devil. Each of the faithful recalls when he came to the waters of baptism, when he received the first seal of the faith and approached the fount of salvation, the words that he pronounced then; he recalls his renunciation of the devil. He promised to resort to none of his pomps and his works and not to submit to any of his servitudes and his pleasures. (*Homilies on Numbers* 12.4)

The renunciation of the devil was a promise (wording based on Num. 21:22). The "first seal of the faith" may be the content of the faith imparted in the preparation for baptism, the confession of faith, or some preliminary signing of the candidate. Origen's wording may reflect the formulas we know from other sources, where we find equivalents of renouncing the devil, his pomps, his works, and his service, but there is no exact equivalent to his fivefold renunciation (most are threefold).

---

99. Georg Kretschmar, *Die Geschichte des Taufgottesdienstes in der alter Kirche* in *Leiturgia*, Vol. 5, nos. 31-34 (1964-1966), pp. 135-136.
100. *Homilies on Exodus* 8.4; Heine, *Origen: Homilies on Genesis and Exodus*, p. 324.
101. *Homilies on Joshua* 26.2; Bruce, *Origen: Homilies on Joshua*, p. 216.

Origen referred to a Christian's renunciations without specific reference to baptism (but in the following passage in a larger baptismal context). He parallels the three days encompassed by Jesus' death, burial, and resurrection with this explanation:

> The first day of death is to have renounced the world; the second is to have renounced the vices of the flesh as well; the third day of the resurrection, however, is the fullness of perfection in the light of wisdom.[102]

Origen several times refers to exorcism, but only one may relate to a preparation for baptism. Christian teachers put to flight innumerable demons (*Homilies on Leviticus* 16.7).

Origen's reference to "agreements" [συνθῆκαι] made at the beginning of the Christian life (*Exhortation to Martyrdom* 12; 17) may indicate simply the renunciations themselves (see above), a *syntaxis* paralleling the renunciations, the combination of the renunciations and the confession of faith, or an ethical promise made at an early stage in the catechumenate.[103] The paraphrase of Joshua 24:15 (*Exhortation to Martyrdom* 17) is probably not meant to be a literal quotation of what was said, whether during the catechumenate or prior to the baptism.

Although again without transmitting a liturgical formula, Origen makes even more frequent reference to confession at baptism. "Faith properly speaking is the acceptance with the whole soul of what is believed at baptism" (*Commentary on John* 10.43 [27].298).[104] The confession was apparently made in question and answer form, as indicated in the quotation from the *Homilies on Numbers* 5.1 at the beginning of this section.[105]

The renunciation of sin has as its counterpart the confession of faith. Origen says that the death to sin in Romans 6:10 and 2 Corinthians 4:10 with the result of Christ living within in Galatians 2:20 is the same as what John writes about confessing Christ's coming in the flesh according to 1 John 4:2.

> Surely in that passage it is not the one who shall have declared these syllables and pronounced them in this common confession that shall seem to be led by the Spirit of God [Rom. 8:14], but the one who has fashioned his life in such a way and has produced the fruit of works.[106]

---

102. *Commentary on Romans* 5.10.4; Schreck, *Origen: Commentary on the Epistle to the Romans*, p. 369.

103. The *syntaxis* following the *apotaxis* (renunciation) is otherwise not attested before the fourth century — Auf der Maur, "Illuminatio," p. 78.

104. Origen continues in this section to say that the perfection of our faith will be given at the great resurrection from the dead of the whole body of Jesus which is his church.

105. Eusebius, *Church History* 7.9.2, quotes from Dionysius of Alexandria, shortly after Origen's time, a passage that indicates the confession at Alexandria was made in response to questions (cited in chap. 24).

106. *Commentary on Romans* 5.8.10; Schreck, *Origen: Commentary on the Epistle to the Romans*, pp. 358-359.

It is notable that the incarnation is here included in the basic confession of the church. In this same work, in the same context as the quotation about renunciation above, Origen again refers to the verbal "confession of the voice" (citing Rom. 10:10).[107] The renunciation and the confession are combined in another passage: "When we come to the grace of baptism," we renounce "all other gods and lords, we confess the only God, Father, Son, and Holy Spirit."[108]

Origen often refers to invoking the Trinity at baptism. The quotation cited under "The Baptisms of John the Baptist and Jesus" from the *Commentary on John* (6.33 [17].166 on John 1:26) attributes the effectiveness of baptism to the "invocations of the worshipful Trinity." To the same import is Origen's appeal to the Trinitarian formula in baptism in his theology of the Holy Spirit:

> [T]he person of the Holy Spirit is of so great authority and dignity that saving baptism is not complete except when performed with the authority of the whole most excellent Trinity, that is, by the naming of Father, Son and Holy Spirit; and that the name of the Holy Spirit must be joined to that of the unbegotten God the Father and his only-begotten Son.[109]

The description of baptism as "saving" is related to the authority of the Trinity. Furthermore, Jesus arose from the dead in order that

> he might make possible for those who had been delivered to be baptized in spirit, soul, and body "into the name of the Father and the Son and the Holy Spirit" [Matt. 28:19], which are the three days eternally present at the same time to those who because of them become the children of light. (*Commentary on Matthew* 12.20)[110]

It is not clear that any of these references indicates a formula spoken by the administrator in addition to or instead of the Trinitarian interrogations of the candidate.

Origen, in commenting on Romans 6:3, "baptized into Christ Jesus," considers why Christ's name alone is mentioned, when "it should not be deemed a legitimate baptism unless it is in the name of the Trinity," according to Matthew 28:19.[111]

---

107. *Commentary on Romans* 5.10.4; Scheck, *Origen: Commentary on the Epistle to the Romans*, p. 369.

108. *Homilies on Exodus* 8.4; Heine, *Origen: Homilies on Genesis and Exodus*, p. 322; cf. 8.5, quoted above on baptism as a marriage — "the grace of baptism, the confession of faith" (p. 327).

109. *On First Principles* 1.3.2; translation by G. W. Butterworth, *Origen on First Principles* (London: SPCK, 1936), p. 30 of the Torchbook reprint (New York: Harper & Row, 1966). This passage exists only in the Latin and the wording is suspect of later updating in the interests of orthodoxy, but the other passages from Origen that survive in Greek attest the essential thought. Another Latin text is "To be baptized in the name of Father, Son, and Holy Spirit" — *Homilies on Ezekiel* 7.4.

110. The context might suggest a *postmortem* baptism of those released from Hades by Jesus, but that would only enhance the value of the testimony to the usual church practice.

111. *Commentary on Romans* 5.8.7; Schreck, *Origen: Commentary on the Epistle to the Romans*, p. 356.

Origen explains that Paul was discussing the death of Christ, so it was not appropriate to mention the Father and the Spirit. Origen speaks of baptism "in the name of Christ" in theological or exegetical contexts, but when referring to the actual rite of baptism he gives the Trinitarian formula.[112]

In the continuation of the commentary on Romans 6:3-4, Origen says we spend three days buried with Christ "when we receive complete knowledge of the Trinity," for all three are associated with light. We "spend three nights when we destroy the father of darkness and ignorance together with the lie."[113] Although Origen associates the three days with the Trinity (as in the *Commentary on Matthew* 12.20 above), he does not relate the three days to a triple immersion (nor in *Homilies on Exodus* 5.2 quoted on the exodus theme), as the fourth-century writers do.

Origen gives no details of the baptismal bath except in his development of the exodus motif as a going down into the water and ascending (*Homilies on Exodus* 5.5 above). By his time λουτρόν had a technical meaning for baptism, as we saw in his frequent use of Titus 3:5 as a key baptismal text. Origen could use words from the *baptizō* family in a metaphorical sense that shows their meaning. He refers to those who have been overwhelmed (καταβεβαπτισμένων) by wickedness (*Commentary on John* 28.9.72 on John 11:45).[114]

Origen does closely associate an anointing with baptism. This association was in keeping with ancient practice where a bath and an anointing were essentially one act. "All of us may be baptized in those visible waters and in a visible anointing, in accordance with the form handed down to the churches."[115] The anointing is closely

---

112. Auf der Maur, "Illuminatio," p. 82.

113. *Commentary on Romans* 5.8.9; Schreck, *Origen: Commentary on the Epistle to the Romans*, p. 357.

114. Origen's student Gregory Thaumaturgus, *Panegyric on Origen* 14, says of him: "He himself would remain on high in safety, and stretching out a hand to others he would save them as if drawing up those submerged [or drowning, βαπτιζομένους]."

115. *Commentary on Romans* 5.8.3; Scheck, *Origen: Commentary on the Epistle to the Romans*, p. 355. Paul F. Bradshaw, "Baptismal Practice in the Alexandrian Tradition: Eastern or Western?" in Maxwell E. Johnson, ed., *Living Water, Sealing Spirit: Reading on Christian Initiation* (Collegeville: Liturgical, 1995), pp. 82-100 (96-97), cautions against assuming this is a postbaptismal anointing, because the same passage speaks of "baptism in the Holy Spirit with the water from above," but the sequence Origen is interested in throughout the section is not the liturgical order but a dying to sin leading to baptism. Similarly *Homilies on Leviticus* 6.2.5, "receive holy baptism and obtain grace of the Spirit" (in the preceding section Origen makes nothing of the anointing of the priests that preceded) is balanced by 6.5.2 (the next quotation in my text). Origen does not give clear evidence in regard to the position of an anointing. Since both the *Commentary on Romans* and *Homilies on Leviticus* give both sequences (anointing or Holy Spirit and water; water and anointing or Holy Spirit), one could as well argue for both a prebaptismal and a postbaptismal anointing as for either of the options about the positioning of a single anointing; but if weight is to be placed on his phrase "in accordance with the form handed down to the churches," preference is to be given to a postbaptismal anointing, as also is implied in my next quotation. Saxer, *Les rites de l'initiation*, pp. 182, 189, 191, excludes the hypothesis that Origen is a witness to a prebaptismal anointing but says that he knew a postbaptismal chrismation, which, however, is not to be understood as "confirmation."

connected with the grace of the baptismal act. The Christian application of the anointing of priests in Leviticus 7:36-37 means, "If the word of the law has washed you and made you clean, and the anointing and grace of your baptism remained uncontaminated."[116] Christ is the fountain from whom rivers of living waters flow, and he is the bread, spikenard, and ointment which makes those anointed to be Christs.[117] All Christians have this sacred anointing and so are priests (*Homilies on Leviticus* 9.9.3). The imparting of the Holy Spirit is not connected with the anointing in Origen's preserved texts.

Origen does connect the imparting of the Holy Spirit with the laying on of hands in dealing with the New Testament texts. He quotes Acts 8:18, "'Through the laying on of the apostles' hands the Holy Spirit was given' in baptism,"[118] but he later makes an explicit distinction based on this text, "The Holy Spirit was bestowed through the laying on of the apostles' hands after the grace and renewal of baptism."[119] Although Auf der Maur and Waldram say that for Origen the imparting of the Holy Spirit was not connected with a specific rite in the baptismal liturgy,[120] this last statement seems to me to reflect church liturgical practice.

Origen mentions the clothing of a priest after his washing (Lev. 8:6-7), but he gives no indication that the newly baptized had special literal clothing to put on after baptism (*Homilies on Leviticus* 6.2.6). Nor does the singing of the song of Moses and Miriam after the crossing of the Red Sea indicate a ritual practice after baptism (*Homilies on Exodus* 5.5). The language in both cases rather seems to refer to the existence of a new person.[121]

The baptismal ceremony proper was followed by a eucharist with the congregation. Origen inserts into his comments on Exodus 19:10-11 a reference to Matthew 22:12: After one has washed his garments he can hear the word of God and "a little while later he shall go in to the wedding dinner, he shall eat from the flesh of the lamb, he shall drink the cup of salvation."[122] Here the sequence is washing and then eating; at another place the sequence is being anointed and eating: "After we have been anointed, that is, after having believed in Christ, we are then ordered to move

---

116. *Homilies on Leviticus* 6.5.2; Barkley, *Origen: Homilies on Leviticus*, p. 125. See Bradshaw's caution in the preceding note; but the same caution applies to concluding there was a prebaptismal anointing based on these passages. The oil of anointing is interpreted as Christ and holy doctrine in *Homilies on Ezekiel* 7.4, so the oil is metaphorical in the further statement, "You are no longer catechumens, you have obtained the 'bath of the second generation' [Tit. 3:5], such a person receives the oil and incense of God."

117. *Commentary on the Song of Songs* 2.9 on Song of Songs 1:12. Cf. *Against Celsus* 6.79.

118. *On First Principles* 1.3.2; Butterworth, *Origen on First Principles*, p. 30.

119. *On First Principles* 1.3.7; Butterworth, *Origen on First Principles*, p. 36. Cf. *On Matthew*, frg. 52 on Matt. 3:13, "The one baptizing is not always superior to the one being baptized. Ananias was not superior to Paul, and although Philip baptized, Peter gave the Holy Spirit through the laying on of hands."

120. Hans Jörg Auf der Maur, "Illuminatio," p. 84.

121. Auf der Maur, "Illuminatio," p. 87 on the song.

122. *Homilies on Exodus* 11.7; Heine, *Origen: Homilies on Genesis and Exodus*, p. 365.

on to the eating of Christ."[123] Origen may have had the eucharist in mind when he interpreted the circumcision of Israel by Joshua and Israel's observance of the passover as referring to their feasting after Jesus' (Joshua's) baptism. "On the day of the baptism into Jesus, . . . Jesus [Joshua] purified the sons of Israel." Israel's passover is then explained in terms of the bread given by Jesus.[124] The association of baptism and eucharist is evident in Origen's reference to those who "reject objects of sense and make no use either of baptism or of eucharist" (*On Prayer* 5.1).

The passages already cited are sufficient to show the importance Origen placed on the moral and spiritual life expected of the one who had been baptized.[125]

123. On the Pasch 25; Daly, *Origen: Treatise on the Passover*, p. 41.
124. *Commentary on John* 6.45 (26).233-236.
125. Hugo Rahner, "Taufe und geistliches Leben bei Origenes," *Zeitschrift für Askese und Mystik* 7 (1932): 205-223, emphasizes that baptism was central to the Christian life for Origen.

26. Syria in the Third Century

Acts of Thomas

The *Acts of Thomas*[1] originated in eastern Syria early in the third century, probably in Edessa and likely in the 220s or 230s.[2] Written in Syriac, the work underwent redactional development. The early Greek translation is regarded by most scholars as nearer the original than the surviving Syriac text, but it too underwent revision so that there are places where the Syriac preserves the original.[3] The principal message of these acts is salvation by return to the original asexual condition of humanity. Hence, the apostle Thomas, presented as the twin brother of Jesus, preaches sexual abstinence. Five accounts of conversion in the *Acts of Thomas* include details of the initiation process.[4]

Thomas presented the heralds of the Savior as proclaiming, "Repent and believe the gospel" (28; cf. Mark 1:15).[5] He prayed for King Gundaphorus in India:

---

1. A. F. J. Klijn, *The Acts of Thomas* (Leiden: Brill, 1962), contains an introduction, text, translation (by W. Wright), and commentary. He reflects on what a second edition would require in "The *Acts of Thomas* Revisited," in Jan N. Bremmer, ed., *The Apocryphal Acts of Thomas* (Leuven: Peeters, 2001), pp. 1-10, and published a second revised edition with the same publisher in 2003.

2. Jan N. Bremmer, "The *Acts of Thomas*: Place, Date and Women," in idem, *The Apocryphal Acts of Thomas*, pp. 74-79.

3. Harold W. Attridge, "The Original Language of the *Acts of Thomas*," in Attridge et al., eds., *Of Scribes and Scrolls* (Lanham, MD: University Press of America, 1990), pp. 241-250; Han J. W. Drijvers, in Wilhelm Schneemelcher, ed., *New Testament Apocrypha*, Vol. 2 (Louisville: Westminster/John Knox, 1992), p. 323. Quotations are from this latter work.

4. Baby Varghese, *Les onctions baptismales dans la tradition syrienne*, Corpus scriptorum christianorum orientalium 512 (Louvain: Peeters, 1989), pp. 3-33, who gives priority in his treatment to the Syriac text. A. F. J. Klijn, "Baptism in the Acts of Thomas," in Jacob Vellian, ed., *Studies on Syrian Baptismal Rites*, Syrian Churches Series, Vol. 6 (Kottayam: CMS Press, 1973), pp. 57-62.

5. Cf. *Acts of Thomas* 58, where the apostle calls on people to turn to God, cease their former works, and "Believe in Christ Jesus, and he forgives you."

"Receive the king and his brother and unite them with thy flock, cleansing them with thy washing [λουτρῷ] and anointing them with thy oil from the error which surrounds them" (25).[6] The order "washing and anointing" is the reverse of that in the remaining accounts and may be for stylistic reasons, if not due to a later revision, rather than representing an actual sequence. The continuation of the narrative highlights the importance of the anointing and introduces the language of the seal for the initiation.

King Gundaphorus and his brother, having been taught to believe in God, asked for "the seal [σφραγῖδα, also used in the other occurrences of seal] of the word," "For we have heard thee say that the God whom thou dost preach knows his own sheep by his seal" (26). Thomas rejoiced and prayed for them to receive the seal and to share in the eucharist. He "commanded them to bring oil, that through the oil they might receive the seal" (26), and the apostle "sealed them" (27). They then heard the voice of the Lord saying, "Peace be with you," but they heard only the voice and did not see his form, "for they had not yet received the additional sealing of the seal [ἐπισφράγισμα τῆς σφραγῖδος]" (27). "The apostle took the oil and, pouring it on their heads, anointed and chrismed [ἀλείψας καὶ χρίσας] them,"[7] invoking the holy name of

---

6. The Greek text mentions only an anointing and the eucharist in this conversion story, unless water is included in the "seal." Susan E. Myers, "Initiation by Anointing in Early Syriac-Speaking Christianity," *Studia Liturgica* 31 (2001): 150-170, takes the account in *Acts of Thomas* 26–27 (Greek) as the point of departure for her argument that early Syriac-speaking Christianity knew an initiation by anointing (which conferred the Holy Spirit) followed by the eucharist with no water baptism.

7. This account and the one in 132 are important texts for Gabriele Winkler's argument, now widely accepted, that the original Syriac practice was only one anointing, a prebaptismal pouring of olive oil on the head (in all the accounts where oil is applied, it is "poured" on the head). See her article, "The Original Meaning of the Prebaptismal Anointing and Its Implications," *Worship* 52 (1978): 24-45; repr. in Maxwell E. Johnson, ed., *Living Water, Sealing Spirit: Readings on Christian Initiation* (Collegeville: Liturgical, 1995), pp. 58-81. Bryan D. Spinks, *Early and Medieval Ritual and Theologies of Baptism* (Aldershot: Ashgate, 2006), p. 23, agrees but finds it difficult to understand why she considers the Synoptic account of the baptism of Jesus as the paradigm for this Syriac pattern. Later an anointing of the whole body was introduced, and eventually a postbaptismal anointing as well. For this outline of the historical development in Syria see Varghese, *Les onctions baptismales*, pp. xxix-xxx. On this scheme, the accounts of Mygdonia (120-121) and Vazan (157) represent a more developed practice with the addition of an anointing of the whole body and also benedictions of oil — Varghese, *Les onctions baptismales*, pp. 5-10. Bryan D. Spinks, "Baptismal Patterns in Early Syria: Another Reading," in Maxwell E. Johnson and L. Edward Phillips, eds., *Studia Liturgica Diversa: Essays in Honor of Paul F. Bradshaw* (Portland: Pastoral Press, 2004), 45-52, suggests that instead of a straight line development there was the co-existence of a diversity of practice.

Winkler objects to the translation "seal," for the Syriac *rushma* ("anointing," from *mesha*, "olive oil," the word used in the Syriac *Acts of Thomas*, not *myron*) meant signing or marking, whereas the word for "seal" (postbaptismal in later Syriac practice) is *hatma*. The similarity of the word for oil with Messiah facilitated an emphasis on the anointing as the key act in identifying a person with Christ. See the summary in her article "The Original Meaning," pp. 58-81 (64-66 on *Acts of Thomas*). I have kept the translation "seal," for I am commenting on the Greek text. For the Syriac *rushma* (*rûšmō*) in the *Acts of Thomas* referring not to the pre-immersion anointing but to the whole baptismal rite, see Varghese, *Les onctions baptismales*, pp. 12-14.

Christ to come upon them. The invocation concluded: "Come, Holy Spirit, and purify their reins and their heart and give them the added seal in the name of Father and Son and Holy Spirit" (27).[8] "When they had been sealed there appeared to them a young man carrying a blazing torch" (27). When dawn came, Thomas "broke bread and made them partakers in the eucharist of Christ" (27). They rejoiced, and many others also who came to faith and were added to their number.

The specific meaning of the seal in the Greek text is not clear.[9] A general reference to the whole rite of initiation might be suggested by the language of "additional sealing," indicating two stages in the rite. A particular association with the anointing is explicit in the phrase that speaks of receiving the seal through the oil. The seal also is associated with the name of Christ. Seal might also stand for baptism, and this is the case in the Syriac text. According to the Syriac the king gave orders that the bath should be closed for seven days, and on the eighth day Judas Thomas, the king, and his brother, "entered into the bath by night that Judas might baptize them."[10] In the places where the Greek says "sealed," the Syriac has "baptized."[11] On this reading, baptism would be "the added seal" in the Trinitarian name.

Only the bread is mentioned in the eucharist (27; 29), and this is in accord with the rest of the *Acts of Thomas*, where the eucharist consists of only bread or bread and water, and wine is not included. That practice agrees with the ascetic thrust of the document.[12]

In an account of Thomas expelling a demon a version of the kerygma is included (47).[13] The woman in whom the demon had dwelt begged the apostle, "Give me the seal, that the enemy may not return to me again!" (49). "Laying his

---

8. This is the only invocation of the Holy Spirit in these accounts — the other prayers, as elsewhere in this account also, call upon the Messiah — Varghese, *Les onctions baptismales*, pp. 24-28, who points out that in the *Acts of Thomas* Christ is in the oil and confers power to the anointed (p. 26) — see the other accounts below.

9. See the discussion in G. W. H. Lampe, *The Seal of the Spirit*, 2nd ed. (London: SPCK, 1967), pp. 187-189. Klijn, "Baptism in the Acts of Thomas," pp. 57-62, who notes that the anointing is very much emphasized in the work, says "seal" originally was used for the anointing only but came to be used for the whole rite; hence a rewriter had to invent a new word, "the added sealing of the seal," for the anointing. He finds the significance of the seal clearly seen in chap. 118 — it has a protective value and is the sign by which it is known that one belongs to God.

10. William Wright, *Apocryphal Acts of the Apostles* (London, 1871; repr. Amsterdam: Philo Press, 1968), p. 166.

11. In addition to this passage, see Wright, *Apocryphal Acts*, pp. 188 (chap. 49), 267 (chap. 132), and 290 (chaps. 157–158), where the Syriac has its regular words for baptism and baptize (meaning to dive, plunge, dip). My thanks to Jeff Childers for verifying the Syriac readings for me.

12. Hans Lietzmann, *Mass and Lord's Supper: A Study in the History of the Liturgy* (Leiden: Brill, 1979), pp. 196-202, collects evidence for a eucharist with bread only or with bread and water. For the *Acts of Thomas*, G. Rouwhorst, "La célebration de l'eucharistie selon les Acts de Thomas," in C. Caspers and M. Schneiders, eds., *Omnes Circumstantes: Contributions towards a History of the Role of the People in the Liturgy* (Kampen, 1990), pp. 51-77.

13. Cf. Justin, *Dialogue with Trypho* 30; 76; 85; *2 Apology* 6:8 for elements of the kerygma included in formulas of exorcism.

hands upon her, [he] sealed her in the name of the Father and of the Son and of the Holy Spirit. And many others also were sealed with her" (49). There followed a eucharist in which only bread is mentioned (49-50). Thomas prayed, marked the cross on the bread, broke it, and distributed it, saying "Let this be to thee for forgiveness of sins" (50).

As far as one can learn from this passage (49), the seal is a blessing with the laying on of hands. We might deduce from other passages, however, that the seal is the application of oil in the Trinitarian name. Baptism might seem less likely in this quite condensed account, but the later Syriac version is explicit: When the woman requested the seal, the apostle "went to a river which was close by there, and baptized her in the name of the Father and the Son and the Spirit of holiness; and many were baptized with her."[14] Notable is the association of forgiveness with the reception of the eucharistic bread.

The account of the initiation of the woman Mygdonia, married to a kinsman of a king, gives more details. Here the sequence is explicit: anointing, baptism, and eucharist. Mygdonia asked of Judas Thomas, "Give me the seal of Jesus Christ" (120). She "stood before the apostle with her head bare; and he taking the oil poured it on her head," speaking a benediction that described the oil as given for sanctification and a mystery in which the cross was shown (121). He told Mygdonia's nurse, Marcia (Syriac Narcia), to unclothe her and put a linen girdle on her, so this was not a completely nude baptism.

> [Going to a spring of water (κρήνη ὕδατος),] the apostle baptized [ἐβάπτισεν] Mygdonia in the name of the Father and the Son and the Holy Spirit. When she was baptized and clothed, he broke bread and took a cup of water, and made her partaker in the body of Christ and the cup of the Son of God. (121)

He explained that she had received the seal and obtained eternal life. Marcia then asked that she too receive the seal, and it was given to her.

The variants in the Syriac are of a different order from those in the first two accounts above. The words spoken at the anointing describe the Lord Jesus as "life, health, and the remission of sins." After casting the oil on Mygdonia's head, Thomas instructed her nurse to anoint her (whole body — this second anointing would have been a later development). Here and in the account in 157 below the Syriac highlights the healing aspect of oil. Then, instead of going to a spring of water, the apostle brought a basin, and, standing over it, he baptized Mygdonia.[15]

Earlier in the narrative Mygdonia had instructed Marcia to bring her wine mixed with water, a loaf of bread, and oil (120), but at the conclusion of the baptism, Thomas "broke bread and took a cup of water" (121 — a cup only in the Syriac).

Thomas then went to the house of Siphor (a general in the Syriac). Siphor, his

---

14. Wright, *Apocryphal Acts*, p. 188.
15. Wright, *Apocryphal Acts*, p. 258.

wife, and his daughter asked for the seal that they might become servants to the true God (131). Thomas spoke to them about baptism:

> This baptism [βάπτισμα] is forgiveness of sins. It brings to new birth [ἀναγεννᾷ, begets] a light that is shed around. It brings to new birth [begets] the new man.... Glory be to thee, hidden power that is united with us in baptism! Glory be to thee, renewal through which are renewed the baptized [βαπτιζόμενοι] who take hold of thee with affection! (132)

Here are expressed some of the fundamental ideas associated with baptism: forgiveness, new birth, enlightenment, and renewal.

Immediately the text continues, "he poured oil upon their heads," with words of glory to the name of Christ. "And he commanded a basin [σκάφην] to be brought, and baptized [ἐβάπτισεν] them in the name of the Father and the Son and the Holy Spirit" (132). "When they were baptized and clothed, he set bread upon the table and blessed it." The blessing included the statement that the bread might become for those who partook forgiveness of sins and again that those who partook might be washed of their sins (133). Once more we have the sequence of anointing (only one), baptizing, and taking a bread eucharist.

The Syriac has several points that bring the account more into line with the catholic church. The words spoken about baptism and the anointing point more to the divine power at work through the actions than to the power in the actions themselves. Instead of a basin, a "large vat" was brought, thus reversing the variation in chapter 121, where the Syriac had a basin instead of a spring. Subsequent to the baptism Thomas brought bread and wine to the table.[16]

Actually the Syriac's "large vat" may better represent what the Greek intended by σκάφη. Although the word can mean a bowl or basin, it more often refers to a trough, tub, or bath and is even used for a grave. There is another reference to bringing a basin of water in an earlier passage (chap. 55) not in a baptismal context (in both Syriac and Greek). A Christian guilty of murder had his hands wither when he took the eucharist. Thomas commanded a basin of water to be brought and told the man to wash his hands in the waters. When he did so, his hands were healed.[17] The word here is λεκάνη, a dish or basin. If a small vessel had been intended in 132, this would have been the word used. The translation "basin" would make an immersion or complete washing impossible, but the correct translation leaves open that possibility. That the persons were unclothed and had to be clothed after the baptism favors a full bath and so a container large enough to permit this. Describing missionary situations, the *Acts of Thomas* does not mention structures specially built for

---

16. Wright, *Apocryphal Acts*, pp. 267–268. One may compare *Acts and Martyrdom of Matthew* 26 for a coffin set up in a bedroom for baptism, but the account proceeds to refer to the baptism in the "sea" (chap. 13).

17. Thomas described it as "waters from the living waters."

baptism; it occurs in a river (49 — Syriac), a spring (121), a bath (27 — Syriac), or a container for collecting water (132, the passage under discussion).

The association of the forgiveness of sins with the eucharist is a special feature. Since the same association is made with baptism, we perhaps should think of the whole rite of initiation and not specifically of its parts, but there may be an increasing idea that communion brought a renewal of the forgiveness initially received in baptism.

The final account of baptism in the *Acts of Thomas* concerns Vazan, son of King Misdaeus. The king accused Thomas of bewitching people with "oil and water and bread" (152),[18] a sequence with which we are now familiar in this work.

Vazan and some women were converted. Vazan was prepared for the baptism before the women were. After praying for them, Thomas instructed Mygdonia to unclothe the women and gird them with girdles. Then the apostle said an extended prayer over the oil, praising its virtues, concluding with the petition: "Jesus, let thy victorious power come, and let it settle in this oil as then it settled in the wood that is its kin . . . , and let it dwell in this oil, over which we name thy holy name!" (157). The apostle poured the oil on the head of Vazan and then on the heads of the women, saying: "In thy name, Jesus Christ, let it be to these souls for remission of sins, and for the turning back of the adversary, and for salvation of their souls" (157).[19] The same effects usually attributed to water baptism are here attributed to the pouring of oil on the head. Then Thomas commanded Mygdonia to anoint the women, and he himself anointed Vazan. After this full anointing, "he led them down to [εἰς] the water in the name of the Father and of the Son and of the Holy Spirit" (157). "When they had come up from the water he took bread and a cup, and blessed" (158). The prayer included the petition, "Let thy body, then, become for us salvation, and thy blood for remission of sins!" (158).

The Syriac is generally rather close to the Greek. It does specify that after they went down into the water they were baptized, and includes the description of the cup blessed with the bread as the "mingled cup."[20]

In addition to the forgiveness of sins a number of gifts are associated with baptism in the *Acts of Thomas*. One of the most important of these is freedom. Also, by baptism one becomes a sheep in the flock of Christ, receives insight (17), becomes a dwelling place of Christ (156); the soul is mingled with the Spirit (121 Greek) and born again (131).[21]

The Greek version of the *Acts of Thomas* gives the impression of preserving in places evidence of an initiation ritual in which the anointing with oil had the central

---

18. The Syriac has "bread and wine" and later in the passage reverses the order found in the Greek to "water and oil and bread and wine" — Wright, *Apocryphal Acts*, p. 285.

19. Franz Josef Dölger, *Der Exorzismus in altchristlichen Taufritual* (Paderborn: Ferdinand Schöningh, 1909), p. 10, refers to this passage for the exorcistic anointing of the body before baptism in relation to Gnostic practice (he identifies the *Acts of Thomas* as Gnostic).

20. Wright, *Apocryphal Acts*, p. 290.

21. Klijn, "Baptism in the Acts of Thomas," pp. 57-62.

place, for which there are indications in the sources for Gnostic practice (chap. 17).[22] Even in the Greek version, and more extensively in the present Syriac version, ideas and practices more in line with catholic Christianity are incorporated. The major differences from Christianity west of the areas influenced by Syriac Christianity are the order of anointing followed by baptism and eucharist and the prominence given to the prebaptismal anointing.[23] The order in Jewish initiation of circumcision, baptism, and sacrifice may have influenced Syriac Christian practice, but the parallel is superficial and the suggestion speculative.

Acts of Xanthippe and Polyxena

I treat this little-known work here because of its dependence on the *Acts of Thomas* (as well as on other apocryphal acts of apostles).[24] The later menologia of the Greek church (tenth century) says Xanthippe lived in the time of the emperor Claudius and was the wife of Probus, ruler of Spain. She had a maiden sister, Polyxena. When Paul came to Spain, they were converted and baptized. Despite the dependence on several western sources and the setting of the beginning of the work in Rome, the author seems to reflect Syrian baptismal practice.

When Xanthippe hears her servant talking about a healer and teacher, she asks what manner of cure he effected.

> The servant says to her, "An invocation of a new name, an anointing of oil, and a bath [λοῦτρον] of water. By this treatment I have seen many with incurable diseases receive healing."

The order of invocation, anointing, and a bath is not the only pointer to Syrian influence.

The account of Xanthippe's conversion is as follows:

---

22. Varghese, *Les onctions baptismales*, pp. 19-24, 28-32, argues this from the Syriac on the basis that all the symbolism of baptism is attached to the oil and none to the immersion or the water, although noting that the anointing was not separated from the immersion. (I wonder if this emphasis on the oil is because the immersion was taken for granted and there was an advocacy for a new practice or a new interpretation?)

23. Georg Kretschmar, "Recent Research on Christian Initiation," *Studia Liturgica* 12 (1977): 87-106 (p. 100), suggests that an analogy to the Syrian sequence of giving the Spirit by anointing followed by baptism is found in the Qumran requirement of inner purification by the Spirit before cultic lustrations (1QS 3, 4-9 — see chap. 3).

24. The Greek text is published by M. R. James in *Texts and Studies* 2.3 (1893): 58-85 with an introduction (pp. 43-57); p. 52 for the use of the *Acts of Thomas*. E. C. Whitaker, *Documents of the Baptismal Liturgy*, rev. and exp. Maxwell E. Johnson (Collegeville: Liturgical, 2003), p. 21, cites with approval James's date of about 250 (p. 54), but actually James's demonstration of the work's use of the apocryphal acts of the apostles only means that it cannot be much earlier than that; but unless use of later material is demonstrated, it probably should not be placed too much later than when the apocryphal acts were most popular.

> She rose up from the ground and said to Paul: "Teacher, why did you leave me desolate? Even now, hasten to give me the seal [σφραγίσαι] so that even if death should overtake me, I should depart to him who is full of mercy and not arrogant.
>
> Immediately therefore the great Paul took her hand and went into the house of Philotheus. He baptized [ἐβάπτισεν] her into the name of the Father and the Son and the Holy Spirit. Next, taking bread and giving thanks, he gave it to her, saying, "May this be to you for forgiveness of sins and for renewal of your soul." Then the blessed Xanthippe, having received the divine gift of holy baptism, went to her house rejoicing and praising God. (13-14)

Although the baptism in the Trinitarian name is not exceptional, the request for the seal and the eucharist in which only bread is mentioned and which is associated with forgiveness of sins could come directly from the *Acts of Thomas*.

The account of the baptism of Probus shows influence from the *Acts of Paul*, even more evident elsewhere in these acts.

> Probus arose early in the morning and went to Paul. He found him baptizing [βαπτίζοντα] many people into the name of the life-giving Trinity. He says, "If, therefore, I am worthy, my lord Paul, to receive baptism [βάπτισμα], now is the time." Paul says to him, "My son, see the water is ready for the cleansing of those coming to Christ." Immediately then, eagerly stripping off his clothes, while Paul held him with his hand, he rushed into the water, saying "Jesus Christ, Son of God and eternal God, may all my sin be covered by this water." And Paul said, "We baptize [βαπτίζομεν] you into the name of Father and Son and Holy Spirit." And then he made him partake of the eucharist of Christ. (21)

The leaping into the water recalls *Acts of Paul* 34 except there it was a self-baptism. The combination of the candidate's confession of faith and a formula pronounced by the administrator is to be noted. Baptism in the triple divine name, as the way to come to Christ, as a cleansing from sin, nudity, and immediate participation in the eucharist are familiar features. Representing a later trend of thought, but not new in this document, is worthiness before receiving baptism.

Didascalia

The *Teaching of the Apostles (Didascalia Apostolorum)* is a church order and pastoral admonition from Syria, written in Greek in the early to mid–third century. The work survives in a Syriac translation, partially in a Latin translation, and some of the Greek can be recovered from the work's incorporation in the fourth-century *Apostolic Constitutions*. There is no independent treatment of the administration of baptism such as is found in other church orders (*Didache* and *Apostolic Tradition*), but quite a bit is said in the treatment of other subjects.

In the context of discussing the reconciliation to the church of Christians who have fallen into sin there is this statement about conversion:

> When the heathen desire and promise to repent, saying "We believe," we receive them into the congregation so that they may hear the word, but do not receive them into communion until they receive the seal and are fully initiated. (10)[25]

Here we have a reference to the practice of excluding non-Christians from the eucharistic service. Those who believed and wanted to repent of their previous life (notice the combination) could come to hear instruction from the scriptures but were dismissed before the communion. The seal here evidently refers to baptism and the whole initiatory ceremony.

An exhortation to the people to respect their bishop refers to the bishop's liturgical activities:

> Hold the bishops in honor, for it is they who have loosed you from sins, who by the baptismal water have given you new birth [regenerated you], who filled you with the Holy Spirit, who reared you with the word as with milk, who established you with doctrine, who confirmed you with admonition, and allowed you to partake of the holy eucharist of God, and made you partakers and joint heirs of the promise of God. (9)[26]

The unifying theme of the passage is the role of the bishop in making one a Christian — pre- and postbaptismal instruction and presiding at the baptismal ceremony and eucharist. The benefits conferred in becoming a Christian are release from sins, regeneration, the gift of the Holy Spirit, enlightenment, and participation in the divine promises.

A passage addressed to the bishop and discussing the need for deaconesses seems to give in sequence the baptismal ritual:

> When women go down into the baptismal water: those who go down into the water ought to be anointed by a deaconess with the oil of anointing; and where there is no woman at hand, and especially no deaconess, he who baptizes must of necessity anoint the woman who is being baptized. But where there is a woman, and especially a deaconess, present, it is not fitting that women should be seen by men, but with the imposition of hand you should anoint the head only . . . whether it be of men or of women; and afterwards, whether you yourself baptize, or you tell the

---

25. Translations are from Sebastian Brock, *The Liturgical Portions of the Didascalia*, Grove Liturgical Study 29 (Bramcote: Grove, 1982), here p. 12. Paul F. Bradshaw, "The Profession of Faith in Early Christian Baptism," *Evangelical Quarterly* 78 (2006): 101-115, notes that the doctrinal instruction came after the baptism (p. 103) and refers to his article "The Gospel and the Catechumenate in the Third Century," *Journal of Theological Studies*, n.s. 50 (1999): 143-152.

26. Brock, *The Liturgical Portions*, p. 12. The bracketed words are the translation of R. H. Connolly, *Didascalia Apostolorum* (Oxford: Clarendon, 1929), p. 94. The word "baptismal" is not in the Syriac here (nor in chap. 16 quoted below) but is a correct expanded translation. Shortly before this passage there is reference to the bishop as the one through whom the Lord gave the Holy Spirit, through whom one learned the word, was sealed, became a son of light, and in baptism by the imposition of hand received the testimony of the Lord.

deacons or presbyters to baptize, let a woman, a deaconess, anoint the women, as we have already said. But let a man pronounce over them the invocation of the divine names in the water. And when the woman who is being baptized has come up from the water, let the deaconess receive her, and teach and instruct her how the seal of baptism ought to be kept unbroken in purity and holiness. (16)

The anointing, as in other testimonies to the Syriac baptismal ritual, preceded the immersion, and there is no postbaptismal anointing.[27] There was both an anointing of the whole body (by a woman in the case of women)[28] and an anointing of the head by the bishop. This latter (in the omitted section) is likened to the anointing of the priests and kings in Israel, which was the common association in early Syriac sources.[29] The male administrator pronounced the divine names at the baptism. A woman deacon received the woman baptizand from the water and took charge of her postbaptismal instruction in the Christian life.

A woman was not to baptize (15). This regulation applied to presiding at the baptism — speaking the words of invocation and anointing the head — and not all the actions involved in the baptizing, for as the subsequent passage quoted above states, the preliminary anointing of a woman was to be done by a woman. The text is not explicit about the dipping, but presumably the male administrator who anointed the head also dipped it under the water.

The single Christian baptism is implicitly contrasted with the multiple washings of Judaism. As part of the work's polemic against observing the Jewish ritual law ("the Second Legislation"), the author refers to the sufficiency of the spiritual circumcision of the heart and then takes up as a further matter the one baptism that completely forgives sins (24).[30]

The author knew that some Jewish purifications required baptism and others sprinkling: From the time of the Second Legislation "were separations, and purifications, and baptisms, and sprinklings [the Latin (50) gives *baptisma et asparsio*]" (26).[31] The distinction is important for word usage: baptism was a complete washing in contrast to a sprinkling, and the word for baptism was used for the Christian rite.

The discussion of Jewish baptisms consistently affirms that Christian baptism

---

27. This feature of the Syriac baptismal practice will be discussed more fully in connection with the fourth century.

28. Epiphanius, *Panarion* 3.79.3.6, repeats the need for deaconesses, so women are not seen naked by men at the time of baptism. Spinks, "Baptismal Patterns in Early Syria," 45-52, says the *Didascalia* may be understood as describing a single prebaptismal anointing of the head and the whole body; if there were no women deacons, the bishop anointed the head only; when the anointing was delegated to deacons, the bishop started the rite with the head and gave the remainder over to male and female deacons.

29. Winkler, "The Original Meaning," pp. 66-70.

30. See the fuller treatment in chap. 16.

31. Connolly, *Didascalia*, pp. 222-223. The passage is missing from the *Apostolic Constitutions*. For the Jewish distinctions see in the Mishnah the tractate *Mikwaoth*, discussed in chap. 4.

brings a complete forgiveness and not a temporary purification that must be repeated with every occasion of impurity (24; 26).[32] The same claim is made elsewhere:

> Sins are also forgiven by baptism to those from the gentiles who draw near and enter the holy church of God. . . . Everyone, therefore, who believes and is baptized has had his former sins forgiven. But after baptism, again, even though he has not sinned some deadly sin or been an accomplice to it, but has just seen or heard or spoken of it, then he is again guilty of sin. (20)[33]

The passage continues by affirming the usual view of the early church that martyrdom was an additional means of forgiveness: "If someone departs from the world by martyrdom for the name of the Lord, . . . their sins are covered." The baptismal forgiveness, however, meant that one should not sin afterward, for the one who does evil after baptism is condemned to the Gehenna of fire (5). Examples of the deadly sins after baptism that all the water in the world would not make clean were adultery and fornication (26).[34]

The contrast with Jewish washings also gives considerable discussion to the baptismal gift of the Holy Spirit as an abiding possession. Those who feel a need for multiple washings imply that the Spirit has left them with every occasion of impurity.

> Let them tell us: on those days and at those hours when they keep themselves from prayer and from receiving the eucharist, or from reading the Scriptures, let them tell us whether they are emptied of the Holy Spirit. For through baptism they receive the Holy Spirit who is continually with those who perform righteousness, and who does not depart from them by reason of natural fluxes and marital intercourse, but is continually and always with those who possess him, and he preserves them. (26)[35]

The author interprets the "waterless places" inhabited by unclean spirits of Matthew 12:43-45 with reference to those who do not go down into the water of baptism. In further discussion of the passage he affirms again the filling with the Holy Spirit at baptism, something which means that one is separated from the unclean spirit:

> The believer is filled with the Holy Spirit, but the unbeliever with an unclean spirit, and his nature does not accept an alien spirit. Therefore the person who has withdrawn and separated himself and departed from the unclean spirit by means of baptism, is filled with the Holy Spirit; and if he performs good works, the Holy

---

32. Connolly, *Didascalia*, pp. 204, 248-250.
33. Brock, *Liturgical Portions*, p. 25, who acknowledges the obscurity of the last sentence. I understand the passage to say that baptism covers not only former sins but also non-deadly sins committed after baptism; cf. Connolly, *Didascalia*, p. 178.
34. Brock, *Liturgical Portions*, p. 33, quoted in chap. 16; the context may indicate that Jewish washings are primarily in view.
35. Brock, *Liturgical Portions*, p. 32.

Spirit abides with him, and he remains filled; and the unclean spirit finds no place with him, for the person who is filled with the Holy Spirit does not accept it. (26)[36]

The author, therefore, does recognize that there are actions that will cause the Holy Spirit to depart, so one must be engaged in good works in order for the Holy Spirit to remain with him. That, however, is not his main concern in this passage. He continues with the affirmation that there is no other power that displaces the unclean spirit except the pure and holy Spirit of God.

The possession of the Holy Spirit had special importance for the author. It was communicated by baptism but could be lost by returning to a life of sin. Such a person was excluded from the communion, even as the heathen was, until the indwelling of the Spirit was restored by the imposition of the bishop's hand. The Christian convicted of sins who repented was received back into the communion of the church by the laying on of the hand of the bishop: "For him the imposition of the hand shall take the place of baptism; for whether it be by the imposition of hand, or by baptism, they then receive the communion of the Holy Spirit" (10).[37]

For the *Didascalia*, as for early Christianity in general, baptism marked the separation of the church from the Gentile world and from the distinctive observances of Judaism. In explaining that the ordinances of the "Second Legislation" had been imposed on the Jews because of the making of the golden calf and idolatry (Exod. 32), the author makes this statement about the significance of baptism: "But you, through baptism, have been set free from idolatry, and you have been released from the Second Legislation which was imposed on account of idols" (26).[38] Baptism was not only a break with idolatry but it also meant that the Christian was not under the ritual laws of the Mosaic covenant, which the Lord "did away with and abolished." But in the gospel he "renewed, fulfilled, and affirmed" what was moral and spiritual in the Law.

The Baptistery at Dura Europus

The earliest dated Christian baptistery was at the Roman garrison town of Dura on the Euphrates River in eastern Syria (Figure 13).[39] Sometime in the 240s the Christian community acquired a private house that was built in 232/3 (dated from a graffito) and remodeled it for their use. Dura was destroyed by the Sassanian Persians in 256.

---

36. Brock, *Liturgical Portions*, pp. 32-33. Dölger, *Der Exorzismus*, p. 8, cites this passage as an indication that the exorcistic character of baptism had gained the upper hand in the first half of the third century. He notes that expelling the devil and receiving the Holy Spirit were inseparable — p. 129.

37. Brock, *Liturgical Portions*, p. 13.

38. Brock, *Liturgical Portions*, p. 31.

39. Carl H. Kraeling, *The Christian Building: The Excavations at Dura Europos,* Final Report 8.2, ed. C. B. Welles (New Haven: Yale University Press, 1967), from which I draw the factual information in this section.

On the south of the central courtyard of the house two rooms were combined and provided with a platform on the east end to make the assembly hall that could accommodate sixty to seventy persons (additional persons could gather in the courtyard). A small room (6.80 by 3.16 meters) on the northwest corner of the courtyard was remodeled as a baptistery and decorated with paintings. The dedication of one room as a baptistery and its extensive artistic program (the only space in the house to receive decorations) show the importance of baptism for the community.

The position of the font on the west (shorter) end of the room was emphasized by the canopy covering it. It was 1.63 meters long north to south, and it had a width of 0.948 meters on its north side and 1.065 meters on its south side. The depth was 0.955 meters. An interior step or ledge runs along the east (front) side of the font and on its north and south ends. On the outside facing the interior of the room there was a rubble step. When water was placed in the font after the excavation, the font was shown to be watertight. The question is sometimes asked if the font was large enough for an immersion, but a negative answer perhaps presupposes laying the body out horizontally (even that position is possible on a diagonal of the font for a person of average height at that time). If the baptizand was seated on the interior ledge, was in a kneeling or squatting position, or leaned forward from the waist there was ample space for an immersion. The depth of the pool compares favorably with many larger pools from a later period seemingly designed for adult immersion. The alternative question to be asked is why the font was as large as it was if only pouring or sprinkling was performed.

The ceiling of the canopy over the font showed a blue sky with many white stars, giving a cosmic setting to the baptismal event (the baptized become part of a new creation?). The picture at the focal point on the west wall behind the baptismal font showed a Good Shepherd carrying a large ram on his shoulders with over twelve rams in the surrounding pasture.[40] The image probably focused on Christ as his people's Savior, who brought forgiveness and deliverance. If the setting is Paradise, then this salvation is eschatological: Christ offers escape from death and a blessed hereafter. There is a niche and ledge on the south wall that may have been used for keeping the oil to be used in anointing; if anointing was a part of the ceremony (as the other Syriac sources indicate), then the analogy of sealing sheep (see above) may have suggested the Good Shepherd as the focal image for the room.

---

40. Johannes Quasten, "Das Bild des Guten Hirten in den altchristlichen Baptisterien und in den Taufliturgien des Ostens und Westens: Das Siegel der Gottesherde," in Theodor Klauser and Adolf Rücker, eds., *Pisciculi: Studien zur Religion und Kultur des Altertums: Franz Joseph Dölger* (Münster: Aschendorff, 1939), pp. 220-244, surveys the baptisteries (of which this is the first) and patristic texts on Christ as the Good Shepherd. The image's relation to baptism was that it represented Christ as Savior; the early Christian designation of baptism as a seal contributed to the imagery, for one of the meanings of a seal was the mark of the owner on his animals (p. 226); Psalm 23 (22) was uniformly given a baptismal interpretation in patristic literature, probably because of its use in the baptismal liturgy (pp. 231-239).

Another artist later added at the bottom left of the picture Adam, Eve, the serpent, and the tree (Gen. 3). Successive events are shown in one scene: picking the fruit (the cause) and wearing aprons (the result). The serpent is on the ground, but the forepart of his body is erect. This recollection of the origin of human sin had the effect of bringing out the baptismal salvation as a forgiveness of sins.

On the north wall nearest the font on the lower register there is a tomb, depicted as a gable-roofed sarcophagus over which are two stars (= angels?), approached by three women bearing torches and bowls of unguents. This scene is likely the front part of a procession that extended to the east wall, where five pairs of feet survive on the same lower level. The reference to the resurrection of Jesus seems most likely. A total of eight persons would connect with the early Christian symbolism of eight for resurrection and the world to come; and it may be that the three women nearest the tomb represent Jesus' three days in the tomb as well as being the women taken from the accounts of Easter morning in the Gospels.

The upper register on the north wall has two scenes: Jesus healing the paralytic, who is lying on his bed and then takes up his bed and walks, and Jesus and Peter walking on the water beside a ship. The healing miracle might be from either John 5:2-9 (where the reference to the pool suggested a baptismal interpretation)[41] or the Synoptics (Matt. 9:2-8; Mark 2:1-12, where the healing of a paralytic is associated with Jesus' power to forgive sins). The discovery of a fragment of Tatian's *Diatessaron* in Greek at Dura would indicate that both the Synoptic Gospels and the Fourth Gospel would have been known at Dura, if not as separate Gospels at least in the harmony by Tatian. Jesus' saving Peter when he began to sink in the water (Matt. 14:28-33) was also given a baptismal interpretation in the early church.[42] These two scenes may be what survives from a cycle of the mighty works of deliverance performed by Jesus.

On the south wall, lower register, there is depicted the woman drawing water at the well of Jacob in Samaria (John 4:4-26; less likely is Rebekah at the well in Gen. 24:15-20). The baptismal use of this scene is probably suggested by Jesus' words about "living water," "springing up to eternal life" (John 4:11, 14).[43]

Another scene of the south wall, poorly preserved but the only scene with names, is David ready to bring the sword down on the neck of the prostrate Goliath. This might be another scene of victory or deliverance, but since the picture is beneath the niche where the anointing oil may have been kept, then the emphasis may have been on David as the Lord's anointed and so the victory of the anointed ones.

Two graffiti in Greek found in the room may be relevant for the religious mentality of the Christian community. "Christ (with you). Remember [plural] Siseos the humble." "Ch(rist) J(esus) be with you. Remember [plural] (Pr)oclus." They may ad-

---

41. Tertullian, *On Baptism* 5.
42. Tertullian, *On Baptism* 11.
43. The Samaritan woman, the starry sky, the Good Shepherd, walking on water, and women at the tomb are all in the program of the Baptistery of San Giovanni in Fonte in Naples (c. 400).

dress the newly baptized or those approaching baptism to remember their teachers. They are a reminder of the central place of Christ in Christian faith.[44]

The medium-sized room on the west side of the house and adjoining the baptistery may have been employed for instruction or for the baptizands' use before and/ or after the baptism, but any proposal is conjectural.

The Mime/Martyr Gelasinus

The *Chronicon Paschale* (seventh century) reports for the year 297 the remarkable "baptism" of the imperial "second mime" Gelasinus in the "Heliopolitan city in [the province] Libansensis" (Lebanon).

> While a public theatrical contest was being held and the populace was watching, the other mimes threw him into a great tub from the bath-house, full of warm water, in mockery of the doctrine of the Christians and holy baptism. And the same Gelasinus, the second mime, after being baptized and coming up from the tub, clad in white robes, no longer tolerated being on stage, saying "I am a Christian; for I saw an awesome glory in the tub, and I will die a Christian."[45]

The people in the theater were enraged and took Gelasinus outside and stoned him to death. His kinsmen built a chapel for him.

The mockery of Christian baptism may have included the baptismal formula ("the doctrine of the Christians"), for the provision of the white robe indicates a miming of the whole baptismal ceremony, except for a throwing in the tub instead of the usual manner of ducking. Gelasinus took the experience as a real baptism. The story has doubtful historical value but may rest on some early remembrance. It is a vivid testimony to baptism understood as a full submersion.

---

44. Othmar Perler, "Deux inscriptions chrétiennes à Doura-Europos," *Revue de théologie et philosophie* 5 (1973): 396. He suggests that Proclus may be the bishop who attended the synod of Antioch in 268 that condemned Paul of Samosata. Othmar Perler, "Zu den Inschriften des Baptisteriums von Dura-Europos," in J. Fontaine and C. Kannengiesser, eds., *Epektasis: Mélanges patristiques offerts au Cardinal Jean Daniélou* (Paris: Beauchesne, 1972), pp. 175-185.

45. PG 92.685A; English translation by Michael Whitby and Mary Whitby, *Chronicon Paschale 284-628 AD*, Translated Texts for Historians 7 (Liverpool: Liverpool University Press, 1989), p. 3.

27. Sources at the Turn to the Fourth Century

The Christian writers considered here, even though dying in the early fourth century, had their intellectual and spiritual formation in the late third century and so are considered in this unit; the same is true for the bishops assembled at Nicaea. I begin with a pagan testimony from the late third century.

Porphyry

The Neoplatonist philosopher Porphyry (234-c. 305) was a strong opponent of Christianity. There is preserved from his treatise *Against the Christians* this criticism:

> We must feel amazed and concerned about our souls, if a man thus shamed and polluted is to stand out clean after a single immersion, if a man whose life is stained by so much debauchery . . . if such a creature, I say, is lightly set free from it all, throwing off the whole guilt as a snake sheds its old scales, merely because he has been baptized and has invoked the name of Christ. Who will not commit misdeeds . . . , if he learns that he can get quit of all these shameful offenses merely by believing and getting baptized, and cherishing the hope that he will hereafter find forgiveness with him who is to judge the living and the dead? . . . They raise it to the rank of a first principle, that a man has no longer to shun godlessness at all — if by the simple act of baptism he gets rid of a mass of innumerable sins.[1]

The attack is an unbalanced and prejudiced reading of Christian teaching, but here as elsewhere Porphyry was well informed about Christianity. The reference to a single immersion, if taken strictly, was incorrect for the usual practice (triple immer-

---

1. Preserved in Macarius Magnes 4.10 — quotation taken from Adolf Harnack, *The Expansion of Christianity in the First Three Centuries*, trans. James Moffatt (London: Williams & Norgate, 1904), Vol. 1, pp. 484-485, n. 1, which translates the whole passage.

sion). Otherwise, Porphyry reports accurately: the connection of baptism (immersion) with the name of Christ, with faith, and with the forgiveness of sins. It is notable that these are the features that stood out to an outsider's perception.

The criticism was repeated later by the emperor (361-363) Julian ("the Apostate"), who ridicules Christian baptism and repentance. Toward the end of Julian's parody on *The Caesars,* Constantine meets in the afterlife Jesus, who is quoted as saying:

> He that is a seducer, he that is a murderer, he that is sacrilegious and infamous, let him approach without fear! For with this water will I wash him and will straightway make him clean. And though he should be guilty of those same sins a second time, let him but smite his breast and beat his head and I will make him clean again.[2]

Here as elsewhere Julian follows Porphyry.

Lactantius

The rhetorician Lactantius from North Africa had more literary and philosophical than liturgical and strictly theological interests. Thus, he gives no indication of the actual ritual of baptism nor symbolic explanation of its rites,[3] but he does formulate the profound transformation effected by it.[4]

Lactantius's principal passage on baptism identifies it with the crucial turning point (conversion) in human life:

> The human being is born mortal. Afterwards he becomes truly immortal when he begins to take his life from God. That means to follow justice, which is comprised in the worship of God, because God lifted human beings up for the contemplation of heaven and of God himself. This occurs when a human being, purified by the heavenly washing [*lavacro,* bath], lays aside his state of infancy with all the pollution of his former life, and receiving an increase of divine strength, becomes a full and complete human being. (*Divine Institutes* 7.5.22)

The idea that God made human beings, unlike animals, to stand upright so that they could look up to heaven and God was a favorite with Lactantius.[5] Appropriate to his presentation of a philosophy of religion, Lactantius's usual word for baptism is

---

2. *Caesars* 336A-B; translation by Wilmer Cave Wright, *Works of the Emperor Julian,* Loeb Classical Library (London: William Heinemann, 1913), Vol. 2, pp. 412-413.

3. *Divine Institutes* 4.28.1, on rejecting the vanities of error, renouncing this life, and being instructed in the rudiments of justice and the practice of true religion, might be an allusion to the renunciations and catechetical instruction associated with baptism; but the passage need not have such a specific reference.

4. Frans Gistelinck, "Lactance et sa théologie baptismale propre son temps," *Questions liturgiques* 55 (1974): 177-193. He explains Lactantius's terminology as borrowed from (Stoic) philosophy and Hermeticism. I follow his theological analysis of baptism in Lactantius.

5. *Divine Institutes* 2.1 quotes Ovid, *Metamorphoses* 1.84-86, on this point. Cf. *On the Workmanship of God* 8.1-3.

"washing" *(lavacrum)* instead of the Christian term, but *lavacrum* (laver, bath), used in the Latin translation of Titus 3:5, was by his time common in the Christian vocabulary of baptism.

Although Lactantius does not use traditional Christian language for the effects of baptism, we can recognize some traditional Christian ideas behind his description. For instance, without using the terminology of regeneration or rebirth Lactantius speaks of a new life that is immortal. The person begins to follow justice, or righteousness, and that means to worship God.

Moreover, the baptismal bath brings forgiveness of sins: one is purified from pollution. Lactantius expresses the thought elsewhere in the context of "the influence exerted on human souls by the precepts of God." He describes various types of sinful persons who are changed into their opposite: "For by one washing [*lavacro*] all wickedness is destroyed" (*Divine Institutes* 3.26.10). This is because the infusion of divine wisdom expels folly, which is the mother of faults. Thus Lactantius sets Christian conversion and baptism in the context of attaining spiritual strength and maturity, attaining immortality, and receiving divine wisdom — ideas associated in early Christianity with the expression "illumination."

Lactantius contrasts Christianity with pagan religious rites.

> They [pagan sinners] come to pray, and they imagine that they piously offer a sacrifice if they wash their skin, as if any streams might wash or any seas purify their minds of wickedness. How very much better it is rather to wash clean the mind, so soiled by evil desires, and by one washing [*lavacro*] of virtue and faith to drive away all vices. Whoever has done this, however much impurity and sordidness his body carries, is sufficiently pure. (*Divine Institutes* 5.19 [20].34)

The theme of the insufficiency of external bathing is common enough in pagan moralists. Lactantius unites the motif with Christian teaching about the necessity of repentance (virtue) and faith accompanying the *one* bath of baptism. He thus continues to draw on the pagan philosophical background to explain Christian attitudes and practice.

More traditional Christian terminology occurs in Lactantius's treatments of the baptism of Jesus by John and the relation of circumcision to baptism. In discussing Jesus' baptism in *Divine Institutes* 4.15.2 (quoted in chap. 7), Lactantius says, "As Jesus saved the Jews by undergoing circumcision, so he might save the Gentiles also by baptism." New was the thought that Jesus' circumcision was for the salvation of the Jews, but more significant for my purposes is the paralleling of circumcision and baptism. And that parallel might account for the novel ascription of saving significance to Jesus' circumcision, or is this Lactantius's reading of Colossians 2:11 and referring to Jesus' death? If one wanted to save Lactantius's reputation as a theologian, one might suggest that he had in mind Jesus identifying himself with Jews by undergoing circumcision as he did with humanity by baptism. Hence, he was interpreting circumcision in terms of Christian baptism.

Two chapters later (*Divine Institutes* 4.17) Lactantius elaborates on the subject of circumcision. The Jews hated Christ because he abolished circumcision along with the Sabbath rest and food laws. The abolition of circumcision was prophesied by Isaiah (he means Jeremiah, for he quotes Jer. 4:3-4) and Moses himself (Deut. 30:6). Circumcision of the flesh is irrational, but was commanded as a figure of the second circumcision, the laying bare of the breast. This circumcision of the heart means repentance, which consists of confession of sins and making satisfaction to God. Lactantius, therefore, does not go beyond paralleling Jesus' baptism to his circumcision to suggest further the equivalence of circumcision and baptism. Rather, the Christian equivalent of fleshly circumcision is the spiritual laying open of the soul. This interpretation we have found to be common Christian teaching.

Methodius

Methodius was an important thinker and bishop at the close of the age of persecution about whom little is known. His one work to survive complete in Greek, the *Banquet*, contains references to baptism in a discourse assigned to Thecla. The ruling motif of the passage is rebirth, but not in terms of the divine begetting; rather, in keeping with the participants in the dialogue being women (although promoting virginity), the image is of the church as mother giving birth.

The woman of Revelation 12 who gave birth to a male child is interpreted as the church.

> The moon upon which she stands [Rev. 12:1] is figuratively, as I think, the faith of those being purified from corruption in the bath [or laver, λουτρῷ]. . . . The church then stands upon the faith and our adoption. . . .[6]
>
> Hence the church must necessarily stand at the bath, giving birth [ἀναγεννῶσα] to those being washed [λουομένους]. In this way her activity with reference to the bath [λουτρὸν] has been called the moon, since those who are being reborn [ἀναγεννώμενος] and have been renewed shine forth a new ray, that is, a new light. Hence, they are also called periphrastically "newly enlightened" [νεοφώτιστοι]. (8.6.186-187)

Central to Methodius is faith, the objective faith that is the basis of the church, but subjectively received and confessed by those being baptized. Titus 3:5 stands behind the terminology of bath and renewal. Only, instead of *palingenesia*, Methodius substitutes *anagennesis*, and it has the meaning of new birth because of the feminine imagery of the church as mother. Methodius provides one of the early attestations of "newly enlightened" for what became a common term in the Greek church for the newly baptized.

6. Alternative translations could be, "our faith and reception [into the church]" (which would have essentially the same meaning) or just possibly, "the faith and our acceptance [of it]," but such an ellipsis is not likely.

Methodius continues by rejecting the interpretation of the male child in Revelation 12 as Christ. The persons holding that interpretation object that the text says a male child, whereas Methodius's view was of a plurality that included women. They described his position this way: "You understand [the text] with reference to those being washed clean, her labor pains being fulfilled in those [feminine] being washed [λουομένας]." Methodius replied (in the person of Thecla): "You must necessarily confess that the church labors and gives birth [γεννῶσαν] to those being ransomed [ἀπολυτρουμένους]" (8.7.188-189).[7]

Methodius then defends the understanding of the church as being the male child that is born on the ground that "the enlightened [φωτιζόμενοι, i.e., the baptized] receive the manliness" of Jesus, when the likeness of the Word is stamped on them. It is "born [γεννωμένης] in them according to the genuine knowledge and faith so that in each one Christ is spiritually born [γεννᾶσθαι]." "Each of the saints by participating in Christ was born a christ," with Psalm 105:15 quoted in support. "Those who have been baptized [βεβαπτισμένων] into Christ have become christs by participation of the Spirit." The church conceives by the word. Methodius then quotes Ephesians 3:14-17 and concludes: "For it is necessary that the word of truth should be stamped and imprinted on the souls of those reborn [ἀναγεννωμένων]" (8.8.190-192). The emphasis on faith and the word of truth continues. Becoming "christs," that is, anointed, is not associated with an anointing but with the baptismal act itself. Baptism into Christ gives one the nature of Christ, and this is effected by the Holy Spirit.

In the following chapter Methodius finds his understanding to be in agreement with the baptism of Christ in the Jordan (included in chap. 7). He makes the application that Christ has never been born in those who never knew the manifold wisdom of God. But "if these perceive the mystery of grace, then also in them, when they are converted and come to faith, Christ is born [γεννᾶται] according to knowledge and understanding" (8.9.193-194).

The work *On the Resurrection* refers to sins done after baptism. "But now, even after believing, and after the time of being touched by the water of sanctification, we are oftentimes found in sin" (1.5).[8] Here is the same emphasis on believing paired with baptism, now described as sanctification (because of the discussion of sin) instead of rebirth.

The *Oration concerning Simeon and Anna* is now acknowledged to be inauthentic, but its understanding of baptism is not inconsistent with what is preserved from Methodius. "For her [Anna's] very name presignifies the church, that by the grace of Christ and God is justified in baptism. For Anna is, by interpretation, grace" (12).[9]

---

7. The witnesses to the text have some form of the word for "ransomed," but one wonders if the reading should be ἀπολουομένους (being washed clean), which occurs earlier in the passage. Indeed, Herbert Musurillo translates "those who are washed in baptism" — *St. Methodius: The Symposium. A Treatise on Chastity,* Ancient Christian Writers 27 (Westminster, MD: Newman, 1958), p. 112.

8. Translation by William R. Clark in A. Roberts and J. Donaldson, *Ante-Nicene Fathers* (repr. Peabody: Hendrickson, 1994), Vol. 6, p. 365.

9. Clark, *Ante-Nicene Fathers,* Vol. 6, p. 392.

Here, too, baptism is in close relationship with the church, and priority is given to the divine initiative; different is the image of justification.

Eusebius of Caesarea

Eusebius's *Church History* has been drawn on for its preservation of material from earlier writers. Selections from his larger corpus now are employed for his own ideas and their testimony to practices at the end of the third and beginning of the fourth century.

Eusebius's argument from the Old Testament prophets in *The Proof of the Gospel* makes allusions to baptism. After quoting Romans 9:17-29 and 11:1-5 for the interpretation of Isaiah 1:9, Eusebius concludes that these words

> imply a rejection of the Mosaic worship and introduce in the prediction about them the characteristics of the covenant announced to all men by our Savior, I mean regeneration by water [τὸν διὰ λουτροῦ παλιγγενεσίας], and the word and law completely new. (*Proof of the Gospel* 2.3.36.65b)[10]

The statement is notable, besides its indication that baptism was the mark of entering the new covenant, for its testimony that Titus 3:5 was by now replacing John 3:5 as *the* baptismal text. Eusebius, nonetheless, interprets Isaiah 1:16 as fulfilled in the Lord's words in John 3:5 (*Commentary on Isaiah* 1:16).

Continuing his argument from prophecy, Eusebius interprets the "two sheep" of Isaiah 7:21 as two orders of disciples: "the one as yet undergoing preliminary instruction, the other already enlightened by baptism [διὰ τοῦ λουτροῦ πεφωτισμένον]" (*Proof of the Gospel* 2.3.71d).[11] We note again the use of *loutron* (bath) for baptism. The association of the idea of enlightenment with baptism here contrasts the full enlightenment of baptism with the prior instruction in first principles.

The "sign" of Isaiah 66:19 is interpreted as "all them that believe in Christ using as a seal the sign of salvation" (*Proof of the Gospel* 6.25.306d). The reference is apparently to the sign of the cross, not to baptism itself as the seal but probably to the sign of the cross made on the one baptized. That would accord with the later statement, "sealed, as is our custom, with the seal of Christ on their foreheads" (*Proof of the Gospel* 9.14.450d). Eusebius's use of "seal" (σφραγίς) for baptism is exhibited in his *Church History* 6.5.6, where he records that the brothers gave the soldier Basilides "the seal in the Lord" the day before his martyrdom.

---

10. I follow the translation of W. J. Ferrar, *The Proof of the Gospel: Eusebius* (London: SPCK, 1920; repr. Grand Rapids: Baker, 1981), here p. 78.

11. Ferrar, *The Proof of the Gospel*, p. 85, translates στοιχειούμενον as "probationary," but I have changed that rendering to bring out more clearly the reference to the prebaptismal instruction given to catechumens.

Eusebius's *Theophania,* another apologetic work, refers to baptism as the "mystery of cleansing" (4.8).[12]

In the *Life of Constantine* Eusebius records the emperor's request toward the end of his life to receive "that seal [σφραγίδος] which confers immortality," the "saving seal [σφργίσματος, properly the impression made by a seal]" — seal here referring to the baptismal ceremony itself. This would permit him, if life was prolonged, "to associate with the people of God and unite with them in prayer as a member of his church" (*Life of Constantine* 4.62).[13] Eusebius then relates that "the prelates performed the sacred ceremonies in the usual manner, and having given him the necessary instructions, made him a partaker of the mystic [ἀπορρήτων] ordinance." Constantine was thus the first of the emperors to be "regenerated [ἀναγγενώμενος]." Having received the "divine seal of baptism" (the third reference to seal in this short passage), he was "filled with heavenly light." He arrayed himself in "shining imperial vestments, brilliant as the light," perhaps an allusion to wearing white, for Eusebius contrasts them with the usual purple.[14] After the ceremony Constantine expressed thanks that he was "counted worthy of immortality" and "made a partaker of divine light" (4.63).

Eusebius's quotations and allusions to Matthew 28:19 were considered in chapter 8. One of his five quotations of the full canonical form of the text occurs in *Against Marcellus* 1.1, Following the quotation, Eusebius says:

> For he alone has favored us with the grace of knowing the Holy Trinity by means of the mystical regeneration [ἀναγεννήσεως], since neither Moses nor any of the prophets supplied this knowledge to the people of the Old Law. . . . This holy, blessed, and mystic Trinity of Father, Son, and Holy Spirit unto hope of salvation through regeneration in Christ the church of God has received and guards.[15]

The passage is an early declaration in the context of Trinitarian discussion that baptism was the occasion and means of revealing the Trinity (based on Jesus' baptismal command and the church's practice at baptism of asking for a confession of the three divine persons) and is another instance of Eusebius's fondness for regeneration as the term for baptism.

---

12. The work survives only in Syriac; English translation by Samuel Lee, *Eusebius: Bishop of Caesarea on the Theophania* (Cambridge: Cambridge University Press, 1843), p. 225.

13. Translations from *The Life of Constantine* are by E. C. Richardson, in Philip Schaff and Henry Wace, *Nicene and Post-Nicene Fathers,* Second Series, Vol. 1 (repr. Peabody: Hendrickson, 1994), p. 556. Studied by E. J. Yarnold, "The Baptism of Constantine," *Studia Patristica* 26 (1993): 95-101.

14. This would seem to be the first reference to wearing a white garment after baptism; if so, the lack of explanation by Eusebius would suggest that the practice was common; or does Eusebius's elaboration, "shining imperial vestments, brilliant as the light," give reason to think that Constantine set a precedent in this regard? See chap. 29, n. 20, on Cyril as an alternative candidate for the first to allude to wearing the white robe after baptism.

15. I have slightly modified the English translation of Bernard Henry Cuneo, *The Lord's Command to Baptise: An Historico-Critical Investigation with Special Reference to the Works of Eusebius of Caesarea* (Washington: Catholic University of America, 1923), p. 82.

Council of Nicaea, 325

Some canons adopted at the first ecumenical council in 325 are relevant to the study of early Christian baptism. Canon 14, in requiring that catechumens who have fallen away and then returned are to spend three years with the "hearers," implies two sorts of catechumens, the "hearers" (who attended the service of the word) and those actually preparing for baptism (later known as *phōtizomenoi* in the East and *competentes* in the West).

Canon 2 directed against rapid advancement of new converts with little instruction from baptism to the presbyterate or episcopate speaks of baptism as the "spiritual washing" (λουτρόν).

Canon 19 later became controversial in regard to "rebaptism," for it required that Paulianists (followers of Paul of Samosata) who came to the Catholic Church must be rebaptized. Athanasius later explained that although the Paulianists baptized in the name of "Father, Son, and Holy Spirit," they, like the Arians, Manichaeans, and Phrygians (Montanists), did not have a right faith about the divine persons.[16]

The earlier council of Elvira is considered in chapter 42 on Spain.

---

16. *Discourses against the Arians* 2.18.42-43. See further in chap. 28.

1. Baptism of Jesus — Jesus ascending from the water. Fresco in Catacomb of San Callisto, Room 1, Crypt of Lucina. Early third century. Photo Credit: Scala/Art Resource, NY.

2. Baptism of Jesus — spray of water surrounds the body. Fresco in Catacomb of San Callisto, Room 21. Third century. Photo courtesy Paul Corby Finney.

3. *Right:* Baptism of Jesus — baptizand is leaning forward. Fresco in Catacomb of San Callisto, Room 12 ("Chapel of Sacraments"). Third century.
Photo courtesy Paul Corby Finney.

4. *Below:* Baptism of Jesus — rays or streams of water, oil, or light descending from dove over the baptizand, with hand of baptizer on his head. Fresco in Catacomb of SS. Pietro e Marcellino, room 43. Fourth century.
Photo Credit: Pontifical Commission for Sacred Archeology.

5. Baptism of a girl (?) with inscription. Gravestone in Aquileia. Museo Paleocristiano, Aquileia. Fourth century. Photograph by author.

6. Baptism of Jesus (on right side) with other scenes. Sarcophagus in Santa Maria Antiqua, Rome. Late third century. Photo Credit: Alinari/Art Resource, NY.

7. Baptismal scene. Left side of sarcophagus from Via della Lungara. Museo Terme (National Museum), Rome. Late third century. Photo Credit: Erich Lessing/Art Resource, NY.

8. Arrest of Peter, and Peter (Moses) striking the rock — among other scenes. The rock produces a stream of water from which two figures drink, a scene given a baptismal interpretation in the early church. Sarcophagus from San Justo de la Vega (León) in the Archaeological Museum, Madrid. No later than 315.
Photograph by author.

9. Baptism of Jesus. Ivory carving. British Museum, London. C. 450.
© The Trustees of the British Museum.

10. Baptism of Jesus — fire on water, which comes to his waist — with other scenes. Detail of miniature illustration in illuminated manuscript Rabbula Gospels, folio 4b. Sixth century.
Carlo Cecchelli, Giuseppe Furlani, and Mario Salmi, *The Rabbula Gospels* (Olten and Lausanne: Urs Graf-Verlag, 1959).

11. Baptism of Jesus — restored in nineteenth century. Mosaic in dome of Baptistery of the Orthodox, Ravenna, Italy. Mid-fifth century.   Photo Credit: Scala/Art Resource, NY.

12. Baptism of Jesus. Mosaic in dome of Baptistery of the Arians, Ravenna, Italy. End of fifth century. Photo Credit: Scala/Art Resource, NY.

13. *Above Left:* Reconstruction of the third-century baptistery from Dura Europos, Syria (detail). Yale University Art Gallery, New Haven, CT.

14. *Above Right:* Octagonal baptismal font from Church at Cenchrea Gate, Corinth, Greece. Early sixth century. Photograph by author.

15. *Below:* Cross-shaped baptismal font from Church of 1000 Gates, Paros, Greece — three interior steps on east end (candidate entered the font on west end and exited on the east). Fourth century. Photograph by author.

16. Baptistery with floor mosaics and baptismal font with six niches from Bishop's Church, Stobi, Macedonia. Fourth/fifth century. Photograph by author.

17. Octagonal baptistery and baptismal font with entrance and exit arms at Church of St. Mary, Ephesus, Turkey. Fourth/fifth century. Photograph by author.

18. Octagonal baptistery and circular font with arms at Church of St. John, Ephesus, Turkey. Fifth-sixth century. Photograph by author.

19. Octagonal font of Church of St. John Lateran, Rome. Original was fourth century.
Photo Credit: Vanni/Art Resource, NY.

20. Font—with conduits for water. Church of S. Thecla, under the Duomo, Milan, Italy. Fourth century. Photograph by author.

21. Octagonal font of Church of St. John, Poitiers, France. Fourth/fifth century. Photo courtesy of SESCM, Poitiers.

22. Font — with drain. Church of St. John, Lyon, France. Fourth/fifth century.
Photograph by author.

23. Font — with concentric circles. Church at the Temple of Jupiter, Cumae, Italy. Fifth/sixth century.
Photograph by author.

24. Author in font — with five steps with two seats (the wooden boards are modern) on level of third seat. Cimiez, France. Fifth century.
Photograph supplied by author.

PART FIVE

The Fourth Century

28. Egypt in the Fourth Century

The fourth century furnishes the fullest information of any of the early centuries on the Christian practice of baptism, as it does on other subjects. From it we have the catechetical lectures of a presbyter or bishop of the important churches of Jerusalem, Antioch, and Milan, the exhortations to baptism of the Cappadocians, and collections of material on church order. None of this, however, comes from Alexandria, so for Egypt we must rely on miscellaneous sources. For the theology and ceremony of baptism we have occasional references in the writings of Athanasius, fuller information in the so-called *Sacramentary* of Serapion, bishop of Thmuis, and the pseudonymous *Canons of Hippolytus*. Didymus of Alexandria (?), *On the Trinity,* provides further information on both the doctrine and practice of baptism, expanding the line of argument found in Athanasius. Papyri add some information.[1]

Athanasius

The writings of Athanasius, the embattled bishop of Alexandria (328-373), mainly concerned the issues, theological and political, in regard to the Godhead occasioned by the conflict between his predecessor Alexander and Arius. These contain incidental references to baptism, employing terminology that shows the centrality and high regard for this rite. Thus Athanasius refers to those who despise "the grace of the font [λουτοῦ χάριν]" and (erroneously) imply that one receives nothing from it (*Letter* 49 [*To Dracontius*].4).

Athanasius in one context uses "baptismal consecration [τελειώσει τοῦ βαπτίσματος]," "holy baptism," and "holy font [λουτρόν]" interchangeably (*Discourses*

---

1. Birger Pearson and Tim Vivian, "On the Epiphany: A Coptic Homily Attributed to St. Peter I of Alexandria," *Coptic Church Review* 13 (1992): 99-116, conclude the attribution is pseudonymous and accept that the homily, also known as "On Baptism," was composed in Coptic in the seventh century.

against the Arians 2.18.41). In this connection he brings baptism in the name of the Father and the Son into the discussion of the Trinity, a practice that became a staple of the Trinitarian arguments by the supporters of the creed of Nicaea.

> When baptism is given, whom the Father baptizes, him the Son baptizes; and whom the Son baptizes, he is consecrated in the Holy Spirit. . . . Where the Father is or is named, there clearly is the Son also. Is the Father named in baptism? Then must the Son be named with him. (*Discourses against the Arians* 2.18.41)

The argument here pertains only to the Father and the Son; later in the fourth century the same line of reasoning was extended to argue for the full deity of the Holy Spirit (see below for Athanasius himself). Shortly afterward Athanasius charges the Arians with not baptizing into Father and Son but into the Creator and a creature, the Maker and the made, the implication that he draws from their doctrine.[2] He then quotes the full formula from Matthew 28:19, while noting that it is prefaced with the command to "teach," or "make disciples." This was because a right faith was necessary as well as the right formula: "That the right faith might follow upon learning, and together with faith might come the consecration of baptism" (*Discourses against the Arians* 2.18.42). Teaching came first, and when it was believed, baptism followed.

Athanasius's further argument refers to sprinkling. He continues by referring to those who use the right words but not with a sound faith.

> In consequence the water which they administer is unprofitable, being deficient in piety, so that he who is sprinkled [ῥαντιζόμενον] by them is rather polluted by irreligion than redeemed. (*Discourses against the Arians* 2.18.43)

This may be a rare reference to sprinkling instead of immersion, or may have sickbed baptism in view. I am inclined rather to think it is a disparaging remark — instead of baptism the deniers of the full deity of Christ are giving only a partial or inadequate baptism, only a sprinkling rather than a full covering with water. Baptism by the Arians is unprofitable.[3]

Athanasius refers in a circular letter dated 339 to the baptistery (βαπτιστήριον)

---

2. So also elsewhere, as in *Defense of the Nicene Definition* 31 that the Lord commanded to baptize "into the name of Father, Son, and Holy Spirit," not into the name of the Unoriginate and Originate, the Uncreate and Creature. Rowan Williams, "Baptism and the Arian Controversy," in Michel R. Barnes and Daniel H. Williams, eds., *Arianism after Arius: Essays on the Development of the Fourth Century Trinitarian Conflicts* (Edinburgh: T & T Clark, 1995), pp. 149-181, notes the use of the Trinitarian formula in creedal statements emphasizing the Three as truly subsistent beings, so Athanasius's interpretation of the unitary divine action in salvation was a counter to a pluralist interpretation; for Athanasius in contrast to Eunomius later (chap. 35) baptism is the unity of God's saving act in which to mention one is to mention all, yet the oneness of the saving God can only be articulated by mentioning all (pp. 159-161, 176).

3. The passage continues by acknowledging that the Arians, as well as Manichees, Phrygians (Montanists), and followers of Paul of Samosata, used the three divine names in baptism, but in Athanasius's view with a heretical understanding.

as a separate structure from the church in Alexandria, where mockers of the Christian rite entered, stripped naked, and acted disgracefully (*Encyclical Letter* 3.3, 5). A separate place for baptisms and the nudity would seem to confirm the usual practice of immersion at Alexandria.

Athanasius's *Letters to Serapion concerning the Holy Spirit* extended the argument from the baptismal formula employed in the *Discourses against the Arians* for the deity of the Son to the deity of the Holy Spirit in opposition to the Tropici or Pneumatomachians, who denied the deity of the Spirit.

> For as the faith in the Triad, which has been delivered to us, joins us to God; and as he who takes anything away from the Triad, and is baptized in the name of the Father alone, or in the name of the Son alone, or in the Father and the Son without the Holy Spirit, receives nothing, but remains ineffective and uninitiated . . . ; so he who divides the Son from the Father, or who reduces the Spirit to the level of the creatures, has neither the Son nor the Father. . . . For as baptism, which is given in Father, Son, and Holy Spirit, is one; and as there is one faith in the Triad . . . ; so the holy Triad, being identical with itself and united within itself, has in it nothing which belongs to things originate. (1.30)[4]

The Trinitarian formula of Matthew 28:19 was so well established in usage that it could be the basis for theological argument about the Godhead.

Athanasius in the *Letters to Serapion* alludes to Acts 8:17 but adapts the wording presumably to fit the practice of his day: "Through the laying on of the apostles' hands the Holy Spirit was given to those who were being regenerated [ἀναγεννωμένοις]" (1.6).

Athanasius's interpretation of Psalm 32:1-2 says that transgressions are forgiven through baptism and sins are hidden through bitter repentance. He continues, "This one is truly blessed who comes to holy baptism with whole heart," for "the one baptized deceitfully will not attain forgiveness but will have judgment" (*Expositions in Psalms*; PG 27.161; cf. *Ep. Marcell.* 18). Later in the same work he interprets the words "sprinkle with hyssop" and "wash" (Ps. 50:9 [51:7]) as baptism, probably following the practice of interpreting any reference to water as baptism rather than being an indication that the sprinkling referred to the usual mode of baptism (PG 27.237).

A story told later about Athanasius's childhood relates a childish parody of Christian baptism. Rufinus, in his continuation of the *Church History* of Eusebius, records an incident typical of stories about great persons who while children acted out their later roles. Bishop Alexander of Alexandria saw at a distance some boys on the seashore playing a game (PG 27.161; cf. *Ep. Marcell.* 18):

> They were mimicking a bishop and the things customarily done in church. Now when he had gazed intently for a while at the boys, he saw that they were also per-

---

4. Translation by C. R. B. Shapland, *The Letters of Saint Athanasius concerning the Holy Spirit* (New York: Philosophical Library, 1951), pp. 139-140.

forming some of the more secret and sacramental things. He was disturbed....
[When the boys were brought to him,] they disclosed in due order what they had
done, admitting that some catechumens had been baptized by them at the hands
of Athanasius, who had played the part of the bishop in their childish game. Then
he carefully inquired of those who were said to have been baptized what they had
been asked and what they had answered, and the same of him who had put the
questions, and when he saw that everything was according to the manner of our
religion, he conferred with a council of clerics and then ruled, so it is reported,
that those on whom water had been poured after the questions had been asked
and answered correctly need not repeat the baptism, but that those things should
be completed which are customarily done by priests. (Rufinus, *Church History*
10.15)[5]

The baptism done by those not clergy (indeed children) in correct form on catechumens was accepted as valid. The baptismal confession was in interrogatory form. The *disciplina arcani* was in force, for the bishop was disturbed that the children were imitating the sacramental actions and words. The baptismal act involved pouring water. This might be taken as evidence that pouring was the normal mode of baptism in Alexandria. A moment's reflection raises the question how Athanasius and his playmates knew what to do. A plausible answer is that they had observed a sickbed baptism (of an adult or a child), where members of the family and others might be present and the usual privacy of a regular baptism could not be observed, performed (as often) by pouring. No age of the catechumens is hinted at; they too were likely children, but, if older, there might have been practical problems in children ducking them. The customary things done by (real) priests to complete the baptism may have included a laying on of hands, an anointing, or signing.

Some Later Athanasian *Spuria*

Many later works were attributed to the illustrious name of Athanasius or were transmitted along with his genuine works. Ascription to Athanasius does not necessarily mean an Egyptian provenance, but for convenience we note here some passages notable for their content.

A sermon *On the Holy Passover*, whose authorship is disputed,[6] connects baptism with the burial and resurrection of Christ and in so doing makes explicit the act of submersion:

In these benefits you were baptized [ἐβαπτίσθης], O newly-enlightened one [νεοφώτιστε]. The initiation in grace, O newly-enlightened one, has become to

---

5. Translated by Philip R. Amidon, *The Church History of Rufinus of Aquileia: Books 10 and 11* (Oxford: Oxford University Press, 1997), pp. 26-27.

6. The *Clavis Patrum Graecorum* II.#2247 lists the work among Athanasius's *Spuria*.

you a guarantee of resurrection; you have baptism [βάπτισμα] as a pledge of life in heaven. In sinking down [καταδύσει] you imitated the burial of the Master; but you rose up [ἀνέδυς] again from there, beholding beforehand the works of the resurrection. (5; PG 28.185)

Undoubtedly spurious is a *Homily on Fasting and the Passion of Christ*, which discusses the question why Christ fasted after his baptism, and the custom of the church was for candidates for baptism to fast before baptism.

The *Questions to the Governor [Ducem] of Antioch* contains a passage that exemplifies the different eastern perspective on children from that of the Augustinian West.

[Question:] Where do believing [πιστά] infants [νήπια] who die go? Into punishment or into the kingdom? And where do infants of unbelievers go? And where are assigned unbaptized infants of believers who die, with believers or with unbelievers?

Answer: Since the Lord said . . . [Matt. 19:14 quoted] and again the apostle spoke . . . [1 Cor. 7:14d quoted], it is evident that the baptized [βεβπτισμένα] infants of believers, being spotless and faithful, enter into the kingdom. But the unbaptized infants and the infants of pagans do not enter the Kingdom, but neither do they go to punishment, for they did not sin. (PG 28.670-672)

No indication is given whether the baptized infants received baptism in illness or as a routine precaution by their Christian parents, but there were small children of Christians who died unbaptized and were therefore a cause for concern. There is no thought of an original sin that needed forgiving or would require punishment, but the necessity of baptism was such that those infants who died without it (whether their parents were believers or not) were excluded from the kingdom (John 3:5).

Another question and answer work, *Questions in the Holy Scriptures,* has several questions pertaining to baptism. The answer to question 45 speaks of "having the seal of holy baptism and the sign of the cross, and the faith in Christ" (PG 28.728). Here baptism is itself the seal, which is distinguished from the sign of the cross made with oil following the baptism.

The answer to question 93 makes explicit reference to immersion of a child:

As Christ died and on the third day arose, so we also dying in baptism arise. For the plunging [καταδῦσαι] of the child in the pool [κολυμβήθρα] and raising the child up [ἀναδῦσαι] three times is evidently the death and resurrection of Christ on the third day. (PG 28.753)

Βαπτίζειν had become so common for the whole action of submerging and raising up that καταδύνω and its opposite had to be used in order to express separately the two different aspects. The statement seems to assume a time when infant baptism had become the norm.

Question 101 dealt with the meaning of 1 Corinthians 10:2. The answer lists different baptisms in Scripture. The first was the flood; the second was that of Moses when Israel crossed the Red Sea (the sea then is the water of baptism now and the cloud then is the Holy Spirit now); the third baptism was the washings the Hebrews had under the law; the fourth was John's; the fifth is Christ's, wholly spiritual, which "we also have"; the sixth is with tears (repentance); the seventh is martyrdom and blood; and the eighth is the final not-saving baptism of fire and unending punishment (PG 28.760-761).

The answer to question 126 accounts for how the righteous before the coming of Christ were saved by baptism: "The ancient and old prophets were baptized from the blood and water that flowed from the side of Christ" (PG 28.769).

Serapion

Serapion (Greek Sarapion) was a friend of Athanasius and bishop of Thmuis (339-363). A collection of thirty prayers (the *Prayer Book* [or *Sacramentary*] of Serapion] is attributed to him, and scholarly opinion in general accepts this attribution, although with some qualifications. The prayers are likely compiled, in part, from earlier groups of prayers. They are all consistent with a mid–fourth-century Egyptian context, and no compelling reason contradicts the ascription to Serapion as their compiler or editor if not author.[7] Seven of the prayers relate to baptism.[8]

There is a prayer for the sanctification of the waters of the baptismal font. It includes this petition:

> Look upon these waters and fill them with the Holy Spirit. May your ineffable Word be in them and transform their energy and prepare them to be productive [γεννητικά], filled with your grace, in order that the mystery [μυστήριον] now being performed may not be found empty in those being regenerated [ἀναγεννωμένοις] and may fill with divine grace all those going down [κατιόντας] and being baptized [βαπτιζομένους]. . . . Form all those being regenerated [ἀναγεννωμένους] into your divine and ineffable form, so that by being transformed and

---

7. Earlier studies are largely superseded by Maxwell E. Johnson, *The Prayers of Sarapion of Thmuis: A Literary, Liturgical, and Theological Analysis* (Rome: Pontificio Istituto Orientale, 1995). His conclusions are on pp. 279-284. He includes an edited text and translation (pp. 46-81); I make my own translation from his text. Also to be noted are the edition of the Greek text with important notes by F. E. Brightman, "The Sacramentary of Serapion of Thmuis," *Journal of Theological Studies* 1 (1900): 88-113, 247-277, and the English translation with commentary by R. J. S. Barrett-Lennard, *The Sacramentary of Sarapion of Thmuis* (Bramcote: Grove, 1993).

8. Studied by Johnson, *Prayers of Sarapion*, pp. 127-143. See also B. Spinks, "Sarapion of Thmuis and Baptismal Practice in Early Christian Egypt: The Need for a Judicious Reassessment," *Worship* 72 (May, 1998): 255-270 and the response by Maxwell E. Johnson, "The Baptismal Rite and Anaphora in the Prayers of Sarapion of Thmuis: An Assessment of a Recent 'Judicious Reassessment,'" *Worship* 73 (March, 1999): 140-168.

regenerated [ἀναγεννωμένους] they may be saved and be worthy of your kingdom. And as your unique [μονογενής] Word came down to the waters of the Jordan and proclaimed them holy, so also may he come down now in these waters and make them holy and spiritual so that those being baptized [βαπτιζομένους] may be no longer flesh and blood but spiritual and able to worship you. (*Prayers* 7)

Several notable aspects of this prayer may be mentioned. Perhaps most notable is the paralleling of the sending of the Holy Spirit and the coming of the Word on the waters.[9] There is further the parallel of Christ's sanctifying of the Jordan at his baptism and the sanctifying of the present baptismal waters. The prayer is that the waters may be generative because filled with God's grace. The effect of baptism is three times described as regeneration. The action is still God's, but the effects are now closely tied to the water itself. Those who are baptized are saved and counted worthy of the kingdom. The baptism presumably takes place in an indoor font or pool. The candidates go down into it (a word not used of the baptismal action) and are baptized (a separate action from entering the pool).[10]

The next prayer in the collection is a prayer for those being baptized (βαπτιζομένων).

We pray that you may count this one worthy of the divine mystery [μυστηρίου] and of your ineffable regeneration [ἀναγεννήσεως]. He is offered to you, the One who loves humanity; we dedicate him to you. Grant him to participate in this divine regeneration [ἀναγεννήσει] in order that he may no longer be led by anyone perverse or evil but may serve you always and observe your commandments. (8)

We find repeated here some ideas from the preceding prayer: being counted worthy, baptism as a "mystery," and regeneration (twice). Regeneration was clearly the primary concept associated with baptism in Serapion's prayers. The baptized person was now devoted to God — delivered from everything evil and pledged to obey the ordinances of God.[11] Although the heading of the prayer uses the plural, the prayer itself is worded in the singular as being made for each candidate individually.

The following prayer is entitled "Prayer after the Renunciation [ἀποταγήν]," which would have been the verbal declaration not to follow the devil and his works. Serapion does not give the wording of the renunciation, but it is perhaps alluded to

---

9. Johnson, *Prayers of Sarapion*, pp. 127-128, cites parallels to the coming of the Logos on the waters in the Coptic Order of Baptism; *Apostolic Constitutions* 7.43; and John Chrysostom, *Catechetical Instructions* 3.3.

10. The prayer accompanying the "Laying on of hands after the blessing of the water and the oil" (6) apparently refers to the oils and waters brought as offerings by the people (5) and not the baptismal water and oil and was a final benediction that the "communion of the body and blood" would continue with the people.

11. Johnson, *Prayers of Sarapion*, pp. 129-131, says the prayer may have belonged to the enrollment for baptism but more likely came at the final scrutiny before baptism. He notes that no formal exorcism is implied.

in the preceding prayer about not following evil and prayer 15 (below) about victory over opposing powers.

> Almighty Lord, seal [σφράγισον] the assent [συγκατάθεσιν] which has now been made to you by this your servant and preserve unchangeably his character and manner of life in order that he may no longer serve worse things but give worship to the God of truth and be a slave to you, the Maker of all things, so as to be declared perfect and genuinely yours. (9)

The renunciation of the Evil One may have been thought to constitute an adhesion to God, or the word "assent" may indicate that a separate expression of adhesion had been made in addition to the renunciation. The language of sealing may imply an imposition of hands accompanying the prayer.[12] The consequences of baptism for the person's way of life are once more highlighted.

The next prayer is headed in the manuscript "Prayer after the Acceptance," but Brightman offers the emendation "After Anointing,"[13] that is, the prebaptismal anointing. He suggests that if the manuscript reading is kept, the meaning might be "after assumption into the baptistery."[14] Other possibilities are the adhesion (a pledge of loyalty to Christ), receiving the creed, or simply being handed over for baptism.

> Savior of all who have made conversion to you, be merciful to your servant here. Lead him by your right hand to regeneration [ἀναγέννησιν]. May your unique Word lead him to the bath [λουτόν]. May his regeneration [ἀναγέννησις] be honored and not be empty of your grace. May your holy Word stand by, may your Holy Spirit be present, driving away and throwing off every temptation. (10)

Especially notable is the association of Word and Spirit in accompanying the baptizand. Once more they jointly participate in the baptismal ceremony. We note the continued description of baptism as regeneration (twice) but its designation also as a bath. The latter term could be influenced by Titus 3:5, but the word for regeneration is different from the word in that verse.

The next prayer is "After Being Baptized and Coming Up." This prayer for blessing and strength summarizes the concerns of the *Sacramentary* (or *Prayer Book*) and the meaning of baptism.

> Bless your servant with your blessing. Declare him pure in the regeneration [ἀναγεννήσει], appoint him a partner with your angelic powers, in order that he

---

12. Johnson, *Prayers of Sarapion*, pp. 131-134, notes that in Chrysostom and Theodore of Mopsuestia a prebaptismal anointing followed the renunciation. Serapion's "Prayer 9 might be simply a reference to an imposition of hands and blessing at the conclusion" of the renunciation and *syntaxis* (p. 134).

13. Brightman, "The Sacramentary of Serapion," pp. 252, 264.

14. Johnson, *Prayers of Sarapion*, pp. 134-135, rejects Brightman's emendation and favors Brightman's alternative interpretation of a reference to a procession of the candidates from the outside to the inside of the baptismal room.

no longer may be called flesh but spiritual by reason of partaking of your divine and beneficial gift. May he be preserved until the end for you the Maker of the universe. (11)

Rendered pure, being regenerated, having fellowship with the angels, and partaking of the divine gift (the Holy Spirit?) — these were the blessings of baptism. The concern for the postbaptismal life is expressed by the petition that the person will be sustained until the end.

Maxwell Johnson concludes that prayers 7-11 allow no place for a postbaptismal anointment. He suggests that prayers 8-11 are collects that conclude separate liturgical units: scrutiny (8), renunciation-*synaxis* (9), entrance into the baptistery (10), and baptism proper (11).[15]

Two prayers among the blessings of the oils are not in the sequence of the baptismal ceremony but do relate to it.[16] The "Prayer in Regard to the Anointing Oil of Those Being Baptized" pertains to a prebaptismal anointing. The title of the prayer is preceded by a heading, "Prayer(s) of Serapion, bishop of Thmuis." This may indicate that this prayer initially stood at the beginning of the collection,[17] or it may indicate that the practice represented by the prayer was new with Serapion.[18] The prayer cites John 20:23 for the power of forgiving sins. Then comes the description of the act and its accompanying petition:

> We anoint with this anointing oil the men and women who are coming to this divine regeneration [ἀναγεννήσει], beseeching that our Lord Jesus Christ may work in the person healing and strengthening power and may make himself known through this anointing oil and may completely cure from their body, soul, and spirit every sign of sin, lawlessness, and Satanic effect. By his own grace may he provide them with forgiveness, in order that "becoming free from sin they might live for righteousness" (1 Pet. 2:24) and having been refashioned through this anointing and "cleansed through the washing" (Eph. 5:26) and "renewed by the Spirit" [Tit. 3:5], they may be fully strengthened to overcome from now on the assaults of the enemy powers and the deceits of this life and thus to be joined and united with the flock of "our Lord and Savior Jesus Christ" (2 Pet. 3:18) and become "fellow-heirs with the saints of the promises" (Heb. 11:9). (15)

---

15. Johnson, *Prayers of Sarapion*, pp. 136-137, 142-143. He cites Georg Kretschmar, "Beiträge zur Geschichte der Liturgie, insbesondere der Taufliturgie in Ägypten," *Jahrbuch für Liturgik und Hymnologie* 8 (1963): 1-54 (43-50), and Paul F. Bradshaw, "Baptismal Practice in the Alexandrian Tradition, Eastern or Western?" in Paul F. Bradshaw, ed., *Essays in Early Eastern Initiation* (Bramcote/Nottingham: Grove, 1988), pp. 5-17 (12-17), for the earlier Alexandrian baptismal liturgy having only a prebaptismal anointing until a postbaptismal anointing was introduced in the mid–fourth century, for which see Prayer 16 below.

16. Johnson, *Prayers of Sarapion*, pp. 138-143, judges prayers 15 and 16 to be later prayers in relation to the baptismal rite reflected in 7-11, which did not have a postbaptismal anointing.

17. G. J. Cuming, "Thmuis Revisited: Another Look at the Prayers of Bishop Sarapion," *Theological Studies* 41 (1980): 568-575 (569-570).

18. Brightman, "The Sacramentary of Serapion," ad loc.

This prayer accommodates the baptismal blessings to the whole ceremony. The persons receiving the anointing are approaching the divine regeneration. The work of healing and strengthening associated with oil is associated with Christ's power to heal and forgive. The baptismal blessings are distributed among the different actions — recreated through the anointing, cleansed through the washing, and renewed by the Spirit. Although the ideas are in the nature of the case more particularly associated with these actions, one should not read too much into this distribution, for the ideas probably belonged to the whole process and would not have been thought of as legalistically divided up. The victory over the opposing powers and the incorporation into the flock of Christ give the prayer an exorcistic nature, but it may be overstating the case to claim that this prayer was specifically for the oil of exorcism.[19]

The second prayer associated with consecration of oil is specifically related to baptism in its title: "Prayer in Regard to the Chrism with Which Those Who Have Been Baptized Are Anointed." The chrism was employed in a postbaptismal anointing and seems to be associated here with the gift of the Holy Spirit. (This collection of prayers is a rare witness to a postbaptismal anointing in Egypt, but rather than being a later insertion Serapion may be a witness to a variety of practice in different churches in Egypt.) The prayer is for the consecration of the oil, not for those to be anointed with it, but the petition very much has the persons in view. The prayer begins with a reference to those who have been converted. Then comes the petition:

> We call upon you that through [the] divine and invisible power of our Lord and Savior Jesus Christ you may work in this chrism a divine and heavenly effect so that those who have been baptized [βαπτισθέντες] and are being anointed with it (by the impress of the saving sign of the cross of your One and Only Son, through which cross Satan and every opposing power is overthrown and triumphed over),[20] as regenerated [ἀναγεννηθέντες] and renewed through "the washing of regeneration [λουτροῦ τῆς παλιγγενεσίας — Titus 3:5]," they may become partakers of "the gift of the Holy Spirit" [Acts 2:38] and being protected by this seal [σφραγῖδι] may remain "steadfast and unmoveable" [1 Cor. 15:58]. (16)

The prayer continues with the petition that by living in faith and knowledge of the truth the baptized persons may await the fulfillment of their hopes for heaven. The consecration of the oil for anointing is a prayer that it will work a heavenly energy. The baptized persons receive an anointing that makes the sign or imprint of the

---

19. Franz Josef Dölger, *Der Exorzismus in altchristlichen Taufritual* (Paderborn: Ferdinand Schöningh, 1909), p. 158, states that prayer over the oil was not to free it from demonic influence but to call for divine power so that the oil could effect exorcism. Johnson, *Prayers of Sarapion*, p. 141, accepts the view that Prayers 15-16 are revisions of earlier prayers. The use of ἄλειμμα and focus on healing and re-creation are earlier features, but the move in the direction of an "exorcisic" interpretation and subordination of this anointing to the bath and postbaptismal anointing are later features.

20. Johnson, *Prayers of Sarapion*, p. 65, n. a, discusses the grammatical difficulties of the section I have put in parentheses and suggests that it was a later "clumsy interpolation added to explain the meaning of the ritual gesture used in the act of anointing."

cross that defeated the powers of evil. Serapion combines the Petrine (1 Pet. 1:23) and Johannine (John 3:5) word for regeneration with the Pauline (Titus 3:5) word apparently without making a distinction in meaning. The regeneration and renewal is associated with the subsequent sharing in the gift of the Holy Spirit and being secured by the seal.

The *Prayer Book* (or *Sacramentary*) of Serapion in its present form reflects a baptismal ceremony that included a sanctification of the waters, a renunciation of the devil, a prebaptismal anointing, baptism in a body of collected water into which and from which one descended and ascended, and a postbaptismal sealing identified with giving the Holy Spirit. All was conducted in an atmosphere of prayer and recognition of the divine activity for salvation (from Jesus' baptism to his cross and the present working of God and the Spirit). The predominant theological idea associated with baptism was regeneration, which involved renewal — being made pure, being healed, and being forgiven. But there was also recognition of the importance of God's grace and human faith, deliverance from the forces of evil, receiving a divine seal, incorporation into the church (which involved fellowship with the angels), and the necessity of continuing in a life devoted and obedient to God while looking forward to the promise of the eternal kingdom. How all of this worked involved a mystery — things unseen but powerfully real because of the working together of God's Word and Spirit.

Canons of Hippolytus

The *Canons of Hippolytus* are a witness to the text of the *Apostolic Tradition* discussed in chapter 20. They are used here for their own sake, but the structure of the rite is quite similar to that in the *Apostolic Tradition*.[21] The document survives in Arabic, which was translated from a Coptic version of a Greek original.[22] It consists of thirty-eight canons. The date favored by recent study is the mid–fourth century; the author (or compiler) was a presbyter or bishop in lower Egypt.[23]

Those who came to the church in order to become Christians were to be examined as to their motives in coming and their occupations and then were to be instructed in the scriptures by a deacon. The document speaks of only forty days of

21. The differences are sufficient enough for Bradshaw to use it along with other sources to argue that the liturgical tradition in Alexandria was neither exclusively western or eastern but is evidence for the variety of local practices; these in the course of time conformed to a more standardized model through mutual borrowing and adaptation — "Baptismal Practice in the Alexandrian Tradition: Eastern or Western?" 5-17, included in Maxwell E. Johnson, ed., *Living Water, Sealing Spirit: Readings on Christian Initiation* (Collegeville: Liturgical, 1995), pp. 82-100 (100), from which latter I cite.

22. I use the translation by Carol Bebawi in Paul F. Bradshaw, ed., *The Canons of Hippolytus* (Bramcote: Grove, 1987).

23. René-Georges Coquin, *Les Canons d'Hippolyte*, Patrologia Orientalis 31.2 (Paris, 1966), pp. 54-60, who favors Alexandria itself. Bradshaw, *The Canons of Hippolytus*, pp. 5-8, surveys the arguments for date, place of origin, and authorship.

catechesis (can. 12). While under instruction, the catechumen was treated as part of the Christian people; and if he was a slave whose master forbade his baptism, the assurance was given that "even if he dies without having received the gift, he is not excluded from the flock" (can. 9), a concession that involved a considerable accommodation to the pagan social order. Canons 11-18, however, detail in a rather thorough way the occupations, circumstances in life, and practices forbidden to Christians. The teacher was to decide whether the break with previous occupations and repentance were sufficient to make the candidate worthy of baptism (can. 12). During the period of the catechumenate the catechumens attended the assemblies of the church to hear the word but did not communicate in the "mysteries," that is, the eucharist (can. 30). A catechumen who was killed for witness to the faith before being baptized was to be buried with the martyrs on account of being "baptized in his own blood" (can. 19).

Canon 19 is a long regulation of the preparation for baptism, the baptism itself, and the postbaptismal activity. Instead of the daily exorcisms in the *Apostolic Tradition*, the *Canons of Hippolytus* refer only to a final scrutiny and exorcism. The catechumen gave an account of his manner of life to the bishop, who approved the person to receive the "mysteries" (here, baptism). Those to be baptized bathed and ate normally on the Thursday and fasted on Friday. Women in their menstrual period had to delay their baptism. On Saturday the bishop exorcised the candidates by prayer and then breathed on their face and signed their breast, forehead, ears, and nose. They spent the night "in the sacred word and prayers."

At cockcrow the candidates took position at "water from a river, running and pure." Baptism was in the nude. Those who replied for little children stripped them of their clothes; children who could answer for themselves were next. Women were baptized last. The bishop blessed the oil of exorcism and gave it to one presbyter and blessed the oil of thanksgiving and gave it to another presbyter. The baptizand turned toward the west and made a renunciation, "I renounce you, Satan, and all your service" (referred to also in can. 38). The presbyter then anointed the person with the oil of exorcism. The candidate next made an adhesion *(syntaxis)*, "I believe, and I submit myself to you and to all your service, O Father, Son, and Holy Spirit."

The person descended into the water. The presbyter placed his hand on the head of the one being baptized. He asked three questions — "Do you believe?" in God the Father, in Jesus Christ, the Son of God (his virgin birth, crucifixion, resurrection, and return as Judge), and in the Holy Spirit ("the Paraclete flowing from the Father and the Son"). With each affirmative answer, "I believe," he immersed the person in the water, "his hand on his head." The presbyter said at each immersion, "I baptize you in the name of the Father, of the Son, and of the Holy Spirit, equal Trinity."[24]

The baptizand came up from the water, and a presbyter with the oil of thanks-

---

24. According to Bradshaw, "Baptismal Practice," pp. 95-96, this is the first evidence of this declaratory formula in Egypt. Here it is combined with the preceding interrogatory form. The declaratory form eventually supplanted the interrogatory form. He likewise sees the postbaptismal anointing as a later addition in Egypt, of which the *Canons of Hippolytus* may mark the beginning of its introduction (pp. 96-98).

giving signed the person's forehead, mouth, and breast and anointed all the body, saying, "I anoint you in the name of the Father, of the Son, and of the Holy Spirit." The person dressed and entered the church.

The bishop laid his hand on all the baptized and offered a prayer that contains a doctrine of baptism:

> We bless you, Lord God almighty, for that you have made these worthy to be born again, that you pour your Holy Spirit on them, and to be the one body of the Church, not being excluded by alien works; but, just as you have granted them forgiveness for their sins, grant them also the pledge of your kingdom; through our Lord Jesus Christ. . . .

Here we have the familiar elements of baptismal theology: in baptism itself a regeneration and forgiveness of sins and following on it the petition for the gift of the Holy Spirit (which would also be the pledge of the kingdom) and membership in the church. Baptism is later called a seal (can. 29).

The bishop signed the forehead of each with oil and gave the kiss, saying, "The Lord be with you." The newly baptized joined the faithful in prayer and received from them the kiss. There followed the eucharist, including milk and honey as the food of little children but also a remembrance of the age to come (the food of the promised land). They are now "complete Christians." A teacher continued their instruction. Indeed, the *Canons of Hippolytus* gave much attention to the subsequent Christian duties, spelled out in the long canon 38.

The baptisms seemingly occurred on a Sunday morning, for the postbaptismal anointing with oil was followed immediately by the eucharistic liturgy, unless this was a special baptismal eucharist. This was apparently not Easter Sunday, for the candidates are said to eat on the Thursday prior to the baptism and the week before Easter was a time of fasting. The fast on the Friday coincided with the community's regular weekly fasts on Wednesday and Friday (can. 20). Coptic tradition claims that in ancient times baptisms were performed in Alexandria on the sixth day of the sixth week of the forty-day fast that began after Epiphany (a separate fast from the pre-Paschal fast).[25] The *Canons of Hippolytus* know a forty-day fast separate from the Paschal season and the Wednesday and Friday fasts (can. 20; 22), so the work may represent a baptism according to this calendar.

Didymus the Blind (?), *On the Trinity*

Didymus (313-398), blind from childhood, lived in Alexandria, where he was a teacher. His biblical commentaries show his adherence to the allegorical method of Origen. A treatise *On the Trinity* is attributed to him. It contains some significant

---

25. Bradshaw, "Baptismal Practice," p. 83. He cites Origen, *Homilies on Leviticus* 10.2 as well as *Canons of Hippolytus* 20 for a forty-day fast.

teaching about baptism and well exemplifies the orthodox argument from the Trinitarian baptismal formula on behalf of the doctrine of the Trinity. The author's treatment emphasizes what the Spirit does in baptism.

Didymus recalls the sign of the cross made on the forehead of catechumens (*Trinity* 2.14 [PG 39.711]).

The baptismal pool is frequently called a κολυμβήθρα, which in secular Greek is a place for diving or a swimming pool. Didymus refers to those persons created spiritually in the "divine κολυμβήθρα" (*Trinity* 2.6.4 [PG 39.520C]) and those purified of sins from the "divine κολυμβήθρα" (2.14 [PG 39.696A]).[26]

The latter passage begins with an extended treatment of biblical texts on water (PG 39.692Cff.), and a survey of this chapter and its context will reveal much of the author's baptismal thought. In necessity, baptism may be performed in any water, even in the sea, for all water has one and the same nature; he quotes Genesis 1:2 and Psalms 29:3 (693A).[27] Among the biblical texts he cites, Didymus gives the "hidden meaning" of the flood. The ark is the church; the dove is the Holy Spirit; the olive is a symbol of peace (696A). The crossing of the Red Sea is "a type of salvation in baptism, where the people are now being enlightened" (696B). Pharaoh is Satan; Moses is a type of Christ; Moses' rod is the cross. The episode of the bitter water (Exod. 15:23-24) recalls the blessing of the water of the κολυμβήθρα (697B). Second Kings 6:4-7 is also given a baptismal interpretation.

"Immortal baptism" came through the Jordan (697C). Hence, there is "the new κολυμβήθρα" and "the faith and benefit through it" (700B). Removing the old clothes, the baptized "put on the gift of new grace and are refreshed from participation in the saving Sprit and from adoption" (700B). This was anticipated in the experience of Naaman, who was commanded to dip (καταβαπτισθῆναι, "to sink" or "be overwhelmed") seven times (700C).

Didymus also makes appeal to the less often used book of Zechariah. The gold lampstand of Zechariah 4 represents the "purest faith." Its seven lamps are the seven spiritual gifts. The two olive trees may be, he suggests, the priesthood and kingship or may be the two peoples of Israel and Christians (704A-B). Zechariah 14:8, "living waters," recalls the κολυμβήθρα in Jerusalem called Bethesda, an image of baptism (708A). An angel moved the water there; after the coming of Christ and the Holy Spirit the waters give healing (708B).

Didymus quotes Psalm 23:1-2 with the sequence of water, oil, and cup. He does not explicitly give this as the baptismal sequence (708B), but the subsequent treatment is structured according to the baptismal ceremony in such a way as to place chrism after baptism. He discusses the chrism with which Aaron was anointed by Moses. All the priests, who are called "christs" from the chrism, bore a type of the sanctified chrism which all Christians receive. Although a bodily act, it benefits spiritually, but "Only if faith concerning the thrice blessed Trinity should come in our

---

26. "Divine" also in 2.12 (PG 39.669A).
27. The passage reminds one of Tertullian, *On Baptism* 4.

hearts, the spiritual word in the mouth, and the seal of Christ in the forehead" (712A). Only when baptism is received and the chrism flows, immediately mercy is found, "which is the nature proper to the Trinity that bestows good" (712A).

With baptism the impure spirits depart. Names are written in the heavenly books. Baptism is the enlightenment of Christians (713A-B). The "ἐπερώτημα [of 1 Pet. 3:21] to God is the confession of the conscience which we set forth, agreeing to be baptized into Father, Son, and Holy Spirit according to the word of the Lord" (716A).

The water of Isaiah 55:1 is the Holy Spirit and the flowing water of the κολυμβήθρα; wine and flesh are "the immortal communion of the body and blood"; we offer faith and not silver (716B). Didymus continues by citing John 7:38 in proof that water is the spirit (716C). "We are enlightened and refreshed by the gift of the Holy Spirit, partaking of the body of Christ and tasting the immortal fount" (716C).

Earlier in the treatise Didymus had used triple immersion as an argument for the Trinity (2.12). Even if some believe and baptize in the name of Father and Son and not equally in the divinity of the Holy Spirit, "they receive in vain the three dippings [καταδύσεις]" (669B-672A).[28] The Pneumatomachians, he claims, transgressed their own confession. In orthodox doctrine the "invisible Spirit of God baptizes into himself and begets again" (672B).

Didymus names Arius, Eunomius, and Macedonius as being like Nicodemus in John 3 in not knowing the Holy Spirit (673B). The words of Jesus, "That which is born of flesh . . ." (John 3:6) "teaches in summary how a person not attaining baptism is fleshly, not sharing in heavenly light . . . but the one who has been baptized is spiritual, sharing in immortal life" (673A). "The Spirit of God begets [γεννᾷ] a spiritual person" (673C).

Baptism in the bare name without true faith is useless. Those baptized in the bare name of the Holy Spirit and not in the name of the divine Spirit have a baptism in bare water and so a senseless hope, being merely dipped [καταδύοντες] in the pool [κολυμβήθρα] (677D-680A).

Christ and the Holy Spirit are linked in the baptismal act, but Didymus's argument with the Pneumatomachians means he gives more prominence to the Holy Spirit. The one baptized is "begotten again and sealed" (680A). That person is clothed with the Savior Christ, and the Holy Spirit begets and seals him or her (680A). One is "begotten again in baptism by the Holy Spirit and sealed by the sanctification" (681B).[29]

On the Trinity 2.12 thus gives an extensive summary of the benefits of baptism as the work of the Holy Spirit: renovates us, brings us back to our pristine beauty, fills us with grace, frees us from sin and death, makes us spiritual persons, sharers in the

---

28. The use of καταδύσεις, a secular term for dipping, instead of βαπτίσματα is a deliberate denial of the sacred character of baptisms by those who denied the deity of the Holy Spirit.

29. In this context it may be noted that the work is an Alexandrian witness to the long ending of Mark — Mark 16:15-16 (683A).

divine glory, makes us sons and heirs, conforms us to the image of the Son of God, and in the divine waters of the baptismal pool extinguishes the inextinguishable fire of hell. When we are immersed in the baptismal pool, we are stripped of our sins, and when we come up from the pool, we put on Christ as a garment. We are now as we were when first made: sinless and masters of ourselves.

The next chapter (2.13) argues that John 3:5 indicates that the water is the Holy Spirit (688C-689A).[30] Didymus refers to the "κολυμβήθρα of the Trinity" (692A). The baptismal pool is the workshop of the Trinity for the redemption of humanity. He elaborates that the κολυμβήθρα is the mother, the Most High is Father, and the Savior who was baptized for us is a brother (692B). This chapter, without making the eucharist explicit, alludes to it, quoting 1 Corinthians 12:13; 10:3-4; and Hebrews 6:14 (689B).

On the Trinity 2.15 argues against those who denied the deity of the Holy Spirit that baptism is in the Spirit as well as in the Father and the Son (717A-B). The Spirit seals the baptizand and restores the first image, so the Lord will recognize his sheep. "In the name of the Father, Son, and Holy Spirit were we both sealed and baptized" (720A). The latter phrase might indicate an anointing followed by baptism, an interpretation supported by the sequence "I will refresh you, having anointed, washed, clothed, . . . and nourished with my body and blood" (2.13; 692B). Yet since Didymus's purpose was doctrinal and not liturgical and he seems to give items in varied orders (as in the quotations above and especially in the treatment of Psalm 23) one should be cautious, remembering that "sealing" could refer to the baptismal act itself.[31]

The author refers to the charge against the Eunomians that they "make one immersion [κατάδυσιν], saying to be baptized only in the death of the Lord" (see chap. 35). Hence, these who come to the orthodox are baptized; "we do not say 'rebaptized,' for they do not have the true baptism" (720A). Otherwise, "Those coming from every heresy are anointed, since they do not have the holy chrism." "Only a bishop performs the chrism in the grace from above" (721A).

The author's argument for the deity of the Holy Spirit and the Spirit's connection with baptism is summarized in this passage:

> If by baptism, together with God and Father and his Son, the Holy Spirit brings us back to the first image; if, by imparting himself to us, he brings about our adoption and our divinization; and if no creature possesses the power to adopt and to deify, how is the Spirit not true God? (*Trinity* 3.2 [PG 39.801D-804A])[32]

---

30. Unlike some modern interpreters who take the water as really meaning the Spirit, Didymus means that the water is really present but indicates the activity of the Spirit.

31. Kretschmar, "Beiträge zur Geschichte der Liturgie," 43-46, argues that Didymus knew no post-baptismal anointing.

32. Quotation from Jules Gross, *The Divinization of the Christian according to the Greek Fathers* (Anaheim: A & C Press, 2002; French original, 1938), p. 198. He cites also 2.14 (716A) that baptism "immortalizes and deifies us" (p. 199).

Papyrus Prayers

A papyrus in Berlin (Papyrus Berolinsis 13415) contains the end of one prayer and a "Sabbath Prayer" complete.[33] The palaeography may date it to the fourth century. Schermann suggests that the prayers were for catechumens preparing for baptism and points to comparable prayers in Serapion (#8 above) and *Apostolic Constitutions* 7.39.3; 8.6.5-8, 10-13 (chap. 35). He argues from the early formulas in the prayers (especially the doxologies) and similarities to the thought of Clement of Alexandria (especially his *Exhortation to Endurance, To the Newly Baptized* — chap. 19) that the prayers were used in the Alexandrian catechetical school in Clement's time. Although the prayers contain early elements, as prayers are accustomed to do, I incline to a date in the later third century or fourth century.

The contents of the prayers would be appropriate for those preparing for baptism. The first prayer refers to forgiveness of sins, to keeping the fasts with a pure heart, being saved from the devices of the devil, being perfected in Christianity, and enduring until the last breath.

The second prayer, entitled "Sabbath Prayer [the Saturday before baptism?]," addresses the God "who turns those seated in darkness and the shadow of death into the straight, firm, and true way." He desires "all persons to be saved and come to the knowledge of truth" (1 Tim. 2:4).

> You have counted us worthy of your holy calling, teaching, and sober thinking, to be instructed in wisdom and understanding, in faith and endurance, in truth and eternal life. You purchased us with the precious and innocent blood of your only Son from deceit, error, and bitter slavery. You ransomed us from the power of the devil into the glory of freedom, from death into the regeneration [ἀναγέννησιν] of spirit, soul and body, from corruption into incorruption.

The prayer continues with petition to be confirmed "in this calling, in this worship," to pay attention to "the holy words of the divine law," and "to be enlightened in all knowledge and piety." God is asked not to remember sins whether conscious or forgotten and not to reckon sins done willingly or unwillingly. The concluding petitions include the following:

> Enlighten us in your exhortation in order that we may be counted worthy of the doctrines preached by your holy apostles and of the noble teaching of the Gospels of our Savior Jesus Christ.

The desire is expressed "to look on the things above, to seek the things above, to contemplate the things above, not the things on the earth."

---

33. Information is taken from Theodor Schermann, "Frühchristliche Vorbereitungsgebete zur Taufe (Papyrus Berolinsis 13415)," *Münchener Beitrage zur Papyrusforschung* (Munich: C. H. Beck, 1917), Vol. 3, pp. 1-32, which contains the text and German translation.

The themes of the prayer — notably forgiveness of sins, enlightenment, regeneration, deliverance from the devil, and petition for faithfulness — might fit other occasions but they were certainly at home in a baptismal context.

29. Jerusalem in the Fourth Century

The influential church at Jerusalem provides fairly detailed evidence for baptismal practice at the mid–fourth century (from its bishop, Cyril of Jerusalem[1]) and at the end of the century (from the report of the pilgrim Egeria[2]). Both sources deal more with the ceremonies but provide information (especially Cyril) on the meaning of baptism.

Cyril of Jerusalem

Cyril was bishop of Jerusalem from about 350 until his death in 387, and he delivered the *Procatechesis* and the eighteen *Catechetical Lectures* either shortly before or (more likely) shortly after becoming bishop. The five *Lectures on the Mysteries* belong some thirty years later (after 382). Strong arguments have been advanced

---

1. A. Paulin, *Saint Cyrille de Jérusalem: Catéchète* (Paris: Cerf, 1959); Hugh M. Riley, *Christian Initiation* (Washington: Catholic University of America Press, 1974); Juliette Day, *Baptism in Early Byzantine Palestine 325-451* (Bramcote: Grove, 1999), with references other than Cyril and Egeria for the period; more fully now in Juliette Day, *The Baptismal Liturgy of Jerusalem: Fourth and Fifth Century Evidence from Palestine, Syria and Egypt* (Abingdon: Ashgate, 2007); Edward J. Yarnold, *Cyril of Jerusalem* (London: Routledge, 2000); Raymond Burnish, *The Meaning of Baptism: A Comparison of the Teaching and Practice of the Fourth Century with the Present Day* (London: Alcuin Club/SPCK, 1985), pp. 1-22; Baby Varghese, *Les onctions baptismales dans la tradition syrienne*, Corpus scriptorum christianorum orientalium 512 (Louvain: Peeters, 1989), pp. 66-80.

2. George E. Gingras, *Egeria: Diary of a Pilgrimage*, Ancient Christian Writers 38 (New York: Newman, 1970); John Wilkinson, *Egeria's Travels to the Holy Land*, 3rd ed. (Warminster: Aris and Phillips, 1999). P. Devos, in a series of articles in *Analecta Bollandiana*, argued successfully to the minds of most for 381-384 as the date for Egeria's travels in the East — "La date du voyage d'Égérie," 85 (1967): 165-194; "Égérie à Édesse," 85 (1967): 381-400; "Égérie à Bethléem," 86 (1968): 87-108 — but E. D. Hunt, "The Date of the *Itinerarum Egeriae*," *Studia patristica* 38 (2001): 410-416, says the date could be in the 390s as well as the 380s.

against their authenticity with Cyril's successor John sometimes assigned their authorship, but the case for Cyril's authorship seems now to be sustained.[3] Cyril has the distinction of offering the first full testimony that survives to the developed baptismal ceremony of the fourth century.

Procedures and Ceremony

Cyril provides little information on what preceded his courses of lectures leading up to baptism. He does refer to members of the church who have spiritually begotten others through "catechizing" them (*Cat.* 15.18).[4] The final instruction during Lent (*Cat.* 4.3; 18.32) preparatory to baptism at passover (*Cat.* 18.33), however, was by a presbyter or bishop. Before this final period the converts were called "catechumens" (κατηχούμενοι). At that time, they heard of hope, but had it not; they heard mysteries but did not understand them; they heard scriptures but did not know their depth (*Procat.* 6). They were now ready to be called "believers" or "faithful" (πιστοί — *Cat.* 1.4; 5.1). In the borderland of transition while they were instructed before baptism, they were called "those being enlightened" (οἱ φωτιζόμενοι). The use of the present participle indicates a process of gradual illumination, which Cyril associates with instruction in the "word of doctrine" (*Cat.* 18.32). Others had used the family of words for enlightenment with reference to baptism itself, and Cyril does too (*Cat.* 18.32, "enlightened by the washing of regeneration"), but for him the words are used primarily for the teaching associated with baptism. The candidates were "disciples of the new covenant and partakers of the mysteries of Christ" by "calling only," but soon they would be that "by grace also" (*Cat.* 1.1).

---

3. Alexis J. Doval, *Cyril of Jerusalem, Mystagogue: The Authorship of the Mystagogic Catecheses*, Patristic Monograph Series 17 (Washington: Catholic University of America Press, 2001). The arguments against the common authorship of the *Catechetical Lectures* and the *Mystagogical Catecheses* by Baby Varghese, *Les onctions baptismales dans la tradition syrienne*, Corpus scriptorum christianorum orientalium 512 (Louvain: Peeters, 1989), pp. 78-80, from different liturgical usage and especially theological differences do not allow for possible changes over a period of time and especially for a common author not discussing in the first set of lectures what he knew would be covered in the latter set and makes overly precise distinctions between whether the Holy Spirit came on Jesus at his baptism or after the baptism. Juliette Day, *The Baptismal Liturgy of Jerusalem*, favors authorship by John. For introduction, text, French translation, and notes, see A. Piédagnel, *Cyrille de Jérusalem, Catéchèses Mystagogiques*, Sources chrétiennes 126 bis (Paris: Cerf, 1988). For English translations, see E. H. Gifford, "The Catechetical Lectures of S. Cyril," in Philip Schaff and Henry Wace, *Nicene and Post-Nicene Fathers*, Second Series, Vol. 7 (repr. Peabody: Hendrickson, 1994), with introduction, i-lvii (including discussion of the liturgy and theology of the sacraments); L. P. McCauley, *The Works of St. Cyril of Jerusalem*, 2 vols., Fathers of the Church 61 and 64 (Washington, D.C.: Catholic University of America Press, 1969, 1970); F. L. Cross, ed., *St. Cyril of Jerusalem's Lectures on the Christian Sacraments: The Procatechesis and the Five Mystagogical Catecheses* (London: SPCK, 1966); and Yarnold, *Cyril of Jerusalem*.

4. The passage also says that fathers who have begotten children according to the flesh should instruct them, but he says nothing about baptizing infants.

Final Instruction and Preparation for Baptism The change from catechumens to entering the state of enlightenment came when the candidates turned in their names, which were inscribed for baptism (*Procat.* 1 and 4). In his first *Catechetical Lecture* Cyril admonishes those being enlightened to be diligent in attending the assemblies of the church and to nourish their souls by reading the scriptures (*Cat.* 1.6). During the lectures and other activities in church the candidates were segregated by sex (*Procat.* 14).

Faith was presupposed, but Cyril often makes mention of it. For instance, in the *Procatechesis,* sins are blotted out "by believing" (8). In his first lecture Cyril calls on his hearers to prepare "through faith for the new birth" and to get the "earnest of the Holy Spirit [2 Cor. 1:22] through faith" so as to be able to enter "the eternal habitations [Luke 16:9]" (*Cat.* 1.2), and declares that the "communion of the Holy Spirit is given in proportion to each person's faith" (1.5). Faith is the ground of forgiveness of sins (2.6; 17.37), makes children of God (7.13), gives regeneration (ἀναγεννηθείσης — 3.4), and saves (5.10 and 13.31 on the thief on the cross). The lecture devoted to baptism (*Cat.* 3) mentions "election according to faith" (*Cat.* 3.1), the soul "cleansed by sincere faith for reception of the Holy Spirit" (3.2), and "drawing near in faith that you may be made faithful" (3.15). In the lecture devoted to faith (*Cat.* 5.10-11) Cyril distinguishes two kinds of faith: dogmatic faith, which is assent to a proposition, and a faith that is a gift of grace enabling one to do things above human power (miracles and visions of God).

Cyril in lecture 4 summarizes the content of the creed that will be expounded and supported from the scriptures in the subsequent lectures. He refers to the practice of delivering the creed to the converts for them to memorize and then recite back (*traditio et redditio symboli* — *Cat.* 4.3; 18.23, 32). The *phōtizomenoi* were not to write down the creed and were to be careful not to recite it in the hearing of the catechumens (*Cat.* 5.12). Perhaps because of this context of delivering the creed that is to be believed and accepted, faith becomes almost "keeping the dogmatic faith," that is, "faithfulness."[5] One misses in the exposition of faith the element of trust evident in the writings of Paul and John in the New Testament, although this is perhaps implicit in the discussion of the faith of Abraham (5.5).

Cyril gives as much attention to the need for repentance. The *Procatechesis* notes that his hearers have forty days for repentance (4). The second *Catechetical Lecture* devotes much of its content to repentance as necessary for forgiveness of sins. There is salvation for those who repent (2.13). Cyril cites biblical examples lest his hearers doubt the power of repentance to bring forgiveness (2.6-17). If God gave pardon to

---

5. Paul F. Bradshaw, "The Profession of Faith in Early Christian Baptism," *Evangelical Quarterly* 78 (2006): 101-115, notes that "the introduction of the recitation of a full creed into the rite" "had the effect of changing the implied character of baptismal faith, from an act of personal commitment to Christ to belief in a body of doctrines as the necessary prerequisite for baptism" (p. 107); and "the original purpose of the act of faith in early baptismal rites . . . seems to have been to articulate the change of ownership and allegiance of the candidate, from the devil to Christ. . . . [I]t came to be seen instead as a vocalization of the content of the candidate's beliefs" (p. 112).

these, "will he not give you, when you repent, the forgiveness of sins and kingdom of heaven, if you live a worthy life?" (2.19). There are many examples of those who have sinned, repented, and been saved (2.20). The lecture on baptism continues the emphasis on repentance: "wash your robes in repentance" (3.2); as Peter offered forgiveness to those who crucified Christ (Acts 2:37-38; 3:15), "Repent and be of good hope, for the same grace is present even now" (3.15). The Lord grants repentance at baptism (λουτροῦ μετάνοιαν — Cat. 4.32). The candidate's confession of faith included belief in the "baptism of repentance" (Mys. 1.9).

Closely connected with Cyril's treatment of repentance is the necessity of confession of sins (the two are virtually equated in Cat. 2.13). He tells his hearers right off that the present is the season for confessing what they have done in word or in deed (Cat. 1.5). David is a biblical example of confession gaining forgiveness (2.6, 11). Confession of sin has power to quench fire and to tame lions (2.15). The examples of those who repented and were saved is the basis of an exhortation to make hearty confession to the Lord (2.20). For those who die in their sins there is no further season for confession (18.14).

Moreover, in this context, it is stated that if they want forgiveness, they must forgive others (1.6; 2.12).

During the forty-day period exorcisms were performed. Cyril urges the candidates to be regular in attendance at the catechizings and to receive with earnestness the exorcisms (Procat. 9; 13-14; Cat. 1.5). The exorcisms were done individually and preceded the catechetical lectures on the days when they were given. Cyril gives little detail but does mention an exsufflation or breathing upon in connection with exorcism and states that those being exorcised had a veil over the face.[6] He does not give the formulas used but says they were collected out of the scriptures (Procat. 9). Without exorcisms, Cyril says, "the soul cannot be purified" (Procat. 9), and he attributes to the breathing of the exorcist the power by the Holy Spirit to consume demons (Cat. 16.19; cf. 16.22 on the power to repel hostile spirits as one of the gifts of the Holy Spirit). He elsewhere mentions the breathing upon by the saints and invocation of God by prayer as the means of driving out evil spirits (Mys. 2.3).

At some point, probably close to the time of the baptism, there was a blessing of the water. Cyril tells his hearers that they should not regard the laver as simple water but consider the spiritual grace that is given with (not by) the water (Cat. 3.3-4).[7] Just as offerings brought to pagan altars become defiled by the invocation of the idols, "so the simple water, having received the invocation of the Holy Spirit, of Christ, and of the Father, acquires a new power of holiness" (Cat. 3.3).[8]

---

6. On *exsufflatio* to expel the devil from the unbaptized see Franz Josef Dölger, *Der Exorzismus in altchristlichen Taufritual* (Paderborn: Ferdinand Schöningh, 1909), pp. 118-130.

7. But shortly after (in 3.5, cited later), Cyril does say grace is given by water.

8. The comparison with the invocation of unclean spirits at idol festivals is also made in regard to the invocation of the Trinity over the bread and wine in *Cat.* 1.7. For the epicleses in Cyril see Doval, *Cyril of Jerusalem*, pp. 88-108 (blessing of font, pp. 95-105). The absence of a blessing of the font in the *Lectures on the Mysteries* is explained by the neophytes not witnessing it and those lectures being con-

Cyril in the *Lectures on the Mysteries* treats the pre-immersion rites, the baptism proper, and the post-immersion chrism in separate lectures (an outline of these is given in *Cat.* 18.33), and we shall follow his lead in the subsequent discussion but include in the first category some items he discusses in his second lecture. To the newly baptized he says that they had been "found worthy of the divine and life-giving baptism" (βαπτίσματος — *Mys.* 1.1). The explanation of the "sacred mysteries" includes the renunciation of Satan, baptism, chrism, and eucharist. We omit the eucharist from our discussion.

Pre-Immersion Rites During the week after baptism Cyril gave lectures on the meaning of the ceremonies the baptizands had experienced. For the first lecture on the renunciation of Satan, the scripture reading was 1 Peter 5:8-11. On the night of their baptism they entered the outer hall (προαύλιον) of the baptistery building and there made their renunciation of Satan.[9] "Facing towards the West you ... stretched forth your hand and as in the presence of Satan you renounced him" (*Mys.* 1.2; cf. *Procat.* 10). The words pronounced were: "I renounce you, Satan, and all your works ['all deeds and thoughts contrary to reason'], and his [sic] pomp ['the madness of theaters, horse-races (circus), hunting (as a sport and gladiator contests), and all such vanity'], and your service [prayer in temples, honors to idols, lighting lamps, burning incense, various forms of divination and magic]" (*Mys.* 1.4-8). The West was symbolically the region of darkness, and the gesture of turning was a visual expression of repentance. The renunciation was a breaking of one's contract with Satan.

The candidates then turned to the East and declared their association with God in the words, "I believe in the Father, in the Son, and in the Holy Spirit, and in one baptism of repentance" (βάπτισμα μετανοίας — *Mys.* 1.9). The renunciation of Satan followed immediately by the profession of belief put together the two essential prerequisites for baptism — repentance and faith.

Cyril's mystagogical lecture on baptism begins with the candidates entering the baptismal room itself. There they removed their clothes: "Having stripped yourselves, you were naked" (*Mys.* 2.2). "Naked" could apply to wearing an undergarment,[10] but Cyril seems to indicate complete nakedness. One must remember that the room was dark and that the separation of the sexes enjoined during the catechetical instruction presumably was still in practice. Cyril saw in the removal of clothing the putting off of the old person (Col. 3:9) and in the nakedness an imitation of Christ on the cross (Col. 2:15) and a restoration of the likeness of Adam in paradise, who was naked and not ashamed (Gen. 2:25) (*Mys.* 2.2; for the gate of para-

---

cerned with what they experienced. Doval notes that in every case Cyril, in explaining the transformation that is effected, brings in a Christological image rather than making reference to the working of the Holy Spirit. Cf. the "Christ-bearing waters" (*Procat.* 15) and Christ imparting the fragrance of his divinity to the waters by his baptism in the Jordan (*Mys.* 3.1)

9. Riley, *Christian Initiation*, pp. 25-26, n. 17, for bibliography and other references in the Fathers to the renunciation.

10. Riley, *Christian Initiation*, p. 145, n. 4.

dise opened, cf. *Procat.* 15–16 and *Mys.* 1.1).[11] A moral interpretation of removing clothing (and receiving a white garment), based on Jesus' parable of the wedding garment (Matt. 22:11-14), is also found in the *Procatechesis* 3–4.

The naked candidates were then anointed with the oil of exorcism "from the very hairs of your head to your feet" (*Mys.* 2.3). The prebaptismal anointing of the whole body was not part of the central rite originally, so in different geographical areas it entered the ceremony at different positions, was given different symbolic interpretations, and had little use of scripture in reference to it.[12] Bathing practices of the ancient world may have influenced the introduction of this anointing into the ceremony, but Cyril offers theological explanations. In keeping with his Christological emphasis, he says the anointed were "made partakers of the good olive tree, Jesus Christ," being cut off from the wild olive tree and grafted into the good one (Rom. 11:17, 24).[13] In addition to the theme of union with Christ, Cyril uses motifs of healing and of combat in interpreting the action. This prebaptismal anointing with olive oil has features similar to anointing of the sick, so it was an effective symbol of healing. Oil was also used in cleansing. By reason of the invocation of God and prayer the exorcised oil had power to cleanse away traces of sin and to chase away the invisible powers of the Evil One. He appealed to the superstitions of the people by describing the exorcised oil as working like a "charm."

The Baptism Proper After the anointing the *phōtizomenoi* were led to the "holy pool [κολυμβήθραν] of divine baptism, as Christ was carried from the cross to the sepulchre that is before our eyes" (*Mys.* 2.4). Cyril, preaching in Jerusalem in the Constantinian basilica of the Holy Sepulchre, had the advantage of an "on the scene" location in explaining the meaning of baptism (see further below on death and resurrection).[14]

In contrast to the declaratory profession of adhesion to God made earlier after the renunciation of Satan, baptism "into Father, Son, and Holy Spirit" (*Cat.* 16.19)

---

11. The paradise motif is prominent in Cyril — *Mys.* 1.4, 9; *Cat.* 1.4; 2.7; 13.31.

12. Riley, *Christian Initiation*, pp. 190-199, on this paragraph. On the exorcistic features of the prebaptismal anointing, see Dölger, *Der Exorzismus im altchristlichen Taufritual*, pp. 137-159 (the introduction of the prebaptismal anointing was the result of considering the unbaptized as sick and possessed morally, of bathing customs, and of the practice of expiatory anointing in Greco-Roman culture — p. 158); cf. Doval, *Cyril of Jerusalem*, pp. 194-198, with reference to *Mys.* 2.3; *Cat.* 4.13; 16.19; and *Procat.* 9. Cyril's term is "exorcistic oil" (cf. "oil of exorcism" in the *Apostolic Tradition* 21.7, 8, 10).

13. Cf. *Mys.* 2.7 for Christ as the true vine with whom one is planted in baptism; cf. *Cat.* 1.4.

14. A. J. Wharton, "The Baptistery of the Holy Sepulcher in Jerusalem and the Politics of Sacred Landscape," *Dumbarton Oaks Papers* 46 (1992): 313-325, favors the south side of the church, where the eleventh-century baptistery complex is located, as the site of the baptistery for the Constantinian basilica over the north side, where a marble basin is located. Alexis Doval, "The Location and Structure of the Baptistery in the *Mystagogic Catecheses* of Cyril of Jerusalem," *Studia patristica* 26 (1993): 1-13, discusses the various proposals for the location and their compatibility with Cyril's account; his book *Cyril of Jerusalem*, p. 86, n. 3, reaffirms the south-side location and gives relevant bibliography. Day, *Baptism in Early Byzantine Palestine 325-451*, pp. 18-24.

continued to be performed as an interrogatory confession. "Each of you was asked concerning belief in the name of the Father, and of the Son, and of the Holy Spirit, and you made that saving confession" (*Mys.* 2.4).

There was a triple immersion, presumably one after each item of faith. The baptizands "descended [κατεδύετε] three times into the water and ascended [ἀνεδύετε] again" (*Mys.* 2.4). They were already in the pool and did not enter it three times, so this statement is not a reference to entering and exiting the pool three times but to the dipping in the water.[15] A full immersion is described in Cyril's explanation of the baptism of the apostles at Pentecost:

> For as the one who plunges into the waters and is baptized is encompassed on all sides by the waters, so were they [the apostles] also baptized completely by the Holy Spirit. The water, however, flows around the outside only, but the Spirit baptizes also the soul within and that completely....
>
> For the house became the vessel of the spiritual water; as the disciples sat within, the whole house was filled. Thus they were entirely baptized according to the promise and invested soul and body with a divine garment of salvation. (*Cat.* 17.14, 15)

Cyril elsewhere speaks of "going down into the water" (καταβαίνειν — *Cat.* 3.4 and 12). The administrators of the immersions ("at the season of baptism") might be "bishops, presbyters, or deacons" (*Cat.* 17.35).

The three immersions are not given a Trinitarian explanation but are related to the burial of Christ for three days in the heart of the earth, each immersion representing one day and night (*Mys.* 2.4). As a person in the night does not see but in the day is in the light, so the person who is under the water is in the night and sees nothing but on ascending out of the water sees clearly in the light of day, another indication of a total submersion.

Postbaptismal Rites   The third of Cyril's *Lectures on the Mysteries* concerns the unction with *myron* (a perfumed oil, different from the prebaptismal oil of exorcism) given immediately after baptism, the fullest exposition of the postbaptismal anointing in the Fathers.[16] Cyril took the anointing of 1 John 2:20-28 literally as pro-

---

15. Riley, *Christian Initiation*, pp. 230-232, on ducking the head three times. The suggestion of Doval, *Cyril of Jerusalem*, p. 145, that this passage implies that the candidates submerged themselves is overinterpretation, unless he means that the candidate ducked the head at the guidance of the administrator's hand.

16. Doval, *Cyril of Jerusalem*, pp. 110-149. Varghese, *Les onctions baptismales*, pp. 75-77, identifies four ideas associated with the act: anointing with the Holy Spirit and participation in the anointing of Jesus at the Jordan, protection against Satan and preparation for combat against him, permitting the giving of the name Christian, and a royal and priestly anointing. E. C. Ratcliff, "The Old Syrian Baptismal Tradition and Its Resettlement under the Influence of Jerusalem in the Fourth Century," in G. J. Cuming, ed., *Studies in Church History*, Vol. 2 (London: Nelson, 1965), pp. 19-37, identifies Cyril and the Jerusalem liturgy as responsible for adding the postbaptismal anointing with myron to the Syrian

viding the text for this act (*Mys.* 3.7). "After you had come up from the pool of the sacred streams, there was given an anointing [χρίσμα], the antitype of that with which Christ was anointed" (*Mys.* 3.1). Note once more the imitation of the experience of Christ. The postbaptismal chrismation was interpreted as a messianic anointing and a strengthening of the neophyte. The ointment was applied (*Mys.* 3.4) to the forehead (so as to remove the shame borne by Adam[17] and to reflect the glory of the Lord — 2 Cor. 3:18), ears (to hear the Lord Jesus in the Gospel — Isa. 50:4; Matt. 11:15), nose (to be the savor of Christ — 2 Cor. 2:15), and breast (with the breastplate of righteousness to stand against the devil — Eph. 6:11, 14). The invocation of the Holy Spirit made the ointment no longer simple or common but Christ's gift of grace fit to impart his divine nature.[18] Although applied to the body, it sanctified the soul by the Holy and life-giving Spirit (*Mys.* 3.3). The ointment may have been applied to the forehead in the shape of a cross (cf. *Cat.* 4.14; 12.8).

The recipients were now "Christians, verifying the name also by your regeneration [ἀναγεννήσις]"; prior to this grace they had no right to the title but were advancing on the way to becoming Christians (*Mys.* 3.5). Earlier Cyril had said that by baptism they had become "partakers of Christ" (Heb. 3:14) and so could rightly be called "christs" (*Mys.* 3.1; cf. *Procat.* 15 on receiving the name of Christ because of the "Christ-bearing waters"). He seems not to have been too concerned with the precise moment but viewed the whole baptismal experience as a unity. The anointed now had received "the seal [σφραγίς] of the fellowship of the Holy Spirit" (*Cat.* 18.33 — see below on the seal). This anointing was prefigured in the anointing of priests after their bathing in water; but the baptizands were now "truly anointed by the Holy Spirit" (*Mys.* 3.6). Unlike earlier sources from Syria but in keeping with western sources, Cyril associates the Holy Spirit with a postbaptismal anointing and not a prebaptismal anointing. This holy anointing was "a spiritual safeguard for the body and salvation for the soul" (*Mys.* 3.7).

The *Lectures on the Mysteries* say nothing about a laying on of hands, but the *Catechetical Lectures* do. In both the Old and New Testaments the Spirit was given by the laying on of hands (Deut. 34:9; Acts 8:18), and "On you also who are about to be baptized, his grace shall come" (*Cat.* 16.26). Whether this was a separate act not dis-

---

rite that previously knew only a prebaptismal anointing (*Didascalia, Acts of Thomas,* and *History of John Son of Zebedee*) along with the addition of the Pauline idea of baptism as sharing in the death and resurrection of Christ, whereas earlier the emphasis was on Christ's baptism as the pattern for Christian baptism (pp. 28-33). He notes that in the West (Tertullian et al.) baptism washes clean to prepare a person to receive the Holy Spirit, but in the East (Syria) the Holy Spirit in the prebaptismal anointing cleanses the person in preparation for baptism (p. 26).

17. Edward Yarnold, *The Awe-Inspiring Rites of Initiation* (Slough: St. Paul, 1971), p. 32, understands this to mean "save from the shame of original sin," but that phrases the statement too much in terms of later western theology.

18. Cyril compares the invocation on the oil to the invocation on the bread of the eucharist (*Mys.* 3.3). Riley, *Christian Initiation,* pp. 370-371, n. 64, says the invocation produces transformation but not transubstantiation.

cussed in the *Lectures on the Mysteries* or Cyril thought the chrismation to involve a laying on of hands is not clear.[19]

Also not discussed in the *Lectures on the Mysteries* is the clothing with a white garment, but it seems to be clearly alluded to (*Mys.* 4.8).[20] The white garment may be related to the description of the newly baptized as "bright in body and radiant in soul" (*Procat.* 15).

As the new Christians entered the church, there was the singing of Psalm 32:1 (*Procat.* 15; *Cat.* 1.1). They then shared in the eucharist, which is the subject of *Lectures on the Mysteries* 4 and 5.

From this whole account it is evident that no infant baptism was in view.

Meaning and Effects of Baptism

Although Cyril does not give the systematic treatment of the meaning of baptism that he does of the ceremony of initiation, there is a rich theology of baptism embedded in his writings.[21]

Christ's baptism instituted our baptism and sanctified the water (*Cat.* 3.11, quoted in chap. 7). No one, therefore, should despise baptism. He, being sinless, did not need forgiveness, but he was baptized that we might become partakers of his presence in the flesh and so of salvation (*Cat.* 3.11). He preached the gospel only after his baptism (*Cat.* 3.14). One is "baptized into Christ" (Gal. 3:27), even as "Christ washed [λουσάμενος] in the river Jordan and imparted the fragrance of his Godhead to the waters" (*Mys.* 3.1; see chap. 7). By our participation in Jesus' baptism we receive "both salvation and honor" (*Cat.* 3.11). Cyril consistently relates the experience of his hearers to that of Christ.

---

19. Another possibility is that the laying on of hands in *Cat.* 16.26 refers to the administrator's hand on the head at the immersions — Doval, *Cyril of Jerusalem*, pp. 143-145.

20. In this passage and in *Mys.* 1.10 and *Cat.* 3.2 Cyril quotes Isa. 61:10: Riley, *Christian Initiation*, p. 350, n. 7, gives considerations favoring the idea that the clothing with a white garment followed the anointing. Cyril may provide one of the first testimonies to what became a general practice by the end of the fourth century of providing the newly baptized with a white robe. John E. Farrell, "The Garment of Immortality: A Concept and Symbol in Christian Baptism" (Diss., Catholic University of America, 1974; Ann Arbor: University Microfilms), pp. 227-262, discusses the ancient preference for white as associated with radiance and radiance with divinity and the significance of linen as associated with sacred functions; pp. 282-303 concludes that the baptismal robe signified restoration to Adam's pre-fall condition, a response of virtuous behavior, and the future resurrection to immortality. Symbolic language about the exchange of clothing and symbolic representation (as in the white garment) were not far distant from each other (p. 269). Cf. other associations in Gerard-Henry Baudry, *Le baptême et ses symboles: Aux sources du salut* (Paris: Beauchesne, 2001), pp. 89-123 (summarized in my chap. 1).

21. Pierre Thomas Camelot, "Note sur la théologie baptismale des Catéchèses attribuées à saint Cyrille de Jérusalem," in Patrick Granfield and Josef A. Jungmann, *Kyriakon: Festschrift Johannes Quasten* (Münster: Aschendorff, 1970), Vol. 2, pp. 724-729, where he finds the more developed theology of the *Mysteries* in comparison to *Cat.* 3 an indication of a later date for the former.

Christ in his baptism not only sanctified water but also by going under the waters of the Jordan he overcame the dragon (Job 40:23, 26; Ps. 74:14), who represented death, and bound the strong one in the waters so that we too could overcome the Evil One (Luke 10:19). "The sting of death [1 Cor. 15:55] is drawn by baptism" (*Cat.* 3.11).

As a result, Cyril defends the appropriateness of water, "the noblest of the four elements," as the means of salvation. He sounds much like Tertullian, as he recalls the place of water in the creation, in the deliverance of Israel through the sea, in the beginning of the gospel at the Jordan, in the making of covenants (Noah after the flood and Israel at Sinai — Heb. 9:19), in Elijah's ascent to heaven after crossing the Jordan, in the washing of Aaron and the priests, and in the laver set up in the tabernacle as a symbol of baptism (*Cat.* 3.5).

Cyril particularly develops the typology of the exodus for the deliverance from the Evil One (*Mys.* 1.2-3; cf. *Cat.* 13.3).[22] He climaxes the parallels (Pharaoh — the devil, Moses — Christ, blood of a lamb — blood of the Lamb) with "The tyrant of old was drowned in the sea; and this present one disappears in the water of salvation."[23] Another type was Joshua (Jesus), who began his rule from the Jordan, as Jesus began to preach after he was baptized (*Cat.* 10.11).

The identification of the baptized with Christ plus the proximity of the church building to the sites of Jesus' crucifixion and burial occasioned extensive use by Cyril of the imagery of death and resurrection with baptism.[24] Romans 6:3-4 was the scripture reading for *Catechetical Lecture* 3 on baptism, and Romans 6:3-14 for the *Lecture on the Mysteries* 2 on baptism. One goes down into the water dead in sins but comes up made alive in righteousness, with Romans 6:5 quoted. "By going down into the water, and being in a manner buried in the waters, as Christ was in the rock, you are raised again 'walking in newness of life' [Rom. 6:4]" (*Cat.* 3.12). This imagery controls the presentation in *Lectures on the Mysteries* 2.4-8, where the parallels of the experience of Christ's sufferings,[25] death, burial, and resurrection and those of the baptizand are elaborated (for burial with Christ and being raised with him see also *Procat.* 2).

---

22. Cyril's comments associated the preliminary rites more than the immersion with the exodus, as other authors did. Doval, *Cyril of Jerusalem*, pp. 163-167.

23. Cf. Ps.-Eusebius of Alexandria, *On Baptism* (PG 86.372D), on trampling on the devil in the water.

24. Doval, *Cyril of Jerusalem*, pp. 145-148, suggests that the emphases in the *Catechetical Lectures* and the *Lectures on the Mysteries* represent a shift in the choice of scriptural models for baptism from Jesus' baptism in the Jordan to his death and resurrection, but he notes that both ideas are present in both sets of lectures and no change in theology was involved. Dana S. Kalleres, "Cultivating True Sight at the Center of the World: Cyril of Jerusalem and the Lenten Catechumenate," *Church History* 74 (2005): 431-459, argues that Cyril directed attention in *Cat.* 13 and 14 to a visualization of the human Jesus, giving prominence to Golgotha (neglected by Constantine's architecture of the site and by Eusebius of Caesarea's account of the site) and pointing past the ornate Anastasis to the original rock-cut tomb.

25. In *Mys.* 2.6 baptism is the "antitype of the sufferings of Christ," apparently with reference to his death (cf. 2.5), but Hugh M. Riley, *Christian Initiation*, pp. 234-241, notes that in spite of Cyril's emphasis on communion with the sufferings of Christ there is no liturgical parallel to them as distinct

Cyril's favorite way of speaking about baptism is to identify it with grace (e.g., *Procat.* 4). Thus he begins his *Catechetical Lectures* by referring to the *phōtizomenoi* as soon by grace to be partakers of the mysteries (1.1). The "grace of God is given through Christ at the regeneration of baptism [λουτοῦ ἀναγεννήσει]" (1.2). God readily gives his grace to those he finds worthy (1.3; cf. 3.13). To receive baptism is to receive grace (1.6; 3.13). The third lecture ("On Baptism") is full of references to grace: "his grace is bountiful," but the clear conscience must agree with the grace (3.2); baptism with water accompanied by reception of the Holy Spirit is to "receive grace in perfection," and the body by water "partakes of grace" (3.4); "grace is given by water" (3.5); "the grace of baptism was great" (3.6); "grace of the Holy Spirit" (3.8); those who are baptized receive a "divine and excellent grace" and become partakers in a "divine grace" (3.11); going down into the water is accompanied by "invocation of grace" (3.12); the grace of forgiveness is present now (3.15).

Cyril often uses the word *loutron* ("washing" or "bath") as simply meaning baptism (*Procat.* 2). Thus, where he speaks of "the repentance of the bath" (*Cat.* 4.32), he refers to his preceding lecture on the bath (λουτρόν), that is, on baptism. In this regard the influence of Titus 3:5 is evident, for the *loutron* is the "bath of regeneration [παλιγγενεσία]" (*Procat.* 11; *Cat.* 18.32, 35), and also of Ephesians 5:26 (quoted in *Cat.* 3.5). The "holy laver of regeneration" (*Mys.* 1.10 and some passages to be cited) shades into a reference to the place as much as to the act of washing. This term calls attention to the cleansing effected by baptism. The water cleanses the body, and the Spirit seals the soul (*Cat.* 3.4; cf. "purified by water" in 3.5). Baptism could cleanse even those guilty of crucifying Christ (*Cat.* 3.15).

More often the cleansing aspect of baptism is expressed in terms of the forgiveness of sins (*Cat.* 1.5, 6; 3.12; 4.32). The grace associated with baptism is the forgiveness of sins (3.2). Against those who suppose baptism only remits sins and gives adoption, Cyril points to other things it does (such as conferring the gift of the Holy Spirit and bringing participation in Christ's sufferings) in addition to purging sins (*Mys.* 2.6).

The creed expounded by Cyril contained in its last article belief "in one baptism of repentance for the remission of sins; and in one holy catholic church, and in the resurrection of the flesh, and in eternal life" (*Cat.* 18.22). The first clause appeared in shortened form in the Nicaeno-Constantinopolitan Creed (chap. 35).

An influential summary of the meaning of baptism occurs toward the conclusion of Cyril's *Procatechesis:*

Great is the baptism that lies before you: a ransom of captives, a remission of sins, a death of sin, a new birth of the soul, a garment of light, a holy indissoluble seal, a

---

from his death, although theologically baptism brings one into contact with his sufferings. Pierre Thomas Camelot, "Note sur la théologie baptismale," p. 728, speaks of the theology of the sacrament expressed by Cyril, "The saving effect of the act of Christ is communicated to us by means of the symbolic (sacramental) imitation of his death and resurrection."

chariot to heaven, the delight of paradise, a welcome into the kingdom, the gift of adoption! (16)

A little later he concludes the address:

> May God grant you forgiveness of your former trespasses; may he plant you into his church, enlist you in his own service, and put on you the armor of righteousness; may he fill you with the heavenly things of the new covenant and give you the seal of the Holy Spirit indelible throughout all ages. (17)

Many passages pick up specifics from these lists and add other benefits of baptism.

Cyril sometimes employs the traditional imagery of regeneration and the new birth. In one passage he connects the death and resurrection motif with that of the new birth in a striking formulation: "At the same moment you were both dying and being born: that water of salvation was at once your grave and your mother" (*Mys.* 2.4). The shift from water as the grave to water as the womb reverses the natural sequence of birth followed by death to death followed by life.[26]

The theme of regeneration is less developed than the death-resurrection motif. The slave of sin receives through faith "the regeneration [ἀναγέννησιν] into freedom and adoption," and baptism is a regeneration (ἀναγέννησις) (*Cat.* 1.2). This regeneration occurs in the holy catholic church (18.26).[27] For the necessity of both the water and the Spirit Cyril quotes John 3:5 (3.4).

Associated with regeneration is the idea of becoming children of God. In contrast to Jesus' Sonship by nature, Christians are adopted. "You do not have the sonship by nature, but you receive it by adoption. He eternally 'is,' but you receive the grace by advancement" (*Cat.* 3.14; cf. *Mys.* 2.6). By likeness of faith to that of Abraham, "we are adopted into the sonship of Abraham" (5.6). With this adoption goes the status of being heirs of eternal life (*Cat.* 4.32).

Cyril has much to say about the Holy Spirit in connection with baptism. His seeming inconsistencies are due to the varied statements in the New Testament and an effort to reconcile these with the liturgical practices of his day. I shall attempt to make an orderly statement of his unsystematized comments.[28]

Reference has been made to Cyril's insistence (in part a moral exhortation to his hearers) that the Spirit and the water are both necessary in baptism. As a human being is body and soul, the cleansing is twofold, by water and Spirit.[29] So one should

---

26. Riley, *Christian Initiation*, p. 302; for baptism as both tomb and womb, Jean Daniélou, *The Bible and the Liturgy* (Notre Dame: University of Notre Dame Press, 1956), pp. 41-49.

27. For παλιγγενεσία see above on *loutron*. Cyril seems to keep the two terms separate, using ἀναγέννησις for the idea of rebirth (although I have kept the translation "regeneration") and παλιγγενεσία in connection with Titus 3:5 and the bath.

28. G. W. H. Lampe, *The Seal of the Spirit*, 2nd ed. (London: SPCK, 1967), pp. 238, 240, concludes from the variety of usage that Cyril by baptism included the whole series of baptismal ceremonies. I rather think that Cyril reflects the Spirit at work in different ways in the varied actions.

29. Doval, *Cyril of Jerusalem*, pp. 171-172, on what he calls Cyril's "theology of double sacramental

"not think of the bare element but look for salvation by the power of the Holy Spirit." Neither being baptized with water but not found worthy of the Spirit nor being virtuous in deeds but not being baptized is sufficient, for "without both you cannot be made perfect" (*Cat.* 3.4; see above). Simon Magus (Acts 8:13-24) was an example of one whose body was dipped [ἔβαψεν][30] in water but whose heart was not enlightened with the Spirit (*Procat.* 2).[31] Similarly, unless one repents, "the water will receive but the Spirit will not accept" (*Procat.* 4)

Christian baptism in contrast to John's "introduces to us the gift of the Holy Spirit" (*Mys.* 2.6). As Jesus was baptized and the Holy Spirit descended on him (*Cat.* 17.9) and the voice from heaven declared him God's Son, "If you too have sincere piety, the Holy Spirit comes down on you also, and a Father's voice sounds over you from on high . . . , 'This one has now been made my son'" (*Cat.* 3.14). So, Cyril seems to have understood a purifying effect in the soul by the Holy Spirit in connection with baptism and a gift of the Spirit bestowed at baptism. Furthermore, Cyril identified the postbaptismal anointing with the Holy Spirit (*Mys.* 3.1).

Cyril understood the prediction that Jesus would baptize with the Holy Spirit and fire (Matt. 3:11) to have been fulfilled in the coming of the Holy Spirit with tongues of fire in Acts 2:2 (*Cat.* 3.9).

References to the Spirit in connection with baptism most often employ the language of a seal (σφραγίς). But "seal" could have multiple usages for Cyril.[32] Once "seal" seems to refer to the creed (*Cat.* 4.17). Sometimes seal is baptism, as in earlier Christian usage, clearly in *Procatechesis* 16, and probably elsewhere: "Where the Lord discerns a good conscience, there he gives the seal of salvation, that wondrous seal that devils tremble at and angels recognize . . . this spiritual and saving seal" (*Cat.* 1.3). This "mystical seal" identifies one as belonging to the Master (*Cat.* 1.2). At other times the seal is associated with the work of the Spirit in baptism (not the Spirit himself given in baptism). Thus, "the Spirit seals the soul" (3.3, 4; but the invocation of grace is also said to seal the soul — 3.12), and the unworthy person does not "receive the seal by water" (3.4); those who have cast off their sins by the repentance of baptism have "received the seal by the Holy Spirit" (4.32). The Spirit "at the season of baptism seals the soul" (4.16); "he seals souls in baptism" (16.24). Or, in another formulation, he leaves a seal on the soul: One should not think of the minister of bap-

---

effect" on body and soul with reference to *Procat.* 2; *Cat.* 3.4, 11; 10.13; *Mys.* 3.3, 7; 4.5. Camelot, "Note sur la théologie baptismale," p. 725, speaks of "a sort of real presence of the Spirit in the baptismal water" for Cyril.

30. It is probably significant that Cyril, after saying "Simon came to the bath [λουτρῷ], was baptized [ἐβαπτίσθη], but was not enlightened," then in the statement referred to in the text above does not repeat the technical word βαπτίζω when he wants to describe a dipping without a spiritual effect.

31. As Simon Magus was regarded as the archheretic from the second century forward, in the fourth century he became typical of the candidate unworthy for baptism — cf. John Chrysostom, *Catechetical Instructions* 5.21.

32. Doval, *Cyril of Jerusalem*, pp. 130-135, lists four uses: (1) in relation to baptism as a sealing by the Spirit, (2) as a visible mark with exorcistic or apotropaic power, (3) as a sign of attestation equal to circumcision, and (4) as a mark of belonging. The great majority of Cyril's uses are in a baptismal context.

tism but of the Holy Spirit, "for he is present in readiness to seal your soul, and he shall give you that seal at which evil spirits tremble, a heavenly and sacred seal" (Eph. 1:13 quoted — *Cat.* 17.35).[33] If one keeps this seal on the soul, no evil spirit will approach, for by the Spirit of God evil spirits are cast out (17.36). On another occasion the oil with which the forehead is anointed seems to be the seal (*Mys.* 4.7).[34] This latter may be the occasion described by the statement, "Be the cross our seal made with boldness by our fingers on our brow," but Cyril goes on to generalize, "and on everything"; hence, "despise not the seal" (i.e., the cross) — *Cat.* 13.36.

The connection of the Holy Spirit, the seal, and circumcision is expressed in a carefully worded statement: "Following upon our faith, we like Abraham receive the spiritual seal, being circumcised by the Holy Spirit through the washing [διὰ τοῦ λουτροῦ], not in the foreskin of the body but in the heart" (Jer. 4:4 and Col. 2:11-12 quoted — *Cat.* 5.6). Spiritual circumcision here is neither baptism nor the gift of the Holy Spirit himself to the baptizand; baptism is the occasion when the Holy Spirit circumcises the heart.

"Baptism is the end of the Old Covenant and the beginning of the New," for its author was John (*Cat.* 3.6). Hence, baptism was a distinctively New Testament institution, and part of its meaning was bringing one into a covenant relationship with God and so a member of the church (*Procat.* 17, quoted above).

All that is said about the meaning and effects of baptism emphasizes its necessity for Cyril. One who does not receive it cannot enter into the kingdom of heaven (*Cat.* 3.6 above). A person enjoys one salvation in the washing (λουτρᾷτῷ; 4.37). To this principle Cyril registers the same reservation concerning martyrs that authors in the age of persecution had made.

> If any one receives not baptism, that person does not have salvation; except only martyrs, who even without the water receive the kingdom. For the Savior, in redeeming the world by his cross, when he was pierced in the side, he shed blood and water [John 19:34], so that men living in times of peace might be baptized in water and in times of persecution in their own blood. [Mark 10:38 and 1 Cor. 4:9] (*Cat.* 3.10)

Cyril noted various interpretations that were offered to the blood and water from the side of Jesus at his crucifixion, one of which repeats the idea advanced in the preceding quotation:

---

33. "This seal did not itself confer the Holy Spirit, but the seal was received through the operation of the Spirit" — Burnish, *The Meaning of Baptism*, p. 6. Cf. *Cat.* 17.26 for the Holy Spirit leaving a seal on the soul of Paul at his baptism.

34. The usage here is likely due to the presence of the word in Exod. 28:26, which is cited. This is a usage in the *Lectures on the Mysteries* different from that in the *Catechetical Lectures* (except for 18.33, a later insertion) and marks a change in use of the term between the early and later Cyril due to a change in rites and not indicating a different author — Doval, *Cyril of Jerusalem*, pp. 137-141, 144. Doval postulates that at Jerusalem in 351 the sealing focused on the water rite, but by the 380s two anointings had become prominent — pp. 136-137.

Since in the Gospels the power of saving baptism is twofold, one which is granted by means of water to the enlightened and a second to holy martyrs in persecutions through their own blood, there came out of that saving side blood and water, in order to confirm the grace of the confession made for Christ, whether in baptism or on occasions of martyrdom. (*Cat.* 13.21)

The common feature uniting baptism and martyrdom that made them means of salvation was the confession of faith in Christ.

The scripture readings in the Old Armenian Lectionary, based on the practices of Jerusalem in the early fifth century, match the scripture readings of Cyril's *Catechetical Lectures*.[35]

Egeria

Egeria was a wealthy ascetic from northwest Spain who made a pilgrimage to the sites of biblical history in the late fourth century. Her account of her travels survives in one manuscript missing the beginning and end and so lacking a title.[36] It is cited today as *Itinerarium Egeriae (Egeria's Travels)*. She was very interested in liturgical practices, especially those in Jerusalem new to her. She gives more information on other activities than on baptism, but even on the liturgy she does not give specifics on the hymns, scripture readings, and prayers, of which she takes frequent note.

What Egeria reports concerning the process of initiation in Jerusalem fits well with what is known from Cyril, but there are some discrepancies. She reports (27.1; cf. 28) an eight-week period of Lent that included forty-one days of fasting (excluding the Saturdays and Sundays). Catechumens enrolled for baptism on the Sunday before the period of fasting began on Monday (45.1-2). On the second day the bishop took his seat in the Martyrium (the main assembly hall of the Church of the Holy Sepulchre) surrounded by the presbyters and other clergy. The candidates were brought individually before the bishop, the men by their "fathers" and the women by their "mothers" (apparently godfathers and godmothers, since small children are not in view). A detailed inquiry was made of the person's neighbors concerning the manner of life and whether serious vices had been engaged in. Those found unsatisfactory were turned away with instructions to amend their lives; the bishop wrote down the names of those accepted for baptism (the inscription of names is not covered by Cyril).

---

35. Conveniently charted along with the whole scheme of the lectionary tables in John Wilkinson, *Egeria's Travels*, pp. 175-194 (194 for the correspondences with Cyril). See also Maxwell E. Johnson, "Reconciling Cyril and Egeria on the Catechetical Process in Fourth-Century Jerusalem," in Paul F. Bradshaw, ed., *Essays in Early Eastern Initiation* (Nottingham: Grove, 1988), pp. 18-30.

36. Text, French translation, and notes in P. Maraval and M. Díaz y Díaz, *Égérie, Journal de Voyage (Itineraire)*, Sources chrétiennes 296 (Paris: Cerf, 1997). English translations with full notes by Gingras, *Egeria*, and Wilkinson, *Egeria's Travels*. My quotations are from Wilkinson.

On the fast days of Lent the clergy exorcised the candidates each morning after the dismissal from the morning office (46.1). Then the bishop's chair was set up in the Martyrium, and he gave catechesis to the candidates and any of the faithful who chose to come (but not catechumens or unbelievers — 46.1-2; cf. 27.6 for the bishop and presbyter preaching on certain days). The teaching was a scriptural syllabus (46.2) covering the whole Bible beginning with Genesis and giving the literal meaning and then explaining the spiritual sense.[37] The instruction lasted for three hours, from 6 to 9 o'clock, each day (46.4).

After five weeks of a biblical survey the creed was delivered, and for two weeks it was expounded article by article in the same way (46.3), literally and spiritually (perhaps referring to the exposition of the scriptural support for each article). At the end of seven weeks, each candidate with their respective godparents came before the bishop to recite the creed (46.5 — not described by Cyril). The bishop then explained that after their baptism during the eight days of Easter the divine mysteries would be interpreted to them (46.6). There was no instruction beyond the regular services during the eighth week, because there were too many services in the week preceding Easter to leave time for it.

Egeria does not describe the baptism itself, perhaps in observance of the *disciplina arcani* ("rule of secrecy") or more likely because she was not actually present and in any case mainly describes what was different or notable to her. She notes (38.1) that after the candidates had been baptized and clothed and left the room of the font, they were led with the bishop straight to the Anastasis (the memorial of Christ's resurrection). She uses the word *infantes* ("infants") for the newly baptized (38.1; also 39.3; cf. 47.2). These were not children, so the word was used in the theological sense of those who had been regenerated.[38]

During Easter week the bishop gave daily explanations of the mysteries (what had taken place in baptism) in the Anastasis to the newly baptized and any of the faithful who wished to hear but with the doors closed to keep out the catechumens (47.1-2). The five days of instruction would correspond to the five *Lectures on the Mysteries* of Cyril. The bishop spoke in Greek, but interpreters translated into Syriac or Latin as needed (47.3-4).

Elsewhere in her travel diary (15.1-2) Egeria notes that she went to see Aenon near Salim, where John the Baptist baptized (John 3:23). She was shown the spring and in front of it a pool. "The holy presbyter also told us that nowadays at Easter the candidates who are to be baptized in the village . . . receive their actual baptism in the spring itself" (15.5).

---

37. For instruction following a biblical history-of-salvation scheme and a twofold approach covering the literal and spiritual meaning, see Everett Ferguson, "Irenaeus' *Proof of the Apostolic Preaching* and Early Catechetical Instruction," *Studia patristica* 18 (1989): 119-140; and Herbert Musurillo, "History and Symbol: A Study of Form in Early Christian Literature," *Theological Studies* 18 (1957): 357-386.

38. This is apparently the use also in the Bordeaux Pilgrim, "a bath where *infantes* are baptized" (*balneum . . . ubi infantes lavantur* — *Corpus Christianorum, Series Latina*, vol. 175, p. 594). The translation "newly baptized" is adopted by Wharton, "The Baptistery of the Holy Sepulcher," p. 315.

30. Writers in Syriac in the Fourth Century: Aphrahat

Our approach is to take an analytical look at the principal Syriac authors of the fourth century. They give a similar picture of the baptismal practice and theology of Syriac-speaking churches, although with characteristic emphases.[1]

Aphrahat (Aphraates in Latin), the "Persian Sage," was later reported to have been bishop at the monastery of Mar Mattai (near modern Mosul, Iraq) in the Adiabene region of Persia. Internal evidence from his writings indicates he was an ascetic, a member of the "Sons of the Covenant" (addressed in *Demonstrations* 6),[2] and probably a bishop (giving instruction to pastors in *Dem.* 10 and writing *Dem.* 14 on behalf of a synod). His literary remains are twenty-three *Demonstrations*, written and preserved in Syriac and early translated (for the most part) into Armenian. His chronological information gives a date of 336/337 for the first ten, 343/344 for the next twelve; number twenty-three would come from 345.

None of Aphrahat's surviving works is devoted to baptism, but he makes enough references to baptism to permit some conclusions about the baptismal rite with which he was familiar and about his theology of baptism.[3]

---

1. B. Botte, "Le baptême dans l'Église syrienne," *L'Orient Syrien* 1 (1956): 137-155, is concerned only with the rite and with Syrian Antioch, so he surveys authors treated in other chapters and does not include Aphrahat and Ephraem.

2. The "Sons of the Covenant" were not identical with those who took a vow of celibacy, for the former could marry — *Dem.* 6.4.

3. E. J. Duncan, *Baptism in the Demonstrations of Aphraates the Persian Sage,* Studies in Christian Antiquity 8 (Washington, DC: Catholic University of America Press, 1945), whose copious references from earlier and contemporary Christian writers demonstrate Aphrahat's continuity with Christian tradition; E. J. Duncan, "The Administration of Baptism in the Demonstrations of Aphraates," in Jacok Vellian, ed., *Studies on Syrian Baptismal Rites,* Syrian Churches Series, Vol. 6 (Kottayam: CMS Press, 1973), pp. 16-36; Baby Varghese, *Les onctions baptismales dans la tradition syrienne,* Corpus scriptorum christianorum orientalium 512 (Louvain: Peeters, 1989); Jaroslav Z. Skira, "'Circumcise Thy Heart': Aphrahat's Theology of Baptism," *Diakonia* 31 (1998): 115-128, which despite its title does not discuss circumcision. For English translations I use (and quote) Kuriakose Valavanolickal, *Aphra-*

Aphrahat makes numerous quotations from the Old Testament. Accordingly, he finds a type of baptism in Israel's crossing the Red Sea.[4] As part of the extensive parallels between Israel's deliverance and Christian salvation Aphrahat says:

> They [the Jews] on the paschal sacrifice went from the slavery of Pharaoh, but we on the day of his crucifixion were redeemed from the slavery of Satan. . . .
>
> Moses was their leader, but for us Jesus was leader and redeemer. Moses divided the sea for them and caused them to pass through. Our redeemer divided Sheol and broke its doors, when he went into its midst and opened them, and besought a way before all those who believed in him. (12.8)

The baptismal connection is soon spelled out: "Israel was baptized in the midst of the sea on that night of the paschal sacrifice, on the day of redemption." Aphrahat continues by noting that it was on the night of the paschal sacrifice that Jesus instituted the true baptism by washing his disciples' feet (discussed below). Aphrahat pointed out the reverse order from the events of the exodus at the last supper: Israel ate the paschal sacrifice and then were "baptized in the clouds and the sea" (with quotation of 1 Corinthians 10:1), but Jesus washed the disciples' feet and then "gave them his body and blood" (12.10).

Aphrahat further connected baptism with Israel's crossing the Jordan River; his main interest here, however, was the discussion of circumcision (the theme of the eleventh *Demonstration*).[5] He mentions the previous covenants that God had changed, including the Mosaic covenant, but the covenant of Jesus will not be changed. "In this testament there is no circumcision of the flesh" (11.11). He continues, "They find life who are circumcised in their hearts and who circumcise themselves a second time on the true Jordan, the baptism of the forgiveness of sins" (11.11). The words "a second time" comes from the biblical text of Joshua 5:2-5, which explains that Israel had practiced circumcision before leaving Egypt (the first circumcision) but not during the years of wilderness wandering, so everyone born during that time had to be circumcised (the second circumcision).

> Joshua the son of Nun circumcised the people a second time with knives of stone when he and his people crossed the Jordan. Joshua [Jesus] our redeemer a second time circumcised the peoples who believed in him with the circumcision of the heart, and they were baptized and circumcised with "the knife which is his word that is sharper than the two-edged sword' [Heb. 4:12]. Joshua the son of Nun led the people across to the Land of Promise; and Joshua our redeemer promised the

---

hat Demonstrations I, Catholic Theological Studies of India 3 (Changanassery, Kerala: HIRS Publications, 1999), for *Dem.* 1–10; Jacob Neusner, *Aphrahat and Judaism: The Christian-Jewish Argument in Fourth-Century Iran* (Leiden: Brill, 1971), for *Dem.* 11–13, 15–19, 21, and 23. French translation in Marie-Joseph Pierre, *Aphraate le Sage Persan: Les exposés*, Vols. 1 and 2, Sources chrétiennes 349, 359 (Paris: Cerf, 1988, 1989).

4. Duncan, *Baptism in the Demonstrations*, pp. 50-56.
5. Duncan, *Baptism in the Demonstrations*, pp. 56-62.

land of the living to whoever passed through the true Jordan, believed, and circumcised the foreskin of his heart [Deut. 10:16]. (11.12)

The crossing of the Jordan apparently suggested baptism to Aphrahat, but his main concern was the reference to circumcision on that occasion.

Aphrahat seems to find in circumcision occurring a second time a double application of the language of circumcision. There was the true circumcision of the heart (Jer. 4:4), and there was the circumcision that occurred in baptism: "Blessed are those whose hearts are circumcised from the foreskin and who are born through water, the second circumcision" (11.12).[6] Christian circumcision, although associated with baptism, is not baptism. Interpreting Exodus 12:44 as the person "who sins, but repents and is bought with the blood of the messiah," Aphrahat then explains, "After he circumcises his heart from evil deeds, then he progresses to baptism, the fulfillment of the true circumcision" (12.9). The circumcision of the heart here is repentance; it is associated with believing in 11.10.[7] What physical circumcision meant for the descendants of Abraham (a sealing and sign — 11.11) is fulfilled in baptism.

Aphrahat also found in the story of Gideon a reference to baptism, something distinctive of him (but see in chap. 31 on the *Hymns on Epiphany*). Of Judges 7:4-8 he says, "This mystery is a great one, which Gideon has foreshown: (it is) a type of baptism and the mystery of the contest" (7.19). How the members of Gideon's army drank water was a "test of the water." Even so, "They shall bring to the waters of baptism those who have been chosen for the contest and they shall be tested. And after baptism they shall look for those who are valiant" (7.21). These words are part of Aphrahat's exhortation to penitents to be ready for battle and not turn back from their commitments.

Priests in the Old Testament bathed, and Aphrahat interpreted the winepress of Isaiah 5:2 as "the baptism of the priests" (5.22). The Pharisees and Sadducees, he says, took pride in their baptisms and other practices, but according to Jesus' teachings there was no profit "in their baptisms and purifications" (15.1).

During Jesus' earthly wanderings with his disciples, "they were baptized with the baptism of the law of the priests, of which John spoke, 'Repent from your sins' [Matt. 3:2]" (12.10). Aphrahat associated John's baptism more with Jewish baptism than with Christian baptism, and in the context distinguished it from the latter: "So know, my beloved, that the baptism of John does not effect the forgiveness of sins but only penitence" (12.10).[8] Nevertheless, the baptism administered by John the Baptist marked a transition. "Elijah divided Jordan (2 Kings 2:8), and John opened up baptism" (6.13).

In an elaborate parallelism of the life of Joseph in Genesis and the life of Jesus, Aphrahat refers to Jesus coming to the Jordan for baptism at the age of thirty, receiv-

---

6. Duncan, *Baptism in the Demonstrations*, pp. 32-36.
7. "There is no profit in circumcision without faith. But anyone who circumcises the foreskin of his heart believes, lives and becomes a son of Abraham" (11.10).
8. Aphrahat quotes Acts 19:3 and 1:5 for the inferiority of John's baptism.

ing the Spirit, and going forth to preach (21.9).[9] Then, in a paralleling of David and Jesus, he says, "Samuel anointed David when he was thirty years old, and Jesus received from John the laying on of the hand when he was about thirty years old" (21.13).[10] The complex of ideas here is that John laid hands on Jesus in immersing him, and this was a spiritual anointing, events linked by the age of David and Jesus.

Christ brought the true baptism. "Many prophets came and they could not bring forth baptism, until the Great Prophet came and he alone opened it up, and baptized in it" (4.6). The New Testament text cited first as the basis for Christian baptism is Mark 16:16, in a listing of Gospel texts on the importance of faith: "When our Lord gave the sacrament of baptism to his apostles, he said to them thus, 'He who believes and is baptized shall live, and he who does not believe shall be judged'" (1.17).

Another text used as a reference to baptism is John 7:37-38. The passage in 4.6 quoted above on Christ as the Great Prophet bringing baptism follows with a quotation of John 7:37. At another place the comparison is made that as Moses brought water from the rock, "our redeemer brought down living waters from his belly" (12.8).

Most distinctive of Aphrahat is his finding the institution of Christ's baptism at his washing of the disciples' feet at the last supper (John 13:3-15).[11]

> Our redeemer washed the feet of his disciples on the night of the paschal sacrifice, [which is] the mystery of baptism. You should know, my beloved, it was on that night that our redeemer gave the true baptism. (12.10).

Aphrahat then summarized the narrative from John 13 and added from the Synoptic Gospels that after resuming his place at table Jesus gave them his body and his blood.[12] (This is the order of the *Diatessaron,* but there is enough intervening material that Aphrahat is not necessarily following it.) The connection of the footwashing with baptism was to have a great future as an explanation of when the apostles were baptized.[13]

Aphrahat's association of the Pasch with the institution of baptism made that season the appropriate time of year for administering baptism. The conclusion of *Demonstration* 12, "On the Paschal Sacrifice," may give a sequence of activities connected with the paschal season and baptism:

---

9. Duncan, *Baptism in the Demonstrations,* pp. 63-67, on the baptism of Jesus in the Jordan as the revelation of Christian baptism.

10. Cf. also *Dem.* 6.13, "John laid his hand on our Savior, and he received the Spirit without measure."

11. Duncan, *Baptism in the Demonstrations,* pp. 67-78, on footwashing as a baptismal rite.

12. The sixth-century illustrated Rossano codex of the Gospels similarly pairs the last supper and the footwashing next to each other on folio 3 — Antonio Muñoz, *Il Codice Purpureo di Rossano e il Frammento Sinopense* (Rome, 1907), plate 5.

13. Harry A. Echle, "The Baptism of the Apostles," *Traditio* 3 (1945): 365-368 (366); Ernest H. Kantorowicz, "The Baptism of the Apostles," *Dumbarton Oaks Papers* 9-10 (1956): 205-251; Simon Legasse, *Naissance du baptême* (Paris: Cerf, 1993), pp. 143-144.

But as for us, it is required that we keep the festival in its time from year to year, fasting in purity, praying firmly, praising diligently, saying psalms as is appropriate, giving the sign [of the cross] and the baptism as is right. (12.13)[14]

For modern scholars the most controversial aspect of Aphrahat's baptismal teaching concerns the possible requirement of celibacy for baptism. The central passage that has fueled the debate occurs in the *Demonstration* "On Penitents." It follows the passage referred to above on the waters of testing in the story of Gideon.

For this reason it befits the blowers on the trumpets, (namely) the preachers of the church, to call out and warn all the covenant of God before baptism, (that is) those who have vowed themselves to virginity and (marital) continence, the young men and virgins and continent, and let the preachers warn them and say:
"He whose heart is set on the state of marriage, let him get married before baptism, lest he fall in the contest and get killed.
"And he who is afraid of this lot of fighting, let him return, lest he break the heart of his brethren, like his own heart. . . .
"While he who has not vowed himself, and has not put on the armor, if he turns back he is not blamed.
"But everyone who has vowed himself and put on his armor, if he turns back from the contest, he becomes a laughing stock. . . ."
And once they have proclaimed and announced and given warning to the whole covenant of God, they shall bring to the waters of baptism those who have been chosen for the contest and shall be tested. And after baptism they shall look for those who are valiant and those who are slack. . . . (7.20-21)

Because of the ascetic requirements in regard to baptism found in Marcion, Tatian, and the apocryphal acts of the apostles, some include Aphrahat as a witness to the requirement of celibacy for baptism in the Syrian church of the fourth century.[15] Because Aphrahat, in spite of his obvious preference for the celibate life over marriage, recognizes married persons as part of the congregation, it has been contended that he sometimes employs material from an older liturgical source, including the requirement for celibacy, that no longer reflected conditions in his own time and his own acceptance of married people for baptism.[16] Another solution is that there was a select group in the Christian community who practiced celibacy (to

---

14. "Let us carry his 'mark' [or sign] on our bodies (Ezek. 9:4) so that we may be delivered from the wrath which is to come (1 Thess. 1:10)" (6.1) may refer to this prebaptismal signing or to baptism itself.

15. F. C. Burkitt, *Early Christianity outside the Roman Empire* (Cambridge: Cambridge University Press, 1902), pp. 50-53; *Early Eastern Christianity* (London, 1904), p. 125; and in other writings.

16. Arthur Vööbus, *Celibacy as a Requirement for Admission to Baptism in the Early Syrian Church* (Stockholm: Estonian Theological Society in Exile, 1951), pp. 7-31 for testimonies to the asceticism of early Syrian Christianity, pp. 35-44 for whether the rule of celibacy was still in effect in the fourth century, pp. 45-48 for Aphrahat's own testimony that marriage was good (*Dem.* 18.8) and virginity was a state chosen voluntarily (*Dem.* 18.12), and pp. 49-57 for this solution to the problem of the apparently contradictory information in *Dem.* 7.18, 20.

which Aphrahat belonged) and Aphrahat calls on candidates for baptism to decide for a single or for a married life.[17] A refinement of this position is that this distinct group took their vows of celibacy when they were baptized and therefore saw baptism as meaning their own self-consecration.[18]

The first *Demonstration*, "On Faith," contains in summary form a statement of faith, perhaps confessed by the candidate before baptism.

> This is indeed the faith: that a man believes in God, the Lord of all, who made the heaven, the earth, the seas and all that is in them. He made Adam in his image. He gave the Law to Moses. He sent from his spirit upon the prophets, again he sent his Christ to the world. That a person should believe in the resurrection of the dead. Again he should also believe in the sacrament of baptism. This the faith of the church of God. (1.19)[19]

The items included here bear some resemblance to the creed on which Cyril of Jerusalem commented (chap. 29). Aphrahat follows this with a long list of things from which a person should abstain — Jewish and pagan religious practices and immoral actions. Faith must precede circumcision (11.2), and so too presumably its Christian counterpart in baptism.

Not only was faith required, but also repentance. Note *Demonstration* 12.9, cited above on repentance preceding baptism. Although *Demonstration* 7, "On Penitents," has in mind ascetics who fell in their combat and should confess to their spiritual fathers,[20] the passage about Gideon and bringing to the waters of baptism those ready for the contest (7.19-21) does have a baptismal setting. Therefore, the vows mentioned in this context have to do with a commitment to a particular kind of life.

Aphrahat gives no information directly relevant to infant baptism. His interpretation of Jesus as the one-year-old lamb of the paschal sacrifice, because "he was a child as to sins," and the quotation of Matthew 18:3 and Isaiah 65:20 (12.5) represent the common view that a child has no sin.

There is an allusion to a blessing of the font:[21] "At that moment when the priests invoke the Spirit, (the Spirit) opens up the heavens, descends and hovers over the water (Gen. 1:2), while those who are being baptized clothe themselves in her" (6.14). The translation reflects the fact that "Spirit" in Semitic languages is feminine. The statement is in the context of the coming of the Holy Spirit on those baptized, of which more below.

---

17. Duncan, *Baptism in the Demonstrations*, pp. 82-103; Skira, "'Circumcise Thy Heart,'" pp. 123-126.

18. Robert Murray, "The Exhortation to Candidates for Ascetical Vows at Baptism in the Ancient Syrian Church," *New Testament Studies* 21 (1974-75): 59-80 (p. 80). Murray starts from the insight of Vööbus and identifies a cycle of themes in Aphrahat, Ephraem, and their forbears which it was proper to mention to candidates for asceticism at their baptism (p. 60).

19. Duncan, *Baptism in the Demonstrations*, pp. 133-134.

20. Murray, "Exhortation to Candidates," p. 60.

21. Duncan, "The Administration of Baptism," pp. 30-34.

If *Demonstration* 12.13 indeed represents a sequence in activities associated with baptism, "giving the sign" preceded baptism.[22] It is not expressly said that this was an anointing, but this is a likely interpretation. Jacob's anointing of a stone pillar (Gen. 28:19) is interpreted of Christians (living stones) receiving an anointing: "For the people who believed in the anointed (Messiah) will be anointed as John said about them, 'God can raise up children for Abraham from these stones' (Luke 3:8)" — 4.5.

The references to the triple divine name in *Demonstration* 23 are uncertain whether applying to anointing or baptism, but 23.3 seems to be the anointing and 23.63 the baptism,[23] and in both cases a declaratory rather than an interrogatory formula. Otherwise, Aphrahat reveals little about the administration of baptism. If we may extrapolate from what is said of John's baptizing Jesus with his hand on his head, this gesture would imply an immersion. "Putting on the Spirit of Christ" implies a covering, as in immersion, which is confirmed by his use of the images of crossing the Red Sea and crossing the Jordan.[24]

There is no indication of a postbaptismal anointing. That a first eucharist and joining in congregational prayer followed on the baptism may be indicated by the association of washing themselves "in the water of baptism" and partaking in "the body and blood of Christ," followed by a mention of prayer (4.19).[25]

Aphrahat offers more information on the meaning of baptism than he does on its ceremony. Baptism brought a forgiveness of sins.[26] The last passage cited declares concerning those who killed Christ:

> They would not be cleansed unless they washed themselves in the water of baptism and partake (in) the body and blood of Christ. Blood is washed through the blood (of Christ), and the body is cleansed through the body (of Christ); sins are washed away in water, then prayer converses with the Most High. (4.19)

---

22. Duncan, *Baptism in the Demonstrations*, pp. 108-123, discusses the meaning of "sign" in Syriac literature and in Aphrahat. Varghese, *Les onctions baptismales*, pp. 37-38, lists different interpretations of "giving the sign" and reports that Aphrahat uses the noun *rûšmô* ("sign") five times for circumcision, once for the sign of Ezek. 9:4-6, and four times in connection with baptism, the only one of which permits a reference to anointing being *Dem.* 23.3; he implies that this refers to a pre-immersion anointing, yet if so, it was not with the sign of the cross, as Duncan thinks (p. 39), but was associated with the Holy Spirit (p. 42). Sebastian Brock, *The Holy Spirit in the Syrian Baptismal Tradition*, The Syrian Churches Series 9, edited by J. Vellian (Kerala: Anita, 1979; 2nd ed. 1998), pp. 22-24, identifies four positions in the baptismal ceremony in which an anointing occurs with a fairly stable terminology in the developed Syrian practice: accompanying the inscription of candidates *(htam)*, after the catechumenate but before the consecration of the water *(rushma)*, following the consecration of the water before the baptism *(mshah)*, and after the baptism before communion *(tba')*. Aphrahat, it seems, refers only to position 2.

23. Duncan, *Baptism in the Demonstrations*, p. 131.

24. Duncan, "The Administration of Baptism," pp. 35-36.

25. Cf. *Dem.* 12.9 on being baptized and being added to the body and blood of the messiah, and *Dem.* 12.10 above on Jesus' washing the disciples' feet and then giving them his body and blood.

26. Duncan, *Baptism in the Demonstrations*, pp. 134-137.

The "second circumcision" is "the baptism of the forgiveness of sins" (11.11). The declaration that the baptism of John did not bring forgiveness of sins, only repentance, implied that Christian baptism did accomplish this, as does the narrative of the footwashing (12.10).

Aphrahat expands on baptism as the occasion of receiving the Holy Spirit.[27]

> Now it is from baptism that we receive the Spirit of Christ . . . [quoted above on the blessing of the font]. The Spirit remains distant from all who are of bodily birth until they come to the birth (that belongs to the baptismal) water: only then do they receive the Holy Spirit. (6.14)[28]

This was true of Christ himself:

> Look, my beloved, at how in the case of our Lord, who was born of the Spirit; he was not tested by Satan until he had received from on high the Spirit at baptism. Only then did the Spirit take him out in order that he might be tempted by Satan. (6.17)

Christ's baptism was the occasion when John laid his hand on him, and he received the Holy Spirit (6.13). Without expressly saying so, Aphrahat, by his comments on spiritual circumcision and the baptismal gift of the Holy Spirit, appears to have understood the Christian equivalent of circumcision as what occurs in baptism rather than baptism per se.[29]

The gift of the Spirit in baptism, however, was not a permanent possession. The Spirit withdraws when a person sins.

> In the case of the person who has preserved the Spirit of Christ in purity, when (this) Spirit goes to Christ, she says to him: "The body to which I went and which put me on from the water of baptism, has preserved me in purity." [So the Spirit will urge Christ to resurrect that body]. . . .
> But in the case of that person who receives the Spirit from the (baptismal) water, and (then) grieves her [Eph. 4:30], she will leave him before he dies and go back to her natural state, Christ. (6.14)

Aphrahat then cites from scripture cases where the Spirit departed from someone who had received her (6.16). She may return, but Satan works at making the person act so wickedly that the Spirit will depart altogether (6.17).

Baptism was a new birth,[30] as indicated in the above quotations, in which context occurs the following explanation:

---

27. Duncan, *Baptism in the Demonstrations*, pp. 137-144; on the theme in general, Brock, *The Holy Spirit*.

28. In the same passage he speaks of our bodies as temples for the Spirit of Christ.

29. Duncan, *Baptism in the Demonstrations*, pp. 32-36; Everett Ferguson, "Spiritual Circumcision in Early Christianity," *Scottish Journal of Theology* 41 (1988): 485-497 (495-497).

30. Duncan, *Baptism in the Demonstrations*, pp. 36-43, 137.

For at (their) first birth they are born with an animate spirit which is created inside a person, which is furthermore immortal, as it is said, "Adam became a living soul" (Gen. 2:7; 1 Cor. 15:45). And at the second birth, which occurs at baptism, they receive the Holy Spirit, from a portion of divinity, and this too is immortal. (6.14)

The second circumcision is to be "born through water" (11.12).

Baptism was furthermore related to the death and resurrection of Christ.[31] The imagery of birth and the passion of Christ are united in one statement: "Those who were born of water and saved by the precious blood" (14.16). The "true baptism" (in contrast to John's) is "the mystery of the passion of our redeemer," followed by a conflated quotation of Romans 6:3-4 and Colossians 2:12 (12.10). Immediately after a summary of the events associated with baptism and reference to the blessings of the Holy One, Aphrahat says:

For our Lord suffered, rose, and again will not die; and death does not rule over him. One who dies for sin dies one time; but the one who lives lives unto God. And also as to us who were dead, he has given us life with him. (12.13)

This involved a defeat of the devil: As "Joshua the son of Nun wiped out unclean peoples, . . . Joshua our redeemer threw down Satan and his host" (11.12).

A favorite image with Syriac authors was clothing.[32] Aphrahat employs this too, especially the imagery of the wedding garment, which he identified with Christ him-

---

31. Duncan, *Baptism in the Demonstrations,* pp. 78-81, on baptism as the sacrament of the passion. Gabrielle Winkler, "Das armenische Initiationsrituale: entwicklungsgeschichtliche und liturgievergleichende Untersuchung der Quelle des 3 bis 10 Jahrhunderts" (Diss., Munich, 1977), which I know only from secondary references, draws a contrast between a *Todes-Mystik* in the West and a *Genesis-Mystik* in Syria and traces a development from an emphasis on the Johannine rebirth motif in baptism to the addition of a Pauline death-resurrection theology of baptism. Rowan Williams, "Baptism and the Arian Controversy," in Michel R. Barnes and Daniel H. Williams, eds., *Arianism after Arius: Essays on the Develpment of the Fourth Century Trinitarian Conflicts* (Edinburgh: T&T Clark, 1993), pp. 149-181 (179), finds this contrast overdrawn, for Cyril of Jerusalem cannot be the source of a death-resurrection theology so widespread a short time after him and Aphrahat does have the paschal death-resurrection theme, for which he cites some of the passages I use. E. C. Ratcliff, "The Old Syrian Baptismal Tradition and Its Resettlement under the Influence of Jerusalem in the Fourth Century," in *Studies in Church History,* Vol. 2 (London, 1965), pp. 19-37, also argued that the old Syrian tradition showed no signs of understanding baptism as death and resurrection: the Jordan and the baptism of Jesus were the archetypes for baptism as a new birth ("You are my Son"); but this tradition was changed by Cyril's *Lectures on the Mysteries* where baptism is the tomb.

32. S. P. Brock, "Clothing Metaphors as a Means of Theological Expression in Syriac Tradition," in Margot Schmidt, ed., *Typus, Symbol, Allegorie bei den östlichen Vätern und ihren Parallelen im Mittelalter* (Regensburg: Friedrich Pustet, 1982), pp. 11-38; reprint in Sebastian Brock, *Studies in Syriac Christianity* (Brookfield, VT: Variorum [Ashgate], 1992), #XI. For the theme in general John E. Farrell, "The Garment of Imortality: A Concept and Symbol in Christian Baptism" (Ph.D. diss., Catholic University of America, 1974).

self, who is put on in baptism.[33] He often alludes to the parables in Matthew 22:1-14 and 25:1-13 (e.g., several times in 6.1). As part of an elaborate development of wedding imagery in reference to the advent of Christ, Aphrahat says, "Light has shone out, resplendent and beautiful, garments not made by (human) hands are in readiness" (6.6). The clothing is described as armor — "Whoever has put on armor from the (baptismal) water, let him not take off his armor" (6.1). Aphrahat could also speak of putting on the Spirit in baptism (6.14).

By putting on Christ in baptism, one was incorporated into the church.[34] The idea is implicit in the use of the requirement of circumcision for eating the paschal sacrifice (12.2) and in baptism followed by prayer (4.19) and the eucharist (12.10). It is stated explicitly that the one who circumcises his heart from evil deeds and is baptized "is joined with the people of God and added to the body and blood of the messiah" (12.9).

---

33. Valavanolickal, *Aphrahat Demonstrations I*, p. 15; Duncan, *Baptism in the Demonstrations*, pp. 43-49, 144-145, on putting on Christ, which entailed the need to preserve baptismal innocence. For Christ himself as the garment of glory that the righteous put on, see *Dem.* 14.39 in a list of Christological titles.

34. Duncan, *Baptism in the Demonstrations*, pp. 145-147.

31. Writers in Syriac in the Fourth Century: Ephraem the Syrian

Ephraem, who was born about 306 and died in 373, is the classic writer of Syriac-speaking Christianity. Baptized as an adult,[1] he became a deacon in Nisibis before Persia took control of the city in 363, when he moved to Edessa. Ephraem's poetic and metaphorical language associates a rich imagery with the meaning of baptism, and his allusions give a confirmation of baptismal practices.[2]

Typology of Baptism

Ephraem's poetic imagination found a continuity of symbolism in nature and in scripture.[3] Representative of his imaginative speech is the statement, "Our Lord lives in the bread, in the baptismal water, and in the stones of the church" (*Hymns against Heresies* 42.9).[4] Two common types of baptism in the early church — the flood and the exodus — are little developed by Ephraem. But with reference to Noah's ark, he says,

---

1. *Hymns against Heresies* 3.13, a triple immersion.
2. Georges Saber, "La typologie sacramentaire et baptismale de saint Ephrem," *Parole de l'Orient* 4 (1973): 73-96; Georges Saber, *La théologie baptismale de Saint Ephrem* (Kaslik, Lebanon: Université Saint-Esprit, 1974); E. Beck, "Le baptême chez Saint Ephrem," *L'Orient Syrien* 1 (1956): 111-136; Baby Varghese, *Les onctions baptismales dans la tradition syrienne*, Corpus scriptorum christianorum orientalium 512 (Louvain: Peeters, 1989), pp. 43-57.
3. Tanios Bou Mansour, *La pensée symbolique de Saint Ephrem le Syrien* (Kaslik, Lebanon: L'Université Saint-Esprit, 1988), especially pp. 353-377 on types and symbols of baptism; Saber, "La typologie sacramentaire et baptismale de saint Ephrem." Note Saber's comment that between nature and the Bible and between the Old Testament and the New Testament each revelation surpasses the preceeding without destroying it but continuing and assuming it (p. 90).
4. Saber, *La théologie baptismale*, p. 31. Unless otherwise credited, I give in English Saber's French translations.

the cross of its steersman, and wood of its sailor who has come to fashion for us a church in the water of baptism: with the three-fold name he rescues those who in her live; in the place of the dove, the Spirit ministers her anointing and the mystery of her salvation. (*Hymns on Faith* 49.4).[5]

In his *Commentary on Exodus,* Ephraem's discussion of the exodus makes much of the cross but little of baptism. The Passover lamb represented Christ crucified (12.2-3) and the rod with which Moses struck the sea is the cross (14.3), but he does not comment on the blood placed on the doorposts and the lintel. He does comment on the prohibition of a stranger eating the Passover as meaning that "No one eats the Body who is not baptized" (12.3).[6] His commentary on 1 Corinthians 10:1-2, prompted by Paul's interpretation, mentions that baptism is followed by the table of the body and blood.[7]

Among practices enjoined in the Law of Moses, Ephraem found three principal types of baptism: circumcision, ceremonial ablutions, and sprinkling of blood and water with hyssop.

Circumcision was put into relation with two characteristics of baptism: a sign of salvation and an invisible seal.[8] "The hidden mark of the Spirit is imprinted by the oil on bodies anointed in baptism and sealed in the dipping" (*Hymns on Virginity* 7.6).[9] Here the anointing with oil and the immersion in water are treated together (as is characteristic for Ephraem), and the decisive work is the interior work of the Spirit. In another passage the parallel is simply between circumcision and baptism because of their common effect of averting death according to one incident:

> If Zipporah has circumcised her son with the temporal circumcision and has averted death [Exod. 4:24-26], will not death with much more reason be banished by the true baptism? The one baptism into Christ puts on the Living One who vivifies the whole world. (*Nisibene Hymns* 72.22)[10]

There was a difference, however, for circumcision was transitory, but Christ's baptism was true, living, and permanent in its effects. As the light of stars disappears

---

5. Translation by Sebastian Brock, *The Holy Spirit in the Syrian Baptismal Tradition,* The Syrian Churches Series 9, edited by J. Vellian (Kerala: Anita, 1979), p. 16; 2nd ed. (1998), p. 33; cf. Saber, *La théologie baptismale,* pp. 38, 51-52. Ephraem's *Commentary on Genesis* in its discussion of the flood does not refer to baptism or mention the dove.

6. Translation by Joseph P. Amar in *St. Ephrem the Syrian: Selected Prose Works,* Fathers of the Church 91 (Washington: Catholic University of America Press, 1994), p. 247.

7. Saber, *La théologie baptismale,* pp. 48-49. The *Hymns on Epiphany* (see below) 1.5-6 do more with the comparison: the cloud was a symbol of the Holy Spirit that overshadows one in baptism; Israel passing through the sea was a symbol of the baptism with which one is washed; Israel did not believe, but Gentiles believe, and when they are baptized they receive the Holy Spirit.

8. Saber, *La théologie baptismale,* pp. 38-43. He cites *Nisibene Hymns* 73.8.

9. Translation by Kathleen McVey, *Ephrem the Syrian Hymns,* Classics of Western Spirituality (New York: Paulist, 1989), p. 294.

10. Saber, *La théologie baptismale,* p. 39.

with the sun, so with the coming of Christ, "Types and symbols ceased. With hidden circumcision visible circumcision was abolished" (*Hymns on Virginity* 9.1).[11] Here, again, the true circumcision is the interior, even if the occasion is the outward act of the baptismal ceremony. The commentary on Colossians 2:11 makes the spiritual contrast: "You have been circumcised in Christ, not the circumcision of the Hebrews by a material instrument, but of the circumcision of Christ, that is, baptism which removes your old humanity."[12] Since the first circumcision could not purify from sin, the "second circumcision," which removes evil works from the heart, replaced it.[13] Christian circumcision appears to be baptism in these statements by Ephraem.

The Jewish ablutions prepared for the baptism of the church.[14] Ephraem's *Commentary on the Diatessaron* 16.12 (on John 3:10) mentions "the cleansing of hyssop, the waters of ceremonial sprinkling, and the baptisms of purification" as types of "the baptism of complete expiation of body and soul."[15] The commentary continues with mention of the washing of Naaman the leper (2 Kings 5:8-14) as "a manifest sign of baptism given to Gentiles" (16.13).[16]

Because of the sprinkling of a mixture of blood and water by hyssop in certain purifications, Ephraem found a type of Christ and baptism in the hyssop. The hyssop (Lev. 14:52) had the power to purify the world (*Hymns on the Nativity* 1.25). Using the language of the Old Testament practice, Ephraem exclaims:

> Purifying Sprinkling, Pardoning Hyssop, Who pardons all their sins in a baptism of water! All the sprinklings of the Levites are unable to pardon one People with their weak hyssops. Blessed are the peoples [whose] hyssosp was the Merciful One, Who purified them with mercy. (*Hymns on Virginity* 31.4).[17]

Christ's baptism put an end to the old bathings and sprinklings (*Hymns on Virginity* 8.10). Hyssop and baptism were compared under the aspect of the power to forgive sins; the blood and water sprinkled by the hyssop suggested the blood of the cross that gave the purifying power to baptism.[18]

---

11. McVey, *Ephrem the Syrian*, p. 301.

12. Saber, *La théologie baptismale*, p. 40. He also refers to the *Sermon on Our Lord* (7) for baptism as the circumcision of the heart.

13. Saber, *La théologie baptismale*, p. 42.

14. Saber, *La théologie baptismale*, pp. 43-45; Saber, "La typologie sacramentaire," p. 87.

15. Translation by Carmel McCarthy, *Saint Ephrem's Commentary on Tatian's Diatessaron*, Journal of Semitic Studies Supplement 2 (Oxford: Oxford University Press, 1993), p. 248.

16. Saber, *La théologie baptismale*, p. 45. *Hymns on Epiphany* 1.2-3 also mentions the priests sprinkling with hyssop and blood and Elisha having Naaman bathe seven times as baptismal symbols; the seven immersions of Naaman represent seven spirits expelled by baptism (cf. 5.6 for baptism cleansing secret misdeeds of the soul as the seven washings cleansed Naaman's leprosy).

17. McVey, *Ephrem the Syrian*, p. 399.

18. Saber, *La théologie baptismale*, p. 47, with reference to *Hymns on Paradise* 4.3-4, where the High Priest (Christ) purifies Adam by hyssop and reintroduces him to paradise, even as under Moses "the priest purifies him [the leper] with hyssop, blood and water" (Sebastian Brock, *St. Ephrem the Syrian: Hymns on Paradise* [Crestwood: St. Vladimir's Seminary Press, 1990], p. 98).

502 | THE FOURTH CENTURY

Some New Testament stories also symbolized baptism. The well of Jacob where Jesus conversed with the woman of Samaria (John 4:1-30)[19] prompted the comments that the holy church is built on the well, and Christ "baptizes with living waters" (John 4:10) (*Hymns on Virginity* 17.10; cf. 18.1).[20] The pool of Bethesda where the paralytic sought healing from the waters when they were stirred (John 5:2-9) was used to make a point about baptism:

> Let the Jews, who do not believe that baptism forgives sins, be put to shame. For, if they believe that an angel can heal illnesses through *the waters of Shiloah* [Siloam], how much more can the Lord of angels purify the stains [of sin] through baptism?" (*Commentary on the Diatessaron* 13.1)[21]

Baptism of Christ

Ephraem identified the institution of baptism with the baptism of Christ and with the water and blood from his side on the cross (John 19:34) rather than with the dominical command of Matthew 28:19. The baptism of Jesus in the Jordan for him was more than a prototype of Christian baptism; it was the foundation of the institution itself.[22]

The role of Christ, however, was placed in continuity with previous salvation history. There was a succession from Moses, on whom God laid his hand at Sinai, through Aaron and the priests of the Old Testament to John the Baptist and to Jesus (who said to John, "Righteousness requires that I am baptized by you in order that the succession may not be lost"), and he transmitted it to the apostles, and this tradition is in the church (*Hymns against Heresies* 22.18-19).[23] In the *Commentary on the*

---

19. Ephraem also brought into his discussion Jacob's watering the sheep (Gen. 29:2-3).

20. Saber, *La théologie baptismale*, pp. 52-53; McVey, *Ephrem the Syrian*, p. 336.

21. McCarthy, *Saint Ephrem's Commentary*, p. 205; Saber, *La théologie baptismale*, p. 109. Ephraem appears to have substituted the name of the pool of Siloam from the story of the healing of the blind man in John 9; the same identification of Siloam with the story in John 5 occurs in *Hymns on Epiphany* 11.6.

22. Saber, *La théologie baptismale*, pp. 70-71; for Christ's baptism and Christian baptism see Sebastian Brock, *The Luminous Eye: The Spiritual World Vision of Saint Ephrem the Syrian*, rev. ed. (Kalamazoo: Cistercian, 1992), pp. 90-94. More on Ephraem's treatment of the baptism of Jesus in chap. 7.

23. Saber, *La théologie baptismale*, pp. 30, 47 (priesthood and baptism were inseparable for Ephraem), and 71. The passage is translated by Brock, *The Holy Spirit*, p. 59. Cf. *Hymns on the Nativity* 3, "He gave imposition of hands to Moses in the Mount, and received it in the midst of the river from John" — trans. by J. B. Morris in *Nicene and Post-Nicene Fathers*, Second Series (repr. Peabody: Hendrickson, 1994), Vol. 13, p. 234. The passage is hymn 4.210 in McVey, *Ephrem the Syrian*, p. 104; henceforth I will give the hymn number in McVey, as the more recent numbering, followed by the *Nicene and Post-Nicene Fathers* numbering in brackets. The imposition of hands on Moses is presumably based on Exod. 33:22 (McVey less plausibly cites Lev. 8). For John's hand on the head of Jesus at his baptism see also *Hymns on Virginity* 15.1-2; Jesus took John's right hand and placed it on his head when

Diatessaron 4.3, Ephraem explained in reference to the baptism of Jesus that the repose of the Spirit on him attested that he was the Shepherd; he had already received the kingdom of the house of David, and he now received through John by his "second birth" prophecy and priesthood.[24]

With this continuity was fulfillment and completion of what had gone before.

> Through baptism [the Lord] assumed the justice of the Old [Testament] in order to receive the perfection of the anointing and give it fully and in its entirety to his disciples. For he put an end to John's baptism and the Law at the same time. . . . Through his justice he dispensed from the Law and through his baptism he abolished [Jewish] baptism. (*Commentary on the Diatessaron* 4.2).[25]

One passage from Ephraem brings together the nature of John's baptism, the reason for Jesus' baptism, and the newness of the baptism instituted by Jesus:

> John had been whitening the stains of debt with common water, so that bodies would be fit for the robe of the Spirit imparted by our Lord. Therefore, since the Spirit was with the Son, he came to receive baptism from John to mix the Spirit, which cannot be seen, with water, which can be seen, so that those whose bodies feel the wetness of the water should be aware of the gift of the Spirit in their souls, and that as the outside of the body becomes aware of water flowing over it, the inside of the soul should become aware of the Spirit flowing over it. (*Sermon on our Lord* 55 [53])[26]

Another passage affirms that Jesus' baptism had a purifying effect on the water and was the institution of Christian baptism:

> Blessed are you, little Jordan River, into which the Flowing Sea descended and was baptized. . . . Blessed are your torrents, cleansed by His descent. For the Holy One, Who condescended to bathe in you, descended to open by His baptism the baptism for the pardoning of souls. (*Hymns on Virginity* 15.3)[27]

---

at the occasion of his baptism he spoke the words of Matthew 3:15 (with Ephraem's explanation that John was the "heel of the Law" but Christ is the beginning of the New Testament) — *Commentary on the Diatessaron* 4.2.

24. Saber, *La théologie baptismale*, p. 71. Brock, *The Holy Spirit*, p. 78, for the Spirit not sanctifying Christ but bearing witness to him. Multiple images were possible: Ephraem suggested that Christ received the priesthood, kingdom, and prophecy at his presentation in the temple — *Sermon on Our Lord* 53 [51]; 55 [53]; and *Commentary on the Diatessaron* — Saber, *La théologie baptismale*, p. 73.

25. McCarthy, *Saint Ephrem's Commentary*, p. 84 (the bracketed word "Jewish" is my addition). (On the terminology, note the use of anointing to designate the baptism of Christ.) Cf. *Sermon on Our Lord* 56 (54) for Jesus' baptism as a fulfillment of Jewish institutions, even though they continued to be practiced — Saber, *La théologie baptismale*, p. 79.

26. Amar, *St. Ephrem*, p. 330. I give the section numbers of his translation with the numbers in the *Nicene and Post-Nicene Fathers* in brackets. The gift of the Spirit in baptism is discussed more below.

27. McVey, *Ephrem the Syrian*, p. 326; cf. *Hymns on Nativity* 18 (13).15 (McVey, *Ephrem the Syrian*, p. 161) for Jesus baptized in the "little waters" of the Jordan, that is, "little" or "small" in contrast to the

The Trinity were involved in Jesus' baptism and were manifest to the senses: the Father by his voice to the sense of hearing, the Son by his power to the sense of touch, and the Holy Spirit by his descent as a dove to the sense of sight — all three baptized Jesus in the Jordan (*Hymns on Faith* 51.7-8).

One passage in Ephraem combines the thought of Christ's conquering the waters with his humility in submitting to baptism and in the process gives an indication of the mode of baptism:

> How wonderful your footsteps, walking on the waters! You subdued the great sea beneath your feet. [Yet] to a little stream you subject your head, bending down to be baptized in it. (*Hymns on Faith* 10.20)[28]

The baptism of Jesus demonstrated his humanity against Marcionite and other dualist heresies, but it also demonstrated his deity, for the coming of the Spirit confirmed his divine status.[29] The Spirit given at his baptism distinguished him from others and was a public manifestation of what was hidden before, not the acquisition of what he did not have. In one passage Ephraem speaks of four begettings of Christ:

> The Father begot Him, and through Him He made all creation. Flesh begot Him, and in His flesh He put passions to death. Baptism begot Him, that through Him it might make (our) stains white. Sheol begot Him to have her treasuries despoiled by Him. (*Sermon on our Lord* 2.5)[30]

The parallel of Jesus' baptism with his conception in the womb of Mary is made elsewhere: "The river in which Christ was baptized conceived him again symbolically, the damp womb of water conceived him in purity and bore him in holinesss, made him rise up in glory" (*Hymns on the Church* 36.3).[31] The baptism, besides being a proclamation of Christ's deity, was paradoxically also a sign of his abasement. It was a paradox that "The Purifier of all was baptized" (*Hymns on Virginity* 15.1).[32] A step

---

great sea measured by the Son (Isa. 40:12), and *Hymns on Virginity* 32.5.7, "Sanctified [was] the river that received Him" (McVey, *Ephrem the Syrian*, p. 405); Saber, *La théologie baptismale*, p. 80.

28. Translation by Robert Murray, "A Hymn of St. Ephrem to Christ on the Incarnation, the Holy Spirit, and the Sacraments: Translation and Notes," *Eastern Churches Review* 3 (1970-71): 142-150 (145).

29. Saber, *La théologie baptismale*, pp. 96-104.

30. Amar, *St. Ephrem*, p. 277. Sections 1 through 2.4 speak of the three births other than baptism.

31. Brock, *The Holy Spirit*, p. 130; 2nd ed., p. 195. The parallel of the incarnation and his baptism is also made in *Hymns on Virginity* 7.10: "Christ, though immortal by nature, clothed Himself in a mortal body; He was baptized (*or* He dived down) — and raised up from the water the treasure of salvation for the race of Adam" (this is the translation of Brock in *The Luminous Eye*, p. 91, which also gives another translation of the passage cited in the text). Cf. *Hymns on the Nativity* 23 (16).14 for his being born again as the means of begetting others. The Word in his incarnation not only put on a body but he also put on the waters of baptism — *Hymns on the Nativity* 23 (16).12.

32. McVey, *Ephrem the Syrian*, p. 326; cf. *Hymns on the Nativity* 23 (16).14, "O Pure One Who was baptized, let Your washing wash us of impurity" (McVey, *Ephrem the Syrian*, p. 190).

on the way from the incarnation to the cross, at the baptism "the pure one was baptized, and the living one dies" (*Hymns on the Resurrection* 18.22). The last strophe of this hymn continues the paradox: "His nativity is our purification [birth was normally considered in the ancient world to cause impurity], his baptism is our expiation; his death is our life; his ascension is our exaltation."[33]

In a different vein, Ephraem offered an explanation of when and how the apostles were baptized that did not entail a literal reception: they were baptized by the word of Christ (cf. John 15:3) — *Commentary on the Diatessaron* 5.15.

John 19:34 provided an association of the water and the blood in human salvation, anticipated already in the purification ceremonies of the Law. Thus in commenting on Jesus' words to the thief on the cross (Luke 23:43), Ephraem said that "It was through the mystery of the water and the blood issuing forth from [the Lord's] side that the robber received the sprinkling which gave him the remission of sins" (*Commentary on the Diatessaron* 20.26).[34] "There came out from [his side] water and blood; Adam washed and lived and returned to paradise" (*Nisibene Hymns* 39.7).[35]

Faith and Repentance

As is implicit throughout Ephraem's writings, baptism as a human response was predicated on faith and repentance. "[The Lord's] baptism forgives freely the debts of those who believe," but there is no forgiveness for the sin against the Holy Spirit (*Commentary on Diatessaron* 10.4).[36] Baptism had no meaning without faith, but conversely faith was without efficacy and subject to error if not sealed by baptism (*Hymns on Faith* 13.3).[37] This faith was particularly the Trinitarian faith: "On these three names depends our baptism; by these three mysteries our faith gleams" (*Hymns on Faith* 13.5).[38] This was what made heretical baptism problematical. The *Hymns on Faith* have this baptismal faith in view. Ephraem seems not to have considered the question of what happens to the catechumen who dies before receiving baptism.

---

33. Saber, *La théologie baptismale*, pp. 103-104. Cf. *Hymns on the Resurrection* 1.16 — "His birth gives us purification, his baptism gives us forgiveness, his death is life to us, his ascension is our exaltation" (Sebastian Brock, *The Harp of the Spirit*, Studies Supplementary to Sobornost 4 [Fellowship of St. Alban and St. Sergius, 1983], p. 29).

34. McCarthy, *Saint Ephrem's Commentary*, p. 307. The "sprinkling" alludes to the sprinkling of blood and water in Old Testament purification.

35. Translation by J. T. Sarsfield Stopford in *Nicene and Post-Nicene Fathers* (repr. Peabody: Hendrickson, 1994), Second Series, Vol. 13, p. 201. The reversed order from the biblical text, "blood and water," likely represented an accommodation to the sacramental symbolism of baptism and eucharist.

36. McCarthy, *Saint Ephrem's Commentary*, p. 166.

37. Saber, *La théologie baptismale*, pp. 56-61.

38. Georges Saber, *La théologie baptismale*, p. 59. Cf. *Hymns against Heresies* 17.2, "The body by baptism comes to faith." On the Trinity as the foundation of faith and of baptism, see Tanios Bou Mansour, *La pensée symbolique*, pp. 123, 166-168, 365-366. See further below on the three divine names in baptism.

Ephraem compared prebaptismal and postbaptismal repentance. The latter was more arduous (*Hymns on Virginity* 46.23), but "Sins committed before baptism can be absolved easily, in baptism, . . . but post-baptismal sins can only be reversed by means of doubled labors" (*Hymns on Virginity*, 46.26).[39] Sin is always possible after baptism, but there is no second baptism, so the Lord grants a pardon after baptism by way of a rigorous exercise of repentance (*Hymns on Virginity* 55.21-22).

Ceremony of Baptism

Hymns on Virginity 7.2, 5-10 shows the sequence in the baptismal ceremony.[40] Baptism was preceded by a period of fasting (a penitential discipline) and was administered in the paschal season.[41] "April gives rest to the fasters, it anoints, baptizes, and clothes in white; it cleanses off the dirt of sin from our souls" (7.2). The minister was the bishop (the high priest), assisted by priests and a "crown of Levites (deacons)" (7.8). "The anointing precedes" the baptism (7.8), but the two acts belong together: "The hidden seal of the Spirit is imprinted by oil on the bodies of those who are anointed in baptism; thus they are marked in the baptismal mystery" (7.6).[42] That the baptism was an immersion is stressed by the phrases and words in strophe 10: "He descends and buries himself in the water," "Once baptized it raises up from the deep," and Christ "was baptized [or dived down], and so raised up from the water a treasure of life for the race of Adam." The triple divine names were pronounced, "the three glorious names of Father, Son, and Holy Spirit" (7.5, cited more fully under regeneration below). There is no trace here or elsewhere in Ephraem of a postbaptismal anointing.[43] The "children" born in baptism are nourished from the altar, eating bread in place of milk (7.8).

39. Brock, *The Holy Spirit*, p. 63; 2nd ed., p. 101, which quotes the whole passage as well as *Hymns on Abraham Qidunaya* 4.2-3 on there being only one baptism but a second means of forgiveness by tears (repentance); Saber, *La théologie baptismale*, pp. 134-135.

40. French translation and discussion in Saber, *La théologie baptismale*, pp. 162-169; English translation by McVey, *Ephrem the Syrian*, pp. 293-296; and by Brock, *The Harp of the Spirit*, pp. 47-51, from whom I quote. We will return later to this important passage for the meaning of baptism.

41. *Hymns on the Fast* 5.1 for baptism following the Fast and being compared to a wedding feast (as in Aphrahat), to which one being baptized comes as a bride — translation in Brock, *The Luminous Eye*, pp. 122-123.

42. E. Beck, *Dorea und Charis. Die Taufe. Zwei Beiträge zur Theologie Ephräms des Syrers* (Louvain: Peeters, 1984), pp. 90, 132, affirms that Ephraem knew a double prebaptismal anointing of the forehead and of the whole body; V. van Vossel, *L'onction baptismale chez St Ephrem*, dissertation (Bagdad: Pontificiae Instituti Orientalis, 1984), pp. 21, 23, 31, argues for an anointing of the whole body as continuation of the anointing of the head. I have not seen these works and know them from Bou Mansour, *La pensée symbolique*, p. 344, n. 51. Varghese, *Les onctions baptismales*, p. 47, concludes that Ephraem probably knew only one anointing of the whole body, which is indicated in *Hymns on Virginity* 7 and *Hymns on Faith* 82.10 cited below.

43. Saber, *La théologie baptismale*, p. 164.

Prior to the baptism occurred a sanctification of the waters.[44] As the fullness of the Spirit was in the Son (*Hymns on Faith* 18.19), so Jesus came to the Jordan in order to mix the Spirit with the water and give to the water the power that it did not have of itself to communicate the Spirit. Ephraem speaks of both Christ and the Holy Spirit being in the water. The Syriac tradition spoke on fire appearing at the baptism of Jesus (chap. 6), and Ephraem associated the Spirit and fire. "[John] baptized the Baptizer Who baptized the Gentiles with a flash of fire and the Holy Spirit" (*Hymns on Virginity* 15.1).[45]

> See, Fire and Spirit in the womb that bore You! See, Fire and Spirit in the river where you were baptized! Fire and Spirit in our baptism; in the Bread and the Cup, Fire and Holy Spirit! (*Hymns on Faith* 10.17).[46]
>
> In fire is the symbol of the Spirit, it is a type of the Holy Spirit who is mixed in the baptismal water so that it may be for absolution, and in the bread that it may be an offering. (*Hymns on Faith* 40.10)[47]

Associated with these ideas was the custom of placing a cross in the water, apparently alluded to in *Hymns on Virginity* 15.6.[48]

Removing clothing for the baptism and being clothed afterward seems to be alluded to in the reference to pearl divers who stripped off their clothes and dived naked to find a pearl: "For clothed bodies were not able to come to thee; they came that were stript as children; they plunged their bodies and came down to thee." Then, "The diver came up from the sea and put on his clothing."[49] The pearl divers stripped and were anointed before diving into the sea: "In symbol and in truth Leviathan is trodden down by mortals: the baptized, like divers, strip and put on oil, as a symbol of Christ they snatched you and came up" (*Hymns on Faith* 82.10).[50]

The sequence of anointing followed by baptism, well-attested in other sources for early Syriac practice,[51] is reflected in Ephraem.

---

44. Sebastian Brock, "The Epiklesis in the Antiochene Baptismal Ordines," *Orientalia Christiana Analecta* 197 (1974): 183-215 (188) identifies four types of epicleses: those with no reference to the Holy Spirit; the Holy Spirit is requested to "come" (older than the next form); the Father or Christ is requested to "send" the Holy Spirit; some other verb is used. Brock, *The Holy Spirit*, pp. 70-75.

45. McVey, *Ephrem the Syrian*, p. 326.

46. Murray, "A Hymn of St. Ephrem," p. 144; fire and Spirit are a theme throughout, and this stanza is something of a summary. Cf. *Hymns on the Nativity* 23 [16].12 for Christ putting on the waters of baptism and from them rays shining forth.

47. Brock, *The Holy Spirit*, p. 11; 2nd edition, p. 27, where he notes that in the Syriac tradition, of the three symbols of the Spirit (fire, dove, and oil), fire is the most important.

48. "Since you set up the cross over the waters!" — Brock, *The Harp of the Spirit*, p. 16.

49. *Hymns on Faith* 85 (The Pearl 5).3 and 4; translation by J. B. Morris in *Nicene and Post-Nicene Fathers* (Peabody: Hendrickson, 1994), Second Series, Vol. 13, pp. 295-296. In addition to the baptismal associations the pearl had multiple symbolisms for Ephraem — paradise, eucharist, faith, virginity, Christ himself (Bou Mansour, *La pensée symbolique*, pp. 92-93).

50. Brock, *The Harp of the Spirit*, p. 33.

51. A summary statement is given by Sebastian Brock, "The Syrian Baptismal Rites," *Concilium*

Other passages stress the Trinitarian nature of baptism: the Trinity acts in baptism. The Trinitarian formula was essential, for the Father signs, one is joined to Christ, and the Holy Spirit sanctifies (*Homilies on Faith* 13.2; cf. 52.3).

> It was not [the pool of] Siloam that opened [the eyes] of the blind man [John 9], just as it was not the waters of the Jordan that purified Naaman [2 Kings 5:14]. It was [the Lord's] command which effected it. So too, it is not the water of our atonement that cleanses us. Rather, it is the names pronounced over it which give us atonement. (*Commentary on the Diatessaron* 16.29)[52]

The Trinity are equal in the administration of baptism (*Hymns on Faith* 77.20-22). Baptism "in his Name" is baptism in the persons and in the naming of Father, Son, and Holy Spirit (*Sermon on Admonition and Repentance* 2). The triune name is frequent in the *Hymns on Faith* — 13.5-6; 23.14; 41.10; 62.13 (which indicates a confession of faith); 65.3; and 67.10 (which seems to insist on the sequence faith and then baptism).[53] The question of the validity of Arian baptism arises because of this connection of the Trinitarian faith with baptism.[54] A triple immersion is indicated in some passages.[55]

---

122 (1979): 98-104 (see chap. 46); Sebastian Brock, "The Syrian Ordines (with Special Reference to the Anointings)," *Studia Liturgica* 12 (1977): 177-183; Sebastian Brock, "The Transition to a Post-Baptismal Anointing in the Antiochene Rite," in Bryan D. Spinks, ed., *The Sacrifice of Praise: Studies on the Themes of Thanksgiving and Redemption in the Central Prayers of the Eucharistic and Baptismal Liturgies in Honour of Arthur Hubert Couratin* (Rome: Edizioni Liturgiche, 1981), pp. 215-225, where he identifies four themes in the prebaptismal anointing (*rushma*, the anointing of the head): mark of ownership, protection, conferring the royal priesthood, and conveying sonship (pp. 217-218). According to the last named work (pp. 222-223), the prebaptismal anointing later became primarily cathartic and protective and the term *rushma* came to be used also for the postbaptismal anointing and the ideas associated with it (notably sonship and royal priesthood) were attributed to baptism itself or to the postbaptismal anointing.

52. McCarthy, *Saint Ephrem's Commentary*, p. 259. In a similar vein Ephraem, in explaining the disciples' baptism, says that the fact that they baptized (John 4:2) was an indication that they had been baptized (or else they would not have been able to baptize) and then offers another explanation: if they were not baptized in water, Jesus' statement "You are clean because of my word" (John 15:3) meant that his word was baptism for them, "since baptism is rendered holy by this same word" (*Commentary on the Diatessaron* 5.15; p. 101).

53. Beck, "Le baptême," 111-136. The threefold name was invoked in the anointing as well as the immersion — "The [anointing] oil has three names, the trumpets of baptism" (*Hymns on Virginity* 4.14; McVey, *Ephrem the Syrian*, p. 279).

54. *Hymns on Faith* 59.2; 65.4; and 41.1, which seems to say Arianism suspends the efficacy of baptism.

55. *Nisibene Hymns* 29.207ff.; *Hymns on Virginity* 7.5 (quoted below on regeneration); 27.4 (which also rejects baptism in only one name).

Meaning of Baptism

Ephraem's understanding of the meaning of baptism can be developed principally in terms of two of the oldest and most stable elements in the theology of baptism — forgiveness of sins and the gift of the Holy Spirit.

Ephraem refers frequently to the baptismal remission of sins.[56] The baptism of Christ had this forgiveness of others in view. "He was baptized in justice because he was sinless, but he baptized in grace because [all others] were sinners" (*Commentary on the Diatessaron* 4.2).[57] "Baptism brought him [Christ] forth, that through him it might wash away stains" (*Sermon on our Lord* 2).[58] The *Commentary on 1 Corinthians* 1:30 states, "We have been justified and sanctified by his death; and by his baptism he has forgiven our sins," and again in the *Commentary on Romans* 8:2 he writes, "The law of the Spirit is the faith of baptism; it is this law that frees you from the law of sin by the baptismal forgiveness."[59] "By baptism he forgives the sins of all human beings" (*Commentary on Romans* 7:13).[60]

Ephraem, furthermore, often connects the forgiveness of sins with the baptismal unction.[61] Reasons for the connection were the forgiveness Jesus pronounced on the sinful woman who anointed his feet (Luke 7:38, 48) — *Hymns on Virginity* 4.11 — and the identity of the name of oil and of Christ — ibid. 7.9. Oil destroys sin as the flood destroyed the impure (*Hymns on Virginity* 4.11) and expels demons (*Hymns on Virginity* 4.13). The explanation for this dual attribution would seem to be the same as the one elaborated below concerning the texts attributing the gift of the Holy Spirit to both the anointing and to the baptism, namely that the baptismal ceremony was viewed as a whole and specific gifts could be attributed to one or another of the parts according to the subject discussed or the point being made.

Although granting that there is no mention of infant baptism by Ephraem nor an express statement of original sin, Georges Saber argues from the presence in Ephraem's writings of the consequences attributed to this doctrine (e.g., loss of the garments of glory and a stain transmitted by generation) that all its elements are there.[62] He seems to me to read too much into the texts cited, for it is death rather

---

56. Saber, *La théologie baptismale*, pp. 107-109. See above on sprinkling by hyssop.
57. McCarthy, *Saint Ephrem's Commentary*, p. 84.
58. Translation by A. Edward Johnston in *Nicene and Post-Nicene Fathers* (repr. Peabody: Hendrickson, 1994), Second Series, Vol. 13, p. 306. Cf. Amar's translation quoted above.
59. Saber, *La théologie baptismale*, p. 138.
60. Saber, *La théologie baptismale*, p. 108.
61. *Hymns on Virginity* 4.9 puts forgiveness in baptism and 4.11 in the oil. Saber, *La théologie baptismale*, pp. 109-111, with reference to *Hymns on Virginity* 4.9; 7.7 and 9 ("the oil destroys sins in baptism"), to which may be added 4.11; 7.12; Varghese, *Les onctions baptismales*, pp. 50-53. For the symbolism of oil in Ephraem, see Bou Mansour, *La pensée symbolique*, pp. 88-91, who observes that the role of oil in forgiveness is a symbolic activity.
62. Saber, *La théologie baptismale*, pp. 111-131. The arguments of Beck, *Taufe*, pp. 171ff., against finding a doctrine of original sin in Ephraem are summarized in Bou Mansour, *La pensée symbolique*, p. 372, n. 81.

than a hereditary culpability for sin that was transmitted to Adam's descendants.[63] Phrases such as the "yeast of Satan," "sign of the first Adam," and "stain of sin" do not necessarily reflect guilt because of Adam's sin. Ephraem affirms the innocence and salvation of children who die young, without making any allusion to their baptism (*Hymns on Paradise* 7.8; 14.10-11); Saber says this presupposes their baptism, although he grants that the baptism of children was probably still the exception in Ephraem's day except for those in peril of death.[64]

The foundation of the baptismal forgiveness of sins was the cross of Christ.[65]

> Let the soul thank you — that filthy thing that You wiped clean of the stains of debts she incurred in her freedom. . . . Whereas [Jewish] priests cleansed with a bird at daybreak, You cleansed the soul that acted foolishly. You bathed it in Your blood, bleached [it] and made it gleam [illumined it]. (*Hymns on Virginity* 37.6).[66]

Two complementary baptisms — the baptism of water and the baptism of the cross — were necessary for salvation:

> There are two baptisms in our Lord, the Purifier of all people: the baptism of water and that of the cross; it is by the baptism of the Passion [Mark 10:38-39] that he makes known the baptism of water. . . . The two baptisms are then necessary for the just and for sinners; if there was only one it would not give life. (*Commentary on the Diatessaron* 21.32).[67]

Ephraem said of his own baptism that he was washed with the water that flowed from the side of Christ on the cross.[68]

Ephraem often expresses the effects of baptism in terms of sanctification, but he

---

63. Passages cited are *Hymns on Paradise* 7.6; 15.5; *Nisibene Hymns* 35.8; 65.23. For an original culpability he cites the *Commentary on Romans* 5:10, "The Lord sows righteousness in our bodies and his fermentation changes our mass, as the first Adam sowed impure sin in pure bodies and the fermentation of malice was buried in our universal mass" (Saber, *La théologie baptismale*, p. 119). If the analogy is to be interpreted as precise, it either says more about the condition of the Christian or less about the consequences of Adam's sin than the doctrines of salvation, on the one hand, or of original sin, on the other hand, would say. I would take the latter option.

64. Saber, *La théologie baptismale*, pp. 129-130. These statements of the innocence of children would presuppose their baptism only if the other passages imply original sin, which is the very point to be proved and not to be assumed here.

65. Saber, *La théologie baptismale*, pp. 132-134.

66. Cf. *Hymns on Virginity* 30.10, "They pierced You with a lance and water flowed forth, as the blotting out of their sins. . . . The Slain One gave water from His blood to His slayers [so that] they would be purified." McVey, *Ephrem Syrian*, pp. 426, 397; cf. Saber, *La théologie baptismale*, pp. 108, 133.

67. I translate the French in Bou Mansour, *La pensée symbolique*, p. 376, of the passage in the Armenian but not in the Syriac. Saber, *La théologie baptismale*, pp. 133-134, understands the baptism of the cross as our taking up our cross in penitence. The primary reference, it seems to me, is to Jesus' cross. Bou Mansour considers the baptism of water and of the cross united in our baptism and rejects a reference to martyrdom in the baptism of the cross (pp. 376-377).

68. Saber, *La théologie baptismale*, pp. 123, 132.

does not develop what sanctification means beyond purification or forgiveness.[69] Ephraem interprets "those who are in Rome and those called to be saints" of Romans 1:7 as two groups: "catechumens and those who have been sanctified by baptism; the baptized are saints thanks to the purification made by baptism."[70] Similarly on Colossians 1:1-2 he identifies believers as catechumens and the saints as the baptized.[71] On 1 Thessalonians 3:13 he exhorts "to remain in the sanctity with which you have been clothed by baptism," and on 2 Thessalonians 2:13 he speaks of "The holiness of the Spirit that you have received in the waters."[72] Ephraem also attributes justification to baptism: "justification by faith" is the baptismal faith: "He justifies them by faith and baptism."[73]

In keeping with baptism's sanctifying effects, Ephraem associates the activity of the Holy Spirit with baptism. "Our Lord heals the whole person and in every respect; he baptizes him in the Holy Spirit" (*Nisibene Hymns* 46.84).[74] "Because the Spirit had come down [on him] at his baptism, the Spirit was given through his baptism" (*Commentary on the Diatessaron* 4.3).[75] Ephraem interpreted John 3:3-7 in terms of baptism as involving water and Spirit:

> [O]ur Lord revealed the baptism of complete expiation for body and soul to him [Nicodemus]....
>
> [B]aptism of water, together with the fellowship of the Spirit, was necessary for the body.... He [the Lord] was instructing him therefore in the faith, indicating that birth from the flesh is visible, but birth from baptism is [from] the Spirit, and this is invisible. (*Commentary on the Diatessaron* 16.12, 14)[76]

Unlike others (and in contrast to *Hymns on Epiphany* 8.16 below), Ephraem in his *Commentary on Genesis* 1.7.1-3 denies that the "wind" of Genesis 1:2 refers to the Holy Spirit hovering on the water.

At other times Ephraem associated the gift of the Spirit with the anointing, and he often expresses the virtue and significance of oil.[77] For instance, oil brings righteousness to sinners (*Hymns on Virginity* 4.10-11). Among the many things oil is said to do in *Hymns on Virginity* 7 are these words:

---

69. Saber, *La théologie baptismale*, pp. 137-139.
70. *Commentary on Romans*; Saber, *La théologie baptismale*, p. 137.
71. *Commentary on Colossians*; Saber, *La théologie baptismale*, p. 138.
72. *Commentary on 1 Thessalonians* and on *2 Thessalonians*; Saber, *La théologie baptismale*, p. 138.
73. *Commentary on Romans* 5:1; Saber, *La théologie baptismale*, p. 138.
74. Saber, *La théologie baptismale*, p. 111. See *Sermon on Our Lord* 55 (53) cited above in connection with Jesus' coming to John's baptism for the Spirit being mixed with the water so that one might be clothed with the Spirit and receive the gift of the Spirit.
75. McCarthy, *Saint Ephraem's Commentary*, p. 85.
76. McCarthy, *Saint Ephraem's Commentary*, pp. 248-249.
77. Saber, *La théologie baptismale*, pp. 160-169; cf. Varghese, *Les onctions baptismales*, pp. 47-49, for oil, "a treasure of symbols" (*On Virginity* 4.2; cf. 5.16; 7.12). Oil is also associated with the eucharist (*Hymns on Faith* 6.4).

Oil is the dear friend of the Holy Spirit, it serves Him, . . . ; for with the oil the Holy Spirit imprints his mark [*rushma*] on His sheep. Like a signet ring whose impression is left on wax, so the hidden seal of the Spirit is imprinted by oil on the bodies which are anointed at baptism.

With the distinctive oil bodies are anointed for forgiveness, bodies that were filled with stains are made white without effort. (7.6-7)[78]

How are the texts assigning the work of the Holy Spirit to the water of baptism and those assigning it to the anointing oil to be reconciled? Saber's observations seem to provide the answer.[79] The unction had a central place in the ceremony and represented it in all its complexity. The Syriac word for baptism was *amad*, which means "to confirm, to stand erect." The Syriac church chose a word to represent baptism that did not express its outward form but that characterized its interior effect. Baptism expressed the confirmation of faith. Ephraem conceived baptism as a whole whose parts may not be dissociated, so he could attribute to the parts of the ceremony the properties of the whole — the forgiveness of sins and the gift of the Holy Spirit. Hence, one part of the ceremony was the equivalent of the other part. The Syriac church had no postbaptismal anointing until later because it attributed to prebaptismal anointing the association with the Holy Spirit that others did to the postbaptismal anointing.

Baptism renewed and regenerated a person to the image of God.

[W]ith oil that all can see is the hidden portrait of our hidden King portrayed on those who have been signed; on them baptism, that is in travail with them in its womb, depicts the new portrait, to replace the image of the former Adam who was corrupted; it gives birth to them with triple pangs, accompanied by the three glorious names of Father, Son, and Holy Spirit. . . .

[T]hey go down sordid with sin; they go up pure like children, for baptism is a second womb for them. Rebirth in the font rejuvenates the old, as the river rejuvenated Naaman." (*Hymns on Virginity* 7.5, 7)[80]

---

78. Brock, *The Harp of the Spirit*, pp. 48-49; cf. Saber, *La théologie baptismale*, p. 162.

79. Saber, *La théologie baptismale*, pp. 164-167; however, his statement that the unction was the culminating point of baptism for the Syrian church may overstate the situation. Brock, *The Holy Spirit*, p. 37, concludes, "The gift of the Spirit is essentially conferred by the rite *as a whole*, and within the rite the anointing and the baptism in water form an inseparable unity." He adds that Syriac texts may focus the gift of the Spirit on one of the anointings, on the water, or on an imposition of hands. Bou Mansour, *La pensée symbolique*, pp. 344-345, concludes that the oil was attached to baptism (and so not to be separated from the baptismal ceremony) but was not confounded with it. Varghese, *Les onctions baptismales*, p. 45, for Christian baptism as consisting of anointing and immersion, so that the oil and water together partake of all the symbolisms of baptism; he affirms that, contrary to the third-century Syrian tradition represented by the *Acts of Thomas*, Ephraem gives equal value to the oil and the immersion (49-50); his observation that the verbs for the anointing (to sign, to mark, to seal, to anoint) are sometimes used for baptism as a whole (pp. 56-57) is also pertinent.

80. Brock, *The Harp of the Spirit*, pp. 48-49; cf. Saber, *La théologie baptismale*, p. 162.

The passage reflects the unity of oil and immersion in baptism. The phrase "womb of water" occurs in *Hymns on the Crucifixion* 3.7.4. The Lord renewed human old age in baptism and built with his blood a temple for God to dwell in (*Hymns on Virginity* 1.2). "You bear the new humanity which has been renewed by baptism and becomes unstained like the image of the Creator" (*Commentary on Colossians* 3:9-10).[81]

In baptism a person — body and soul — puts on Christ. "The body confesses you, Lord, . . . The soul adores you. . . . The body and soul all together exalt you because they were baptized in you and have put you on" (*Hymns against Heresies* 17.5).[82] "Thou wast baptized from the water; thou hast put on Christ in his naming; the seal of the Lord is on thy person and his stamp on thy forehead" (*Sermon on Admonition and Repentance* 2).[83] Thus one is clothed with the garments of glory. Ephraem made a succinct parallel of the incarnation with the baptismal clothing: "Our body became your garment, your Spirit became our robe" (*Hymns on the Nativity* 22 [15].39.3).[84]

That the church derives from baptism is indicated in passages already referred to (*Hymns on Virginity* 17.10; and *Hymns on Faith* 49.4).

Hymns on Epiphany Attributed to Ephraem

There are doubts about authenticity of the fifteen *Hymns on the Epiphany*.[85] For this reason and because of their abundant information about baptism due to their subject matter (the Epiphany of Christ was his baptism in the Greek and eastern churches) I give these hymns separate treatment.

These hymns begin with a hymn that elaborates on a great number of baptismal

---

81. Saber, *La théologie baptismale*, p. 142.

82. Saber, *La théologie baptismale*, p. 146; Sebastian Brock, "Clothing Metaphors as a Means of Theological Expression in Syriac Tradition," in Margot Schmidt, ed., *Typus, Symbol, Allegorie bei den östlichen Vätern und ihren Parallelen im Mittelalter* (Regensburg: Friedrich Pustet, 1982), pp. 11-38; repr. in Sebastian Brock, *Studies in Syriac Christianity* (Brookfield, VT: Variorum [Ashgate], 1992), #XI, pp. 13, 18-21. He cites *Hymns on the Nativity* 23 (16).13 as summing up the four scenes of the drama of salvation in which the imagery of clothing was employed: Adam and Eve clothed in "garments of glory" or "of light"; these stripped off at their fall; Divinity putting on Adam at the incarnation (including the depositing of the robe of glory in the baptismal waters — Christ "was baptized for Adam's sin"); and when one is baptized one picks up the robe of glory left in the water by Christ. He notes a contrast between Greek writers, who speculated on what was "taken off," and Syriac ones, who emphasized what garments were "put on" (p. 22).

83. Translation by A. Edward Johnston in *Nicene and Post-Nicene Fathers* (repr. Peabody: Hendrickson, 1994), Second Series, Vol. 13, p. 320.

84. Quoted by Brock, "Clothing Metaphors," p. 18.

85. Brock, *The Holy Spirit*, p. 28, "unlikely to be by Ephrem himself." Bou Mansour, *La pensée symbolique*, pp. 356-361, 363-364, 368-371, 373-374, 376, sees the hymns as developing Ephraem's ideas, and Varghese, *Les onctions baptismales*, p. 46, n. 18, judges that the hymns contain authentic texts of Ephraem alongside others that are not. I quote the translation by A. Edward Johnston in *Nicene and Post-Nicene Fathers*, Second Series, Vol. 13, pp. 265-289.

symbols: Elisha's (Naaman's) bathing seven times in the river (1.2-3 — 2 Kings 5:1-14), the hyssop and the blood (1.3 — Lev. 14:52), Moses' sweetening the bitter waters (1.4 — specified as "a sign of baptism"; cf. 2.25 — Exod. 15:22-25), the cloud and sea of the exodus (1.5-6 — Exod. 14:19-25), the proclamation of light by John the Baptist (1.17-18 — John 1:6-9), the gifts of the Magi (1.19 — Matt. 1:11), and the heavenly voice at Jesus' baptism 1.10-20 — Matt. 3:17). The second hymn refers to the footwashing: "He washed men's feet and cleansed men's souls" (2.7 — John 13:1-20).

The third hymn is an extended praise of oil that confers the seal, making reference to the many incidents in scripture in which oil has a place. The relation of the chrism and the water is expressed according to the imagery of birth: "Christ and chrism are conjoined; . . . the chrism anoints visibly, Christ seals secretly, . . . for he engendered it of the chrism, and he gave it birth of the water" (3.1), a clear indication that the anointing preceded the immersion. With reference to the anointing of Jesus' feet by the sinful woman (Luke 7:36-50), the hymn says, "Christ by the hand of his servants seals and anoints your bodies. It befits him, the Lord of the flock, that in his own person he seal his sheep" (3.2). The statement that "by chrism [your bodies] are sealed as holy" (3.9) may allude to an anointing of the whole body. Circumcision as the seal that distinguished among peoples is paralleled, not with baptism or the interior work of the Spirit, but with the anointing (which could be thought of as the exterior sign of the Spirit): "From the peoples he separated the People [Israel] by the former seal of circumcision; but by the seal of anointing, the peoples [Gentile Christians] he separates from the People" (3.4; cf. 3.13 for Jewish circumcision a sign of Christians' sealing). The principle is expressed in words that may give the sequence of the initiation ceremony: "The type has passed and the truth is come; lo! with chrism you have been sealed, in baptism you are perfected, in the flock you are intermixed, from the Body you are nourished" (3.17). Here as elsewhere anointing precedes the baptism, and no mention is made of a postbaptismal anointing. After baptism one is part of the church and partakes of the eucharist.

Types of baptism and anointing recur in other hymns of the collection. Both occur in hymn 5. In addition to Elisha cleansing Naaman[86] and Moses baptizing in the midst of the sea,[87] there is the water that flowed from the rock when struck by Moses' rod (a baptismal symbol in early Christian art; Exod. 17:1-7):

> By the water that flowed from the rock, the thirst of the People was quenched. Lo! in the fountain of Christ, the thirst of the peoples is quenched.
> The rod of Moses opened the rock, and streams flowed forth. . . .
> Lo! from the side of Christ flowed the stream that bestowed life. (5.12-14)

Hymn 7 draws baptismal lessons from a huge number of references to water in the scriptures, from which we select a few.[88] The flock watered by Jacob (Gen. 30:38) are

---

86. He cleansed him of leprosy; "in baptism are cleansed the secret misdeeds in the soul" (5.6).
87. Moses' baptism did not wash the heart — 5.7.
88. There are also several scriptural types of baptism found in hymn 8.

"the sheep of Christ" who "stand round the laver of baptism; in the water they put on the likeness of the living and goodly cross" (the rods placed by Jacob are a figure of the cross) — 7.1-3. The story of Gideon appears with a similar function to what it had in Aphrahat (7.8).[89] The linen girdle buried by Jeremiah at the River Euphrates (Jer. 13:1-11) represented Israel that grew old and decayed, but the nations "that were decayed and marred, by the waters have been clad in newness" (7.12). The clothing metaphor is used in the next strophe (with reference to 1 Kings 1:38-39), "Through the pure waters you have been clad in the purity of heaven" (7.13). Natural phenomena are appealed to as well: The sweat of the body protects against fever; "the fountain of baptism is set to protect against the flame. This is the water that avails for the quenching of Gehenna" (7.16). "Again the diver brings up out of the sea the pearl. Be baptized and bring up from the water purity that therein is hidden" (7.18). As a seaman keeps a store of fresh water on board ship, "So amidst the floods of sin, keep you the water of baptism" (7.19). From the New Testament the author interprets John 4:14 as holy baptism after which one will never be thirsty "so that you should come to another baptism" (7.21). The blind man who washed in the "baptism of Siloam" (John 9:7) was "enlightened by the water" and even so the baptized "from the water" were "clad in light" (7.22).[90] Peter's net caught "150 fishes [153 — John 21:11]";[91] but "there were taken by his preaching, out of the bosom of baptism, ten thousands and thousands," giving life to those that were about to die (7.24-25). In addition to this allusion to the preaching that preceded baptism there may be an allusion to a postbaptismal ceremony, "You baptized, receive your lamps, like the lamps of the house of Gideon; conquer the darkness by your lamps [Judg. 7:4-20]" (7.9).

The clothing imagery for baptism is expressed in hymn 4: "You too in the water receive from him the vesture, that wastes not or is lost, for it is the vesture that vests them that are vested in it forever" (4.3). This thought is related to the theme of putting on Christ and so putting on sonship and freedom: "For the bondman who has put on him who makes all free in the waters, though bondman he be on earth, is son of the free on high, for freedom he has put on" (4.7; cf. 4.1, 10, 13, 17 for putting on Christ in baptism and 5.1 below for putting on the Holy Spirit).

The metaphor of clothing, particularly putting on Christ, probably prompted by the putting on of new clothing after baptism, finds frequent expression in the *Hymns on Epiphany*.[92] The glory that Adam lost in the garden is received again from

---

89. "From the water Gideon chose for himself the men who were victorious in the battle. You have gone down to the 'victorious' waters; come up, and be glorious in the contest. Receive from the water reconciliation and from the contest, crowning" — Murray, "The Exhortation to Candidates," pp. 63-64.

90. Cf. Ephraem, *Hymns on Faith* 83.2, for the Ethiopian treasurer (Acts 8:27-39) shining with joy after his baptism.

91. Ephraem, *Hymns on Virginity* 33.8, also gives the number as 150.

92. "Having gone down, been baptized and put on the single 'Only One' [Only-begotten]. . . . For whoever is baptized and puts on the Only One, the Lord of the many . . . , for Christ becomes his great treasure" (8.16-17 [17-18]) — Murray, "The Exhortation to Candidates," p. 64. Jesus mingled his might

the water of baptism: "He put it on and went up and was adorned therein" (12.1). What was lost through Satan's envy (Wis. 2:24) God's grace restores in baptism (12.2). Instead of "leaves of necessity," God clothes "with glory in the water" (12.4). There may be an allusion to putting on white garments after baptism in 9.12. The Lord's "worshippers are made white like his garments" at the transfiguration (Mark 9:2-3): "the garments in Tabor and the body in the water." Yet, "instead of garments the peoples are made white." There may also be an allusion to giving the baptized crowns to wear (12.3). Shining garments and crowns that do not fade are combined with the imagery of the bridal chamber for those "who come up from Jordan's river" (13.1-3, 5-6, 11-13, 21-22), but the language of "armor of the Holy Spirit" and "armor of victory" (13.2, 7) cautions against too ready acceptance of a literal allusion.

There are treasure houses in the water (4.9). The Trinity "has laid up treasures in baptism. Descend, you poor, to its fountain" (12.7).

The response to the verses in hymn 4 is, "Blessed is he that blots out in water misdeeds that are without measure!" and the response to the verses in hymn 5 is "Blessed is he that ordained baptism for the atonement of the sons of Adam!" Along with this affirmation of forgiveness in baptism, hymn 5 is especially notable for its (characteristically Syrian) association of the Holy Spirit and fire with baptism (more below) and the linking of oil and water (characteristic of Ephraem):

> Descend, my brethren, put on from the waters of baptism the Holy Spirit; be joined with the spirits that minister to the Godhead!
>
> For lo! He is the fire that secretly seals also his flock, by the Three spiritual Names, wherein the Evil One is put to flight.
>
> . . . .
>
> This is he that testified of our Savior, that with fire and the Spirit he should baptize. Lo! the fire and the Spirit, my brethren, in the baptism of truth.
>
> For greater is baptism than Jordan that little river; for that in streams of water and oil, the misdeeds of all men are washed out. (5.1-2, 4-5)

The theme of forgiveness continues in the response for hymn 6, "Blessed is he who was baptized that he might baptize you, that you should be absolved from your offenses." And this theme is in the content of the hymn:

> The baptized when they come up are sanctified; the sealed when they go down are pardoned. They who come up have put on glory; they who go down have cast off sin. Adam put off his glory in a moment; you have been clothed with glory in a moment. (6.9)

The baptized are like sheep who have been sealed (6.6), but the pardon comes in baptism. The leprosy of Naaman was washed away in the water, as transgressions are

---

with the water, so those who are baptized put him on and are to have their soul as well as body washed (9.5); the response for hymn 11, "Let the bodies rejoice which the Evil One made naked, that in the water they have put on their glory!"

in baptism (6.12). "Today, lo! your offenses are blotted out, and your names are written down. The priest blots out in the water; and Christ writes down in heaven" (6.13). Atonement is received from the water (7.8). Baptism is a washing away of sins, but the hearers are warned not to turn again to uncleanness, "for there is but one cleansing of your bodies" (8.10).

The sealing would be related to the Spirit, and the special emphasis of hymn 6 is the necessity of sanctification of the water by the Spirit. "The Spirit came down from on high and hallowed the waters by his brooding" (6.1). Without this coming of the Spirit the waters of the sea are not sufficient to bring forgiveness: "While the fountains are full of water, it is the water of baptism that alone is able to atone. Mighty is the water in the seas, yet is it too weak for atonement" (6.4).

This coming of the Holy Spirit effects a new birth and a sanctification in baptism. "In the baptism of John [the Spirit] passed by the rest and abode on One: but now he has descended and abode on all that are born of the water" (6.1).

> The angels and the watchers rejoice over that which is born of the Spirit and of water: they rejoice that by fire and by the Spirit, the corporeal have become spiritual. . . . (T)hey who are made holy have been increased.
> . . . Baptism is bringing forth the heavenly from the earthly! (6.7-8)

Teaching was necessary for these things to come about. Hymn 6 expresses this blessing: "(T)o the teacher who has toiled with voice, be forgiveness through grace! to the priest who has toiled in baptizing, let there come the crown of righteousness!" (6.19).

The association of fire and the Holy Spirit with baptism (found above in hymn 5) is developed in hymn 8.[93] "Our bodies which in the water with the fire of the Holy Spirit have been mingled" (8.4). The three Hebrew youths in the fiery furnace (Daniel 3) are said to have been baptized in its fire, for the fire pointed to the Holy Spirit that is hidden and mingled in the water (8.5-6). As the Holy Spirit hovered over the waters at creation (Gen. 1:2), she hovers over the water of baptism (8.16). Hymn 8 concludes with reference to God as fire (Isa. 30:27) and then gives a summary of the acts of initiation: "With the unction you have been anointed; you have put him on in the water; in the bread you have eaten him; in the wine you have drunk him" (8.22).

The water of baptism is a womb: "(O)ut of the water is the birth whereof the spiritual are worthy" (8.9). There is a robe of glory for those who have "the birth that is from the water" (13.20).[94] Baptism gives life. It is called "the well-spring of life, which the Son of God opened by his life; and from his side [John 19:34] it has brought forth streams" (12.5). The opposite follows from this affirmation: "All that are not baptized in the waters that give life to all, they are dead invisibly" (8.20).

The baptism of Christ was an act of his condescension (8.1). Moreover, it sancti-

---

93. Cf. Hymn 14.32.
94. See the quotations above for "born of the water" (6.1) and "born of Spirit and water" (6.7). For baptism as "new birth," see 15.26.

fied the water: the response for hymn 9 is, "Blessed is he who came down and sanctified the water for the remission of the sins of the children of Adam!"[95] The Spirit rested on the head of the Son:

> The head of the Highest went down and was baptized and came up to be Head on earth! Children of the Spirit you have thus become, and Christ has become for you the Head: you also have become his members. (9.1)

Baptism is our Jordan: "Instead of the river Jordan you have glorious baptism" (9.2).[96] The baptism of Christ paralleled his birth and his resurrection: all were for the restoration of humanity to God (10.2-3, 9). "He came down and sanctified the water for our baptism" (10.2). "But if he, the All-cleanser, was baptized, what man is there that shall not be baptized? for grace has come to baptism to wash away the foulness of our wound" (10.11). The Lord's baptism in the Jordan opened up baptism for those who followed (11.2). The response for the short hymn 12 is: "Blessed is he who went down and was baptized in Jordan and turned back the People from error!" The long hymn 14 enlarges on the conversation between John, protesting against baptizing Jesus, and Jesus, explaining the reasons for his baptism — in which the meaning of baptism is elaborated. In connection with Jesus' baptism by John reference is made to laying a hand on the head to effect the baptism (14.37 and 42).

The Trinitarian aspect of baptism is expressed in the following imagery: "The Father has sealed *Baptism* to exalt it; and the Son has espoused it to glorify it; and the Spirit with threefold seal has stamped it, and it has shone in holiness" (12.7). For the Trinitarian formula, note hymn 11.8.[97]

The illumination theme was naturally associated with Epiphany. Baptism is "with understanding"; "rich are the fountains of its rays," so "the darkness that is on the mind departs" (9.9).[98]

Through baptism the Evil One is subdued (13.19-20).

The fourth-century writers in Syriac differed from their Greek and Latin contemporaries principally in the importance they attached to the prebaptismal anointing, with the absence of a postbaptismal anointing, and in the nature and variety of symbolism, often expressed allusively, in interpreting baptism.

---

95. Cf. 14.32, "The waters in my baptism are sanctified, and fire and the Spirit from me shall they receive."

96. Varghese, *Les onctions baptismales*, p. 50, cites this as the first explicit allusion in the Syrian tradition to the equality between baptismal water and the Jordan. Cf. 13.2, "In the likeness of angels, you have come up, beloved, from Jordan's river in the armor of the Holy Spirit."

97. Trinitarian expressions also in 13.13, 14.

98. The enlightenment theme is developed in regard to Jesus' birth in hymn 15.

32. The School of Antioch: Theodore of Mopsuestia

We turn from Syriac-speaking (east) Syria to Greek-speaking (west) Syria. I begin with Theodore of Mopsuestia as a connecting link geographically and linguistically between the different parts of Syria.

Theodore was a presbyter in Antioch before becoming bishop of Mopsuestia in 392. He delivered sixteen *Catechetical Homilies* in Greek that survive only in a Syriac translation.[1] If preached while he was in Antioch, they belong before 392; but if in Mopsuestia, then any time before his death in 428 is possible. The majority opinion seems to be for Antioch,[2] but some contend for Mopsuestia and the later date.[3] I place the discussion of his information before that of John Chrysostom not out of conviction for an earlier date but because of his connections with Syria (discussed in the last chapter) — his work was preserved in Syriac, and it was the Syriac-speaking Church

---

1. The Syriac translation was made shortly after his death, but survives only in a fourteenth-century manuscript. I use the English translation of A. Mingana in *Woodbrooke Studies,* vols. 5 and 6 (Cambridge: W. Heffer & Sons, 1932, 1933), which contains the Syriac text as well. See also the translation and study in Edward Yarnold, *The Awe-Inspiring Rites of Initiation* (Slough: St. Paul, 1971); the study by Hugh M. Riley, *Christian Initiation,* Studies in Christian Antiquity 17 (Washington, D.C.: Catholic University of America Press, 1974); the study of the anointings in Baby Varghese, *Les onctions baptismales dans la tradition syrienne,* Corpus scriptorum christianorum orientalium 512 (Louvain: Peeters, 1989), pp. 92-104; and the survey of the theology and liturgy of baptism in Theodore by Raymond Burnish, *The Meaning of Baptism: A Comparison of the Teaching and Practice of the Fourth Century with the Present Day* (London: Alcuin Club/SPCK, 1985), pp. 49-77.

2. R. Tonneau and R. Devreesse, eds., *Les Homélies Catéchétiques de Théodore de Mopsuestia,* Studi e Testi 145 (Vatican City: Apostolic Library, 1949), p. xvi, date the homilies between 381 and 392 in Antioch; pp. xxviii-xxxi of the introduction discuss baptism. Victor Saxer, *Les rites de l'initiation chrétienne du IIe au VIe siècle: Esquisse historique et signification d'après leur principaux témoins* (Spoleto: Centro italiano di studi sull'alto medioevo, 1988), p. 267, places the homilies in Antioch before 392.

3. Hans Lietzmann, *Die Liturgie des Theodor von Mopsuestia* (Berlin, 1933), p. 3; accepted by Riley, *Christian Initiation,* p. 16.

of the East that highly honored him as its premier theologian (considerations that might favor the origin of the homilies in Mopsuestia, but not necessarily so).

The *Catechetical Homilies* are in two sets: the first ten discourses are an exposition of the "Nicene Creed" (actually an Antiochian recension of the Niceno-Constantinopolitan Creed)[4] and the remaining six are one on the Lord's Prayer, three on baptism, and two on the eucharist and the liturgy.[5] Internal indications are that all but the last two were delivered to the candidates before their baptism. The contents indicate a liturgy similar to that in John Chrysostom's *Baptismal Instructions* and somewhat less so that of the *Apostolic Constitutions*;[6] the interpretation of the ceremonies has points of contact with Cyril of Jerusalem and John Chrysostom.

The Process of Initiation

Theodore summarized in this way the early stages of initiation about which he had spoken:

> From what we have previously said, you have sufficiently understood the ceremonies [things] which are duly performed, prior to the sacrament, and according to an early tradition, upon those who are baptized. When you go to be enrolled in the hope of acquiring the abode and citizenship of heaven, you have, in the ceremony of exorcism, a kind of law-suit with the Demon, and by a divine verdict you receive your freedom from his servitude. And thus you recite the words of the profession of faith and of prayer, and through them you make an engagement and a promise to God. . . . After you have been taken away from the servitude of the Tyrant by means of the words of exorcism, and have made solemn engagements to God along with the recitation of the creed, you draw nigh unto the sacrament itself. (*Cat. hom.* 13; Vol. 6, pp. 35-36).[7]

Theodore considered himself to be commenting on an ancient, not a modern liturgy.

The period of preparation for baptism began with the candidate coming to the church (12, pp. 23-24), where a "duly appointed person" inscribed the name in a

---

4. Saxer, *Les rites de l'initiation*, p. 269.

5. The last five are preceded by short statements that are often interpreted as a very old liturgical source that Theodore used when he composed these homilies. Recent study indicates that these texts are excerpts made later and were based on the Syriac translation of the homilies — Clemens Leonhard, "Ṣūrat Ktāb: Bemerkungen zum sogennanten 'Rituale' des Theodor von Mopsuestia am Beginn der Katechetische Homilien 12-16," *Vigiliae Christianae* 56 (2002): 411-433; a version of the same, "Did Theodore of Mopsuestia Quote an Ancient Ordo?" *Studia Liturgica* 34 (2004): 191-204.

6. Mingana, *Woodbrook Studies*, vol. 6, p. xvi, concludes that Theodore's shorter ritual is older than that of the *Apostolic Constitutions*.

7. I cite the homilies by their consecutive numbering (unlike Mingana) and then the page number of Mingana's translation; homilies 1-10 are in vol. 5; 6-16 in vol. 6. I have Americanized his spelling and eliminated capitalization not in accord with current usage.

book (pp. 25-26). Another person, designated a "godfather" or "sponsor" (p. 25),[8] testified to the candidate's manner of life. The diligent inquiry of whether the person was ready to leave the service of the devil was necessary because of being enrolled as the citizen of another kingdom — "we expect to be enrolled in heaven through the gift of the holy baptism" (p. 30).

Theodore says that his lectures on the faith deal with the creed of the bishops at Nicaea, but his exposition includes phrases that were part of the creed associated with the Council of Constantinople in 381. The words "I believe" give occasion for a description of faith (*Cat. hom.* 1, Vol. 5, pp. 22-24); since the creed is the theme of the first ten homilies, it is evident that faith had to do primarily with the content of the faith that "has been handed down." These homilies, nonetheless, have quite a bit to say about baptism, for the "profession of faith" is made "before Christ our Lord at the time of our baptism" (1, p. 21).

Near the beginning Theodore cites John 3:5, which gave him his favorite description of a "second birth" (1, pp. 20-21).[9] The foundational text for Theodore's exposition, however, is Matthew 28:19, because it gave a scriptural basis for the Trinitarian faith of the creed that was confessed at baptism (2, pp. 27-28; and frequently thereafter — e.g., 8, pp. 91-92; 9, pp. 95-96; 10, pp. 111-112). Thus Christ "called God the Father in whom they had to believe and in whose name they had to be baptized" (2, p. 30). Matthew 28:19 is, furthermore, a proof text for the deity of the Holy Spirit (9, p. 94).

One of the lectures on the humanity of Jesus enlarges on the creed's affirmations by including his baptism. Theodore offers explanations of why Jesus was baptized (see our chap. 7).[10] He freed us from the Law and gave us a symbol of our own baptism.

> It is with justice, therefore, that he paid the debt of the law, received baptism, and showed the new economy of the gospel, which is the symbol of the world to come, so that we also, who believed in Christ and became worthy of baptism, through which we received the symbol of the world to come, should live according to his commandments. (6, p. 70)[11]

---

8. Mingana uses these alternative translations in the passage, but the Syriac is the same in both instances.

9. Jeff Childers informs me that the Syriac here is literally "spiritual birth." Most instances of "second birth" in Mingana's translation represent the Syriac "birth again/anew." The phrase comes probably from John 3:3, 7 (Peshitta); the later, more literal Harclean version opted for the alternative meaning of the Greek, "from above." The Peshitta makes no effort to distinguish the *palingenesia* of Titus 3:5, using the same word, "birth again/anew," as in John 3, so this verse too could be behind Theodore's terminology.

10. Cf. *Cat. hom.* 14, pp. 65-66, He "was baptized by John, but not in the baptism of John, which was that of repentance for forgiveness of sins."

11. Burnish, *The Meaning of Baptism*, p. 51, discusses the different translation by R. Tonneau. Cf. *Cat. hom.* 6, p. 71, "we become strangers to all the observances of the law"; p. 70, "We also when we are baptized show the symbol of the world to come."

The symbol of the world to come is to die and rise. This eschatological dimension of baptism, so prominent in Theodore's thought, is discussed further below, as is the correlative thought of attaining "new life in the baptismal birth" (p. 71).

As part of the proof of the divinity of the Holy Spirit from Matthew 28:19, Theodore speaks of "the communion of the ineffable divine benefits" that "accrue to us through baptism" (9, p. 95). This occurs because we are baptized in the divine nature (p. 96). It is folly to call the Holy Spirit a creature and a servant, since the mention of his name "frees us from death and corruption through baptism, and renews us" (p. 101). We are "born of baptism by the power of the Holy Spirit . . . through whom we were reborn and by whom we obtained the gift of being one body of Christ" (p. 103). There is one nature of the Father, Son, and Holy Spirit, "in which we are initiated to our faith and which we have agreed to name at baptism" and which accomplishes "the grace of our second birth" (p. 103).

The Nicaeno-Constantinopolitan Creed includes in its third article a confession of "one baptism for forgiveness of sins." Theodore alludes again to Matthew 28:19 as indicating that baptism (as following on "make disciples") "should be the end of catechumenate" (10, p. 111). He affirms again that "faith is professed at baptism" and the divine names "are pronounced at baptism" (p. 112).[12] Theodore says, "Each of us declares: 'I will believe and be baptized in the name of the Father, and of the Son, and of the Holy Spirit through one holy catholic church'" (p. 114), but this statement may characterize the baptismal act and not be words actually spoken.

The article on the Holy Spirit refers to many of the benefits of baptism (on which more below). Baptism puts one in the church, "the congregation of the faithful." This incorporation in the one body of Christ (the church) occurs "at the second birth from holy baptism" (p. 113).[13] Dying and rising with Christ in baptism symbolizes the relationship with the divine nature (p. 113). The "remission of sins" meant not a simple remission of sin "but its complete abolition" (p. 114). The conclusion of the doctrinal exposition speaks again of the "grace of baptism" and "grace of the second birth" (p. 116). Thus the homilies on the Nicene Creed give a rather full doctrine of baptism, echoed in the subsequent homilies on the ceremonies of initiation.

After instruction in the creed the candidates were taught the words of the Lord's Prayer "so that it should be learned and kept in memory by those who come near unto the faith of baptism" (11, p. 1). In addition to accurate doctrine of the creed, through prayer they can "possess that perfection which is required of those who receive the gift of baptism, and through which they are counted in the number of the citizens of the heavenly life" (p. 16).

During the period of instruction, exorcisms were performed on the candidates.

---

12. Reference to the profession of faith made at baptism occurs again on p. 115. This connection of the profession of faith with baptism agrees with the conclusion that "There is no question in Theodore of the children's baptism" — Mingana, *Woodbrooke Studies*, vol. 6, p. xiii, n. 1.

13. Mingana uses "regeneration" also in this passage — "regeneration of baptism" (p. 113; again in Vol. 6, p. 43), but the Syriac both times is the same phrase elsewhere rendered "second birth" (or, literally, "birth that is again/anew").

[The exorcists] ask in a loud and prolonged voice that our enemy should be punished and by a verdict from the judge be ordered to retire and stand far, so that no room and no entry of any kind might be left to him from which to inflict harm on us, and so that we might be delivered for ever from his servitude, and allowed to live in perfect freedom, and enjoy the happiness of our present enrollment. (12, p. 31)[14]

The candidates "stand perfectly quiet" "with outstretched arms in the posture of one who prays, and look downward" (p. 31). They then removed their outer garment and stood barefooted, showing their state of servitude to the devil and their need for the divine mercy. They stood on sackcloth so that their feet might be pricked as a reminder of their sins and an expression of repentance (p. 32).[15] Then they kneeled with the rest of the body erect and their arms outstretched to God while looking toward heaven and praying (13, p. 36). The posture of kneeling represented the fallen state of humanity and also a confession of Jesus (Phil. 2:10-11) (13, pp. 36, 45). The attendants then came to assure the candidates that their prayers were heard and to raise them up as a sign of moving from slavery to freedom.[16]

The time was to be spent in meditation on the creed so that it might be "deeply fixed in [the] mind" and they would be able to recite it by heart (p. 32). There was apparently a time at which the candidates recited before the priest the words of the creed as a profession of faith and the words of the Lord's Prayer (12, pp. 33-34; 13, p. 35) in addition to their declaration of association with God discussed below.

Persons were considered to have been previously in a pact with the devil (13, p. 38). That pact was broken in an act of abjuration of the devil. Deacons prepared the candidates to recite the words. The synopsis that precedes homily 13 gives the words as: "I abjure Satan and all his angels, and all his works, and all his service, and all his deception, and all his worldly glamor" (p. 35).[17] As quoted in the text of the homily, the abjuration lacks "all his works" (p. 37), perhaps because Theodore did not comment on it. He explains the other items in the list. The devil was the cause of "numerous and great calamities" that brought injury to people, yet previously they were afraid to renounce him because of their servitude to him (pp. 37-38).

Satan's angels are interpreted as men used by Satan to serve his will — pagan poets and philosophers, heretics, Judaizers, and advocates of immorality (pp. 39-41).

---

14. John Bowman, "Exorcism and Baptism," in R. H. Fischer, ed., *A Tribute to Arthur Vööbus: Studies in Early Christian Literature and Its Environment, Primarily in the Syrian East* (Chicago: Lutheran School of Theology, 1977), pp. 249-263 (258-263 on exorcism in Theodore of Mopsuestia as distinct from the adjuration of the devil). Theodore explains the exorcisms on the analogy of a courtroom scene — Riley, *Christian Initiation*, p. 53.

15. Riley, *Christian Initiation*, p. 32. Theodore is the earliest witness to standing and kneeling on sackcloth (*cilicium*, rug of goat's hair) — Johannes Quasten, "Theodore of Mopsuestia on the Exorcism of the Cilicium," *Harvard Theological Review* 35 (1942): 209-219.

16. Riley, *Christian Initiation*, pp. 70-74.

17. Variations in the wording of the renunciation in different sources connected with Antioch may reflect different communities within the metropolis or the lack of fixity in its wording.

"All his service" includes everything dealing with paganism, Judaism, or heresy (pp. 41-42). "Deception" is whatever leads people to impiety. "All his worldly glamor" includes "the theater, circus, race-course, contests of athletes, profane songs, water-organs, and dances" introduced by the devil "under the pretext of amusement" (p. 43). The abjuration, therefore, meant one was to to have no association any more with Satan.

The abjuration was immediately followed by words of engagement and promise to God: "I engage myself, and believe, and am baptized in the name of the Father, and of the Son, and of the Holy Spirit" (pp. 37, 43). Theodore underscores that faith is necessary so that there is no doubt about the existence of God and the good things, although invisible, he has prepared for believers (p. 44). To faith is added the declaration of baptism. Theodore speaks of the "birth of holy baptism" (p. 41), the "regeneration [or, more literally, "the birth again"] of baptism" (p. 43), and "another birth" (p. 44). He combines with the Johannine language of rebirth the Pauline imagery of death and resurrection: "to be reborn and to die with Christ" and to "have risen also with Christ through baptism, and [to] have received the symbol of the new birth" (p. 44).

The candidates made their "promises and engagements" in the same posture of knees bowed and hands outstretched. The priest, now clothed in radiant linen, came and signed their foreheads with holy chrism, saying, "So-and-so is signed in the name of the Father, and of the Son, and of the Holy Spirit" (13, pp. 45-46). Theodore illustrates the signing by referring to the mark of ownership placed on a lamb and the stamp placed on the hand of a soldier at his enlistment. The godfather then placed a linen *orarium* (a prayer stole) on the candidate's head and raised him up (p. 47). This was a mark of freedom and one's confidence before God (3, pp. 46-47; 4, p. 49).[18]

It is notable that the language and imagery of the seal are applied now not to baptism (as in second-century authors) but to the anointing of the forehead.[19] Ideas associated with baptism became increasingly differentiated according to the accompanying ceremonies. Theodore's explanation of this symbolic act showed it as giving meaning to the renunciation of Satan and association with Christ. Theodore (as Chrysostom, next chapter) interpreted this signing with oil as indicative of belonging to Christ (the owner), as appointment to a life task, and as assurance of final victory.[20]

---

18. On the confidence (Greek, *parrhēsia*) of the Christian as a citizen of heaven, see Riley, *Christian Initiation*, pp. 125-131, following W. Van Unnik, "*Parrhēsia* in the 'Catechetical Homilies' of Theodore of Mopsuestia," in *Mélanges offertes à Chr. Mohrmann* (Utrecht, 1963).

19. Riley, *Christian Initiation*, p. 112; cf. the conclusions of J. Ysebaert, *Greek Baptismal Terminology: Its Origins and Early Development* (Nijmegen: Dekker & Van de Vegt, 1962), pp. 419-421, on the variety of applications of the language of the seal; G. W. H. Lampe, *The Seal of the Spirit*, 2nd ed. (London: SPCK, 1967), pp. 202, 270, 299.

20. Riley, *Christian Initiation*, pp. 115, 118-119, 122-131. He points out that what Cyril of Jerusalem says of the postbaptismal anointing, Theodore says of the prebaptismal anointing of the forehead — pp. 384-385. Varghese, *Les onctions baptismales*, pp. 93-94, identifies the principal ideas as the mark of a sheep and of a soldier (13.17), so attachment to Christ; protection against Satan (13.18-20); and a royal mark (14.1). The Syriac words used mean "to sign" or "to seal," and the material used was olive oil (not myron, as in Chrysostom).

The candidate then removed his clothing, becoming naked as Adam was in paradise (14, p. 54). Garments represented one's mortality, and removing them expressed that one was now receiving immortality. The priest (bishop) began the anointing of the body, saying, "So-and-so is anointed in the name of the Father, and of the Son, and of the Holy Spirit," and others (deacons?) completed it so that the whole body was covered (the anointing taking the place of clothes) as a sign of immortality to be received in baptism (p. 54).[21]

The baptismal water was previously "consecrated by the benediction of the priest." Since the water could not give "the second birth" except "through the coming of the Holy Spirit," the priest "made use of clear words, according to the rite of the priestly service, and asked God that the grace of the Holy Spirit might come on the water and impart to it the power of conceiving that awe-inspiring child and becoming a womb to the sacramental birth" (14, pp. 54-55).

The candidate descended into the water. The priest placed his hand on the person's head and said, "So-and-so is baptized in the name of the Father, and of the Son, and of the Holy Spirit." He did not say, "I baptize," in order to show that as a human being he was not able to confer the benefits that only divine grace could give. This grace comes equally from all three divine persons, who are the cause of these good things (pp. 58-59). In further explanation of baptism in the triple name, Theodore says that the singular "name" before all three persons shows the one eternal nature, and baptism derives its benefits from calling on the Trinity (pp. 60-61).

Theodore gives precision to the manner in which the triple immersions were performed. The priest's hand rested on the baptizand's head, and as he pressed the head down, the person being baptized ducked his head under the water.

> The priest places his hand on your head and says "of the Father," and with these words he causes you to immerse yourself in water, while you obediently follow the sign of the hand of the priest and immediately, at his words and at the sign of his hand, immerse yourself in water. By the downward inclination of your head you show as by a hint your agreement and your belief that it is from the Father that you will receive the benefits of baptism. (14, p. 62)

The process was repeated with the words "of the Son" and "of the Holy Spirit," the priest pressing the head down into the water and the person immersing himself by bowing his head each time (p. 63). Only after three identical immersions did one leave the water.

Theodore explained that by inclining one's head, one subscribed to the things said by the priest (pp. 62-63). The administrator pronounced the Trinitarian formula instead of the baptismal confession being made in response to interrogations. Rather than connecting the three immersions to the three days of Jesus in the tomb, as Cyril did, Theodore brings out the Trinitarian significance. He does connect the immersion with the death, burial, and resurrection of Jesus. "When I plunge my

---

21. Riley, *Christian Initiation*, pp. 203-205.

head, I receive the death of Christ our Lord, and desire to have his burial, and because of this I firmly believe in the resurrection of our Lord; and when I rise from the water I think that I have symbolically risen a long time ago" (14, p. 52).

After emerging from the baptismal water the initiate put on a radiant garment (14, p. 68). The radiant garment in Theodore's mystagogy is given an eschatological interpretation as a sign of resurrection and union with Christ, with no mention of purity of life (as is done by Cyril and Chrysostom).[22] Putting on a white garment after baptism involved giving a symbolic meaning to a functional act, the reclothing after the baptism.

The priest then signed the person again on the forehead, saying, "So-and-so is signed in the name of the Father, and of the Son, and of the Holy Spirit" (p. 68). This postbaptismal signing (not explicitly an anointing) is compared to Jesus' anointing with the Holy Spirit after his baptism and looks to one's future immortality.[23]

"After you have received in this way a sacramental birth through baptism, you draw nigh unto an immortal food, consonant with your birth, with which you will be nourished" (14, p. 69), food that maintains the existence given in baptism (15, p. 73), "the sacramental food of immortality" (p. 74). This bread and wine were received "as if the body and blood" of Jesus (p. 75). Theodore drew a parallel between baptism and the eucharist as both symbolically related to immortality received by the grace of the Holy Spirit through those chosen as priests. Only those who had been baptized could partake of the eucharist (16, p. 108).

The Doctrine of Baptism

More attention in secondary literature has been given to Theodore's liturgical information than to his doctrine of baptism, and in this latter regard the main interest has been his sacramental theology. Frederick G. McLeod is correct to take an intermediate position between those who would see Theodore's view as assigning to the sacraments only a bare symbolism of a future heavenly fulfillment and those who advocate dynamic or realistic benefits received from the sacraments.[24] Theodore's view of the two natures of Christ which differentiated between the One who assumed and the one who was assumed (*Cat. hom.* 8) was not congenial, on the one hand, to a realistic

---

22. Riley, *Christian Initiation*, pp. 434-438.

23. Riley, *Christian Initiation*, pp. 380-88. Varghese, *Les onctions baptismales*, pp. 97-99, argues against the authenticity of this passage as a sixth-century Syrian interpolation to bring it into harmony with later practice. This is plausible and has points in its favor, but the argument perhaps depends too much on assumptions of a uniform (even if general) absence of a postbaptismal unction in early Syrian practice and that an author in the same homily could not put the coming of the Spirit on Jesus both at the time of his baptism and at the time of his coming out of the water (would writers before the development of a separate rite of confirmation have felt a problem with such a lack of precision?).

24. Frederick G. McLeod, "The Christological Ramifications of Theodore of Mopsuestia's Understanding of Baptism and the Eucharist," *Journal of Early Christian Studies* 10 (2002): 37-75 (especially 65-72).

union of the divine and the material in the sacraments. On the other hand, Theodore's understanding of "symbol," "type," and "participation" did mean that there was such a union that the sacraments had spiritual benefits in the present age.[25]

The content of the lectures on the creed and the citations above about the ceremony of baptism already give some indication of the doctrinal ideas Theodore associated with baptism. One of his homilies on baptism lists the benefits of baptism:

> Second birth, renewal, immortality, incorruptibility, impassibility, immutability, deliverance from death and servitude and all evils, happiness of freedom, and participation in the ineffable good things which we are expecting. (14, p. 62)

Shortly therafter Theodore described the benefits of baptism as the grace of adoption as children, a second birth, a burial and sign of resurrection, becoming a new person, and participation in incorruption (p. 67).

An important theme in Theodore's homilies is the escape from the tyranny of the devil. This naturally comes out in the discussion of the exorcisms and renunciation of the devil. "Through the gift of the holy baptism you are separating yourselves from the servitude of the Tyrant, which all our fathers from the time of Adam downwards received, and in which they lived" (12, p. 30). This concern with deliverance from Satan leads Theodore to include the temptations of Jesus in the treatment of the parallel between Jesus and his followers (12, 30-31).

There is a strong emphasis by Theodore on the Trinitarian aspects of baptism, and not only in his exposition of the formula in the account of the baptismal ceremony noted above. Theodore had a special concern, because of recent theological controversy, in affirming the deity of the Holy Spirit alongside that of the Father and of the Son. He makes frequent reference to Matthew 28:19 (see some of the references given above). All the benefits of baptism come from Father, Son, and Holy Spirit (14, p. 62).[26] Theodore, in contrast to Serapion and Cyril of Jerusalem, has an epiclesis of the grace of the Holy Spirit to come upon the water.[27]

---

25. McLeod, "The Christological Ramifications," p. 73. Cf. pp. 62-63: "Theodore conceived of the real relationship existing in general between a type and its archetype and specifically between baptism and the eucharist as sacramental types that are related to their heavenly archetypes. For Theodore the type and its archetype are historical realities with the presence of a real bond uniting them and with a guarantee that the archetype will be fulfilled. When applied to baptism and the eucharist, this means that both sacraments have a real relationship and are, therefore, really bonded with the spiritual realities that they foreshadow." Tonneau and Devreesse, *Les Homélies Catéchétiques*, p. xxxii, summarize Theodore's view of the eucharist as a memorial, a nourishing presence, and a figure. Varghese, *Les onctions baptismales*, pp. 100-101, notes the usage of the word "mystery" for baptism in homilies 12 and 14 and also for the two prebaptismal anointings (the word can be used of the whole ceremony or in the plural for its different parts); on p. 102 he counts twenty-eight times that Theodore uses the word "figure" in the three baptismal homilies (12-14).

26. The Trinity is the cause and agent of renewal, as of all good things — Tonneau and Devreesse, *Les Homélies Catéchétiques*, p. xxxi.

27. Johannes Quasten, "The Blessing of the Baptismal Font in the Syrian Rite of the Fourth Century," *Theological Studies* 7 (1946): 309-313. He attributes the change from an emphasis on the working

One of these benefits derived from the whole Trinity is "the grace of the second birth" (14, p. 62). Among the benefits expected from baptism was "the second birth, the second creation" (p. 64). The language of (new) birth in connection with baptism is quite prevalent in Theodore.[28] John 3:5 is explained this way: "[The Lord] mentioned the method by saying 'of water,' and he revealed the cause by the mention of 'the Spirit,'" so in Jesus' further words to Nicodemus he does not mention the water, since the active agent is the Spirit (14, pp. 50-51).[29] The water does not possess the power of new birth or the other attributes of baptism by itself (p. 56). The water is the womb into which the grace of the Spirit comes to fashion a second birth (p. 55). As in human birth, the potentialities are there, but the one who is born again must develop and mature into an immortal nature (pp. 55-56). Beyond this, Theodore grants that human beings cannot grasp how the second birth in water changes people.[30]

Related to the imagery of birth is the separate imagery of adoption, which Theodore sometimes uses to the same effect. God "grants us through baptism the adoption of children" (14, p. 64). The baptism of Jesus is the confirmation of his disciples' adoption as children. One goes out of the water having received "the grace of the adoption of children in the name of the Father, the Son, and the Holy Spirit," comparable to the voice at Jesus' baptism proclaiming him God's Son (14, p. 67). In baptism one receives the symbol of the eschatological adoption (Rom. 8:23) as children (14, p. 53).

Baptism is, furthermore, a dying and rising with Christ.[31] Near the beginning of the first homily on baptism, quoting Romans 6:3-4, Theodore declares,

> [Paul] clearly taught here that we are baptized so that we might imitate in ourselves the death and the resurrection of our Lord, and that we might receive from our remembrance of the happenings that took place the confirmation of our hope in future things. (12, p. 20)

Baptism was an imitation of the past resurrection and a sign of the future resurrection (see further below).

Although the effective agent in baptism is the Holy Spirit (indeed, the whole

---

of Christ in the baptismal water to the controversy in the later fourth century over the deity and personality of the Holy Spirit.

28. Riley, *Christian Initiation*, pp. 328-341.

29. Theodore, *Commentary on Ephesians* 4:5 (H. B. Swete, *Theodori Episcopi Mopsuesteni in epistolas B. Pauli commentarii*, Vol. 1 [Cambridge: Cambridge University Press, 1880], p. 164), says "regenerated by the Spirit."

30. McLeod, "Christological Ramifications," p. 70.

31. Riley, *Christian Initiation*, pp. 286-288; according to Sebastian Brock, "The Transition to a Post-Baptismal Anointing in the Antiochene Rite," in Bryan D. Spinks, ed., *The Sacrifice of Praise: Studies on the Themes of Thanksgiving and Redemption in the Central Prayers of the Eucharistic and Baptismal Liturgies in Honour of Arthur Hubert Couratin* (Rome: Edizioni Liturgiche, 1981), pp. 215-225 (221-22), Theodore was the first in the Syrian area "to lay great stress on the Pauline view of baptism as a death and resurrection."

Godhead), water was necessary. Theodore uses the illustration of a potter, who uses water in reshaping a vessel. Even so, "We were by nature made of clay, that we fell and sin corrupted us, that because of this we received the sentence of death, but that we were renewed and remodeled by divine grace" (14, p. 57).[32] "We perform the symbols and the signs (of these things) in water, and are renewed and reconstructed according to the working of the Spirit on it" (14, p. 57).[33] Theodore draws the conclusion: "As we do not expect a second renewal, so we do not expect a second baptism" (p. 58).

Theodore carries the illustration from the making of pottery further to include the place of the furnace. As the soft clay is baked in fire,

> So also we, who are in a mortal nature, rightly receive our renewal through baptism and are refashioned through this same baptism and receive the grace of the Holy Spirit, which hardens us more than any fire can do. (14, p. 58)

Theodore found the importance of water also in making a connection between baptism and the eucharist.

> As we received the second birth in water, which is useful and necessary to life in this world — so much so that we are not even able to make bread without water — so also we take our food in bread and in wine mixed with water, as they eminently fit this life and sustain us to live in it. (15, p. 74)[34]

There is a pervasive eschatological emphasis. This begins with the understanding of the registration for baptism as an enrollment as a citizen of heaven and carries throughout the interpretation of the ceremonies and their meaning.

> The power of the holy baptism consists in this: it implants in you the hope of the future benefits, enables you to participate in the things which we expect, and by means of the symbols and signs of the future good things, it informs you with the gift of the Holy Spirit, the firstfruits of whom you receive when you are baptized. (14, pp. 53-54).

Baptism as a second birth and as a dying and rising are both given a primarily eschatological reference. The real second birth is the rebirth to immortality at the end of the ages; the baptismal rebirth is a symbol of this future birth. "You will in reality receive the true second birth only after you have risen from the dead" (14, p. 49). One receives the symbols and signs of "the awe-inspiring sacrament [of baptism] so that you may not question your participation in future things" (p. 50). Theodore ex-

---

32. Riley, *Christian Initiation*, pp. 336-338.
33. Tonneau and Devreesse, *Les Homélies Catéchétiques*, p. xxx, for baptism of water as the sign and Holy Spirit as the active agent.
34. Theodore refers again to the use of water in making bread and the customary practice of mixing water with wine on p. 78, where he states that water is a symbol of the birth in baptism and the wine mixed with water is a symbol of Christ's blood.

plains that there are two ways in which one may receive the new birth of John 3:3. One way, which the Lord did not explain to Nicodemus because he knew that the Jewish teacher could not receive it, is at the resurrection. The other is by being born of water and the Spirit. The Lord "called baptism a second birth because it contains the symbol of the second birth, and because through baptism we participate as in symbol in this second birth" (14, pp. 50-51).[35] The real new birth is eschatological; the baptismal rebirth is a symbol of and the means of participating in it.[36]

Similarly, the true resurrection is the eschatological one at the end of the ages, and the baptismal act is a symbol and anticipation of this real resurrection. Whereas Cyril and Chrysostom thought of the baptismal death and resurrection as bringing salvation primarily by imitation of Christ's death and resurrection, Theodore saw it primarily as looking to the future.[37] Theodore continues in the same context about rebirth, and after quoting Romans 6:3-5, with these statements:

> We know that death has been abolished a long time ago by Christ our Lord, and we draw near to him and are baptized with such a faith because we desire to participate in his death, in the hope of participating also in the resurrection from the dead, in the way in which he himself rose. . . .
>
> The working of the Holy Spirit is that it is in the hope of the future things that you receive the grace of baptism, and that you draw near unto the gift of baptism in order to die and to rise with Christ so that you may be born again to the new life. (14, p. 52).

Theodore follows Paul in associating baptism with dying with Christ and referring the resurrection to the future. Baptism is a great symbol of the coming reality of entering into the likeness of Christ's resurrection. In commenting on the eucharist Theodore again quotes Romans 6:3-5, making a similar point:

> [Paul] shows here that resurrection was made manifest in the death of Christ our Lord, and that we are buried with him in baptism, and after we have been here partakers of his death in faith, we shall also participate in the resurrection. (15, p. 72)

As we have seen above, Theodore makes much of the Holy Spirit's activity in baptism. The Holy Spirit is also received in baptism and now resides in the baptized.[38] As quoted above, baptism shapes one with the gift of the Holy Spirit, who is the firstfruit (Rom. 8:23) received when one is baptized (14, pp. 53-54). The Holy Spirit, who is then with the person, works the change into incorruptibility (14, pp. 53-54). John the Baptist could not confer the Spirit, but Christ could, and this gift of

---

35. Cf. in reference to the resurrection, p. 52, "After having been led by these symbols to the participation in the realities, you will perform the symbol of that true second birth," and p. 69, "a second birth from dust."

36. Riley, *Christian Initiation*, pp. 325-328, 382.

37. Burnish, *The Meaning of Baptism*, p. 72.

38. Tonneau and Devreesse, *Les Homélies Catéchétiques*, p. xxxi.

the Spirit in baptism (by way of the word "firstfruits") also had an eschatological meaning:

> It belonged to our Lord to confer the Spirit, whom he conferred now upon us in baptism as the firstfruits of the future benefits, which he will confer upon us in their entirety at the time of the resurrection. (14, p. 66)

Several motifs are brought together in the following statement:

> And because we are born now symbolically through baptism, in the hope of that other birth which we are expecting, we receive at present, in form of an earnest, the firstfruits of the grace of the Holy Spirit, which will then be given to us, as we expect to receive it fully in the next world through the resurrection. (15, p. 72)

The postbaptismal anointing was a sign of this imparting of the Holy Spirit but is not said to have directly bestowed the Spirit:

> [The anointing] is an indication and a sign to you that it is in the name of the Father, Son and Holy Spirit that the Holy Spirit descended on you also, and you were anointed and received grace; and he will be and remain with you, as it is through him that you possess now the firstfruits. (14, p. 68)[39]

Theodore does not say much about the forgiveness of sins except in his interpretation of this element in the Nicaeno-Constantinopolitan Creed. He does interpret Matthew 3:14-15 as meaning that righteousness is fulfilled by the grace of baptism (14, p. 65). He also speaks of the holiness received from the Holy Spirit, when "born in baptism of the grace and coming of the Holy Spirit" (16, p. 109).

Another feature of Theodore's exposition of baptism is its function of incorporating one into the body of Christ, the church.[40] Christ's body is "more than a corporate body made up of church members. Rather it signifies that those who are united to Christ are bonded together in some sort of 'physical' organic body." Thus a member of the body of Christ "can participate in the spiritual blessings that Christ's human nature now enjoys because of its union with the Word's divine nature."[41] Union with the church and with Christ's body in some sense transforms one's life by freeing one from sin and giving assurance of the blessed afterlife.

With reference to Ephesians 4:4-6, Theodore affirms,

> In [the one Godhead] we believe and are baptized and through it we become one body, according to the working on us of the Holy Spirit, in baptism, which makes us children of God and one body of Christ our Lord, whom we consider our head. (14, p. 64).

---

39. Lampe, *The Seal of the Spirit*, pp. 202, 299.
40. Riley, *Christian Initiation*, pp. 288-290; McLeod, "Christological Ramifications," pp. 57-60.
41. McLeod, "Christological Ramifications," p. 68.

He adds that the faith is one, because the Godhead is one, baptism by which the second birth is received is one, and we become "one body of Christ" (14, pp. 64-65). This feature is particularly evident in the treatment of the eucharist. Through the one new birth of baptism all are joined in a close union; the taking of flesh and blood more strongly unites all in the "single body of baptism" (15, p. 92).

> As through the second birth and through the Holy Spirit all of us become one body of Christ, so also by the one nourishment of the holy sacrament, through which the grace of the Holy Spirit feeds us, all of us are in one fellowship with Christ our Lord. (16, p. 110).[42]

Theodore was aware of and accepted deathbed baptism and infant baptism, but he had some negative things to say about those who acquired the "grace of baptism" at the time of death in old age after a life of luxury and about those who received "the grace of baptism in infancy" but in whom the love for good did not follow. They needed to understand the reason why baptism was given. The gift of baptism was no benefit to Simon (Acts 8), since, by reason of his wicked purpose, the Spirit did not rest on him; but the robber entered into paradise although he had not received baptism (Luke 23:39-43). Theodore explains, "I say this not for the destruction of baptism," but because of those who are negligent in regard to it. "Baptism is great because it contains such great goods."

> The gift of baptism is able to confer great benefit to those receiving it. Not the nature of water, but faith by those receiving it is accustomed to draw the complete generosity of God to baptism.[43]

Here once again is expressed in strong language Theodore's thought that baptism is the occasion of great blessings, but these are dependent on the disposition of the recipients which conditions the divine activity.

Theodore has a rich theology of baptism, characterized by some distinctive emphases — particularly with regard to the divine working of the Holy Spirit in baptism and the heavenly orientation of the imagery associated with baptism. It is a participation in real benefits without losing its symbolic character.

---

42. As all "have been perfected into one body in the likeness of the second birth, so also they may be knit here as if into one body by the communion of the flesh of the Lord" (16, p. 104).

43. Theodore, *Commentary on 1 Timothy* 3:2 (Swete, *Theodori Episcopi*, Vol. 2 [1882], pp. 106-108).

33. The School of Antioch: John Chrysostom — I

John Chrysostom was a presbyter in Antioch from 386 to 398, when he became bishop of Constantinople. His twelve *Catechetical Instructions,* or *Baptismal Instructions* (by which name I will cite them), which have come down to us in different manuscripts, are in three overlapping series that belong to the period in Antioch, probably from two different years, 388 and perhaps 390.[1]

Baptismal Instructions 1 and 9 were preached in different years ten days after Lent began, thirty days before Easter (cf. *Bapt. Instr.* 9.29). Numbers 10 and 12 were delivered twenty days after Lent began, again in different years. The eleventh instruction came on holy Thursday (11.19) and concluded the prebaptismal catechesis; the

---

1. Studies include Edward Yarnold, *The Awe-Inspiring Rites of Initiation* (Slough: St. Paul, 1971); Hugh M. Riley, *Christian Initiation,* Studies in Christian Antiquity 17 (Washington, D.C.: Catholic University of America Press, 1974); Raymond Burnish, *The Meaning of Baptism: A Comparison of the Teaching and Practice of the Fourth Century with the Present Day* (London: Alcuin Club/SPCK, 1985); Raymond Burnish, "Baptismal Preparation under John Chrysostom," in Stanley E. Porter and Anthony R. Cross, eds., *Baptism, the New Testament, and the Church: Historical and Contemporary Studies in Honour of R. E. O. White* (Sheffield: Sheffield Academic Press, 1999), pp. 379-401; Baby Varghese, *Les onctions baptismales dans la tradition syrienne,* Corpus scriptorum christianorum orientalium 512 (Louvain: Peeters, 1989), pp. 81-91; J. Knupp, *Das Mystagogieverständnis des Johannes Chrysostomus* (Munich, 1995); and especially Thomas M. Finn, *The Liturgy of Baptism in the Baptismal Instructions of St. John Chrysostom,* Studies in Christian Antiquity 15 (Washington, D.C.: Catholic University of America Press, 1967); Philippe de Roten, *Baptême et mystagogie: Enquête sur l'initiation chrétienne selon s. Jean Chrysostome,* Liturgiewissenschaftliche Quellen und Forschungen 91 (Münster: Aschendorff, 2005); and Paul W. Harkins, *St. John Chrysostom: Baptismal Instructions,* Ancient Christian Writers 31 (Westminster: Newman, 1963) with translation and copious notes. My quotations are from Harkins, and citations follow his numbering. Their sequence in the order of the baptismal liturgy was different, and he recommends reading them in the order 1, 9, 2, 10-12, and 3-8 (p. 202, n. 23). The Greek texts are available in A. Wenger, *Jean Chrysostome: Huit catéchèses baptismales inédites,* Sources chrétiennes 50 and 50b (Paris: Cerf, 1957, 1970); A. Piédagnel, *Jean Chrysostome: Trois catéchèses baptismales,* Sources chrétiennes 366 (Paris: Cerf, 1990); and Reiner Kacynski, *Johannes Chrysostomus: Catecheses Baptismales (Taufkatechese) I-II: Griechisch-Deutsch,* Fontes Christiani 6.1-2 (Freiburg: Herder, 1992).

"Second Instruction" also was given shortly before baptism in a different year. Catechesis number 3 was given on Easter morning shortly after baptism and eucharist. Numbers 4 through 8 followed on successive days (beginning either later on Sunday or on Monday) of the week after Easter.

We also have from Chrysostom an Epiphany sermon, *On the Baptism of Christ*,[2] preached in 387, and his homilies on many of the New Testament texts mentioning baptism, some of which belong to his time in Constantinople.

Nontechnical Word Usage

John Chrysostom's extensive literary corpus includes several nonbaptismal uses of βαπτίζω found in pre-Christian secular authors. Thus he speaks of swimmers "swamped [or drowned, βαπτίζονται] by waves" (*Homilies on John* 33.1 [PG 59.187D]). A ship sailing with fair winds "is not hindered or sunk [βαπτισθῆναι]" (*Homilies on Hebrews* 34.3 [7] [PG 63.235B]). The whole body of anything which is hollow (or concave) is submerged (βαπτίζεται) up to (ἐπὶ) (the level of) the waters, as with regard to (the hold of) a ship; when the whole body that has been made convex is above, only the extremities (the rim) rest upon the waters (*Homilies on Ephesians* 19.3 on Eph. 5 [PG 62.131D]). The strengthened compound form of the verb occurs with reference to a boat sinking and alludes to a metaphorical use:

> Even as a boat filled with water is quickly submerged [καταβαπτίζεται] and is under water, so also a person, whenever he gives himself to gluttony and drunkenness, . . . causes his reason to be under water. (*Homilies on Genesis* 10.2 [PG 53.84])

With reference to a sword thrust, Chrysostom says that David did not plunge (βαπτίσαι) the sword into Saul (*On David and Saul* 3.7 [PG 54.704C]). Absalom wanted to plunge (βαπτίσαι) his right hand (= sword) into David's neck (*Expositions on Psalms* 7.14 [PG 55.103C-D]). Similarly, "You plunge [βαπτίζεις] your right hand into the neck" (*Homilies on Hebrews* 25.3 [6] [PG 63.176B]). In talking about Abraham's sacrifice of Isaac, he says that the knife "both touched, passed through, was made crimson, and was immersed [ἐβαπτίσθη, in intention or metaphorically], but was not immersed [ἐβαπτίσθη, literally, since the act was not carried out]" (*Homilies on 2 Corinthians* 3.6 [PG 61.414D]). He continues, God did not allow Abraham's "right hand to be bathed [βαπτισθῆναι, immersed (with blood)]" (415B). There is a similar usage in a passage that alludes to Christian baptism in discussing John 5: We wash away (ἀπονιψώμεθα) everything at baptism (βαπτίσματος), for he leads the man to the pool (κολυμβήθραν) of waters. Then, in describing the cures of Jesus, Chrysostom says that they did not involve fire, iron plunged

---

2. Everett Ferguson, "Preaching at Epiphany: Gregory of Nyssa and John Chrysostom on Baptism and the Church," *Church History* 66 (1997): 1-17 (8-16 on Chrysostom).

(βαπτιζόμενον) in, or flowing (ῥέον) blood (*On the Paralytic Let Down through the Roof* 3–4 [PG 51.53A; 55B]).

The literal meaning in these passages easily passed into related metaphorical applications. In comparing life to sailing on the sea, Chrysostom thinks of a ship sinking and speaks of "not being swamped [or drowned, βαπτίζεσθαι] by reverses and despondencies of life" (*Homilies on John* 1.3 [5] [PG 59.23C]). If one has accurate reasoning, "the waves do not overwhelm [βαπτίζει] you" (*Homily on Lazarus* 6.5 [PG 43.1034A]). In discussing anger Chrysostom says "that we should plunge [βαπτίζωμεν] the sword into the breast of the devil; there bury the sword to the hilt, if you will, even the hilt itself and never draw it out again" (*Homilies on Ephesians* 14.2 [PG 62.102C]). "To baptize" here is equivalent to "to bury," and the preposition indicating the matter into which the baptizing is done, as normal, is εἰς. A metaphorical use of "to dip [βαπτίσαι] his own hands" is parallel to an earlier statement about a physician who (literally) thrusts [καθίησι] his fingers into a wound (*Homilies on 1 Thessalonians* 5.3 [PG 62.427b]).

Immersion applied to sleep had classical antecedents: "The devil plunged Eutychus into sleep" (*Homilies on Acts* 43.1).[3] A metaphorical use further removed from the literal applications refers to a "soul immersed in numberless vices" (*Homilies on Acts* 47.4), or "concerning us who have been immersed in countless sins" (*Homilies on Genesis* 33.5 on Gen. 13 [PG 53.312C]). We are immersed or drowned (βεβαπτισμένοι) in wickedness, so we could not be purified but are in need of regeneration (ἀναγεννήσεως); this is declared to be the παλιγγενεσία of Titus 3:5, so Chrysostom took the two words to be equivalent (*Homilies on Titus* 5.3 [PG 62.692A-B]). "The ears of those immersed [βεβαπτισμένων] in the depth of sin have been made deaf" (*On Repentance* 7.4 [PG 49.329A]). Particularly descriptive for the meaning of the word is the statement, "You brought up out of the depth of evil his soul which had been overwhelmed [βεβαπτισμένην] and indeed had become submerged [ὑπβρύχια]" (*Homilies on Genesis* 43.4 [PG 54.401D]).[4] A parallel usage referred to being overwhelmed with cares: Not overwhelmed (βαπτίζεται) by present disasters (*On Psalms* 114 [116].3 [PG 55.319B]); not overwhelmed (βαπτίζεται) in the pains of the present life (*Homilies on 1 Corinthians* 8.5 [PG 61.69C]). A figurative use makes a comparison based on the literal meaning: The rich man, as if to overwhelm (βαπτιζεῖν) the soul of Lazarus with successive waves (*Homily on Lazarus* 1.10 [PG 48.977A]). These statements are comparable to the secular usages surveyed in chapter 3 and show that the Christian use of the *bapt-* words had not lost or changed their ordinary meaning.

---

3. *Homilies on 1 Corinthians* 12.11, "plunged [βαπτιζόμενοι] in deep sleep."
4. Metaphorical use of περικλύζω ("to wash all around, swamp, overwhelm"), a word sometimes used in connection with βαπτίζω, is comparable: "washing all around the tongue with water" with reference to speech (*Hom. in Mt.* 51.4 on Matt. 15; PG 58.516A); "like covering in warm water with praises" (*Hom. in 1 Cor.* 44.4; PG 61.379).

Administration of Baptism

Chrysostom's vocabulary does not have a technical terminology to distinguish those preparing for baptism from catechumens in general.[5] The period of preparation for baptism coincided with Lent, and the baptism itself occurred on Easter.[6] Chrysostom saw this as the fitting season for initiation, since this was the season when Christ won his victory over sin, death, and the devil; but he affirms that baptism may occur at any season, for God gives the same grace (*Bapt. Instr.* 10.5-7).[7] The period began with enrollment for baptism, interpreted as enlistment for military service and a spiritual betrothal (1.1).[8] The candidates were accompanied throughout the period by "sponsors," also called "spiritual fathers," whom Chrysostom directly addressed at one point concerning the seriousness of their responsibility in giving surety and providing instruction for the candidates (2.15-16).[9] During the time leading up to baptism the candidates were expected, but not required, to fast, drink only water, and not bathe (3.1-5). This was a time of repentance and confession of sins.[10] Chrysostom refers to the catechumens bowing their heads and the congregation praying for them (*Homilies on 2 Corinthians* 2.10).

Chrysostom calls for attention to his discourses by making a play on the root from which the word *catechesis* comes ("echo"):

> For I do not speak only that you may hear, but that you may remember what I said.... This is why my discourse is called a catechesis, so that even when I am not here my words may echo in your minds. (*Bapt. Instr.* 12.1)[11]

Unlike Cyril and Theodore's catechetical lectures, those that survive from Chrysostom do not give systematic instruction on the creed. Nevertheless, there are references to such instruction and to the importance of faith. In one of his postbaptismal lectures Chrysostom refers to his previous instruction (6.1).[12] There was a

---

5. De Roten, *Baptême et mystagogie*, pp. 137-216, on catechumens and the catechumenate. Chrysostom calls those preparing for baptism κατηχούμενοι or οἱ μέλλοντες φωτίζεσθαι — de Roten, *Baptême et mystagogie*, p. 137 — but (unlike Cyril of Jerusalem and the *Apostolic Constitutions*) not φωτιζομένοι — p. 150.

6. De Roten, *Baptême et mystagogie*, pp. 153-173, on Lent.

7. Cf. *Homilies on Acts* 1 (PG 60.24D) for an exhortation to those who would delay baptism not to wait for Lent since there is danger of not living until the usual time for baptism.

8. For the enrollment and the images used for it, see Finn, *The Liturgy of Baptism*, pp. 50-54, and for sponsors, pp. 54-58.

9. For the prebaptismal activities of enrollment and sponsors, exorcisms, renunciation of Satan and covenant with Christ, and anointing of the candidate, see P. W. Harkins, "Pre-Baptismal Rites in Chrysostom's Baptismal Catecheses," *Studia patristica* 8 (1966): 219-238.

10. *Diab.* 2.6 (PG 49.463B-464B) lists five ways of repentance: condemnation of sins, forgiving others, prayer, alms, and humility.

11. On the catechumens (Chrysostom uses the term in 10.16 and 18) and their division into two classes (those remotely and those proximately preparing for baptism), see Finn, *The Liturgy of Baptism*, pp. 31-42. The former are the "uninitiated" (11.18); the latter, "those about to be initiated."

12. He complains of those who this day deserted the instruction to attend the chariot races; cf. a

special training program for catechumens lasting thirty days that Chrysostom compares to the exercises in a wrestling school (9.29; cf. 9.2 on the thirty days). To be able to make "a strong confession of faith" required not only speaking words with the lips but also an understanding of the heart and "solid resolution of the mind" (Rom. 10:10 quoted — 1.19).

Something of the dogmatic content of the instruction is found in the succeeding summary of the Trinitarian faith (1.20-24) that serves as "the foundation of piety" (1.20). "You must have these articles of faith accurately fixed in your minds" so as to avoid the deceits of the devil (1.22). Matthew 28:19 is quoted to support the equal dignity of the Spirit with the Father and the Son (1.23). Chrysostom says that he leaves to the teacher (the bishop?) the instruction on faith (11.18). His failure to refer explicitly to a recitation of the creed by the catechumens[13] may also be due to the bishop's role in hearing it.

The surviving *Baptismal Instructions* show Chrysostom the preacher and pastor giving more attention to moral instruction. The six chapters on the faith in the "First Instruction" are followed by twenty-three on attitudes and conduct — accepting the invitation of Christ (Matt. 11:28-29 — 1.25-29); humility (1.30-33); the true adornment of a woman (1.34-38); against omens, oaths, and spectacles (1.39-43); and doing honor to the name "Christian" (1.44-47). Similar themes recur in the "Twelfth Instruction": the true adornment of women (12.42-47); against omens, charms, and incantations (12.53-61). Other concerns are almsgiving (12.7), avoiding sins of the tongue (12.16) and of the eyes (12.17-18), and getting rid of evil habits (12.21-24). Sins of speech, especially the swearing of oaths, was a special concern of Chrysostom's (9.30-47; 10.1-4, 18-30). Chrysostom's descriptions of the new life and exhortations to the newly baptized will return to moral concerns (chap. 34).

The uninitiated were not present for the later stages of the preparation for baptism (11.18). "After this daily instruction, we send you along to hear the words of the exorcists" (2.12-14; exorcisms are described also in 9.11 and 10.14-17). Chrysostom does not explain who performed the exorcisms, only saying "those appointed to this task" (2.12). Nor does he quote the words, which the catechumens would hear, but he describes them as "frightening and horrible words" (10.16).[14] The candidates heard the exorcists' words barefoot and "naked except for a short garment" (9.11; 10.14).[15] They stood with arms outstretched and hands upturned (10.14; 2.14). The lack of at-

---

similar complaint in *Bapt. Chr.* 1 (PG 49.363), which gives a summary of subjects on which one must be instructed (49.364D).

13. Perhaps alluded to in 11.15, "I entrust nothing else to you until you shall say 'I believe.'" See n. 22.

14. "Frightening" also in 10.17; "awesome words" and "awesome formula" in 2.12; "awesome and wonderful invocations" in 2.14; "dread formula" in 10.17. For the exorcisms, de Roten, *Baptême et mystagogie*, pp. 191-197.

15. Is it possible that the nakedness at the immersions (below) meant the same attire in underwear as here? Laurie Guy, "'Naked' Baptism in the Early Church: The Rhetoric and the Reality," *Journal of Religious History* 27 (2003): 133-142 (p. 140).

tire was a reminder of their captivity to the devil (2.14) and that they were now captives of Christ, a captivity that (unlike human captivity) "changes slavery into freedom" (10.15). The purpose of the exorcisms was to cleanse the mind by banishing the demons and so make the heart worthy for "the King of heaven to dwell within you" (2.12). They also served to make the heart contrite and by routing the demons to prepare the soul to receive its King.[16]

On Good Friday at three o'clock in the afternoon occurred the renunciation (ἀποταγή) of the devil and the adherence (συνταγή) to Christ (11.19).[17] The catechumens were gathered together and prayed while kneeling with hands outstretched to heaven (2.18; 11.21). The posture agrees with what Theodore says but differs from Cyril (and Ambrose), for whom the candidates are standing and turn to the west. The posture of kneeling expressed the former condition of slavery to Satan and present submission to Christ (11.22; 2.18) and the confession of Christ as Lord (based on Phil. 2:10 — 11.22). That all kneel together expressed that now there was no distinction among them (based on Gal. 3:28 — 11.21; cf. 2.13).[18] The priest has the persons say: "I renounce thee, Satan, thy pomps, thy service, and thy works" (2.20; cf. 11.22, 24-25; 12.48, 60).[19] This was apparently done in question and answer form (11.19). To renounce Satan was an expression of repentance so as never to return to him (12.22).

Chrysostom's "pomps" correspond to Theodore's "worldly glamor."

> What are the pomps of the devil? Every form of sin, spectacles of indecency [the theater], horse racing, gatherings filled with laughter and abusive language. Portents, oracles, omens, observances of times, tokens, amulets, and incantations — these too are pomps of the devil. (11.25)

Another passage includes in the pomps of Satan "the madness to be adorned with pearls" (12.48), for one receives gold not to put on the body but to feed the poor. It continues with the listing: "theaters, racecourses, every sinful observance of days, presages contained in chance utterances, and omens" (12.52).[20]

---

16. Harkins, "Pre-Baptismal Rites," p. 228; Finn, *The Liturgy of Baptism*, p. 82.

17. On the renunciation see Riley, *Christian Initiation*, pp. 50-53, 64-68, 92-94, 96-101; de Roten, *Baptême et mystagogie*, pp. 256-267. Finn, *The Liturgy of Baptism*, pp. 88-89, adopts the solution that 2.14 places the renunciation on Saturday because Chrysostom was there recalling his own baptism but in 11.19 the practice in his own day when the ceremony had been moved to a day earlier. On the essentiality of the renunciation and adhesion to the baptismal ceremony see 9.9 and my discussion in chap. 39 on Chrysostom.

18. The *Homilies on 1 Corinthians* 10:1 (PG 51.247) associates the lack of distinctions among baptizands with baptism itself: everyone "going into the bath [κολυμβήθραν] of waters" is equal and initiated in the same way.

19. Harkins, "Pre-Baptismal Rites," p. 231, notes that Chrysostom, *Homilies on Colossians* 6.4 on Col. 2 (PG 62.342C), substitutes "angels" for "works," probably because that was the formula of Constantinople, where his commentary on Colossians was produced. *Homilies on 2 Corinthians* 2.9 summarizes that the candidate renounced the devil's rule, bent the knee, deserted the devil for the King, and uttered fearful words.

20. Finn, *The Liturgy of Baptism*, p. 101, notes that earlier the pomps of the devil were associated

After the renunciation the priest had the persons say, "And I enter into thy service, O Christ" (2.21; 11.24).[21] By these words one confessed Christ's sovereignty and attached oneself to him (2.22).

There may have been a prebaptismal confession of faith at some point in the service. A passage that connects the renunciation and the confession of faith may have in mind a prebaptismal confession of the creed rather than the adhesion to Christ, for the confession seems to be something additional to the enlistment in the service of Christ (see further in the next chapter on faith and confession under the interpretation of baptism).

> What is more beautiful than the words with which we renounce the service of the devil and enlist in the service of Christ, than both the confession which is before the laver [λουτροῦ] and that which is behind the laver [λουτρόν]? Let us consider how many of us corrupted our baptism.[22]

If this passage had been written at an earlier time, the confession after baptism might have been in reference to martyrdom, but more likely in this place Chrysostom refers to a returning to Christ after postbaptismal sin.

Chrysostom frequently interprets the renunciation and adhesion as a contract on the analogy of contracts in the secular world.[23] "This contract is also called faith," and "The words which you utter here are registered in heaven" (2.17; carried to heaven by the angels according to 2.20). The words are the terms of an agreement (2.21); the candidates present their contracts to the Master (11.19). The contract is not written on paper with ink but by the Spirit through the words of the tongue (2.17; 3.20; 4.31). Chrysostom emphasizes that the contract is voluntarily entered into; Christ does not force or compel one into it, but out of gratitude one freely enrolls in his service (12.49-50). He likens the contract to entering into a marriage (11.23, 26). Thereafter the neophytes are exhorted to keep their contract with Christ in mind, to keep it completely, and to flee the devil's pomps (4.32; cf. 3.20).

---

with idolatry, but in Chrysostom, Theodore, and Cyril the association is more with immoral aspects of paganism. On horse racing, cf. *Homilies on Genesis* 6 on Gen. 1 (PG 53.55-56).

21. Cf. the summary statement, "I renounce Satan and I ally myself with Christ" — *Homilies on Colossians* 6.4.

22. *Homilies on Ephesians* 1.3 on Eph. 1:6 (trans. modified from that in *Nicene and Post-Nicene Fathers* (repr. Peabody: Hendrickson, 1994), First Series, Vol. 13, p. 53. Chrysostom makes no express statement about a delivering and reciting of the creed. Finn, *The Liturgy of Baptism*, p. 112, thinks the *redditio symboli* took place at the close of the renunciation and profession on Good Friday rather than at the last instruction on Holy Thursday. De Roten, *Baptême et mystagogie*, pp. 207-216, discusses the difficulties in knowing when and how exactly the rendition of the faith took place in Antioch. Paul F. Bradshaw considers the options in "The Profession of Faith in Early Christian Baptism," *Evangelical Quarterly* 78 (2006): 101-115 (pp. 105-107).

23. Finn, *The Liturgy of Baptism*, pp. 93-95, counts more than twenty uses of "contract" (συνθήκη) in the *Baptismal Instructions*. Cf. *Homilies on Colossians* 6.4 on the renunciation and allegiance to Christ as not a bond but a covenant.

At the conclusion of the renunciation and adhesion occurred an anointing on the forehead, a symbolic expression of their significance, for one now belonged to Christ and received his protection.

> The priest anoints you on the forehead with the oil [myron] of the spirit and signs you, saying: "So-and-so is anointed in the name of the Father, and of the Son, and of the Holy Spirit." (2.22)

It seems that this anointing is the same as what is called the "unguent of the Spirit" (10.17). The chrism was a mixture of olive oil and unguent (myrrh?), because the oil was used by an athlete and the unguent by a bride (11.27). The anointing was with the sign of the cross (11.27).[24] This sign makes the Enemy turn away (2.23; 11.27; 12.60). The person anointed is now "a combatant chosen for the spiritual arena" (11.22).[25] The symbolisms associated with the anointing are athletic, nuptial, and identification with Christ, but not exorcistic or pneumatological.[26]

Next, "in the full darkness of the night" (presumably Saturday night) occurred the full body anointing.[27] "He strips off your robe," and "he causes your whole body to be anointed with that olive oil of the spirit" (2.24; cf. 11.27).[28] "It is not a man but God himself who anoints you by the hand of the priest" (11.27).[29] This act too is seen as a protection that holds the devil in check (11.27; 2.24). Neither prebaptismal anointing is associated by Chrysostom with the gift of the Spirit.

The same kind of oil was likely used for both the anointing of the forehead and the anointing of the body. Chrysostom was the first Antiochian witness to "myron" (perfumed oil) used for the prebaptismal anointing.[30] Signing of the forehead and

---

24. Cf. *Homilies on Philippians* 13 (PG 62.277) for the anointing making the cross visibly present in baptism.

25. On the two anointings (below) see de Roten, *Baptême et mystagogie*, pp. 268-282, and Finn, *The Liturgy of Baptism*, pp. 119-146, who suggests they were originally united but in Chrysostom's description separated in time (the first after the renunciation and profession on Friday and the second during the Easter vigil immediately before baptism) but not distinct in symbolism or effect. He notes that Chrysostom emphasizes the protective character of Christ's ownership — p. 135. Riley, *Christian Initiation*, p. 114, sees this first anointing as illustrative, and not causative, of the implications of the renunciation and adhesion. Varghese, *Les onctions baptismales*, pp. 86-87, denies that this anointing was the conclusion of the rite of renunciation as Riley proposed, for it was a preparation for the future.

26. Varghese, *Les onctions baptismales*, pp. 85, 88-90.

27. This time the anointing was more than on the head — *Homilies on Colosians* 6.4. In 11.28-29 the removal of clothing is somewhat inconsistently mentioned after the anointing but probably because Chrysostom wants there to develop the theme of baptism as a return to the innocence of paradise — Finn, *The Liturgy of Baptism*, pp. 122, 147-149.

28. In addition to "oil of the Spirit," Chrysostom speaks of the "oil of gladness" (Ps. 45:7) — 3.9 — chrism (χρίσμα) — 11.27 — and "spiritual myron" — 2.22. See Finn, *The Liturgy of Baptism*, pp. 130-135.

29. Harkins, "Pre-Baptismal Rites," p. 237, suggests that the anointing of women was probably done by deaconesses.

30. Chrysostom uses ἀλείφω, χρίω, σφραγίζω, and ἐντυπῶ for the anointing of the forehead and ἀλείφω for the anointing of the body. Varghese, *Les onctions baptismales*, pp. 83-84.

anointing the whole body plus a postbaptismal anointing, this last absent in Chrysostom, became the norm later in Syriac churches.[31]

There is no mention of the blessing of the font, probably because the candidates were not involved in it. This act is implied, however, in the phrase "it is the grace of the Spirit which sanctifies the nature of the water" (2.10 — the passage, which deals with the effect of baptism, is quoted more fully in the next chapter). Chrysostom makes frequent reference to "flowing waters" (τὰ νάματα — 2.25, 27, 29; 3.26; 7.10; 11.28), but the language may be figurative and not an indication that an effort was made to provide running water into the font. Chrysostom calls the baptismal pool a *kolymbēthra* (κολυμβήθρα — swimming or diving pool) in 11.28 (cf. chap. 34, n. 4) or *namata* (νάματα — which evokes the idea of running water), but his usual term is *loutron* (λουτρόν — e.g., 9.13, 16).

The anointing of the whole body was followed immediately by the baptism.[32] The priest led the person still naked into the water.[33] Walls and/or curtains may have preserved a measure of modesty, and those actually present were only the candidates (separated by sexes), sponsors, and clergy.[34] The nakedness recalled Adam and Eve in Paradise, but the bath was better than the garden, for there was no serpent now and although the beautiful trees could not be seen spiritual favors could be (11.28-29).[35]

The priest pronounced the formula, "So-and-so is baptized in the name of the Father, and of the Son, and of the Holy Spirit."[36] He did not say, "I baptize so-and-so." Chrysostom offers the same explanation as Theodore does for the passive in-

---

31. Georg Kretschmar, "Recent Research on Christian Initiation," *Studia liturgica* 12 (1977): 87-106, observes that in Antioch (and elsewhere in the East) the pattern of baptism, consignation, and eucharist occurs not at the beginning but at the end of a development, so he concludes that liturgical conformity is by no means a sign of great antiquity but may result from later development (p. 92).

32. Finn, *The Liturgy of Baptism*, pp. 149-152, suggests there was probably a baptismal profession of faith in question-and-answer dialogue form, perhaps alluded to in 2.26 and *Homilies on 1 Corinthians* 40.2 (PG 61.347). The former passage may simply mean that baptism in the Trinitarian name is the profession of faith. The latter passage is better support for the idea, for it says that when we are about to be baptized we add "I believe in the resurrection of the dead," words that were part of the Nicaeno-Constantinopolitan Creed (for the context of the passage see chap. 34, n. 14). De Roten, *Baptême et mystagogie*, p. 288, sees Chrysostom's invitation to candidates to pray during their immersion as likely excluding a confession of faith spoken during the immersion.

33. The ordinary minister at baptism was the bishop but could be a presbyter or deacon.

34. Chrysostom's *Letter to Innocent* 1.3, quoted in Palladius, *Dialogue on the Life of Saint John Chrysostom* 2, refers to women unrobed for baptism when a disturbance forced them to flee naked without being allowed to clothe themselves as womanly decency requires. The text is somewhat ambiguous, for the "unrobed for baptism" and "clothe themselves as womanly decency requires" could mean that some undergarments were worn: Guy, "'Naked' Baptism," p. 140, argues that such was meant by "naked."

35. *Homilies on Colossians* 6 on Col. 2:13-15 (PG 62.342) gives a different interpretation, namely that one is naked so that one may be set free from sin (unlike in the Garden); the passage proceeds to recall the nakedness of the athlete and of the baby at birth.

36. Chrysostom takes the phrase "with the word" in Eph. 5:26 as the Trinitarian formula of Matt. 28:19 that accompanies the washing with water.

stead of the active form: "In this way he shows that it is not he who baptizes but those whose names have been invoked" (11.14). The priest is "only the minister of grace," and it is the undivided Trinity that fulfills all things (2.26).[37]

When the priest pronounces the formula, "he puts your head down into the water three times, and three times he lifts it up again." "For it is not only the priest who touches the head, but also the right hand of Christ," followed by the explanation cited at the end of the preceding paragraph (2.26).[38] The priest's hand on the head was functional for dipping the head under the water and was not a separate act, but it was also indicative of the invocation of the triune God, who actually does the baptizing.[39]

The argument is made that baptisteries excavated in Syria (see further chap. 53) were not deep enough to submerge an adult. It should be remembered, however, that persons were not as tall then as today and that a kneeling posture might have been employed.[40] The further contention that Chrysostom's terminology does not exclude the possibility of a partial immersion completed by an infusion of water on the head is contradicted by Chrysostom's descriptions of baptism cited above. His terminology, καταδύ(ν)ω/ἀναδύ(ν)ω ("plunge" or "duck"/"emerge"),[41] in reference to

---

37. On the formula see de Roten, *Baptême et mystagogie*, pp. 290-294. Finn, *The Liturgy of Baptism*, pp. 129-130, 170-173, sees the formula used in the anointing (above) as parallel to the baptismal formula and suggests that Chrysostom and Theodore changed an earlier active to the passive wording as a result of the Trinitarian controversies in order to assert the unity and equality of the Three Persons as well as to focus attention on the divine action by making the ministers instrumental. *Homilies on John* 78.3 says that the Trinity is included in baptism, for each of the Three is able to effect the whole of the act.

38. Elsewhere Chrysostom refers to the individual who is baptized submerging the head in the water: the old person is buried in a tomb, sunk forever, and entirely hidden; as he raises the head, the new person rises; this is done three times — *Homilies on John* 25.2 on John 3:5. As Theodore made explicit, there was a cooperation so that the administrator guided the head down and the baptizand followed the lead in dipping and raising the head. That it is actually God who performs the baptism was an important concept for Chrysostom; cf. also 2.10-11 and 11.12-13, discussed in the section on the interpretation of baptism in the next chapter, and *Homilies on Romans* 16 on Rom. 9:9, discussed on regeneration there; *Homilies on Matthew* 50.3 explains that although the priest acts, it is really Christ's hand that is stretched out, and that the priest does not baptize, but God gives the heavenly power.

39. The importance of the priest's hand on the head of the baptizand led Chrysostom to say John's hand was on Jesus' head at the latter's baptism, a detail not in the Gospel accounts — *Bapt. Instr.* 11.13. Finn, *The Liturgy of Baptism*, pp. 174-181, discusses the importance Chrysostom gives to the imposition of the bishop's hand in the administration of the dipping. He assigns two reasons for the emphasis: In the controversies over the validity of baptism by heretics and by unworthy priests Chrysostom required their faith in the Trinity but affirmed the validity of baptism independent of the moral qualities of the minister (*Homilies on John* 86.4 [PG 59.472] — the priests lend hand and tongue, but the Father, Son, and Holy Spirit give all; *Homilies on 2 Timothy* 2.4 — God works through worthy and unworthy priests in the laver and in the mysteries); and the imposition of the hand witnessed to the conferral of the Holy Spirit in baptism (2.10). See also de Roten, *Baptême et mystagogie*, pp. 288-290.

40. The suggestion that a kneeling posture was unworthy of baptism (de Roten, *Baptême et mystagogie*, p. 251, n. 219) might prompt the opposite conclusion.

41. In addition to the *Baptismal Instructions* cited above, see *Homilies on 1 Corinthians* 40.1-2 (on

one standing in the water (although not necessarily requiring that all the body is under the water but surely implying it) is inconsistent with pouring water on the head, as is the hand of the administrator on the head of the candidate.[42] The complete body anointing would have had as its counterpart the covering of the whole body with water.

Chrysostom addresses the question of baptism by unworthy priests, and in so doing appeals to his point that God is the real baptizer, with these words:

> God is accustomed to work even through unworthy persons, and the grace of baptism is harmed in no way by the life of the priest. Or else the receiver would suffer loss.... For man introduces nothing into the things set before us, but everything is the work of the power of God. He is the one who initiates you. (*Homilies on 1 Corinthians* 8.1 [PG 61.69B-C])

Chrysostom agrees with the earlier Syrian tradition and, unlike Theodore, makes no reference to a postbaptismal anointing.[43]

Not explicitly mentioned, but alluded to elsewhere and perhaps implied in Chrysostom's frequent reference to the clothing imagery, was the putting of a white robe, which was worn for seven days, on the neophyte after his emerging from the baptism.[44] "Your shining robe now arouses admiration in the eyes of all who behold you, and the radiance of your garments proves that your souls are free from every blemish" (7.24). He continues with the paraenesis that prayer and almsgiving preserve the luster of this spiritual garment (7.24-27). As this quotation shows, one meaning of the radiant robe was the symbolism of forgiveness of sins: the baptized person "has put off the old garment of sin and has put on the royal robe" (2.25). Related to this idea was the robe as a symbol of purity of life. "Guard the spiritual garment bestowed on you, keeping it clean and spotless," so as to "show a far-reaching

---

1 Cor. 15:29 — see quotation in chap. 34, at n. 11) and *Homilies on John* 25.2 (on John 3:5) quoted below. The meaning "to hide" or "to cover" for καταδύω is a secondary meaning derived from the result of the action in the primary meaning.

42. Pouring was employed in clinical baptism — chap. 39. One passage that might refer to an infusion is *Homilies on Matthew* 30.6 about a woman who has Christ as head, "Do you not remember the water splashed around [περικλύσαντός] your face, the sacrifice which adorns your lips, the blood that reddens your tongue?" The passage is directed against women's cosmetics and is worded accordingly. Περικλύζω means "to wash around" and metaphorically "to overwelm." In this passage it could as well refer to water splashing around the head dipped in the water as to water poured over the head.

43. Finn, *The Liturgy of Baptism*, pp. 139-146, on the absence of a postbaptismal anointing in Chrysostom as reflecting earlier Syrian practice. Theodore and the *Apostolic Constitutions* reflect a change in that tradition. For Chrysostom the Spirit is conferred in the baptismal action itself — see next chapter.

44. Riley, *Christian Initiation*, pp. 421-433; Finn, *The Liturgy of Baptism*, pp. 191-197; de Roten, *Baptême et mystagogie*, pp. 302-309, for the clothing symbolizing the change of condition that baptism represents (union with Christ and incorruptibility), and pp. 309-312, for the brightness of the neophytes (compared to stars).

change in our lives" (5.24).⁴⁵ These passages point to Chrysostom's interpretation of baptism as a putting on of Christ (Gal. 3:27), for which see the next chapter. The neophytes may also have been given candles to carry in procession into the church.⁴⁶

The only postbaptismal act expressly described in the *Baptismal Instructions* is the kiss. "As soon as they come forth from those sacred waters, all who are present embrace them, greet them, kiss them, rejoice with them, and congratulate them" (2.27). Then they are led to the "royal table," the "awesome table," where they "taste of the Master's body and blood" (2.27).⁴⁷ Thus the neophytes were welcomed into the fellowship of the congregation. The kiss described in 11.32-34 may be a separate kiss, the ritual exchange of peace as part of the eucharistic liturgy.⁴⁸

The words about the bridal feast lasting seven days (6.24) perhaps allude to the period of instruction in the mysteries for seven days after baptism.⁴⁹ Chrysostom often uses μυσταγωγία (always a liturgical celebration and most often baptism or eucharist) and μυστήριον (more often in the plural, which is used of the eucharist, not baptism per se).⁵⁰

Another topic related to the administration of baptism but also important for Chrysostom's understanding of the benefits of baptism is the practice of infant baptism. In a homily likely given on Easter morning after the baptism and eucharist, he says:

> You have seen how numerous are the gifts of baptism. Although many men think that the only gift it confers is the remission of sins, we have counted its honors to the number of ten. It is on this account that we baptize even infants, although they are sinless, that they may be given the further gifts of sanctification, justice, filial adoption, and inheritance, that they may be brothers and members of Christ, and become dwelling places for the Spirit. (3.6)

An allusion to infant (or child) baptism relates it to circumcision:

> Our circumcision, I speak of the grace of baptism, has painless healing and becomes the patron of a myriad good things to us, even a filling of the grace of the Holy Spirit to us, and has no boundary of time, but it is possible to receive this cir-

---

45. Cf. "Keep the marriage robe in its integrity" (6.24); keep "your royal robe shining even more brightly than it now does by your godly conduct and your strict discipline" (4.18); "make this spiritual robe of ours more brilliant . . . careful to keep this bright robe of ours without spot or wrinkle" (4.31-32).

46. Finn, *The Liturgy of Baptism*, pp. 190-191.

47. See Finn, *The Liturgy of Baptism*, pp. 199-207, for references in the *Baptismal Instructions* to the eucharist.

48. De Roten, *Baptême et mystagogie*, pp. 313-319, discusses the kiss and argues that there was a separate kiss of peace of the newly baptized before the eucharistic kiss; so Riley, *Christian Initiation*, pp. 351-352.

49. De Roten, *Baptême et mystagogie*, pp. 335-337, for the paschal octave.

50. De Roten, *Baptême et mystagogie*, pp. 47-107.

cumcision without hands which occurs in very young age, middle age, or old age itself. (*Homilies on Genesis* 40.4 [PG 53.373D])

Chrysostom exhorts parents to take to heart the religious formation of their children, but he says nothing about their need to have them baptized.[51] Infants were signed with the cross on their foreheads; since this was the mark of entrance into the catechumenate, this act may have been an alternative to baptism.[52] Are the infant baptisms defended by Chrysostom, therefore, emergency baptisms? He himself was probably baptized at about age 18.[53]

Chrysostom does not explain what accommodations, if any, were made for infants in the ceremony of baptism, so obviously constructed for those of responsible age. Indeed, in another reference to infant baptism he expressed his concern that "those who have been enlightened [baptized], whether because they received it as children or having received it in sickness [chap. 39] and recovered," often had no desire to make an earnest business of living to the glory of God.[54] There is allusion to sponsors answering and acting on behalf of children: Many are profited by alms done by others; if this were not so, "how are children saved?"[55] Chrysostom testifies to the common association of baptism with the forgiveness of sins. In asserting that infants have no sins, Chrysostom states the usual eastern view on human nature and thus the justification of infant baptism on other grounds. In this regard he distinguishes himself from the Augustinian tradition in the West that associated infant baptism with original sin.[56] In his extensive discussion of God's treatment of Adam, Chrysostom says nothing indicative of original sin (2.1-8). Indeed, an unbaptized deceased infant is not lost.[57]

In the passage quoted above, Chrysostom lists six gifts of baptism in addition to remission of sins. However, in the preceding paragraph he does have ten blessings, although with some overlapping: free citizens of the church, holy, just, sons, heirs,

---

51. De Roten, *Baptême et mystagogie*, p. 12. *Homilies on 1 Thessalonians* 6.2 speaks of a widow bringing up her children in the fear of God, but there is no mention of baptism. The closest approximation to an obligation in this regard is *Homilies on Ephesians* 8.5, where the jailor in Acts 16 is said to be unlike those who allow slaves, wives, and children to go unbaptized.

52. *Homilies on Mattthew* 54.4 refers to making the sign of the cross on the forehead of infants, but is this the sign of the cross after baptism? De Roten, *Baptême et mystagogie*, p. 140.

53. De Roten, *Baptême et mystagogie*, p. 14.

54. *Homilies on Acts* 23.3 (PG 60.182A). One should note the linking of child baptism and sickbed baptism.

55. *Homilies on Acts* 21.4 on Acts 9:26-27 (PG 60.168).

56. Augustine could accept the statement of Chrysostom as applying to actual sins but not to sin inherited from Adam. See the note in Harkins, *St. John Chrysostom: Baptismal Instructions*, pp. 232-233, n. 12.

57. De Roten, *Baptême et mystagogie*, p. 13, with references. *Homilies on Acts* 21.4 on Acts 9:26-27 states there is nothing to condemn in a little child who dies, and the newly baptized (neophyte) who dies is in the same condition as a little child (PG 60.168). *Homilies on 1 Corinthians* 12.13 refers to the many untimely deaths of babies; *Homilies on Colossians* 8.6 says a child who dies goes to heaven, but it is not said whether the child is baptized.

brothers of Christ, joint heirs, members, the temple, and instruments of the Spirit (3.5).[58] There are other shorter listings by Chrysostom.[59]

These listings lead to a consideration of the meaning of baptism according to Chrysostom (next chapter).

---

58. Harkins, *St. John Chrysostom: Baptismal Instructions*, p. 232, n. 9, gives the scriptural basis of each, and in n. 11 references to other listings in Chrysostom. A listing of nine items occurs in *Homilies on 1 Corinthians* 7 on 1 Cor. 2:6-7 quoted in the next chapter in a note on faith.

59. Outside the *Baptismal Instructions*, note *Homilies on Romans* 11 on Rom. 6:5: "For as [Christ's] body, by being buried in the earth brought forth as the fruit of it the salvation of the world; thus ours also, being buried in baptism, bore as fruit righteousness, sanctification, adoption, countless blessings. And it will bear also hereafter the gift of the resurrection" (tr. J. B. Morris, W. H. Simcox, and George B. Stevens, "St. John Chrysostom: Homilies on Romans," *Nicene and Post-Nicene Fathers* [repr. Peabody: Hendrickson, 1994], First Series, Vol. 11, p. 408. Also, *Homilies on Matthew* 11 — forgiveness of sins, pardon from punishment, righteousness, sanctity, redemption, filial adoption, brotherhood, sharing in the inheritance, and abundant outpouring of the Holy Spirit — and *De gloria in tribulationibus* (PG 49.226D) — God has made us just, holy, sons by adoption, heirs of the kingdom, joint heirs with Christ.

34. The School of Antioch: John Chrysostom — II

In this chapter we turn from word usage and the administration of baptism to the interpretation of baptism by John Chrysostom.

The *Baptismal Instructions* contain some briefer listings of the benefits of baptism that incorporate items mentioned at the close of the preceding chapter.

> You are called "faithful" [in contrast to the catechumens] both because you believe in God and have as a trust from him justification, sanctity, purity of soul, filial adoption, and the kingdom of heaven. (12.6)[1]

Chrysostom continues that the baptized were called "newly illumined" because their soul was "illumined and becomes brighter from the grace it has received from the Spirit" (12.10).[2] Another notable statement is that "They not only are cleansed but become holy, too, and just" (9.18).

Christ's Baptism

Chrysostom presented what happened to the body of Christ in his baptism in the Jordan as comparable to what happens when one is baptized now and so as the model for Christian baptism (3.13; 5.27). He describes the baptism of Christ in terms of the theological point he wants to make about Christian baptism, namely that it is not a human being but God who administers baptism and so bestows its blessings:[3]

> Although John appeared to be holding his body by the head, it was the divine Word which led his body down into the streams of Jordan and baptized him. The

---

1. I continue to quote and use the numbering system of Paul W. Harkins, *St. John Chrysostom: Baptismal Instructions*, Ancient Christian Writers 31 (Westminster: Newman, 1963).
2. Baptism as enlightenment is discussed further below.
3. For the context, see the quotation of 11.12 below.

Master's body was baptized by the Word, and by the voice of his Father from heaven which said: *This is my beloved Son,* and by the manifestation of the Holy Spirit which descended upon him. This also happens in the case of your body. The baptism is given in the name of the Father and of the Son and of the Holy Spirit. Therefore, John the Baptist told us, for our instruction, that man does not baptize us, but God: [Luke 3:16 quoted]. (11.13)

When Chrysostom preached *On the Baptism of Christ,* however, he was concerned to distinguish Christ's baptism from Christian baptism by making the express reservation that Jesus had no need of repentance, forgiveness, or supply of the Spirit, which blessings pertain to Christian baptism. Jesus received neither Jewish nor Christian baptism but John's; he was, nonetheless, himself incomparably greater than John (*Bapt. Chr.* 3 [PG 49.367-368]; see our chap. 7).

A homily *On John the Precursor* ascribed to Chrysostom but printed among the *dubia et spuria* of his works contains an imaginative recreation of Jesus' words to persuade John to baptize him, in which he correlates Jesus' baptism with his death:

> I receive this baptism in order that I may provide for my disciples the baptism of regeneration [παλιγγενεσίας]. . . . I accept the cross because of sinners; shall I avoid the bath that has no danger? I am going to endure death three days; shall I not make the descent [κατάδυσιν] that is without pain? I urge myself to go down to the very depth of Hades; will I not embrace the flowing river? Then baptize [βάπτισον] me who am going to baptize and save those who are willing. Baptize me who am going to raise the nature of human beings immersed [βεβαπτισμένη] in sins to heavenly height. Baptize me as a man below who is praised above by the angels as God. (PG 59.803)

The reader notes Jesus' mission as bringing regeneration and forgiveness to save those who are willing. Notable for the meaning of "baptize" and so for the action of baptism is the parallel of the metaphorical meaning ("immersed in sins") with the baptism requested from John, the synonym "descent" ("dipping") for baptism, and the description of going down to the very depth of Hades as equivalent to "baptize" (in the flowing river).

Images of Baptism

Chrysostom employs images to convey the significance of baptism. A favorite image is that of marriage. The catechumens are told, "Behold, . . . the days of your spiritual marriage are close at hand" (1.1). He elaborates on the image explaining that the heavenly Bridegroom does not choose his bride for her beauty (1.3-6), but the catechumen like a bride forsakes her family and past to be united with the Bridegroom (1.11-15; cf. 3.19). He combines this image with that of a contract by speaking of the marriage contract (1.16-18; cf. 11.26). On the last day of instruction, Chrysostom tells the candidates that in two days "the Bridegroom is coming" and they are to be watchful as they await the bridal procession (11.1). The bridal clothing is given spiritual interpretation (11.6-10).

The preacher combines the marriage imagery with military imagery. The catechumens' spiritual marriage was a "military enlistment" (1.1). Unlike those who recruit human armies, the King of heaven receives all into his army; he does not recruit them for the service they will give, but "he leads his troops into a spiritual battle" (12.30-32).

This spiritual battle is a combat with the devil and demons, who are behind pagan religion and immorality (1.5). Chrysostom more often employs the image of an athletic contest to describe this combat. The parallels are worked out according to the school for training, stripping and anointing, the spectators, and the crown; a point of contrast is that the judge of our contest (Christ) does not stand aloof but is on our side (3.8-11; cf. 12.33-37). The athletic imagery then shades into the military imagery of armor and weapons (3.11). The thirty days of instruction before baptism are likened to the exercises in the wrestling school; after the baptism our combat with the demon is like a boxing or wrestling match (9.29).

Chrysostom relates the combat with the devil at baptism to the exodus of Israel from Egypt.

> Now you shall see greater and much more brilliant [miracles] than those seen when the Jews went forth from Egypt. You did not see the Pharaoh and his armies drowned, but you did see the drowning of the devil and his armies. The Jews passed through the sea; you have passed through the sea of death. They were delivered from the Egyptians; you are set free from the demon. They put aside their servitude to barbarians; you have set aside the far more hazardous servitude to sin. (3.24)[4]

The events connected with the exodus provided Chrysostom with the comparison of the blood of the Passover lamb with the blood of Christ. Just as the destroying angel saw the blood on the doorposts and passed by, so the devil restrains himself all the more when he sees the blood of Christ on the faithful (3.12-15).

At baptism one responds to the invitation of Christ (Matt. 11:28-29) and takes his yoke (1.25-33). The language of a contract employed for the renunciation of Satan

---

4. Harkins, *St. John Chrysostom: Baptismal Instructions*, p. 240, n. 52, cites parallels in *Homilies on Matthew* 39 (PG 57.437C) and *Nolo vos ignorare* (PG 51.247D-50C). Cf. *Homilies on Colossians* 7 on Col. 3:2-4 cited below on baptism as a death and resurrection. In addition to the Red Sea other types of baptism were Elisha's axe that floated, Naaman, and from the New Testament the paralytic healed at the pool — *Homilies on John* 26.2. Chrysostom contrasts the healing at the pool in John 5:2 with Christ's baptism: "Only one person a year was healed, but grace came.... An angel descended into the pool [κολυμβήθραν] and troubled the water, and one was healed. The Master of angels went down into the Jordan and troubled the water, and he healed the whole earth" (*Resurrection of Christ* 4 [PG 50.439D-440A]). *Pascha* 5 (PG 52.771A) contrasts the waters at creation that produced irational creatures with the waters that now give out spiritual gifts.

and adhesion to Christ (chap. 33) is also used more broadly. By sin human beings were debtors to the devil, but this old contract was nailed to the cross of Christ (Col. 2:14). He did not just erase it, but he tore it to pieces (3.20-22). Chrysostom exhorted neophytes to keep "their contract with the Master, which you wrote not with ink nor on paper, but with faith and in confession" (4.31). The contract with Christ belonged in the whole context of the baptismal ceremony.

Grace, Faith, and Repentance

The attentive reader will notice how often the word "grace" occurs in the passages quoted about the various themes related to baptism in Chrysostom's exposition.[5] This word sums up the divine activity in baptism. The human response is faith and repentance.

The themes of faith and repentance are integral to the baptismal context. Chrysostom insists on the necessity of faith for baptism.[6] Those who enrolled for baptism "bring forward a generous faith and a strong reason" (*Bapt. Instr.* 2.9). Chrysostom could summarize what must be done in order to be saved as, "Believe and be baptized."[7] Faith in the sense of being convinced, however, is not sufficient, for God must confer the mysteries.[8] What takes place in baptism "requires faith and the eyes of the soul," because what occurs is invisible to the eyes of the body. "This is faith: to see the invisible as if it were visible" (2.9). In another homily Chrysostom elaborated on the difference between what the eyes of the flesh and the eyes of faith see:

> The eyes of the flesh see water; the eyes of faith behold the Spirit. Those eyes see the body being baptized; these see the old man being buried. The eyes of the flesh see the flesh being washed; the eyes of the spirit see the soul being cleansed. The

---

5. Raymond Burnish, *The Meaning of Baptism: A Comparison of the Teaching and Practice of the Fourth Century with the Present Day* (London: Alcuin Club/SPCK, 1985), pp. 31-34, on baptism as a gift in Chrysostom; Philippe de Roten, *Baptême et mystagogie: Enquête sur l'initiation chrétienne selon s. Jean Chrysostome*, Liturgiewissenschaftliche Quellen und Forschungen 91 (Münster: Aschendorff, 2005), pp. 356-370, on the gifts and effects of baptism as Chrysostom assigns them to the action of the Father, the cross of Christ, or the gifts of the Spirit.

6. De Roten, *Baptême et mystagogie*, p. 34.

7. Homilies on Ephesians 8 on Eph. 4:1-2 (PG 62.68). Chrysostom refers to the question asked by the Philippian jailer in Acts 16:30 and the Jews on Pentecost in Acts 2:37. The translation in the *Nicene and Post-Nicene Fathers*, First Series, Vol. 13, p. 93, gives the response as "Repent and be baptized," although the Greek has "Believe and be baptized." The translator followed Peter's answer in Acts 2:38 and may have thought the Greek text was a mistake, a view possibly supported by "believers" already being mentioned in the sentence. However, it may be that Chrysostom did say "believe" as a conflation of Paul's answer to the jailer (Acts 16:31) and "be baptized" from Peter's answer on Pentecost (Acts 2:38).

8. De Roten, *Baptême et mystagogie*, p. 148. Cf. *Pentecost* 1.2 (PG 50.456D), "We sent up faith, and we received grace gifts from above; we sent up obedience, and we received righteousness."

eyes of the body see the body emerging from the water; the eyes of faith see the new man come forth brightly shining from that sacred purification. Our bodily eyes see the priest as, from above, he lays his right hand on the head and touches; our spiritual eyes see the great High Priest as he stretches forth his invisible hand to touch his head. For, at that moment, the one who baptizes is not a man but the only-begotten Son of God. (11.12)[9]

This faith is in the Trinity, in whose name the baptism is given (11.13-14). "It is faith in this Trinity which gives the grace of remission from sin; it is this confession which gives to us the gift of filial adoption" (2.26). This faith must indeed be confessed; the candidates must say, "I believe" (11.15). "You who are coming to God, first believe in God and then speak out that word loud and clear" (11.16). With the lips are made a "strong confession of faith" that represents "the resolution of the mind" and understanding (1.19). The confession included not only faith in the triune God but also in the resurrection (*Homilies on 1 Corinthians* 40.2 on 1 Cor. 15:29).[10] When one has believed and confessed in words, God gives full assurance, for the baptism itself is God's assurance of the resurrection (on which see more below).

> How and in what manner? By the water. For the being baptized and immersed [καταδύεσθαι] and then emerging [ἀνανεύειν, rising up] is a symbol of the descent into Hades and return thence. [Rom. 6:4, quoted for Paul calling baptism a burial.] . . . For the blotting out of sins is a much greater thing than the raising up of a body.[11]

He continues that God does so in the laver in regeneration. The passage is a clear indication that the baptism was a full submersion.

Those who "put on Christ" will "henceforth through the kindness of God" "be called a Christian and one of the faithful" (1.44). They will wear the name "faithful" because they believe things their bodily eyes cannot see (11.11), and they are called Christian because they belong to Christ.[12] Chrysostom also calls them "newly illuminated" (9.12; 12.10-12) and once "newly initiated" (4.24; cf. 9.2-3, 10).

---

9. Cf. the similar contrast in *Homilies on 1 Corinthians* 7 on 1 Cor. 2:6-7 — An unbeliever "hearing of a laver [λουτρόν] counts it merely as water; but I behold not simply the thing which is seen, but the purification of the soul which is by the Spirit. He considers only that my body has been washed; but I have believed that the soul also has become both pure and holy; and I count it the sepulchre, the resurrection, the sanctification, the righteousness, the redemption, the adoption, the inheritance, the kingdom of heaven, the full effusion of the Spirit" (trans. by J. Keble and T. W. Chambers, "St. John Chrysostom Homilies on 1 Corinthians," *Nicene and Post-Nicene Fathers* [Peabody: Hendrickson, 1994], First Series, Vol. 12, p. 34).

10. In this passage Chrysostom interpreted the verse to mean baptized "for dead bodies," which would be raised.

11. *Homilies on 1 Corinthians* 40.1 on 1 Cor. 15:29 (PG 61.348C-D; trans. Keble and Chambers in *Nicene and Post-Nicene Fathers*, First Series, Vol. 12, p. 245. Chrysostom presumably used "baptism" for the whole ceremony, which included the immersion and emersion.

12. On the name Christian see *On the Beginning of Acts* 2 (PG 51.86D); *On the Statues* 14.16 (PG

Addressing those about to be baptized, Chrysostom says, "We must repent and keep far away from our former sins and in this way approach to grace" (12.22). In discussing God's remaking of human nature in baptism, Chrysostom declares that if one afterwards slips into sin, "He can lead us back through sincere repentance to our former state" (9.26).[13]

Doctrinal Meaning of Baptism

Death, Burial, and Resurrection

Quite prominent in Chrysostom's mystagogy is the identification of the baptizand with the death, burial, and resurrection of Christ.[14] He states the interpretation succinctly: "Baptism is a burial and a resurrection. For the old man is buried with his sin and the new man is resurrected, 'being renewed according to the image of his Creator' [Col. 3:10]" (*Bapt. Instr.* 2.11). In the same homily, he states,

> The priest makes you go down into the sacred waters, burying the old man and at the same time raising up the new, who is renewed in the image of his Creator. . . . Instead of the man who descended into the water, a different man comes forth. (2.25)

Or again, "For in baptism there are both burial and resurrection together at the same time," for Paul "calls baptism a resurrection" (10.11).[15] As might be expected, a fuller statement is found in his homily on Romans 6:3-4.

49.176B-D). Contrary to the usage of Cyril and Augustine, who give the name to catechumens, Chrysostom limits it to the baptized — Thomas M. Finn, *The Liturgy of Baptism in the Baptismal Instructions of St. John Chrysostom*, Studies in Christian Antiquity 15 (Washington, D.C.: Catholic University of America Press, 1967), pp. 182-184. Note, however, that he says that he calls them "brothers even before your birth" (9.1).

13. That there is no second baptism for postbaptismal sins, see below on the forgiveness of sins.

14. Hugh M. Riley, *Christian Initiation*, Studies in Christian Antiquity 17 (Washington, D.C.: Catholic University of America Press, 1974), pp. 261-279, considers this "his principal interpretation of the meaning of the baptismal act" (p. 261). He notes that Finn, *The Liturgy of Baptism*, p. 158, counts thirteen times that Chrysostom cites Rom. 6:1-13 and Col. 2:12-15; 3:1-4. Cf. de Roten, *Baptême et mystagogie*, pp. 295-299.

15. Chrysostom continues that "our death, burial, and resurrection [are] all at the same time" (10.12), but Christ's resurrection was delayed for three days in order to establish proof of a genuine death and resurrection. In his *Homilies on Romans* 11 on Rom. 6:5 he acknowledges that Paul does not make a clear statement in Rom. 6 about our resurrection but only about the way of life after baptism. Cf. what Chrysostom says in *Homilies on Colossians* 6 on Col. 2:12: Baptism is not only a burial. All is of faith. "You believe God is able to raise the dead, and so you were raised." In *Homilies on John* 25.2 on John 3:5, he says, "In baptism are fulfilled the pledge of our covenant with God; burial, death, resurrection, and life — this takes place all at once," and continues by asserting that as it is easy for us to dip the head in the water and lift it again, so it is easy for God to bury the old and show forth the new. In preaching on 1 Cor. 15:29, Chrysostom notes the Marcionite practice of baptizing on behalf of the dead

What does being "baptized into his death" mean? That it is with a view to our dying as he did. For baptism is the cross. What the cross then, and burial, is to Christ, that baptism has been to us, even if not in the same respects. For he died himself and was buried in the flesh, but we have done both to sin. Wherefore, he does not say, planted together in his death, but in the likeness of his death.[16]

Chrysostom continued the thought in his next homily on Romans 6:5:

> Here then he says there are two mortifyings and two deaths, and that one is done by Christ in baptism, and the other it is our duty to effect by earnestness afterwards. For that our former sins were buried, came of his gift. But the remaining dead to sin after baptism must be the work of our own earnestness, however much we find God here also giving us large help.... Since then we were buried in water, he in earth, and we in regard to sin, he in regard to his body....[17]

Baptism marked a person's death to the world (7.20-23). With reference to Colossians 3:3, Chrysostom comments, "You are corpses as far as sin is concerned. Once and for all you have renounced the present life" (7.21).

> After you have died and become dead to sin once and for all by your baptism, accordingly have nothing to do with the passions of the flesh and the affairs of the world. (7.22)

New Creation

Baptism was not only a death, but it also represented a new creation (*Bapt. Instr.* 4.12-16). Quoting 2 Corinthians 5:17, and observing persons no longer living for pleasures and no longer worshipping idols, Chrysostom asks,

> Did you see how a new creation has truly taken place? The grace of God has entered these souls and molded them anew, reformed them, and made them different from what they were. It did not change their substance, but made over their will. (7.14)

Faith in Christ and a return to virtue constitute a new creation (7.16).

---

and offers his interpretation that baptism is based on the recitation of the confession, "I believe in the resurrection of the dead," so baptism is for the resurrection of dead bodies (*Homilies on 1 Corinthians* 40.2). That baptism is an assurance of our resurrection, see the quotation above under faith and confession. For baptism and the cross see below.

16. *Homilies on Romans* 10 on Rom. 6:3-4. Translation by J. B. Morris, W. H. Simcox, and George B. Stevens, "St. John Chrysostom Homilies on Romans," in *Nicene and Post-Nicene Fathers* (repr. Peabody: Hendrickson, 1994), First Series, Vol. 11, p. 405.

17. Chrysostom, *Homilies on Romans* 11 on Rom. 6:5; *Nicene and Post-Nicene Fathers*, First Series, Vol. 11, p. 408.

Elsewhere Chrysostom does speak of the new creation in terms of a renewal of human nature (9.21-26).[18] The bath is paradoxically also a furnace.

> God plunges [this nature of ours] into the waters as into the smelting furnace and lets the grace of the Spirit fall on it instead of the flames. Then he brings us forth from the furnace, renewed like newly-molded vessels. (9.22)

He proceeds to bring in the image of God as a potter (9.24) who is able to reshape a vessel.

Baptism is both a destruction of sin and a generation of life.

> Our first man is buried: buried not in earth but in water; not death-destroyed but buried by death's destroyer, not by the law of nature but by the governing command that is stronger than nature.

The symbol of this was the Red Sea, where the Egyptians sank beneath it and the Israelites went up out of it. "In the same act he buries the one, generates [γεννᾷ] the other. Marvel not that generation [γένεσις] and destruction take place in baptism."[19]

In discussing the cross in relation to baptism Chrysostom does not speak so much as a theologian making a doctrinal point about the relation of the cross of Christ to baptism as he does as a pastor making a moral point to the effect that the converts should place their lives on the cross. He calls on his hearers, "Be crucified yourself through your baptism," for baptism is a cross and a death" (10.7).[20] There follows a discussion of baptism in relation to the cross. Baptism is both the death of sin and the cross because of Romans 6:3 and 6 (10.8). Chrysostom further cites Jesus' words in Luke 12:50 and a conflation of Matthew 20:22 and Mark 10:38 to the effect that Jesus called his baptism a cross (10.9). The cross has "the strength of a wonderful amulet and a mighty incantation" to drive away the devil (11.25).

Chrysostom does expound on the power of the blood of Christ to drive away the devil and to save (3.12-15). The blood of the lamb on the doorposts of the Israelites (see above on the exodus) was able to save, "Not because it is blood, but because it prefigures the Master's blood" (3.14). Chrysostom, in keeping with the catechetical instruction, interpreted the blood not in terms of the doctrine of the atonement but as an expression of the eucharist. He found a lesson in the water and blood from Jesus' side when he was dead on the cross (John 19:34). He reverses the order of the

---

18. Cf. *Homilies on Acts* 23 (PG 60.181C), "Truly great is the power of baptism; it makes those who share in the gift different from what they were."

19. *Homilies on Colosians* 7.2 on Col. 3:2-4 (trans. rev. by John A. Broadus, "St. John Chrysostom: Homilies on Colossians," *Nicene and Post-Nicene Fathers* [repr. Peabody: Hendrickson, 1994], First Series, Vol. 13, p. 290).

20. Cf. 9.12, where baptism is called a cross with the quotation of Rom. 6:6. The *Commentary on Galatians* 2:20 takes the verse as an allusion to baptism. Baptism is also called a cross in *Homilies on John* 25.2 with quotation of Mark 10:39 and Luke 12:50. Cf. *Homilies on Philippians* 13 on Phil. 3:18-21 — "Baptism is through the cross, for we must receive that seal. The laying on of hands is through the cross."

biblical text, because "first comes baptism and then the mysteries [the eucharist]" (3.16). As these derive from Christ, so too "It is from his side that Christ formed his church" (3.17).[21]

Regeneration

In keeping with the new creation theme in baptism, Chrysostom speaks of baptism as a regeneration.[22] The water and the blood from the side of Christ produce the church through "'the bath of regeneration and renewal by the Holy Spirit' [Titus 3:5] through baptism and the mysteries" (3.17). Chrysostom often cites this biblical text, but without elaborating on it. In his homilies on Titus he interpreted the παλιγγενεσία ("regeneration") of the verse as ἀναγεννήσια ("regeneration").[23] "Bath of regeneration" is one of the names he cites for baptism (9.12). He alludes to the "bath of baptism" (1.17), the "bath of regeneration" (3.23), and "the regeneration that comes from the water and the Spirit" (11.29), and he calls the baptismal experience simply "regeneration" (10.14).[24] In one passage Christ is the one who begets (3.19); in another God begets (*Homilies on Matthew* 50 [PG 58.597D]). Or, expounding on Isaac being begotten by the promises of God, he says that it is the words of God that beget:

> Thus are we also gendered by the words of God. Since in the pool of water it is the words of God which generate and fashion us. For it is by being baptized into the name of the Father and of the Son and of the Holy Spirit that we are engendered, and this birth is not of nature, but of the promise of God.... [E]ven in nature itself the generation by means of baptism from above was sketched out beforehand.[25]

---

21. Cf. 3.18, "As God took the rib of Adam and formed a woman, so Christ gave us blood and water from his side and formed the church."

22. Riley, *Christian Initiation*, pp. 313-324. Finn, *The Liturgy of Baptism*, pp. 162-163, notes the association of the Pauline symbolism of the tomb and the Johannine symbolism of birth in *Homilies on Colossians* 7.2 (PG 62.346) and for baptism as a birth *Homilies on Colossians* 6.4 (PG 62.342); *Homilies on John* 26.1 (PG 59.153); *Homilies on Ephesians* 20.3 (PG 62.139); and *On the Beginning of Acts* 6 (PG 51.96).

23. *Homilies on Titus* 5 on Tit. 3:5. Chrysostom uses "baptize" in the passage in a metaphorical sense drawn from the word's literal meaning, "baptized [βεβαπτισμένοι, 'drowned'] in wickedness."

24. "How lowly born you were before regeneration." Another citation of Titus 3:5, "God granted to us renewal through 'the washing of regeneration,'" is in *Homilies on Genesis* 40.4 (PG 53.373).

25. *Homilies on Romans* 16 on Rom. 9:9 (trans. in *Nicene and Post-Nicene Fathers*, First Series, Vol. 11, p. 463). Chrysostom also employs the story of Sarah and Isaac in a similar way in his *Commentary on Galatians* 4:28 — "So also in our regeneration [ἀναγεννήσεως] it is not nature but the words of God spoken by the priest (the faithful know them), which in the bath [κολυμβήθρα] of water is a sort of womb, form and regenerate [ἀναγεννᾷ] the one who is baptized." Similarly, in *Homilies on John* 26.1 on John 3:6 the analogy is drawn that what the womb is to the embryo, water is to the believer, for in it he/she is fashioned and formed, but unlike the long period of human gestation all is done in a single moment.

Chrysostom, as others, based the necessity of baptism for salvation on John 3:5.[26] His homily on John 3:5 asserts that water is necessary and indispensable to the new birth. Like the first creation from clay, he does not understand how it is done but he does not disbelieve; so one accepts the fact of the new birth on faith. The Spirit is present in the water. In his further exposition he associates the passage with the theme of death and resurrection and confirms details of how the baptism was performed.

> Divine symbols are celebrated in the water: burial and death, resurrection and life, and all these occur together. For when we sink [καταδυόντων] our heads in the water as in a kind of tomb, the old person is buried, and sinking down [καταδὺς] beneath it is completely hidden all at once. Then when we raise the head [ἀνανευόντων], the new person comes up again.

He then adds that this is done three times so that we may learn the power of the Father, Son, and Holy Spirit.[27]

Chrysostom uses the image of the church as a mother, who gives birth to children in baptism.[28] Addressing the neophytes shortly after their baptism, he comments on the great numbers baptized: "See how many children this spiritual mother [the church] has brought forth suddenly and in a single night!" (*Bapt. Instr.* 4.1).[29] Chrysostom elsewhere contrasts the physical and spiritual birth:

> O birth pangs that are [ceremonially] pure! O spiritual births! O new offspring! There is conception without a womb, there is birth without a belly, there is childbearing without flesh, a spiritual childbearing, childbearing by the grace and kindness of God, a childbearing that is filled with joy and gladness.[30]

Forgiveness of Sins

Chrysostom put more emphasis on the positive effects of regeneration than on the negative aspects of forgiveness:

> And why, someone will say, if the bath takes away all our sins, is it not called the bath of the remission of sins, or the bath of cleansing, rather than the bath of regeneration [Titus 3:5]? The reason is that it does not simply remit our sins, nor does it simply cleanse us of our faults, but it does this just as if we were born anew.

---

26. De Roten, *Baptême et mystagogie*, p. 11, n. 27, for references in Chrysostom and others; pp. 380-381 for baptism as a birth used as often as baptism as adoption.

27. *Homilies on John* 25.2 (PG 59.151A-B). For the piscina as a tomb see the discussion of baptism as a burial.

28. Allusions to the church as mother in 6.20; 10.15; and *Bapt. Chr.* 1 ("the common mother of all, I mean the church" — PG 49.364).

29. Cf. *Bapt. Chr.* 1, "the church gives birth to so many children" (PG 49.363).

30. *On the Beginning of Acts* 3 (PG 51.96D), translation in Harkins, *St. John Chrysostom: Baptismal Instructions*, p. 245, n. 6, where the whole passage is translated.

For it does create us anew and it fashions us again, not molding us from earth, but creating us from a different element, the nature of water. (*Bapt. Instr.* 9.20)

Nevertheless, as indicated in the discussion of infant baptism in the last chapter, Chrysostom recognized the common association of baptism with the forgiveness of sins. This is almost something that Chrysostom takes for granted in the *Baptismal Instructions* as understood by his hearers in regard to baptism ("Not only is it wonderful that he forgives us our sins" — 12.36), but he often refers to it elsewhere.[31] He does explicitly say that remission of sins is received in baptism (*Homilies on Ephesians* 11 on Eph. 4:4-7). The forgiveness of sins removes the judgment and pain of conscience against us (1.28; cf. 9.12-15). Thereby one is justified "without labor, sweat, or good works," because "when all human wickedness falls into the bath of divine waters, it is drowned and disappears" (9.19). Unlike the body when it grows old and ugly, the soul can be returned to its former beauty and innocence (5.15). He uses an illustration that was to have a great future in Syria. As one recasts iron or gold in a furnace of fire, so "the Holy Spirit recasts the soul in baptism as in a furnace and consumes its sins."[32]

For postbaptismal sins there is forgiveness "but not a second remission by baptism." Just as there is no second cross, there is no second forgiveness by the bath of regeneration (3.23).[33] God does away with sin by the laver [λουτροῦ] and by repentance (*Homilies on Ephesians* 4 on Eph. 2:10).

Our discussion of Chrysostom's defense of infant baptism noted his affirmation that infants do not have sins. The forgiveness of sins and the cleansing of the conscience, however, distinguished the Christian bath from the Jewish bath.

> The washing which is common to all men is that of the baths, which usually cleanses away the filth of the body. There is also the washing of the Jews, which is

---

31. The passage later indicates that in baptism God forgives sins without requiring a public confession of them. In *Bapt. Chr.* 1 (PG 49.364) Chrysostom puts baptism and forgiveness of sins together in a listing of the topics on which he preached. A typical statement is, "[He] granted remission of sins by the laver of regeneration" — *Homilies on John* 28.1. Baptism forgives even murder and adultery — *Homiles on Acts* 1.6 (PG 60.22D). Note the associated ideas: "If God gave his Son for our sins, if he granted us the gift of baptism, if he gave the forgiveness of previous sins, if he prepared the way of repentance for us" (*Homilies on Genesis* 34.5 on Gen. 13 [PG 53.313D]). De Roten, *Baptême et mystagogie*, p. 373, declares that the two gifts of baptism Chrysostom mentioned the most as summarizing the others are forgiveness and adoption (pp. 373-378 on forgiveness, pp. 378-380 on adoption, noted often in passages we have quoted).

32. *Homilies on 1 Corinthians* 40.2.

33. There is no second baptism (*Homilies on Ephesians* 2 on Eph. 1:14), no "fresh baptism" (*Homilies on Ephesians* 5 on 2:16). Concerning those who have contracted the filth of sin after their baptism Chrysostom urges "to cleanse [it] away by confession, tears, and most exact repentance" (6.23). There is remission of sins for those who fall after baptism — *Homily on Repentance* 1 ("When He Returned from the Countryside"), 4.26 (tr. Gus George Christo in Fathers of the Church 96 [Washington: Catholic University of America Press, 1998], pp. 11-12); "[Peter] performed a second baptism with the tears from his eyes. By crying bitterly, he wiped away his sin" — *Homily on Repentance* 3 ("Concerning Almsgiving and the Ten Virgins"), 4.20 (Christo, p. 40). Burnish, *The Meaning of Baptism*, p. 28.

> more solemn than that of the [secular] baths, but much inferior to the bath of grace. While this bath cleanses bodily filth, it does not merely remove the uncleanness of the body but also that which clings to a weak conscience.... The bath of grace, however, does not remove such a stain [of ceremonial uncleanness] but the real uncleanness of the body and the stain which has been put upon the soul. Even if a person be effeminate, or an adulterer, or an idolater, or has done some dread deed, or dwells with all human wickedness, after he goes down into the bath of waters, he comes forth from the divine waters purer than the rays of the sun. (*Bapt. Instr.* 9.13, 16)

Chrysostom continues by quoting 1 Corinthians 6:9-11 in support of baptism's cleansing power with regard to all sins (9.17-18). He employs similar wording in his *On the Baptism of Christ*.

> The Jewish baptism that removes bodily filth was not removing the sins of the conscience. For if one did adultery, if one dared theft, if one transgressed in any other such way, it did not remove him from these reproaches. But if anyone touched the bones of the dead, ... he washed and was unclean until evening and then was purified....
>
> The Jewish purifications did not remove sins, only bodily filth, but our purification is not like that, being full of much grace by very much more. It removes sins, wipes clean the soul, and gives an abundance of the Spirit. (*Bapt. Chr.* 2-3 [PG 49.366])[34]

Accordingly, Jewish baptism ceased when Christian baptism brought the dignity of adoption, the removal of evil, and the granting of all good things.[35]

Christian baptism is, moreover, superior to the baptism administered by John the Baptist. John's baptism was superior to Jewish purifications, but was a transition to Christian teachings. His was a baptism of repentance, but it "did not give the Holy Spirit, nor did it provide forgiveness through grace" (*Bapt. Chr.* 3 [PG 49.367]).[36] That John's baptism did not bestow the Holy Spirit was a standard part of the contrast Christians made between it and their baptism, but the explanation that "it was not able properly to forgive" is somewhat puzzling in view of Mark 1:4. Presumably Chrysostom meant either that John's baptism pointed toward the real forgiveness offered by Christ or that it gave a forgiveness premised on the works of repentance

---

34. Cf. Chrysostom, *Homilies on Romans* 19 on Rom. 11:27, where, commenting on Paul's conflation of Isa. 59:20 and Jer. 31:31, 34, he says that forgiveness of sins was promised to the Jews but had not yet happened, "nor have they ever enjoyed the remission of sins by baptism" (*Nicene and Post-Nicene Fathers*, First Series, Vol. 11, p. 493).

35. *Homilies on Matthew* 12 (PG 57.206A).

36. *Homilies on John* 17.1-2 explains that the One able to wash away sins did not come to John to confess sins; Jesus' baptism is to cleanse all and give the power of the Comforter, but John's was to manifest Jesus to Israel and could not give the Holy Spirit. For the comparison of John's baptism with the baptism given by Christ, see *Homilies on Matthew* 10.2; 11.6; 12.1-2.

and not on grace. The preacher interpreted the baptism with the Holy Spirit and fire that John said the Messiah would administer (Mark 1:8 and parallels) as referring to Acts 2:3-4.

Holy Spirit and Baptism

Previously cited passages have noted the activity of the Holy Spirit in baptism.[37] The Spirit is the real power in the water (*Bapt. Instr.* 11.12) and sanctifies the water:

> When you see the bath of water and the hand of the priest touching your head, you may not think that this is merely water, nor that only the hand of the bishop lies upon your head. For it is not a man who does what is done, but it is the grace of the Spirit which sanctifies the nature of the water and touches your head together with the hand of the priest. (2.10)

Moreover, the Holy Spirit descends on the person at baptism.[38] When the old self is buried in the water and the new self is raised, "It is at this moment that, through the words and the hand of the priest, the Holy Spirit descends upon you" (2.25). The threefold immersion in the triple divine name prepares one "to receive the descent of the Spirit" (2.26). Those who had recently "put on Christ" also "received the descent of the Spirit" (8.25). Those who have Christ dwelling in their souls have with him also the "Father and the manifestation of the Holy Spirit" (4.17). Thus, although Chrysostom agreed with earlier practice in Syria of prebaptismal anointing, he differed in attributing the coming of the Holy Spirit not to an anointing but to the water bath itself.

Seal and Circumcision

Accordingly, the language of the seal applies to baptism, or what is done in baptism.[39] "For the catechumen is a sheep without a seal" (10.16). And the possession of the Spirit is the true circumcision. One of the names Chrysostom gives to baptism is circumcision, with quotation of Colossians 2:11 (9.12). His commentary on that pas-

---

37. For the work of the Holy Spirit in baptism see also *Homilies on John* 26.1, where the birth of baptism is by "the grace of the Spirit," and *Homilies on Acts* 1.5, where it is stated that the essential part of baptism is the Spirit, "through whom water has its operation." This passage explains that in the case of the apostles the water and the Spirit were separated — they received water baptism from John and Spirit baptism later on Pentecost, but "in our case both take place under one act, but then they were divided." *Homilies on Acts* 24 says that as Cornelius in Acts 10 received the most essential part (the Holy Spirit), so Peter commanded that he receive the water also.

38. *Homilies on Matthew* 12.3 on Matt 3:16 says that the Spirit came on Jesus at his baptism to point out the Son of God to those present and to John and also to teach "you that at your baptism the Spirit comes."

39. In *Homilies on Hebrews* 13.9, "counted worthy of the seal," the seal is baptism; it is also applied to the mark of the Spirit received in baptism (see below). The seal was a mark of protection and a sign of belonging to Christ — de Roten, *Baptême et mystagogie*, pp. 273-276.

sage is more precise, identifying the circumcision not with baptism per se but with what the Spirit does in baptism:

> No longer, says St. Paul, is circumcision accomplished by the knife, but in Christ himself, for the hand does not perform the circumcision as in the old law, but the Spirit circumcises not a part but the whole person. There was a body there, and there is a body here; but that body was circumcised in the flesh, this body in the Spirit.... When and where? In baptism.[40]

In one of his homilies on 2 Corinthians Chrysostom gives a series of contrasts of the Old Testament with the New, including the simple counterpart, "Instead of circumcision [there is] baptism."[41] Earlier in these homilies, however, he had given more nuance to the relationship. Explaining 2 Corinthians 1:21-22, he said: "And what is 'anointed' and 'sealed'? The giving of the Spirit by whom he did both these things." The anointing with the Spirit made Christians prophets, priests, and kings (the functionaries who received anointing in the Old Testament). "You are made kings, prophets, and priests in the bath [λουτρῷ]" (*Homilies on 2 Corinthians* 3.7). The giving of the Spirit and the anointing as spiritual priests and kings that characterized earlier Syriac sources are assigned by Chrysostom to baptism.[42] As a seal is put on a soldier, the Spirit is the seal put on the faithful. "The Jews had circumcision for a seal, but we the earnest of the Spirit."[43] The Christian circumcision for Chrysostom, then, is not properly baptism, but what takes place in baptism; the seal is either the Spirit himself or the spiritual circumcision he imparts in connection with baptism.

Enlightenment

Another name that Chrysostom acknowledges for baptism is "enlightenment," quoting Hebrews 10:32 and 6:4-6 (*Bapt. Instr.* 9.12).[44] He explains to those about to be

---

40. *Homilies on Colossians* 6.2 on Col. 2:11 (PG 62.340A); translation (slightly modified) by Harkins, *St. John Chrysostom: Baptismal Instructions*, p. 292, n. 35.

41. *Homilies on 2 Corinthians* 11.4 on 2 Cor. 5:18 (PG 61.476). The passage quoted in chap. 33 on infant baptism (*Homilies on Genesis* 40.4) similarly identified "our circumcision" with "the grace of baptism," but the continuation of the passage is more precise: "They [Jews] received the sign of circumcision.... We receive the circumcision through baptism once" (PG 53.374B). *Homilies on Genesis* 39.5 — as circumcision separated Jews from Gentiles, circumcision by (or through) baptism distinguished believers and nonbelievers; *Homilies on 1 Corinthians* 29.2.

42. Gabriele Winkler, "The Original Meaning of the Prebaptismal Anointing and Its Implications," in Maxwell E. Johnson, ed., *Living Water, Sealing Spirit: Readings on Christian Initiation* (Collegeville: Liturgical, 1995), pp. 58-81 (73).

43. *Homilies on 2 Corinthans* 3.5, 7 on 2 Cor. 1:21-22 (PG 61.411, 417, 418).

44. Baptism is simply called "illumination" in *Homilies on Romans* 10 on Rom. 6:3-4; the two words are equivalent in *Homilies on Acts* 20 on Acts 9:10-12 (PG 60.131D-132A); *Homilies on Hebrews* 13.10 contrasts the "enlightened and catechumens." See de Roten, *Baptême et mystagogie*, p. 149, n. 93, for other references where baptism is called illumination, and p. 150 for the baptized called "the en-

baptized that they will be called "newly illumined" because their "light is always new" (12.10), supported by quotation of John 1:5. The soul is "illumined and becomes brighter from the grace it has received from the Spirit" (12.10).

> Whenever grace comes and drives out the darkness from our mind, we learn the exact nature of things; what frightened us before, now becomes contemptible in our eyes. We no longer are afraid of death after we have learned carefully from this holy initiation that death is not death but a sleep and repose which lasts but for a time. (12.12)

Enlightenment is here related both to the spiritual effects of the working of the Holy Spirit and to learning the instruction that accompanied baptism.

Clothing with Christ

As indicated by his treatment of the baptismal robe (chap. 33), quite meaningful for Chrysostom was the imagery of baptism as putting on Christ. Inspired by Galatians 3:27 and Colossians 3:9-10, Chrysostom used the imagery of clothing for union with Christ and putting on a new person.

> [You] have put off the burden of your sins and put on the shining robe — and what do I mean by the shining robe? — do you, who have put on Christ himself and have received the Master of all things to dwell within you, show forth a conduct worthy of him who dwells within you? (*Bapt. Instr.* 5.18)[45]

Or again,

> We put off the old garment, which has been made filthy with the abundance of our sins; we put on the new one, which is free from every stain. What am I saying? We put on Christ himself. [Gal. 3:27 quoted.] (2.11)

The person who has identified with Christ is a "new creature," because of putting on a "new and shining cloak, this royal robe," so that "a new creation has truly taken place," with reference made to 2 Corinthians 5:17 (4.12, 14). Chrysostom exhorts those "who have recently put on Christ":

> Each day look to the luster of your garment, that it may never receive any spot or wrinkle, either by untimely words, or idle listening, or by evil thoughts, or by eyes which rush foolishly and without reason to see whatever goes on. (8.25)

---

lightened." The baptistery is called φωτιστήριον ("place of enlightenment") in *Post reditum* 2 (PG 52.444B).

45. The neophytes "have put on Christ himself, wherever they go they are like angels on earth, rivaling the brilliance of the rays of the sun" (2.27; cf. 4.4 on the "luster of the garment" and 8.25, quoted below).

With reference to Galatians 3:27 Chrysostom says that the garment of salvation is not of grace alone, but requires faith and after faith, virtue (*Exposition in Psalms* 44:10 [PG 55.190D]).

Even as baptism put one into Christ, so it put one into the church. Neophytes were now "citizens of the church" (3.5). Chrysostom exhorts, "Avoid all these wicked snares of the devil and hold nothing in greater honor than your entrance into the church" (1.46).

Moral Consequences and Faithfulness

The predominant concern of the *Baptismal Instructions* is with the consequences from baptism for one's conduct.[46] Chrysostom uses all aspects of his interpretation of baptism, especially its forgiving and renewing qualities, as bases for exhortations to new converts to abstain from sin. "The bath takes away the sins, but you must correct the habit" (*Bapt. Instr.* 12.24). "Let those of us who received this gift [God's grace] in the past show a far-reaching change in our lives" (5.24).

A special concern expressed by Chrysostom was the swearing of oaths (1.42; 9.30-47; 10.1-4, 18-30). Even true oaths were to be avoided (9.39). Superstitious and magical practices from the pagan past were also common among the converts (1.39-40, 42; 11.25; 12.53-61). The people frequented the chariot races at the hippodrome instead of attending church (1.43; 6.1; cf. 6.14 on the racecourse and spectacles as "worldly amusements"). "Drunkenness is a self-chosen demon" ("the demon of drink" — 5.9), but there is also a drunkenness of the passions that does not come from wine (5.4-8). He asks, "What is more dishonorable than dancing" (10.21) and proceeds to discuss it (10.22-23).

Chrysostom laid out a daily program for new Christians that included gathering at church at dawn for prayer and confession, being watchful of one's conduct in daily work, at evening asking for pardon, spending the night soberly, and on days dedicated to the martyrs[47] to remember their instruction (8.16-18). The Christian must "hold spiritual things of greater importance than all the goods of this life" (8.16), place the care of the soul first (8.19-25), and use leisure time for what is spiritual (8.20). Prayer and almsgiving are given a prominent place as means of keeping one's baptism pure (7.24-27; cf. 12.6-7).[48] Fasting is good, but true fasting is to abstain from sin (5.1-3).

The baptized were given the name "faithful," and they were expected to live up

---

46. Among the principal passages concerning the life expected of the neophyte are the following: 4.17-33; 5.4-14; 6.14-20; 9.30-47; 12.15-24, 53-61.

47. *Bapt. Instr.* 7 discusses the martyrs as examples of seeking heavenly goods and being dead to the world but does not make the theological connection between martyrdom and baptism (but see 10.8-10 discussed above on the relation of baptism to the cross and the blood of Jesus).

48. Cornelius in Acts 10 is discussed as an example of prayers and almsgiving and not with regard to his baptism. Note the definition of prayer as "nothing more than conversation with God" (7.25).

to this quality of faithfulness (12.4-9). The very word "faithful" gives an exhortation to virtue (12.6). As God has entrusted believers with many blessings, so believers entrust to God "almsgiving, prayers, temperance, and every other virtue" (12.6). There is an indissoluble connection between grace, faith, and baptism (*Exposition in Psalms* 44:10).

Faithfulness at an earlier time might have resulted in martyrdom, and Chrysostom makes the (by his time) traditional identification of martyrdom with baptism. He makes the identification on the basis of the similar benefits that are involved:

> Do not be surprised if I call martyrdom a baptism. For here also [in martyrdom as in baptism] the Spirit hovers above with much fullness, and there is a taking away of sins and a certain wonderful and marvelous cleansing of the soul. Even as those who are baptized in water, so those who bear witness as martyrs are washed in their own blood.[49]

The distinctive benefits of baptism (and martyrdom) are stated in terms of the activity of the Holy Spirit and the forgiveness of sins.

---

49. *Homily on the Martyr St. Lucius* 2 (PG 50.522D). Since Tertullian martyrdom was seen as a baptism. After martyrdom was a thing of the past, the language of martyrdom could be applied to the initiation of every Christian — Gordon Jeanes, "Baptism Portrayed as Martyrdom in the Early Church," *Studia liturgica* 23 (1993): 158-176 (p. 174).

35. Miscellaneous Sources: Church Orders and "Eunomian" Baptism

Apostolic Constitutions

The compiler/editor of the *Apostolic Constitutions* was active in the last quarter of the fourth century, probably in western Syria, although Asia Minor or Constantinople are also suggested. His doctrinal affiliation is not completely clear but a moderate Arian or even Neo-Arian position seems likely; however, these sentiments do not affect the rites themselves.

The first six books of the *Apostolic Constitutions* are based on the *Didascalia*, the seventh book on the *Didache*, and the eighth book on the *Apostolic Tradition* and other materials; at the end are appended the *Apostolic Canons*.[1] The compiler/author has so rewritten his sources as to give his own presentation and interpretation; nevertheless, inconsistencies (or apparent inconsistencies) remain that are likely due to the incorporation of different sources. There are two principal accounts of the ritual of baptism — *Apostolic Constitutions* 7.1-28, a rewriting of the *Didache*, and 7.39-45, an elaboration of the *Apostolic Tradition*. Because of the way the sources are used, there is no systematic treatment of the ceremony and doctrine of baptism that the author knew or was advocating. From the varied and frequent references it is possible to reconstruct the author's views on baptism. There is little indication, however, of the sequence of events in the initiation procedures — except for the central acts of anointing with oil, immersing, and anointing with ointment — so I have arranged the items culled from the different parts of the work according to the sequence attested in other sources.[2] The pre-

---

1. Greek text and French translation in Marcel Metzger, *Les constitutions apostoliques*, 3 vols., Sources chrétiennes 320, 329, 336 (Paris: Cerf, 1985-1986).

2. Baby Varghese, *Les onctions baptismales dans la tradition syrienne*, Corpus scriptorum christianorum orientalium 512 (Louvain: Peeters, 1089), pp. 105-112. With reference to 7.39-45, the position has been taken that the redactor did not present an actual rite but his idea of an ideal rite — E. C. Ratchliff, "The Old Syrian Baptismal Tradition and Its Resettlement under the Influence of Jerusalem in the Fourth Century," in G. J. Cuming, ed., *Studies in Church History*, Vol. 2 (London, 1965), pp. 19-37.

scriptions may promote an ideal rite more than a living rite, but there is close similarity to the baptismal rite of Jerusalem as found in the *Lectures on the Mysteries* of Cyril of Jerusalem (chap. 29).

Baptismal Ceremony

There was an examination of the candidates for baptism to determine their worthiness. The compiler elaborates on the instructions in regard to different circumstances in life and restrictions on occupations found in *Apostolic Tradition* 15–16 with some modifications to fit the late fourth century (8.32).[3]

The necessity of repentance is underscored from the examples of Matthew, Zacchaeus, and the soldiers and tax collectors addressed by John the Baptist in the Gospels. Repentance for postbaptismal sins is compared to repentance before baptism:

> Life is not refused to the heathen, if they repent and reject their unbelief. . . . If one [who has sinned] repents, when they want to repent and to turn from their error, we receive into the church, even as we receive the heathen, to hear the word but not to share in communion until they receive the seal [baptism] and are made complete. (2.39.6)

Penitents, like catechumens, departed from the services after the reading of the Law, the Prophets, and the Gospel and before common prayer until they showed the fruit of repentance (2.39.6). The catechumens preparing for baptism must "purify the heart of all perversity of mind and all spot and wrinkle before participating in the mysteries" (7.40.1).

The following directions are given: "Receive those who repent, 'for this is the will of God in Christ' [1 Thess. 5:18]. After instructing the catechumens in the basic principles, baptize them" (6.18.1). The first sentence may refer to penitents coming for baptism. If it refers to receiving penitents who sinned after baptism, then the passage would have two different groups in mind. In either case, the second sentence underscores the necessity for instruction prior to baptism. The catechumens were a recognized part of the church community, but could not participate in the common prayer and eucharist, which were for the faithful (2.57.14; 8.6.14).[4]

One remained in the status of a catechumen for three years but might be admitted to baptism sooner if the manner of life justified it (8.32.16). During this period instruction in Christianity was given. The teacher might be a layman, if he was experienced in the word and serious in manner of life (8.32.17). This teacher is presumably the person described as "the one who lays hand on" the catechumen in blessing

---

3. Alan Kreider, "Military Service in the Church Orders," *Journal of Religious Ethics* 31 (2003): 415-442 (428-430), discusses the changes in instructions to soldiers.

4. A prayer for catechumens in 8.6 is almost identical to one in John Chrysostom, *Homilies on 2 Corinthians* 2.5-8.

during this period (7.39.4). The *Apostolic Constitutions* provides a summary of the instruction to be given before baptism. The material covered doctrinal points, a survey of biblical history, and the moral life pleasing to God (7.39).[5]

Before the baptism the candidates were to fast (7.22.4). It is explained that the Lord fasted after his baptism, because he had no need of cleansing or fasting; but the person being initiated ought to fast beforehand and not afterward, since it would not be proper for the one who experienced burial and resurrection with Christ to appear downcast.

The catechumen awaiting baptism was taught about the renunciation (ἀποταγή) of the devil and adherence (συνταγή) to Christ (7.40.1). The one being baptized made a more expanded renunciation than in most sources with these words: "I renounce Satan, his works, his pomps, his services, his angels, his inventions, and all things under him" (7.41.2). Elsewhere it is said that the one being baptized was to be free from all iniquity, "one who has renounced Satan, all his demons, and his deceits" (3.18.1).

The adherence to Christ begins, "I associate myself with Christ," and continues, "I believe and am baptized." It is expanded into a full creedal statement (drawn from the creed of Nicaea with elements from Antioch and Jerusalem), elaborating on the nature of the only true God, on the nature and incarnate and eschatological history of Christ, and on the ministry of the Holy Spirit to all those who believe in the church, the resurrection, the forgiveness of sins, the kingdom of heaven, and life in the world to come (7.41).

The oil, the water, and the ointment used in the ceremony were blessed. The oil "is blessed by the priest for the remission of sins and preparation for baptism" (7.42.2). He calls upon God to "sanctify the oil in the name of the Lord Jesus, to give it spiritual grace, effective power, forgiveness of sins, and preparation for the confession of baptism" so that the one being anointed might "become worthy of initiation" (7.42.3).

The prayer over the water begins with an extended blessing and glory to God for what he has done in Christ for human salvation. The priest then prays:

> Look down from heaven and sanctify this water; give grace and power. May the one being baptized according to the command of your Christ be crucified, die, be buried, and be raised with him to the adoption which is in him, to be dead to sin and alive to righteousness. (7.43.5)[6]

A shorter combined blessing for water and oil is found elsewhere (8.29), where it is pronounced by the bishop, if he is present; if not, by a presbyter. Since this water and oil were offered by a man or woman and since the prayer is followed by prayers for

---

5. Everett Ferguson, "Irenaeus' *Proof of the Apostolic Preaching* and Early Catechetical Instruction," *Studia patristica* 18.3 (1989): 119-140 (121-123), for the pattern of instruction based on biblical history.

6. A prayer that includes praise to God for creation, in apparent allusion to Gen. 1:6-7, says that God put a living spirit in the waters (7.34.1).

firstfruits, tithes, and other oblations (8.30-31), it seems that they were not for the baptismal service.

At some point, apparently after the renunciation and adherence, the candidates were taught to say the Lord's Prayer, "saying as from the common congregation of the faithful" (3.18.1). A prayer of blessing by the bishop on those being baptized is recorded in 8.8(7).4-5.

There appear to be three prebaptismal anointings with "holy oil": of the forehead by a deacon, of the whole body by a deacon (of males) or a deaconess (of females), and of the head by the bishop.[7] For the anointing of the whole body, in the case of women, a deacon anointed the forehead and a deaconess (ἡ διάκονος) completed the anointing, "for there is no need for women to be seen by men" (3.16[15].2). The anointing of the head of men and women with "holy oil" just before the baptism was done by the bishop, "for a type of the spiritual baptism" (3.16[15].4). I take this phrase to mean the anointing with oil was a type of the Spirit's baptizing the person. This anointing is called a laying on of hand by the bishop (3.16[15].3). The Old Testament precedent was the anointing of priests and kings, not because the baptized are appointed priests but as sharing in the anointing of Christ they become a royal priesthood (1 Pet. 2:9).[8]

Either the bishop or a presbyter did the baptizing. "Speaking the holy invocation over them and pronouncing the name of Father, Son, and Holy Spirit, you will dip [βαπτίσεις] them in the water" (3.16.4).[9] The appended *Apostolic Canons* give more information. A bishop or presbyter was not to rebaptize someone who had true baptism or fail to baptize someone who was polluted by the ungodly (i.e. someone regarded by the author as heretical) — canon 47. Canon 49 may be directed against Nicenes (baptism into the Father, the Son, and the Holy Spirit is not baptism into "three beings without beginning") and Monarchians (nor is it baptism "into three Sons or into three Comforters"). These formulations would not represent anyone's actual liturgical practice but is the author's interpretation of teaching he rejected.

Canon 50 then specifies the necessity of three immersions:

> If any bishop or presbyter does not perform three immersions [βαπτίσματα] of the one initiation [μυήσεως], but one immersion [βάπτισμα] that is given into the death of the Lord, let him be deprived. For the Lord did not say, "Immerse [βαπτίσατε] into my death," but "Go and make disciples of all the nations, immersing [βαπτίζοντες] them into the name of the Father and the Son and the Holy Spirit."

---

7. Varghese, *Les onctions baptismales*, pp. 105-106. The first, however, may not be a separate act but only a token beginning of the full body anointment performed by a deaconess on women.

8. Other references to prebaptismal anointing are 7.22, commented on below in connection with the postbaptismal anointing, and 7.41-42, the prayer of consecration of the oil quoted above.

9. Cf. 7.22.1, where the three are identified as "the Father who sent, the Christ who came, and the Paraclete who testified," and a similar characterization in 3.17.2, 4; cf. also 7.44.1.

Apparently there were some (see below) who used a single immersion into the death of Christ, contrary to the usual custom of the church in the later fourth century. The persons behind the *Apostolic Canons* took Matthew 28:19 as authorizing a triple immersion.

The *Apostolic Constitutions* opposed the practice of women administering baptism.

> Concerning women baptizing, we make known to you that there is no small danger to women who undertake this. Therefore, we counsel against this, for it is dangerous, or rather unlawful and impious. (3.9.1)

We may safely assume that what someone forbids, someone else is doing. That the prohibition was controversial is indicated by the compiler proceeding to argue extensively his reasons: Man is head of woman (1 Cor. 11:3); he is appointed to the priesthood; it is not right to set aside the order of creation; woman was taken from the side of man; man will rule over her (Gen. 3:16); if a woman was not permitted to teach, neither should she perform the office of a priest (as was the practice in Gentile religion); if women were to baptize, the Lord would have been baptized by his mother and not by John; and the Lord gave no authorization for women to baptize (something not fitting according to nature). Although the author's position on this practice is given extended justification, he states more briefly the prohibition of a layman performing any priestly function (sacrifice, baptism, laying on of hands, blessing — 3.10) and the prohibition of the lesser clergy baptizing (something to be done only by bishops or presbyters assisted by deacons — 3.11.1).

The document warns against the delay of baptism. The author quotes some as saying, "When I am dying, I will be baptized so that I will not sin and defile my baptism." He responds that such a person is ignorant of God and forgetful of his own nature, "for you do not know what the next day will bring forth" (6.15.6).

The author also expressly enjoins the baptism of infants, something not found in the previous church order literature or earlier authors: "Baptize [βαπτίζετε] your infants, and 'bring them up in the instruction and admonition of God' [Eph. 6:4]." He cites Matthew 19:14 in support of his command (6.15.7).

A male deacon received the man and a female deacon the woman on their leaving the water, "so that the conferring of this inviolable seal [baptism?] might be done with fitting propriety" (3.16.4). The bishop then anointed with ointment (*myron*, μύρῳ) those who had been immersed (βαπτισθέντας).[10] The prayer for the ointment

---

10. Varghese, *Les onctions baptismales*, p. 106, affirms this as the first appearance in the Syrian tradition of the postbaptismal unction with *myron*, but he notes that little importance was given to it in comparison to the prebaptismal anointing that was compared to the anointing of kings and priests. A. H. B. Logan, "Post-Baptismal Chrismation in Syria: The Evidence of Ignatius, the *Didache* and the *Apostolic Constitutions*," *Journal of Theological Studies*, n.s. 49 (1998): 92-108, argues, in part on the basis of *Apostolic Constitutions* 7.27, that the compiler discovered the postbaptismal rite in the *Didache*'s ointment prayer and Ignatius, *Ephesians* 17.1, and considered it apostolic; and so instead of introduc-

is given in connection with its actual application, with the petition that "the sweet odor of Christ might remain [with the baptized person], who having died with Christ may rise and live with him" (7.44.2).

The prebaptismal anointing with oil, the baptism in water, and the postbaptismal application of *myron* involved a laying of hands (χειροθεσία) on the initiates, an act which was intimately connected with prayer. Invocation (ἐπίκλησις) to God in regard to the elements applied to the initiates gave efficacy to the laying on of hands in each case.[11]

> Let [the priest] say these and like things, for the power of the laying on of hands in each case is this [prayer]. Without the invocation by the pious priest upon each one of these [elements], the person baptized only goes down into the water like the Jews, and only puts away the filth of the body, not the filth of the soul. (7.44.3)

The invocation of the divine power and not the elements themselves gave to them their effectiveness. There was thus a laying on of hands associated with the immersion, as the art shows (chap. 7), as well as in the pre- and postbaptismal anointings.[12] The bishop's laying on of hands associated with the application of the ointment is perhaps the laying on of hands interpreted as imparting the Holy Spirit in 2.32.3, quoted below, but in view of our next quotation (7.22.3) it could be any of these three impositions of hands.[13]

Earlier, in a passage developing *Didache* 7 (but without its permission of pouring as a substitute for immersion), the author had given a summary of the three central acts of the initiation and given priority to the water baptism as the principal ceremony, by itself alone sufficient.

> You will anoint first with holy oil, then you will baptize [βαπτίσεις] in water, and finally you shall seal [σφραγίσεις] with ointment, so that the anointing [χρῖσμα]

---

ing it as a novelty from the outside rediscovered the practice of some groups in Syria in the second century that had not spread or was replaced by the prebaptismal anointing. Joseph G. Mueller, "Post-Baptismal Chrismation in Second-Century Syria: A Reconsideration of the Evidence," *Journal of Theological Studies*, n.s. 57 (2006): 76-93, finds Logan's evidence insufficient.

11. D. Van den Eynde, "Baptême et confirmation d'après les Constitutions apostoliques, VII, 44, 3," *Recherches de science religieuse* 27 (1937): 196-212, whose translation and argument I follow; also Paul Galtier, "Imposition des mains et bénédictions au baptême," *Recherches de sciences religieuse* 27(1937): 464-466. Other passages where the ceremonies of initiation are the oil, the water, and the myron are 3.16.2-4; 3.17.1; and 7.22.2-3.

12. The imposition of the hand at the immersion is likely referred to in 2.32.3 (below) and 2.41.2; other references in patristic literature are in Van den Eynde, "Baptême et confirmation," pp. 209-210.

13. The prebaptismal oil is identified with the Holy Spirit in 3.17 and 7.22.3, and this leads Varghese, *Les onctions baptismales*, p. 111, to deny that the postbaptismal myron was put in relation to the gift of the Holy Spirit. The compiler continues the Syrian association of the gift of the Holy Spirit with the prebaptismal oil but includes a postbaptismal anointing under the influence of Jerusalem, according to E. C. Ratcliff, "The Old Syrian Baptismal Tradition and Its Resettlement under the Influence of Jerusalem in the Fourth Century," in G. J. Cuming, ed., *Studies in Church History* 2 (London: Nelson, 1965), pp. 19-37 (33-35).

may be a participation in the Holy Spirit, the water a symbol of death, and the ointment a seal of the covenants. If there is neither oil nor ointment, the water is sufficient for the anointing, the seal, and the confession of the one who died [Christ] or is indeed now dying together with [the baptizand]. (7.22.2-3).

The seal here is not the baptism itself (as it was in the *Didascalia* 16) but the postbaptismal anointing, a seal of the contract with Christ (a function given by Theodore to the prebaptismal anointing). An alternative translation of the last clause would interpret the words as applying to the baptizand: "the confession by the one who is dead or is dying together [with Christ.]"[14]

After the postbaptismal anointing, the baptizand stood and facing the east prayed "the prayer which the Lord taught us" (7.45[44].1-2) and then said another prayer (7.45.3).[15]

The unbaptized were not admitted to the eucharist (2.39.6; 2.57.14).

Doctrine of Baptism

Several general statements explain the meaning of the baptismal ceremony. A passage that characterizes the Father, Son, and Holy Spirit gives this further interpretation:

> Baptism then is given into the death of Jesus. The water is in the place of the burial, the oil in the place of the Holy Spirit, the seal in the place of the cross, the ointment is the confirmation of the confession. . . . The descent [into the water] is dying together [with Christ]; the ascent is rising together [with him]. (3.17)

The summary of the teaching given to catechumens says that the teacher thanks God for sending Christ:

> that he might save humanity, wiping away their transgressions, forgive their ungodliness and sins, "cleanse from every defilement of flesh and spirit" [2 Cor. 7:1], sanctify humanity according to the good pleasure of his kindness, give understanding of his will, "enlighten the eyes of the heart" [Eph. 1:18], . . . , that they might hate every way of wickedness and walk in the way of truth, be counted worthy of "the bath of regeneration" [Tit. 3:5] "to the adoption in Christ" [Eph. 1:5], "being planted together in the likeness of the death of Christ" [Rom. 6:5] in hope of sharing in his glory, may be dead to sin and alive to God. . . . (7.39)[16]

---

14. This is the understanding of the translation in the *Ante-Nicene Fathers* (repr. Peabody: Hendrickson, 1994), Vol. 7, p. 469. The inclusion of the confession along with the anointing oil and the seal of the ointment may be an indication that the compiler here includes an acceptance of deathbed baptism as effective without the subject being able to verbalize the confession of faith — see chap. 39.

15. The *Apostolic Constitutions* is unusual in having the neophyte recite the Lord's Prayer after baptism, but in John Chrysostom, *Homilies on Colossians* 6 (PG 62.342), preached in Constantinople, reference is made to this practice.

16. For the latter items cf. the prayer of sanctification of the water in 7.43.5 quoted above.

The bishop's prayer for those to be baptized addresses God as the "one who appointed spiritual regeneration in Christ" and petitions him:

> Bless and sanctify them and prepare them to be worthy of your spiritual gift and your true adoption, your spiritual mysteries, to be gathered together with those saved through Christ our Savior. (8.8.5)

The scriptural basis for baptism was Christ's command in Matthew 28:19 (7.22.1; 7.40.3). Other basic texts were John 3:5 and Mark 16:16. On the basis of these two texts the compiler says, "The person who out of contempt does not want to be baptized will be condemned as an unbeliever and will be reproached as ungrateful and senseless" (6.15.5). The Old Testament text cited as foretelling baptism was Isaiah 1:16 (8.8.5).

Jesus' baptism was also a basis of Christian baptism. He was baptized not because he needed cleansing but in order "to testify to the truth to John and to furnish us an example" (7.22.5).[17]

Although some, as indicated above, made baptism into the death of Jesus their central conception, the editor of the *Apostolic Constitutions* himself considered this important in the understanding of baptism. As it was for Chrysostom, this idea served for moral exhortation:

> Let it be known to you, beloved, that "those who have been baptized into the death of the Lord Jesus" [Rom. 6:3] ought no longer to sin. For, even as those who have died are incapable of sin, so those who died with Christ do not practice sin. (2.7.1)

Those who sin after baptism are warned that if they do not cease they shall be condemned to Gehenna (2.7.2). The baptism into Christ's death also involved rising with him (7.22.6; 7.43.5).

A favorite concept with the compiler was regeneration. Those to be baptized were to be deemed worthy of the "bath of regeneration" (Titus 3:5 — 7.39.4).[18] A related phrase is "one washed [λουσάμενον] with the bath of life [τὸ τῆς ζωῆς λουτρόν]" (2.7.2). The "baptism of regeneration" (τὸ βάπτισμα τῆς παλιγγενεσίας) is a type of the cross (7.43.3). *Palingenesia* (Παλιγγενεσία) is primarily an eschatological word for the compiler.[19]

The compiler also uses the *anagennesis* family of words. The bishop is described as a father to his people after God, "having begotten you again [ἀναγεννήσας] to adoption 'through water and the Spirit' [John 3:5]" (2.26.4).[20] Those being baptized "were appointed for spiritual regeneration [ἀναγέννησιν] through Christ" (8.8.5).

These passages about the bishop as figuratively the begetter of spiritual children

---

17. Cf. 7.36.2, "he manifested himself in his baptism."
18. The phrase also in 8.6.6 in a prayer for catechumens.
19. 7.33.3; 7.34.8; 8.12.20; cf. 5.7.14 of the Phoenix bird.
20. Cf. 2.33.3, "your spiritual parents . . . who begat you again through water."

in baptism remind the reader of the centrality of the bishop in the community, which included the initiation process and its blessings.

> [Through the bishop] the Lord gave the Holy Spirit among you by the laying on of hands. Through him you learned the sacred doctrines, have known God, have come to believe in Christ, have been known by God. Through him you were sealed with "the oil of gladness" [Ps. 45:7] and the ointment of understanding. Through him you were declared "sons of light" [John 12:36], and through him the Lord at your illumination gave testimony to you by the laying on of the bishop's hand. (2.32.3)[21]

The laying on of hands mentioned first could be the pre- or the post-baptismal anointing. The second mention may refer to the same, but the association with illumination likely indicates the imposition of hand at the immersions.

The regeneration in baptism is combined with the analogy of adoption (2.26.4; 7.39.4; 8.8.5 — quoted above). The adoption is eschatological in 7.43.5; 8.9(8).5; and 5.1.2 (of martyrs) and is related to praying the Lord's Prayer three times daily (7.24.2).

The language of illumination is preserved in reference to baptism. The baptismal ceremony is called "illumination [φωτισμός]" (2.32.3) or "being illuminated [φωτίζεσθαι]" (3.16[15].2). Those undergoing the preparation for baptism are "the ones being illuminated [οἱ φωτιζόμενοι]" (8.8[7].2, 6; in 8.35.2 distinguished from catechumens). The bishop prayed that they might be enlightened (or illuminated) in their hearts (7.39.4 quoted above).[22] Illumination or enlightenment is primarily associated with instruction and learning (2.5.7; cf. "illuminated us with the light of knowledge" in 8.37.6). Through the Holy Spirit "every one of the faithful received the illumination of the glory of the gospel [2 Cor. 4:4]" (5.1.2). Apart from these contexts this family of words is used most often for the illumination provided by the cloud in the exodus from Egypt (6.3; 6.20.6; 8.12.26).

The language of a seal (σφραγίς), as shown by the passages already quoted and others, is used in various ways: of baptism itself (2.14.8; 2.39.6), of the post-baptismal anointing with ointment (7.22.2), and of both the prebaptismal anointing with oil and the postbaptismal ointment (2.32.3). Some passages are ambiguous: 3.16.4 appears to be a reference to baptism, but immediately after (3.17.1) the seal stands for the cross — apparently distinct from the water, the oil, and the ointment — and so possibly a reference to the bishop making the sign of the cross with his hand on the forehead. Similarly, in 7.22.3 the seal may be the ointment of the preceding passage or may be a distinct act, such as making the sign of the cross.

The *Apostolic Constitutions* gives more indirect, almost perfunctory, attention to

---

21. Cf. 2.33.2 for the bishop regenerating by water, filling with the Holy Spirit, nourishing by teaching, and imparting the body and blood of the eucharist.

22. Cf. the deacon's prayer for catechumens in 8.6.5, "Illumine them and give them understanding, instruct them in the knowledge of God."

two staples of the earlier teaching about the benefits of baptism: the forgiveness of sins (2.33.2; 6.15.3 [those not baptized do not receive remission of sins]; 7.41.8 [quoting the creed]; 7.43.2 [part of the purpose of Christ's coming]) and the gift of the Holy Spirit (2.33.2; 2.32.3 [by the laying on of the bishop's hand — cf. 2.41.2 and 5.7.3 of the apostles]; 3.17.1 and 4 and 7.22.2 [by anointing]. The forgiveness of sins is associated with the anointing with oil in preparation for baptism in 7.42.2-3 and with taking the eucharist in 8.12.39 and 8.14.2. "Every one who has been baptized according to the truth is separated from the diabolical spirit and is placed within the Holy Spirit; and the Holy Spirit remains with the one who does good" (6.27.5). References to the Holy Spirit occur most often in the Trinitarian baptismal formula and even more frequently in prayers (especially in book 8).

The *Apostolic Constitutions* rejects a second baptism but gives an even stronger rejection to baptism by heretics.

> Be satisfied with one baptism only, which is given into the death of the Lord, not the baptism by despicable heretics but that given by blameless priests "into the name of the Father and the Son, and the Holy Spirit." Let not that which comes from the ungodly be acceptable to you, and let not that which comes from holy persons be rejected in its validity by a second [baptism]. For as there is one God, one Christ, one Paraclete, and one death of the Lord in the body, so let there be given one baptism into him. Those who receive what is polluted from the ungodly will become partners in their opinions. . . . Those who were baptized by them are not initiated, but remain polluted, not receiving the forgiveness of sins but the bond of impiety. Rather, do not those who attempt to baptize a second time those already initiated crucify the Lord again? (6.15.1-4)

The phrase about baptism "into the death of the Lord" recalls the polemic of *Apostolic Canons* 50 against a single immersion and makes the reader wonder, therefore, if this passage was originally directed against more than one immersion and not against the second conferral of baptism. If not such a thorough rewriting occurred as this possibility suggests, there may have been the addition either of "into the death of the Lord" or of the Trinitarian formula, by one side or the other.

For those who sinned after baptism, repentance was the essential element in their return to the church (2.7.2; 2.12.1; 2.16; 2.38; 2.41). Those seeking reconciliation to the church are those "who are repenting" (2.12.1; 2.57.14) or those who are "in repentance" (8.9.11).

The Nicaeno-Constantinopolitan Creed

The creed approved at the ecumenical council of Constantinople in 381 (and now generally called the "Nicene" Creed) included in its last article, "We acknowledge one baptism for remission of sins." This statement summarizes the universal understanding of the early church about the purpose of baptism as being directed "unto the forgiveness of sins." The "one baptism" was certainly not a reference to a single as opposed to a triple immersion, and it seems unlikely to be a rejection of a second baptism for a heretic entering the catholic church (for there appears to be no western influence on the formulation and eastern practice was mixed on this question). Rather, the affirmation was that there is no second baptism for sins committed after the first baptism (for these sins there must be another remedy).[23]

Council of Laodicea and the Origin of a Postbaptismal Anointing in the East[24]

Sixty (the last of which is of doubtful genuineness) canons are preserved from a synod at Laodicea in Phrygia Pacatiana of uncertain date in the latter half of the fourth century. Three of these pertain to baptismal practice. "They who are to be baptized must learn the faith [Creed] by heart and recite it to the bishop or to the presbyters on the fifth day of the week" (probably referring to Thursday of Holy Week before their baptism at the Pasch) — can. 46.[25] "They who are baptized in sickness and afterwards recover must learn the creed by heart and know that the divine gifts have been vouchsafed to them" (can. 47). This canon accords with the emphasis placed on the ordinary necessity of verbal confession even in sickbed baptism (chap. 39). "They who are baptized must after baptism be anointed with the heavenly chrism and be partakers of the kingdom of Christ" (can. 48).

This last quoted canon (48) promotes the postbaptismal anointing not everywhere practiced in the East before the late fourth century. Such a canonical regulation implies an act not being done and thus may witness to an effort to generalize a new practice.

Canons 7 and 8 of the same synod distinguished heretics who must be rebaptized from those who, on renouncing their error, were admitted to communion upon receiving an anointing with "holy chrism." It thus joins two other sources from Asia Minor that enjoined an anointing of certain heretics reconciled to the church — Basil, *Letter* 188 (First Canonical Letter to Amphilochus, dated 374), 1; Constantinople, canon 7 (actually from a fifth-century letter of Constantinople to Martyrios of Antioch). These sources speak of chrismation as a perfecting of faith or of baptism (cf. *Apostolic Constitutions* 3.17).[26] There was the further notion that the Holy Spirit was the principle of baptismal perfection.

---

23. David Wright, "The Meaning and Reference of 'One Baptism for the Remission of Sins' in the Niceno-Constantinopolitan Creed," *Studia patristica* 19 (1989): 281-285; David Wright, "One Baptism or Two? Reflections on the History of Christian Baptism," *Vox evangelica* 18 (1988): 7-23.

24. Varghese, *Les onctions baptismales*, pp. 113-133, on which this section is based.

25. Quotations are taken from Henry R. Percival, *The Seven Ecumenical Councils, Nicene and Post-Nicene Fathers* (repr. Peabody: Hendrickson, 1994), Second Series, Vol. 14, p. 154.

26. Varghese, *Les onctions baptismales*, pp. 124-126, for other texts using the language of chrismation as a perfecting of baptism.

Hence, the hypothesis may be advanced that the anointing already applied to schismatics was ready to assume the significance of imparting the Holy Spirit in the baptismal rite. After its introduction in Asia Minor it spread to Syria. The employment of a perfumed oil *(myron)* was encouraged by the theological ideas associating the Holy Spirit and Christ with a sweet perfume of heavenly aroma. Perfumed oil was used in Gnostic baptism (chap. 17). Thus what had been figurative language about anointing in the New Testament and the earliest Christian writers became an actual rite of postbaptismal anointing in the baptismal ceremony of churches in the East in the fourth century as it had already been in the West.

When considering all parts of the early Christian world, one finds that greater variety characterized anointing than other parts of the baptismal ceremony. Some anointings were before baptism; others after. Some applied to the whole body, others to the head or forehead only. Different substances were applied — olive oil and/or *myron*. Accompanying gestures might vary — the laying on of hands, making the sign of the cross. Different theological interpretations were given: the anointing of kings and priests, protection from demons, preparation for athletic combat or for a spiritual marriage, a sealing with the Holy Spirit. This variety indicates that the practice of anointing was not of apostolic appointment but was a later development (although still quite early), put at different places in the ceremony and given different theological meanings.

Eunomian Baptism

Eunomius was a leader of those called Neoarians who made a sharp distinction in substance between God and Christ. The late canon 7 ascribed sometime after 560 to the Council of Constantinople (381) provided for Arians to be received into the catholic church on a renunciation of their errors but treated Eunomians, "who are baptized with only one immersion," as pagans who had to be baptized.[27] Epiphanius said concerning Eunomius:

> He rebaptizes [ἀναβαπτίζει] those already baptized [βαπτισθέντας], . . . even those from Arians themselves. He rebaptizes them in the name of the uncreated God and in the name of the created Son and in the name of the sanctifying Spirit who is created by the created Son. (*Panarion* 76.54.32-33)[28]

---

27. For this section I follow M. F. Wiles, "Triple and Single Immersion: Baptism in the Arian Controversy," *Studia patristica* 30 (1997): 337-349. The fifth-century *Life of Porphyry* (of Gaza) 57 describes the conversion of an Arian boat captain who was not rebaptized but signed, blessed, and given communion. More on this work in chap. 45.

28. Translation by Philip R. Amidon, *The Panarion of St. Epiphanius, Bishop of Salamis: Selected Passages* (Oxford: Oxford University Press, 1990), p. 338. For more on Eunomian baptism see from Theodoret in chap. 46.

This would not have been the actual formula used but the orthodox interpretation of the way Eunomians understood the three beings,[29] and so is evidence that Eunomius continued to use the traditional triple invocation at baptism. The historians Socrates and Sozomen are probably to be trusted, therefore, that it was among followers of Theophronius and Eutychius, the former ejected by the Eunomians and the latter who withdrew from them, that the practice arose sometime between 381 and 394 of not baptizing in the name of the Trinity but into the death of Christ.[30] Sozomen adds that some attributed to Eunomius the substitution of one immersion (μιᾷ καταδύσει) for three in performing divine baptism but considers it more accurate that it was Theophronius and Eutychius that did so and baptized in the name of the death of Christ.[31] These accounts seem to be more precise than the generalization voiced by some of the orthodox that Eunomians must be baptized on coming to the catholic church because they practiced a single immersion into the death of Christ.[32]

If a single immersion was introduced by schismatics from the Eunomian community, this context would account for canon 50 of the *Apostolic Constitutions*. That work is now generally thought to represent the views of a Neoarian, or specifically a Eunomian. The features of baptism in the main body of the work correspond with what may be concluded about early Eunomian practice: use of the Trinitarian formula combined with the understanding of baptism as entering into the death of Christ, a hierarchical view of the Trinity with each person having different roles, and the rebaptism of converts from the catholic church. Yet canon 50 cannot be a Nicene interpolation.[33] The canons as a whole show the same style and language and breathe the same spirit as the *Constitutions*.[34] Hence, a reasonable hypothesis is that the polemic of canon 50 is directed against schismatics from the Eunomian fellowship who instituted a different baptismal practice.[35]

---

29. As Wiles, "Triple and Single Immersion," p. 341, points out, this is what Athanasius did in regard to the Arian view (*Against Arians* 2.42-43) — see chap. 28.

30. Socrates, *Church History* 5.24.

31. Sozomen, *Church History* 6.26 (PG 67.1361C); cf. 7.17. He adds that they "rebaptize [ἀναβαπτί-ζοντες] those they persuade, thinking them to be unbaptized [ἀβάπτιστος]" (1364C).

32. Didymus the Blind, *On the Trinity* 2.15 (see chap. 28); Theodoret, *Fables of Heretics* 4.3 (PG 83.420B — quoted in chap. 46); from the other side, Philostorgius, *Church History* 10.4 (but the comment may be Photius's, from whose summary the text comes).

33. Rowan Williams, "Baptism and the Arian Controversy," in Michel R. Barnes and Daniel H. Williams, eds., *Arianism after Arius: Essays on the Development of the Fourth Century Trinitarian Conflicts* (Edinburgh: T&T Clark, 1995), pp. 149-181 (161-170).

34. C. H. Turner, "Notes on the *Apostolic Constitutions*, II: The Apostolic Canons," *Journal of Theological Studies* 16 (1915): 523-538 (533-536).

35. This is the hypothesis advanced by Wiles, "Triple and Single Immersion," pp. 345-346, with the further conclusion that this would confirm a date for the *Apostolic Constitutions* and canon 50 in the 380s.

Asterius the Homilist

A set of thirty-one anonymous homilies on Psalms 1–15 and 18 is preserved among the works of John Chrysostom. Their modern editor identified the author as Asterius the Sophist of Cappadocia, who lived from about 270 until the 340s, a thinker who influenced Arius, Aetius, and Eunomius.[36] Some of the contents seemed to require a rethinking of the origins of "Arianism," but a recent study makes a better case for assigning these homilies to an otherwise unknown author writing between 385 and 410 in Antioch or its environs, which is the view adopted here.[37]

The dating is important because of "Asterius's" endorsement of infant baptism in three passages.[38] The later date coincides with the command of the *Apostolic Constitutions* for parents to present their children for baptism (see above). The principal passage discusses baptism in the context of the number eight (in the title of the Psalm) as the day of the Lord's resurrection, the number of souls saved in Noah's ark, and especially the eighth day for circumcision. The passage is notable for bringing the resurrection, circumcision, and baptism together by means of Colossians 2:11-12 and using the parallel with circumcision as a warrant for infant baptism.

> If the circumcision of the Jew was given early and quickly, immediately after swaddling clothes, to the infant, how much more ought the circumcision of Christ, which is by baptism, be given more quickly to the infant for safety.[39]

Three aspects of the infant's safety are noted: protection against demons, avoidance of heresy, and the precautionary concern with the possibility that illness would overtake the life of the child (but the passages do not deal with baptisms of necessity).[40] It is possible that another motive was the possible moral and spiritual consequences of a delay in baptism. The passage continues with the parallel that under the Law one not circumcised was accursed and now one not baptized is a foreigner. And John 3:5 is quoted in support of infant baptism. Neither here nor elsewhere is there any mention of original sin as a motive for baptism.

Another passage encourages child baptism. The author likens the seven days of creation to the seven ages of life. "The first day is the day of infants [i.e., in ancient

---

36. Marcel Richard, *Asterii Sophistae commentariorum in psalmos* (Oslo, 1956), whose text I use.

37. Wolfram Kinzig, *In Search of Asterius: Studies on the Authorship of the Homilies on the Psalms* (Göttingen: Vandenhoeck & Ruprecht, 1990). K.-H. Uthemann gave a long critical review in *Vigiliae Christianae* 45 (1991): 194-203, to which Kinzig replied in the same journal, "Asterius Sophista oder Asterius Ignotus? Eine Antwort," pp. 388-398.

38. J.-C. Didier, "Le pédobaptisme au IVe siècle: Documents nouveaus," *Mélanges de science religieuse* 2 (1949): 233-246, written under the persuasion of a date in the early fourth century for the homilies.

39. Asterius, *Hom.* 12, *In Ps.* 6 (Richard, p. 83).

40. Didier, "Le pédobaptisme," pp. 238-239. He notes that it is striking that two eastern advocates of infant baptism, our author and the compiler of the *Apostolic Constitutions* (two works we now regard as contemporary), were more or less Arian (p. 238).

thought, until about age seven], in order that you may be enlightened [φωτισθῇς] in baptism immediately."[41] The first day of creation, when light was created, means that the beginning of life is time for enlightenment in baptism.

When the baby was presented for baptism, the priest required the sponsor (ἀνάδοχος, one who gives security for another) to respond for the baby that the infant renounced Satan and identified with Christ.

> Someone presents the suckling child to be baptized, and the priest asks the unsteady age of life and the guarantor of the infant for promises and agreements. He receives the sponsor and inquires, "Does he renounce Satan?" And the priest does not say, "Does he renounce Satan at the end [of life?], does he give adherence to Christ at the end?" but he asks directly at the beginning of life for the renunciations and promises.[42]

The sponsor spoke for the infant the words that the infant could not say. This modification in how the renunciation of Satan and profession of Christ, still considered essential, were expressed was an important accommodation of the baptismal ritual to infants.

A further connection with the *Apostolic Constitutions* is the warning that a person baptized into a heresy was not baptized.[43] Notable is the reference to the heresy of Arius and Eunomius.[44]

A homily on the newly baptized speaks of them as "wet, bedewed" (δροσιζόμενοι), because of the image of a tree rather than an indication of the mode of baptism. The author does refer to the baptismal pool (κολυμβήθρα).[45] Baptism makes a person "white,"[46] and Easter week is called "the shining week," for the newly baptized wore white all week.[47]

In spite of the emphasis on infant baptism, the sequence expected by the homilist is "to teach, to catechize, to baptize, to fill the churches."[48] "We enter the church through baptism."[49] Baptism is to put on Christ.[50]

One homily discusses the benefits of baptism in traditional terms.[51]

---

41. *Hom. 21 in Ps. 11*, hom. 2 (Richard, p. 163).
42. *In Psalm 14*, hom. 2.2 (Richard, p. 215).
43. *Hom. 12, In Ps. 6* (Richard, p. 83).
44. *Hom. 26, In Ps. 14*, hom. 1 (Richard, pp. 206-207).
45. *Hom. 14, In Ps. 8*, hom. 1.
46. *Hom. 26, In Ps. 14*, hom. 1 (Richard, p. 206).
47. *Hom. 12, In Ps. 6* (Richard, p. 83).
48. *Hom. 16, In Ps. 8*, hom. 3 (Richard, p. 121).
49. *Hom. 26, In Ps. 14*, hom. 1 (Richard, p. 210).
50. *Hom. 30, Hom. in feriam 5* (Richard, p. 240).
51. *Hom. 15, In Ps. 8*, hom. 2 (Richard, pp. 110-111).

Opus Imperfectum in Matthaeum

This work preserved in Latin (PG 56.611-946; CCL 87B) is probably from the early fifth century. It has long been identified as coming from an Arian, but it has been argued that there are even more contacts with Pelagianism.[52] The unknown author speaks of five baptisms: in the word (instruction in the faith), in water (which removes sins committed up to this point), in the Spirit (which fortifies the soul and neutralizes carnal concupiscence), in fire (which progressively burns away the roots of concupiscence), and in death (which brings the final deliverance). The common motif is cleansing: from the filth of ignorance, from sin, from the power of concupiscence, from the roots of concupiscence, and from death itself. Water washes away past sins; the Spirit drives away present concupiscence; and fire fortifies against the future.

In all five the initiative is from God, but each (except for death) requires the human will to act. There is no treatment of infant baptism in the work, but there was no necessity in the author's system for it.

Testament of the Lord

The *Testament of the Lord,* like *Apostolic Constitutions* book 8, is among the documents dependent on the *Apostolic Tradition.* The *Testament of the Lord* is often placed in the fifth century in Syria, but its latest English translator places it in the late fourth century in Asia Minor.[53] The work was composed in Greek but survives in Syriac, Ethiopic, and Arabic versions. Unlike the *Apostolic Constitutions* it has a strong anti-Arian Trinitarian theology. The work gives a fairly detailed liturgy for baptism but offers only the basics of a theology of baptism. The baptismal ceremony lacks the distinctive features of Syrian practice but has similarities to the baptismal rite of the *Apostolic Constitutions* and Theodore of Mopsuestia.

After the catechumens had prayed, the bishop or a presbyter laid a hand on them and said a prayer for them, followed by their dismissal (2.5). If a catechumen was condemned to tortures and requested the bath (baptism), the bishop was not to hesitate to give it. If, however, the catechumen became a martyr before being baptized, baptism in his own blood provided justification (2.5).

Those to be baptized were first tested as to their conduct during their catechumenate and had to be approved by the testimony of those who sponsored

---

52. Fredric W. Schlatter, "The Pelagianism of the *Opus Imperfectum in Matthaeum*," *Vigiliae Christianae* 41 (1987): 267-284, whose discussion of baptism in the work (pp. 273-275) I follow in this section.

53. Grant Sperry-White, *The Testamentum Domini: A Text for Students, with Introduction, Translation, and Notes* (Bramcote/Nottingham: Grove, 1991). He translates the seventh-century Syriac version, but he does not translate the whole document and arranges selections topically. My quotations are from his translation.

them for baptism (2.6). Each day of preparation for baptism they were to hear the gospel, have a hand laid on them, and be exorcized individually by the bishop.[54] A person with an "impure spirit" was rejected for baptism. Those about to be baptized received instruction, washed, and sprinkled their heads on Thursday. Menstruating women were to delay their baptism. The candidates fasted on Friday and Saturday (2.6).

On the Sabbath the bishop gathered those to be baptized, had them kneel, placed a hand upon them, and said a long prayer of exorcism (which is quoted). The prayer toward the close refers to their coming baptism "in the Trinity, in the Name of the Father and of the Son and of the Holy Spirit," with the heavenly beings as witnesses (2.7). After the bishop's prayer of exorcism, the priest exorcized them, breathed on them, and signed them "between their eyes, on the nose, on the heart, on the ears" (2.7).

Baptism occurred in the middle of Saturday night (2.8). The water was to be "pure and flowing" (2.8). The size of the "house for baptism" *(baptisterion)* and its location in the front court of the church building are specified (1.19). The order of persons to be baptized was infants, men, and women, except that a person pledged to virginity was to be baptized first (2.8). Children who were able to do so were to make their own responses to the priest; parents or someone from their families replied on behalf of those who could not answer for themselves (2.8). Women were to loose their hair, and all were to remove any gold from their person (2.8). The oil for the exorcism of catechumens was exorcized, and thanks was given for the oil for anointing at the baptism (2.8).

Each candidate turned to the west and was asked to say, "I renounce you, Satan, and all your service, and your theatres, and your pleasures, and all your works" (2.8).[55] After the renunciation and confession of sin, the candidate was anointed with the exorcized oil (2.8). Turned to the east, the candidate said, "I submit to you, Father and Son and Holy Spirit, from whom all nature quakes and trembles. Grant that I may do all your wishes, without fault" (2.8).

The candidates then stood naked in the water, a deacon (or minister) entering the water with them, while the priest led the interrogations (2.8).

> Let him who baptizes say thus as he lays his hand upon him:
> "Do you believe in God the Father omnipotent?"
> And let the one being baptized say, "I believe." Let him baptize him immediately one time.
> Let the priest again say:

---

54. The various exorcisms in the *Testamentum Domini* are studied by Henry Ansgar Kelly, *The Devil at Baptism: Ritual, Theology, and Drama* (Ithaca: Cornell University Press, 1985), pp. 139-141, 192-193.

55. "Theatres" is included in the "pomp" of the renunciation in Cyril, *Lectures on the Mysteries* 1.6, and John Chrysostom, *Baptismal Instructions* 12.52, and the "worldly glamor" of Theodore of Mopsuestia.

"Do you believe in Christ Jesus, the Son of God, . . . ?"
And when he says, "I believe," let him baptize him a second time.
And again let him say,
"Do you believe in the Holy Spirit in the holy church?"
And let him who is being baptized say, "I believe," and thus let him baptize him a third time. (2.8)

When the person came up out of the water, he was anointed with the oil of thanksgiving by the presbyter, who said, "I anoint you with oil in the name of Jesus Christ" (2.8). The women were anointed by widows, with the presbyter reciting over them. Similarly, in the baptismal profession and the renunciations, the widows received the women under a veil while the bishop pronounced the words (2.8).

The newly baptized were led into the church, where the bishop laid a hand on them and prayed. This prayer incorporated the principal items in the meaning of baptism. The recipients of baptism were deemed worthy "of forgiveness of sins through the washing of rebirth" (Titus 3:5). They were removed from "the gloom of error and darkness of unbelief." The bishop, moreover, prayed that they be made "worthy to be filled with your Holy Spirit." The bestowal of God's grace would permit them to "perform your commandments in holiness" and do "always those things which are of your will" so that they might enter "your eternal tabernacles" (2.9).

The bishop poured out oil and placed a hand on the baptizand's head, saying, "Anointing, I anoint you in almighty God and in Christ Jesus and in the Holy Spirit, that you may be for him a laborer who has perfect faith . . . a vessel pleasing to him" (2.9). Having sealed him on the forehead, the bishop then gave the kiss of peace (2.9).

From that time the baptized could pray with the people and share in the eucharist. The cup was wine mixed with water to typify the blood and the bath (2.10).

A closing note adds that in the absence of a presbyter, "a deacon may, of necessity, baptize" (2.10).

36. Cappadocia: Basil the Great

The three major Cappadocian theologians — Basil the Great, his friend Gregory of Nazianzus, and his brother Gregory of Nyssa — have much in common in their teaching about baptism as in other things, but I will discuss them separately so as to detect their individual nuances. By the latter third of the fourth century the delay of baptism was a problem, so all three (along with others) preached exhortations to baptism that are rich sources of information for the practice and especially the theology of baptism.[1] These sermons will be drawn on in each chapter for the preachers' general baptismal teaching and in chapter 39 for their information on sickbed or deathbed baptism.

Basil was a presbyter from about 362 and bishop of Caesarea in Cappadocia from 370 to 379. From him, in addition to his *Homily* 13, *Exhortation to Baptism* (PG 31.423-444), we have another work, *On Baptism*, and important references to baptism in *On the Holy Spirit* and in several of his *Letters*.[2]

---

1. Everett Ferguson, "Exhortations to Baptism in the Cappadocians," *Studia patristica* 32 (1997): 121-129.

2. For Basil's *Exhortation* see my "Basil's Protreptic to Baptism," in John Petruccione, ed., *Nova & Vetera: Patristic Studies in Honor of Thomas Patrick Halton* (Washington, D.C.: Catholic University of America Press, 1998), pp. 70-83; J. Gribomont, "Saint Basile: Le Protreptique au Baptême," in G. J. Békés and G. Farnedi, eds., *Lex Orandi Lex Credendi: Miscellanea in onore di P. Cipriano Vagaggini* (Rome: Anselmiana, 1980), pp. 71-92, who dates the work to January 7, 371 or 372. Translations from this work *(Exh.)* are my own, but there is also an English translation by Thomas Halton in André Hamman, ed., *Baptism: Ancient Liturgies and Patristic Texts* (Staten Island: Alba House, 1967), pp. 75-87. Quotations from *On Baptism (Bapt.)* follow M. Monica Wagner, *Saint Basil: Ascetical Works*, Fathers of the Church 9 (New York: Fathers of the Church, 1950), pp. 339-430; critical edition (adopting Neri's text [below] with small changes) and French translation by J. Ducatillon, *Basile de Césarée, Sur le baptême*, Sources chrétiennes 357 (Paris: Cerf, 1989) — pp. 46-56 on the treatise's baptismal doctrine. Questions about this work's authenticity are resolved in its favor by U. Neri, *Basilio di Cesarea, Il battesimo: Testo, traduzione, introduzione e commento* (Brescia, 1976), esp. pp. 31-53. The translation of *On the Holy Spirit* and the *Letters* is that of Blomfield Jackson in *Nicene and Post-Nicene Fathers* (repr. Peabody: Hendrickson, 1994), Second Series, Vol. 8.

Nontechnical Word Usage

In one passage Basil combines a literal and a metaphorical usage of *baptizō*, both usages well attested in classical authors. He refers to persons more pitiable than those tempest tossed in the deep whom the waves submerged (ἐπιβαπτίζοντα); so are the souls overwhelmed (βεβαπτισμέναι) in wine (*Homily 14, On Drunkards* 4). A little later he says that wine overwhelms (καταβαπτίζει) the reason (14.7). Related to the first image is the reference to a person who, as a skillful pilot, preserved the soul uncapsized (ἀβάπτιστον) (*On the Martyr Julitta* 4). As to the metaphorical use for drunkenness, Basil says, "You carry about a soul immersed [βεβαπτισμένην] in wine" (*Commentary on Isaiah* 5.178; PG 30.417B). The action involved in dyeing material is described as "wool immersed [βαπτισθὲν] in dye [βάμματι]" (*On Baptism* 1.2.10). These uses illustrate the literal meaning of *baptizō*.

Baptismal Ceremony

Basil affirms the day of the Pascha, as the memorial of the resurrection, to be the most suitable time for baptism, "but every time is suitable for salvation through baptism, whether night, day, hour, or moment of time" (*Exh.* 1; PG 31.423C-D). The immediate preparation for baptism began with the candidates turning in their names to be enrolled (*Exh.* 7; PG 31.440A).[3] It was now time for catechumens to be weaned from the words of catechesis in order to be given a taste of the solid nourishment of doctrines (*Exh.* 1; PG 31.425A). They were to learn the gospel way of life (*Exh.* 7; PG 31.440A). Repentance was necessary, and Basil warns against delaying repentance until it is too late to benefit from it (*Exh.* 7; PG 31.441A).[4]

Because of his involvement in doctrinal controversies about the Trinity, Basil emphasized the connection of baptism with confession of the faith of the church. Faith and baptism belong together, and confession precedes baptism:

> Faith and baptism are two kindred and inseparable ways [τρόποι, modes of expression] of salvation: faith is perfected through baptism, baptism is established through faith, and both are completed by the same names [Father, Son, and Holy Spirit].... First comes the confession, introducing us to salvation, and baptism follows, setting the seal upon our assent. (*Holy Spirit* 12.28)

If baptism is in the name of Father, Son, and Holy Spirit, "so we are under obligation to believe [and] make our confession in like terms as our baptism" (*Holy Spirit* 27.67).[5] In the treatise *On Baptism* Basil makes a point of the order in Matthew

---

3. His analogies are the registration of a soldier, enrollment of an athlete in competition, and registration of a citizen — so as to be enrolled in heaven.

4. The definition of virtue is also a definition of repentance: "Virtue is the turning away from evil and doing good" (*Exh.* 5; PG 31.456B).

5. The same thought in *Letter* 251.4, "As we are baptized, so we make profession of our faith"; the

28:18-20 that making disciples (teaching) precedes baptism, since a disciple is "one who comes to the Lord for the purpose of following him, and so of hearing his words, believing in him and obeying him (1.1).[6]

Among the customs without the written authority of Scripture Basil mentions the blessing of the water of baptism, of the oil of the chrism, and of the catechumen who is going to be baptized; the anointing itself[7] and the triple immersions; the renunciation of Satan and his angels (*Holy Spirit* 27.66). The position of the last shows that the order of mention did not follow the liturgical sequence,[8] so we should be cautious about concluding that the anointing preceded the immersions.[9] In commenting on Matthew 6:17, "anoint your head and wash your face," Basil reverses the order and says, "Wash [ἀπόπλυνε] your soul from sins and anoint [χρῖσαι] your head with holy chrism in order that you may become a partner of Christ."[10]

The benefits of baptism came not from the nature of the water, for "if there is any grace in the water, it is . . . of the presence of the Spirit" (*Holy Spirit* 15.35). The baptism was with trine immersion. "In three immersions [καταδύσεσι, "dippings" or "plungings"] and with three invocations the great mystery of baptism is performed" (*Holy Spirit* 15.35). The immersions fulfilled the figure of Jesus' three days in the tomb and are our way of making the descent into Hades and so imitating his burial

---

mention of baptism before the confession is not the sequence of events but is dictated by the argument: the baptismal formula requires that the faith professed be the same (and for Basil that meant three equal persons constituting one God). Cf. *Letter* 226.3, "We have made profession of our faith in the Father, Son, and Holy Spirit, and we are baptized in the name of Father, Son, and Holy Spirit," and *Holy Spirit* 10.26 for preserving in the confession of faith and in doxology the doctrine taught in baptism. J. Ducatillon, *Basile de Césarée, Sur le baptême*, p. 53, affirms that faith and baptism are strictly connected for Basil.

6. Wagner, *Saint Basil*, pp. 339-341; cf. *Bapt*. 1.2, which states that "instruction is necessary before we are worthy to receive" baptism (Wagner, *Saint Basil*, p. 349; repeated, p. 383). *Exh*. 6 says about the Ethiopian eunuch of Acts 8:26-40: "Having been taught the gospel of the kingdom, he received the faith in his heart and did not put off the seal of the Spirit" (PG 31.437A).

7. *Letter* 10 refers to someone, "the wings of whose soul" Basil "anointed with the sweet oil of God." *Exh*. 7 (PG 31.441B), in the application of the parable of Matthew 25:1-13, warns his hearers who postpone baptism about "not receiving the oil [ἔλαιον] that nourishes light." The wording may be dictated by the parable and not by an allusion to an anointing in the baptismal rite.

8. The sequence "confess safely, reach agreement with God, renounce the Enemy" in reference to a deathbed baptism adds mention of an association with God, but placing it before the renunciation does not agree with the sequence in other sources (*Exh*. 5; PG 31.436D) — a passage treated more fully in chap. 39. Freeing oneself from the tyranny of the devil is associated with renouncing the world and its concupiscences (*Bapt*. 1.1; Wagner, p. 347).

9. As does Jean Daniélou, "Chrismation prébaptismale et divinité de l'Esprit chez Grégoire de Nysse," *Recherches de science religieuse* 56 (1968): 177-198 (p. 187), by stopping his listing before the renunciation.

10. *Homily 1 on Fasting* 2 (PG 31.165A). That there was only a prebaptismal anointing in Basil's church is argued by Georg Kretschmar, *Die Geschichte des Taufgottesdienstes in der alten Kirche*, in K. F. Müller and Walter Blankenburg, eds., *Leiturgia: Handbuch des evangelischen Gottesdienstes* (Kassel, 1970), Vol. 5, pp. 167-169, as well as by Daniélou, "Chrismation prébaptismale," pp. 186-187, but it would seem without considering all Basil says that might be relevant.

(*Holy Spirit* 15.35). "It is impossible for any one to be immersed [βαπτισθῆναι] three times, without emerging three times" (*Letters* 236.5), a statement which makes explicit that the baptism was indeed a dipping.[11] As the statements already quoted make clear, the three invocations of the baptismal formula were "Father, Son, and Holy Spirit." Thus Basil repeatedly quotes Matthew 28:19 to the effect that baptism is not in one of the names but in all three.[12] The passages that speak of being baptized into Christ (Gal. 3:27; Rom. 6:3) imply the Father and the Spirit, "For the naming of Christ is the confession of the whole, showing forth, as it does, the God who gave, the Son who received, and the Spirit who is the unction," with reference to Acts 10:38 and Isaiah 11:1 for God's anointing the Son with the Spirit (*Holy Spirit* 12.28).

After becoming children of God in baptism, "We require to be nourished with the food of eternal life" (*Bapt.* 1.3; Wagner, p. 387), a statement followed by a collection of texts on the eucharist. The baptismal eucharist is also implied in the statement, "Israel ate the bread of angels [Ps. 78:25] after baptism [the Red Sea deliverance]; how will you eat the living bread if you do not first receive baptism?" (*Exh.* 2; PG 31.428B).

The practice of taking a new name at baptism seems to be alluded to in *Letter* 10. The new name signaled the new life. The thrust of *On Baptism* is that the baptized are obligated to live a certain way. This fact is summed up in the statement:

> It has been clearly demonstrated, then, that all who have received the one baptism, as it is written [Eph. 4:5], are equally bound to fulfill in the manner of him who died for us and rose again the words of the apostle [2 Cor. 5:14-15].... Such a one has indeed concluded an inviolable agreement to follow the Lord in all things. (*Bapt.* 2.1; Wagner, p. 392)[13]

Baptismal Theology

With reference to the baptismal formula, Basil distributed the principal benefits of baptism among the three divine persons:

> Thus, baptized in the name of the Holy Spirit, we were born anew. Having been born, we were also baptized in the name of the Son, and we put on Christ. Then, having put on the new man according to God, we were baptized in the name of the Father, and called sons of God. (*Bapt.* 1.3; Wagner, pp. 386-387)

---

11. Note the statement, "For the bodies of the baptized are, as it were, buried in the water" (*Holy Spirit* 15.35). Basil found in the fire kindled from the water that Elijah commanded to be poured three times on the altar (1 Kings 18:33-35) a demonstration of the strength of baptism (*Exh.* 3; PG 31.429A). The connection of the story with baptism came from the water and the number three, not from the pouring itself.

12. In addition to references cited at nn. 5 and 7, *Holy Spirit* 10.24; 14.31; 25.60; *Bapt.* 1.2 (Wagner, p. 376). Baptism into the name of Father, Son, and Holy Spirit was an important part of Basil's argument for the divinity of the Holy Spirit.

13. See also the description of the Christian life in *Exh.* 7 (PG 31.440B).

The unusual reverse order of the names does not reflect an alternative baptismal practice but serves a rhetorical purpose, for Basil precedes this statement with the affirmation, "By the blood of Christ, through faith, we have been cleansed from all sin, and by water we were baptized in the death of the Lord," so that we might become dead to sin and alive to righteousness (1 Pet. 2:24) (*Bapt.* 1.3; Wagner, p. 386). This leads to the declaration of the new birth by the Spirit, and the statement about becoming children of God leads into the quotation above about the need to be nourished with the food of eternal life. Hence, the natural progression of thought is dictated by other considerations than the liturgical sequence of the immersions.

These characteristics set Christian baptism apart from the baptisms of the Jews and of John the Baptist. The baptism of John was superior to the purifications under Moses' law because it recognized no distinction of sins, required no variety of sacrifices, did not involve strict rules or observance of days and seasons, and did not involve any delay in receiving pardon (*Bapt.* 1.2; Wagner, p. 355).[14] Christ is greater than John, and his baptism is superior to John's, for "The Holy Spirit is as far superior to water as he who baptizes in the Holy Spirit obviously is to him who baptizes in water" (*Bapt.* 1.2; Wagner, p. 355).[15] "John preached a baptism of repentance. . . . The Lord preaches a baptism of adoption." John's baptism was introductory, the Lord's is perfective (*Exh.* 1; PG 31.425A).

Nevertheless, Christian baptism was adumbrated in the Old Testament.[16] Israel's exodus from Egypt (1 Cor. 10:2) was a "shadow and type" (*Holy Spirit* 14.31). In this passage Basil reverses the order of treatment from "cloud and sea" (1 Cor. 10:2) to sea and cloud, not because he considered the bestowal of the Holy Spirit as a separate act following water baptism, but because in his typology of the event the sea represents the death of the old nature and the cloud represents the Spirit who gives new life to the believer in baptism (see further below on *Holy Spirit* 15.35).[17] A similar development of the typology is found in a nonpolemical but hortatory context in the *Exhortation to Baptism*:

> Israel was baptized into Moses in the cloud and sea, delivering to you the types and characterizing the truth to be received at the end of the ages. But you flee baptism, not typified in the sea but fulfilled in truth; not in the cloud but in the Spirit; not into Moses a fellow slave but into Christ the Maker. Israel, if it had not crossed the sea, would not have escaped from Pharaoh. And you, if you do not cross through the water, will not escape the painful tyranny of the devil. (*Exh.* 2; PG 31.428B)

---

14. Christians do not wash themselves at each defilement, as the Jews do, because the "baptism of salvation" is "one" (Eph. 4:5), understood as administered once (*Holy Spirit* 15.35).

15. Also, *Holy Spirit* 15.36.

16. Two types are taken from Elijah — see notes 11 and 18.

17. Michael A. G. Haykin, "'In the Cloud and in the Sea': Basil of Caesarea and the Exegesis of 1 Cor. 10:2," *Vigiliae Christianae* 40 (1986): 135-144, who sets Basil's exposition in the context of the Pneumatomachian arguments made by Eustathius of Sebaste.

An encomium on baptism gives an impressive list of its blessings:

> Baptism is a ransom to captives, a forgiveness of debts, the death of sin, regeneration [παλιγγενεσία] of the soul, a shining garment, an unassailable seal, a chariot to heaven,[18] the agent of the kingdom, the gift of adoption. (*Exh.* 5; PG 31.433A).

Characteristic of Basil is the way he brings together the traditional ideas of forgiveness (Acts 2:38), death to sin (Rom. 6:2), and regeneration (Titus 3:5). He explains the meaning of "anew" ("again") in John 3:3, 5 as entailing the remission of sins, and he continues that "the manner of our being born anew of water" is explained by Paul as a dying and rising with Christ in baptism, quoting Romans 6:3-11 (*Bapt.* 1.2; Wagner, pp. 356-359). That Basil thought of these passages as related and mutually interpreting is shown in his quoting consecutively as giving the same teaching John 3:5; Romans 6:3-4; Galatians 3:27-28; and Colossians 2:11-12 (*Bapt.* 2.1; Wagner, p. 391).

Basil liked the phrase "baptism of salvation" (i.e., "saving baptism").[19] He often affirms the forgiveness of sins in connection with baptism, but this is not separated from the blood of Christ and faith (*Bapt.* 1.3, quoted above).[20] Whether one's sins are many and great or few and slight, grace is available.[21] Sins are forgiven by the grace of Christ: the corollary of Christ dying once for sin (Rom. 6:10) is that "we who have died once and for all to sin by the baptism of water, which is an image of the cross and of death, should . . . return no more to sin" (*Bapt.* 1.2; Wagner, p. 371). To be baptized into the death of the Lord is to die to sin (*Bapt.* 1.2; Wagner, p. 362).

As these passages indicate, grace is a prominent word with Basil in connection with baptism.[22] To be baptized is "to receive grace" (*Exh.* 5; PG 31.437A). Paradoxical, then, are the expressions "to be made worthy to be baptized" and "to merit to receive the great grace" (*Bapt.* 1.2; Wagner, p. 379). Basil, furthermore, introduces a number of metaphors for the grace of forgiveness: healing of illness, a distribution of gold, emancipation from slavery, adoption as sons, made a citizen of heaven, cancellation of debts.[23]

The association of baptism with the death and resurrection of Christ is promi-

---

18. 2 Kings 2:6-11. The association of the chariot to heaven with baptism comes from the preceding crossing of the Jordan, whose waters were parted by Elijah's mantle allowing a crossing on dry land, as in the exodus across the Red Sea and the entrance into Canaan through the Jordan.

19. *Holy Spirit* 15.35 (cited in n. 14); *Letters* 91; 105.

20. *Letters* 199.20 says the forgiveness of sins results from faith but is connected with being received into the church at baptism.

21. *Exh.* 4 (PG 31.432A-B).

22. Also, *Exh.* 3 (PG 31.429B); 5 ("do not bargain over grace" — PG 31.436A; "experience the grace" — PG 31.437A); 6 ("grace is bounteous" — PG 31.437B); *Bapt.* 1.1 — "receiving so great a grace" (Wagner, p. 347). In *Homily on Ps.* 28 (Eng. 29:3) he explains that the "grace of baptism" is called a flood, because the soul is washed from sins, cleansed from the old person, and made fit as a habitation of God in the spirit.

23. *Exh.* 2 (PG 31.428A); 3 (PG 31.429A-432A). On healing, cf. the restoration of youth and health in *Exh.* 5 (PG 31.432D-433A).

nent. It is a central theme of *On Baptism*. Baptism of water is a "promise to be crucified, to die, to be buried with him, and so on" (Rom. 6:4-11 — *Bapt.* 1.1; Wagner, pp. 346-347). The one "who desires to receive purification through faith in the power of the blood" of Jesus "will be cleansed from every iniquity and sin." Then, "baptized in the death of the Lord, he will desire to be conformed to his death, which is to die to sin, to himself, and to the world." "He who is dead must be buried, and he who is buried in the likeness of death must rise again by the grace of God in Christ" (*Bapt.* 1; Wagner, pp. 362-363). Basil further elaborates on the concept. Quoting Romans 6:6, he points out that the one who is buried with Christ is first crucified with him (*Bapt.* 1; Wagner, p. 368).[24] "Baptism is an image of the cross, of death, burial, and resurrection from the dead" (*Bapt.* 1; Wagner, p. 369).[25] "We will assuredly be raised up together with Christ," but in the present life we are to live in newness of life and obedience (*Bapt.* 1; Wagner, p. 370). Baptism is an imitation of the death and burial of Christ. "How then do we achieve the descent into hades? By imitating, through baptism, the burial of Christ" (*Holy Spirit* 15.35).

Death to sin and burial with Christ is "in order that we might live." "Let us be buried with Christ, who died on behalf of us, in order that we also might rise with him who secured the resurrection for us" (*Exh.* 1; PG 31.424B-C). Only those planted in the likeness of Jesus' death will become partners of his resurrection (*Exh.* 2; PG 31.428A). Basil puts the death and life associated with baptism together in this striking formulation:

> Baptism is a type of the resurrection of the dead. For this cause the Lord, who is the dispenser of our life, gave us the covenant of baptism, containing a type of life and death, for the water fulfills the image of death, and the Spirit gives us the earnest of life. Hence it follows that the answer to our question why the water was associated with the Spirit is clear: the reason is because in baptism two ends were proposed; on the one hand, the destroying of the body of sin, that it may never bear fruit unto death; on the other hand, our living unto the Spirit, and having our fruit in holiness; the water receiving the body as in a tomb figures death, while the Spirit pours in the quickening power, renewing our souls from the deadness of sin unto their original life. (*Holy Spirit* 15.35)

The giving of life by the Holy Spirit in baptism leads into the development of baptism as regeneration. Thus the passage just quoted continues: "This then is what it is to be born again of water and of the Spirit [John 3:5], the being made dead being effected in the water, while our life is wrought in us through the Spirit" (*Holy Spirit* 15.35). John 3:5 is quoted among the passages indicating the "indispensable require-

---

24. So, Basil calls on his hearers, "Die to sin, be crucified with Christ" (*Exh.* 7; PG 31.440B). Ducatillon, *Basile de Césarée, Sur le baptême*, p. 48, lists six passages in this one work on the theme.

25. The same statement except translated "type" occurs in *Bapt.* 1.2 (Wagner, p. 384); in both cases the Greek word is "likeness." The Greek words for "image" and "type" occur with the same referent in *Holy Spirit* 15.35.

ments for entrance into the kingdom of heaven" (*Bapt.* 1.2; Wagner, pp. 350-351).[26] The one born of the Spirit becomes spirit and walks by the Spirit (*Bapt.* 1.2; Wagner, p. 377), or, more boldly, becomes like God.[27] For Basil baptism in water is baptism in the Holy Spirit, and the emersion from the water is linked with John 3:5.[28] The blessings of baptism are the working of the Holy Spirit:

> Through the Holy Spirit comes our restoration to paradise, our ascension into the kingdom of heaven, our return to the adoption of sons, our liberty to call God our Father, our being made partakers of the grace of Christ, our being called children of light, our sharing in eternal glory, and, in a word, our being brought into a state of all "fullness of blessing." (*Holy Spirit* 15.36)

It is in terms of regeneration that Basil sets forth his understanding (which he considers the general Christian understanding) of the relationship of grace, faith, and baptism.

> Whence is it that we are Christians? Through our faith would be the universal answer. And in what way are we saved? Plainly because we were regenerate (ἀναγεννηθέντες) through the grace given in our baptism. How else could we be? (*Holy Spirit* 10.26)

He continues that this salvation comes through Father, Son, and Holy Spirit. Because of the profession of faith, "Baptism was the beginning of life, and that day of regeneration [παλιγγενεσίας] the first of days" (*Holy Spirit* 10.26). Regeneration (παλιγγενεσίας) is the "beginning of a second life" (*Holy Spirit* 15.35).[29]

According to Basil's exposition, John 3:5 is associated with the circumcision of Colossians 2:11:

> The Jew does not defer circumcision . . . , but you delay the circumcision not made with hands in the stripping off the flesh, which circumcision is performed in baptism, having heard the Lord himself. . . . (*Exh.* 2; PG 31.428A)

There follows the quotation of John 3:5 and Romans 6:4-5. Basil does not equate baptism with circumcision; rather, the circumcision made without hands occurs in baptism, and according to the subsequent quotations is understood to be the work of the Spirit and the burial with Christ.[30]

---

26. The other passages are Matt. 5:3, 10; 25:34-35; Luke 6:20; 12:32-33; Matt. 18:3; Mark 10:15. John 3:3, 5 are again quoted, leading into the quotation of Matt. 28:19 (*Bapt.* 1.2; Wagner, p. 356) and alluded to in the phrase, "born again [ἀναγεννᾶται] without a mother" (*Exh.* 5; PG 31.433A).

27. *Exh.* 1; PG 31.424B — "to be born by the Spirit"; 425A — "John's baptism was a means of retreat from sin; the Lord's is a becoming like to God"; 3; PG 31.429A — "through baptism the one approaching becomes like God."

28. Ducatillon, *Basile de Césarée, Sur le baptême*, pp. 46 and 48.

29. Basil seems to use ἀναγέννησις and παλιγγενεσία as synonyms, but the associations of the latter with a new age may be in the background.

30. Colossians 2:11-12 about circumcision is cited for the understanding of baptism as the "put-

Baptism is itself, as in earlier Christian usage, the seal.[31] Baptism of water and the Spirit is the seal of faith.[32] Various words are used in one passage to describe baptism as the distinguishing sign of the Christian:

> No one will know whether you are ours or the enemies' if you do not possess the likeness of the mystical signs [συμβόλοις], if the light of the face of the Lord is not signified [σημειωθῇ] on you. How will your angel . . . deliver you if he does not recognize the seal [σφραγῖδα]? How will you say, "I am God's," if you do not bear the marks [γνωρίσματα]? Or, are you ignorant that the Destroyer passed over the houses that were sealed [ἐσφραγισμένας] but killed the firstborn in those not sealed [ἀσφραγίστοις; Exod. 12:21-30]? . . . The unmarked [ἀσημείωτον] sheep is plotted against without danger. (*Exh.* 4; PG 431.B-C)

The lack of technical terminology reflects the different images evoked as well as the fact that Basil was addressing the unbaptized, but the subject is the baptism itself rather than another part of the ceremony. "We were sealed through the grace of baptism into the Father and the Son" (*Against Eunomius* 2.22; PG 29.620C).

The allusion in *Exhortation* 4 above to the light of the Lord's face recalls the motif of enlightenment in connection with baptism. This theme was especially associated with the instruction accompanying baptism: "By the delivery of the divine knowledge the baptized may have their souls enlightened" (*Holy Spirit* 15.35). Basil reminds his hearers that "Ignorance of God is the death of the soul; and the one not baptized has not been enlightened" (*Exh.* 1; PG 31.424C). Through baptism "pure and heavenly light shines in the souls of those drawing near through faith in the Trinity" (*Exh.* 3; PG 31.429A).

In *On Baptism* Basil interpreted the baptism of fire as moral teaching about the duties of a Christian leading not just to understanding but also to doing. Jesus' teachings do what fire does, and the word of the Savior necessarily precedes water baptism, so the baptism of fire concerned catechumens. In *On the Holy Spirit*, however, Basil gives a more traditional interpretation associating fire with judgment.[33]

In dealing with baptisms by heretics, Basil appealed to the practice of his predecessors. That precedent was "to reject the baptism of heretics altogether, but to admit that of schismatics on the ground that they still belonged to the church" (*Letters* 188.1). Heresies were those alienated in matters relating to the faith: he names from the past Manichaeans, Valentinians, Marcionites, Montanists (*Letters* 188.1). The key factor here was not only use of the proper Trinitarian formula but also having the right understanding of the divine persons (cf. *Letters* 199.47). The Novatianists

---

ting off of the works of the flesh" (*Holy Spirit* 15.35). On baptismal circumcision in Basil, cf. Ducatillon, *Basile de Césarée, Sur le baptême*, p. 50.

31. *Exh.* 5, quoted above in the encomium on baptism, and 6, quoted in note 6.

32. Ducatillon, *Basile de Césarée, Sur le baptême*, p. 53.

33. Ducatillon, *Basile de Césarée, Sur le baptême*, pp. 50-53, with the observation that the two interpretations are not mutually exclusive.

(Cathari) had been the subject of different practices, but Basil treats them in their origin as schismatics. The precedents established meant that a valid faith was necessary for a valid baptism. Hence, "Whether a person have departed this life without baptism, or have received a baptism lacking in some of the requirements of the tradition, the loss is equal" (*Holy Spirit* 10.26), a strong affirmation of the necessity of (a correct) baptism.[34]

Nevertheless, Basil recognized the circumstance of martyrdom taking the place of water baptism:

> There have been some who in their championship of true religion have undergone death for Christ's sake, not in mere similitude [baptism], but in actual fact, and so have needed none of the outward signs of water for their salvation, because they were baptized in their own blood. Thus I write not to disparage the baptism by water, but to overthrow the arguments of those who exalt themselves against the Spirit. (*Holy Spirit* 15.36)

The statement occurs in the context of discussion of Matthew 3:11 and 1 Corinthians 3:13, apparently taking martyrdom as a baptism of fire, as part of an argument against those who denied the full divinity of the Holy Spirit.

---

34. For the question of Eunomian baptism, contemporary with Basil, see chap. 35.

37. Cappadocia: Gregory of Nazianzus

Gregory alternated between leadership of churches in Nazianzus (Cappadocia) and the imperial capital of Constantinople and periods of retirement. This study will concentrate on his *Orations* 39 ("On the Holy Lights" — preached on Sunday, January 5, on the baptism of Christ) and especially 40 ("On Holy Baptism," preached on the following day), probably in the year 380.[1] The latter is the most elaborate of the exhortations to baptism of the period, expanded into a rather full theology of baptism.[2] Although both sermons were delivered during his brief tenure as bishop of Constantinople (379-381), Gregory's intellectual and spiritual formation was in Cappadocia, and their many similarities in contents to Basil and Gregory of Nyssa justify placing discussion of him at this point.

1. J. M. Szymusiak, "Pour une chronologie des discours de S. Grégoire de Nazianze," *Vigiliae Christianae* 20 (1966): 183-189 (184-185).

2. Heinz Althaus, *Die Heilslehre des heiligen Gregor von Nazianz* (Münster: Aschendorff, 1972), pp. 153-180, on baptism as the subjective appropriation of Christ's salvation; D. F. Winslow, "Orthodox Baptism — A Problem for Gregory of Nazianzus," *Studia patristica* 14 (1976): 371-374; Everett Ferguson, "Exhortations to Baptism in the Cappadocians," *Studia patristica* 32 (1997): 121-129. I use but modify for both orations the translation by Charles Gordon Browne and James Edward Swallow in *Nicene and Post-Nicene Fathers* (repr. Peabody: Hendrickson, 1994), Second Series, Vol. 7, pp. 352-377; Greek text and French translation in C. Moreschini and P. Gallay, *Grégoire de Nazianze Discours 38-41*, Sources chrétiennes 358 (Paris: Cerf, 1990), who consider 39 and 40 more likely to have been delivered in 381, the date given by Browne and Swallow. Althaus, p. 153, gives 380; he says that Epiphany was the name for the feast of the incarnation; when Christmas was introduced, it became Epiphany, and Gregory Nazianzus introduced the name "Lights" for the festival on January 6. Gabriele Winkler, "Die Licht-Erscheinung bei der Taufe Jesu und der Ursprung des Epiphaniefestes: Eine Untersuchung griechischer, syrischer, armenischer und lateinischer Quellen," *Oriens Christianus* 78 (1994): 177-229 (pp. 221-222), notes the use of Epiphany and Theophany for the manifestations of the divinity of Jesus (at his birth and his baptism) and suggests Gregory's name "Lights," for the festival may go back to older conceptions of the appearance of light at Jesus' baptism. Justin Mossay, *Les fêtes de Noël et d'Épiphanie d'après les sources littéraires Cappadociennes du IVe siècle* (Louvain: Abbaye du Mont César, 1965), pp. 21-30 on the names of the feasts, pp. 31-44 on their celebration, pp. 45-65 on their ideological and theological context, and p. 65 for conclusions.

Baptismal Ceremony

Gregory's idealized record of his father's baptism is the closest we have from him to an account of the ceremony of baptism.

> [B]ending his knee, he received the form of admission to the state of a catechumen . . .
>
> He was approaching that regeneration [ἀναγεννήσει] by water and the Spirit, by which we confess to God the formation and completion of the Christlike person, and the transformation and reformation from the earthy to the Spirit. He was approaching the bath with warm desire and bright hope, after all the purgation possible, and a far greater purification of soul and body than that of the people who were to receive the tables from Moses [Exod. 19:10, 15]. . . . The whole of his past life had been a preparation for the enlightenment, and a preliminary purification making sure the gift, in order that perfection might be entrusted to purity, and that the blessing might incur no risk in a soul which was confident in its possession of the grace. And as he was ascending out of the water, there flashed around him a light and a glory worthy of the disposition with which he approached the gift of faith. . . . To the baptizer and initiator it was clear . . . that he was anointing with the Spirit his own successor. (*Oration* 18.12-13)

Even here the main characteristic is the theological themes associated with baptism that are expressed, anticipating nearly all those to be commented on below: regeneration by water and Spirit, confession to God, transformation into the likeness of Christ, purification of body and soul, enlightenment, gift of faith, grace, and anointing with the Spirit.

The catechumens were "in the porch," and Gregory invites them to come inside (*Oration* 40.16). "It is better to be baptized with Christ, to rise with Christ on the day of his resurrection [Pasch]," but because of the uncertainties of life, "Do not delay in coming to grace" (*Oration* 40.24).[3] The forty days of fasting during Lent were a symbol of dying with Christ and a purification in preparation for the Pasch (*Oration* 40.30). The preparation for baptism involved "vigils, fasts, sleeping on the ground, prayers, tears, pity for and almsgiving to those in need" (*Oration* 40.31). There were also confessions of sins and exorcisms (*Oration* 40.27).

One should not ask for the credentials of the administrator of baptism, for anyone of the same faith and not a stranger to the church may administer it. One person may be holier in life than another, but "the grace of baptism is the same" (*Oration* 40.26); yet Gregory anticipates that he himself will do the baptizing (*Oration* 40.41).[4]

Gregory of Nazianzus gives great importance to the confession of faith. He

---

3. "Every time is suitable for your ablution, since any time may be your death" — (*Oration* 40.13); note 40.11 quoted in chap. 39 for elements of the baptismal ceremony.

4. Cf. *Oration* 40.44, "My reward for . . . consecrating you by baptism," and "I lend my hands to the Spirit," who is the real baptizer.

summarizes the initiation process as, "Having spoken, be baptized; and having been baptized, be saved" (*Oration* 40.26). This necessity of a confessed faith in connection with baptism made sickbed baptism problematical (chap. 39), if one was impeded in speaking the "sacramental words" (*Oration* 40.11) and required special consideration in regard to infant baptism (see below on *Oration* 40.28).

Gregory spells out what must be believed in a paraphrased Credo (*Oration* 40.45). He explains that this summary is what can be spoken of the mystery (his regular word for "sacrament") for anyone to hear, but the rest will be learned within the church and must be kept secret (*Oration* 40.45).[5] Gregory, preaching in the context of the Trinitarian controversies of the late fourth century, makes much of baptism in the Triune name (*Oration* 40.41-42, 44-45) and calls on his hearers, "Be baptized with this faith" (*Oration* 40.44). Gregory perhaps has both subjective and objective faith in mind when he says that his father as a reward for his conduct "attained to the faith" (*Oration* 18.6).

As might be expected in an exhortation to baptism, Gregory makes frequent reference to the "font" or the "bath" (λουτρόν) (e.g., *Oration* 40.4, 21, 22, 28, 35).[6] As Peter and John ran to Jesus' tomb and his resurrection, "let us hasten to the font" (*Oration* 40.25). Immersion is implicit in the description of baptism as a burial (discussed below on the theology of baptism). Gregory of Nazianzus once uses καταβαπτίζω (literally, "dip or plunge down," so "sink") in reference to Arian baptism (*Oration* 33.17) as aberrant, not because of a different action involved, but because of a wrong faith. *Baptizō* could be used by him in the secular sense of drowning, but the relevant passage may have been influenced by the exodus typology: in relating a series of events at the exodus from Egypt, he says the sea will be parted, Pharaoh will be drowned (βαπτισθήσεται), and bread will rain down (*Oration* 45.21).

Gregory refers to the robe worn after baptism (*Oration* 40.25) and the reception of the newly baptized into church:

> The Psalmody with which you will be received is a prelude of the heavenly hymnody. The lamps which you will light are a sacrament [mystery] of the illumination in heaven with which we shall meet the Bridegroom . . . with the lamps of our faith shining. (*Oration* 40.46)[7]

He gives no indication of post-immersion rites and goes directly from his account of baptism to the eucharist.

Special attention falls on Gregory's treatment of infant baptism.

> Have you an infant child [νήπιον]? Do not let sin get any opportunity, but let the child be sanctified from childhood [βρέφους]; from the very tenderest age

---

5. The preliminary, public instruction was "elementary initiation of the word" (*Oration* 39.10).
6. See also *Oration* 18.13.
7. The allusion to lamps reflects the practice at Constantinople — Victor Saxer, *Les rites de l'initiation chrétienne du IIe au VIe siècle: Esquisse historique et signification d'après leur principaux témoins* (Spoleto: Centro italiano di studi sull'alto medioevo, 1988), p. 327.

[ὀνύχων] be consecrated to the Spirit. . . . [Instead of amulets and incantations], give your child the Trinity, that great and noble Guard. (*Oration* 40.16)

This is one of the early surviving encouragements from a leading churchman for infant baptism.[8] It occurs in a context encouraging people, whether old or young, to be baptized.

Gregory gives a fuller discussion later that puts some qualifications on what he said. Baptism is to be given to those who ask for it, but someone may inquire:

"What have you to say about those who are still children [νηπίων] and conscious neither of the loss [sin] nor of the grace? Are we to baptize them too?"[9] Certainly, if any danger threatens. For it is better that they should be unconsciously sanctified than that they should depart unsealed and uninitiated.

A proof of this is found in the circumcision on the eighth day [Gen. 17:12], which was a sort of typical seal and was conferred on those who did not have the use of reason. And so is the anointing of the doorposts, which preserved the firstborn, though applied to things which had no consciousness [Exod. 12:22-23, 29]. But in respect of others [not in danger] I give my opinion to wait till the end of the third year, or a little more or less, when they may be able to listen and to answer something about the sacrament [mystery]; that, even though they do not perfectly understand it, yet at any rate they may know the outlines [may receive at least an impression]; and then to sanctify them in soul and body with the great sacrament [mystery] of our consecration. For this is how the matter stands; at that time they begin to be responsible for their lives, when reason is matured, and they learn the mystery (for of sins of ignorance owing to their tender years they have no account to give), and it is far more profitable on all accounts to be fortified by the font [λουτρῷ, "bath"], because of the sudden assaults of danger that befall us. (*Oration* 40.28)

Gregory clearly does not reject, but even encourages, baby baptism; yet neither does he recognize it as the normal practice, and he knows questions about it, factors that do not encourage the thought that it was a long-standing routine practice. His defense of infant baptism applies primarily to emergency situations where the child is in danger of dying, something known as early as Tertullian (chap. 21). He was troubled about administering baptism where there was a lack of consciousness in the recipient, and so he makes a new application of the analogy from circumcision. His preference was to delay baptism to an age when the child had some understanding of the words and what was done. (He was rather more optimistic about the degree of development of reasoning powers in a three-year-old than modern parents are likely to have.) Gregory thought some understanding, if not absolutely necessary, was at

---

8. About the same time, *Apostolic Constitutions* 6.15.7, quoted in chap. 35.
9. In *Oration* 40.23 Gregory refers to those not in a position to receive baptism by reason of infancy, perhaps in the sense of not being able to ask for baptism and dependent on others to bring them to the font.

least desirable. His discussion here is another indication of the importance he attached to the confession of faith in connection with baptism. For him children were not guilty of sin, but baptism was necessary as a seal of belonging to Christ.[10] He divided those persons who were not baptized into three classes: those who despise baptism will be punished; those who honor baptism but put it off will have to suffer but less than the first class; and those who because of infancy or some involuntary circumstance are prevented from receiving it will be neither glorified nor punished (40.23).[11] Gregory's proposal of baptism after three years of age makes more sense as a response to a recent practice of infant baptism in nonemergency situations than as an effort to modify a long-established custom. Could the choice of age have had something to do with a three-year catechumenate? The recommendation seems not to have had an impact.

To the objection against Gregory's urging people to hasten to baptism that Christ was thirty years old when he was baptized, the preacher responds that since Christ was divine there was no danger in his putting off baptism: his hearers had no small danger in delaying (*Oration* 40.29).

Baptismal Theology

In contrast to the limited liturgical information in Gregory of Nazianzus, he offers a rich theology of baptism. *Oration* 39 identifies five kinds of baptism:

> Moses baptized but it was in water [e.g., Lev. 11], and before that in the cloud and in the sea [1 Cor. 10:2]. This was typical, as Paul says: the sea of the water and the cloud of the Spirit, the manna of the bread of life, the drink of the divine drink. John also baptized; but this was not like the baptism of the Jews, for it was not only in water but also "unto repentance." Still it was not wholly spiritual, for he does not add "and in the Spirit." Jesus also baptized, but in the Spirit. This is the perfect baptism. And how is he not God, if I may digress a little, by whom you too are made God? I know also a fourth baptism — that by martyrdom and blood, which also Christ himself underwent — and this one is far more august than all the others, inasmuch as it cannot be defiled by after-stains. Yes, and I know of a fifth also, which is that of tears, and is much more laborious, received by him who washes his bed every night and his couch with tears. (*Oration* 39.17)

---

10. Althaus, *Die Heilslehre*, pp. 164-165.

11. The sentiment expressed here, that unbaptized infants who die are "worthy neither of the kingdom nor punishment," was often repeated in the Byzantine church (see the quotation from Pseudo-Athanasius in chap. 28), in contrast to the Augustinian position that they went to a place of milder punishment (chap. 52). See Jane Baun, "The Fate of Babies Dying before Baptism in Byzantium," in Diana Wood, ed., *The Church and Childhood*, Studies in Church History 31 (Oxford: Blackwell, 1994), pp. 115-125, who explains that Byzantine canonists did not address their condition because before being baptized and receiving a name (given at baptism) the infant for the Greeks had no identity at all.

Gregory combines the purificatory washings of the Law of Moses with the typical baptism of crossing the Red Sea into one Old Testament predecessor of baptism. The baptism administered by Christ in the Spirit is probably to be identified with Christian baptism into the triune name (otherwise unmentioned in the listing) rather than considered a different baptism.[12] The "baptism of tears" was otherwise treated in the early church as a "second repentance."

In his "Funeral Oration on his Sister Gorgonia" Gregory alludes to her baptism when she "obtained the blessing of cleansing and perfection, which we have all received from God as a common gift and foundation of our second life" (*Oration* 8.20). He further refers to her receiving "regeneration [ἀναγεννήσεως] from the Holy Spirit," and this "mystery" was a "seal" (*Oration* 8.20). These terms recur in Gregory's baptismal theology.

Gregory begins *Oration* 40 by indicating that his discourse will concern "baptism and the benefits which accrue to us" from it (*Oration* 40.1). Because, as he says, the preceding day was "the festival of the Holy Lights," he begins by talking about baptism as enlightenment (φώτισμα) — *Oration* 40.1 — and describes its meaning:

> Enlightenment is the splendor of souls, the conversion of life, the pledge of the conscience to God [1 Pet. 3:21]. It is the aid to our weakness, the renunciation of the flesh, the following of the Spirit, the fellowship of the Word, the improvement of the creature, the overwhelming of sin, the participation of light, the dissolution of darkness. It is the carriage to God, the dying with Christ, the perfecting of the mind, the bulwark of faith, the key of the kingdom of heaven, the change of life, the removal of slavery, the loosing of chains, the remodeling of the whole person. (*Oration* 40.3)

The baptism of Christ brought enlightenment and purification (*Oration* 39.1).[13] The name "Enlightenment" is given to baptism because of its splendor (*Oration* 40.4).

The praise of light is developed from the description of God as Light (*Oration* 40.5) to the manifestations of light in Scripture (*Oration* 40.5-6). "Light is in a special sense the enlightenment of baptism . . . , which contains the great and marvelous sacrament [mystery] of our salvation" (*Oration* 40.6). The theme continues throughout the discourse. Among the blessings of the bath is to be "enlightened by Christ" (*Oration* 40.10).[14] "In the Lord's light see light" (Ps. 36:9), and in God's Spirit to be enlightened by the Son — a threefold and undivided Light (*Oration* 40.34).[15]

---

12. Althaus, *Die Heilslehre*, pp. 173-180, discusses the baptism of Christ as the pattern for Christian baptism and Christ as the giver of baptism.

13. Althaus, *Die Heilslehre*, pp. 157-162, discusses Gregory's doctrine of the essence and effects of baptism under these two rubrics — purification from sin (the prerequisite) and enlightenment (an imparting of the divine essence, which is light).

14. See also *Oration* 40.22, 24, 36-37, 38, 46 (lamps given to the newly baptized — see above). For enlightenment in general, note *Oration* 39.8; it was clearly a favorite theme with Gregory — he includes himself among those "who are charged with the enlightenment of others" (*Oration* 2.36).

15. Cf. *Oration* 39.11 — "When I speak of God you must be enlightened at once by one flash of light and by three. Three in individualities or hypostases . . . but one in substance."

"The light of God is marked upon him [Ps. 4:7, Greek], that is, the signs of the illumination given are impressed upon him and recognized" (*Oration* 40.36). *Oration* 39.14 exhorts to baptism with a comparison to the baptism of Christ: "Christ is enlightened, let us shine forth with him. Christ is baptized, let us descend with him that we may also ascend with him."[16]

In the manner of Clement of Alexandria, Gregory gives a listing of the names of baptism: "We call it gift, grace, baptism, enlightenment, anointing, clothing of immortality, bath of regeneration [Titus 3:5], seal, everything honorable" (*Oration* 40.4).

That baptism is a gift from God is frequent.[17] "Enlightenment is the best and most magnificent of God's gifts" (*Oration* 40.3). Baptism is named a gift, "because it is given to us in return for nothing on our part" (*Oration* 40.4). Therefore, "What folly it is to put off the gift" (*Oration* 40.27) and what importance there is to preserve the forgiveness "you have received as a gift" (*Oration* 40.34). "Let us hasten to salvation. Let us arise to baptism. The Spirit is eager, the consecrator is ready, the gift is prepared" (*Oration* 40.44).

The gift came because of God's grace, another pervasive word in connection with baptism.[18] With it comes "the grace of new creation" (*Oration* 40.2). Baptism is named grace "because it is conferred even on debtors" (*Oration* 40.4.). "Such is the grace and power of baptism" that it brings "a purification of the sins of each individual and a complete cleansing from all the bruises and stains of sin" (*Oration* 40.7). The grace reaches to the depth of the soul (*Oration* 40.11). Yet Gregory can speak of "the right disposition for grace" (*Oration* 40.27). Since one is dealing with grace, Gregory (like Basil) warns against trying to make a trade in regard to Christ (*Oration* 40.11).

Gregory alludes to the literal meaning of baptism in specifying one important aspect of its doctrinal significance: The name "baptism" is given "because sin is buried with it in the water" (*Oration* 40.4).[19] Hence, he exhorts, "Let us then be buried with Christ by baptism that we may also rise with him; let us descend with him, that we may also be exalted with him" (*Oration* 40.9).

It is notable that Gregory of Nazianzus identifies baptism as the anointing (χρῖσμα). This name makes it "priestly and royal, for such were they who were anointed" (*Oration* 40.4).

The name "clothing" of incorruption is given to baptism "because it hides our

---

16. For the baptism of Christ as the foundation of Christian baptism cf. also *Oration* 39.15, quoted in our chap. 7.

17. Baptism is simply called "the gift" in *Oration* 40.11-12, 16, 18, 21, 22, 23, 25 (plural), and 44, in addition to texts cited — many of these chapters having more than one reference to gift.

18. In addition to passages cited in the text, baptism is designated "grace" in *Oration* 40.12, 20, 24 (cited above on when to be baptized), 25, 26 (cited above on the administrator of baptism), 28 (cited on infant baptism), 34 ("the measure of grace"), 44.

19. This description is the nearest Gregory Nazianzus comes to describing the action of baptism. Cf. "dying with Christ" in *Oration* 40.3, quoted above, and "rise with Christ" in *Oration* 40.24, quoted above on the Pasch.

shame" (*Oration* 40.4), a description that alludes to the theme prominent in the Syriac tradition that in baptism one is restored to the condition humanity had in paradise. With reference to Galatians 3:27, Gregory encourages providing clothing for the naked "in honor of your own garment of incorruption, which is Christ" (*Oration* 40.34). Related to this is the idea of the "restoration of the image which had fallen through sin" (*Oration* 40.7). By baptism, also designated the seal (see below), one is in the image of God, has put on Christ, and is transformed into Christ (*Oration* 40.10).[20] Baptismal enlightenment is a "remodelling" (*Oration* 40.3) or, in a combination of related terms, "a regeneration [ἀναγεννήσεως], a remaking, a restoration to our former state" (*Oration* 40.8).

Baptism is called the "laver" or the "bath" (λουτρόν), "because it washes us" (*Oration* 40.4). The cleansing waters of baptism are superior to the purifications of the Old Testament law, for the latter were a temporary cleansing of the body, had to be repeated, and did not provide a "complete removal of sin" (*Oration* 40.11).[21] The theme of forgiveness of sins is prominent.[22] "The font [bath] does not wipe away good deeds as it does sins" (*Oration* 40.22). Gregory refers to "baptized souls, whose sins the font [bath] has washed away" (*Oration* 40.35). The laver (or bath) is "not merely a washing away of sins in you, but also a correction of your manner of life" (*Oration* 40.32).

Baptism is the seal, "because it preserves us and is an indication of dominion" (*Oration* 40.4). Gregory here alludes to the double significance of a seal — in the passive sense as the imprint it is protected and in the active sense that one who possesses a seal has authority. The seal is a popular image of baptism for Gregory.[23] The unbaptized are "unsealed" (*Oration* 40.23). Like Basil he uses the illustration of a seal (or a brand) on a sheep: "A sheep that is sealed is not easily snared, but that which is unmarked is an easy prey to thieves" (*Oration* 40.15). In the same context Gregory treats the seal, being signed, and an anointing as equivalent: "[F]ortify yourself beforehand [before death] with the seal, and secure yourself for the future with the best and strongest of all aids, being signed both in body and in soul with the anointing, as was Israel" (Exod. 12:22) — *Oration* 40.15.

20. Cf. "Let the bath be not for your body only but also for the image of God in you" — *Oration* 40.32. On the day when one is remade, the old marks are effaced, and Christ is put on one so as to escape future shame — *Oration* 40.27. For the restoration of the condition of Adam, see *Oration* 39.2, quoted below on the new birth.

21. Cf. the cleansing of the soul in *Oration* 40.13; becoming "white in soul" in 40.26; "washed" in *Oration* 17.32; "baptismal purity" in *Oration* 8.14. Gregory correctly uses "sprinklings" when referring to the application of the ashes of a heifer under the Law — *Oration* 39.3.

22. *Oration* 40.3 (quoted above on enlightenment), 7 (quoted above on grace), 34 (partially quoted above on gift); 10 simply refers to the things granted by the laver. The statement that Christ "was baptized as a human being, but he remitted sins as God" (*Oration* 29.20) implies that baptism was for the forgiveness of sins.

23. *Oration* 40.7, 10 (see above on image), 17, 18. A literal use of seal occurs in *Oration* 40.26, and circumcision was a seal in a typical sense according to *Oration* 40.28. Secret matters of Christian doctrine are to be kept within oneself as under a seal — *Oration* 40.45.

Another theme for baptism is regeneration and new birth.[24] Although not listed separately in his names for baptism, it is referred to in the phrase "bath of regeneration" (*Oration* 40.4). He refers to three births: the natural birth, the birth of baptism, and the birth of the resurrection. Christ honored all of these — by breathing life into human beings (Gen. 2:7), by himself becoming incarnate and being baptized, and by his resurrection (*Oration* 40.2-3). The feast of Epiphany initiated a special season:

> It is a season of new birth, let us be born again. It is a time of reformation, let us receive again the first Adam. Let us not remain what we are, but let us become what we once were. (*Oration* 39.2)

The Spirit's role in baptism is affirmed. Important for Gregory in the Trinitarian debates was the consideration, "If [the Holy Spirit] is not to be worshipped, how can he deify me by baptism?" (*Oration* 31.28). To deify meant to confer immortality. The passage continues, "From the Spirit comes our regeneration [ἀναγέννησις], and from the regeneration our new creation" (*Oration* 31.28; cf. 41.14 for the Spirit effecting regeneration). To be baptized is to be consecrated by the Spirit (*Oration* 40.17).[25] The Spirit transforms the soul through water (*Oration* 7.15). The Spirit is connected with the theme of light (above) as "Light and Lightgiver" (*Oration* 41.9). To those who want to be baptized by an important bishop, as at Jerusalem, Gregory interposes, "Grace does not come of a place but of the Spirit" (*Oration* 40.26). The one who baptizes is the instrument of the Spirit, who is always ready (*Oration* 40.44).

Since a human being is both body and soul, the one part visible and other part invisible,

> [S]o the cleansing also is twofold, by water and the Spirit; the one received visibly in the body, the other concurring with it invisibly and apart from the body; the one typical, the other real and cleansing the depths. (*Oration* 40.8)

Gregory gives primacy to the inner cleansing by the Spirit, of which the outward washing with water is only a type; but he does not separate the two cleansings, for they are simultaneous.

Gregory considered the water and the Spirit to continue to work together for the Christian's protection. When the Tempter assails the Christian, Gregory says, "Defend yourself with the water; defend yourself with the Spirit" (*Oration* 40.10). They quench the fiery darts of the wicked (Eph. 6:16).

These words are a reminder that baptism was a deliverance from the Evil One.

> The unclean and malignant spirit is gone out of you, being chased by baptism. He will not submit to expulsion . . . [and returns. However,] [h]e fears the water; he is choked with the cleansing, as the Legion were in the sea [Mark 5:13]. (*Oration* 40.35)

---

24. *Oration* 40.8, quoted above in regard to restoration to our former state.
25. Cf. *Oration* 40.43, "Baptism consecrating me through the Spirit."

Baptism is a deliverance from slavery to sin and the Evil One (*Oration* 40.3). How foolish it is "to seek for freedom from earthly slavery, but not to care about heavenly freedom" (*Oration* 40.13).

Gregory employs the imagery of healing to baptism:

> Why wait for a fever to bring you this blessing, and refuse it from God? . . . Heal yourself before your extremity; have pity upon yourself the only true healer of your disease; apply to yourself the really saving medicine. (*Oration* 40.12).

These words are not a contradiction to what he said earlier about grace. His point here is that only the person concerned can make the move to accept baptism. Human beings need healing (*Oration* 40.26). The healing imagery is elaborated in *Oration* 40.34.

The power of baptism is to be understood as "covenants [συνθήκας] before God for a second life and a purer manner of life" (*Oration* 40.8).

As some of the quotations have shown, sacrament [μυστήριον, mystery] is a common word in Gregory in reference to baptism.[26] With reference to the robe given the newly baptized, he says, "The sacrament is greater than the things seen" (*Oration* 40.25), and he refers to the "power of the sacrament" (*Oration* 40.43).

Because the connotations of the word "mystery" from Greek religions were strong, Gregory was careful to explain that he was not concerned with these "mysteries" (*Oration* 39.4-6). The ceremonies and mysteries, he says, were to him nonsense (*Oration* 39.3).

Consistent with Gregory's emphasis on confession in connection with baptism, he picks up this idea in saying that baptism made a person one of the "faithful." One of the considerations he advances for not waiting and having to receive sickbed baptism is to be made one of the faithful (πιστός) — *Oration* 40.11. To the catechumens he says, "Do not despise to be and to be called faithful" (*Oration* 40.16). To be baptized was to become a "Christian" (*Oration* 40.16).

Gregory recognized the baptism of martyrdom (*Oration* 39.15 and see above). There also remains a "last baptism," the baptism of fire that lasts longer and is more painful than one's penance for sins (*Oration* 39.19).

Among the excuses advanced for the delay of baptism was the equal reward for the laborers who worked in the vineyard all day or only one hour according to Jesus' parable (Matt. 20:1-16). Gregory gave an extended discussion of the parable, including the point that those who labored only one hour responded when they were called (*Oration* 40.20). Another argument was that God in his mercy would take the desire of baptism for baptism. Gregory exposes the folly of such reasoning:

---

26. "Sacrament of our salvation," above under enlightenment (*Oration* 40.6); the infant being able to answer something about the sacrament (*Oration* 40.28), which is "the great sacrament of perfection" (*Oration* 40.28). For other occurrences, the word is used in the same context for a child understanding the "mystery" (sacrament?), of "the sacrament of the Passover" (eucharist) in *Oration* 40.30, and of the lamps given the newly baptized as a "sacrament of the enlightenment" in heaven (*Oration* 40.46).

> [W]hat you mean is that because of God's mercy the unenlightened is enlightened in his sight; and he is within the kingdom of heaven who merely desires to attain to it but refrains from doing that which pertains to the kingdom. (*Oration* 40.22)

Does one really desire what one is negligent about? Gregory then analyzes different kinds of persons and different circumstances and reasons why someone does not receive baptism. Persons do not think about other things the same way as they do about substituting the desire for baptism for the act itself:

> If you judge the murderously disposed person by his will alone, apart from the act of murder, then you may reckon as baptized him who desired baptism apart from the reception of baptism. But if you cannot do the one, how can you do the other? I cannot see it. . . . If desire in your opinion has equal power with actual baptism, then judge in the same way in regard to glory, and you may be content with longing for it, as if that were itself glory. And what harm is done you by your not attaining the actual glory, as long as you have the desire for it? (*Oration* 40.23)

Gregory is arguing from the objector's own viewpoint, not according to how God judges murderous thoughts (Matt. 5:21-22). God will not honor the intention, only the fact of baptism (contrast Ambrose on the "baptism of desire" in chap. 40).

Baptism was extremely important for Gregory of Nazianzus, but it was only one step on the road to salvation, a beginning (*Oration* 40.7) that one must continue to pursue (*Oration* 40.12, 14, 22).[27]

---

27. Winslow, "Orthodox Baptism," pp. 371-374. His use, however, and selective translation of *Oration* 32.33 (p. 374) in order to imply that Gregory did not draw the conclusion of the necessity of baptism for salvation lifts his words out of context. See the translation of the whole sermon by Martha Vinson, *St. Gregory of Nazianzus: Select Orations*, Fathers of the Church 107 (Washington, DC: Catholic University of America Press, 2003), pp. 191-215 (the passage under discussion is on pp. 214-215).

38. Cappadocia: Gregory of Nyssa

Gregory, brother of Basil, was bishop of Nyssa from 372 until his death about 395. Three works are especially relevant for the study of baptism: the *Catechetical Oration* 33-36, 38-40;[1] the liturgical sermon *On the Day of Lights* or *On the Baptism of Christ*;[2] and the protreptic sermon *Against Those Who Defer Baptism*.[3]

Baptismal Ceremony

Gregory of Nyssa refers to those who have grown old and are still "dismissed with the catechumens . . . when the mystery is going to be spoken about" (*Defer,* PG 46.421C).[4] He invites his hearers,

> Give me your names so that I can inscribe them in the visible books, and I will write them in ink; God has marked them in the invisible tablets and written them

---

1. Translations from Gregory of Nyssa are my own. The Greek text is by Ekkehard Mühlenberg, *Gregorii Nysseni Oratio Catechetica, Opera Dogmatica Minora, Pars IV* in *Gregorii Nysseni Opera*, III, Pars IV (Leiden: Brill, 1996), pp. 82-105; cited *GNO,* page, and line. Studies by Reinhard Jakob Kees, *Die Lehre von der Oikonomia Gottes in der Oratio Catechetica Gregors von Nyssa* (Leiden: Brill, 1995); Everett Ferguson, "The Doctrine of Baptism in Gregory of Nyssa's *Oratio Catechetica*," in Stanley E. Porter and Anthony R. Cross, eds., *Dimensions of Baptism: Biblical and Theological Studies* (London: Sheffield Academic Press, 2002), pp. 224-234; Salvatore Taranto, "Il Cristo e i sacramenti in Gregorio di Nissa: il battesimo," in M. Girardi and M. Marin, *Origene e l'Alessandrinismo Cappadoce (III-IV secolo)* (Bari: Edipuglia, 2002), pp. 171-201, whose thesis is that for Gregory baptism cannot be separated from the incarnation and the mediatorial work of Christ and the church.

2. Greek text by E. Gebhart *GNO,* Vol. 9: *Sermones* I (Leiden: Brill, 1967), pp. 221-242. Studied in my "Preaching at Epiphany: Gregory of Nyssa and John Chrysostom on Baptism and the Church," *Church History* 66 (1997): 1-17.

3. Not yet in *GNO;* PG 46.416C-432A. Studied in my "Exhortations to Baptism in the Cappadocians," *Studia patristica* 33 (1997): 121-129.

4. The catechumens were outside paradise (*Defer,* PG 46.417C); on paradise see also 420C.

with his own finger, as he at one time wrote the law for the Hebrews. (*Defer*, PG 46.417C)

The preparation for baptism was a time of penitence leading up to the death of sin in the water (see further below). The break in the continuity of evil in one's life is effected by repentance and death to sin:

> Two things concur for the removal of sin: repentance by the transgressor and imitation of death. By these means a person is in some measure freed from the natural tendency to evil. By repentance one advances to a hatred and aversion toward evil, and by death one effects the destruction of evil. (*Catechetical Oration* 35, GNO 89, 9-14)

The imitation of death occurred in baptism in water (more below). Gregory gives a variation in his statement of the three requirements for baptism (below), substituting repentance for faith: mystic water, invocation of divine power, and the correction of repentance (*Catechetical Oration* 35, GNO 91, 19-23).

The break with sin (and the devil) was expressed in exorcism. Gregory ascribes to Gregory Thaumaturgus an expulsion of a demon from a lad by taking the linen cloth off his shoulders, breathing on it with his mouth, and placing it over the lad; he explains that breath from the saint's mouth was sufficient for deliverance from demons. The account, however, is not in a baptismal context and is only one of several miracles of exorcism recounted, so (although breathing on the person was a part of some baptismal exorcistic rituals) we must be cautious about concluding that such was part of Gregory of Nyssa's baptismal ceremony.[5]

In defending the divinity of the Holy Spirit Gregory has a passage concerned with Jesus' anointing with the Holy Spirit that may have relevance to an anointing prior to baptism in Gregory's ceremony.[6]

> For as between the body's surface and the liquid of the oil nothing intervening can be detected . . . so inseparable is the union of the Spirit with the Son; and the result is that whoever is to touch the Son by faith must needs first encounter the oil in the very act of touching; there is not a part of Him devoid of the Holy Spirit. Therefore belief in the Lordship of the Son arises in those who entertain it, by means of the Holy Spirit.[7]

The claim is that Gregory refers to a full bodily anointing that conferred the Holy Spirit (so no part of the body is naked of the Holy Spirit) and made possible the bap-

---

5. *Life of Gregory Thaumaturgus* 11.77.

6. Such is argued by Jean Daniélou, "Chrismation prébaptismale et divinité de l'Esprit chez Grégoire de Nysse," *Recherches de science religieuse* 56 (1968): 177-198, but the case is inferential and not conclusive.

7. *On the Holy Spirit* (GNO 3.1). I have adapted the translation of William Moore and Henry Austin Wilson in *Nicene and Post-Nicene Fathers* (repr. Peabody: Hendrickson, 1994), Second Series, Vol. 5, p. 321.

tismal confession of faith in Christ (referred to later in the passage — see below). The interpretation is possible, but persuasiveness depends on Cappadocia and Pontus following the Syrian baptismal practice. Another interpretation is possible, namely that the oil is metaphorical for the Spirit (who makes possible an approach to the Son) and the one not devoid of the Spirit is the Son (not the believer), as in the translation quoted (Him, not him).[8]

Gregory of Nyssa gave more prominence to faith as a necessity for baptism. He expresses three requirements for Christian baptism — invocation of heavenly grace, water, and faith. In responding to the doubts of unbelievers about how a new birth to immortal life can occur, he mentions the means employed: "Prayer to God and invocation of heavenly grace, water, and faith are the means through which the mystery of regeneration [ἀναγεννήσεως] is accomplished" (*Catechetical Oration* 33, GNO 82, 15-17).[9] Gregory discusses these three prerequisites in this order, but our comments will follow the initiatory sequence of faith, invocation, and water.

Instruction in the word of God produces faith. The *Catechetical Oration* was a catechesis (κατήχησις — 1, GNO 1, 8 and 40; GNO 42, 5), written for the teachers who would prepare candidates for baptism.[10] Gregory related the conversion of the Ethiopian treasurer (Acts 8:26-40), who learned from the evangelist Philip to understand the prophecy of Isaiah and requested baptism. He recognized that any water is suitable, "if only it finds faith in the one receiving it" (*Defer*, PG 46.421C-D). Christ is present with those who believe he is God, and it is a matter of faith in the divine promise that grace is present in those baptized (*Catechetical Oration* 34, GNO 84, 16-21; 85, 20 — 86, 4). To believe is a matter of free choice. Unlike in natural birth, "in the spiritual regeneration [ἀναγέννησιν]" one "has the power to become whatever (s)he chooses to be." "The spiritual birth depends on the power of the one being born," for "this offspring has the power to choose his/her own parents."[11]

Hence, it is important that one places trust in the right objective faith. "Of necessity what is born is of the same nature as that of the parents" (*Catechetical Oration* 39, GNO 100, 7-8). The convert chooses from whom he is begotten and so of what sort of child he is (*Catechetical Oration* 38, GNO 98, 19-20).

> Since then in the Gospel [Matt. 28:19] are delivered the three Persons and the names through which the birth to believers occurs, the one who is begotten in the Trinity is begotten equally by the Father, the Son, and the Holy Spirit. (*Catechetical Oration* 38, GNO 99, 13-16)

---

8. Daniélou makes much of Gregory's doctrine that the Holy Spirit precedes a confession of faith (pp. 190, 192ff.), but this doctrinal affirmation need not require a liturgical expression.

9. Cf. *Catechetical Oration* 36, GNO 92, 13-25, "calling upon his life giving power, ... faith and water." See Kees, *Lehre*, pp. 164, 167-168.

10. Kees, *Lehre*, pp. 6 (intended for catechists), 10 (keeping the ones to be instructed in view).

11. *Catechetical Oration* 38, GNO 98, 20-21, 39; GNO 98, 23-24 and 99, 4-5. Cf. *Life of Moses* 2.13 (GNO 7.1.34–8.14) for choosing one's own parents and *Homilies on Ecclesiastes* 6 on Eccl. 3:2 (GNO 5.380, 1-11) for becoming one's own parents through the choices made.

By faith one makes the choice of the kind of birth to be received and so of one's spiritual nature. "The one who confesses the uncreated holy Trinity enters into the unchanging and unalterable life," but the one who sees the Son and Spirit as created is baptized into creatures and is "begotten to a changeable and alterable life" (*Catechetical Oration* 38, *GNO* 100, 2-7).[12] The person who considers the Son and/or Spirit as created, places the "hope of salvation in himself and not in the divine" and "has a birth from below and not from above" (*Catechetical Oration* 38, *GNO* 101, 4–6 and 101, 23–102, 2).

Gregory gives prominence to calling upon the divine in prayer as giving effectiveness to baptism. He may have in mind the blessing of the water, the calling on the threefold divine name at the actual baptism, or both. At some point prior to the baptism there was "prayer and the invocation of divine power upon the water" (*Catechetical Oration* 33, *GNO* 82, 20-21).[13] There was also the pronouncing of the threefold divine name by the baptizer, explicit in the statement: "We do not receive the sacrament [mystery] in silence, but there are pronounced over us the [names of the] three holy Persons, into whom we have believed" (*Lights, GNO* 9.228, 23-25).

The incarnation and miracles of Christ are a proof that "Deity, when called upon, is present for the sanctification of the things done [in baptism]," and this is true "every time he is called upon" (*Catechetical Oration* 34, *GNO* 84, 6-14). Christ "has promised to be always present with those who call upon him, to be in the midst of believers, and to remain and to be with them collectively and individually"; so he is certainly present in baptism also (*Catechetical Oration* 34, *GNO* 84, 16-20). The divine power brings about human birth, even when parents do not ask for it. "How much more in the spiritual mode of generation" will this power be effective, "since God has promised to be present in what is done and has put his own power in the work," while we according to our faith add our prayer and will to what is undertaken (*Catechetical Oration* 34, *GNO* 85, 10-16). "The invocation by prayer precedes the divine dispensation" (*Catechetical Oration* 34, *GNO* 85, 3-4).

The candidates' confession of the faith in the triune God is indicated expressly by the phrase, "confessing the uncreated holy Trinity" (*Catechetical Oration* 39, *GNO* 100, 3). It is perhaps referred to in Gregory's exhortation: "Be joined to the mystical people and learn the secret words. Speak with us those words which the six-winged Seraphim speak and hymn with the initiated Christians" (*Defer*, PG 46.421C). Those words suggest a possible liturgical sequence involving the baptismal confession and singing the Trisagion. The next statement may refer to the eucharist, "Desire the nourishment that strengthens the soul. Taste the drink that rejoices the heart" (*Defer*, PG 46.421C).[14] Gregory does expressly refer to the baptizer's words in the passage quoted above about pronouncing the names of the three holy Persons (*Lights, GNO* 9, 228, 23-25).

---

12. Cf. *Lights, GNO* 9, 228, 22–229, 18 for the same argument that the baptismal formula means the equal deity of all three persons.

13. See also *Defer*, PG 46.421D, cited on the water below.

14. See further on the triple immersion below.

The three requirements for baptism stated in the *Catechetical Oration* are found also in the exhortation to baptism: "Every place belongs to the Master, and all water is suitable for the use of baptism, if only it finds faith in the one receiving it and the blessing of the priest who sanctifies it" (*Defer*, PG 46.421D). Although any water would do, Gregory's church had a baptistery (βαπτιστήριον — *Defer*, PG 46.420A).

Gregory describes those who administer baptism as "those who wash away [ἀποκλύζοντας] the blemish of sins with mystical water," "those who administer grace," and lavers or bathtubs [λουτῆρας] "to those who share in the free gift."[15]

Baptism involved three dippings (καταδύσεις — *Lights*, GNO 9, 228, 7). The three immersions represent "the grace of [the Savior's] resurrection on the third day" (*Lights*, GNO 9, 228, 21-22). The *Catechetical Oration* also refers to "the descent into the water and being in it three times" (35, GNO 86, 6-7) and likewise understands that the "three movements are an imitation of the three days of the grace of the resurrection" (35, GNO 88, 11-12). The descent here is clearly the dipping and not the entering the baptistery.

This last passage contains a statement that might incorrectly be interpreted as referring to the application of water by pouring. The one who is joined to Christ "instead of earth, water is poured [ἐπιχεάμενος] over him" (*Catechetical Oration* 35, GNO 88, 10). A little later Gregory repeats the thought:

> We imitate the transcendent Power in so far as the poverty of our nature allows, being poured over [ἐπιχεάμενοι] with water and again coming up from the water, we interpret [or enact a correspondence to] the saving burial and resurrection which occurrred on the third day. (*Catechetical Oration* 35, GNO 89, 10-24).

The action described as receiving a pouring could refer to water being scooped by the administrator over the exposed part of the body while the candidate stood in the baptistery or to water flowing over the body if the baptism took place in a river or other natural body of water. However, since the comparison is with a burial in which after the body is lowered into the grave earth was "poured" or "spread" over it, it seems likely that Gregory refers to the person being dipped into the water, which then flowed or spread over the body. In that case the pouring was not what the administrator did with the water (which Gregory does not say occurred) but what the person being baptized experienced, comparable to what happens to a body being buried. Such a reading is encouraged by the facts that the word for "poured over" had as one of its meanings (in the passive) "to be drowned" and the express statement in the former passage that the result of "being poured over" with water was that one "goes down into" (ὑποδύς) or "submits" to the element (*Catechetical Oration* 35, GNO 88, 10-11). Moreover, in the sermon *On the Day of Lights* Gregory in the same comparison says that just as in the Savior's burial, "we conceal [or hide, ἐγκρύπτομεν] ourselves" in the water (GNO 9, 268, 20). The result, therefore,

---

15. *Life of Moses* 2.185 (GNO 7.1, 96, 7-13). He refers to John the Baptist, Peter, and Philip as biblical persons who performed baptism.

whether the water artificially or naturally flowed over the person, was that the whole body was covered.

Gregory of Nyssa identifies six objects or persons that are changed when sanctified to a special purpose by a benediction (*Lights, GNO* 9, 225, 10–226, 8). In response to the question why the Spirit alone was not sufficient to effect regeneration, Gregory points to seemingly insignificant things that by a blessing become different.

> The Spirit blesses the body that is baptized and the water that baptizes. Therefore, do not despise the divine washing nor disparage it as something ordinary because of the use of water, for what is accomplished is great, and marvelous things are performed by it. (*Lights, GNO* 9, 225, 10-14)

Similarly, the stone of the altar and the bread and wine are ordinary, but when they receive blessing they are consecrated to the service of God. "Even so the mystical oil.... Before the blessing it is something insignificant, but after the sanctification by the Spirit" it effects its own operation (*Lights, GNO* 9, 225, 23-25). Persons who are ordained, although in appearance the same, are transformed in soul for better things.

The treatment of the eucharist in the middle of the discussion of baptism in *Catechetical Oration* 37 implies that it was connected with the initiation ceremony. But what about the oil? Gregory does not give separate treatment to it, and its location in the homily on *Lights* among the objects of little importance in themselves given a special meaning by benediction does not necessarily indicate a use in the baptismal ceremony nor, if so, its position in the order of activities, mentioned after the water and the bread and wine.

Baptismal Theology

Gregory of Nyssa introduced his discussion of baptism in the *Catechetical Oration* 32 by identifying as part of the "mystical teachings" "the dispensation with reference to the washing [λουτρόν], whether one wishes to name it baptism [βάπτισμα], enlightenment [φώτισμα], or regeneration [παλιγγενεσίαν]" (*GNO* 82, 1-4). Besides the word "baptism" itself, Gregory's favorite name for baptism in this work is "bath" or "washing," taken from Titus 3:5,[16] and one of his favorite concepts was regeneration, except that in discussing regeneration in the *Catechetical Oration* he prefers the wording of 1 Peter 1:3 and 23 (ἀναγέννησις)[17] and especially of John 3:3-7 (regeneration or birth from above by the Spirit)[18] over that of Titus 3:5 (παλιγγενεσία). These

---

16. Used seven times for baptism — *GNO* 82, 2; 91, 4, 9 ("grace from the bath"; cf. *Lights, GNO* 9, 223, 2, "grace of the bath"); 16; 103, 2, 5, and 20.

17. *GNO* 91, 4-5 rephrases the λουτρὸν παλιγγενεσίας of Titus 3:5 as λουτρὸν ἀναγεννήσεως. For other uses see *GNO* 82, 17; 83, 12; 85, 23; 99, 17-18; 102, 9 and 24; and 104, 11 with reference to John 1:12-13.

18. *GNO* 99, 14-18; 101, 19–102, 3; 102, 21; cf. 104, 10-12; 85, 10-11; 98, 18-19; 100, 18-19.

terms for regeneration (ἀναγέννησις and παλιγγενεσία), apparently used interchangeably, are his favorite descriptions of baptism in the sermon *On the Day of Lights*, together occurring fifteen times.[19] The exhortation *Against Those Who Defer Baptism* refers to the "washing of regeneration" (PG 46.429C) and speaks of "the grace of regeneration" (PG 46.425B), in both cases *palingenesia*.

Gregory of Nyssa grounded the concept of regeneration in the incarnation of Christ.[20] The incarnation occurred for the sake of salvation. The birth of Christ makes possible and guarantees the new birth to those who are baptized. As an illustration of how new life can come through the process of initiation Gregory appeals to the analogy of physical birth. "Show me the manner of the generation according to the flesh, and I will explain the power of regeneration according to the soul"; as to how, he appeals to the incomprehensible power of God (*Lights*, GNO 9, 227, 7-26). One cannot perceive a connection between the moist seed (sperm) and the resulting human person endowed with all the attributes of reason, yet if divine power can change that visible underlying matter into a human being, it is nothing marvelous for the divine power to bring about regeneration through the "mystical dispensation."[21] Even as the power of God takes the moist sperm and makes a human being, so the power of God uses the water of baptism to make a corruptible human being into an incorruptible person. The reverse is also true: even as the moist seed without the divine power is inactive, so the material element of water alone is ineffectual for regeneration.[22]

Following on Christ's incarnation was his baptism. The sermon on the feast celebrating the baptism of Christ noted why he was baptized: "In order to cleanse the defiled, to bring the Spirit from above, and exalt humanity to heaven, in order to raise up the fallen and bring to shame the one who cast humanity down" (*Lights*, GNO 9, 223, 14-16).[23] By reason of what Christ did, "Baptism is a purification of sins, a forgiveness of trespasses, a cause of renewal and regeneration [ἀναγεννήσεως]" (*Lights*, GNO 9, 224, 4-5). He explains that the regeneration does not affect the external appearance but brings the person back to the status of a newborn:

> The old person is changed into a child, . . . the one grown old in evil habits is brought back to the innocence of a baby. For as a newborn child is free from accusations and penalties, so too is the child of regeneration. (*Lights*, GNO 9, 224, 8-15)

---

19. Ἀναγέννησις occurs eight times (GNO 9, 224, 5, 6, 15; 227, 6, 9; 237, 9; 239, 2; 240, 16) and παλιγγενεσία seven times (GNO 9, 227, 13; 230, 11; 232, 11; 233, 9; 235, 14; 236, 10; 237, 23). In this sermon "baptism" occurs twenty-one times, "water" twenty-nine times (because of the use of Old Testament episodes and the argument for the use of material elements), and "bath" only four times.

20. See my "Doctrine of Baptism," pp. 225-227.

21. *Catechetical Oration* 33-34, GNO 82, 23–84, 5 and 85, 5–86, 1.

22. *Catechetical Oration* 33, 34, 40, GNO 83, 15-16; 85, 9-10; 103, 9-10. For the contrast in the spiritual birth that one gets to choose one's parents, see above on faith as a free choice.

23. Christ is a rich spring from which flows a stream that washes the whole world (*Defer*, PG 46.420D).

The regeneration in baptism was to result in a changed moral life. Some are reborn "only in appearance and not in reality. For the transformation of our life that occurs through rebirth would not be a transformation if we should remain in the state in which we were" (*Catechetical Oration* 40, *GNO* 102, 4-11).[24] Referring to Christ as "firstborn" (see next paragraph), Gregory presents Christ as the guide in the birth of the water and the Spirit, for in the Jordan he brought down the grace of the Spirit (*On Perfection, GNO* 8.1, 202, 6-8).[25] He makes the fact that "through the same manner of new birth through water and the Spirit we became brothers of the Lord" the basis for an exhortation to imitate his purity (*On Perfection, GNO* 8.1, 203, 8–204, 8).[26]

Gregory was fond of the idea that Christ had three births, suggested by the biblical descriptions of him as "firstborn" in relation to "creation" (Col. 1:15), "among many brethren" (Rom. 8:29), and "from the dead" (Col. 1:18). To these correspond three births by Christians — in the body, in regeneration, and in the resurrection of the dead.[27]

Christ brought salvation and life, deifying flesh by assuming it; but he also brings life through the resurrection. Alongside regeneration and rebirth, Gregory gives equal (or greater) attention to baptism as an identification with the death, burial, and resurrection of Christ. The effectiveness of baptism is rooted not only in the incarnation but also in the death and resurrection of Christ. As the "Pioneer of our salvation" (Heb. 2:10) Christ makes possible human escape from the "prison house of death" (*Catechetical Oration* 35, *GNO* 87, 13).

Gregory asserts that earth and water are kindred elements: of the four elements (the other two are air and fire), they alone have weight, move downward, can exist in one another, and can be contained in one another (*Catechetical Oration* 35, *GNO* 87, 20–88, 2). He then parallels the burial of Christ with Christian baptism as its imitation: "Since then the death of him who is the Author of our life occasioned his burial under the earth according to our common nature, the imitation of his death that we perform is represented in the kindred element [of water]."[28] Or again, "We die together with the One who died willingly, being buried through baptism in the mysti-

---

24. Gregory expresses the same concern in *Lights, GNO* 9, 237, 23–238, 11. See further below.

25. Cf. *Refutation of the Confession of Eunomius* 80 (*GNO* 2, 345, 6-17) — Christ by his baptism drew down upon the water the Holy Spirit so that people can be changed from corruption to incorruption by the birth from above by water and the Spirit.

26. Brothers of Christ also in 202, 10.

27. *Against Eunomius* 3.2.45-54 (*GNO* 2, 67, 64-70); *Refutation of the Confession of Eunomius* 79-81 (*GNO* 2, 344, 20–346, 5); *Homilies on Canticles* 13, on Cant. 5:10 (*GNO* 6, 389, 19–390, 6); *On Perfection* (*GNO* 8.1, 200, 4–204, 9). Regeneration is a new creation (*On Perfection, GNO* 8.1, 202, 15-17).

28. *Catechetical Oration* 35, *GNO* 88, 2-5. The same comparison of the burial of Christ in the earth and burial in water in baptism is found in *Lights, GNO* 9, 228, 13-26. See further above on triple immersion, and cf. "Becoming dead to earthly life, immediately on receiving the word they were buried with Christ through baptism" — *Homilies on Canticles* 14 on Cant. 5:13 (*GNO* 6, 405, 14-15), with reference to the household of Cornelius in Acts 10.

cal water . . . in order that the imitation of his resurrection might follow the imitation of his death" (*Against Apollinaris, GNO* 3.1, 227, 4-9).

The baptismal death, burial, and resurrection are not an exact imitation; otherwise, there would be "not an imitation but an identity." In the water of baptism there occurs "not a complete destruction but a certain rupture of the connection of evil." The image of death in the water is an image of the destruction of evil, but it is not a complete destruction. The complete likeness must await the end time. In the process of the dissolution of a human being in death, evil flows out of a person. That makes possible a reconstitution of human nature purified of evil at the resurrection (*Catechetical Oration* 35, GNO 89, 5-17).

Christ's resurrection has consequences for baptism and human resurrection:

> We rehearse beforehand in the water the grace of the resurrection so that we might know that to ascend [ἀναδῦναι, the word for ascending from the baptistery] again from death is equally easy for us as to be baptized in water. (*Catechetical Oration* 35, GNO 90, 13-16).

Another important motif associated with washing in water for Gregory was cleansing, and this too had an eschatological dimension.

> For common sense and the teaching of the Scriptures show that it is impossible for one not thoroughly cleansed of every evil spot to enter the divine presence. . . . The salvation of those who are in need is characteristic of the divine activity. This becomes effective through the cleansing in water. The one who has been purified will participate in Purity, and the Deity is truly pure. (*Catechetical Oration* 36, GNO 92, 8-20)

The language of washing is associated with purification or cleansing in other contexts as well.[29] This experience points to the moral change in the lives of the baptized: "As the prophet says [Isa. 1:16], when we are 'washed' in this mystic 'bath,' we become pure in our wills, are washed clean of our souls' evils, and are changed for the better" (*Catechetical Oration* 40, GNO 103, 2-5).

The elements of water and fire have in common a purifying quality. Those who receive the cleansing in water do not require the cleansing power of fire. At the resurrection not all rise to the same life:

> The distance is great between those who have been purified and those in need of purification. Those whose purification through the bath has preceded in this life will return to a kindred state [of purity and impassibility]. But those to whom no cleansing of their defilement was applied . . . will be in a corresponding state [of impurity].

---

29. *Catechetical Oration* 35, GNO 88, 23–89, 14 (especially line 7); 91, 14-18; "cleansing of sins" (*Defer*, PG 46.416C, quoted below on grace; "wash away your sins" (*Defer*, PG 46.429D). The kindred image of pardon or forgiveness for sins is found in *Defer*, PG 46.424B and 429C.

For those latter the proper condition will be the furnace of fire:

> When the evil mixed with their nature is melted away, the pure nature is saved to God at the end of long ages. Since then there is a certain cleansing power in fire and water, those washed clean of evil's stain by the mystical water have no need of another kind of cleansing; but the uninitiated in this cleansing necessarily are purified by fire. (*Catechetical Oration* 35, *GNO* 91, 10–92, 8)[30]

Although Gregory can affirm, "Water, although it is nothing other than water, renews a human being into a spiritual regeneration, when the grace from above blesses it" (*Lights*, *GNO* 9, 227, 5-7), the renewal and cleansing are not effected by water as water without the divine blessing. The activity of the Holy Spirit is required.

> The water does not grant the benefit [of regeneration] . . . but the ordinance of God and the intervention of the Spirit coming mystically to set us free. But the water serves to exhibit the cleansing. For since we are accustomed by washing in water to make our body clean when it is soiled by dirt or filth, we apply it also to the mystical action. (*Lights*, *GNO* 9, 224, 17-24)

John 3:5 speaks of "water and the Spirit" because the human being is a compound and healing must apply to both aspects:

> Water, an element that can be sensed, [is assigned] to the visible body; but to the invisible soul, the unseen Spirit [is] summoned by faith that is inexpressibly present. (*Lights*, *GNO* 9, 225, 6-8)

Hence, Gregory can insist:

> If the bath was applied to the body, and the soul did not cleanse itself of the stains of its passions but after the initiation the life corresponds to the uninitiated life, even if it is bold to say it, I will say it and will not turn away from it, in these persons the water is water, since the gift of the Holy Spirit is in no way manifest in what occurred. (*Catechetical Oration* 40, *GNO* 102, 24-103, 10)[31]

A similar argument occurs on behalf of the divinity of the Holy Spirit.

> In holy baptism there is a participation in a life no longer subject to death. . . . Is that life-giving power in the water itself that is employed to convey the grace of baptism? Or is it not rather clear to every one that this element is only employed as a means in the outward ministry, and of itself contributes nothing toward the

---

30. Here we are introduced to Gregory's teaching on ἀποκατάστασις, the restoration of all things after a period of purifying fire: Jean Daniélou, "L'apocatastase chez saint Grégoire de Nysse," *Recherches de science religieuse* 30 (1940): 328-347; Abraham J. Malherbe and Everett Ferguson, *Gregory of Nyssa: Life of Moses* (New York: Paulist, 1978), p. 168, n. 102.

31. The reverse argument for the necessity of water as well as the Spirit occurs in *Lights*, *GNO* 9, 224, 25–225, 14.

sanctification, unless it be first transformed itself by the sanctification? What gives life to the baptized is the Spirit. [John 6:63a quoted.] But for the completion of this grace he alone, received by faith, does not give life, but belief in our Lord must precede, in order that the gift of life may come upon the believer.[32]

Through the power of the Spirit Christ "furnishes through baptism [λουτροῦ] to those who are worthy a pledge of immortality."[33]

"Water that has been blessed cleanses and enlightens a person" (*Lights, GNO* 9, 227, 14-15). Enlightenment is another key aspect of Gregory's baptismal theology,[34] although not developed as much as might be expected in his sermon *On the Day of Lights*. His consciousness of the motif is shown by his including in the Old Testament prophecies of baptism two passages that do not refer to water: Psalm 34:5 in the Greek (33:6) commands, "Come to him and be enlightened, and let not your faces be ashamed" (*Lights, GNO* 9, 235, 18-19); and Zechariah 3:3-4 describes the priest Joshua [Jesus] "adorned with a pure and shining garment" (*Lights, GNO* 9, 236, 3-7).[35]

The unbaptized is "an unenlightened [ἀφώτιστον] soul, not adorned with the grace of regeneration [παλιγγενεσίας]" (*Defer*, PG 46.424B). Receiving this grace makes one a debtor to the giver: "When we are enlightened [φωτισθῶμεν] in baptism, we are in debt to the Benefactor for his benevolence" (*Defer*, PG 46.432A). Christ came to "call sinners to repentance, whom he made by the bath of regeneration [Titus 3:5] to shine as lights [Phil. 2:15], having washed their darkened form in water" (*Homilies on Canticles* 2 on Cant. 1:5 [*GNO* 6, 49, 2-4]).

The words "grace" and "gift" have appeared frequently in the quotations already given, and this is only a small sampling of their frequency in Gregory's discussions of baptism. To take only the protreptic *Against Those Who Defer Baptism*, I count fifteen occurrences of "grace" and five of "gift."[36] Gregory begins the sermon by designating the season as the "day of salvation," when the custom was to "call strangers to adoption, those in need to a participation in grace, those filthy in transgressions to the cleansing of sins" (*Defer*, PG 46.416C) and concludes it by defining grace as "a gift of the Master" (*Defer*, PG 46.429D). To "baptize" is to "give grace" (*Defer*, PG 46.424D), and baptism is a "river of grace" that brings the "fruits of the Spirit" (*Defer*, PG 46.420C-D).[37] Gregory offers the same warning as his two episcopal colleagues, "Do not traffic in grace" by delaying baptism (*Defer*, PG 46.420B).

Gregory of Nyssa shares with his fellow Cappadocians the use of the imagery of the seal on sheep. He exhorts his hearers as "sheep" to prepare "for the seal and the

32. *On the Holy Spirit* (*GNO* 3.1, 105, 19–106, 11). I have adapted the translation of William Moore and Henry Austin Wilson in *Nicene and Post-Nicene Fathers*, Second Series, Vol. 5, p. 322.
33. *On the Christian Institution* (*GNO* 8.1, 44, 11-13).
34. See enlightenment as a name for baptism in *Catechetical Oration* 32 (*GNO* 82, 3), cited at the introduction to Gregory's theology of baptism.
35. See further below on the clothing imagery.
36. Grace — PG 46.416C; 420A, B, C; 424A, B (twice), D; 425A, B, D; 429B, C (twice), D (twice). Gift — PG 46.420B, C; 424B; 425B; 429D.
37. Cf. *Defer*, PG 46.421B, for becoming "children of the Spirit."

sign of the cross that protects against evils" (*Defer*, PG 46.417B). He asks how the angels will know "the unsealed person who does not carry the sign of the Master" (*Defer*, PG 46.424B). "The seal of the Spirit" is given "through baptism" (*On the Christian Institution* [*GNO* 8.1, 58, 12-13]).

Gregory exhorts his hearers to "take off the old self, as a filthy garment" and to "receive the garment of immortality [or incorruption] that Christ, having unfolded, holds out to you" (*Defer*, PG 46.420C; also in 429D). Modifying Isaiah 61:10, he speaks of the Lord clothing one with the "robe of salvation and the garment of joy" and being crowned with a mitre as a bridegroom (*Lights*, *GNO* 9, 241, 23-25). Those who "wash away the filth of the soul in the bath of the word [Eph. 5:26]" remove the garment of skin put on at the first sin and are clothed with Jesus himself (*Homilies on Canticles* 11 on Cant. 5:3 [*GNO* 6, 327, 14–328, 11]). Christ himself during his passion was clothed with purple, but he "grants immortality to those who are regenerated through water and the Spirit" (*Sermon V on the Resurrection of the Lord* [*GNO* 9.1, 317, 20-22]).

To come to baptism is to escape from the devil. "Flee the devil as a bitter jailer" (*Defer*, PG 46.417C). With reference to the exodus, Gregory declares the devil and his servants to perish in the water of regeneration (*Lights*, *GNO* 9, 233, 9-14).[38] At baptism Christ takes away the flock of Satan (*Lights*, *GNO* 9, 232, 20-22). Gregory knew that the devil would continue "fiery temptations," but his response was to quote Romans 6:4 and its consequence that sin was to be henceforth a corpse (*Lights*, *GNO* 9, 239, 20-24; 240, 2-6).

The exodus is only one of many types of baptism that Gregory finds in the Old Testament. These are multiplied in the sermon *On the Day of Lights*, each focused on persons in the biblical narratives: (1) An angel showed Hagar and Ishmael a well of water (Gen. 21:15-19) so that "by means of living water there was salvation for him who was perishing" (*GNO* 9, 230, 19–231, 9); (2) A wife for Isaac was found at a well, and Isaac digged wells (Gen. 24:15-20; 26:18-22; *GNO* 9, 231, 10-22); (3) Jacob met his wife at a well and laid three rods near the watering trough where the flocks mated (Gen. 29:9-10; 30:37-38; *GNO* 9, 231, 23–232, 22); (4) Moses as a babe was placed in a basket beside the river (Exod. 2:2-4), occasioning the remark that the daily sprinklings of the Hebrews pointed to the perfect baptism, and Moses led the people through the Red Sea (Exod. 14 and 1 Cor. 10:1-2; *GNO* 9, 232, 23–233, 14); (5) Joshua set up twelve stones at Israel's crossing of the Jordan (Josh. 4:9), anticipating the twelve apostles, "the ministers of baptism" (*GNO* 9, 233, 15-24);[39] (6) Elijah, in his contest with the prophets of Baal on

---

38. Gregory develops the typology of the crossing of the Red Sea in *Life of Moses* 2.121-129 (*GNO* 7.1, 70, 17–74, 10): the staff of faith leads the way: the cloud gives light; the enemy's army drowns in the water, but the water gives life to those who find refuge in it; the "saving baptism," also called the "mystical baptism," means that the passions must be put to death in the water and must not continue after emerging from the water.

39. Gregory's exhortation to baptism adds another type and continues with an application of the crossing of the Jordan: "[The river of grace from Christ] brings pleasure in the manifestation of the Spirit, as the spring of Merra [Marah] at the placing of the wood [Exod. 15:22-25] was fordable to

Mount Carmel, had water poured three times on the altar before he prayed for fire from heaven to consume the sacrifice (1 Kings 18:30-40), the fire kindled from water by prayer representing the "mystagogy of baptism," which includes the Spirit, water, and the word of prayer (*GNO* 9, 233, 24–235, 4); (7) Elisha cured Naaman of leprosy by having him dip in the Jordan (2 Kings 5:1-14; *GNO* 9, 235, 5-12).

Gregory follows these Old Testament types "in deed and act of regeneration by baptism" with "prophecies of it in words and speech": Isaiah 1:16; Psalm 34:5 (33:6 — enlightenment); Ezekiel 36:25-27; Zechariah 3:3 (clean and bright clothing); Isaiah 35:1-2; Psalms 143:6 (142:6) and 42:2 (41:3) quoted together; Psalm 1:3; Psalm 29:3-4 (28:3).

Furthermore, Gregory draws on illustrations from secular life to convey the significance that was involved in baptism. He begins his sermon *Against Those Who Defer Baptism* by employing several of these. Items I have not mentioned elsewhere are: release to those in bonds, remission to debtors,[40] healing (Gregory elaborates on this, in keeping with his fondness for medical imagery), and receiving royal gifts (*Defer*, PG 46.417A-B). Adoption of strangers as sons is mentioned at the beginning and again later (*Defer*, PG 46.416C; 425B).[41] Near the conclusion he declares, "The rights of citizenship are the proper reward" (*Defer*, PG 46.429D). No longer under the rule of the devil, the Christian is a citizen of heaven.

Similarly, in the sermon *On the Day of Lights* Gregory early gives a list of the blessings conveyed by the grace of baptism: forgiveness of punishments, release from bonds, kinship with God, a free person's boldness of speech, in place of a servile humiliation an equal honor with the angels" (*Lights, GNO* 9, 222, 23–223, 1).

The last quoted passage is preceded by mention of those "initiated" (*Lights, GNO* 9, 222, 22). Gregory, like other writers of his time, freely uses the words for "mystery" in reference to baptism (and other sacred actions and objects), as seen in several passages already cited. The *Catechetical Oration* does so frequently. For instance, the descent into the water and the triple immersion are said to involve a "mystery" (35, *GNO* 86, 6-7). Baptism employs "mystic water" (35, *GNO* 91, 21 and 92, 5; cf. 40, *GNO* 103, 2). This common usage in the late fourth century prepared for "mystery" to become the word in the Greek church roughly equivalent to what the Latin church came to call "sacraments."

Gregory of Nyssa has a great deal to say about the moral implications of baptism.[42] He devotes the last chapter of the *Catechetical Oration* to this subject (40,

---

the pious but deep and inaccessible to the profane. Imitate Joshua son of Nun. Take up the Gospel, as he did the ark. Leave the wilderness, sin. Cross the Jordan. Hasten to the Christian way of life" (*Defer*, PG 46.420D-421A).

40. Cancellation of debts and freedom are mentioned also in PG 46.424B.

41. Also in *Lights, GNO* 9, 239, 20.

42. See my "The Doctrine of Baptism," pp. 231-233; for Gregory's interest in the Christian moral life cf. my article, "Some Aspects of Gregory of Nyssa's Moral Theology in the Homilies on Ecclesiastes," in Stuart G. Hall, ed., *Gregory of Nyssa: Homilies on Ecclesiastes* (Berlin: W. de Gruyter, 1993), pp. 319-336.

GNO 102, 4 — 106, 18). Employing the motifs of rebirth and cleansing, Gregory sums up his point pithily, "What you have not become, you are not" (40, GNO 104, 10).[43] The sermon *On the Day of Lights* also speaks to "the change in your ways that should follow" "the mystical grace" of "regeneration" and appeals to several biblical examples (Zacchaeus, Matthew, Paul) of change in life (GNO 9, 227, 23–239, 19). It is necessary for those who have received the grace of the Spirit and been begotten again by the power of God to grow into perfect maturity.[44] This spiritual growth is necessary because, "Baptism destroys sins but not the inclination to them."[45]

Implicit in Gregory's doctrine of baptism is that, properly received and with proper results, it is necessary to salvation. In some places he states this explicitly. With reference to baptism as regeneration, he declares, "It is not possible apart from the regeneration in the bath for a person to be in the resurrection" (*Catechetical Oration* 35, GNO 91, 4-5). The same result derives from the view of baptism as a cleansing (see the passage quoted above on the necessity for cleansing in order to enter the divine presence — *Catechetical Oration* 36, GNO 3.4, 92, 8-11). Baptism is the means of accomplishing this task. The river of Christ's grace surrounds the whole world and carries into paradise; "it washes the whole world" (*Defer*, PG 46.420C-D). Baptism is necessary but not alone sufficient for salvation.[46] The benefits of baptism are received in the water, but not from the water. They come from invoking the divine power and require the faith and repentance of the recipients.[47]

---

43. Cf. *Catechetical Oration* 40, GNO 102, 24-103, 10 quoted above.
44. *On the Christian Institution* (GNO 8.1, 43, 8–47, 23 [44, 26–45, 2]).
45. Taranto, "Il Cristo e i sacramenti," p. 194.
46. Taranto, "Il Cristo e i sacramenti," p. 205.
47. See the summary of Gregory's theology of baptism in Ferguson, "The Doctrine of Baptism," p. 234.

39. The Delay of Baptism: Sickbed Baptism, Believers' Baptism, and Infant Baptism

The importance of receiving baptism before death was felt early in Christian history. It was suggested in chapter 23 that this practice was a key factor in the origin of infant baptism. Cyprian (chap. 22) in the third century justified abridgements in the baptismal ceremony for those baptized in extreme circumstances. An example of deathbed baptism is provided by an inscription from Macedonia dated to the third century.[1] The deceased, Nikandros, is perhaps described as a "neophyte" (newly baptized) according to a possible restoration of the damaged beginning of the inscription, and, seriously ill, he is said to have "received [baptism or grace] at the end of life."[2] Awaiting the resurrection, he is "pure since desirously he has attained divine washing [λουτροῦ]."

The policy instituted by Constantine of favoring the church was advanced by his successors, with a brief interruption under Julian, until Theodosius made Christianity the official religion of the empire. Hence, an affiliation with the church was advantageous for those politically and socially ambitious, but not all were willing to undertake full responsibilities of church membership. Moreover, the spiritual benefits of baptism in the forgiveness of all sins and guarantee of entrance into the kingdom of heaven promoted in the theology of the church made it seem desirable in the minds of many to delay reception of such a powerful sacrament until death approached so as to gain maximum benefits from it without risking the loss of those benefits by further sin.[3]

---

1. S. R. Llewelyn, "Baptism and Salvation," in S. R. Llewelyn, ed., *New Documents Illustrating Early Christianity* (North Ryde, N.S.W.: Macquarie University, Ancient History Documentary Research Centre, 1998), Vol. 8, pp. 176-179, based on D. Feissel, *Recueil des inscriptions chrétiennes de Macédoine* 5 (Paris, 1983), pp. 25-27.

2. Based on the common terminology in inscriptions of using the word "received" as shorthand for receiving baptism or grace, my translation departs from Llewelyn's "has accepted the end of life."

3. Hugh M. Riley, *Christian Initiation*, Studies in Christian Antiquity 17 (Washington, D.C.: Catholic University of America Press, 1974), p. 213, observes that the postponement of baptism threatened

Whether from delay of baptism or other considerations, some were caught in severe illness before receiving baptism. And this circumstance caught the attention of bishops even before the delay of baptism became a widespread problem. The Council of Arles in 314 had decreed, "Concerning those who are in an infirm condition and wish to profess belief, we decided that hands should be laid upon them" (can. 6).[4] This canon apparently refers to those too sick to receive baptism. The laying on of hands was presumably for admission to the catechumenate; what other benefits the bishops thought this substitution conferred are not stated.

Other factors could enter in. The fifth-century historian Socrates mentions the custom of the churches in Thessaly to baptize at the Easter season only, with the result that many died without receiving baptism (*Church History* 5.22).

The opportunities afforded for missionary work could result in the opposite tendency to speedy baptism. Socrates records that in the fifth century the Burgundians, desirous of the help of the God of the Romans, embraced the faith of Christ and went to a bishop in Gaul requesting Christian baptism. He instructed them to fast for seven days, during which time he instructed them in the elementary principles of the faith, and he baptized them on the eighth day (*Church History* 7.30).

Sickbed Baptism

The misunderstanding and abuse of baptism in its deliberate delay led preachers to deliver exhortations to catechumens to enroll for the instruction leading up to baptism at Easter. In these they often described in an unfavorable way the circumstances frequently surrounding a sickbed or deathbed baptism.[5] Hence, allowance must be made for rhetorical exaggeration in these accounts, because the preachers were attempting to motivate their hearers to respond to the call to baptism now rather than waiting for an emergency later. With that understanding these accounts can be quite revealing about the practice of clinical baptism and about what elements were considered so essential to baptism that they could not be omitted even in an emergency situation.

Basil the Great

In warning against the delay of baptism, Basil in his *Homily* 13, *Exhortation to Baptism* gives his most detailed account of the normal baptismal ceremony:

---

to give baptism a purely eschatological orientation and make it highly individual rather than an ecclesial concern. The clinical baptism of children had a similar implication.

4. Mark Edwards, *Optatus: Against the Donatists* (Liverpool: Liverpool University Press, 1997), p. 187 (translation of Optatus's Appendix 4). Cf. the Council of Elvira, can. 39, in chap. 42.

5. Everett Ferguson, "Exhortations to Baptism in the Cappadocians," *Studia patristica* 32 (1997): 121-129.

> Why do you wait for a fever for baptism to become a gift to you? When you are not able to utter the saving words nor are inclined to hear purely (when the sickness dwells in the head itself), nor lift the hands to heaven nor stand upon the feet, nor to bend the knee in worship, nor to be taught profitably, nor to confess safely, nor to reach agreement with God, nor to renounce the enemy, nor to follow intelligently being initiated, when those present are doubtful that you experience the grace or have feeling of the things happening. But when you receive the grace knowingly, then you possess the talent and do not threaten the activity. (*Exh.* 5; PG 31.436C-437A)

This passage brings together, but perhaps not in exact sequence, items mentioned elsewhere in Basil's writings (see chap. 36) and adds details not otherwise attested. Basil does not specify with what actions the different postures of raising hands, standing, and kneeling were associated.[6] He indicates that his church knew a renunciation of the devil and an adhesion to God as part of the baptismal ceremony. Basil underscores by repetition the important place he gives to the teaching associated with baptism — hearing what is said and being taught — and of the candidate's verbal participation — repeating the saving words and making confession. Basil has apparently participated in administering clinical baptism and so was not willing to reject it. Nevertheless, he expresses the doubts that were felt about the practice. In order to discourage the delay of baptism he emphasizes the desirability of being able to follow intelligently the procedure and to experience what was going on. The inability to do so, he implies, might threaten the validity of the baptism.[7] The clinical baptism of those unable to make the responses was given to those who would have wanted to be baptized, that is, catechumens, and so their assent could be assumed even if not verbally expressed. This extenuating circumstance would not cover those who had not entered the catechumenate or otherwise affiliated in some way with the church.

In order to encourage his hearers to act in the present, Basil describes a worst case scenario:

> There may be difficulty everywhere and inconsolable affliction, the physicians and relatives having given up hope; when you are constrained by short, dry breaths; when you are consumed with a burning fever on the inside and you sigh deeply from within your heart, yet you will find no one to share your grief. You will utter something faint and feebly, but no one will understand; everything you say will be dismissed as delirium. Who will give you baptism then? Who will seek to extend consciousness for one in a stupor from suffering? Those close to you are fainthearted; others despise the suffering. Your friend hesitates to make a suggestion, as causing confusion, or perhaps even the physician deceives; and you yourself do not despair on account of the natural love of living. It is night, and there are no

---

6. Cf. Cyril of Jerusalem, Theodore of Mopsuestia, and John Chrysostom.
7. One naturally then raises the question what effect this principle would have on infant baptism.

helpers. No one to administer baptism is present. Death has come near; the pallbearers approach. Who is the Deliverer? Only God, whom you despised? But will he listen to you then, for you do not listen to him now. (*Exh.* 7; PG 31.441B-C)

The concern to die baptized and the distress of not receiving baptism or not receiving it properly testify to the importance of baptism.

Gregory of Nazianzus

Gregory of Nazianzus describes a similar scene of commotion that could be a paraphrase of Basil (in part word for word) in trying to dissuade his hearers from a delay of baptism until their deathbed.

> Let us be baptized today . . . nor wait till we get more wicked that more may be forgiven us. . . . While you are still master of your thoughts, run to the gift. While you are not yet sick in body or in mind, nor seem so to those who are with you (though you are really of sound mind); while your welfare is not yet in the power of others, but you yourself are still master of it; while your tongue is not stammering or parched, or (to say no more) deprived of the power of pronouncing the sacramental words [words of mystagogy]; while you can still be made one of the faithful, not conjecturally but confessedly; and can still receive not pity but congratulation; while the gift is still clear to you, and there is no doubt about it; while the grace can reach the depth of your soul, and it is not merely your body that is washed for burial; and before tears surround you announcing your decease — and even those restrained perhaps for your sake — and your wife and children would delay your departure, and are listening for your dying words; before the physician is powerless to help you, and is giving you but hours to live — hours which are not his to give — and is balancing your salvation with the nod of his head . . . ; before there is a struggle between the man who would baptize you and the man who seeks your money, the one striving that you may receive your viaticum [provision for a journey], the other that he may be inscribed in your will as heir — and there is no time for both.
>
> . . . Why will you receive the blessing of force and not of free will; of necessity rather than of liberty? (*Oration* 40.11-12)[8]

Gregory refers to one of the less worthy motivations in postponing baptism — to gain the maximum forgiveness from it. Consistent with his preference that the baptizand know what is being done and in keeping with his (and Basil's) emphasis on the confession of faith (chap. 37), he wants baptism to be a conscious choice verbally participated in. Accordingly, he indicates that there were ambivalent feelings

---

8. In an unquoted part of the passage there is a figurative use of *baptizō* as a play on words, as Gregory warns against being sunk or overwhelmed (βαπτίζεσθαι) and making shipwreck of grace (40.11).

about deathbed baptism. Not all acknowledged it, for, as only a likeness of the real thing, one could only conjecture its validity. One should receive baptism when it was evident and not uncertain.

Gregory intimates that the deathbed baptism might be a decision made by others (one's welfare in the hands of others and receiving baptism not of free choice). That was not a desirable situation but one comparable to infant baptism (*Oration* 40.28). The comparison indicates Gregory did not reject sickbed baptism any more than he did infant baptism; but both practices were an anomaly in his basic understanding of the baptismal rite.

Neither Gregory nor Basil indicates whether any accommodation in the application of the water was made in sickbed baptism, but there are possible hints in Gregory of Nyssa and clear indications in John Chrysostom and Epiphanius that such was the case.

Gregory of Nyssa

Like his fellow Cappadocians, Gregory of Nyssa in his sermon *Against Those Who Defer Baptism* draws an unfavorable picture of the circumstances surrounding a sickbed baptism.

> [When it is said "this night your soul is released from the body"], then there is tumult and a cry. And all is sought quickly in the crisis of time: the vessels, the water, the priest, the word that makes ready for grace. Necessity requires it and sickness overshadows, causing sudden and unyielding shortness of breath. And there is no less tumult than in the encounter of a battle. All those meeting one another in the house break out into passionate words, and there is jostling, disorder, and mournful and indistinct noise, when slaves, kinfolk, friends, children, and the wife are entangled with one another as if in a night battle. As it is still now a time of peace, let us arrange wisely our affairs. (*Defer*, PG 46.425A)

Gregory describes a scene that (no doubt intentionally) would hardly seem consonant with the solemnity normally accompanying baptism in church. He is distinctive in comparing the confusion to the noise of a battlefield.

The account, perhaps designedly, includes a listing of what was essential for baptism. What the vessels were and what their purpose was, however, are unexplained. Were they perhaps containers for pouring the water over the body of the sick person? Did they contain oil for an anointing? If the latter, does the order indicate a prebaptismal anointing? Did they carry the bread and wine for a baptismal eucharist? Or, did they serve several purposes, including something I have not suggested? The possibilities are intriguing, but any explanation is hypothetical.

The need for water is obvious in a baptism, but the setting suggests something brought in rather than that to which the person is taken and so other than a baptismal pool. The expectation is for a priest (ἱερεύς) to perform the ceremony.

The presence of the "word which makes ready for [the] grace [of baptism]" accords with emphases in Basil and the other Gregory, but there is some ambiguity about which word the Nyssene has in mind. Is it the word of prayer by which the priest consecrated the water?[9] Is it the formula pronounced by the priest over the baptizand? Or is it the word of faith confessed by the latter? The prominence given to this confessed faith by the other Cappadocians might favor this interpretation, but the context of things sought for the baptism would favor a reference to words spoken by the priest.

John Chrysostom

John Chrysostom's account of sickbed or deathbed baptism occurs not in an exhortation to baptism but in one of his *Baptismal Instructions*.[10] He congratulates those preparing for baptism that they "do not approach baptism at your final gasp" (9.4).[11] He contrasts the joy of those who receive baptism in normal circumstances in church with the lament of those on their deathbed:

> Even if the grace is the same for you and for those who are initiated on their deathbeds, neither the choice nor the preparations are the same. They receive baptism in their beds, but you receive it in the bosom of the common mother of us all, the church; they receive baptism amidst laments and tears, but you are baptized with rejoicing and gladness; they are groaning, while you are giving thanks. . . . (9.5)[12]

Chrysostom continues in the vein of the Cappadocians by referring to the "tumult and confusion" of the scene (9.8). The arrival of the priest is a greater source of fear than the fever itself, for the coming of this person who should represent eternal life is a symbol of death.

Then Chrysostom indicates what he considers the essentials in the baptismal rite by raising doubts about the effectiveness of the rite when they are absent. While preparations for the baptism and for the death of the sick person are in progress, it often happens that the soul departs (or appears to depart) the body:

---

9. He had referred to the blessing of water by the priest earlier in 421D — see chap. 38.

10. Philippe de Roten, *Baptême et mystagogie: Enquête sur l'initiation chrétienne selon s. Jean Chrysostome*, Liturgiewissenschaftliche Quellen und Forschungen 91 (Münster: Aschendorff, 2005), pp. 7-10.

11. The same phrase occurs in the warning to catechumens against postponing salvation "until the last gasp" (*Homilies on John* 18 [PG 59.115B]; again in *Homilies on Acts* 23.3 [PG 60.182]; and 1.7 [PG 60.24A] — this was not a time for giving the mysteries but for making wills); *Homilies on Hebrews* 13.9 (PG 63.108A-B) speaks of those who wait to "receive baptism at the last gasp" but often do not receive it.

12. Translation by Paul W. Harkins, *St. John Chrysostom: Baptismal Instructions*, Ancient Christian Writers 31 (Westminster MD: Newman, 1963), p. 133.

When the man who is going to be baptized is unconscious and lies as inert as a log or stone, differing in no way from a corpse, when he does not recognize those who are present, nor hear what they say, when he cannot make the responses by which he will enter into the blessed contract with the common Master of us all, what benefit does he get from his initiation?

One who is about to approach those sacred rites and awesome mysteries ought to be alert and wide-awake. . . . (9.9-10)[13]

Chrysostom refers to the words of renunciation of the devil and of adhesion to Christ (described in 2.20-21; 11.19-25; see chap. 33), which he regularly describes as a contract.[14] The preacher does not answer his question; having planted the doubt in his hearers' minds, he accomplished his hortatory purpose. But the question implies greater doubt about the effectiveness of clinical baptism than was expressed by the Cappadocians, perhaps because Chrysostom considers the explicit circumstance of unconsciousness. The consciousness and active participation of the baptizand in the ceremony was certainly considered the norm if not an absolute necessity.

The statement above about receiving baptism in bed likely includes the application of water by pouring, and such is made explicit in another discussion of deathbed baptism with close parallels to this passage. Chrysostom speaks of the "noise and tumult" and observes, "Sometimes it is upon the dead that the water has been poured [ἐπεχύθη] and holy mysteries flung upon the ground."[15] His warning about delay of baptism evokes a circumstance of which he apparently had knowledge of the baptism not being completed before the person expired.

Chrysostom responds to the excuses given for delaying baptism.[16] He warns that the person baptized at the point of death departs without good works. Baptism is given, "not that we should receive and depart, but that we should show fruits of it in our later life." A person's last illness is not a time for giving the mysteries but for making wills. "The time for mysteries is in health of mind and soundness of soul." In affairs of the world, the law does not recognize a will when a person is not of sound mind. "Why delay?" A person taken away unbaptized has "intolerable punishments."[17] God gave baptism to do away with our sins (see chap. 34 on forgiveness in baptism according to Chrysostom), not to increase them (by postponing baptism).[18]

---

13. Harkins, *St. John Chrysostom: Baptismal Instructions*, p. 134.

14. Hans Kirsten, *Die Taufabsage: Eine Untersuchung zur Gestalt und Geschichte der Taufe nach den altkirchlichen Taufliturgien* (Berlin: Evangelische Verlagsanstalt, 1960), pp. 134, 136, concludes that for the ancient church in general the renunciation and adhesion were considered a unity with baptism and if not essential to it were central to it (p. 77).

15. *Homilies on Acts* 1.8 on Acts 1:4-5 (PG 60.26). Translation here and following is by George B. Stevens et al. in *Nicene and Post-Nicene Fathers* (repr. Peabody: Hendrickson, 1994), Second Series, Vol. 11, p. 10.

16. Roten, *Baptême et mystagogie*, pp. 15-27.

17. *Homilies on Acts* 1. Translation by Stevens et al., *Nicene and Post-Nicene Fathers*, Second Series, Vol. 11, p. 9.

18. *Homilies on Hebrews* 13.9 (PG 63.108A-B).

Marcianus the Ascetic

Marcianus the Ascetic from Cyrus is described by Theodoret in his *Religious History* 3 (PG 82.1325-1340) and mentioned in his *Church History* 4.25 as notable for the practice of asceticism in the region of Antioch in the late fourth century. Nine opuscula and some fragments preserved in Syriac have been attributed to him.[19] One of these, the third in J. Lebon's edition, is "On Baptism." It is an exhortation to baptism addressed to those who were deferring baptism until their deathbed and comparable to the exhortations given by the three Cappadocians and Chrysostom.

The author asks, "Why do we put off receiving the gift of God?" "Why do we want to live in evil and wait for the time of our departure to approach the grace of God and be justified?" (3). He responds to similar concerns addressed in the works examined above. He asks, Why put off baptism under the pretext that we are not pure? Why be concerned to leave the world simply pure and not also full of fruits? (5). If "we say, 'Let us do all we want and when we have done it, then let us receive his gift and have our sins removed,'" we "despise the gift of God" (6).

Marcianus encourages his hearers by the assurance that the gift of God makes the sinner pure in an instant. Angels rejoice because one not only repents (Luke 15:10) but is regenerated (7). We have been purified; let us not be soiled again (8). But he knows that one concern was that a fall might occur after baptism, so he affirms that the way of penitence will still be open. The Good Shepherd will carry us on his shoulders and introduce us again into his sheepfold (9). There is remission of sins after baptism according to Luke 15:11ff. and 1 Corinthians 5:1ff. (10). Will not God be merciful to those who pray to him and confess his name? (11).

"On Baptism" begins with a high doctrine of the benefits conferred by baptism. The Lord engenders anew by holy baptism and makes those dead by sins to be alive (1). But evil concupiscence causes us to outrage the gift of the Holy Spirit. We must turn to penitence, for John 3:5 means that anyone without baptism is without the kingdom of heaven (2). Matthew 28:19 and the accounts in Acts show the importance of baptism (4). Those without baptism are not Christians, for they are sheep not branded, are strangers to the flock of Christ, and lack remission of sins (5). Purification of sins and regeneration are recurring themes (7). There is perhaps allusion to the confession of faith in the statement, "Baptism is confirmation of our faith" (6), and reference to a renunciation in the declaration, "We have renounced the Adversary and cursed all his works" so let us not give him opportunity or power against us (8). Other notable statements are that since the Adversary is defeated, "death is dead" (7), and "We were slaves to sin, but we have been set free" (8).

---

19. J. Lebon, *Le moine Saint Marcien: Étude critique des sources: Edition de ses écrits*, publ. Albert Van Roey (Leuven: Spicilegiumsacrum Lovaniense, 1968), gives the Syriac text and French translation. The third opusculum, "On Baptism," is discussed on pp. 136-142, the Syriac text given on pp. 170-175, and the French translation on pp. 225-229. My references are to the twelve paragraphs of his translation.

Epiphanius of Salamis

Epiphanius passes on a report he had heard from Josephus of Tiberias (born during the old age of the emperor Constantine), a Jew converted to Christ. This Josephus was close to the Jewish patriarch in Tiberias, Ellel, who asked for Christian baptism as he approached death.

> When Ellel was dying he asked the bishop who then lived near Tiberias for holy baptism, and he received it from him *in extremis* for allegedly medical reasons. For he had sent for him, as though for a doctor, Josephus, and he had the room cleared and begged the bishop, "Give me the seal in Christ!" The bishop summoned the servants and ordered water prepared, as though intending to give the patriarch, who was very sick, some treatment for his illness with water. They did what they were told, for they did not know. But pleading indulgence for his modesty the patriarch sent them all out, and was allowed the laver and the holy mysteries. . . .
>
> "I peeped in through the cracks in the doors and saw what the bishop was doing to the patriarch. . . . When this was over and the doors were opened, the patriarch's visitors asked him how he felt after his treatment, and he replied, 'Great!' He knew what he was talking about!"[20]

This was a baptism that apparently could not have been by immersion. Hence, the modifications made in cases of sickbed baptism attested by Cyprian in the third century for the West apparently obtained, at least in some places, in the East in the fourth century. Presumably the water was poured over the whole body, which (if the reference to modesty is to be given full force) was nude (as in normal baptism).

We note that "seal" is used in this account for the baptism itself.

A Report by Socrates

Sickbed baptism did not always entail water being brought to the sickbed. Socrates Scholasticus tells the story of a notable conversion of a Jew who was paralytic. Medical treatment and prayers by his fellow Jews failed to effect a cure, so he resorted to Christian baptism. The bishop instructed him in the first principles of Christian truth and then directed that he should be taken in his bed to the font. "The paralytic Jew receiving baptism with a sincere faith, as soon as he was taken out of the baptismal font [βαπτιστήριον], found himself perfectly cured of his disease."[21] Death was not imminent, and nothing hindered a full immersion in the font. Instruction and faith are duly noted as preceding the baptism.

---

20. Epiphanius, *Panarion* 30.4.3-7 and 30.6.1-4. Translation by Frank Williams, *The Panarion of Epiphanius of Salamis* (Leiden: Brill, 1987), pp. 122-124.

21. Socrates, *Church History* 7.4; translation by A. C. Zenos in *Nicene and Post-Nicene Fathers* (repr. Peabody: Hendrickson, 1994), Second Series, Vol. 2, p. 155.

Inscriptions

See chapter 23 for inscriptions recording the emergency baptisms of children and chapter 24 for an adult baptized as death presumably approached. There are other epitaphs of adults who received late baptism, probably at the onset of death, giving inscriptional support to the literary sources indicating that such was not an isolated phenomena.[22]

Sponsors and Instruction

As was earlier specified in the baptism of infants (chap. 20), provision was made for sponsors to give the answers to the baptismal questions for those adults who had earlier indicated a desire for baptism but became too ill to speak for themselves.[23]

The Council of Laodicea (chap. 35) decreed not only that those to be baptized must learn the faith (creed) by heart and recite it (can. 46) but also that someone baptized in sickness (and so with an abbreviated ceremony for an emergency situation) who then recovered must similarly memorize the creed by heart and know the divine gifts granted to them (can. 47). This is another indication of the importance attached by the bishops noted above to faith (albeit now creedalized) in connection with baptism.

Believers' Baptism in Christian Families

A separate phenomenon from emergency or sickbed baptism of those who deliberately delayed baptism until the end of life was baptism on reaching a responsible age by those whose parents (one or both) were Christians. This is not the same question as the origins of infant baptism (chap. 23), nor is it properly "delay of baptism." The assumption of the general practice of infant baptism has obscured the significance of the fact that, although we know the names of many children of Christian parents in the fourth century not baptized until their teens or later, explicit testimony is lacking that would permit us to name the first Christian baptized as an infant whose baptism was not a case of clinical baptism. Indeed, what we know of the ages at which those from strong Christian families who became leaders in the church in the

---

22. S. R. Llewelyn in *New Documents Illustrating Early Christianity*, Vol. 8 (North Ryde, N.S.W.: Macquarie University, Ancient History Documentary Research Centre, 1998; Grand Rapids: Eerdmans, 1997), p. 176 with reference to Feissel, *Recueil des inscriptions chrétiennes de Macédoine* 5, p. 120. The examples cited are *Inscriptiones Christianae urbis Romae* VII, 19820 (Rome); *Inscriptiones Latinae selectae* 9481 (Salona), and Feissel, *Recueil*, no. 123.

23. Paul F. Bradshaw, "The Profession of Faith in Early Christian Baptism," *Evangelical Quarterly* 78 (2006): 101-115 (p. 113, n. 44), cites the Council of Hippo, 393, can. 36; First Council of Orange, 441, canon 12; Cyril of Alexandria, *Commentary in John* 11:26; and others.

fourth century were baptized offers no certain examples of baptism in childhood.[24] The list includes Ephraem the Syrian, Basil of Caesarea, Gregory of Nyssa, Gregory of Nazianzus, John Chrysostom,[25] Ambrose, Jerome, Rufinus, Paulinus of Nola, and Augustine.[26] To these may be added Ambrose's brother Satyrus, Gregory of Nazianzus's father Gregory, sister Gorgonia, and brother Caesarius, Jerome's friends Heliodorus and Rufius, Paulinus of Nola's brother, and Rufinus of Aquileia.[27] The practice is so extensive that we cannot put it down as a new tendency; where is the evidence that the practice was ever different?

Nor do the individuals involved fit the profile of those who did not take their Christianity seriously. For example, Gregory of Nazianzus speaks glowingly of his pious upbringing by his mother and his father (who was a bishop) but has no word about infant baptism or criticism for it not being given. He himself did not oppose the practice (chap. 37) but does not treat it as normal. Basil the Great and Gregory of Nyssa traced their ancestry on their father's side to one of the early converts in Cappadocia by Gregory the Wonderworker and on the mother's side to a martyr in the persecution by Diocletian — not the kind of people to neglect a fundamental Christian duty.

Infant Baptism: The Fourth Century and Beyond

Emergency baptism of children had begun at the latest by 200 (chap. 23), and after Tertullian we do not hear of opposition to infant baptism. However, if children were healthy, there is no evidence that their parents presented them for baptism. The instruction to parents to baptize their children begins in the late fourth century (*Apostolic Constitutions* and Asterius — chap. 35), and the routine baptism of babies belongs to the fifth century and after, when evidence for accommodations of the baptism ceremony to the presence of infants begins to appear (chaps. 44, 45, 46, 48,

---

24. See chap. 23 and David F. Wright, "At What Ages Were People Baptized in the Early Centuries?" *Studia patristica* 30 (1997): 389-394. For believer's baptism in general, Steven A. McKinion, "Baptism in the Patristic Writings," in Thomas R. Schreiner and Shawn D. Wright, eds., *Believer's Baptism: Sign of the New Covenant in Christ* (Nashville: Broadman and Holman, 2006). A different perspective is found in Eduard Nagel, *Kindertaufe und Taufaufschub: Die Praxis vom 3.-5. Jahrhundert in Nordafrika und ihre theologische Einordnung bei Tertullian, Cyprian und Augustinus* (Frankfurt, 1980).

25. John Chrysostom was not unrepresentative in being given a biblical education as a youth (in his case by his Christian mother, a widow), but he is special in that we are told the age at which he was baptized: At the age of eighteen he was "admitted to the mystery of the washing of regeneration" — Palladius, *Dialogue on the Life of St. John Chrysostom* 5.

26. This is the list in Joachim Jeremias, *Infant Baptism in the First Four Centuries* (London: SCM, 1960), p. 88. H. Thurston, "When Baptism Was Delayed," *Month* 152 (1928): 529-541, also distinguishes the delay of baptism among those from Christian families.

27. Wright, "At What Ages Were People Baptized in the Early Centuries?" p. 393, repeats Jeremias's list with these additions. Augustine, *Against Julian* 1.4.14 reports the rumor that his Pelagian opponent, Julian of Eclanum, was baptized as an infant.

49, 52). The history of baptism begins again in the West with Augustine (chap. 52), and under his influence infant baptism became the norm there.[28]

Two developments in the fourth century closely related to the material covered above and in chapter 23 and supportive of the latter's conclusions are pertinent. The imperial favor for Christianity led many to enroll as catechumens but delay their baptism until the approach of death. In this way they could claim identification with the church but not assume full responsibilities of church membership. Such a powerful sacrament as baptism that brought forgiveness of all sins was not to be wasted on one's youth! Such unworthy motives, however, do not apply to children who grew up in strong Christian families and whose parents were leaders in the church and yet did not have their children baptized in childhood (noted above). The church fathers of the fourth century, who were not themselves baptized as infants but never before Augustine reproached their parents for not having them baptized as children, nonetheless urged that baptism could be administered at any age. Infant baptism became a normal practice in the West after Augustine (chaps. 50 and 52).

As an alternative to infant baptism some parents vowed their children to the service of God and/or enrolled them as catechumens.[29] Jerome wrote to Laeta "to instruct you how to bring up our dear Paula, who has been consecrated to Christ before her birth and vowed to his service before her conception" (*Letters* 107.3). Pope Siricius (384-399) decreed that "whoever has vowed himself to the services of the church from his infancy must be baptized before the years of puberty and join the ministry of lectors" (*Letters* 1.9.13), an indication of how little infant baptism was common in Rome at this time.

Basil of Caesarea speaks of a "catechumen since infancy" (*Homilies* 13.1). The best-known example of enrollment as a catechumen after birth is Augustine (*Confessions* 1.11; 6.4). This may have been the norm. For the continuation of the practice in the Greek church, note the apparent alternatives expressed by Cyril of Alexandria in his comments on John 11:26, "When a newborn baby is brought to receive the chrism of the catechumenate or the chrism of perfection in holy baptism. . . ."

The distinction of being the first person baptized as an infant in a non-emergency situation whose name we know may belong to the future emperor Julian. According to the fifth-century historian Sozomen, Julian "was initiated in infancy according to the custom of the church," but earlier sources for his baptism are indef-

---

28. David F. Wright, "Augustine and the Transformation of Baptism," in Alan Kreider, ed., *The Origins of Christendom in the West* (Edinburgh: T&T Clark, 2001), pp. 287-310, and our chapter 51 below on Augustine. Epiphanius's statement about Hieracas that he "does not accept children who die before reaching the age of reason" (*Panarion* 67.2.7) presumably means that he did not accept them for baptism, and probably for the same considerations that prompted Pelagius, before he was pressed by Augustine (chap. 52), to deny the necessity of baptism for infants.

29. David F. Wright, "Infant Dedication in the Early Church," in Stanley E. Porter and Anthony R. Cross, eds., *Baptism, the New Testament and the Church* (Sheffield: Sheffield Academic Press, 1999), pp. 352-378.

inite as to the time and the reference, if not Sozomen's own interpretation, may be to enrolling him as a catechumen.[30]

It seems that in the West as in the East the baptism of infants may not have been general before the sixth century.[31] Many of the cases of infant baptism and references to the practice in the third to fifth century may indeed have been to emergency or clinical baptism.[32] There were voices urging the baptism of children: Isidore, presbyter at Pelusium in Egypt (d. c. 435), said, "We are surrounded with evils; let us hasten to baptize our children" (*Letters* I.125 [PG 78.265]). The fifth-century canons of councils (Milevis, 416, and Carthage, 418), excommunicating "any who deny the necessity of baptism for the newborn," are directed against the Pelagians and should not be generalized as requiring infant baptism (see chap. 50 where the canon at Carthage is quoted). In the sixth century Caesarius of Arles beseeches his hearers to bring a son or slave to baptism and not postpone doing so. This was to be done at Lent in order to receive the sacrament of baptism in proper manner (at Pasch?). He refers to some women reluctant to bring their babies to baptism (*Sermon* 84.6).[33]

An inscription from southern Gaul dated to the fifth century records the plaintive emotions of parents who affirmed the innocence of their deceased infant, whom they did not succeed in bringing to the font before death.

> Worthy child, circled round by the rampart of the cross, innocent, undarkened by the filth of sin, little Theudosius, whose parents in purity of mind intended to bury [*tingui*, immerse — EF] him in the holy baptismal font, was snatched away

---

30. Sozomen, *Church History* 5.2; earlier sources for his baptism are Gregory of Nazianzus, *Oration* 4.52 and Cyril of Alexandria, *Against Julian* 1, pref. 3. David F. Wright, "The Baptism(s) of Julian the Apostate Revisited," *Studia patristica* 39 (2006): 145-150, canvasses the sources and wonders "whether, after all, we can be sure that Julian ever was baptized" (p. 150).

31. Jean-Charles Picard, "Ce que les textes nous aprennent sur les équipements et le mobilier liturgiques nécessaires pour le baptême dans le sud de la Gaul et l'Italie du Nord," *Actes du XIe Congrès International d'Archéologie Chretienne, Lyone, Vienne, Grenoble, Genève et Aoste, 21-28 septembre 1986* (Vatican, 1989), Vol. 2, p. 1454, asserts that up to the sixth century without doubt baptism concerned in most cases adults. With this conclusion concurs A. Piédagnel, ed., *Jean Chrysostome: Trois catéchèses baptismales*, Sources chrétiennes 366 (Paris: Cerf, 1990), pp. 256-257. He attributes this to the influence of churches of Spain and Gaul where this practice was widespread, and cites Caesarius of Arles, *Sermon* 84.6. The passage, however, applies only to Gaul and indicates that infant baptism was not routine; see below.

32. Mark Searle, "Infant Baptism Reconsidered," in M. E. Johnson, ed., *Living Water, Sealing Spirit: Readings on Christian Initiation* (Collegeville: Liturgical, 1995), pp. 365-409 (367), observes that too little consideration has been given to the relationship between infant baptism and clinical deathbed baptism. (This would apply to both the liturgy and the circumstances of administration.) Searle adds that the Gelasian *Order for the Making of a Catechumen or for Baptizing* was nothing other than a rite for baptizing the dying.

33. For Caesarius's information on baptism see Victor Saxer, *Les rites de l'initiation chrétienne du IIe au VIe siècle: Esquisse historique et signification d'après leur principaux témoins* (Spoleto: Centro italiano di studi sull'alto medioevo, 1988), pp. 512-525, and on Gregory of Tours, for whom the catechumenate has disappeared, pp. 525-528.

by shameless death; yet the ruler of high Olympus will give rest to any member lying beneath the noble sign of the cross, and the child will be heir to Christ.[34]

The allusion to God as "ruler of high Olympus" shows the continuation of pagan classical language. The parents appear to cling to the conception of the innocence of children in spite of (or in contradiction to or ignorance of) the teaching of original sin and so to reflect the earlier sentiment of the necessity nonetheless of baptism, perhaps reinforced in their case by a superstitious (unless we read too much into the pagan description of God) view of the efficacy of baptism.

A law preserved in the Codex of Justinian is sometimes cited for the legal requirement of infant baptism:

> It is fitting that those not yet counted worthy of venerable baptism make themselves manifest . . . and approach the most holy church together with their wives, children (παισὶ), and everyone in their house to be taught the true faith of Christians, and so having been taught and thoroughly rejecting their former error to be counted worthy of saving baptism. . . .
>
> We establish the law that their children (τέκνα) who are of young age immediately and without delay receive the saving baptism, even as is required of those who have already reached the age to attend regularly the most holy churches and to be instruct in the divine canons and divine scriptures so as to lay hold of genuine repentance and shaking off the old error to receive venerable baptism. (*Codex* 1.11.10.1, 5).[35]

The context is household conversion, including the children of whatever age and slaves, and does not refer to children of Christian parents but presupposes their baptism. The passage specifically refers to Manichaeans and imposes economic penalties against those who do not comply.

The prevalence of infant baptism in the sixth century brought an end to the catechumenate and as a corollary the cessation of the "rule of secrecy."[36] Basilicas built after the sixth century in the East as a rule no longer had a separate baptistery but had fonts built just for infants. The role of sponsors for the candidates for baptism changed to "godparents." Otherwise, the new situation of infant baptism as the usual practice did not change the rite of baptism.[37]

---

34. *Corpus Inscriptionum Latinorum* XII.5750; translation by Peter Cramer, *Baptism and Change in the Early Middle Ages c. 200-c. 1150* (Cambridge: Cambridge University Press, 1993), p. 131.

35. Greek and Latin text in Paul Krueger, *Corpus Iuris Civilis*, Vol. 2: *Codex Iustinanus* (Berlin: Weidmann, 1954), p. 64.

36. Saxer, *Les rites de l'initiation*, p. 626 and passim, for the catechumenate on the way to disappearance in the sixth century with the disappearance of adult converts, and p. 636 for only the ritual aspects remaining.

37. With reference to the Orthodox Church, see Lothar Heiser, *Die Taufe in der orthodoxen Kirche: Geschichte, Spendung, und Symbolik nach der Lehre der Väter* (Trier: Paulinus, 1987), pp. 229-235, who describes the ceremonies. He explains that from the Orthodox perspective participation in the death

The evidence of liturgical practice, as noted in preceding chapters, demonstrates the priority, temporally and theologically, of the baptism of adults. The medieval western baptismal liturgies continued to demonstrate the point.[38] Everything in the *Sacramentarium Veronense* is for full-grown candidates and nothing is said about minors, although at the time of its redaction the majority of baptizands in fact were children.[39] The *Gelasianum* contains an old form of baptism adapted to minor children, mostly by shortening.[40] The *Ordo Romanus XI* has only minor children in view, but the rite represents the usage of a totally different situation.[41] The prevalence of infant baptism meant a change from Easter and Pentecost as the times for baptism.[42] The age of Charlemagne saw the definitive legal enforcement of infant baptism in the West.[43]

The answers to the questions about renouncing the devil and about confessing the faith were so essential to the rite of baptism that they could not be abandoned. For the infant unable to give the answers, the solution was for the words to be spoken by the parents or godparents. Infant baptism from the beginning sought and found its justification in parents or others who brought them and spoke for them the words of renunciation and confession of faith. These words were initially in the third person, "[The child] believes," but soon the majority of liturgies had the parents (or others) use the first person, "I believe."[44]

The displacement of dipping by pouring lay a millennium in the future.[45] The explanation may not apply to this late date, but one wonders if the prevalence of deathbed baptism and the acceptance of pouring in such cases was not a factor in the eventual acceptance of pouring or sprinkling as a normal way of administering baptism, even as deathbed baptism had earlier been the principal factor in the rise of infant baptism.

The historical evidence of an absence of explicit reference to infant baptism before the end of the second century is thus supported by the evidence from liturgical

---

and resurrection of Christ and the imparting of the Holy Spirit did not depend on the receptivity of the recipient (p. 231).

38. Burkhard Neunheuser, "Die Liturgie der Kindertaufe: Ihre Problematik in der Geschichte," in Hans Jörge Auf Der Maur and Bruno Kleinheyer, eds., *Zeichen des Glaubens: Studien zu Taufe und Firmung: Balthasar Fischer zum 60. Geburtstag* (Freiburg: Herder, 1972), pp. 319-334, surveys the evidence. A. S. Yates, *Why Baptize Infants? A Study of the Biblical, Traditional and Theological Evidence* (Norwich: Canterbury Press, 1993), p. 161, acknowledges that infant baptism was somehow fitted into the adult rite without a rite being designed for the young child.

39. Neunheuser, "Die Liturgie der Kindertaufe," p. 324.
40. Neunheuser, "Die Liturgie der Kindertaufe," p. 325.
41. Neunheuser, "Die Liturgie der Kindertaufe," pp. 326-327.
42. Neunheuser, "Die Liturgie der Kindertaufe," p. 329.
43. Neunheuser, "Die Liturgie der Kindertaufe," pp. 329-330.
44. Neunheuser, "Die Liturgie der Kindertaufe," p. 330. See further chapters 51 and 52 on Augustine.
45. The end of the fifteenth or beginning of the sixteenth century according to Neunheuser, "Die Liturgie der Kindertaufe," p. 332.

practice and the history of baptismal theology (which becomes even more evident in the fourth to fifth centuries) that shows the secondary development of infant baptism. The liturgies of baptism were clearly designed for those of responsible age, and only at the end of the fourth century (apart from the *Apostolic Tradition*) are there indications of minor but telling accommodations to fit those who could not speak for themselves. The theology of baptism applied to those of responsible age and only with Augustine's developed doctrine of infant participation in the guilt of Adam's sin did a theological justification of infant baptism gain favor, and then only in the West. The lack of an agreed theology of infant baptism between the Greek (e.g., Chrysostom) and Latin (e.g., Augustine) churches at a time when the practice came under discussion (late fourth and early fifth century) argues strongly against infant baptism having been a common or standard practice for the preceding centuries.[46]

In both the East and West there remained the memory that infant baptism was a later development. The late *Life of Severus of Antioch* (who himself lived 465-538) by Robert Bishop of the Arabians states:

> Severus earnestly desired to receive baptism there and also to become, he, too, a signed one among the lambs of the house of God. For this Mother [faith] had still not been acquired by him, because in the country of his people, they used to baptize none except [grown] men.[47]

Macarius, bishop of Memphis in Egypt in the tenth century, wrote:

> In the first generation one did not baptize infants, but those who attained a proper age were called catechumens. It is to these that one preached baptism and taught the Christian religion for three years, and they were baptized.[48]

He later explains that baptism of adults was rejected and it was given to those born in the faith of Christ, the children of the faithful.[49] Macarius may have known the three-year catechumenate from the Egyptian Church Order (*Apostolic Tradition* 17), but if so, his testimony becomes all the more significant since the *Apostolic Tradition* provided for the baptism of children who could not speak for themselves as well as of adults.

In the West Walahfrid Strabo in the ninth century wrote in *De exordiis et incrementis quarundam in observationibus ecclesiasticis rerum* 27 that originally baptism was not given to children:

---

46. Wright, "Augustine and the Transformation of Baptism," p. 305.

47. Translation by Kathleen McVey, "The Life of Severus of Antioch by Robert Bishop of the Arabians" (Ph.D. dissertation, Harvard University, 1977), p. 95.

48. I have given in English the French translation of Louis Villecourt, "La lettre de Macaire, évêque de Memphis, sur la liturgie antique du chrême et da baptême à Alexandrie," *Le Muséon* 36 (1923): 33-46 (p. 34). At another point Macarius says, "Baptism was for those who were adults who believed, were instructed for three years and then were baptized" — Louis Villecourt, "Le livre du chrême: Ms. Paris arabe 100," *Le Muséon* 41 (1928): 49-80 (p. 57). See further in chap. 44,

49. Villecourt, "La lettre de Macaire," p. 35.

Next it must be noted that at first the traditional grace of baptism was given only to those who had already matured in both body and mind, they would be able to know and understand what effort must follow after baptism, what must be confessed and believed; in short, what must be observed by those reborn in Christ.

Then he explains that people came to understand original sin. Reversing Augustine's argument from infant baptism to original sin (chap. 52), he argued from original sin to infant baptism:

[Hence, it was] ruled that infants must be baptized for remission of sins; they may perish if they die without the remedy of regenerating grace.

With infant baptism came godfathers and godmothers, who received the infants from the font. When children reached a sensible age, they made their own avowal of belief.

Consequently, not only those who are old enough to speak and to understand what is happening, but also those who are unable to speak by themselves for themselves must be baptized.[50]

In the same passage Walahfrid Strabo testifies to immersion as the practice in baptism, with pouring allowed when necessary. "It should be understood that at first believers were simply baptized in rivers and fountains." The ceremony became more elaborate in time. Anointing with chrism and exorcisms were added. Either three immersions or one was acceptable. "It should be noted, however, that many have been baptized not by immersion, but by pouring water over from above. They can still be baptized this way if necessary." He gives as an example when a person's size keeps him from being immersed in smaller basins.[51]

Some confirmation for Strabo may be found in Ireland where there is evidence that the older practice of adult immersion survived when it had gone out of fashion on the continent. This conclusion is based on both early medieval literary sources and the holy wells which were clearly suited for baptizing adults.[52]

---

50. Alice L. Harting-Correa, *Walahfrid Strabo's* Libellus de exordiis et incrementis quarundam in observationibus ecclesiasticis rerum: *A Translation and Liturgical Commentary* (Leiden: Brill, 1996), pp. 177-181.

51. Harting-Correa, *Walahfrid Strabo's* Libellus de exordiis et incrementis, pp. 171, 173, 177.

52. Eoin de Bhaldraithe, "Some Evidence from Ireland: Adult Baptism in the Early Church," *Anabaptism Today* (June 1997): 10-15. Niam Whitfield, "A Suggested Function for the Holy Well," in A. Minnis and J. Roberts, eds., *Text, Image, Interpretation: Studies . . . in Honour of Éamonn Ó Carragáin* (Turnhout: Brepols, 2007), pp. 495-513, supports the idea that the wells were baptisteries.

40. Milan: Ambrose

Ambrose went from being a Roman provincial governor and unbaptized catechumen to being bishop of Milan in 374. Two sets of instructions that he gave in his latter capacity to the newly baptized — *On the Sacraments* and *On the Mysteries* — are his principal works of interest to this study.[1] They were given in the latter part of his episcopate (d. 397), perhaps around 390.

The stylistic differences appear not to indicate separate authorship: *On the Sacraments* has the marks of actual oral delivery only lightly retouched, whereas *On the Mysteries* is a more polished literary presentation of the material. *On the Sacraments* is a fuller but not so well-organized account. The differences in content are not so great, but may reflect lectures given in two different years. Both works have their setting in the postbaptismal instruction given in the week after

---

1. Text and French translation by B. Botte, *Ambroise de Milan: Des Sacrements, Des Mystères, Explication du Symbole*, Sources chrétiennes 25 bis (Paris: Cerf, 1961); text and German translation by Josef Schmitz, *Ambrosius: De Sacramentis, de Mysteriis; Über die Sakramente, Über die Mysterien*, Fontes Christiani 3 (Freiburg: Herder, 1990). I use but revise the translation (with useful introduction and notes by J. H. Srawley) by T. Thompson, *St. Ambrose: "On the Mysteries" and the Treatise "On the Sacraments" by an Unknown Author* (London: SPCK, 1919). Studies of Ambrose's baptismal theology and liturgy include Johannes Quasten, "Baptismal Creed and Baptismal Act in St. Ambrose's De mysteriis and De sacramentis," in *Mélanges Joseph de Ghellinck S.J.*, Vol. 1: *Antiquité* (Gembloux: J. Duculot, 1951), pp. 109-120; L. L. Mitchell, "Ambrosian Baptismal Rite," *Studia liturgica* 1 (1962): 241-253, reprinted in L. L. Mitchell, *Worship: Initiation and the Churches* (Washington, DC: Pastoral Press, 1991), pp. 75-89, including a comparison with the later Ambrosian liturgy; E. J. Yarnold, "The Ceremonies of Initiation in the 'De Sacramentis' and 'De Mysteriis' of St. Ambrose," *Studia patristica* 10 (1970): 453-463; Hugh M. Riley, *Christian Initiation*, Studies in Christian Antiquity 17 (Washington, D.C.: Catholic University of America Press, 1974), passim; William Ledwich, "Baptism, Sacrament of the Cross: Looking behind Ambrose," in Bryan D. Spinks, *The Sacrifice of Praise* (Rome: Edizioni Liturgiche, 1981), pp. 199-211; Everett Ferguson, "Catechesis and Initiation," in Alan Kreider, ed., *The Origins of Christendom in the West* (Edinburgh: T&T Clark, 2001), pp. 229-268 (248-256). For Augustine's references in his *Confessions* to baptismal practice in Milan see chap. 51.

Easter to the newly baptized, explaining to them the significance of what they had experienced.[2]

Baptismal Ceremony

Ambrose's treatise *On Repentance* (which deals with repentance for sins committed after baptism and not with conversion repentance) refers to the delay of baptism that was the subject of the last chapter. "If there were no place for penitence, everyone would defer the grace of cleansing by baptism to old age." But since penitence is available, "it is better to have a robe to mend, than none to put on."[3] He exhorted catechumens against the delay of baptism: "If anyone has not been baptized, let him with all the greater security be converted, receiving the remission of his sins. . . . why do you hesitate, why do you delay?"[4]

Ambrose summarized the preliminaries, comparing candidates for baptism to athletes:

> You have given your name for the contest of Christ, you have signed for the competition for the crown; take thought, exercise yourself, anoint yourself with the oil of gladness, cleanse yourself from ointment. (*On Elijah and Fasting* 21.79)[5]

In Ambrose's church catechumens enrolled for baptism at Epiphany,[6] and were signed with the cross.[7] During the subsequent weeks Ambrose discoursed daily on "right conduct," basing his instruction on readings from Genesis and Proverbs.[8] The surviving works of Ambrose that give moral and spiritual teaching from the lives of the patriarchs may be written versions of sermons given during Lent to candidates for baptism (the *competentes*). *On Abraham* contains three direct addresses to those "who are proceeding to the grace" of baptism.[9] On Saturdays scrutinies or exorcisms

---

2. Ambrose offered two explanations for withholding explanation until after baptism: only after initiation in the mysteries should their full secrets be revealed — to do otherwise would be a betrayal of them; and one could understand them better after experiencing the rites than was possible from only hearing about them (*Mys.* 1.2).

3. *On Repentance* 2.11.98 (tr. H. De Romestin in *Nicene and Post-Nicene Fathers* [repr. Peabody: Hendrickson, 1994], Second Series, Vol. 10, p. 357). Ambrose exhorts not to delay baptism in *Exposition of the Gospel according to Luke* 4.76 and 7.221.

4. *On Elijah and Fasting* 22.83. English translation by Mary Joseph Aloysius Buck, *S. Ambrosii De Helia et ieiunio: A Commentary; with an Introduction and Translation*, Patristic Studies 19 (Washington, D.C.: Catholic University of America Press, 1929), p. 107.

5. Buck, *S. Ambrosii De Helia et ieiunio*, p. 105.

6. *Exposition of the Gospel according to Luke* 4.76; cf. *Sacr.* 3.2.12.

7. *Mys* 4.20; cf. *Sacr.* 2.4.13.

8. *Mys.* 1.1. William Harmless, *Augustine and the Catechumenate* (Collegeville: Liturgical Press, 1995), p. 106, presents in chart form Ambrose's sermons with reference to the catechumenate, his Lenten sermons, *traditio symboli*, and mystagogical works.

9. *On Abraham* 1.4.25; 1.7.59; 1.9.89. Some of his other works on the patriarchs are translated by

were held to determine the fitness of the candidates for baptism.[10] On the Sunday before Easter, after the scripture readings, sermon, and dismissal of the catechumens, Ambrose delivered the creed to the *competentes* and then proceeded to celebrate the eucharist.[11] The sermon *Explanation of the Symbol* was perhaps given at such an occasion of the delivery of the creed *(traditio symboli).*[12]

The ritual of initiation proper began on Holy Saturday night at the door of the baptistery with the ceremony of *ephphatha* or *aperitio,* the "opening of the ears," in which the bishop touched the ears and nose of the baptizand.[13] The name was taken from Mark 7:34, the healing of a man deaf and dumb, where Jesus said in Aramaic, "Be opened." Ambrose explains that the priest touched the ears so that they would be open to his words.[14] This was done so that "Each one who is coming to grace might know what he is asked, should be bound to remember what he answered,"[15] already an indication of the prominence Ambrose would give to the candidate's renunciation of the devil and profession of faith.

The candidate entered the baptistery (the "holy of holies"), where a deacon and presbyter anointed his body as an athlete being prepared to wrestle.[16] Then followed the renunciation of the devil. The bishop asked, "Do you renounce the devil and his works?" The candidate replied, "I renounce." "Do you renounce the world and its pleasures." "I renounce."[17] The candidate was apparently facing west, renouncing the devil "to his face." Then he turned to the east to look at Christ face to face.[18] No words of association with Christ are given, but the renunciation is described as a promise and a contract.[19]

Michael McHugh, *Saint Ambrose: Seven Exegetical Works,* Fathers of the Church 65 (Washington, D.C.: Catholic University of America Press, 1972).

10. Alluded to in *Explanation of the Symbol* 1.

11. *Letter* 20.4.

12. Text and translation by R. H. Connolly, "The Explanatio Symboli ad initiandos, a Work of St. Ambrose," *Texts and Studies* 10 (1952). Chapters 9 and 11 refer to the candidates signing themselves before reciting the symbol.

13. *Sacr.* 1.1.2-3; *Mys.* 1.3-4.

14. He further explains that, although in the Gospel Jesus touched the dumb man's mouth, it was inappropriate to touch a woman candidate's mouth, and touching the nose symbolized receiving the sweet odor of Christ (2 Cor. 2:15). E. J. Yarnold, "The Ceremonies of Initiation," pp. 454-455, suggests that Ambrose may not have mentioned the use of spittle on the ears and nostrils out of delicacy.

15. *Mys.* 1.3.

16. *Mys.* 2.5; *Sacr.* 4.1.2 for a parallel reference to the baptistery; *Sacr.* 1.2.6, 8 for the anointing of the athlete. Yarnold, "The Ceremonies of Initiation," pp. 455-456, sees it as typical of Ambrose's delicacy that he does not mention the removal of clothes nor the anointing of the whole body, but the taking off of clothes is referred to in *On Psalms 61, Homily* 2.

17. *Sacr.* 1.2.5; *Mys.* 2.5 ("renounce the devil and his works, the world and its luxury and pleasures"), 8 ("the high priest questioning"); *Hexaemeron* 1.4.14 (renounce "you, devil, your angels, your works, and your rule").

18. *Mys.* 2.7. Yarnold, "The Ceremonies of Initiation," p. 457, finds the turning to Christ in the east implied in the words of promise or bond (*Sacr.* 1.4, 6, 8).

19. *Sacr.* 1.2.5-6, 8. The answers (to the questions of the renunciation, or to the adherence?) are kept in the "book of the living" (*Mys.* 2.5).

The candidate's seeing the water of the font is the occasion for Ambrose to mention the consecration of the baptismal water by the bishop. When the priest (bishop) enters, "he makes an exorcism over the element of water, afterwards he offers an invocation and a prayer that the font may be consecrated, and the presence of the eternal Trinity may come down."[20] The prayer involved a calling on the Trinity: "The priest comes; he says a prayer at the font; he invokes the name of the Father, the presence of the Son and of the Holy Spirit; he uses heavenly words."[21] The heavenly words are explained by quoting Jesus' command in Matthew 28:19 about baptizing in the name of the three divine persons. The consecration may have involved the making of the sign of the cross on the water.[22]

Ambrose would likely have been baptized in the baptistery of Santo Stefano, which according to its reconstruction was an octagon of about two meters in diameter and one meter in depth.[23] Ambrose himself was probably responsible for the baptistery of San Giovanni alle Fonti adjoining the church of St. Thecla in Milan. Its baptismal pool has been definitely dated to the time of Ambrose (Figure 20).[24] It is sunk in the ground, but the remains do not show how high a wall might have risen above ground. The diameter of the pool, 5.16 meters (over sixteen feet) across, is ample for immersions.[25] It was eight-sided. The text of an inscription placed around the font, now lost, is preserved in a ninth-century manuscript in the Vatican (the so-called *Sylloge Laureshamensis* — Codex Vaticanus palat. 833). The inscription was perhaps placed around the font in the rebuilding at the end of the fifth century by Bishop Laurentius, but Ambrose is commonly regarded as the author. The eight distiches are divided into two strophes, the first on death and resurrection and the

---

20. *Sacr.* 1.5.18. The presence of the divinity was necessary for the divine effects of baptism — *Mys.* 3.8. Ambrose interpreted the angel troubling the water in the pool (John 5:4) as a type of the descent of the Holy Spirit to consecrate the waters when invoked by the prayers of the priest (*On the Holy Spirit* 1.7.88).

21. *Sacr.* 2.5.14.

22. *Mys.* 3.14, with reference to Exod. 15:23-25, "For water without the proclamation of the Lord's cross serves no purpose of future salvation; but when it has been consecrated by the mystery of the saving cross, then it is fitted for the use of the spiritual laver and the cup of salvation. . . . [T]he priest casts the proclamation of the Lord's cross into this font, and the water becomes sweet unto grace." The statement would be satisfied by reference to the cross in the prayer of consecration (see *Mys.* 4.20, "For what is water without the cross of Christ?" for the association of the cross with baptism) but may have been prompted by some visual representation of the cross in the ceremony.

23. Silvia Lusuardi Siena and Marco Sannazaro, "I battisteri del complesso episcopale Milanese alla luce delle recenti indagini archeologiche," *L'edificio battesimale in Italia: Aspetti e problemi: Atti dell'VIII Congresso Nazionale di Archeologia Cristiana . . . 21-26 settembre 1998* (Bordighera: Istituto Internazionale di Studi Liguri, 2001), pp. 647-674 (653).

24. M. Mirabella Roberti, *Il battistero Ambrosiano di San Giovanni alle Fonti* (Milan, 1974).

25. S. Lusuardi Siena and Marco Sannazaro, "I battisteri del complesso episcopale Milanese," 657-670, give the diameter as 5.50 meters and the present depth as 80 centimeters. They correlate the Ambrosian literary descriptions of the practice of baptism with the archaeological data, suggesting that because the basin was not deep the baptizand was laid flat on the bottom as a dead person in a tomb; but this is unnecessary if the walls originally extended higher.

second an exhortation not to defer baptism but to approach it joyfully. The inscription expresses Ambrose's baptismal theology and connects the octagonal shape with baptism.

> With eight chapels [niches] the temple rises high for holy use,
>   the font is eight-cornered, which is appropriate for its gift.
> With this number [eight] it was fitting the hall of holy baptism
>   to erect, by which true salvation returned to the peoples
> in the light of the rising Christ, who releases from the prison
>   of death and raises up the dead from their graves,
> and freeing from the stain of sin the guilty who make confession,
>   he washes them with the clear flowing water of the font.
> Here, whoever wants the sins of a shameful life
>   to lay aside, may bathe the heart strings and have a pure soul.
> To this place may they eagerly come: however dark he may be
>   who has the courage to approach, he departs whiter than snow.
> To this place may they hurry to be holy: without these waters
>   no one is holy, in them is the kingdom and counsel of God,
> the glory of righteousness. What is more divine than this,
>   that in a brief moment the guilt of the people perishes?[26]

After the anointing and consecration of the water, the baptizand descended into the pool, attended by the bishop, presbyter, and deacon.[27] The baptism itself was a triple immersion accompanying a triple interrogatory confession:

> You were asked, "Do you believe in God the Father Almighty?" You said, "I believe," and you dipped [*mersisti*, sank down], that is, you were buried. Again you were asked, "Do you believe in our Lord Jesus Christ, and in his cross?" You said, "I believe," and dipped; therefore, you were also *buried with Christ* [Rom. 6:4; Col. 2:12]; for he who is *buried with Christ* rises again with Christ. A third time you were asked, "Do you believe also in the Holy Spirit?" You said, "I believe," and dipped a third time, that the triple confession might absolve the manifold fall of your former life. (*Sacr.* 2.7.20)

The action is summarized shortly thereafter: "Believing in the Father and the Son and the Holy Spirit, we are received, and plunged [*demergimur*, submerged], and emerge [*surgimus*, rise], that is, we are raised up [*resuscitamur*]" (*Sacr.* 3.1.1). The "dipping" was a burial (*Sacr.* 2.6.19 and 2.7.23).

---

26. The translation is mine from G. B. De Rossi, *Inscriptiones christianae urbis Romae* (Rome: Libraria Pontificio, 1857-1888; repr. Vatican City, 1922-), II.1, p. 161 (= E. Diehl, *Inscriptiones latinae christianae veteres*, 2nd ed. [Berlin: Weidmann, 1961], #1841). The inscription is studied in relation to the theology of Ambrose by F. J. Dölger, "Zur Symbolik des altchristlichen Taufhauses. I. Das Oktogon und die Symbolik der Achtzahl," *Antike und Christentum* 4 (Münster: Aschendorff, 1934), pp. 153-165.

27. *Sacr.* 1.5.18; 2.6.16.

The parallel in *On the Mysteries* 5.28, as is characteristic, is briefer and does not quote exact words (perhaps, as written for wider circulation, preserving the *disciplina arcani*). Both accounts are unique in adding to what is known of other confessions the phrase "in his cross" to the second article. "You did descend, then; remember what you did answer, that you believe in the Father, you believe in the Son, you believe in the Holy Spirit," a "pledge made with your own voice."[28] Ambrose's baptismal confession, unlike others of the time, made no addition to the "Holy Spirit" in its third member, not even in the fuller statement of *Sacraments* above. The preceding words, "Believe, therefore, that invoked by the prayers of the priests the Lord Jesus is present" (with Matt. 18:20 quoted), may refer to the consecration of the water (above, as effecting the divine presence); but in view of the context here the invocation is likely the baptismal profession of faith, put in question form by the bishop.

The baptizand then ascended from the font and came to the bishop, who anointed the head.[29] The bishop's words are quoted in *On the Sacraments*:

> Therefore you dipped, you came to the priest. What did he say to you? "God the Father Almighty," he says, "who has regenerated you by water and the Holy Spirit" and has forgiven you your sins, himself anoint you unto eternal life. (2.7.24)

The unction on the head was with *myron*.[30] This anointing is associated with eternal life, an enrichment of human faculties by grace, and the priestly and royal anointings of the Old Testament but (notably) not with the giving of the Holy Spirit.[31]

The distinctively different element in the baptismal ceremony of Ambrose's Milan was a footwashing, accompanied by the reading of John 13.[32] Ambrose interpreted the footwashing as removing hereditary sins (with allusion to Gen. 3:1, 15), while baptism remitted a person's own sins, an interpretation that had no future.[33] The act was begun by the bishop but carried through by the presbyters. Ambrose knew the rite was not practiced in Rome and was interpreted only as an act of hu-

---

28. *Mys.* 5.28, which continues with the note that "in his cross" was added to the confession of Christ. Cf. *Mys.* 4.21 where baptism in the name of the Trinity is accompanied by a confession of Father, Son, and Holy Spirit. The emphasis on confession is also evident in *On the Holy Spirit* 2.10.105, "In the mysteries the threefold question is put, and the threefold answer made, and no one can be cleansed but by a threefold confession." There is no indication of a triple declaration in addition to the triple interrogatory confession. Quasten, "Baptismal Creed and Baptismal Act in St. Ambrose's De mysteriis and De sacramentis," pp. 223-234, compares the procedure and the wording of the confession at Ambrose's Milan with that at other places.

29. *Mys.* 6.29. Mitchell, "Ambrosian Baptismal Rites," pp. 248-249.

30. *Sacr.* 3.1.1. Eccl. 2:14 is quoted, as also more accurately in *Mys.* 6.30, in reference to the unction.

31. *Mys.* 6.30; *Sacr.* 4.1.3.

32. The practice was continued in the Ambrosian rite and is known in some medieval service books.

33. *Mys.* 6.31-32. *Sacr.* 3.1.7 gives more nuance to the thought: "In baptism all guilt is washed away," but "because Adam was tripped up by the devil, and poison was poured over his feet," the feet are washed in order "to wash off the poison of the serpent" and as a lesson in humility.

mility (as in welcoming a guest), but he defends it as a sacrament and means of sanctification.[34]

The newly baptized were clothed in white garments. This custom was a sign of forgiveness of sins, of union with Christ, and of purity of life. The baptizands had put off the covering of sins and put on the garments of innocence.[35]

The newly baptized then received the "spiritual seal," identified with the sevenfold gifts of the Spirit in Isaiah 11:2 and with the sealing, confirmation, and earnest of the Spirit in 2 Corinthians 1:21-22, which had been in the reading for the day.[36] This spiritual seal, distinct from the postbaptismal unction, was for the perfecting of what occurred in the font and took place at the invocation by the bishop that the Holy Spirit be given, the listing of the seven gifts perhaps being part of the formula used in the prayer.[37] This communication of the Spirit seems to have been accomplished by making the sign of the cross (on the forehead):

> It is God who *anointed* you, and the Lord *signed* you, and put the Holy *Spirit* in your *heart* [2 Cor. 1:21-22]. . . .
>
> How? Because you were signed with the image of the cross itself into his passion, you received a seal into his likeness, that you may rise into his image and live after his pattern . . .[38]

It is to be noted that there is no mention of oil in connection with this signing.[39]

The new Christians went to the altar for the eucharist and joined in the Lord's Prayer.[40] There was a daily eucharist in the week following the Easter baptism,[41] during which time Ambrose's explanations of the sacraments (mysteries) occurred.

---

34. *Sacr.* 3.1.4-6.

35. *Mys.* 7.34-41; only alluded to in *Sacr.* 5.3.14; 4.2.5-6. Riley, *Christian Initiation*, pp. 438-445.

36. *Mys.* 7.42. For being sealed with the Spirit by God in the heart (although visible in the body, but an act distinct from baptism), see Ambrose, *On the Holy Spirit* 1.6.79; for "spiritual seal" see *Sacr.* 6.2.8 and other passages to be cited.

37. *Sacr.* 3.2.8. The seven gifts are seven virtues, "when you are sealed" — *Sacr.* 3.2.10.

38. *Sacr.* 6.2.6-7.

39. Since Ambrose professes his rite to be the same as Rome's (except for the footwashing), the absence from Ambrose's account of a laying on of hands and second anointing by the bishop (characteristic of Rome) poses a problem. Either Ambrose covers the difference in practice by a reference to the prayer for the Spirit, or Ambrose's "spiritual seal" referred to these Roman rites, or Rome had not yet adopted or had newly adopted the second chrismation and episcopal laying on of hands. See Maxwell E. Johnson, *The Rites of Christian Initiation: Their Evolution and Interpretation* (Collegeville: Liturgical, 1999), pp. 137-140, who inclines to the last explanation, noting that Ambrose gives no clue about any gesture associated with the spiritual seal and that later Milanese liturgies preserve nothing of this seal. Cf. also Riley, *Christian Initiation*, pp. 354-356, n. 30. Mitchell, "Ambrosian Baptismal Rites," pp. 251-252, compares Ambrose and the *Apostolic Tradition* on the postbaptismal rites.

40. *Mys.* 9.50-59; *Sacr.* 5.3.12–6.1.4. Ambrose, *Letter* 41.14-15, refers to the eucharistic kiss, and *Sacr.* 5.5 probably does also and not to a postbaptismal kiss.

41. Mitchell, "Ambrosian Baptismal Rites," p. 252. The quotation of Song of Songs 5:1 in *Sacr.* 5.15-17 may imply the use of milk and honey in the baptismal eucharist.

Baptismal Typology

On the Mysteries develops several traditional typologies of baptism, taking them up in their biblical order. The mystery of baptism was prefigured in the creation, when the Spirit of God moved upon the waters (Gen. 1:2).[42] The flood in the days of Noah combined the elements of water ("in which the flesh is plunged"), wood (the olive branch for the cross), dove for the Holy Spirit, and the raven for sin (Gen. 8:7-8, 11).[43] The exodus from Egypt (1 Cor. 10:1-2) offered the parallels of guilt and error being drowned and destroyed in the water and the cloud representing the presence of the Holy Spirit (Exod. 15:10 also quoted).[44] The "font of Marah" had bitter water until Moses made it sweet by casting wood into it (Exod. 15:23-24); even so the "proclamation of the Lord's cross" sweetens the water for grace.[45] Naaman was a favorite with Ambrose (2 Kings 5:1-14). It was not the water but the grace when he obeyed the command to dip seven times in the Jordan that brought cleansing; the captive maiden that directed Naaman to the prophet Elisha stands for the church from the Gentiles.[46] Ambrose treated Naaman's dipping in the Jordan in terms of Christian baptism. It signified for him the spiritual mysteries of the baptism of salvation. A leper when he plunged *(merserat)*, he was one of the faithful when he emerged *(emersit)*. When the body is washed *(abluitur)*, the heart *(adfectus)* is washed.[47]

On the Sacraments adds other types. Elijah called down fire from heaven on the altar (1 Kings 19:38); when Elisha called on the name of the Lord, the axe head that had sunk came up out of the water (2 Kings 6:4-6), representing human beings weighed down like iron and their weakness raised when the wood of the cross is cast into the water.[48] To these Old Testament figures there is added Jesus' healing of the paralytic at the pool (John 5:4), where the angel who troubled the water is a figure of Christ.[49]

---

42. *Mys.* 3.9. That the Spirit not only moved but also worked is supported by the citation of Ps. 33:6.

43. *Mys.* 3.10-11; *Sacr.* 1.6.23; 2.1.1; alluded to in *Sacr.* 2.3.9. Cf. the different combination in Justin, *Dialogue with Trypho* 138, of water, faith, and wood of the ark.

44. *Mys.* 3.12-13. Cf. *Sacr.* 1.6.20-22 for the Holy Spirit and the water at the crossing of the Red Sea as "a type of baptism"; simply listed in 2.3.9. Cf. "The Lord removes sins, passes over iniquities, and buries them in the depth of the sea. That can be applied to baptism in which the Egyptian is submerged and the Hebrew is raised up" (*Letter* 70.24).

45. *Mys.* 3.14; cf. *Mys* 4.20 (quoted in n. 22) and *Sacr.* 2.4.12-13 (water without the cross cannot take away sin).

46. *Mys.* 3.16-18; *Sacr.* 2.3.8; *On Repentance* 2.2.12 (it appears impossible that water should wash away sin or cleanse leprosy, but God makes it possible).

47. *Exposition of the Gospel according to Luke* 4.51.

48. *Sacr.* 2.4.11. *On Duties of the Clergy* 3.18.102-108, in developing the association of fire with the Holy Spirit (John 1:33 and elsewhere), mentions the typologies of Elijah calling down fire on the altar as well as the crossing the Red Sea and the flood of Noah.

49. *Sacr.* 2.2.3-5. In *Mys.* 4.22 the counterpart of the angel is the Holy Spirit.

Ambrose concludes that if the figures could accomplish as much as they did, "how much more can baptism in reality do?"[50]

Baptismal Theology

Although Ambrose draws many types from the Old Testament, he sharply distinguishes Christian baptism from Jewish washings. "The baptism of the unbelievers does not heal, does not cleanse but defiles. The Jew *baptizes pots and cups* [Mark 7:4], as if inanimate things were capable of sin or grace."[51] The baptisms of the Jews were either superfluous or figurative.[52] The "baptisms" of Hebrews 6:2 are explained as the baptisms or washing under the law, but "The whole of the washings under the law are done away with, and there is one baptism in the sacraments of the church."[53] The Gentiles too had "baptisms," but, properly speaking, "They are baths, baptisms they cannot be. The flesh is washed, but guilt is not washed away."[54] Many kinds of baptism preceded the true sacrament of baptism in the water and Spirit that redeems the whole person; even so the circumcision of many preceded the circumcision of the Lord's passion.[55]

Ambrose relates baptism closely to the Trinity. The Father, the Son, and Holy Spirit each forgives; but the three are "one name" (Matt. 28:19), indicating that they are "one substance, one divinity, one majesty."[56] He proceeds to overcome the seeming contrast that baptism in the book of Acts was often in the name of Christ by affirming that the one name is the same as the name of Christ, "wherein all must be saved" (Acts 4:12). Although "there is a distinction of persons," "the whole mystery of the Trinity is bound up together."[57]

Jesus' baptism offered lessons for Christian baptism. Jesus descended, as the Spirit also descended on him like a dove at his baptism; and as the dove represents innocence, those who are baptized are to have innocence, not in appearance but in reality.[58] Christ did no sin, so he needed no washing away of sins; but we do need the washing, so Christ descended into the water so that our flesh might be cleansed. His baptism to "fulfill all righteousness" (Matt. 3:14-15) means that "all righteousness is based on baptism."[59] Jesus was baptized in order to purify the waters; washed by the

---

50. *Sacr.* 2.4.13.
51. *Sacr.* 1.4.23.
52. *Sacr.* 2.1.2.
53. *On Repentance* 2.2.11 (tr. De Romestin, *Nicene and Post-Nicene Fathers,* Second Series, Vol. 10, p. 346).
54. *Sacr.* 2.1.2.
55. Ambrose, *Letter* 72 (16).18. For the Lord's passion as circumcision, cf. Col. 2:11.
56. *Sacr.* 2.7.22; on the one Name, *Holy Spirit* 1.13.132. Ambrose often refers to baptism in the name of the Trinity — e.g., *On Faith* 1.4.31; 5.9.115.
57. *Sacr.* 6.2.8.
58. *Mys.* 4.24-25.
59. *Sacr.* 1.5.15-16.

flesh of Christ, which knew no sin, the waters now have the right of baptism. Whoever comes to the bath of Christ puts away sin.[60] The Trinity was present in the baptism of Christ, for the Spirit descended as a dove and the Father spoke from heaven.[61]

Ambrose frequently explained baptism in terms of the death, burial, and resurrection of Christ.[62] The baptistery was like a tomb in shape.[63] In the manner of Gregory of Nyssa, Ambrose sees a similarity of water and earth, but he develops the symbolism in his own way. An actual burial in the earth would destroy physical life, so there was substituted a burial in water (*mergeretur in fontem*, "immersed into the font"), by which one symbolically returns to the earth. In a creative combination of Genesis 3 and Romans 6:4-6 Ambrose recalls the punishment on Adam and Eve of death for disobedience and a returning to the earth (Gen. 2:17; 3:19) and declares that dipping (*mergis*) in the water fulfilled the sentence of death and was the means of rising again to life. "What is water, but from the earth?" "The font is, as it were, a burial."[64]

The second immersion (*Sacr.* 2.7.20, quoted above) was a burial with Christ. "When you dip, you take on the likeness of death and burial, you receive the sacrament of that cross, because Christ hung on the cross."[65] "In baptism you are, as it were, specially crucified with Christ."[66] While the imagery of immersion symbolized burial and resurrection, no liturgical action was a symbol of crucifixion, so Ambrose's connection of baptism with the cross was theological. Christ died in reality; the baptizand died in similitude.[67]

Ambrose affirmed that both the first and second immersions were a burial, with the second immersion elaborated as a burial with Christ, but he gave no separate interpretation to the third immersion.[68] Rather, he explains the triple dipping as a triple confession that absolves "the manifold fall of your former life." The threefold action represents the completeness of the correction of a person's life. Ambrose drew a parallel with Peter's fall and restoration by Christ's asking him three times if he loved him. "He said it three times that he might be three times absolved."[69]

Ambrose associated the resurrection with the coming up from the dipping. As cited above (*Sacr.* 3.1.1), "We are plunged [*demergimur*] and emerge [*resurgimus*],

---

60. *Exposition of the Gospel according to Luke* 2.83.
61. *Sacr.* 1.5.19; *Mys.* 5.26 (but not as explicitly stated).
62. Riley, *Christian Initiation*, pp. 242-250. See *On Repentance* 2.2.8-9 in addition to passages referred to below.
63. *Sacr.* 3.1.1.
64. *Sacr.* 2.6.17-19.
65. *Sacr.* 2.7.23. Riley, *Christian Initiation*, pp. 250-255, for the association of baptism with the cross.
66. *Sacr.* 6.2.8. Cf. 6.2.7, "Your *old man* plunged into the font was *crucified* to sin, but rose again to God."
67. *Sacr.* 2.7.23.
68. *Sacr.* 2.7.20 above. Riley, *Christian Initiation*, pp. 255-259.
69. *Sacr.* 2.7.21. A cleansing by a threefold confession is also affirmed with reference to Peter in Ambrose's *On the Holy Spirit* 2.10.105.

that is, we are raised up." So, he adds, "in baptism, since there is a likeness of death, without doubt when you dip [*mergis*, sink down] and rise again [*resurgis*], there is made a likeness of the resurrection" (*Sacr.* 3.1.2).[70]

This same passage introduces in connection with baptism the idea of regeneration, a favorite word with Ambrose.[71] Using the quotation of Psalm 2:7 in Acts 13:33 and the words of Colossians 1:18 for the language of begetting in relation to Christ's resurrection, Ambrose connects baptismal resurrection with regeneration:

> What is regeneration? ... [Since there is in baptism a likeness of the resurrection,] rightly, therefore, according to the interpretation of the apostle Peter [does he mean Paul?], as that resurrection [Christ's] was a regeneration, so also is this resurrection [in baptism] a regeneration. (*Sacr.* 3.1.2)

Christ's resurrection was a new begetting, and the same is true for converts to Christ.

Ambrose brought Genesis into connection with this concept, as he had done with the death and burial motif. At the creation living creatures were born in the water by the word of God (Gen. 1:11, 20). We continue to live in a world that figuratively is characterized by heavy waves and fierce storms. God does not take Christians out of the world any more than fish are taken out of water, but as the fish swim in the sea and do not drown, so the world loses its destructive force for Christians.[72]

Ambrose began the treatise *On the Mysteries* by telling the newly baptized that "after being renewed by baptism" they should "continue to practice the life that is fitting for the regenerate" (1.1). He concluded the treatise by picking up the theme of regeneration and connecting it with the Spirit's effecting the virgin birth of Jesus. "Let us recognize that we are regenerate." Someone might object, as Nicodemus did (John 3:4), that the usage of nature is not observed since one does not enter again the mother's womb.

> [I]t is not always the usage of nature that produces birth; we confess that Christ the Lord was born of a virgin, and we deny the order of nature. ... [Matt. 1:18 and Luke 1:35 are quoted for Mary not conceiving from a man.] If, then, *the Holy Spirit coming upon* the virgin effected conception and fulfilled the work of generation, surely we must not doubt that, coming upon the font or upon those on whom baptism is conferred, he effects the reality of regeneration.[73]

As the Spirit accomplished the virgin birth of Jesus, the Spirit regenerates human beings in baptism. Ambrose does not decide whether that power of regeneration is to

---

70. Riley, *Christian Initiation*, p. 259, is in error when he takes the coming out of the pool and not the coming up from the immersion as the likeness of the resurrection.

71. Riley, *Christian Initiation*, pp. 305-312, on the motif of new birth in Ambrose. Note *Mys.* 6.29, "souls regenerated today"; *Sacr.* 3.1.5, where sacrament, baptism, and regeneration seem to be equivalent. The related imagery of "the grace of adoption" occurs in *On the Holy Spirit* 1.6.80.

72. *Sacr.* 3.1.3. Riley, *Christian Initiation*, p. 309.

73. *Mys.* 9.59.

be associated with the Spirit's coming on the font in the consecratory prayer over the water or with his coming as a gift on those who are baptized. He probably thought that both were true. "The water does not cleanse without the Spirit."[74] The water heals only when the Spirit descends and consecrates it.[75] In contrast to John, Christ baptizes in the Spirit and dispenses grace.[76] Although baptism is in the water and the Spirit, their functions are different:

> [W]e are buried in the element of water that we may rise again renewed by the Spirit. For in the water is the representation of death, in the Spirit is the pledge of life, that the body of sin may die through the water, which encloses the body as it were in a kind of tomb, that we, by the power of the Spirit, may be renewed from the death of sin, being born again in God.[77]

Indeed, "the water, the blood, and the Spirit" (1 John 5:7) were all three necessary for baptism. The water without the blood has no "sacramental effect." "Nor again is there any mystery of regeneration without water," followed by a quotation of John 3:5. Unless there is a baptism in the name of Father, Son, and Holy Spirit, one "cannot receive the remission of sins nor imbibe the gift of spiritual grace."[78]

As this last quotation indicates, the usual association of baptism with forgiveness of sins is not lacking: The water in which the flesh is plunged "washes away every sin of the flesh; every wrong act is buried there."[79] In this way one is released from the bondage to the devil.[80]

Baptism also justifies. It renders one innocent and just. In commenting on Luke 7:29, Ambrose plays on the wording of the text, exhorting to justify the Lord (by being baptized) so that we may be justified by the Lord.[81]

To summarize, Ambrose attributed the efficacy of baptism sometimes to the

---

74. *Mys.* 4.19.
75. *Sacr.* 1.5.15.
76. *On Elijah and Fasting* 22.84.
77. *On the Holy Spirit* 1.6.76 (tr. De Romestin, *Nicene and Post-Nicene Fathers*, Second Series, Vol. 10, p. 103).
78. *Mys.* 4.20. The combination water, blood, and Spirit also occurs in *Exposition of the Gospel according to Luke* 10.48 for a similar purpose. Cf. *On the Holy Spirit* 1.6.77, explaining from 1 John 5:8 that the water is a witness of burial, the blood a witness of death, and the Spirit a witness of life, and adding that any grace in the water comes from the presence of the Holy Spirit.
79. *Mys.* 3.11. Cf. the remarkable statements, "You have put off the old age of sins, you have taken the youth of grace; this the heavenly sacraments bestowed on you. . . . You are eagles, renewed by the washing away of sin" (*Sacr.* 4.2.7). No specific confession of sin was called for in the baptismal ceremony, yet one "makes a complete confession of all sins by the very fact of asking to be baptized in order to be justified, that is, pass from guilt to grace" (*Sacr.* 3.2.12). In commenting on Luke 7:29-30 Ambrose associated confession and forgiveness of sins in baptism (*Exposition of the Gospel according to Luke* 6.3). In baptism sin is forgiven, but it does not remove the impediment of a second marriage to ordination — *Duties of the Clergy* 1.50.257; reaffirmed in *Letter* 63.63.
80. *Sacr.* 2.6.18-19.
81. *Exposition of the Gospel according to Luke* 6.2.

cross,[82] sometimes to Christ,[83] sometimes to the name of the Trinity,[84] and sometimes to the Holy Spirit.[85] Obviously these are interrelated concepts. And it is in such contexts that we are to understand his praise of water.[86]

Baptism was a mark of faith and gave the title "faithful" to those who received it.[87] Thus Ambrose, as others surveyed, set baptism in the context of faith. And, as others in the "Arian" controversy of the late fourth century, he used the baptismal faith in the three divine persons to argue for the co-equality of Father, Son, and Holy Spirit. The renunciation of the devil, a verbal expression of repentance, was a promise, a bond.[88]

Baptism introduced one into the church and formed a bond of unity: "Good will expands in the body of the church by fellowship in faith, by the bond of baptism, by kinship through grace received, by communion in the mysteries."[89] One must be in the church in order to be saved, yet Ambrose as a pastor was perhaps the first to set forth the possibility of salvation through a baptism of desire:

> But I hear that you are grieving because he did not receive the sacrament of baptism. . . . Has he not then the grace which he desired, has he not the grace which he requested? Surely because he asked, he received."[90]

In another context he applied John 3:5 absolutely but suggested that an infant dying unbaptized was in an intermediate state. After quoting the verse, he declared:

> It makes no exception — not an infant, not one in some way prevented by necessity. Nevertheless, they have a hidden place exempt from punishment, yet I do not think they have the honor of the kingdom.[91]

The terms "mysteries" and "sacraments" appear to have been used interchangeably. Their presence in the titles of the works forming the basis of this chapter indi-

---

82. *Sacr.* 2.2.6; 3.4.11-13; and cf. the addition of "and in his cross" to the second baptismal interrogation (*Sacr.* 2.7.20; *Mys.* 5.28).

83. *Sacr.* 2.2.7; 2.7.23.

84. *Sacr.* 2.3.9; 2.4.10-13; 2.5.14; 2.7.20-22.

85. *Sacr.* 2.5.15; *Mys.* 4.19.

86. *Exposition of the Gospel according to Luke* 10.48.

87. *Sacr.* 1.1.1.

88. *Sacr.* 1.2.8. The statement about "not in baptism alone but also in repentance" occurs the destruction of the flesh (*On Duties of the Clergy* 3.18.108) probably refers to postbaptismal repentance.

89. *On the Duties of the Clergy* 1.33.170 (tr. De Romestin, *Nicene and Post-Nicene Fathers*, Second Series, Vol. 10, p. 29).

90. *On the Death of Valentinian* 51. English translation by T. A. Kelly, *Sancti Ambrosii Liber de consolatione Valentiniani: A Text with a Translation, Introduction, and Commentary*, Patristic Studies 58 (Washington, D.C.: Catholic University of America Press, 1940), p. 217.

91. *On Abraham* 2.11.84. *On Abraham* 2.11.81 referred to the command to circumcise as exempting "neither old man, proselyte, nor infant of the household," because as every age is guilty of sin every age has the same sacrament. *Letter* 44 speaks of infants' "regeneration on the eighth day," which may point to their baptism on the eighth day after birth, unless Ambrose is using "eighth day" in a symbolic sense for their regeneration through the resurrection of Christ with a view to the world to come.

cates how much the ideas of secret and initiation from the language of the Greek mysteries had come to identify practices that the Latin church since Tertullian had described as sacraments, oaths, or pledges.[92] The rites had hidden meanings that were communicated only to the initiated.

---

92. J. D. B. Hamilton, "The Church and the Language of Mystery: The First Four Centuries," *Ephemerides theologicae lovanienses* 53 (1977): 479-494.

41. Other North Italians

The information for Milan and Ambrose is similar to that provided by other bishops in north Italy.

Zeno of Verona

Zeno was bishop of Verona from about 362 to about 370/71. The ninety-two homilies (only about thirty complete) surviving from him are grouped in two books of sixty-two and thirty texts respectively. Eight of these are summaries, outlines, or fragments of sermons addressed to catechumens giving "invitations to the font,"[1] comparable to the exhortations to baptism found in contemporary Greek preachers. Although Zeno does not give the systematic, detailed account that Ambrose does, much of the Easter baptismal ceremony at Verona can be reconstructed from his allusions.

Activities preparatory for baptism included fasting (1.24.1) and penitence (see below). Zeno appears to be the earliest writer to use *competentes* (co-petitioners) for the candidates preparing for baptism.[2]

The "consecrated oil" of 2.13 appears to be a prebaptismal anointing, for it precedes reference to the immersion.[3] It may have accompanied the renunciation,

---

1. Text by B. Löfstedt in *Corpus Christianorum, Series latina*, Vol. 22 (Turnhout: Brepols, 1971); English translation of seven of these by Thomas P. Halton in A. Hamman, ed., *Baptism: Ancient Liturgies and Patristic Texts* (Staten Island: Alba, 1967), pp. 64-66; study by Gordon P. Jeanes, *The Day Has Come! Easter and Baptism in Zeno of Verona* (Collegeville: Liturgical, 1995), who translates all the paschal homilies (pp. 54-99) and from whom I quote; Gordon P. Jeanes, "Paschal Baptism and Rebirth: A Clash of Images?" *Studia patristica* 26 (1993): 41-46.

2. Jeanes, *The Day Has Come!* p. 166. He reconstructs and discusses the paschal baptismal liturgy on pp. 149-214.

3. Jeanes, *The Day Has Come!* pp. 239-241, understands the statement in this passage as connecting forgiveness of sins with the prebaptismal anointing, but in spite of parallels in other authors he

which is indicated in several passages (2.11.5; 1.37.10 and 12). *Sermons* 1.37 may reflect the formula, "the devil, his angels, and the world."[4] The renunciation was an expression of repentance, which is implied in the exhortation to "throw off that old self of yours with its filthy garments" (1.49) and the declaration that "you flee the world's snares, guilt, wounds, and death" (2.23).

The candidates entered the baptistery singing Psalm 42 (1.23; cf. 2.10 and 14). The blessing of the font (perhaps alluded to in 1.23) had occurred earlier. The water is described as "warmed" (1.23; 1.32),[5] a change from the earlier preference for water in its natural temperature.

The candidates stripped naked (cf. 1.49) for the baptism. "You will indeed go down [*demergitis*, "plunge"] naked into the font" (1.23). The baptism was an immersion, described from the candidates' perspective as immersing themselves in the water: "plunge into the life-giving vessel of the everlasting waters [*gurgitis alueo genitali condentes*]" (1.49); "Immerse yourselves staightway [*Vos constanter inmergite*]" (2.23). From another perspective: "Immerse yourselves with all haste in the wave, let its stream run [flow] over you [*superfluentis amnis undae subiecti*]" (1.12). In spite of this language, there may not necessarily have been provision for flowing water into the font. The mention of "living water" *(aqua uiua)* does not refer to running water but to the life-giving effect of the water by reason of the work of the Holy Spirit (1.23). This passage (1.23) speaks of the water as blended "with the Holy Spirit and fire," indicating that he understood Christ's baptism with Holy Spirit and fire (Matt. 3:11) as effected in water baptism.

The baptismal faith in "Father, Son, and Holy Spirit" (1.13.13) was confessed in response to "sacred questions" (2.11.5) by which one was spiritually bound. Zeno gives prominence to faith.[6] The candidates' faith gives birth to them (2.23). By reason of their faith, the generative wave conceived them (2.28). Their faith meant they ought to come to the font, and their beatitude will be according to their faith (1.55). The more one believed, the nobler the one was, and so "steadfastly and faithfully" one was invited to baptism (1.49).

There was a postbaptismal anointing and sealing. The "anointing" *(unctui)* in 1.23, in spite of being mentioned before the "washing," is postbaptismal, because of its association with the bath attendant (*balneator* — bishop or deacon?) prepared to dry off the baptizand.[7] The comparison to "a golden denarius sealed with triple ef-

---

probably overinterprets; we should rather, as he does with the gift of the Holy Spirit (pp. 250-251), see the ceremony as all one event that brings forgiveness.

4. Jeanes, *The Day Has Come!* p. 172, with the modification that Zeno usually speaks of *saeculum* instead of *mundus*, as here. He shows that in the West there was no separate formula of adhesion, which was part of the meaning of the interrogatory formulae at the immersions.

5. Jeanes, *The Day Has Come!* p. 178.

6. Jeanes, *The Day Has Come!* p. 219, notes that throughout the ceremonies Zeno presupposes the faith of the candidates, referring to 1.2.25; 1.55; 2.28. Jeanes, "Paschal Baptism," p. 46, notes that in both Pacian and Zeno passivity is not enough, for the candidates make a renunciation and a confession.

7. See the discussion in Jeanes, *The Day Has Come!* pp. 179-182.

figy" (1.23) may refer to the usage of the triple divine name in this anointing, in the baptism, or in both.[8]

Different ages received baptism. "Though differing in age, sex, and state in life, you are soon going to be joined in unity" (1.55). How young some were is not made known. All are identical in baptism (1.41). Baptism was unrepeatable (1.12; 2.14).

When they emerged from the font, the baptized were "robed in white, dressed in heavenly vesture," with the promise that if they did not soil the baptismal garment they would possess the kingdom of heaven (1.23). They were "robed in white" (1.49).[9] Zeno interpreted the procession from the font into the church as an entry to paradise or heaven.[10] The baptized heard the singing of a hymn (2.26.1 and 3 and 1.28).[11] There may be an allusion to the baptized carrying lights (2.6.8).

Zeno preached, and led the paschal eucharist (1.24; 1.32). The statement that they would "be babes at the breast together" (2.28) may refer to drinking milk as part of the baptismal eucharist or may simply have been a further figurative development of the theme of new birth.

Indeed, Zeno's favorite imagery for baptism was language drawn from the reproductive process.[12] "Hasten to the fountain of the sweet womb of your ever-virgin mother" (1.55). The mother is the church, an image that Zeno uses often (1.32; 2.28). The font is the singular womb in which the new birth of many takes place.

> The sweet crying of infants is heard. Behold, from the single womb of their parent proceeds a dazzling throng. It is a new thing, that each one is born [*nascatur*] in a spiritual manner. (2.28)

He can boldly speak of the "life-giving [*genitalis*, generative or reproductive] font" (1.12).[13] The wave or the water itself is described with same word *(genitalis)*, generative or reproductive, bestowing a new birth (2.28).

Although using the language of birth, Zeno contrasts the spiritual with physical birth.

> Not in the manner in which your mothers bore you when they brought you into the world, themselves groaning with birth pains and you wailing, filthy, done up

---

8. Jeanes, *The Day Has Come!* pp. 182-186, favors interpreting the denarius as chrism.
9. Cf. 1.38.3; 2.6.8.
10. 1.46B.3 (cf. 1.49 on baptism as entering the heavenly gates); 1.44.2; 2.26.3.
11. Psalm 32?
12. G. de Paoli, "L'iniziazione cristiana nei Sermoni di S. Zenodi Verona," *Rivista liturgica* 54 (1967): 405-417, groups the material under the themes of regeneration, baptism and faith, baptism and penitence, and baptism and the Holy Spirit. I know the work from Jeanes, *The Day Has Come!* p. 216, who follows a different approach from this and from mine in describing Zeno's theology of baptism (pp. 215-257), but who says that regeneration is the dominant theme in Zeno (pp. 251-252).
13. The same phrase in a closely similar passage in 2.14. Cf. 1.38.3 on birth of baptizands. Jeanes, "Paschal Baptism," pp. 44-46, observes that Zeno's description of the font is as a womb, not a tomb, and that despite the paschal setting of baptism, dying and rising with Christ is not integrated into the rite of immersion according to Zeno's exposition.

in filthy swaddling clothes and surrendered to this world, but with joy and gladness and freed from all your sins, and she feeds you not in a stinking cradle but with delight from the sweet smelling rails of the holy altar. (1.32)

Varying the image, Zeno begins the passage by saying, "Now our mother adopts you so that she may give birth to you" (1.32). "Oh what a marvellous and truly divine, most blessed honor, in which she who gives birth does not groan, and the one born [*renascitur*] never cries!" (1.55).

The day on which the new people "was quickened by the heavenly seed" was the day on which the resurrection was celebrated (1.16.2). Thus baptism is a renewal *(renouatio)*, resurrection, and eternal life (1.55). It means a putting off of the old person (1.49 above), a death of the old person in order to be victorious (2.23). When the "old self" is "buried in the wave of the sacred waters," one is quickened and tastes "the privileges of the resurrection" (2.29.1). All is a matter of grace (1.49).

Zeno exhorts his hearers to fly to the faithful or sacred *(pius)* water *(gurgitem)* of the font (2.23). "Now the saving warmth of the everlasting font invites you" (1.32). "Hurry, hurry for a good wash [*loturi*], brothers" (1.23). Zeno treats water as bringing refreshment (1.12; 2.28), washing (1.23; 1.49), forgiveness (2.1-2), and as a burial (2.10.2 — "our water receives the dead"; 2.29.1).[14]

The presence of the Holy Spirit is communicated through the water. The water is "living with the Holy Spirit and warmed with the sweetest fire" (1.23; cf. 1.33.2). Those who have been renewed *(nouelli)* "are all rich with the gift of the Holy Spirit" (1.49). Zeno can also associate the Spirit with the pre- and postbaptismal anointings and signing with the cross.[15] All are viewed as part of one event.

Baptism places one in the church. The church as mother "incorporates us in one body after assembling us from every race and every nation" (1.55).

Maximus of Turin

Maximus was bishop of Turin from about 390 to between 408 and 423. We have a large number of short sermons surviving from him.[16] He was much dependent on Ambrose. Although he lived into the fifth century, I treat him under the fourth century because his baptismal thought is mostly traditional (although with distinctive emphases) and his concerns are those of the fourth century.

---

14. Jeanes, *The Day Has Come!* pp. 247-250. He notes that for Zeno the candidate is already dead when entering the font, which is the place of burial, but there are exceptions where death occurs in the font (2.23).

15. Jeanes, *The Day Has Come!* p. 251 cites 1.13.10 and 1.3.21.

16. English translation by Boniface Ramsey, *The Sermons of St. Maximus of Turin*, Ancient Christian Writers 50 (New York: Newman, 1989), from which I quote. Georg Langgärtner, "Die Taufe bei Maximus von Turin," in Hans Jörg Auf Der Maur and Bruno Kleinheyer, eds., *Zeichen des Glaubens: Studien zu Taufe und Firmung: Balthasar Fischer zum 60. Geburtstag* (Freiburg: Herder, 1972), pp. 71-81.

In some of his sermons Maximus directly addresses catechumens.[17] But he was also aware of those who postponed baptism: "A catechumen becomes worthless and goes to ruin when he remains a catechumen a long time, for he deteriorates within himself." With the quotation of John 3:5 he concludes, "The one who does not enter into the kingdom, however, necessarily remains in hell" (*Sermon* 65.2).

The period of preparation for baptism corresponded to the forty days of fasting, *quadragesima*, leading up to Easter:

> So that we also who are fasting during the course of these forty days might merit the spiritual rain of baptism. . . . With these fasts of forty days God is appeased, the heavens are opened, and hell is shut. (35.4)[18]

This was also a period of prayer: "Hence we also, observing the same fasts as Elijah, with our attentive prayers open a closed heaven to those requesting baptism [*competentibus*]"; by the prayers of those fasting "either the world is renewed or their brethren are reborn" (52.2).

The Pasch, or Easter, was the time for receiving baptism. "On this day . . . the earth is renewed by the church's neophytes, and heaven is unlocked by the Holy Spirit" (53.1). The newly baptized are called neophytes because on the Pasch "they cast off the stains of oldness and receive the grace of simplicity" (55.1). Maximus correlates the Pasch and Pentecost, incidentally giving an answer to the question of the baptism of the apostles: "At Easter all the pagans are usually baptized, while at Pentecost the apostles were baptized" (44.4).[19]

The baptizands received baptism nude: "We are born naked in the world, naked we come to be washed" (48.3). This feature was a characteristic of immersion, and Maximus makes several references to this practice. "We must be dipped in the same stream as Christ was so as to be able to be what Christ was" (13.2; see further below on the baptism of Christ). Our sins are "drowned in the water in which his holiness was submerged" (13.1).

> The Savior plunged into the waters . . . so that . . . it is not so much the waters of this world that cover [the one baptized in the name of the Lord] but the waters of Christ that purify him" (13A.3).

Maximus expresses several times the connection of baptism with the Trinitarian name. At the baptism of Christ, since God is invisible, the presence of the Spirit took the form of a dove and God's voice was heard (64.2; cf. 13.3; 13A.2-3). It was not remarkable, he explains, that the mystery of the Trinity was present at the Lord's washing, "since the sacrament of the Trinity makes our washing complete" (64.1).

---

17. *Sermon* 13.1, 4; 65.1 and 2; 111.3. Other references to catechumens in 33.5; 89.2.

18. In this passage the precedents for the forty days of fasting were Elijah (1 Kings 19:8), Moses (Exod. 24:18), and Jesus (Matt. 4:2) — *Sermon* 35.3-4. This fast is discussed with other biblical instances of forty days also in 50.2-3.

19. The allusion would be to their baptism in the Holy Spirit — Acts 1:5; 2:2.

That the neophytes "have laid aside their old vesture . . . and have put on the new clothing of holiness" (55.1) likely alludes to their putting on a white garment after baptism.

Maximus employs the familiar Old Testament types of baptism (52.2-4). The appearance of the dove at the baptism of Christ reminds him that "The very dove that once hastened to Noah's ark in the flood now comes to Christ's church in baptism" (64.2; cf. 50.2 on the flood). As was true with regard to Noah, "baptism is a flood to the sinner and a consecration to the faithful"; "by the Lord's washing, righteousness is preserved and unrighteousness is destroyed" (50.2). Maximus invokes Paul in 1 Corinthians 10:1-2 for understanding Israel's passing through the Red Sea as a "kind of baptism": "a cloud covered the people and water carried them" (100.3).

Similarly, Israel's coming to the streams of the Jordan parallels the Christian people's coming to the streams of baptism:

> In the one case when the Israelite went into the deeps of the river the water avoided him, while in the other when the Christian goes down into the font the sins of his evil deeds are scattered. (67.3)[20]

Elijah at the Jordan is a type in *Sermon* 35.4.

Maximus repeats the contrast of Christian with Jewish baptisms but goes further in denigrating the latter. The water of the synagogue "does not wash away sins by its baptism but begets them, which does not purify a person by its washing but makes him dirty" (28.3). One purpose of Jesus' baptism was to fulfill the Law (Matt. 3:15) that had ordained its commandments (13.4). Hence, even John's baptism is superseded by Christ's. "As the brightness of a lamp is done away with by the coming of the sun, so also John's baptism of repentance was rendered void when the grace of Christ overtook it" (62.3).

It belonged to the nature of the liturgical year that most of the references to baptism are prompted by comments on the baptism of Christ at Epiphany. Frequently recurring themes for Maximus are brought together in one of his Epiphany sermons.

> The Lord Jesus, then, came today to baptism, and he wanted his holy body to be washed with water. Perhaps someone should say: "Why did one who is holy want to be baptized?" Listen, then! Christ is baptized not that he might be sanctfied by the waters but that he himself might sanctify the waters and purify with his own purification the steams that he touches. For Christ's consecration is greater than that of the element. For when the Savior is washed all water is cleansed for our baptism, and the source is purified so that the grace of the washing might be ministered to the people who would follow after. Christ underwent baptism first, then, so that after him the Christian people might confidently follow. (100.3)

---

20. The passage also invokes the imagery of crossing the Red Sea.

That Christ had no need to be purified by water was the occasion for frequent comment. The paradox was that Christ was "purer than the font," so he purified (sanctified, cleansed, consecrated) the water, which did "not so much wash Christ as submit to being washed" (13A.3). He had no sin, but he was baptized for the sake of others.

> The Lord came to the washing not so that he himself might be purified by the water but so that the streams of waters might purify us, for he went down into the waters thereby destroying the sins of all believers" (64.1)

By his baptism the Lord cleansed all water. "In order to be dipped in the same water" it is not necessary to go to the Jordan, "for now Christ is everywhere and the Jordan is everywhere" (13.2).

Christ's baptism was an example to be followed by others. In his baptism the Lord demonstrated "first in himself what he would afterwards demand of the human race" (64.1).

Maximus cited Psalm 114:3 on the waters of the Jordan turning back, but he declares as even more marvelous that "now sins are turned back" (64.3).[21]

The water received grace from Christ so that it might give blessing to Christians (13.1). Indeed, Christians' baptism is more grace filled than was Christ's. The latter's baptism was administered by John, but the former is administered by Christ (13.2), and Maximus continues with a contrast of Christ's baptism with that of Christians, showing the blessings conferred in Christian baptism.

Nonetheless, the benefits of Christian baptism derive from Christ's baptism. And, as the passages already cited show, Maximus most often refers to baptism in terms of forgiveness of sins.[22] Christ's baptism "purges away sins" and "remits sins" (13A.1). The "water of Christ" "vivifies souls and extinguishes sins" (22A.3). The water cleanses the spiritual stains on souls; even though it is material, it reaches the conscience (13B.2). The baptized leave their filth and soiled consciences behind (67.3).

The work of the Holy Spirit in baptism is less prominent but is expressed, especially in connection with the Lord's baptism. The Holy Spirit, who was present with Christ in the womb, at his baptism "sanctifies the running waters for him" (13A.2). And so, "the Lord was both born and baptized through the Holy Spirit" (13A.2). "In the baptism of Christ, then, both heaven and the underworld are opened — the former so that the Holy Spirit might come, the latter so that the mercy of the Savior might penetrate" (22A.3). Only with baptism does the Holy Spirit come from heaven and enliven hearts (52.2).

Maximus refers to the familiar motif of baptism as a death and burial. "Baptism, therefore, is Christ's burial place for us, in which we die to sins, are buried to

---

21. Cf. 67.3 on the waters of the Jordan turning back when Israel crossed them into the promised land.

22. Maximus also attributes forgiveness to almsgiving, but this is for sins committed after baptism (22A.4). Martyrdom is a baptism (9.2).

evil deeds, and are restored to a renewed infancy" (59.4). The passage continues by talking about receiving "a new life," for this burial "both cleanses the sinner and gives life to the dying."[23] "For we die to our sins through the bath, but we are reborn to life through the Spirit," followed by quotation of Colossians 3:3 and Romans 6:4 (35.1). Thus Maximus combines the imagery of death and burial with that of new birth: "This second birth signifies that the former life has come to an end" (35.1). The "conscience of the old man" is "dissolved in us for the sake of another birth" (59.4).

Maximus more often employs the imagery of new birth than that of death and burial for baptism. Christ's baptism was "another kind of birth" for him (13A.2), and this second birth was "more noble" than the first (13A.2). Christ by his baptism was "reborn on the Epiphany" (65.3). Similarly, Christians are "born again into childhood" and, even if old, are "turned into babes" (55.1).[24] They are restored to their "infant beginnings" (67.3). Hence, Maximus exhorts the catechumens to "hasten to the grace of the second birth," followed shortly thereafter by a quotation of John 3:5 (111.3).

Maximus employs the language of enlightenment in reference to baptism. In his development of the typology of the flood he says, "The saving washing might enlighten us in baptism" (50.2), or similarly with reference to Elijah, "The rain of the saving washing may enlighten them" (52.2).

Other benefits of baptism are alluded to. Heaven is opened, and the fires of Gehenna are extinguished (22A.3). Heaven is closed before baptism but opened when the divine mysteries of the Trinity are revealed (52.3).

Drawing lessons from the story of David and Goliath, Maximus speaks of "the sign of salvation" and the "Savior's seal" (85.3), but the context does not reveal what Maximus had in mind — baptism, an anointing, sign of the cross, the Holy Spirit, or something else?

Maximus often speaks of grace in connection with baptism. "The grace of baptism" is a frequently recurring phrase (e.g., 22A.3; 52.2; 55.1; 35.4 — "baptismal grace"). Baptism bestows grace on believers (13.3; cf. 13.1, cited above).

The human corollary of divine grace is faith. Like Israel in crossing the Red Sea, the Christian has "faith in the washing" and walks with faith (100.3). The appearance of the dove and the sounding of the voice of the Father at the baptism of Christ was to build up human faith (64.2).

Maximus illustrates the wide variety of the ways the words "sacrament" and "mystery" were used by his time. Among these is the "mystery of baptism" (100.3). There are several instances of the use of "sacrament" or "mystery" in reference to baptism (13.2-3; 13B.1 — "mysteries of the sacraments"; 64.1 — both terms with reference to the Trinity in baptism).

23. Cf. 52.2, with reference to the rain in answer to Elijah's prayers: "The water of baptism moistens the human race so as to bring to life the dead hearts of souls."

24. This passage develops the theme of renewal from Ps. 103:5, "renewed like an eagle." For the correlation between Jesus' birth from the virgin and his baptism (e.g., 13A.1) see Georg Langgärtner, "Die Taufe," p. 73. Other references to rebirth are in 2.3; 31.2; 33.5.

Chromatius of Aquileia

His Writings

Chromatius was born in Aquileia and became the city's bishop in 388, consecrated by Ambrose. He was closely associated with Rufinus and Jerome. His surviving literary output includes over forty sermons and some sixty tractates on Matthew.[25] He died in 407 or 408.

Chromatius does not give a systematic account of the baptismal rite, but he makes several allusions to it.[26] There was a renunciation before the baptism.

> Before you came to baptism, one asked you if you renounced the world, its pomps, and its works. And you responded that you renounced them. And so you came to the grace of eternal baptism. Your words are preserved before God. Your response is written in heaven. (*Sermon* 14.4)

The exact words of the formula of renunciation may not be preserved, for it is to be doubted that the devil or Satan would have been omitted.[27]

The following words may still refer to the renunciation or may refer to a separate confession.

> You made a sworn promise of your faith to God. You swore your promise in the presence of angels, because angels are present when you are asked about your faith. See what you did. If something promised to a human being is binding, what about that which is solemnly pledged to God? (*Sermon* 14.4)

A footwashing preceded the baptism, as at Milan. Chromatius bases his treatment on John 13 but cites other instances in scripture of footwashing (Gen. 18:4; Judg. 6:11-18, but not mentioned in the text). Like Ambrose, he associates the footwashing with removal of the vestiges of the sin of Adam (*Sermon* 15.6). Peter's desire for his hands and head also to be washed anticipated the complete cleansing of baptism (*Sermon* 15.5).

> The Lord washed the feet of his servants, whom he invited to the grace of saving baptism. And if the similar deed appears to be performed by human beings, it is nevertheless the work of the author of this gift. He himself does what he instituted. We show forth the deed, but he grants the gift. (*Sermon* 15.6).

---

25. I use the edition of Joseph Lemarié and French translation of Henri Tardif, *Chromace d'Aquilée, Sermons*, 2 vols., Sources chrétiennes 154 and 164 (Paris: Cerf, 1969, 1971).

26. Especially in *Sermons* 14 ("On the Healing of the Paralytic and on Baptism") and 15 ("On the Washing of Feet"). Lemarié, *Chromace d'Aquilée*, Vol. 1, pp. 97-103, describes the baptismal rite on the paschal night in comparison with the rite at Milan. For his baptismal liturgy, supplemented from Rufinus, see also Victor Saxer, *Les rites de l'initiation chrétienne du IIe au VIe siècle: Esquisse historique et signification d'après leur principaux témoins* (Spoleto: Centro italiano di studi sull'alto medioevo, 1988), pp. 349-364.

27. Lemarié, *Chromace d'Aquilée*, Vol. 1, p. 98.

Baptism involved a triple immersion in the three divine names.

> Our flesh by nature is something worthless but becomes precious by the change effected by grace, when we, like a spiritual purple cloth, are dipped three times [*trifarie tingatur*] in the mystery of the Trinity. (*Sermon* 19.2)

Tingere, used as a synonym for *baptizare*, is Chromatius's regular word for baptism.[28] Chromatius elsewhere relates the effectiveness of baptism to the Trinity:

> We cannot be made clean and be purified from sins except by the mystery of the Trinity. In the name of Father, Son, and Holy Spirit is given the grace of baptism which purifies us from all the filth of sin. (*Sermon* 3.8)

Or, again, this effectiveness is related to faith in the Trinity. "There is no true baptism nor true remission of sins where there is not the truth of the Trinity, nor is it possible for remission of sins to be given where the perfect Trinity is not believed" (*Sermon* 34.2).[29]

Quoting Ecclesiastes 9:8, Chromatius alludes to the baptizand being clothed in a white garment and being anointed with unction: "We always have white garments if we keep the grace of baptism intact. We always have oil on the head, if we preserve the saving chrism that we have received" (*Sermon* 14.4). Chromatius makes another allusion to the white garment. He interpreted the nuptial robe of Matthew 22:12 as "the grace of saving baptism, which shines not in the brightness of wool but in the whiteness of faith." "We receive the snow white garment of Christ by the grace of baptism" and "by faith in Christ," with Galatians 3:27 quoted (*Sermon* 10.4).[30]

The continuation of the passage quoted above about footwashing that emphasizes the divine action in the ceremonies of initiation adds the detail of imposition of hands to confer the Holy Spirit.

> We wash the feet of the body; he [the Lord] washes the footprint of souls. We dip the body in water; he forgives sins. We dip; he sanctifies. We, on the earth, lay on hands; from heaven he gives the Holy Spirit. Hence, my children, catechumens, you must hasten to the grace of baptism, so that you may lay aside the filth of sin. (*Sermon* 15.6)

Those words may provide a transition to the doctrinal meaning of baptism set forth in Chromatius's *Sermons*.

A fairly set phrase with Chromatius is "the grace of baptism" (e.g., *Sermon* 14.4, three times and "grace" twice to stand for baptism). Thus he says, "Abundant is the

---

28. Cf. *Sermon* 14.2 (twice) and the note by Lemarié, *Chromace d'Aquilée*, pp. 40-41.

29. See further below on *Sermon* 18.4. Other references to the Trinity not cited in my text are *Sermons* 15; 40; 44.

30. The whiteness resulting from baptism is compared to milk in *Sermon* 14.2. This fits the new birth imagery (below); does Chromatius allude to milk in the baptismal eucharist?

grace of the church's baptism" (*Sermon* 14.3). In contrasting the piscina called Bethsaida (Bethesda or Bethzatha — John 5:2) with the "grace of saving baptism," of which it was an image, Chromatius lists some of the graces of baptism.

> The water of this piscina [of Bethsaida] was stirred only once a year; but the water of the church's baptism is always ready and stirred. That water was stirred in only one place, but this is stirred through all the world. To that one an angel came down; here the Holy Spirit. There was the grace of an angel; here the mystery of the Trinity. There the water healed only one person a year; here daily people are saved. The water of that pool healed only the body; these waters save both body and soul. That one freed only the body from infirmity; this frees body and soul from sin. (*Sermon* 14.1)[31]

The effects of baptism are the working of the Trinity that brings salvation of body and soul and deliverance from sin.

In explicating the Lord's Prayer Chromatius relates sanctifying the name of God to what baptism does. "We ask that his name may be sanctified in us, so that we who were sanctified in baptism may persevere in that which we began to be" (*Sermon* 40.2).

Chromatius's favorite language for the effects of baptism are regeneration and new birth by which human beings are renewed and become like children. Commenting on John 5:14, he says to his hearers, "Whatever sins you had are forgiven; you are healed from every infirmity of sin; . . . you are raised a new person from the bath of regeneration [*regenerationis*]" (*Sermon* 14.4). One of his sermons on the Paschal night declares that "In this time the world is renewed, since on this day the whole human race is renewed" (*Sermon* 17.3). He continues:

> Innumerable are the people throughout the whole world who today are raised in "newness of life" [Rom. 6:4] by the water of baptism, with the old life of sin removed. . . . At this time the church of God like a spiritual ewe gives birth [*procreat*] to a flock of the faithful even as sheep for Christ. . . . The church is shown by the bath as having just delivered, because by the grace of baptism it gives birth to sons for God. (*Sermon* 17.3)

Chromatius had one sermon "On Nicodemus and on Baptism." By the words of John 3:5-6,

> The Lord clearly shows to Nicodemus that there are two births: one earthly, the other heavenly; one fleshly, the other spiritual. The birth of the Spirit is much superior to that of the flesh. . . .
>
> Fleshly then is the birth from a human being; spiritual is the birth from God. . . . That one gives birth [*procreat*] to a person in the world; this one generates [*generat*] for God. . . . This spiritual birth is accomplished altogether invisibly,

---

31. A similar summary in 14.3.

even as that birth is visible. Now it is certainly seen that one who is baptized is dipped and is seen to come up from the water. But what is done in that bath is not seen. The church of the faithful alone understand spiritually that a sinner goes down into the font but comes up clean from all sin.... Those who are regenerated [*regenerantur*] by baptism are reborn [*renascuntur*] in innocence, having put away the old error and malice of sin. For it is the spiritual womb of the church that conceives and bears sons for God. (*Sermon* 18.2-3)

The one baptized is now worthy to enter the kingdom of heaven (John 3:5). This sermon concludes by drawing a parallel between the first creation as the work of the Trinity and the second creation ("our spiritual birth") in baptism as a work of the Trinity, for "The Father does nothing without the Son nor without the Holy Spirit" (18.4). The special concern here is that "our spiritual birth is not without the Holy Spirit" (18.4).

Chromatius thus freely interchanges the male and female terms for procreation in describing what takes place in baptism. He ascribes the maternal role to the church. What takes place invisibly during the visible immersion is the work of the divine Trinity.

The sermon "On the Epiphany of the Lord" brings several of these motifs together. The washing of baptism is given only once, and it makes one pure and new, whiter than snow (34.2). This sermon adds the idea of dying and rising with Christ.[32]

> Our Lord came to give a new baptism for the salvation of the human race and forgiveness of all sins. First he considered it appropriate for himself to be baptized, not to put away sins, since he had done no sin, but he sanctified the waters of baptism in order to destroy the sins of all believers by the baptism of the reborn. He was baptized in water so that we by baptism might be washed from all sins....
>
> [Gal. 3:27 and Rom. 6:4 quoted.] Thus by baptism we die to sin, but we live with Christ; we bury our old life, but we are raised to a new life; we take off the error of the old person, but we take on the clothing of the new person. Therefore, the Lord in baptism fulfilled all righteousness. He wanted to be baptized so that we might be baptized; he received this "washing of regeneration" [Titus 3:5] so that we might be reborn in life. (*Sermon* 34.3)

We note Chromatius's linking of the new birth motif with the death and resurrection motif and with the forgiveness of sins; he interchanges the language of regeneration and new birth. All is rooted in and anticipated by Christ's baptism that sanctified the waters. Missing here is prominence to the work of the Holy Spirit in baptism, attested in other quotations above.

Chromatius continues in the passage with the suggestion that Jesus' baptism

---

32. It is cited above (34.2) for the presence of the Trinity in baptism. Chromatius interprets the opening of the heavens at the baptism of the Lord to mean that in the bath of regeneration the kingdom of heaven is open to believers according to John 3:5 (34.2).

had the effect of baptizing John and forgiving his sins (*Sermon* 34.3). The grace of Jesus' baptism was mystically prefigured in Israel's crossing the Jordan into the promised land; even so, thanks to the same river, there is opened a way into the blessed land of promise, the kingdom of heaven (*Sermon* 34.3).

The church of Christ is "white and brilliant, having the splendor of heavenly life and the brightness of saving baptism [*baptismi salutaris*]" (*Sermon* 3.6).

The recipients of baptism with these great benefits must be careful to preserve it from sin, because it is given only once.

> The baptism in the church is one and true, because it is given only once. The person who is dipped on the one occasion is made pure and new — pure because of putting away the filth of sins, new because raised in a new life, having put away the oldness of sin. For this washing of baptism makes a person whiter than snow, not in the skin of the body but in the spendor of the mind and purity of the soul. (*Sermon* 34.2)

"Watch so that you do not return to your former sins and incur danger of death, because the grace of baptism is given only once" (*Sermon* 14.4).

Chromatius makes a modification of the uniqueness of baptism in regard to martyrdom. In the last-quoted sermon Chromatius had earlier declared that "martyrdom signifies baptism" and quoted Luke 12:50 as referring to "the baptism of the Lord's passion" (*Sermon* 14.2). He then explains,

> The baptism of water is certainly good, but much better and superior is the baptism of martyrs. That gives pardon, but this a reward. That is a remission of sins; this obtains a crown of virtues. (*Sermon* 14.2)

Archaeological Evidence

The restored hexagonal baptismal pool presently visible to the west and on the same axis of the patriarchal basilica at Aquileia belongs to the medieval church (either the work of the patriarch Poppo in the eleventh century or Maxentius in the early ninth century), the latest of three fonts on the site.[33] Beneath it was an octagonal pool (of the late fourth or second half of the fifth century). When the two parallel halls (connected by a transversal hall on their west ends) of the first independent church were built by Bishop Theodore at the beginning of the fourth century, the baptistery was located in the open space within the U-shape of the halls. The first font was rectangular and may have been a bathtub in the Roman house on the site that preceded the Christian building. Its dimensions were 1.73 meters long, 0.84 meters wide, and 0.94 meters deep. The shape and dimensions are comparable to those of the font at the

---

33. Gabriella Brumat Dellasorte, *Ancient Aquileia* (Venice: Storti, 1993-1995), pp. 57-78 (60). Almost everything about the archaeological history of the basilica is subject to different scholarly opinions.

Dura house church. The font was then made round and surrounded by a hexagonal parapet.[34] In the mid–fourth century, probably under Bishop Fortunatianus, who enlarged the north hall, the baptistery was relocated nearer it and provided with a hexagonal font (Ristow #334).[35] Chromatius enlarged the south hall and had a large new baptistery built in alignment with it, housing the first of three fonts at the location of the medieval fonts (Ristow #335), although some scholars date this work to the period after devastation caused by Attila the Hun in the fifth century. This hexagonal font had a six-columned ciborium and a depth of 1.60 meters.

Aquileia is the site of an inscribed gravestone containing a scene often cited as depicting an affusion (Figure 5).[36] It has a circle representing heaven in which is portrayed a dove and from which streams (of water, oil, or light?) descend surrounding what appears to be a young girl (note the pearl necklace, hence not the baptism of Jesus, despite the presence of a dove) standing in a shallow basin. The baptizer dressed as a shepherd lays a hand on her head, so he is not pouring water. On the other side of the girl a man with a nimbus extends a hand toward her. The accompanying inscription reads, "To Innocent, whose spirit the Lord chose [or, To the innocent spirit whom the Lord called]; rests in peace, a believer. August 23." Thus she likely died shortly after her baptism, and we may have here an example of the emergency baptism of a child. If the lines descending around the baptizand are meant to represent water, which is uncertain in view of the nearest iconographical parallel in the catacomb painting from SS. Pietro e Marcellino discussed in chapter 7, then they may suggest the presence of flowing water rather than an affusion.

An iconographical parallel is a glass fragment found in Rome.[37] It depicts an

---

34. S. Anita Stauffer, *On Baptismal Fonts: Ancient and Modern*, Alcuin Club 29-30 (Bramcote: Grove, 1994), p. 42, with picture showing steps at one end. G. C. Menis, "La liturgia battesimale ad Aquileia nel complesso episcopale del IV secolo," *Antiquité Tardive* 4 (1996): 61-74 (on p. 61 it summarizes and on p. 71 it diagrams a proposed itinerary through the episcopal complex by catechumens during the baptismal ceremony on the night of the Pascha in the fourth century, which he considers an important clarification of the distinctive use of the fourth-century double church; he includes a picture of the funerary eipgraph from Aquileia discussed below); also his "Il battesimo ad Aquileia nella prima metà del IV secolo," *L'edificio battesimale in Italia: Aspetti e problemi: Atti dell'VIII Congresso Nazionale di Archeologia Cristiana . . . 21-26 settembre 1998* (Bordighera: Istituto Internazionale di Studi Liguri, 2001), pp. 685-708.

35. Lemarié, *Chromace d'Aquilée*, p. 99, n. 1, identifies this as the baptistery contemporary with Chromatius and gives the upper diameter of the font as 2.20 meters. Baptismal fonts are identified by their number in Sebastian Ristow, *Frühchristliche Baptisterien, Jahrbuch für Antike und Christentum*, Ergänzungsband 27 (Münster: Aschendorff, 1998).

36. It is often reproduced, as in the guidebook by B. Forlati Tamaro and L. Bertacchi, *Aquileia: Il Museo Paleocristiano* (Padova: Antoniana, 1962), p. 38. Fabrizio Bisconti, "L'iconografia dei battisteri paleocristiani in Italia," in *L'edificio battesimale in Italia: Aspetti e problemi: Atti dell'VIII Congresso Nazionale di Archeologia Cristiana . . . 21-26 settembre 1998* (Bordighera: Istituto Internazionale di Studi Liguri, 2001), p. 419, describes it as an immersion; reproduction of the scene on p. 418; G. C. Menis, "Il battesimo ad Aquileia," p. 705, also understands the scene as an immersion (and reproduces it on 707) but interprets the hand on the head not as baptismal but as an unction.

37. Franz J. Dölger, "Die Firmung in den Denkmälern des christlichen Altertums," *Römische*

upside down jar from which (presumably) water streams down to the head of a clothed young woman named Alba while a dove with an ivy leaf in its beak approaches from above her on the right. A large nimbed figure on the left named Mirax gestures with the right arm extended toward the woman. On the right is shown a forearm with the right hand touching the woman's head. A dotted background surrounds the woman. De Rossi interpreted the scene as an already completed baptism, alluded to by the water flowing from the container, with the person clothed in white *(alba)*. The nimbed figure is the baptizer, and the person laying on a hand is a godfather or deaconess who assisted at the baptism. Garrucci, on the other hand, interprets what flows from the container as not actually water but the saving grace effected by baptism. The dove represents the imparting of the Holy Spirit in confirmation. Mirax is a saint chosen as a godfather, and the one laying on a hand is the human godfather.

There are difficulties in both de Rossi's interpretation of the scene as baptism and Garrucci's as confirmation, notably the lack of support in literary sources for a godfather laying on a hand. The baptismal interpretation has in its favor that the laying on of hands coincided with the baptismal confession and immersions. That the figure is clothed supports a laying on of hands at the subsequent anointing of the head with oil, representing the imparting of the Holy Spirit. We likely have here a composite scene, for the water baptism and the anointing were viewed as one ceremony and not distinguished as separate sacraments of baptism and confirmation.

Neither the gravestone from Aquileia, the glass from Rome, nor the painting in the Catacomb of Peter and Marcellinus (chap. 7) can properly be invoked in support of pouring as the mode of baptism, for even if the streams coming down represent water, the administrator has his hand on the head of the baptizand and is not pouring the liquid, which comes from another source.

Quartalschrift 19 (1905): 1-41 (21-25) with picture, on whom the following discussion is based. The glass is also reproduced (in support of an aspersion) in Clementina Rizzardi, "La decorazione musiva del battistero degli ortodossi e degli Ariani a Ravenna: Alcune considerazione," in *L'editicio battesimale in Italia: Aspetti e problemi: Atti dell'VIII Congresso Nazionale di Archeologia Cristiana . . . 21-26 settembre 1998* (Bordighera: Istituto Internazionale di Studi Liguri, 2001), p. 922, along with another reproduction of the grave slab on p. 923. I have not seen R. Garrucci, *Storia dell' arte cristiana nei primi otto secoli della chiesa* 6 (Prato, 1880), pp. 90-91, plate 462.8; p. 152, plate 487.26; p. 93, plate 464.1.

42. Spain

Information about baptism before the Middle Ages is sparser for Spain than some other regions, but there are indications of distinctive features, in some respects perhaps preserving earlier practices that were superseded elsewhere. In the period covered by our study single immersion was the normal practice; chrismation and blessing of oil was done by presbyters; and the rise of infant baptism took longer than at many places.[1]

Council of Elvira

Bishops and presbyters from Spain met at Elvira (vicinity of Granada) in the first decade of the fourth century. They took a strict approach to the problems posed by a superficial Christianization of converts. The eighty-one canons they adopted deal with disciplinary matters, and a few are relevant to baptismal practices.[2]

The canons throughout concern adolescents or adults. Catechumens *(catechumeni)* who had served as pagan priests *(flamines)* but without performing sacrifices could be admitted to baptism *(baptismum)* after a period of three years (can. 4).

When at sea or where a church was not near, a believer who had held fast to his baptism *(lavacrum)* and had not married a second time could baptize *(baptizare)* a catechumen in case of necessity caused by illness *(infirmitatis)*. If the neophyte sur-

---

1. These are the conclusions of Christian David McConnell, "Baptism in Visigothic Spain: Origins, Development, and Interpretation" (Ph.D. diss., University of Notre Dame, 2005), p. 1; for single immersion, pp. 209-219; chrismation, pp. 197-209; infant baptism, pp. 191-197; my summary at the end of this chapter. He covers the period from the fourth century to 711.

2. The canons pertaining to baptism are found in André Benoit and Charles Munier, *Le baptême dans l'Église ancienne*, Traditio Christiana 9 (Bern: Peter Lang, 1994), pp. 250-253, and in English in E. C. Whitaker and Maxwell E. Johnson, *Documents of the Baptismal Liturgy*, rev. ed. (Collegeville: Liturgical, 2003), pp. 154-155.

vived, he was to be taken to a bishop, who would perfect *(perfici)* his initiation by laying on of a hand (can. 38).

Canon 39 dealt with another case of emergency. If a pagan was ill and desired a hand to be laid on him, if his life was upright, a hand was to be laid on him and he was to be made a Christian. This canon may refer to admission to the catechumenate (by the imposition of a hand) as "being made a Christian" (same usage later in Augustine), or the (less likely) imposition of a hand may be shorthand for the giving of emergency (sickbed) baptism. The canon is problematic, for (unless the latter interpretation is correct) if admission to the catechumenate was thought to assure salvation, why was emergency baptism practiced?[3]

Canon 42 clarifies the usual procedure recognized in the churches represented at the council. Those who come to the first profession of faith *(primam fidem credulitatis)* and have good conduct ought to be admitted to the grace of baptism *(baptismi gratiam)* after two years. An exception was made in cases of necessity by reason of illness and the person asking for grace. The designation of baptism as grace is terminology often found by this time. The two-year catechumenate was less than the three years required in some sources.[4] Emergency baptism was a recognized practice but one still calling for justification.

Catechumens were not always exemplary in their conduct. If one for a long time had not attended church, there was a question about administering baptism. It was decided that if one of the clergy knew the person to be a Christian (indicating the use of the term for a catechumen, so a believer but not yet baptized), or if some of the faithful *(fideles,* the baptized and faithful) could attest the person's manner of life, baptism was not to be denied if it was evident that the person had abandoned the old way of life (can. 45).

The custom had grown up of those who were baptized to make a payment of money to the clergyman, but the council said this should not be done (can. 48). It was also said in this canon that their feet should not be washed by priests. The import of this canon in connection with payment for a baptism is not clear. The rite of footwashing in connection with baptism is known from later in the fourth century at Milan (see on Ambrose, chap. 40); and if that is the reference here, the practice was known in Spain.[5]

It was agreed that when a baptism was performed by a deacon in the absence of a bishop or presbyter, it was the duty of a bishop to perfect *(perficere)* the person. But if the person died before this could be done, he was assured of being justified by virtue of his faith (can. 77). Here is another use of "perfect," or "complete," for the bishop's imposition of hand as completing the action of baptism and of the association of faith (the "faithful") with baptism.

3. McConnell, "Baptism in Visigothic Spain," pp. 128-29.
4. McConnell, "Baptism in Visigothic Spain," p. 125, suggests that the two years was a lengthening rather than a shortening.
5. One reading forbids the practice by priests or clerics; another reading forbids it to be done by priests but not by clerics.

Gregory of Elvira

Gregory's life spanned much of the fourth century. His writings draw heavily from his predecessors, but they give a rare look at baptismal practice in fourth-century Spain.[6]

Gregory interpreted the three decks of Noah's ark (Gen. 6:16) as three periods: the catechumenate in general, the preparation for baptism, and receiving the sacrament.[7] The catechumenate concerned moral, intellectual, and existential formation. It included penitence, confession of sin, and satisfactions for sins (e.g., alms).

The blessing of the water for baptism was rooted in the baptism of Christ. Baptism was administered by the bishop.[8] Gregory compared the confession of the Trinitarian faith to the oath of soldiers. He does not say anything about the manner of administering baptism. He uses various expressions for baptism: *lavacrum vitae* ("bath of life"), *flumen lavacri et aqua baptismatis* ("river of washing and water of baptism"), *lavacrum aquae salutaris* ("bath of saving water"), *divinum lavacrum* ("divine bath"), *in piscina lavacri* ("in the pool of washing").[9]

Scripture and daily life provided a varied symbolism for baptism to Gregory. Baptism is a liberation from the pagan world by which people are reunited in the church. It is a new passage of the Red Sea in which the devil (Pharaoh) is submerged. As water washes, baptism purifies and sanctifies. On the basis of Exodus 17:6 and John 7:38 baptism is the source of living waters. As the potter makes a new vessel (Jer. 18), baptism makes a new creation. Baptism integrates one into the church. It transforms the soul (using John 2:1-12). As Moses was saved from the water (Exod. 2:1-10), in baptism the believer finds Christ.[10]

For the description of the postbaptismal rites Gregory borrows from Tertullian, *On the Resurrection of the Flesh* 8.3. After the *lavacrum*, the baptizand's head was anointed with perfumed oil, an act compared to the consecration of priests and kings of the Old Testament. The anointing indicated the conferring of spiritual gifts by Christ; it represented a spiritual force strengthening the Christian athlete and was a medicine to the soul. The anointing was followed by an imposition of both hands (not one hand as in Tertullian and other sources). Then came the eucharist.[11]

---

6. Philippe Beita, "L'Initiation chrétienne dans une communauté espagnole du IV siècle," *Bulletin de littérature ecclesiastique* 96 (1995): 83-95, whom I follow in this section and who provides references in Gregory's writings.

7. Beita, "L'Initiation chrétienne dans une communauté espagnole du IV siècle," pp. 85-86.

8. Beita, "L'Initiation chrétienne dans une communauté espagnole du IV siècle," p. 88.

9. Beita, "L'Initiation chrétienne dans une communauté espagnole du IV siècle," p. 89.

10. Beita, "L'Initiation chrétienne dans une communauté espagnole du IV siècle," pp. 89-91. McConnell, "Baptism in Visigothic Spain," notes that the later writers in Spain (Isidore and Ildefonsus) develop the Exodus motif more than do others — pp. 219ff.

11. Beita, "L'Initiation chrétienne dans une communauté espagnole du IV siècle," pp. 92-94.

Pacian of Barcelona

Pacian died between 379 and 392 as bishop of Barcelona. Among his sparse literary remains is a sermon, *On Baptism*.[12] It is filled with biblical passages, some quoted loosely.

Pacian's opening of that sermon expresses his concern for the "candidates for baptism" (1.1).[13] And near the conclusion he says, "We renounce the devil and all his angels" (7.2). The context would not of itself suggest a formal renunciation of the devil in the baptismal ceremony. Yet that is apparently the allusion, although Pacian is not following the sequence of events, for the sentence begins, "Freed therefore from our chains, when through the sacrament of baptism we come unto the sign of the Lord, we renounce. . . ." Earlier there is a reference to "the sacraments of baptism and chrism at the hands of the bishop" (6.2), indicating a postbaptismal anointing (see further below).

That last section contains a passage that brings together some of Pacian's key thoughts in regard to baptism: new birth, faith, and Holy Spirit.

> And so the seed of Christ, that is, the Spirit of God, produces through the hands of the priests the new man, conceived in the womb of our [spiritual] mother and received at birth at the baptismal font, with faith still attending as the nuptial protectress. For neither will someone appear attached to the church who has not believed, nor will someone be born from Christ who has not received his Spirit. We must believe therefore that we can be born again. (6.2)[14]

Then Pacian emphasizes the importance of faith by combining nuptial imagery with birth imagery by referring to faith as the *pronuba*, the woman who prepared the bride for marriage (6.3).[15]

Pacian had earlier laid out the human condition that made a new birth necessary. He described the death to which human beings were subject before their coming to baptism (1.2-2.1). Adam was condemned to everlasting death, and this decree held sway over all his descendants (Rom. 5:14). Human beings are all held under slavery to sin, "that is, for impure acts under the influence of wicked angels." Adam's condemnation to death (Gen. 3:19) "was transmitted to the whole human race." "For

---

12. G. P. Jeanes, "Paschal Baptism and Rebirth: A Clash of Images?" *Studia patristica* 26 (1993): 41-46. I quote the English translation by Craig L. Hanson, *Iberian Fathers*, Vol. 3, *Pacian of Barcelona; Orosius of Braga*, Fathers of the Church 99 (Washington, D.C.: Catholic University of America Press, 1999); there is also an English translation by Thomas Halton in André Hamman, *Baptism: Ancient Liturgies and Patristic Texts* (Staten Island: Alba House, 1967), pp. 67-73.

13. His work on *Penitence* refers to catechumens, penitents, and faithful as making up the community — McConnell, "Baptism in Visigothic Spain," pp. 21-22.

14. Hanson, *Pacian of Barcelona*, p. 92.

15. Jeanes, "Paschal Baptism," pp. 42-44, expects too much literal consistency in figurative language in suggesting a shift from birth imagery to the nuptial in the passage; even the literal minded can associate a birth with a preceding wedding.

all sinned, with nature itself now impelling them to it" (Rom. 5:12 quoted). This passage is easily read in view of later theological developments as expressing original sin understood to be "the sin of Adam as having been passed down to all of his descendants."[16] Actually Pacian's words are that death, the punishment for sin, not Adam's sin and its guilt, passed to all human beings. The sin that is talked about here is the sin of individuals. "Without the Law [man] perished because he could not recognize sin; and under the Law he perished because he rushed into that very sin which he saw." Later, Pacian does say, "The sin of Adam had passed on to the whole human race" (5). He proceeds to quote Romans 5:12, but he draws the conclusion, "Therefore, the righteousness of Christ must pass on to the whole human race" (Rom. 5:19, 21). His exposition of Romans 5 may not be carefully stated, for if he really meant "original sin" derived from Adam, he would have to mean "universal righteousness" derived from Christ. So, the reader must be careful not to make Pacian say more than Paul says in his Adam-Christ typology.

Nonetheless, sin is universal and human beings could not free themselves from it, but God's grace provided a remedy (Rom. 7:24-25). Grace is God's gift to needy humanity. Grace "is the remission of sin; that is, a gift" (3.1). Hence, Pacian expounds on "what faith offers and what indulgence baptism grants" in contrast to paganism (1.1).

Christ defeated the devil by not sinning (4). He set people free from the powers of darkness and broke the chains of sins (7.2). Accordingly, the baptizands are to put aside their former errors and follow the new ways in Christ (6.2).

Despite the Paschal observance of the death and resurrection of Jesus,[17] Pacian features the new birth imagery for baptism. He begins his sermon by expressing his desire "to reveal in what way we are born in baptism" (1.1). Conception is in the "womb of our [spiritual] mother," stated twice (6.1 as well as the quotation above from 6.2). I take the mother to be the church and not the baptismal font, for it is mentioned separately in the quotation above. "We are born of Christ" (stated twice in 6.1). From the marriage of Christ and the church "is born the Christian people, with the Spirit of the Lord coming from above" (6.1). The whole person is "born again and renewed in Christ" (6.2).

Pacian related the forgiveness of sins to baptism. In his *Letter* 3 dealing with the Novatianists he declares that, while a person is sealed by an anointed priest, it is not the human administrator but "God alone, who in baptism both forgives the offense and does not reject the tears of the penitents" (3.7.3).[18] In the sermon *On Baptism* the forgiveness of sins in baptism is supplemented by a further detail of the baptismal ceremony that relates the gift of the Holy Spirit to an anointing: "For by baptism sins are washed away; by chrism the Holy Spirit is poured out" (6.2).

Pacian admonishes the baptizands not to sin any more, for "only once are we

---

16. Hanson, *Pacian of Barcelona*, p. 88, n. 5.
17. *Letter* 3.9.3 quotes Rom. 6:3-4 on baptism.
18. Hanson, *Pacian of Barcelona*, p. 47.

washed; only once are we set free; only once are we admitted into the eternal kingdom; just once" is Psalm 32:1 applicable (7.3).

Pacian's *Letter* 1 says that bishops (like the apostles) baptize, confer the Spirit, and cleanse nations of sins. The position of the middle term suggests a baptismal conferral of the Spirit, not a separate liturgical act.[19]

Some Later Developments in Spain

Martin of Braga (bishop 556-579) attests to controversy in the Iberian peninsula over three immersions or one and in the case of the former whether there was a single confession of the Trinitarian faith or it was distributed among the three immersions.[20] A Bishop Boniface had written Martin that he had heard that priests baptized not in the singular name but in the plural names of the Trinity, and Martin says the report was false. The practice was to dip three times in the single name of the Trinity (*Triple Immersion* 2).

Martin then discusses a single versus a triple immersion. Some, he says, hear "one baptism" (Eph. 4:5) and refer it to one immersion rather than to the unity of Catholic practice of a single manner of baptizing. They changed the "ancient tradition" to one immersion in a single name to avoid Arianism, not realizing that a single immersion (he says) was a Sabellian practice (*Triple Immersion* 3-4). One should not reject a triple immersion because the Arians practiced it. The single profession of the name expressed the oneness of God, and the triple immersions his threeness.

The single immersion, however, appears to have been the norm in Spain and to have prevailed in spite of Martin's advocacy of three immersions.[21] Isidore of Seville (ca. 560-630) prescribed one immersion, citing a letter of Gregory the Great to Leander of Seville approving a different practice in Spain because of the special circumstances there that associated triple immersion with Arianism.[22]

Indeed, a distinctive liturgical tradition developed in Spain.[23] Two other points are notable in this development in contrast to the information in Gregory of Elvira:

---

19. McConnell, "Baptism in Visigothic Spain," pp. 17-18, concludes that Pacian refers to the water rite and chrismation together as a unit, noting that his word is *chrismatis*, not confirmation.

20. Martin of Braga, "Triple Immersion," translated by Claude W. Barlow in *Iberian Fathers*, Vol. 1, Fathers of the Church 62 (Washington, D.C.: Catholic University of America Press, 1969), pp. 99-102.

21. McConnell, "Baptism in Visigothic Spain," pp. 40-46, on Martin of Braga. McConnell contends that the argument for single immersion as distinguishing orthodox from Arian baptism was an explanation after the fact in favor of continuing single immersion rather than the reason for its origin — pp. 209-219.

22. Gregory the Great, *Letters* 1.43, dealing specifically with the baptism of infants, by the time of the late sixth century the norm.

23. T. C. Akeley, *Christian Initiation in Spain c. 300-1100* (London: Darton, Longman, and Todd, 1967), mainly deals with the sixth century and later, especially later liturgical manuscripts, so a period beyond the scope of this book, but we summarize some of his points that seem to derive from earlier times and that offer perspective relative to other regions.

the functions of presbyters and bishops appear not to have been distinguished in the administration of baptism (with the presbyter sometimes performing all the ceremonies), and there are no signs that consignation received an independent liturgical status (the gift of the Spirit is sometimes placed after baptism and at other times associated with the water itself). The baptismal chrismation was not the same as the second anointing in Roman practice that became the sacrament of confirmation.[24]

There was a shift from adult baptism at Easter as normal to infant baptism at any time. Corresponding to this development was the shift from baptism generally performed by bishops to baptism generally performed by presbyters. Infant baptism was taking effect by the beginning of the seventh century, but adult baptism was far from being in decline yet. Isidore had to explain infant baptism, and he defended its "profitability" in terms of original sin, but for Idelfonsus infant baptism was normal.[25] We cannot tell whether pouring or dipping was usual.[26] There was a variety of practice on many matters.

Some baptisteries survive from the period of my interest. All seem to call for the baptizand to stand in water no more than a meter in depth.[27] That accords with the size of many baptisteries elsewhere and would be consistent with an immersion by bending forward from the waist or kneeling or with a partial immersion by scooping water over the exposed part of the body. One must not think in terms of the height of persons today in determining the mode of baptism in these pools and must also reckon with the increasing frequency of infant baptism. The rectangular shape may be suggestive of a tomb but might have been employed for utilitarian and not theological reasons.

One of the poems by the late fourth/early fifth-century Spanish poet Prudentius, *On the Martyrs' Crown* 8, is dedicated to a baptistery built at Calagurris (Calahorra) on the site of several martyrdoms.[28] A number of baptisteries were located at martyr sites, so people may have gone to such sites to be baptized. The parallel of baptism and martyrdom is frequent in martyr literature. Both were viewed as a

---

24. McConnell, "Baptism in Visigothic Spain," pp. 197-209, contends that although chrismation and confirmation are theologically equivalent (as associated with the bestowal of the Spirit), they are structurally different, for chrismation is inseparable from baptism and may be given by a presbyter but confirmation (involving a second anointing and handlaying) was separable from baptism and was normally reserved to the bishop.

25. McConnell, "Baptism in Visigothic Spain," pp. 191-196.

26. Akeley, *Christian Initiation in Spain*, p. 64.

27. Akeley, *Christian Initiation in Spain*, p. 54. Thilo Ulbert, *Frühchristliche Basiliken mit Doppelapsiden auf der iberischen Halbinsel: Studien zur Architektur und Liturgiegeschichte* (Berlin: Gebr. Mann, 1978), p. 160, criticizes Akeley on baptisteries on account of the limited number of baptismal structures utilized resulting in mistaken interpretation of the archaeological finds; most of the baptisteries from Spain are from the sixth century and later. For more on the baptisteries in Spain see chap. 54.

28. Translated by M. C. Eagen, *The Poems of Prudentius*, Fathers of the Church 43 (Washington, D.C.: Catholic University of America, 1962), pp. 180-181. Cf. *Hymn* 1.30 for souls baptized in blood. For other references to baptism in Prudentius, see McConnell, "Baptism in Visigothic Spain," pp. 27-34.

washing or cleansing, one by water and the other by blood. Both represented rebirth. The depiction of martyrs in white clothes paralleled neophytes' putting on white garments after baptism. The baptismal motif in martyrdom had its reverse aspect in that baptism was a "dying with Christ."

The first documents of major importance for baptismal practice in Spain are from the seventh century: Isidore of Seville, *De origine ecclesiasticorum officiorum* 2.21-27, and Ildephonsus of Toledo, *De cognitione baptismi*.[29] Both are traditional, especially Isidore, who synthesizes patristic thought and earlier liturgical usages, so there is a question of how much they reflect actual practice in Spain. For that they must be compared with the two baptismal rituals in the Visigothic *Liber ordinum* (the manuscripts are ninth century but the elements are much older). The results do not carry us with certainty any earlier than the sixth century, so I do not include these materials for study but only note them for completing the history of baptism in the Iberian peninsula before the Middle Ages.

---

29. Victor Saxer, *Les rites de l'initiation chrétienne du IIe au VIe siècle: Esquisse historique et signification d'après leur principaux témoins* (Spoleto: Centro italiano di studi sull'alto medioevo, 1988), pp. 539-544 on Isidore and pp. 545-551 on Ildephonsus; McConnell, "Baptism in Visigothic Spain," chap. 3 on Isidore and chap. 4 on Ildefonsus.

43. Some Other Latin Authors

Hilary of Poitiers

Hilary corresponds to many Christian writers of the fourth century in coming from a good (in his case pagan) family, well educated, and receiving baptism as an adult. He was bishop of Poitiers, France, from about 353 until his death about 367. His literary remains do not contain a special treatment of baptism,[1] but he mentions it with some frequency in his doctrinal and exegetical works. He was indebted to ideas found in Origen and other Greek authors as well as his Latin predecessors. His treatment of the baptism of Jesus in his *Commentary on Matthew* was summarized in chapter 7.

In a manner similar to Gregory of Nyssa and others, Hilary speaks of multiple "births" of Christ. In addition to his eternal generation as divine Son of God, the incarnation, baptism, and resurrection of Christ are presented as births, a description prompted by the language of scripture. The three are brought together in his *Commentary on Psalms* 2.27, 29, where Christ's baptism is said to have made him a perfect Son in his humanity (2.29).[2]

Hilary relates baptism to circumcision, also with reference to Christ's incarnation. Quoting Colossians 2:11-12, he explains:

---

1. His *Treatise on the Mysteries* does not concern the sacraments and Christian initiation (as Ambrose's does) but is a spiritual, figurative interpretation of persons from the Old Testament. Kilian McDonnell and George T. Montague, *Initiation and Baptism in the Holy Spirit: Evidence from the First Eight Centuries* (Collegeville: Liturgical, 1991), pp. 122-157, mainly treats the spiritual gifts in Hilary.

2. In addition to the *Commentary on Matthew* 2.5-6 (chap. 7) Hilary refers to the "birth that took place in his baptism" as a "perfect and true birth" in *On the Trinity* 8.25. For this work I quote the translation of Stephen McKenna, *Saint Hilary of Poitiers: The Trinity*, Fathers of the Church 25 (New York: Fathers of the Church, 1954), here p. 294. For the resurrection as a birth, see also *Commentary on Psalms* 53.14.

We are circumcised, therefore, not by a carnal circumcision, but by the circumcision of Christ, that is, we have been born again into the new man. Since we are buried together by his baptism, we must die to the old man, because the regeneration of baptism is the power of the resurrection. And this circumcision of Christ is not by having the flesh of the foreskin removed, but by dying entirely with him and thereby living afterwards entirely with him. We rise again in him through faith in his God, who raised him from the dead.[3]

The "circumcision of Christ" is not, strictly speaking, baptism but death to the old self and being born again to the new life of the resurrection.[4] Christ accomplishes these things through human identification with him in baptism, so one could speak of baptism as the occasion of the circumcision administered by Christ. The passage introduces other themes important in Hilary's understanding of baptism — regeneration and burial and resurrection with Christ.

The association of baptism with regeneration is expressed elsewhere in *On the Trinity*. "Do not all have the power to be born as sons of God through the sacrament of regeneration?" (6.36). The mysteries of human salvation are accomplished in us "through the power of regeneration into the life of the Father and the Son" (5.35). The baptismal connection of the thought is made explicit in the closing words of the work: "That I may always hold fast to that which I professed in the creed of my regeneration when I was baptized in the Father, Son, and the Holy Spirit" (12.57).

In allusion to the baptismal renunciations Hilary speaks of rejecting the devil, the world, and sins.[5] Baptism involved a confession of faith: "Those coming to baptism first confess faith in the Son of God, in his passion and resurrection" (*On Matthew* 15.8).

Baptism in the name of the Trinity is an important part of the argument in Hilary's *On the Trinity*, as it was in other defenses of the creed of Nicaea in the fourth century. In Hilary's outline of the contents of the treatise he highlights baptism in the three divine names (1.21). He opens book two by emphasizing that "the confession of the Origin, the Only Begotten, and the Gift" made at baptism contains the whole mystery of human salvation. Everything is complete in the Lord's commission of Matthew 28:19-20 — "the meaning of the words, the efficacy of the actions, the order of procedure, and the concept of the nature" (2.1).[6]

---

3. *On the Trinity* 9.9 (McKenna, *Saint Hilary of Poitiers: The Trinity*, p. 330).

4. Cf. *Trinity* 1.13, where instead of bodily circumcision Christ obliges us "in order that the spirit, when it had been circumcised from vices, might cleanse every natural necessity of the body by the purification from sin," followed by a reference to the burial in baptism quoted below.

5. *Commentary on Psalms* 14.14.

6. M. Milhau, "Hilaire de Poitiers, De Trinitate, 2,1: Formule baptismale et foi trinitaire," *Studia patristica* 38 (2001): 435-448, for theological and rhetorical commentary on the passage; Matthew 28:19 was for Hilary a "rapid and accessible presentation of the Trinity." Matthew 28:19 is quoted also in *On the Synods* 1.11; 12.29 (alluded to in 12.32) to the same import. In 27.85 he refers to the Lord's command and to the apostles' baptizing in the name of Jesus only as one of several apparent contradictions in Scripture that do not lead to the conclusion that we should abolish the holy Gospels.

This Trinitarian baptism is the "one baptism" of Ephesians 4:4-6. The one baptism, one faith, one Lord, and one God belong together as involved in the Christian confession (*Trinity* 11.1). This text was another important proof-text for Hilary, since it expressed the unity of the faith (*Trinity* 8.7, 8, 34, 40). Through the one faith confessed at baptism a person is reborn.[7] It is the "symbol of my regeneration when I was baptized in the Father, Son, and Holy Spirit" (*Trinity* 12.57). Through the one baptism all become one in Christ (Gal. 3:27-28 quoted).[8]

Hilary makes reference to an anointing after the water bath on the analogy of the Spirit coming down on Jesus at his baptism (*On Matthew* 2.6). He also refers to bestowing the Holy Spirit through laying on of hands and prayer, but it is not clear that he is referring to baptism (*On Matthew* 19.3). Hilary does think of two elements in the initiation ceremony, water and fire (= Holy Spirit), and speaks of the "sacraments of baptism and the Spirit" (*On Matthew* 4.10 and 4.27).

The connection of baptism with the death and resurrection of Christ is affirmed elsewhere.[9] Following a quotation of Colossians 2:8-15, Hilary comments on 2:12:

> By his death we would be buried together in baptism that we might return to eternal life, while death after life would be a rebirth to life, and dying to our vices we would be born again to immortality." (*Trinity* 1.13)

Here again the motifs of resurrection and rebirth are linked, the common feature being the new life given to the baptized.

Baptism is an illumination of the soul (*On Psalm 118*, prologue 4). "By the sacrament of baptism and 'precept of God' we are illuminated" (*On Psalm 118* 3.9).

In a passage reminiscent of Origen, but lacking the latter's problematic thoughts, Hilary says that the baptism of the Holy Spirit awaits Christians in cleansing fire either after death or in the purification of martyrdom.[10] Here he identifies the baptism in fire and the Holy Spirit as one act of cleansing after death; martyrdom was itself a baptism of fire, so martyrs were already purified and did not need to pass through the purifying fire after death. In a similar passage (*On Psalm 118* 3.5) Hilary says that if one thinks there is perfect purity from the sacrament of baptism, he should remember Matthew 3:11 about the baptism of fire and the Holy Spirit. After water baptism there is a purification pertaining to perfect purity when one is sanctified by the coming of the Holy Spirit, and the fire of judgment purifies the harshness of union with the body of death. The passion of martyrdom washes in blood sanctified by faith.

---

7. *Trinity* 8.7 — "baptism of rebirth"; those reborn are "one in the regeneration of the same nature."
8. *Trinity* 8.8.
9. Hilary quotes Rom. 6:4 on dying and being buried with Christ in *On Psalms 118* 15.13.
10. *Commentary on Psalms* 135.3; 137.2-3.

Optatus of Milevis

Very little is known of the life of Optatus. He was bishop of Milevis in the province of Numidia in North Africa and wrote an important work *Against the Donatists* (also known as *Against Parmenian,* Donatist bishop of Carthage, 362-392).[11] It was perhaps issued in two editions, first in the mid-360s and the second c. 384. This work comprises seven books plus a collection of ten official documents in appendices. Book 5 discusses the different views of Donatists and Catholics on baptism. Drawing on earlier arguments against rebaptism, Optatus anticipated some of the arguments made later by Augustine (chap. 52).

Optatus considers baptism to be the substance of the dispute and charges the Donatists with repeating what Christ said was to be done once (since they rebaptized those they converted from catholicism). He cites Parmenian's arguments for the oneness of true baptism, which he accepts but turns against the Donatist interpretation. Parmenian had affirmed that there were two waters, one true and the other false.[12] Parmenian held that "the baptism of Christians had been foreshadowed in the circumcision of the Hebrews" (5.1 [p. 96]). Optatus agrees that circumcision was a type of baptism: when done once it preserved health, but if done again it might bring ruin. "So too the baptism of Christians, jointly performed by the Trinity, confers grace; if it is repeated it causes life to be cast away" (5.1 [p. 97]).

The flood too was an image of baptism, but Optatus insists that it was no proof of true and false water, for it occurred once and there was only one ark and one dove (5.1 [p. 98]; also 1.5). Parmenian's praise of water that brought forth living creatures according to Genesis 1:20 omitted that the waters did not do this of their own accord but only by the working of the Trinity (5.2 [p. 99]).

The praise Parmenian bestowed on baptism reflected what the two parties held in common:

> (B)aptism is the life of the virtues, the death of crimes, the birth of immortality, the means of imparting the heavenly kingdom, the port of innocence and, as you have said yourself, the shipwreck of sinners. (5.1 [pp. 98-99]).

Optatus counters Parmenian with the argument that "the heavenly gift is conferred on every believer by the Trinity, not by a human" (5.3 [p. 99]). Baptism is to be conferred only once, regardless of the administrator. Jesus's words at the footwashing in John 13:10, "He who is once washed has no need to be washed again," is given a baptismal interpretation, as referring to the baptism commanded in Matthew 28:19, a washing through the Trinity. The word "once" forbids the repetition of baptism. "This is the reason why we [Catholics] have accepted those who come from you

---

11. My quotations are from Mark Edwards, *Optatus: Against the Donatists,* Translated Texts for Historians 27 (Liverpool: Liverpool University Press, 1997).

12. *Against the Donatists* 5.1 (p. 96). I will henceforth cite the book and section number of the treatise with the page number of Edwards's translation in parentheses.

[Donatists] without reservation" (5.3 [p. 101]). Optatus, as others before him, appeals also to Ephesians 4:5, maintaining that there may as well be another God, Christ, and faith, as to be another baptism (5.3 [p. 102]).

Optatus makes an important contribution to sacramental theology in his definition of three aspects essential to a valid baptism:

> In the celebration of this sacrament of baptism, there are three aspects, which you will not be able to augment, diminish or omit. The first aspect concerns the Trinity, the second the believer and the third the agent. (5.4 [p. 102])

The three aspects do not have equal weight. The first two are necessary, but the third is changeable and temporary.

The Trinity "holds the prime place" (5.4 [p. 102]). "(T)he person of the agent can change, while the Trinity cannot change" (5.4 [p. 103]). The "sacraments are holy through themselves," not through the human beings who administer them, because "God, not man, does the washing" (5.4 [p. 103]). Optatus formulated the Donatist position as, "Those who deem themselves holy will wash them"; against this position he insists that "God is the giver," citing Isaiah 1:18 and John 4:13 (5.4 [p. 104]). Optatus frequently adverts to the role of the Trinity in baptism. Baptism is founded on the Trinity (5.1 [p. 98]). The name of Father, Son, and Holy Spirit sanctifies, and not the act of baptism itself (5.7 [p. 109]). It is "the faith of the believer and the Trinity" and not "the agent of the rite" that guarantees the blessings of baptism "to every believer" (5.1 [p. 99]).[13]

Optatus has less to say about the necessity of the faith of the recipient because this was not at issue with the schismatic but nonheretical Donatists. But he does speak about "the merit of the believer" and refers to those incidents when miracles of healing occurred not on the basis of Christ's holiness and majesty but required that there be faith on the part of those who made a request on behalf of others or who sought healing for themselves (a confusion or conflation of Luke 7:11-17 with 8:49-55 and Mark 7:29; Matt. 8:13; Luke 8:43-48 and parallels). These incidents refuted the Donatist claim that "It belongs to the giver, not the receiver" (5.8 [pp. 110-112]). Optatus refers to the renunciation of the devil and confession of faith in God, etc., at baptism, when the proselyte says, "I renounce him and believe" etc. (5.7 [p. 108]).[14]

Optatus was particularly concerned to refute the Donatist insistence that the merits of baptism depended on the administrator (the agent) of the rite. The Donatists picked up the contention of Cyprian and were fond of saying, "He who has nothing to give, how can he give?" (5.6 [p. 107]).[15] Optatus replies that it is absurd to claim that "This gift of baptism belongs to the giver, not the receiver" (5.7

---

13. Optatus says in 2.10 that where the Trinity meets faith, there is spiritually a new birth.

14. There is another allusion to the renunciation: "(Y)ou had renounced the devil at one time" (5.10 [p. 114]).

15. Optatus in 1.10 refers to the Donatist position that one who is stained cannot wash away sins in a baptism that to them was not a baptism.

[pp. 107-108]). Just as one who dyes wool does not effect the change in color but the pigments do, so the agent of baptism can give nothing from himself without the Trinity (5.7 [p. 108]). The Savior commanded the form of baptism, but he did not define who was to be the agent for performing it (5.7 [pp. 108-109]). Optatus offers an interesting interpretation of 1 Corinthians 3:6. Paul showed that the whole sacrament of baptism belongs to God: when he said, "I planted," that meant, "I made a catechumen of a pagan"; when he said, "Apollos watered," that meant "he baptized the catechumen"; but Paul indicated that neither amounted to anything, but everything is of God (1 Cor. 3:7) — 5.7 (pp. 109-110).

Our polemicist had to deal with the one case of rebaptism in the New Testament, that involving disciples of John the Baptist in Acts 19:2-4. He explains that they were rebaptized because they received baptism after the law of Jesus' baptism went into effect, a law that nullified previous baptisms. The error in their baptism was in its factual nature, not in the person who baptized them. Hence, their case was different from the rebaptism administered by Donatists (5.5 [pp. 106-107]). John's baptism was different from Christian baptism because it lacked the Trinity, specifically Christ and the Holy Spirit (5.5).

Optatus distinguished heretics from schismatics with reference to baptism. "Heretics cannot possess the gifts of the church" (1.10 [p. 9]). Heretics are the only ones with false baptisms; this cannot be said of schismatics (1.12). The Donatists wanted to treat both the same and deny the baptism of both; the Roman church agreed with the first part of the approach but with the opposite policy of accepting the baptism of both. Optatus's distinction between the baptisms of schismatics and those of heretics had good company in the East, but was not the way the western church was to go.

Optatus asserts that catholics are baptized the same way Donatists are (3.9). Some aspects of the baptismal ceremony appear in the course of the argument. Optatus notes that even someone born of Christian parents is not without an unclean spirit that must be driven out before receiving the bath of salvation. "This is the work of exorcism, by which the unclean spirit is expelled and driven into desert places" (4.6 [p. 90]). Part of the formula of exorcism is quoted as in effect said by Donatists of God: You by rebaptizing say to the indwelling God, "Accursed one, go out" (4.6 [p. 90]).

Optatus indicates a consecration of the font in his interpretation of Christ as the Fish of Tobias (Tob. 6:3-6). He is placed in the waters of the font (which accordingly is known as a *piscina*) by the invocation of God (3.2).

In disputing Parmenian's interpretation of Ecclesiastes 10:1 that the Catholics were the dying flies that corrupt the odor of the oil, Optatus refers to the anointing oil of the baptismal ceremony. The oil that "is seasoned in the name of Christ" is designated chrism (7.4 [p. 142]).

> (W)hen refined, [oil] is now called chrism,, and contains the sweetness which soothes the skin of conscience by expelling the pain of sins, and produces a new

ease of mind which prepares a seat for the Holy Spirit, so that, bitterness having been ousted, he may gladly deign to dwell there by invitation. (7.4 [p. 143])

Optatus thus associates the anointing (postbaptismal) with the removal of the sense of guilt for sins and with the conferring of the Holy Spirit, but apparently not as the means of the latter but as the preparatory occasion. The anointing oil was placed on the head (4.7). Optatus's accusatory description of Donatist practice reflects the order of the Catholic baptismal ceremony as well: "You have seduced people, you have rebaptized them, you have anointed them again" (4.7). The baptism of Jesus reflected the order of water before the oil. After his baptism, the anointing oil was replaced by the dove descending on him, so he was anointed by God; the imposition of hand (after the baptism) was replaced by the voice of God, "This is my Son" (4.8).

In adducing Galatians 3:27 for those who are baptized being clothed with the robe of Christ, Optatus says that it fits all ages and types — infants, youths, and women (5.10 [p. 113]) — a likely reference to infant baptism.

Optatus's views on original sin, however, had not attained the clarity that Augustine's would. His comments on Parmenian's discussion of the baptism of Christ does not reject the latter's statement of the universal sinfulness of human flesh and may imply acceptance of it. His main concern, however, is to correct other aspects of Parmenian's language. Parmenian had said that "that sinful flesh of Christ, when submerged in the flood of the Jordan, was cleansed from universal impurity." Optatus finds the statement inept in several respects. The flesh of the whole human race was not included in Christ's baptism, and although all human beings have flesh each person has his particular flesh. "Everyone who believes is baptized in the name of Christ, not in the flesh of Christ, which belonged peculiarly to him." His flesh could not be bathed for the remission of sins, since he had committed no sin. Parmenian's word "submerged" applied to Pharaoh and his people, who sank in the Red Sea and remained there (Exod. 15:5); Christ rather descended into the Jordan and then ascended. By this descent he cleansed the water rather than being cleansed by it (1.8 [pp. 6-7]). Elsewhere Optatus does deny that anyone other than the Savior is perfect (2.20 [p. 48]).

On the other side, Optatus in the last-cited passage also says, "to will is ours and to make progress." Furthermore, he affirms that Adam's offense did not accrue to Seth (7.1 [p. 133]). So, even if he accepted an inherent sinfulness in human beings, "he had not yet arrived at Augustine's notion of a biological transmission of sin from Adam to all his posterity."[16]

Jerome

Jerome was born about 347 in Stridon (of uncertain location, perhaps northern Dalmatia) and died 419/420 in Bethlehem. He was baptized as a teenager during his

---

16. Edwards, *Optatus*, p. xxiv, n. 67.

student years in Rome.[17] Jerome's references to baptism are mostly subordinate to other subjects but for that reason are all the more revealing of the commonly held views.

Jerome's most extended discussion of baptism occurs in his *Dialogue against the Luciferians*. The followers of Lucifer of Cagliari refused to accept bishops who came over to the Catholic church from the "Arian" position, although they accepted laymen who had been baptized by those bishops. The rationale was that there was a difference between those who in simplicity received Christian baptism without knowing the views of the administrator and the bishops who understood the teaching and accepted it. The "orthodox" spokesman in the dialogue argued the inconsistency of the Luciferian position. If the baptisms administered by Arian bishops are valid, then so is their episcopal rank; if the Arian bishops are not true bishops, then their baptisms are invalid.

> The point in dispute is . . . whether a heretic has received valid baptism. If he has not . . . how can he be a penitent [in coming to the Catholic church], before he is a Christian? . . . But if he is not a Christian, if he had no priest to make him a Christian [the implication of the Luciferian position], how can he do penance when he is not yet a believer? (*Dialogue against the Luciferians* 13).[18]

Jerome argued that even teachers with more serious doctrinal errors were not rebaptized (*Dialogue against the Luciferians* 23).

Central to this issue was the conviction that there is no baptism without the Holy Spirit. On this both parties agreed; hence the Luciferians received a lay penitent from heretics with the laying on of hands and prayer for the Holy Spirit. The orthodox spokesman then pressed the point by associating the gift of the Holy Spirit with the forgiveness of sins.

> For seeing that a person, baptized in the name of the Father and the Son and the Holy Spirit, becomes a temple of the Lord . . . how can you say that sins can be remitted among the Arians without the coming of the Holy Spirit? How is a soul purged from its former stains which has not the Holy Spirit? For it is not mere water which washes the soul, but it is itself first purified by the Spirit that it may be able to spiritually wash the souls of people. . . . [Quoting Gen. 1:2], from which it appears that there is no baptism without the Holy Spirit. (*Dialogue against the Luciferians* 6)[19]

---

17. Jerome, *Letters* 16.2.1, "I received the garment of Christ in Rome." He provides comparable testimony about Rufinus, who "has but now bathed, he is clean and white" (*Letters* 4.2.2). Translation by Charles Christopher Mierow, *The Letters of St. Jerome*, Vol. 1, *Letters 1-22*, Ancient Christian Writers 33 (Westminister, MD: Newman Press, 1963), pp. 74 and 36.

18. The translation by W. H. Fremantle, *The Principal Works of St. Jerome*, Nicene and Post-Nicene Fathers (repr. Peabody: Hendrickson, 1994), Second Series, Vol. 6, pp. 320-334 (326), is used for my quotations from this work.

19. Cf. *Homilies on Psalm* 76 (77) on Gen. 1:2 as indicating that there could not be true baptism without the Spirit.

Appealing to the baptism of Christ as precedent, Orthodoxus explains that the Lord did not need to receive the Spirit but the Spirit came to show that the Spirit belongs with true baptism. He continues, "So then if an Arian cannot give the Holy Spirit, he cannot even baptize, because there is no baptism of the church without the Holy Spirit" (*Dialogue with the Luciferians* 6).[20]

In view of this argument the orthodox representative has a problem with the baptism practiced by John the Baptist, for it did not give the Holy Spirit but was said to be "for forgiveness of sins" (Mark 1:4). The explanation offered is that a future forgiveness of sins was intended that would come through the sanctification offered by Christ (*Dialogue with the Luciferians* 7). Hence, it is further asserted that John "did not forgive sins, for no one has sins remitted without the Holy Spirit" (7). Moreover, "(N)o baptism can be called perfect except that which depends of the cross and resurrection of Christ" (7). Although framed in a polemical context, the arguments do show the intimate connection between forgiveness of sins and the gift of the Holy Spirit in the theology of baptism.

The *Dialogue with the Luciferians* reveals some aspects of the baptismal ceremony. There was an expanded interrogatory confession of faith: "It is the custom at baptism to ask, after the confession of faith in the Trinity, do you believe in holy church? Do you believe in the remission of sins?" (12).[21] The baptism could be performed by presbyters, deacons, or "even laymen" in necessity; afterward the bishop laid on hands and invoked the Holy Spirit (9).[22] The Luciferian explains, and no objection is made on the point, that the laying on of hands after baptism and the invocation of the Holy Sprit is a "custom of the churches." He then adds,

> For many other observances of the churches, which are due to tradition, have acquired the authority of the written law, as for instance the practice of dipping the head three times in the laver, and then, after leaving the water, of tasting mingled milk and honey in representation of infancy. . . . (8)

This testimony about triple immersion,[23] baptismal laying on of hands, and milk and honey at the baptizand's first eucharist agrees with what Tertullian nearly two

---

20. The other side of the argument is that the convert from Arianism could not receive the Holy Spirit from the church when that one had not obtained forgiveness through the prior baptism (administered by one not considered a true bishop) — *Dialogue with the Luciferians* 9. The arguments are designed to refute the Luciferian practice and not to confirm the Catholic practice, to which they apply only by implication.

21. The chapter earlier refers to one who "sincerely believed in the Father, and the Son, and the Holy Spirit, and therefore obtained baptism." See further below.

22. Jerome elsewhere speaks of an anointing following baptism: "When you descend into the lifegiving font with the Savior . . . (A)nd after baptism you are anointed" *(Homily on Mark 13:32-33)*. Translation by Marie Liguori Ewald, *The Homilies of Saint Jerome*, 2 vols., Fathers of the Church 48 and 57 (Washington, D.C.: Catholic University of America Press, 1964, 1966), Vol. 2, p. 190.

23. Jerome, *Commentary on Ephesians* 2:4, comments on the "one baptism" of Eph. 4:5, "We are immersed three times that there may appear one sacrament of the Trinity."

centuries before had said and affirms the common experience that traditional customs lacking scriptural authority yet assume a status equal to written law.[24]

The *Dialogue* further expresses some baptismal themes common elsewhere. Baptism conferred a "lay priesthood," Revelation 1:6 and 1 Peter 2:9 cited (4). The story of Noah's ark provided baptismal lessons: "(I)n the church's baptism . . . [like the raven that did not return to the ark] the devil is expelled, and the dove of the Holy Spirit announces peace to our earth" (22).

Jerome refers to the renunciation of the devil but giving its content in different forms: "you, the devil, your pomps, your vices, and your world" (*Commentary on Matthew* 5:27); "you, the devil, your age, your pomps, and your works" (*Letter* 130.7).

Jerome, while discussing another question, argues from the premise that in baptism all sins are washed away and a person is made new (*Letter* 69, e.g., 69.2). This letter has a long section adducing Old Testament passages as praises of water and baptism (*Letter* 69.6). These include Genesis 1:2 ("the infant world [is] a type of the Christian child that is drawn from the laver of baptism"[25]); Ezekiel 1:29 ("believers soar out of the laver with wings to heaven") and 47:1, 8; the flood (Gen. 8:8-11);[26] crossing the Red Sea (Ps. 74:13-14); the waters of Marah (Exod. 15:23-27 — "so the cross makes the waters of the law life-giving"); the wells in the narratives about the patriarchs Abraham, Isaac, Jacob, and Moses. He then turns to water in the New Testament: Christ's "baptismal immersion" began his ministry and cleansed the Jordan;[27] his first miracle was turning water into wine; he met the Samaritan woman at a well; he spoke the words of John 3:5 to Nicodemus; there came from his side blood and water ("twin emblems of baptism and martyrdom"). Several of the baptisms in Acts are mentioned. Jerome refers several prophecies to the "grace of baptism," concluding with Micah 7:19, which means that "All sins are drowned in the baptismal laver" (*Letter* 69.7).

That baptism removes sins is often expressed. For instance, "In baptism our guilt is taken away" and "Happy is the person whose sins are forgiven in baptism."[28] A comparable statement is the report that the miracles of the monk Chariton "induced an innumerable crowd of pagans and Jews to receive the saving bath" (*Life of Chariton* 14). This association leads Jerome to express other thoughts. Thus he says to catechumens, "No one, indeed, would think of approaching baptism to have his

---

24. According to Jerome's *Commentary on Zechariah* 3:14, Easter and Pentecost were the seasons for baptism. I owe this reference to Walter J. Conway, *The Time and Place of Baptism: A Historical Synopsis and a Commentary*, The Catholic University of America Canon Law Series 324 (Washington, D.C.: Catholic University of America Press, 1954), p. 6.

25. The Christian becomes as a child in baptism, not a reference to child baptism. Translations from this letter by W. H. Fremantle, *The Principal Works of St. Jerome*, pp. 145-146.

26. Cf. *Letter* 10.1.2, where the flood is called a baptism that cleansed the world.

27. Cf. the quotation below from *Homily for Epiphany*.

28. *Homilies on Psalms*, Second Series, *On Psalm 84 (85)*. For the homilies on Psalms I quote (but sometimes slightly modify) the translation of Marie Liguori Ewald, *The Homilies of Saint Jerome*, 2 vols., Fathers of the Church 48 and 57 (Washington, D.C.: Catholic University of America Press, 1964, 1966); here, Vol. 2, p. 51.

sins forgiven without first forgiving his brother" *(Homily on Mark 11:15-17)*.[29] Jerome repeated against the Pelagians the argument of Augustine (chap. 52) that infants who had done no sin were baptized for the forgiveness of the Adamic sin (*Dialogue against the Pelagians* 3.17-19).

Jesus came to be baptized "as though he were a sinner" *(Homily on Mark 1:1-12)*.[30] "In the baptism of the Lord all sins are forgiven," yet "true remission of sins is in the blood of Christ, in the mystery of the Trinity" *(Homily on Mark 1:1-12)*.[31] Indeed, the mystery of the Trinity was present in the baptism of Jesus: he was baptized; the Spirit descended as a dove; and the Father spoke from heaven (*Homily on Mark 1:1-12*; also the next homily cited).

Jesus' baptism is commemorated on Epiphany, for it was his "manifestation" to the world *(Homily for Epiphany)*.[32] His baptism was a paradox:

> He is holier than the one who baptizes. He is purified by John in the flesh, but he purifies John in the spirit. The waters that had been accustomed to cleanse others are now purified by the cleansing of our Lord. *(Homily for Epiphany)*

Jerome involves God the Father as well as Christ and the Holy Spirit in the sanctifying work of baptism. He offers the prayer for the catechumens that God Almighty would "descend upon you in baptism; may he sanctify the waters that you may be sanctified" *(Homily on Mark 11:15-17)*.[33] Among the consequences of Jesus' baptism are that the demons are now destroyed and the fire of hell is extinguished *(Homily for Epiphany)*.[34]

The saving aspect of baptismal forgiveness involves other associations. Jerome interprets the purification of lepers by sprinkling blood with water and hyssop in Leviticus 13–14 by referring to those being healed "through the blood of Christ and through baptism"; only by coming to the blood and the water can one be saved *(Homily on Psalm 84 [85])*.[35] Another application of water and blood (this time the water and blood from the wounded side of Jesus) is to the building of the church: by baptism sins are forgiven and the blood of martyrs crowns the building of the church *(Homily on Psalm 88 [89])*.[36] Jerome interprets the deer of Psalm 42:1 as a catechumen who desires to come to Christ, in whom is found the source of light, and having been purified he receives the gift of the Holy Spirit *(Homily on Psalm 41 [42])*.

John's baptism was given in repentance, but the baptism instituted by the Savior is given in grace *(Homily on Mark 1:1-12)*.[37] One passage brings together various descriptions of this grace: "O happy you, who are to be reborn in Christ, who are going

---

29. Ewald, *The Homilies of Saint Jerome*, Vol. 2, p. 184.
30. Ewald, *The Homilies of Saint Jerome*, Vol. 2, p. 128.
31. Ewald, *The Homilies of Saint Jerome*, Vol. 2, p. 129.
32. Ewald, *The Homilies of Saint Jerome*, Vol. 2, p. 229.
33. Ewald, *The Homilies of Saint Jerome*, Vol. 2, p. 185.
34. Ewald, *The Homilies of Saint Jerome*, Vol. 2, p. 230.
35. Ewald, *The Homilies of Saint Jerome*, Vol. 1, p. 131.
36. Ewald, *The Homilies of Saint Jerome*, Vol. 2, p. 65.
37. Ewald, *The Homilies of Saint Jerome*, Vol. 2, p. 123.

to receive the garment of Christ, who are to be buried with him that you may rise again with him!" *(Homily on Mark 11:15-17).*[38] Regeneration is through baptism *(Homily on Psalm 77 [78]).*[39]

Those once washed in Christ do not need to wash again (John 13:10) — *Letters* 14.10.3. Hence, Jerome warns against those who receive baptism insincerely, as did Simon the magician *(Homily on Psalm 80 [81]).*[40] For those who sin after baptism, repentance, when they are washed with tears, is as a baptism to them *(Homily on Mark 1:13-31).*[41] Showing an influence from Origen, Jerome says that those who are defiled after being baptized by the Spirit are in need of the cleansing of baptism by fire *(Letters 18a.11.3).*[42]

Jerome gives prominence to the necessity of faith: "They who are going to be baptized must believe in the Father, the Son, and the Holy Spirit" *(Homily on Mark 13:32-33).*[43] Baptism with its confession of faith was an oath of allegiance, comparable to joining the army: "Remember the day of your enlistment when, buried with Christ in baptism, you took the oath of allegiance" *(Letters 14.2.2).*[44] After baptism one is called a "believer," one of the "faithful" *(Homily on Psalm 91 [92]).*[45]

> If we are Christians (we, who have received the baptism of Christ, are, indeed, Christians and not only confess but profess that we are), because we are Christians, we must believe the evangelists. *(Homily on Psalm 77 [78])*[46]

Jerome's *Commentary on Matthew* 28:19 contains a declaration about the priority of faith that hardly accords with his acceptance of infant baptism (above), but such dual perspectives reflecting the normal missionary situation of the early church and the newer reality of infant baptism were not uncommon.

> First they teach all nations, then they dip in water those taught. For it is impossible for the body to receive the sacrament of baptism unless the soul has previously received the truth of the faith.[47]

In common with others Jerome insisted on the manner of life to follow baptism: "the washing of sins, grace of baptism, and more advanced doctrines do not suffice for us unless we also have works" *(Letter 64.20)*.

---

38. Ewald, *The Homilies of Saint Jerome*, Vol. 2, p. 184. In *Letter* 64.19 Jerome brings together the themes of forgiveness and clothing and alludes to the white garment worn after baptism.
39. Ewald, *The Homilies of Saint Jerome*, Vol. 1, p. 86.
40. Ewald, *The Homilies of Saint Jerome*, Vol. 1, p. 98.
41. Ewald, *The Homilies of Saint Jerome*, Vol. 2, p. 146.
42. Mierow, *The Letters of St. Jerome*, p. 90.
43. Ewald, *The Homilies of Saint Jerome*, Vol. 2, p. 186.
44. Mierow, *The Letters of St. Jerome*, p. 60.
45. Ewald, *The Homilies of Saint Jerome*, Vol. 2, p. 91.
46. Ewald, *The Homilies of Saint Jerome*, Vol. 1, p. 80.
47. Émile Bonnard, *Saint Jerome Commentaire sur S. Matthieu* II, Sources Chrétiennes 259 (Paris: Cerf, 1979), pp. 316-317.

Paulinus of Nola

Paulinus of Nola's life overlapped the fourth and fifth centuries (355-431). No attempt is made to survey baptism in his writings (see chap. 7 for his statement about the baptism of Jesus sanctifying the waters), but an inscription he suggested about 403 for a baptistery built by Sulpicius Severus in southwest France is significant for baptismal thought.

> Here the birth-giving spring *(fons)* of souls to be restored pushes the river alive with divine light. Down into the pool comes the Holy Spirit from heaven and marries the holy waters to the heavenly spring. The flow conceives God and in these maternal waters God's beneficence brings forth a holy progeny from the eternal seed. Wonderful is the goodness of God. The sinner is immersed *(mergitur)* in the waves, and soon emerges from the same water justified. So it is that man undergoes a happy fall and rises from it; dies to the things of the world, and rises to things everlasting. Blame perishes, but life returns; the old Adam is buried and the new is born to eternal empires.[48]

Paulinus blends allusions to the baptism of Jesus with the present experience of those baptized. His poetry combines the themes of new birth/new life, coming of the Holy Spirit on the water, and forgiveness/justification.

---

48. The Latin text and an English translation are taken from Peter Cramer, *Baptism and Change in the Early Middle Ages c. 200-c. 1150* (Cambridge: Cambridge University Press, 1993), pp. 272-273.

PART SIX

The Fifth Century

44. Egypt: Cyril of Alexandria and the Coptic Rite

As was done for the fourth century, in this unit we begin a circuit around the Mediterranean, beginning with Egypt.

Cyril of Alexandria

Cyril was bishop of Alexandria from 412 to 444. Much indebted to the theology of Athanasius, Cyril is best known for his role in the Christological controversies of the fifth century. He had some important things to say about the doctrine of baptism.

The baptism of Christ was a major event in salvation history for Cyril.[1] His commentary on the event is the longest in patristic literature, and he sees it as of central importance in the divine economy of salvation.[2] Cyril defends the baptism of Jesus against Adoptionistic and Arian arguments.

As does the Gospel of John, Cyril focuses not on the baptism itself but on the descent of the Spirit on Jesus. The divine inbreathing in Genesis 2:7 imparted the Holy Spirit and the divine characteristics in Adam. Adam's sin not only brought death but also began a process of the progressive loss of the divine Spirit by human beings. "For Cyril, the recovery of the divine image in us is not simply the recasting

---

1. His view is summarized in chap. 7 in the context of patristic interpretations of the baptism of Jesus. Robert L. Wilken, *Judaism and the Early Christian Mind: A Study of Cyril of Alexandria's Exegesis and Theology* (New Haven: Yale University Press, 1971), pp. 132-141; Daniel A. Keating, "The Baptism of Jesus in Cyril of Alexandria: The Re-creation of the Human Race," *Pro Ecclesia* 8 (1999): 201-222, where the main interest is not baptism itself but the theological and soteriological aspects; Daniel A. Keating, *The Appropriation of Divine Life in Cyril of Alexandria* (Oxford: Oxford University Press, 2004), esp. pp. 20-39, which I follow in this section.

2. *Commentary on John* 1:32-33. English translation by P. E. Pusey and Thomas Randell, *Commentary on the Gospel according to St. John by S. Cyril, Archbishop of Alexandria*, 2 vols. (Oxford: James Parker, 1874; London: Walter Smith, 1885).

of our deformed nature; it necessarily involves the reacquisition of the divine life through the Spirit which was given in the original creation."[3] The baptism of Jesus was decisive for the reacquisition of the Spirit by human beings.

The centerpiece of Jesus' baptism was not the revelation of the Trinity, as often expressed in other writers, but the plan of redemption. Christ received the Spirit not for himself, since he already had the Spirit from the incarnation, but for us and "as one of us." Such a declaration was a traditional idea, but Cyril incorporated it into his particular and overriding theology of the return of the Spirit and with him of the divine life to the human race that was lost as a consequence of sin. The coming of the Spirit on Jesus was not a one-time event, but the Spirit remained on him (John 1:32-33). The baptism of Jesus, set in the context of his incarnation and death, "reveals the goal and strategy of the eternal plan of God."[4] This correlation of the return of the Spirit with the first creation fits an Adam-Christ typology.

Cyril's commentary on Luke similarly responds to Arian arguments and views the baptism of Jesus as a revelation of the plan of redemption.[5] The divine Word had no need of baptism or of the Holy Spirit but received them for the sake of the economy of salvation. When Jesus received the Spirit — since he is the representative human being and the second Adam — the Spirit can rightly be said to have been poured out on "all flesh" (Joel 2:28).

Cyril introduces additional ideas in the commentary on Luke. John the Baptist's promise that Christ would baptize in the Holy Spirit is interpreted to mean that he bestows "the indwelling of the Holy Spirit."[6] Christ gives the Holy Spirit to "them that believe in him."[7] "What is it that we gain by holy baptism? Plainly the remission of our sins. But in Jesus there was nothing of this."[8] He had no sins needing forgiveness; nor was he in need of the Holy Spirit. "He had no need of holy baptism, being wholly pure and spotless. . . . Nor had he need of the Holy Spirit," for the Spirit is his as well as the Father's.[9] Picking up the idea that Christ was baptized as part of accomplishing the economy of salvation, Cyril enumerates the effects of the church's baptism.

---

3. Keating, *Appropriation of the Divine Life*, pp. 24-25. Wilken, *Judaism and the Early Christian Mind*, p. 135, also notes that Cyril's discussion of the baptism of Jesus centers on the descent of the Spirit.

4. Keating, *Appropriation of the Divine Life*, pp. 27, 28. P. 29, n. 21 refers to Cyril's *Commentary on Isaiah* 11:1-3 and *Commentary on Joel* 2:28-29 for the feature of Jesus' baptism resulting in the Spirit remaining on him.

5. *Homily* 11, *On Luke* 3:21-22. Keating, *Appropriation of Divine Life*, pp. 31-36. English translation of the Syriac by R. Payne Smith, *Commentary on the Gospel of S. Luke by Saint Cyril of Alexandria* (New York: Studion, 1983; repr. in 1 vol. of the original 2 vols. [Oxford: Oxford University Press, 1859]).

6. *Homily* 10, *On Luke* 3:15-17 (Payne Smith, *Commentary on Luke*, p. 75; henceforth page numbers are to his translation)).

7. *Homily* 10, *On Luke* 3:15-17 (p. 76).

8. *Homily* 11, *On Luke* 3:21-23 (p. 78).

9. *Homily* 11, *On Luke* 3:21-23 (p. 80).

Faith in the Triune God is confessed before many witnesses, the filth of sin is washed away, we are enriched by participation (μέθεξιν) in the Holy Spirit, we are made "partakers of the divine nature" [2 Pet. 1:4], and we receive the grace of adoption (υἱοθεσίας).[10]

Moreover, Christ set an example. Besides being the representative of the human race, Jesus is also the model for receiving baptism (another traditional theme) and the Holy Spirit. From Christ's baptism we learn "how much we gain by approaching so great a grace."[11] Since Jesus was praying when he was baptized (Luke 3:21), he is an example of the need for constant prayer.

As the Spirit descended at the first creation (Gen. 1:2), so the Spirit "again came down as at a second commencement of our race." Thus Christ received the Spirit "not so much for his own sake as for ours." Hence, Cyril gives the exhortation, "Having taken, therefore, Christ as our pattern, let us draw near to the grace of holy baptism."[12]

Cyril recapitulates, connecting Jesus' reception of the Spirit with believers' "regeneration that is by water and Spirit" in baptism, receiving sonship, and becoming "partakers of the divine nature" through participation in the Holy Spirit.[13] He continues that Christ was the first to receive the Spirit that "the grace of fellowship with the Holy Spirit might reach us by his means." Quoting Hebrews 2:12, Cyril affirms, "He is sanctified with us, although he is himself the Sanctifier of all creation."[14]

The flesh of the Word (not the Word himself) required sanctification by the Spirit, and the testimony to this sanctification was the descent of the Spirit at his baptism. The baptism of Jesus, therefore, was a sign, revealing that "the reacquisition of the Spirit" meant "the sanctification of the human race in Christ."[15] "Because Christ is the model for us, our spiritual sanctification is effected by the gift of the Spirit in baptism."[16]

These features of the baptism of Christ prepare for Cyril's treatment of baptism in the church.[17] The gift of the indwelling Spirit marked the difference between the Old and New Covenants. This difference is represented by the contrast between fleshly and spiritual circumcision (see further below). Cyril drew on the typology of Israel's baptism in the cloud and the sea (1 Cor. 10:2) to make a further contrast. "Those who by faith in Christ mount up to sonship with God are baptized, not into one of the things made, but into the Holy Trinity itself." Hence, by baptism, "We who have received the

---

10. I quote here Keating, *Appropriation of the Divine Life*, pp. 32-33, for the indication of underlying Greek words; slightly different in Payne Smith's translation of *Homily* 11 (p. 80).

11. *Homily* 11, *On Luke* 3:21-23 (p. 81).

12. *Homily* 11, *On Luke* 3:21-23 (p. 81).

13. *Homily* 12, *On Luke* 4:1-2 (p. 86).

14. *Homily* 12, *On Luke* 4:1-2 (p. 86).

15. Cyril, *Commentary on John* 17:18-19; Keating, *Appropriation of the Divine Life*, pp. 36-39 (38).

16. Cyril, *Commentary on John* 17:18-19; Keating, *Appropriation of the Divine Life*, p. 91.

17. *Commentary on John* 1:12-14a; Keating, *Appropriation of the Divine Life*, pp. 54-57 (especially 56).

regeneration [ἀναγέννησιν] by the Spirit through faith, are called and are begotten of God."[18] Cyril understood John 1:13b, "born of God," as the new birth by the Spirit in baptism. It is notable that Cyril gives prominence to the Holy Spirit in a text that does not mention the Spirit. "Cyril's commentary on John 1:12-14a, then, links baptism and the gift of the Spirit as the means by which we receive divine sonship through Christ, and identifies this event with the fulfilment of 2 Peter 1:4 in us."[19]

Cyril had no doubt of the baptismal reference in John 3:5, but he focuses on the spiritual rather than the material aspects of the passage.[20] The adverb ἄνωθεν (John 3:3) is read as "from above." This agrees with Cyril's theological emphasis that receiving the divine life can only be a work of God. The divine power works through a material element, water. The Spirit sanctifies and heals the human spirit, and water (through the working of the Spirit) sanctifies and heals the human body. Since a human being is a combination of a perceptible body and an intellectual soul, the regeneration (ἀναγέννησιν) of healing must include both: "The spirit of a person is sanctified by the Spirit, and the body by the sanctifying water." He offers this illustration:

> In the same manner as water poured into cauldrons by the power associated with it extinguishes the flames of fire, so through the working of the Spirit the perceptible water by a certain divine and ineffable power transforms and sanctifies.[21]

The contrast yet relationship of Spirit and flesh is developed by Cyril in regard to circumcision in an excursus on John 7:23-24.[22] Cyril's treatment of circumcision in the Spirit amounts to a commentary on Romans 2:25-29. Circumcision was a fleshly act in order to teach that the flesh must be purified. Spiritual circumcision comes from the working of the divine Word in the human heart. Circumcision was performed only on the eighth day, "that is, the day of the resurrection of our Savior, taking this as a sign that circumcision of the Spirit is of the giver of life."[23]

Spiritual circumcision not only cleanses from defilement, but it also gives new life. The agent of this new life is the indwelling Holy Spirit, or, put another way, Christ himself circumcises human hearts by the Holy Spirit.[24] The connection with baptism is that as Joshua circumcised the people of Israel after crossing the Jordan (Josh. 5:1-7), so circumcision of the Spirit requires passing through the waters of baptism.[25] Cyril, however, does not explicitly connect the circumcision of the Spirit with a postbaptismal anointing, but he rather treats baptism and the gift of the

---

18. *Commentary on John* 1:12-14a; Keating, *Appropriation of the Divine Life*, p. 56.
19. Keating, *Appropriation of the Divine Life*, p. 57.
20. *Commentary on John* 3:3-6; Keating, *Appropriation of the Divine Life*, pp. 57-59.
21. *Commentary on John* 3:5.
22. *Commentary on John* 7:24; Keating, *Appropriation of Divine Life*, pp. 59-62.
23. *Commentary on John* 7:24; Keating, *Appropriation of Divine Life*, p. 60.
24. *Commentary on John* 7:24; Keating, *Appropriation of Divine Life*, p. 61.
25. In addition to *Commentary on John* 7:24 the typological connection of crossing the Jordan and circumcision with baptism and circumcision of the Spirit is made in *Commentary on John* 6:35 and *Commentary on Luke* 2:21-24.

Spirit as one united reality.[26] Similarly, there is celebrated the Passover (Josh. 5:10-11), an implied allusion to the eucharist, only after crossing the waters and receiving circumcision by the living Word.[27]

Cyril summarized the effects of spiritual circumcision in terms used for the effects of baptism:

> Conceiving it not in a Jewish way, we will understand circumcision on the eighth day as the cleansing through the Holy Spirit, in faith and in the resurrection of Christ, the casting away of all sin, the destruction of death and corruption, the giving of sanctification and intimate relationship (οἰκειότητος) with Christ, the way and the door to close friendship (οἰκειώσεως) with God.[28]

Cyril's commentary sees in all three texts (John 1:12-14a; 3:3-6; and 7:24) the same reality described of the new birth in the Holy Spirit through baptism. The indwelling Holy Spirit is prominent as Christ's agent who accomplishes in human beings the fruits of Christ's redemption. And in each case the gift of the Spirit is related to baptism.[29] In many other texts Cyril links the gift of the indwelling Holy Spirit with baptism.[30] *On Right Faith to Theodosius* 38 quotes Acts 2:38; John 20:22; and Romans 8:9-10 in developing human participation in the Spirit through baptism.[31] In his *Commentary on Isaiah*, Cyril says:

> The grace in holy baptism does not occur in us without the Spirit. For we have been baptized [βεβαπτίσμεθα] not in mere water, nor have we been sprinkled [ἐρραντίσμεθα] with the ashes of a heifer for the cleansing of the flesh, as the blessed Paul says [Heb. 9:13 with reference to Num. 19:9, 17-18], but in the Holy Spirit and a divine fire . . . consuming away the pollution of sin.[32]

Cyril apparently understood the baptism "in the Holy Spirit and fire" of Matthew 3:11 as one act accompanying Christian water baptism.[33]

The *Commentary on John* 19:34 found a basis for baptism in the "blood mixed with water" from the side of Jesus at his crucifixion. This was an image "of the mystic

---

26. Keating, *Appropriation of Divine Life*, pp. 61-62.

27. Cf. *Commentary on John* 20:17, where Cyril interprets Jesus' command that Mary Magdalene not touch him to mean that one must receive the Holy Spirit in baptism before handling the body of Christ in the eucharist. Keating, *Appropriation of Divine Life*, p. 91, for Christ giving life not only through the Spirit in baptism but also through his flesh in the eucharist.

28. Keating, *Appropriation of Divine Life*, p. 62.

29. Keating, *Appropriation of Divine Life*, p. 63.

30. Keating, *Appropriation of Divine Life*, p. 91, n. 41, lists *Commentary on Matthew* 3:11; 12:31-32; 20:1-16; *Commentary on Luke* 2:21; 4:1-2; *Commentary on John* 3:29; 7:39; 9:6-7; 13:8; *Commentary on Romans* 1:3-4.

31. Keating, *Appropriation of Divine Life*, p. 91.

32. Cyril, *Commentary on Isaiah* 1.3 on Isa. 4:4. Note may be made of his use of "baptize" (immerse) for the Christian rite and "sprinkle" for a contrasting rite of purification in the Old Testament.

33. Cf. *Worship in Spirit and Truth* 12, "For we have not been baptized into a fire perceptible to the senses but in the Holy Spirit, like fire consuming the pollution in souls" (PG 68.821B).

blessing and of holy baptism," for "holy baptism is truly Christ's and from Christ, and the power of the mystic blessing arose for us from his holy flesh" (book 12; PG 74.677B).

Cyril found a baptismal reference in the man bearing a jar of water (Luke 22:10-11). "There Christ will lodge, for he removes us from all filth."[34]

The effects of baptism include being "purified through holy baptism" and "those who have been baptized and sealed [κατασφραγισμένων] through grace" (*On Worship in Spirit and Truth* 7; PG 68.532A). Grace and enlightenment are connected in the following passage: "Those who through instruction [κατηχήσεως] have tasted the doctrines concerning Christ and keep the enlightenment [φωτισμὸν] through the Spirit and the grace through baptism" (*Embellishments on Exodus* 2; PG 69.432A).

With regard to the ceremony of baptism Cyril cites the text of the renunciation: "I renounce you, Satan, all your works, all your angels, all your pomps, and all your worship" (*Commentary on Psalms* 45.11; PG 69.1044). He refers to the confession of faith made in response to questions at baptism:

> It is indeed necessary for you to know that it is to God that we make confession of faith, even though questioned by men who fill the office of the priesthood, when we say the "I believe" at the reception of holy baptism. (*Commentary on John* 11:26)

There would have been three interrogations, for Cyril parallels the baptismal questions with the three questions the resurrected Jesus asked Peter (*Commentary on John* 21:15-17).

Cyril's commentary on the healing of the man born blind (John 9:6-7) indicates a prebaptismal anointing. Jesus' anointing of the man's eyes with spittle gave contact with the life-giving power of Christ's body. Cyril identified it with the anointing and enlightenment that led to baptism, which is prefigured in the command to wash in the pool of Siloam.[35]

Cyril speaks of two anointings: the "the chrism of catechesis" and that "of perfection at holy baptism" (*Commentary on John* 11:26). The anointing at baptism is referred to in the *Commentary on Isaiah* 25.6-7. "We anoint with myron especially at the time of holy baptism, making the chrism a symbol of the partaking of the Holy Spirit" (PG 70.561D). Also in the *Commentary on Joel* 2:21-24, "Oil contributes to perfection to those being justified in Christ through holy baptism" (PG 71.373B).

Cyril alludes to the new clothing of neophytes: "It is fitting and quite reasonable to say to those who have been baptized what was said through the voice of the prophet [Isa. 61:10 quoted]" (*On the Pascha* 24; PG 77.897D).

Cyril's *Letter* 55, "On the Creed," section 27 (35), quotes Ephesians 4:5, highlighting the centrality and relationship of the Lord, faith, and baptism. "Who is the Lord,

---

34. *Fragment in Luke* 22:8 (PG 72.904C-D).
35. Keating, *Appropriation of Divine Life*, p. 92.

whom we have believed in and been baptized into?" The word of God's "lordship over us" is matched by "faith on our part." Baptism is characterized as "saving baptism," "the power of holy baptism," and the "grace of holy baptism." "Into his [the Word's] death we have been baptized, his who suffered humanly in his own flesh" (55.28 [38]).[36]

Cyril summarizes and paraphrases Paul by saying that people "are justified, not by works of law, but through faith and baptism." Isaiah 1:16 prefigured "the grace that is through holy baptism" (*Commentary on Isaiah* 1.1 on Isa. 1:16).

Cyril represents the tendency to add oil to the traditional water, bread, and wine as elements through which God works spiritual blessings. He gives a sacramental interpretation of Joel 2:21-24.

> For he has given to us as rain the living water of holy baptism, as in the wheat the bread of life and as in wine the blood. He added beforehand also the use of oil that completes the initiation of those justified in Christ through holy baptism. (*Commentary on Joel* 32 [PG 71.373A-B])

The intimate connection of a subsequent anointing with baptism has continued in Greek Orthodox practice.

A Prebaptismal Anointing Formula

A papyrus in the John Rylands Library contains a pre-immersion formula of anointing that was used in eastern baptismal liturgies of the late fourth century.[37] The text is: "The holy oil of gladness against every adverse Power and for the grafting of thy good olive tree of the catholic and apostolic church. . . . Amen."[38] The papyrus represents the adoption of this formula from the ceremony of prebaptismal anointing (cf. the Coptic Rite as cited below) in fourth-century Egypt for use as an amulet in the fifth century.

Der Balyzeh Papyrus

A papyrus dated to the sixth-seventh century contains a profession of faith that could come from any century in early Christianity.[39] It is suggested that the text is a

---

36. Lionel R. Wickham, ed. and trans., *Cyril of Alexandria: Select Letters* (Oxford: Clarendon Press, 1983), pp. 126-127.

37. Theodore de Bruyn, "P. Ryl. III.471: A Baptismal Anointing Formula Used as an Amulet," *Journal of Theological Studies*, n.s. 57 (2006): 94-109.

38. The translation is that of the original editor, C. H. Roberts, as quoted by de Bruyn, "P. Ryl. III.471."

39. I use and translate from the text in C. H. Roberts and B. Capelle, *An Early Euchologium: The Der Balyzeh Papyrus Enlarged and Reedited* (Louvain, 1949).

baptismal creed, but the declaratory form is unusual for an early baptismal confession. The profession might be the formula of adherence following a renunciation, but the items included would be unusual in that setting. The liturgical context of the confession must remain uncertain.

> One confesses the faith thus: I believe in one God the Father Almighty and in his only Son our Lord Jesus Christ and in the Holy Spirit and in the resurrection of the flesh and the holy catholic church.

The addition of the resurrection and the church to the Holy Spirit agrees with the Latin version of the *Apostolic Tradition* (except that the latter's order is "the holy church and the resurrection of the flesh").

An Epiphany Hymn

A hymn celebrating the baptism of Christ is incompletely preserved on a papyrus of the fifth/sixth century.[40] Forty-five lines of the text are extant.

> . . . .
> And he rejoiced at the holy font,
> confessing the Christ in the presence of earth and heaven
> and thoroughly defeating the Enemy. . . .
> For the glory of the Lord surrounded him
> and his power overshadowed you.
> Shout to the Lord, all the earth,
> because God the Word who existed before the ages appeared on the earth.
> Come, let us meet the Bridegroom in Bethlehem,
> the One who with the Father and the Holy Spirit
> was invited to the marriage feast as a human being and turned the water
>   into wine,
> who gave sight to the blind at Siloam,
> who cleansed the leper with a word,
> fed five thousand with five loaves.
> He came to the waters of the Jordan,
> the Lamb of God who takes away the sins of the world,
> to be baptized by the forerunner.
> A voice from the Father said,
> "This is my Beloved Son in whom I am well pleased."
> When we beheld the Jordan, we were filled with great joy,
> since the one born on the earth as a human being arrived in it,

---

40. K. Treu, "Neue berliner liturgische Papyri," *Archiv für Papyrusforschung* 21 (1971): 62-65 and plate 3, from whose restoration I translate. It is Papyrus 1163 of the Berlin collection.

and the forerunner himself heard your voice saying,
"Let us fulfill the dispensation of the Father."
As the Lord willed, John said,
When you, Christ, came down into the waters,
the mountains skipped like rams and hills like little lambs of the sheep.
When you came up out of the Jordan,
a voice came to you out of heaven,
"This is my Beloved Son in whom I am well pleased."
    Fear him.

The hymn makes an association between the birth of Jesus and his baptism, as several authors did, no doubt because of double liturgical significance of January 6. The paradox of the one with miraculous power submitting to the baptism commanded of penitent sinners is also a familiar motif (see chap. 7). The declaration of the heavenly voice serves as something of a refrain. Baptism as the time of confessing Christ and as the overthrow of the devil further resonated with the significance of Christian baptism. The Trinitarian presence is rather artificially introduced. The going down into the Jordan and coming up out of it also corresponded to the Christian act.

The Coptic Rite

Although manuscripts of the Coptic baptismal rite are later, it is argued that the similarities and in some cases identical wording of prayers in the Coptic and Greek rites indicate an origin before 451.[41] The Coptic and Greek (Melchite) churches later looked back on the decisions at the Council of Chalcedon as the occasion of their division. The separation, however, was gradual, and they continued for some time to be parties struggling for control of one church. Hence, parallel developments and direct liturgical borrowings continued well after the mid–fifth century, so common elements do not necessarily establish a date prior to 451. Nevertheless, the Coptic baptismal rite has elements in common with other rites, so we may assume at least in broad outline an origin no later than the fifth century for its main features. I note here mainly the features with parallels in other rites.

Two prayers connected with the catechumenate express something of the theology of baptism.

---

41. O. H. E. Khs-Burmester, "The Baptismal Rite of the Coptic Church (A Critical Study)," *Bulletin de la societé d'archéologie Copte* 6 (1945): 27-80 (27), that I follow in this section. Georg Kretschmar, "Beiträge zur Geschichte der Liturgie, insbesondere der Taufliturgie, in ägypten," *Jahrbuch für Liturgik und Hymnologie* 8 (1963): 1-54, compares different sources for the development of the baptismal liturgy in Egypt and Alexandria (charts on pp. 25-27, 33-35 [baptism in the fourth to sixth century]). I have not had access to W. Hassab Alla, *Evolution historique du rite et de la pratique du baptême dans l'Église copte orthodoxe d'Alexandrie* (Panazol, 1988).

> Confirm the profession of these Thy servants; let power dwell in them that they turn not back again to those things which they have left. Strengthen their faith that nothing may separate them from Thee.[42]
>
> On these, O Lord, who also are Thy creation, have mercy; deliver them from the slavery of the enemy; receive them into Thy kingdom. Open the eyes of their heart, that they may be enlightened with the light of the gospel of Thy kingdom.... Cast out of their heart every unclean spirit, and the wicked spirit which troubleth their heart.... And make them sheep of the holy fold of Thy Christ, purified members of the Catholic Church, purified vessels, sons of light, heirs of Thy kingdom; in order that they may live according to the commandments of Christ, and may keep the seal inviolate.[43]

The priest's prayer for himself contains the petition, "May Christ take form in those who are about to receive the baptism of the new birth through me."[44]

The consecration of the water includes instructions for the priest to breathe upon the water three times in the form of the cross.[45] The long prayer of consecration recalls much of the biblical typology of baptism: Moses' "baptism" of Israel at the Red Sea (1 Cor. 10:1-2), the water from the rock (Exod. 17:6), the changing of bitter waters into sweet (Exod. 15:24), crossing the Jordan under Joshua (Josh. 3:14-17), Elijah pouring water on the altar (1 Kings 18:31-38), Naaman cleansed by the Jordan (2 Kings 5:14).[46] The invocation on the water asks that the Lord give to the the water "the grace of the Jordan, and the power and the strength of heaven; and by the descent of Thy Holy Spirit upon it hallow it with the blessing of the Jordan." The prayer continues with petitions that it become "water of life," "holy water," "water washing away sins," "water of the laver of regeneration," "water of sonship," "a garment of incorruption," and "a renewing of the Holy Spirit." Further,

> Grant unto this water that there remain not in it, nor descend into it with him who is about to be baptized therein, any evil spirit, or any unclean spirit ... let them be crushed before the sign of Thy cross, and of Thy Holy Name which we invoke.... That they who are about to be baptized therein, may put off the old man which is corruptible according to the deceitful lusts, and put on the new man which shall renew again according to the image of him that created him; and may the light of truth give light within them through the Holy Spirit, that they may gain eternal life and the blessed hope; and may stand before the Judgment seat of Christ, and receive the heavenly crown and forgiveness of their sins.[47]

---

42. Khs-Burmester, "Baptismal Rite," p. 28.
43. Khs-Burmester, "Baptismal Rite," pp. 30-31.
44. Khs-Burmester, "Baptismal Rite," p. 33.
45. Khs-Burmester, "Baptismal Rite," p. 34.
46. Khs-Burmester, "Baptismal Rite," p. 39.
47. Khs-Burmester, "Baptismal Rite," pp. 41-43, 72-74.

There were two prebaptismal anointings. The first, the oil of catechesis, involved anointing the forehead of the catechumens, with the priest saying, "We anoint thee, N., with the oil of catechesis of the One Holy Catholic Apostolic Church of God. Amen." He then anointed the breast, hands, and back, saying, "May this oil bring to nought all the opposition of the adversary. Amen."[48]

There followed a prayer of exorcism, exorcism with imposition of hands, complete undressing of the candidates, who turned to the west and with right hands extended pronounced the renunciation of Satan, "or, if he be an infant, his father, mother, or sponsor shall say it for him." The renunciation, repeated three times, was, like the entire rite, much elaborated beyond earlier formularies:

> I renounce thee, Satan, and all thy unclean works and all thy wicked angels and all thy evil demons, and all thy power, and all thy abominable service, and all thy evil cunning and error, and all thy host, and all thy authority, and all the rest of thy impieties.

Then the priest breathed upon the face of the one to be baptized and said three times, "Come forth, unclean spirit."[49]

The candidates turned to the east and with both hands uplifted declared their profession: "I profess Thee, Christ my God, and all Thy saving laws and all Thy vivifying service, and all Thy life-giving works." The priest asked each one three times to confess a short form of the creed, "Do you believe," and each answered, "I believe." Note that the interrogations occurred before the baptism and not in the water (as was the case in western sources). Then came a prayer for the catechumens to be confirmed in their allegiance to Christ.[50]

A prayer of exorcism asked that "all magic, all sorcery, all working of Satan" be driven out of the candidates. Then occurred a second anointing, designated the oil of exorcism. The priest anointed the breast, arms, the front of the heart to the back, and middle of the hands with the sign of the cross, saying this formula,

> Thou, N., art anointed with the oil of gladness, availing against all the workings of the Adversary, unto the grafting into the sweet olive tree of the Holy Catholic Apostolic Church of God. Amen.[51]

The priest laid hands on the candidates and prayed.

The priest poured pure oil into the font in the form of the cross and said a

---

48. Khs-Burmester, "Baptismal Rite," p. 52, with the note that this unction of the oil of catechesis does not occur in the Greek rite.

49. Khs-Burmester, "Baptismal Rite," pp. 44, 52-53, 65-66.

50. Khs-Burmester, "Baptismal Rite," pp. 44, 53, 66-68; Kretschmar, "Beiträge zur Geschichte der Liturgie," p. 42, for Syrian use of a positive confession *(syntaxis)* after the renunciation, western use of baptismal questions and answers in the water, and Alexandrian use of questions and answers at the place of the adhesion to Christ in the Syrian order.

51. Khs-Burmester, "Baptismal Rite," pp. 37, 54, 68-69.

prayer. This was followed by readings of Titus 2:11–3:7; 1 John 5:5-13; Acts 8:26-39; Psalm 32:1-2; and John 3:1-21.[52] There were other prayers, including a prayer of exorcism of the waters, "Sanctify this water . . . ," accompanied by his breathing on the water three times in the form of the cross and reciting Matthew 28:19. Then occurred the "Prayer of Sanctification of the Waters of the Font," cited above for the theology of baptism. Other prayers and recitations from the Psalms ensued.[53]

> The priest . . . shall baptize him thrice, and after each immersion he shall raise him up and shall breathe in his face, saying:
> "I baptize thee, N., in the Name of the Father,
> At the second immersion: and of the Son,
> At the third immersion: and of the Holy Spirit. Amen."[54]

The first-person-active formula, "I baptize," was used in the Coptic and Latin rites, whereas the Greek and Syrian rites used the third-person-passive form, "N. is baptized."[55]

The postbaptismal anointing with holy chrism is much elaborated. The priest said a prayer over the chrism, not to consecrate it (for it had been consecrated on the preceding Thursday) but to invoke on it the gift of the Holy Spirit: "Bestow the Holy Spirit in the outpouring of the holy chrism." The priest anointed the one who had been baptized on the forehead and eyes, saying, "In the Name of the Father and of the Son and of the Holy Spirit. Amen. An unction of the grace of the Holy Spirit. Amen." With the anointing of the nostrils and mouth he said, "An unction of a pledge of the kingdom of heaven. Amen." With the anointing on the ears he said, "An unction of a fellowship of life immortal and eternal. Amen." An anointing of both sides of the hands was accompanied by the priest saying, "A holy unction of Christ our God, and a seal that shall not be broken. Amen." With the anointing of the breast he said, "The perfection of the grace of the Holy Spirit, and a breastplate of faith and truth. Amen." At the anointing of the knees, the instep of the feet, the back, the arms, and the front of the heart, he said, "Thou, N., art anointed with holy oil, in the Name of the Father, and of the Son, and of the Holy Spirit. Amen." Then the priest laid hands on the baptized and pronounced a blessing. Breathing on the face of the baptized, the priest said, "Receive the Holy Spirit."[56]

Those who had been baptized were clothed in white garments to the words, "A garment of life eternal, imperishable, and immortal. Amen." Then the priest placed crowns on the heads and girdles around the waist of those who had been baptized

---

52. Khs-Burmester, "Baptismal Rite," pp. 45, 54-55, p. 70. This part of the service appears to come from the final editing of the rite.
53. Khs-Burmester, "Baptismal Rite," pp. 55-57.
54. Khs-Burmester, "Baptismal Rite," pp. 57, 75.
55. Kretschmar, "Beiträge zur Geschichte der Liturgie," pp. 39-40, 41-42, for the passive versus active formulae.
56. Khs-Burmester, "Baptismal Rite," pp. 58-59, 76-77.

accompanied by further words of blessing. Meanwhile the people sang, "Receive the Holy Spirit, O thou who hast received holy baptism. . . ."[57]

Then the priest administered to those who had been baptized the sacrament. He prayed,

> Blessed art Thou, Lord God Almighty. . . . Who has made his servants worthy of the laver of regeneration and of the forgiveness of sins . . . and the gift of Thy Holy Spirit. . . . make them worthy of the communion of the holy body and of the precious blood of Thy Christ.

Note the combination of regeneration, forgiveness of sins, and the gift of the Holy Spirit. Afterwards he laid his hand on their heads and spoke further words of blessing.[58]

The adaptation to infant baptism included the omission of instructions given to adults, and the various exorcisms, exsufflations, and unctions were contracted into a single introductory ceremony.[59]

A late report (from the tenth-century bishop of Memphis, Macarius) assigns to the patriarch Theophilus of Alexandria (385-412) the change from an annual administration of baptism at the Pasch at the hand of the patriarch at his church, because children might die beforehand, to baptism "at any time, in any place, and at the hand of any priest" in cases of necessity, which custom prevailed thereafter. Theophilus also gave the instructions concerning the ingredients for preparing the oil of unction at baptism.[60]

---

57. Khs-Burmester, "Baptismal Rite," pp. 60, 78-79.
58. Khs-Burmester, "Baptismal Rite," pp. 60, 79-80.
59. Khs-Burmester, "Baptismal Rite," p. 61.
60. Louis Villecourt, "Le livre du chréme: Ms. Paris arabe 100," *Le Muséon* 41 (1928): 49-80 (pp. 57-59). Paul F. Bradshaw, "Baptismal Practice in the Alexandrian Tradition: Eastern or Western?" in Maxwell E. Johnson, ed., *Living Water, Sealing Spirit: Reading on Christian Initiation* (Collegeville: Liturgical, 1995), pp. 82-100 (p. 87), cites an earlier confirmation of the change in time and circumstances of baptism from the "Canonical Responses" attributed to Timothy of Alexandria but probably from the fifth century as indicating that candidates for baptism were now infants rather than adults, so baptism was administered by a priest and not restricted to any one season.

45. Writers and Writings in Syriac and Armenian

Syriac Acts of John

The *Syriac Acts of John*, actually entitled in the manuscripts *The History of John the Son of Zebedee*, is different from the second-century *Acts of John* (chap. 13). This text exists only in Syriac and dates from the late fourth or more likely the early fifth century. There are three fairly detailed accounts of conversion in the text, and in their main outline they exhibit the Syrian baptismal ritual.[1]

The first account of baptism concerns a procurator and his nobles. John made the sign of the cross over the oil, saying, "Glory be to the Father and to the Son and to the Spirit of holiness for ever, Amen" (3, p. 39). Fire blazed forth from the oil but did not consume the oil, for angels spread their wings over it and pronounced the Trishagion. John then signed the water, saying, "In the name of the Father and of the Son and of the Spirit of holiness, for ever, Amen" (8, p. 39). The people stretched out their hands to heaven and said, "Great is the mystery! We believe in the Father and in the Son and in the Spirit of holiness" (14, p. 39).

John instructed the procurator to remove his clothes, made the sign of the cross on his forehead, and anointed his whole body (15, p. 40). John told him to descend, and, stretching out his hands to heaven, the procurator said, "I believe in the Father and in the Son and in the Spirit of holiness" (19, p. 40).

John placed his hand on the head and dipped him once, saying: "In the name of the Father." A second time: "In the name of the Son." A third time: "In the name of the Spirit of holiness." (20-21, p. 40)

---

1. William Wright, *Apocryphal Acts of the Apostles*, Vol. 1: *Syriac Text*, and Vol. 2: *The English Translation* (London, 1871), pp. 3-60. I quote from A. F. J. Klijn, "An Ancient Syriac Baptismal Liturgy in the Syriac Acts of John," *Novum Testamentum* 6 (1963): 216-228, citing Klijn's section number and the page number of Wright's translation.

The procurator was clothed in white garments and given a kiss of peace. The document places the meaning of the baptism on the lips of the procurator:

> When I was (first) dipped, I opened my eyes and saw, not that I was going down, but that I was going up to heaven. And the second time, I looked and opened my eyes, and saw a right hand holding a reed and writing. And the third time, I heard a voice saying: "The sinner, the sheep which was lost, is found; let him come in." (25, p. 42)

The baptism of the procurator's nobles is summarized, "John anointed them, and baptized them in the name of the Father and of the Son and of the Spirit of holiness" (26, p. 42).

The second account of conversion concerns the priests of Artemis. The priests said, "We renounce this Artemis, in whom there is no use," and beat their faces (27-28, p. 46). John kneeled, prayed, and directed them to look to the east. "John arose and signed them with the sign of the cross" (31, p. 47), and the priests confessed, "We have sinned and done wrong.... Have mercy on us, Lord! ... for henceforth we abjure all idols" (32, p. 48). They arose and lifted their hands to heaven, saying, "Glory unto thee, God, the Maker of heaven and earth! ... We confess Thee and there is no other God, but Thee" (34-37, p. 48). John then expounded the Law and the Prophets and taught concerning the Lord Jesus (38, p. 48).

The third account, the baptism of people assembled in the theatre, is the fullest. John called on the people to rise in prayer, and they looked to the east and fell on their faces, saying, "Lord have pity upon us" (39-41, p. 50). "The people stood barefooted and girded with sackcloth, dust on their heads," and they called on God to have pity on them, confessing "We have sinned" (42-43, p. 50). John then prayed for God to have pity on them. He "made the sign of the cross upon the forehead of each of them" (48, p. 51). They confessed their faith in the "one God, who created the world," and in "His only and beloved Son, our Lord, Jesus the Messiah, who put on the body from the holy Virgin Mary" (50, p. 52). John spoke the word of God to them, interpreting it and exhorting them (51, p. 53).

After a doxology, John expressed something of the meaning of baptism in a prayer:

> Lord God Almighty, let Thy Spirit of holiness come, and rest and dwell upon the oil and upon the water; let them be bathed and purified from uncleanness; and let them receive the Spirit of holiness through baptism; and let them henceforth call Thee: "Our Father who art in Heaven." Yea, Lord, sanctify this water with Thy voice, which resounded over the Jordan and pointed out our Lord Jesus (as) with a finger (saying) ... [Matt. 3:17]. Thou art here who wast on the Jordan. (55, pp. 53-54)

Fire blazed over the oil, and angels spread their wings over it. The people confessed, "We believe in the name of the Father and the Son and the Spirit of holiness, and we will never know aught else" (pp. 54, 56-59). "John anointed them with oil" and "baptized them in the name of the Father and the Son and Spirit of holiness for the forgiveness of debts and the pardon of sins" (60-61, p. 54).

Putting the accounts together, Klijn presents a reconstruction of the baptismal liturgy. The preparation for baptism followed this order: confession of guilt and asking for mercy in sackcloth by the candidates, an intercession by the administrator, signing with the cross, a renunciation of sin and idolatry, confession of faith (standing), and an exposition of the scriptures. The baptism proper included the following: doxology, consecration of the oil, appearance of fire and angels with singing of the Trishagion, consecration of the water, confession of the Trinity, removing garments, signing of forehead and anointing of whole body, descent into the water, confession of Trinity, threefold immersion with administrator's hand on the head, giving white garments, kiss of peace, salutation as bridegroom and youth.[2]

These accounts have features that were not unique to Syrian sources: a renunciation (but not fully developed here), a confession of faith, consecration of oil and water (but no fixed form is in evidence), nudity, triple immersion with the administrator's hand on the head, white garments. As in other Syriac sources, anointing with oil preceded the baptism and there was no postbaptismal anointing. The prominence of the anointing is shown by the appearance of angels in two accounts, in both of which fire appears on the oil, not on the water as in earlier Syrian sources. Notable is the confession of sins and the frequency with which the three divine names are mentioned. Exorcisms are absent from the accounts. Instruction from the scriptures accompanied the baptism. The baptismal ceremony brought pardon for sins, the gift of the Spirit of holiness, recording of one's name in heaven, and the right to address God as "Father." Much of this may reflect earlier practices.[3]

Narsai

Narsai was an adherent of the dyophysite (two-nature) Christology (not too accurately called Nestorianism) of Theodore of Mopsuestia. He was a teacher at Edessa and later at Nisibis. His literary activity began in 437, and he died at an advanced age in 502. His homilies exhibit the weaving together of the rich imagery characteristic of Syriac authors. *Homilies* 17, 22, 21, and 32 are "Liturgical Homilies."[4] *Homily* 22 on

---

2. Klijn, "Ancient Syriac Baptismal Liturgy," pp. 220-221.
3. Klijn, "Ancient Syriac Baptismal Liturgy," pp. 222-228.
4. I cite the English translation by R. H. Connolly, "The Liturgical Homilies of Narsai," *Texts and Studies* 8 (Cambridge University Press, 1909), with introduction (ix-lxxvi), translation (1-74), notes (75-84), and appendices (85-163). I give the page number in Connolly and his reference to the page number of the text by A. Mingana, which he translates. *Homily* 17 (35), "Expositions of the Mysteries," is not a genuine work of Narsai — see Luise Abramowski, "Die liturgische Homilie des Ps. Narses mit dem Messbekenntnis und einem Theodor-Zitat," *Bulletin of the John Rylands Library* 78.3 (1996): 87-100; it paraphrases the baptismal creed of Antioch (called the Symbol of the 318 Fathers, confirming the broader use of the name Nicene to include creeds with other wording than the one adopted at Nicaea), which included belief in "one baptism for remission of sins."

anointing belongs before 21 on baptism and eucharist, so there was no postbaptismal anointing.[5] These two homilies are dated about 450 or later.

The baptismal ceremony in Narsai followed this sequence: renunciation of Satan, confession of faith, endorsement by a sponsor of the candidate, the latter's kneeling on sackcloth, blessing of oil, signing on forehead, anointing of whole body (these items in *Homily* 22), baptism, and eucharist (these in *Homily* 21).[6]

An enrollment or turning in one's name for baptism may be alluded to in the words about writing "body and soul in the book of life" (*Homily* 22, p. 36; 359). The statement that "In the books the priest enters the name of the lost one . . . and places it in the archives of the King's books" (p. 40; 363) occurs in the context of signing the candidate with oil, and so may refer to inscribing one in the rolls of the church rather than the enrollment for baptism.

The priest says to the candidates, "Renounce the Evil One and his power and his angels and his service and his error" (p. 36; 359). The devil's angels are identified as human teachers of error: Mani, Valentinus, Arius, Eunomius, Apollinarius, Paul of Samosata, and Eutyches (p. 37; 360). The circus, the stadium, and the theaters are his invention.[7] "His error are soothsayings and witchcrafts of all sorts" (p. 38; 361). In this context Narsai recalls the repentance of the prodigal son (Luke 15) (p. 39; 362).[8] The renunciation is to reject "the standard of the Evil One, and his power and his angels" and receive "the standard of the King" (p. 44; 367).

The counterpart of the renunciation is to confess the name of the Creator (p. 36; 359). After the renunciation the candidate comes to the confession of the faith (p. 38; 361). The renunciation of the Evil One and confession of allegiance to God belong together:

> They confess and they renounce — the two in one, without doubting — (making) a renunciation of the Evil One, and a confession of the heart in the name of the Divinity. By the hand of the priesthood they make a covenant with the Divinity that they will not again return to Satan by their doings. They give to the priest a promise by the words of their minds. (P. 44; 367)

Narsai does not give the liturgical words of the confession but expresses their meaning as becoming a servant and soldier of the heavenly kingdom.

The initiate, "as an exile," "stands naked, without covering" (p. 38; 362). By the

---

5. Connolly, "Liturgical Homilies," p. xlvi. These two homilies are studied by Marcia A. Kappes, "The Voice of Many Waters: The Baptismal Homilies of Narsai," *Studia Patristica* 33 (1997): 534-547. A. Guillaumont, "Poème de Narsaï sur le baptême," *L'Orient Syrien* 1 (1956): 189-207, gives a French translation of *Homily* 22 that tries to bring out the poetic structure of the homily.

6. Connolly, "Liturgical Homilies," pp. xlii-xlix. Bryan D. Spinks, "The Rise and Decline of Sin and the Devil in the East Syrian Baptismal Tradition," *Studia patristica* 26 (1993): 67-74, gives much attention to Narsai, especially to exorcism and renunciation.

7. Connolly, "Liturgical Homilies," p. 38, n. 1, cites the similar words of Cyril, *Lectures on the Mysteries* 19.6.

8. The parable is alluded to in *Homily* 21, p. 53; 348, where conversion is a repentance.

wretched plight of nakedness, he seeks to win pity from the Judge (p. 39; 363). "He bends his knees and bows his head," and spreads sackcloth (p. 39; 363). The kneeling represents the fallen human condition and the making payment as a debtor.

A sponsor accompanied the initiate to "bear witness to his preparation and his sincerity" (p. 40; 363).

After the renunciation of the dominion of the Evil One and the confession of the power of the Creator, the priest (bishop) blessed oil by invoking the Trinity.

> The three names he casts upon the oil, and consecrates it, that it may be sanctifying the uncleanness of men by its holiness. With the name hidden in it he signs the visible body; and the sharp power of the name enters even unto the soul. (p. 42; 365)

(We will read below a similar statement about casting the word upon the water.) The priest then traced "the image of the Divinity [the cross] upon [the candidate's] forehead" (p. 36; 359). Narsai describes this signing as a "spiritual stamp" on the forehead "bright before angels and men" (p. 43; 366). The persons are like a flock of sheep, signed "with the sign of its Lord" (p. 40; 363-364), sealed with "the signet of His name" (p. 35; 358-359). They are signed with the Trinity (p. 41; 365). The priest "mixes the name of the Divinity in his hands with the oil; and he signs and says 'Father' and 'Son' and 'Holy Spirit'" (p. 44; 367).

> The priest does not say "I sign," but "is signed"; for the stamp that he sets is not his, but his Lord's. He is (but) the mediator who has been chosen by a favor to minister; and because it is not his it drives out iniquity and gives the Spirit. By the visible oil he shows the power that is in the names, which is able to confirm the feebleness of men with hidden (powers). (Pp. 44-45; 367)

The third-person formula repeated the emphasis found earlier in Theodore of Mopsuestia and John Chrysostom. It coincided with the theology attributing the power of the act to the divine working (next paragraph).

There followed (immediately) the anointing of the whole body. The passage continues:

> The three names [the priest] recites, together with (the rubbing of) the oil upon the whole man; that hostile demons and vexing passions may not harm him. It is not by the oil that he keeps men from harms; it is the power of the Divinity that bestows power upon (its) feebleness. The oil is a symbol which proclaims the divine power; and by outward things He (God) gives assurance of His works (done) in secret. By His power body and soul acquire power; and they no more dread the injuries of death.... This power the oil of anointing imparts: not the oil, but the Spirit that gives it power. (P. 45; 367-368)

Here is expressed the sacramental theology of Narsai and the Syriac church. The same thought will be expressed about the water in baptism (below). The material element is not what conveys the spiritual benefit, but the divine Persons work through the material element on the occasion of its application to effect the spiritual change. A visible physical act is the means of an invisible spiritual blessing.

In addition to the imagery of sealing sheep (noted above) Narsai used other imagery in reference to the anointing: a physician healing (p. 42; 366), the athlete rubbed with oil before the contest in the arena (p. 45; 368), the brand of soldiers in warfare against the Evil One and his demons (p. 45; 368 and p. 43; 366).

Narsai often mentions "oil and water" together (and always in this order) as the instruments of God's blessings. Liberty comes with "oil and water" (p. 40; 363). Oil and water are the foundation of the change in human beings into "pure gold" (p. 42; 365). The "mysteries of the oil and water" are armor against evil spirits (p. 43; 366 — quoted below). In keeping with his theological emphasis, Narsai adds that the "renewal of our race" is by "oil and water and the invincible power of the Spirit" (*Hom.* 21, p. 46; 341).

As part of an extended praise of the priesthood, Narsai says that the Spirit teaches it to "bestow power upon common water" (*Homily* 21, p. 47; 342). The priesthood does this by writing "the three names over the water" (*Homily* 21, p. 47; 342). Or, in another image, the priest casts his word as a seed "into the bosom of the waters; and they conceive and bring forth a new" birth (p. 50; 345). More literally, "with the three Names, he consecrates the water, that it may suffice to accomplish the cleansing of the defiled" (p. 50; 345). After this consecration "The power of the Divinity dwells in the visible waters, and by the force of His power they dissolve the might of the Evil One and of Death" (p. 50; 345). Thus the priests "have the key of the divine mercies . . . placed in their hands, and according to their pleasure they distribute life to men" (p. 48; 343).

Baptism itself involved the invocation of the Trinity. The priest made mention of the Divinity, "and he says three times: 'Father and Son and Holy Spirit, one equality'" (p. 51; 346). The names are repeated "with the voice openly." The priest does not say, "I baptize," but "Such a one is baptized in the name of the Father and the Son and the Spirit" (p. 51; 346). The same explanation for the passive formula is given as was stated in regard to the anointing. It is not the priest who baptizes, "but the power that is set in the names." "The names give forgiveness of iniquity, not a man; and they sow new life in mortality" (p. 51; 346). In the discussion of the anointing Narsai brings the formula in the two actions together: "With the name of the Father and of the Son and the Spirit he seals his words; and he confirms him that is being baptized with their names" (*Homily* 22, p. 43; 366).

The baptizand assents to the three Names. "Three times he bows his head at Their names, that he may learn the relation — that while They are One They are Three" (*Homily* 22, p. 43; 366). Narsai relates the dipping into the baptismal font three times not only to the Trinity but also to the three days the Redeemer was in the tomb (p. 43; 366).[9] The action of immersion is carried through in the interpretation given by Narsai: "[Our Lord] buried it [death] in the water" of baptism (p. 46; 341; see further below).

---

9. Connolly, "Liturgical Homilies," p. 51, n. 2, suggests that this was copied from Cyril, *Catechetical Lectures* 20 (*Lectures on the Mysteries* 2).4.

Narsai describes the reception of the newly baptized in terms of the treatment of a newborn baby, but likely reflects actual baptismal practice.

> As a babe from the midst of the womb he looks forth from the water; and instead of garments the priest receives and embraces him. He resembles a babe when he is lifted up from the midst of the water; and as a babe every one embraces and kisses him. Instead of swaddling-clothes they cast garments upon his limbs, and adorn him as a bridegroom on the day of the marriage-supper. (*Homily* 21, p. 52; 346)

The newly baptized person is welcomed by the priest and the church with hugs and kisses. The garments with which the person is clothed are not said to be white, but "by his adornment he depicts the glory that is prepared for him." The language of "the glorious robe of baptism," drawn from Luke 15:22, may be baptism itself or again may allude to a white robe given after baptism (p. 53; 348).

More certain is that baptism was followed by the eucharist. Developing the birth imagery of baptism, Narsai says that the spiritual mother (the church) puts into the mouth of the newborn child not breasts but the body and blood (p. 52; 347). As with the oil and water, "The priest calls upon the Hidden One to send him hidden power, that he may give power in the bread and wine to give life" (p. 56; 351, as part of an extended discussion of the eucharist following on the discussion of baptism).

Narsai found no tension between the death/resurrection motif and the new birth motif in explaining the meaning of baptism. Both images imply submersion in the water.

> The waters become fruitful, as a womb; and the power of grace is like the seed that begets life. Body and soul go down together into the bosom of the water and are born again, being sanctified from defilement. (*Homily* 32, p. 66; 148).

Narsai immediately shifts his comparison from the womb to the tomb and back again:

> [God] buries men in the bosom of the waters, as in a tomb, and brings back and quickens to new life them that were dead in iniquity. By the power of the Creator he buries the dead and quickens the dead; and as from the womb he begets men spiritually. (p. 66; 148)

"Death and life is the mystery of baptism" (*Homily* 22, p. 41; 364). The initiate dies "in the midst of the waters," yet life is given "by the water" (p. 41; 364). "The resurrection of the body and the redemption of the soul are preached" in baptism (*Homily* 21, p. 50; 345). In baptism, "as in a tomb, body and soul are buried, and they die and live (again) with a type of the resurrection that is to be at the end" (pp. 50-51; 345). "In the grave of the water the priest buries the whole man; and he resuscitates him by the power of life that is hidden in his words" (p. 51; 345). The person dies in the water but quickly comes to life again (p. 51; 345-346). In the three divine names the person "that is baptized is baptized (and buried) as in a tomb; and they call and raise him up from his death" (p. 51; 345-346).

In baptism there is a representation of the Redeemer's death and resurrection. The person "verily dies by a symbol of that death which the Quickener of all died; and he surely lives with a type of the life without end" (*Homily* 21, p. 51; 345-346). The same context combines this imagery with the clothing metaphor: "Sin and death he puts off and casts away in baptism, after the manner of those garments which our Lord departing left in the tomb" (p. 51; 345-346). Baptism depicts the death of Jesus and his coming to life again, and "After they have died with Him they have risen and have been resuscitated mystically" (p. 54; 348-349). And so they now travel with him in the new life of the resurrection.

The resurrection and new birth themes are combined also in reference to eschatology:

> Mystically he dies and is raised and is adorned; mystically he imitates the life immortal. His birth (in baptism) is a symbol of that birth which is to be at the end, and the conduct of his life of that conversation which is (to be) in the kingdom on high. (*Homily* 21, p. 52; 347)

As the quotations already given indicate, the imagery associated with birth is a somewhat more pervasive theme. Baptism is "the womb of waters" that brings forth spiritually (*Homily* 21, p. 53; 348). Narsai combines the male and female aspects of the birth process in talking about baptism and delights in the paradoxes suggested by his imagery. It was a divine invention "that without seed man should beget (children) from the midst of the water. Where ever had the like been done or achieved — that the bosom of the waters should bring forth without wedlock?" (*Homily* 21, p. 46; 341). In the ordinary course of nature, creatures reproduce after their kind. But in this case a "senseless nature" (baptism) brings forth the rational or spiritual (p. 46; 341).

Another astonishing thing to Narsai is that "the womb of the water should conceive and bring forth babes full grown" (*Homily* 21, p. 46; 341). Moreover, "It is altogether a new thing . . . that within an hour should be accomplished the period of conception and birth" (p. 46; 341). In the interests of his paradox, Narsai omits the usual earlier interpretation that would bring the sowing of the seed of the word that produces faith during the period of the catechumenate into relation with the baptismal birth.

> Come, O hearer, listen to the wonder of the new birth, the conception whereof and the bringing forth are accomplished in one hour. . . . (W)hile yet the word lingers in the mouth (the birth) has come forth from the womb. . . . Come, ye mortals, and look upon a nature full of mortality that puts off its passions in baptism and puts on life. Come, let us examine exactly the mystery of our renewal; and let us learn concerning the power that is hidden in the visible waters. (p. 47; 342)

The person was baptized in order to become an "heir, son, and citizen" (*Homily* 22, p. 40; 363). A frequently recurring motif is freedom from the forces of evil.

Baptism is a "new creation," founded in "the deep of the waters," whereby the handiwork of God's creation might be restored (*Homily* 22, p. 41; 364).

For Narsai, as for Syrian authors before him, a favorite image, itself rather paradoxical, of the renewal in baptism is a furnace. "As in a furnace He re-cast our image in baptism; and instead of our clay He has made us spiritual gold" (*Homily* 22, p. 33; 356).

> The furnace of the waters His purpose prepared mystically; and instead of fire He has heated it with the Spirit of the power of His will. His own handiwork He made a craftsman over His creation, that it should re-cast itself in the furnace of the waters and the heat of the Spirit. (p. 41; 364)

"As in a furnace he re-casts bodies in baptism; and as in a fire he consumes the weeds of mortality." The Spirit is cast "into the water, as into a furnace; and he purifies the image of men from uncleanness" (p. 48; 313).

Narsai elaborates on the clauses of the Nicene Creed as recited in the service. It included a confession of "one bath and baptism, wherein we are baptized unto pardon of debts and the adoption of sons" (*Homily* 17, p. 6; 274-275). Continuing the concern with evil spirits, Narsai mentions the signing of the forehead as "for the confusion of the devils," and then adds that it is on account of these devils that the "mysteries of the oil and the water" are performed (*Homily* 22, p. 43; 366).

The deliverance from the rule of demons and the promise of the kingdom of heaven mean that the baptizands "enter and rest" in the "holy church" (*Homily* 21, p. 55, 350).

Narsai's notable imagery in developing his themes in the baptismal homilies includes God as an artisan, the wiping away of the rust of iniquity, the priest as a pen writing in the oil and water, a lawcourt (setting of the renunciation), the Son of God and Christians as athletes.[10] Some basic themes recur throughout: God's loving act of creation, the Holy Spirit's power to re-cast human beings, the role of the priest, oil and water as symbols in baptism, and the call for the baptized Christian to be an active participant in God's ongoing work.[11] Some readers would see a weakness in Narsai's attention to the Spirit and priests at the expense of reference to Christ and his church.[12]

The Teaching of Saint Gregory

Christianity in Syria had a great influence on the development of the faith in Armenia. *The Teaching of Saint Gregory* (attributed to Gregory the Illuminator, missionary to Armenia, who converted its king early in the fourth century) is a catechism composed in Armenian with three main facets: doctrinal instruction based on a creed; exposition of the types and prophecies of the Old Testament as a proof of the New; and moral ex-

---

10. Kappes, "The Voice of Many Waters," p. 541.
11. Kappes, "The Voice of Many Waters," pp. 540-541.
12. Kappes, "The Voice of Many Waters," p. 542. She notes striking parallels to Narsai's language in the Zoroastrian *Gathas* as providing the cultural and religious context of his homilies.

hortation to repentance.[13] Exposition of scripture takes a prominent place. Like Irenaeus, whose *Demonstration of the Apostolic Preaching* survives only in Armenian, the author presents doctrinal and moral teaching in the framework of an exposition of the biblical history of salvation. The author was familiar with Greek and Syriac sources, showing an indebtedness particularly to Cyril of Jerusalem and John Chrysostom. He belonged to the circle of intellectuals responsible for the remarkable flourishing of Armenian literature in the fifth century. *The Teaching of Saint Gregory* cannot be earlier than the 430s or 440s. The pseudonymity had the purpose of giving the authority of Gregory the Illuminator to the theology of the Armenian church of the time.

The Teaching of Saint Gregory sets baptism in relation to the doctrine of creation. The following passage includes several themes characteristic of the work.

> And because He made the first earth emerge from the waters [Gen. 1.9] by his command, and by water were fattened all plants and reptiles and wild animals and beasts and birds, and by the freshness of the waters they sprang from the earth; in the same way by baptism He made verdant the womb of generation of the waters, purifying by the waters and renewing the old deteriorated earthly matter, which sin had weakened and enfeebled and deprived of the grace of the Spirit. Then the invisible Spirit opened again the womb of visible water, preparing the newly born fledglings for the regeneration of the font [Titus 3.5], to clothe all with robes of light who would be born once more. (412)[14]

John the Baptist served for the author as the connecting link between the Old Testament and the New. The anointings with oil in the Old Testament were types of the anointing of Christ (431-432). Priests, prophets, and kings received an anointing. This was passed on in the seed of Abraham until John, a priest, prophet, and baptist. As a keeper of the tradition, John "gave the priesthood, the anointing, the prophecy, and the kingship to our Lord Jesus Christ" (433).[15]

John gave the "baptism of repentance" to the crowd, but he recognized that Jesus "must increase and I decrease" (John 3:30)" (442). "John came and washed the people with repentance, in order that when the Son of God should appear they might be ready to approach with worthiness and hear [his] teaching" (409). Jesus came at age thirty to John the Baptist, the greatest of the prophets, and submitted to baptism. John's baptism of repentance was like Moses' command to the people to wash and purify themselves (Exod. 19:10) in preparation for "the revelation of the divine glory." But his baptism was "not the baptism of the divine mark [the seal conferred by baptism] of illumination of eternal life" (408).

---

13. Robert W. Thomson, *The Teaching of Saint Gregory: An Early Armenian Catechism* (Cambridge: Harvard University Press, 1970), p. 10. I follow his introduction (pp. 1-38), and my quotations are from his translation. There is a revised edition (New Rochelle, NY: St. Nersess Armenian Seminary, 2001).

14. I place in parentheses the section number of citations from Thomson's translation. For baptism as a womb, compare 679 quoted at the end of this section on *The Teaching of St. Gregory*.

15. This motif was characteristic of Syriac Christianity.

This Armenian catechism gives Christ's baptism by John much attention. It repeats the traditional motif that Christ's baptism sanctified the waters: "He came down to the waters and sanctified the lower waters of this earth, which had been fouled by the sins of mankind" (413). Or, in other words, "He Himself came down upon the waters, and made the waters at once purifying and renovating" (411). The result is that the waters now give life to those who follow Christ's example: "And at his baptism He vivifies all baptized by having Himself received baptism, and He made baptism honorable by his own descent to baptism" (415). After quoting several Old Testament passages about the waters, the author affirms that Christ's purity cast out impurity: "For He who is pure and clean has entered it [water] to cast out the impure and execrable" (552).

Several themes are brought together in a basic passage on the baptism of Christ:

> Then He came and was Himself baptized by John; undertaking to write an eternal covenant and sealing it with his own blood [Heb. 13:20], to give life to all by the illuminating and life-giving baptism, He ordered all men born from the earth, all humans, to imitate the divine image of salvation. Then He came to the seal-giver John to be baptized by him [followed by quotation of Matthew 3:14-15]. (410)

Baptism, as in earlier Christian teaching (and in 408 above), is both life-giving and illuminating. Therefore, the author of the catechism calls on people to imitate Christ in baptism, but he expresses the command in a distinctive way. To be baptized is "to imitate the divine image of salvation." In the immediate context the baptism of Christ is this image of salvation, that is, to be baptized would be to identify with Christ and his salvation; but one wonders if there was not in the back of the author's mind the action of baptism as representing death, burial, and resurrection — but this latter is language he otherwise does not employ for baptism. Apparently unique to this document is the description of John as "the seal-giver," his baptism being regarded as conferring a seal.[16]

His baptism was Jesus' revelation as Son of God, declared "by the voice of the Father and the descent of the Spirit" (416), when he "was made known to all" (417). The Spirit came in the likeness of a dove because the dove is a symbol of purity, and one can approach the Son of God only in sinlessness and holiness (418).

Christ's baptism showed others that in the same way they become pleasing to the Father and receive the blessing of the Spirit. He "fulfilled the covenant of the fathers" and established baptism for all people.

> The Son of God, therefore, came and was baptized, to establish the baptism of all who would be baptized, that handing on this tradition He might reveal salvation to all. (420)

---

16. Thomson, *The Teaching of Saint Gregory*, p. 88, note ad loc., observes that "seal" was usually reserved for Christian baptism; see 408 quoted above.

Thus the baptism of Christ connects with the mission he gave to the apostles. Following a quotation of Matthew 28:19-20, the catechism says:

> He gave them knowledge of the truth of the Trinity . . . that according to this pattern they might make disciples of all men, and baptize them in the name of the Father, Son, and Holy Spirit. (662)

This mission of the apostles leads to a comprehensive statement of the blessings of Christianity, represented in baptism:

> Thus they preached throughout the world "to illumine all men who were to come into the world [John 1.9]," to give repentance of salvation to all, to wash all men and deliver them from the bonds of darkness by baptism, to stamp all nations as the band of Christ, to make the Spirit of God dwell in men's hearts, to unite and join them to the love of the Son of God . . . that the name of bondage might be taken away, and the name of adoption be placed on them by the grace of Christ; to enable them to eat the flesh of the Son of God and drink the life-giving blood. (690)

To summarize, the apostles' mission brought illumination, saving repentance, washing, deliverance from bondage, the seal of Christ, the indwelling Spirit, adoption, and access to the eucharist — although baptism is mentioned only once in the passage, all of these items are connected in Christian teaching with baptism.

The apostles' mission involved the Spirit and fire as well as water.

> The apostles brought forth the whole world afresh by water and the Spirit. They seasoned everyone by fire [Mark 9:49]. . . . They were joined indissolubly to the Godhead and illumined. They made the world rejoice and showered [all] with gifts. For who have been baptized into Christ have put on Christ and his Spirit [Gal. 3.27]. (681)

The Spirit is here linked with water and with baptism into Christ, so that he is added to the quotation from Galatians 3:27. Fire suggests the imagery of refashioning in the furnace of fire[17] that we have encountered elsewhere in Syriac baptismal teaching. "The just have been plunged into the furnace of righteousness and dyed in the hues and colors of the Holy Spirit" (682).

The author brings together "believe and be baptized" but not in reference to belief in Christ but to belief in the message of the apostles. Catechumens are instructed:

> Hear them and believe in the truth of the gospel of your salvation; believe in them and be baptized into the Spirit of the gospel of holiness, who is the guarantee of our inheritance [Eph. 1.14]. (691)

The passages quoted in regard to the baptism of Christ and the mission of the apostles show the meaning of baptism for the Armenian church, as represented in

---

17. See 639 also on the furnace.

The Teaching of Saint Gregory. Additional aspects are also found. The Savior orders that we "renew ourselves" (Titus 3:5) and "strip off" the old person (Col. 3:9). The context gives no indication that this was a ritual action as well as a moral exhortation.

The water and the Spirit are brought together in another statement about Christ sanctifying and purifying the waters. Alluding to the creation, the author says:

> And just as formerly the Spirit moved over the waters [Gen. 1:2], in the same way He will dwell in the waters and will receive all who are born by it. . . . He made these waters just as those, because He Himself came down to the waters, that all might be renewed through the Spirit by the waters . . . and the same Spirit might bring all to adoption [Rom. 8.15, 23; 9.4; Gal. 4.5; Eph. 1.5] by the waters for ever. (414)

Renewal is by the Spirit, but baptism is the means by which the renewal takes place. The author uses the imagery of birth by the waters and of adoption by the Spirit as equivalent.

After quoting the Lord's "decree" in John 3:5, the author declares, "And he will not be renewed a second time" (454).

The preference for the birth analogy to baptism is evident in an important text, influenced by John 3:5 and reiterating some ideas already expressed.

> God descended to earth and raised mankind to heaven. . . . He renewed and rejuvenated creation once and for all. He opened the womb of baptism that they might be renewed and born again as children of the kingdom by baptism. For the apostles acted as the womb of baptism, they gave birth to all the world again and brought them to the innocence of children's unadulterated milk, to make them all sons of God and heirs of the salvation of Christ. (679)

Here are found the document's common ideas of renewal, birth from the womb of baptism, entering the kingdom of God, and becoming children and heirs of God.

Armenian Ritual of Baptism

The liturgy of the Armenian church belongs outside the time frame of this study, but since it is sometimes cited for preserving early features I include a brief summary of its baptismal ceremony.[18]

There were prayers on the eighth and fortieth day for a child, designated a catechumen (pp. 86-88). Then the ritual gives the baptismal rite for children and those

---

18. I use the English translation of F. C. Conybeare, *Rituale Armenorum* (Oxford: Clarendon, 1905), giving in parentheses the page numbers of this book. The standard study of Armenian initiation is Gabriele Winkler, *Das Armenische Initiationsrituale: Entwicklungsgeschichtliche und liturgievergleichende Untersuchung der Quellen des 3. bis 10. Jahrhunderts*, Orientalia christiana analecta 217 (Rome, 1982).

of full age (pp. 89ff.). There was the ancient practice of a triple renunciation and a triple confession (p. 92). Priests, kings, and prophets of the Old Testament were anointed, and there is a prayer for the "oil of grace of the all-Holy Spirit" (p. 93). The water was consecrated by a petition to "send the Holy Spirit into the water and cleanse it as thou didst cleanse Jordan by entering it," prefiguring the font of baptism and regeneration of all men (p. 95). The doctrinal meaning of baptism was remission of sins, reception of the Holy Spirit, adoption as sons, and inheritance of the kingdom of heaven (p. 95). Baptism was received nude. Water was poured on the head three times, and then the baptizand was plunged three times for Jesus' three days in the grave (p. 96). There followed an anointing of various parts of the body (p. 98). The neophyte wore white and stayed in the church eight days in prayer and partaking of the body and the blood (p. 100). A later alternative order of baptizing involved pouring water three times over a child's head (p. 105).

Later Syrian Baptismal Liturgies

The formative period of the Antiochene services was the fifth to seventh centuries.[19] The four Syrian services (Church of the East, Syrian Orthodox, Maronite, and Melkites), although the East Syrian rite stands somewhat apart, show the same basic structure: initial ceremonies of the catechumenate, one or two anointings, baptism by immersion or affusion using a passive formula, postbaptismal anointing (*myron* in the west and oil in east Syria), communion. Prior to the fifth century there was only one anointing, and that before baptism; originally it was on the forehead, but it was extended to the whole body, thus giving rise to two prebaptismal anointings. The basis was Christ's baptism, his anointing as King and Priest. His presence sanctified the water. By grace Christians become kings and priests at baptism. By rebirth

---

19. Sebastian Brock, "The Syrian Baptismal Rites," *Concilium* 122 (1979): 98-104, whom I follow in this section. In addition to his works footnoted in chaps. 30 and 31: Sebastian Brock, "Studies in the Early History of the Syrian Orthodox Baptismal Liturgy," *Journal of Theological Studies*, n.s. 23 (1972): 16-64 (on the manuscript tradition); Sebastian Brock, "Studies on Syrian Baptismal Rites," in J. Vellian, ed., *Studies on Syrian Baptismal Rites*, The Syrian Churches Series 6 (Kottayam: CMS Press, 1973); Sebastian Brock, "Baptismal Themes in the Writings of Jacob of Serugh," *Orientalia christiana analecta* 205 (1978): 325-347. Other works: B. Botte, "Le baptême dans l'Église syrienne," *L'Orient Syrien* 1 (1956): 137-155 (concerned only with the rite and with Syrian Antioch, introducing the following article); G. Khouri-Sarkis, "Prières et cérémonies du baptême selon le rituel de l'Église syrienne d'Antioche," *L'Orient Syrien* 1 (1956):156-184 (French translation of a Syriac text), to which B. Botte added "Note sur la prière de signation d'un enfant," pp. 185-188; G. DeVries, "Théologie des sacrements chez les Syriens monophysites," *L'Orient Syrien* 8 (1963):261-288 (immersion was usual, but sometimes infusion; must be accompanied by holy chrism; refused to recognize baptism by laity; baptism of infants has Monophysite origins; necessity of baptism based on John 3:5); Aloys Grillmeier, "Die Taufe Christi und die Taufe der Christen: Zur Tauftheologie des Philoxenus von Mabbug und ihrer Bedeutung für die christliche Spiritualität," in H. J. Auf der Maur et al., *Fides sacramenti sacramentum fidei* (Assen: Van Gorcum, 1981), pp. 137-175.

the robe of paradise lost by Adam is put on. At the end of the fourth century new prominence began to be given to death and resurrection; hence the prebaptismal anointing began to be interpreted as cathartic and protective and the postbaptismal anointing was introduced and given the charismatic character formerly ascribed to the prebaptismal anointing. There is a richness of symbolism in the Syriac rites: the womb of Mary, the Jordan, and Sheol. The gifts of the Spirit at baptism are sonship, becoming a limb of the body, a lamb branded with the mark of Christ. Distinctive of the Syriac tradition are putting on the "robe of glory" (Isa. 61:3), the typological use of John 19:34, and the return to paradise (present and eschatological).

46. Greek-Speaking Syria

Theodoret

Theodoret was born in Antioch in 393. He became bishop of Cyrus in 423 and died sometime around 460.

His *Fables of Heretics (Haereticarum fabularum compendium)* contains a section "On Baptism" that expresses the same line of thinking as John Chrysostom.

> Instead of the Jews' vessels for sprinkling, there suffices for believers the gift of most holy baptism. It not only gives forgiveness of old sins, but it also inspires the hope of good things promised. It establishes participants of the Lord's death and resurrection; it grants a share of the gift of the Holy Spirit; it declares the sons of God, and not only sons but also heirs of God and fellow heirs of Christ. For it is not as the mindless Messalians [chap. 47] think that baptism is only a razor removing previous sins. It grants this out of its abundance. For if this was the only work of baptism, why do we baptize infants, who have never tasted of sin? The mystery [sacrament] promises not only this but also greater and more perfect things. For it is the down payment of good things to come — a type of the future resurrection, fellowship of the Lord's passion, a sharing of the Lord's resurrection, a garment of salvation, a clothing of joy, a luminous cloak, or rather light itself.... [Gal. 3:27 and Rom. 6:3-5 quoted] The divine apostle taught us to think this way about most holy baptism, because having been buried with Christ we shall share in his resurrection. (*Fables of Heretics* 5.18; PG 83.512A-C)

Theodoret, like Chrysostom, separates infant baptism from the forgiveness of sins. Both of these Greek theologians speak only of actual sins; they show no concept of an inherited Adamic sin, nor do they relate infant baptism to such a concept. They rather justify the practice from the many other blessings associated with baptism. This approach reflects a quite different perspective from that championed by Theodoret's contemporary Augustine in North Africa.

In the same work Theodoret passed on reports about the practice of baptism by Eunomians. After mentioning the theological "blasphemies" of Eunomius, he repeats the charge of a single baptism into the death of Christ (chap. 35) and proceeds to describe other aberrations by some of the Eunomians.

> [Eunomius] overturned the custom of holy baptism established by the Lord and delivered by the apostles, and he laid down opposite laws. He said not to use three dippings [τρὶς καταδύειν] of the one being baptized [βαπτιζόμενον] nor to invoke the Trinity, but to baptize once [ἅπαξ βαπτίζειν] into the death of Christ. In baptizing they drench in the water down to the chest, but they forbid the water to the other parts [genitalia] of the body as bearing a curse. On account of this, when they baptize [ἐβάπτιζον] in a bathtub, they stand the man outside it and bring his head once down to the breast into the water. Since there occurs some injury to the head when it beats against the tub, they invented another form of baptism. Extending the person face forward on some step and hanging his head outside (it), they pour [καταχέουσετό] water, which touches no other part of the body. Some of them also seek out another form of baptism. Preparing a very broad band and dedicating it, they wind this around the person up to the finger nails, beginning from the breast. And so they apply the pouring of the water. Those who have fled their impiety and have joined the flock of our Savior and God reveal these things. (*Fables of Heretics* 4.3; PG 83.420B-C)

Theodoret describes these practices because they departed from the church's usual manner of administering baptism. The accuracy of the reports may be questioned, and even if they are accurate, the frequency of what is described may be further doubted. Theodoret's own word usage is notable: in the early part of the passage "to baptize" (βαπτίζειν) is "to dip" (καταδύειν), and later in the passage the pouring is described as inventing "another form of baptism." The practices appear to be almost a parody of orthodox baptism. The bending of the head forward was the usual practice; the difference in what is reported here is that the baptizand stood outside the pool instead of in it. Hence, the dipping did not wet the whole body, but only from the chest up.[1] Theodoret's word for "parts" of the body was used for the genitalia, and that is apparently what is intended here. Only the upper part of the body, and not its lower parts, was worthy of being baptized. Whatever one makes of the reason advanced to explain changing the dipping of the head to a pouring, this too had a precedent in the orthodox practice of sickbed baptism (chap. 39), only substituted here for well persons.

A nonsacramental use of the *bapt-* family of words shows the continued recog-

---

1. This practice could explain what Epiphanius reports: "Some people have declared that he [Eunomius] baptizes those whom he rebaptizes upside down, their feet up and their heads down" (*Panarion* 76.54.34) — translation by Philip R. Amidon, *The Panarion of St. Epiphanius, Bishop of Salamis: Selected Passages* (Oxford: Oxford University Press, 1990), p. 338. The difficulty alone of doing this disqualifies it as an accurate report, but it could be a garbled version of what Theodoret describes.

nition of their literal meaning. In his *Church History* Theodoret reports of Diodore in Antioch (he was later bishop of Tarsus) that "in the great storm he preserved the ship of the church from sinking [ἀβάπτιστον, 'unsubmerged']" (5.4).

Theodoret's *Cure of Pagan Maladies* gave little occasion to speak of baptism, but what he says shows his view of baptism. The "baptism [βάπτισμα] of immortality and regeneration [παλιγγενεσίας]" is indicated by Isaiah 1:16 (7.29).[2] Theodoret contrasts "all holy baptism" with the "habitual sprinklings" of the Law (7.30). And he speaks of "the forgiveness of sins, which [God] gave through all holy baptism," citing Isaiah 43:25 (7.32).

If the current attribution of *Questions and Answers to the Orthodox* to Theodoret is correct, it adds important information from him about baptism. Question 14 raises the problem that if the baptism of heretics is false and vain, why do the orthodox not baptize the heretic who flees to orthodoxy but allow the spurious baptism as if it were true? The answer given is: "When the heretic comes to orthodoxy, the error is set right: the bad opinion by a change of thinking, and the baptism by the application of the holy *myron*" (PG 6.1261C-D). The practice of recognizing baptism given among heretics apparently continued to pose a difficulty, but the catholic policy adopted in the third and fourth centuries prevailed. Presumably, it was assumed that the proper Trinitarian formula had been employed. The question no doubt still reflected a real situation.

Question 37, in contrast, raised a theoretical concern with regard to John's baptism: If the baptism of John was not according to the Law (as it was not), was not receiving it against the Law? The response is this:

> The baptism of John was the preamble to the gospel of grace. Therefore, it went beyond the Law. For it was not possible to those who sinned according to the Law. By it forgiveness is received through repentance and faith in Christ. (PG 6.1284A-B)

The answer is important as an explicit linking of the effectiveness of baptism with repentance and faith. That it is said with reference to John's baptism might imply that those who received John's baptism of repentance before the institution of Christ's baptism needed only to add faith in Christ without being rebaptized to receive salvation (would this have been the case with the apostles?)

Question 56 is important for showing Greek thinking on infant baptism that was quite different from what in the same period Augustine (chap. 52) was developing in the Latin church:

> If infants who die have no praise or blame from their works, what is the difference in the resurrection of those who have been baptized by others and have done nothing and those who have not been baptized and likewise have done nothing?

---

2. Theodoret's *Commentary on Isaiah* 1:16 (PG 81.229B-C) emphasizes the need for moral purification, which he opposes to the ritual ablutions, but keeps the significance of baptism as the "washing of regeneration."

The answer is the following:

> This is the difference of those infants baptized and those not baptized: those infants attain the good things through baptism; those not baptized do not attain them. The former are considered worthy of the good things through baptism by the faith of those who bring them to baptism. (PG 6.1297C-D)

This answer was closer to Pelagius's position. The orthodox spokesman refers to the positive, good things associated with baptism, as did Chrysostom (chap. 33), and not to the removal of sins. The reference to the faith of parents or sponsors is a point in common between the Greek and Latin authors.

With reference to the baptismal anointing, Question 137 observes that Mary (unnamed in the Gospels) anointed Jesus with *myron* before his passion and raises the question:

> Why are we anointed with oil and then, having performed the symbols of the Lord's passion and resurrection in the baptismal pool, afterward sealed with *myron*? Is this not a contradiction to what was done to the Lord, since he was first anointed with *myron* and afterward suffered? And is it not superfluous to apply the anointing of oil to those going to be baptized, since the Lord was anointed with only *myron* at his passion? (PG 6.1389C)

The first part of the question may reflect the old Syrian practice of only a prebaptismal anointing and have behind it a scriptural justification that was found for the practice; the second part queries the seemingly extraordinary use of two anointings.

The reply calls attention to Jesus' word "beforehand" (or, "in anticipation") in Mark 14:8. Theodoret explains that this word stands for "before the proper time she gave *myron* to my body." Hence, what was done by Mary presents no contradiction, for "what was done to the Lord before the time is done to those being baptized at the proper time." The use of oil in the prebaptismal anointing and the use of *myron* in the postbaptismal anointing have different meanings. The significance of oil, as in the old anointings of the Jews, was "so that we might become christs." The *myron* is a memorial of what the Lord himself considered an anointing for burial (PG 6.1389C-1392A).

In his *Commentary on Hebrews* 6:1, Theodoret relates believing with baptism and appears to connect the laying on of hands with the baptism itself and not with a separate act:

> Those who have believed submit to holy baptism, . . . and through the hand of the priest they receive the grace of the Spirit, and by holy baptism . . . they await the common resurrection of all and the coming judgment. (PG 82.716)

Mark the Deacon, *Life of Porphyry*

The *Life of Porphyry* ascribed to Mark the Deacon records events of the late fourth and early fifth century, but the dependence of the present form of the Greek text on Theodoret among other things indicates that our surviving Greek text was written after the mid–fifth century at the earliest.[3] I include the work in this chapter because the Greek text is the form in which it is best known, but there is an internal indication that the original may have been in Syriac (chap. 68). A recent study finds evidence that the Syriac source of the Georgian version was translated from a Greek text like our Greek text,[4] but the latter likely contains interpolations not in the original work.

The text contains numerous accounts of conversions to Christianity. The first of these occurs in chapter 21, where 78 men, 35 women, and 14 children are sealed with the seal of Christ. Although "to seal" could be used of baptism, the usage here and elsewhere in the work seems to refer to signing with the cross for admission to the catechumenate. This is clearly the usage in chapters 30–31. A pregnant woman through the prayer of Porphyry gave safe delivery of the child, who was in breach position. The people, impressed with the outcome, were commanded to believe on Christ. Porphyry then sealed them and made them catechumens. After instructing them, he baptized them, together with the mother and child. These 64 persons are identified as "they that were enlightened," the author's designation for those who were baptized.

Seven days after the empress Eudoxia gave birth to Emperor Theodosius II they were given the seal of the cross (chap. 45). The young emperor was then said to have been baptized or enlightened, the two words used interchangeably (46–47). There is reference to the white garment worn for a week after the baptism (49). This and the preceding account clearly include infant baptisms along with predominantly adult baptisms.

Chapters 56–57 tell the story of the conversion of a shipowner from Arian to Catholic Christianity (referred to in chap. 35). When he renounced the Arian heresy, the bishops on board the ship sealed him again (language used twice — 56 and 57), prayed with him, and had him partake of the divine mysteries. It has been argued that "sealed again" meant "rebaptized," or if only the giving of the sign of the cross, then the communion was in anticipation of his orthodox baptism. The usage of

---

3. There is an old English translation of a corrupt Greek text by G. F. Hill, *Mark the Deacon: Life of Porphyry, Bishop of Gaza* (Oxford: Clarendon, 1913). A critical Greek text and French translation was done by Henri Gregoire and M.-A. Kugener, *Vie de Porphyre, évêque de Gaza* (Paris: Belles lettres, 1930). An English translation taking into account the quite different Georgian version, translated from Syriac, is being prepared by Claudia Rapp and Jeff Childers for the series Translated Texts for Historians.

4. J. W. Childers, "The *Life of Porphyry*: Clarifying the Relationship of the Greek and Georgian Versions through the Study of New Testament Citations," in J. W. Childers and D. C. Parker, eds., *Transmission and Reception: New Testament Text-Critical and Exegetical Studies,* Texts and Studies, Third Series 4 (Piscataway, NJ: Gorgias, 2006), pp. 150-178.

sealed elsewhere in the work, however, argues that we should read this in a straightforward way, as accepting the person's Arian baptism and receiving him into communion by the sign of the cross, prayer, and eucharist.

In chapter 62 there are 31 men and 7 women who believed, were "added to the fold of Christ," and were sealed. In chapter 74 Porphyry received those that desired to be enlightened and instructed them before baptizing them; 300 were added to the fold of Christ. Chapter 85 refers to certain persons but lately enlightened. In chapter 91 there are those who "repented and were enlightened."

Chapter 100 gives a fairly full account concerning a girl of 14, her aunt, and her grandmother that shows the normal sequence and terminology of the document. Bishop Porphyry sealed them with the sign of the cross. Then there was a time of prayer and the instruction of catechumens, and this was followed by baptism. This account seems to certify the interpretation given above of sealing and to outline the normal pattern of conversion according to the author's various accounts: believing/repenting, reception into the catechumenate, prayer and instruction, baptism/enlightenment.

Pseudo-Dionysius the Areopagite

Around the year 500 there flourished a writer in Greek, probably of Syrian origin, whose works became enormously influential in Christian mystical theology. He put forth his writings under the name of Paul's convert in Athens, Dionysius, a member of the court of the Areopagus. The forgery succeeded, and the claim to the authority of a learned and philosophical convert of Paul's added to the writings' influence. Pseudo-Dionysius was much indebted to Neoplatonism, and he makes much of the themes of illumination and divinization. His *Ecclesiastical Hierarchy,* chapter 2, includes a description of the rite of baptism and a contemplation on its ceremonies.[5] The rite of baptism described by Pseudo-Dionysius contains the elements characteristic of its observance in Greek and eastern churches in the fifth century.

The "starting point" toward the goal of union with God is "to dispose our souls to hear the sacred words as receptively as possible" and to accept the "most divine and sacred regeneration [ἀναγεννήσεως]" (*Ecclesiastical Hierarchy* 2.1). Catechumens formed a distinct group. The deacons gave them instruction in the scriptures, and degrees of progress on the road to sanctity are described (6.1.1). Catechumens are like fetuses not yet brought to the divine birth (3.3.6). They, like the penitents and those possessed, could listen to the singing of the Psalms and the reading of the scriptures but were excluded from the eucharistic liturgy (3.3.6).

5. I quote the translation by Colm Luibheid, *Pseudo-Dionysius: The Complete Works,* Classics of Western Spirituality (New York: Paulist, 1987), pp. 200-208. See also Thomas L. Campbell, *The Ecclesiastical Hierarchy* (Washington, DC: University Press of America, 1981). Victor Saxer, *Les rites de l'initiation chrétienne du IIe au VIe siècle: Esquisse historique et signification d'après leur principaux témoins* (Spoleto: Centro italiano di studi sull'alto medioevo, 1988), pp. 451-464. Paul L. Gavrilyuk, "Did Pseudo-Dionysius Live in Constantinople?," *Vigiliae Christianae* 62 (2008): 505-514, argues on the basis of the similarities in the baptismal ritual (see my pp. 752-755) that the author lived in Constantinople.

A person came to a member of the church (an "initiate") and requested that he take charge of his training and serve as a sponsor in bringing the candidate to the "hierarch" (bishop — 2.2.2-5). The latter gives thanks and prostrates himself before God, who calls and saves (2.2.3). The candidate confesses sin and receives instruction in the divine life. The hierarch asks the "postulant" if he wishes to live the "God-possessed life." On the reply, "Yes," the hierarch "places his hand upon his head, marks him with the sign of the cross," and instructs the priests to enroll the person and the sponsor (2.2.5; 2.3.4 on the spiritual meaning of what is described in this paragraph).

After prayer a deacon removes the person's garments (so he is "naked and barefoot") and turns him to the west (2.2.6; 5.1.6). The hierarch has the candidate stretch out his hands in a gesture of abhorrence, and "Three times he bids him breathe his rejection of Satan and his abjuration of him. Three times he speaks the words and the other repeats them" (2.2.6). A deacon then turns the person to the east. The hierarch commands the candidate "with eyes raised and hands lifted to heaven" "to submit to Christ" (2.2.6; 2.3.5 on the meaning of the renunciation and "sacred vows" "to look up to the divine Light"). These words and actions represent the "sustained effort" necessary "to reach the One" (2.3.5).

The candidate three times makes a profession of faith, and the hierarch prays, blesses, and lays on hands (2.2.7). The deacons completely strip him, and the priests bring the holy oil. It had been consecrated by prayer (4.2). "The ointment is made up of a mixture of fragrant substances" (4.3.4). The bishop begins the process of anointing by making a threefold sign of the cross, and the priests anoint the rest of the body (2.2.7). This prebaptismal anointing of the body prepares the person as an athlete for "the sacred contests" (2.3.6).

The bishop sanctifies the water by pouring the holy oil into it three times, each time in the form of the sign of the cross (2.3.6). This action intimates that one is baptized into Jesus' death (4.3.10). The priests bring the person to the water and hand him over to the bishop, who is standing on a more elevated spot. The hierarch "immerses three times the initiate." "Each time the initiate is plunged into the water and emerges, the hierarch invokes the three persons of the divine blessedness" (2.3.6).[6]

The priests take the newly baptized to his sponsor, and together they reclothe him and bring him back to the bishop. The white garments put on the baptized person mean that light is to shine through all his life (2.3.8).

"Using the most potently divine ointment he makes the sign of the cross on him and proclaims him ready to participate in the sacredly initiating eucharist" (2.2.7). The postbaptismal anointing "joins the initiates together with the Spirit of the Deity" (2.3.8) and is associated with the coming of the "divine Spirit" (4.3.11). The description of the rite of anointing the deceased recalls the double baptismal anoint-

---

6. Pseudo-Dionysius speaks of pouring oil in the water; if he had understood baptism as an infusion of water he could have used the same word for baptism, but instead he speaks clearly of plunging the candidate into the water.

ings: "The first participation in this sacred symbol, the oil of anointing, was given to the initate during the sacred divine birth, before the actual baptism and after he had exchanged his old clothes for the new" (7.3.8).

One was now called to "the most sacred eucharist," and granted communion in "the mysteries which will perfect him" (2.3.8). The "sacred ointment" consecrated the eucharistic altar as it did the baptismal water (4.3.12). The eucharist is the "sacrament of sacraments" (3.1).

Pseudo-Dionysius describes the eucharist as "the rite of the synaxis" in chapter 3 and "the rite of the ointment" in chapter 4. This departure from the liturgical order perhaps reflects an order of priority and even the later addition of the ointment to the baptismal ceremony.

The ceremony was clearly designed for persons able to speak and act for themselves. Pseudo-Dionysius, however, accepted infant baptism and offered an explanation for it.

> You might say, however, that what could really earn the ridicule of the impious is the fact that infants, despite their inability to understand the divine things, are nevertheless admitted to that sacrament of sacred divine-birth and to the sacred symbol of the divine communion. . . . And a further cause for laughter is the practice whereby others speak the ritual renunciations and the sacred promises on behalf of the infants. (7.3.11)

Pseudo-Dionysius reflects infant communion as well as infant baptism, a consistent position. He attributes the objections to infant baptism to the "impious" (pagans, or other Christians?), but the fact of his dealing with the question indicates that this was a real objection, to which he devotes an appendix to the section under consideration. That the objections may come from Christians is perhaps indicated by Pseudo-Dionysius continuing with an explanation of how the bishop is to refute the objections.

Pseudo-Dionysius appeals to tradition in support of baptizing children but on the condition that they will be raised in holiness.

> Our divine leaders decided it was a good thing to admit children, though on the condition that the parents of the child would entrust him to some good teacher who is himself initiated in the divine things and who could provide religious teaching as the child's spiritual father and as the sponsor of salvation. Anyone thus committed to raise the child up along the way of a holy life is asked by the hierarch to agree to the ritual renunciations and to speak the words of promise. (7.3.11)

Pseudo-Dionysius thus reflects the importance fourth-century church leaders had placed on the words of repentance and faith as integral to the baptismal ceremony. He proceeds to note the further words of reproach that it is really the sponsor who is being initiated. He responds:

[The sponsor] does not say, "I am making the renunciations and the promises for the child," but "the child himself is assigned and enrolled." In effect what is said is this: "I promise that when this child can understand sacred truth I shall educate him and shall raise him up by my teaching in such a way that he will renounce all the temptations of the devil, that he will bind himself to the sacred promises and will bring them to fruit." (7.3.11)

Although affirming that the child makes the renunciations and promises, the author does not advocate the fiction that the parents or God-parents are speaking for the child but explains that they are promising to train the child so that at an appropriate age the child will make his/her own renunciation of the devil and promise of faithfulness.[7]

Under the heading of "Contemplation" Pseudo-Dionysius sets forth the meaning of baptism.[8] The subtitles of sections 1 and 2 of the chapter on baptism are headed "The Rite of Illumination" and "The Mystery of Illumination," and in the context of the author's mystical theology illumination is an important concept. The theme of light is developed in relation to baptism in *Ecclesiastical Hierarchy* 2.3.3-4. It is the privilege of the "divine hierarch" to enlighten the initiates (2.3.3-4). Baptism "introduces the light," so it is "the source of all divine illumination" and is given "the designation of what it achieves, that is, illumination" (3.1). Illumination will bring persons "to perfection" (3.3.6).

The author's most frequent designation in the chapter, however, is "divine birth [θεία γέννησις],"[9] but he does not elaborate this theme.

Rather, the divine birth is presented as a purification. It is a "physical cleansing by water," a "cleansing of the whole body by water," but the accompanying "holy instruction" also "teaches a holy way of life" and thus together there is proposed "a complete purification of an evil way of life" (2.3.1). The perceptible ceremonies are to lead the way to spiritual things (2.3.2).

The person dies to sin in baptism so that "one could say mystically that he shares in the death of Christ himself" (2.3.6). The complete covering of the body by water is an image of death and burial. The triple immersion and emersion imitates Jesus' three days and nights in the tomb (2.3.7).

---

7. For infants who died without baptism, see Jane Baun, "The Fate of Babies Dying before Baptism in Byzantium," in Diana Wood, ed., *The Church and Childhood*, Studies in Church History 31 (Oxford: Blackwell, 1994), pp. 113-125; chap. 37, n. 11.

8. R. Roques, "Le sens du baptême selon le Pseudo-Denys," *Irénikon* 31 (1958): 427-449.

9. *Ecclesiastical Hierarchy* 2.1 (twice and "divine regeneration" once — see above); 2.3.1 ("sacred divine birth"); 2.3.8; also 3.1; 3.3.6; 4.3.10 (twice) and 11; 7.3.8.

47. Baptism in the Messalian Controversy

Messalianism

The name "Messalians" is from the Syriac for "Those Who Pray" or "People of Prayer"; in Greek their name was "Euchites." The persons involved represented more of a tendency than an organized sect. The movement began in northern Mesopotamia (North Syria) in ascetic circles in the late fourth century and spread to Asia Minor. The Messalians, according to their opponents in the orthodox church, taught an extreme asceticism and heightened spiritual experience. They held that only intense and ceaseless prayer could eliminate the passions by which demons held power over a person; hence, they did not work and lived on alms so as to devote themselves to prayer. Their opponents charged that their views denigrated the effects of baptism, for they said that the demon was chased away from a person by prayer and not by baptism.

The study of Messalianism has been complicated by uncertainty in the attribution of authorship to certain treatises and by the paucity of works supporting the Messalian practices. The *Homilies* attributed in the manuscript tradition to Macarius of Egypt or to Symeon of Mesopotamia (now designated Pseudo-Macarius) have been central to modern studies (see further below). These studies have brought some clarity and precision to what Messalianism meant in its historical context, but many points remain unclear.[1]

---

1. J. Gribomont, "Le Dossier des origines du Messalianisme," in J. Fontaine and C. Kannengiesser, eds., *Epektasis: Mélanges patristiques offerts au Cardinal Jean Daniélou* (Paris: Beauchesne, 1972), pp. 611-625; Columba Stewart, *"Working the Earth of the Heart": The Messalian Controversy in History, Texts, and Language to AD 431* (Oxford: Clarendon, 1991); K. Fitschen, *Messalianismus und Antimessalianismus* (Göttingen: Vandenhoeck & Ruprecht, 1998); Marcus Plested, *The Macarian Legacy: The Place of Macarius-Symeon in the Eastern Christian Tradition* (Oxford: Oxford University Press, 2004). Brief introductions in English are by Andrew Louth, "Messalianism and Pelagianism," *Studia patristica* 17.1 (1982): 127-135, and Paul Blowers, "The Bible and Spiritual Doctrine: Some Controversies within the Early Eastern Christian Ascetic Tradition," in Paul Blowers, ed., *The Bible in Greek Christian Antiquity* (Notre Dame: University of Notre Dame Press, 1997), pp. 229-255 (237-246 on the Messalian

The late compilation by John of Damascus, *Heresies*, in chapter 80 (PG 94.728-737) contains "Summaries of the Impious Doctrine of the Messalians, Taken from Their Book." The book was perhaps their lost *Asceticon*, or excerpts from it prepared for and condemned at the Third Ecumenical Council, Ephesus in 431. Or, alternatively, the *Asceticon* was the name given to the writings of Pseudo-Macarius, and the excerpts were drawn directly from him. More likely, however, the book was compiled by Messalians under the influence of Pseudo-Macarius and contained Macarian material, from which opponents made excerpts.[2] If drawn directly or indirectly from Pseudo-Macarius, they represent propositions circulating at an early phase of the controversy, although the form taken in the condemnations belong to a later stage. Items four through seven in John's list of erroneous teachings relate to baptism.

4. That baptism does not make a man perfect, nor does participation in the sacred mysteries cleanse the soul, but only prayer, to which they sedulously apply themselves.
5. That man is all bespattered with sin, even after undergoing baptism.[3]
6. That it is not by baptism that the believer receives the true and incorruptible garment, but by prayer.
7. That it is one's duty to obtain freedom from the passions, and to partake of the Holy Spirit by actual sensation and with full assurance [ἐν πάσῃ αἰσθήσει καὶ πληροφορίᾳ].[4]

These points focus the issues in the Messalian controversy as pertaining to baptism and will be found in the earlier documents that are of concern in this chapter. The

---

Controversy) — both with additional bibliography. A summary of this chapter in E. Ferguson, "Baptism in the Messalian Controversy," *Studia Patristica* 46 (2010): 353-58.

2. On the *Asceticon* see Fitschen, *Messalianismus*, pp. 45, 48, 86, 88. He suggests that Messalians in Asia Minor/Pamphylia prepared the *Asceticon* as an ascetic handbook in the tradition of exegesis of Ps.-Macarius begun by Adelphius (p. 218; cf. 214, an early collection from Ps.-Macarius strongly shaped into Messalian form).

3. The Syriac *Liber graduum*, generally identified with Messalianism or its milieu, says baptism does not eliminate vices, but there remains a deposit of sin that can coexist with the Spirit in the baptized — Columba Stewart, "Working the Earth," p. 89, with reference to col. 344.4-5. Klaus Fitschen, *Messalianismus*, pp. 108-128, has an extended comparison of the *Liber graduum*, which he dates in the first half of the fourth century, with Messalianism, especially pointing out differences.

4. Translation by George L. Marriott, "The Messalians; and the Discovery of Their Ascetic Book," *Harvard Theological Review* 19 (1926): 191-198 (193-194). The similar list in the earlier (c. 600) Timothy of Constantinople (PG 86.45-52) states: "They [Messalians] say that holy baptism contributes nothing to the driving out of this demon; nor is holy baptism sufficient to cut out the roots of sins that have coexisted from the beginning in people." Stewart, "Working the Earth," Appendix 2, pp. 244-277, has a "Synopsis of Anti-Messalian Lists" in Theodoret of Cyrus, Timothy of Constantinople, and John of Damascus (cited passage, pp. 247, 251), with discussion of contents, pp. 58-65; cf. Fitschen, *Messalianismus*, 61-88. Timothy's list may be associated with a synod at Constantinople in 426 and John's with material prepared for Ephesus in 431 (Stewart, pp. 54-55; overlapping but different conclusions on the relation of the anti-Messalian lists to one another are found in Fitschen, pp. 87-88).

phrase translated "by actual sensation and with full assurance" (ἐν πάσῃ αἰσθήσει καὶ πληροφορίᾳ) occurs repeatedly in the literature associated with Messalianism.[5] The "garment" was a popular image in Syriac Christianity for the blessings conferred in baptism (chaps. 30 and 31). The denigration of baptism, stated or implied by Messalian teaching, was a major objection raised by the movement's opponents.

The first written notice of the Messalians comes from Ephraim the Syrian, *Against Heresies* 22.4 between 363 and 373, who simply lists them with other heresies.[6] Shortly thereafter (377) Epiphanius of Salamis also notes the early phase of Messalianism.[7] His main treatment, *Panarion* 80, seems not to be well acquainted with them, for he associates their practices with those of non-Christian groups. He records some of their practices — praying, chanting, renouncing the world, not working but begging, not fasting, wearing sackcloth and long hair but cutting off their beards, abstaining from sexual relations — but does not give their reasons for them. In particular, he says nothing about baptism in his account. Thereafter the Messalians were condemned by several church councils, beginning at Side and Antioch (between 383 and 394).[8]

The fifth-century author Theodoret of Cyrus (chap. 46), who had access to sources in Antioch, reports in his *Church History* (written in the 440s) the rise of the Messalians in the late fourth century but knows them at an intermediate stage of development. He devotes a chapter in his *Fables of Heretics* (A.D. 453) to "Messalians, Euchites, and Enthusiasts." He reports as follows:

> They say baptism . . . removes the judgment of former sins but does not cut off the root of sin. Unceasing prayer pulls up by the roots the source of sin and drives out of the soul the evil demon assigned from the beginning. For they say a demon immediately accompanies each person who is born and this demon excites the per-

---

5. Stewart, *"Working the Earth"*, studies these words in Pseudo-Macarius: πληροφορία, πληροφορέω ("assurance" associated with faith, but more often "fullness" as descriptive of experienced perfection, which is the goal achieved in confidence of hope — pp. 97-116); αἴσθησις, αἰσθάνομαι (intense "feeling" of grace working in the soul — pp. 116-138). He points out that Ps-Macarius's favorite combination of words for the apprehension and experience of divine reality in the soul is αἴσθησις and πληροφορία (p. 155); cf. Fitschen, *Messalianismus*, pp. 190-193.

6. For a fuller history of the controversy see Stewart, "Working the Earth," pp. 12-52, and Fitschen, *Messalianismus*, pp. 18-60. Stewart marks out three phases in the controversy: (1) emergence to public view in texts from the 370s; (2) condemnation by local councils in the 380s and 390s; (3) intense anti-Messalian activity in 420s-430s ratified by the synod at Constantinople in 426 and the ecumenical council at Ephesus in 431. Fitschen, *Messalianismus*, p. 19, puts Ephraim's reference before 363.

7. His *Ancoratus* 13.6, perhaps written before 374 (an outline of the *Panarion*), also notes them. *Panarion* 75 calls a disciple of Eustathius who practiced asceticism a Messalian. Fitschen, *Messalianismus*, pp. 89-92, discusses Epiphanius's report; pp. 95-96 give a reconstruction of the pre-history of Messalianism.

8. Most historians put the synod at Side first, because Photius mentions it first (*Library* 52), but Stewart, "Working the Earth," pp. 24-39, thinks that the synod at Antioch may have preceded, and Fitschen, *Messalianismus*, p. 36, concurs; at any rate Flavian of Antioch (below) was the key ecclesiastical figure in the condemnation of Messalianism in the second phase of the controversy (380s-390s).

son to improper deeds. Neither baptism nor any thing else is able to drive this demon from the soul, only the activity of prayer.[9]

Bishop Flavian of Antioch (381-404) judged this teaching to be heresy.

Theodoret records a meeting of Flavian with one of the Messalian leaders, Adelphius,[10] whose position was as follows:

> No benefit accrues to the recipients of holy baptism, in that it is only by earnest prayer that the in-dwelling demon is driven out, for that every one born into the world derives from his first father slavery to the demons just as he does his nature; but that when these are driven away, then comes the Holy Spirit giving sensible and visible signs of his presence, at once freeing the body from the impulse of the passions and wholly ridding the soul of its inclination to the worse; with the result that there is no more need for fasting that restrains the body, nor of teaching or training that bridles it and instructs it how to walk aright.[11]

Flavian (and Theodoret) considered this position self-condemned. Viewing the soul as possessed by demons through inheritance from Adam, baptism as only a prayer, and the coming of the Holy Spirit as occurring later and recognized in an experiential way were extremes that opponents of the Messalians sought to correct or modify.

Severus of Antioch, about 600, knew of the proceedings at Antioch against Adelphius.

> That the Messalians think that abominable idea [of substantive indwelling evil] is known from the memoranda which [were] written against Adelphius. In them is found a notice from Euprepius, bishop of Paltus, to Flavian, who was bishop of Antioch after the great Meletius. In it are written these things: "They say that after Adam transgressed the commandment, evil was by nature like an entity; that by no other way than by prayer can a man be freed from evil; baptism is for purifying men, for the sins done by the living, but does not extinguish the source of evil thoughts; prayer frees from the sufferings of [evil] thoughts.[12]

The convergence in content of these statements gives a basis for judging the extent of Messalian content in other sources.

---

9. Theodoret, *Fables of Heretics* 4.11 (PG 83.429B-C). For baptism as a razor that shaves but does not cut out the roots, see Fitschen, *Messalianismus*, pp. 64-65. Theodoret, *Religious History* 3.16, says of the monk Marcianus that he completely rejected those called Euchites, who hid under a monastic form the disease of the Manichaeans (an association likely made because of the activity of evil in a person).

10. Fitschen, *Messalianismus*, pp. 25, 27-28, 342, identifies Adelphius as the one who gave amorphous groups of ascetics their profile and doctrinal basis.

11. Theodoret, *Church History* 4.10. Translation by Blomfield Jackson in *Nicene and Post-Nicene Fathers* (repr. Peabody: Hendrickson, 1994), Second Series, Vol. 3, p. 115. Fitschen, *Messalianismus*, p. 68, considers it highly probable that Theodoret's sources included Flavian's *Hypomnemata*, compiled in connection with the hearing on Adelphius.

12. Translation by Stewart, "Working the Earth," p. 35.

Pseudo-Macarius: A Moderate Voice

The writings ascribed to "Macarius" probably come from the 380s and show contacts with both Syria and Asia Minor. They survive in four collections of logoi and homilies, giving the instructions of a spiritual elder to his disciples. Logia 1 of Collection I is the *Great Letter,* a treatise on the Christian life. The best-known collection is II, fifty *Spiritual Homilies* in Greek. Collection III has forty-three logoi, about half unique to it. Collection IV has twenty-six logoi, wholly contained in Collection I.[13] In the author's thought, there is a progression from a heart possessed by evil (because of Adam's disobedience), to a heart in which both sin and grace live, to finally a heart from which sin has been expelled by a cooperation of human will and the divine Spirit. The primary concern is with experiential reality.[14]

The relation of Pseudo-Macarius to Messalianism is formulated in different ways by recent scholars. Pseudo-Macarius was a moderate spiritual teacher acquainted with and influenced by some features of Messalianism but correcting its extreme expressions.[15] Or, alternately, the *Homilies* perhaps derived from Symeon the Mesopotamian, a leader of the Messalian movement of the fourth century, and were then purged of extreme Messalian errors and attributed to the holy and orthodox Macarius of Egypt.[16] Or, more likely, Pseudo-Macarius came from the same ascetic milieu that produced Messalianism but preceded its more extreme developments, which drew from him.[17] Regardless of ancestry, the spiritual teaching of

---

13. Stewart, *"Working the Earth,"* pp. 70-74; Plested, *The Macarian Legacy,* pp. 9-12; Fitschen, *Messalianismus,* pp. 145-175, who gives a history of scholarship on the authorship of Ps.-Macarius (pp. 145-158), suggests Edessa, Samosata, or Melitene as satisfying the requirements of location for the author (p. 170), and dates his work between 360 and 390 (170).

14. Stewart, *"Working the Earth,"* pp. 74-75.

15. John Meyendorff, "Messalianism or Anti-Messalianism: A Fresh Look at the Macarian Problem," in Patrick Granfield and Josef F. Jungmann, eds., *Kyriakon: Festschrift Johannes Quasten* (Münster: Aschendorff, 1970), Vol. 2, pp. 585-590; Gribomont, "Le dossier," pp. 611-625 — the *Homilies* borrowed from Messalianism but were not Messalian; Plested, *The Macarian Legacy,* pp. 46-49, 57-58, 255-256 — Macarius contradicted the Messalian propositions in Timothy of Constantinople and John of Damascus; his points of contact with Messalianism come from a shared ascetic milieu; and Macarius sought sympathetically to channel their energies into the broader church structures.

16. George A. Maloney, *Pseudo-Macarius: The Fifty Spiritual Homilies and the* Great Letter, Classics of Western Spirituality (New York: Paulist Press, 1992), pp. 8-9. His translation is quoted. It may be that Symeon of Mesopotamia was himself a more moderate Messalian than the position represented by the errors that drew conciliar condemnation.

17. Fitschen, *Messalianismus,* pp. 176-238, after an extensive comparison of Ps.-Macarius with the lists of Messalian propositions in John of Damascus and Timothy of Constantinople, concludes that the Messalians were a group that grew out of the ascetic context of Ps.-Macarius and shared and radicalized his views. Ps.-Macarius was no Messalian heresiarch or Messalian theologian; the leader and theologian of the Messalian movement was Adelphius of Edessa. Ps.-Macarius played a great role in the Messalian movement, but he was radically reinterpreted. He already knew some of the radical tendencies, represented by the "praying ones" noted by Ephraim and Epiphanius, that were reshaped later by Adelphius into Messalianism proper (pp. 218, 238, 342).

"Macarius" had great influence in eastern and western spirituality.[18] Fortunately for my purposes it is not necessary to disentangle the relationship of Pseudo-Macarius and Messalianism but only to select some of the accessible passages on baptism.[19]

The *Great Letter* stands at the head of Collection I. References to baptism in it are concentrated near its beginning. Baptism involved a confession of the Trinity. After referring to "the three hypostases of the one deity," Pseudo-Macarius states, "Even so in the holy mystery of baptism we piously confessed the good confession before many witnesses [1 Tim. 6:12]."[20] It brings to believers a down payment or pledge of the Lord's working:

> At the holy baptism of the blessed Trinity those who have believed receive the guarantee [ἀρραβῶνα] of the inexpressible activity of the Lord Jesus Christ for growth and progress of the perfect inheritance.[21]

Sincerity as well as faith is necessary to receive the Holy Spirit in baptism:

> The divine and comforting Spirit which was given to the apostles and through them to the only true church of God, having been supplied from the hour of baptism in many and various forms according to one's measure of faith, coexists with each person who comes with a sincere faith to baptism.[22]

John 3:5 continued to influence baptismal language: "The person born [γεννώμενος, or generated] from above of water and the Spirit ought not to remain in the childhood state of spiritual growth."[23] Here is the special concern of the author. The Holy Spirit given in baptism as a seal is the means of spiritual growth: "[The apostle Paul] implores those counted worthy of the seal of the Spirit of promise through baptism to make growth in spiritual progress."[24] Pseudo-Macarius thus employs traditional

---

18. His vocabulary and themes of his spirituality are set in the context of other Greek Christian writers and shown to have more affinities with the Syriac tradition by Stewart, *"Working the Earth,"* pp. 70-240. Fitschen, *Messalianismus*, p. 14, questions Stewart's basic thesis that Syriac vocabulary and imagery were misunderstood in the Greek world, although finding his outline of the history and his word studies helpful. Plested, *The Macarian Legacy*, traces the Macarian influence in Mark the Monk, Diadochus of Photice, Abba Isaiah, and Maximus the Confessor.

19. V. Desprez, "Le baptême chez le Pseudo-Macaire," *Ecclesia orans* 5 (1988): 121-155.

20. Translations from the *Great Letter* are my own from the edition of Werner Jaeger, *Two Rediscovered Works of Ancient Christian Literature: Gregory of Nyssa and Macarius* (Leiden: Brill, 1954), here p. 234, lines 18-20.

21. *Great Letter* (p. 236, 1-3). Collection III, 28.3, also refers to the *arrabon*: "The soul that lives a virgin life in Christ, even if it receives the *arrabon* through baptism . . . and after baptism immediately receives many gifts, . . . should not be counted worthy of union with the incorruptible bridegroom . . . and does not recognize the wedding garment in the spiritual gifts, but in the adoption itself in which is unchangeable love. Therefore, having the *arrabōn* of baptism, you have the perfect talent" (Greek text in Fitschen, *Messalianismus*, p. 189).

22. *Great Letter* (p. 236, 6-11).

23. *Great Letter* (p. 236, 18-20).

24. *Great Letter* (p. 248, 14-16).

baptismal concepts, even though his special interest is in the struggle to make progress in the spiritual life after baptism.

The fifty *Spiritual Homilies*, Collection II, likewise lack the negative, or restricted, view of baptism charged against the Messalians. The impression from these homilies that Macarius marginalizes the sacraments is corrected by the other collections (including the *Great Letter*).[25]

Pseudo-Macarius, nevertheless, does employ the language of rebirth in a distinctive way in reference to the Holy Spirit. The Lord, in fulfillment of the history of salvation, came to earth and died on the cross, "so that he might beget from himself and his very own nature children from his Spirit," that is, those "born from his seed of the Godhead." Those who are willing are "born of the womb of the Spirit of the Godhead."[26]

Pseudo-Macarius declares that "By the power of the Spirit and the spiritual regeneration, man not only comes to the measure of the first Adam, but he also reaches a greater state than he possessed," for one is divinized.[27] In most patristic writers, such a statement would refer to baptism, but in the case of Pseudo-Macarius the claim to a superiority over Adam through divinization indicates that a more extended spiritual experience was in mind.[28]

The true priesthood, according to Pseudo-Macarius's appropriation of a central motif of Syriac Christianity, has now passed from the Jewish priests to the church: "Now there is a baptism of fire and the Spirit and we are given a certain circumcision of the heart. The divine and heavenly Spirit abides within the mind."[29] Another kinship with the traditions of Syriac Christianity is the numerous images of Christ's *descensus ad inferos;* the descent was a dipping, as in baptism.[30]

Nevertheless, these perfect ones, as long as they live in the flesh, are subject to temptation. Pseudo-Macarius refers to the presence of sin after baptism in a manner similar to the view mentioned by John of Damascus (item 5 quoted above). He is correcting those who saw baptism as annulling the continuing power of sin:

> But if you insist that through the coming of Christ sin was condemned and after baptism evil has no more power of suggestion within the human heart, then you ignore the fact that from the coming of the Lord up to this day the many who have been baptized, have they not, thought evil things at some time? . . . Or do we not find that after baptism many commit many sins and many live in error?[31]

---

25. Plested, *The Macarian Legacy*, pp. 38, 85.
26. *Homilies* 30.2 (Maloney, *Pseudo-Macarius*, pp. 190-191).
27. *Homilies* 26.2 (Maloney, *Pseudo-Macarius*, p. 164).
28. Fitschen, *Messalianismus*, pp. 188, 195-196; see n. 34 below. The view of two stages in which the Spirit works (in baptism and in the later perfecting of a person) could have been a modification of Messalianism or a teaching developed in a radical way by Messalians.
29. *Homilies* 26.23 (Maloney, *Pseudo-Macarius*, p. 172).
30. Martin Illert, "Zum descensus ad inferos bei Makarios," *Vigiliae christianae* 53 (1999): 321-322.
31. *Homilies* 15.14 (Maloney, *Pseudo-Macarius*, p. 113). Plested, *The Macarian Legacy*, p. 256, points out that Mark the Monk and Diadochus revised Macarius's theory of the coexistence of sin and grace in the baptized person.

The author, however, worked for a different result.

In a contrast of things done under the Law with things under Christ, the author says:

> They were manifested as the people of God from the circumcision. But here the people of God, being very special, receive the sign of circumcision inwardly in their heart. For the heavenly knife cuts away the excess portion of the mind, that is, the impure uncircumcision of sin. With them was a baptism sanctifying the flesh, but with us there is a baptism of the Holy Spirit and fire [Matt. 3:11].[32]

The passage may be read as saying that Christian baptism involves the Holy Spirit and fire in addition to the water,[33] which alone Jewish baptisms had; but in other statements (next paragraph) it seems that the baptism of the Holy Spirit is separated from water baptism.

Pseudo-Macarius uses the language of "baptism of the Holy Spirit" to describe the progressive inward purification from the roots of sinfulness effected by the indwelling Holy Spirit in response to the individual's pursuit of the love of Christ. The end result is that "Christians, having been baptized in the Holy Spirit, have no experience of evil."[34]

More explicit affirmations of the value of water baptism occur in the other Macarian collections.

> God gave the Holy Spirit to the holy catholic church, ordaining that he be present at the holy altar and in the water of holy baptism. . . . [F]rom baptism, the altar, the eucharist of bread, and from all the mystical worship that is in the church, believing hearts might be powerfully acted upon by the Holy Spirit. . . . [And the Holy Spirit is present in] all the mystagogy of holy baptism.[35]

Macarius related baptism to the forgiveness of sins and the gift of the Holy Spirit. The latter, however, was granted according to the recipient's measure of faith, and so there was a progressive manifestation of baptismal grace:

> The grace already laid down at baptism wishes to visit every soul richly and desires that the perfection of the divine power be given speedily — but participation

---

32. *Homilies* 47.1-2 (Maloney, *Pseudo-Macarius*, p. 232).

33. For the Syriac *Liber graduum* 12.1.4 visible baptism may also be Spirit and fire baptism — Fitschen, *Messalianismus*, p. 126.

34. *Homilies* 43.3 (Maloney, *Pseudo-Macarius*, p. 220; see his introduction, p. 19); cf. Fitschen, *Messalianismus*, p. 188. Fritschen thinks that Ps.-Macarius, in contrast to Hieronymus of Jerusalem (below), by "new birth" did not mean baptism but an act on the way to perfection that is not imparted to all the baptized and indeed has nothing to do with baptism (p. 265). This is an overstatement and overlooks the use of John 3:5 in reference to baptism in the *Great Letter*. K. T. Ware, "Baptism and the Ascetic Life in Mark the Monk," *Studia patristica* 10 (1970): 441-452 (p. 449), concludes that Ps.-Macarius in the *Homilies* seems to mean by being born of the Spirit not sacramental baptism but a more advanced stage of "spiritual" baptism.

35. Collection I, 52.1.4-5, quoted by Plested, *The Macarian Legacy*, pp. 39, 40.

in grace comes about according to the varying measure of faith and piety of each. [The grace of baptism] grants forgiveness of sins to all equally, but grants the capacity to receive the Spirit according to the measure of faith, waiting for and encouraging all men to come, through progress in the virtues and an excellent manner of life . . . , to perfect liberation from the passions and the complete and active indwelling of the Holy Spirit.[36]

Pseudo-Macarius, therefore, posits a gift of the Spirit at water baptism and a future (progressive) working of the Spirit that perfects the person who pursues spirituality and that can be described in baptismal language.

Diadochus of Photice: A Later Moderate Voice

Diadochus was bishop of Photice in Greece after 451 (but before 457) until his death, perhaps 468 but before 486. His principal literary work is *One Hundred Chapters on Spiritual Perfection*, on which rests his importance as a spiritual teacher in eastern Christianity.[37]

Diadochus shows a number of points of contact with Pseudo-Macarius.[38] Some scholars see Diadochus's spirituality as primarily under the influence of Evagrius and find his teachings to be directed against Pseudo-Macarius. Others place him as a forerunner of a reformed Messalianism and hold that the influence of Pseudo-Macarius on him was more important than that of Evagrius. It may be that both Evagrius and Pseudo-Macarius were known by him and that he attempted a synthesis of elements from both.[39]

Diadochus refuted the views of those who depreciated the value of baptism because evil continued to be at work in human beings after baptism. These opponents

---

36. Collection I, 25.2.4-5 — quoted by Plested, *The Macarian Legacy*, pp. 86-87.

37. Édouard des Places, *Diadoque de Photicé: Oeuvres spirituelles*, 3rd edition, Sources chrétiennes 5 (Paris: Cerf, 1966). I have not seen J. Rutherford, *One Hundred Practical Texts of Perception and Spiritual Discernment from Diadochos of Photike: Text, Translation and Commentary* (Belfast, 2000).

38. Édouard des Places, "Diadoque de Photice et le Messalianisme," in Patrick Granfield and Josef A. Jungmann, eds., *Kyriakon: Festschrift Johannes Quasten* (Münster: Aschendorff, 1970), Vol. 2, pp. 591-595, examines the differences between Diadochus and Ps.-Macarius. Fitschen, *Messalianismus*, pp. 257-264, notes his clear and numerous references to Ps.-Macarius but describes in detail his differences, including on baptism. Fitschen thinks he may not have had conflict with or dependence on Messalians and considers those he writes against not to be represented by a literary corpus but to be actual opponents (p. 259).

39. Kallistos Ware, "Diadochus von Photice," in *Theologische Realenzyklopädie* (Berlin: de Gruyter, 1981), Vol. 8, pp. 617-620 (p. 619); Theodoritus Polyzogopoulos, "Life and Writings of Diadochus of Photice," *Theologia* (1984): 772-800 — Diadochus mediates between Evagrius and Ps.-Macarius but is closer to the latter (p. 782); Plested, *The Macarian Legacy*, pp. 133-175, compares Macarius and Diadochus, finding the latter's spiritual teaching a creative synthesis of Macarius and Evagrius (p. 134) and his anti-Messalianism, "such as it is," to be a development and refinement of Macarius (p. 174).

are usually identified with Messalians but may have been others (see on Hieronymus of Jerusalem below). He was an enemy of extreme Messalianism but was under its influence. An indication of Diadochus's engagement with Messalian concerns is his frequent use of the phrase "in all spiritual perception and full assurance" (ἐν πάσῃ αἰσθήσει καὶ πληροφορίᾳ).[40]

For Diadochus baptism purifies wholly and perfectly from the guilt and stain of sin but does not heal the duality of the human will. On this point he agrees with Augustine (chap. 52) and differs from Mark the Monk (below). With the latter he shares the view that through baptism the devil is driven from the depth of the soul and grace is hidden in it. When by right use of free will one cooperates with grace, this indwelling grace comes to consciousness.[41]

Diadochus refers to those who think that grace and sin, the spirit of truth and the spirit of error, coexist in the mind of those who have been baptized. He replies that the scriptures and experience give a different understanding:

> Before baptism grace exhorts the soul to the good from the outside, but Satan hides in its depths. . . . But in the very hour in which we are regenerated [ἀναγεννώμεθα] the demon passes to the outside and grace is inside. Hence we find that, as at one time error ruled over the soul, even so after baptism the truth ruled over it. Nevertheless, after this Satan continues to work on the soul, . . . but he does not coexist with grace — may it not be thought! . . . God allows him to use the irrational pleasures. . . .
>
> Grace, as I said, from the very instant we are baptized is hidden in the very depth of the mind.[42]

Thus Diadochus gives a different explanation for the continuing presence of inclinations to sin in the baptized. Sin and grace have changed places at baptism. After baptism the demon attacks from without rather than ruling from within. This explana-

---

40. *Chapters* 40, 44, 68, 90, 91, 94. For Messalian use, see John of Damascus, *Heresies* 80.7 (above); cf. Ps.-Macarius, *Homilies* 26.2; 37.7. Des Places, *Diadoque de Photicé*, pp. 20-21 and 38, understands the phrase in Diadochus to mean "a total perception of fullness," seeing in πληροφορίᾳ more the meaning completeness than certitude; cf. n. 5 above. Polyzogopoulos, "Life and Writings of Diadochus of Photice," pp. 782-790, identifies his opponents as extreme Messalians.

41. Ware, "Diadochus," p. 618.

42. *Chapters* 76–77. Discussed in comparison to Ps.-Macarius by Fitschen, *Messalianismus*, p. 262, and Plested, *The Macarian Legacy*, pp. 150-156. The latter explains that Ps.-Macarius had used the theme of the coexistence of sin and grace in the intellect to contradict the Messalian view that grace drives out sin entirely. In contrast, Diadochus distinguished two gifts in baptism — the actuality of the renewal of the divine image by effacing sin and the potentiality of acquiring the divine likeness which requires our cooperation (i.e., forgiveness and the gift of the Holy Spirit — EF); Plested says this is a criticism of Ps.-Macarius's view of the coexistence of sin and grace and not a criticism of Messalianism. May it not be a criticism of both (although capable of harmonization with Ps.-Macarius), either a partial appropriation of Messalianism, or better an alternative explanation of the relation of grace and sin in the Christian prompted in part by Messalianism and revising Macarius?

tion corrects the Messalian error of confusing grace with feelings of grace and sin with temptations to sin.[43]

Moreover, Diadochus preserves the traditional meaning of baptism. Because of the effects of Adam's sin, he explains, "the holy Word of God became incarnate."

> He granted to us the water of salvation through his own baptism as God for regeneration [ἀναγέννησιν]. We are then regenerated [ἀναγεννώμεθα] through the water by the working of the Holy and Life-giving Spirit. Wherefore, if one comes to God with a complete inclination, we are immediately purified in soul and body, since the Holy Spirit dwells in us and puts sin to flight.[44]

He continues his polemic by claiming that it is impossible for two opposite entities to remain in one soul.

> When divine grace attaches itself to the soul through holy baptism . . . where is there room for the evil being? . . . Therefore, we believe that the multiform serpent is cast out of the treasure rooms of the mind through the bath [λουτροῦ] of incorruption.[45]

We should not, however, be astonished if after baptism we think evil thoughts along with the good. "For the bath of holiness removes from us the filth of sin, but the duality of our will is not changed, nor are the demons hindered from warring against us and speaking words of error to us."[46] "Satan is chased from the soul by holy baptism," but he is permitted to work on the soul through the bodily desires. "The grace of God dwells in the very depth of the soul, that is, the mind."[47]

Grace hides its presence in the baptized. When one makes progress in keeping the commandments and ceaselessly calls on the Lord Jesus, then holy grace consumes the evil and resists demonic attacks.[48] Grace enlightens all the deeper feelings and enables the heart to think on spiritual things in peace and no longer to think according to the flesh.[49]

---

43. Polyzogopoulos, "Life and Writings of Diadochus of Photice," pp. 784-86. Louth, "Messalianism and Pelagianism," pp. 132-133, citing I. Hausherr. Louth distinguishes Augustine from the Messalians, for the former found sin in the depth of the heart but the latter said demons attack from without. Diadochus would qualify that interpretation, for he understands his opponents (Messalians?) as placing the demons within the soul even after baptism.

44. *Chapters* 78. The passage explains that baptism frees from the "defilement of sin," but in contrast to Mark the Monk, for whom baptism returns one to the situation of Adam in Paradise (below), the "duality of the will" inherited from Adam's fall remains in the baptized.

45. *Chapters* 78. Polyzogopoulos, "Life and Writings of Diadochus of Photice," p. 787.

46. *Chapters* 78.

47. *Chapters* 79.

48. *Chapters* 85.

49. *Chapters* 88.

Hieronymus (Jerome) of Jerusalem: A Messalian Voice?

One of three fragments ascribed to Hieronymus of Jerusalem is entitled *On the Effect of Baptism* (PG 40.860-865). There is uncertainty about the date of the work. In part because John of Damascus cites a work by a Hieronymus, identified as a presbyter of Jerusalem, some date the work to the seventh or eighth century.[50] Older works gave a date in the fourth or fifth century.[51] The images and principal biblical citations are found in Symeon the New Theologian (tenth to eleventh century), and on this basis it is possible that the opuscules of Jerome are later than Symeon,[52] but there is no convincing reason why the relationship is not the reverse. The late date was also argued on the basis of indications of anti-Islamic statements in the other fragments, which are ascribed to a dialogue with a Jew.[53] There is real doubt, however, if the fragment *On the Effect of Baptism* belongs to the same work as the other fragments printed together by Migne, or if it even belongs to the same author.[54] Nothing distinctively Muslim or even Jewish characterizes the author's opponents, whose rivals are other versions of Christianity. An important factor in dating involves the document's probable association with Messalianism. The similarities of the ideas in the tract with Pseudo-Macarius and with ideas modified or corrected by Diadochus of Photice (above) and Mark the Monk (below) favor a fifth-century date.[55] My impressions on the attitudes toward infant baptism also point to the fifth century.

On the Effect of Baptism comes from a monastic context. This is indicated by the concessionary tone about married people receiving the grace of the Holy Spirit (864A-B). The author distinguishes himself from the "many who live in the world" and from both "those who attend the altar and those who come to participate in the mysteries" (864B), which (if I am reading the implication correctly) would make the

---

50. G. Röwekamp, "Jerome of Jerusalem," in Siegmar Döpp and Wilhelm Geerlings, *Dictionary of Early Christian Literature* (New York: Crossroad, 2000), p. 323. Lampe's *Lexicon* accepts an eighth-century date.

51. William MacDonald Sinclair, "Hieronymus (3)," in William Smith and Henry Wace, eds., *Dictionary of Christian Biography*, Vol. 3 (London: John Murray, 1882), pp. 28-29, says fourth century. Migne, *Patrologiae Graecae*, Vol. 40, cols. 845-846, assigns a date c. 400, but the index volume gives sixth century.

52. Jean Darrouzes, "Jérôme le Grec," in *Dictionnaire de spiritualité* (Paris: Beauchesne, 1974), Vol. 8, col. 919.

53. E. Amann, "Jérome de Jérusalem," *Dictionnaire de théologie catholique* (Paris: Letouzey et Ané, 1934), Vol. 8, cols. 983-985, following P. Batiffol, "Jérome de Jérusalem," *Revue des questions historiques* 39 (1886): 248-255.

54. M. Geerard, ed., *Clavis patrum Graecorum*, Vol. 3 (Turnhout: Brepols, 1979) #7817, lists the work as *spuria* to Hieronymus of Jerusalem.

55. I. Hausherr, "Les grands courants de la spiritualité orientale," *Orientalia christiana periodica* 1 (1935): 114-138 (pp. 126-128 on this point). Fitschen, *Messalianismus*, pp. 264-266, discusses Hieronymus in comparison to Ps.-Macarius (see my criticism above under Ps.-Macarius, n. 34); he considers his charismatic theology of experience wholly different from that of Ps.-Macarius and finds Rahner's dating (n. 56) unacceptable.

identification of the author with the presbyter of Jerusalem quoted by John of Damascus problematic.

On the Effect of Baptism combines a high doctrine of baptism with an overriding emphasis on perceptible experiences of grace. The work may represent an effort at compromise between Messalians and the orthodox, by keeping some features of both sides. These features, however, are compatible with a Messalian origin,[56] and it is more likely that they give us the Messalian position without distortion from the orthodox, who reported only on the negative implications of Messalianism.

The tract is in the literary form *erotapokrisis* (question and answer), which attained popularity in the fifth century. The third question leads into the heart of the discussion: "How do you know that you were baptized at all?" (40.860C). The answer is, "From the effects" (860D). The author continues with a strong asseration that performing "all the commands and righteous deeds of God" is not sufficient, for only those who receive the divine life "through the water and the Spirit [John 3:5] and maintain undefiled purity" attain "such grace and activity" as to feel the working of the Holy Spirit (861B).

This internal test of the Holy Spirit living within is the "true and unerring demonstration" that one is a Christian (861C-D). The experience of the Holy Spirit is shown through "tears, rejoicings, consolation, and happiness" (864A). These feelings are manifest especially at the time of the liturgical gatherings of the church. The author singles out particularly the eucharist as a time for the experience of "grace, activity, sweetness, or compunction" (864B). The experience of the Holy Spirit applies to men and women, to priests and laity alike (864A-B).

The tract makes the astonishing claim that "The Holy Spirit's grace and working hidden in the heart of the Christian" is more important than the faith, the church, and the scriptures, for others than true Christians may have these externals (864C-D).[57] Yet, the author repeats that this internal working of the Holy Spirit comes only to the person properly baptized into the name of the Father, Son, and Holy Spirit (864D).

The author contrasts this true sign of a Christian with external marks: going to church, making the sign of the cross, partaking of the eucharist. "The Gospels, prophets, teachers, and apostles" teach by words, but God teaches by his own actions in the soul (865A-B). The tract concludes with a stirring appeal to "feel within . . . [this] sign, gift, grace, and treasure" (865B) and to hold on to this unique gift until death.

Some interesting aspects of this text may be noted that accord with traditional baptismal teaching. There is a strong doctrine of baptismal regeneration. In the bap-

---

56. Karl Rahner, "Ein Messalianisches Fragment über die Taufe," *Zeitschrift für Katholische Theologie* 61 (1937): 258-271 (p. 262, 265-268), who concludes for a date "at the latest at the turn from the fourth to the fifth century" (p. 271).

57. A longer list referring to non-Christians or to those not counted by the author as orthodox mentions scriptures, churches, sacrifices, teachers, books, divine knowledge, good deeds, feasts, changes of garments, prayers, vigils, priest (864C).

tism of water and the Spirit there is the birth of the spiritual life and the beginning of the indwelling of the Holy Spirit.[58] Although the language of new birth predominates in the description of baptism, baptism is also named "enlightenment" (861A; possibly 864A).

The author assumes the practice of infant baptism. It is sufficiently long-standing to be normal practice but recent enough that one cannot automatically assume that parents presented the child for baptism and recent enough that practical questions are raised. There is the possibility of a child being abandoned by the parents without having been baptized (860C-D). One ought not to depend on what parents or others tell him about his baptism, but ought to have the evidence of the Holy Spirit within (861C). Instead of baptism itself being evidence that one is a Christian, the situation now was such that one must find evidences that one has been baptized.

The central doctrinal affirmation of the tract is the indwelling of the Holy Spirit in the person who has been baptized. The author offers as proof that one is a Christian the internal activity of the Holy Spirit. The workings of the Holy Spirit in the heart that provide this internal test are described as "joy, happiness, and rejoicing" (861A) but include also "tears" (864A). There is "compunction" as well as "sweetness" (864B) and "consolation" (864A).

"Hieronymus" employs the analogy of the woman who knows she is pregnant by the movements of the babe in the womb. Just as a woman knows from the movements in her womb that it contains a new life, so persons from the internal experience of the Holy Spirit are fully assured in the heart of their baptism. Although the quoted scriptural basis for the analogy is Isaiah 26:18,[59] the author's frequent mention of "leapings" (σκιρτήματα — 861A; 861C; 864A) for the movements of the Holy Spirit within is perhaps influenced by Luke 1:41, the leaping of John the Baptist in the womb of Elizabeth on her meeting Mary. The descriptions of the movements of the Holy Spirit are based primarily on this analogy of physical pregnancy: leapings, pokings, and throbbings (861A).

Quite impressive is the large number of scriptures used in support of the doctrine of the indwelling of the Holy Spirit received at baptism. Some of these we expect, but some are unusual, such as Matthew 13:44 (864D): the "treasure hidden in a field" is the invisible work of the Holy Spirit in the human heart. There is no indication of an anointing or any later act than baptism that confers the Holy Spirit. This theme of the secret indwelling of the Spirit occurs frequently in the writers surveyed in this chapter.

Hieronymus's response to his (unidentified) religious rivals is to make a strong assertion of the uniqueness of Christianity in regard to the inner working of the

---

58. "Conceived the divine Spirit in baptism" (861A); this "gift received in baptism" (861B); "only those correctly baptized" receive "the Spirit's grace" (864D); "the Holy Spirit hidden in us on the day of divine baptism" (864D); "what God gave in baptism" (865B).

59. Gregory of Nyssa, *Life of Moses* 1.11, gives a different use of the Greek translation of Isaiah 26:18, speaking of "always in labor but never giving birth." Hieronymus, however, takes πνεῦμα not as "wind" but as the Holy Spirit, for the Old Greek actually reads the "spirit of your salvation."

Holy Spirit, for "no other faith on the earth possesses" this (865B; cf. 864D). The modern reader, however, may ask, "Is the subjective test of one's feelings any more distinctive of the true believer than the external practices the author finds shared with others?" Certainly others have felt the full assurance of faith in their beliefs.

Mark the Monk: An Anti-Messalian Voice

Uncertainty surrounds the exact identity of Mark the Monk (or Hermit), but a date in the middle third of the fifth century is likely,[60] and both earlier[61] and later[62] dates have been proposed. Mark the Monk's long work *Answer to Those Who Doubt concerning Divine Baptism* also employs the question and answer format.[63] The author was not a great stylist or the clearest thinker, but because of his repetitiveness the main points stand out. He seems to appropriate words and phrases characteristic of Messalianism in order to give them a new meaning or to refute Messalian practices.[64] Yet his opponents cannot be said to be Messalians in the full sense, and Mark the Monk controverts only individual points and not the Messalian system.[65] The lack of

60. George-Matthieu de Durand, "Études sur Marc le Moine," I. "L'Epitre à Nicolas," *Bulletin de littérature ecclésiastique* 85 (1984): 259-278 (the letter is inauthentic); II. "Le traité sur l'Incarnation," 86 (1985): 5-23 (the treatise is genuine; hypothesis for a date 437-438); III. "Marc et les controverses occidentales," 87 (1986): 163-188 (use of his works in the Reformation; parallel to Augustine he accepted that *fomes peccati* remain after baptism, but for Mark the *fomes* is not sinful in itself, for it was present in Adam before the fall — pp. 173-174, 184).

61. Otmar Hesse, "Marcus Eremita," in G. Krause, G. Müller et al., eds., *Theologische Realenzyklopädie* (Berlin: de Gruyter, 1977–), Vol. 22, pp. 101-104, puts him in Egypt between 381 and 431.

62. Plested, *The Macarian Legacy*, pp. 75-76, places him in the latter two-thirds of the fifth century. Henry Chadwick, "The Identity and Date of Mark the Monk," *Eastern Churches Review* 4 (1972): 125-130, suggests that the author known as Mark the Monk may be Mark the presbyter and head of a monastery near Tarsus addressed by Severus of Antioch (between 515 and 518). Chadwick characterizes Mark as "writing in a *milieu* with a powerful Messalian presence," to which his attitude "was one of conciliatory moderation as well as of courteous criticism" (p. 128); Severus wanted Mark to be more aggressive. O. Hesse, "Was Mark the Monk a Sixth-Century Higumen near Tarsus?" *Eastern Churches Review* 8 (1976): 174-178, raises doubts about Chadwick's suggestion.

63. Critical edition and French translation by G. M. de Durand, *Marc le Moine: Traités*, 2 vols., Sources chrétiennes 445 and 455 (Paris: Cerf, 1999, 2000). My references will be to Migne, PG column and section numbers.

64. Unlike Chadwick (n. 62), Erik Peterson, "Die Schrift des Eremiten Markus über die Taufe und die Messalianer," *Zeitschrift für die neutestamentliche Wissenschaft* 31 (1932): 273-288, saw Mark as a strong opponent of Messalianism. Babai the Great (seventh century), *Commentary on the Centuries of Evagrius* 3.85, read him the same way: "Blessed Mark confounded this impious heresy [Messalianism] with a treatise on baptism" — quoted by Fitschen, *Messalianismus*, p. 246, but he points out that we do not know that the opusculum of Mark the Monk is the same work Babai referred to. For other writers who understand Mark the Monk as a strong anti-Messalian, see Ware, "Baptism and the Ascetic Life," p. 442, n. 2; Ware's paper compares Mark the Monk on baptism with Gregory of Nyssa and Ps.-Macarius (pp. 447-451).

65. Fitschen, *Messalianismus*, pp. 247-256, who concludes that more cannot be proved than that there is a possibility that Mark the Monk knew part of the Ps.-Macarian tradition and dealt with ascet-

exact agreement of Hieronymus of Jerusalem and Mark the Monk with the earlier Messalian and anti-Messalian statements may reflect later stages in the conflict or the transmutation of the arguments to new movements or situations.[66]

Some points regarding Mark the Monk's general theological position may be noted as the context of his arguments in regard to baptism. The central issue addressed in *Answer to Those Who Doubt concerning Divine Baptism* is why persons sin after baptism has supposedly destroyed sin. "Why," they say, "if sin is abolished in baptism, does it again work in the heart?"[67] Since sin remained active after baptism, his opponents doubted some of the claims made for the effectiveness of baptism and maintained that people must root out sin, including the sin of Adam, by their own effort (985A; 988A).

Mark the Monk replied to the question about sin continuing to be active in those baptized and needing to be eliminated through ascetic works by saying, "If we say sin is destroyed by works, then 'Christ died in vain' [Gal. 2:21]" (988A).[68] The consequence of his opponents' view is that "The grace of God is no longer grace but the reward of our efforts." His own position on grace and works relates human works to the commands of God; works are not so much our own efforts but are a response of faith and freedom to God's grace: "If [overcoming sin] is by grace, the work is not work but a command of the one who set us free and is a work of liberty and faith" (988A). For Mark the Monk, "Faith is not only to be baptized into Christ but also to do his commands" (985D), and not to do them is to show oneself unfaithful (985C). "We are obligated to believe completely in Christ and to do all his commands, receiving the power of doing so from him" (1004C). God's commands are not in contradiction to freedom, for "The commands of Christ given after baptism are a law of liberty [James 2:13]" (988B-C) and obedience to them proceeds from freedom. Moreover, "The commands do not cut off sin (for this has already been done through the cross), but they guard the boundaries of the freedom given to us" (992A).

His opponents and Mark the Monk agreed in an emphasis on free will. "They

---

ics who stood in the influence of the Messalian stream and that he was more an anti-Messalian than an anti-Macarian. Plested, *The Macarian Legacy*, pp. 75-132, compares Mark the Monk with the Macarian writings and concludes that Mark belongs to the Macarian spiritual tradition but on some points enters into constructive dialogue with Macarius; he compares the two on baptism on pp. 81-90 and on p. 81 records different views on the purpose of Mark's treatise on baptism. I have not seen O. Hesse, "Markos Eremites und Symeon von Mesopotamien: Untersuchung und Vergleich ihrer Lehren zur Taufe and zur Askese" (Ph.D. diss., Göttingen, 1973).

66. Fitschen, *Messalianismus*, pp. 273-285, notes the general lack of reference to the Ps.-Macarian writings after the sixth century and the lack of continuity in "Messalianism" after the condemnation of 431. He thinks that there was a transformation of components of the Messalian system by new ascetic movements but that no actual Messalian was known after the sixth century; "Messalian" became a label of reproach designating "heresy."

67. Mark the Monk, *Answer to Those Who Doubt concerning Divine Baptism* (PG 65.992A). Future references will be given only to the column and section numbers of Migne, PG 65.

68. Cf. "[God] nullified sin by the cross" (989C). Mark says that it is not what was removed that works after baptism, which gives complete release, but the passions chosen by free will (902B).

say" that human beings "have been enslaved to sin by free will" (988A). Mark the Monk concurs: "If after baptism we are held in the power of sin, it is not as if baptism is imperfect but that we neglect the commandment and are addicted to pleasures by free will"; one turns to sin by the choice of free will (988B). "We have authority to incline to whatever we will, whether to good or to evil" (989A; cf. 1016B — to incline to the devil's suggestion or to the command of God). "According to one's own will, even if baptized, he abides in what he loves on account of free will" (989B). "To abide or not to abide in the commandments is conceded to our own free will" (989C). It is not through any deficiency in baptism that people sin after baptism but because of the choice of their free will (992B).

The debate over why persons sin after baptism occasions reference to the effects of Adam's sin. Contrary to his opponents Mark the Monk considered baptism to set one free from "the paternal sin" and so the slavery to sin (988C). Here we encounter different eastern perspectives in contrast to Augustine's doctrine of original sin (chap. 52).[69] Neither side, it seems, held to an inheritance of the guilt of Adam's sin, but the opponents did subscribe to an inherited sinful human nature; Mark the Monk rather understood inherited human nature to have a propensity to sin.[70] The opponents held that the presence of evil reasonings after baptism was "a remnant of the sin of Adam" (992C) and that even after baptism "the sin of Adam works without [our] cause" (996D). Mark the Monk replies in each case that the godlessness proceeds from ourselves and cannot be blamed on Adam (992C; 996D).[71] The Lord said that the evil reasonings "proceed not from Adam but from the heart, and on account of this they defile a person [Matt. 15:18-19]" (1000D).[72]

Neither the necessity of divine grace for salvation nor the effects of Adam's sin conflicted in Mark's mind with the exercise of free will in faith and obedience. "No one cuts off the sin of Adam but Christ alone according to the degree of faith in him" (1012B). "Neither God nor Satan compels the will and baptism" (988B). The things which his interlocutor said were the sin of Adam, Mark the Monk said were errors of

---

69. Ware, "Baptism and the Ascetic Life," p. 444, for Mark's difference from Augustine.

70. On universal sinfulness in other writings by Mark the Monk, see Ware, "Baptism and the Ascetic Life," p. 443. Plested, *The Macarian Legacy*, p. 80, does find the implication of an element of inherited guilt in Macarius and Mark but says they differed in that Mark held that the effects of original sin were entirely removed at baptism but for Macarius this was done later through the power inherent in baptism (p. 89) — this importing of western terminology into the discussion requires giving "original sin" a broader sense than the more precise Augustinian doctrine. Other than this difference, he finds Mark's teaching on baptism to be fundamentally that of Macarius.

71. Cf. 996A for the opponents urging the destruction of the sin of Adam by efforts (struggles) and "not by the grace of God that is in us secretly by baptism," and 997A and 1013A (quoted below) for "evil reasonings are the sin of Adam"; Mark the Monk's reply is that "you are the cause of their activity, not Adam" (997A) and that the sin is not of Adam but of the one doing it (997D; also 1004C).

72. Cf. 997A for love of pleasure from lack of faith as the cause of evil reasonings, not Adam; 1017C for sin not the result of the transgression of Adam but the reproach of each one's passion; 1020D for the soul darkened by love of pleasure and vainglory falling into ignorance through little faith and neglect of the commands.

human free will (1012C). Transgression is not by necessity derived from Adam but from free will (1017C); we transgress the same way Adam did, by will (1025C). Hence, we should not blame Satan or the sin of Adam but ourselves (1012D).

> You say the changeable reasonings are the sin of Adam. . . . If these things are not of our will but of the tyranny of Satan and a remnant of the sin of Adam, why are we who are involuntarily influenced by sin and under the tyranny of Satan charged by scripture? And are we going to be punished without cause? Or is God perhaps unjust, commanding things beyond our nature . . . ? But this is not possible. (1013A)

Is the compulsory nature of evil thinking something said by the opponents or the author's interpretation of their position? Surely the implication that God is the cause of evil thinking is the author's conclusion about the opponents' position.

Human beings, Mark the Monk says, have the same nature as Adam; neither he nor we transgress the command by necessity of nature (1013C). The transgression of Adam was not transmitted to us, for we do not sin in the likeness of his transgression (Rom. 5:14) (1017C and D). "We succeeded only to the death of Adam" (1025D; also 1024D). Every effect from Adam's sin was destroyed by Christ (1028A). The causes of evil thoughts are not derived in a compulsory manner from Adam, or else "all would be affected similarly and be controlled inevitably" (1020D). Human beings are necessarily attacked by Satan, but the attack is not itself sin (1020A stated twice; cf. 992B for sin as only the yielding to the attack), only a proving of our free will.

The number of scriptural quotations is notable. The debate was carried on by scriptural interpretation. Frequently cited is Romans 5:14.

In the context of this theology of the human condition Mark the Monk makes frequent reference to baptism, both in brief and in longer statements. The treatise, *Answer to Those Who Doubt concerning Divine Baptism*, begins with a question contrasting baptism as perfection, quoting Acts 22:16 and Isaiah 1:16 and so indicating perfection as the removal of sins, with the requirement to purify oneself according to 2 Corinthians 7:1 (984A). The description of baptism as "perfection" ("For holy baptism is perfection [τέλειον]" — 984C) was particularly problematic to Mark's opponents in view of the continued presence of sin in the lives of the baptized, so Mark immediately qualifies his statement: "But it does not perfect the one who does not do the commands" (984A).[73] The opponents said that "They have perfection from their efforts [struggles]" (988A), which view Mark saw as denigrating what was done in baptism. Rather, perfection is received mystically (sacramentally) in baptism (1028A). The presence of sin does not mean that baptism is imperfect (see 988B above). "Holy baptism is perfect in us, but we attain imperfectly to it" (1005A). The

---

73. His thought seems to be that baptism gives perfection, but the person must then fulfill it in obedience to the commands. God "gave commands in order that, having done them, we may find the perfection that has been given to us" (985D-988A). "The cleansing by baptism occurs mystically but is realized effectively by [keeping] the commands" (988C).

person baptized may not know what is received, being imperfect in faith and deficient in work, yet God grants his blessing perfectly (1028A), and the grace that was given through baptism does not come from the outside but continues to work secretly from within (1000A).

The discussion above indicates the importance to Mark the Monk of grace, which he saw threatened by the opponents' emphasis on human ascetic disciplines. He combines the theme of perfection with grace in the description of "holy baptism" as "perfect, the grace of Christ hidden in secret" (993C). The opponents, however, agreed that grace is received through baptism (1020B), but they said that we must "destroy the sin of Adam by struggles and not by the grace of God which is in us secretly by baptism" (996A). Mark speaks of the grace given mystically (sacramentally) through baptism and that now indwells secretly (1001B; cf. 993C; 996A; 1004B); "apart from the grace of Christ given through baptism it is impossible to prevail over sin" (993A). He underscores that "perfect grace is given us through baptism" (992D). Those baptized are "set free by the grace of Christ" from the slavery of sin (988C-D).[74]

Although human beings are dependent absolutely on divine grace for deliverance from sin, there is a cooperation on their part. Grace does not obviate the necessity of obedience: "The perfect grace of God has been given to us for the fulfilling of all the commands" (1004B; cf. 1008C below on the Holy Spirit). If one does not do the commands, the grace that has been given does not come to manifestation (1008B).

Grace given in baptism is particularly associated with the Holy Spirit. "The grace of the Spirit is received sacramentally from baptism" (993B). The grace of the Holy Spirit is in us from baptism (1001D; 1005C). "Christ . . . has given perfectly the grace of the Spirit to the baptized" (1028B). Bringing together his key ideas, Mark says that one is given the perfect grace of the Spirit (the "grace of the Spirit" should be taken as an objective genitive, i.e., the Spirit is the grace), and this is "for the fulfilling of all the commandments" (1008C).

Baptism gave the Holy Spirit. The Holy Spirit is the "treasure" (Matt. 13:44) hidden in the heart of believers (1005D; so also, from baptism, Christ is hidden within — 1005D).[75] He is the "one who indwells" (1005B [or is this Christ? for this is also said of Christ — 996C; 1008B]). The indwelling of the Spirit from baptism is a first-fruit, not some part of the whole (1009D), so from baptism the Spirit makes one capable of all activities and gifts, but he does not work his gifts in everyone equally (1012A). "Inasmuch as we believe and do the commands, by so much the Holy Spirit produces his own fruit in us" (1004D-1005A). "We are influenced by sin on our own account, and we are set free from enforced slavery by the Spirit" (1000B). Mark says repeatedly that one receives the power to keep the commands (e.g., 1004B-C; 1005B; 1008C). Indeed, the grace of the Spirit is given, as cited above (1008C), for the pur-

74. Cf. "set free according to the gift of Christ" — 989B.
75. Matthew 13:44 is given the same interpretation by Hieronymus of Jerusalem (above).

pose of fulfilling the commands. The indwelling of the grace of the Spirit is given "mystically" or "secretly" in baptism, but Christians must work together with God by fulfilling the commandments in order to become "actively" and "clearly" conscious of this grace.[76] Mark uses the Messalian phrase ἐν πάσῃ πληροφορίᾳ καὶ αἰσθήσει ("in full assurance and perception") to describe the experienced result (1004D, added to a quotation of Eph. 3:14-17).[77]

By receiving the Holy Spirit through baptism one also received through the Spirit the Father and the Son (1008D). Mark the Monk also says that what one "received mystically through baptism is Christ [Gal. 3:27]" (1028B). Christ in himself is present from baptism. "We have been mystically buried with him through baptism, and he raised us with him, and he seated us in the heavenly places [Rom. 6:4; Eph. 2:6]" (985D). "Through baptism one is clothed with Christ [Gal. 3:27]" (997A). Christians are spiritually Jews, having received the circumcision of the heart, and "the heavenly lawgiver, Christ, wrote the spiritual law itself through the Spirit on believers'" hearts (993B).

The divine presence works regeneration, a key concept with our author. As with other writers of the patristic age, Mark combines the terminology of 1 Peter 1:23 and Titus 3:5, "The heavenly Jerusalem, our mother, has given to us new birth [ἀναγεννῶσα] through the 'washing of regeneration [λουτροῦ τῆς παλιγγενεσίας]'" (993C). "The Lord himself made us alive through the washing of regeneration and granted the grace of the Spirit" (1008C), thus reversing the death received from Adam. "The Lord came so that he might make us alive through the washing of regeneration and reconcile to God what he had made" (1017D). "If having been begotten again [ἀναγεννηθέντες] we offer anything to him, this has already been hidden [in us] by him" (1028C). That which is hidden within human hearts (grace, the Holy Spirit, Christ) must come to fruition through living by the commands of God; the keeping of the commands, however, is not a human originated work but a free and faithful response to God's gifts, only possible because of the divine working within.

Other imagery used for the effects of baptism is liberty and purification by the gift of Christ (988C; 1001B-C). People are purified and renewed through baptism (1025A-B).[78]

Little is said in the treatise about the ceremony of baptism. Mark the Monk does relate baptism to faith: he refers to "the beginning of faith through baptism" (1001).[79]

---

76. Ware, "Baptism and the Ascetic Life," p. 445: "a progress from baptismal grace present μυστικῶς to baptismal grace experienced ἐνεργῶς."

77. Ware, "Baptism and the Ascetic Life," p. 447.

78. Cf. 988C quoted in note 73. See Ware, "Baptism and the Ascetic Life," pp. 443-444, for purification and liberty conferred in baptism according to Mark the Monk.

79. The disciples of John at Ephesus in Acts 19:2-6 are said to have been baptized without faith (1004A).

Immediately from baptism the Holy Spirit is given to those who firmly believe, but to those who are unbelieving and those believing wrongly and those who have not been baptized, he is not given. (1004B)

Baptism is also connected with repentance: "We do not say everyone baptized and receiving grace is finally immutable and no longer needing repentance" (1004B).

Baptism is the work of the Trinity; by the saying of the name of either one, the whole Trinity is named (1009A). Baptism is in the catholic church (1001B), and by it the Lord "places us in the paradise of the church" (1025B).

The point about baptism not cutting out the root of sin is attested in the anti-Messalian lists noted above,[80] but other arguments found in *Answer to Those Who Doubt concerning Divine Baptism* are not represented in the anti-Messalian lists. Mark the Monk is like Pseudo-Macarius in presupposing spiritual progress,[81] but against any misunderstanding about the priority of baptismal grace Mark the Monk declares that whatever comes later is already hidden in us.

The fact that much of the controversy in regard to Messalianism and its spiritual teaching was carried out in terms of baptism and the implications of that teaching and accompanying ascetic practices for baptism testifies to the centrality of baptism in the religious life of eastern Christianity in the fifth century.

---

80. Fitschen, *Messalianismus*, p. 254, notes Timothy of Constantinople's item 3 and Theodoret, *Fables of Heretics* 2 and 3.

81. Ps.-Macarius, *Homilies* 15.41. Fitschen, *Messalianismus*, p. 254.

48. Asia Minor and Constantinople

Two very rhetorical homilies on the baptism of Christ may be surveyed for information on early Byzantine baptismal practice and thought before turning to evidence for the rite in Constantinople from a church historian, from a fifth-century bishop of the city, and from a later liturgical text incorporating early materials.

Theodotus of Ancyra

Theodotus (d. before 446) was bishop of Ancyra. There is attributed to him a homily "On the Holy Theophany," although there are doubts about the attribution.[1] This sermon on the Lord's baptism takes its text from Matthew 3:12-17.[2] The treatment of the Lord's humility is an example of Theodotus's rhetorical style:

> The Master comes to the servant, the King to the soldier, the One who needs nothing to the one in need, the Giver to the borrower, the Reality to the shadow, the Word to the voice [John 1:23], the express image to the type. (5)

The significance of the baptism of Christ is announced in the beginning of the homily:

> The fountains are purified, the rivers are washed clean, the Lamb [John 1:29, 36] is washed [λουόμενον] and the world is thoroughly washed [ἀποπλυνόμενον],

---

1. It is Homily 7 of Theodotus of Ancyra in Codex Parisianus gr. 1171 (tenth century), ff. 240r-245r. I use the Greek text and French translation of Michel Aubineau, "Une homilie grecque inédite attribuée à Theodote d'Ancyre, sur le baptême du Seigneur," in ΔΙΑΚΟΝΙΑ ΠΙΣΤΕΩΣ (1969), pp. 3-28 (text and translation on pp. 10-21).

2. For earlier treatments of the baptism of Christ see chaps. 6 and 7. The name "Theophany" for the baptism of Christ accords with the usage of Constantinople — Justin Mossay, Les fêtes de Noël et d'Épiphanie d'après les sources littéraires Cappadociennes du IVe siècle (Louvain: Abbaye du Mont César, 1965), p. 23, on the usage of Proclus and likely Basil of Caesarea.

thirsty Adam is given to drink of the forgiveness of trespasses, and Eve is washed clean of the lamentations for the ancient grief. (1)

Theodotus expresses the significance of the baptism of Christ in terms of the practice of baptism that he knew:

> See today to how many sons grace gives birth [ἔτεκεν] and what children the nature of the waters begets [ἀνεγέννησεν], a nature sanctified by the manifestation of the Master. (3)

He draws on Old Testament typology and texts:

> Today the bodiless Pharaoh [the devil] sinks in the deep [Exod. 15:4], today the army of demons drowns, today the spiritual Moses [Christ] leads the people through the waters of the nations, today humanity is set free from the brick-making of pleasures [Exod. 5:7-8]. . . . David worthily proclaimed when he spoke the truth saying, "Wash [Πλυνεῖς] me, and I will be whiter than snow" [Ps. 51:7]. For truly today Christ by being baptized [βαπτιζόμενος] in the waters thoroughly washes [ἀποπλύνει] and makes us whiter than snow. (4)

(Theodotus provides an instance of using the verb for washing, or thoroughly washing, in connection with immersion, to sink in the deep.) "The salvation of human beings is provided for" (5). Jesus' coming to the Jordan was "the invisible grace of regeneration [ἀναγεννήσεως]" (6).

The preacher contrasted the baptism of John with the baptism of Christ, ascribing the following words to John:

> "My baptism [βάπτισμα] is exhortation, yours is forgiveness. My baptism is not able to bury sins, for it is not mixed with Spirit and fire [Matt. 3:11]. Your word is release from all iniquity." (8)

Theodotus evidently understood Christian water baptism as involving also the baptism in the Spirit and fire that Jesus would administer. John continued, addressing Jesus, "In baptizing others, I made mention of you, but in baptizing you on whom shall I call?" (8).

There are perhaps allusions to features of the baptismal ceremony in the preacher's elaboration of what Jesus meant by "fulfilling all righteousness" (Matt. 3:15).

> To seek and save the lost [Luke 19:10], to clothe in white the naked, to make the poor rich with the kingdom, to anoint the fallen for the contest, to honor the captive with adoption to sonship . . . to incline the head in baptism. (9)

"John allowed the water to the condescension of the Savior" (10). When Jesus came up from the water, "he rained forgiveness upon the world" (10). Heaven was opened, the Spirit came down, and the Father testified to "the teaching of the Savior which he sealed" (10). In summary, "The creation was washed clean [ἀπελούετο] in the waves of the Jordan, . . . all life had the leprosy of sin washed off [ἀπενίπτετο]" (11).

Pseudo-Gregory Thaumaturgus, *On the Holy Theophany*

Gregory the Wonderworker (third century) was a student of Origen, missionary to Cappadocia and Pontus, and bishop of Neocaesarea. Among the later works ascribed to him are four homilies, three "On the Annunciation to the Holy Virgin Mary" and one "On the Holy Theophany, or on Christ's Baptism." The last also carries the title "On the Holy Lights." It belongs at the earliest to the late fourth century (from which time we have sermons with this title by the two Cappadocian Gregories [chaps. 37 and 38]), but more likely the fifth century, if not later.

The author's rhetorical elaboration of the conversation between John the Baptist and Jesus includes these words ascribed to Jesus, which give information on baptismal practice and theology:

> There is a mystery which gives to these waters the representation of the heavenly streams of the regeneration of humanity. . . . It becomes me to be baptized with this baptism for the present, and afterwards to bestow the baptism of the consubstantial Trinity upon all persons. Lend me, therefore, O Baptist, your right hand for the present economy, even as Mary lent her womb for my birth. Immerse me in the streams of Jordan, even as she who bore me wrapped me in children's swaddling clothes. Grant me your baptism even as the Virgin granted me her milk. Lay hold of this head of mine that the seraphim revere. With your right hand lay hold of this head that is related to yourself in kinship. Lay hold of this head that nature had made to be touched. . . . Baptize me who am destined to baptize those who believe on me with water, with the Spirit, and with fire: with water, capable of washing away the defilement of sins; with the Spirit, capable of making the earthly spiritual; with fire, naturally fitted to consume the thorns of transgressions.[3]

Baptism is presented as bringing regeneration and forgiveness of sins. The baptism with the Holy Spirit and fire is understood as occurring in water baptism. The right hand of the administrator was on the head of the one baptized (as shown in earlier and contemporary art). The baptism was an immersion, the water covering the body as the swadding clothes covered the newborn infant. It was administered to all believers and was related to the "consubstantial Trinity."

---

3. I have modified the translation by S. D. F. Salmond in *Ante-Nicene Fathers* (repr. Peabody: Hendrickson, 1994), Vol. 6, p. 70.

Socrates on Paul the Novatian

Socrates the church historian tells the story of a Jew who pretended to be a convert to Christianity and obtained a large amount of money by being baptized often by different Christian sects. When he approached Paul, bishop of the Novatians in Constantinople (early fifth century), Paul said that he must first be instructed in the fundamentals of the faith and required him to fast and pray many days. At the Jew's urging, Paul expedited the baptism, purchasing a white vestment for him, and had the font filled with water. When they approached the font for the baptism, the water suddenly disappeared. Since it was thought that the water had escaped through the drains, they were more carefully closed. On the second occasion before the baptism could be performed, the water in the font disappeared again. On being recognized by one of the witnesses as someone previously baptized by the orthodox bishop Atticus, the Jew was exposed as an imposter (*Church History* 7.17). The tale is useful for its details of the preliminaries of instruction in faith, prayer, and fasting and for its incidental information about a baptistery that was filled with water from an outside source and drained by channels underneath.

Proclus

The only catechetical discourse on baptism preserved from the church in Constantinople is *Homily* 27 of Proclus, bishop from 434 to 446.[4] It is the jewel in the collection of his homilies. Proclus's sermon takes the form of a dramatized dialogue alternating between the words of the preacher and words ascribed to the catechumens. The contents emphasize theological confession of the three divine Persons and ethical imperative derived from renunciation of Satan and allegiance to Christ as Lord and Savior.

After introductory words of praise to God, the catechumens' renunciation of Satan is repeated: "I renounce you, Satan, and your pomp and your cult [service] and your angels and all your works" (*Homily* 27.2.3). These are common elements in the formula of renunciation, although not in this order. Proclus spells out what Satan had caused people to do: blaspheme, pursue pleasure, do evil deeds, cause harm, accept idolatry (27.2.4-8). He elaborates on what the renunciation means: not to commit adultery, act with envy, become drunk, steal, lie, practice prostitution, engage in magic to obtain health (27.2.9-10). Proclus then declares, "This you called

---

4. For introductory material and translation I use J. H. Barkhuizen, "Proclus of Constantinople, Homily 27: μυσταδωγία εἰς τὸ βάπτισμα," *Acta patristica et Byzantina* 14 (2003): 1-20. Other homilies of Proclus are cited from his work, *Proclus Bishop of Constantinople: Homilies on the Life of Christ*, Early Christian Studies 1 (Brisbane: Australian Catholic University, 2001). For the liturgy of baptism in Proclus see Victor Saxer, *Les rites de l'initiation chrétienne du IIe au VIe siècle: Esquisse historique et signification d'après leur principaux témoins* (Spoleto: Centro italiano di studi sull'alto medioevo, 1988), pp. 333-340.

out in words. Demonstrate it with your deeds! Sanction your confession with your conduct. . . . Do not return to the place whence you ran away" (27.3.11-12). The devil is the "enemy from whom you have fled" (27.9.53).

The renunciation was followed by a declaration of allegiance: "I swear allegiance to you, O Christ!" (27.3.13, 14).

Immediately there was delivered "the symbol of faith," and the catechumen confessed, "I believe" (27.9.55; 27.8.47; to believe is important in statements additional to those explaining the confession of the creed — 27.7.44; 27.9.55). To acknowledge God is to profess him as Father, Son, and Holy Spirit (27.5.25). The first article of faith is, "I believe in one and only true God!" (27.4.16, 19, 20, 21; 27.9.55), "I believe in the Almighty Father" (27.9.55). Proclus elaborates on what it means to confess God as Creator, Infinite One, Invisible One, Ineffable One, One not containable (4.16) and then gives a long description of what God has done in creation and providence (27.4.20-23), followed by an affirmation of God's one nature "considered indivisibly in a trinity" (27.4.24-26).

The second article of faith is, "I believe in the Lord Jesus Christ, the Son of God" (27.9.56). The confession of the Son is developed in terms of his nature rather than his works (27.5.27-6.40). Reflecting the Christological debates of his time, Proclus explains that the Son is

> God in so far as he was from above, born of the Father;
> Man according to his birth in the flesh from a mother.
> I allot to each nature what is true and fitting, and proclaim the unity of person.
> (27.6.31)

In a more striking fashion, Proclus formulates the nature of Christ this way: "For as God He is from the Father, as man He is from a mother. Therefore He is without a father as one recently born, and without mother as one who is before the ages" (27.6.38-39).

The confession, "I believe in the Holy Spirit" (27.9.56), is developed in terms of the Spirit's works: he re-creates, forms anew, seals, anoints, cleanses, wakens (27.7.43).

The candidates for baptism are called on to "Throw away the robe of corruption. Press on naked as one (fleeing) from captivity" (27.8.48). (The nakedness is referred to again in 27.8.49 [twice] and 27.8.50.) They are instructed: "Incline towards the earth as one who is condemned, and stretch out your hand toward heaven, and beg for pity as suppliant" (27.8.48; raise hands to heaven also in 27.8.50). Mourning for sins in penitence is alluded to in 27.8.49.

At some point the Lord's Prayer was delivered to the candidates. This was an act of anticipation: By addressing God as "Father," they were honored before their birth; "You have been made his own before you have been born" (27.9.54). This is the first attestation of the use of the Our Father in baptism in the East.

Further features of the baptismal ceremony are probably reflected in the references to perfume (that gives "the sweet smell of virtues"), the oil (that "makes you bright"), the baptismal font (a "tomb"), being "raised to life through the Spirit," being clothed with "bright clothes," and holding lamps (revealing "the illumination of the soul") (27.8.50). The order here indicates a prebaptismal anointing; no postbaptismal application of oil is indicated unless it is alluded to in the sealing and anointing referred to above among the works of the Spirit (27.7.43).

Proclus says much about the meaning of baptism in his language of instruction and admonition. Christ is described as present and distributing heavenly gifts: "participation in immortality; enjoyment of sonship, possession of a kingdom, joy of a heavenly wedding, . . . illumination (by) (of) a divine love for mankind" (27.10.62). The baptismal fonts are "fountains of salvation" (28.4.23).

The theme of illumination is prominent. The catechumens acknowledge, "The radiance of the light has shone on me" (27.3.14). "Whenever I believe, I have understood. Whenever I desire, I have drawn near. Whenever I wish, I have been enlightened" (27.4.18). The person who had been in filth was "made brilliant" (27.9.57). (See above in 27.8.50 on shining forth with oil and in 27.8.51 on the lamps.) Related to illumination is the theme of acquiring knowledge (27.8.44, 46). Those approaching baptism are exhorted, "Shine forth as persons being present in the light," and "Be radiant as people in a bride-chamber" (27.10.60). Another exhortation is, "Come, . . . let us be enlightened in our minds, and though we have sinned, let us repent. Let us confess our sins" (28.11.70).[5]

Baptism is the time of "the birth of adoption as son through the Trinity," so one is to "endure as one who is born" (27.8.44). Through the Spirit one receives life and becomes a new person (27.8.50). The only Son of the Father "granted through baptism sonship to those who believe" (7.5). "(T)he baptismal font has many children" (28.2.9).[6] Proclus can speak paradoxically of the "painless birth pangs of the baptismal font" (33.16.61). "You were deemed worthy to call Him Father and Lord through your confession concerning the truth, having through grace been made his son" (27.9.55). The confession of Christ was a symbol of brotherhood with him (27.9.56). Hence, "Become like a newborn babe towards virtue" (27.9.52). "Leave . . . the person that you were. Be the person that you (now) have" (27.10.61)

Except for the quotation of Psalm 32:1 (27.8.51), forgiveness of sins is expressed in other terms. The Lord now accepts one "as without sins" (27.8.50). "This knowledge of your confession wipes out for you the record of debt" (27.8.46). The candidates are to confess their "debt as before a judge" and "Let go the practice of sin" (27.9.52). "You were justified as blameless; you who have become rich while you were before in great debt" (27.9.57).[7]

Through confession of the Holy Spirit one "received participation in sanctification" (27.9.56).

The baptismal confession was a "symbol of freedom" (27.8.46). One moved

---

5. Cf. 28.11.72, "(T)he Lover of mankind gave us repentance and confession as healing."
6. Likewise, 5.3, "The baptismal font unceasingly gives birth."
7. See further below on *Homily* 28 on the baptism of Christ.

away from slavery towards a Liberator (27.8.47). "You who have been freed while being in bonds" (27.9.57).

Proclus discussed the baptism of Christ in *Homilies* 7 and 28, "On the Holy Theophany." The feast of Epiphany celebrated "the epiphany of God" (7.1). It was a "consecration of the waters and the womb of baptism" (3.4). By his baptism Christ "unbinds the bonds of our sins" (7.1). "He grants salvation through baptism" to all (Jews and pagans), "presenting baptism as universal good" (7.2). Christ came to baptism as if a sinner, but he had no need of purification (7.3).[8] John the Baptist protested, "How shall I, defiled man that I am, sanctify God?" (7.5). His baptism, however, served two purposes: "in order that he may grant grace that sanctifies the waters, and urge every person on to be baptized" (7.3). Proclus contrasted the flood in the time of Noah with the baptism of Christ. "There the waters of the flood killed the human race, but here the waters of baptism through the one baptized brought life to those who died." "There a dove was carrying an olive branch, . . . but here the Holy Spirit, coming in the form of a dove, reveals the compassionate Lord" (7.3).

Homily 28 repeats motifs from *Homilies* 7 and 27. Christ is pure; we are the ones who have sinned; yet he is baptized (28.8.55). He was born and baptized "in order that he might destroy the deceit of the devil, and reveal the truth" (28.8.56). Christ's baptism "has cleansed us" and "crushed *the heads of the invisible snakes* [Ps. 74:13]" (28.2.7). "Here the waters were blessed," and here there is enlightenment (28.2.8). "The Lord came to be baptized, wishing to wash out Adam's *record of debt* [Col. 2:14]" (28.3.18). Christ "is covered in the waters of the Jordan, in order that he may bury our sins in water" (28.3.20); he "appears in a river in order that he may wash away the rivers of our sins" (28.3.21). Christ's baptism is described in the language of Christian baptism. He was "illuminated" (28.3.21), and so the celebration of his baptism is an exhortation, "Let us be illuminated" (28.6.48; 28.7.50). Since "Christ is baptized because of you. . . . Christ is being illuminated," Proclus presses his hearers how they can be indifferent and exalt themselves as if they were pure (28.7.51). Proclus also projects current baptismal practice back on the baptism of Christ: He "is stripped naked, in order that he may clothe the naked ancestor with a robe of incorruption" (28.3.19); "he is stripped naked on account of us, the naked ones, in order that he may clothe all in a robe of incorruption" (28.3.21). "Spiritual lamps" (alluding to Matt. 25:1-13) may reflect baptismal practice (28.6.44; see above) as well as the language of illumination.

Proclus based baptism not only on the baptism of Christ but also on his death — the water that gushed from his side is a symbol of baptism (36.61) — and the commission of Matthew 28:19 (36.45).

Paschal Sunday gave Proclus occasion to refer to the Exodus typology but developed in Proclus's characteristic way of antitheses between "there" (then) and "here" (now), which include the following:

---

8. Cf. *Homily* 26.5.18 — Christ's baptism indicated purification.

There Pharaoh was drowned together with his own terrifying army, but here the spiritual Pharaoh is submerged with all his power through his baptism.

There the Hebrews, having crossed the Red Sea, were singing the victory song to the benefactor, saying: . . . [Exod. 15:1]. Here those deemed worthy of baptism sing in a mystical way the victory song, saying: "One is holy. One Lord Jesus Christ, to the glory of God the Father. Amen."[9] . . .

The Hebrews, having crossed the Red Sea, used to eat manna in the desert. But now those coming from the baptismal font eat the bread that came down from heaven. (14.2)

In addition to the traditional motif of baptism (specified here as Christ's) drowning the spiritual foes, there are allusions to the liturgical elements of song and the eucharist.

Homily 16, "On Holy Pentecost," discusses "the grace of the Holy Spirit." Proclus parallels the coming of the Spirit on the apostles in Acts 2:3 with his coming on the Savior at his baptism (16.2). He concludes with the prayer, "And may he also now come upon us and bless us. For he is blended with the water, and melts away our sins like a fire, and shines on the newly enlightened like a light" (16.2).

In view of the blessings asociated with baptism, Proclus exhorts:

Become immortal in virtue.
Become a genuine son with a view to righteousness.
Become a perpetual king.
Become an undefiled bridegroom
Be radiant without stain. (10.63)

Barberini Euchologion

A Greek manuscript written in 790 preserves the oldest document of the *Ordo of Constantinople*, which likely goes back at least to the time of Bishop Proclus.[10]

Folios 260 and following contain the rite of renunciation *(apotaxis)* and adherence *(syntaxis)*. The renunciation occurred on the Friday before Easter Sunday at noon (Chrysostom puts it at 3:00 p.m. — see chap. 33). The archbishop (patriarch)

---

9. From the liturgy of Chrysostom.

10. Greek text with English translation in F. C. Conybeare, *Rituale Armenorum* (Oxford: Clarendon, 1905), pp. 389-405; French translation in Antoine Wenger, *Jean Chrysostome: Huit catécheses baptismales*, Sources chrétiennes 50 (Paris: Cerf, 1957; 2nd edition, 50b, 1970), pp. 83-90; and Greek text in S. Parenti and E. Velkovska, *L'Eucologio Barberini gr. 336*, Bibliotheca "Ephemerides liturgicae" subsidia (Rome, 1995). English translation of parts relevant to baptism in E. C. Whitaker, *Documents of the Baptismal Liturgy*, revised and expanded edition by Maxwell E. Johnson (Collegeville: Liturgical Press, 2003), pp. 109-123, and for the rite of renunciation Thomas M. Finn, *The Liturgy of Baptism in the Baptismal Instructions of St. John Chrysostom*, Studies in Christian Antiquity 15 (Washington, D.C.: Catholic University of America Press, 1967), pp. 114-118.

directed the candidates to sign themselves and remove their (outer?) clothing and shoes. He then instructed them that by word and action they were going to make a contract of faith, comparable to a person about to die making a will. He explained what they were going to do with all the powers of heaven present.

Turning to the west and raising their hands, the candidates repeated after the archbishop: "I renounce Satan and all his works and all his service and all his angels and all his pomps." This was done three times, and indeed everything was said three times. The archbishop asked three times, "Have you renounced Satan?" and they replied each time, "We have renounced him." To the Greeks saying or doing something three times indicated that one really meant it. They were instructed as an act of defiance to blow on the devil, who is described as dismayed at their escape to freedom.

The candidates then turned to the east, lowered their hands, and made their *syntaxis*. The archbishop asked them again to repeat after him: "I adhere to Christ, and I believe in one God the Father Almighty [continuing with the remainder of the Niceno-Constantinopolitan Creed]." This too he said three times with all responding. And he asked three times, "Have you adhered to Christ?" and they replied, "We have adhered."

After a brief prayer, the archbishop continued with admonition, picking up on the theme of a contract. At its conclusion the candidates raised their hands, the archbishop spoke topics for prayer, and to each the candidates responded, "Lord, have mercy." The archbishop signed the people, said another prayer, and told the candidates to put on their clothes.

The baptism is described as the "holy enlightening," and the candidates are "those being enlightened." One of the prayers includes the petitions, "(G)ive them new birth into eternal life, and fill them with the power of the Holy Spirit, unto the praise of your Christ: that they may be no longer children of the body but children of your kingdom." Those being enlightened came forward, bowed their heads, and received the laying on of hands and further prayers of blessing.

Another part of the manuscript (fol. 170ff.) contains a prayer for an infant when he receives his name on the eighth day, after which the infant is sealed on forehead, breast, and mouth.[11] The following prayer in the manuscript is for when the infant comes into the church on the fortieth day. It prays for the child "that, coming to the washing of immortality, he may become a child of light and day; that he may attain to a portion of the heritage of your elect and partake of your precious Body and Blood."

The next prayer is for the making of a catechumen, who removes his clothes and shoes and faces east. The officiant breathes on him three times and seals his forehead, mouth, and breast. He prays, "I set my hand upon this your servant . . . (G)rant that he may go forward in all your commandments . . . write his name in your book of life: and unite him to the flock of your inheritance."

There are prayers to accompany three exorcisms. The first begins, "The Lord rebuke you, O devil, the Lord who came into the world . . . to destroy your tyranny." It is structured by the phrase "I adjure you," by God or Christ stated three times ac-

---

11. Whitaker, *Documents*, p. 114; pp. 114-123 for what follows.

companied by the command to "depart" five times. The second exorcism declares that "God commands you and all your companions to depart from these who are but lately sealed in the name of our Lord Jesus Christ." "I adjure you" occurs twice and the command to "depart" three times, the last of which says, "Go out and depart from these who are making ready for the holy enlightening." The third exorcism is shorter than the other two and worded differently but is still premised on the divine power. "(L)ook upon your servants; seek, search out and drive away from them all the operations of the devil. Rebuke the base and unclean spirits, pursue them and cleanse the works of your hands."

After a prayer for the one approaching baptism, the bishop breathes on him three times and seals his forehead, mouth, and breast. He prays, "Drive away from him every evil and unclean spirit."

The candidate is stripped of clothes and shoes and turned to the west. The priest says three times, and the candidate or his sponsor repeats each time, "I renounce Satan, and all his works and all his service and all his angels and all his pomp." There follows, as in the other part of the manuscript, the triple question, "Have you renounced Satan?" the response, "We have renounced," and the command to blow on him. Turned to the east, the candidate repeats three times "I adhere to Christ" and "I believe in one God" and the rest of the creed. Again the priest asks, "Have you adhered to Christ?" and they answer "We have adhered." There follows the same prayer referred to above in the last paragraph on the other part of the manuscript.

The priest calls for prayer to the Lord:

For the sanctification of these waters by the indwelling and power of the Holy Spirit . . .

That the Lord may send upon them the grace of redemption, the blessing of Jordan . . .

For the descent upon these waters of the kindly cleansing of the supersubstantial Triad.

The priest then says a prayer silently for himself and then aloud that God would make the water "a fount of purity, a gift of sanctification, a way of deliverance from sins, a protection against disease, a destruction to demons, . . . filled with angelic power."

Next he breathes into the water three times, signs it with his finger three times, and offers another prayer. This prayer gives a full theology of baptism:

(L)et no evil spirit go down with him at his baptism. . . . (D)eclare this water to be a water of rest, water of redemption, water of sanctification, a cleansing of the pollution of the body and soul, a loosening of chains, forgiveness of sins, enlightenment of souls, washing of rebirth, grace of adoption, raiment of immortality, renewal of spirit, fount of life. . . . You have given us the new birth from above by water and Spirit. Be present, Lord, in this water and grant that those who are baptized therein may be refashioned . . . and put on the new man, who is restored after the image of him that created him. . . .

The prayer continues by looking forward to the resurrection and to guarding the gift of the Holy Spirit.

The deacon holds a vessel of olive oil, and the priest breathes on it three times and seals it three times. He prays to God:

> (B)less even this oil with the power and operation and indwelling of your Holy Spirit so that it may be a chrism of incorruption, a shield of righteousness, a renewal of soul and body, turning away every work of the devil, unto deliverance from all evil for those who are anointed in faith.

The priest makes three crosses with the oil in the water.

The one to be baptized is brought to the priest, who takes the holy oil on his finger and makes the sign of the cross on the forehead, breast, and back of the baptizand. "So and so is anointed with the oil of gladness into the name of Father, Son, and Holy Spirit." Then a deacon anoints his whole body.

The priest baptizes the candidate with the formula, "So and so is baptized in the name, etc." After the baptism the singer begins Psalm 32:1.

A deacon recites a prayer, and then the priest says a prayer that includes the following words expressing the meaning of the baptism:

> (T)o us unworthy [you] have given the blessed cleansing of his holy water and divine sanctification in the life-giving chrism: who even at this moment has been pleased to give new birth to these your servants newly enlightened, by water and Spirit, and has bestowed upon them forgiveness of their sins, both willingly and unwillingly committed: therefore, Master most benevolent, give them also the seal of the gift of your holy and all-powerful and worshipful Spirit, and the communion of the Holy Body and Precious Blood of your Christ.

Here are the traditional concepts of new birth, enlightenment, forgiveness of sins, and the gift of the Holy Spirit.

The priest next anoints the baptized with *myron*, making the sign of the cross on the forehead, eyes, nostrils, mouth, and both ears, saying, "The seal of the gift of the Holy Spirit." The priest enters the church with the neophytes, and the divine liturgy begins.

With this *Ordo* the baptismal liturgy of the Greek church reached its completed form. It incorporates, but elaborates on (especially in the frequent prayers), the long traditional elements designed for adult converts: catechumenate, renunciation of the devil, adherence to Christ, confession of the creed, prebaptismal anointing (partial by the priest, complete body by a deacon), baptism proper, postbaptismal sealing, and eucharistic liturgy. Infant baptism was recognized, but minimal accommodations were made to adjust to this phenomenon, which was on its way to becoming the normal practice.

49. Ravenna and Rome

Ravenna was the meeting place of East Rome and West Rome in the fifth century. For its baptismal practice we have the sermons of one of its bishops, Peter Chrysologus, and two important surviving baptisteries. Surviving liturgical sources for Rome prior to the sixth-century *Gelasian Sacramentary*, which preserves some earlier practices, are sparse. We note here some papal pronouncements and the rather full information from John the Deacon. Siricius restated the Roman position on baptism by heretics and the method of receiving them into the Catholic Church. The ruling of Innocent I contributed to the development of confirmation as a separate sacrament from baptism in the West. Leo I offers a rich theology of baptism with his own stamp. John the Deacon provides a description of the ceremony of baptism. The earliest surviving baptistery from Rome is that of the Lateran.

Peter Chrysologus of Ravenna

Peter Chrysologus was metropolitan bishop of Ravenna from approximately 431 until probably 451. His numerous sermons give information on the liturgical year, but make only occasional references to baptism.[1]

Peter Chrysologus contrasts John's baptism with Jewish cleansings and in turn with Christian baptism:

> [John] went to the Jordan, because a water jar could no longer wash away the filth of the Jews, but only a river could.... [John 2:6 quoted]. He went to the Jordan, in

---

1. I quote the translations of George E. Ganss, *St. Peter Chrysologus: Selected Sermons,* Fathers of the Church 17 (New York: Fathers of the Church, 1953), and William B. Palardy, *St. Peter Chrysologus: Selected Sermons,* Vols. 2 and 3, Fathers of the Church 109 and 110 (Washington, D.C.: Catholic University of America Press, 2004, 2005). All references are to the number of his sermons in these translations.

order to give the penitents water and not wine to drink. . . . Pardoning was within John's power, but not without repentance; there was forgiveness, but acquired by sorrow; . . . there was a baptism to remove the fault, but not to blot out the lingering sense of guilt.

. . . By means of John's baptism the human being was being purified for repentance, but not advanced to grace. But, by contrast, Christ's baptism regenerates, transforms, and makes a new person out of the old one. (*Sermon* 137.4)[2]

These are familiar points of ceremonial cleansing versus forgiveness, outward forgiveness versus removal of guilt, and purification versus regeneration. Peter is especially concerned to bring out the relation of John's baptism with repentance and to emphasize that the baptism instituted by Christ goes beyond purification to bring the grace of transformation. In reference to Mark 7:2, 5 he further declared that the Pharisees were ignorant of the one baptism that not only cleanses but renews souls and bodies, that doesn't wash off the skin but washes off the conscience for salvation (171.2).

The Epiphany sermons make several references to the baptism of Jesus. The connection of Jesus' birth with his baptism (a rebirth according to the Christian doctrine of baptism) is expressed this way: "During Epiphany Christ entered the basin of the Jordan to consecrate our baptism, in order that those whom he had assumed by being born of earth, he would raise up to heaven by being reborn," free those who were captives, bring life to those made mortal by guilt, and make partners in heaven those the devil made exiles on earth (157.6). Another benefit of baptism that is the result of Jesus' baptism comes out in another Epiphany sermon: "Today Christ entered the River Jordan to wash away the sins of the world" (160.3). A description of the baptism of Jesus brings out the paradox of the Lord's identification with humanity:

> [The son of Zechariah] submerges [*demergit*] his Lord in the baptism of repentance, washes him for the forgiveness of sins, because the Fountain wanted to be washed, the Advocate wanted to receive pardon, and the Judge himself wanted to undergo his own sentence. (*Sermon* 90.3)

Nonetheless, Christ is not a servant to his baptism but has authority over it (Ps. 29:3) (160.5).

Peter gives a common sacramental interpretation of John 19:34 in his allusion to the wounds of Jesus, "which have already shed water for the baptismal bath and blood for the redemption of humanity" (84.9).

The quotation of Romans 6:3-4 leads to the explanation that "The three days the Lord spent in the grave are represented by the triple immersion [*trina demersione*] in baptism" (113.5).

---

2. *Sermon* 137.12 promised a more extensive comparison of John's and Christ's baptism, but it is not extant.

Jesus' words about his death being a baptism (Luke 12:50) provokes this statement:

> Christ is baptized in his own blood, so that whatever he assumed from our flesh he would wash clean, renew, and restore completely into the form of his divine majesty. Christ is baptized with the baptism of his passion, since the sin of the whole world could not be destroyed except by him who had made the world. (164.6)

Here the familiar associations of baptism, death (martyrdom), blood, and forgiveness are woven together with the incarnation and destruction of sin by the Creator.

In a Lenten sermon on Psalm 29 (Latin and Greek 28), Peter issues this invitation:

> Bring to the Lord those who are to be baptized; bring those whom faith and not flesh conceives; bring those whom the grace of God and not earthly nature generates. . . . Bring, yes, bring those whom necessity prevents from coming of their own accord, or age hinders, or ignorance detains, or vices restrain, or sins delay, or appearance deceives, or poverty tricks and confuses. Entice the willing, compel the unwilling. (10.5)

The words may allude to bringing small children and the sick and aged. The sermon continues with a master bringing his slave, a father his son, a husband his wife, and a believer those of old age, a friend a friend, a citizen a foreigner. This statement does not indicate the age of the father's son to be brought. Although Peter elaborates on compelling the unwilling, he does not really specify the means to be employed, but he does not neglect to set his words in a context of grace and faith.

Peter Chrysologus preached sermons on the creed (55-62a) and on the Lord's prayer (67-72) that may have been part of instruction preparatory for baptism.

Baptisteries of Ravenna

Both the Baptistery of the Orthodox and the Baptistery of the Arians are octagons (Ristow #s 397-399).[3] So too is the present font in the Baptistery of the Orthodox, but it was presumably round in its first phase (end of fourth century) and certainly in phase two (459-460). The present octagonal font measures 3.45 meters wide and 0.84 meter deep. Later restorations limit the confidence to be placed in these dimensions, but excavation has revealed that the restored font rests on the fifth-century foundations and the pulpit for the administrator on one of the eight sides is likely fifth century, so the font as visible today may not be too far off from its early dimensions and appearance.[4] The font is not preserved in the Baptistery of the Arians (c. 500), but its round shape is evident from the building's floor.

---

3. Baptisteries are identified by their number in Sebastian Ristow, *Frühchristlich Baptisterien*, Jahrbuch für Antike und Christentum, Ergänzungsband 27 (Münster: Aschendorff, 1998).

4. Spiro K. Kostof, *The Orthodox Baptistery of Ravenna* (New Haven: Yale University Press, 1965),

The Baptistery of the Orthodox was built under Bishop Ursus in the first quarter of the fifth century; its mosaics were added under Bishop Neon in the mid–fifth century (Ristow #s 398-399). The Baptistery of the Arians belongs to about 500 (Ristow #397). As octagons both buildings convey the symbolism of the world to come associated with the number eight.[5] The following discussion will concern the decorations in the Baptistery of the Orthodox other than the dome mosaic (discussed in chap. 7; Figure 11) that have a special relevance for baptism.

On the arches of four niches in the interior walls of the baptistery are biblical quotations/paraphrases in Latin that go back to Neon's baptistery but are in part restored.[6] The texts are Matthew 14:29-32 (excerpts from); Psalms 32:1-2; John 13:4-5; Psalms 23:2. All had a long history of association with baptism. Four of the slabs on the interior of the font are inscribed: one in Greek has John 3:6; the other three are in Latin — Galatians 3:27; Acts 2:38; and there is a nonbiblical dedicatory inscription ("Ursus, pontiff of Ravenna, dedicated to John, son of Zechariah and forerunner of Christ"). The present location presumably was not original, nor may the inscriptions themselves be.[7]

In the zone above these arches above four of the aedicules are reliefs depicting biblical scenes: Jonah and the great sea monster; Christ carrying a cross and an open book treading on a lion and a snake (Ps. 91:13; Luke 10:19); the seated Christ giving the law to Peter on his right while Paul on his left makes a gesture of acclamation; and Daniel and the lions.[8] Christ's victory over evil and his commission to the apostles gave the assurance of deliverance of which the Old Testament scenes were types.

The procession of the apostles formed a circle around the central dome mosaic of the baptism of Christ. The next circle of mosaics around the dome showed alternating representations of four empty thrones (of Christ) with his cross and four altars with an open Bible.[9] The baptizand on looking up beheld not only the baptism of Christ but a triumphant picture of heavenly glory.

---

pp. 139-140; for the art note Peter van Dael, "Purpose and Function of Decoration Schemes in Early Christian Baptisteries," in H. J. Auf der Maur et al., eds., *Fides sacramenti sacramentum fidei* (Assen: Van Gorcum, 1981), pp. 113-135.

5. The number "eight" was important in early Christianity: Jesus' resurrection on the eighth day, eight periods of history in some apocalyptic schemes of history, eight saved in the ark of Noah, circumcision on the eighth day, David the eighth son of Jesse, Jesus' eight beatitudes, the ogdoad in Gnosticism — Everett Ferguson, "Octagon," in Paul Corby Finney, *Encyclopedia of Early Christian Art and Archaeology* (Grand Rapids: Eerdmans, forthcoming); Paul A. Underwood, "The Fountain of Life in Manuscripts of the Gospels," *Dumbarton Oaks Papers* 5 (1950): 80-87.

6. Kostof, *The Orthodox Baptistery of Ravenna*, 58-62, figures 103-106, quotes and pictures the present form of the inscriptions and translates them.

7. Text in Kostof, *The Orthodox Baptistery*, 139-140.

8. Kostof, *The Orthodox Baptistery*, pp. 66-71, figures 75, 76, 79-82.

9. Hans-Peter L'Orange, "Bemerkung zu einem zentalen Thema des Mosaikschmucks im Kathedral-Baptisterium in Ravenna," in Otto Feld and Urs Peschlow, eds., *Studien zur spätantiken und byzantinischen Kunst*, Vol. 2 (Bonn: Rudolf Habelt, 1986), pp. 163-165, interprets the altars with Bibles as the spiritual kingdom, in each case flanked by a throne and a crown as representing the earthly empire, doubled because of its division into two parts (east and west Rome).

Siricius of Rome

Although the papacy of Siricius falls within the fourth century (384-399), his declarations on baptism are related to the positions of his fifth-century successors. His letter to Himerius of Tarragona deals with practical questions related to the administration of baptism.[10] Against those who wanted to rebaptize persons baptized by Arians he declares that "We bring them into the Catholic fold . . . simply by the invocation of the sevenfold Spirit and the laying on of the bishop's hand" (*Letter* 2.2). He adds (with exaggeration) that "This is the custom observed throughout East and West."

Against performing baptisms at Christmas, Epiphany, and feasts of the apostle or martyrs, he affirms the privilege alone of the Pasch and secondarily of Pentecost. The "elect" are to give their names forty days or more in advance. During that period they are to be "expiated by exorcism and daily prayer and fasting" (*Letter* 2.3). An exception was made for "infants who cannot yet speak because of their age and those who because of some distress need the water of sacred baptism"; they "should come with all haste" to "the saving font" lest they should depart this life and "lose the kingdom and life" (2.3). This statement has been cited as evidence that infant baptism was common at Rome and in Spain and as implying that in Spain it was not widespread. Since Siricius is addressing exceptions to the preferred times for baptism, especially in cases of emergency baptism (which already had two centuries of precedent), conclusions about the general practice of infant baptism are dubious.

Innocent I and Gelasius

Innocent I was bishop of Rome from 402 to 417. Of his thirty-six letters, the one to Bishop Decentius of Gubbio in 416 (*Letter* 25) is important for distinguishing the postbaptismal rites that became confirmation from baptism.

The relevant section begins with an allusion to infant baptism: "Regarding the signing of infants, this clearly cannot be done validly by anyone other than the bishop" (25.3).[11] That bishops alone should "sign or give the comforting Spirit" is affirmed on the basis of ecclesiastical custom and the precedent of Acts 8:14-18, where Peter and John gave the Spirit to those who had been baptized. Innocent applied the laying on of hands in Acts 8 to the "signing." He explains that

---

10. English translation of sections 2 and 3 in Gordon P. Jeanes, *The Origins of the Roman Rite* (Bramcote/Nottingham: Grove, 1991), p. 8, from which I quote.

11. I use the translation of Martin F. Connell, *Church and Worship in Fifth-Century Rome: The Letter of Innocent I to Decentius of Gubbio* (Cambridge: Grove Books, 2002). He notes that in Innocent's time most initiates were adults (p. 10) and that some interpret "infants" as a metaphorical reference to neophytes but nothing suggests another meaning than literal infants (p. 29). I think it unlikely that the signing referred to admission to the catechumenate. Another translation and study is Gerald Ellard, "How Fifth-Century Rome Administered Sacraments," *Theological Studies* 9 (1948): 5-11.

(P)resbyters are allowed to anoint the baptized with chrism. But they are not allowed to sign the forehead with the same oil consecrated by the bishop, for that is used by the bishops only when they give the Spirit. (25.3)

This ruling by Innocent was to be often repeated in support of associating the postbaptismal laying on of hands and anointing with the conferral of the Holy Spirit by the bishop.[12]

A Roman synod under Innocent in 402 says that persons baptized in childhood who have remained chaste and those baptized as adults who were married only once may become ecclesiastics.[13] This ruling reflects a time when infant and adult baptism were both present.

Elsewhere Innocent declares baptism to be unrepeatable (*Letter* 2.8). In *Letter* 17.10 he discusses the different treatment of the Novatianists and Paulianists, the latter of whom were required to be rebaptized, by the Council of Nicaea (can. 8 and 19); he comments on Acts 8:17 and 19:2-6 with the explanation that in the case of the latter there is a difference between being washed in water and baptism in the name of the Father, Son, and Holy Spirit.

Later in the fifth century Gelasius, bishop of Rome (492-496), forbade presbyters from making the chrism or applying the episcopal consignation, except perhaps with his command.[14] The distinction in functions meant that the postbaptismal signing was often separated in time (sometimes for an extended period) from the baptism.[15] In this respect western practice differed from eastern, where the presbyter who baptized gave the anointing also as part of one rite.

Leo I

Leo I the Great was bishop of Rome from 440 to 461. Better known for other things, he had occasion to address matters relative to baptism with some frequency.[16]

---

12. Franz J. Dölger, "Die Firmung in den Denkmälern des christlichen Altertums," *Römische Quartalschrift* 19 (1905): 1-41, quotes an inscription from the fourth or beginning of the fifth century mentioning the right hand of the chief shepherd signing *(signat)* the person baptized in order to impart the Holy Spirit (p. 16).

13. C. J. Hefele, *A History of the Councils of the Church,* tr. H. N. Oxenham (Edinburgh: T&T Clark, 1896), Vol. 2, p. 429.

14. Quoted in Connell, *Church and Worship,* p. 32.

15. Gregory I (in 593) reaffirmed the practice of presbyters giving the prebaptismal anointing on the children's breast but bishops giving the postbaptismal anointing on the forehead (*Letter* 4.9, to Januarius), but he later (594) conceded that in the absence of a bishop, even presbyters could anoint the baptized on their foreheads (*Letter* 4.26, to Januarius). Both Gelasius and Gregory required that the presbyters use oil consecrated by the bishop (Connell, *Church and Worship,* p. 33). Innocent's position remained the norm.

16. Victor Saxer, *Les rites de l'initiation chrétienne du IIe au VIe siècle: Esquisse historique et signification d'après leur principaux témoins* (Spoleto: Centro italiano di studi sull'alto medioevo, 1988), pp. 584-588.

Leo's *Letter* 16, "To the Bishops of Sicily," objected to their practice of baptizing at Epiphany. He claimed apostolic authority for making Easter and Pentecost the principal times for baptism. The festivals of the worship of Jesus by the wise men and of his resurrection were distinct and should be kept distinct in their celebration.

Leo affirms,

> It is appropriate that the power of baptism should change the old into the new creature on the death-day of the Crucified and the Resurrection-day of the Dead: that Christ's death and his resurrection may operate in those being reborn. (*Letter* 16.4)[17]

He supports this with the quotation of Romans 6:3-5. Hence, the Pachal season is "the time chosen for regenerating the sons of men and adopting them among the sons of God" (16.4). "Death ensues through the slaying of sin, and threefold immersion imitates the lying in the tomb three days,[18] and the raising out of the water is like him that rose again from the tomb" (16.4). The associations of regeneration (and related ideas) with death to sin and resurrection to new life are central baptismal motifs for Leo.

The example of Peter (Acts 2:37-41 quoted) in baptizing at Pentecost, which occurs on the same day of the week as Easter, makes that a suitable time also for baptizing (*Letter* 16.5). The ordinary routine of the church does not mean, however, that baptism is refused when someone is in peril of death, at a time of siege, in the distress of persecution, or in terror of shipwreck (16.6). Leo ascribed baptismal exorcism to apostolic times (16.6).

The baptism of Jesus was the time when he was revealed more openly (*Letter* 16.3). There is such a difference between his baptism and baptism in the church that his baptism does not make Epiphany a usual time for baptism.[19] He needed no forgiveness of sin or to be reborn of the Holy Spirit. Jesus received baptism, as he did circumcision, because of his identification with human beings and to fulfill the law. He ratified the power of rebirth when there flowed from his side (John 19:34) the "the blood of ransom and the water of baptism" (16.7).[20] Without the reality of the incarnation there would be no regeneration in the water of baptism nor redemption in the blood of his passion (*Sermon* 69.5).

The flood and the ark of Noah show the restoration that takes place in baptism and the salvation on the wood of the cross (*Sermon* 60.3.1). Human beings are renewed in holy baptism (*Sermon* 18.1).

---

17. Unless otherwise noted, I use (and sometimes adapt) the translation of Charles Lett Feltoe, "The Letters and Sermons of Leo the Great," in *Nicene and Post-Nicene Fathers* (repr. Peabody: Hendrickson, 1994), Second Series, Vol. 12, p. 28 here.

18. Other references cited below.

19. *Letter* 168 rebukes the practice of baptizing on saints' days instead of limiting the normal practice to Easter and Pentecost.

20. Also in *Letter* 28.5, where they are the font and the cup, and *Sermon* 34.4.2.

Leo brings together the essential elements of the baptismal ceremony at Rome in the following passage:

> (R)emain firm in that faith which you have professed before many witnesses and in which you were reborn through water and the Holy Spirit and received the anointing of salvation and the seal of eternal life. (*Sermon* 24.6)

Profession of faith, baptism in the water and the Holy Spirit, and chrism constituted the heart of the baptismal ceremony for Leo. Another important element in baptism was the renunciation of the devil (*Sermon* 41.2). The baptismal ceremony is alluded to in the following statement that introduces frequently recurring motifs:

> For the renunciation of the devil and belief in God, the passing from the old state into newness of life, the casting off of the earthly image, and the putting on of the heavenly form — all this is a sort of dying and rising again, whereby he that is received by Christ and receives Christ is not the same after as he was before he came to the font, for the body of the regenerate becomes the flesh of the Crucified. (*Sermon* 41.2)

A reference to the threefold immersion speaks of "the mystery of regeneration, where the destruction of sin means life for the reborn and the triple immersion follows the pattern of our Lord's three-day death" (*Sermon* 70.4).[21]

The Spirit, water, and blood of 1 John 5:8 are identified as the Spirit of sanctification, the blood of redemption, and the water of baptism. These three are "one and undivided" (*Letter* 28.5).

In a passage that affirms the transmission of original sin and repeats that the water and blood flowing from Christ's side was the "mystery of redemption and regeneration," Leo speaks of "the very condition of a new creature which at baptism puts off not the covering of true flesh but the taint of the old condemnations" and makes one become the body of Christ (*Letter* 19.4).

A passage that has the celebration of Easter as its context speaks of "whole tribes of the human race brought in afresh to the adoption of God's sons, and offspring of the new birth multiplied through the virgin fertility of the church" (*Sermon* 49.3). Rebirth is an important theme for Leo (see more below), but he employs other motifs as well. The passage continues by declaring that the devil sees himself robbed of his tyrannical power, as thousands of either sex — old, young, middle-aged — receive justification from sin, whether his own sin or original sin (*Sermon* 49.3).

The rebirth of baptism makes one a partaker of the birth of Christ, which was free from the curse on human flesh. Leo goes beyond likening the font to a womb to identify it with the virgin Mary's womb:

---

21. Translation by Jane Patricia Freeland and Agnes Josephine Conway, *St. Leo the Great: Sermons*, Fathers of the Church 93 (Washington, D.C.: Catholic University of America Press, 1996), p. 308.

> And each one is a partaker of this spiritual origin in regeneration; and to every one when he is reborn, the water of baptism is like the virgin's womb; for the same Holy Spirit fills the font, who filled the virgin, that the sin, which that sacred conception overthrew, may be taken away by this mystical washing. (*Sermon* 24.3)

Here Leo combines forgiveness of original sin, regeneration, and likeness to Jesus' birth on the basis of the common activity of the Holy Spirit.[22] The same thought appears in the next sermon in the collection:

> He placed in the font of baptism that very origin which he had assumed in the virgin's womb. He gave to the water what he had given to his mother. For, the same "power of the Most High" and "overshadowing Holy Spirit" [Luke 1:35] that caused Mary to bear the Savior makes the water regenerate the believer. (*Sermon* 25.5)[23]

Christ left both a "sacrament and an example." We apprehend the sacrament (mystery) by being reborn, and we follow the example by imitation (*Sermon* 63.4). The idea of rebirth[24] or regeneration[25] is common.

"By the birth of baptism an innumerable multitude of sons are born to God" (*Sermon* 63.6).[26] By faith they are adopted as sons of promise. Regeneration occurs "by the faith of all the newborn" (*Sermon* 63.6). It is notable how often Leo links faith with the theme of the new birth.

Baptism is not only an identification with Christ's birth; it is also an identification with his death.[27]

> The entire body of the faithful being born in the font of baptism is crucified with Christ in his passion, raised again in his resurrection, and placed at the Father's right hand in his ascension, so with him are they born in this nativity. For any believer in whatever part of the world that is reborn in Christ quits the old paths of his original nature and passes into a new man by being reborn. (*Sermon* 26.2)

The two ideas of regeneration and the forgiveness of sins are often combined. In the baptism of regeneration all stain of sin is washed away (*Sermon* 7.1). Remission of sins comes to those reborn in holy baptism (*Sermon* 44.1). Sins are washed in holy

---

22. For the Holy Spirit in baptism according to Leo (in comparison with Cyril of Alexandria) see Daniel A. Keating, *The Appropriation of Divine Life in Cyril of Alexandria* (Oxford: Oxford University Press, 2004), pp. 269-270.

23. Freeland and Conway, *St. Leo the Great*, p. 103.

24. "Rebirth through baptism" — *Sermon* 36.3.1; reborn in the baptism of the Holy Spirit (I understand this to be a reference to Christian water baptism in which the Holy Spirit is at work) — *Sermon* 45.1.

25. "Regeneration of baptism" — *Sermon* 43.3; "divine regeneration" — *Sermon* 41.2; "baptism of regeneration" — *Sermon* 9.4.

26. Baptism as new birth: *Sermons* 4.3.22; 5.5.22; 50.5.74.

27. Baptism as death and resurrection: *Sermons* 6.2.22; 57.4.74.

baptism (*Sermon* 49.6); the water of baptism forgave those who poured out the Savior's blood (Acts 2:23, 36-38, but not cited — *Sermon* 67.3).

Baptism made one a temple of the Holy Spirit. Leo says, "By the mystery of baptism you were made the temple of the Holy Spirit," and proceeds with an admonition not to put him to flight by sinful acts and to become again a servant of the devil (*Sermon* 21.3).

Leo admonishes, "Let all those reborn through water and the Holy Spirit consider the one whom they have renounced," for they have shaken off the yoke of tyrannical domination (*Sermon* 57.5.2).[28] Similarly, he speaks of those who abandon the profession of faith uttered at the time of rebirth and forget that divine promise, adhering to what they had renounced (*Sermon* 66.3.1).

Leo insisted that baptism was to be administered only once, citing Ephesians 4:5. Those who out of fear or a mistake repeated their baptism, on realizing their mistake, were to be received in communion by penitence and the imposition of the bishop's hands (*Letter* 159.7). These may have been baptized in the church and then were induced by heretics to be baptized again. The following section considers those who received baptism from heretics but had not been previously baptized in the church. They are to receive imposition of hands and invocation of the Holy Spirit "because they have received the bare form of baptism without the power of sanctification" (159.8).[29] If Leo intended a contrast between the preceding persons who were to be received by penitence and the imposition of hands and these who were received by imposition of hands with invocation of the Holy Spirit, then those interpreters who see in the latter class a reference to "confirmation" would be more likely correct than those who interpret the latter case as the reception of penitents also. In both cases he did not want "the font once entered to be defiled by repetition" (159.8).

Leo, however, made an important exception to his ruling in regard to cases that betrayed one of the problems with infant baptism. Some had been carried into captivity at a young age and on their return had no recollection of being baptized. In response to their craving "the healing waters of baptism," certain brethren hesitated to baptize them lest they violate the rule against rebaptism. Leo's answer is that their case was different from those forced by heretics into the font a second time, "since what is not known to have been done at all cannot come under the charge of repetition" (*Letter* 166.1).[30] Similarly, if children have been left by Christian parents but there is no proof among kinsfolk, clergy, or neighbors of their baptism, "steps

---

28. Freeland and Conway, *St. Leo the Great*, p. 247.

29. Similarly, *Letter* 166.2 considers baptism by heretics not to confer the power of the Holy Spirit, yet the "mystery of regeneration" is not to be repeated and the deficiency is to be supplied by imposition of the bishop's hands. Those who came from Africa or Mauretania, where Donatism was strong, and were doubtful about the faith of those who baptized them were not to be baptized but were to receive imposition of hands and invocation of the Holy Spirit's power, "which they could not receive from heretics" (*Letter* 167.18).

30. Leo deals with the same circumstance in *Letter* 167.17. Those baptized in infancy and carried off by Gentiles who have lived as Gentiles, are received back with public penitence (167.19).

should be taken for their regeneration" (*Letter* 167.16). The tone of uncertainty in these two letters suggests that infant baptism could by no means be assumed as routine in Rome in the mid–fifth century.

John the Deacon

John was a deacon in the church at Rome at the end of the fifth and beginning of the sixth century; some identify him with the John who later became pope (523-526). About the year 500 he wrote a letter to a certain Senarius responding to questions raised by the latter concerning baptismal practice at Rome. It is a major source of information about the baptismal ritual at Rome at the end of the period chosen for my study.[31]

The candidate for baptism began as a catechumen. During this time of instruction the person was blessed by "frequent laying on of the hand," as the blessing of the Creator was "called over his head three times in honor of the Trinity" (3). One was progressively delivered from the power of the devil by exorcisms. These involved exsufflation and adjurations for the devil to depart. The catechumen was given salt as a reminder that as flesh is preserved by salt so the mind is preserved by wisdom and the preaching of the word of God. One is delivered from the devil by renouncing him as part of "the first beginning of faith with a true confession" (3). Without this one cannot be "reborn in Christ" and "approach the grace of the saving laver" (3).

The candidate, after renouncing the works and pomps of the devil, received the words of the Symbol of the Apostles.[32] The catechumen was now called one of the *competentes* (those requesting baptism) or *electi* (chosen for baptism), "For he was conceived in the womb of Mother Church and now he begins to live, even though the time of the sacred birth is not yet fulfilled" (4). The scrutinies followed: an examination of the candidates' hearts. This was to determine "whether since the renunciation of the devil the sacred words have fastened themselves" on their minds; "whether they acknowledge the future grace of the Redeemer"; "whether they be-

---

31. I use the translation in E. C. Whitaker, *Documents of the Baptismal Liturgy*, revised and expanded by Maxwell E. Johnson (Collegeville: Liturgical Press, 2003), pp. 208-212. The letter's baptismal ceremony is summarized by G. G. Willis, *A History of Early Roman Liturgy to the Death of Pope Gregory the Great* (London: Henry Bradshaw Society, 1994), p. 118, who concludes that the change from an interrogatory to a declarative creed at the administration of baptism in Rome occurred two or three centuries after Gregory the Great (p. 129). The letter's information on the admission to the catechumenate (by imposition of the hand, exsufflation, exorcism, sign of the cross, and tasting salt) is studied by Antoine Chavasse, "Les deux rituels romain et gaulois de l'admission au catécuménat que renferme le sacramentaire gélasien (*Vat. Reg.* 316)," *Études de critique et d'histoire religieuses* (Lyon: Facultés Catholiques, 1948), pp. 70-98 (79-83). Chavasse finds the same ritual in the *Gelasian Sacramentary* 1.30-32; it differed from the fourth-century practice in Gaul, where admission to the catechumenate was by laying on of hands (Arles, can. 6; Sulpicius Severus, *Dialogues* 2.4.8; *Life of St. Martin* 13 — p. 95).

32. Willis, *A History of the Early Roman Liturgy*, p. 123, places the change at Rome from use of the Apostles' Creed to use of the Nicene Creed between 500 and 550.

lieve in God the Father Almighty" (4). Infants too were "scrutinized three times before the Pascha" (2), but no indication is given as to how this was done.[33]

The ears were touched with "the oil of sanctification" so that faith might enter through them and they might be sealed against the entrance of anything harmful (4). The nostrils also were touched so that as long as they drew the breath of life they might abide in the service of God, perceiving the spiritual odor of divine sweetness and giving no admittance to the pleasures of the world (4-5). The breast next was anointed with the oil, for "with a firm mind and a pure heart" the person promised to follow the commandments of Christ (6).

The person approached baptism completely naked, "having put aside the carnal garments of mortality" (6). At this point John says, "The church has ordained these things with watchful care over many years, although the old books may not show traces of them" (6). How much John included in this statement of what preceded him is not clear, but it is a striking acknowledgment that the baptismal ceremony, although quite traditional by the time John wrote, contained much that lacked attestation in the earliest sources.

Consecration in baptism occurred in the "one laver" by a "threefold immersion." The threefold immersion signified the Trinity in whose name the baptism was performed, and acknowledged the one who upon the third day rose from the dead (6).

The one baptized was then clothed in a white garment, and "his head [was] anointed with the unction of the sacred chrism" (6). This anointing was associated with the anointing of kings and priests. The idea of priesthood was further expressed by dressing the head with linen. The white garments on the neophytes prefigured the resurrection. The old clothing represented the error that darkened the first birth, but the clothing of the second birth displayed "the raiment of glory, so that, clad in a wedding garment," one may "approach the table of the heavenly bridegroom as a new man" (6).

John the Deacon affirms that "all these things are done, even to infants, who by reason of their youth understand nothing" (7). He offers this justification: "When they are presented by their parents or others, it is necessary that their salvation should come through other people's profession, since their damnation came by another's fault" (7).[34] He thus takes a different approach to infant baptism from Pseudo-Dionysius in two respects: He sees the parents or sponsors as making a profession on behalf of the child instead of promising to train the child (although this was likely implied as well), and he justifies this vicarious profession as parallel to original sin (see chap. 52 on Augustine). His wording seems to indicate that the bap-

---

33. Willis, *A History of the Early Roman Liturgy*, p. 120, states that candidates for baptism in the first five centuries were normally adults but after c. 500 they were almost exclusively children of Christian parents and the rites in John the Deacon and later are designed for children.

34. J.-C. Didier, "Une adaptation de la liturgie baptismale au baptême des enfants dans l'église ancienne," *Mélanges de science religieuse* 22 (1965): 79-80, endorses the view that the change from the baptismal interrogations to a declaratory formula, effected at Rome in the seventh century, was a consequence of the general practice of infant baptism (pp. 79, 82).

tismal questions were put to the sponsors in the second person and, as in adult baptism, answered in the first person.[35]

Milk and honey were offered along with the sacrifice of bread and wine at the Pascha. The milk and honey represented the land of promise (Lev. 20:24), which is interpreted as the land of resurrection to eternal bliss. This sacrament was "offered to the newly baptized so that they may realize that no others but they who partake of the body and blood of the Lord shall receive the land of promise" (12). They who have received the second birth are nourished on their journey with the food of little children.

Gelasian Sacramentary

The Vatican manuscript of the *Gelasian Sacramentary* is mid–eighth century, but it is a composite document. The baptismal ritual reflects the period after the Byzantine reconquest of Rome in the sixth century and is in direct continuity with baptismal usages of the fourth and fifth centuries.[36] Since the *Gelasianum* is later than the period of this study, I take only summary notice of it, but I do so because of its confirmation of earlier features and its importance in the history of practice at Rome.

From the prayers the following sequence of the baptismal ritual may be discerned: inscription of candidates for baptism; prayers for the *electi* (those to be baptized); blessing of salt given to the catechumens and blessing of the candidate after giving the salt; three scrutinies and three exorcisms on the third, fourth, and fifth Sundays of Lent; *traditio* of the Gospels (a new rite created at Rome in the sixth century); *traditio symboli* (no longer the Apostles' Creed, as still in John the Deacon but the Niceno-Constantinopolitan Creed); *traditio* of the Lord's Prayer; on holy Saturday an exorcism, opening of ears, prebaptismal anointing with oil of exorcism and renunciation of Satan, *redditio* of the Symbol, imposition of hand; at the Paschal vigil a blessing and signing of the font with an epiclesis of the Spirit on the font; baptismal interrogation and triple immersion; signing with chrism on the neck by priest, signing by bishop on forehead with imposition of hand and prayer; kiss of peace; mass of the resurrection.

The minister was a presbyter, but the bishop confirmed the candidate. Distinctive elements of the Roman ritual of initiation were the terminology of *electi* instead of *competentes* usual in other parts of the West, the *redditio symboli* in public, three scrutinies, and the distinctive place of the bishop (baptism and consignation by a priest, but the consignation and imposition of hand with invocation of the Holy Spirit only by a bishop).

---

35. Didier, "Une adaptation," pp. 85-87, who contrasts this Roman wording with the African, Gallican, and Visigothic custom in the fifth to seventh centuries of interrogations to the sponsors and answers by them with reference to infants in the third person; the Roman custom prevailed in the Carolingian period, but traces of the other custom may be found (pp. 88-89).

36. Saxer, *Les rites de l'initiation chrétienne du IIe au VIe siècle*, pp. 597-623, from whom I take the following information. There is a summary in Bryan D. Spinks, *Early and Medieval Rituals and Theologies of Baptism* (Aldershot: Ashgate, 2006), pp. 111-114.

The Lateran Baptistery in Rome

The octagonal baptistery adjoining the Lateran basilica constructed under the auspices of Constantine had in its second phase a circular baptismal font with a depth of 91 centimeters below floor level (Ristow #403).[37] This Lateran baptistery was reconstructed under Sixtus III (432-440), and the font was given its present octagonal shape (Ristow #404; Figure 19). The baptismal pool was 8.5 meters (about 28 feet) in diameter, and so designed for multiple immersions. Sixtus placed a Latin inscription over the eight sides of the entablature of the colonnade surrounding the room. It sets forth his baptismal theology:

> Here is born from life-giving seed a people, consecrated to another city,
>   whom the Spirit brings forth from the fertile waters.
> To plunge [*mergere*] in the holy purifying flood the sinner,
>   whom the wave receives as old but gives forth as new.
> None reborn is different from those it makes one,
>   One font [*fons*], one Spirit, one faith.
> Mother church as a virgin brought forth those who are born,
>   whom she conceived by the divine breath and brought into being in the
>   flowing water.
> The person who wants to be innocent is here made clean by washing,
>   whether from the guilt of the first parent or one's own.
> Here is the font of life which bathes the whole world,
>   its ultimate source the side of Christ wounded.
> Reborn in this font for the kingdom of heaven,
>   the blessed life does not receive those born only once.
> Be not afraid of the number or kind of your sins,
>   for the one born in this river will be holy.[38]

Other baptisteries in Rome will be noted in chapter 54.

---

37. For the successive baptisteries at the Lateran see Underwood, "The Fountain of Life," pp. 41-138 (44-45, 50-51, 53-61). Marina Falla Castelfranchi, "L'edificio battesimale in Italia nel periodo paleocristiano," in *L'edificio battesimale in Italia: Aspetti e problemi: Atti dell'VIII Congresso Nazionale di Archeologia Cristiana . . . 21-26 settembre 1998* (Bordighera: Istituto Internazionale di Studi Liguri, 2001), 267-301, suggests that the Constantinian baptistery at the Lateran was the model for the octagonal baptisteries at other places in the fourth and fifth centuries (270-271).

38. Text in Hugo Brandenburg, *Ancient Churches of Rome from the Fourth to the Seventh Century: The Dawn of Christian Architecture in the West* (Turnhout: Brepols, 2004), p. 324, chap. 2, n. 32; for the English translation given there I have substituted a more literal rendering. Underwood, "The Fountain of Life," pp. 50-61, also gives the text and translation, and he suggests the future bishop Leo as the author of the anonymous inscription. Giuseppe Cuscito, "Epigrafi di apparato nei battisteri paleocristiani d'Italia," in *L'edificio battesimale in Italia* (n. 37), 441-466, gives the Latin text of seventeen inscriptions, including this one (462-466).

50. Gaul and North Africa: Gennadius of Marseilles, Some African Councils, and Quodvultdeus of Carthage

Gennadius of Marseilles

To Gennadius, presbyter in Marseilles at the end of the fifth century, is usually attributed the work *De ecclesiasticis dogmatibus*. Its chapter 74 (PL 58.997) contains a strong statement of the necessity of baptism for salvation and refers to affusion as an alternative to immersion.

> We believe in the act of baptism for salvation. We believe that no catechumen, although dying in good works, has eternal life, except by martyrdom, where the whole sacrament of baptism is completed. The one being baptized confesses his faith before the priest and answers when questioned. The martyr also does this before the persecutor: he both confesses his faith and answers when questioned. After the confession, he is either sprinkled *(aspergitur)* with water or immersed *(intingitur);* the martyr indeed is either sprinkled *(aspergitur)* with blood or overcome *(contingitur)* with fire. He receives the Holy Spirit by the imposition of hand of the bishop.

The passage goes on to talk about the martyr having the equivalent of the eucharist, confession, renunciation, and sins forgiven. Because of the strong statement about the necessity of baptism and the elaboration of martyrdom bringing the equivalent of baptism, I wonder if the reference to aspersion has sickbed baptism in view.

Some African Councils

A supposed synod at Carthage in 398, whose canons are included in a later compilation, says that widows or virgins consecrated to God who are employed at the baptism of women must be competent to instruct ignorant women how to answer at their baptism and how to live afterward (can. 12).[1] Another canon, however, says, "A woman may not baptize" (can. 100).[2] "Those who desire to be baptized must give their name, and when they have been proved by abstinence from wine and flesh and by repeated imposition of hands, they shall be baptized" (can. 85), and after baptism they are to abstain for a time from luxurious feasts, the theatre, and intercourse with their wives (can. 86).[3] The repeated imposition of hands may refer to exorcisms or blessings; the length of the period for abstinence after baptism is not specified.

A council in Carthage in 401 directed that "Children of whom it is uncertain whether they have been baptized shall be baptized without delay" (can. 7).[4] Unfortunately we do not know the circumstances to give a context for this ruling, but the canon shows that one could not automatically assume the baptism of children.

The Council of Carthage in 418 fully supported Augustine in the Pelagian controversy (chap. 52).

> If any man says that new-born children need not be baptized or that they should indeed be baptized for the remission of sins, but that they have in them no original sin inherited from Adam which must be washed away in the bath of regeneration, so that in their case the formula of baptism "for the remission of sins" must not be taken literally, but figuratively, let him be anathema. (can. 2)[5]

Some manuscripts add as the third canon a further denial of teaching associated with the Pelagians:

> If any man says that in the kingdom of heaven or elsewhere there is a certain middle place, where children who die unbaptized live in peace, whereas without baptism they cannot enter into the kingdom of heaven, that is, into eternal life, let him be anathema.[6]

These positions are further explicated in chapter 52.

Quodvultdeus

Quodvultdeus became a deacon in the church of Carthage about 420 and its bishop in 437. Banished by the Vandals two years later, he went to Naples. He was dead by 457. His three homilies on the creed, *De symbolo* 1–3, were preached as a deacon in

---

1. C. J. Hefele, *A History of the Councils of the Church*, tr. H. N. Oxenham (Edinburgh: T&T Clark, 1896), Vol. 2, p. 412.
2. Hefele, *A History of the Councils*, p. 417.
3. Hefele, *A History of the Councils*, p. 417.
4. Hefele, *A History of the Councils*, p. 424 (with the note that the canon is #72 in the collection of Dionysius Exiguus and #6 in Pseudo-Isidore).
5. Hefele, *A History of the Councils*, p. 458.
6. Hefele, *A History of the Councils*, p. 459.

the 430s.[7] They were delivered on the Sunday a week before Easter, likely in three successive years, to those preparing for baptism.

As other sources indicate, catechumens, "hearers," gave their name to the bishop at Epiphany, or the start of Lent, to indicate that they desired baptism at the coming Easter. Those approved to receive baptism were now called *competentes*, "those seeking together" for baptism. The details of the period of preparation for baptism in North Africa are known especially from Augustine, and their description will be given in the next chapter.

During the Saturday vigil two weeks before Easter the *competentes* were delivered the creed *(traditio symboli)* to be memorized during the following week. On the next Saturday night they recited the creed, the articles of which Quodvultdeus expounded in sermons on Sunday. In these sermons Quodvultdeus referred to three other events of the preceding night that were "pivotal rites" in the conversion process preparatory to baptism.[8]

There was a scrutiny to determine readiness for baptism, described in *De symbolo* 1.1.5-10. Each person was presented before the entire church with head bowed and standing barefoot on goatskin. An exorcism was performed to root out the devil and free each from his dominion.[9] All chanted psalms, saying, "Probe me, Lord, and know my heart" (Ps. 139:3). All — rich and poor, master and slave — were equal in this ceremony designed to remove pride and produce humility. After the chanting of the psalm, they received the creed; the "sacrament of the symbol" and "the banner of the cross" would serve as protection against the "diabolical adversary."

The second rite was the renunciation of the devil. The *competentes* renounced aloud "the devil, his pomps, and his angels" (1.1.11) and also "his works" (1.1.13). "The names of those making the profession were inscribed in the book of life," by a "heavenly power," as "soldiers of Christ" (1.1.12-13).[10] The devil's weapons are pleasure and fear (1.1.16). Quodvultdeus spends much time describing the spectacles (chariot races in the circus, mimes and pantomimes in the theater, and wild animal contests in the amphitheater) that the devil used to entice people to pleasure (1.1.17-1.2.28). The second homily on the creed is briefer on the renunciation of "the devil, his pomps, and angels," explaining the pomps of the devil as "illicit desires," illustrated by 1 John 2:16, "carnal pleasures, lust of the eyes, and worldly ambitions" (2.1.3-6).

---

7. I follow Thomas Macy Finn, *Quodvultdeus of Carthage: The Creedal Homilies*, Ancient Christian Writers 60 (New York: Newman Press, 2004), pp. 1-22, and my quotations are from his translation. The homilies are studied by J. R. Simone, "The Baptismal and Christological Catecheses of Quodvultdeus," *Augustinianum* 25 (1985): 265-282. For the baptismal liturgy to be found in him see Victor Saxer, *Les rites de l'initiation chrétienne du IIe au VIe siècle: Esquisse historique et signification d'après leur principaux témoins* (Spoleto: Centro italiano di studi sull'alto medioevo, 1988), pp. 401-416.

8. Finn, *Quodvultdeus*, pp. 6-8.

9. The third homily on the creed alludes to exorcism by saying that the hearts of the *competentes* were prepared to receive the creed because their enemy had been driven from them (3.1.7). It refers also to breathing on the candidates (3.1.3), which Quodvultdeus does not comment on.

10. Finn, *Quodvultdeus*, pp. 95-96, n. 12, points to the parallels to Quodvultdeus's language in the procedures for enlistment in the Roman legions.

The person who conquers these three things conquers the devil, who seduces the world through pride. Quodvultdeus was concerned that his initiates renounce not only with their voices but also in their conduct (3.1.10).

The third crucial rite of the night was the profession of faith in the creed, the event that provides the text for Quodvultdeus's three sermons. Before commenting on the creed, I note Quodvultdeus's summary listing of the pivotal experiences on the night before his sermons on the creed: "exorcism, prayers, spiritual songs, insufflations, the goatskin, bowed necks, bare feet — this trembling endured for the gift of full peace of mind" (3.1.3).

The importance of believing the content of the creed in becoming a baptized Christian is evident in the amount of attention Quodvultdeus gave to its exposition. If one comes to baptism without this faith, the door of remission of sins is closed (1.10.1). Faith leads to understanding (Isa. 7:9 in Quodvultdeus's and Augustine's Latin text), and one must seek to understand what one believes (2.2.2). Faith is also necessary for sight and for the vision of God, which only comes later. "Faith is work; vision is God's reward" (3.2.1-2). By deferring the vision, God trains people and increases their desire (3.2.4).

The explanation of the baptismal creed, article by article, occupies the largest part of all three sermons, hence their designation, *De symbolo*.[11] Quodvultdeus states, "(W)e are about to explain the sentences of the most holy creed, that we may impress deeply on your understanding the content of each" article (3.1.7). The renunciation of allegiance to the devil prepared the hearts for reception of a new contract, the content of which was the creed. All three homilies are concerned with an orthodox exposition of the Trinity, especially against the Homoian form of Arianism. The second homily is also concerned to refute idolatry (2.2.4-2.3.14). Quodvultdeus also has his eye on Jews and Judaism.[12]

My special concern here is with the article on the remission of sins (1.10.1; 2.10.1; 3.10.1). "Holy baptism completely destroys all sins, both original and personal: things said, things done, things thought, things known, things forgotten" (2.10.1).[13] That "souls were snatched from the burden of sins" happens in no other way than through the incarnation of the Son of God (1.10.2).

Otherwise, Quodvultdeus's favorite imagery for baptism was new birth. The *competentes* whom he was addressing were "not yet reborn through holy baptism" (1.1.3). Rather, through the sign of the cross they were now conceived in the womb of the church, who as a mother carries them and nourishes them until she can rejoice in their birth (1.1.3).[14] The same imagery occurs in *De symbolo* 3.1.1 — "Holy Mother

---

11. Saxer, *Les rites de l'initiation*, pp. 410-411, reconstitutes the Symbol, which was given orally and was to be memorized.

12. Finn, *Quodvultdeus*, pp. 10-20, surveys the treatment of Jews, pagans, and heretics.

13. The forgiveness of original sin is particularly important for Augustine and will be discussed more fully in chap. 52.

14. The earlier perspective would have identified conception with reception of the word of God in faith — in the New Testament, James 1:21; 1 Pet. 1:23; cf. Heb. 4:2.

the Church . . . has conceived you in the womb through this most holy sign of the cross."[15] They will be "reborn through the washing"; meanwhile she carries them "to the day of birth." They will be "reborn from baptism," when the Mother will show them to Christ (3.1.3).[16] The creed was a "protection against the poison of the serpent for those in the process of birth" (3.1.4).[17] The remission of sins means, "He who created the person makes him anew . . . for grace precedes even this second infancy" (2.10.2). Baptism gave a "new state" or condition to replace the old state that had been forsaken (3.10.1).

Nearly as prominent is the motif of deliverance from the devil into a new life of freedom. By the "second infancy" one was "liberated through Christ," so that "those who were once captives in Adam and bound by the devil are free" (2.10.2). The soul "unburdened of its baggage of sins" and "adorned with the freedom of a new life" may with divine help conquer the devil (3.10.2).

The cross of Christ was the source of baptism and the eucharist.

> (T)he church was formed from the side of Christ, hanging on the cross. For his side was pierced, as the gospel says [John 19:34], and immediately there flowed out blood and water, which are the twin sacraments of the church: the water, which became her bath; the blood, which became her dowry. (1.6.5)

Another work by Quodvultdeus refers to the gift of the Holy Spirit through baptism (*Against the Jews* 19.6).

Quodvultdeus refers to the Arian (Homoian) practice of rebaptizing catholic Christians (1.13.6), something done by Donatists as well.

The *Book of the Promises and Predictions of God* is now assigned to Quodvultdeus.[18] This work cites Matthew 19:14 in connection with infant baptism: "(L)ittle children also, when consecrated by his [Christ's] baptism, are buried with him in death so that the body of sin may be destroyed" (2.5.8). The author opposes Pelagius for having two baptisms, since Pelagius accepted infant baptism but for another purpose than the forgiveness of sins; he asserts, "the one baptism is for remission of sins" (2.6.11). Here is an indication of an argument Augustine developed more fully.

Christ consecrated the river at his baptism (*In baptismo*, 2.31.68).

The *Book of Promises* also affirms that baptism sets one free from demons (2.9.16). This is associated with the frequent use of the crossing of the Red Sea as a figure of baptism (1.33.45; 1.37.54; 2.11.21). The author further connects baptism with

---

15. The sign of the cross refers to the rite of entry into the catechumenate — Finn, *Quodvultdeus*, p. 93, n. 3, and p. 121, n. 1.

16. Cf. "reborn in heaven" — 1.2.21, a passage to which Finn, *Quodvultdeus*, p. 100, n. 25, compares the Roman birth ritual according to which the father lifted up the infant and accepted the child as his own.

17. Finn, *Quodvultdeus*, p. 122, n. 4, suggests that Quodvultdeus may here refer to the practice of taking a pharmacological poison to induce abortion.

18. R. Braun, *Livre des promesses et des prédictions de Dieu*, I-II, Sources chrétiennes 101-102 (Paris: Cerf, 1964).

Israel's crossing of the Jordan and the administration of circumcision. "In baptism is the circumcision of the heart" (2.14.27). The boat in the water in which the baby Moses was placed was a figure of the cross and baptism (1.33.45). Another Old Testament type of baptism was Naaman's washing in the Jordan, but Christian baptism is in the name of the Trinity (2.31.69).

Christians are sons of God reborn by baptism (2.17.31). Rebirth is made possible by the blood of Christ: "reborn in baptism by the sign of his blood" (2.14.26). One is dipped in the blood of Christ by baptism, and this thought finds a parallel in martyrdom. "Martyrs were dipped [or dyed, *tinguntur*] a first time in the blood of Christ by baptism; they were dyed [*retincti*] again by the shedding of their own blood" [2.2.3].

51. North Africa: Augustine of Hippo — I

Augustine was born of a Christian mother (Monnica) and a pagan father (Patricius) in 354 in Thagaste in the province of Numidia, North Africa. Pursuing a career as a rhetorician, he received appointment in 384 to teach rhetoric in Milan. Listening to Ambrose's sermons removed the intellectual difficulties Augustine had with the Christian faith. That and other factors led to his conversion in 386 and his receiving baptism at age thirty-two from Ambrose on Easter Sunday, 387.[1] Returning to Thagaste, he gathered some friends in a monastic-like community, but the life of contemplative piety was not to last long. Ordained presbyter at Hippo in 391, he did most of the preaching, became co-bishop of the city in 395 and sole bishop the following year. Augustine's enormous literary output accompanied an active pastoral life until his death in 430.

Augustine's Own Experience with Baptism

Augustine's experience in the delay of baptism was not unlike many of his age in the late fourth and early fifth century.[2] Shortly after his birth, his mother had him en-

---

1. That Ambrose administered the baptism is stated in *Letter* 147.52.

2. For this chapter I am much indebted to William Harmless, *Augustine and the Catechumenate* (Collegeville: Liturgical Press, 1995), and his summaries of "Baptism" and "Catechumens, Catechumenate" in Allan D. Fitzgerald, ed., *Augustine through the Ages: An Encyclopedia* (Grand Rapids: Eerdmans, 1999), pp. 84-91, 145-149. Also helpful are R. De Latte, "Saint Augustin et le baptême: Étude liturgico-historique du rituel baptismal des adultes chez Saint Augustin," *Questions liturgiques* 56 (1975): 177-223; Vittorino Grossi, *La catechesi battesimale agli inizi del V secolo: Le fonti agostiniane* (Rome: Institutum Patristicum "Augustinianum," 1993), an expanded and updated version of his *La liturgia battesimale in S. Agostino: Studio sulla catechesi del peccato originale negli anni 393-412* (Rome: Institutum Patristicum "Augustinianum," 1970), and his summary, "Baptismus," in E. Mayer et al., *Augustinus Lexikon* (Basel: Schwabe & Co., 1990), Vol. 1, cols. 583-591; and in Latin, Benedictus Busch, "De initiatione christiana secundum sanctum Augustinum," *Ephemerides liturgicae* 52 (1938): 159-178, 385-483.

rolled as a catechumen but not baptized. "I was already signed with the sign of the cross and seasoned with salt from the time I came from my mother's womb."[3] While a small boy an illness caused Augustine to beg for baptism.

> [Monnica] hastily made arrangements for me to be initiated and washed in the sacraments of salvation, confessing you, Lord Jesus, for the remission of sins. But suddenly I recovered. My cleansing was deferred.[4]

Augustine relates the reasoning of his mother and others that it was better, in view of the temptations of adolescence, to delay baptism until later, since the guilt would be greater for sins committed "after that solemn washing." Augustine comes close to rebuking his mother's decision by expressing the view that it would have been better to take action for the healing of his soul.[5] On a later occasion of illness he "had no desire for your baptism."[6]

At the beginning of Augustine's teaching career in Thagaste he had an unnamed friend from a Catholic family whom Augustine influenced with Manichaean teaching. When the friend fell deathly ill, his family had him baptized, although he was unconscious. On his recovery, Augustine attempted to joke with him about a meaningless baptism received while "far away in mind and sense." The friend, however, took offense at this levity and severely rebuked Augustine for not taking what had happened seriously. The fever returned, and he died a few days later.[7]

Other references to baptisms in the *Confessions* are to conversion baptisms: Monnica's hope for Augustine (6.13.23), the baptism of Victorinus (8.2.3-5), Verecundus's deathbed baptism (9.3.5), Nebridius (like Augustine a convert back to Catholicism from Manichaeism — 9.3.6), Alypius along with Augustine and Augustine's son Adeodatus (9.6.14), Evodius (a member of Augustine's circle — 9.8.17), his

---

3. *Confessions* 1.11.17. For the *Confessions* I quote the translation by Henry Chadwick, *Saint Augustine Confessions*, World's Classics (Oxford: Oxford University Press, 1991), here p. 13. Mark Searle, "Infant Baptism Reconsidered," in M. E. Johnson, ed., *Living Water, Sealing Spirit: Readings on Christian Initiation* (Collegeville: Liturgical, 1995), pp. 365-409 (367), observes that in the fourth and fifth centuries Christian parents frequently enrolled their children as catechumens but postponed their baptism indefinitely while the children were healthy. David F. Wright, "Infant Dedication in the Early Church," in S. E. Porter and A. R. Cross, eds., *Baptism, the New Testament and the Church* (Sheffield: Sheffield Academic Press, 1999), pp. 352-378, cites the experience of Augustine among considerable evidence for infant dedication but not baptism.

4. *Confessions* 1.11.17.

5. *Confessions* 1.11.18. David F. Wright, "Augustine and the Transformation of Baptism," in Alan Kreider, ed., *The Origins of Christendom in the West* (Edinburgh: T&T Clark, 2001), p. 289, speaks more strongly of Augustine's "censure of his mother's negligence," with the observation that Augustine alone of the church leaders of the time not baptized in infancy has any word of criticism of their parents for this neglect (p. 290), but he notes that Augustine's censure was not for failing to have him baptized as a baby but for not carrying through with the baptism he had urgently requested (p. 291).

6. *Confessions* 5.9.16 (p. 83). He adds, "I did better as a boy when I begged for it from my devout mother."

7. *Confessions* 4.4.8.

father Patricius at the end of his life (made a catechumen earlier — 2.3.6, so his may be another case of sickbed baptism — 9.10.22), and Monnica at an unstated time (9.13.34).[8]

Augustine's account of his baptism, in which he was joined by his friend Alypius and his fifteen-year-old son Adeodatus, is brief and, as is characteristic of the *Confessions*, dwells more on his inner state than on what the ceremonies entailed.[9] After his experience in the garden, Augustine went into retirement, resigned his position as teacher of rhetoric in Milan, and notified Ambrose of his change with a request for recommended reading.[10] He writes:

> Your [God's] will was brought home to me in the depths of my being, and rejoicing in faith I praised your name. This faith did not allow me to be free of guilt over my past sins, which had not yet been forgiven through your baptism.[11]

Augustine does mention that "When the time came for me to give in my name for baptism, we left the country and returned to Milan."[12] Of the immediate preparation for baptism and the baptism itself he only says, "We were baptized, and disquiet about our past life vanished from us."[13]

Baptismal Ceremony in Hippo

Augustine's usual word for baptism was *baptismus*, the Latinized form of the Greek. Less often occurs *tinctio/ intinctio* (verbs *tinguere/intinguere* — "to wet by plunging into a liquid"). Where a distinction is observed, the verb *baptizare* refers to the inner purification by Christ and *intinguere* to the ritual action. *Lavacrum*, meaning purification, occurs in reference to Titus 3:5 and Ephesians 5:25-27.[14] Once he uses *submersio*, so he presumably employed an "authentic immersion."[15]

---

8. Wright, "Augustine and the Transformation of Baptism," p. 290.

9. For the baptismal ritual at Milan see chap. 40. Pamela Bright, "En-Spirited Waters: Baptism in the *Confessions* of Augustine," in Abraham J. Malherbe, Frederick W. Norris, and James W. Thompson, eds., *The Early Church in Its Context: Essays in Honor of Everett Ferguson* (Leiden: Brill, 1998), pp. 48-58, considers the baptismal language of the *Confessions*, especially in the meditation on Genesis in books 12-13.

10. *Confessions* 9.5.13.

11. *Confessions* 9.4.12 (p. 163).

12. *Confessions* 9.6.14 (p. 163).

13. *Confessions* 9.6.14 (p. 164). He refers to his receiving the washing of regeneration from Ambrose in *On Marriage and Concupiscence* 1.35.40.

14. Grossi, "Baptismus," cols. 585-586; Grossi, *La catechesi battesimale*, pp. 101-103, gives sample references for each.

15. Against other opinions, such is the conclusion of De Latte, "Rituel baptismal des adultes," p. 211, and Busch, "De initiatione christiana," p. 460 ("veram immersionem"), who suggests that adults by bending forward or kneeling could be immersed in pools said to be too small for an immersion (citing *On Baptism* 5.9.11 for Christ kneeling at his baptism). *Submersio* occurs in *Exposition of the Gospel of John* 81.2; *submergere* in *Against the Letters of Petilian* 2.83.184. Cf. Sermon 229A.1 for "plunged" in

Although lacking the systematic account of baptism given by Ambrose at Milan, Augustine's prolific writings say enough to permit a reconstruction of the rite at Hippo.

Augustine used the Latinized Greek word for catechumens, whom he defined as "hearers."[16] The catechist interviewed the person, or usually the sponsor, to determine the readiness to receive instruction in Christianity. The catechist gave a preliminary introduction to Christianity. Augustine's *On Catechizing the Uninstructed* fulfilled a request for a sample of such an instruction, in both a long and a short form.[17] Augustine used a survey of biblical history as the framework for remarks about topics most needed by the hearers.[18]

If the person declared faith in the preliminary instruction and a willingness to live accordingly, formal admission to the catechumenate occurred. It included being signed with the cross, receiving a laying on of hands, and tasting salt.[19] The sign of the cross was made on the forehead with the invocation of God and Christ, an action that brought a safeguard against evil and a consecration to God.[20] There may have been an exorcism at this point.[21] The laying on of hands accompanied a prayer of benediction.[22] Augustine treated the salt as a sacrament, a symbol of a preservative against corruption and of wisdom.[23] The person was now considered a Christian but

---

the font. Harmless, *Augustine*, p. 309, n. 39, notes passages where Augustine uses *conspergere* ("to sprinkle" or "to cover with small drops"). Augustine's description of Peter pouring water from his eyes and so baptizing his conscience (*Sermon* 229P.4) is a reference to his repentance and would seem to have no relevance to the method of baptism, but if it does, the result was the immersion of the conscience regardless of how the water came to cover it. A better explanation, however, is probably that this passage, like Peter's "baptism of tears" in *Sermon* 229O.1, is metaphorical — the language of baptism with its result (forgiveness) being transferred to another means of forgiveness (repentance).

16. *Sermon* 132.1.

17. J. Belche, "Die Bekehrung zum Christentum nach Augustins Büchlein De catechizandis rudibus," *Augustiniana* 27 (1977): 26-69, 333-363; 28 (1978): 255-287; 29 (1979): 247-279; Harmless, *Augustine*, pp. 107-155.

18. On the use of biblical history in catechetical instruction, see my "Irenaeus's *Proof of the Apostolic Preaching* and Early Catechetical Instruction," *Studia patristica* 18.3 (1989): 119-140. For Augustine's catechetical instruction in general in comparison to preceding practice see my "Catechesis and Initiation," in A. Kreider, ed., *The Origins of Christendom in the West* (Edinburgh: T&T Clark, 2001), pp. 229-268 (250-265 on Augustine).

19. *On Catechizing the Uninstructed* 26.50 (signed and dealt with according to the custom of the church); *The Punishment and Forgiveness of Sins and the Baptism of Little Ones* 2.26.42 (catechumens are sanctified by the sign of Christ and the prayer of imposition of hands). On Augustine himself see *Confessions* 1.11.17, quoted above.

20. *On Catechizing the Uninstructed* 20.34; *Sermon* 215.5; 306B (Denis 18).8; *Exposition of the Gospel of John* 11.3, 4; 50.2; *Explanations of the Psalms* 36.2. De Latte, "Rituel baptismal des adultes," pp. 182-184.

21. De Latte, "Rituel baptismal des adultes," pp. 186-187, with reference to *To Cresconius* 2.5, 7; *Against Julian, an Unfinished Work* 3.164; *On the Creed* 1.1.

22. *On Baptism* 3.16.21, which asks rhetorically, "What is the laying on of hands if not a prayer over a person?"

23. *On Catechizing the Uninstructed* 26.50; *Explanations of the Psalms* 101, 2.2. De Latte, "Rituel baptismal des adultes," pp. 188-189.

not a full member of the church.[24] Treating baptism as the new spiritual birth, Augustine likened admission to the catechumenate to conception.[25]

There began now a period of apprenticeship in Christian living.[26] Catechumens attended the scripture readings, sermons, and singing of the Psalms at regular Christian assemblies. Augustine emphasized the scriptures as the textbook for instruction.[27] Although we do not have a complete course of instruction (if there was such) from Augustine, several of his works contain material addressed to catechumens.[28] Augustine several times refers to the practice known as the *disciplina arcani* ("rule of secrecy") by which the unbaptized were not told about the mysteries of initiation. He understood the practice as having a pedagogical purpose, for one has an increased desire for what is hidden.[29] Catechumens were dismissed before the eucharist and baptism.[30]

One of Augustine's letters (dated 428) replies to a catechumen's arguments to delay baptism.[31] His reasons were that the burden of the baptismal life was too heavy (chap. 4), his delay showed reverence for the mysteries (chap. 6), and one must await the will of God (chap. 7). Augustine answered these objections and urged baptism on his correspondent (chaps. 3 and 11), for he needed the "grace of rebirth" (chap. 7).

Since the Pasch was the primary, but not exclusive, time for baptism, the season of Lent was the period for intense preparation for baptism.[32] Those desiring baptism turned in their names to the bishop.[33] Augustine implies a procedure for excluding unworthy candidates.[34] Those undergoing immediate preparation for baptism were no longer ordinary catechumens but were known as *competentes* ("petitioners").[35]

---

24. Sermon 294.14; 132.1; 301A.8; *Exposition of the Gospel of John* 44.2; 11.3-4 in discussing John 3:5 draws a clear line between catechumens and the baptized.

25. Sermon 260C.1.

26. *Faith and Works* 6.9.

27. Harmless, *Augustine*, p. 236, "Scripture was his catechumenate's textbook." Sermon 95.1.

28. E.g., Sermon 132; *Explanations of the Psalms* 81 (Latin 80); *Exposition of the Gospel of John* 4; 10; and 11. Harmless, *Augustine*, pp. 156-193, discusses Augustine's preaching to catechumens; his chart 7 (pp. 191-192) lists works addressed to catechumens, including many passages giving admonitions to seek baptism.

29. *Exposition of the Gospel of John* 96.3; the *disciplina arcani* is referred to in *Explanations of the Psalms* 48.3 (Eng. 49:2); 80:8 (Eng. 81:5); Sermons 49.8; 131.1.

30. Sermon 49; Letter 126.

31. Letter 2* (Divjak). Translation by Roland Teske, *Letters 211-271, 1*-29**, The Works of Saint Augustine: A Translation for the 21st Century (Hyde Park: New City Press, 2005), Vol. II/4.

32. Sermon 210.2. In case of necessity baptism could be performed at any time of the year.

33. Sermon 132.1; 213.1; 335H3; Letter 258.4-5; *Care of the Dead* 12.15; *Exposition of the Gospel of John* 10.10; 11.1-6; *On Faith and Works* 6.8.

34. *On Faith and Works* 6.8; 10.16; 13.19; 17.31; 18.33 for refusing baptism to those who resisted correction and admitting others.

35. Augustine distinguished them from ordinary catechumens — Sermon 392.1; *On Faith and Works* 6.9 (*competentes* are those who have given their names for baptism). Harmless, *Augustine*, p. 247. Sermon 216.1 explains the meaning, "asking together, and aiming at one and the same thing" (see next note for translation used, p. 167); *Faith and Works* 6.9. Augustine also called them "those to

Augustine offers a striking analogy of conversion in the process of baking bread, which summarizes the main steps in the baptismal ceremony.

> Unless wheat is ground, after all, and moistened with water, it can't possibly get into this shape which is called bread. In the same way you too were being ground and pounded, as it were, by the humiliation of fasting and the sacrament of exorcism. Then came baptism, and you were, in a manner of speaking, moistened with water in order to be shaped into bread. But it's not yet bread without fire to bake it. So what does fire represent? That's the chrism, the anointing.[36]

During Lent the *competentes* fasted until 3:00 p.m. each day.[37] They abstained from meat, wine, bathing, and from sexual relations.[38] They often attended all-night prayer vigils and gave alms.[39] Augustine employed athletic and military imagery familiar from other catechists in order to encourage the candidates in these ascetic disciplines.[40] His distinctive imagery for this period of time was to compare it to pregnancy.[41]

In summary, Augustine says the catechumens were catechized, exorcized, and scrutinized.[42] The petitioners were present for Augustine's Lenten sermons. We have several of these sermons preserved.[43] Augustine was concerned about both doctrinal and moral instruction. His treatise *On Faith and Works* was occasioned by those who would teach catechumens only about the faith and reserve instruction in morals and the requirements of the Christian life until after baptism; they seem to have been motivated by the desire to admit those in adulterous marriages

---

be baptized" *(baptizandi)* — *On Faith and Works* 7.11 (where catechumens seems to include the *competentes*) and passim.

36. *Sermon* 227. Quotations from the sermons on the liturgical seasons (numbers 184-229Z) are taken from the translation of Edmund Hill, *Sermons III/6*, The Works of Saint Augustine: A Translation for the 21st Century (New Rochelle: New City Press, 1993), here p. 254; other sermons in other volumes. The same illustration from making bread is used in *Sermon* 229.1; 229A.2; 272. See Harmless, *Augustine*, Chart 17, p. 343, for Augustine's various applications of the imagery of baking bread for the stages of initiation.

37. *Letter* 54.7.9. "Put on sackcloth, and humble your soul with fasting" — *Sermon* 216.10 (p. 173). Augustine noted the objection that Jesus fasted after his baptism, but in the church the fast preceded the baptism, and he explained that Jesus' example was not a rule to be followed in this regard — *Sermon* 210.2-3.

38. *On Faith and Works* 6.8; *Sermon* 207.2; 210.9. Harmless, *Augustine*, p. 248, cites Augustine's various summary listings of activities by catechumens in Lent; pp. 251-260 describes the Lenten discipline. *Sermon* 351.2.2 notes that only infants were exempt from this penitence, since they did not yet have exercise of free will.

39. *Sermon* 206.2; 210.12 on remembering the poor.

40. E.g., *Sermon* 216.6.

41. *Sermons* 216.7; 228; *Exposition of the Gospel of John* 12.3 (see below on new birth). Harmless, *Augustine*, pp. 244-299, on Lent as "time in the womb."

42. *On Faith and Works* 6.9.

43. *Sermons* 205-211; 211A; 216. Harmless, *Augustine*, p. 297, gives a chart of Augustine's sermons to the *competentes,* and p. 298, a list of his passing references to them.

to baptism. Catechumens, Augustine says, should hear both what the faith is and what the pattern of the Christian life is, both the rule of faith and morals; the candidate for baptism must be instructed in what to believe (faith) and how to live (i.e., repentance).[44]

Exorcisms were part of the Lenten experience of the *competentes*, but Augustine gives no indication of their frequency.[45] One sermon, "To the *Competentes*," refers to a scrutiny, exorcism, and standing on sackcloth (goatskins) at the renunciation of the devil.[46] The purpose was to sanctify the catechumens by freeing them progressively from the dominion of evil and transferring them to God's dominion in preparation for becoming sons on the day of baptism.[47]

At some point, perhaps eight days before Easter, there was a major scrutiny.[48] It involved a physical exam to determine if there were signs on the body that would indicate that one was still under the power of Satan. Curses were pronounced on the devil, and there was a breathing on (or hissing at — *exsufflatio*) the candidate to expel the devil.[49] The exorcism was made in the name of Christ.[50] Augustine brings together a reference to the exorcisms and a call for the *competentes* to make their own scrutiny of their hearts in anticipation of the renunciation of the devil:

> What we are doing for you by invoking the name of your redeemer, you must complete by thoroughly scrutinizing and crushing your hearts. We block the wiles of the ancient and obstinate enemy with prayers to God and with stern rebukes; you must stand up to him with your earnest prayers and contrition of heart, in order to be snatched from the power of darkness and transferred into the kingdom of his glory.... We heap curses on him, appropriate to his vile wickedness; it is for you, rather, to join glorious battle with him by turning away from him and devoutly renouncing him....
>
> And you indeed, while you were being scrutinized, and that persuader of flight and desertion was being properly rebuked by the terrifying omnipotence of the Trinity, were not actually clothed in sackcloth, but yet your feet were symbolically standing on it....
>
> From these we have just now found you to be free; we congratulate you, and exhort you to preserve in your hearts the health that is apparent in your bodies.[51]

Two weeks before Easter Augustine delivered to his candidates the baptismal creed *(traditio symboli)*. It was not written down, but delivered orally, and the candi-

---

44. *On Faith and Works* 6.9; 7.11; 27.49.
45. Augustine refers to the fasts and exorcisms of the *competentes* in *Sermons* 227 and 229.1.
46. *Sermon* 216.10, included in the quotation below at n. 51.
47. On the scrutinies and their components, Grossi, *La catechesi battesimale*, pp. 50-60.
48. *Sermon* 216. Harmless, *Augustine*, pp. 260-274.
49. *Against Julian: Unfinished Work* 1.50; 1.60; 2.181; 3.82; 3.182; 4.77; *Against Julian* 1.4.14; 3.3.8; *On Marriage and Concupiscence* 2.18.33; *On the Creed* 1.2; *Letter* 108.1.3.
50. *Explanations of the Psalms* 48, 2.1 (English 49:14); *On Baptism* 5.24.34.
51. *Sermon* 216.6, 10, 11 (pp. 171, 173, 174).

dates were expected to memorize it.⁵² Augustine describes it as a brief summary of what was heard and taught in the scripture readings and sermons in church. Quoting Romans 10:9-10, he says that the Symbol is "what you must both believe and confess, so that you may be saved."⁵³ Augustine compares the profession of faith to a commercial contract and calls it a "rule of faith" that serves as a sign or mark of identity like a password.⁵⁴ The *competentes* individually recited the creed to the bishop a week before Easter as a rehearsal for its formal repetition *(redditio symboli)* at the Pasch.⁵⁵ Augustine also delivered to the *competentes* the Lord's Prayer, which he expounded in a series of sermons; it was rendered back collectively.⁵⁶ The daily recitation of the Lord's prayer was "as if a daily baptism" because of its petition for forgiveness of sins.⁵⁷

52. Harmless, *Augustine*, pp. 274-286; on p. 299 a chart quotes the creeds found in Augustine's sermons. Grossi, *La catechesi battesimale*, pp. 60-74 — the creed was used exclusively in the baptismal liturgy, but the Lord's Prayer was daily; it served as a rule of faith, life, and salvation. Sermons 212-214 were preached at the handing over of the creed and summarize its content. See *On Faith and Works* 9.14 and 11.17 for committing the creed to memory and repeating it from memory. "And in no way are you to write it down, in order to retain the same words; but you are to learn it thoroughly by hearing it, and not write it down either when you have it by heart, but keep it always and go over it in your memory" (*Sermon* 212.2; p. 138; cf. 214.1). De Latte, "Rituel baptismal des adultes," p. 201, notes that in this passage Augustine bases the prohibition against writing down the creed not on the rule of secrecy but on Jer. 31:33, "written on the heart."

53. *Sermon* 214.1 (p. 150); cf. 213.2, "once you have believed, you must confess" (p. 142).

54. *Sermon* 212.1 on a contract; 213.2 on "rule of faith"; and 214.12 for password.

55. *Sermon* 213.11. He consoles and warns, "If any of you get the words wrong, at least don't get the faith wrong" (p. 147). *Sermon* 215 was preached at the giving back of the creed and summarizes its contents. *Sermon* 58.1.

56. *Sermons* 56-59. The Lord's Prayer was delivered a week later than the Symbol; Augustine explained from Romans 10:14-15 that it is those who believe in the Lord who can call upon him in prayer — *Sermon* 213.1. Harmless, *Augustine*, pp. 286-292, and Grossi, *La catechesi battesimale*, pp. 74-77, on the "Our Father." The latter notes that the rite of delivery of the "Our Father" in relation to baptism seems to have been an African tradition, later transmitted to other churches (p. 74).

57. *Sermon* 213.9. Ekkart Sauser, "Baptismus-Baptismus cottidianus — und Sündenvergebung in der Theologie des hl. Augustinus," in H. Auf Der Maur and B. Kleinheyer, eds., *Zeichen des Glaubens: Studien zu Taufe und Firmung: Balthasar Fischer zum 60 Geburtstag* (Freiburg: Herder, 1972), pp. 83-94, discusses the one-time baptism whose effects are renewed daily by the petition of the Lord's Prayer for forgiveness. Cf. *On the Creed* 7.14 for sins once washed away in baptism daily washed away by prayer; 8.16 says there are three ways sins are remitted by the church — by baptism, prayer, and penance; but these are only to the baptized. So, prayer was not an independent means of forgiveness but had its basis in baptism, which was a unique event but its effects were renewed daily in the Lord's Prayer, whose power was promised only to the baptized. This forgiveness comes through identification with the death of Christ (*Enchiridion* 52.14; *Sermon* 169.13.16) and the indwelling Holy Spirit (*Sermon* 99.9). Passages linking baptism and the petition of the Lord's Prayer for forgiveness include *Sermon* 58.10 (when praying the Lord's Prayer daily one becomes as when baptized); 59.4; 261.10; *Exposition of the Gospel of John* 56.4 (the prayer is a daily footwashing); 124.5; *On Marriage and Concupiscence* 1.33.38 (the Lord's Prayer a daily cleansing). The petition for forgiveness is discussed in *City of God* 21.27. Other means besides prayer of extending the postbaptismal forgiveness are penance (*On Romans* 19) and alms and charity (*On Marriage and Concupiscence* 1.33).

On holy Thursday before Easter Sunday the *competentes* broke their fast and had a bath.[58] On Saturday there was a final catechesis on baptism.[59] Augustine, like Theodore of Mopseustia and John Chrysostom but unlike Cyril of Jerusalem and Ambrose, gave instruction on the meaning of baptism and eucharist before baptism instead of waiting until the week after its reception to do so.

The *competentes* recited the creed individually either on Saturday or during the Saturday night vigil as part of the preliminaries to the immersion proper.[60] Children over seven years of age also made the recitation of the creed.[61] Augustine recounts a dramatic occasion of the *redditio symboli* at Rome by the learned pagan rhetorician and philosopher Victorinus, whose conversion made an impression on Augustine.

> Finally the hour came for him to make the profession of faith which is expressed in set form. At Rome these words are memorized and then by custom recited from an elevated place before the baptized believers by those who want to come to your grace.[62]

The presbyters at Rome gave Victorinus the opportunity to make his profession in private, as they were accustomed to do for those who felt embarrassed or afraid. He declined the offer, for "he preferred to make profession of his salvation before the holy congregation." He explained that as he had taught publicly so he should make his profession of faith in public.

At some point there was a renunciation of the devil and an adhesion to Christ, of which Augustine has little to say. He does refer to "renouncing the devil . . . and withdrawing your minds and hearts from his parades [pomps] and his angels."[63] Also, the water of the font was consecrated, but Augustine does not say whether this was in the presence of those to be baptized or not.[64] The consecration was done by the sign of the cross and invocation of the name of Christ.[65]

---

58. *Letter* 54.7.10.

59. Alluded to in *Sermon* 229A.1.

60. Received collectively, the creed was recited one by one — *Sermon* 215.1. Cf. *Sermon* 59.1, "You have given back what you are to believe, and you have heard how you are to pray" (III/3, p. 126). Augustine is the first western writer to mention the *redditio*.

61. *On the Soul and Its Origin* 1.10.12; 3.9.12.

62. *Confessions* 8.2.5 (p. 136).

63. *Sermon* 215.1; 216.6. The facing west for the renunciation and turning east for swearing allegiance seem to be alluded to in *Explanations of the Psalms* 102.19 (Eng. 103:12). On the renunciation see further on accommodations made for infant baptism.

64. *Sermon* 213.9, "you are going to come to the holy font," may imply a consecration before the catechumens came to the font (so De Latte, "Rituel baptismal des adultes," p. 207), but "holy font" may be a set phrase.

65. *Exposition of the Gospel of John* 118.5 mentions the sign of the cross over the forehead of believers, over the water which serves for regeneration, over the oil of anointing, and over the sacrifice with which one is nourished (eucharist). The divine invocation is alluded to in *On Baptism* 3.10.15, and prayer over the water of baptism in *On Baptism* 5.20.28; *Sermon* 352.3. Augustine did not attach sacramental value to the water (*On Baptism* 6.25.47 — De Latte, "Rituel baptismal des adultes," p. 208).

At Hippo, as elsewhere, baptism except in cases of emergency was normally at Easter at the climax of the preceding Saturday night vigil.[66] Following the recitation of the creed, there was a procession of the *competentes* and the officiating clergy to the baptistery accompanied by the singing of Psalm 42 (Latin 41).[67]

Excavations have revealed the baptistery at the episcopal church in Hippo.[68] The baptistery room was square on two sides and semicircular on the other. The room was 4.80 meters by 4.00 meters. On one side was a room possibly for the catechumens to assemble, and on another side a chapel, where the anointing and other postbaptismal ceremonies perhaps occurred, and that communicated with the basilica. In the center of the baptismal room was the rectangular font with exterior dimensions of 2.55 by 1.95 meters. Marble columns to a height of 2.40 meters at the four corners perhaps supported curtains around the font. Access to the pool was by three steps on one of the short sides. The pool had a depth of 1 meter and floor dimensions of 1.35 by 1.10 meters. Next to but independent of the font on one of its long sides was a small rectangular basin, 0.24 by 0.41 meter and 0.45 meter deep, perhaps used for foot washing (see below).

The baptizands stripped and entered the font. There is indication of a separation of the sexes for their baptism.[69] Augustine makes a point of the baptizands stepping down into the font as an indication of humility.[70]

Augustine gave "capital importance" to the profession of faith "for the efficacy of the sacrament." This was "considered indispensable" even in cases of sickbed and infant baptism (see further below).[71] The baptism was in the name of the Trinity.[72] Against the Donatists he declares, "I know only one baptism consecrated and marked by the name of Father, Son, and Holy Spirit; it is necessary that I approve this form wherever I find it."[73] He affirms the necessity of both water and the word of God: "What is the baptism of Christ? The bath of water in the word. Take away the water; there is no baptism. Take away the word; there is no baptism."[74] Or again,

---

66. *Sermon* 210.2 — baptism coincides with Easter day, but there is the difference that the anniversary of the Lord's passion can be celebrated only at Easter, but baptism can be received on any day; *Letter* 55.2-3. *Sermons* 219-223K belong to the Easter vigil. Harmless, *Augustine*, pp. 302-313, for the Easter vigil, and p. 340 for a chart listing sermons for the Easter vigil.

67. *Explanations of the Psalms* 41 [Eng. 42].1.

68. E. Maroo, *Monuments chrétiens d'Hippone* (Paris: Arts et métiers graphiques, 1958), pp. 105-112; photograph on p. 103; Sebastian Ristow, *Frühchristliche Baptisterien*, Jahrbuch für Antike und Christentum, Ergänzungsband 27 (Münster: Aschendorff, 1998), #70.

69. *City of God* 22.8.

70. *Sermon* 125.6; cf. 258.2.

71. De Latte, "Rituel baptismal des adultes," pp. 209, 211. Cf. *Sermon* 212.2 for "baptized believers" (p. 138).

72. *Against the Letters of Petilian* 3.8.9; *Sermon* 215.8; *Explanations of the Psalms* 77.2 (Eng. 78:1) — baptism in the Trinity is the laver of regeneration.

73. *Letter* 23.4 (see further on Donatism in chap. 52). *Letter* 54.1.1 says baptism is a sacrament because it is made sacred by the name of the Trinity. Other references to the Trinitarian formula include *On Baptism* 3.15.20; *Against the Letters of Petilian* 2.81.178.

74. *Exposition of the Gospel of John* 15.4.

"Take away the word, and the water is neither more nor less than water. The word is added to the element, and there results the sacrament, as if itself also a kind of visible word."[75] Augustine does not elaborate on the manner of the confession, but instead of a declaratory formula he indicates that the triple immersions were in response to triple interrogations.[76]

There was a postbaptismal chrismation and laying on of hands. In a passage about the baptism of a baby Augustine refers to the usual rites: "He was baptized, sanctified; he received the holy anointing and the imposition of hands; then, when all the rites were completed, his life departed."[77] It appears that only the head was anointed on this occasion.[78] In keeping with his broad usage of the word "sacrament" for anything that conveys a spiritual benefit, Augustine calls the unction or chrism a sacrament.[79] It expresses the royal priesthood of the church and incorporation into the body of Christ, the Anointed One.[80] The visible anointing is a sacrament of the spiritual anointing with the Holy Spirit.[81]

The laying on of hands was the rite especially associated with the gift of the Holy Spirit. "The Holy Spirit is given in the Catholic church only by the imposition of hands."[82] The laying on of hands represented a prayer, and this prayer was specifically for the imparting of the seven gifts of the Spirit (Isa. 11:2).[83] Augustine listed the water, oil, eucharist, and laying on of hands (in reconciliation of penitents?) as occasions of sacramental prayer.[84] Augustine's reference to the stamp *(characterem)* with which the neophytes were sealed may refer to baptism, the postbaptismal anointing and imposition of hands, or all the rite.[85]

---

75. *Exposition of the Gospel of John* 80.3. Cf. *Sermon* 227 for the word of God sanctifying the bread and wine as it did the baptismal waters.

76. *Sermon* 294.12; *On Faith and Works* 9.14 refers to questions and the answers to be given by the one to be baptized.

77. *Sermon* 324.

78. *Against the Letters of Petilian* 2.104.237.

79. *Against the Letters of Petilian* 2.105.239.

80. *Sermon* 351.5.12; *City of God* 17.4.9.

81. *Sermon* 227. For Augustine's rich mind the oil also symbolizes love (*Exposition of the Gospel of John* 6.20) and peace (*Explanations of the Psalms* 127.13 [Eng. 128:3]).

82. *On Baptism* 3.16.21. See also *Sermon* 266.3-6, "The Holy Spirit comes on a person only when hands are imposed." Cf. *Against the Letters of Petilian* 2.35.81; *On the Trinity* 15.26.46; *On the Letter of John* 6.10.

83. The laying on of hands was defined as a prayer — *On Baptism* 3.16.21 (see above at n. 22); seven gifts of the Spirit — *Sermon* 249.3; cf. 229M.2, "the sevenfold Spirit who is also called down upon the newly baptized" (III/6, p. 317). See De Latte, "Rituel baptismal des adultes," pp. 216-217, for differing views on Augustine's statements in relation to the sacrament of "confirmation." Augustine does not distinguish the postbaptismal anointing and laying on of hands from baptism by a special terminology, so he had to deal with the Donatist objection that Catholics repeated the postbaptismal rites but not baptism itself.

84. *On Baptism* 5.20.28.

85. *Sermon* 229O.3.

The newly baptized, called by Augustine *infantes*,[86] were given new white robes to wear during the following week.

> These infants, whom you behold outwardly clothed in white, inwardly cleansed and purified, the brilliance of their garments representing the splendor of their minds, were once darkness . . . But now they have been washed clean in the bath of amnesty.[87]

Their heads were covered.[88] A footwashing is alluded to.[89]

The baptismal eucharist expressed incorporation into the church. It involved the consecration of the bread and wine, the saying of the Lord's Prayer, Augustine's proclamation "Peace be with you," the exchange of the kiss of peace, and distribution of the elements. Later in the day the new faithful joined the church in the Sunday eucharist and received instruction from Augustine about it.[90] With reference to the body of Christ, he called on his hearers, "Be what you see, and receive what you are."[91]

A number of Augustine's sermons to the neophytes preached during the week following Easter Sunday (the Easter octave, *Octavae infantium*) are preserved.[92] They deal with the preceding Easter vigil, the sacraments, and the Gospel readings of the paschal week.[93] After this week the *infantes* fully mingled with the faithful.

Augustine dealt with some modifications in the ceremony required by sickbed and infant baptisms. These were administered when the occasion required. Abandoning his youthful disparagement of baptism given to those not conscious because of illness (see above), he said that it was better to baptize the unwilling than to withhold baptism.

> Therefore, if catechumens are at the end of this life, whether they be stricken by disease or some misfortune, and if they cannot request baptism for themselves or answer questions, although they still are alive, let baptism be administered to them, because the disposition of their will toward Christianity has long been known. Let them be baptized after the manner of infants, whose will, to be sure, is not yet in evidence. . . .

86. *Sermons* 229A.1; 228.1, 3 (see below on new birth); 228B.1; 226.

87. *Sermon* 223.1 (III/6, p. 209). Other references to the white clothing include *Sermon* 120; 146.2; 260C.7

88. *Sermon* 376A.2.

89. *Letter* 55.18.33 says that some did this on different days out of concern that it might seem to belong to the sacrament of baptism and raise the question whether this was a custom; *On Agreement among the Evangelists* 2.30.75.

90. For the sequence, see *Sermon* 229.3; sermons explaining the eucharist — 227 (a daily eucharist); 228B; 229; 229A. In *Sermon* 228.3 Augustine says he owes the "infants" a sermon on the "sacrament of the altar," even as he had explained to them in earlier sermons the "sacrament of the symbol," the "sacrament of the Lord's Prayer," and the "sacrament of the font and baptism." *Sermon* 174.7.

91. *Sermon* 272.

92. *Sermons* 229E-O, R-V. Their theme is Jesus' resurrection and his appearances after his resurrection.

93. De Latte, "Rituel baptismal des adultes," p. 222; Harmless, *Augustine*, pp. 324-330, 345.

Therefore, in deference to [Matt. 7:6] they dare not baptize those who are unable to answer for themselves, lest, perhaps, the decision of their will be contrary. This cannot be said of children, in whom there is not yet the use of reason. However, it is not alone incredible for a catechumen not to wish to be baptized at the end of this life but, even if his will is uncertain it is much more satisfactory to give it against his will than to deny it to him when he desires it.[94]

Augustine continued that it is easier to conclude that if he could speak he would desire to receive the sacraments, which he already believed were necessary.

Infant baptism, although not yet the norm, was common, especially emergency baptisms. Indeed, Augustine in an early work alludes to the fact that most infants who receive baptism die before knowing anything of it.[95] There is hardly any explicit mention of baptizing healthy infants.[96]

The ritual was essentially the same for infants as for adults, but there were some accommodations.[97] Infants were exorcized.[98] Indeed, Augustine saw in this a proof of

---

94. *On Adulterous Marriages* 1.26.33. Translation by Roy J. Deferrari, *Saint Augustine: Treatises on Marriage and Other Subjects*, Fathers of the Church 27 (New York: Fathers of the Church, 1955), pp. 98-99. Cf. 1.28.35 in regard to one in an adulterous marriage. The words "after the manner of infants" indicates a special form of the ritual for them — Robert De Latte, "Saint Augustin et le baptême: Étude liturgico-historique du rituel baptismal des enfants chez saint Augustin," *Questions liturgiques* 57 (1976): 41-55 (p. 44). Note *Sermon* 393.1 for sick adults carried to the church for emergency baptism and dying before even leaving the premises.

95. *On Free Will* 3.23.67, clearly indicating that these were emergency baptisms. *Sermon* 293.10; *Letter* 166.7.21; 166.8.23; and *On the Letter of John* 4.11 speak of the faithful hastening with their infants to baptism, words that imply an emergency situation (in the last passage the practice is taken as an indication that infants are born with sin). *On the Literal Interpretation of Genesis* 10.11.19 seems to have emergency baptism in mind in saying that the church maintains that parents should hasten with their babies while they are still alive to baptism, since when they have died, nothing will do any good. That some died on the way to baptism is mentioned in *Letter* 217.6.19; *Gift of Perseverance* 13.31. Other references to infant baptism: *Sermon* 323; 324; *Explanations of the Psalms* 50.10 (Eng. 51:5); *Exposition of the Gospel of John* 38.6; *The Punishment and Forgiveness of Sins and the Baptism of Little Ones* 1.18.23; *Against Julian* 1.7.31; *On the Gift of Perseverance* 12.31; *On the Deeds of Pelagius* 1.2.4 (countless multitude of baptized infants). On infant baptism see further on the Pelagian controversy (chap. 52).

96. William Harmless, "Christ the Pediatrician: Infant Baptism and Christological Imagery in the Pelagian Controversy," *Augustinian Studies* 28 (1997): 25. He cites *Sermon* 115.4 as the clearest example. The passage exhorts, "Let the babies come," quoting Luke 18:16. Augustine continues with points to be met again in our exposition: infants have no evil but what they contracted from their source, and the church is told, "Speak for those who can't, pray for those who can only cry."

97. De Latte, "Rituel baptismal des enfants," p. 43; p. 51 for the great majority of infant baptisms being emergency baptisms. J.-C. Didier, "Une adaptation de la liturgie baptismale au baptême des enfants dans l'église ancienne," *Mélanges de science religieuse* 22 (1965): 79-80, states that the baptismal ritual was originally constituted for adults only (p. 79); accommodations were made in the new concept of sponsors, reorganization of the scrutinies, and the baptismal profession of faith (p. 81). Pelagius claimed to perform the baptism of children with the same words as for adults — *On the Grace of Christ and Original Sin* 1.32.35-1.33.36; 2.5.5.

98. *The Punishment and Forgiveness of Sins and the Baptism of Little Ones* 1.34.63; *On the Creed* 1.2; *Letter* 194.10.46 (exorcism and exsufflation); *Against Julian* 3.5.11; 6.5.11; *Against Julian: Unfinished*

his doctrine of original sin as guilt, for the babies were implicitly viewed as in the hold of the devil. Adults or others[99] spoke for the children the renunciation and profession of faith.[100] Augustine quotes a part of the interrogations on faith: "One asks, 'Does [the infant] believe in Jesus Christ?' The response is, 'He believes.'"[101] Indeed, even the baptism of infants could be described as a "believers' baptism" according to this rationale, for the sponsor affirms that the baby believes. What infants were not yet able to do through their own faith was done for them by those who love them.[102] The baptismal questions were addressed to those who brought the baby, but the questions and the answers were framed in the third person. Without the words of the profession of faith there could be no baptism at all, so Augustine resorts to the faith of others to justify infant baptism.[103] There is no reason to believe that the immersion of infants was different from that of adults.[104] As adults had responded for the child with the words of the symbol (creed), so they also did with the words of the Lord's Prayer. These vicarious affirmations mean that his correspondent should not be upset with the words of the Lord's Prayer, "Forgive us . . ." being attributed to the infant.[105]

The children received an anointing (chrismation) and laying on of hands (consignation).[106] They also participated in the baptismal eucharist, taking both the bread and wine.[107]

Work 1.117; 2.181; 3.144, 164. Franz Josef Dölger, *Der Exorzismus in altchristlichen Taufritual* (Paderborn: Ferdinand Schöningh, 1909), p. 43, concludes that exorcism in the ritual of infant baptism was simply taken over from the baptism of adults and that the doctrine of original sin did not ground exorcism in infant baptism but that in the Pelagian controversy (chap. 52) exorcism was an argument for infant baptism.

99. De Latte, "Rituel baptismal des enfants," p. 52, for different terms (with the references) used by Augustine for those who brought babies for baptism. He never used the word *patrinus* (godparent).

100. "It is true, then, and in no way false, that the devil's power is exorcized in infants, and that they renounce him by the hearts and mouths of those who bring them to baptism, being unable to do so by their own; in order that they may be delivered from the power of darkness and be translated into the kingdom of their Lord" — *On Marriage and Concupiscence* 1.20.22. For the renunciation and the profession of faith in the creed (including its clause about the forgiveness of sins) spoken by the sponsors — *The Punishment and Forgiveness of Sins and the Baptism of Little Ones* 1.34.63 (cited in chap. 52 on the Pelagian controversy); *On Baptism* 1.13.21; 4.24.32; *Letter* 98.5, 7; 5*.2; *Sermon* 294.12. See further below on the works of the devil destroyed in infant baptism.

101. *Sermon* 294.12. De Latte, "Rituel baptismal des enfants," p. 47, understands the use of the third person to indicate that the function of the sponsor (godparent) was not to be a substitute but to inform; cf. Didier, "Une adaptation," p. 84.

102. *On the Literal Interpretation of Genesis* 10.14.25 — Baptism absolves them from the punishment of original sin, so it is right and proper to baptize them.

103. Didier, "Une adaptation," pp. 82-83. See further chap. 52.

104. De Latte, "Rituel baptismal des enfants," p. 48.

105. *Letter* 5*.2. The words would apply to original sin in the case of the infant. The responses by those who presented infants for baptism was the surety of faith and gave the baptism its effectiveness — *On the Soul and Its Origin* 2.12.17.

106. *Sermon* 323.3; 324, cited above on the usual ceremony of baptism.

107. *Letter* 217.5.16.8; *Sermon* 174.7 says infants are members of Christ and receive the sacraments, including sharing in his table.

Augustine's Traditional Baptismal Theology

Augustine repeated much of the traditional doctrine of baptism. He often made use of the Exodus typology.[108] He made an argument from the analogy of circumcision for the necessity of each individual being baptized: just as the son of a circumcised man had to be circumcised, so the son of one baptized must also receive baptism.[109] Baptism is unrepeatable, just as was circumcision.[110] He explained to the Manichaean Faustus that Christians are not circumcised because what it prefigured is fulfilled in Christ. Circumcision is a type of the removal of the fleshly nature, which is fulfilled in the resurrection of Christ. The sacrament of baptism looks forward to human resurrection; baptism thus substitutes for circumcision in this secondary sense.[111]

The baptism administered by John did not bring regeneration, for it was by the water alone and not by the Holy Spirit. Christ submitted to his baptism, not because of any sin needing to be washed away but to manifest his humility in submitting to the plan of God.[112] Jesus' baptism, moreover, serves as an example; indeed, it is more needful for human beings than for him to be baptized.[113] Jesus' baptism was not only exemplary of Christian baptism but also was revelatory of who Christ is.[114] Christian baptism is better than John's baptism, because Christ baptizes the Christian.[115]

The baptism of the apostles, especially of Peter, is dealt with in *Letter* 265. Augustine explains that the apostles were baptized with water but not with the Holy Spirit until Acts 2.[116] John 13:10 indicates that Peter had been baptized. He interprets John 4:1-2 to mean that the sacrament of baptism is the Lord's, but the ministry of

---

108. E. g., *Sermon* 213.9; 223E.2; *On Catechizing the Uninstructed* 20.34; *Explanations of the Psalms* 80.8 (Eng. 81:5) — crossing the Red Sea equals the passage of the faithful through baptism; 106.3 (Eng. 107:3) — by baptism consecrated with the blood of Christ sins (the Egyptians) are washed away; *Exposition of the Gospel of John* 11.4 (crossing the Red Sea and eating the manna represent baptism and eucharist); *On Faith and Works* 11.17 (the Red Sea signifies baptism). Grossi, *La catechesi battesimale*, pp. 103-106, on the typology of the Exodus and of crossing the Jordan and circumcision.

109. *The Punishment and Forgiveness of Sins and the Baptism of Little Ones* 2.25.40. The comparison to circumcision is also in *On Baptism* 4.31.

110. *Letter* 23.4.

111. *Against Faustus* 19.9.

112. *Enchiridion* 14.49.

113. *The Punishment and Forgiveness of Sins and the Baptism of Little Ones* 2.24.38. Jesus was baptized to show humility and show others that they should be baptized — *On Baptism* 4.22.30; *Exposition of the Gospel of John* 4.13; *Sermon* 210.2; *Explanations of the Psalms* 90.14 (Eng. 91:11).

114. *Exposition of the Gospel of John* 5.3, which includes the statement that Jesus' baptism shows his servants that they must eagerly run to baptism. See further below on the gift of the Spirit at baptism.

115. *Sermon* 210.3.

116. *Letter* 265.3; cf. *Exposition of the Gospel of John* 6.11. It seems to me that this explanation (anticipated in the treatise *On Rebaptism* [chap. 24]), that the apostles received water baptism from John (or Jesus) and what was lacking (the Holy Spirit) was completed on Pentecost in Acts 2, offers the most likely answer to the question about their baptism.

baptizing belonged to his disciples. It is more worthy of belief that the apostles were baptized by Christ than that they were baptized by John.[117]

Augustine listed what baptism does as "our being born again, cleansed, justified by the grace of God."[118] In regard to cleansing, he repeated the connection of baptism with forgiveness of sins. He emphasized that Acts 2:38 meant the forgiveness of *all* sins.[119] (More of this in the next chapter on the Pelagian controversy.) Formerly in darkness, people were now light[120] because of the forgiveness of their sins.[121] Augustine cites approvingly the custom of the Christians of Carthage to call baptism "salvation."[122] The forgiveness of sins is the beginning of the renovation of human beings, but all of the old infirmity is not destroyed.[123]

Baptism is the means of entering into the death, burial, and resurrection of Christ, and this is connected with forgiveness of sins. In explaining Romans 6:1-11, Augustine says that the "mystery of holy baptism" is "bound up with the cross of Christ."

> [Paul makes] us understand baptism in Christ as nothing but an image of Christ's death, and that Christ's death on the cross is nothing but an image of the remission of sin. Just as real as was his death, so real is the remission of our sins; and just as real as was his resurrection, so real is our justification.[124]

---

117. *Letter* 265.5.

118. *Against the Letters of Petilian* 3.50.62.

119. *Sermon* 229E.2 (even the sin of killing Christ — also in *On the Creed* 15); cf. *Enchiridion* 17.64; *Sermon* 213.9; 223E.2 (all our sins drowned in baptism); 56.13 (all debts forgiven); *Exposition of the Gospel of John* 4.13 (all sins remain unless one comes to saving baptism); *On the Creed* 7.15 (baptism was devised for all sins, which are cleansed but once by baptism and then are cleansed daily by prayer); *Letter* 153.5.15 (after the destruction of sins in baptism, the way of forgiveness of sins is by "sacrifices of mercy"); *Letter* 194.10.45. The "bath of rebirth and word of sanctification" (with reference to Eph. 5:25-27) forgives past and future sins ("what good would penance do either before baptism, if baptism did not follow, or after baptism, if it did not come first?" — *On Marriage and Concupiscence* 1.33.38; the baptismal bath (again with reference to Eph. 5:26-27) forgives future as well as past sins of the faithful — *Letter* 185.9.39-40; in baptism is renewal by remission of all sins — *Trinity* 14.17; see Sauser, "Baptismus," in n. 57.

120. *Sermon* 225.4; cf. 135.1, "be baptized in order to be enlightened" (III/145, p. 346). See further chap. 5a on infant baptism.

121. *Sermon* 226. With reference to Ps. 103:2-5, Augustine says forgiveness is in the sacrament of baptism — *Spirit and the Letter* 33.59. Baptism is the sacrament of the forgiveness of sins — *On Baptism* 5.21.29.

122. *The Punishment and Forgiveness of Sins and the Baptism of Little Ones* 1.24.34.

123. *The Punishment and Forgiveness of Sins and the Baptism of Little Ones* 2.7.9; *Sermon* 131.6 — all sins are erased in the sacrament of baptism, but there is still a feebleness to be healed in the church; *Explanations of the Psalms* 102.5 (Eng. 103:3-5) — complete forgiveness, but we still carry a weak body. See further chap. 52 on concupiscence.

124. *Enchiridion* 14.52; tr. Louis A. Arand, *Saint Augustine: Faith, Hope, and Charity*, Ancient Christian Writers 3 (Westminster, MD: Newman, 1955), p. 55. Cf. also *Sermon* 229A.1 for baptism ("immersion") as being buried with Christ, and *Sermon* 210.3 for baptism as "the sacrament of Christ's resurrection"; *Sermon* 228A; *Letter* 55.2-3; *Exposition of the Gospel of John* 11.4.

Augustine continues with Paul's point in Romans 6 that those dead to sin are not to practice it. The crucifixion, burial, resurrection, and ascension of Christ are a model for the Christian life — crucifying the flesh, buried in baptism, resurrection to a new life, seeking the things above where Christ is (*Enchiridion* 14.53). "You believed, you were baptized, your old life died, slain on the cross, buried in baptism. The old, which you lived so badly, has been buried; let the new life arise."[125]

Persons participate in eternal life, which is Christ himself, through baptism.[126] The baptized were now members of the body of Christ.[127] Those cleansed by baptism are incorporated into the unity of his body.[128] The church is formed from Christ's side by faith in his death and in baptism (John 19:34).[129]

The language of new birth was a favorite with Augustine:

> You see, you have begun to have God for your Father, and you will have him so when you are born anew. But even now, before you are born, you already have been conceived by his seed to be duly brought forth from the womb of the church, so to say, in the font.[130]

Those who before were "petitioners," "agitating their mother's womb, asking to be born," were now "called infants [*infantes*] because they have just now been born to Christ."[131] Conceived in faith, the catechumens are to be brought forth in baptism and nourished on the eucharist.[132] With reference to the Pelagians, Augustine said, "Will any Christian tolerate hearing that someone can attain eternal salvation without being reborn in Christ, which is brought about by baptism?"[133] To be "born again in baptism" was a set phrase.[134] To be baptized was "to be born of God the Father and the mother church."[135] The new birth occurs invisibly by the

---

125. *Sermon* 229E.3 (p. 282).

126. *Exposition of the Gospel of John* 19.11-13. *City of God* 21.19-20, 25 refers (disapprovingly) of those who say the persons who receive baptism and eucharist will receive eternal life no matter how badly they lived.

127. *Sermon* 224.1.

128. *On Agreement among the Evangelists* 4.6.7. In the passage Augustine deals with those outside the church who live better than some who are within it.

129. *On Genesis, against the Manichees* 2.24.37.

130. *Sermon* 56.5 (III/3, p. 97).

131. *Sermon* 228.1 (p. 257); "born again of water and the Spirit" — *Sermon* 228B.1 (p. 261). Those "who have been baptized in Christ and born again" — *Sermon* 224.1 (p. 242); the newly baptized "have been born again through the blood of Christ" — *Sermon* 224.3 (p. 244). They were children of God, sons by adoption — *Sermon* 216.8; cf. "regenerated, adopted, and redeemed by the holy washing" — *Against Two Letters of the Pelagians* 3.3.5.

132. *Exposition of the Gospel of John* 12.3.

133. *The Punishment and Forgiveness of Sins and the Baptism of Little Ones* 1.18.23. Translation adapted from Roland J. Teske, *Answer to the Pelagians*, The Works of Saint Augustine I/23 (Hyde Park: New City Press, 1997), p. 46, from which other translations of the anti-Pelagian works are taken.

134. E.g., *On Baptism* 1.10.13.

135. *Sermon* 260C.1. Cf. *Sermon* 213.8 (the church as a virgin mother gives birth); also 223; 228B.1 (born again of water and the Spirit); *Enchiridion* 14.49 (born of water and the Spirit); *Sermons* 228.1

Spirit.[136] For the theme of newness resulting from baptism see *Sermon* 229A.1. He connected regeneration with the forgiveness of sins as the work of the Holy Spirit: "This spiritual regeneration where all sins are removed is effected by the Holy Spirit."[137] The Holy Spirit works remission of sins.[138] The role of the Holy Spirit in conferring forgiveness was developed by Augustine out of John 1:33, where the agency of Christ in conferring baptism is connected with the Holy Spirit.[139]

The Holy Spirit is given to those baptized.[140] Augustine explained that Christ did not really receive the Spirit at his baptism (for he already possessed the Spirit), but the descent of the Spirit prefigured the church's reception of the Spirit at baptism.[141] In scripture water (symbolizing cleansing) and oil (symbolizing joy and the fire of love) are signs that designate the Holy Spirit.[142]

Martyrdom is counted as baptism.[143] Against those who used the thief on the cross (Luke 23:39-43) as an argument against the necessity of baptism for salvation, Augustine cited Cyprian for the view that the thief's confession placed him among the martyrs. Augustine goes on to say that nobody can prove that the thief was not baptized previously.[144]

---

and 224.1 (to be baptized is to be born again); *The Punishment and Forgiveness of Sins and the Baptism of Little Ones* 1.16.21 (born again in baptism); 2.28.45 (born again); *On the Letter of John* 2.9. John 3:5 was an exceedingly popular text; so too the "washing of regeneration" of Titus 3:5. John 3:5 meant that there was no salvation without baptism — *Exposition of the Gospel of John* 11.1; he continues, explaining that "In the Spirit we are born by word and sacrament" — 12.5. Harmless, *Augustine*, pp. 233-234, on *Exposition of the Gospel of John* 11.4-12.3. See more on the Pelagian controversy (chap. 52).

136. *Exposition of the Gospel of John* 12.5.

137. *Sermon* 71.12.19 (III/3, p. 257); cf. *Sermon* 229E.2 for all sins forgiven in the "washing of rebirth" (Titus 3:5). See *The Punishment and Forgiveness of Sins and the Baptism of Little Ones* 2.9.11 for being renewed by the Spirit through the remission of sins. For regeneration: *On Marriage and Concupiscence* 1.33.38; *Against Two Letters of the Pelagians* 3.3.5; *On the Merits and Forgiveness of Sins and on Infant Baptism* 1.22.31 (saved by the washing of regeneration); *On Faith and Works* 6.9 ("cleansing waters of regeneration"); and often.

138. *On Baptism* 1.11.15, but only in the Catholic church (see chap. 52 on the Donatist controversy).

139. J. Patout Burns, "Christ and the Holy Spirit in Augustine's Theology of Baptism," in Joanne McWilliam, ed., *Augustine: From Rhetor to Theologian* (Waterloo: Wilfrid Laurier University Press, 1992), pp. 161-171 (162). Christ baptizes true and feigned converts through good and evil ministers, while the Holy Spirit cleanses and sanctifies the good convert through saints and spiritual persons (pp. 163, 167).

140. *On Nature and Grace* 53.61.

141. *On the Trinity* 15.26.46.

142. *Explanations of the Psalms* 108.26 (Eng. 109:24).

143. *Letter* 265.4; *City of God* 13.7 — for the unbaptized who die confessing Christ their confession has the same efficacy for remission of sins as for baptism. Cf. *Against the Letters of Petilian* 2.23.51-52 for the language of sprinkling with the baptism of blood.

144. *On the Soul and Its Origin* 1.9.11. Less convincingly, he cites the view that the thief was sprinkled with water that issued from the wounded side of Jesus and that this counted as a baptism. The explanations of the thief on the cross are more fully developed in *On the Soul and Its Origin* 3.9.12, and see further in chap. 52 on the treatise *On Baptism*. Martyrs are exempted from the requirement of John 3:5 — *On the Soul and Its Origin* 2.12.17.

As other preachers before him, Augustine used the season of baptism as the basis for an exhortation.[145]

Augustine's special contributions to the theology of baptism will be discussed in the next chapter.

---

145. Note especially *Sermon* 224, "On the Octave of Easter"; 272.

52. North Africa: Augustine of Hippo — II

Augustine developed his distinctive contributions to later baptismal thought in the Donatist and Pelagian controversies. The Donatist controversy about the role of the minister in conferring baptism contributed profoundly to sacramental theology and ecclesiology; the Pelagian controversy on original sin and the baptism of babies developed sacramental doctrine and theological anthropology.[1] Against both Donatists and Pelagians, Augustine appealed to the custom of the church — in one case to accept baptism administered by non-Catholics and in the other the baptism of babies.[2]

The Donatists and the Indelible Character of Baptism

Baptism was central to the Donatist position and so to the controversy between them and the Catholics. Augustine charged the Donatists with three fundamental sins: they broke the unity of the church, profaned the inheritance of Christ, and rejected baptism by Christ. In reply he insisted on the absolute objective validity of the sacrament: its holiness was in the rite itself, not in the administrator or the recipient.[3] Augustine built on the insistence of earlier Catholics in opposition to schismatics that there is only one baptism and that the Godhead is the true minister of this act, not the human administrator. In explaining this he developed the idea that God imparted an indelible character or mark at baptism so that, although the baptism became effective only in communion with the Catholic church, the act itself did not need to be repeated.

---

1. Vittorino Grossi, *La catechesi battesimale agli inizi del V secolo: Le fonti agostiniane* (Rome: Institutum Patristicum "Augustinianum," 1993), pp. 99, 159; see chap. 51, n. 2. He states the principal goal of his research to be an examination in Augustine's catechetical sources of the doctrine of original sin as a baptismal motif at the beginning of the Pelagian controversy (p. 153).

2. Grossi, *La catechesi battesimale*, p. 12.

3. Grossi, *La catechesi battesimale*, p. 126.

Augustine laid out the Donatist position and his response especially in his *On Baptism, Against the Donatists* and *Against the Letters of Petilian,* Donatist bishop of Cirta, both written about 400 or shortly thereafter. *On Baptism* is in seven books and is more *Against the Donatists* than strictly on the subject of baptism.[4] *Against the Letters of Petilian* is in three books and quotes short passages from Petilian each followed by Augustine's answer.

Augustine characterizes Petilian's argument from Matthew 7:16-18 and 12:35 as the one "who is baptized is made to partake of the character of him by whom he is baptized."[5] The Donatists insisted that Catholic bishops were tainted by their communion with those who surrendered copies of the scriptures to the authorities in the persecution under Diocletian and so their sacraments were invalid. They argued that their practice of rebaptizing converts from Catholicism was not a violation of the one baptism of Ephesians 4:5; in Petilian's words, "For when you [catholics] in your guilt perform what is false, I do not celebrate baptism twice, which you have never celebrated once."[6]

In support of rebaptism the Donatists cited Paul baptizing the disicples in Ephesus who had received John's baptism (Acts 19). Augustine's reply gives a large discussion of John's baptism, including his baptism of Christ.[7] The baptism commanded by Christ cleanses the church, so no second baptism is required, but John's baptism had to be repeated.[8] Here Augustine offered his explanation that John's "baptism of repentance for forgiveness of sins" (Mark 1:4) merely brought an expectation of forgiveness to be given in Christ's baptism, yet he allowed for the view of those who said there was a real forgiveness in John's baptism.[9] That Paul ordered the baptism of John's disciples in Ephesus meant this was a baptism different from John's baptism.[10] John's baptism itself was not repeated; but since it was different from Christ's baptism, even if it were repeated, this was not to be done in the case of the baptism commanded by Christ.[11]

When schisms occurred in the Donatist ranks, as with Maximianus, the

---

4. J. Patout Burns, "Christ and the Holy Spirit in Augustine's Theology of Baptism," in Joanne McWilliam, ed., *Augustine: From Rhetor to Theologian* (Waterloo: Wilfrid Laurier University Press, 1992), pp. 161-171, studies especially *On Baptism.*

5. *Against the Letters of Petilian* 3.50.61. J. R. King and Chester D. Hartranft translated this work (and *On Baptism*) in *Nicene and Post-Nicene Fathers* (reprint Peabody: Hendrickson, 1994), First Series, Vol. 4, p. 622. See chap. 43 under Optatus for more on the Donatist position.

6. *Against the Letters of Petilian* 2.25.58 (p. 545); cf. 2.2.4, "Those who have polluted their souls with a guilty laver, under the name of baptism, reproach us with baptizing twice" (p. 530). Augustine discusses rebaptism in *Letter* 108.1-20.

7. *On Baptism* 5.9.10-11; 5.13.15.

8. *On Baptism* 5.9.11.

9. *On Baptism* 5.10.12.

10. *On Baptism* 5.11.13. Cf. *Against the Letters of Petilian* 2.34.79-80; *Letter* 93.11.47-48 says that baptism is conferred by Christ and the (re)baptism of Acts 19 occurred because the prior baptism was John's and not Christ's.

11. *On Baptism* 5.12.14; 5.15.17.

Donatists did not rebaptize his followers nor those baptized by them who later identified with the main body.[12] Augustine exploited this situation, reasoning that according to their own practice the grace of baptism could be retained and could be given outside the church.[13]

At the the heart of Augustine's case was the argument that Christ, not the purity of the minister, made baptism effective. Hence, Catholics did not rebaptize converts from a heresy or a schism who had been baptized in the Trinitarian name. Baptism is not a schismatic's or heretic's, but is God's and the church's.[14] Christ's baptism is holy; although it may exist among heretics or schismatics, it does not belong to the heresy or the schism.[15] "The baptism of Christ, consecrated by the words of the gospel, is necessarily holy, however polluted and unclean its ministers may be."[16] "Baptism in the name of the Father and of the Son and of the Holy Spirit has Christ for its authority, not any man, whoever he may be."[17] The merit of baptism is in the Trinity, not the administrator.[18]

Not rebaptizing heretics on their conversion to the Catholic church was not a recognition of heretical baptism, for the baptism was Christ's, even if given among evil men.[19] In baptism it is not a matter of "who gives, but what he gives; not who receives, but what he receives; not who has, but what he has."[20] This "what" is baptism itself, not the blessings of baptism, for these can be received only in the communion of the church. Heretics cannot give forgiveness of sins, but they can give baptism.[21] Baptism is the sacrament or outward sign of grace, not grace itself.[22]

Augustine argued that the Donatists ought to apply their position in regard to heretical and schismatical baptism to persons of moral turpitude as well.[23] Jesus said

---

12. *On Baptism* 1.1.2.

13. *On Baptism* 1.5.7. He points out the inconsistency in the treatment of Catholics and of those in communion with Maximianus in *Against the Letters of Petilian* 1.11.12.

14. *On Baptism* 1.14.22. Christ is the minister of the sacraments — *To Cresconius* 4.16.19; *Exposition of the Gospel of John* 6.7.

15. *On Baptism* 1.19.29.

16. *On Baptism* 3.10.15 (p. 439); 6.25.47. Christ, not the purity of the minister, made baptism effective — *Exposition of the Gospel of John* 5.15.

17. *Against the Letters of Petilian* 2.24.57 (p. 545); cf. 2.2.5, "When the water of baptism is given to any one in the name of the Father, and of the Son, and of the Holy Spirit, it is neither ours [Catholics] nor yours [Donatists]" (p. 530). On the Trinitarian formula in baptism, see chap. 51, and on the argument from it see below at nn. 37 to 39.

18. *Against the Letters of Petilian* 2.35.82; cf. *Exposition of the Gospel of John* 5 for the minister and the true power of baptism.

19. *On Baptism* 4.4.6-7. Against the Donatist position that a true baptism is given by a righteous person, Augustine says that not the human minister but Christ baptizes — *Letter* 89.5.

20. *On Baptism* 4.10.17 (pp. 453-454).

21. *On Baptism* 5.20.30. Cf. 1.12.18 — baptism is for forgiveness, but it avails for this only when one is reconciled to the unity of the church; 3.13.18 — there is remission of sins but the sins return again unless one returns to the peace of the church.

22. *On Baptism* 7.19.37.

23. E.g., *On Baptism* 6.34.66; 6.41.80.

not only, "Except one is born of water and the Spirit" (John 3:5), but also, "Except your righteousness exceed that of the scribes and Pharisees, you shall not enter the kingdom of heaven" (Matt. 5:20), a pairing he often made.[24]

Yet Donatists did not insist on rebaptizing those baptized by those who were immoral. Augustine says that the implication of the Donatist position is that if the baptizer is a sinner, then the baptism is in vain.[25] He reduces the Donatist position to absurdity by reasoning that if there is hatred in the baptizer, or any other bad quality, then that is imparted to the one baptized.[26] Augustine's position is that baptism by an unrighteous man does not make an unrighteous baptism.[27] The Donatist position that baptism was dependent on the baptizer would introduce uncertainty about everyone's baptism.[28] That position had the effect of requiring that one put faith in a man (the baptizer) and not the Lord.[29]

Augustine leads off his reply to Petilian by quoting the latter's statement: "What we look for is the conscience of the giver to cleanse that of the recipient"; and again, "He who receives faith from the faithless receives not faith but guilt."[30] But what if the recipient is ignorant of concealed evil and faithlessness in the giver of baptism? Augustine presents a dilemma to his opponent: If the latter's guilty conscience does not affect the recipient when he is unaware of it, then one can receive faith from the faithless and the efficacy of baptism is not dependent on the giver; if the recipient receives guilt from the giver regardless of whether the guilt is concealed, then there is no assurance of salvation and there must be constant rebaptizing.[31] The Donatists were unwilling to rebaptize those of their own party, so Augustine concludes, "The purity therefore of baptism is entirely unconnected with the purity or impurity of the conscience either of the giver or the recipient."[32]

The practice of the church was that a sinful person or an apostate not be rebaptized on returning to the church.[33] One born in baptism need not be born again.[34]

---

24. In the anti-Donatist writings *On Baptism* 4.21.29; *Against the Letters of Petilian* 3.56.68. In the latter he comments on the two verses: "The form of the sacrament is given through baptism, the form of righteousness through the gospel. Neither one without the other leads to the kingdom of heaven" (p. 626). Also *Letter* 2*.6.

25. *Against the Letters of Petilian* 1.9.10.

26. *Against the Letters of Petilian* 2.6.13.

27. *Against the Letters of Petilian* 2.33.78.

28. *Against the Letters of Petilian* 1.4.5.

29. *Against the Letters of Petilian* 2.102.233; 3.28.33.

30. *Against the Letters of Petilian* 1.1.2-1.2.3 (p. 520).

31. Augustine reverts to the argument often: whence can a person be cleansed who receives baptism from one of whose polluted conscience he is ignorant? — *Against the Letters of Petilian* 2.35.82; 3.19.22-3.20.33; 3.27.32; 3.33.38; 3.48.58-3.49.59. Augustine was pushing for the admission that the effectiveness of baptism came from God (or an angel, Petilian allowed as a possible escape from his dilemma — 3.48.58-3.49.59) and not the minister, but all Petilian could reply was that the candidate ought to examine carefully the baptizer — 3.27.32; 3.33.38.

32. *Against the Letters of Petilian* 2.35.82 (p. 551).

33. *On Baptism* 5.15.20.

34. *On Baptism* 1.14.22.

The same principle distinguishing the act of baptism from its blessings applied to those baptized in the church but who renounced the world only in words and not in deeds: baptism is of no profit to a robber, a covetous person, and the like until they give up these practices.[35]

Augustine dealt with the seeming implication that his position did not matter whether one was baptized within or outside the church. The one baptized outside the church was worse off, not because of his baptism, but for two other reasons — his being outside the Catholic church and whatever error attached to the party outside the church. He considered the case of someone holding erroneous ideas about Christ baptized in that heresy and of someone holding the same ideas baptized in the Catholic church while thinking those ideas were orthodox. Augustine considered the latter person not a heretic unless when he was better instructed he deliberately chose to reject the truth. In the case of the other person, it was not only erroneous opinion but also schism that needed correcting. But in neither case is the sacrament to be repeated.[36]

The water of baptism was sanctified even if the words spoken by an unskillful priest were faulty. The succeeding discussion indicates Augustine had in mind the formula of baptism, not the prayer consecrating the water.

> Generally the fault of the prayer is more than counterbalanced by the intent of him who offers it; and those fixed words of the gospel [Matt. 28:19], without which baptism cannot be consecrated, are of such efficacy that, by their virtue, anything faulty that is uttered in the prayer contrary to the rule of faith is made of none effect, just as the devil is excluded by the name of Christ.[37]

Augustine continues that if a wicked man offers a correct prayer, "it does not follow that because the prayer is right the man himself is also right." God upholds the words of the gospel; Christ consecrates his sacrament in the recipient, who before, when, or in the future turns in truth to God so that it becomes effective for salvation. "There is no baptism of Christ, if the words of the gospel in which consists the outward sign" are not used. "Every baptism consecrated in the words of the gospel is everywhere the same and cannot be vitiated by perversity on the part of any men." In explaining this, Augustine testified that even heretics used the formula of Matthew 28:19 in baptizing, which is what gave the baptism its validity (see above).[38] Hence, the church is correct in not rebaptizing those baptized by heretics:

> The baptism of Christ, consecrated by the words of the gospel, is necessarily holy, however polluted and unclean its ministers may be; because its inherent sanctity

---

35. *On Baptism* 4.4.6-7.
36. *On Baptism* 4.16.24.
37. *On Baptism* 6.25.47 (p. 491).
38. *On Baptism* 3.15.20 names Marcion, Valentinus, Arius, and Eunomius as using these words. *Explanations of the Psalms* 77.2 (Eng. 78:1) says that heretics and false brothers have the same baptism as the church.

cannot be polluted and the divine excellence abides in the sacrament, whether to the salvation of those who use it aright, or to the destruction of those who use it wrong.[39]

Although the integrity of the sacrament was recognized, regardless of the administrator and the community in which it was given, the baptism availed for forgiveness of sins only in the unity of the church.[40] The water of faith, salvation, and holiness is only in the church.[41] Augustine used the flood in the days of Noah as an illustration. The same water that saved those in the ark from a sinful world destroyed those who were outside the ark. So it is with baptism and the church; baptism saves those in the church, but it is for the condemnation of those outside the church.[42]

Augustine unhesitatingly gave his preference to the pious but as yet unbaptized catechumen over the baptized heretic, and he acknowledged that some catechumens were better and more faithful than some baptized persons. Cornelius even before his baptism (Acts 10) was superior to the baptized Simon (Acts 8); but he received no better sacrament than Simon did, and his virtues did not mean that the sacrament of the catechumen (the giving of salt on admission to the catechumenate) was to be preferred to the sacrament of baptism, nor that baptism was to be despised. The lack of baptism was supplied invisibly when its administration was prevented not by contempt but by the necessity of the moment, as in the case of the thief on the cross. Indeed, baptism might have seemed superfluous in the case of Cornelius who was baptized in the Holy Spirit, but he was commanded to be baptized and would have been convicted of contempt if he refused baptism. Moreover, quoting John 3:5, Augustine asserts that baptism is of "no avail for salvation," unless one "be incorporated into the church."[43] Baptism and conversion are different, but they are made complete together. The situation is different if one of them is absent intentionally from the case of an absence due to circumstances.[44]

Baptism performed in the name of the Trinity, Augustine insisted, conferred an indelible character *(character indelibilis)*. This was bestowed regardless of the minister and remained with a person, so regardless of what happened later the person on return to the fellowship of the Catholic church was not rebaptized.[45] He used the illustration of a military mark (a tattoo or brand),

---

39. *On Baptism* 3.10.15 (p. 439).

40. *On Baptism* 3.17.22.

41. *On Baptism* 4.2.2.

42. *On Baptism* 5.28.39; also 6.40.78; for the point cf. 4.10.17. The wood of the ark was saving — *On Catechizing the Uninstructed* 19.32.

43. *On Baptism* 4.21.29-4.22.30 (p. 460).

44. *On Baptism* 4.22.30; 4.25.33. To the suggestion in the former passage that faith and conversion of heart as well as martyrdom could supply what was wanting of baptism (as in the case of the thief on the cross) Augustine offered the correction that the thief may have been previously baptized — *Revisions [Retractions]* 1.25.62 and 2.18.44; and see chap. 51 on *On the Soul and Its Origin* 1.9.11 for other discussions of the thief's case.

45. *Letter* 185.3; 173.3; *On Baptism* 1.4.5; *Against the Letter of Parmenian* 2.13.

which, though it can both be retained, as by deserters, and, also be received by those who are not in the army, yet ought not to be either received or retained outside its ranks; and, at the same time, it is not changed or renewed when a man is enlisted or brought back to his service.[46]

Accordingly, a baptism could be valid without the implication that the position of those administering it was acceptable, since they should return to Catholic truth.

In keeping with this teaching on the formal character of baptism, Augustine, characteristically exploring several kinds of circumstances, even considered the possible validity of baptism administered in jest.[47] But basically he distinguished baptism's validity from fruitfulness. Hence, Donatists did not have to be rebaptized, but in order to receive the benefits of baptism they had to end their schism from the Catholic church and return to the unity of love. He offered this summary of his position:

> I should have no hesitation in saying that all men possess baptism who have received it in any place, from any sort of men, provided that it were consecrated in the words of the gospel, and received without deceit on their part with some degree of faith; although it would be of no profit to them for the salvation of their souls if they were without charity, by which they might be grafted into the Catholic church.[48]

The Donatists made much of Cyprian, the great father of the African church, who had argued for the rebaptism of those baptized in schism or heresy when they came to the church. Augustine had to explain Cyprian in a way that preserved his reputation but avoided the conclusions drawn from him by the Donatists. The views of Cyprian provide the framework of *On Baptism*, books 2-5, and the responses of the eighty-seven bishops at the Council of Carthage in 256 under the presidency of Cyprian are the subject of books 6-7.

Cyprian, according to Augustine, was wrong on the subject of rebaptizing converts from a heresy or a schism, but he was right in not severing communion with those who disagreed. His being wrong on one thing showed the truth of his charity even more clearly.[49] The Donatists appealed to the authority of Cyprian in favor of rebaptism; they should follow his example in the preservation of unity rather than in altering the custom of the church, now sanctioned by general councils of the church

---

46. *On Baptism* 1.4.5 (p. 414); also in *Exposition of the Gospel of John* 6.15; *Letter* 185.6.23; *On the Creed* 8.16 (heretics too have the soldier's mark, *characterem*). Cf. the Lord's mark on sheep — *Letter* 173.3.

47. *On Baptism* 7.53.101.

48. *On Baptism* 7.53.102 (p. 513). Augustine charged that the Donatists by creating a schism sinned against brotherly love. Cf. *Exposition of the Gospel of John* 32.8, "One possesses the Holy Spirit in the measure to which he loves the church of Christ."

49. *On Baptism* 1.18.27. Burns, "Christ and the Holy Spirit in Augustine's Theology of Baptism," pp. 165-168, for Augustine going beyond Cyprian in teaching that the charity which unites the saints is the power to forgive sins, a power exercised through prayer.

(Arles and Nicaea).[50] Cyprian himself recognized that the custom of the church was against his position, and the bishops in Cyprian's council testified that the custom was different.[51] Cyprian's mistake was in not distinguishing the sacrament from its effect.[52]

Augustine granted that the Donatists were sound in most things, but by schism they sinned against charity and needed to be healed of that.[53] Near the beginning of *On Baptism* he set forth the propositions in dispute: That baptism exists in the Catholic church, is rightly received in the Catholic church, and not rightly received in the Donatist schism; all three "we assert and they deny." On one thing both sides agree: That baptism exists among the Donatists.[54] Augustine deals theoretically with what may actually have occurred: Some took the practice that both sides agreed on, namely that baptism exists in the Donatist church, and received baptism there and then came to the Catholic church. "I prefer, the person says, to receive Christ's baptism where both parties agree that it exists."[55] Coming to the Catholic church, however, showed that the persons really believed the Catholics to be right, so they should be baptized there.

Hence Augustine says to the Donatists, Do not abstain from giving baptism, but "Abstain from giving it in schism." Nor does he say to those about to be baptized, "Do not receive the baptism," but rather, "Do not receive it in schism,"[56] unless there is an urgent necessity and no Catholic is available to give baptism. But if one is delivered from death, he should seek out a Catholic congregation, for baptism is of no profit as long as one remains in heresy or schism.

Augustine's *On Baptism* discusses infant baptism and shows his settled position with which he approached the question in the Pelagian controversy.

> But as in the thief [Luke 23:39-43], to whom the material administration of the sacrament was necessarily wanting, the salvation was complete, because it was spiritually present through his piety, so, when the sacrament itself is present, salvation is complete, if what the thief possessed [confession] be unavoidably wanting. And this is the firm tradition of the universal church, in respect of the baptism of infants, who certainly are as yet unable "with the heart to believe unto

---

50. *On Baptism* 2.7.12; 2.9.14.
51. *On Baptism* 3.5.7-3.9.12.
52. *On Baptism* 6.1.1. Since the effect and use of the sacrament were not among heretics, Cyprian concluded that the sacrament itself was not among them; but the church universal decided for the original custom that those baptized by heretics did not need rebaptism. In this passage Augustine repeats his insistence that the baptism of Christ is not rendered void by any perversity in the administrator or recipient.
53. *On Baptism* 1.8.11.
54. *On Baptism* 1.3.4 (p. 413).
55. *On Baptism* 1.5.6.
56. *On Baptism* 1.2.3 (pp. 412-413). Note the summary of his position in 6.3.5-6.5.7 — bad men, whether in or out of the church, can have, confer, and receive baptism, for they do not affect its holiness; but sins are actually forgiven only in the bond of charity and peace.

righteousness and with the mouth to make confession unto salvation" [Rom. 10:10], as the thief could do; nay, who even, by crying and moaning when the mystery is performed upon them, raise their voices in opposition to the mysterious words, and yet no Christian will say that they are baptized to no purpose.[57]

One or the other of the essentials of baptism — the water or the confession of faith — might be absent in any given case because of necessity, yet the salvation was complete by reason of the words of the Lord (spoken directly in the case of the thief or spoken representatively by sponsors and by invocation of him in infant baptism). Augustine continues by answering those who seek divine authority for infant baptism: "What is held by the whole church, and that not as instituted by councils but as a matter of invariable custom, is rightly held to have been handed down by apostolical authority."[58] Augustine thus admits implicitly the lack of clear scriptural authorization and explicitly the lack of conciliar authorization. Instead he makes an argument from the parallel of circumcision. He cites examples where the order in which things are received differs: Abraham was justified by his faith and then circumcised; Cornelius was sanctified by the gift of the Holy Spirit before his baptism; male children (e.g., Isaac) were circumcised on the eighth day before they could believe.

> So in infants, who are baptized, the sacrament of regeneration is given first, and if they maintain a Christian piety, conversion also in the heart will follow, of which the mysterious sign had gone before in the outward body.[59]

In the baptism of infants the grace of God supplies the lack of personal confession, which is made for them by others, who make the vows that they cannot answer for themselves, so that the sacrament may be complete. This practice does not apply to those who are able to answer for themselves.

In another anti-Donatist writing Augustine appeals to the standard texts of Job 14:4-5 and Psalm 51:5 to explain why people hasten "even with infants to seek remission of their sins."[60]

Pelagianism, Infant Baptism, and Original Sin

The objective necessity of baptism developed in the Donatist controversy provides the context for Augustine's arguments against the Pelagians. The sacrament works

---

57. *On Baptism* 4.23.31 (p. 461). Augustine takes the crying by infants as witness to their wretchedness and request for baptism — *Sermon* 293.10; but he could also take it as a resistance to baptism — *The Punishment and Forgiveness of Sins and the Baptism of Little Ones* 1.25.36. He refers to infants crying and struggling when they are baptized also in *On Grace and Free Will* 22.44. *Letter* 187.7.25 absolves them from blame since they do not know what they are doing.
58. *On Baptism* 4.24.32 (p. 461). See n. 44 on the thief's case.
59. *On Baptism* 4.24.32 (pp. 461-462).
60. *Against the Letters of Petilian* 2.102.232 (p. 589).

what it signifies.[61] Unlike the Donatist controversy, where baptism was at the heart of the dispute, in the Pelagian controversy Augustine and his associates introduced baptism, specifically infant baptism, as a central argument on behalf of original sin. Before the Pelagian controversy Augustine was not much occupied in his catechesis with the remission of original sin, although it was implicit in his teaching.[62] It is typical that one responds to what is challenged and that opposition forces one to draw out implications of a position; even so, for Augustine the necessity of baptism because of original sin comes to special notice with the Pelagian controversy. His coupling of infant baptism and original sin was the foundation of his reconstruction of baptismal doctrine and practice that was to dominate the western church for subsequent centuries.

The same doctrine of baptism expounded in the Donatist controversy occurs in the Pelagian controversy, only now specifically applied to infants. Augustine reasoned, What is regeneration in baptism except renovation from the corruption of the old person? How is one renovated if sins are not forgiven? If one is not regenerated, neither has one put on Christ.[63] One who has put on Christ passes from darkness to light.[64] If one baptizes infants, baptism must have the same significance for them; therefore, they are born in need of regeneration, renovation from corruption, forgiveness, and enlightenment.

In the context of the Pelagian controversy Augustine repeated his emphasis that all past debts are forgiven in baptism.[65] He can take it for granted that "among us" no

---

61. Grossi, *La catechesi battesimale*, pp. 127-128, 156 (the doctrine of the sacraments from the Donatist controversy now applied to original sin).

62. Grossi, *La catechesi battesimale*, pp. 19, 144-145, 154-155 (although he may be reading the rites of the church too much in terms of their Augustinian interpretation), 157 (Pelagianism the occasion for a clear systematization of arguments). He finds anticipations in *On Catechizing the Uninstructed* 26.52; *Exposition of the Gospel of John* 3.12; and *Against the Letter of Parmenian* 2.7.14 — pp. 39-45; and he observes that whereas Augustine's comments in his sermons on the delivery of the Symbol only hint at original sin, comments on the Lord's Prayer speak of it more directly — pp. 70-76. In the early work *On Free Will* Augustine saw human beings, because of the sin of Adam, in a state of punishment but not of sin (3.10.31; 3.19.54; 3.20.56ff.), a view in accord with much of earlier Christian thought, and he argued that the soul by virtue could overthrow the sin of Adam; but he defended the usefulness of infant baptism (3.13.67) — Eduard Nagel, *Kindertaufe und Taufafuschub: Die Praxis vom 3.-5. Jahrhundert in Nordafrika und ihre theologische Einordnung bei Tertullian, Cyprian und Augustinus* (Frankfurt am Main: Peter D. Lang, 1980), pp. 119-132.

63. *On Baptism* 1.11.16. For the significance of the Pelagian controversy on Augustine's doctrine of infant baptism see David F. Wright, "Augustine and the Transformation of Baptism," in Alan Kreider, ed., *The Origins of Christendom in the West* (Edinburgh: T&T Clark, 2001), pp. 287-310. On the whole subject of infant baptism in Augustine see J. C. Didier, "S. Augustin et le baptême des enfants," *Revue des études augustiniennes* 2 (1956): 109-129; J. C. Didier, *Le baptême des enfants dans la tradition de l'Église: Dossier rassemblé et annoté* (Tournai, 1959), pp. 55-116; J. C. Didier, *Faut-il baptiser les enfants? La réponse de la tradition* (Paris, 1967), pp. 119-189; briefly but insightfully Gerald Bonner, "Baptismus paruulorum," in C. Mayer et al., *Augustinus Lexikon* (Basel: Schwabe, 1990), Vol. 1, cols. 592-602.

64. *On Baptism* 1.12.19.

65. *On the Perfection of Human Righteousness* 7.16; in 15.35 he applies Eph. 5:26 (washing of water with the word) to the cleansing of the church from past sins and driving away the dominion of wicked

one denies that the sins of all persons are remitted in the "laver of regeneration."⁶⁶ But in this polemical situation Augustine goes further to specify the forgiveness of original sin. The children of even the regenerate are born in sin.⁶⁷

Augustine dealt with infant baptism apart from the Pelagian controversy in his *Letter* 98 to Boniface, bishop of Cataqua in Numidia, although the degree to which that controversy was in the background of the letter depends in part on whether the date of the letter is 408 or 413/414.⁶⁸ Boniface had asked Augustine some questions: Can evil committed by parents harm their small children? If not, how can the faith of parents help their children? Do sponsors not lie when they respond for the infant claiming that the infant believes, since they cannot predict what the child will believe when grown up? Boniface apparently knew that Augustine denied the first question and affirmed the second, and so he asks for a justification of this distinction.

Augustine replies that the power of the sacrament of "baptism unto salvation" is so great that someone "reborn through the spiritual will of others" cannot be harmed by "another's sinfulness, if he has not consented to it."⁶⁹ "The soul of the infant, however, contracted from Adam the sin that is removed by the grace of that sacrament." The child contracted guilt "because it was one with Adam and in Adam."⁷⁰ After birth the child became another individual from the parent and was not involved in the sins of the parent.

"The child can be reborn through the act of another's will," because this rebirth is "the work of the one Spirit." John 3:5 indicates that the rebirth is not from the will of the parents or the faith of the godparents or ministers, but "The water externally presents the sacred sign of grace, and the Spirit internally produces the benefit of grace."⁷¹ Parents who involve their children in demonic rites sin against the children but do not make them sinful.

Boniface should not be disturbed, Augustine says, because some do not bring

---

angels. (Against the Donatists, who applied the passage to the visible church of saints, Augustine applied it to the eschatological church — Grossi, *La catechesi battesimale*, pp. 162-163). *Against Two Letters of the Pelagians* 1.13.26, "I say that baptism gives forgiveness of all sins"; 4.7.17, "all sins," also using Eph. 5:26-27; 3.3.5. "Only baptism brings about the full and complete forgiveness of sins" — *The Punishment and Forgiveness of Sins and the Baptism of Little Ones* 2.27.44 (translation modified from Roland J. Teske, *Answer to the Pelagians*, The Works of Saint Augustine I/23 [Hyde Park: New City Press, 1997], p. 109, from whom translations of the anti-Pelagian works are taken). *On the Good of Marriage* 21; *On Holy Virginity* 48.

66. *On the Deeds of Pelagius* 12.28; cf. "all sins" washed away in the "laver of regeneration" — *On the Grace of Christ and Original Sin* 2.40.44-45.

67. *On the Grace of Christ and Original Sin* 2.39.44-45.

68. Tarsicius J. van Bavel, "Augustine on Baptism: *Letter* 98," *Augustinian Heritage* 39 (1972): 191-212; Nagel, *Kindertaufe und Taufaufschub*, pp. 133-144; Grossi, *La catechesi battesimale*, pp. 146-152, who dates the letter to 413 and places it in the Pelagian controversy. Quotations are from the translation by Roland Teske, *Letters II/1, 1-99*, The Works of Saint Augustine: A Translation for the 21st Century (Hyde Park: New City Press, 2001), pp. 426-432.

69. *Letter* 98.1 (p. 426).

70. *Letter* 98.1 (p. 427).

71. *Letter* 98.2 (p. 427). Cf. *Sermon* 294.12 quoted below.

their little ones to baptism with faith in its proper purpose but out of superstitious expectation of healing or protection against illness.[72] Through the "actions of the minister and the words of the mysteries" the sacrament has an objective effectiveness apart from the intentions of those who present the child. It is not just the parents or sponsors who are involved but the "universal society of the saints and believers" who present the child. "The whole church, our mother, which exists in the saints, does this, because the whole church gives birth to each and every one." Since the sacrament is one and the same, "it has such power, even among heretics, and suffices for the consecration of the infant to Christ, although it does not suffice for the reception of eternal life" outside the communion of the catholic church.[73] Hence, it is not, as Boniface suggested, that "Just as the parents were the sources of their condemnation, so they are justified through the faith of their parents," but others than parents may present the child for baptism.[74]

Boniface's last question began with the observation that, if asked, one cannot say how a little child will live when grown up, or what its thoughts are. Augustine quotes him:

> "If, then, you do not dare to promise anything certain about his future conduct nor about his present thoughts, why is it that, when infants are presented for baptism, the parents reply on their behalf as responsible for them and say that they do what infants at that age are incapable of thinking. . . . For we ask those who present the children and say, 'Does he believe in God?' And concerning the child at that age at which it does not know whether God exists, they reply, 'He believes.' And they reply in that way to each of the rest of the questions that are asked."[75]

Boniface was an honest man, who felt the practice was inconsistent. He wanted a reasoned answer and not just an appeal to the tradition of the church.

Augustine acknowledged that this was a difficult question. His reply pointed to the use of accommodative language in reference to sacraments in the church. We say that "The passion of the Lord is tomorrow," referring to the celebration of something that happened many years ago; or on the Lord's day we say, "Today the Lord has risen," although it happened many years ago.

> For, if the sacraments did not have some likeness to those events of which they are sacraments, they would not be sacraments at all. But because of this likeness they

---

72. Augustine himself refers to miraculous cures occurring at baptism — *City of God* 22.8.
73. *Letter* 98.5 (p. 429). Augustine had earlier asserted that the grace of the Almighty supplied any lack of personal faith in a baptized child who died before reaching the age of reason — *On Baptism* 4.24.32; here he advances the view that the faith of the whole church guaranteed the faith of the infant so that the Spirit conferred grace in the water (for the faith of the church standing behind the faith of infants note *The Punishment and Forgiveness of Sins and the Baptism of Little Ones* 1.38).
74. *Letter* 98.6 (p. 430).
75. *Letter* 98.7 (p. 430).

generally receive the name of the realities themselves. Just as, then, in a certain way the sacrament of the body of Christ is the body of Christ and the sacrament of the blood of Christ is the blood of Christ, so the sacrament of the faith is the faith. To believe, however, is nothing else than to have faith. And for this reason when the answer is given that the little one believes, though he does not yet have the disposition of faith, the answer is given that he has faith on account of the sacrament of the faith.[76]

Later with specific reference to the Pelagian controversy, Augustine affirmed that infants were not only believers, "because they in some sense profess the faith by the words of their parents," but also "repentant, since we see that they renounce the devil and this world by the words of these same parents."[77]

Augustine concludes his response by acknowledging the difference between adult and infant baptism but affirming what they have in common:

> And so, even if that faith that is found in the will of believers does not make a little one a believer, the sacrament of the faith itself, nonetheless, now does so. For, just as the response is given that the little one believes, he is also in that sense called a believer, not because he assents to the reality with his mind but because he receives the sacrament of that reality. But when a human being begins to think, he will not repeat the sacrament, but will understand it and will also conform himself to its truth by the agreement of his will.[78]

Personal faith and commitment, in other words, may follow as well as precede baptism. Augustine then summarizes the effects of infant baptism: It gives protection from the power of evil; it brings release from the condemnation that entered the world through Adam; and it affords the loving support of the church community. Someone who does not believe this, even if he has received the sacrament of faith, is actually an unbeliever; the baptized infant is better off than this person, for although lacking faith in the mind this little one has not placed an obstacle against it. For Augustine, although maintaining faith as a personal profession by those old enough to make it, in the case of infants faith was conferred on the infant by baptism and was not the personal allegiance it had been in the early days of Christianity.

Augustine thus marked out a defense of infant baptism in relation to faith by pointing to the faith of parents, godparents, and the church that brought the infant to baptism and especially to baptism's objective character as a sacrament of faith. He,

---

76. *Letter* 98.9 (p. 431).

77. *The Punishment and Forgiveness of Sins and the Baptism of Little Ones* 1.19.25 (p. 47). The passage is notable for its conjunction of faith and repentance in children by reason of the profession of faith and the renunciation of the devil. Cf. *Letter* 184A.1.2 — when infants are baptized they are counted among the faithful, and if it were not true that they believed they would be condemned; *Sermon* 174.7 — "Believing infants" are those who have been baptized in Christ.

78. *Letter* 98.10 (p. 432).

furthermore, in this passage alluded to the forgiveness of original sin that he was to develop most fully in the Pelagian controversy and was to become in the Middle Ages the major support for the practice.

When Augustine wrote his *Enchiridion* in 421/422, he very much had the issues of the Pelagian controversy on his mind, although he makes no reference to Pelagianism in the work. Thus his treatment of Romans 6:1-11 includes infants in the meaning of baptism.

> If, then, the fact that we are baptized in the death of Christ shows that we are dead to sin, then surely infants, too, at their baptism in Christ die to sin, because in his death they are baptized. No exception was made in the statement, *All we, who are baptized.* . . . [Rom. 6:3][79]

The passage continues with Augustine's conclusion, "But to what sin do infants die in their regeneration other than that which they bring with them at birth?"[80] Looking at matters from the standpoint of original sin, Augustine declares that the gift of baptism "is an antidote against original sin, so that what is contracted by birth should by a second birth be taken away."[81]

Augustine's arguments on behalf of original sin and the necessity of infant baptism were presented most fully in his three books on *The Punishment and Forgiveness of Sins and the Baptism of Little Ones* written in 411 at the beginning of the Pelagian controversy, but they recur in other anti-Pelagian works.[82] This work has already been cited on some points in our exposition, and it brings together much of his thought expressed elsewhere. He later wrote of the work, "I discussed in particular the baptism of infants because of original sin, and grace by which we are justified."[83] The work makes an organic connection between original sin and baptism: birth in Adam brings eternal death; rebirth in Christ brings eternal life.[84] Augustine makes a

---

79. *Enchiridion* 14.52; tr. Louis A. Arand, *Saint Augustine: Faith, Hope, and Charity,* Ancient Christian Writers 3 (Westminster, MD: Newman, 1955), pp. 55-56.

80. *Enchiridion* 14.52 (p. 56). Augustine summarizes at the end of the section, "And so to those baptized in Christ's death, in which not only adults but also infants are baptized" (p. 57). Earlier in the work he declared, "For, as no one, from the infant newly born to the old man bent with age, is to be barred from baptism, so there is no one who in baptism does not die to sin. But infants die to original sin only, while adults die also to all those other sins which by their evil lives they have added to the sin they contracted at birth" (13.42; p. 50). He refers to infant baptism also in 17.66.

81. *Enchiridion* 17.64 (p. 65).

82. Nagel, *Kindertaufe und Taufaufschub*, pp. 145-161; Grossi, *La catechesi battesimale*, pp. 123-146. Grossi summarizes the work in three points: every person is born a sinner, an heir of the guilt and punishment of Adam; baptism frees from death; and the liberation from sin by baptism works in adults and children (p. 131).

83. *Revisions* [*Retractationes*] 2.59; tr. Mary Inez Bogan, *Saint Augustine: The Retractions,* Fathers of the Church 60 (Washington, D.C.: Catholic University of America Press, 1968), pp. 187-188.

84. "For only original sin is contracted through birth in the flesh, but through rebirth in the Spirit we have forgiveness, not only of original sin, but also of voluntary sins" (1.15.20; Teske, p. 45). Grossi, *La catechesi battesimale*, pp. 154, 156.

threefold intertwined argument from scripture, the authority and tradition of the church, and the meaning of the rite of baptism.

On the basis of John 3:5; 1:29; and Luke 2:11 Augustine presents Christ as the Savior of infants, but from what does he save if not original sin? And no salvation is promised without baptism.[85] Augustine readily agreed that infants have never committed any offense, and it is for this reason that everyone is in the habit of calling them innocent.[86] He collects testimonies from scripture that he sees as indicating infants will perish if they are not baptized, for instance, "Since little ones begin to belong to his sheep only by baptism, they will certainly perish, if they do not receive it."[87] Central to Augustine's argument was the inheritance of the guilt of original sin that made baptism of infants necessary.

> Just as the birth of sinful flesh through the one Adam brings to damnation all those who are born in that way, so the birth of the Spirit by grace through the one Jesus Christ leads to the justification of eternal life all those who have been predestined and reborn in that way. The sacrament of baptism is, of course, the sacrament of rebirth [regeneration]. . . . [After quoting John 3:5, he proceeds:] Even a little one, then, must be immersed in the sacrament of rebirth [regeneration] to avoid departing from this life without it in an evil state. And this is done only for the forgiveness of sins. . . . (I)nfants, then, are conformed to the death of Christ through the sacrament of baptism . . . [and] set free from the bite of the serpent.[88]

More briefly, he states, "No one is born from Adam through the process of generation without the sin on whose account it is necessary even for infants to be reborn in Christ through the grace of rebirth."[89]

Pelagius and his supporters refused to accept the transmission of original sin by sexual reproduction. They denied that infants have "original sin and the need of its remission by the sacrament of baptism."[90] "The Pelagians state that the words said in sacred baptism to remove sins offer no help to infants, since they have no sins."[91]

---

85. *The Punishment and Forgiveness of Sins and the Baptism of Little Ones* 1.23.33.
86. *The Punishment and Forgiveness of Sins and the Baptism of Little Ones* 1.35.65.
87. *The Punishment and Forgiveness of Sins and the Baptism of Little Ones* 1.27.40 (p. 57).
88. *The Punishment and Forgiveness of Sins and the Baptism of Little Ones* 2.27.43 (p. 108). *Letter* 143.6 says little ones have sinful flesh, and so are baptized.
89. *Letter* 202A.8.17 (Teske, *Letters* II/3, 156-210 [2004], p. 369). The same thought is found in *Letter* 166.3.6; 186.4.11. *Explanations of the Psalms* 50.10 (Eng. 51:5) quotes the usual proof texts for original sin applied to forgiveness of sins.
90. *On the Soul and Its Origin* 2.12.17 (trans. rev. by Benjamin B. Warfield, *Saint Augustin's Anti-Pelgian Works*, Nicene and Post-Nicene Fathers, First Series, Vol. 5 [repr. Peabody: Hendrickson, 1994], p. 339); similarly in *The Punishment and Forgiveness of Sins and the Baptism of Little Ones* 1.9.9. The anathema of the 16th Council of Carthage (418) of those who maintain that the newborn have no need to be baptized (can. 2, quoted in chap. 50) is directed against the Pelagian denial of original sin.
91. *Against the Two Letters of the Pelagians* 2.2.3 (p. 143); "those who say that infancy has nothing in it for Jesus to save" are denying that Christ is Savior — *Sermon* 174.4 (Edmund Hill, *Sermons* III/5,

The Pelagians, however, accepted the church's custom of baptizing infants.[92] Augustine quotes his Pelagian critic Julian,

> "We confess," he says, "that the grace of Christ is necessary for all, both for adults and for little ones, and we declare anathema those who say that one born of baptized parents need not be baptized."

He says that this was learned from Pelagius, namely that "baptism is necessary for little ones, not for the sake of the forgiveness of sins, but for the sake of the kingdom of heaven." Augustine replies, "In the church of the savior little ones believe through others, just as from others they contracted those sins which are forgiven them in baptism."[93] Although Augustine admits the Pelagians did not say it in so many words, he asserts that their position made infant baptism superfluous while leaving the infants more destitute than orphans since the grace of Christ which they cannot ask for themselves was denied them.[94] Because of an absolute reading of John 3:5, the Pelagians had to accept the necessity of baptizing infants.[95] The issue became the purpose of infant baptism: admission to the kingdom of heaven (granted by both sides) or also the forgiveness of original sin (denied by Pelagians).[96] When pressed on the baptismal confession that included belief in the forgiveness of sins, Pelagians offered two different explanations: either that it referred

---

The Works of Saint Augustine: A Translation for the 21st Century [Hyde Park: New City Press, 1992], p. 261).

92. *Sermon* 294.1.2; *On Grace of Christ and Original Sin* 1.35.

93. *Against the Two Letters of the Pelagians* 1.22.40 (p. 137); similar words (perhaps from Celestius) in 2.5.10 and 2.6.11. For Celestius cited explicitly as rejecting original sin — *On the Grace of Christ and Original Sin* 2.4.4 and *Letter* 157.3.22 (he had to admit that infants must be baptized but he refused original sin and said the baptism was for redemption; but Augustine asks from what is one redeemed if not the power of the devil, which is because of sin); and Pelagius not rejecting infant baptism — *On the Grace of Christ and Original Sin* 2.17-18.19. Baptism for the sake of the kingdom of heaven — *The Punishment and Forgiveness of Sins and the Baptism of Little Ones* 1.18.23 (those who say newborn infants receive baptism not for remission of sins but for entrance into the kingdom of heaven and to be made children and heirs of God — see n. 95). Augustine's reply asserts that there is no salvation without being born again in baptism, and Christ died for the ungodly (= all, including children); he applies the same reasoning to the necessity of taking the eucharist in *The Punishment and Forgiveness of Sins and the Baptism of Little Ones* 1.20.26-27.

94. *The Punishment and Forgiveness of Sins and the Baptism of Little Ones* 3.13.22.

95. *The Punishment and Forgiveness of Sins and the Baptism of Little Ones* 1.30.58 — except for the authority of this passage the Pelagians would be of the opinion that infants ought not to be baptized at all. Augustine gives the Pelagian interpretation as distinguishing the kingdom of heaven from salvation and eternal life, so infants dying unbaptized, since they have no sin, do receive salvation and eternal life. Augustine replied that renewal implies an old condition that needs changing and that only through the remission of sins does one reach the kingdom of God. He rejects the Pelagian distinction between the kingdom of heaven and eternal life in *Sermon* 294.2.3.

96. *On the Grace of Christ and Original Sin* 2.19.21. Since Pelagius affirmed that the one baptism "ought to be administered to infants in the same sacramental formula as it is to adults," Augustine concluded that, since this included the confession of baptism "for the forgiveness of sins," Pelagius too baptized infants to receive forgiveness of sins — *On the Grace of Christ and Original Sin* 1.32.35; 2.1.1.

to sins children committed after being born, or that infants were neither sinners nor righteous and needed baptism to be made righteous. Refuting these interpretations, Augustine concluded that nothing remained but original sin, which was forgiven in baptism to infants.[97]

The inconsistency of accepting infant baptism and denying original sin was pressed by Augustine.

> (T)hose people grant that little ones should be baptized, because they cannot stand up against the authority, which was beyond any doubt, given to the whole church through the Lord and the apostles. They should, then, also grant that they need these benefits of the mediator so that, washed by the sacrament, . . . they might be reconciled to God. Thus they would become in him living, saved, set free, redeemed, and enlightened. From what, save from death, . . . guilt, . . . and darkness of sins? And since they committed at that age no sin in their own life, there remains only original sin.[98]

Personal faith was an issue for some. Augustine refers to those who grant infants must be baptized and says for them to hear, "One who does not believe . . ." (Mark 16:16b). As they admit infants are reborn by the ministry of others, so let them "admit that they also believe through the hearts and lips of those who make the responses." If there is no original sin, they cannot dare say God will condemn them in their innocence.[99] For Augustine the intrinsic efficacy of sin and of grace is independent of the knowing cooperation of individuals.[100]

The Pelagians argued with reference to Romans 5:12-17, a favorite Augustinian text, that, according to the wording, if Adam's sin injured even those who do not sin, then Christ's righteousness also profits even those who do not believe.[101] Augustine does not really meet the objection but only asserts the difference between what is said of Adam and what is said of Christ and exploits the Pelagian inconsistency in accepting infant baptism without the Augustinian rationale.

Some argued that since sinners beget sinners, then the righteous should beget righteous children.[102] Augustine rejected this reasoning, because the sinful nature, although coming through the parents, does not come from them but from Adam. He explained the necessity of baptizing the children of believers by saying that these

---

97. *The Punishment and Forgiveness of Sins and the Baptism of Little Ones* 1.17.22-19.24; 1.34.63-64. Since [little ones] "are not yet held guilty of any sins from their own lives, the illness stemming from their origin is healed in them by the grace of him who saves them through the bath of rebirth [the washing of regeneration — Titus 3:5]" (*The Punishment and Forgiveness of Sins and the Baptism of Little Ones* 1.19.24 [p. 47]; cf. 1.26.39 for original sin as the only sin left from which to be saved in baptism). He later refutes the possibility of sins in a previous existence (1.22.31).
98. *The Punishment and Forgiveness of Sins and the Baptism of Little Ones* 1.26.39 (p. 56).
99. *Letter* 194.10.46 (Teske, *Letters* II/3, 156-210 [2004]).
100. Grossi, *La catechesi battesimale*, p. 135.
101. *The Punishment and Forgiveness of Sins and the Baptism of Little Ones* 3.2.2.
102. *The Punishment and Forgiveness of Sins and the Baptism of Little Ones* 2.9.11.

parents convey their carnal birth, not their spiritual birth, to their children.[103] In the baptized the guilt of concupiscence and any previous sins resulting from it are forgiven, but concupiscence itself remains and must be gradually removed by the new life of the Spirit.[104] Pelagians argued from 1 Corinthians 7:14 that the holiness of children of a believer made baptism unnecessary for them. Augustine replied with his usual approach of the inconsistency of the Pelagian practice and further insisting that whatever the sanctification intended in the passage, baptism was still necessary.

> [Whatever the sanctification of 1 Cor. 7:14,] it is unable to make them Christians and to forgive sins, unless they become believers by the teaching and sacraments of Christ and the church.... And no matter how holy and righteous the parents are who begot them, little ones are released from the guilt of original sin, only if they have been baptized in Christ.[105]

Augustine used other descriptions in addition to sinfulness to describe the condition of infants, for he applied the whole doctrine of baptism to infant baptism.[106] Infants were in darkness without baptism. Infants who resist baptism are an evidence that they are not enlightened; yet they are baptized even if they resist.[107] Infants by reason of baptism have the Son of God, who destroys the works of the devil (1 John 3:8).[108] Not only baptism but the exorcism performed on infants in the baptismal ceremony implied their need to be released from the devil. "What does my exorcism do for the child, if he is not held in servitude to the devil?"[109] Augustine continues that the sponsor renounced the devil for him — how is this possible if no devil is in him? Similarly, how can the sponsor announce he believed in the remission of sins if no sins were attributable to him? Baptism, moreover, brought reconciliation and salvation to infants.[110] If, as the Pelagians said, infants were already in

---

103. *On Marriage and Concupiscence* 1.32.37; cf. *The Punishment and Forgiveness of Sins and the Baptism of Little Ones* 2.27.44 for parents begetting children from the remains of their old nature and not from their renewed nature; *On the Grace of Christ and Original Sin* 2.39.44.

104. *The Punishment and Forgiveness of Sins and the Baptism of Little Ones* 1.39.70; 2.4.4; 2.28.45-46; *Against Two Letters of the Pelagians* 1.13.27-14.28; *Letter* 2*.10 (there remains concupiscence in the baptized).

105. *The Punishment and Forgiveness of Sins and the Baptism of Little Ones* 3.12.21 (pp. 134, 135); 2.25.41; cf. 2.26.42 for degrees of sanctification — catechumens are sanctified but if not baptized this does not avail for entrance into the kingdom of heaven and the remission of sins — and the assertion that 1 Cor. 7:14 has nothing to do with baptism or the origin and remission of sin.

106. Cf. the quotation of *The Punishment and Forgiveness of Sins and the Baptism of Little Ones* 2.27.43 at n. 88.

107. *The Punishment and Forgiveness of Sins and the Baptism of Little Ones* 1.25.35-36. See n. 57.

108. *The Punishment and Forgiveness of Sins and the Baptism of Little Ones* 1.27.42.

109. *The Punishment and Forgiveness of Sins and the Baptism of Little Ones* 1.34.63 (p. 71); exorcism a proof of original sin — *On Marriage and Concupiscence* 1.20.22 ("In all truth, then, and not by any false rite, the power of the devil is exorcised in little ones, and they renounce him through the hearts and lips of their sponsors, because they cannot do so through their own" — Teske, p. 43); 2.29.50; 2.40.45; *Letter* 194.10.46; and see chap. 51 on the baptismal ceremony applied to infants.

110. *The Punishment and Forgiveness of Sins and the Baptism of Little Ones* 1.27.44.

Christ, why then baptize them? If they are not baptized, they are not with Christ; but how can they be against Christ if not by sin?[111] Redemption can be understood in no other way than as a forgiveness of sins.[112] Christ is the physician needed by the sick, not the healthy; accordingly infants have the disease of original sin.[113]

Baptized infants were counted among the "faithful."[114] Augustine declares that no one in the church would hesitate to use this designation, for it did not derive from the act of believing, but the name was given "through the power of the sacrament [of baptism] and the responses of those who present them."[115] The normal sequence was to hear the word, believe, and be baptized.[116] According to Mark 16:16, to believe is to be baptized and not to be baptized is to disbelieve; hence those not baptized are reckoned unbelievers.[117]

Augustine claimed that infant baptism was apostolic.[118] His claim that the universal church "from its earliest days" believed "believing little ones have received the forgiveness of original sin through Christ's baptism" attributes his deductions from the biblical texts to the early church.[119] Against the Pelagians he repeatedly insisted that infant baptism was for the remission of sins.[120] Original sin excludes from the kingdom of heaven;[121] infants inherit original sin, but baptism incorpo-

---

111. *The Punishment and Forgiveness of Sins and the Baptism of Little Ones* 1.28.55.

112. *The Punishment and Forgiveness of Sins and the Baptism of Little Ones* 1.34.63.

113. *The Punishment and Forgiveness of Sins and the Baptism of Little Ones* 1.18.23-1.19.24. This was a frequent image in Augustine: William Harmless, "Christ the Pediatrician: Infant Baptism and Christological Imagery in the Pelagian Controversy," *Augustinian Studies* 28 (1997): 7-34, with other reference to Christ as a physician to infants. He observes that even in the fourth century infant baptism was emergency baptism; this was not the pastoral norm, but that does not mean it was rare, for the infant mortality rate was high in the ancient world (pp. 24-25).

114. *The Punishment and Forgiveness of Sins and the Baptism of Little Ones* 1.20.28.

115. *The Punishment and Forgiveness of Sins and the Baptism of Little Ones* 1.33.62; cf. 1.25.38 (the faith of the church is spoken through the mouth of the godparent) and 1.19.25 (confession of faith is constitutive of the sacrament but not spoken by the infant). The baptized infant is a believer through the confession of faith of the church — *Letter* 217.5.16.

116. *The Punishment and Forgiveness of Sins and the Baptism of Little Ones* 1.22.31.

117. *The Punishment and Forgiveness of Sins and the Baptism of Little Ones* 1.27.40 and 1.33.62. A child is born an unbeliever but becomes a believer through baptism — 3.9.17.

118. *The Punishment and Forgiveness of Sins and the Baptism of Little Ones* 1.24.34 — an "ancient and apostolic tradition" that without baptism and partaking of the supper one cannot attain the kingdom and eternal life; cf. 1.26.39 (the authority of the universal church handed down by the Lord and his apostles); and *On the Grace of Christ and Original Sin* 2.39.45 for the church baptizing infants on the "authority of very ancient tradition"; *On the Literal Interpretation of Genesis* 10.23.59 — an apostolic tradition.

119. *The Punishment and Forgiveness of Sins and the Baptism of Little Ones* 3.4.9 (p. 125). The earliest person he cites for the view is Cyprian — *The Punishment and Forgiveness of Sins and the Baptism of Little Ones* 3.5.10; otherwise he cites Jerome and his North African colleagues — 3.6.12-7.14; also Reticius of Autun and Ambrose (*Against Julian* 1.7 and 10). As Augustine found original sin implicit in the practice of infant baptism, one might find implicit in its absence at least a lack of recognition of original sin; the exhortations against a delay of baptism are silent on original sin as a reason not to postpone baptism.

120. See at notes 60 and 66; cf. chap. 51 on the doctrine of baptism.

121. *The Punishment and Forgiveness of Sins and the Baptism of Little Ones* 1.12.15.

rates them in the church.[122] The sin contracted from Adam is washed away by the bath of rebirth.[123]

Augustine dealt with the dilemma: either God forces souls to become sinful or he punishes the innocent, yet the soul of the unbaptized infant is carried off to condemnation.[124] Because of original sin unbaptized infants were not saved, but Augustine posited a mild punishment for them.[125] Pelagius denied that unbaptized infants went either to eternal death or to the kingdom of heaven but professed ignorance on where they did go.[126] And Augustine himself was troubled by the implications of his doctrine, but he retreated to his doctrine of predestination in response to the seeming injustice of some children saved by baptism and others lost by not receiving it.[127] His consistent position was that infants are to be baptized although their only sin is what they contracted from their condemned root, a sin washed away in the bath of rebirth. Why this rebirth is given to some but not others in the case of both adults and infants falls under the inscrutable judgment of God.[128]

A certain Victor, although not a Pelagian since he accepted the doctrine of original sin, nonetheless affirmed that infants prevented by death from being baptized entered paradise and the kingdom of heaven.[129] Among other arguments, Augustine believed that John 3:5 refuted this idea.[130] Augustine was aware of some who were unwilling to ascribe sin in a strict sense until puberty in the fourteenth year. He

---

122. *The Punishment and Forgiveness of Sins and the Baptism of Little Ones* 3.4.7.

123. *Letter* 2*.10.

124. *Letter* 166.4.10.

125. An infant is condemned by original sin alone, if the bath of rebirth is not received — *Letter* 215.1. The unbaptized infant cannot enter the kingdom of God or have eternal life — *The Punishment and Forgiveness of Sins and the Baptism of Little Ones* 3.4.8. *On the Literal Interpretation of Genesis* 10.15.26 — 10.16.29 discusses those who die in infancy; 10.16.28 says they need baptism because of the contagion of sin; they are judged on the basis of the kind of life they would have lived if they had survived (also *Letter* 217.5.16.8). For milder punishment — *The Punishment and Forgiveness of Sins and the Baptism of Little Ones* 1.16.21, "little ones who leave the body without baptism will be under the mildest condemnation of all" (p. 45); *Enchiridion* 23.93; *Against Julian* 5.11.44; *Letter* 184A.1.2 says unbaptized infants have the slightest punishment and cites Matt. 10:15 in support of differences in punishment.

126. *On the Grace of Christ and on Original Sin* 2.21.23; cf. *The Punishment and Forgiveness of Sins and the Baptism of Little Ones* 1.18.23.

127. He asks about the divine justice in damning an unbaptized child (*Letter* 166.6-10) but resigns himself to the will of God (*Letter* 190.12). *On Predestination of the Saints* 24 rejects divine foreknowledge of future merits as the explanation why some infants receive baptism and others die without it — Wright, "Augustine and the Transformation of Baptism," p. 295. *The Gift of Perseverance* 12.31 explains that, when the parents and minister are ready but for some reason the child dies before receiving baptism, God does not choose it to occur. An earlier statement on predestination is found in *Against the Letters of Petilian* 2.6.11-2.7.14.

128. *Letter* 2*.10.

129. *On the Soul and Its Origin* 1.9.10-11; 3.13.19. In 3.9.12 Augustine said that if anyone wished to be Catholic, he must refrain from believing, saying, or teaching that infants without baptism may obtain forgiveness of original sin. In *Letter* 182.5 he writes against those who preach that infants can be given eternal life without the grace of baptism, which he says would be without rebirth.

130. *On the Soul and Its Origin* 2.10.14-12.16.

pointed out that there were other sins than sexual sins that manifest themselves at a younger age, and he reaffirmed original sin, the penalty of which was wiped out in infants by baptism.[131]

Augustine in 413 preached his *Sermon* 294 in Carthage against the Pelagians and those who say there is no need to baptize babies. A survey of its contents summarizes much of his thought on the matter. Pelagians agree that babies are to be baptized; the issue is why. They say for eternal life and the kingdom of heaven but not for forgiveness. Augustine asks, Is there salvation apart from the kingdom? He asserts that there is no middle place between the kingdom and damnation (Matt. 25:37, 41).[132] In dealing with the condemnation of unbaptized babies, Augustine acknowledged that the mystery of election is inexplicable from a human standpoint, and he resorts to Romans 11:35-36 in response to the problem.[133] Depending on John 3:5, he concludes that only those in Christ go up to heaven (John 3:13).[134]

Crying by infants is their asking for help. "They believe by means of others, because they sinned by means of others."[135] John 3:36 allows only two categories, believers and unbelievers. The custom of the church is to call baptized babies "believers."[136] In regard to original sin Augustine says, "What was in Adam a matter of fault, not of nature, has now become for us, his progeny, a matter of nature."[137]

In explaining why a child of righteous persons is not born righteous, Augustine argues that the offspring of a circumcised man was not born circumcised; likewise the offspring of a baptized man cannot be born baptized because one cannot be born again before being born.[138] Some argued that if Adam harmed those who have not sinned, Christ ought to benefit even those who have not believed. Yet, they dare not say Christ does not benefit baptized babies. In further response, Augustine adds that if infants are cleansed by the faith of parents, they are defiled by the sin of parents.[139] He takes up 1 Corinthians 7:14, pointing out that the unbelieving husband sanctified in the wife yet perishes if he is not baptized; same is true for the child.[140]

Augustine's theology dominated western thought in the succeeding centuries. In particular, he advanced the theological arguments that connected original sin and infant baptism, a linking that would be followed thereafter in the western church.[141]

---

131. *On the Literal Interpretation of Genesis* 10.13.23-25.
132. *Sermon* 294.2-3.
133. *Sermon* 294.6-7.
134. *Sermon* 294.8, 10.
135. *Sermon* 294.12 (Hill, *Sermons III/8* [1994], p. 188); also 294.17 below.
136. *Sermon* 294.14.
137. *Sermon* 294.14 (Hill, *Sermons III/8* [1994], p. 189).
138. *Sermon* 294.16.
139. *Sermon* 294.17. But Augustine does not deal with the fact that the parents are not the same in the two instances.
140. *Sermon* 294.18.
141. Burkhard Neunheuser, "Die Liturgie der Kindertaufe," in Hansjörge Auf Der Maur and Bruno Kleinheyer, eds., *Zeichen des Glaubens: Studien zu Taufe und Firmung: Balthasar Fischer zum 60. Geburtstag* (Freiburg: Herder, 1972), pp. 319-334 (p. 331).

It is notable, however, that in contrast to later thinkers, Augustine reasoned from infant baptism to original sin, not the other way around. Since Pelagius accepted infant baptism but not original sin, Augustine was able to argue from the accepted doctrine of baptism for the forgiveness of sins to establish original sin as the only sin applicable to infants. Once original sin was established as the basic framework for thinking, then it was natural for it to become the principal reason for infant baptism.

Much in Augustine is traditional, although passed through the genius of his thought. Yet it is also true that the history of baptism in western Christianity begins a new chapter with him.

PART SEVEN

Baptisteries

53. Baptismal Fonts: East

Introduction to Baptismal Fonts

When Christians built special buildings and basins for performing baptisms, they employed various names for these places.[1] From secular usage they adopted βαπτιστήριον (swimming bath; the less frequent βαπτιστήρ is new), κολυμβήθρα (place for swimming; reservoir or cistern), λουτρόν (bath, place for bathing, water for washing; but rarely λούτρων, bath house), *piscina* (fish pond or swimming pool), *fons* (spring, fount, or source, from which is derived font, and probably resulting from the custom of baptizing in springs) — the usual word from the fifth century on, *balneum* (a room or place for bathing), and *lavacrum* (washing, bath). A distinctively Christian usage for baptistery was φωτιστήριον, the place of enlightenment. I will follow the modern convention of using baptistery (from βαπτιστήριον) for the building (room or rooms) where baptisms were performed and piscina or font (κολυμβήθρα) for the pool or basin in which the actual baptisms occurred. The large number of special structures for baptism built in the fourth to sixth centuries testifies to its importance in the church.

The literary sources give two principal symbolisms for the baptismal font — the tomb of death and resurrection and the womb of new birth.[2] The former symbolism was reinforced by variations on a cross shape, which became fairly common in the fifth and sixth centuries. Both baptisteries and basins in the shape of a hexagon may have alluded to Jesus' death on the sixth day of the week; the octagon to his resurrection on the eighth day or at any rate to the idea of resurrection and eternal life.[3] The

---

1. F. W. Deichmann, "Baptisterium," in Theodor Klauser, ed., *Reallexikon für Antike und Christentum* (Stuttgart: Hiersmann, 1950), Vol. 1, cols. 1157-1167 (1158), for the names and references.

2. W. M. Bedard, *The Symbolism of the Baptismal Font in Early Christian Thought* (Washington, D.C.: Catholic University of America, 1951).

3. F. J. Dölger, "Zur Symbolik des altchristlichen Taufhauses," *Antike und Christentum* 4 (1934): 153-187; Paul A. Underwood, "The Fountain of Life in Manuscripts of the Gospels," *Dumbarton*

latter was explicit in the case of the octagonal baptismal font in Milan (see chap. 40 on the Ambrosian font). Even the frequency of three steps for the entrance and three for the exit of pools may have had symbolic worth (three days in the tomb), and the practice of sinking the font below floor level may have enhanced the association with a tomb. The rectangle may have alluded to a tomb, and the circle may have alluded to the womb or to eternity; or they could have been merely utilitarian. Often symbolic considerations must finally remain in the realm of speculation.[4]

The study of early Christian baptismal fonts is greatly facilitated by the corpus of baptisteries and fonts compiled by Sebastian Ristow (n. 4). He lists 1,061 objects known from archaeological finds or (a few) from detailed written accounts. He groups them in three categories: certain/probable baptisteries (#s 1-788); possible baptisteries (#s 789-934); and uncertain and doubtful finds (#s 935-1,061). The chronological span is from Dura Europus in the third century (240s) to the ninth century; even approximate dating is often problematic. The geographical coverage is the lands surrounding the Mediterranean Sea and adjacent to them.

Baptisteries may be found at small towns, pilgrim sites, monasteries, and castles, and some cities had several, so their presence is not necessarily a sign of a bishop's church.[5] More than two-thirds of the baptisteries were added to or built into the church's assembly room, but there is no rule as to the location or the orientation of the baptismal room. Stand-alone baptisteries were often to the west or southwest of the church building, but there are regional variations. Only a few baptisteries cannot be brought into relation with a known church building, and a distance of twenty to twenty-five meters distance is the rare exception.[6] There were often other rooms than the room with the font as part of the baptistery complex, but in most cases it is almost impossible to verify suppositions about which might be a catechumenorum, an unclothing room, and a consignatorium. The greatest number of these rooms were on the west of the baptistery, and a clear majority of baptisteries had the entrance on the west;[7] these arrangements would fit what the literary sources tell us about the preliminaries to the baptism proper.

The piscinae were usually in the center of the baptismal room, and the central position was sometimes emphasized by a ciborium, columns, or pillars; next in frequency was a location at the east side of the room.[8] About thirty percent of the baptismal piscinae are round, sixteen percent are cross-shaped, fourteen percent are

---

Oaks Papers 5 (1950), Appendix B on "The Six and the Eight in Baptisteries and Fonts: Archeological Evidence."

4. Sebastian Ristow, *Frühchristliche Baptisterien,* Jahrbuch für Antike und Christentum, Ergänzungsband 27 (Münster: Aschendorff, 1998), pp. 77-81, for various factors involved in the symbolism of different shapes and the caution necessary in the absence of explicit explanations.

5. Ristow, *Frühchristliche Baptisterien,* p. 2.

6. Ristow, *Frühchristliche Baptisterien,* pp. 15-17.

7. Ristow, *Frühchristliche Baptisterien,* pp. 23-25.

8. Ristow, *Frühchristliche Baptisterien,* p. 17; p. 28 gives the number 365 out of 592 where the location of the piscina can be determined as being in the center of the room.

rectangular, eleven percent are octagonal, nine percent are square, and five percent hexagonal. Several have a mixed form, and it is not unusual for an internal shape to be different from the external form.[9] Already in the fourth century the most important different ground plans are found: round (earliest certain example is the Constantinian Lateran baptistery in its phase two); rectangular (in the third century at Dura and in the fourth century at Poreč, phase one) and square (Geneva phase one); octagon (Nea Anchialos, but most are fifth century); cross-shaped (earliest certain examples are fifth century); hexagonal (Salona, phase one); and quatrefoil (first in the first half of the fifth century).[10]

The dimensions of the fonts are generally not under one meter by not over three meters. Their depth is not under thirty centimeters and rarely over 1.80 meters.[11]

My attention will be given to the piscinae and not to the baptismal buildings. Ristow gives the depth of these fonts where the archaeological reports record this information, but unfortunately only rarely are the length and width (of rectangular fonts) or diameter (circular, polygonal fonts) given. I will take note of those fonts which belong (with a few exceptions) before the sixth century (in keeping with the period covered in this study) and where the depth is given. The number of surviving baptismal fonts increases from the fourth to the sixth centuries.

This chapter will deal with those baptismal pools in the East; the next chapter with those in the West. The arrangement of the material follows roughly the geographical expansion of Christianity and then the approximate chronological order within each country. The piscinae are identified by the numbers in Ristow. At the conclusion of the next chapter some evaluation will be given of Ristow's generalizations about the implications of the sizes of fonts for the administration of baptism and for its symbolism.

Israel[12]

There survive from Israel several baptismal pools of some size and a few smaller ones. Few of the fonts go beyond one meter in depth (three examples) with a maximum of 1.3 meters. The majority measure between 60 and 90 centimeters, and the minimum depth is 30 (three examples). The largest fonts have an average internal measurement of 1.80 meters across. Many measure internally from .60 to 1.0 meter.[13]

---

9. Ristow, *Frühchristliche Baptisterien*, p. 28.
10. Ristow, *Frühchristliche Baptisterien*, pp. 61-68.
11. Ristow, *Frühchristliche Baptisterien*, p. 28. A meter is a fraction more than 3 feet and 3 inches.
12. Malka Ben-Pechat, "The Paleochristian Baptismal Fonts in the Holy Land: Formal and Functional Study," *Liber annus studii biblici franciscani* 39 (1989): 165-188 and plates 27-34, a summary of his doctoral dissertation, *L'architecture baptismale de la Terre Sainte du IVème au VIIème siècle: Étude historique, archéologique et liturgique* (Paris: Nanterre, 1985), 3 vols. This article studies fifty-three fonts before the ninth century and distinguishes nine different types according to the shape of the font's rim.
13. Ben-Pechat, "The Paleochristian Baptismal Fonts," p. 169. See further on the significance of the dimensions in chap. 54.

More than half the fonts have some variation of the cross shape.[14] Unlike the central location in the baptismal room common elsewhere, the usual location of fonts in the Holy Land was at one end of the room, preferably at the east.[15]

At El-Burdsch (Dor) there is a rectangular piscina of the fourth century (Ristow #304) with two steps giving entrance to the pool. Its depth is 97 centimeters. This figure corresponds with what appears to be the most common depth for fonts of about one meter. In a second phase from the early fifth century (Ristow #305) the depth was reduced to 77 centimeters. This accords with a common pattern that remodeling made a later font smaller than its predecessor.

The baptismal font at Magen in its first phase at the end of fourth or beginning of the fifth century (Ristow #315) was a square with a depth of approximately one meter.[16] Four steps on the north side gave access. In the second phase (Ristow #316), dated fifth/sixth century, the font was given a cross shape and its depth reduced to 80+ centimeters.

The Eleona church in Jerusalem had a piscina of the fourth or fifth century (Ristow #308). The square pool had one step and a depth of approximately 80 centimeters.

At Evron, five kilometers north of Akko, the baptistery can be dated at 442/443 (Ristow #306), the earliest in Israel with an absolute date. The font is unusual in being a trapezoid; its depth is approximately 50 centimeters.

At the house of Peter in Capernaum there is a fifth-century font in the shape of a rectangle (Ristow #323). It has two steps on both the north and south, and the depth is 70 centimeters.

From Nessana in the Negev there is found an impressive font dated 464 to 527/65 (reign of Justinian) (Ristow #318). It was of composite shape (semicircle within a square) and was entered by two steps each on the north and west. Its depth is approximately one meter, and it had a ciborium.

Also in the Negev is the font at Kurnub (Mampsis) (Ristow #313). The date given is fifth/sixth century.[17] Its cross form within a rectangle had five steps on the north, south, and west. The depth is one meter,[18] and the ciborium has four columns. There is a smaller secondary piscina nearby. Many sites have such secondary piscinae, and their function is not clear (perhaps different at different locations) — footwashing, receptacle for oil of anointing, and infant baptism are the leading suggestions, but since footwashing is not attested as a baptismal rite in the East and

---

14. Ben-Pechat, "The Paleochristian Baptismal Fonts," p. 184.
15. Ben-Pechat, "The Paleochristian Baptismal Fonts," p. 184.
16. Juliette Day, *Baptism in Early Byzantine Palestine 325-451* (Bramcote: Grove, 1999), p. 36, makes the claim that the font was only deep enough for an adult to sit, not stand. A depth of one meter was common and ample for a dipping, as shown by Jewish mikwaoth.
17. Ben-Pechat, "Paleochristian Baptismal Fonts," p. 172, gives early fifth century on the basis of archaeological evidence.
18. Ben-Pechat, "The Paleochristian Baptismal Fonts," p. 173, gives the depth as 1.10 meters. (It will be noted that Ristow rather frequently gives smaller dimensions than other reports.)

some of the containers are connected to the larger font, infant baptism is more likely.[19] The presence of small piscina(e) adjacent to a larger one perhaps testifies(y) to a time when adult and child baptism co-existed.

A comparable beautiful and well-preserved font is at the north church of Abdat (Eboda, Oboda) in the Negev, possibly the second half of the fourth century (Ristow #300).[20] It too is cross-shaped (but within a semicircle) and has a nearby smaller secondary piscina. The main piscina is monolithic and has a depth of 1.10 meters.[21] No steps are preserved; they may have been of wood, or access may have been by a movable ladder.[22]

West Jordan and Jordan

On the West Bank of the Jordan, under Israeli control at the time of writing, there are several baptisteries to be noted because many have rather shallow fonts. At the Octagonal Church in Garizim, south of Nablus, which can be dated to 485, there is a font in the shape of a hexagon (Ristow #772). It had one step on both the northeast and southwest. Its depth was 40+ centimeters.

At Horvat Beit Loya (five kilometers south of Beth Guvrin), phase one of the piscina (second half of the fifth century) is round (Ristow #773). Its depth is 40 centimeters, but the diameter is 1.60 meters. Phase two (Ristow #774) represents one of the few instances when the later font is enlarged. In the sixth century the depth is recorded as 100+ centimeters (1 meter).

The baptistery at Khirbet el-Merd, 492 to seventh century, has a quite small round font for the period: its depth is approximately 32+ centimeters and its inner diameter is 57 centimeters (Ristow #776).

The Church of the Nativity in Bethlehem had a baptistery in the fourth century, but information on it is lacking (Ristow #764). In phase two (Ristow #765) during the reign of Justinian (sixth century) the piscina was a quatrefoil and octagon with two single steps. Its depth was approximately 75 centimeters.

Quite remarkable is the sixth-century piscina from Tekoa (Ristow #781). Its shape is round on the inside and octagonal on the outside, marked with a cross. The one interior step gives a smaller circumference to the lower part than the upper part of the font. The depth of 112 centimeters is greater than the diameter.

In present-day Jordan at Gerasa there is a font from the end of the fifth century located in an apse at the east of the baptistery (Ristow #439). This font is oval with four steps on both the north and south; its depth is 80 centimeters. As the rectangular shape suggested a tomb, the oval shape may have been evocative of the womb.

19. So Ben-Pechat, "Paleochristian Baptismal Fonts," pp. 177-179.
20. Color photograph in Lothar Heiser, *Die Taufe in der orthodoxen Kirche: Geschichte, Spendung, und Symbolik nach der Lehre der Väter* (Trier: Paulinus, 1987), Plate XII.
21. Ben-Pechat, "Paleochristian Baptismal Fonts," p. 173, gives 1.20 meters.
22. Ben-Pechat, "Paleochristian Baptismal Fonts," p. 176.

The church at Petra, excavated in 1993 and 1996, contained one of the best-preserved baptisteries of the Syro-Palestinian region (cf. Ristow #443a, "monastery").[23] The baptistery, dated mid to late fifth century, is the almost square room X. The adjoining rooms XI and IX on a straight axis with room X could have served for prebaptismal and postbaptismal rites respectively. At room X's center is the externally quadrangular font, 2 meters by 2.3 meters. Four columns at the corners of the platform supported a canopy.

Within the quadrangle is a centrally sunk but nonsymmetrical cruciform basin. The main access to the font was the south arm of the cross. The west and north arms have a single external step. The opening of the cross at the top of the platform measures 1.46 meters east-west and 1.4 meters north-south. The marble walls rise between 0.57 meter and 0.62 meter above floor level. The central basin is surrounded by an internal step on all four sides. The lowest part of the basin is a central square, 0.7 by 0.72 meter and 0.35 meter high to the step. At the level of the step the opening is a square of about 0.9 meter. The bottom is 1.22 meters below the top of the platform and 0.6 meter below the level of the room's floor. (This feature of part of the depth below floor level and part above demonstrates the error of taking only one of these dimensions in incompletely preserved or imperfectly excavated fonts.) No traces of a means of water conduction and evacuation have been found, but this was common in the region's baptisteries, which must have been filled and emptied by jars.[24]

This font has one of the deeper and larger basins in the region. "It is generally acknowledged that even the largest main fonts could not accommodate standing adults for the required rite of total immersion and that individuals must have adapted their posture accordingly."[25] This statement could actually accord with an immersion by ducking the head of a standing person or bending forward the person who may have been sitting or kneeling. On the north side of the southwest column there is a large stone jar with a diameter of about 0.46 meter and a depth of 0.6 meter. "The stone jar in Petra would allow for convenient and safe infant immersion, assuming that the infant was lowered vertically into the jar."[26]

Syria and Lebanon

The earliest securely dated Christian baptistery was discovered at Dura Europos in Syria (Ristow #617; Figure 13) and was discussed in chapter 26 on third-century Syrian sources. Other finds from Syria are significantly later and represent fonts of shallower depth.

23. Z. T. Fiema, C. Kanellopoulos, T. Waliszewski, and R. Schick, *The Petra Church* (Amman: ACOR, 2001). Z. T. Fiema's chapter, "Reconstructing the History of the Petra Church: Data and Phasing," pp. 45-49, describes the baptistery and its baptismal font.
24. So also Ben-Pechat, "Paleochristian Baptismal Fonts," p. 176.
25. Fiema, *The Petra Church*, p. 48.
26. Fiema, *The Petra Church*, p. 48.

The piscina at Qal'at Sim'ān, phase one, is dated to c. 491 (Ristow #631). It was round with four steps on the north and on the south, with a depth of 70 centimeters. Phase two (Ristow #632) from the sixth century was oval with a depth of 50 centimeters.

The East Church at Halabiyya, about 500, had a piscina in the shape of a cross in an octagon (Ristow #618). Its depth was approximately 60 centimeters.

At Khirbet Sarkiyeh the font is dated as fifth/sixth century (Ristow #624). It was round within a square, with a ciborium of four columns. The depth was approximately 75 centimeters.

Also of the fifth/sixth century is the East Cathedral at Al'at al-Mudīq (Ristow #628). The baptismal pool in its first phase was round within a quatrefoil and had a depth of 80 centimeters.

In Lebanon one baptistery is given an early date, c. 389 (Ristow #486). It is located at Zahrani (eight kilometers south of Sidon). The piscina is half-round in shape, with a depth of 20+ centimeters. If the date and dimensions hold up, it is most unusual. Two baptisteries of fifth-century date are more representative. Hössn Niha (south of Baalbek) has a round piscina of a depth of one meter (Ristow #484). At Sūr, Tyre, at the church founded in 316, is a baptistery from a later period containing a piscina in the shape of a cross with two sets of two steps (Ristow #485). The depth is 92 centimeters.

Egypt and Libya

The extensive and impressive remains at Abū Mīnā include at the Menas Church a baptistery that went through three phases of development from the fifth to eighth centuries (Ristow #s 3-5). Phase one, dated to 400-410, is a round piscina with four steps on the east and west. Phase two belongs to the reign of Justinian in the sixth century. For this period we have the depth of the round piscina with its steps as 1.15 meters. The third phase in the eighth century kept the same dimensions but added a ciborium.

The West Church at Quft (Koptos/Kebt) has a baptistery of the fifth (?) century (Ristow #52) with a large piscina.[27] It is an octagon within a cross shape. There are four outside steps and inner steps — three on the south, and two on the north, south, and east — and a ciborium. The depth of the piscina is 1.40 meters.

At Sūhāğ a piscina of the mid–fifth century (Ristow #55) has three steps on the east and west and a depth of 78 centimeters.

Within the modern country of Libya the ancient city of Sabratha provides two churches whose baptisteries went through two phases of construction. Church III had a baptistery from the end of the fourth century (Ristow #498). It is a trapezoid in shape with one step on the north and east and two steps on the west. Its depth was

27. A. Weil, "Koptos," *Annales du service des antiquités de l'Egypte* 11 (1911): 131-134.

75+ centimeters. In phase two of the church (sixth century) a larger baptistery was located on the opposite side of the church (Ristow #499 and plate 16a). The new piscina was a rectangle with four steps on the west and two (or four?) on the east; it had a depth of 1.10 meters. Church I at Sabratha in its first phase (fifth century?) had a piscina that was a square in a rectangle (Ristow #496). There were two steps on the north, south, and east, and the depth was 90 centimeters. Phase two in the second half of the sixth century was made more impressive as a cross in an octagon with a ciborium (Ristow #497). It too was enlarged — four steps on north, south, and west, and the depth was 141 centimeters.

The cross shape became popular. At Chafagi Aamer the fifth/sixth-century (?) piscina was a cross with four sets of three steps and a depth of 120 centimeters (Ristow #489). Church A at Latrun, fifth/sixth century, also has a cross-shaped piscina, but it is smaller — one step on north and south and half the depth at 60 centimeters (Ristow #494).

Turkey

The country of Turkey provides several examples within our time period of pools with considerable depth. In Ephesus there are two prominent baptisteries, both set into the ground. The earlier is at the Church of St. Mary. Phase one (Ristow #659; Figure 17) is perhaps from the second half of the fourth century and is the stage exhibited at the site. The centralized baptistery has eight niches that give an octagonal appearance. The baptismal pool is round with extensions on the west and east for four steps each. The depth of 115 centimeters provided the potential for water to reach the chest of a grown person. Phase two (Ristow #660) of the fifth (?) century was a dodecagon with one step on both the east and west and a depth of 60 centimeters.

The huge St. John Church, Selçuk — Ephesus — from the reign of Justinian, has to its north an eight-sided baptistery that is dated from the mid–fifth to the mid–sixth century (Ristow #686; Figure 18). The baptismal room itself has adjoining rooms on the east and west. The piscina is round with long arms east and west containing three steps each and the cross arms rounded. Its depth is 84 centimeters. There are two rectangular secondary piscinas, one on the north and one on the south, 50 centimeters deep.

A baptistery in what had been the Asklepieion in Pergamum is dated from the fourth to the sixth century (Ristow #648). Its cross-shaped font had three steps on both the east and west, and its depth was 112 centimeters.

At the Babylas sanctuary in Antioch (fifth century) there is a half-round piscina with a depth of 60 centimeters (Ristow #644).

The cloister complex of Alahan Manastiri contains a baptistery dated to the end of the fifth century (Ristow#643). It may have served for the baptism of pilgrims. The pool is in the shape of a cross with three steps on each of its four arms. It has a remarkable depth of 1.35 meters (approximately four feet, seven inches, approaching shoulder height).[28]

At Aslan Burnu a font of the fifth/sixth century (?) is an oval within a cross (Ristow #647). It has two sets of three steps and a depth of 98 centimeters.

The baptistery at Güllbahçe near Izmir is dated fifth or sixth century (Ristow #664). The octagon-shaped pool has two steps and a depth of 1 meter.

Possibly fifth century is the baptistery of the Chalkopraten Church in Istanbul (Ristow #670). Its round/oval piscina has a depth of 105 centimeters.

Note may also be made of the more famous but later Hagia Sophia, built under Justinian (527-565) in Istanbul (Ristow #668). The oval/rectangle font continues the practice of a deep pool — 111 centimeters.

Cyprus

The large baptismal complex of several rooms at Carpasia is dated to the fifth century (Ristow #784). The baptismal room itself is small but is dominated by the piscina in the center. Its dimensions are 175 by 60 centimeters, with a depth of 90 centimeters. Its form is rectangular, and the five entrance steps on the east and west give it the shape of a cross.

At Kourion the baptistery is located on the northwest side of the Episcopal Church of Zenon (Church I or A). The piscina of the first phase (fifth century, but sometimes dated fourth century) of the baptistery (Ristow #785) is in the shape of a cross with three steps on the east and west and a standing place for the administrator on the north. The breadth of the cross arm is 1.53 meters, and the depth is 1.12 meters. The cruciform font is in a cruciform building and is located in an apsidal recess in south wall of the hall.[29]

Church C (= Gamma) at Paphos belongs to the second half of the fifth century (Ristow #787). The piscina is a quatrefoil(?)/rectangle. It is 1.30 by 1.50 meters, but the depth is only 50+ centimeters.

For comparison refer to Church B at Salamis from the sixth century (Ristow #788). It, like Kourion, is a cross with three steps on the east and on the west and a step for standing for the baptizer on the north. The cross arms are each 70 by 85 centimeters, and the depth is 120+ centimeters. There are two small piscinae in the north corners approximately 40 by 40 centimeters.

---

28. Heiser, *Die Taufe in der orthodoxen Kirche*, plates XIII-XV.

29. Kyriakos Nicolaou, "Archaeological News from Cyprus, 1974," *American Journal of Archaeology* 80 (1976): 361-375, described briefly with a picture of the font on p. 371; Heiser, *Die Taufe in der orthodoxen Kirche*, plate XVI.

Greece

Greece offers a large number of surviving baptismal fonts, and there is a comprehensive corpus of its baptisteries written in Greek.[30]

The oldest surviving baptismal pool in Greece is at Epidauros in the Peloponnesus.[31] It belongs to the end of the fourth century (Ristow #242 gives fourth/fifth century). The interior shape is round, the external form a square. The upper diameter of the pool is 1.45 meters; a step gives to the lower part a diameter of 0.95 meter. The depth is about 0.75 meter (Ristow gives 0.70).

Corinth and vicinity provide five examples.[32] On Acrocorinth are some remains of a baptistery of the fifth century (Ristow #247) with a square *kolumbēthra*. Basilica B (Kraneion, Cenchrea) has a baptistery dated 500-550/551 (Ristow #248; Figure 14). The octagonal *kolumbēthra* extends 0.57 meter below ground, and Volanakis supposes that with its height above ground the total depth would have been 0.77 or 0.87 meter. There is one step on the east and west. The huge basilica D (Lechaion) of c. 500 has an extensive baptismal complex that is older than the basilica. The *kolumbēthra* lies in the center of the baptismal room *(phōtistērion)*. It is an octagon with four arms that give a cross-shape. Two steps are in the east and west arms. The octagon is 1.10 meters across, but with the cross arms this extends to 1.77 meters. The preserved depth is approximately 0.48 meter, but the original depth would have been about 0.80 meter. A secondary piscina in the southeast niche is 0.74 meter by 0.67 meter, but it has a depth of 1.02 meters; it too has a step. Basilica C or Gamma (Skoutela) has a baptistery of the early sixth century (Ristow #250). The *kolumbēthra* is a Greek cross with two steps on each of its four arms. Basilica E on the outskirts of Corinth has a baptistery of the fifth century (Ristow #251), but Volanakis lists it as doubtful.

Sikyon has a baptistery of the fifth century (Ristow #293). The exterior of the piscina is round and the interior a decagon. Ristow does not give the dimensions, but Volanakis does.[33] The cylindrical-shaped pool has a diameter of 55 centimeters at the bottom, 90 centimeters at the middle, and 120 centimeters at the top. The depth is 110 centimeters. There are two steps.

On mainland Greece at Amphissa in Phocis there is an early baptistery dated to the end of the fourth century (Ristow #233). This piscina is half round with one step on the south and on the north. The depth is 90 centimeters. At Eleusis, Church of St. Zechariah, there is a fifth-century baptistery (Ristow #241). The piscina is a cross of equal arms with an inner circle of a diameter of one meter. The whole length of the

---

30. ΙΩΑΝΝΟΥ ΗΛ. ΒΟΛΑΝΑΚΗ, ΤΑ ΠΑΛΑΙΟΧΡΙΣΤΙΑΝΙΚΑ ΒΑΠΤΙΣΤΗΡΙΑ ΤΗΣ ΕΛΛΑΔΟΣ, ΒΙΒΛΙΟΘΗΚΗ ΤΗΣ ΕΝ ΑΘΗΝΑΙΣ ΑΡΧΑΙΟΛΟΓΙΚΗΣ ΕΤΑΙΡΕΙΑΣ 84 (ΑΘΗΝΑΙ, 1976) = Ioannis Volanakis, *The Early Christian Baptisteries of Greece* (Athens, 1976). I shall follow his geographical grouping but not his alphabetical order within the groups.

31. Volanakis, *The Early Christian Baptisteries of Greece*, pp. 30, 60-61.

32. Volanakis, *The Early Christian Baptisteries of Greece*, pp. 61-66, 69-70.

33. Volanakis, *The Early Christian Baptisteries of Greece*, p. 68.

arms of the cross is about three meters. The total depth is about 75 centimeters.[34] At Aigosthena there is a baptistery from the end of the fifth century (Ristow #232). The piscina has a square exterior, and the interior is octagonal at the top (diameter 70 centimeters) and hexagonal for the bottom 22 centimeters (diameter 38 centimeters). The preserved depth is about 55 centimeters.[35]

In Thessaly the Damakrotia Basilica at Demetrias went through several building phases (Ristow #s 238-239). Phase one of Basilica A belongs to the second half of the fifth century. The piscina is round within a hexagon and has one step and a ciborium. The depth is 76 centimeters. In the second phase the shape became an oval and the depth was reduced to 32(?) centimeters. Volonakis gives different dimensions.[36] According to him, the lower part of the piscina (round) has a diameter of 1.20 meters and a depth of 0.45 meter; the upper part is a hexagon with its greatest diameter as 1.95 meters and its least diameter as 1.70 meters. He gives the total depth of the *kolumbēthra* as 0.97 meter. In the southeast corner of the baptistery room there is a second *kolumbēthra* in the shape of an ellipsis with a depth of 0.70.

Nearby Nea Anchialos has three baptisteries. At Basilica A the *phōtistērion* is dated about 470 (Ristow #272). The *kolumbēthra* is octagonal at the upper part and round at the lower part. The diameter of the latter is one meter. The depth of the lower round part is 35 centimeters, and the preserved part of the upper octagon adds another 10 centimeters, giving a depth of 45 centimeters; but uncertainty whether the octagon originally extended higher means the actual depth of water possible cannot be determined accurately.[37] Basilica B is dated to the end of the fifth century (Ristow #273), but dimensions are not provided for its piscina. Basilica C (Gamma) belongs to the first half of the sixth century (Ristow #274). Its *kolumbēthra* is a quatrefoil within a square (1.42 meters by 1.42 meters). Damage prevents accurate knowledge of the depth.[38] An octagonal baptistery of the mid–fourth century at Hagios Petros in Nea Anchialos included by Ristow (#271) is not mentioned by Volanakis.

In Greek Macedonia a baptistery at Dion (Pieria), outside the atrium of Basilica B, is dated by Ristow as sixth century (#240) but by Volanakis as mid–fifth century.[39] The font is a Maltese cross within an octagon. The total length is 2.70 meters. The preserved depth is 50 centimeters, but it appears that the original depth was 70 to 80 centimeters.

---

34. Volanakis, *The Early Christian Baptisteries of Greece*, p. 74.
35. Volanakis, *The Early Christian Baptisteries of Greece*, p. 71.
36. Volanakis, *The Early Christian Baptisteries of Greece*, pp. 79-81. Ristow, *Frühchristliche Baptisterien*, pp. 153-154, gives other dimensions cited by A. Khatchatrian, *Les Baptistères paléochrétiens* (Paris, 1962); also A. Khatchatrian, *Origine et typologies de baptistères paléochrétiens* (Mulhouse: Centre de culture chrétienne, 1982).
37. Volanakis, *The Early Christian Baptisteries of Greece*, p. 82. Ristow gives as the depth only the 35 centimeters of the lower part.
38. Volanakis, *The Early Christian Baptisteries of Greece*, pp. 82-85.
39. Volanakis, *The Early Christian Baptisteries of Greece*, pp. 91-92. There is a good picture in the frontispiece of F. M. Buhler, *Archeologie et baptême* (Mulhouse: Centre de Culture Chrétienne, 1986).

On the island of Thasos Ristow (#293) includes at Alyki a fifth-century baptistery with a round piscina 45 centimeters deep that is not discussed by Volanakis. At Hebraiokastron there is a fifth- or sixth-century baptistery (Ristow #595) with a square piscina.[40]

At Philippi the important octagonal church just east of the Roman Forum has in the middle of its baptistery a *kolumbēthra* in the shape of a Maltese cross (Ristow #281). Ristow gives a date in the first half of the sixth century, but Volanakis argues for a fifth-century date.[41] One arm has three steps, and the others two each. The breadth across the arms is 2.20 meters. The depth is approximately 80 centimeters. Church B at Philippi is sixth century (Ristow #280). It has a square piscina.

At the northwest corner of the Church of St. Demetrius in Thessalonica are rooms built at the site of Roman baths that probably formed the church's baptistery in the fifth century (Ristow #296).[42] The font was a hexagon with one step. Beside the later Church of Hagia Sophia there is the tetraconch baptistery of St. John the Baptist (Ristow #297). The piscina is a large hexagon with six sets of two steps alternating with six semicircular insets.[43]

The Greek islands of the Aegean furnish many early Christian baptisteries. On Samos at Heraoin there is a baptistery of the beginning of the fifth-century (Ristow #289). The *kolumbēthra* is a circle within a square with columns to support a ciborium at the four corners. The diameter of the circle is 2.80 meters.[44] At Kedros there is a baptistery of the fifth/sixth century (Ristow #290). The cross-shaped piscina has a step on the east arm. The preserved depth is 27 centimeters,[45] but this is unlikely to be the original size.

At Milos in the Cyclades the Church of Panagia (North Church), Kepos, there is a fifth-century baptistery (Ristow #266). The breadth of the cross-shaped piscina (four sets of two steps) is 1.75 meters. The preserved depth is given by Volanakis as 46 centimeters with the observation that originally it would have been much greater,[46] and indeed Ristow gives it as 110 centimeters.

On Paros the Katapoliani Church has an impressive baptistery (Ristow #279; Figure 15). On-site information gives a fourth-century date, but Volanakis says fifth century,[47] and Ristow says sixth century with a question mark. The pool is in the shape of an equal-armed cross (total breadth 2.95 meters), and it has three steps on the east and west. The depth is approximately 95 centimeters, about half of which is

---

40. Volanakis, *The Early Christian Baptisteries of Greece*, pp. 92-93.
41. Volanakis, *The Early Christian Baptisteries of Greece*, pp. 96-98 (98 on the date).
42. Volanakis, *The Early Christian Baptisteries of Greece*, pp. 99-100, includes it as doubtful but gives arguments for the baptistery interpretation.
43. Pictured in E. Ferguson, et al., eds., *Encyclopedia of Early Christianity*, 2nd edition (New York: Garland [Taylor and Francis], 1997), p. 165.
44. Volanakis, *The Early Christian Baptisteries of Greece*, p. 105.
45. Volanakis, *The Early Christian Baptisteries of Greece*, p. 106.
46. Volanakis, *The Early Christian Baptisteries of Greece*, p. 109.
47. Volanakis, *The Early Christian Baptisteries of Greece*, pp. 111-112.

above floor level and half beneath, a fact which cautions against drawing conclusions where above-ground walls survive only partially or not at all or the below-ground depth has not been excavated. Byzantine crosses within circles decorate the outside walls of the font.

Not included in Ristow or Volanakis is a circular pool that may be a baptismal font on the island of Delos, off Mykonos. It has a depth of 38 inches, approximately 1 meter.

In the Dodecanese[48] the island of Cos contains several baptisteries dated fifth/sixth century. At Zepari the Church of St. Paul has an interesting font (Ristow #259).[49] The lower part of the interior is in the shape of a square; in the middle it is an octagon; and the upper part is a cross (the whole inner breadth of the arms is about 1.80 meters). The preserved depth is 0.70 meter (Ristow gives 0.56+). At Zepari-Kapama the central part of the piscina is square, but the exterior and interior is an equal-armed cross with a combined breadth of 2.13 meters (Ristow #252).[50] Each arm of the cross has three steps. The depth of the pool is one meter (Ristow gives 80+ centimeters).

At Kephalos on Cos there is a baptistery at the Church of St. Stephen (Ristow #253).[51] The piscina is square at the bottom, becomes an octagon, and finally is cross-shaped at the top. There are two steps at the east arm. Volanakis gives the depth as approximately 82 centimeters, but Ristow as 40+. At Masticari the piscina is a square in a cross (Ristow #258). Each arm of the cross has two steps. There is a width of 1.54 meters and a depth of one meter (Ristow gives 92 centimeters).[52]

In the city of Cos itself there are four baptisteries. In the West Baths (Ristow #255)[53] there is a polygonal font with an inner diameter of 1.20 meters and exterior diameter of 1.76 meters. The depth is 125 centimeters (Ristow gives only 90+ centimeters). There are three steps on the east and west. On opposite sides are two smaller circular basins with a diameter of 48 centimeters each and a depth of 38 centimeters for one and 35 centimeters for the other. At the harbor of Cos there is a baptistery with a piscina in the shape of a cross with four sets of two steps (Ristow #254). The preserved depth of the piscina is 80+ centimeters, but Volanakis estimates the origi-

---

48. A. C. Orlandos, "Les baptistères du Dodécanese," in *Actes du Ve Congrès international d'archéologie chrétienne: Aix-en-Provence, Sept. 1954,* Studi di antichità cristiana 22 (Rome, 1957), pp. 199-211, studies eleven baptisteries (with complete plans) in the Dodecanese dated fifth/sixth century. The fonts take various shapes, but the most common is a cross. They were all constructed of bricks covered with marble and located in the center of a room. The depth below the floor of the room does not exceed 24 centimeters, but the sides are always elevated above the floor 30 centimeters. In this basin the neophyte received triple immersion, but where there is no trace of a conduit he concludes there was a triple effusion on the head (an unnecessary conclusion, since there were other ways of filling and emptying the basin).

49. Volanakis, *The Early Christian Baptisteries of Greece,* pp. 115-116.
50. Volanakis, *The Early Christian Baptisteries of Greece,* pp. 117-118.
51. Volanakis, *The Early Christian Baptisteries of Greece,* pp. 118-119.
52. Volanakis, *The Early Christian Baptisteries of Greece,* pp. 124-126.
53. Volanakis, *The Early Christian Baptisteries of Greece,* pp. 119-121.

nal depth to have been about one meter.[54] In Psalidi, the Church of St. Gabriel has a piscina in the shape of a cross (Ristow #256). It has four sets of two steps. The depth is approximately 80 centimeters (Ristow gives 67+). In the Lampi district, in the garden of the Hotel Atlantis, there is another cross-shaped baptistery (Ristow #257). The total breadth across the cross is 2.05 meters. There are two steps on the west arm, and the depth is 81 centimeters. On the northwest corner of the cross there is a second basin, a rectangle of 41 by 38 centimeters with a depth of 25 centimeters.[55]

The large island of Rhodes also provides several baptisteries, but I limit the listing to those of a date relevant to this study. In the city of Rhodes at the New Stadium there is a *kolumbēthra* beside the basilica of the fifth century (Ristow #288). It was cross-shaped, but unfortunately the remains of the basilica and the baptistery were covered over after their discovery.

An interesting baptistery is found at the north end of the island on the acropolis of Ialysos (medieval Filerimos) on the ruins of a temple of Athena (Ristow #283).[56] Dating has varied from the fourth to the fifth/sixth century. The font is in the shape of a cross: the east-west arms extend a total of 2.72 meters, and the north-south arms 2.52 meters. The east and west arms have three steps. The depth is 67 centimeters below the floor and 20 centimeters above, giving a total depth of 87 centimeters (Ristow gives 80).

Mesanagros, Rhodes, has a monolithic cross-shaped piscina of the fifth/sixth century (Ristow #287). Two arms are rounded. The inner width is 80 centimeters, and the depth is 42 centimeters. Another monolithic cross piscina of the fifth/sixth century was found at Kalathos (Ristow #284). There are two steps east and west, and its depth is 60+ centimeters.

The baptisteries of Greece are numerous enough to permit some generalizations, and these apply for the most part to those found elsewhere.[57] The baptisteries in general had two rooms, a foreroom and the principal room in which the font appeared; sometimes there was a third or even a fourth room for the different pre- and postbaptismal rites. The piscinae were customarily in the center of the room. In the sixth century there began to appear monolithic baptismal basins. The baptismal piscinae appear in different forms: cross, round, square, octagon, and hexagon. The depth, breadth, and general construction of the piscinae make evident that the baptism was a dipping under and emergence from the water. Infant baptism's prevalence from the end of the sixth century and beginning of the seventh century corresponds to the setting up of monolithic baptismal fonts. Most baptisteries in Greece were destroyed in the seventh and eighth centuries. The best preserved are in the Dodecanese. Volonakis often gives a greater depth to the piscinae than does Ristow; preference is to be given to the former as having personally examined them.

54. Volanakis, *The Early Christian Baptisteries of Greece*, p. 122.
55. Volanakis, *The Early Christian Baptisteries of Greece*, pp. 122-123.
56. Volanakis, *The Early Christian Baptisteries of Greece*, pp. 127-128.
57. Volanakis, *The Early Christian Baptisteries of Greece* [Greek], pp. 139-140, gives a summary in German that is the basis of this paragraph.

Balkans

In Macedonia the bishop's church at Stobi provides an impressive baptistery, the floor mosaics of which are preserved (Ristow #514; Figure 16).[58] The mosaics include two pairs of deer, each pair facing from opposite sides a large kantharos full of water, two pairs of peacocks, each facing a vase, and other birds and plants.[59] In its first phase at the end of the fourth century the piscina was round with four half-circle niches and four sets of three steps. The depth was 1.33 meters. In the second phase (Ristow #515) at the end of the fifth century the piscina became an oval within a dodecagonal shape, and a ciborium with six pillars was added. The arrangement of four sets of three steps was kept, but the depth became 1.20 meters. The later baptistery of the North Church at Stobi has a polygonal font with cross arms. The depth permitted water to reach between an adult's waist and breast. At Ohrid there is a piscina of the second half of the fifth century (Ristow #511). It is an oval within a cross and has two steps on both the south and east. The depth is 75 centimeters. At Studenčište a cross-shaped piscina of the fifth/sixth century has a depth of 60 centimeters (Ristow #516).

In Sofia (ancient Serdica), Bulgaria, there is before the east gate beside two churches a baptistery (fourth/fifth century) that contains an oval piscina with a secondary piscina nearby (Ristow #137). The primary piscina has two steps on the east and west. The rotunda of the fourth century at the Roman baths in Sofia became the church of St. George in the fifth century. Other early baptisteries in Bulgaria are late fifth century. At Krivina there is a square piscina with a standing place for the baptizer and a depth of 70 centimeters (Ristow #128). At Sliven there is a round piscina within a cross; it has three steps east and west and a depth of 110 centimeters (Ristow #136). There is a second piscina nearby. The baptistery at Svištov is dated fifth/sixth century. It has a quatrefoil piscina and a depth of approximately 90 centimeters.

There is preserved in the Varna Museum a font for infant baptism (Ristow #121), equipped with the means of heating the water.[60] It comes from the village of Galata, south of Varna, and was found at the entrance to the nave of the church. The font including the stand is 99 centimeters high, but the bowl itself is rather shallow and has a diameter of 69 centimeters. Its use is dated from the beginning of the fifth century to the end of the sixth. A Greek inscription on the rim reads, "The font of . . . and his fellows. . . ." In the north part of the narthex of the church is a square font for adult baptism.

---

58. John F. Cherry, "Baptismal Rites in an Early Christian Basilica at Stobi, Macedonia," *Baptist Quarterly* 25 (1974): 350-353, in need of correction at some points.

59. Heiser, *Die Taufe in der orthodoxen Kirche*, plate XXI.

60. Historical Museum, Varna, inventory #3.298. For this paragraph see the entry on "Bulgaria," in Paul Corby Finney, *Encyclopedia of Early Christian Art and Archaeology* (Grand Rapids: Eerdmans, forthcoming), and Renate Pillinger, "The Significance of Early Christian Monuments for the Study of Liturgy: The Example of Baptism," *Studia liturgica* 25 (1995): 32-50 (48-50) = "Die Bedeutung frühchristlicher Denkmaler für die gegenwärtige Liturgie — veranschaulicht am Beispiel der Taufe," *Heiliger Dienst* 48 (1994): 293-307 (304-306).

The surviving baptisteries of Bosnia-Herzegovina are from the latter part of the period of interest of this study. From the end of the fifth century comes the baptistery at Klobuk (Ristow #107), whose piscina is quatrefoil with three steps on the north and a depth of 70 centimeters. The fifth/sixth-century piscina at Bare is a cross with an octagon in the middle (Ristow #99). It has two steps north and south and a depth of 125 centimeters. The fifth/sixth-century piscina at Cim is an oval (Ristow #101). It has more steps than the one at Bare, three each on north and south, but less than half the depth at 60 centimeters. Church 1 at Mogorjelo, in the first phase of its baptistery (also fifth/sixth century), has a cross-shaped piscina (Ristow #111). Each arm has one step, and the depth is 85 centimeters. Similarly dated is the baptistery at Žitomislići (Ristow #119) with three steps and a depth of 105 centimeters.

The active archaeological history of Croatia has uncovered many baptisteries. Forty-seven assured baptisteries dated between the fourth and seventh centuries have been found in the region of Dalmatia, including Salona.[61] In addition to baptisteries at the bishop's church there was a multiplication of baptisteries in secondary urban churches, funerary churches, and rural churches. Fonts were generally located in the center of the room and came in all the main shapes represented elsewhere. The median depth was about one meter. The mean of interior surfaces was between 50 and 100 centimeters square, so the mean capacity for a font one meter deep was one cubic meter. The dimensions indicate that at least theoretically baptism of adults was by total immersion in the fifth and sixth centuries. Some very late fonts did not permit immersion of adults, for which 50 to 60 centimeters of water is necessary; the late reductions in size and changes in the approach to the fonts may be explained by the introduction of the baptism of infants and the reduction in the number of adult converts. That the baptism of adults became rare does not imply the abandonment of immersion. Aspersion or affusion was reserved, it seems, for the sick or for emergencies and was done outside a baptistery.[62]

Much excavated and studied is the orthodox church complex at Salona, near modern Split in Dalmatia.[63] The baptistery of phase one (Ristow #473) was built in the Roman baths and is dated to the fourth century. It was a hexagon with a depth of 70-80 centimeters. Phase two (Ristow #474) belongs to the sixth century. The hexagonal shape was kept, and there are two steps on the north. The greater depth, 100 centimeters, is perhaps explained by the reuse of the Roman bath. To complete the history of the baptistery, phase three (Ristow #475) in the sixth/seventh century has a

---

61. Pascale Chevalier, *Ecclesiae Dalmatiae: L'Architecture paleochrétienne de la province romaine de Dalmatia (IVe-VIIe S.) [En dehors de la capitale, Salona]*, Collection de l'École Française de Rome 194/2, Salona II (Rome: École française de Rome; Split: Musée Archéologique de Split, 1995). This paragraph is based on Tome II — Illustrations and conclusions, pp. 158-180 (p. 159).

62. Chevalier, *Ecclesiae Dalmatiae*, II, especially pp. 171-176, 179.

63. E. Dyggve, "Le baptistère de la basilica urbana à Salone d'après les fouilles de 1954," in *Actes du Ve Congrès international d'archéologie chrétienne: Aix-en-Provence, Sept. 1954*, Studi di antichità cristiana 22 (Rome, 1957), pp. 189-198, who notes that the basins in all phases permitted immersion (p. 197).

cross-shaped piscina with four steps on the west and a depth of 110 centimeters. The fourth phase (Ristow #476) of the seventh century or later keeps the four steps but has a depth of 95 centimeters.[64] In this case the second and third phases brought a greater depth and the last phase did not bring a significant reduction in the depth of the baptismal pool.

Also notable is Church A (the first cathedral) at Poreč in Istria from the end of the fourth century (Ristow #468). Its piscina was a quadrangle with three steps on the west and two on each of the other three sides. The baptistery of Church B (the second cathedral) goes back to the fifth century but was incorporated into the sixth-century rebuilding of the episcopal complex under Bishop Eufrasius c. 550 and is preserved today (Ristow #469). The hexagonal font has a place for the baptizer on the west and two entrance steps on the west; its depth is given as 70 centimeters.

At Hvar-Stari Grad, St. John's Church has a baptismal font in its first phase from the fifth century in the shape of an octagon (Ristow #462). The depth of the font is reported only for the second phase in the sixth century (Ristow #463): one meter with two entrance steps on the north and on the south. Deep fonts continued to be built in the sixth century. Two at Brac have the same depth. In Lovrecino (sixth century?) the font is a cross/rectangle with two steps on the north and west and one on the south; the depth is 120 centimeters (Ristow #455). In Povlja (sixth century) the font is cross-shaped with two steps on the north and south; the depth is 115 centimeters. The baptistery at Zadar (Zara) was destroyed by bombing in 1944 (Ristow #483). Its font was cross-shaped, and it had a depth of 1.50 meters. Ristow gives the date as sixth century, but Cambi dates it fifth century.[65]

In Slovenia two early fifth-century baptisteries are reported. At Celje (Celeia) the piscina, dated c. 400, is an octagon with two steps north and south and a ciborium, but the dimensions are not given (Ristow #557). The size and shape are similar to the nearly contemporary baptismal font in Ljubljana at the South Basilica, whose octagonal piscina is dated 408-423. It has two steps east and west and a depth of 67 centimeters (Ristow #558).

---

64. The literature distributed on site gives a briefer and slightly different architectural history. The urban or episcopal basilica of the fifth century had next to it a square baptistery with a hexagonal font; in the sixth century Bishop Honorius made the baptistery into a monumental octagon with the font a cross. Ema Višić-Ljubić, *Salona* (Split: Split Archeological Museum, n.d. [my visit to the site was in June, 2004]).

65. N. Cambi, "Nuove scoperte di archeologia cristiana in Dalmazia," in *Atti del XIe Congrès international d'archéologie* (Vatican City, 1989): 2389ff.

54. Baptismal Fonts: West

Italy

Italy is home to a fairly large number of early baptisteries.[1] Some of the most important of these have been discussed already because of their connection with literary sources: Lateran, Rome (chap. 49), Milan (chap. 40; Figure 19), and Aquileia (chap. 41; Figure 20).[2]

There is shown under St. Mark's in Venice a baptistery claimed to be of the third century.

The piscina of the baptistery at Aosta reveals four phases of development (Ristow #s 328-331). These illustrate the common shapes of baptismal fonts: (1) round/polygonal in phase one (end of fourth century); (2) cross within a circle with one step on each side (fifth/sixth century); (3) octagon (sixth century?); and (4) square (? — seventh-ninth century). The progressive reduction in size from an exterior diameter of nearly 3 meters and interior diameter of over 2.40 meters to an interior dimension of 1.80 meters may reflect increased use of affusion or the decline of adult baptism. A secondary font, square in shape, in an annex may reflect the great number of baptisms at the paschal season in the fifth and sixth centuries that required the bishop to have two baptisteries at his disposal or the use of separate fonts for men and women.[3]

---

1. Eugenio Russo et al., *L'edificio battesimale in Italia: Aspetti e problemi: Atti dell'VIII Congresso Nazionale di Archeologia Cristiana . . . 21-26 settembre 1998* (Bordighera: Istituto Internazionale di Studi Liguri, 2001), 2 vols., has mainly other interests but contains some information on baptismal basins. Vincenzo Fiocchi Nicolai and Sauro Gelichi, "Battisteri e chese rurali (IV-VII secolo)," in that work catalog fifty-five rural baptisteries in Italy (303-384).

2. S. Anita Stauffer, *On Baptismal Fonts: Ancient and Modern* (Bramcote/Nottingham: Grove Books, 1994), gives a popular survey of nearly fifty western fonts; significant criticism and corrections are found in the review by Noël Duval, "Architecture et liturgie," *Revue des études Augustiniennes* 42 (1996): 121-127.

3. Charles Bonnet and Renato Perinetti, *Aoste aux premiers temps chrétiens* (Aosta: Musumeci, 1986), pp. 24-30, with pictures and plans.

At Noli in Liguria beneath the Romanesque church of San Paragorio there is a fifth-century font, octagonal on the exterior and a circle on the interior with a diameter of 1.26 meters and a depth of about 1.60 meters. It shows successive reductions in size. There was a system for channeling water in and out of the basin.[4]

Ambrose's baptismal font at Milan (chap. 40; Figure 20) was doubtless the inspiration for many octagonal baptisteries and fonts in northern Italy, for instance, at the cathedral of Novara in Lombardy. The edifice of the baptistery is an octagon with a maximum diagonal of 10.50 meters to be dated probably not after the mid–fifth century. In the center is the ancient piscina with one step and a depth of about 60 centimeters (Ristow #391 gives 55+ meters). In the early Middle Ages a circular funerary monument was placed inside the basin as a new, smaller baptismal font.[5]

Also in Lombardy at Isola Comacina there is an octagonal piscina of the fifth/sixth century with a depth of 50+ centimeters (Ristow #370). But other shapes were employed in northern Italy. At Sabiona in the region of Trent there is a round piscina within a polygon from the beginning of the fifth century; it has a depth of 50 centimeters (Ristow #418).

The baptistery at Albenga (Ristow #326) is notable for its mosaics, c. 500 or earlier.[6] The vault of the eastern apse shows three superimposed chi-rho monograms each flanked by alpha and omega, encircled by doves, and with star-filled surroundings. On the interior arch two large sheep and smaller sheep face a cross. On the outer arch there is a mosaic inscription now much damaged. Without depicting a human figure the mosaics have an emphasis on Christ (chi-rho and alpha-omega), the Holy Spirit (doves), salvation by the cross, and the promise of heaven (stars) and paradise for the Lord's sheep. The piscina is a large octagon with a ciborium of eight columns. The diameter at the base is 1.58 meters, and the upper diameter including the step is 2.26 meters. There is one step 0.584 meters above the base and a total depth of approximately 0.90 meters. A later piscina in the northeast niche of the building (to the left of the apse mosaic) was perhaps for footwashing or for infant baptism.

The cathedral baptisteries at Grado show similarities to those at neighboring

---

4. Alessandra Frondoni, "Battisteri ed *ecclesiae baptismales* della Liguria," in *L'edificio battesimale in Italia: Aspetti e problemi: Atti dell'VIII Congresso Nazionale di Archeologia Cristiana . . . 21-26 settembre 1998* (Bordighera: Istituto Internazionale di Studi Liguri, 2001), 749-791 (752-763).

5. Umberto Chierci, *Il battistero del duomo di Novara* (Novara: Banca Popolare di Novara, 1967), pp. 23, 30, 37. From the plan of the fifth-century structure on p. 74 I estimate the width of the ancient basin at a little over two meters. Pictures of the piscina are on pp. 115-116. Umberto Chierci, "Il battistero di Novara alla luce delle recenti indagini," in *Atti del VI Congresso Internazionale di Archeologia Cristiana: Ravenna 23-30 Settembre 1962* (Rome: Pontificio Istituto di Archeologia Cristiana, 1965), pp. 673-682, does not discuss the piscina. Luisella Pejrani Baricco, "Chiese battesimali in Piemonte: Scavi e scoperte," in *L'edificio battesimale in Italia: Aspetti e problemi: Atti dell'VIII Congresso Nazionale di Archeologia Cristiana . . . 21-26 settembre 1998* (Bordighera: Istituto Internazionale di Studi Liguri, 2001), 542-52, gives the early Christian phase of the cathedral at Novara as fifth/sixth century and notes that the sides of the octagon were 1.25 to 1.30 meters long.

6. M. Marcenaro, *Il battistero paleocristiano di Albenga: Le origini del cristianesimo nella Liguria Marittima* (Genoa: Le Mani, 1994), pp. 129-191 on the mosaics, 282-285 on the piscina.

Aquileia (chap. 41), but discarding of early materials and reconstructions make correct evaluation difficult (Ristow #s 361-363). The building is an octagon, and the piscina of the first phase, dated to the fifth century, was round in a hexagon and had one step on the west and south; phase two, sixth century, was a hexagon with two (?) steps; phase three, medieval, is round. There is another baptistery in Grado at Sta. Agatha/St. John the Evangelist — the first phase of its piscina from the fifth century was square (Ristow #364). At Trieste there is a hexagonal font with one step, dated c. 400 (Ristow #428).

A late baptistery may be noted for its indication of changes prompted by the general practice of infant baptism. The baptistery at Piacenza is dated by Ristow as early Middle Ages (Ristow #865).[7] The font is circular on the inside. It is not possible to be precise on its depth, but perhaps it is 56 centimeters. The diameter is 98 centimeters. This font was for children. A later reduction in size perhaps served as a basin for aspersion.

The baptisteries in Ravenna were considered in chapter 49. They are best known for their spectacular mosaics featuring the baptism of Christ (chap. 7; Figures 11 and 12).

In Rome, besides the important episcopal baptistery at the Lateran (chap. 49; Figure 19), many other baptisteries have been excavated in recent years. During the fifth century it seems that each *titulus,* or parish church, received its own baptistery.[8] I will mention a few as representative.

An impressive baptismal font at San Marcello is dated in its first phase to the late fourth or beginning of the fifth century at the time of a Christian adaptation of a house to a church building (Ristow #411). The font is a hexagon reveted with marble slabs on the interior but with its niches a dodecagon on the exterior. The interior is 2.5 meters across. Three steps lead down into the pool.[9]

The baptistery at the church of Santa Croce may date to the fifth or sixth century.[10] In addition to serving local pastoral needs, it may have been constructed for pilgrims who sought baptism at a holy site, as was the case at other pilgrimage centers. The baptistery is an apsidal room with a font in the center of the room. The font is circular with a diameter of four meters.

Sta. Cecilia in Trastevere, in phase one (fourth/fifth century) had a round piscina in a hexagon and was covered with a ciborium (Ristow #407). Dating from the fifth

---

7. Paolo Piva, "Il battistero paleocristiano di Piacenza," *Antiquité Tardiv* 5 (1997): 265-274, on whom the following description is based (especially p. 272).

8. Hugo Brandenburg, *Ancient Churches of Rome from the Fourth to the Seventh Century: The Dawn of Christian Architecture in the West* (Turnhout: Brepols, 2004), pp. 165, 251-252. Ristow lists the following for the fifth century (or possibly) in addition to those discussed below: Lateran — #s 403-404; S. Agatha (498-514) — #405; S. Anastasia (c. 402) — #406; S. Lorenzo fuori le mura — #410; S. Maria Maggiore — #413; S. Sabina (422-32) — #414; S. Vitalis — #416.

9. Picture in Brandenburg, *Ancient Churches of Rome,* p. 298; description on p. 165.

10. Brandenburg, *Ancient Churches of Rome,* p. 108; ground plan of the church, including the baptistery, on p. 283.

century is San Lorenzo Outside the Walls (Ristow #410). Its piscina is round with the entrance on the southwest, and there is a nearby secondary piscina. A piscina from the second half of the fifth century at San Crisogono was destroyed in the twelfth century (Ristow #409). It was round with entrances from the southeast and southwest. San Stefano in Via Latina has a piscina from the fifth century or later. It is round in a square and has a ciborium and one step on the northwest and southwest. Its depth is 90 centimeters.

Excavations in 1993-1995 at San Clemente uncovered a baptistery for which the excavators in their preliminary report were uncertain of the date (fifth or sixth century).[11] It contained a large pool that perhaps was a fountain or basin going back to the third century.[12] This pool was polygonal on the outside, six flat sides alternating with six concave sides, and circular on the inside. The pool's internal diameter, which must be extrapolated since the whole is not visible, would have been 2.15 meters. The depth is 1.16 meters, 34 centimeters below the level of the pavement and 82 centimeters above.[13] The excavators point to other titulary churches with comparable baptisteries — San Crisogono, San Marcello, Santa Cecilia, and San Lorenzo in Lucina, and perhaps San Marco.[14]

At Naples the cathedral baptistery, San Giovanni in Fonte, was built c. 400 (Ristow #385). The piscina is round with one step and has a depth of 45 centimeters according to Ristow and 61 centimeters according to Massimo d'Antonio and a diameter of 2 meters.[15] This baptistery is famous for its mosaics, executed at the end of the fourth or the first decade of the fifth century, although some date them later. At the center of the dome is a staurogam (cross with vertical beam curved to form a rho) surrounded by stars. The dome mosaics depict many scenes associated with baptism in the early church or found in the decorations of other baptisteries:[16] the Samaritan woman at the well and Jesus turning water into wine at Cana; Christ beside the Sea of Galilee full of fish; Christ giving the law to Peter; the Good Shepherd with sheep (twice); a shepherd between two deer drinking (twice);[17] a

---

11. Federico Guidobaldi, "Gli scavi del 1993-1995 nella basilica di S. Clemente a Roma e la scoperta del battistero paleocristiano: Nota preliminare," *Rivista di archeologia cristiana* 73 (1997): 459-491 plus plates.

12. Guidobaldi, "Gli scavi del 1993-1995 nella basilica di S. Clemente," p. 489.

13. Guidobaldi, "Gli scavi del 1993-1995 nella basilica di S. Clemente," pp. 477, 479.

14. Guidobaldi, "Gli scavi del 1993-1995 nella basilica di S. Clemente," pp. 487-488.

15. Massimo d'Antonio, "L'edificio battesimale in Campania dalle origine all'altomedioevo," in *L'edificio battesimale in Italia: Aspetti e problemi: Atti dell'VIII Congresso Nazionale di Archeologia Cristiana . . . 21-26 settembre 1998* (Bordighera: Istituto Internazionale di Studi Liguri, 2001), 1003-1036 (1032 — a useful chart of baptisteries and their basins in Campania).

16. J.-L. Maier, *Le baptistère de Naples et ses mosaïques: Étude historique et iconographique* (Fribourg: Editions Universitaires, 1964).

17. Johannes Quasten, "Das Bild des Guten Hirten in den altchristlichen Baptisterien und in den Taufliturgien des Ostens und Westens: Das Siegel der Gottesherde," in Theodor Klauser and Adolf Rücker, eds., *Pisciculi: Studien zur Religion und Kultur des Altertums: Franz Joseph Dölger* (Münster: Aschendorff, 1939), p. 221.

woman at the tomb; apostles with crowns; and figures from the Apocalypse (representing the evangelists?).

The San Gennaro Catacomb at Naples has a round piscina with one step and a depth of 91 centimeters (Ristow #384). It is dated 762-766 and so illustrates that later piscinae were not always smaller.

Paulinus of Nola, *Poem* 28, lines 180-195, speaks of the baptistery at Cimitile, but it does not survive.

In the Zeus (Jupiter) temple at Cumae in Campania there is a round piscina with a ciborium of the fifth/sixth century (Ristow #345; Figure 23). The piscina is formed by three progressively wider concentric circles, giving the appearance of steps all the way around. The external diameter is 3 meters; the internal is 2.40 meters. Ristow gives the depth as only 38 centimeters, but this must be for only the bottom circle, for the height of the top circle is waist high on an adult, and if the person is sitting on the middle step the height reaches to the breast. Massimo d'Antonio records the depth as 45 centimeters below the pavement and 70 centimeters above, giving a complete depth of 1.15 meters.[18]

At Egnazia in Puglia (Apulia) the North Church, phase two, has a rectangular piscina (Ristow #351). Four steps are located on the south, east, and west sides, and there was a ciborium. The depth is approximately 1.20 meters. The same depth holds for phases three and four (Ristow #s 352-353); in the last phase a secondary piscina was introduced nearby.

The church of San Giusto in the same region has a splendid baptistery of the mid–fifth century attached to Church A, excavated in 1995-1997.[19] The building is a large circle with a diameter of about 16 meters. Within it there is a wide base (1.4 to 1.6 meters), a circle on the outside and an octagon on the inside, with a total diameter of nine meters, for columns supporting a circular cupola that would have risen higher than the outer walls of the baptistery. The area around the columns was an ambulatory. At the center of the room under the cupola was the basin, an irregular circle on its outside (an octagon in the reconstruction) and a quadrilobe on the inside. The three lobes on the east, south, and west have two steps. Particularly well preserved are two channels, one for bringing in water and the other for evacuating it. The steps result in a square bottom to the pool on three sides and the curve of one lobe on the north side. From the plans and pictures I estimate the font to be about two meters across at its maximum width and one meter or more in depth.

On the island of Sardinia at Cornus phase one of the baptistery (fifth/sixth century) contained a rectangular piscina (Ristow #421). It has three steps on the north

---

18. M. d'Antonio, "L'edificio battesimale in Campania," 1005-1011.

19. Annalisa Biffino, "Il battistero," in G. Volpe, ed., *San Giusto: La villa, le ecclesiae* (Bari: Edipuglia, 1998), pp. 101-114; color reconstruction in figures 323-326, pp. 278-279; Giuliano Volpe, Annalisa Biffino, and Roberta Giuliani, "Il battistero del complesso paleocristiano di San Giusto (Lucera)," in *L'edificio battesimale in Italia: Aspetti e problemi: Atti dell'VIII Congresso Nazionale di Archeologia Cristiana . . . 21-26 settembre 1998* (Bordighera: Istituto Internazionale di Studi Liguri, 2001), 1089-1130.

and the south and a ciborium with six columns. The depth is 80 centimeters. In phase two, sixth century (Ristow #422), the shape was changed to a cross in an octagon, the three steps were on the east and west, and the pool was deepened slightly to 90 centimeters.

Large octagonal baptismal pools continued to be built in Italy. These include in Tuscany the existing fonts in Pisa (sixth century — Ristow #395) and Pistoia (1226). The no-longer-extant Romanesque font in Florence is frequently described as octagonal, but it was a square immersion font with an octagonal screen around it.[20] In Verona the octagonal font of 1135 (Ristow #432) has a depth of 135 centimeters.

Tunisia

Extensive archaeological work in Tunisia has brought awareness of many baptisteries from late antiquity. None of those in the environs of Carthage can be brought into the time of the early history of the church in Carthage. The earliest surviving font in Carthage is in the church complex at Damous el-Karita, Carthage, dated to the end of the fourth century (Ristow #722). It is round within a hexagon with three entrance steps on the southeast and on the southwest and a ciborium of six columns. The diameter is 250 centimeters, and the depth is 110 centimeters. The so-called Church of St. Cyprian is dated to the second half of the fifth century (Ristow #719). The font is round on the interior, has a ciborium (four columns), and is 75 centimeters deep. At Dermech immediately outside the walls of Carthage there is a large baptistery dated after 533 (Ristow #720). It is an octagon in a cross with four sets of five steps, has a ciborium with eight columns, and has a depth of 110 centimeters. Also in Dermech is the baptistery at Basilica 1 from the second half of the sixth century (Ristow #723). Its piscina is round in a hexagon, and it has two entrances from the southeast and northwest, a ciborium of four columns, and a depth of 115 centimeters.

Relatively early is the baptistery at Kélibia — in its first phase from the end of the fourth century (Ristow #727). The piscina is oval in a rectangle with two steps on the east and has a depth of 90 centimeters. Phase two from the second half of the sixth century (Ristow #728) changed the shape to round within a quadrilobe and increased the depth to 104 centimeters.[21]

Sbeitla has baptisteries attractively decorated with mosaics. The baptistery of Church I (Jucundus) from the fourth/fifth century (Ristow #740) has a mosaic in the east apse depicting a kantharos. The piscina is in an irregular cross shape, has a ci-

---

20. The proposal of Franklin Toker, "A Baptistery below the Baptistery of Florence," *Art Bulletin* 58 (1976): 157-167, is that the stone octagon previously identified as an unusually large font and whose date has been debated between early Christian and Romanesque was actually the foundation of the early Christian baptistery building, not a font. The outline of the Romanesque octagonal screen that preserved the shape of the earlier baptistery is clearly marked on the floor of the present baptistery.

21. The spectacular mosaics may be seen in the color plate in Stauffer, *On Baptismal Fonts*, plate 1.

borium, and is entered by three steps on the north and on the south. The rectangular bottom of the pool is approximately 1.45 meters by 0.95 meter. The depth is approximately 1 meter. The baptistery of Church II (Vitalis) was built in the church's second phase in the fifth/sixth century (Ristow #741). Surviving mosaics show a cross and a crowned chi-rho monogram with pendant alpha and omega on the floor of the font. It is similar to Church I's piscina in being an irregular cross in an oval, having two sets of three steps, and having a ciborium of four columns. Its depth is slightly greater at 113 centimeters.[22] At the rim its dimensions are 2.95 meters by 1.10 meters, and the rectangular bottom is 1.25 meters long. Church III's (Servus) piscina is also fifth/sixth century (Ristow #742). It is a hexagon (almost round), has two steps east and south, and is 130 centimeters deep.

Baptismal fonts in Tunisia dated fourth/fifth century include the following: (1) Henchir el-Farouar, Basilica 1, phase one (Ristow #708), a quatrefoil with a depth of 50+ centimeters; (2) Henchir el Farouar, Basilica 2, phase one (Ristow #710), a cross with a depth of 75+ centimeters; (3) Henchir ez-Zouitina, fourth/sixth century (Ristow #712), a rectangle in a hexagon, with two steps and a ciborium, and a depth of 133 centimeters.

The baptisteries of the fifth/sixth century have rather uniformly deep fonts. The piscina of the baptistery at Djerba is now in the Bardo Museum, Tunis (Ristow #702). It is a square in a cross, and it has four sets of two steps, a ciborium, and a depth of approximately 120 centimeters. The piscina at Hanchir Kasabat (Ristow #715) has an oval interior, four sets of three steps, and a depth of 115 centimeters. The piscina at Makhtar, Basilica 3, in its second phase (Ristow #734), is a square with an entrance step on all but the east side, a ciborium, and a depth of 125 centimeters. At Sidi Abiche (Ristow #746) there is a square font in a quatrefoil, a ciborium, three steps, and a depth of approximately one meter. At Sidi Jedidi (Ristow #747) the piscina is round in a six-foil exterior, has three steps and a ciborium of six columns, and is 140 centimeters deep.

Algeria

In Algeria pride of place as to date and importance belongs to the baptistery at Hippo Regius discussed in chapter 51 in connection with Augustine (Ristow #70). A comparably early baptistery, dating to the end of the fourth century (or early fifth), belongs to the West Church at Timgad (outside the walls) in ancient Numidia, possibly Donatist (Ristow #94). The piscina is three concentric hexagons of decreasing diameter as one descends into it. The depth is one meter. Dated fourth/fifth century is the baptistery at Bou Ismail (Castiglione) (Ristow #73). Its piscina is round/quatrefoil, has four single steps, and is 70 centimeters deep. Also fourth/fifth century

---

22. Color plate in Stauffer, *On Baptismal Fonts*, plate 2; she gives the depth as 116 centimeters — p. 41.

is the cathedral baptistery at Tipaza (Tipasa) (Ristow #95). The square building has a round piscina, which was entered by two steps and had a depth of one meter.

From the first half of the fifth century is the baptistery at Djemila (Cuicul in ancient Numidia) (Ristow #75). It contains a quatrefoil piscina, four sets of three steps, and a ciborium of four columns. The baptistery at Tebessa (Theveste) in its first phase is dated fifth century (Ristow #88). The piscina has a ciborium and is round with twelve niches, two steps, and a depth of 70 centimeters. Phase two, fifth/sixth century (Ristow #89), is slightly less deep at 65 centimeters. The font at Tigzirt belongs to the fifth/sixth century (Ristow #90). It is round and has one step, a ciborium, and a depth of 80 centimeters. The fifth/sixth-century font at Ksar Belezma (Ristow #79) is a quatrefoil. It is exceptional for the early Christian fonts in North Africa by having a reported depth of only 42 centimeters.

France

Southern France has a large number of early Christian baptisteries, most of which have been well studied.

The baptistery of St. Stephen beside St. John in Lyon was constructed near the end of the fourth century (Ristow #192; Figure 22).[23] It contains a large eight-sided piscina that has in part been restored. The pool was entered by three steps and had an exterior diameter of 3.66 meters and a depth of 86 centimeters. In phase two of the fifth century or later (Ristow #193) the depth was reduced nearly in half to 47 centimeters.

The baptistery at Grenoble, phase one, is dated c. 400 (Ristow #174). No depth is given for its oval piscina, but in phase two of the early Middle Ages (Ristow #175) the piscina became an octagon with a depth of 50 centimeters.

At Fréjus there is an octagonal baptistery of the fifth/sixth century, whose interior has four apses alternating with four flat niches (Ristow #173).[24] The piscina is round within an octagon and has a standing place for the baptizer on the west. It has two steps and is surrounded by eight columns for a ciborium. The depth is sunk 82 centimeters below the floor. At the surface the diameter is 1.35 meters; the circular bottom level is 90 centimeters across.

The well-preserved baptistery in Aix-en-Provence went through three phases of development (Ristow #s 154-156). The development began in the first half of the fifth century with an octagonal piscina having two steps, a depth of 83 centimeters, and a diameter of 160 centimeters. In phase two of the fifth to eighth centuries the depth was reduced slightly to 75 centimeters. The imposing ciborium of eight columns is a medieval addition.

The baptistery at Cimiez (Ristow #199; Figure 24) was built over Roman baths in

---

23. See also Jean-François Reynaud, *Lyon aux premiers tempts chrétiens: Basiliques et nécropoles* (Lyon: Ministère de la Culture et de la Communication, 1986), pp. 99-106, for plans and pictures.

24. P.-A. Février and M. Fixot, "Fréjus: Cathédrale, baptistère," in *Atlas archéologiques de la France: Les premiers monuments chrétiens de la France* (Paris, 1995), Vol. 1, pp. 155-164.

439, and the channel for bringing warm water from the hypocaust is still clearly visible. There was an altar on its east side. The font is a hexagon 160 centimeters across at the top level and sunk in the ground to a depth of 86 centimeters. It is a rectangle at the bottom (54 by 50 centimeters; its depth is 50 centimeters). The pool is set within a cross and is entered by five (Ristow says three, but this applies only to the lower rectangle and not the whole pool) steps on the inside (north), and there are two seats on the level of the second step down. The contention that water filled only the lower rectangle and the administrator stood on the second level down so that the baptism was by effusion and not immersion is arbitrary.[25] The pool would have been covered by an octagonal canopy. Smaller columns surround the piscina inside a circle of larger columns.

The baptistery at Marseilles was built not before the fifth century (Ristow #194).[26] It has an octagonal piscina with a depth of 70 centimeters.

The baptistery and piscina at Poitiers are well preserved (Ristow #s 201-202; Figure 21).[27] Whether it was a baptismal font in origin is disputed. Phase one of the fourth/fifth century has a piscina formed of five concentric octagons (serving as steps) of decreasing diameter from top to bottom. The large piscina has a total depth of 142 centimeters. Phase two of the sixth/seventh century had only three steps but kept the same depth.

At Civaux (Fanum) in the region of Vienne there is a baptistery of the middle third of the fifth century (Ristow #166). Its hexagonal piscina has a depth of 119 centimeters.

France preserves several relatively early piscinae that are rather shallow. Le Teil-Mélas (fifth century or later) is the site of a square piscina with a depth of 40 centimeters (Ristow #189). An uncertainly dated baptistery at Loupian (fourth [?]-sixth century) has a hexagonal piscina with one step, a ciborium, and a depth of 50+ centimeters (Ristow #191). Similarly uncertain in date is the baptistery at Meysse, phase one (fourth to sixth century); its piscina is an octagon with one step on the west and a depth of 35+ centimeters (Ristow #195). The shallowness of these fonts likely argues for the later date. Somewhat nearer the normal depth is the hexagonal font at Portbail, fifth century (?), with one step and a depth of 60 centimeters. The well-preserved baptistery at Riez (Ristow #211) has been restored several times since the twelfth century, so

---

25. Fernand Benoît, "Le baptistère de Cimiez," in *Atti del VI Congresso Internazionale di Archeologia Cristiana: Ravenna, 23-30 Settembre 1962* (Rome: Pontificio Istituto di Archeologia Cristiana, 1965), pp. 147-158 (p. 156 and drawing on p. 151). The use of only the lower rectangle might apply to infant baptism, but the whole design of the rest of the font suggests other possibilities — the candidate either standing on the bottom of the font or seated on a step and then bent forward in the immersion (the smaller dimensions of the lower part of the font where the candidate's lower extremities were would have conserved water, and the larger dimensions of the upper part allowed for an immersion).

26. I have not seen F. Roustan, *La major et le premier baptistère de Marseille* (Marseilles: Aubertin & Rolle, 1905).

27. I have not seen these studies: C. de la Croix, "Étude sommaire du baptistère Sanit-Jean de Poitiers," *Memoires de la societé des antiquaires de l'ouest*, 2e Ser., 27 (1903): 285-414; F. Eygun, "Le baptistère Saint-Jean de Poitiers," *Gallia* 1 (1964): 137-171.

its early history is difficult to evaluate. A colonnade of eight columns surrounds the central font. The diameter is 110 centimeters, but the depth of 62 centimeters possibly (but not necessarily) implies affusion or infant baptism (but at what date?).

From the island of Corsica three sites come under purview. At Pianottoli-Caldarello, the square piscina of phase one is dated c. 370 or later (Ristow #183). Its depth is given as approximately 40 centimeters. At Mariana there is a cross-shaped piscina dated c. 500 (Ristow #179). It has a step and a depth of 50 centimeters. Quite in contrast is the fifth/sixth-century piscina at Golo (Ristow #177). Its cross-shaped piscina has a depth of approximately 100 centimeters. The later phase two (from the sixth/seventh century to the Middle Ages) made a drastic reduction in depth to 24 centimeters (Ristow #178).

From northern France note may be taken of the baptistery for the cathedral at Rheims in its three phases (Ristow #s 208-210). The development began at the end of the fourth century with a rectangular font having four sets of four steps, for which a depth is not given but the brim was three meters long. It is stated that in the second phase (fifth/sixth century) the dimensions of the piscina were reduced in length and breadth to 85 by 90 centimeters. In the third phase (Middle Ages?) the font became a round polygon of 30 centimeters diameter.

Switzerland[28]

Six phases are distinguished in the history of the baptistery under the Cathedral of St. Peter in Geneva (Ristow #s 540-545). The old baptistery, phase one, is dated 370-380. Its piscina was square with edge dimensions of 120 centimeters. Phase two was c. 400 and kept the square shape. Phase three, the middle baptistery, was also c. 400. Its piscina was a square in an octagon, and it had steps, an eight-column ciborium, and dimensions greater than the piscina at Milan. In phase four (sixth century) the diameter of the octagon of the piscina was reduced from 280 centimeters to 180. In phase five (sixth/seventh century) the round piscina had one step, the ciborium had five supports, and the depth was 48 centimeters. Phase six is the new baptistery (sixth/seventh century) in octagonal form.[29] A baldachin of eight columns surrounded the font about A.D. 400; this became a covered ciborium in the sixth century. A second basin was installed. The stucco on the interior wall of the circular font would not hold water for long, so baptism by immersion was no longer current at this time.

At Martigny the baptistery is dated fourth/fifth century (Ristow #546). The piscina is horseshoe shaped and has two steps on the west. The depth is 40+ centimeters.

---

28. O. Perler, "Frühchristliche baptisterien in der Schweiz," *Zeitschrift für Schweizerische Kirchengeschichte* 51 (1957): 81ff.

29. Charles Bonnet, *Genève aux premiers temps chrétiens* (Geneva: Fondation des Clefs de Saint-Pierre, 1986), pp. 24-28, 34-37, provides plans and pictures; he gives five phases: mid–fourth century, second half of fourth century, about 400, fifth century, and sixth/seventh century. The remainder of the paragraph is drawn from this work.

The impressive baptistery at Riva San Vitale, one of the best-preserved fifth-century baptisteries, had three phases of development (Ristow #s 547-549).[30] The building was four-sided but became an octagon on the interior with four half-round niches. The font from the first phase at the end of the fifth century was an octagon entered by two steps on the west with the platform for the baptizer on the east. Its diameter was 2.1 meters, and its depth was 66 to 70 centimeters. The inference of affusion from the depth to the first tread of 40 centimeters appears to be the result of an arbitrary limitation on the depth of the water. In the second phase, perhaps not many years later, the depth became 57 centimeters. The third phase in the seventh-ninth century with the disappearance of adult baptism saw the pool become round and the depth reduced slightly further to 55 centimeters.

The baptistery at Zurzach (Ristow #s 554-556) was built in the fifth century.[31] A fireplace in the room was perhaps for warming the water. The font was 110 centimeters square, but reduced in size twice. The depth was 60 centimeters. On the west three steps on the outside and two on the inside gave access; on the east there were two exterior steps, but none on the interior. Phase two, fifth/sixth (?) century, produced a slight reduction in depth to 56 centimeters.

Perler gives a date of fifth century for the second baptistery at Saint-Maurice (Agaunum) and second half of the sixth century for the third (last).[32] The piscina is the best-preserved part, and it was changed in size three times. Originally it was an oval with a square projection on the south and north for steps. The overall dimensions were 1.4 meters by 1.56 meters, with a depth of 65 centimeters. Perler notes that the second smaller piscina still presupposed immersion of infants, which was the rule up to the late Middle Ages. The liturgy at Saint-Maurice included footwashing.

Austria, Lichtenstein, Germany, and England

Two fifth-century fonts in Austria have shallow depths. At Duel (Ristow #518), the piscina from the second half of the century is a quatrefoil with a depth of 42 centimeters. At Lavant (Ristow #521) the piscina is perhaps fifth century. It is a rectangle with one step each on east and west, a ciborium, and a depth of 35 centimeters.

There is a fifth-century font at Schaan in Lichtenstein (Ristow #504). It is round with a size more nearly approaching the average, being 80 centimeters deep.

The baptisteries noted for Germany are assigned later dates than have sometimes been suggested. The cathedral at Cologne originated in the fourth century,

---

30. Perler, "Frühchristliche baptisterien in der Schweiz," pp. 89-94; R. Cardani, *Il battistero di Riva San Vitale: L'architettura, i restauri e la decorazione pittorica* (Locarno, 1995).

31. Perler, "Frühchristlichen Baptisterien in der Schweiz," pp. 81-89; he suggests that since the baptizand stood in water 60 centimeters at its highest, we can speak of a combination of immersion baptism (to that height) and infusion or aspersion baptism (p. 86). He cites in a postscript a study that dates the Zurzach church to the fifth century and the baptismal complex to c. 500 or early sixth century.

32. Perler, "Frühchristlichen baptisterien in der Schweiz," pp. 94-110.

and a pool could have been in Christian use in the fourth-fifth century in connection with the water course on the site, but there is no proof.[33] The baptistery building was constructed on a cruciform plan at the beginning of the fifth century, but the pool is on the same level and line with the sixth-century ambo of the church and so is assigned by Ristow (#s 142-144) to phases 3, 4, and 5 of the church (sixth to seventh centuries). The font was an octagon with a ciborium and was entered by two steps on two of the sides. Its depth was originally 80 centimeters according to information given on site, but Ristow says 60+ centimeters.

The model of the baptismal font from the Castle Church of St. Goar at Boppard in the Römisch-Germanische Zentralmuseum in Mainz dates it fourth century and identifies it as from the oldest baptistery in Germany. Ristow (#140), however, assigns it also to the sixth century. The piscina is round within a heptangular exterior. It has one step, a ciborium, and a depth of 60+ centimeters.

At Augsburg there is well shaft to a Roman house that tradition says was used as a baptistery in the time of St. Afra (d. A.D. 304), but the tradition cannot be verified.

One certain baptistery in England belongs to the period of this study. It is located in the Roman fort at Richborough in Kent and is dated fifth/sixth century (Ristow #151). The hexagonal piscina had a depth of 75 centimeters and measures two and a half meters by two meters.

The discovery of a possible baptistery at Bradford-on Avon, England, has been announced recently.[34] Set within the walls of the principal room of building 1 is a circular curb of stone blocks, five meters in diameter. The curb supported a low wall, probably little more than one meter high. In the southeast arc there is a drain. The construction belongs to a post-Roman date of fifth/sixth century but at a time when the Roman house was still standing. The excavator supposes that a font of stone, lead, or wood was set into the floor and of a size to allow initiates to stand knee-deep while the priest poured water on their heads. Since no trace of the font survives, this is speculation.

I leave out of considertation the lead tanks with Christian emblems that have been found in England, because their baptismal use is disputed.

Spain

Spain offers many examples of sixth-century baptisteries, but attention here is largely limited to those with a possibility of being earlier.[35]

---

33. Sebastian Ristow, "Das baptisterium im osten des Kölner Domes," *Kölner Domblatt: Jahrbuch des Zentral-Dombau-Vereins* 58 (1993): 291-312, with pictures and plans, identifies the octagonal pools in the first two phases as secular and dates the piscina of the third phase most probably to the sixth century.

34. Mark Corney, "The Roman Villa at Bradford-on Avon: Investigations at St. Laurence School," *ARA: The Bulletin of the Association for Roman Archaeology* 16.1 (2004): 10-13, 15.

35. Thilo Ulbert, *Frühchristliche Basiliken mit Doppelapsiden auf der iberischen Halbinsel: Studien zur Architektur und Liturgiegeschichte* (Berlin: Gebr. Mann, 1978), pp. 139-181, locates eighteen baptisteries on the peninsula and five on the Balearic Islands (map, p. 139). His special concern is the basili-

In Seville at the Alcazar there is a baptistery dated fourth/fifth century (Ristow #592). The piscina is square, with entrance on the west; its depth is 88 centimeters. At Tarragona the baptistery comes from the beginning of the fifth century (Ristow #595). The piscina is a rectangle with two steps each on the north and south; its depth is 69 centimeters. The baptistery at Gerena in the region of Seville in its first phase is possibly mid–fifth century (Ristow #575). The piscina is in the shape of a cross and has two steps on the south and one on the west, and its depth is 30+ centimeters. At Las Vegas de Pedraza in the region of Segovia there is a baptistery whose phase one is possibly fifth century (Ristow #578a). The font is a rectangle; it has three steps each on the east and west, and a depth of approximately 120 centimeters. The font kept the same depth in phase two of the sixth/seventh century (Ristow #578b).

Several baptisteries are assigned a date of fifth/sixth century. El Bovalar has a rectangular font entered by three steps on the north (Ristow #571).[36] It was covered by a ciborium, and its depth was 80 centimeters. San Pedro de Alcántara has a font that is a rectangle within a quatrefoil (Ristow #589).[37] There are three steps on the south and on the north. Its depth is 110 centimeters. There is also a smaller rectangular piscina with a depth of 60 centimeters and one step. Both were contemporary, and the smaller is reasonably interpreted as for infant baptism. The baptistery at San Pedro de Mérida is one of a group in southwest Spain with a long, narrow rectangular font (in this case one side is rounded — Ristow #590).[38] The dimensions are 165 by 35 centimeters and the depth is 100 centimeters (Ristow gives 93). There are four steps on the east and on the west. At Terrassa (or Tarasa) in the region of Barcelona the Church of Sta. Maria has a font that in phase one was a square entered by two steps with a ciborium and had a depth of 70 centimeters (Ristow #596).

Baptismal fonts in Spain represent extremes in depth. The font at the basilica of Villa of Fortunatus at Fraga is reported to be a mere 10 centimeters, too shallow for immersion even of an infant.[39] On the other extreme is the font at Casa Herrera near Mérida with a depth below floor level of 150 centimeters.[40] The length of this large rectangular basin is 3.4 meters, and its width is 0.52 meter. On each small side there are seven steps to the floor of the piscina. On the north and south of this large basin at a later time two smaller basins were built. The one on the north is an oval, one meter by 40 centimeters across, with a depth of 65 centimeters and three steps into it; the south basin is 70 by 35 centimeters with a depth of 55 centimeters and two steps. The basilica at Casa Herrera was built about 500.[41] Its baptistery and the contempo-

---

cas in the southwest — in the province of Lusitania and adjoining Baetica. Ristow records several not included in his study.

36. Ulbert, *Frühchristliche Basiliken*, pp. 146-147, says not later than the beginning of the sixth century.
37. Ulbert, *Frühchristliche Basiliken*, pp. 84-85, plate 12b.
38. Ulbert, *Frühchristliche Basiliken*, pp. 140, 148.
39. Ulbert, *Frühchristliche Basiliken*, p. 145, n. 26.
40. Ulbert, *Frühchristliche Basiliken*, pp. 19-22, 140-145, 154-156, plate 3.
41. Ulbert, *Frühchristliche Basiliken*, pp. 99, 182.

rary one at Torre de Palma (Portugal) are central to the thesis of Ulbert that baptisteries with multiple fonts were employed for both adult and infant baptism at the same time.[42] The dimensions of the large basin are 2.90 meters long, 0.50 meter wide, and one meter deep, and it had two sets of four steps.[43] There was a smaller basin of 0.60 meters in depth, with two steps. The smaller basins at Torre de Palma and San Pedro de Alcántra (above) are said to be earlier than the larger basins built in the mid–sixth century;[44] this would raise the question of why there would be an increase in adult baptisms at this later date. Are the examples of larger fonts in Spain and North Africa in the sixth century due to Byzantine influence?

Evaluation of the Evidence of Baptismal Fonts

The predominant number of baptismal fonts permitted immersion, and many were so large as to defy any reason for their existence other than for immersion. The fonts in which an immersion is problematic or impossible require special consideration.

Sebastian Ristow, whose corpus of early Christian baptisteries has formed the basis for our chapters 53 and 54,[45] notes the tendency to reduce the size of piscinae in later periods (although, as we have found, there are exceptions to this tendency, as in Spain) and to erect a second pool nearby. Both changes occurred chiefly in the second half of the fifth century and in the sixth century, and further reductions in size occurred in the seventh and eighth centuries. The addition of a secondary piscina is largely a phenomenon of the sixth century. These secondary piscinae were, as a rule, between 30 and 60 centimeters in depth. The first set of changes belongs to a time when the baptism of a large number of catechumens at one time was declining (and, I would add, when infant baptism was becoming increasingly common). The great part of the later reductions fall in the time of the general spread of infant baptism.[46]

The depth of piscinae in the fourth and early fifth century was customarily in the area of one meter (approximately waist high for most grown persons). The tendency of fifth-century piscinae was to be smaller in diameter and depth. After the sixth century a piscina over one meter in depth is extremely rare.[47] My conclusion is

---

42. Ulbert, *Frühchristliche Basiliken*, pp. 157-159, 179, passim.

43. Ulbert, *Frühchristliche Basiliken*, pp. 148, 152-153.

44. Ulbert, *Frühchristliche Basiliken*, p. 142. He notes that according to literary sources for Spain (*Liber ordinum*, Isidore of Seville, Idelfonse of Toledo) there was only adult baptism at the beginning of the sixth century with few exceptions, both adult and infant baptism from about the mid–sixth century, and exclusively infant baptism in the seventh century (p. 176); the baptismal structures at Casa Herrera correspond to this sequence (p. 177).

45. Sebastian Ristow, *Frühchristliche Baptisterien*, Jahrbuch für Antike und Christentum, Ergänzungsband 27 (Münster: Aschendorff, 1998).

46. Ristow, *Frühchristliche Baptisterien*, pp. 43, 45-49. He says infant baptism was practiced from the third century and displaced adult baptism in the seventh or at the latest the eighth century — p. 84.

47. Ristow, *Frühchristliche Baptisterien*, pp. 50-52.

that, rather than the practice of perfusion (although this may have occurred), infant baptism would seem to be the primary factor in the smaller size of piscinae and in the erection of secondary piscinae.

Ristow, in spite of the pattern he describes, nevertheless thinks perfusion or affusion was common. A principal consideration is the size of baptismal fonts. He asserts that in most communities the size of the piscina appears to make a complete submersion of an adult improbable or impossible; hence a half immersion of the person standing in the water and water then poured over him/her must be assumed as a rule. A piscina of a depth of 30 to 80 centimeters allows no other kind of baptism than an *infusio* or *perfusio*. An immersion or submersion could have been employed at only a minority of piscinae.[48]

The chronology Ristow himself follows places few of the shallow baptisteries in the fourth and fifth centuries; most are later. Those who have witnessed total immersions in bathtubs and shallow streams would change his limit for an immersion from 80 centimeters to around 50 or 60, depending on the size of the person and diameter of the font. Ristow says nothing about the posture of the baptizand. The argument against immersion from the size of some early fonts may have in mind the practice of some modern religious groups of laying the person back horizontally. If while the person is standing the head is bent forward, a much smaller diameter is required. If the person is kneeling or sitting, an immersion is permitted in a body of water less deep than might be thought practical. There is also the possibility that the walls of piscinae were higher than what is preserved in a given case.

The literary sources that have constituted the majority of the present study, when they describe the baptismal action, uniformly describe an immersion or imply it as the norm. Ristow cites several passages as instances of pouring or sprinkling.[49] *Didache* 7 (chap. 12) allowed pouring water over the head in the absence of sufficient water for an immersion — clearly a secondary alternative in an emergency situation. The *Sibylline Oracles* 7.83-84, in apparent allusion to the baptism of Christ (the Logos), says, "Sprinkling [ῥαίνων] with pure water your baptism [βάπτισμα] through which you shone out of fire," and lines 87-88, "Taking the head of this man, sprinkle [ῥάνας] with water; pray three times; call fervently to your God." This figurative, poetic passage (quoted more fully in chap. 6) from an uncertain group is of dubious value for determining usual baptismal practice. Gregory of Nyssa, *Catechetical Oration* 35, is discussed in chapter 38, where the meaning, to be consistent with Gregory's other descriptions, would be a reference to the water pouring over a person in immersion and not to the administrator pouring water over the baptizand. Cyprian's defense of pouring or sprinkling in cases of sickbed baptism (Ristow says *Letter* 59, but he means 69) is discussed in chapter 22 (and the later

---

48. Ristow, *Frühchristliche Baptisterien*, pp. 82-83, 91. He frequently gives smaller dimensions than those given in other detailed studies, notably for Israel and Greece.

49. Ristow, *Frühchristliche Baptisterien*, pp. 83-84.

practice in chap. 39). Clinical baptism, although establishing the acceptability in the church's eyes of pouring, was always recognized as exceptional and for many persons as being of doubtful validity (to what extent the mode entered into these doubts is not clear). It was not considered normal practice, and, since usually done at home, was irrelevant to the practice at the church's baptisteries.

Ristow further invokes representations of baptism in art as support for pouring.[50] He refers to the spoon from Aquileia, now lost, for which we are dependent on a possibly unreliable drawing, and to a glass fragment from Rome. The gravestone from Aquileia (chap. 41) has the administrator's hand on the head of the baptizand and so not pouring the running water that is depicted. The pouring shown in the representation of the baptism of Christ in the dome of the Orthodox Baptistery in Ravenna is now recognized as the work of the nineteenth-century restorer. Similar scenes on sarcophagi are also the work of restorers. The ancient depictions of baptism in art almost uniformly show the hand of the administrator on the head of the baptizand and not as pouring water on the head.

The contributors to *Gottesdienst der Kirche: Handbuch der Liturgiewissenschaft* also argue for infusion as the normal mode of baptism. Johannes H. Emminghaus claims that of over 100 piscina he has examined only in two or three is full immersion of an adult possible but even there is hardly practical.[51] He must not have examined many of those surveyed above and in chapter 53, or have preconceived ideas about the manner of immersing or the size required, or neglected to pay attention to the dates of the fonts. B. Kleinheyer interprets *immersio* as to stand in water and claims the practice was an *infusio* but not a *submersio*. He says architecture and literature do not attest total immersion but the opposite.[52] Readers of the evidence in this book may judge for themselves the accuracy of his claims.

A. Nestori proposes that the glass plate naming Alba and showing water from a jug but the hand of the administrator on the head and the inscription from Aquileia represent a union of two ceremonies — by immersion and by infusion. He refers to a later sculpture on the altar of San Ambrogio, Milan, in which the baptizand stands naked in an octagonal pool to his hips; the bishop on the left has a hand on the baptizand's head while on the right a deacon (?) pours water from an amphora on his head. He suggests there was a baptism by infusion immersion.[53]

A different interpretation is offered by two important regional studies. Malka Ben-Pechat offers these conclusions based on a detailed study of the baptismal fonts in the Holy Land:

50. Ristow, *Frühchristliche Baptisterien*, p. 83. The art evidence is discussed in my chap. 7.
51. "Der gottesdienstliche Raum und seine Ausstatung," *Gestalt des Gottesdienstes, Gottesdienst der Kirche: Handbuch der Liturgiewissenshaft* 3.6 (Regensburg: Friedrich Pustet, 1987), p. 402, n. 55.
52. *Sakramentliche Feiern*, I: *Die Feiern der Eingliederung in die Kirche, Gottesdienst der Kirche: Handbuch der Liturgiewissenschaft* 7.1 (Regensburg: Friedrich Pustet, 1989), pp. 60, 62-63. He cites in support W. Gessel, "Baptisterien der alten Christenheit," *Klerus-Blatt* 65 (1985): 176-181.
53. A. Nestori, "L'acqua nel fonte battesimale," in *Studi in memoria di Giuseppe Bovini*, Biblioteca di Felix Ravenna 6 (Ravenna, 1989), Vol. 2, pp. 419-427 (424-25).

The major authors of the east, since the fourth century up to the thirteenth, insisted in their writings on baptism by the triple, and total immersion. . . . Baptism by infusion was, on the other hand, mentioned only in exceptional cases and could not have been the usual practice. However, none of the fonts in the Holy Land was deep enough to permit total immersion of a standing adult. . . .

Consequently I have come to the conclusion that an adult of average height should have adapted himself, helped by the priest, to the dimensions of the font and to its internal design by taking an appropriate position which would have enabled him to dip and rise [sic] his head without losing his balance. Either bending his knees, kneeling, or sitting, an adult could have been totally immersed as required in fonts from 1.30 m to 60 cm deep. . . .

Under 60 cm by depth the fonts were probably used for child baptism only.[54]

Jean-Charles Picard, working with the literary texts but correlating them with archaeological sources for southern France and northern Italy, concludes that the authors who furnish details of the baptismal rite speak only of immersion. *Tinguere, mergere,* and *submergere* seem to imply a total immersion, and he observes that there is no ancient representation where the celebrant pours water on the head of the baptized. Where water falls in a cascade into the font, this evoked living water, and the baptized person was not pushed under the cascade but dipped in the piscina. The smaller fonts were sufficient for a total immersion of a young child. Rituals of the end of the eighth century prescribe that priests and deacons descend into the piscina in order to plunge the infants in the water. He suggests that where two fonts were in use at the same time — as at Geneva, Aosta, and Milan — one may have been for the baptism of men and one for the baptism of women. Fonts were often below floor level so that the candidates descended into the water.[55]

---

54. Malka Ben-Pechat, "The Paleochristian Baptismal Fonts in the Holy Land: Formal and Functional Study," *Liber annus studii biblici franciscani* 39 (1989): 165-188 (pp. 180-181).

55. Jean-Charles Picard, "Ce que les textes nous aprennent sur les équipements et le mobilier liturgiques nécessaires pour le baptême dans le sud de la Gaul et l'Italie du Nord," in *Actes du XIe Congrès International d'Archéologie Chrétienne, Lyone, Vienne, Grenoble, Genève et Aoste, 21-28 septembre 1986* (Vatican, 1989), Vol. 2, pp. 1451-68 (1455, 1457, 1459, 1462-63).

55. Conclusions

Origin of Baptism

Early Christians commonly based their practice of baptism on the dominical command of Matthew 28:19 and on the Lord's example (Matt. 3:13-17 and parallels). Historically considered, Christian baptism had its precedent in the baptism administered by John the Baptizer, which seemingly was engaged in also by Jesus and his disciples (John 3:26; 4:1-2). Christian baptism was distinguished from John's in its call for faith in Jesus, its being administered in Jesus' name, and in its connection with the Holy Spirit. John's baptism, in its turn, had its background in Jewish religious washings but differed from them in its eschatological call for repentance, its one-time exercise, and its being administered by John and not self-administered.

Christians found lessons applicable to their practice in certain Old Testament events involving water — notably the crossing of the Red Sea at Israel's exodus from Egypt and the flood in the days of Noah (both already in the New Testament — 1 Cor. 10:1-4 and 1 Pet. 3:20-22 respectively). These and other events as well as prophetic texts were interpreted in the light of Christian practice as providential preparations for Christian baptism.

There seems little to associate Christian baptism with pagan religious washings, a parallel drawn by some Christians in the second century for apologetic purposes. The verb for "baptize" (βαπτίζω) was not a religious term in pagan usage but kept its basic secular meaning of "plunge" or "dip" in Christian usage. Christians adopted for the noun (βάπτισμα), a word different from the word used for pagan and Jewish dippings (βαπτισμός).

Doctrine of Baptism

François Bovon identifies these common elements in early baptismal theology: baptism is a work of God and of humans and a sign of the covenant; baptism is a sign of the work of Christ, an actualization of the redemptive work of Christ; and it was an efficacious sign.[1]

Although in developing the doctrine of baptism different authors had their particular favorite descriptions, there is a remarkable agreement on the benefits received in baptism. And these are present already in the New Testament texts. Two fundamental blessings are often repeated: the person baptized received forgiveness of sins and the gift of the Holy Spirit (Acts 2:38). The two fundamental doctrinal interpretations of baptism are sharing in the death and resurrection of Christ, with the attendant benefits and responsibilities (Rom. 6:3-4), and regeneration from above (John 3:5), with its related ideas.

Other features (with their New Testament basis) that are commonly present include: clothing with Christ (Gal. 3:27), deliverance from Satan's bondage to freedom in Christ (Col. 1:13), and enlightenment (Heb. 6:4?). Less frequently mentioned are the motifs of marriage to Christ (Eph. 5:25-27) and a contract (more often associated with the renunciations and confession of faith — 1 Pet. 3:21).

Building on Paul's imagery of the gift of the Holy Spirit as the Christian's equivalent for circumcision as the seal of the covenant (2 Cor. 1:22; Eph. 1:13), those who brought spiritual circumcision into relation to baptism made the equation most often not of baptism itself with circumcision but saw baptism as the occasion for the inward circumcision by the Spirit. A common term for baptism was "seal," but it was also applied to the anointing and the laying on of hands, actions also related to the Holy Spirit.

The New Testament and early Christian literature are virtually unanimous in ascribing a saving significance to baptism.[2] If anything, the early church exaggerated this aspect of baptism's significance. John 3:5 was taken outside its context in the Fourth Gospel and given an absolute sense. Only a few (fringe) heretics of the ancient church tried to dehydrate the new birth. The main variation among mainstream Christian authors was in how strongly different individuals affirmed the necessity of baptism for salvation. The major explicit exception to this requirement was for martyrs who died for a confession of faith prior to receiving baptism.

Baptism, however, was not seen as a human work but as God's work, and the salvation in baptism was premised on the saving effect of Christ's death on the cross and his victorious resurrection.

Water was indispensable to baptism, and the use of water naturally gave the association of baptism with the motif of cleansing. The provision for other applications of water than by immersion (on which more below) and the extension of baptism to babies lest they die unbaptized (also discussed below) testify to the sense of necessity to receive baptism for salvation.

---

1. François Bovon, "Baptism in the Ancient Church," *Sewanee Theological Review* 42 (1999): 429-438 (435-436).

2. Cf. Albrecht Oepke, "βάπτω, βαπτίζω (et al.)," in Gerhard Kittel, ed., *Theological Dictionary of the New Testament*, tr. Geoffrey W. Bromiley (Grand Rapids: Eerdmans, 1964), Vol. 1, pp. 540-543, for the saving significance of baptism into Christ.

Baptismal Ceremony/Liturgy

The New Testament texts indicate immediate baptism of those converted to faith in Christ and give little indication of accompanying ceremonial actions. Most of the early converts came from Judaism or from Gentiles already exposed to the teachings of the Old Testament. As the situation changed, more teaching was found necessary; consequently a longer period of preparation for converts was considered helpful. The ceremony of baptism was elaborated to give enacted expressions to features of the meaning of baptism (e.g., the new birth motif), and actions accompanying the baptism (like unclothing and reclothing) were given a symbolic meaning — these too perhaps as teaching devices.

Essential to baptism were faith (expressed in a verbal confession apparently from the beginning) and repentance (this too required at the beginning but soon finding verbal expression in a renunciation of the devil). These features continued to be considered minimum necessities to the water rite even in situations of emergency baptism. Hence, the importance of accompanying instruction in faith and morals was evident.

Since baptism was a bath of cleansing for the whole person, nudity (partial, or likely complete) was the practice from quite early times. Although nudity is not mentioned in the earliest sources, it may have been present. Although there are notices in the context of the time of immersions while clothed, other factors would have contributed to nude baptism: Jewish washings for ceremonial purposes, secular bathing customs, and various doctrinal motifs (innocence of childhood, return to the pre-fall condition of paradise).

Triple immersion became the nearly universal custom from the third to fifth centuries. Whether it too was practiced but not mentioned earlier cannot be determined. Several authors (Tertullian, Jerome) recognized it as a custom without explicit scriptural attestation.

A laying on of hands accompanied baptism from a quite early time. Doubt remains whether individual references to the gesture apply to a prayer of blessing at the time of the baptism, the functional imposition of a hand at the immersion, an accompaniment to a postbaptismal prayer for the imparting of the Holy Spirit, the means of anointing with oil or marking with the sign of the cross, or some combination of these.

The anointing with oil of a part of the body, the whole body, or both as separate acts is one of the early additions to the baptismal rite without express literal mention in the New Testament, but it is attested before the end of the second century. The different applications of oil and/or *myron* and the different placement of the action (pre- or postbaptismal or both) in different liturgies would seem to indicate a lack of apostolic pattern. The association of oil with the Holy Spirit assured its acceptance as an important part of the baptismal ceremony, rivaling if not equaling the application of water for some church leaders (and among some Gnostics it had superiority over the water rite). The secular uses of oil (in bathing, in athletics, in medicine), reinforced by the religious significance of anointing of religious leaders (priests, kings, prophets) in the Old Testament, gave occasion for development of symbolic significance to the gesture in baptism.

From the mid–second century at least the baptismal ceremony was followed (or concluded) by the newly baptized joining in the congregational celebration of the eucharist. This expression of admission to the fellowship of the church was natural when the baptism occurred on a Sunday.

Other elements gave dramatic expression to the theology of baptism in some rites, as the taking of milk and honey (and sometimes water also) with the bread and wine of the eucharist. The milk and honey had the double significance of food for the newborn child and, according to the biblical description, the food of the promised land. Removal of clothing suggested abandoning the former manner of life, and reclothing suggested putting on a new self. Clothing with a white garment after rising from the baptismal water was a fourth-century development. It was prompted by the normal procedure of reclothing after the baptismal washing and carried the significance of purity, being clothed with Christ, and the eschatological meaning of heavenly clothing.

In general we can say that there was a great deal of similarity in the baptismal rites during the patristic period. Major items on which there were differences or the beginning of differences include the following: (1) the West was beginning to separate the postbaptismal rites that became confirmation from baptism; (2) the Syrian practice was an unction associated with the Holy Spirit before baptism, whereas the principal anointing elsewhere was after the baptism; (3) the liturgy at Milan included an "opening of the ears" *(ephphatha)*; (4) the liturgy in the East included a spitting in the renunciation of the devil; (5) in Milan and Spain there was a footwashing; (6) in a few places catechesis on the sacraments preceded baptism, but at other places it followed the experience itself.[3]

Origin and Progress of Infant Baptism

There is general agreement that there is no firm evidence for infant baptism before the latter part of the second century. This fact does not mean that it did not occur, but it does mean that supporters of the practice have a considerable chronological gap to account for. Many replace the historical silence by appeal to theological or sociological considerations.

Arguments against the originality of baby baptism, in addition to its lack of early attestation, include: the essential nature ascribed to verbal confession and re-

---

3. This list is elaborated from Bovon, "Baptism in the Ancient Church," p. 431. He affirms that baptism in the New Testament and the Fathers has "a coherence of being the same plant in the same soil" (p. 430), but he is wrong in saying that there was triple immersion in the East and triple aspersion in the West (p. 433).

pentance; the liturgy designed for persons of responsible age; size of baptisteries; and the lack of an agreed theology to support it (Chrysostom and the eastern churches vs. Augustine).

The most plausible explanation for the origin of infant baptism is found in the emergency baptism of sick children expected to die soon so that they would be assured of entrance into the kingdom of heaven. There was a slow extension of the practice of baptizing babies as a precautionary measure. It was generally accepted, but questions continued to be raised about its propriety into the fifth century. It became the usual practice in the fifth and sixth centuries.

In the Augustinian-Pelagian controversy infant baptism was a principal support for the doctrine of original sin, rather than the other way around, since baptism was universally recognized as for forgiveness of sins. With the victory of Augustine's arguments original sin became *the* reason for infant baptism in the western church.

The development of the view of baptism as objectively effective paralleled the development of infant baptism. If baptism is defined as consisting of water and the Trinitarian formula, then conscious faith and obedience become less important. In the absence of a personal confession of faith and renunciation of the devil other justifications were offered — the faith of the church; the guarantee by the sponsors that the child would be raised in the church; the child considered a believer by reason of receiving the sacrament of faith (baptism).

Mode of Baptism: Immersion with Exceptions

Those who approach the study of baptism from the standpoint of archaeology tend to find greater probability that affusion, or perfusion, was a normal practice; those who come from the literary evidence see a greater likelihood of immersion, or submersion, being the normal practice. The comprehensive survey of the evidence compiled in this study gives a basis for a fresh look at this subject and seeks to give coherence to that evidence while addressing seeming anomalies. The Christian literary sources, backed by secular word usage and Jewish religious immersions, give an overwhelming support for full immersion as the normal action. Exceptions in cases of a lack of water and especially of sickbed baptism were made.

Submersion was undoubtedly the case for the fourth and fifth centuries in the Greek East and only slightly less certain for the Latin West. Was this a change from an earlier practice, a selection out of options previously available, or a continuation of the practice of the first three centuries? It is the contention of this study that the last interpretation best accords with the available facts. Unless one has preconceived ideas about how an immersion would be performed, the literary, art, and archaeological evidence supports this conclusion. The express statements in the literary sources, supported by other hints, the depictions in art, and the very presence of specially built baptismal fonts, along with their size and shape, indicate that the normal procedure was for the administrator with his head on the baptizand's head to bend the upper part of the body forward and dip the head under the water. Whether the person was standing, kneeling, or sitting may have varied in different instances, but in the art the one baptized is standing.

The only viable alternative interpretation of the evidence that would account for the fonts is a partial immersion in which the baptismal candidate stood in water and the administrator poured water over the upper part of the body, but this is largely conjectural. This interpretation is not really supported by paintings and sculpture (where the few cases of streams, which may not represent water, coming from above proceed not from the administrator, whose hand is on the head of the baptizand, but from another source; and the sometimes shallow amount of water reaching only to the ankles or knees is allusive and not descriptive) and with little (and that dubious) literary support. A pouring or sprinkling did occur in two special circumstances: a lack of water and (more often) sickbed or deathbed conversions. Both were treated as exceptional, second choice, and undesirable alternatives.

There are, of course, other ways than mine of reading the evidence, in whole or in part. I will take for examination one of those: although old, it makes a total case and presents arguments often made by others.[4] A review of its arguments will respond to the main points brought up in opposition to my conclusions about the evidence.

Stommel contends that bathing customs in the ancient Near East involved pouring water over the body and not a submersion of the body.[5] Since ancient pictures of bathing show a variety of postures and applications of water, and some descriptions of Roman baths speak of submersion of oneself or swimming in the baths, it would not be proper to generalize to a single standard procedure (chap. 2). He makes the connection between bathing customs and Christian baptism by the

---

4. Eduard Stommel, "Christliche Taufriten und antike Badesitten," *Jahrbuch für Antike und Christentum* 2 (1959): 5-14. A more recent taking up of the same lines of argument is found in Renate Pillinger, "The Significance of Early Christian Monuments for the Study of Liturgy: The Example of Baptism," *Studia liturgica* 25 (1995): 32-50 = "Die Bedeutung frühchristlicher Denkmaler für die gegenwärtige Liturgie — Veranschaulicht am Beispiel der Taufe," *Heiliger Dienst* 48 (1994): 293-307. Although granting that the sepulchral representations offer no clues about the manner of baptizing (pp. 38-39), she concludes from the iconographic and monumental evidence as well as some literary sources that it was usual for the baptizand to stand in water knee to hip-deep and have water poured over him by the baptizer (p. 50). The case for affusion as the usual method of administering baptism was argued from the archaeological evidence over a century ago by C. F. Rogers, "Baptism and Christian Archaeology," *Studia biblica et ecclesiastica* 5 (1903): 239-358 (supplemented and corrected in "Baptism by Affusion in the Early Church," *Journal of Theological Studies* 6 [1905]:107-110). Claiming that literature and the church orders represent the ideal and archaeology the average, Rogers examines the artistic representations in various media and baptismal fonts. His work is now quite dated, especially in dates assigned to the items examined, is replaced by later, more complete knowledge, and includes many items later than the period of my study.

5. According to this line of reasoning, the different practices of oiling the body either before or after the bath would account for the different placement of anointings in Christian rituals, but Georg Kretschmar, "Recent Research on Christian Initiation," *Studia liturgica* 12 (1977): 87-106 (p. 98), disagrees and looks to the sacral oil rites of Old Testament ritual for kings and priests as behind Christian practice.

common motif of cleansing, which he sees as the original motif in Christian baptism. Since cleansing is a natural motif to associate with water, I observe that it would have been a normal motif to attribute to baptism and need not derive from any connection with bathing customs. The original association of cleansing with baptism was already in the spiritualized sense of inner forgiveness of sins, made especially by John the Baptist. Stommel cites Cyprian's argument for sickbed affusion (see chap. 22), but Cyprian's comparison with ordinary bodily washing is an "after the fact" justification, not the basis of the action.

Stommel seeks to avoid the meaning of the Greek βαπτίζειν (chap. 3) by arguing that the word in the New Testament derived its meaning from Jewish proselyte baptism, which he claims was not a dipping under the water but a bath in the water (p. 9). Here he not only assumes an early date for proselyte baptism but also is wrong on the manner of the Jewish practice (chap. 4). He reasons further that John's baptism with water according to the Gospels and Acts is grammatically parallel to the baptism with the Holy Spirit, and the latter (Acts 2:17, 32f.) was effected by pouring (pp. 10-11). Stommel here confuses the manner in which the Holy Spirit was said to fill the room with the resultant baptism (chap. 10), even as there is no correlation between the manner in which water fills a font and the subsequent baptism.

The *Didache*'s instructions (chap. 12) are understood to mean that if there is not either cold or warm water in which the baptizand can stand, then the pouring can be done without standing in the water (p. 11),[6] but the plain reading of the text is that the pouring is distinguished from the "baptizing." He and Pillinger (who says the contrast was between pouring over the whole body and pouring over the head)[7] are both subject to the same criticism that if water was poured in both cases (7.1-2 and 7.3), why is a distinction in verbs made? Stommel then cites other supposed examples of sprinkling or pouring for baptism (pp. 11-12), but some of these are instances of the usual ancient interpretive method of giving any mention of water a baptismal meaning without any suggestion that the manner of application was the same.

Patristic interpretations of baptism as a death and burial are understood to mean entering and exiting the baptismal pool and not going under and coming up from the water (pp. 12-13). Theodore of Mopsuestia, for one (chap. 32), refutes this as being always the case. For Stommel, the pouring of water was understood as the immersion (p. 13). He sees the general adoption of submersion to coincide with the decline of adult baptism and infant baptism becoming the rule (p. 13); the spread of infant baptism, however, at other periods has had the opposite effect. He appeals to depictions of baptism in art (see my explanations in chap. 7) and the size of fonts (the argument from size of fonts is examined in chapter 54 in connection with Ristow's position). He doesn't really deal with the hand on the head in the art, except

---

6. It occurs to me that the practice of partial immersion, that is, standing in water and having it poured over the head (in imitation of running water), which could have been a way of covering the body with water, might have led to simple pouring or sprinkling by not having the person stand in water as formerly, but this is hypothetical.

7. Renate Pillinger, "Die Taufe nach der Didache," *Wiener Studien*, n.s. 9 (1975): 152-162 (p. 160).

to explain that at the Lateran baptistery the administrator by laying on of hands in connection with the questions and answers guided the head three times under the water flowing into pool. The western church, he says, kept any application of water as decisive (p. 14), whereas the eastern church changed the action to an immersion; but this hardly agrees with the general trend in size from larger baptismal fonts to smaller fonts, and the main exceptions (oddly enough) are precisely in the West (North Africa and Spain). Moreover, the usage of pouring in sickbed baptism seems to have been no more characteristic of one part of the church than the other.

The conclusions of Lothar Heiser on the administration of baptism after examining the literary and pictorial evidence accord with mine: the water customarily reached to the hips of the baptizand; after calling on the triune God, the priest bent the baptizand under so as to dip him in water over the head; in the cases of pouring in the *Didache* and in sickbed baptism the one baptized did not stand in the font.[8]

The theology of baptism, the elaborations in the liturgy of baptism, the permission of infant baptism (especially in cases of serious illness), and the accommodations made in sickbed baptism all testify that the church of the early centuries gave great importance and centrality to baptism.

---

8. Lothar Heiser, *Die Taufe in der orthodoxen Kirche: Geschichte, Spendung, und Symbolik nach der Lehre der Väter* (Trier: Paulinus, 1987), pp. 101-102. He acknowledges that in the present practice of infant baptism in the Greek church the priest holds the child as far under the water as possible and scoops water over the head so as to be fully covered with water (pp. 300-301).

Index of Biblical Passages

OLD TESTAMENT

Genesis

	635, 778n.9
1	539n.20
1:1-2	111n.54, 256, 337
1:2	101, 242, 256nn.31-32, 310, 344, 404, 407, 468, 494, 511, 517, 641, 678, 680, 689, 712
1:6-7	566n.6
1:7	310
1:9	709
1:11	644
1:20	246-247, 644, 674
2:7	348, 497, 600, 687
2:10	353n.13
2:15	417
2:17	643
2:25	124n.67, 477
3	643
3:1	639
3:15	639
3:16	568
3:19	643, 666
3:22	211
6–9	404
6–8	337, 347
6:1–8:22	62
6:5	190
6:11-13	190
6:14	404
6:16	665
8:7-8	641
8:8-11	101, 680
8:11	641
13	535, 557n.31
17:9-14	76
17:12	595
18:4	66n.34, 656
21:15-19	614
22:2	101
22:3-4	316
22:12	316
22:18	316
24:15	442
24:15-20	614
26:18-22	614
28:19	495
29:2-3	502n.19
29:9-10	614
30:37-38	614
30:38	514
48:14	344
49:11	196

Exodus

2:1-10	665
2:2-4	614
4:24-26	500
5:3	401, 415
5:7-8	746
12:13	355n.26
12:21-30	590
12:22	46, 599
12:22-23	595
12:29	595
12:44	491
12:48-49	76
13:19	152n.13
13:21	152n.13
14:1–15:21	62, 614
14:16	152n.13
14:19-20	415
14:19-25	514
14:19-29	152
14:26-31	337
15:1	752
15:4	746
15:5	677
15:10	641
15:22-25	514, 614n.39
15:22-26	337
15:23-24	468, 641
15:23-25	114, 637n.22
15:23-27	680
15:24	696
15:25	346
15:27	109
16:29	168n.6
17:1-7	212, 514
17:6	114, 128, 337, 665, 696

19:10	76n.89, 593, 709	14:52	501, 514	**Joshua**	
19:10-11	411, 427	15	71n.67	3	402
19:15	593	15:5-13	61n.9	3:11	128
21:22-25	421	15:11-12	61n.9	3:14-17	696
24:5	76n.89	15:13	95n.55	3:15	46
24:8	76n.89	15:16	66, 77, 250	3:16	128
24:18	652n.18	15:16-18	61n.9	4:9	614
28:26	486n.34	15:18	66	4:14	403
30:30	343	15:19-24	250	5:1-7	690
32	273, 440	15:19-27	61n.9	5:2	273, 416
33:22	502n.23	15:32-33	250	5:2-5	490
35:5ff.	47	16:23-24	317, 321	5:5	76n.89
		19:23	315n.46	5:9	402, 404
Leviticus	61n.4	19:25	315n.46	5:10-11	691
1:9	404-405	20:24	768	6:10	168n.6
4:3	343			8:32	370
4:5	343	**Numbers**		24:15	424
4:6	46	5:17	62, 204n.14		
4:17	46	8:5-7	355	**Judges**	
7:36-37	427	15:14-15	76n.89	6:11-18	656
8	502n.23	19	212	7:4-8	491
8:6	188n.5	19:8	355	7:4-20	515
8:6-7	427	19:9	355, 691		
8:30	188n.5	19:12	355	**Ruth**	
9:9	46n.34	19:13	355	2:14	46
11	596	19:14-20	77		
11:24	61, 77	19:17	62, 95n.55, 204n.14	**1 Samuel**	
11:24-25	275	19:17-18	691	14:27	46
11:28	61n.6	19:17-20	47, 61		
11:32	47, 61	19:18	46	**1 Kings**	
11:39-40	61n.6	19:19	275	1:38-39	515
12:2-7	368	20:2-13	212	18:30-40	615
12:3	370, 371	20:7-11	337	18:31-38	696
12:8	368	20:11	128	18:33-35	585n.11
13-14	681	21:22	423	19:8	652n.18
14:5	62	31:21-24	405n.16	19:38	641
14:5-6	95n.55, 204n.14			22:11	85n.13
14:6-7	46n.34	**Deuteronomy**			
14:6-8	62, 188n.5	10:16	306, 491	**2 Kings**	
14:9	62n.10	18:15-20	260	2:6-11	587n.18
14:15-16	62, 188n.5	21:4	95n.55	2:8	403, 491
14:16	46n.33	23:1	172n.21	2:9	404
14:26-27	62n.10	28:10	188	2:12	404
14:50	204n.14	30:6	273, 447	2:14	403
14:50-52	95n.55	32:11	101n.5	5	403-404
14:50-53	62	33:24	46	5:1-14	63n.16, 514, 615, 641
14:51	46n.34, 62n.10, 204n.14	34:9	480	5:8-14	501
				5:9	404

Index of Biblical Passages

5:10	57n.53, 404	49:2 (Lt. 48:3)	780n.29	143:6 (Gk. 142:6)	615
5:14	57n.53, 305, 508, 696	49:14 (Lt. 48:15)	782n.50	**Proverbs**	635
6:4-7	346, 468, 641	51:5 (Gk. & Lt. 50:7)	368, 413n.56, 788n.95, 803, 809n.89	9:17	319
8:15	46	51:6-11 (50:8-13)	62n.11	**Ecclesiastes**	
10:19	168n.6	51:7 (50:9)	88, 457, 746	2:14	639n.30
Job		51:10 (51:12)	88	3:2	605n.11
9:31	46, 57	68:23 (Gk. 67:24)	47	9:8	657
14:4	368, 405n.16	69:2 (Gk. 68:3)	57, 140n.29	10:1	676
14:4-5	367, 368, 369n.18, 413n.56, 803	69:15 (68:16)	140n.29	**Song of Songs**	
40:23	121, 482	74:13-14 (73:13-14)	121, 482, 680, 751	1:5	613
40:26	482	77 (Lt. 76)	678n.19	1:11	401n.5
Psalms	698, 720	77:16 (76:17)	334	1:11-12	405
1	212	78 (Lt. 77)	682	1:12	427n.117
1:1	211	78:1	799n.38	1:13	411n.44
1:3	211, 353n.13, 615	78:15-17	212	4:12	390
1:3-4	127	78:25	585	4:15	390
1:3-6	211	81 (Lt. 80)	682, 780n.28	5:1	640n.41
2:7	101-102, 103n.13, 104, 106, 118-120, 644	81:5 (Lt. 80:6)	780n.29, 790n.108	5:3	614
4:6 (Gk. 4:7)	598	85 (Lt. 84)	681	5:10	610n.27
18:4 (17:5)	140n.29	88:6-7 (87:7-8)	140n.29	5:13	610n.28
23 (Gk. 22)	128n.83, 441n.40, 470	89 (Lt. 88)	681	**Isaiah**	
23:1-2	468	89:29 (88:30)	106	1:9	449
23:2	759	91:11 (Lt. 90:11)	790n.113	1:15-16	67n.41, 271
29 (Lt. & Gk. 28)	758	91:13 (90:13)	759	1:15-17	84n.6
29:3	468, 587n.22, 757	92 (Lt. 91)	682	1:15-20	273
29:3-4	615	102 (Lt. 101)	779n.23	1:16	88, 242, 243, 267, 268, 449, 571, 611, 615, 693, 717, 741
32 (31)	650n.11	103:2-5 (102:2-5)	791n.121	1:16-17	62n.11
32:1	481, 668, 750	103:3-5 (Lt. 102:3-5)	791n.123	1:16-19	334
32:1-2	457, 698, 759	103:5 (102:5)	655n.24	1:16-20	28, 241
33:6 (32:6)	641n.42	103:12 (Lt. 102:12)	784	1:18	675
34:5 (Gk. 33:6)	613, 615	104:4 (103:4)	112n.56	2:3-4	271
36:9 (35)	597	105:15 (104:15)	448	4:4	305n.20, 691n.32
37:17 (36)	779n.20	107:3 (Lt. 106:3)	790n.108	5:2	491
42 (Lt. & Gk. 41)	649, 681, 785	107:16 (Gk. 106:16)	211	7:9	773
42:1 (41:2)	127, 681, 785n.67	109:24 (Lt. 108:24)	793n.142	7:21	449
42:2 (Gk. 41:3)	615	114:3	121n.56, 334, 654	11:1	585
42:7 (41:8)	140n.29	114:3-8	128, 130n.94	11:1-3	110, 688n.4
45:7 (Gk. 44)	540n.28, 572	114:5	121n.56, 334, 654	11:2	105, 106n.24, 112, 117, 640, 786
46:4 (Gk. 45)	334, 403	116 (Gk. 114)	535	16:1-2	211
		118 (Lt. 117)	673n.9, 673	20:2	85n.13
		118:26	182n.42	21:4	57
		128:3 (Lt. 127:3)	786		
		132:14 (131:14)	106		
		139:3 (138:3)	772		

864 | INDEX OF BIBLICAL PASSAGES

26:18	737	31:31-32	272	Zechariah	468
30:27	517	31:33	783n.52	3:3	615
30:27-28	140n.29	31:34	558n.34	3:3-4	613
33:16-18	211	38:22 (Gk. 45:22)	57	4	468
35:1-2	615			7:10	168n.6
40:1-5	90	Ezekiel	246	13:1	88
40:1-17	242	1:29	680	14:8	468
40:3	87, 93	4:1-8	85n.13		
40:3-5	91	9:4	196, 493n.14	Malachi	
40:12	504n.27	9:4-5	355	3:1-6	91
42:1	101, 103n.13	9:4-6	355n.26, 495n.22	3:1–4:6	88
42:2-5	91	16:4	411	4:1	91
42:10	402	20:6	211		
43:2	140n.29	20:15	211	**APOCRYPHA/**	
43:18-20	357	23:15	47	**DEUTEROCANONICAL**	
43:18-21	272, 353n.13	23:31-35	140n.29	**LITERATURE**	
43:25	717	36:22-33	84n.6		
44:3	88	36:25	188n.5	Tobit	
45:2-3	211, 213n.48	36:25-26	62, 355	2:5	65
48:21	272, 353n.13, 357	36:25-27	143, 615	6:3-6	676
50:4	480	47:1-12	211		
51:17	139n.29	47:12	353n.13	Judith	
51:21	139n.29			12:7	57
52:10–54:6	267-268	Daniel	326	14:10	77
53:7-8	172, 605	3	517		
55:1	321, 469	5:21	47	Wisdom	
55:3-5	267	7:9-10	91n.43	2:24	516
56:3-5	172n.21			7:27	106
59:20	558n.34	Hosea			
61:1	101, 105, 117	2:14-15	90	Sirach	
61:3	714			3:30	361
61:10	481n.20, 614, 692	Joel		24:7	106
63:3	196	2	175	34:30 (25)	57
65:20	494	2:13	274		
66:19	449	2:21-24	692-693	Daniel	
		2:28-29	688n.4, 688	13:15	326
Jeremiah	409n.34, 413	2:28-32 (Gk. 3:1-5)	167	13:17	326
2:12-13	211	2:32	169		
2:13	268			1 Maccabees	
4:3-4	272, 273, 274, 447	Micah		10:63	168n.6
4:4	369n.18, 486, 491	7:19	680		
13:1-11	515			**NEW TESTAMENT**	
14:9	188	Habakkuk			
18	665	2:16	140n.29	Matthew	102n.10, 105, 132-137, 182n.42, 656
25:15	139n.29				
25:27-29	139n.29	Zephaniah		1:11	514
27:2	85n.13	3:19	211	1:18	644
31:31	558n.34				

Index of Biblical Passages

1:20b-21	134n.8	7:22-23	386	18:10	412
2:8	136	8:4	137	18:20	342, 639
2:13	137	8:5-6	137n.17	19:13-15	138, 369
2:20	137	8:13	675	19:14	364-365, 369, 459,
3:1-12	90-91, 93	8:24	338n.10		568, 774
3:2	88n.30, 491	9:2	338	19:28	163, 409n.36, 412
3:3	87n.21	9:2-8	442	20:1-16	370, 601, 691n.30
3:7	88n.31	9:6	137	20:22	554
3:7-10	94-95	9:13	136	21:9	182n.42
3:7-12	85n.12, 88n.30	9:22	338	21:23-27	90
3:8	94n.54	9:35	137n.17	21:25	92, 337
3:8-10	127	10:7	136	21:32	102n.8
3:10-12	111n.54	10:15	814n.125	22:1-14	259, 498
3:11	88n.29, 92n.46, 94,	10:20	117	22:11-14	478
	99, 153n.17, 272-	10:32	208, 418	22:12	427, 657
	273, 337, 357, 406,	10:41	182n.43	22:20-21	283
	409n.36, 412, 422,	10:42	182n.43	22:30	415
	485, 591, 649, 673,	11:4	136	23:9-10	138
	691, 731, 746	11:11	92	23:25	139n.23
3:11-12	242	11:12-15	242	23:25-26	94, 95
3:12-17	745	11:15	480	24:5	182n.44
3:13	114, 427n.119	11:28-29	549	25:1-13	498, 584n.7, 751
3:13-14	172n.23	11:28-30	134n.8	25:34-35	589n.26
3:13-15	99n.2	12:18	102n.10, 103n.13	25:37	815
3:13-17	102-103, 853	12:28	102n.10	25:41	91n.43, 815
3:14-15	531, 642, 710	12:31-32	691n.30	26:23	139
3:15	109-110, 117, 287,	12:35	796	26:26-30	132n.1
	406, 503n.23, 653,	12:40	155n.26	26:28	92n.45, 110
	746	12:43-45	439	27:52	106, 226
3:16	88n.28, 95, 124,	13:30	91n.43	28:7	136
	559n.38	13:42	91n.43	28:16-20	132-138
3:16-17	107, 320	13:44	737, 742	28:18-20	138, 583-584
3:17	119n.46, 261, 313,	14:21	171n.17	28:19	13, 130, 134,
	514, 701	14:28-33	442		182n.43, 182-183,
3:21	83n.3	14:29-30	338		203, 207n.24, 235,
4:2	652n.18	14:29-32	759		256, 282, 304n.12,
4:23	137n.17	15	535n.4		307, 316, 326, 342-
5:3	589n.26	15:2	139n.23		343, 349, 352n.9,
5:3-10	134n.8	15:18-19	740		359n.49, 387, 412,
5:6	102n.8	16:19	347		414, 425, 450, 456,
5:10	102n.8, 589n.26	16:21-23	102		457, 502, 521-522,
5:20	798	17:5	103		527, 537, 541n.36,
5:21-22	602	17:11-13	242		568, 571, 585,
5:34	254	17:27	136		589n.26, 605, 624,
6:17	584	18:2-4	369		637, 642, 672, 674,
6:33	102n.8	18:3	138, 240, 310, 320,		682, 698, 751, 799,
7:6	788		494, 589n.26		853
7:16-18	796	18:5	182n.44	28:19-20	141, 251, 711

866 | INDEX OF BIBLICAL PASSAGES

Mark	138-141, 182n.42	10:38-39	139, 510	3:21-22	101-102, 688n.5
1:1-8	89-90	10:39	554n.20	3:22	119n.46, 120, 410
1:1-12	681	11:15-17	680-681, 682	3:23-38	307
1:4	85, 88n.29, 89n.32, 92, 93, 99, 105, 110, 558, 679, 796	11:19	182n.42	4:1	411
		11:27-33	90	4:1-2	691n.30
		11:30	92	4:2	120n.52
1:5	88n.29, 89n.32, 95, 100, 236	13:6	182n.44	4:16-21	101
		13:32-33	679n.22	4:18	195n.30
1:7	89n.35	14:8	718	4:40	174n.29
1:7-8	99n.1	14:20	139	6:20	589n.26
1:8	88n.29, 89n.36, 92n.46, 153n.17, 406	14:51-52	140	7:11-17	675
		16:5	140	7:20	83n.3, 91
		16:8	140n.32	7:28	92
1:9	95	16:9-20	140-141	7:29-30	92, 207, 645n.79
1:9-11	100-101	16:15-16	140, 469n.29	7:33	91
1:10	88n.28, 95	16:16	207n.24, 492, 571, 811, 813	7:36-50	514
1:13-31	682			7:38	509
1:15	429	16:17	182n.42	7:47	273
2:1-12	128n.84, 442	16:18	174n.29	7:48	509
5:13	600	16:19	141	8:31	402
6:5	174n.29			8:43-48	675
6:14	83	Luke	141-142, 164	8:49-55	675
6:24	83	1:33	106	9:19	91
6:25	83n.3	1:35	101, 644, 764	9:48	182n.44
7:2	757	1:41	737	9:49	182n.42
7:3	139n.24	1:59	182n.44	10:17	182n.42
7:4	138-139, 642	1:77	92n.45	10:19	121, 482, 759
7:5	757	2:11	809	10:49	122
7:29	675	2:21	691n.30	11:1	87n.23
7:32	174n.29	2:21-24	690n.25	11:38	141
7:34	636	2:22	120n.52, 367, 368	12:32-33	589n.26
8:23	174n.29	2:25-28	227n.18	12:49-52	141, 296
8:25	174n.29	3:1-4	422	12:50	140, 141, 278n.9, 279, 349, 360, 408n.33, 417, 418, 554, 660, 758
9:2-3	516	3:1-20	91-92		
9:37	182n.44	3:3	85n.11, 93, 105, 133, 168, 410		
9:38	182n.42				
9:39	182n.44	3:7-8	422	13:13	174n.29
9:41	182n.42	3:7-9	94-95	13:35	182n.42
9:49	711	3:7-17	85n.12	15	703
10	140	3:8	495	15:10	624
10:13-14	172n.23	3:14	86n.17	15:11ff.	624
10:13-16	138	3:15-16	407n.25, 409	15:22	348
10:15	589n.26	3:15-17	688n.6	16:9	475
10:32-34	141	3:16	88n.29, 92n.46, 99n.1, 153n.17, 166-167, 406, 409, 548	16:10-12	207-208
10:35-40	140			16:16	92, 242
10:38	110, 141, 278n.9, 279, 417, 418, 486, 554			16:24	141, 145
		3:16-17	88n.30	18:15-17	138
		3:21	175, 689	18:16	788n.96

Index of Biblical Passages | 867

19:10	746		521n.9, 530,	3:31	143
20:1-8	90		589n.26, 690	3:34	356
20:4	92	3:3-5	142-145, 241	3:36	144, 815
21:8	182n.44	3:3-6	691	4	162n.43
22:8	692n.34	3:3-7	511, 608	4:1-2	103, 143, 790, 853
22:10-11	692	3:4	240, 644	4:1-30	502
23:39-43	532, 793, 800, 802	3:5	4, 119, 124n.66, 162,	4:2	337, 406, 508n.52
23:43	360, 505		163, 184, 188, 217-	4:4-26	442
24:45-49	167		218, 226, 236, 240,	4:7-15	142
24:47	92n.45, 133, 168,		256-257, 261-262,	4:10	169, 502
	182n.44, 235		282, 307n.35, 310,	4:13	675
24:49	148n.5, 169n.12		320, 337, 339, 347,	4:14	442, 515
28:18	174n.29		349, 359n.50, 369,	5	502n.21, 534
			378, 392, 408, 411-	5:1-7	142
John	142-145, 164, 226,		414, 449, 459, 465,	5:2	549n.4, 658
	240		470, 484, 521, 528,	5:2-9	337, 442
1:5	561		542n.38, 543n.41,	5:2-16	128n.84
1:6-9	514		552n.15, 556, 571,	5:4	337, 637n.20, 641
1:9	711		577, 587, 588-589,	5:4-9	344
1:12	182n.43		612, 624, 645, 646,	5:14	658
1:12-13	143n.42, 144		652, 659, 659n.32,	5:43	182n.42
1:12-14a	690, 691		680, 690, 712, 729,	6:35	690n.25
1:13b	690		731n.34, 736,	6:53	273
1:14	193		780n.24, 793n.135,	6:63	143, 613
1:19-37	93		793n.144, 797-798,	7:23-24	690
1:23	745		800, 805, 809, 810,	7:24	691
1:24-27	406		814, 815, 854	7:37-38	492
1:25-31	242n.20	3:5-6	272, 273, 357,	7:37-39	353n.13
1:26	88n.29, 143, 425		359n.49, 658	7:38	354n.22, 469, 665
1:26-34	99n.1	3:5-8	142n.41	7:38-39	142n.37, 154n.22,
1:29	103, 106, 745, 809	3:6	469, 555n.25, 759		194, 413
1:29-34	687	3:6-12	143	7:39	306n.23, 691n.30
1:31	103, 144	3:7	521n.9	7:53	168n.8
1:31-34	116-117	3:8	143, 144	8:12	241n.11
1:32-33	687n.2, 688	3:10	501	8:41	143n.42
1:33	92n.46, 102n.12,	3:11	144	9	502n.21, 508
	103, 143, 144,	3:13	815	9:1-17	142
	153n.17, 406,	3:14	143	9:2	143n.42
	641n.48, 793	3:18	182n.43	9:6-7	691n.30, 692
1:34	103	3:22-23	103, 143	9:7	307, 515
1:36	745	3:23	88n.28, 93, 95, 488	9:19	143n.42
2:1-12	665	3:23–4:2	145	9:20	143n.42
2:6	756	3:25	93	9:32	143n.42
2:23	182n.43	3:25-26	143	9:34	143n.42
3	469	3:26	93, 103, 853	10:40	93
3:1-21	698	3:27-30	93	11:26	626n.23, 628, 692
3:3	240, 320, 411-412,	3:29	691n.30	11:45	426
		3:30	709	12:36	572

868 | INDEX OF BIBLICAL PASSAGES

12:42-43	143n.42	1:5	91n.44, 153n.17, 166,	3:15	476
13	270n.10, 639, 656		177, 184, 491n.8,	3:26	168
13:1-20	514		652n.19	4:7	182n.42
13:3-15	492	1:8	169, 171	4:10	182n.42
13:4-5	759	1:14	167	4:12	167n.3, 642
13:5	305n.20	1:21-22	89n.37	4:17	182n.44
13:5-10	142	1:22	100, 174n.28, 184	4:18	182n.44
13:8	405, 691n.30	2	175, 177, 183n.48,	4:27	195n.30, 344
13:10	336n.5, 338, 405,		184, 345n.37, 347,	5:14	170n.15, 185n.51
	674, 682, 790		479, 551n.12, 790	5:28	182n.44
13:26	141n.36, 145	2:1-2	170	5:31	92n.45, 168n.5
14:13	182n.42	2:1-4	167, 177	5:32	169, 184
14:14	182n.42	2:1-5	169, 177	5:40	182n.44
14:17	195	2:1-13	117	6:1-6	170
14:26	182n.42, 195	2:1-45	92	8	179, 181, 183n.48,
15:3	162n.43, 505,	2:2	485, 652n.19		387, 532, 800
	508n.52	2:2-4	91	8:4-20	13
16:7	117	2:3	752	8:4-25	170-172
16:21	143n.42	2:3-4	112n.56, 559	8:12	185
16:23	182n.42	2:4	184	8:12-16	408
16:26	182n.42	2:6	184	8:13	171
17:11	182n.42	2:14-36	170	8:13-19	411
17:12	182n.42	2:16	92	8:13-24	485
17:18-19	689nn.15-16	2:17	169, 859	8:14	171, 177n.35
18:37	143n.42	2:17-18	154n.21, 177	8:14-18	760
19:11	143	2:21	167, 169, 175	8:15	169
19:30	194	2:23	765	8:15-17	171n.19
19:34	142, 143n.43, 194,	2:32-33	859	8:15-18	92
	349, 486, 502, 505,	2:33	154n.21, 169	8:16	182n.43, 184
	517, 714, 757, 762,	2:36	167, 169	8:17	169, 457, 761
	774, 792	2:36-38	765	8:17-18	184, 187
19:35	194	2:37-38	476, 550n.7	8:18	427, 480
20:17	691n.27	2:37-41	170, 762	8:18-19	171
20:21-22	358	2:38	85, 92n.45, 94, 133,	8:19	169
20:21-23	133, 391		150, 168-170, 171,	8:20	169
20:22	125, 169n.11, 691		175, 176, 182n.44,	8:26-39	698
20:22-23	145, 410		183, 184, 185,	8:26-40	172-173, 584n.6,
20:23	463		214n.50, 275,		605
20:31	182n.42		305n.20, 347, 353,	8:27-39	515n.90
21:11	515		464, 587, 759, 791,	8:36	172
21:15-17	692		854	8:37	158, 172, 175
		2:38-39	167-170	8:38-39	173, 213n.47, 218
Acts	8, 142, 150, 233,	2:39	147	8:39	229
	624, 642, 680	2:40	190n.11	9	183n.48
1-2	166-170	2:41	169	9:1-19	173-174, 175
1:3	120n.52	2:41-47	170	9:6	339
1:4	169n.12, 185n.51	2:47	170n.15	9:10-12	560n.44
1:4-5	166, 623n.15	3:6	182n.42	9:12	184

Index of Biblical Passages | 869

9:14	167n.3	16	92, 179, 545n.51	5:14	666, 741
9:17-18	174, 184	16:12-15	179	5:19	667
9:18	185, 339	16:15	178	5:21	667
9:21	167n.3	16:16-34	179-180	6	4, 149, 348, 552n.15
9:26-27	545n.55, 545n.57	16:30	550n.7	6:1	421
9:28	182n.42	16:30-34	179	6:1-11	155-158, 791-792, 808
10–11	173	16:31	178, 550n.7		
10	135, 183n.48, 303, 387, 388, 559n.37, 562n.48, 610n.28, 800	16:40	179	6:1-13	552n.14
		17:11-12	180	6:3	411, 425, 554, 571, 585, 808
		18:8	178, 180, 185		
		18:24-26	92	6:3-4	19, 156, 159, 287, 402, 408, 412, 414, 415, 426, 482, 497, 528, 552, 553n.16, 560n.44, 587, 667n.17, 757, 854
10:1-48	176	18:24–19:7	180-182		
10:1–11:18	175-178	18:25	181, 182n.40		
10:14	177	19	183n.48, 796		
10:23	185	19:1-3	87n.23		
10:36-42	176	19:1-7	13, 92, 389		
10:37	89n.37, 100	19:2-3	89n.36, 184	6:3-5	282, 530, 715, 762
10:38	101, 103, 176, 195n.30	19:2-4	676	6:3-11	587
		19:2-5	407	6:3-14	482
10:43	92n.45, 168n.5, 177, 305	19:2-6	743n.79, 761	6:4	157, 348, 409n.36, 412, 482, 551, 614, 638, 658, 659, 673n.9, 743
		19:3	491n.8		
10:44	411	19:3-5	406		
10:44-46	169	19:4	85n.11, 89n.35, 92, 181		
10:44-48	92, 176-177			6:4-5	589
10:45	185	19:5	181, 182n.43	6:4-6	643
10:46	184	19:6	181, 184, 187	6:4-11	588
10:47	169, 172n.23, 177, 184	21:5	185n.51	6:5	482, 546n.59, 552n.15, 553, 570
		21:8	173n.25		
10:48	182n.42, 185	22:3-21	174-175	6:5-6	157, 368
11:1-18	177	22:12-16	174-175	6:6	554, 588
11:4-17	176	22:13	174	6:8	157
11:12	185	22:14-15	174n.28, 175	6:8-10	422
11:14	176, 177	22:16	89n.34, 135, 150, 175, 183, 741	6:9-10	157
11:15	177			6:10	424, 587
11:15-16	166	26:16-18	174n.28	6:11	157
11:16	91n.44, 153n.17, 177, 184	26:18	92n.45	7:13	509
		26:20	227	7:24-25	667
11:17	169, 177			8:2	509
11:18	177	**Romans**	155-158	8:9-10	691
11:24	170n.15	1:3-4	691n.30	8:14	411, 424
13:24	85n.11, 89n.37, 92, 93	1:7	511	8:15	712
		2:25-29	690	8:23	528, 530, 712
13:33	120n.52, 644	2:28-29	159	8:29	120, 610
13:38	92n.45	3:21–5:21	155	9:9	542n.38, 555n.25
14:1	180	5	667	9:17-29	449
15:7-11	176	5:10	510n.63	10:8-10	162n.43
15:20	258	5:12	667	10:9-10	158, 783
15:29	258	5:12-17	811	10:10	425, 537, 803

10:14-15	783n.56	10:7-10	151	3:14	169n.12
11:1-5	449	10:11	151	3:22	147
11:17	478	11:3	568	3:23-28	314
11:24	478	12	169	3:26	147
11:27	558n.34	12:3	153n.18	3:26-27	160, 184, 320
11:35-36	815	12:9	153n.18	3:26-29	147-148
13:11	158	12:12-13	152, 161	3:27	154, 156n.27, 481, 544, 561, 562, 585, 599, 657, 659, 677, 711, 715, 743, 759, 854
		12:13	146, 147, 152-154, 156, 158, 184, 314, 320, 470		
1 Corinthians	149-155, 185				
1	152				
1:2	167n.3	14:16	153n.18		
1:12-17	149	14:18-19	420n.83	3:27-28	161, 587, 673
1:13	153, 182n.43	14:20	308	3:28	153, 158, 538
1:13-17	13	14:35	343	4:1-7	147
1:14	180, 320	15	349	4:5	712
1:15	182n.43	15:10	303	4:6	147, 184
1:16	178	15:12	157n.29	4:19	421
1:17	340	15:29	154-155, 277, 280, 299, 319, 349, 543n.41, 551n.11, 552n.15	6:17	283
1:18-24	149				
2:6-7	546n.58, 551n.9			**Ephesians**	161-162
3:1-3	315			1:5	570, 712
3:6	676	15:32	231n.36	1:6	539n.22
3:7	676	15:45	497	1:13	159n.36, 162, 189, 208n.31, 486, 854
3:13	591	15:49	306		
4:8	157n.29	15:55	121, 482	1:14	557n.33, 711
4:9	486	15:58	464	1:18	570
5:1ff.	624			2:4-6	161
5:4	182n.42	**2 Corinthians**	149, 155	2:6	743
6:9-10	347	1:21	8, 159n.36, 195n.30	2:10	557
6:9-11	149-150, 273, 309, 319, 358, 558	1:21-22	155, 560, 640	2:11-22	161
		1:22	208n.31, 475, 854	2:15	402
6:11	153n.18, 182n.42, 304, 321	2:15	480, 636n.14	2:16	557n.33
		3:18	480	3:7	169
7:12-16	150-151	4:4	572	3:10	247
7:14	459, 812, 815	4:10	424	3:14-17	448, 743
10	189n.9	5:14-15	585	4:1-2	550n.7
10:1	490	5:17	553, 561	4:3	161
10:1-2	62n.15, 128n.77, 149, 359, 500, 614, 641, 653, 696	5:18	560n.41	4:4-6	153, 161, 385, 531, 673
		7:1	570, 741		
				4:4-7	557
10:1-3	151-152	**Galatians**	147-148	4:5	280, 336n.5, 349, 385, 585, 586n.14, 668, 675, 679n.23, 692, 765, 796
10:1-4	402, 853	2:16	147		
10:1-6	160	2:20	424		
10:2	403, 460, 586, 596, 689	2:21	739		
		3:2	169n.11	4:7	169
10:3-4	470	3:6-9	147	4:8	410
10:4	114, 337	3:7	147	4:22	414
10:6	151, 359	3:11	147	4:24	402, 414

Index of Biblical Passages | 871

4:30	159n.36, 162, 208n.31, 496	2:12	497, 552n.15, 638, 673	2:11	163
5	534	2:12-13	161	2:11–3:7	698
5:8	312	2:12-15	552n.14	3:4-7	162-163
5:14	316	2:13-14	347	3:5	184, 163, 247, 275, 306, 307, 321, 326, 335, 347, 353, 402, 407, 409n.36, 412, 414, 426, 446, 447, 449, 462, 463, 465, 483, 484n.27, 521n.9, 535, 555, 556, 570, 571, 581, 587, 598, 608, 613, 659, 709, 712, 743, 778, 793n.135, 793n.137, 811n.97
5:20	182n.42	2:13-15	541n.35		
5:25-27	162n.43, 778, 791n.119, 854	2:14	550, 751		
		2:15	158, 477		
5:26	5, 13, 109n.48, 150, 161-162, 162n.43, 163, 353, 463, 483, 541n.36, 614, 804n.65	2:16	159		
		2:17	159		
		2:18-23	383		
		2:20–3:17	160		
		3:1	161		
5:26-27	326n.6, 805n.65	3:1-4	552n.14		
6:4	568	3:2-4	549n.4, 554n.19		
6:10-17	209n.35	3:3	553	3:5-6	154n.21
6:11	480	3:9	477, 712		
6:12	415	3:9-10	124n.67, 414, 513, 561	**Hebrews**	186-188, 196
6:14	480			1:5	120n.52
6:14-17	316	3:10	552	1:6	120
6:16	600	3:11	147, 153	1:9	195n.30
				2:10	610
Philippians		**1 Thessalonians**		2:12	689
2:10	182n.42, 538	1:3	210n.37	3:14	480
2:10-11	523	1:10	493n.14	4:2	773n.14
2:15	613	2:12	161	4:12	490
3:3	159	3:13	511	5:5	120n.52
3:18-21	554n.20	5:8	210n.37	6:1-2	186-187
3:21	409n.36, 412	5:18	565	6:2	642
				6:1-6	13
Colossians	158-160	**2 Thessalonians**		6:4	169, 241, 854
1:1-2	511	2:13	511	6:4-6	187, 216, 560
1:13	854	2:14	161	6:10	182n.43
1:14	92n.45	3:6	182n.42	6:14	470
1:15	120, 610			9:10	186
1:18	120, 610, 644	**1 Timothy**		9:13	691
2	538n.19	2:4	471	9:13-14	192n.24, 267
2:8	158	2:12	301	9:14	187
2:8-15	673	3:4	164	9:19	482
2:9-10	158	6:12	729	9:24	191
2:9-12	417			10:2	188
2:11	306, 405, 446, 501, 559, 560n.40, 589, 642n.55	**2 Timothy**		10:10-12	188
		2:18	157n.29	10:19-20	188
		2:22	167n.3	10:21	188
2:11-12	486, 577, 587, 671	**Titus**	162-164	10:22	109n.48, 405
2:11-13	159	1:6	164	10:22-23	158, 188
2:11-14	158n.34	2:2	210n.37	10:24	188

10:26-27	216	2:24	191, 463, 586	2:29	195n.31
10:32	187n.3, 560	3:4	190n.14	3:8	812
11:7	244n.26	3:15	189, 192	3:9	195, 321
11:9	463	3:16	192	3:11	195
13:20	710	3:18-22	189-193	4:1-6	195
		3:20-21	13, 62n.13, 158n.34, 244n.25, 390, 404	4:2-3	193
James	188-189			4:2	195, 424
1:18	188-189	3:20-22	853	4:6	195
1:21	189, 773n.14	3:21	189-193, 282, 342n.27, 405, 469, 597, 854	4:7	195
2:7	7, 182n.44, 188			4:15	158
2:13	739			5:1	195
5:10	182n.42	4:2	193	5:4	195
5:14	182n.42	4:4	190n.14	5:5-8	193
		4:14	182n.42	5:5-13	698
1 Peter	151n.11, 164, 186, 189-193, 196	4:16	182n.42	5:6	349
		5:8-11	477	5:6-7	143n.43
1:2	188n.6, 193			5:7	645
1:3	163, 192-193, 240, 244n.25, 247, 608	**2 Peter**		5:8	8, 194, 321, 409n.33, 645n.78, 763
		1:4	689, 690		
1:5	191, 193	1:17	103n.13	5:13	182n.43
1:7	193	2:5	190n.11	5:18	195
1:9	191, 193	3:18	463		
1:13	192			**2 John**	
1:18	191	**1 John**	143n.42, 193-195	7	193
1:18-19	193	1:1-4	195		
1:21	192, 193, 244n.25	1:5	195	**Revelation**	142, 196
1:22	193	1:5-7	241n.11	1:5	307
1:23	124n.66, 163, 188, 193, 240, 247, 320, 412, 465, 608, 743, 773n.14	1:7	194	1:6	680
		2:2	194	3:2	196n.32
		2:7	195	7:3	196n.32
		2:9	195	9:4	218n.68
1:25	193	2:12	195	12	447-448
2:1	191n.20	2:16	772	12:1	447
2:1-3	193	2:19	194	14:1	196n.32, 355n.26
2:2	191, 412	2:20-24	195	19:13	141n.36, 196
2:8	190n.14	2:20-28	479	20:13	168n.8
2:9	567, 680	2:22-23	193	22:1-2	353n.13
2:19	192	2:24	8, 195	22:4	196n.32
2:22	410	2:27	8, 195		

Index of Greek and Roman Authors and Writings

Achilles Tatius
Leucippe and Clitophon
1.3.3	54
2.11.4-5, 8	44
2.14.4	50
2.31.2	54
3.10.1	54
3.1.3, 5	50
3.21.4	50
4.10.1	54
4.18.6	50
6.19.5	54
7.2.1	54

Aelius Aristides
Orations
3.8	48n.36
39	26n.7
48.71, 74-76, 80	26

Aelius Gellius
Attic Nights
5.14.5-30	231

Aeschylus
Agamemnon
612	42

Libation Bearers
1011	43

Prometheus
863	39

Aesop
Fable 75 (= 363 = 324 = 305 = 73)
Dolphin and the Ape version 1, ll. 14-15   48

Fable 122 (= 77 = 34 = 120)
Gardener and His Dog version 1, l. 3   48

Fable 223 (= 275 = 311 = 207)
Shepherd and the Sea version 3, l. 5   48

Alexander of Aphrodisias
Problems
1.16, 17, 28, 38	55
2.38	55

Antiphanes
25	40n.7

Apollonius Rhodius
Argonautica
4.156ff	45

Apuleius
Metamorphoses (or *Golden Ass*)
11.16, 21, 23-24	**31-32**

Aratus
Phaenomena
858	41

873

874 | INDEX OF GREEK AND ROMAN AUTHORS AND WRITINGS

951	40-41

Aristophanes   41
The Acharnians
| 1.112 | 43 |

Birds
| 287 | 43 |

Clouds
| 150 | 39 |

Ecclesiazusae
| 216 | 43 |

Knights
| 523 | 43 |

Lysistrata
| 51 | **43n.18** |

Peace
| 959-960 | 39 |
| 1176 | 43 |

Plutus
| 530 | 43n.18 |
| 656-657 | **26n.6** |

Aristophon
Philinides
| 11, 472d | 54 |

Aristotle
History of Animals
5.15, 547a	44
7 [8].2, 592a.18	40
7 [8].26, 605a.29	40

On Marvellous Things Heard
| 136.844a | 48-49 |

Mechanical Problems
| 28, 357a | 40 |

On the Soul
| 3.12, 435a.2 | 40 |

Politics
| 7.14, 1334a | 42 |

Arrian
Discourses of Epictetus
| 2.9.19-21 | 42, **78-79** |

3.21.14, 16	29

Athenaeus
Learned Banquet
4 (11), 133d	51
5, 221a	54
7, 307f fragment 68	54
9, 385d	42
9, 409b	51
9, 472d?	54
11, 472d	54
11, 480e	45
14, 645c	42

Augustan History,
Alexander Severus   35n.54

Babrius
| 71.2 | **39n.4** |

Celsus
De Medicina
| 1.4.3 | **35-36** |

Chariton of Aphrodisias
Chaereas and Callirhoë
2.4.4	55
3.2.6	54-55
3.4.6	54

Corpus Hermeticum
| 4.4 | **55-56** |
| 4.6 | **55-56** |

Demosthenes
Aristogeiton
| 1.41, 782 | 48 |

Dio Cassius
Roman History
37.58.3	51
38.27.2	**51n.39**
41.42.5	51
50.18	51
50.32.6 & 8	51n.38
50.35.3	51
74.13.3	**51n.39**

Index of Greek and Roman Authors and Writings

Diodorus Siculus
Library
1.36.9	49
1.73.6	53
5.30.1	44
16.80	49

Diogenes Laertius
Lives of Philosophers
8.33	28

Dionysius of Halicarnassus
Roman Antiquities
5.15.2	41

Dioscorides
Medical Matters
5.121	41

Epictetus   50, 78

Eubulus
Nausikla   54

Eupolis
Baptae   34, 48

Fragment 363, 434   43

Euripides
Hecuba
610	39

Hippolytus
123	39

Ion
94-97	**26n.9**

Orestes
707	39

Phoenician Maidens
1578	39

Galen
De alimentorum facultatibus
6, 538, 1	41-42
6, 539, 2	42n.12
6, 636, 2	42n.12
6, 716, 14	42n.12

De compositione medicamentorum
12, 407, 16	42
12, 437, 7	44
12, 502, 8	44n.26
12, 588, 14	50
12, 603, 11	42
12, 603, 15	**42n.15**
12, 622, 14	42n.15
12, 645, 10	**42n.15**, 50
12, 694, 10	42n.13
12, 809, 2	**42n.15**
12, 813, 13	41
12, 814, 1-2	42
12, 817, 6	**42n.15**
12, 863, 3	**42n.12**
12, 875, 4	**42n.12**
12, 906, 10	**44n.26**
12, 958, 15	42n.14
12, 991, 14; 999, 5	**42n.12**
13, 357, 4	42n.12
13, 733, 4	42
13, 858, 1	42n.14
13, 987, 17	**44n.26**

De marcore
7, 698, 2	42n.12

De methodo medendi
10, 447, 1, 10-11	50
10, 717, 7-11	41n.10
10, 718, 16	41
10, 722, 6	**41n.11**
10, 722, 15	**41n.11**

De sanitate tuenda
6, 51, 15	41

De venae sectione
11, 215, 1	42n.12

In Hippocratis
15, 890, 11	**42n.12**
16, 581, 3	**44n.26**
17b, 271, 13	44n.26

Greek Anthology
14.71	**26-27**
14.74	**27n.10**
16.388, line 4	**53n.44**

Antipater of Sidon
6.206, 4 **45n.31**

Archias
6.192, line 5 **53n.44**

Crinagoras
6.229, 2 45n.31

Evenus
11.49 53

Leonidas of Tarentum
Epigram
9.326 45

Leo the philosopher
9.214, 2 **46n.32**

Lucian
11.408 45n.31

Lucillius
Epigram
11.42, line 3 45-46
11.67, 4 45n.31
11.68 45
11.398, 1 & 3 45n.31

Heliodorus
Ethiopian Story
1.39.3 51
2.3.4 55
4.17.3; 20.1 55
5.16.2 55
5.27.5 51

Hermeneumata 35

Herodotus
Histories
2.47 25, 55
2.64 25
7.67 43

Hippocrates 39
De affectionibus interioribus
7, 13-14 39
9, 23 40n.6
28, 34 39
30, 27 39
52, 12 40

De capitis vulneribus
21, 14 & 19 40n.6

De diaeta acutorum
20, 9 42n.12
79, 9 40n.6

Epistulae
17, line 243 48

De humidorum usu
5, 5 40n.6

De moribus popularibus
2, 14, 17 40
2, 22, 5 39
2, 26, 18 39
2, 26, 30 40n.6
2, 31, 4 40n.6
2, 43, 9 39
2, 54, 26 39
5, 63, 5 48

De mulierum affectionibus
39, 23 39
74, 49-51 39
122, 4 44

Homer/Pseudo-Homer
The Battle of the Frogs and Mice
v.220 45

Hymn to Demeter
98-107 30n.23

Iliad
18.329 45

Odyssey
9.392 39, 42

Horace
Epode
17.56-57 **34n.44**

Iamblichus
Life of Pythagoras
18 **40n.7**

Inscriptions
Corpus Inscriptionum Latinarum
6.510 33

Inscriptiones Graecae
IV.1 #126   26n.7

Inscription of Maximus   **27**

Sylloge Inscriptionum Graecarum
III 982   25-26
III 983, 1042   26
At Thebes   34

Juvenal
Satires
2.91-92   **34n.44**
6.522-525   **31**
14.104   79

Livy
History of Rome
39.9.4   30

Lucian of Samosata
Dionysus
7   54

Fisherman
6   45n.27

Hall
11   45n.27

The Ignorant Book-Collector
27   34n.43

Lexiphanes
5   41

Timon
44   **50**

Trials by Jury
8   45n.27

True Story
1.17   45
2.4   50

Marcus Aurelius
Meditations
3.4.3   45
5.16.1   45
6.30.1   45
8.51.1   45

Menander
Anger
fragment 303.4 [363.4]   44

Epitrepontes (The Arbitrants)
III, 861   49

Orpheus
Argonautica
512   27n.11, 51
1230-1233   29

Ovid
Fasti
2.35-38   28
2.45-46   26, 28

Metamorphoses
1.84-86   445n.5

Papyri Graecae Magicae (PGM)   56n.51
IV. 43-45   27
V.66-68   56
VII.441-442   56

Papyrus Paris 47   **53**

Pausanias
Descriptions of Greece
1.38.6   30n.23
4.33.4   30n.23
5.13.3   26n.6
9.20.4   30

Pindar
Pythian Odes
2.80   48

Plato
Euthydemus
7, 277D   53

Laws
8, 847C   **44n.20**

Republic
1.17, 344d   34-35
4.429D-E   **43-44**

Symposium
176B   53

Timaeus
73e   40

Pliny the Younger
Epistles (Letters)
2.17.11   49
5.6.25   49-50
9.36   **35n.54**

Plotinus
Enneads
1.4.9   55
1.6.7   **330n.27**
1.8.13   55
6.9.8   55

Plutarch   51-53
Moralia
  Advice about Keeping Well
  25 (= 136A)   43
  Beasts Are Rational
  7 (= 990E)   51
  Causes of Natural Phenomena
  10 (= 9114D)   52
  Cleverness of Animals
  23 (= 975C)   53
  35 (= 983C)   52
  Education of Children
  13 (= 9B)   **52**
  Is Fire or Water More Useful?
  9 (= 957D)   204n.15
  Greek and Roman Parallel Stories
  3 (= 306C)   52
  Obsolescence of Oracles
  41 (= 433A)   43n.16
  On the Control of Anger
  10 (= 458E)   41
  Precepts of Statecraft
  27 (= 820C)   **51n.42**
  Principle of Cold
  2, 20 (= 946C, 954C)   43

  Sayings of Kings and Commanders
  23 (= 178F)   44
  Sign of Socrates
  24 (= 593f)   53
  Summary of Comparison between Aristophanes and Menander
  1 (= 853B)   53
  Superstition
  3 (= 166A)   27
  Table Talk
  3.8.2 (= 656d)   53
  6 intro (= 686b)   53
  6.2 (= 688F)   44n.24
  8.5 (= 725C)   44
Parallel Lives
  Agesilaus
  30.3 (= 612d)   **44n.24**
  Alexander
  67.2 (= 702C)   52
  Artaxerxes
  22 (= 1022B)   41
  Caesar
  49.4 (= 731)   **52**
  Galba
  21.2 (= 1062C)   53
  Marcellus
  15.2 (= 306)   51
  Philopoemen
  9.3 (= 360F)   44n.24
  Phocion
  28.3 (= 754C)   29n.22, 44n.24
  Sulla
  21.4 (= 466)   52
  Theseus
  24.5 (= 11)   52

Polyaenus
Stratagems
4.2.6   50-51

Index of Greek and Roman Authors and Writings | 879

Polybius
History
1.51.6-7	49
3.72.4	49
5.47.2	49
8.6(8).4	49
16.6.2	49
34.3	49
34.7	49

Porphyry
Against the Christians **444**

Soranus
Gynaeciorum
4.11.5	**50**

Sophocles
Ajax
95	39
651	42

Women of Trachis
574	43
580	43

Statius
Achilleid
1.134	36
1.269.270	36-37

Stobaeus
Gnomologium
47 (82)	50n.37

Strabo
Geography
1.2.16	49
4.4.5	**44n.23**
5.4	49
6.2.9	49
12.2.4	49
13.4.14	44
14.3.9	49
15.1.30	44
15.1.58	**44n.23**
16.2.42	49
16.4.10	41

Theocritus
Idyl
5.127	40

Theophrastus
Characters
9.8	40
16.2,13	28

De causis plantarum
1.22.5	42

Enquiry into Plants
3.7.4	40
3.8.6	44
3.13.6	29n.19
3.14.3	44
3.18.5	44
4.6.5	**44n.21**
4.6.8	**44n.21**

On Stones
42	40

Tibullus
Poems
1.3.25	32n.32

Vergil
Aeneid
2.717-720	26
9.815-818	26n.4

Georgics
3.45	119n.44

Index of Jewish Authors and Writings

MISHNAH
63-65, 204n.14

Zeraim
Berakoth
3.5   63n.17

Shebi'ith
10.9   79n.104

Mo'ed
Shabbath
9.3   81n.125
18.3-19.6   81n.125

Pesahim
8.8   76n.90, 77n.94

Yoma
3.3-4   63n.19

Hagigah
2.6   63n.18, 69n.52

Nezikin
'Eduyyoth ('Eduyyot)
5.2   77, 77n.95

Qodashim
Hullin
10.4   79n.104

Kerithoth
2.1   78

Tohoroth   63
Nega'im
14.10   63n.17

Parah
8.8-11   64n.21
8.10   89
12.11   63n.17

Mikw(v)aoth   63-65, 438n.31
2.2   64
5   64n.21
6.1-2, 5-6   139n.22
6.7-9   64
7.7   139n.22
8.5   64
8.5-9.7   81n.122
9.1-4   64n.23
10.1, 5   139n.22

TOSEFTA

t. Shabbath
15.9   76n.90

t. Pesahim
7.13 (167)   77n.94

t. 'Abodah Zara
3.12   76n.90

Index of Jewish Authors and Writings | 881

t. Yadayim
2.20   72n.74

BABYLONIAN TALMUD
79n.105

b. Berakoth
22a   64n.26, 72n.74, 205n.19
52a   72n.74

b. Shabbath
145b-146a   79n.108

b. Pesahim
92a   77n.94

b. Yebamoth
22a, 23a   79
40b   81n.123
46a   79, **80**
46a-b   80
46b-47b   81n.121
47a   80n.115, **86n.18**
47a-b   78n.97, 81n.119, 81n.123
47b   79n.109
62a   79n.105
71a   80n.116, 80n.118
78a   81n.126
97b   81n.124

b. Kethuboth
11a   **81n.128**

b. ʿAbodah Zara
59a   80n.118

b. Kerithoth
8b   78n.98
8b-9a   76n.89
9a   76n.90

b. ʿErubin
4b   64n.23
14b   64n.24

b. Baba Qamma
82a-b   81n.122

JERUSALEM TALMUD

y. Berakoth
3.6c   72n.74

y. Pesahim
8.36b   77n.94

y. Qiddushin
3.13 (64d)   80n.118

y. Bikkurim
3.3   80n.112

OTHER RABBINIC LITERATURE

Gerim
1.1   78n.97, 79n.110, 81n.120
1.1-4   81n.123
2.5   78n.98, 80n.112

Mekhilta
on Ex. 13–14   152n.13

Pesiqta
40b   63n.18

Sifre Numbers
108   76n.90

Midrash Rabbah to Ecclesiastes
1.8.4   80

DEAD SEA SCROLLS
68-71, 93-94

Community Rule   70n.54
1QS
ii.4-10   69n.50
ii.25-iii.4   69n.50
ii.25-iii.9, vv. 7-15   70n.54
iii.4-9   435n.23
iii.4-9, 13   **68-69**
iv.19-22   87
iv.21-22   69
v.8-11   69
viii.13-14   87

Damascus Document
CD
x.10-14 **71**
xi.21 71n.64
xi.1-2 71n.65

4Q271
fr. 2 70

Halakic Letter
4QMMT (4Q395) 70
B55-58 70

Ordinances c
4Q514 70n.55
1.i.5-7 69n.50

Purification Rules
4Q274
i.1-9 70
ii.1.1-9 70n.61

Temple Scroll
11Q19
xlv.7-15 70
xlix.16-21 70n.56
xlix-li 69n.49

4Q265
vii.3.8-9 70n.61
fr. 7, ii 70n.63

4Q284, 5 **69n.49**

4Q397 70n.60

4Q414
xiii.1-10 70n.61

JOSEPHUS
70n.54, 72, 77, 87, 93-94, 175

Against Apion
2.23.198 66n.35
2.24.203 66n.35

Antiquities
3.102 (36.1) 47
3.263 (3.11.4) 66
4.81 (4.4.6) 47, 58, 61n.8
9.212 (9.10.2) 58
10.169 (10.9.4) 59
15.55 (3.3) 58
18.19 (1.5) 86n.15
18.116-117 (5.2) 58, **84-85**, 87n.20
20.34-53 (2.3-5) 77n.92

Jewish War
1.437 (1.22.2) 58
1.490 (24.7) 47
1.535 (1.27.1) 59
2.129 (8.5) 68n.46
2.138 (8.7) 68, 87n.20
2.149 (8.9) 68n.46
2.150 (8.10) 68n.46
2.161 (8.13) 68n.46
2.476 (18.4) 59
2.556 (20.1) 58
3.196 (3.7.15) 59
3.368 (3.8.5) 58
3.423 (9.3) 58
3.525 (10.9) 58
3.527 (10.9) 58
4.137 (3.3) 59
4.563 (9.10) 47

Life
3.15 58
11 [2] 68, 204n.16

PHILO
57, 60, 76-77

Allegorical Laws
3.[6].18 57

Cherubim
[28] 95 **28**

Contemplative Life
5.46 57

Life of Moses
2.143 [28.157] **65n.30**

Migration of Abraham
37.204 57

On Providence
67 58

On Special Laws
1.24.119 65n.32

1.48.257-258 66n.33
1.48.261–1.49.263 66
3.10.63 66n.33

Questions and Answers on Genesis
4.5 66

The Unchangeablemess of God
7 28n.18
[2] 8 **28**
9 28n.18

The Worse Attacks the Better
48.176 57-58

TRANSLATORS

Aquila 57

Symmachus 57

Theodotion 47, 326

PSEUDEPIGRAPHA

4 Baruch
 221
6.25 221

Joseph and Aseneth
14.12, 15 (17) 77
18.8-9 77n.93

Jubilees
21.16 **66**

Life of Adam and Eve
(Apocalypse of Moses)
6-7 (29.11-13) 67
37.3 **67**, 225n.13

Sibylline Oracles
1.332 108
1.339-341 67
1.341-343 67n.42
3.591-593 66
4 67, 85
4.162-170 **67**
5.478 **66n.39**

Testaments of the Twelve Patriarchs
Testament of Levi
2.3 B 1-2 65
8.5 **65n.30**
9.11 65

Index of Non-Canonical Christian Authors and Writings

Boldface indicates significant quotations or the treatment in detail of an author or work.

Acts and Martyrdom of Matthew	
8	234-235
26	235, 433n.16

Acts of Andrew	232-234

Acts of Andrew and Matthias	
32	**233**

Liber de virtutibus sancti Andreae apostoli	
4	233
10	233
22	233

Passion of Andrew	
10	233
11	233

Acts of Barnabas	235
1	235
13	235
17	235
26	235

Acts of John	232
57	232
84	**232**

Acts of Justin and His Companions	
4	239n.6, 363

Acts of Paul	229-232, 436
6	229
25	229
34	**230**, 436
40	230
Hamburg Papyrus	299n.29
P 1	231
P 4-5	**231**
Episode 10, p7	299n.29
Coptic papyrus	**231-232**

Martyrdom of the Holy Apostle Paul	
5	232

Acts of Paul and Thecla (Acts of Thecla)	229

Acts of Peter	228-229, 232
5	**228**

Acts of Pilate	106-107

Acts of Philip	178n.38, 234, 235
29.24 = II.24	**234n.53**
36.7 = III.19	234
44.8 = IV.6	**234n.53**
58, 63	178n.38
63.19 = V.25	234

884

Index of Non-Canonical Christian Authors and Writings | 885

86.23 = VI.22	**234n.51**
117.3 = Martyrdom 11	234
134.28 = Martyrdom 28	234
140 = Martyrdom 34	234
144 = Martyrdom 38	234
147 = Martyrdom 41	234n.51

Acts of Thaddaeus

1	235
4	235
7	236

Acts of Thomas

	9, 221, 429-435, 436, 480n.16, 512n.79
12	288n.40
17	434
25-26	430
27	430-431, 434
28	429
29	431
47	431
49	431, 434
49-50	431-432
55	433
58	429n.5
120-121	430n.7, 432
121	**432**, 433-434
124	288n.40
131	432-433, 434
132	430n.7, **433**, 433-434
133	433
152	434
156	434
157	430n.7, 432
158	434

Acts of Xanthippe and Polyxena 435-436

13-14	**435-436**
21	**436**

Adelphius of Edessa 725n.2, 727, 728n.17

Ambrose 7, 14, 602, 627, 634-647, 648, 651, 656, 664, 671n.1, 776, 778-779, 784, 813n.119, 820, 837

Explanation of the Symbol 636

1	636
9	636
11	636

Exposition of the Gospel according to Luke

2.83	114n.7, 643
2.91	114n.9
4.51	641
4.76	635n.3, 635n.6
6.2, 3	645n.79, 645n.81
7.221	635n.3
10.48	645n.78, 646

Hexaemeron

1.4.14	**636n.17**

Letters

20.4	636
41.14-15	640n.40
44	**646n.91**
63.63	645n.79
70.24	**641n.44**
72 (16).18	642
147.52	776

On Abraham 635

1.4.25	635
1.7.59	635
1.9.89	635
2.11.81, 84	**646, 646n.91**

On the Death of Valentinian

51	**646**

On the Duties of the Clergy

1.33.170	646
1.50.257	645n.79
3.18.102-108	641n.48, 646n.88

On Elijah and Fasting

21.79	**635**
22.83	635
22.84	645

On Faith

1.4.31	642n.56
5.9.115	642n.56

On the Holy Spirit

1.6.76	**645**
1.6.77	645n.78
1.6.79	640n.36
1.6.80	644n.71
1.7.88	637n.20
1.13.132	642n.56

2.10.105	639n.28, 643n.69	2.1.2	642
On the Mysteries	634, 641, 644	2.2.3-5	641
1.1	635, 644	2.2.6, 7	646
1.2	635n.2	2.3.8	641n.46
1.3	636	2.3.9	641nn.43-44, 646
1.3-4	636n.13	2.4.10-13	646n.84
2.5	636, **636n.17**, 636n.19	2.4.11	641
2.7, 8	**636n.17**, 636	2.4.12-13	641n.45
3.9, 10-11	641	2.4.13	635n.7, 642
3.11	645	2.5.14	637, 646n.84
3.12-13	641	2.5.15	646
3.14	**637n.22**, 641	2.6.16	638n.27
3.16-18	641	2.6.17-19	643
4.19	645, 646n.85	2.6.18-19	645
4.20	635n.7, **637n.22**, 641n.45, 645	2.6.19	638
4.21	639n.28	2.7.20	**638-639**, 643, 646n.82
4.22	641n.49	2.7.20-22	646n.84
4.24-25	642	2.7.21	643
5.26	643n.61	2.7.22	642
5.28	639, 646n.82	2.7.23	638, 643, 646n.83
6.29	639, 644n.71	2.7.24	**639**
6.30	639nn.30-31	3.1.1	638, 639n.30, 643-644
6.31-32	639n.33	3.1.2	**644**
7.34-41, 42	640	3.1.3	**644**
9.50-59	640	3.1.4-6	640n.34
9.59	**644**	3.1.5	644n.71
On Psalm 61, Homily 2	636n.16	3.1.7	**639n.33**
		3.2.8, 10	640n.37
On Repentance	635	3.2.12	635n.6, **645n.79**
2.2.8-9	643n.62	3.4.11-12	646n.82
2.2.11, 12	641n.46, 642	4.1.2	636n.16
2.11.98	635	4.1.3	639n.31
On the Sacraments	634, 639, 641	4.2.5-6	640n.35
1.1.1	646	4.2.7	**645n.79**
1.1.2-3	636	5.3.12–6.1.4	640n.40
1.2.4	636n.16	5.3.14	640n.35
1.2.5-6	636	5.5	640n.40
1.2.6	636n.18	5.15-17	640n.41
1.2.8	636n.18, 646	6.2.6-7	**640**
1.4.23	642	6.2.7	**643n.66**
1.5.15	645	6.2.8	642, 643
1.5.15-16	642	*Paradise*	
1.5.16	115-116	31	365n.7
1.5.18	637, 638n.27		
1.5.19	643	**Ambrosiaster**	
1.6.20-23	641nn.43-44	*Questions*	
2.1.1	641n.43	80.2	365n.7

Index of Non-Canonical Christian Authors and Writings | 887

Aphrahat	489-498, 506n.41
1–10	490n.3
1	
"On Faith"	494
1.17	492
1.19	**494**
4.5	495
4.6	492
4.19	**495**, 498
5.22	491
6	489
6.1	493n.14, 498
6.6	498
6.13	491, **492n.10**, 496
6.14	494, **496-497**, 498
6.16	496
6:17	**106n.25, 496**
7	
"On Penitents"	493
7.18	493n.16
7.19	491
7.19-21	494
7.20	493n.16
7.20-21	**493**
7.21	491
10	489
11–13	490n.3
11	490
11.2	494
11.10	**491n.7**
11.11	490, 491, 496
11.12	**490-491**, 497
12	
"On Paschal Sacrifice"	492-493
12.2	498
12.5	494
12.8	**490**, 492
12.9	491, 494, 495n.25, 498
12.10	490, 491, **492**, 495n.25, 496, 497, 498
12.13	**493**, 495, **497**
14	489
14.16	497
14.39	498n.33
15–19	490n.3
15.1	491
18.8, 12	493n.16
21	490n.3
21.9, 13	492
23	490n.3
23.3	495n.22, 495
23.63	495

Apocalypse of Peter	67n.44, 225
14	**225**

Apocalypse of Sedrach	221-222
11.8	222n.3
14.3, 5-6	**222**

Apostolic Constitutions	18, 366, 436, 520, 536n.5, 543n.43, 564-573, 577, 578, 627
2.5.7	572
2.7.1	**571**
2.7.2	517, 573
2.12.1	573
2.14.8	572
2.16	573
2.26.4	571, 572
2:32	102n.7
2.32.3	569n.12, **572**, 573
2.33.2	572n.21, 573
2.33.3	**571n.20**
2.38	573
2.39.6	**565**, 570, 572
2.41	573
2.41.2	569n.12, 573
2.57.14	565, 570, 573
3.9.1	**568**
3.10, 11.1	568
3.16.(15)2	567, 572
3.16.(15)3	567
3.16.2-4	569n.11
3.16.4	567, 568, 572
3.17	569n.13, **570**, 574
3.17.1	569n.11, 572
3.17.2, 4	567n.9
3.18.1	567
5.1.2	572
5.7.3	573
5.7.14	571n.19
6.3	572
6.6.4	73n.75
6.6.5	72

888 | INDEX OF NON-CANONICAL CHRISTIAN AUTHORS AND WRITINGS

6.15.1-4	**573**	8.8.5	**571**, 572
6.15.3	573	8.9(8).5	572
6.15.5	571	8.9.11	573
6.15.6	568	8.12.20	571n.19
6.15.7	138n.19, 595n.8, 568	8.12.26	572
6.18.1	565	8.12.39, 14.2	573
6.20.6	572	8.29	566
6.27.5	573	8.30.31	567
7	206	8.32	565
7.1-28	564	8.32.16, 17	565
7.22	567n.8	8.35.2	572
7.22.1	**567n.9**, 571	8.37.6	572
7.22.2	573		
7.22.2-3	569n.11, **569-570**, 572	**Apostolic Canons**	564
7.22.3	569	canon 47	567
7.22.4	566	canon 49	567
7.22.5	571	canon 50	**567-568**, 573, 576
7.22.6	571		
7.24.2	572	**Aristides**	
7.27	568n.10	*Apology*	
7.33.3	571n.19	15.11	365n.7
7.34.1	566n.6		
7.34.8	571n.19	*Ascension of Isaiah*	
7.36.2	**571n.17**	3.17-20	**135**
7.39-45	364		
7.39	566, **570**	*Asceticon*	725
7.39.3	471		
7.39.4	565-566, 571, 572	**Asterius the Homilist**	577-578, 627
7.40.1	565, 566	Homily 12, *In Ps. 6*	**577**, 578
7.40.3	571	Homily 14, *In Ps. 8*, hom. 1	578
7.41	566	Homily 15, *In Ps. 8*, hom. 2	578
7.41-42	567n.8	Homily 16, *In Ps. 8*, hom. 3	578
7.41.8	573	Homily 21, *In Ps. 11*, hom. 2	578
7.42.2-3	566, 573	Homily 26, *In Ps. 14*, hom. 1	578
7.43.2	573	Homily 27, *In Ps. 14*, hom. 2.2	578
7.43.3	571	Homily 30, *Hom. in feriam 5*	578
7.43.5	**566**, 570n.16, 571, 572		
7.44.1	567n.9	**Athenagoras**	
7.44.2, 3	**569**	*On the Resurrection* 14	365n.7
7.45(44).1-2, 3	570		
8	573, 579	**Athanasius**	116n.27, 455-458, 687
8.6	565n.4	*Discourses (Orations) against the Arians*	
8.6.5	572n.22	1.12.47-48	116
8.6.5-8	471	2.18.41	**456**
8.6.6	571n.18	2.18.42-43	399, 451, 456
8.6.14	565		
8.8(7).4-5	567		
8.8(7).2, 6	572		

2.18.43	**456**	1.7.31	788n.95
2.42-43	576n.29	1.10	813n.119
Defense of the Nicene Definition		3.3.8	782n.49
31	456n.2	3.5.11	788n.98
		5.11.44	814n.125
Expositions in Psalms		6.5.11	788n.98
PG 27.161, 237	457	*Against Julian, an Unfinished Work*	
Encyclical Letter		1.50, 60	782n.49
3.3, 5	457	1.117	788n.98
		2.181	782n.49, 788n.98
Letter 49 (to Dracontius).4	455	3.82	782n.49
Letters to Serapion concerning the Holy Spirit		3.144	788n.98
		3.164	779n.21, 788n.98
1.6	457	3.182	782n.49
1.30	**457**	4.77	782n.49
		Against the Letter of Parmenian	
Pseudo Athanasius	596n.11	2.7.14	804n.62
On the Holy Passover		2.13	800n.45
5 (PG 28.185)	**458-459**	*Against the Letters of Petilian*	796-798
Homily on Fasting and the Passion of Christ	459	1.1.2–1.2.3	798
		1.4.5	798
Questions to the Governor (Ducem) of Antioch	459	1.9.10	798
		1.11.12	797n.13
PG 28.670-672	**459**	2.2.4	**796n.6**
		2.2.5	**797n.17**
Questions in the Holy Scriptures		2.6.11–2.7.14	814n.127
45 (PG 28.278)	459	2.6.13	798
93 (PG 28.753)	**459**	2.23.51-52	793n.143
101 (PG 28.760-761)	460	2.24.57	797
126 (PG 28.769)	460	2.25.58	796
		2.33.78	798
Augustine	3, 4, 5, 14, 353n.17, 379, 391, 545, 627, 628, 631n.44, 632, 664, 674, 677, 681, 715, 717, 733, 734n.43, 740, 767, 772, 773n.13, 776-816, 842, 857	2.34.79-80	796n.10
		2.35.81	786n.82
		2.35.82	797, 798
		2.81.178	785n.73
		2.83.184	778n.15
To Cresconius (Against Crescens)		2.102.232	803
2.5, 7	779n.21	2.102.233	798
3.3.3	381n.4	2.104.237	786
4.16.19	797n.14	2.105.239	786
		3.8.9	785
Against Faustus		3.19.22–3.20.33	798n.31
19.9	790n.111	3.27.32	798n.31
Against Julian		3.28.33	798n.29
1.3	371n.25	3.33.38	798n.31
1.4.14	627n.27, 782n.49	3.48.58–49.59	798n.31
1.7	813n.119	3.50.61	796

3.50.62	791	23.93	814n.125
3.56.68	**798n.24**	52.14	783n.57

Against (Answer to) the Two Letters of the Pelagians

Explanations of the Psalms

		36.2.4	779n.20
1.13.26	**805n.65**	41.1 (Eng. 42:1)	785
1.13.27–14.28	812n.104	48, 2.1 (Eng. 49:14)	782n.50
1.22.40	**810**	48.3 (Eng. 49:2)	780n.29
2.2.3	809	50.10 (Eng. 51:5)	788n.95, 809n.89
2.5.10	810n.93	77.2 (Eng. 78:1)	785n.72, 799n.38
2.6.11	810n.93	80 (Eng. 81)	780n.28
3.3.5	**792n.131**, 793n.137, 805n.65	80.8 (Eng. 81:5)	780n.29, 790n.108
4.7.17	805n.65	90.14 (Eng. 91:11)	790n.113
		101, 2.2	779n.23

Care of the Dead

12.15	780n.33	102.5 (Eng. 103:3-5)	791n.123
		102.19 (Eng. 103:12)	784n.63

City of God

		106.3 (Eng. 107:3)	790n.108
13.7	793n.143	108.26 (Eng. 109:24)	793
17.4.9	786n.80	127.13 (Eng. 128:3)	786n.81
21.19-20, 25	792n.126		
21.27	783n.57	*Exposition of the Gospel of John (Tractates on John)*	
22.8	785, 806n.72		
		3.12	804n.62

Confessions

	634, 777n.3, 778	4	780n.28
1.11	628	4.13	790n.113, 791n.119
1.11.17	777, 779n.19	5	797n.18
1.11.18	777n.5	5.3	790
2.3.6	778	5.15	797n.16
4.4.8	777	6.7	797n.14
5.9.16	**777n.6**	6.11	790n.116
6.4	628	6.15	801n.46
6.13.23	777	6.20	786n.81
8.2.3-5	777	10	780n.28
8.2.5	784	10.10	780n.33
9.3.5, 6	777	11	780n.28
9.4.12	**778**	11.1	793n.135
9.5.13	778	11.1-6	780n.33
9.6.14	777, 778	11.3-4	779n.20, 780n.24
9.8.17	777	11.4	790n.108, 791n.124
9.10.22	778	11.4–12.3	793n.135
9.13.34	778	12.3	781n.41, 792
12–13	778n.9	12.5	793n.135-136
		15.4	**162n.4**, 785

Enchiridion

	808	19.11-13	792
13.42	808n.80	32.8	**801n.48**
14.49	790, 792n.135	38.6	788n.95
14.52	**791**, 808	44.2	780n.24
14.53	792	50.2	779n.20
17.64	791n.119, 808	56.4	783n.57
17.66	808n.80		

Index of Non-Canonical Christian Authors and Writings | 891

80.3		162n.43, 786	
81.2		778n.15	
96.3		780	
118.5		784	
124.5		783n.57	
Letters			
1*-29*		780n.31	
2*		780	
2*.6		798n.24	
2*.10		812n.104, 814	
5*.2		789n.100, 789n.105	
23.4		785, 790	
54.1.1		785n.73	
54.7.9		781	
54.7.10		784	
55.2-3		785n.66, 791n.124	
55.18.33		787	
89.5		797n.19	
93.11.47-48		796n.10	
98 "To Boniface"		805	
98.1, 2		805	
98.5		806	
98.5, 7		789n.100	
98.6		806	
98.7		**806**	
98.9		806-807	
98.10		**807**	
108.1-20		796n.6	
108.1.3		782n.49	
126		780n.30	
143.6		809n.88	
153.5.15		**791n.119**	
166.3.6		809n.89	
166.4.10		814	
166.6-10		814n.127	
166.7.21		788n.95	
166.8.23		788n.95	
173.3		800n.45, 801n.46	
182.5		814n.129	
184A.1.2		807n.77, 814n.125	
185.3		800n.45	
185.6.23		801n.46	
185.9.39-40		791n.119	
186.4.11		809n.89	
187.7.25		803n.57	
190.12		814n.127	
194.10.45		**791n.119**	
194.10.46		788n.98, 811, 812n.109	
202A.8.17		809	
210.3		790	
211-271		780n.31	
215.1		814n.125	
217.5.16		813n.115	
217.5.16.8		789, 814n.125	
217.6.19		788n.95	
258.4-5		780n.33	
265		790	
265.3		790	
265.4		793	
On Adulterous Marriages			
1.26.33		**787-788**	
1.28.35		788n.94	
On Agreement among the Evangelists			
2.30.75		787n.89	
4.6.7		792	
On Baptism, against the Donatists		793n.144, 796, 801-803	
1.1.2		797	
1.2.3		802	
1.3.4		802	
1.3.12		381n.4	
1.4.5		800n.45, 801	
1.5.6		802	
1.5.7		797	
1.8.11		802	
1.11.15		793	
1.11.16		804	
1.12.18		797n.21	
1.12.19		804	
1.13.21		789n.100	
1.14.22		797, 798	
1.18.27		801	
1.19.29		797	
Books 2–5		801	
2.7.12		802	
2.9.14		802n.50	
3.5.7–3.9.12		802	
3.10.15		784n.65, 797, **799-800**	
3.13.18		797n.21	
3.15		277n.2	
3.15.20		278n.8, 785n.73, 799	
3.16.21		779, 786nn.82-83	
3.17.22		800	
4.2.2		800	
4.4.6-7		797, 799	

4.6	381n.4	18.33	780n.34
4.10.17	797, 800n.42	27.49	782n.44

On Free Will

4.16.24	799
4.21.29	798n.24
4.21.29–4.22.30	800
4.22.30	790n.113, 800
4.23.31	**802-803**
4.24.32	789n.100, 803, 806n.73
4.25.33	800n.44

3.10.31	804n.62
3.13.67	804n.62
3.19.54	804n.62
3.20.56ff	804n.62
3.23.67	788

On Grace and Free Will

4.31	790n.109
5.9.10-11	796
5.9.11	778n.15

22.44	803n.57

On Genesis, against the Manichees

5.10.12	796
5.11.13	796

2.24.37	792

On Holy Virginity

5.12.14	796
5.13.15	796n.7
5.15.17	796n.11

48	805n.65

On Marriage and Concupiscence (Desire)

5.15.20	798
5.20.28	784n.65, 786
5.20.30	797
5.21.29	791n.121
5.24.34	782n.50
5.28.39	800
6–7	801
6.1.1	802
6.3.5–6.5.7	802n.56
6.7.10	356n.29
6.25.47	784n.65, 797n.16, **799**

1.20.22	789n.100, **812n.109**
1.32.37	812n.103
1.33	783n.57
1.33.38	783n.57, **791n.119**, 793n.137
2.18.33	782n.49
2.29.50	812n.109
2.40.45	812n.109

On Nature and Grace

53.61	793

On Predestination of the Saints

6.34.66	797n.23
6.40.78	800n.42
6.41.80	797n.23
7.19.37	797
7.53.101, 102	801

24	814n.127

On Romans

19	783n.57

On the Creed

On Catechizing the Uninstructed   779

19.32	800n.42
20.34	779, 790n.108
26.50	779
26.52	804n.62

1.1	779n.21
1.2	782n.49, 788n.98
7.14	783n.57
7.15	791n.119
8.16	783n.57, 801n.46
15	791n.119

On Faith and Works   781

On the Deeds (Proceedings) of Pelagius

6.8	780, 781
6.9	780n.26, 780n.35, 781, 782, **793n.137**
7.11	781n.35, 782n.44
9.14	783n.52, 786n.76
10.16	780n.34
11.17	783n.52, 790n.108
13.19	780n.34
17.31	780n.34

1.2.4	788n.95
12.28	805

On the Gift of Perseverance

12.31	788n.95, 814n.127
13.31	788n.95

On the Good of Marriage

21	805n.65

On the Grace of Christ and Original Sin

1.32.35	810n.96
1.32.35–1.33.36	788n.97
1.35	810n.92
2.1.1	810n.96
2.4.4	810n.93
2.5.5	788n.97
2.17–18.19	810n.93
2.19.21	810
2.21.23	814
2.39.44	812n.103
2.39.44-45	805
2.39.45	**813n.118**
2.40.44-45	805n.66

On the Letter of John

2.9	793n.135
4.11	788n.95
6.10	786n.82

On the Literal Interpretation of Genesis

10.11.19	788n.95
10.13.23-25	815
10.14.25	789
10.15.26–10.16.29	814n.125
10.23.59	813n.118

On the One Baptism

13.22	381n.4

On the Perfection of Human Righteousness

7.16	804
15.35	**804n.65**

On the Soul and Its Origin

1.9.10-11	814
1.9.11	793, 800n.44
1.10.12	784
2.10.14–12.16	814
2.12.17	789n.105, 793n.144, 809
3.9.12	784n.61, 793n.144, 814n.129
3.13.19	814n.129

On the Trinity

14.17	791n.119
15.26.46	786n.82, 793

The Punishment (Merits) and Forgiveness of Sins and the Baptism of Little Ones 808

1.9.9	809n.90
1.12.15	813
1.15.20	**808n.84**
1.16.21	793n.135, **814n.125**
1.17.22–19.24	811
1.18.23	788n.95, 792, 810n.93, 814n.126
1.18.23–1.19.24	813
1.19.24	**811n.97**
1.19.25	807, 813n.115
1.20.26-27	810n.93
1.20.28	813
1.22.31	793n.137, 811n.97, 813
1.23.33	809
1.24.34	791, 813
1.25.35-36	812
1.25.36	803n.57
1.25.38	813n.115
1.26.39	811n.97, **811**, 813n.118
1.27.40	809, 813
1.27.42, 44	812
1.28.55	813
1.30.58	810
1.33.62	813, 813n.117
1.34.63	788n.98, 789n.100, 812, 813
1.34.63-64	811n.97
1.35.65	809
1.38	806n.73
1.39.70	812
2.4.4	812n.104
2.7.9	791
2.9.11	793n.137, 811
2.24.38	790
2.25.40	790
2.25.41	812n.105
2.26.42	779n.19, 812n.105
2.27.43	**809**, 812n.106
2.27.44	**805n.65**, 812n.103
2.28.45	793n.135
2.28.45-46	812n.104
3.2.2	811
3.4.7	814
3.4.8	814n.125
3.4.9	813
3.5.10	813n.119
3.6.12–7.14	813n.119

3.9.17	813n.117	213.11	783
3.12.21	812	214.1	783nn.52-53
3.13.22	810	214.12	783n.54
		215	783n.55
Revisions (Retractions)		215.1	784n.60, **784n.63**
1.25.62	800n.44	215.5	779n.20
2.18.44	800n.44	216 "To the *Competentes*"	781n.43, 782
2.59	808	216.1	780n.35
		216.6	781n.40, 782, 784n.63
Sermons		216.7	781
49	780	216.8	792n.131
49.8	780n.29	216.10	781n.37, 782
56–59	783	216.11	782
56.5	**792**	219-223K	785n.66
58.1	783n.55	223	792n.135
58.10	783n.57	223.1	**787**
59.1	**784n.60**	223E.2	790n.108, 791n.119
59.4	783n.57	224 "On the Octave of Easter"	794n.145
71.12.19	793	224.1	792, **792n.131**, 793n.135
95.1	780n.27	224.3	**792n.131**
99.9	783n.57	225.4	791
115.4	788n.96	226	787n.86, 791
120	787n.87	227	781, 782n.45, 786n.75, 786n.81,
125.6	785		787n.90
131.1	780n.29	228	781n.41
131.6	791n.123	228.1	787n.86, 792, 792n.135
132	780n.28	228.3	787n.86, 787n.90
132.1	779, 780n.24, 780n.33	228A	791n.124
146.2	787n.87	228B	787n.90
169.13.16	783n.57	228B.1	787n.86, **792n.131**, 792n.135
174.4	**809n.91**	229	787n.90
174.7	787n.90, 789n.107, 807n.77	229E-O, R-V, the Easter octave	787
184-229Z	781n.36	229.1	781n.36, 782n.45
205-211	781	229.3	787n.90
206.2	781	229A	787n.90
207.2	781n.38	229A.1	778n.15, 784n.59, 787, 793
210.2	780, 785, 790n.113	229A.2	781n.36
210.2-3	781n.37	229E.2	791, 793n.137
210.3	791n.124	229E.3	792
210.9	781n.38	229M.2	**786n.83**
210.12	781n.39	229O.1	779n.15
211A	781n.43	229O.3	786
212-214	783n.52	229P.4	779n.15
212.1	783	249.3	786n.83
212.2	783n.52, 785n.71	258.2	785n.70
213.1	780n.33, 783n.56	260C.1	780, 792
213.2	783nn.53-54	260C.7	787n.87
213.8	792n.135	261.10	783n.57
213.9	783, 784, 790n.108, 791n.119		

Index of Non-Canonical Christian Authors and Writings | 895

266.3-6	786n.82	13.1 (PG 31.424B-C)	588, 589n.27
272	781n.36, 787, 794n.145	13.1 (PG 31.424C)	590
273.12	115n.22	13.1 (PG 31.425A)	583, 586, **589n.27**
293.10	788n.95, 803n.57	13.2 (PG 31.428A)	587n.23, 588, **589**
294	815	13.2 (PG 31.428B)	585, **586**
294.1.2	810	13.3 (PG 31.429A-432A)	587n.23
294.2-3	815	13.3 (PG 31.429A)	585n.11, 589n.27, 590
294.2.3	810n.95	13.3 (PG 31.429B)	587n.22
294.6-7	815	13.4 (PG 31.432B-C)	590
294.8, 10	815	13.4 (PG 31.432A-B)	587n.21
294.12	786n.76, 789n.100-101, 805n.71, 815	13.5 (PG 31.432D-433A)	587n.23
294.14	780, 815	13.5 (PG 31.433A)	**587**, 590n.31
294.16	815	13.5 (PG 31.436A)	**587n.22**
294.17	815n.135, 815	13.5 (PG 31.436C-437A)	**618-619**
294.18	815	13.5 (PG 31.436D)	584n.8
301A.8	780n.24	13.5 (PG 31.437A)	587
306B.8	779n.20	13.6 (PG 31.437A)	**584n.6**, 590n.31
323	788n.95	13.6 (PG 31.437B)	587n.22
323.3	789	13.7 (PG 31.440A)	583
324	786, 788n.95, 789n.106	13.7 (PG 31.440B)	585, 588
335H3	780n.33	13.7 (PG 31.441A)	583
351.2.2	781n.38	13.7 (PG 31.441B-C)	**619-620**
351.5.12	786		
352.3	784n.65	*Homily 14, On Drunkards*	
378A.2	787	14.4, 7	583
392.1	780n.35	*Homily on Ps. 28*	587n.22
393.1	788n.94		

The Spirit and the Letter
33.59	791n.121

Babai the Great (7th cent.)
Commentary on the Centuries of Evagrius
3.85	**738n.64**

Basil of Caesarea   582-591, 598, 603, 613, 618-620, 622, 624, 627, 745n.2

Against Eunomius
2.22 (PG 29.620C)	590

Commentary on Isaiah
5.178 (PG 30.417B)	583

Homily 1, On Fasting
2 (PG 31.165A)	584n.10

Homily 13 (PG 31.423-444)   582
Exhortation to Baptism
13.1	628
13.1 (PG 31.423C-D)	583

Letters   582
10 (PG 31.441)	584n.7, 585
91, 105	587n.19
188	399n.66
188.1	574, 590
199.20	587n.20
199.47	590
226.3	**584n.5**

On Baptism   582, 585, 588, 590
1	588
1.1	583-584, 584n.8, 587n.22
1.2	**584n.6**, 585n.12, 586, **587**, 589
1.2.10	583
1.3	**585**, 586, 587
2.1	**585**, 587

On the Holy Spirit   582, 590
10.24	585n.12
10.26	584n.5, **589**, 591
12.28	**583**, 585
14.31	585n.12, 586

15.35	584-585, **586n.14**, 586, 587n.19, **588**, 589, 590	19.2	**657**
		34 "On the Epiphany of the Lord" 659-660	
15.36	586n.15, **589, 591**	34.2	657, 659, **660**
25.60	585n.12	34.3	**659**, 660
27.66	584	40	657n.29
27.67	583	44	657n.29

On the Martyr Julitta
4   583

Chronicon Paschale   443
PG 92.685A   **443**

Book of the Resurrection of Jesus Christ   227-228

21.4-6	228
22.10	228n.25
23.2	228

Clement of Rome
(1 Clement)   206-209, 248

7.6, 7	207
9.4	207
35.1-2	207
36.1-2	207
42.4	206, 207n.26
59.2	207

Books of Jeu   296, 297-299

2.43 (102)	**297**, 298
2.44 (105)	297
2.45 (106-108)	**297**
2.46 (111-112)	**298**
2.47 (113-114)	**298**
2.48, 49	**298**

2 Clement   207-209, 218

3.1–4.1	208
6.7, 9	207
7.6	208, 219n.70
8.6	207-208, 219n.70
9.3	208n.30
14.1-4	208

Bordeaux Pilgrim   **488n.38**

Caesarius of Arles   629n.33
Sermon 84.6   629

Clement of Alexandria   210, 249n.3, 280, 299-300, 309-321, 363, 598

Excerpts from Theodotus   280-283

Chromatius of Aquileia   656-662
Sermons

3.6	660
3.8	**657**
10.4	657
14 "On the Healing of the Paralytic and on Baptism"	656n.26
14.1	**658**
14.2	657n.28, 657n.30, 658, **660**
14.3	658
14.4	**656**, 657, 658, 660
15 "On the Washing of Feet"	656n.26, 657n.29
15.5	656
15.6	**656**, 657
17.3	**658**
18 "On Nicodemus and on Baptism"	658-659
18.2-3	**658-659**
18.4	657n.29, 659

18	317n.59
21	288n.40
22	**280-281**, 288n.40, 318-319
35-36	288n.40
36.2	319
64-65	288n.40
72-75	282
74.2, 75.1	282
76.1-77.3	**282**, 319
76	319
76.1-3	282, 314, 316
77-78	319
77.2-3	282, 316n.52, 319
78	318
78.1-2	282, **281**
79-80.1	296n.83
80.1-2	**282-283**
80.2-3	282, 312n.30, 316, 318, 319

81	310n.11, 319	1.6.50	312, 316n.56
81.2-3	**283**	1.7.53.1	365n.7
82	319	1.12.98.2	310
82.1-2	281, 282, 318	2.2	309
83	312n.30, 318	2.2.19.4	319
83–84	281	3.11.59.2	128n.80, 363, 310n.10
85	318, 319	3.11.63.1	319
85.1	314n.37		
86	312n.30, 318	*Miscellanies (Stromata)*	
86.2	**283**	1.5.31.5	313
		1.19.96.3-4	319, 380
Exhortation (Protrepticus)		1.21.145-146	**300**
1.3	309	2.3.11.2	313, 314, 316n.53
6.70	66n.38	2.8.38.1	319
9.82.4	310n.10	2.9.43.5	313n.31
9.84.2	317	2.9.44.1-3	317
10.94.1-2	309, 321	2.18	315n.46
10.99.3	317	2.20.114.3-6	310n.11
11.116.4	316	3.12.82.6	317
12.118.4	**318**	3.12.83	310n.9
12.120.1-2	**318**	3.12.83.1	311n.12
		3.12.88.1	310n.9
Exhortation to Endurance,		4.18.116.2	**313n.33**
to the Newly Baptized	316, 471	4.22.141.4–142.3	317
Hypotyposes		4.22.143.1	315
Book 5	319-320	4.24.153.3	314
On I John 3:9	321	4.24.154.3	314n.42, 320
On I John 5:8	321	4.25	378n.49
		4.25.160.1-2	363, 365n.7
Instructor (Paedagogus)		4.25.160.2	310
1.5-7	363	5.6.39.3-4	317
1.6	316	5.10.64.4	311n.17
1.6.25	102n.7, 124n.66	5.10.66.2	315
1.6.25.1	311, 312	5.11.73.2	316
1.6.25.3–26.1	**313**	6.6.45.4	317n.59
1.6.26.1, 2, 3	309, 311-312	6.6.46.1-2, 5	317n.59
1.6.27.2-3	311, 312n.25, **314n.40**	6.12.104.1	313
1.6.28.2	312	6.14.109.3	320n.74
1.6.29-30	**312**	6.15.120.1	315
1.6.29.2	**314n.40**	7.14.86.4-5	321
1.6.30.2	314		
1.6.31-35	124n.66	*Prophetic Eclogues*	
1.6.32.1	311, **314**	1-26	314n.38
1.6.32.4	311	5	310
1.6.36.2-4	315	7-8	310
1.6.36.3	315n.49	7	310n.11
1.6.38	315, 316n.56	7.1	256n.31, 314n.38
1.6.39-40, 42-43	316n.56	7.2	314
1.6.46, 47, 49	316n.56	12.9	313n.31

898 INDEX OF NON-CANONICAL CHRISTIAN AUTHORS AND WRITINGS

14-16	316
15.2	320
25-26	314n.39
25.1	**312n.30**
28.3	315
Quotations from *Secret Mark*	319

Who Is the Rich Man That Is Saved?

23.2	310
34	309, 316n.53
39.1	313n.31
40.1, 6	320
42.4	313, 315
42.14-15	320

Cologne Mani Codex

94,1–95,14	74

Commodian

Instructions 46, 51	**371n.26**

Coptic Baptismal Rite	693, 695-699, 695n.41
pp. 28, 30-31, 41-43	**696**
pp. 52-53, 68-69	**697**
pp. 72-74	**696**
p. 75	**698**
pp. 79-80	**699**

Cornelius

Letter to Fabius of Antioch	**381-382**

Council of Arles (314)	801-802
canon 6	**618**, 766n.31
canon 9 (8)	399

Council of Carthage (256).
See *Judgments of the 87 Bishops*

Council of Carthage (401)	
canon 6	771n.4
canon 7	771
canon 72	771n.4

Council of Carthage (418)	629
canon 2 (quoted in ch. 50)	629, **771**, 809n.90
canon 3	**771**

Council of Chalcedon (451)	695

Council of Constantinople (381)	483, 521, 768
canon 7	574, 575
Nicaeno-Constantinopolitan Creed	**522, 573-574**

Council of Elvira	451, 663-664
canon 38	382n.10, 663-664
canon 39	618n.4, 664
canons 42, 45, 48, 77	664

Council of Ephesus (431)	725, 726n.6

Council of Hippo (393)	
canon 36	626n.23

Council of Laodicea	574-575
canons 7, 8	574
canons 46, 47	574, 626
canon 48	574

Council of Milevis (416)	629

Council of Neocaesarea	
canon 12	382n.9

Council of Nicaea in 325	399, 451, 521, 801-802
canon 2	451
canon 8	761
canon 14	451
canon 19	399, 451, 761
Nicene Creed	521, 702n.4, 708, 766n.32

Council of Orange, First (441)	
canon 12	626n.23

Cyprian, bishop of Carthage	6, 9, 16, 272-273, 351-361, 365, 378, 379, 380, 382, 383, 388-399, 617, 625, 675, 793, 801-802, 813n.119

To Demetrianus

15	351n.4
23	355

To Donatus (Letter 1)

4	**357**
3	359
5	351n.4, **361n.60**

Index of Non-Canonical Christian Authors and Writings | 899

14	**361n.60**	70 (69).2.1	352n.7, **352n.8**
15	358n.42	70 (69).2.2	353
		70 (69).2.3	353n.15, 391n.40
To Fortunatus		70 (69).3.1	389-390, **392**
Pref. 4	**360**	71 (70).1.2	381n.4, 385
7	352n.6, 359n.52	71 (70).1.3	385, 391
Letters	352n.5	71 (70).2.1	384n.16
8 (2).3.1	351n.2	71 (70).2.1-2	389
11 (7).1.2	352n.6	71 (70).2.3	391n.40
13 (6).2	361n.61	71 (70).3.1	384n.16, 394n.53
13 (6).5.3	352	71 (70).3.2	**390n.35**
18 (12).2.2	351n.2	71 (70).4.1	381n.4. 384n.17
29 (23)	351nn.2-3	72 (71).1.1	353, 354n.21, 391n.40
30 (30).3.1	360n.54	72 (71).1.2	360n.56
55 (51).22	360n.53	73 (72).1.2	**385n.22**
57 (53).3.1	352n.6	73 (72).2.1	381
63 (62).8	16, 357n.36	73 (72).2.2	**390n.34**
63 (62).8.1	353	73 (72).3.1	381n.4, 384n.17
63 (62).8.3	354	73 (72).3.2	351n.3
63 (62).8.4	358	73 (72).4	277n.2
64 (58).2-6 *(to Fidus)*	370-371	73 (72).4.1	278, 353n.10
64 (58).3, 4	370	73 (72).4.1-2	395n.55
64 (58).5	**371**	73 (72).4.2	352, **390n.39**
69 (75) *(to Magnus)*	355-356, 390, 850	73 (72).5.2	384n.21
69 (75).1.1-3	389	73 (72).5.3	390
69 (75).2.1	390	73 (72).6.2	354n.21, 355, 387n.28, 392
69 (75).2.2	355n.24, 390	73 (72).6.2–7.1	358n.43
69 (75).2.3	390	73 (72).7.1	358
69 (75).3.1	389-390	73 (72).7.2	**391**
69 (75).4.2	390n.34	73 (72).8.2	391n.40
69 (75).5.1	390n.34, 391n.40	73 (72).9.2	355
69 (75).5.2	390	73 (72).10.1	391n.40
69 (75).7.1	352n.7, 382n.11	73 (72).10.3	353n.13, 390n.37
69 (75).7.2	352, 390	73 (72).11.2	358n.40
69 (75).10.2–11.1	**391**	73 (72).12.1	359n.48
69 (75).11.1	358	73 (72).12.2	358n.43
69 (75).11.3	354n.21, 358, 392	73 (72).13.1	**384n.16**
69 (75).12	358n.41	73 (72).13.3	384n.16, 390-391
69 (75).12.1-3	**355-356**, 382n.9	73 (72).14.3	384n.20
69 (75).13.1	356n.30	73 (72).16.1	353n.12
69 (75).13.3	356n.28, 356n.30	73 (72).16.1-2	384n.20
69 (75).14.1	356n.31, 392	73 (72).17.1	358n.43, 384n.20
69 (75).15	**352n.5**, 359	73 (72).17.2	353n.12, **357n.37**
69 (75).15.2	351n.4	73 (72).18.1	384n.20, 385n.21
69 (75).16.1	359	73 (72).18.2-3	**358n.40**
70 (69) *(of the 32 bishops)*	351n.5, 391	73 (72).21.1-2	360n.57, 389n.31
70 (69).1.2	381n.4, 391, 384n.17	73 (72).21.2	353n.15, 390
70 (69).1.3	351, 358n.40, **391**	73 (72).21.3	389n.33, 392

73 (72).22.1-2	351n.2	75 (74).18.1	384n.19
73 (72).22.2	360, 389	75 (74).18.1-2	395
73 (72).23.1	389	75 (74).19.1	395
73 (72).24.1-3	389	75 (74).19.1-2	384n.16
73 (72).24.3	**390n.35**	75 (74).19.3, 4	395
73 (72).25.1	389	75 (74).21.1	396
73 (72).25.2	391	75 (74).24.2	394
74 (73) *(to Pompey)*	357-358, 383-385	*Advantage of Patience*	
74 (73).1.2	**383**, 384	12	352n.6
74 (73).2.2	384n.17, 385	*Dress of Virgins*	
74 (73).3.1	384n.16, 385	2	**358n.44**
74 (73).4.1	385	7	352n.6
74 (73).4.2	391n.41	23	**358**, 359n.49
74 (73).5	16	*Jealousy and Envy*	
74 (73).5.1	**354**, 357, **384**	11	352n.6
74 (73).5.2	357, **358n.42**	13	**359n.49**
74 (73).5.3	357	14	**359n.46**
74 (73).5.4	354n.22, 357-358, **359**, 387n.28, **392**	*Lapsed*	
74 (73).6.1	358, 359	2	352n.6, 353
74 (73).6.1-2	353n.14	8	352n.6
74 (73).6.2	357-358	9	372
74 (73).7	277n.2	25	372
74 (73).7.1-2	354n.23	*Lord's Prayer*	
74 (73).7.2	358, 390	9	**359n.49**
74 (73).7.3	384	10	359
74 (73).8.2	385	10-11	361
74 (73).9.2	384	12	361
74 (73).11.1	385	13	352n.6
74 (73).11.3	358, 385, **390n.38**	17	359
74 (73).12	389	19	352n.6
75 (74) *(from Firmilian)*	394-396, 399	28	360
75 (74).5.2, 6.1	395	*Morality*	
75 (74).6.2	394, 396	26	352n.6
75 (74).7.3, 4	395	*Testimonies against Jews*	272-273
75 (74).8.1, 2	395	1-2	272-273
75 (74).9.1	**395**	1.8	357n.36
75 (74).9.2	395	1.11	273
75 (74).10.2-5	396	1.12	272, 357
75 (74).10.5–11.1	352n.7	1.24	273, 357
75 (74).11.1	396	2.22	355n.26
75 (74).12.1	396	3	273
75 (74).13.1	396	3.11	352n.6
75 (74).14.1	396	3.25	359n.49, 273
75 (74).15.1-2	396	3.65	358, 273
75 (74).15.2	**396n.56**	3.116	358, 273
75 (74).17.1	394		
75 (74).17.2	394, 396		

Unity of the Church
6   389
390n.36

Works and Alms
2   **358n.40**, 360, **361**

Pseudo-Cyprian
Against the Jews   271
3   271
6   271
7   271
8   271
9   271
10.79-82   **271**

De singularitate clericorum
1.4   353n.16

On the Glory of Martyrdom
30   360n.58

Cyril of Alexandria   116n.27, 687-693
Against Julian
1, pref.   629n.30

Comentary on Psalms
45.11 [PG 69.1040]   692

Commentary on Isaiah
1.1 on 1:16   693
1.3 on 4:4   **691**
on 11:1-3   688n.4
25.6-7 [PG 70.561D]   692

Commentary on Joel
32 on 2:21-24 [PG 71.373A-B]   692, **693**
on 2:28-29   688n.4

Commentary on Matthew
3:11   691n.30
12:31-32   691n.30
20:1-16   691n.30

Commentary on Luke
2:21   691n.30
2:21-24   690n.25
3:21   114n.13
4:1-2   691n.30
Frag. 22:8 [PG 72.904C-D]   692

Commentary on John
1:12-14a   689, 690-691
1:32-33   687

2:1   116
3:3-6   690-691
3:29   691n.30
5:2   118
6:35   690n.25
7:24   690-691
7:39   691n.30
9:6-7   691n.30, 692
11:26   626n.23, 628, **692**
13:8   691n.30
17:18-19   689
19:34 (bk. 12; PG 74.677B)   691-692
20:17   691n.27
21:15-17   692

Commentary on Romans
1:3-4   691n.30

Embellishments on Exodus
2 [PG 69.432A]   692

Homily 10, On Luke 3:15-17   688

Homily 11, On Luke 3:21-23   688, 689

Homily 12, On Luke 4:1-2   689

Letter 55 "On the Creed"
55.27 (35)   692-693
55.28 (38)   693

On the Pascha
24 [PG 77.897D]   692

On Right Faith to Theodosius
38   691

On the Trinity
5.591   118n.43

On Worship in Spirit and Truth
7 [PG 68.532A]   692
12 [PG 68.821B]   **691n.33**

Cyril of Jerusalem   18, 450n.14, 473-487, 494, 497n.31, 520, 524n.20, 525, 526, 527, 530, 536, 536n.5, 539n.20, 619n.6, 709, 784
Procatechesis   473
1   475
2   482, 483, 485, 485n.29
3-4   478
4   475, 483, 485

6	474	4.37	486
8	475	5.1	474
9	476, 478n.12	5.5	475
10	477	5.6	484, 486
11	483	5.10-11, 12	475
13-14	476	6.19	478n.12
14	475	7.13	475
15	477n.8, 480, 481	10.11	482
15-16	478	10.13	485n.29
16	**483-484**, 485	12.8	480
17	**484**, 486	12.15	130n.94
		13-14	482n.24
Catechetical Lectures	473, 483	13.3	482
1	475	13.21	**486-487**
1.1	474, 481	13.31	475, 478n.11
1.2	475, 483, 484, 485	13.36	486
1.3	485	15.18	474
1.4	474, 478n.11, 478n.13	16.19	476, 478
1.5, 6	475, 476, 483	16.22	476
1.7	476n.8	16.24	485
2	475	16.26	480, 481n.19
2.6-17	475	17.9	485
2.7	478n.11	17.14, 15	**479**
2.11, 12	476	17.26	486n.33
2.13	475, 476	17.35	479, 486
2.15, 19, 20	476	17.36	486
3	475, 481n.21, 482	17.37	475
3.1	475	18.14	476
3.2	475, 476, 481n.20	18.22	483
3.3	476, 485	18.23	475
3.3-4	476	18.26	484
3.4	475, 479, 483, 484, 485	18.32	474, 475, 483
3.5	161n.41, 482, 483	18.33	474, 477, 480, 486n.34
3.6	483, 486	18.35	483
3.8	483		
3.9	485	*Lectures on the Mysteries*	
3.10	**486**	*(Mystagogic Catecheses)*	473-474, 476n.8,
3.11	115, **121**, 481, 482, 483, 485n.29		477, 480-481, 481n.21, 488,
3.12	479, 482, 483, 485		497n.31, 565
3.13	483	1.1	477, 478
3.14	481, 484, 485	1.2	477
3.15	475, 476	1.2-3	482
4	475	1.4	478n.11
4.3	474, 475	1.4-8	477
4.13	478n.12	1.6	580n.55, 703n.7
4.14	480	1.9	476, 477, 478n.11
4.16	485	1.10	481n.20
4.17	485	2	482
4.32	476, 484, 485	2.2	124n.67, 477

Index of Non-Canonical Christian Authors and Writings | 903

2.3	476, 478	*Didascalia Apostolorum*	
2.4	478, 479, 484, 705n.9	*(Teaching of the Apostles)*	273-275,
2.4-8	482		436-440, 480n.16, 564
2.6	482n.25, 483, 484, 485	5	439
2.7	478n.13	9	**437**
3	479-480	10	**436-437**, 440
3.1	118, 477n.8, 480, 481, 485	15	438
3.3, 4, 5, 6	480	16	**437-438**, 570
3.7	479-480, 485n.29	24	274, 438-439
4	481	26	273-274, 438-440, **439**
4.7	486	50	438
4.8	481		
5	481	**Didymus the Blind**	467
		On the Trinity	467-470
Diadochus of Photice	729n.18, 730n.31,	2.6.4 (PG 39.520C)	468
	732-734	2.12 (PG 39.669A)	468n.26
One Hundred Chapters on		2.12	469-470
Spiritual Perfection	732	2.12 (PG 39.669-681)	469
40, 44, 68	733	2.12 (PG 39.683)	469n.29
76-77	**733**	2.13 (PG 688-692)	470
78	**734**	2.14	468-469
79, 85, 88	734	2.14 (PG 39.692-711)	468
90, 91, 94	733	2.14 (PG 39.712-716)	469
		2.14 (PG 39.716A)	**470n.32**
Didache	13, 19, 201-206, 213-214, 237, 244,	2.15	470, 576n.32
	255, 436, 564, 860	2.15 (PG 717, 720-721)	470
1–6	202, 203n.8	3.2 (PG 39.801D-804A)	**470**
1–4	204		
4.9	203	**Dionysius of Alexandria**	381n.6, 384n.15,
4.10-11	204		396-398, 399, 424n.105
6	341	*Letters*	397-398
6.3	204	*On the Trinity*	455
7	202, 569		
7.1	135, 135n.10, 206	**Dionysius Exiguus**	771n.4
7.1-2	129, 205, 223, 341, 859		
7.1-4	**202**	Egeria	473, 487-488
7.2-3	206	*Itinerarium Egeriae (Egeria's Travels)*	
7.3	205, 205n.18, 850, 859	15.1-2, 5	488
7.22	206	27.1	487
9–10	203	27.6	488
9.3	204	28	487
9.5	135n.10, 203	38.1	488
10.3	204	39.3	488
10.3–12.2	202	45.1-2	487
15.3	168n.6	46.1-6	488
16.2, 5	203n.9	47.1-4	488

904 | INDEX OF NON-CANONICAL CHRISTIAN AUTHORS AND WRITINGS

Ephraem the Syrian 494n.18, 499-518, 627, 728n.17

Commentary on Genesis
1.7.1-3   500n.5
    511

Commentary on Exodus
12.2-3   500
14.3   500

Commentary on the Diatessaron   503n.24
4.1   114, 123n.62
4.2   **503, 503n.23,** 509
4.3   119n.46, 502-503, 511
5.15   505, **508n.52**
10.4   505
13.1   **502**
16.12-14   501, **511**
16.29   **508**
20.26   505
21.32   **510**

Commentary on Romans
1:7   511
5:1   511
5:10   **510n.63**
7:13   509
8:2   509

Commentary on 1 Corinthians
1:30   509

Commentary on Colossians
1:1-2   511
3:9-10   513

Commentary on 1 Thessalonians
3:13   511

Commentary on 2 Thessalonians
2:13   511

Homilies on Faith
13.2   508
52.3   508

Hymns against Heresies
3.13   499
17.2   505n.38
17.5   513
22.4   726
22.18-19   502
42.9   499

Hymns on Abraham Qidunaya
4.2-3   506n.39

Hymns on the Church
36.3   504
36.3-6   120

Hymns on the Crucifixion
3.7.4   513

Hymns on the Epiphany   491, 513-518
1   513-514
1.2-3   501n.16, 514
1.5-6   500n.7, 514
2.7   514
3   514
4   515-516
5   501n.16, 514, 516
5.1-2, 4-5   **516**
5.12-14   **514**
6   516-517
6.7-8   **517**
6.9   **516**
7   514-515
7.8   515, 517
8   514n.88, 517
8.16-18   511, 515n.92, 517
9   518
9.1   **518**
9.5   516n.92
10.2-3, 9, 11   518
11   **516n.92**
11.2   518
11.6   502n.21
11.8   518
12   516-518
13   516
13.2   516, **518n.96**
13.13, 14   518n.97
13.19-20   518
13.20   517
14   518
14.32   517n.93, **518n.95**
15   518n.98
15.26   517n.94

Hymns on Faith   505
6.4   511n.77
10.17   120n.52, **507**
10.20   **504**

13	505, 508	7.5-7	500, 506, 508n.55, 509n.61, **512**
18.19	507	7.9	509
23.14	508	7.10	**504n.31**
40.10	**507**	7.12	509n.61, 511n.77
41.1	508n.54	8.10	501
41.10	508	9.1	501
49.4	499-**500**, 513	15.1-2	502n.23, 504, 507
51.7-8	504	15.3	**503**
59.2	508	15.6	507
62.13	508	17.10	502, 513
65.3	508	18.1	502
65.4	508n.54	27.4	508n.55
67.10	508	30.10	**510n.66**
77.20-22	508	31.4	**501**
82.10	506n.42, 507	32.5-7	504n.27
83.2	515n.90	33.8	515n.91
85.3-4	507n.49	37.6	**510**
		46.23, 26	506
Hymns on the Fast		55.21-22	506
5.1	506n.41		
		Nisibene Hymns	
Hymns on the Nativity		29.207ff	508
1.25	501	35.8	510n.63
4 (3).210	**502n.23**	39.7	505
18 (13).15	503n.27	46.84	511
22 (15).39.3	513	65.23	510n.63
23 (16).12	504n.31, 507n.46	72.22	**500**
23 (16).13	513n.82	73.8	500n.8
23 (16).14	504n.31, 504n.32		
		Sermon on Admonition and Repentance	
Hymns on Paradise		2	508, 513
4.3-4	501n.18		
7.6	510n.63	*Sermon on Our Lord*	
7.8	510	1-2	120, 504n.30, 509
14.10-11	510	2.5	**504**
15.5	510n.63	7	501n.12
		53 (51)	503n.24
Hymns on the Resurrection		55 (53)	**503**, 503n.24, 511n.74
1.16	505n.33	56 (54)	503n.25
18.22	505		
		Epiphanius of Salamis	248f, 263-264, 274-275, 625, 728n.17
Hymns on Virginity			
1.2	513	*Anacephalaiosis*	
4.2	511n.77	1.17	72n.70
4.9	509n.61	2.30.4	**264n.63**
4.10-11	511	3.42.3	277n.5, 278n.9
4.11, 13	509	53.1.1-9	**73n.77**
4.14	508n.53	53.1.7	74n.83
5.16	511n.77		
7	506n.42, **506**, 511-512		
7.2-8	506		

906 | INDEX OF NON-CANONICAL CHRISTIAN AUTHORS AND WRITINGS

Ancoratus		*Epistle of Barnabas*	210-214, 231,
2.30.4	250n.5		259-260, 267, 268
13.6	726n.7	1.3, 4, 6	212n.44
17	72	4.3	213n.46
		4.8	212n.44, 214
Panarion		6	212-214
1.9.3.6	275	6.8-11	223
1.19.5.4-7	72n.68	6.8-19	212f
1.17.1.2-3	72n.70	6.11	212, 365n.7, 214
1.17.2.4	**275**	6.17	223, 343n.30
1.40.2.6, 8, 9	301	8.3	211-212, 212n.45, 214
1.42.4-5	278	8.5	**212n.41**, 212n.44
2.1-2	72n.70	9	214
2.28.6.4-5	299	10.12	214n.52
2.30.2	264, 275n.20	11-12	211
2.30.15.1, 3	263	11	212-214, 223, 266
2.30.16	263-264	11.1-11	**210-211**
2.30.16.1	**264**	11.6-8	127, 212n.44
2.30.21.1-2	264n.63	12	211, 212n.44
2.30.26.1-2	264n.62	13.1, 6	213n.46
2.30.28.1-9	264n.62	14.5	213n.46
2.30.32, 33, 34	264	15.8-9	244n.24
3.6	74	16	212-214
3.42.3.6-10	278	16.1, 2	212n.44
3.79.3.6	438n.28	16.7-10	212f
6.1-4	625	17.1	212n.44
11	73n.76	18-21	214
19.1.4–19.5.1	73n.77	18-19	241n.11
19.1.7	74	19.7	212n.44
30	263		
30.3.2	73n.77	*Epistle of Titus*	**229n.30**
30.4.3-7	**625**		
30.13.4-5, 6, 7-8	**104**	Eusebius of Alexandria (Pseudo-Eusebius)	
30.15.3	250n.5	*On Baptism* (Sermon 11)	121, 334n.47
34.19.4-6	279n.12	86.372C-D	121-122, 482n.23
36.2.5	280n.14	86.373A-376A	121-122
67.2.7	628n.28	86.376C-377D	122
72.3	332n.35		
75	**726n.7**	*On the Coming of John into Hades,*	
76.54.32-33	**575**	*and on the Devil* (Sermon 13)	121n.57
76.54.34	**716n.1**		
80	726	*On the Devil and Hades*	
		(Sermon 15)	121n.57
Epistle of the Apostles	225-228		
17.1	227n.18	Eusebius of Caesarea	134, 482n.24
24	**226**	quotations from Mt. 28:19	133-135, 450
24.2	227		
41-42	**225**	*Against Marcellus*	
		1.1	**450**

Index of Non-Canonical Christian Authors and Writings | 907

Church History	449, 457
3.26.2	299
4.22.7	72, 73n.75
4.26.2	245n.27
6.5.6	449
6.43.14-15	**381-382**
6.43.17	382n.9
7.2-3	384nn.15-16
7.5	397
7.5.5	397
7.8	**381n.6**, 397, 398n.60
7.9.1-5	398
7.9.2	397n.59, 398n.60, 424n.105

Commentary on Isaiah	
1.16	449

Life of Constantine	
4.62-63	450

Preparation for the Gospel	
8.14 (399a)	58n.55

The Proof of the Gospel	449
2.3.36.65b	**449**
2.3.71d	449
6.25.306d	449
9.14.450d	449

Theophania	
4.8f	134n.6, 450

Eznik
De Sectis 4	277n.5, 278n.6

Firmilian — see Cyprian Letter 75

Flavian of Antioch	723, 726n.8, 727
Hypomnemata	727n.11

Gelasius, bishop of Rome (492-496)	761
Gelasian Sacramentary	7, 631, 756, **768**
Order for the Making of a Catechumen or for Baptizing	379n.50, 629n.32
1.30-32	766n.31

Gennadius of Marseilles
De ecclesiasticis dogmatibus 74	**770**

Gospel of Bartholomew	227

Gospel of the Ebionites	102n.7, 104, 110-111, 263
Frag. 1-3	**104**

Gospel of the Hebrews	**105-106**

Gospel of the Nazarenes	104-105, 106n.24, 112n.56

Gospel of Nicodemus	106, 226-227
18.2.1	**106-107**
19	**226**
27	**227**

Acts of Pilate	
18.3	106

Gregory of Elvira	**665**, 668
Tractate 15	128n.82

Gregory I, the Great	15, 766n.31
Letter 1.43	668
Letter 4 (to Januarius).9, 26	761n.15

Gregory the Illuminator	708-709
The Teaching of Saint Gregory	708-712, 709n.14
408-413	709-710
410	**710**
412	**709**
414	**712**
415-418	710
420	**710**
431-433	709
454	712
552	710
662	**711**
679	709n.14, **712**
681-682, 690, 691	**711**

Gregory of Nazianzus	316n.57, 582, 592-602, 613, 620-621, 622, 624, 627, 747

Orations	
2.36	597n.14
4.52	629n.30
7.15	600

8 "Funeral Oration on His Sister Gorgonia"	597	40.24	593, 597n.14, 598n.18, 598n.19
8.14	599n.21	40.25	594, 598n.17, 598n.18, 601
8.20	597	40.26	593-594, 598n.18, 599n.21, 599n.23, 600, 601
11.23	365n.7	40.27	593, 598, 599n.20
17.32	599n.21	40.28	594, **595**, 598n.18, 599n.23, 601n.26, 621
18.6	594		
18.12-13	**593**	40.29	596
18.13	594n.6	40.30, 31	593
29.20	114n.7, **599n.22**	40.32	**599n.20**, 599
31.28	600	40.34	597, 598, 598n.18, 599, 599n.22, 601
32.33	602n.27	40.35	594, 599, **600**
33.17	594	40.36	598
38.16	114	40.36-37, 38	597n.14
39 "On the Holy Lights"	592	40.41-42	593, 594
39.1	597	40.43	600n.25, 601
39.2	599n.20, **600**	40.44-45	**593n.4**, 594, 598, 599n.23, 600
39.3	599n.21, 601	40.46	**594**, 597n.14, 601n.26
39.4-6	601	41.9, 14	600
39.8	597n.14	45.21	594
39.10	594n.5		
39.11	**597n.15**	**Gregory of Nyssa**	582, 603-616, 621-622, 624, 627, 643, 671, 738n.64, 747
39.14	598	*Against Apollinaris*	
39.15	114, 115, 598n.16, 601	GNO 3.1,277,4-9	610-611
39.16	122	*Against Eunomius*	
39.17	**596**	3.2.45-54 (GNO 2.67-70)	
39.19	601	[PG 45.633-637]	120n.51, 610n.27
40 "On Holy Baptism"	592, 597-602	*Against Those Who Defer Baptism*	603, 609, 613
40.1	597		
40.2	120n.51, 598	PG 46.416C	611n.29, 613, 615
40.2-3	600	PG 46.416C-432A	603n.3
40.3	**597**, 598, 598n.19, 599, 599n.22	PG 46.417	**603-604**, 613-615
40.4	594, 597, 598-599, 600	PG 46.420	603n.4, 607, 609n.23, 613, 614, 616
40.5-6	597, 601n.26		
40.7	598, 599, 599nn.22-23, 602	PG 46.420D-421A	615n.39
40.8	599, 600n.24, **600**, 601	PG 46.421	603, 605, 606, 607, 613n.37, 622n.9
40.9	598		
40.10	597, 599, 599nn.22-23, 600	PG 46.424	611n.29, 613, 614, 615n.40
40.11-12	593n.3, 594, 598, 599, **601**, 602, **620**	PG 46.425	609, 613n.36, 615, **621**
40.13	599n.21, 601	PG 46.429	609, 611n.29, 613, 614, 615
40.14	602	PG 46.432A	613
40.15	599	*Catechetical Oration*	603, 607, 608
40.16	593, **594-595**, 598n.17, 601	1 (GNO 1,8, 40, 42)	605
40.17-18	599n.23, 600	32 (GNO 82,1-4)	608, 613n.34
40.20	598n.18, 601	33 (GNO 82,15-21)	605, 606, 608n.17, 609n.22
40.21	594, 598n.17		
40.22	594, 597n.14, 598n.17, 599, **602**		
40.23	595n.9, 598n.17, 599, **602**		

33-34 (GNO 82,23–86,1)	609n.21	GNO 9,225-227	608, 609, 612, 613, 616
34 (GNO 84,6–86.4)	605, 606, 608nn.17-18, 609n.22	GNO 9,225,6-8	**612**
		GNO 9,225,10-14	**608**
35	850	GNO 9.228,7	606, 607, 610n.28
35 (GNO 86,6–88,12)	607, 610, 615	GNO 9,230-233	609n.19, 614
35 (GNO 88,23–89,14)	611n.29	GNO 9,235-238	115, 609n.19, 610n.24, 613, 615
35 (GNO 89,5-24)	**604, 607,** 611		
35 (GNO 90,13-16)	**611**	GNO 9,239-241	609n.19, 614, 615n.41
35 (GNO 91,4-9)	608nn.16-17, 616	GNO 9,268,20	607
35 (GNO 91,10–92,8)	**611-612**	*On the Holy Spirit*	
35 (GNO 91,14-18)	608n.16, 611n.29	GNO 3.1	**604**
35 (GNO 91,19-23)	604, **615**	GNO 3.1,105,19–106,11	**612-613**
35 (GNO 92,5)	604, **615**		
36 (GNO 92,8-25)	605n.9, **611**, 616	*On Infants Who Die Prematurely*	
37	608	PG 46.177D	365n.7
38 (GNO 98,18–99,18)	605, 608nn.17-18	*On Perfection*	
38 (GNO 99,13-16)	**605**	GNO 8.1,200,4–204,9	610, 610nn.26-27
39 (GNO 100,2–102,2)	605-606, 608n.18	*Refutation of the Confession of Eunomius*	
40 (GNO 102,4–104,12)	608nn.17-18, 609n.22, 610, 611, **612,** 615-616	79-81 (GNO 2.344.20–346.5)	
		(PG 45.501B-504A)	**120,** 610n.27
		80 (GNO 2,345,6-17)	610n.25
Homilies on Ecclesiastes		*Sermon V on the Resurrection of the Lord*	
6 (GNO 5,380,1-11)	605n.11	GNO 9.1,317,20-22	614
Homilies on Canticles			
2 (GNO 6,49,2-4)	613	**Gregory Thaumaturgus**	604, 627
11 (GNO 6,327,14–328,11)	614	*Panegyric on Origen*	
13 (GNO 6,389,19–390,6)	610n.27	14	**426n.114**
14 (GNO 6,405,14-15)	**610n.28**		
Life of Gregory Thaumaturgus		**Pseudo-Gregory Thaumaturgus**	747
11.77	604	"On the Annunciation to the Holy Virgin Mary"	747
Life of Moses			
1.11	**737n.59**	"On the Holy Theophany or on Christ's Baptism" or "On the Holy Lights"	**747**
2.13	605n.11		
2.121-129	**614n.38**	**Gregory of Tours**	629n.33
2.133-134	109n.45	*Liber de virtutibus sancti Andreae apostoli*	
2.185	607n.15	4, 10, 22	233
On the Christian Institution			
(GNO 8.1)	613, 614, 616n.44	**Hegemonius**	
On the Day of Lights		*Disputation of Archelaus with Manes*	
(On the Baptism of Christ)	603, 608, 609, 613, 614, 615	50	114-115
GNO 9,222-224	608n.16, 609, 612n.31, 615	**Hegesippus**	72, 73n.75
GNO 9,223,24–235,4	615		
GNO 9,224,8-15	**609**	**Hermas**	67n.44, 208, 214-220, 221-222, 225, 241, 317
GNO 9,224,17-24	**612**		

910 | INDEX OF NON-CANONICAL CHRISTIAN AUTHORS AND WRITINGS

Visions
1.1.2 (= 1.2)	218
1.1–3.1 (= 1.3–9.5)	216n.60
3.1–3.6 (= 9.9–14.5)	215nn.56-57
3.3 (= 11)	**215**
3.7 (= 15)	**215**
4.1.3 (= 22.3)	216n.60
5.3, 7 (= 25.3, 7)	216n.59

Mandates
2.1 (= 27.1)	365n.7
2-12 (= 27–46) (various)	216n.60, 219n.72
4.3.1-4, 6 (= 31.1-4, 6)	**216**

Similitudes
5.6.2-3 (= 59.2-3)	217
5.7.3-4 (= 60.3-4)	216n.60
8.2, 6 (= 68, 72)	218, 218nn.68-69
8.6.3 (= 72.3)	**219**
9.12.4 (= 89.4)	217n.62, **217n.64**
9.13.2 (= 90.2)	218n.66, 218n.69, 219
9.13.3 (= 90.3)	215n.56
9.13.6–14.3	219
9.15.2 (= 92.2)	217n.62, 218n.66, 219
9.16.1-7 (= 93.1-7)	**217**, 218-219, 317n.59, 378n.49
9.17.4 (= 94.4)	218, 218n.69, **219**
9.26.6 (= 103.6)	94n.54
9.29, 31 (= 106, 108)	365n.7
10.2.2-3 (= 112.2-3)	216n.60

Hieronymus (Jerome) of Jerusalem 731n.34, 733, 735-738, 739, 742n.75

On the Effects of Baptism
[PG 40.860-865]	735, 736
860C-D	736, 737
861	736-737
861B	**737n.58**
864	735-738
865A-B	736, **737n.59**, 738

Hilary of Poitiers 18, 671-673
Commentary on Psalms
2.27, 29	671
2.29-30	120n.50
14.14	672
53.14	671n.2
135.3	673n.10
137.2-3	673n.10

Commentary on Matthew 119-120, 671
2.5-6	118n.42, 119-120, 671n.2
2.6	673
4.10	673
4.27	673
15.8	672
19.3	673

On Psalm 118
prologue 4	673
3.5, 9	673
15.13	673n.9

On the Synods
1.11	672n.6
12.29, 32	672n.6
27.85	**672n.6**

On the Trinity 672
1.13	**672n.4, 673**
1.21	672
2.1	672
5.35	672
6.36	672
8.7, 8	673
8.25	120n.50, **671n.2**
8.34, 40	673
9.9	**671-672**
11.1	673
12.57	672, 673

Treatise on the Mysteries 671n.1

Hippolytus 325
Against Noetus 325, 326
14	326

Apostolic Tradition 3, 6, 9, 16-17, 305, 315n.46, 325, 327-333, 340, 342, 343, 364n.6, 366-367, 393n.48, 420, 436, 465, 466, 564, 579, 632, 694
15-16	565
15, 17, 18	329
16.1-4	127
17	632
19.1-2	329, 366
20.1-9	329
21	330
21.1-3	129n.88, 330, 414

21.4-5	330, **366**	*Trallians*	
21.6-18	126n.71, 330, 331, 342, 478n.12	2.2–3.1	209n.34
21:19-21.38	332-333, 353n.17	7.2	209n.34
On Christ and Antichrist	325, 326	*Smyrnaeans*	
6	333n.40	1.1	109
59	326	6.2–7.2	209n.34
Refutation of All Heresies	73n.77, 325nn.1-2	7.1	210n.36
5.6-11 (5.1-6)	300n.101	8.1, 2	**209**
5.9.22 (5.4)	300	13.1	**178n.38**
5.27 (5.22)	**300-301**	*Polycarp*	
6.41.2 (6.36)	**279n.11**	6.1, 2	**209-210**
6.41.4 (6.36)	281n.18	8:2	**178n.38**
7.20-27 (7.8-15)	300	*Philadelphians*	
7.35 (23).2	119n.45	2.1	209n.34
9.12 (7).25f	380-381	4	209n.34
9.13.4 (9.8)	73	4.1	210n.36
9.14, 16 (9.9, 11)	74n.81	8.1	209n.34
9.15 (9.10)	73		
9.15.3-6	275n.20	**Innocent I**	756, 760-761
10.14 (10.10)	300n.100	*Letters*	
10.23 (19).2	119n.45	2.8	761
10.29.1-3 (10.25)	74n.81	17.10	761
		25	760, **761**
Canons of Hippolytus	455, 465-467	25.3	760, **761**
canon 9, 11-18	466	Synod at Rome (402)	761
canon 12	465-466		
canon 19	466-467, **467**	**Inscriptions**	372-377, 626
canon 20, 22, 29	467	Baptistery Inscriptions	
canon 30	466	Dura Europus graffiti	**442**
canon 38	466, 467	Lateran	**769**
		Ravenna, Orthodox	759
Commentary on Daniel	325-326	Santa Stefano, Milan	637-638
Susanna 15, 17	326	Sulpicius Severus	**683**
		Varna Museum #3.298	833
Idelfonsus of Toledo	665n.10, 669		
De cognitione baptismi	670	*Corpus Inscriptionum Graecarum*	
		(CIG)	376n.35
Ignatius	109-110, 113, 209-210	III.6408	375-376
Ephesians		IV.9727	**376-377**
5.2-3	209n.34	IV.9810	**376**
17.1	209, 568n.10	IV.9815	**376**
18.2	109, 209	IV.9817	**376**
20.2	209n.34, 209, 210n.36	IV.9855	**376**
Magnesians		*Corpus Inscriptionum Latinorum*	
4	209n.34	XII.5750	**629-630**
6.1–7.2	209n.34		
6.2	168n.6		

Inscriptiones christianae
urbis Romae 638n.26
II.1 **637-638**
VII, 19820 626n.22

Inscriptiones latinae christianae veteres
(ILCV) 372n.29, 638n.26
1343 **373**, 377n.41
1477, 1478 375
1484C, 1488B 375
1508, 1509A 377n.42
1509B **373n.31**, 377n.42
1524, 1525, 1529 374
1531, 1532 373
1533 374-375
1539, 1549 374
1841 **637-638**
2155 372
3315 373

Inscriptiones Latinae selectae 9481 626
Miscellaneous Inscriptions
Epitaph of Abercius **312n.30**
From Aquileia 128, 661
From Hippo 375
From Macedonia 376n.38, 617n.1, 626n.22
Others 626n.22, 761n.12

Irenaeus 107-108, 194, 278-281, 286n.32
Fragment 34 **305**, 307n.34, 308n.43

Against Heresies (Adversus haereses)
1.2.5-6 280n.15
1.7.1-2 107, 194n.28, 288n.40
1.9.4 304
1.10.1 304, **308n.42**
1.14.6 307n.30, 308n.43
1.15.3 108
1.16.2 107n.31
1.21.1-4 **279**, 287n.38, 307, 308n.40, 308n.43
1.24.4 194n.28
1.23.5 299
1.26.1 107, 194
1.30.12-14 107, 194n.28
2.2.4 363
2.22.4 **308**
3.3.4 194n.26
3.4.2 304n.10
3.9.3 **117n.36**, 305n.18
3.10.5 141

3.12.2, 7 305
3.12.8 172
3.12.15 303
3.17.1 304n.12, 307, 308n.40
3.17.1-2 117, 308n.40, 378n.49
3.17.2 128n.85, 306
3.17.3 306n.25
3.18.3 117
3.22.4 **307**
3.23.3 304n.8
4.2.7 304
4.16.1 306
4.20.11 196n.34
4.22.1 305n.20
4.23.2 303
4.24.1-2 303
4.27.2 **305n.21**
4.28.3 308, 365n.7
4.33.4, 11 307
4.38.2 305n.17, 308n.44
4.40.1 304n.8
4.41.3 304n.8
5.2.2 307n.39
5.11.2 303, 306
5.15.1 307n.39
5.15.3 307
5.16.2 304n.8
5.18.2 306n.23

Demonstration (or *Proof*) *of*
Apostolic Preaching 304n.6, 709
3 304, 306, 307
6-7 304n.9
7 304, 306n.26, 307
24 306n.29
35 303n.7
41 117, 306
42 306
46 109n.45
47 305n.18
52-53 303n.7
53 **117n.36**
89 306n.26
100 **304n.13**

Isidore of Seville 665n.10, 668, 669
De origine ecclesiasticorum officiorum
2.21-27 670

Index of Non-Canonical Christian Authors and Writings | 913

Isidore of Egypt
Letters I.25 (PG 78.265) 629

Jerome 341n.25, 627, 656, 677-682, 813n.119, 855
Translations of Origen 409n.35

Against the Pelagians
3.2 **105**

Commentary on Zechariah
3:14 680n.24

Commentary on Matthew
5:27 680
28:19 **682**

Commentary on Ephesians
2:4 679n.23

Dialogue against the Luciferians 678-680
4 680
6 **678**, 679
7 679
8 **679**
9 679n.20, 679
12 679
13 **678**
22 680
23 678

Dialogue against the Pelagians
3.17-19 681

Homily for Epiphany 680n.27, **681**

Homily on Mark 1:1-12 681

Homily on Mark 1:13-31 682

Homily on Mark 11:15-17 681, 682

Homily on Mark 13:32-33 679n.22, 682

Homilies on Psalms 680n.28
41 (42) 681
76 (77) 678n.19
77 (78) **682**
80 (81) 682
84 (85) 680, 681
88 (89) 681
91 (92) 682

In Isaiah
4 **105-106**

Letters
4.2.2 **678n.17**
10.1.2 680n.26
10.3 682
14.2.2 682
16.2.1 **678n.17**
18a.11.3 682
64.20 682
69.2, 6, 7 680
107.3 628
130.7 680

Life of Chariton
14 680

Lives of Illustrious Men
61 326

John Chrysostom 18, 462n.12, 519, 524, 526, 530, 619n.6, 621, 622-623, 624, 627, 704, 709, 715, 718, 752n.9, 784, 857

Baptismal Instructions
(or *Catechetical Instructions*) 520, 533-534, 537, 539n.23, 547
1 533, 537
1.1 536, 548-549
1.3-6 548
1.5 549
1.11-18 548
1.17 555
1.19 537, 551
1.25-33 537, 549
1.39-43 537, 562
1.42-47 537, 551, 562
2 534
2.1-8 545
2.9 550
2.10 541, 542nn.38-39, **559**
2.11 542n.38, **561**
2.12-14 537, 537n.14, 538
2.15-16 536
2.17-21 538, 539, 623
2.22 539, **540**, 540n.28
2.23, 24 540
2.25 541, **552**, 559
2.26 541n.32, 542, 551, 559
2.27 541, 544, 561n.45
2.29 541

3	534	8.25	559, **561**
3.1-5	536	9	533
3.3	461n.9	9.1	**552n.12**
3.5	546, 562	9.2	537
3.6	**544**	9.2-3	551
3.8-11	549	9.4	622
3.9	540n.28	9.5	**622**
3.12-15	549, 554	9.8	622
3.13	547	9.9-10	538n.17, **623**, 551
3.14	554	9.11	537
3.16, 17	555	9.12	551, 559
3.18	**555n.21**	9.12-15	557
3.19	548, 555	9.13, 16	541, **557-558**
3.20	539	9.17-18	558
3.20-22	550	9.18	547
3.23	555, 557	9.19	557
3.24	**549**	9.20	**556-557**
3.26	541	9.21-26	552, 554
4	534	9.22	**554**
4.1	556	9.29	533, 537, 549
4.4	**561n.45**	9.30-47	537, 562
4.12-16	553, 561	9.39	562
4.17	559	10	533
4.17-33	562n.46	10.1-4	537, 562
4.18	**544n.45**	10.5-7	536
4.24	551	10.7-9	554
4.31-32	539, **544n.45**, 550	10.8-10	562n.47
5	534	10.11	552
5.4-14	562	10.12	**552n.15**
5.15	557	10.14	537, 555
5.18	**561**	10.14-17	537
5.21	485n.31	10.15	538, 556n.28
5.24	562	10.17	537n.14, 540
5.27	547	10.16	536n.11, 537, 559
6	534	10.18	536n.11
6.14-20	562n.46	10.18-30	537, 562
6.20	556n.28	10.21, 22-23	562
6.24	**544n.45**, 544	11	533
7	534, 562n.47	11.1, 6-10	549
7.10	541	11.11	551
7.14	**553**	11.12	547n.3, **550-551**, 559
7.16, 20-23	553	11.12-13	542n.38
7.22	**553**	11.13	542n.39, **547-548**
7.24	543, 562	11.13-14	542, 551
7.24-27	543	11.15	**537n.13**, 551
7.25	**562n.48**	11.16	551
8	534	11.18	536n.11, 537
8.16-25	562	11.19	533

Index of Non-Canonical Christian Authors and Writings | 915

11.19-25 (various)	538-539, 623	40.4 (PG 53.373D, 374B)	**544-545, 555n.24, 560n.41**
11.22	540	43.4 (PG 54.401D)	535
11.25	554, 562	*Homilies on Psalm 1–15, 18*	577
11.26	539, 548		
11.27	540	*Homilies on Matthew*	
11.28-29	124n.67, 540n.27, 541	10.2	558n.36
11.29	555	11	546n.59
11.32-34	544	11.6	558n.36
12	537	12 (PG 57.206A)	558n.35
12.1	**536**	12.1-2	558n.36
12.4-9	563	12.3	122-123, 559n.38
12.6	**547**, 563	28.3	365n.7
12.6-7	562	39 (PG 57.437C)	549n.4
12.7	537	50 (PG 58.597D)	555
12.10	547, 561	50.3	542n.38
12.10-12	551	51.4 (PG 58.516A)	**535n.4**
12.12	**561**	54.4	545n.52
12.15-24	562n.46		
12.16, 17-18, 21-24	537	*Homilies on John*	
12.22	538, 552	1.3 (5) (PG 59.23C)	535
12.24	562	17.1-2	558n.36
12.30-32, 33-37	549	18 (PG 59.115B)	622n.11
12.36	557	25.2 (PG 59.151A-B)	542, 543n.41, **552n.15**, 554n.20, **556**
12.42-47	537	26.1 (PG 59.153)	555n.22, 555n.25, 559n.37
12.48	538	26.2	549n.4
12.49-50	539	28.1	**557n.31**
15.52	538, 580n.55	33.1 (PG 59.187D)	534
12.53-61	537, 562n.46	78.3	542n.37
12.60	538, 540	86.4 (PG 59.472)	542n.39
Commentary on Galatians		*Homilies on Acts*	623n.17
2:20	554n.20	1 (PG 60.24D)	536n.7, 623
De diabolo tentatore		1.5	**559n.37**
2.6 (PG 49.463B-464B)	536n.10	1.6 (PG 60.22D)	557n.31
De gloria in tribulationibus		1.7 (PG 60.24A)	622n.11
PG 49.266D	546n.59	1.8 (PG 60.26)	623
Expositions on Psalms		20 (PG 60.131D-132A)	560n.44
7.14 (PG 55.103C-D)	534	21.4 (PG 60.168)	545n.55, 545n.57
44.10 (PG 55.190D)	562, 563	23 (PG 60.181C)	**554n.18**
114 (116).3 (PG 55.319B)	535	23.3 (PG 60.182A)	545n.54, **622n.11**
Homilies on Genesis		24	**559n.37**
6 (PG 53.55-56)	539n.20	43.1	535
10.2 (PG 53.84)	**534**	47.4	535
34.5 (PG 53.313D)	557n.31	*Homilies on Romans*	
35.5 (PG 53.312C)	535	10	**553**, 560n.44
39.5	560n.41	11	**546n.59, 552n.15, 553**
		16	542n.38, **555**

19	**558n.34**	*Homilies on 2 Timothy*	
Homilies on 1 Corinthians		2.4	542n.39
7	551n.9	*Homilies on Titus*	
	546n.58, **551n.9**	5	555n.23
8.1 (PG 61.69B-C)	**543**	5.3 (PG 62.692A-B)	535
8.5 (PG 61.69C)	535	*Homilies on Hebrews*	
10.1 (PG 51.247)	**538n.18**	13.9 (PG 63.108A-B)	**559n.39, 622n.11**, 623
12.11	535	13.10	560n.44
12.13	545n.57	25.3 (6) (PG 63.176B)	534
On 15:29	277n.5	34.3 (7) (PG 63.235B)	534
29.2	560n.41	*Homily on Lazarus*	
40.1 (PG 61.347, 348C-D)	542n.41, 551n.11	1.10 (PG 48.977A)	535
40.2 (PG 61.347)	541n.32, **553n.15**, 557	6.5 (PG 40.1034A)	535
44.4 (PG 61.379)	535n.4	*Homily on the Martyr St. Lucius*	
Homilies on 2 Corinthians		2 (PG 50.522D)	**563**
2.5-8	565n.4	*Homily on Repentance* 3	
2.9	538n.19	4.20	557n.33
2.10	536	*Letter to Innocent*	
3.5, 7 (PG 61.411, 417, 418)	560n.43	1.3	541
3.6 (PG 61.414D)	534	*Nolo vos ingnorare*	
3.7	560	PG 51.247D-50C	549n.4
11.4 (PG 61.476)	560	*On the Baptism of Christ*	534
Homilies on Galatians		1 (PG 49.363-364)	537n.12, **556n.28,**
4.28	**555n.25**		**556n.29**, 557n.31
Homilies on Ephesians		2 (PG 49.365-366)	115, 116-117
1.3	**539**	2-3 (PG 49.366)	**558**
2, 4, 5	557n.33, 557	3 (PG 49.367-368)	116-117, 548, 558
8 (PG 62.68)	**550n.7**	3-4 (PG 49.368-369)	117
8.5	545n.51	*On the Beginning of Acts*	
11	557	2 (PG 51.86D)	551n.12
14.2 (PG 62.102C)	535	3 (PG 51.96D)	**556**
19.3 (PG 62.131D)	534	6 (PG 51.96)	555n.22
20.3 (PG 62.139)	555n.22	*On David and Saul*	
30	162n.42	3.7 (PG 54.704C)	534
Homilies on Philippians		*On John the Precursor*	548
13 (PG 62.277)	540n.24, **554n.20**	PG 59.803	548
Homilies on Colossians		*On the Paralytic Let Down through the Roof*	
6 (PG 62.342)	541n.35, **552n.15**, 570n.15	3 (PG 51.53A)	535
6.2 (PG 62.340A)	**560**	4 (PG 51.55B)	535
6.4 (PG 62.342)	538n.19, **539n.21**, 539n.23,	*On Repentance*	
	540n.27, 555n.22	7.4 (PG 49.329A)	535
7.2 (PG 62.346)	549n.4, 554, 555n.22		
8.6	545n.57		
Homilies on 1 Thessalonians			
5.3 (PG 62.427B)	535		
6.2	545n.51		

On the Statues
14.16 (PG 49.176B-D)   551n.12

Pascha
5 (PG 52.771A)   549n.4

Pentecost
1.2 (PG 50.456D)   **550n.8**

Post reditum
2 (PG 52.444B)   561n.44

Resurrection of Christ
4 (PG 50.439D-440A)   **549n.4**

John of Damascus   728n.15, 728n.17, 730, 736

Heresies (De haeresibus)
80 (PG 94.728-737)   725
80.7   733n.40

John Moschus
Spiritual Meadow
5.176 (PG 87.3045CD)   320

John the Deacon   756, 766-768
Letter to Senarius   766-767
2   767
3   766
4   766-767
5, 6, 7   767

Judgments of 87 Bishops   392-394, 801
1 Caecilius of Bilta   352n.7, 352n.9, 393n.48, 394, **394n.51**
4 Novatus   393
5 Nemesianus   354n.21, **359n.50**, 393, **394nn.49-51**
7 Lucius   352n.9
8 Crescens   351n.4, 393
9 Nicomedes   393
10 Munnulus   **359n.49**, 393, 394
11 Secundinus of Cedias   **393n.47**
12 Felix of Bagai   393
14 Thogenes of Hippo Regius   393, 394
15 Dativius   393n.45
16 Successus   393
18 Sedatus   352n.5, 394
22 Cassius   **393**
24 Secundinus of Carpi   394
25 Victoricus   393n.45
26 Felix of Uthina   393
27 Quietus   393n.46
30 Libosus   394
31 Lucius of Thebeste   393n.48
35 Adelphinus   394
37 Vincentius   351n.4, 393, 394
39 Sattius   393n.46
40 Victor of God   393n.45
41 Aurelius   393n.45
46 Felix of Marazana   394
48 Pomponius   393n.45
53 Marcellus   393n.45
63 Felix of Bussacene   394
64 Saturninus   393
72 Peter of Hippo Diarrhytus   394
79 Clarus   394
80 Secundianus of Thambei   393n.45, 393

Julian the Apostate   628
The Caesars
336A-B   **445**

Justin the Gnostic
Baruch   300

Justin Martyr   6, 73n.75, 111, 136, 237-246, 255, 258n.37, 267-269, 270n.10, 271, 272, 273, 292
1 Apology   237-242, 243n.21, 244
14.2-4   239
15.6   363
44.3-4   241n.16
49.5   239
61   378n.49, 241n.15, 244, 258n.37
61.1-3   238-239, 240
61.1-13   **237-238**
61.5   240-241
61.6-8   241
61.10   238-240
61.11, 13   239
61.14   109n.44
62   241
62.1   **28**, 241-242
62.3   242n.17
64   241
64.1-4   242
65   239-240

65.1	**238**, 238-239, 240n.8	Justinian	
66.1	240, **242**	*Codex* 1.11.10.1, 5	**630**
2 Apology		Lactantius	445-447
6.6	239n.7	*Divine Institutes*	
6:8	431n.13	2.1	445
		3.26.10	446
Dialogue with Trypho	242-244, 267-269	4.15	102n.7
8.1	241n.12	4.15.2	**118**, 446
12-14	267	4.17	447
12.3	243n.22, 267	4.28.1	445
13.1	241n.16, **267**	5.19 (20).34	**446**
14.1-2	**268**	7.5.22	**445**
14.2	**241n.16**		
18.2	**241n.16**, 243	*On the Workmanship of God*	
19.2	214n.52	8.1-3	445n.5
19.2-3	**268**		
29.1	214n.52, 243, **269**	*Letter of Abgar*	
30	431n.13	8	236
30.3	239n.7		
39.2	241n.10, 241n.13	Leo I	14, 756, 761-766
43.2	**243**, 269	*Letters* 16 "To the Bishops of Sicily"	762
44.4	**243n.22**	16.3-7	762
46.2	267	16.4	**762**
49.3, 5	242	19.4	763
50.2–51.3	242	28.5	762n.20, 763
51.2, 3	242n.19	159.7, 8	765
52.4	110n.51	166.2	765n.29
76	431n.13	167.16	766
76.6	239n.7	167.17, 19	765n.30
80.4	72	167.18	765n.29
83.3	241	168	762n.19
84.4	242n.19		
85	431n.13	*Sermons*	
85.2	239n.7	4.3.22	764n.26
86	244	5.5.22	764n.26
86.6	**243**	6.2.22	764n.27
87.2	110n.51	7.1	764
88.2-4	**110**	9.4	764n.25
88.3	241	18.1	762
88.7	242	21.3	765
88.8	102n.7, 110n.51, 111	24.3	**764**
103.6	102n.7, 111n.53	24.6	**763**
116.1-2	239n.7	25.5	**764**
122.5	241n.13	26.2	**764**
138	128n.81, 240n.8, 641n.43	34.4.2	762n.20
138.1-3	**244**	36.3.1	764n.24
138.3	240n.8	41.2	**763**, 764n.25
		43.3	764n.25

44.1	764	**Mark the Deacon**	
45.1	764n.24	*Life of Porphyry*	719-720
49.3	763	21, 30-31	719
49.6	764-765	45, 46-47, 49	719
50.5.74	764n.26	56-57	575n.27, 719
57.4.74	764n.27	62, 74, 85, 91	720
57.5.2	765	100	720
60.3.1	762		
63.4, 6	764	**Mark the Monk**	729n.18, 730n.31, 733, 735, 738-744
63.7	765		
66.3.1	765	*Answer to Those Who Doubt concerning Divine Baptism* (PG 65)	738-739
69.5	762		
70.4	763	902B	739n.68
		984A, C	741
Leontius of Constantinople	333n.43	985	739, 743
		988A, B	739, 740, 741
Liber Graduum	725n.3	988C	739, 740, **741n.73**, 743
12.1.4	731n.33	988C-D	742
		989	739n.68, 740, 742n.74
Life of Polycarp		992A	739
19	**363**	992B	739, 740, 741, 742
		993	742, 743
Liturgies, miscellaneous		996A	740, **740n.71**, 742
Armenian Ritual of Baptism	712-713	997	740nn.71-72, 743
Egyptian Church Order	632	1000	740, 742
Medieval service books	639n.32	1001	742, 743, 744
Milanese liturgies	640n.39	1004A	743n.79
Old Armenian Lectionary	487	1004B	742, **744**
Ordo Romanus XI	631	1004C	739, 740n.71, 742
		1004D-1005	741, 742, 743
Sacramentarium Veronense	631	1008	742, 743
Syrian Baptismal Liturgies	713-714	1009	742, 744
Visigothic *Liber ordinum*	670	1012	740, 741, 742
		1013A	**741**
Macarius Magnes		1017	740n.72, 743
4.10	**444**	1020D	740n.72, 741, 742
		1024	741
Macarius, bishop of Memphis (10th cent.)	**632**, 699	1025	741, 743, 744
		1028	741-742, 743
Macarius of Egypt	724, 728		
		Martin of Braga	668
Marcellus of Ancyra	332n.35	*Triple Immersion*	
		2, 3-4	668
Marcianus the Ascetic (the Monk)	624, 727n.9		
Third opusculum "On Baptism"	624	*Martyrdom of Polycarp*	
1-11	624	9.3	363

920 | INDEX OF NON-CANONICAL CHRISTIAN AUTHORS AND WRITINGS

Martyrdom of Saints Perpetua and Felicitas
3	379
7-8	226n.15

Maximus of Turin 651-655
Sermons
2.3	655n.24
9.2	654n.22
13.1-3	652, 654, 655
13A.1-3	**652**, 654, 655
13A.2-3	652
13B.1-2	654, 655
13.4	652n.17, 653
22A.3-4	654, 655
28.3	653
31.2	655n.24
33.5	652n.17, 655n.24
35.1	655
35.3	652n.18
35.4	652n.18, **652**, 653, 655
44.4	652
48.3	652
50.2-3	652n.18, 653, 655
52.2	652, 654, 655
52.2-4	653
52.3	655
55.1	652, 653, 655
59.4	654-655
62.3	653
64.1	652, **654**, 655
64.2	652, 655
64.3	654
65.1	652n.17
65.2	652
65.3	655
67.3	**653**, 654n.21, 655
85.3	655
89.2	652n.17
100.3	**653**, 655
111.3	652n.17, 655

Maximus the Confessor 729n.18
Scholion on Dionysius
the Areopagite **365n.7**

Melito of Sardis 41n.8, 51n.40, 245-246
On Baptism 245

Frg. 8	122, **245**

On Pascha 245
14	246
15	246
16	246
67	246
103	246
Fragment 6	118n.42
Fragment 12	246
Fragment 15	122

Methodius 447-449
Banquet
8.6.186-187	**447**
8.7.188-189	448
8.8.190-192	448
8.9.192-193	119
8.9.193-194	448

Oration concerning Simeon and Anna
12	448

On the Resurrection
1.5	448

Minucius Felix
Octavius 2.1 365n.7

Nag Hammadi 276, 278, 283-299
On the Anointing, NHC XI 2a 283

Apocalypse of Adam, NHC V 5
78,18–79,18	290
83,4-6	290
84,5-20	290, 292n.61
85,19-31	290
85,30	293n.64

Apocryphon of John
NHC II 1 (& III 1)	293-294
II 6,23-33	294n.71
II 31,22-25	294
III 2,3-4	294
III 9,24–10,9	294n.71

On Baptism A, NHC XI 2b
(40,30–41,38)	283
40,38	283n.21
41,11,21-22	283
42,38-39	283n.21

Index of Non-Canonical Christian Authors and Writings | 921

41,36-37	283
On Baptism B, NHC XI 2c (42,1–43,19)	283
42,11,36-37	283
Book of Thomas the Contender II 7	
144,1	**291n.52**
On the Eucharist A-B, NHC XI 2d-e	283
Gospel of the Egyptians,	
NHC III 2 & IV 2	292-293, 298
III 49,23–50,9	293
III 53,16–54,6	293
III 55,12	293n.69
III 55,12-16	293n.62
III 55,19–56,3	293
III 61,24–62,11	293
III 62,24–64,9	292
III 63,3	293n.69
III 63,9-19	290n.50
III 64,9–65,26	292
III 65,23-25	292
III 65,26–66,8	298n.94
III 66,2-8	**293**
III 66,3	293n.69
III 66,8-22	293
III 66,22–67,4	293
III 66,22–68,1	298n.94
III 67,4–68,1	293
III 67,6-9, 22-23	293
IV 58,6	293n.69
IV 59,1,27	293n.69
IV 59,13-29	293
IV 78,1-10	293
Gospel of Philip	
NHC II 3	280, 284-288, 285n.27
60; II 67,27-30	285
22; II 57,23-28	285
37; II 61,12-20	286
47; II 63,25-30	286
51; II 64,22-31	**286**
53; II 65,11	287n.37
55; II 66,16-19	**286n.34**
58; II 67,3-6	285
59; II 67,9-27	287
59; II 67,16	287n.37
59; II 67,19-20	287
59; II 67,19-22	285, 286
60; II 67,30	287n.37
67; II 69,4-14	287
68; II 69,23-27	**287**
68; II 69,24-37	287n.37
68; II 69,27	288n.39
70; II 70,18-21	287n.37
71; II 70,33	287n.37
72; II 70,34–71,3	**286**
73; II 71,7	286
73; II 71,7-9	287n.37
78; II 72,29–73,1	287
79; II 73,1-8	**287**
80; II 73,17	286n.31
83; II 74,12-15	285
83; II 74,12-22	285-286
83; II 74,21	288n.39, 287n.37
84; II 74,29–75,1	286
86; II 75,14-24	286
92; II 77,7-11	287
102; II 82,17,23	287n.37
105; II 85,21	287n.37
107; II 85,33	287n.37
107; II 86,6-7	288
Gospel of Truth, NHC I 3 & XII 2	284n.26
I 13-31	285n.29
I 19-20	**285n.29**
I 38,7–39,28	287n.36
I 38,36-37	287n.36
Melchizedek IX 1	294
7,27–8,9	290n.49
7,28	294
8,1-5	294-295
14,15–18,24	294
14,23–16,11	294n.73
16,12-15	293n.66, 294
16,12-16	294n.73
16,13-14	295
16,16–18,23	294n.73
On the Origin of the World, NHC II 5	
and XIII 2 (or *Writing Without Title*)	288
II 5,122,13-16	288
Paraphrase of Shem, NCH VII 1	
30,22-27	291
36,28–38,27	**291**
Testimony of Truth, NHC IX 3	288-290
30,20-29	**289**
31,22–32,3	**287n.35**

39,23–40,7	289	*Homilies*	
45,14-18	289n.45	17 (35) "Expositions of the	
55,4-15	289	Mysteries"	702, 708
69,7-26	**289**	21	702-703, 705, 706-707, 708
		p. 47; 342	**707**
Trimorphic Protennoia		p. 52; 346-347	**706, 707**
NHC XIII 1	291, 293, 294	22	702-705, 706, 707-708
36,4-27	298n.94	p. 41; 364	**708**
37,2	291	p. 44; 367	**703, 704**
41,20-24	291	p. 45; 367-368	**704**
44,32	291	32	702, 706
45,12-20	291	p. 66; 148	**706**
47,35–48,35	292		
49,30-31	292	**Novatian**	381-383, 399
50,9-11	**292n.57**	*Chastity*	
		2	383
Tripartite Tractate, NHC I 5		*Jewish Meats*	
122,13-35	284n.25	5	383
127,25-34	**284**		
128,1-18, 24-33	284	*On the Trinity*	
128,33-35	288n.39	1	352n.7, 382n.11
129,1-4	284	5	382n.11
129,7-15	284	9	352n.7
129,32-36	284	10	382
		29	352n.7, 382n.11, 383
Zostrianos, NHC VIII 1	160n.39, 291n.53	*Public Shows*	
5,14–7,21	**295**	4	382
6,7–7,21	**295**		
6,13	296n.86	**Odes of Solomon**	108n.37, 120-121, 222-224
6,14	295n.77, 296n.86	11.2, 3, 4	223
17,4-16	295	11.6-7	**223**
22,4-15	298n.94	11.9, 10, 12, 14	223
23,2-20	295n.81	17.6-16	213n.48
23,3-20	298n.94	19.1	**223**
24,17–25,20	296n.86, 298n.94	22.5	121
25,11-16	295	24.1, 7	121
57,11,20,24	295n.77	39.5-13	**223-224**
58,13,25	295n.77	42.10-11	**224**
60,23	296	42.11	121
61,13,23	296	42.14-16, 19-20	**224**
62,13-15	296		
129,13-14, 15	296n.86	**On Rebaptism**	111-112, 354n.21, 384,
129,14	295n.77		385-388, 790n.116
129,6-16	296n.86	1	**386**, 387
131,2	291	2	387
131,2-10	**296**	4	382n.10, 387
		5	388
Narsai	17, 702-708	6	**386**, 387

Index of Non-Canonical Christian Authors and Writings | 923

7	**386**, 387
10	352n.7, 386, 386nn.25-26, **387-388**
11	388
12	386n.25
13	387
14, 15	388
16-17	112
18	388

Optatus of Milevis 14, 674-677, 796n.5
Against the Donatists
(Against Parmenian) 674

1.5	674
1.8	677
1.10	675n.15, 676
1.12	676
2.10	675n.13
2.20	677
3.2, 9	676
4.6	676
4.7, 8	677
Book 5	674
5.1	**674**, 675
5.2	674
5.3	674, 675
5.4	**675**
5.5, 6, 7, 8	675, 676
5.10	**675n.14**, 677
7.1	677
7.4	**676-677**

Opus imperfectum in Matthaeum
PG 56.611-946; CCL 87B	579
1.1.15.	114n.14

Ordo of Constantinople
Barberini Euchologion 752-755
Folio 170	753-755
Blessing of Oil	**755**
Blessing of Water	**754**
Prayer after Adherence	**754**
Prayer after Immersion	**755**
Folio 260	752-753, 754

Origen 13, 280, 367-370, 371, 378, 400-428, 467, 671, 673, 682, 747

Against Celsus
1.7	421n.95
1.40-48	102n.11
2.4	420
2.72	119n.46
3.15	421n.95
3.49	419
3.51	**419**
3.59-60, 69	420n.82
4.13	408n.32
5.15	408n.32
6.27	**300n.102**
6.79	427n.117

Commentary on Genesis
Book 3	417

Commentary on the Song of Songs
2.8	401n.5, 405
2.9	427n.117
2.10	411

Commentary on Matthew
12.20	**425**, 426
13.16	369
13.27	412
15.6-9	369-370
15.23	408n.32, **409n.36**, 412, 414n.62
15.36	370
16.6	114, **418**
Ser. 33 (852)	421n.95
Frag. 49	**406**
Frag. 52	**427n.119**

Commentary on John 369, 402, 406, 407n.27
1.7 (9).40	407
1.32	102n.7
1.204 (29)	119n.46
1.182	414n.62
6.22 (13).120-136 (20).183	406
6.28.144	420n.85
6.23 (13).125	406
6.32 (17).162	**406**
6.33 (17).165	**422**
6.33 (17).166-167	**407**, 411n.42, 425
6.33 (17).168-169	404, **407**, 412n.53
6.42 (25).220	406
6.43 (26).226-248 (29).249	401
6.43 (26).223-224	408, 409n.33
6.43 (26).227	401
6.44 (26).228-230	402-403

6.44 (26).232	417	30	**418**
6.45 (26).233-236	428	39	418
6.46 (27).238-239	403	50	419
6.47 (27).242-245	404	*Homilies on Genesis*	401n.5, 404n.14
6.48 (29).250	**404**	10.5	416, 422
6.50 (31).260-263	406	13	411
6.54 (36)	419n.81		
6.56 (37).290-291	417	*Homilies on Exodus*	401
10.43 (27).298	424	5.1-2	128n.77, 401-402, 415, 426
10.231-232, 243	414n.62	5.4-5	**402**, 415, 426, 427
28.9.72	426	8.4	411n.45, 423, 425
32 (15-16).187-193	421n.95	8.5	411n.45, **416**
50 (31).260-263	406	10.4	411n.45, 412n.52, 421
Frag. 36	369, **413-414**	11.7	411, 427
Frag. 6-55	413	*Homilies on Leviticus*	368, 405n.16,
Commentary on Romans	368, 404n.15,		426n.115
	426n.115	1.4.6	405
2.1.2	419	2.4.4-5	419
2.12.4	**416**	2.4.6	411
2.13.8-33	405	5.10.3	420
2.13.32	**405**	6.2.4	**421n.89**
3.1.11	404n.15	6.2.5	411, **420**, **426n.115**
3.1.12	411n.45, **415**	6.2.6	427
5.2.11	412	6.5.2	**420n.89**, 426n.115, 427
5.8.2	**414**	8.3.5	**368**, 411n.43
5.8.3	**408**, 426	9.4.4	411
5.8.6	406	9.9.3	427
5.8.7	425	10.2	467n.25
5.8.8	**421**	15.3	408n.32
5.8.10	**414**, **424**	16.7	424
5.8.12, 13	**414**	*Homilies on Numbers*	
5.9.2	415n.63	3.1	411, 420n.83
5.9.11	**368**-69	5.1	423, 424
5.10.2	422	7.2	402
5.10.4	**424**, 425	10.2	419n.81
8.5.3	**412**	12.4	**423**
13.2	**416**	15.4	414n.62
Commentary on 1 Corinthians		18.4	119n.46
1.7	408	22	152n.13
Frag. 63	420n.83	25.6	405n.16, **409n.34**
Commentary on Ephesians		26.4	403
4:5	280, 408n.31	*Homilies on Joshua*	**402**
Dialogue with Heraclides	422n.95	1.6	416-417
		1.7	416
Exhortation to Martyrdom	418	4.1-2	403, **413n.57**, **420**
12	418, 424	5.1-3	403, **420**
17	424	5.5-6	416

5.9	402
9.4	370, 412
10.3	413n.57
15.7	411
26.2	423

Homilies on Judges
5.6	420
7.2	414n.62, 415, **418-419**

Homilies on Jeremiah
1.16.2	415
2.3.1-2	**409**
2.5	415
5.13	421n.95
5.14	369n.18
16.5.2	413
Frag. 26	413

Homilies on Ezekiel
5.1	409
6.3	119n.46
6.5, 7	411
7.4	**425n.109, 427n.116**

Homilies on Luke 367, 404n.13
7.1	406
14.1	417
14.3-4	114, 368
14.5	**367**, 368
14.6	409
21.3	422
21.4	**410**
22.5, 6, 8	**422**
24.2	**409**
26.3	**409-410**
27.5	119n.46, **410**
28.4	119, 412
29.2	411
33.5	**404**

On First Principles 425n.109
1.3.2	411n.45, **425**, 427
1.3.7	427
2.10.4	408n.32

On the Pasch 412n.54
4.29-36	412
25	427-428

On Prayer
5.1	428

Pacian **14, 649n.6**, 666-668

Letters
1	668
3.7.3, 9.3	667

On Baptism
1.1	666, 667
1.2–2.1	666
3.1	667
4, 5	667
6.1-3	**666**, 667
7.2	666, 667
7.3	667-668

Penitence 666n.13

Palladius
Dialogue on the Life of Saint John Chrysostom
2	541n.34
5	627n.25

Papias
Frag. 8	**365n.7**

Papyrii
Der Balyzeh Papyrus	**693-694**
Papyrus Berolinesis 13415	471
2nd prayer *Sabbath Prayer*	**471**
Berlin collection 1163	
An Epiphany Hymn	**694-695**
Hamburg Payrus	
Episode 10	229n.29
John Rylands Library	
P. Ryl. III.471	693

Oxyrhynchus Papyrus 840 104n.16, 269-270, 271
ll. 14-16	**270**
ll. 24-28	**270**
ll. 34-35	**270**
ll. 42-43	**270**

Paulinus of Nola 627, 683
Inscription	**683**
Poem 28, lines 180-195	840

Peter Chrysologus 756-758
Sermons 756n.1

10.5	**758**	Homilies	
55–62a	758	3.4	751
67–72	758	7.1, 2, 3	751
84.9	757	7.5	750, 751
90.3	**757**	10.63	**752**
113.5	757	14.2	**752**
137.4	**756-757**	16.2	752
137.12	757n.2	26.5.18	751n.8
157.6	757	27.2.3, 4-8, 9-10	748
160.3	757	27.3.11-12, 13	749
160.5	757	27.3.14	749, 750
164.6	**758**	27.4.16	749
171.2	757	27.4.18	750
		27.4.19-26	749
		27.5.25, 27-6.40	749
		27.6.31	**749**
		27.6.38-39	749

Philostorgius
Church History
10.4   576n.32

Photius   576n.32
Library 52   726n.8

Physiologus   236
6, 11   236

Pistis Sophia   296-297
1.7, 57, 61-62 (12, 111, 122-125)   296
2.63, 86 (128, 197)   297
2.91 (209)   **297n.90**
3.112 (290)   297n.91
3.115 (296-299)   297
3.116-117 (299-301)   296
3.122 (310)   297
3.128 (324, 325)   297, 297n.91
3.133 (347-348)   296n.88
4.141 (368)   296n.88, 297
4.142 (372)   297
4.143 (372-374)   297n.89

The Preaching of Paul   112

The Preaching of Peter   249n.3

The Preachings of Peter
(Kerygmata Petrou)   249n.3, 256n.30,
              256n.33, 256n.35, 258nn.37-38

Proclus   745, 748-752

27.7.43, 44	749, 750
27.8.44, 46	750
27.8.47	749, 751
27.8.48, 49	749
27.8.50	749, 750
27.8.51	750
27.9.52	750
27.9.54	749
27.9.55, 56	749, 750
27.9.57	750, 751
27.10.60, 61, 62	750
28	750n.7
28.2.7, 8	751
28.2.9	750
28.3.18, 19, 20, 21	751
28.4.23	750
28.5.3	**750n.6**
28.6.44, 48	751
28.7.50, 51	751
28.8.55, 56	751
28.11.70	750
28.11.72	**750n.5**
33.16.61	750
36.45, 61	751

Homily on the Holy Epiphany
(PG 65.757C-D)   115

Prudentius
Hymn
1.30   669n.28

Index of Non-Canonical Christian Authors and Writings | 927

On the Martyrs' Crowns (Peristephanon)
8   669
10.1006-1050   33

Pseudo-Clement   16, 248-263, 266
Epistle of Clement to James
13, 14, 15   254n.24

Contestatio (Epistle of Peter to James)
1 (= 4.1)   254, 263n.58

Degrees (Ascents) of James   263

Homilies   248, 254
1.22   254-255
2.23   72
3.29   255n.29
3.71, 73   254
5.30   249n.4
7.4   258n.38
7.5   251
7.8   **258**
7.12   251
8.2   250n.7
8.15   260n.48
8.22   **259**
8.23   258n.38, 259
9.9-10   251n.13
9.19   254, **259**
9.23   249n.5, **253**, 254n.26
10.1   249n.5
10.26   249n.5, 250
11   256n.30
11.1   249n.5
11.21-33   256nn.30-31
11.24   **258n.37**
11.25   **261n.54**
11.26   254n.26, 261n.53
11.26-27   **255-256**, 261
11.27-30, 33   258n.38, 250, **250n.8**
11.35, 36   **252, 252n.14**
12   363
12.6   260n.48
13.4   **252**, 254n.26, 363
13.9   253n.17
13.10   **260**
13.11, 12   253
13.13   258n.39, 259
13.20   **258**
13.21   **261n.54**

13.30   255
14.1, 3   250n.7
15.1-2   363
17.7   251
19.23   **257nn.36-37**
20.23   251

Peregrinations of Peter   263

Recognitions   248, 254
1.19   255n.29
1.27-71   260
1.37   260n.47
1.39   254n.27, **260**
1.48   **261**
1.54, 55   254, 261
1.55.3-4   260
1.60   261
1.63, 69   254n.26, **262**
1.69.4   260
1.73   254
2.19   **257n.37**
2.33   260n.45
2.70-72   255n.29
2.71   253n.22
3.67   251, 254n.26
3.72   251
3.75   **258n.37**
4.3   249n.5
4.32   254n.26, 259
4.35   **259n.41**
4.36   258n.38
4.37   255n.29
5.36   250n.6
6.6-14   256n.30
6.7   256n.31
6.8   **257**
6.9   254n.26, 256-257, 261n.53
6.10-11   257, 258n.38
6.15   252
7.29   **252**, 254n.26, 363
7.34   **252-253**
7.35   260n.44
7.38   255, 258n.39, 259
8.1   249n.5, **250n.7**
8.53   263
9.7   257
9.31   257n.36
10.1-4   363

10.49	258	43.3	731
10.68	251	47.1	275
10.71-72	251n.11, 253	47.1-2	**731**
		Collection III	728
Pseudo-Dionysius the		III, 28.3	**729n.21**
Areopagite	16, 720-723, 767	Collection IV	728
Ecclesiastical Hierarchy		*The Questions of Bartholomew*	227
2.1, 2	720-721, 723	5.8	227
2.3	721-723		
3	720, 722-723	**Quodvultdeus**	771-775
4	721-722, 723n.9	*Against the Jews*	
5.1.6	721	19.6	774
6.1.1	720		
7.3.8	722, 723n.9	*Book of the Promises and*	
7.3.11	**722, 723**	*Predictions of God*	
		1-2	774-775
Pseudo-Hippolytus		*De symbolo 1–3*	771-772
On the Holy Theophany	325-326, 333-335	1.1	772
2	128n.78, 334	1.1.3	773
4	121n.57, 334	1.2.21	774n.16
5	115n.22, 334	1.6.5	**774**
6	334	1.10.1, 2	773
7	124n.66, 334	1.13.6	774
8-10	334	2.1.3-6	772
10	**335**	2.2-3	773
		2.10	773-774
Pseudo-Isidore	771n.4	3.1.1-4	773-774
		3.1.3, 7	772n.9, 773
Pseudo-Macarius	725, 728-732, 732n.39,	3.1.10	773
	733n.42, 735, 738nn.64-65,	3.2	773
	739nn.65-66, 740n.70, 744	3.10	774
Collection I			
Logia 1 *Great Letter*	728, 729n.20, 730,	*In baptismo*	
	731n.34	2.31.68	774
p. 234, lines 18-20	729		
p. 236, lines 1-3, 6-11	**729**	***Revelation (Apocalypse or Vision)***	
p. 236, lines 18-20	729	***of Paul***	227
p. 248, lines 14-16	729	22	225n.13, **227**
25.2.4-5	73		
52.1.4-5	**731**	**Rufinus**	627, 656, 678n.17
Collection II: *Spiritual Homilies*	724, 728,	*Church History*	
	730	10.15	**457-458**
15.14	**730**	*Commentary on the Apostles' Creed*	332n.35
15.41	744n.81	Translations of Origen	368, 400n.3
26.2	730, 733n.40	Translation of *Recognitions*	248, 260n.46
26.23	730		
30.2	730	*Secret Mark*	140, 319
37.7	733n.40		

Index of Non-Canonical Christian Authors and Writings | 929

Sentences of the 87 Bishops.
See *Judgments of the 87 Bishops*

Serapion 460-465, 527
Sacramentary (or *Prayer Book*) 455, 460-465
5, 6 461n.10
7 Sanctification of Waters **460-461**, 463
8 For Those Being Baptized **461**, 463, 471
9 After the Renunciation **462**, 463
10 After the Acceptance **462**, 463
11 After Being Baptized and
Coming Up **462-463**
15 Of Anointing Oil of Baptizands 462, **463**, 463n.16, 464n.19
16 Regarding the Chrism 463nn.15-16, **464**, 463n.16, 464n.19

Severus of Antioch 727

Sibylline Oracles 110
6.3-7 **108**
7.66-67 109
7.81-84 **109**
7.83-84, 87-88 850
8.245-247 109
8.271 109

Siricius, Pope (384-399) 756, 760
Letters 1.9.13 628
2.2-3 760

Sixtus III (432-440)
Baptistery inscription **769**

Socrates Scholasticus 745, 748
Church History
5.22 618
5.24 576
7.4 **625**
7.17 748
7.30 618

Sozomen 628-629
Church History
5.2 628-629
6.26 (PG 67.1361C) 576
7.17 (PG 67.1364C) **576n.31**

Stephen, bishop of Rome 380, 383-385, 387n.28, 397-398

Sulpicius Severus
Dialogues
2.4.8 766n.31
Life of St. Martin
13 766n.31

Sylloge Laureshamensis
(Codex Vaticanus palat. 833) **637-638**

Symeon of Mesopotamia 724, 728, 735

Symeon the New Theologian 735

Synods
Antioch 726n.8
Carthage 398 770-771
canon 12, 85, 86, 100 771
Constantinople 426 725n.4, 726n.6
Side 726n.8
Rome under Innocent 402 761

Syriac Acts of John (History of John the Son of Zebedee) 700-702
3, 8, 14, 15, 19 700
20-21 **700**
25 **701**
26-41 (various) 701
55 **701**
60-61 702

Tatian 246, 493
Diatessaron 111, 246, 442, 492
Oration 5 **246**

Tertullian of Carthage 6, 9, 13, 18, **272**, 273, 305, 326, 328, 329n.21, 331n.32, 336-350, 352n.6, 353n.15, 362, 363-366, 379, 387, 480n.16, 482, 563n.49, 595, 627, 679-680, 855
Answer to the Jews (Against the Jews) 272
3, 6 272
8 338, 272
8.14 113, 337n.9
9 272

930 | INDEX OF NON-CANONICAL CHRISTIAN AUTHORS AND WRITINGS

13	337, **346**	12.1	349
		12.1-2	337-338
Against Marcion		12.3-4	170n.14, 336n.5
1.14.3	277n.2, **277**, 345	12.3-5, 6, 8-9	338
1.23	277n.2	13.1-4	339
1.28.2-3	341n.24, **346**, 348, 349	13.3	342-343, 349
1.29.1	**277**	14.2	340
3.22	277n.2	15.1-2	336n.5, 349, 380
4.9	337	15.3	336, 347
5.10	277n.4	16.1-2	142n.39, 349
		17	278
Against Praxeas		17.1-5	343
26	342	17.4-5	229n.28, 230
Against the Valentinians		18	**364**, 365nn.8-9
1	284n.24	18.1	348
		18.5	138n.19, 340
Apology		18.6	**339n.17**, 348
18.4	340	19.1-3	345
50.15	350	20	344
		20.1	340
On Baptism	301, 336, 346n.38	20.4	337
1.1	**336n.2**, 340, 346, 347, 349	20.5	**336n.2**, 347, 348
1.2-3	128n.80, 301, 349	*On the Crown*	
1.10	347	3	340, 341, 342, 345, **363n.4**
2.2	347		
3	334n.47, 337, 348	*On Fasting*	
3.6	301-302	8	340n.19
4	256n.31, 334n.47, 348, 468n.27	*On the Flesh of Christ*	
4.1, 3-5	114, 340, 341, 346	17	347
5	334n.47, 347, 348, 442n.41		
5.1-3	**32**, 336, 346	*On Idolatry*	329
5	127	6	349
5.5-6	128n.84, 337, 346-347		
5.7	347	*On Modesty*	
6	127, 348	9	342n.27
6.1	337, 338, 342, 344, 347, 348n.41	9.9	**344n.34**
6.2	342	9.11	348
7	118, 310n.11	10	**339n.14**
7.1	341, 343	16.5	347
7.2	344, 347	18.15	347
8	310n.11, 337, 348	19.5	347, 348
8.1-3	125n.70, 337, 344	19.20	347
8.4	347	21.12	347
9.1	128n.77, 337, 347	22	142n.39, 349
9.2-4	114, 337	22.4, 9-10	350
10.2-3	337, 346n.38		
10.5-7	337, 338	*On Repentance*	347, 348
11	442n.42	4-6	338
11.1-4	337, 346	6-7	347
12	378n.49		

Index of Non-Canonical Christian Authors and Writings | 931

6	**341n.23**, 348n.41, 364n.5
6.16-17, 20	**338-339**
7	339
7-12	338
12	**339n.15**

On the Resurrection of the Flesh

8	**344**
8.3	665
47	348
48	349, 277n.4
48.11	**342n.27**

On the Shows

	329
4	340, 342, 348n.41, 349
24	**342n.26**, 348n.41

On the Soul

1.4	**344n.34**
11	365n.8
16	365
35.3	340n.20
39-41	365n.8
41	**347**

Prescription against Heretics

23	**339n.16**
36	338, 348n.41
36.5	345
40	**32n.35**, 345n.36

Scorpiace

6	350
12.10	**349n.46**

Testimony of the Soul

1	**340n.18**
3.2	365n.8
39-41	346

To the Martyrs

3	349

Veiling of Virgins

2	349n.45

Testament of the Lord 579-581

2.5	579
2.6, 7	580
2.8	**580-581**
2.9, 10	581

Testaments of the Twelve Patriarchs 108

Testament of Levi

18.6-7	101n.6, **108**

Testament of Judah

24.2	108

Testament of Asher

7.3	108

Theodore of Mopsuestia 15, 18, 462n.12, 519-532, 536, 539n.20, 541-542, 543, 570, 579, 580n.55, 619n.6, 702, 704, 784, 859

Catechetical Homilies 116n.24, 519-520

1-10	520n.7
1, 2, pp. 20-30	521
3, 4, pp. 46-47, 49	524
6, pp. 63-71	116n.24, **521, 521n.11**, 522
8, pp. 91-92	521, 526
9, pp. 94-96, 101, 103	521, 522
10, pp. 111-116	521, 522
11, pp. 1, 16	522
11-16	520n.7
12	527n.25
12, p. 20	**528**
12, pp. 23-26	520-521
12, p. 30	521, 527
12, p. 31	**523**, 527
12, pp. 32, 33-34	523
13	527n.25
13, pp. 35-36	**520**, 523
13, pp. 37-44	523, 524, 522n.13
13.17, 18-20, pp. 45-49	523, 324
14	527n.25
14, pp. 49-51	528, 529-530
14, p. 52	525-526, **530n.35, 530**
14, pp. 53-57	525, 528-530
14, pp. 53-54, 57-58	**529**
14, pp. 60-63	**525, 527**, 528
14, pp. 64-67	116, **521n.10**, 527, 528, **531**, 532
14, pp. 68-69	526, 530n.35, **531**
14.1	524n.20
15, pp. 72-78	526, **529, 530, 531**
15, p. 92	532
16, pp. 104, 108-109	526, 531, **532**

Commentary on Ephesians

4:5	528

INDEX OF NON-CANONICAL CHRISTIAN AUTHORS AND WRITINGS

Commentary on 1 Timothy
3:2   532n.43

On Psalms
50.7   365n.7

Theodoret of Cyrus   575n.28, 715-718,
                          719, 725n.4

Church History   726
4.10   **727**
4.25   624
5.4   717

Commentary on Isaiah
1:16 (PG 81.229B-C)   717n.2

Commentary on Titus 3:5   **163n.47**

Commentary on Hebrews
6:1 (PG 82.716)   **718**

Cure of Pagan Maladies
7.29, 30, 32   717

Fables of Heretics
2, 3   744n.80
4.3 (PG 83.420B-C)   576n.32, **716**
4.11 (PG 83.429B-C)   **726-727**
5.18 (PG 83.512A-C)   **715**

Questions and Answers to the Orthodox 717
14 (PG 6.12.61C-D)   717
37 (PG 6.12.84A-B)   **717**
56 (PG 6.1297C-D)   **717-718**
137 (PG 6.1389C-1392A)   **718**

Religious History
3 (PG 82.1325-1340)   **624**
3.16   **727n.9**

Theodosian Code
16.6.1-7   278n.9

Theodotus of Byzantium   119, 278, 280-283

Theodotus of Ancyra   280, 745-747
Homily 7 "On the Holy
Theophany"   745
1   **745-746**
3   **746**
4   **746**
5   **745**, 746

6   746
8   **746**
9   **746**
10   746-747
11   747

Theophilus of Alexandria (385-412)   699

Theophilus of Antioch   246-247
To Autolycus   246
1.8   247
1.12   247
2.16   378n.49, **247**

Timothy Aelurus of Alexandria   398
"Canonical Responses"   699n.60

Timothy of Constantinople   728n.15,
                                     728n.17
PG 86.45-52   **725n.4**, 744n.80

Walahfrid Strabo
*De exordiis et encrementis quarundam
in observationibus ecclesiasticis*
"rerum 27"   **632-633**

Zeno of Verona   648-651
Sermons
1.2.25   649n.6
1.3.21   651n.15
1.12   650, 651
1.13.10   651n.15
1.13.13   649
1.16.2   651
1.23   649-650, 651
1.24   650
1.28, 32   649, **650-651**
1.33.2   651
1.37   648-649
1.38.3   650n.9, 650n.13
1.41   650
1.44.2   650n.10
1.46B.3   650n.10
1.49   649, 650n.10, 651
1.55   649n.6, 650, 651
2.1-2   651
2.6.8   650
2.10   649

2.10.2	651	2.26.1	650
2.11.5	648, 649	2.26.3	650
2.13	648, 649	2.28	649, **650**, 651
2.14	649, 650, 650n.13	2.29.1	651
2.23	649, 651		

Index of Modern Authors

Abrahams, I., 64n.22
Abramowski, Luise, 339nn.16-17, 702n.4
Adamik, Tomas, 231n.39, 232n.40
Adler, Nikolaus, 171n.18
Adurgal, Ekrem, 26n.8
Agourides, S., 222n.2
Akeley, T. C., 668n.23, 669nn.26-27
Aland, Kurt, 362n.1, 369n.19, 376n.37, 378
Alla, W. Hassab, 695n.41
Allert, Craig D., 240n.8, 241n.16
Althaus, Heinz, 592n.2, 596n.10, 597nn.12-13
Amann, E., 735n.53
Amar, Joseph P., 500n.6, 503n.26
Amidon, Philip R., 458n.5, 575n.28, 716n.1
Amsler, Frédéric, 234n.49
Arand, Louis A., 791n.124, 808n.79
Ash, Anthony, 92n.47, 180n.39
Attridge, Harold W., 160n.39, 186n.1, 284n.23, 285n.29, 429n.3
Aubineau, Michel, 745n.1
Audet, J. P., 206n.22
Auf der Maur, Hans Jörg, 400n.1, 414n.61, 420n.82, 421n.93, 424n.103, 426n.112, 427nn.120-121
Austin, C., 34n.43, 48n.36
Avemarie, Friedrich, 141n.34, 166n.1, 171n.18, 172nn.22-23, 173nn.26-27, 174n.30, 176n.33, 181n.39, 182n.41, 183n.48, 185nn.50-53

Badia, Leonard F., 87n.25

Baily, D. R. Shackleton, 37n.57
Bamberger, B. J., 76n.87, 77n.92, 78n.98, 79n.103, 80n.114, 80n.117
Bammel, E., 110n.50, 242n.20
Baricco, Luisella Pejrani, 837n.5
Barkhuizen, J. H., 748n.4
Barkley, Gary Wayne, 405n.16
Barlow, Claude W., 668n.20
Barnard, L. W., 210n.39
Barrett-Lennard, R. J. S., 460n.7
Baudry, Gerard-Henry, 19-20, 148n.7, 241n.10, 481n.20
Baun, Jane, 596n.11, 723n.7
Beall, Todd S., 68n.48, 70n.54
Beasley-Murray, G. R., 60n.3, 100n.3, 102n.9, 103n.15, 115n.21, 133n.4, 137n.16, 139n.29, 146nn.1-2, 148n.4, 152n.14, 154n.20, 156n.27, 158n.32, 164n.48, 182n.40, 184n.48, 185n.51, 189n.8, 190n.15, 191n.16, 195n.29, 197, 198n.39
Beck, E., 506n.42, 508n.53, 509n.62
Bedard, W. M., 819n.2
Beita, Philippe, 665nn.6-11
Belche, J., 779n.17
Benoît, André, 22, 201n.2, 203n.8, 207n.25, 207nn.27-28, 208n.29, 209n.33, 213n.47, 214n.52, 215n.54, 218n.69, 219n.72, 237n.1, 238n.3, 239n.7, 241n.10, 269n.7, 303n.1, 306nn.24-25, 308n.44, 663n.2
Benoît, Fernand, 844n.25
Ben-Pechat, Malka, 821nn.12-13, 822nn.114-

15, 822nn.17-18, 823n.19, 823nn.21-22, 824n.24, 851-852
Bernard, J. H., 222n.5
Bertacchi, L., 661n.36
Bertrand, Daniel Alain, 103n.14, 104n.16, 112n.58
Bethge, Hans-Gebhard, 288n.43
Betz, Hans Dieter, 146n.2, 155n.26, 157n.31
Betz, Otto, 69n.54
Bévenot, Maurice, 343n.28, 390n.35
Bierma, Lyle D., 277n.2
Biffino, Annalisa, 840n.19
Bigg, C., 119n.44, 204n.12
Billerbeck, Paul, 63n.18, 76n.87, 139n.22
Bingham, D. Jeffrey, 267n.3
Bisconti, Fabrizio, 123n.63, 661n.36
Blanc, Cécile, 400n.1, 405n.20, 407n.26
Blowers, Paul, 724n.1
Böcher, Otto, 158n.34
Boeckh, A., 376n.35
Bogan, Mary Inez, 808n.83
Böhlig, Alexander, 292n.59
Bonnard, Émile, 682n.47
Bonner, Gerald, 804n.63
Bonnet, Charles, 836n.3, 845n.29
Bornemann, J., 113n.1
Botte, Bernard, 118n.39, 327, 343n.32, 344n.33, 489n.1, 634n.1, 713n.19
Bou Mansour, Tanios, 499n.3, 505n.38, 506n.42, 509nn.61-62, 510n.67, 512n.79, 513n.85
Bouvier, Bertrand, 234n.49
Bovon, François, 234nn.49-50, 269n.9, 276n.1, 853-854, 856n.3
Bowman, John, 523n.14
Bradshaw, Paul F., 239n.7, 327, 330n.24, 331n.32, 332n.37, 341n.25, 345n.37, 366n.11, 367n.14, 426n.115, 427n.116, 437n.25, 463n.15, 465nn.21-467n.25, 475n.5, 539n.22, 626n.23, 699n.60
Brandenburg, Hugo, 769n.38, 838nn.8-10
Brandt, Wilhelm, 72n.67, 76n.87
Braun, R., 774n.18
Brent, Allen, 325nn.1-3, 326n.4, 327nn.13-14, 328
Bright, Pamela, 417n.79, 778n.9
Brightman, F. E., 460n.7, 462nn.13-14, 463n.18

Broadus, John A., 554n.19
Brock, Sebastian, 273n.13, 437n.25, 439n.34, 495n.22, 496n.27, 497n.32, 500n.5, 501n.18, 502nn.22-23, 503n.24, 504n.31, 505n.33, 506nn.40-41, 507n.44, 507n.51, 512n.79, 513n.82, 513n.85, 528n.31, 713n.19
Brooks, O. S., 146n.1
Brown, Colin, 90n.39
Brown, Raymond E., 87n.19, 194nn.27-28, 195n.29
Brown, Scott, 140n.30
Browne, Charles Gordon, 592n.2
Bruce, Barbara J., 402n.8, 403n.12
Bruns, Gerda, 34n.46
Buck, Mary Joseph Aloysius, 635n.4
Buckley, Jorunn Jacobsen, 74n.84
Buhler, F. M., 829n.39
Burkert, Walter, 29n.21
Burkitt, F. C., 493n.15
Burnish, R. F. G., 364n.6,
Burnish, Raymond, 473n.1, 486n.33, 519n.1, 521n.11, 530n.37, 533n.1, 550n.5, 557n.33
Burns, J. Patout, 383n.12, 793n.139, 796n.4, 801n.49
Busch, Benedictus, 776n.2, 778n.15
Butterworth, G. W., 425n.109

Cambi, N., 835n.65
Camelot, Pierre Thomas, 12, 113n.2, 114n.6, 115n.21, 481n.21, 483n.25, 485n.29
Camp, Ashby L., 168n.8
Campbell, Thomas L., 720n.5
Capelle, B., 693n.39
Carlson, Stephen C., 140n.30
Carson, Donald A., 143n.44
Casey, Robert Pierce, 280n.17
Castelfranchi, Marina Falla, 769n.37
Cerfaux, L., 69n.54, 71n.67
Cerrato, J. A., 325n.1
Chadwick, Henry, 738n.62, 738n.64, 777n.3
Chadwick, John, 38n.2
Chambers, T. W., 551n.9
Charlesworth, James H., 87n.19, 121nn.54-55, 223n.6
Chase, F. H., 134n.6, 135n.10
Chavasse, Antoine, 766n.31
Cherix, Pierre, 228n.24
Cherry, John F., 833n.58

Chevalier, Pascale, 834nn.61-62
Chevallier, M.-A., 99n.2
Chierci, Umberto, 837n.5
Childers, Jeff, 431n.11, 521n.9, 719nn.3-4
Chilton, Bruce, 83n.1, 87n.23, 90n.41
Choufrine, Arkadi, 311n.17, 311n.20, 313n.36, 317n.59
Christiansen, Ellen Juhl, 343n.29
Christo, Gus George, 557n.33
Cirillo, L., 256n.30, 256n.34
Clark, William R., 448n.8
Clarke, G. W., 352n.5, 353n.15, 354n.19, 354n.21, 356nn.32-33, 370n.22, 381n.5, 382n.10, 383n.13, 384n.20, 385n.23, 389n.32, 394n.52
Clauss, Manfred, 33nn.37-38
Cohen, Shaye J. D., 76n.87, 77n.95, 78nn.96-97, 80n.117, 81n.129
Collins, A. Y., 61n.4
Collins, J. J., 67n.42, 108n.38
Conant, T. J., 38n.1
Connell, Martin F., 760n.11, 761n.14
Connolly, R. Hugh, 274n.14, 327, 438n.31, 439n.32, 636n.12, 702n.4, 703nn.5-7, 705n.9
Conway, Agnes Josephine, 763n.21
Conway, Walter J., 341n.22, 345n.37, 680n.24
Conybeare, F. C., 134n.6, 398n.61, 712n.18, 752n.10
Cook, David, 190n.14
Copenhaver, Brian P., 56n.50
Coquin, René-Georges, 465n.23
Corblett, Jules, 1-2, 362n.1
Corney, Mark, 847n.34
Cosentino, Augusto, 112n.57, 276n.1
Cramer, Peter, 17, 630n.34, 683n.48
Crehan, Joseph, 135n.9, 149n.8, 150n.9, 162n.45, 167n.3, 175n.32, 192n.21, 208n.32, 348n.44, 352n.7
Cross, Anthony R., 186n.1
Cross, F. L., 474n.3
Crouzel, Henri, 400nn.1-3, 413nn.59-60, 415n.64, 415n.67, 418n.80
Cullmann, Oscar, 102n.9, 139n.27, 146n.1, 172n.23, 252n.16
Cuming, G. J., 154n.21, 463n.17, 569n.13
Cuneo, Bernard Henry, 134n.7, 450n.15
Curley, M. J., 236n.55

Cuscito, Giuseppe, 769n.38

Dahl, Nils A., 60n.1, 161n.40
Dale, James W., 38n.1
Dalton, William Joseph, 189n.10
Daly, Robert, 412n.54
Danby, Herbert, 63n.20
Daniélou, Jean, 400n.3, 401n.4, 402n.9, 404n.14, 416, 484n.26, 584nn.9-10, 604n.6, 605n.8, 612n.30
d'Antonio, Massimo, 839n.15, 840
Darrouzes, Jean, 735n.52
Dassmann, Ernst, 15-16, 123n.63
Davis, J. C., 168n.10
Day, Juliette, 473n.1, 474n.3, 478n.14, 822n.16
de Bhaldraithe, Eoin, 633n.52
de Bruyn, Theodore, 693nn.37-38
deBruyne, L., 123n.63, 125n.70, 128n.87
DeConick, April D., 285n.28, 288n.41
de Durand, George-Mattheiu, 738n.60, 738n.63
Deferrari, Roy J., 788n.94
Deichmann, F. W., 127n.73, 127n.75, 128n.79, 819n.1
Dekkers, Eligius, 352n.7, 391n.43
de la Croix, C., 844n.27
Delaine, Janet, 35n.51
De Latte, Robert, 776n.2, 778n.15, 779nn.20-21, 779n.23, 783n.52, 784nn.64-65, 785n.71, 786n.83, 787n.93, 788n.94, 788n.97, 789n.99, 789n.101, 789n.104
Dellasorte, Gabriella Brumat, 660n.33
Delling, Gerhard, 85n.10, 88n.26, 139n.26, 143n.43, 146nn.1-2, 152n.14, 157n.29, 159n.35, 163n.46, 164n.49, 166n.1, 167n.4, 175n.32
DeMaris, Richard E., 154n.24
Denney, James, 133n.5
de Paoli, G., 650n.12
De Romestin, H., 635n.3, 645n.77, 646n.89
De Rossi, G. B., 638n.26, 662
de Roten, Philippe, 533n.1, 536nn.5-6, 537n.14, 538n.17, 539n.22, 540n.25, 541n.32, 542n.37, 542nn.39-40, 543n.44, 544nn.48-50, 545nn.51-53, 545n.57, 550nn.5-6, 550n.8, 552n.14, 556n.26, 557n.31, 559n.39, 560n.44, 622n.10, 623n.16
des Places, Édouard, 732nn.37-38, 733n.40

Desprez, V., 729n.19
Devos, P., 473n.2
Devreesse, R., 519n.2, 527n.25, 529n.33, 530n.38
DeVries, G., 713n.19
Díaz y Díaz, M., 487n.36
Didier, J.-Ch., 363n.1, 367n.13, 369n.19, 577n.38, 577n.40, 767n.34, 768n.35, 788n.97, 789nn.102-103, 804n.63
Diehle, E., 372n.29, 638n.26
Dirksen, Aloys H., 85n.11, 339n.14
Dittenberger, W., 26n.2
Dix, Gregory, 327
Doignon, Jean, 118n.42, 119n.48
Dölger, Franz Josef, 53n.46, 62n.15, 207n.28, 252n.13, 281n.20, 310n.11, 393n.48, 434n.19, 440n.36, 464n.19, 476n.6, 478n.12, 638n.26, 661n.37, 761n.12, 789n.98, 819n.3
Donfried, Karl Paul, 207n.27, 208n.29
Doval, Alexis J., 474n.3, 476n.8, 478n.12, 478n.14, 479nn.15-16, 481n.19, 482n.22, 482n.24, 484n.29, 485n.32, 486n.34
Draper, Jonathan A., 202n.5
Drijvers, Han J. W., 111n.54
Drower, E. S., 75n.86
Ducatillon, J., 582n.2, 584n.5, 588n.24, 589n.28, 590n.30, 590nn.32-33
Duensing, Hugo, 227n.20
Duncan, E. J., 489n.3, 490nn.4-5, 491n.6, 492n.9, 492n.11, 494n.17, 494nn.21-495n.24, 495n.26, 496n.27, 496nn.29-30, 497n.31, 498nn.33-34
Dunderberg, Ismo, 278n.10
Dunn, James D. G., 148n.6, 153n.16, 153n.20
Duthoy, R., 33n.41
Duval, Noël, 836n.2
Dyggve, E., 834n.63

Eagen, M. C., 669n.28
Echle, Harry A., 309n.6, 312n.29, 313n.31, 313n.34, 318n.64, 320n.72, 492n.13
Edelstein, Emma J., 26nn.6-7
Edelstein, Ludwig, 26nn.6-7
Edsman, Carl-Martin, 91n.43, 408n.32
Edwards, Mark, 618n.4, 674n.11, 677n.16
Ehrhardt, Arnold, 192n.22
Ellard, Gerald, 760n.11
Emminghaus, Johannes H., 851
Engelmann, H., 34n.47

Escher, 37n.57
Evans, Craig A., 83n.1
Evans, Ernest, 336n.1, 337n.8, 339n.17, 340n.20, 341n.22, 341n.25, 343n.31, 346n.38, 348n.44
Ewald, Marie Liguori, 679n.22, 680n.28
Eygun, F., 844n.27

Farmer, William R., 140n.32
Farrell, John E., 148n.5, 330n.26, 332n.39, 481n.20, 497n.32
Fascher, E., 1
Fausone, A. M., 123n.63, 127n.76
Fee, Gordon D., 153n.20
Feissel, D., 376n.38, 617n.1, 626n.22
Feldman, Louis H., 86n.15
Feltoe, Charles Lett, 762n.17
Ferguson, Everett, 20, 22, 29n.21, 115n.18, 121n.57, 123n.63, 126n.70, 153n.16, 171n.19, 187n.2, 210n.39, 212n.42, 214n.52, 227n.19, 239n.5, 239n.7, 248n.1, 269n.7, 328n.19, 331n.33, 363n.1, 365n.7, 367n.15, 372n.30, 378n.48, 400n.1, 415n.67, 416n.74, 488n.37, 496n.29, 534n.2, 566n.5, 582nn.1-2, 603nn.1-3, 609n.20, 612n.30, 615n.42, 616n.47, 618n.5, 634n.1, 725n.1, 759n.5, 830n.43
Ferrar, W. J., 449n.10
Février, P.-A., 843n.24
Fiema, Z. T., 824n.23, 824nn.25-26
Finkelstein, L., 76n.91
Finn, Thomas Macy, 4, 19, 21, 318n.67, 533n.1, 536n.8, 536n.11, 538nn.16-17, 538n.20, 539nn.22-23, 540n.25, 540nn.27-28, 541n.32, 542n.37, 542n.39, 543nn.43-44, 544nn.46-47, 552n.12, 552n.14, 555n.22, 752n.10, 772nn.7-8, 772n.10, 773n.12, 774nn.15-17
Finney, Paul Corby, 833n.60
Fischer, Joseph A., 391n.42
Fitschen, Klaus, 724n.1, 725nn.2-4, 726nn.5-8, 727nn.9-11, 728n.13, 728n.17, 729n.18, 730n.28, 731nn.33-34, 732n.38, 735n.55, 738nn.64-65, 739n.66, 744nn.80-81
Fixot, M., 843n.24
Flemington, W. F., 146n.1
Freeland, Jane Patricia, 763n.21
Fremantle, W. H., 678n.18, 680n.25

Flusser, David, 134n.6, 134n.8, 136n.11, 201nn.2-3, 202n.4, 205n.19
Froidevaux, L. M., 307n.31
Frondoni, Alessandra, 837n.4
Funk, Wolf-Peter, 294n.72

Gagé, J., 375n.34
Galtier, Paul, 569n.11
Ganss, George E., 756n.1
Garrucci, R., 662
Gärtner, Michael, 362n.1
Gaselee, S., 54n.48
Gaudette, Pierre, 354n.23, 357n.35, 358n.38, 359n.47, 360n.59, 361n.64
Gavin, F., 60n.1
Gebhart, E., 603n.2
Geerard, M., 735n.54
Gelichi, Sauro, 836n.1
George, A. M., 146n.1
Gero, Stephen, 202n.7
Gessel, W., 851n.51
Gianotto, Claudio, 294n.72
Gieschen, Charles A., 136n.13, 162n.42, 196n.32
Giet, S., 218n.67
Gifford, E. H., 474n.3
Gingras, George E., 473n.2, 487n.36
Gistelinck, Frans, 445n.4
Giuliani, Roberta, 840n.19
Giversen, Søren, 289n.44, 294n.72, 294n.74
Gnilka, Joachim, 70n.54, 86n.16, 89n.33
Grant, Robert M., 245n.28
Green, H. B., 134n.8
Green, Joel B., 178nn.36-37
Gregoire, Henri, 719n.3
Grenfell, B. P., 269n.8
Gribomont, J., 582n.2, 724n.1, 728n.15
Griffiths, J. Gwyn, 31nn.30-31, 32n.33, 330n.27
Grillmeier, Aloys, 713n.19
Groff, Kent I., 140
Gross, Jules, 470n.32
Grossi, Vittorino, 776n.2, 778n.14, 782n.47, 783n.52, 783n.56, 790n.108, 795nn.1-3, 804nn.61-62, 805n.65, 805n.68, 808n.82, 808n.84, 811n.100
Guida, A., 316n.57
Guidobaldi, Federico, 839nn.11-14

Guillaumont, A., 703n.5
Guy, Laurie, 330n.28, 537n.15, 541n.34

Häkkinen, Sakari, 248n.1
Hall, Stuart George, 118n.42, 122nn.58-60, 245n.28, 246n.30, 383n.14
Halton, Thomas P., 21, 582n.2, 648n.1, 666n.12
Hamilton, J. D. B., 647n.92
Hamman, Adalbert, 219n.71
Hamman, André, 21-22
Hammerich, Holger, 256n.30, 339n.14, 364nn.5, 365n.6, 372n.30, 382n.8
Hanson, Craig L., 666n.12
Hanssens, Jean Michel, 327, 329n.23
Harkins, Paul W., 533n.1, 536n.9, 538n.16, 538n.19, 540n.29, 545n.56, 546n.58, 547n.1, 549n.4, 556n.30, 622n.12, 623n.13
Harmless, William, 635n.8, 776n.2, 779n.15, 779n.17, 780nn.27-28, 780n.35, 781n.36, 781n.38, 781n.41, 781n.43, 782n.48, 783n.56, 785n.66, 787n.93, 788n.96, 793n.135, 813n.113
Harnack, Adolf von, 122n.59, 142n.41, 143n.43, 276n.2, 310n.8, 444n.1
Harrill, J. Albert, 349n.45
Harris, M. J., 168n.10
Harting-Correa, Alice L, 633nn.50-51
Hartman, Lars, 88n.27, 90n.40, 136nn.11-12, 148n.4, 182n.41, 182n.45, 183n.47, 197, 215n.54
Hartranft, Chester D., 796n.5
Hastings, James, 1
Hausherr, I., 734n.43, 735n.55
Hawthorne, Gerald F., 246n.29
Haykin, Michael A. G., 586n.17
Hefele, C. J., 761n.13, 771nn.1-6
Heggelbacher, Othmar, 11-12
Heine, Ronald E., 401n.5, 407n.27, 413
Heiser, Lothar, 3, 12, 115n.21, 125n.69, 630n.37, 827nn.28-29, 833n.59, 860
Henrichs, A., 56n.51
Herter, Hans, 365n.7
Hesse, Otmar, 738nn.61-62, 739n.65
Hill, Charles E., 107n.30
Hill, Edmund, 781n.36, 809n.91
Hill, G. F., 719n.3
Hoffmann, Adolf, 26n.8

Index of Modern Authors | 939

Hoffmann, R. Joseph, 277n.3, 278n.8
Hort, F. J. A., 190n.15
Houssiau, A., 303n.1, 304n.13, 305n.18, 306n.22, 307n.30
Hubaux, J., 34
Hubbard, B. J., 133n.3
Hug, Joseph, 140n.32
Hull, Michael F., 154n.23
Hunt, A. S., 269n.8
Hunt, E. D., 473n.2
Hunt, John, 76n.91
Hvalvik, Reidar, 210n.38, 214n.52

Illert, Martin, 730n.30

Jackson, Blomfield, 582n.2, 727n.11
Jaeger, Werner, 729n.20
James, M. R., 225n.11, 435n.24
Janssens, Yvonne, 292n.56
Jeanes, Gordon P., 563n.49, 648nn.1-3, 649nn.4-6, 650n.8, 650nn.12-13, 651nn.14-15, 666n.12, 666n.15, 760n.10
Jeffery, Peter, 140n.30
Jefford, Clayton N., 202n.6
Jensen, Robin M., 123n.63, 129n.90
Jeremias, Joachim, 76n.88, 81n.127, 178n.37, 269n.8, 362n.1, 369n.19, 373n.32, 376nn.36-37, 377-378, 627nn.26-27
Jilek, August, 16
Johnson, Maxwell E., 3-4, 20-21, 327, 332n.37, 345n.37, 366n.11, 435n.24, 460nn.7-8, 461n.9, 461n.11, 462n.12, 462n.14, 463, 464nn.19-20, 487n.35, 640n.39, 663n.2, 766n.31
Johnson, M. D., 67n.43
Johnson, S. E., 221n.1
Johnston, A. Edward, 509n.58, 513n.83, 513n.85
Jones, Larry Paul, 142n.40, 144n.46
Jones, Christopher, 26n.8
Jones, F. Stanley, 202n.7, 249n.3, 254nn.27-28, 257n.36, 258n.39, 260nn.46-47, 261n.49, 261n.53, 262nn.55-56
Jones, William H., 170n.16
Jonge, Marinus de, 67nn.43-44, 225n.13

Kacynski, Reiner, 533n.1
Kaetli, Jean-Daniel, 228n.24

Kalleres, Dana S., 482n.24
Kanellopoulos, C., 824n.23
Kantorowicz, Ernest H., 492n.13
Kappes, Marcia A., 703n.5, 708nn.10-12
Kassel, Rudolf, 34n.43, 48n.36
Kasser, Rodolphe, 231n.36, 301n.105
Keating, Daniel A., 687n.1, 688nn.3-5, 689n.10, 690n.19, 691nn.26-31, 764n.22
Keble, J., 551n.9
Kees, Reinhard Jakob, 603n.1, 605nn.10-11
Kelhofer, James A., 140n.32
Kelly, Henry Ansgar, 16-17, 329n.22, 340n.20, 580n.54
Kelly, J. N. D., 332n.35
Kelly, T. A., 646n.90
Kertelge, Karl, 132n.2, 134n.6
Khatchatrian, A., 829n.36
Khouri-Sarkis, G., 713n.19
Khs-Burmester, O. H. E., 695nn.41-699n.59
King, J. R., 796n.5
Kingsbury, Jack Dean, 133n.3
Kinzig, Wolfram, 332n.36, 577n.37
Kirchner, Hubert, 383n.12
Kirsten, Hans, 340n.20, 623n.14
Klauser, Theodor, 204n.13
Kleinheyer, B., 851
Klijn, A. F. J., 73n.77, 74n.80, 104nn.17-18, 105n.23, 111n.54, 429n.1, 429n.4, 434n.21, 700n.1
Knupp, J., 533n.1
Kollwitz, Johannes, 123n.63
Kosmala, Hans, 134n.8
Kostof, Spiro K., 129n.91, 758n.4, 759n.6, 759n.8
Kötzsche-Breitenbruch, Lieselotte, 129n.89
Kovacs, , David, 39n.3
Kraeling, Carl H., 86n.16, 440n.39
Kraft, H., 363n.1
Kraft, Robert A., 221n.1
Kreider, Alan, 565n.3
Kretschmar, Georg, 5, 7-9, 157n.30, 158n.34, 162n.44, 207n.28, 328n.19, 330n.25, 331n.30, 332n.34, 332n.38, 333n.41, 366n.12, 367n.13, 382n.10, 423n.99, 435n.23, 463n.15, 470n.31, 541n.31, 584n.10, 695n.41, 697n.50, 698n.55, 858n.5
Krueger, Paul, 630n.35
Kugener, M.-A., 719n.3

Kruger, Michael J., 269n.8
Kühn, C. G., 41n.9
Kuss, Otto, 147n.3, 160, 196-197

Lake, Kirsopp, 1
Lamb, W. R. M., 53n.45
Lampe, G. W. H., 269n.5, 312n.29, 348n.40, 348n.42, 354n.23, 382n.10, 431n.9, 484n.28, 524n.19, 531n.39, 735n.50
Lane, Anthony N. S., 362n.1, 363n.4, 377n.39
Langgärtner, Georg, 651n.16, 655n.24
Laporte, Jean, 368n.17
LaSor, William L., 64n.27
Lawrence, Jonathan D., 60n.2, 64n.27, 68n.48, 70n.54, 70nn.57,61, 71n.66, 266n.1
Layton, Bentley, 285n.27, 288n.43, 291n.54, 295n.79
Lebon, J., 624
Leclercq, H., 123n.63, 312n.30
Ledwich, William, 634n.1
Lee, Samuel, 134n.6, 450n.12
Légasse, Simon, 19, 74n.85, 76n.88, 82n.130, 83n.1, 87n.23, 87n.25, 96n.57, 115n.21, 320n.72, 492n.13
Leipoldt, Johannes, 25n.1, 30n.25, 33n.39, 76n.87, 79n.111, 86n.16, 378n.45
Lemarié, Joseph, 656nn.25-27, 657n.28, 661n.35
Leonhard, Clemens, 520n.4
Lewis, Jack P., 201n.1
Lichtenberger, Hermann, 68n.45, 84n.9, 87n.25
Lienhard, Joseph T., 367n.15, 404n.13, 409n.35, 417n.77
Lietzmann, Hans, 431n.12, 519n.3
Lightfoot, J. B., 363n.2
Lindsay, Jack, 31n.31
Littré, É., 39n.5
Llewelyn, S. R., 376n.38, 617nn.1-2, 626n.22
Löfstedt, B., 648n.1
Logan, Alastair H. B., 202n.7, 279n.13, 294n.71, 568n.10
Lohmeyer, Ernst, 83n.1, 86n.17
L'Orange, Hans-Peter, 759n.9
Louth, Andrew, 724n.1, 734n.43
Louw, J. P., 21
Luibheid, Colm, 720n.5

Lukken, G. M., 369n.19
Lundberg, Per, 11, 120n.53, 121n.56, 139n.28, 151n.11, 189n.10, 210n.39, 212n.42, 213n.48, 224n.9, 402n.9
Luomanen, Petri, 105n.19
Lupieri, Edmondo F., 74n.84, 83n.1, 86n.15
Luttikuizen, Gerard P., 74n.82

McCarthy, Carmel, 501n.15
Macartney, Thomas, 45n.29
McCauley, L. P., 474n.3
McConnell, Christian David, 663n.1, 664nn.3-4, 665n.10, 668n.19, 668n.21, 669nn.24-25, 669n.28, 670n.29
MacDermot, Violet, 296n.87, 297n.92
MacDonald, Dennis, 233nn.43-44
McDonnell, Kilian, 17-19, 102n.7, 105n.21, 112n.57, 113n.1, 115n.21, 117n.33, 120n.52, 344n.35, 402n.9, 414n.62, 671n.1
McHugh, Michael, 635n.9
McIntyre, Luther B., Jr., 168n.7
McKenna, Stephen, 671n.2
McKinion, Steven A., 627n.24
McLeod, Frederick G., 526, 527n.25, 528n.30, 531nn.40-41
MacRae, George W., 285n.29, 290n.49
McVey, Kathleen, 500n.9, 502n.20, 502n.23, 506n.40, 508n.53, 510n.66, 632n.47
Maertens, Th., 2-3, 183n.46, 364n.6, 367n.13
Magen, Y., 64n.27
Magness, J. Lee, 140n.32
Magness, Jodi, 69n.49, 71n.66
Mahé, Jean-Pierre, 294nn.72-73, 295n.76
Maier, J.-L., 839n.16
Malherbe, Abraham J., 231n.36, 612n.30
Malina, Bruce J., 137n.14
Maloney, George A., 728n.16
Manson, T. W., 194n.25
Mantey, J. R., 168n.9
Marcenaro, M., 837n.6
Marcovich, Miroslav, 73n.77, 279n.11
Marcus, Ralph, 168n.10
Marec, E., 785n.68
Markschies, Christoph, 328
Marriott, George L., 725n.4
Marsh, H. G., 318n.64
Marshall, I. Howard, 59n.56
Martin, Hubert, Jr., 27n.11

Maraval, P., 487n.36
Mather, P. Boyd, 133n.3
Mattei, Paul, 386n.24, 387n.27
Meeks, Wayne, 285n.28
Meier, John P., 133n.3
Ménard, Jacques, 283n.21
Menis, G. C., 130n.93, 661n.34, 661n.36
Merkelbach, R., 34n.47
Metzger, Bruce M., 231n.36
Metzger, Marcel, 327n.14, 564n.1
Meyendorff, John, 728n.15
Meyer, Marvin, 301n.105
Michaélides, D., 348n.44
Michaelis, Wilhelm, 138n.20, 169n.13, 178n.37
Mielke, U., 123n.63
Mierow, Charles Christopher, 678n.17
Milavec, Aaron, 201nn.2-3, 202nn.4-7, 203n.8, 203n.10, 204n.11, 205n.17, 205n.19, 206nn.22-23
Milhau, M., 672n.6
Mingana, A., 116n.24, 519n.1, 520n.6, 521n.8, 522nn.12-13, 702n.4
Minge, J. P., 735, 738n.63, 739n.67
Mirecki, Paul Allen, 141n.32, 202n.7
Mitchell, Leonel L., 330n.25, 634n.1, 639n.29, 640n.39, 640n.41
Mitchell, Nathan, 201n.2, 206n.22
Mohrmann, Christine, 374n.33
Molland, Einar, 250n.6, 250n.9, 252n.16, 253n.21, 255n.29, 256n.34, 258n.38, 261n.50
Montague, George T., 17-18, 344n.35, 671n.1
Moore, Joseph R., Jr., 378n.46
Moore, William, 604n.7, 613n.32
Morard, Francoise, 290n.50, 295n.78
Morris, J. B., 502n.23, 546n.59, 553n.16
Mossay, Justin, 592n.2, 745n.2
Mueller, Dieter, 284n.23
Mueller, Joseph G., 569n.10
Mühlenberg, Ekkehard, 603n.1
Müller, C. Detlef G., 225n.12, 225n.14, 226n.15
Munier, Charles, 22, 213n.47, 332n.38, 663n.2
Muñoz, Antonio, 492n.12
Murray, Robert, 494n.18, 504n.28, 515n.89, 515n.92
Mussner, Franz, 188n.7

Musurillo, Herbert, 488n.37
Myers, Susan E., 222n.5, 430n.6
Myllykoski, Matti, 107n.30

Nagel, Eduard, 365nn.8-9, 370nn.23-24, 371n.27, 627n.24, 804n.62, 808n.82
Nardi, Carlo, 310n.12, 313n.31, 314nn.38-39, 315n.46, 316, 320n.76
Neri, U., 582n.2
Nestori, Aldo, 123n.64, 851
Netzer, Ehud, 64n.27
Neunheuser, Burkhard, 12-15, 388n.29, 631nn.38-45, 815n.141
Neusner, Jacob, 63n.20, 490n.3
Nicolai, Vincenzo Fiocchi, 836n.1
Nicolaou, Kyriakos, 827n.29
Niederwimmer, Kurt, 206n.22
Nock, Arthur Darby, 25n.1, 26n.3, 27, 29n.19, 31n.31, 32n.35, 85n.13

O'Ceallaigh, G. C., 106n.27
Oepke, Albrecht, 25n.1, 38n.1, 79n.102, 83n.2, 88n.29, 148n.7, 150n.10, 378n.45, 854n.2
Oldfather, W. A., 29n.20
Orbe, A., 309n.6, 311n.13, 312n.23, 313n.35
Orlandos, A. C., 831n.48
Osborn, Eric F., 239n.4
Osburn, Carroll D., 141n.36, 168n.6, 196n.33
Osiek, Carolyn, 215n.53, 215nn.55-56
Ostmeyer, Karl-Heinrich, 151n.11, 189n.9, 190n.12, 191n.17, 191n.19
Outler, Albert C., 421n.94

Pagels, Elaine, 284n.26, 286nn.32-33, 288n.42
Palardy, William B., 756
Parenti, S., 752n.10
Paton, W. R., 45n.30
Paulin, A., 473n.1
Payne Smith, R., 688nn.5-6, 689n.10
Pearson, Birger A., 289n.44, 294n.72, 294n.74, 299n.97, 455n.1
Preisendanz, K., 56n.51
Pelikan, Jaroslav, 369n.19
Peradse, Gregor, 205n.18
Percival, Henry R., 574n.25
Perinetti, Renato, 836n.3

Perler, Othmar, 443n.44, 845n.28, 846
Pernveden, Lage, 215n.54, 215n.58, 218n.69, 219n.73
Petersen, William L., 111n.55
Peterson, Erik, 225n.13, 738n.64
Phillips, L. Edward, 327, 366n.11, 397n.57
Picard, Jean-Charles, 629n.31, 852
Piédagnel, A., 474n.3, 533n.1, 629n.31
Pierce, Mark, 222n.5
Pierre, Marie-Joseph, 490n.3
Pillinger, Renate, 204n.13, 205n.21, 833n.60, 858n.4, 859
Piva, Paolo, 838n.7
Plested, Marcus, 724n.1, 728n.13, 728n.15, 729n.18, 730n.25, 730n.31, 731n.35, 732n.39, 733n.42, 738n.62, 739n.65, 740n.70
Polyzogopoulos, Theodoritus, 732n.39, 733n.40, 734n.43, 734n.45
Porter, Stanley E., 175n.31
Power, David N., 303n.1
Preisendanz, K., 56n.51
Prigent, Pierre, 212n.42
Prostmeier, Ferdinand R., 210n.38, 214n.49
Purintun, Ann-Elizabeth, 221n.1
Pusey, Karen, 76n.91
Pusey, P. E., 687n.2

Quasten, Johannes, 128n.83, 441n.40, 523n.15, 527n.27, 634n.1, 639n.28, 839n.17
Quesnel, M., 183n.48
Quinn, Frank C., 328n.19

Raeder, Maria, 155n.25
Rahner, Hugo, 428n.125
Rahner, Karl, 216n.61, 735n.55, 736n.56
Räisänen, Heikki, 277n.2
Ramsey, Boniface, 651n.16
Randell, Thomas, 687n.2
Rapp, Claudia, 719n.3
Ratcliff, E. C., 479n.16, 497n.31, 564n.2, 569n.13
Razette, Jean, 336n.1, 337n.6, 346n.38, 347n.39, 348n.40, 348n.43
Reich, Ronny, 64n.27, 71n.66
Reicke, Bo, 189n.10, 190n.15, 191n.16, 192n.21, 192n.23
Reinink, G. J., 73n.77, 74n.80, 111n.54
Reitzenstein, R., 53n.46

Reynaud, Jean-François, 843n.23
Reynders, D. Bruno, 305n.14
Rhodes, James N., 212n.43
Ricciardi, Monica, 126n.72
Richard, Marcel, 577n.36
Richardson, Alan, 139n.27
Richardson, E. C., 450n.13
Ries, J., 73n.79
Riggenbach, E., 134n.6
Riley, Hugh M., 473n.1, 477nn.9-10, 478n.12, 479n.15, 480n.18, 481n.20, 482n.25, 484n.26, 519n.1, 519n.3, 523nn.14-16, 524nn.18-20, 525n.21, 526nn.22-23, 528n.28, 528n.31, 529n.32, 530n.36, 531n.40, 533n.1, 538n.17, 540n.25, 543n.44, 544n.48, 552n.14, 555n.22, 617n.3, 634n.1, 640n.39, 643n.62, 643n.65, 643n.68, 644nn.70-72
Ristow, Günter, 123n.63
Ristow, Sebastian, 661n.35, 758n.3, 785n.68, 820-21, 822n.18, 828-32, 838, 840, 844, 847n.33, 849-851
Rizzardi, Clementina, 129n.92, 662n.37
Roberti, M. Mirabella, 637n.24
Roberts, C. H., 693nn.38-39
Robinson, J. Armitage, 136n.11, 307n.31
Robinson, James M., 285n.29
Roey, Albert Van, 624n.19
Rogers, C. F., 64n.22, 130n.93, 858n.4
Roques, R., 723n.8
Rordorf, Willy, 201n.2, 202n.4, 204n.12, 205n.18
Roustan, F., 844n.26
Rouwhorst, G., 431n.12
Röwekamp, G., 735n.50
Rowley, H. H., 86n.16, 87n.25
Rudolph, Kurt, 71n.67, 72n.69, 73n.75, 73n.78, 74n.84, 77n.91, 79n.100, 88n.29, 283n.22
Russo, Eugenio, 836n.1
Rusten, Jeffrey, 40n.7
Rutherford, J., 732n.37

Saber, Georges, 499nn.2-4, 500n.5, 500nn.7-8, 501n.14, 502nn.21-22, 503n.24, 504n.27, 504n.29, 506nn.39-40, 506n.43, 509-510, 511n.77, 512
Sabou, Sorin, 156n.26

Sagnard, François, 318n.67
Salmond, S. D. F., 334n.45, 747n.3
Sanders, E. P., 64n.27
Sannazaro, Marco, 637n.23, 637n.25
Santos Otero, Aurelio de, 227n.20, 229n.30
Sauser, Ekkart, 783n.57, 791n.119
Saxer, Victor, 9-11, 218n.67, 219n.69, 280n.17, 315n.46, 320n.74, 351n.1, 352n.6, 352n.8, 353nn.16-17, 354n.20, 360n.56, 360n.58, 400n.1, 420n.83, 426n.115, 519n.2, 520n.4, 594n.7, 629n.33, 630n.36, 656n.26, 670n.29, 720n.5, 748n.4, 761n.16, 768n.36, 772n.7, 773n.11
Schäferdiek, Knut, 232nn.41-42
Scheck, Thomas P., 368n.16, 404n.15
Scheidweiler, Felix, 106n.28, 226n.17, 227n.22
Schenke, H.-M., 288n.40
Schenkl, H., 50n.37
Schermann, Theodor, 471n.33
Schick, R., 824n.23
Schiller, Gertrud, 123n.63
Schlarb, Robert, 156n.26
Schlatter, Fredric W., 579n.52
Schmidt, Carl, 230n.34
Schmitz, Josef, 634n.1
Schnackenburg, Rudolf, 146n.2, 149n.8, 151n.12, 152nn.14-15, 153n.19, 155n.26, 156nn.27-28, 159nn.36-37, 165n.50
Schneemelcher, Wilhelm, 104n.18, 105n.23, 228n.27, 229n.29, 269n.8
Schoedel, William R., 109n.49, 209n.34, 210n.37
Schoeps, Hans Joachim, 248n.1, 250n.9, 260n.48, 263
Schwartz, Eduard, 327
Scobie, C. H. H., 83n.1, 84n.5, 88n.26
Scott, John A., 45
Scroggs, Robin, 140
Searle, Mark, 369n.19, 379n.50, 629n.32, 777n.3
Sebastian, J. Jayakiran, 383n.12, 389n.32, 393n.44
Segelberg, E., 75n.86, 284n.26, 285n.29, 288n.40
Selwyn, E. G., 191n.19
Sevrin, Jean-Marie, 288n.39, 290nn.47-48, 290n.50, 291n.54, 292nn.58-60, 293nn.62-63, 293n.65, 294n.71, 294n.75, 295n.81, 296n.84, 296n.86, 298n.93, 299n.95
Shapland, C. R. B., 457n.4
Sieber, John N., 291n.53, 295n.80
Siena, Silvia Lusuardi, 637n.23, 637n.25
Silverstein, Theodore, 227n.21
Simcox, W. H., 546n.59, 553n.16
Simone, J. R., 772n.7
Sinclair, William MacDonald, 735n.51
Skarsaune, Oskar, 80n.114, 204n.13, 212n.40, 212n.42, 241n.14
Skira, Jaroslav Z., 489n.3
Smith, Daniel A., 117n.34
Smith, Derwood, 76n.88
Smith, Joseph P., 304n.6, 306n.26
Smith, M. A., 237n.2
Smith, Morton, 140, 319n.71
Smith, Robert Harry, 137n.15
Smyth, Herbert Weir, 137n.18
Spencer, W. G., 36n.55
Sperry-White, Grant, 579n.53
Spinks, Bryan D., 4-5, 430n.7, 438n.28, 460n.8, 703n.6, 768n.36
Squarciapino, Maria Floriani, 33n.36
Srawley, J. H., 634n.1
Stander, H. F., 21, 124n.65
Stanley, D. M., 146n.1
Stauffer, S. Anita, 661n.34, 836n.2, 841n.21, 842n.22
Steely, John E., 277n.2
Stegemann, Hartmut, 87n.25
Stenzel, Alois, S. J., 5-7, 158n.33
Stevens, George B., 546n.59, 553n.16, 623n.15
Stewart, Columba, 724n.1, 725nn.3-4, 726nn.5-6, 727n.12, 728nn.13-14, 729n.18
Stewart-Sykes, Alaistair, 328
Stommel, Eduard, 34, 36, 205, 858-860
Stone, Darwell, 1
Stopford, J. T. Sarsfield, 505n.35
Story, Cullen I. K., 241n.15
Strack, Herman L., 63n.18, 76n.87, 139n.22
Strecker, Georg, 105n.23, 249nn.3-4, 254n.27, 256n.30, 256nn.32-35, 258n.37
Suchla, B. R., 333
Swallow, James Edward, 592n.2
Szymusiak, J. M., 592n.1

Tamaro, B. Forlati, 661n.36
Tannehill, Robert C., 155n.26
Taranto, Salvatore, 603n.1, 616nn.45-46
Tardif, Henri, 656n.25
Taylor, Joan E., 70n.54, 83n.1, 84n.5, 84n.9, 94n.52
Taylor, T. M., 76n.91
Teske, Roland J., 780n.31, 792n.133, 805n.65
Thiering, B. E., 94n.50
Thomas, Joseph, 67n.41, 71n.67, 72n.72, 74n.84, 84n.9, 85n.14, 86n.15, 87n.23, 248n.2, 249n.4, 250n.9, 263n.61
Thomassen, Einar, 278n.10, 284n.26, 289n.46
Thompson, T., 634n.1
Thomson, Robert W., 709nn.13-14, 710n.16
Thurston, H., 627n.26
Tiddia, Fabrizio, 311n.17
Toker, Franklin, 841n.20
Tonneau, R., 519n.2, 521n.11, 527n.25, 529n.33, 530n.38
Treu, K., 694n.40
Trigg, Joseph W., 408
Tripp, D. H., 284n.26, 286n.31
Turner, C. H., 576n.34
Turner, John D., 288n.40, 290n.47, 291nn.51-52, 292n.59, 293n.68, 295n.77, 295n.79, 296n.85

Ulbert, Thilo, 669n.27, 847n.35, 848nn.37-41, 849nn.42-44
Underwood, Paul A., 759n.5, 769n.38, 819n.3
Uthemann, K.-H., 577n.37

Valavanolickal, Kuriakose, 489n.3, 498n.33
Van Bavel, Tarsicius J., 805n.68
van Dael, Peter, 759n.4
Van Damme, Dirk, 271n.11
Van den Eynde, D., 569nn.11-12
van de Sandt, Huub, 134n.6, 136n.11, 201nn.2-3, 202n.4, 205n.19
van Unnik, W. C., 330n.29, 524n.18
van Vossel, V., 506n.42
Varghese, Baby, 429n.4, 430n.7, 431n.8, 435n.22, 473n.1, 474n.3, 479n.16, 489n.3, 495n.22, 499n.2, 506n.42, 511n.77, 512n.79, 513n.85, 518n.96, 519n.1, 524n.20, 526n.23, 527n.25, 533n.1, 540nn.25-26, 540n.30, 564n.2, 567n.7, 568n.10, 569n.13, 574n.24, 574n.26
Velkovska, E., 752n.10
Vermaseren, Maarten J., 33nn.40-41
Vermes, Geza, 69n.50
Vielhauer, Philipp, 105n.19, 105n.23
Vigne, Daniel, 87n.24, 102n.7, 105nn.22-23, 106n.26, 110n.50, 112n.56, 114n.6, 117n.33, 120n.52, 299n.97, 300n.98, 300n.100
Villecourt, Louis, 632nn.48-49, 699n.60
Vinson, Martha, 602n.27
Vinzent, Markus, 332n.36
Višič-Ljubić, Ema, 835n.64
Vivian, Tim, 455n.1
Voicu, S. J., 333n.43
Volanakis, Ioannis, 828-832
Volpe, Giuliano, 840n.19
von Allmen, Jean Jacques, 166n.1, 170n.15, 184n.49, 185n.51
Vööbus, Arthur, 493n.16, 494n.18

Wagner, Günther, 29n.19, 155n.26
Wagner, M. Monica, 582n.2, 584n.6
Waldram, Joop, 400n.1
Waliszewski, T., 824n.23
Wall, William, 1
Wallis, Ernest, 386n.25, 393n.44
Ware, Kallistos T., 731n.34, 732n.39, 733n.41, 738n.64, 740nn.69-70, 743nn.76-78
Warfield, Benjamin B., 809n.90
Waszink, J. H., 340n.20, 365n.8
Weatherly, Jon A., 184n.48
Webb, Robert L., 65n.29, 68n.45, 70n.54, 77n.91, 83n.1, 84n.5, 84n.9, 87n.23, 87n.25, 90n.41, 93n.48, 95n.56
Wedderburn, A. J. M., 146n.2, 155n.26
Weil, A., 825n.27
Wenger, Antoine, 533n.1, 752n.10
Werblowsky, Reuben J. Zwi, 80n.111, 328n.20
Westra, Liuwe H., 332n.37
Wharton, A. J., 478n.14, 488n.38
Whitaker, E. C., 4, 20-21, 435n.24, 663n.2, 752n.10, 753n.11, 766n.31
Whitby, Mary, 443n.45
Whitby, Michael, 443n.45
White, L. Michael, 67nn.43-44, 225n.13

Whittaker, Molly, 246n.31
Wickham, Lionel R., 693n.36
Wiles, M. F., 575n.27, 576n.29, 576n.35
Wilken, Robert L., 113n.1, 115n.16, 115n.21, 116n.27, 687n.1, 688n.3
Wilkinson, John, 473n.2, 487nn.35-36
Williams, Frank, 264n.65, 625n.20
Williams, George H., 237n.1, 239n.7, 242n.17, 243n.21
Williams, Michael A., 290n.47
Williams, N. P., 369n.19
Williams, Rowan, 456n.2, 497n.31, 576n.33,
Willis, G. G., 766nn.31-32, 767n.33
Wilson, Henry Austin, 604n.7, 613n.32
Windisch, Hans, 138n.19, 365n.7
Winkler, Gabriele, 430n.7, 438n.29, 497n.31, 560n.42, 592n.2, 712n.18
Winslow, D. F., 592n.2, 602n.27
Wisse, Frederik, 291n.51, 292n.59, 294n.70
Witherington, Ben III, 146n.1
Wright, David F., 138n.19, 150n.10, 226n.15, 362n.1, 366n.10, 378, 379n.51, 379n.52, 574n.23, 627n.24, 627n.27, 628nn.28-29, 629n.30, 632n.46, 777n.3, 777n.5, 804n.63, 814n.127
Wright, William, 431nn.10-11, 433n.16, 700n.1
Wright, Wilmer Cave, 445n.2
Wood, B. G., 71n.66
Wood, H. G., 1
Wurst, Gregor, 301n.105

Yarnold, Edward J., 450n.13, 473n.1, 474n.3, 480n.17, 519n.1, 533n.1, 634n.1, 636n.14, 636n.16, 636n.18
Yates, A. S., 362n.1, 631n.38
Yegül, Fikret, 35n.50, 35nn.52-54, 36nn.55-56
Ysebaert, J., 12, 25n.1, 38n.1, 60n.2, 142n.41, 146n.1, 163n.46, 202n.7, 208n.28, 240n.9, 241n.10, 310n.8, 311n.17, 312n.26, 524n.19

Zenos, A. C., 625n.21
Zuntz, G., 30n.28

Index of Subjects

accounts of baptism, 228-231, 235, 430-434, 450, 487-488, 593, 700-702, 784. *See also* ceremony of baptism; conversion accounts; emergency baptism
adherence (to God/Christ), 335, 539, 566, 703, 752-753. *See also* confession of faith; interrogatory confession
administrator of baptism, 75, 88, 102, 103, 458, 547-548, 622, 675-676, 678, 758, 827; actions of, 351-352, 391-392, 524-526, 541-542, 580-581, 697-699; female, 230, 277-278, 343, 437-438, 567-568, 581, 770-771; hand on head of baptizand, 125-126, 226, 331-333, 466, 525, 542, 662, 747, 857-858; irrelevance of, 149, 353, 674-676, 797; qualified, 209, 479, 593, 663, 760-761; unqualified, 387, 543, 797-798. *See also* self-administered
adolescent baptism, 373, 376, 663, 677, 720, 777-778, 814
adoption, 334, 484, 528, 557n.31, 750
adult baptism, 21, 366, 631-633, 669, 755, 761, 807, 823, 836, 846
age of baptizand 178, 203, 315, 363-364, 370, 372-378, 595-596, 626-627, 632-633, 814-815; any age, 650, 677, 763. *See also* adolescent baptism; children, baptism of; infant baptism
amount of water, 64, 71, 81, 205, 357, 834, 840, 860. *See also* size of baptismal fonts
anointing 247, 353-354, 426-427, 566, 575, 692, 718, 855; full body, 540-541, 543, 567, 700, 704, 755; Old Testament significance, 118, 567, 598, 709; pre-baptismal, 478, 567, 559, 697, 721, 755; post-baptismal, 479-480, 531, 639, 698, 760-761, 786. *See also* Holy Spirit; oil; ointment
apostles' baptism, 297-298, 319-320, 337-338, 491, 505, 652, 790-791
Apostles' Creed, 332n.35, 766, 768
apotaxis. See renunciation
archaeology, 30, 34, 64-65, 128-131, 170, 372-377, 626, 633, 758-759, 819, 852, 857. *See also* baptisteries
Arius, 451, 456, 575, 703, 758-759, 799n.38
art, 34, 123, 131, 837, 857; images associated with baptism, 127-130, 441-443, 661-662, 759, 833, 837, 839-840, 841-842; portrayals of baptism, 126-131, 661-662, 838, 851, 857
ascent, 101, 462-463. *See also* descent
asceticism, 230-231, 287-288, 431, 739-742, 771. *See also* celibacy
aspersion. *See* sprinkling
athletic imagery, 247, 537, 549, 636, 708, 781

baptism available to all, 255, 650, 677, 736, 763. *See also* worthy
baptism. *See* accounts of; benefits of; ceremony; doctrinal summaries; efficacy of; mock; multiple; names for; self-administered; substitutes for; time appropriate for; validity of; vicarious

baptisma, 83-84, 110, 139, 237, 267f
baptismal fonts, 441, 607, 633, 832, 834; secondary fonts, 785, 822-823, 836, 837, 846, 848, 849-850, 852. *See also* kolombēthra; mikvaoth; size of fonts
baptismos, 83-84, 139-140, 160, 186-187
baptisteries, 440-443, 477, 542, 637, 643, 660-661, 669, 769, 785, 832; *baptistērion*, 245, 456, 819
baptizare, 2, 229, 341, 778
baptizō, 139-140, 148n.7, 149, 205, 237, 270, 341, 583, 716; drown/sink, 48-49, 51, 58, 309, 534, 594; grammatical voice, 88n.29, 141; intoxicated, 54, 59, 309, 534; overwhelm, 53, 57-58, 140, 243, 309, 535; plunge, 50, 55, 534-535. *See also* passive baptismal formula; temper
baptō (to dip or soak), 25, 78, 139, 141, 242; *See also* dye; temper
bath, 68, 238, 245, 326, 558; *lavacrum*, 31-32, 118, 341, 445-446; *loutron*, 28, 60, 114, 267-268, 541, 594, 819. *See also* Roman baths
bathing customs, 34-36, 68, 70, 330, 341-342, 426, 478, 858
belief. *See* faith
believers (the faithful), 374, 420, 474, 511, 547, 601, 813. *See also* catechumens
benefits of baptism, 255, 357-358, 462-464, 469-470, 545-546, 587, 597, 711, 715, 807, 854. *See also* efficacy of baptism
birth, 193, 195, 447-449, 605; first birth, 257, 359, 497, 650-651; multiple births of Christ, 120, 504, 600, 610, 671; second (rebirth), 33, 411-414, 524, 667, 763-764, 769, 808. *See also* new creation; regeneration; womb. *See also* life
blood, 33, 44, 59, 267, 349, 501, 549, 774, 775; baptism of, 357, 360, 563
bread 282, 432, 499. *See also* Eucharist

calling on the name of, 174-175, 606. *See also* name of, in the
Callistus, 123, 325n.1, 373, 380
catechumens, 8, 351, 437, 449, 466, 559, 565-566, 630, 720, 800; *competentes* or *phōtizomenoi*, 474-478, 520-521, 566, 583, 648, 766, 780-781; enrollment of, 419-421, 721, 753, 779; length of catechumenate, 329, 465, 565, 603; martyrdom of, 389, 579. *See also* believers; instruction; newborns; preparation for baptism; worthiness of candidate
celibacy, 232, 277, 493, 735, 761
ceremony of baptism, 197-198, 244, 298, 330-333, 393-394, 477-481, 579-581, 633, 668-669, 679, 702, 766-768, 784-787; instructions for, 202, 460-465. *See also* accounts of baptism; conversion accounts; infant baptism
children, 169, 185n.51, 212-213, 238, 363, 404; innocence of, 308, 364, 367-368, 372, 494, 512, 545, 629-630. *See also* infants
children, baptism of, 2, 75, 81, 171, 340, 366, 378, 466, 577-578, 771, 777, 784, 823; fonts for, 2, 824, 832-834, 838, 845, 849-850, 852. *See also* age of baptizand; infant baptism
Christ's baptism, 333-334, 502-505, 547-548, 609, 687-689, 710-711, 745-746, 747; in art, 123-131, 838, 851. *See also* Epiphany; purification of water; sinlessness of Christ
church, 215, 352, 389-391, 440, 448, 681; and Holy Spirit, 387, 731; as mother, 447, 556, 651, 658-659, 769, 806; consisting of the baptized, 160, 176, 417, 498, 562; giving baptism, 356, 382, 390, 556, 799-800. *See also* womb
circumcision, 267-269, 272, 405, 500-501, 559-560, 671-672; and baptism, 159, 262-263, 274, 416, 446-447, 674, 790; and infant baptism, 21, 370, 577, 803; Jewish practice, 76, 81, 177, 400-401; as a seal, 486, 514, 559-560; spiritual, 243, 589, 690-692, 730-731
cleansing, 275, 407. *See also* bath; purification
clinical baptism. *See* emergency baptism
clothing, 68, 126-127, 411, 515-516, 614, 650, 706-707, 714, 767; after baptism, 131, 450, 524, 543, 578, 670, 698; as baptism, 219, 259, 339, 598-599, 678n.17; with Christ, 147, 497-498, 513, 561-562, 677; sackcloth, 523, 701, 704, 782; of Spirit, 494, 503;

white linen, 31, 75, 297-298, 332n.39, 432, 524
community, 86n.17, 188, 202-203. *See also* church
competentes. *See* catechumens
confession of faith, 304, 366, 424, 487, 551, 583, 785-786. *See also* adherence; creed; interrogatory confession
confession of sin, 339n.14, 536; *See also* repentance
confirmation, 12, 17, 343, 633, 760-761, 768. *See also* anointing, post-baptismal; laying on of hands
conversion, 19, 146, 184-185, 314, 445, 720, 800, 803
conversion accounts, 166-185, 234-236, 251-253, 429-436, 719-720, 777-778; mass conversions, 170, 171, 432, 680, 701. *See also* accounts of baptisms
creed, 332, 488, 521-523, 574, 594, 773. *See also* symbolo; specific creeds
Creed of Antioch (Symbol of 318 Fathers), 520, 702n.4
cross, 11, 139, 159, 210-211, 468, 500, 554, 820, 822. *See also* sign of cross
custom. *See* tradition

dead. *See* righteous dead
dead, baptism for. *See* vicarious baptism
death, 217, 347, 482, 553, 604
death and resurrection of Christ, 159-160, 522, 552-553, 570-571, 587-588, 610, 654-655, 764. *See also* descensus ad inferos
deathbed baptism. *See* delay of baptism; emergency baptism
delay of baptism, 568, 601-602, 776-777, 780; reasons for, 348, 364, 466, 595-596; warnings against, 256, 382. *See also* moral living
demons, 233, 241-242, 281-282, 336, 415, 726-727. *See also* exorcism; Satan
descensus ad inferos, 11, 120-122, 213, 223-224, 226, 415, 730
descent, 213, 290, 516, 525, 548, 785, 852; into and ascent from water, 110, 213, 216-218, 290, 317, 426, 479, 677; of Holy Spirit, 112, 296, 559, 687-689, 793. *See also* pouring out of Spirit

disciples' baptism. *See* apostles' baptism
disciplina arcani, 7, 423, 458, 630, 780
doctrinal summaries, 213-214, 219-220, 253, 263, 319, 334, 382-383, 389, 396, 467, 711
dove, 118, 653, 710, 751; in art, 125-126, 130, 661-662, 837
dye, 39, 47-48, 286, 676, 775

ears, 636, 755, 767
Easter. *See* Pasch
eight, 442, 637-638, 690, 712-713, 759, 837
efficacy of baptism, 346, 353, 355, 384, 422, 605, 736, 799-801, 806
emergency baptism, 343, 532, 661, 760, 787-788, 858; examples of, 372-377, 381, 619-620, 625, 777, 786; validity questioned, 355-357, 382, 851. *See also* infant baptism
enlightenment, 109, 241, 292, 311-312, 471, 560-561, 613, 819; *phōtizomenoi*, 238, 451, 474-475, 572. *See also* light; neophyte
Epiphany, 115-117, 333-335, 635, 653, 695, 757
eschatology, 85, 141, 197, 408-410, 415, 529-530, 611
eternal life. *See* life
Eucharist, 240, 264, 333, 427-428, 481, 530, 581, 640, 699, 721-722, 736; children's participation, 372, 722, 789; closed 437, 526, 565, 720; who may partake, 203, 242. *See also* bread; milk (and honey)
Eunomius, 456n.2, 575-576, 703, 799n.38
exorcism, 329, 476, 522-524, 537-538, 697, 753-754, 782. *See also* demons; Satan

faith, 160, 164, 260, 314-315, 421, 475, 532, 666, 743-744; belief (personal faith), 180, 422; content of, 339nn.16-17, 394; importance of, 304, 387, 550. *See also* adherence; confession of faith; creeds; doctrinal summaries
fasting, 31, 202, 459, 562, 760, 781, 784; before baptism, 251-252, 281, 506, 566. *See also* catechumens, *competentes*; Lent; preparation for baptism
fideles. *See* believers
fire, 261, 282-283, 314, 406-407, 517, 611-612, 711; of Gehenna, 360, 439; on water, 108, 110-112, 130

fire baptism, 90-91, 288, 297-298, 408-410, 417, 730
fish, 301, 347, 644, 839
fons. See baptismal fonts
footwashing, 492, 639, 656, 787, 846; fonts for, 785, 822, 837
forgiveness of sins, 210-212, 216-217, 296-298, 314-315, 346, 393, 417-418, 419, 483, 505, 509, 556-559, 809; and Holy Spirit, 358, 396, 679; in John's baptism, 83, 84, 337. *See also* Jewish ceremonial washings; post-baptismal sin
formula for baptism, 172, 203, 352n.7, 383-384, 799. *See also* Trinitarian formula
freedom, 282, 434, 515, 521, 645, 666-668, 774. *See also* Satan
free will, 239, 365, 422, 605, 739-740, 814

gift of the Holy Spirit, 337, 439-440, 496, 509, 530-531, 651, 689, 736, 765
gifts of the Holy Spirit, 18, 110, 406, 742, 786
Gnosticism, 276-302, 318-319
godparents, 487, 630. *See also* sponsors
Good Shepherd, 125, 127, 441, 839
good works. *See* righteous deeds
grace, 358-359, 550, 553, 587, 598, 613, 654-655, 681-682, 731-732, 733-734, 739-740, 803

hands. *See* administrator; laying on of hands
hands of baptizand, 344, 348, 477, 524, 619, 753. *See also* position of baptizand
heretical baptism, 380-400, 469-470, 573, 678-679, 717. *See also* schismatic baptism; validity of baptism
holiness, 403, 531, 543-544, 638, 722. *See also* keeping one's baptism; moral living
Holy Spirit, 116-117, 283, 344, 559, 673, 688-690, 736; and anointing, 117-118, 305, 511-512, 531, 560, 855; in church, 208, 387, 392, 731; descent of, 112, 296, 559, 687-689, 793; and forgiveness, 358, 396, 679; gifts of, 18, 110, 406, 742, 786; indwelling (gift) of, 337, 439-440, 496, 509, 530-531, 651, 689, 736, 765; and laying on of hands, 184, 427, 440, 572, 679; pouring out of, 108, 154n.21, 162-163, 177, 392; and seal, 162, 382, 640, 705; and water, 163-164, 393, 407-408, 484f, 517, 559, 651. *See also* gift(s) of Holy Spirit
Holy Spirit baptism, 90, 184, 269, 387
hope, 212, 259-260
household conversions, 176-178, 179-180, 233, 235, 253, 630

illumination. *See* enlightenment
imagery (figures) of baptism, 1-2, 15-16, 123-125, 151-152, 442, 513-516, 641-642, 680, 708. *See also* art; Old Testament figures of baptism
imitate, 610-611, 710
immersion, 70, 188, 213, 341, 663, 832, 850, 857; partial, 49, 542, 669, 858; substitutes for, 355-358, 770; total (submersion), 37, 64, 286, 443, 458-459, 778, 824, 852. *See also baptize; mergere;* triple immersion
incarnation, 114-120, 194, 513, 606, 609-610, 762
indwelling of Holy Spirit. *See* gift of the Holy Spirit
infants, 421, 488, 680, 787, 792; condition of, 151, 372-377, 459, 545, 629-630, 646, 715, 717-718, 809, 814-815. *See also* children; original sin
infant baptism, 1, 17, 81, 138, 169, 308, 363-366, 370-372, 423, 532, 594-596, 627-633, 663, 681, 722, 755, 760-761, 765-766, 787-789, 802-803, 832, 856-857; ceremony for, 366-367, 580, 712-713, 722-723, 755, 767-768, 787-788, 803; emergency, 372-376, 509-510, 595-596, 627, 629, 788; necessity of, 373-374, 459, 568, 627, 630, 771, 810; routine, 164, 627, 629-630, 669, 715, 737, 755, 832. *See also* age of baptizand; children, baptism of
initiation, Christian, 18, 251-255, 318, 423, 520-526. *See also* ceremony of baptism; conversion
initiation, Jewish, 69, 78, 80, 86-87. *See also* proselyte baptism
initiation, pagan (mystery religions), 29-31, 34, 317-318, 330, 378, 647
innocence of children. *See* children; infants
instruction, 80, 82, 281, 314-315, 420-422, 437, 533-534, 782; for *competentes*, 474f,

488, 536-537, 583, 605, 635; pre-baptismal, 251, 340, 397, 520-522, 618, 779; post-baptismal, 137, 186-187, 303, 467, 634-635, 667-668. *See also* catechumens; *disciplina arcani*; moral living
interrogatory confession, 80, 332, 352n.7, 466, 478-479, 580-581, 692

Jewish ceremonial washings, 63-67, 71n.67, 80, 84-89, 138, 186-187, 266-267, 273-275, 501; contrasted with Christian baptism, 260, 266, 273, 438-439, 557-558, 642, 653; daily, 66, 72-73, 75, 87, 249-250, 264, 275. *See also* proselyte baptism
John the Baptizer, 99, 266, 488, 565, 694-695
John's baptism, 167, 181-182, 485, 653, 717, 756, 853; compared to Jewish and Christian, 558, 586
Jordan River, 75, 128-130, 221, 410, 461, 503, 653
Jesus' baptism. *See* Christ's baptism

keeping one's baptism pure, 207, 227, 229, 409, 660. *See also* holiness; moral living; seal, keeping
kingdom of heaven/God, 85, 217, 307, 375
kiss (of peace), 240, 333, 370, 467, 581
kolumbēthra, 330, 468-470, 478, 541, 819

laying on of hands, 125-126, 184, 187, 281, 329, 344, 354-355, 568-569, 618, 855; completing baptismal ceremony, 384, 387-388, 567, 664, 718; on penitents and returning heretics, 383-384, 440, 765. *See also* Holy Spirit
legal language, 331n.32, 365, 539, 549-550, 613; *stipulatio*, 192, 349n.45, 367. *See also* oaths
Lent, 474, 487-488, 533-534, 593. *See also* fasting; liturgical calendar; Pasch
life, 204; eternal (immortality), 231, 306, 445, 497, 525; living (running) water, 71n.67, 77, 202-204, 256, 466; new, 79, 217. *See also* new creation
light, 314, 426, 597-598, 600, 683, 750; fire on water, 108, 110-112. *See also* enlightenment

liturgy, 11, 19, 123, 189, 487, 631-632, 712-714. *See also* ceremony
liturgical calendar, 300, 345, 395, 618, 762. *See also* time appropriate for baptism

Marcion, 276-278, 384, 395, 799n.38
marital imagery, 161, 224, 279, 285-288 passim, 346, 416, 427, 498, 516, 548-549, 614, 666, 694
martyrdom, 350, 417-419, 486-487, 562n.47, 591, 669-670, 673. *See also* blood
mass conversions, 170, 171, 235, 251, 432, 680, 701, 719
mergere, 2, 31, 36-37, 338, 341, 638, 683, 852
mikvaoth, 63-65, 70, 170, 205, 269-270
military imagery, 209-210, 498, 516, 524, 549, 781, 800; oath of soldiers, 349, 403, 665, 682
milk, 315-316, 650; and honey, 213, 333, 345, 768
mock baptism, 443, 457-458, 801
mode of baptism, 2, 21, 95-96, 203, 625, 631, 669, 834, 845, 850-852
moral living 242, 360-361, 414, 615-616, 780-782; exhortations to, 207, 216-217, 410-411, 537, 660, 748-749, 752; required after baptism, 202, 348, 428, 462-463, 610-611, 799. *See also* delay of baptism; righteous deeds
multiple baptisms, 278, 297, 460, 579, 596. *See also* Jewish ceremonial washings; rebaptism
mysteries or sacraments, 13-14, 17, 348-349, 403, 550, 646-647, 655; baptism, 404, 601, 615; Eucharist, 264
mystery, 321, 460, 647
mystery religions, 28-34, 155n.26, 317-318, 601, 647. *See also* initiation, pagan

naked, 81, 36, 330, 432-433, 477-478, 507, 537, 541, 652, 703-704, 767, 855; baptizand in art, 123-124, 127
names for baptism, 238, 284, 309, 372-373, 403, 608, 715. *See also* specific names
name of, in the, 135-136, 384, 386, 395, 469; Jesus Christ, 7, 89, 148, 171; the Lord, 214, 223-224; Trinity, 505, 551, 585, 705, 800. *See also* calling on the name of

necessity of baptism, 215-218, 349, 378-379, 486-487, 591, 804, 860; exceptions to, 258, 337-338, 360-361, 579, 793, 854. *See also* infant baptism
neophyte, 372-376, 447, 539, 543-544, 562, 635, 787
newborn, 2, 79, 247, 628-629, 370, 375, 378, 609, 706, 747, 750; enrollment as catechumen, 628-629, 712, 719, 753, 777
new creation, 212, 553-555, 762. *See also* life
new name, 235, 286, 585, 753
Nicene Creed, 456, 573, 708, 766n.32
Niceno-Constantinopolitan Creed, 520-521, 573-574, 753, 768

oath, 69, 87, 254, 424, 647; of soldiers, 349, 403, 665, 682. *See also* adherence
oil, 35, 279-280, 326, 434-435, 441-442, 463-465, 509, 514, 657, 693, 700, 755. *See also* anointing
ointment (*myron*), 479-480, 540, 568-570, 575, 718, 755. *See also* anointing
Old Testament figures of baptism, 207, 210-212, 400-405, 468-469, 614-615, 696
one baptism, 317, 349, 388, 660; conversion immersion, 266, 273-274, 347, 674; single immersion 575-576, 668, 444
original sin, 365n.8, 371, 633, 677, 740, 763, 771, 804, 808-816. *See also* children, innocence of; infants, condition of

pagan religious washings, 26-28, 242, 446, 853. *See also* mystery religions
paradise, 122, 124, 417, 541, 599, 650, 707, 714
Pasch, 326, 492-493, 536, 658, 699. *See also* Lent; liturgical calendar; time appropriate for baptism
passion, 256, 282; of Christ, 109, 139, 346, 417
passive baptismal formula, 7, 174-175, 541-542, 704-705, 755
Passover. *See* Pasch
penitents 380, 383-384, 389, 451, 494, 565, 678, 765, 798-799. *See also* post-baptismal sin
Pentecost 166-170, 345, 652, 762
perfect, 312-313, 417, 574, 616, 664, 741
perfusion. *See* pouring

phōtizomenoi. *See* catechumens
pomps of devil, 538, 748, 752-753, 772-773
position of baptizand, 2, 95, 126, 344, 441, 669, 850, 857-858. *See also* hands of baptizand
post-baptismal sin, 216-217, 278, 320, 338-339, 361, 417-418, 440, 506, 571, 635, 682, 733-734, 740. *See also* holiness; moral living; penitents
pouring (perfusion), 118-119, 205-206, 607, 661-662, 850; substitute for immersion, 355-356, 713, 716, 836, 858
pouring out of Holy Spirit, 108, 154n.21, 162-163, 176, 392. *See also* descent, of Spirit
prayer, 471-472, 606, 689, 697, 724-727, 754-755, 786; Lord's Prayer, 522-523, 567, 695-696, 749, 768, 783, 789; in baptismal ceremony, 434, 460-465, 471-472, 566-567, 640, 701; by baptizand, 344, 471, 579, 652, 760, 781; for baptizand, 461, 566-567, 571, 681, 696, 753, 768
preparation for baptism, 254, 303, 314, 316, 329, 466, 475-477, 766, 780. *See also* catechumens
proselyte baptism, 86-88, 159, 177, 266, 377-378, 859
purification, 26-28, 70-72, 93, 315, 368-369, 511. *See also* Jewish ceremonial washing; pagan religious washings
purification of water; for baptismal ceremony, 340, 391, 414, 460-461, 476, 507, 754; by Christ, 113-115, 121, 314, 481, 517-518, 653-654; by Spirit, 517, 559

rebaptism, 9, 73, 278, 451, 470, 674, 760-761, 765, 796
regeneration, 162-163, 240, 307-308, 309-311, 334-335, 462, 555-556, 571-572, 588-589. *See also* birth; life; new creation
regula fidei, 421-422. *See also* tradition
renunciation (of Satan), 335, 366, 423, 461-462, 523-524, 631, 721. *See also* adherence; pomps of Devil; repentance
repentance, 80, 85, 87, 207, 314-315, 338-340, 410, 422, 447, 475-476. *See also* confession of sin; post-baptismal sin; renunciation

resurrection, 287, 415. *See also* death and resurrection of Christ
righteous dead, 106, 217-218, 225, 317. *See also descensus ad inferos*
righteous deeds (good works), 207, 257, 260, 333, 361, 424, 440, 557, 623, 682, 739. *See also* moral living
rite of baptism. *See* ceremony
rock (stone), 114, 482, 499, 514, 608
Roman baths, 35-36, 830, 833, 834, 843. *See also* bathing customs
rule of secrecy. *See disciplina arcani*

sacraments. *See* mysteries
salt, 766, 768, 777, 779
salvation, 163, 215, 221-222, 413, 425, 434, 710
sanctification, 448. *See also* purification; purification of water, for baptismal ceremony
Satan (devil), 120-121, 279, 334, 523-524, 703, 812; baptism releases from, 359, 600-601, 614, 645, 733-734. *See also* demons; exorcism; freedom; pomps of devil; renunciation
schismatic baptism, 352, 590-591, 676, 761, 799. *See also* validity of baptism
scrutinies 419-420, 487, 579-580, 766-767, 768, 772, 782
seal, 8, 218-220, 283, 297-298, 316, 348, 354-355, 485-486, 559-560, 572, 599, 786; anointing, 514, 569-570, 649, 698; baptism, 234, 257-258, 312-313, 338-339, 449, 590; conversion accounts, 229-230, 430f, 625; Holy Spirit, 162, 382, 640, 705; keeping the seal, 207-208, 233, 462; sheep, 516, 524, 559, 599, 613-614; signing forehead, 7, 196, 524, 459, 753. *See also* keeping one's baptism
self-administered baptism, 57, 75, 88, 95, 230, 250-201, 305
sequence of baptismal ceremony, 4, 232, 251, 271, 353, 697, 768; Gnostic, 281-282, 286, 289, 299; Syrian, 433, 435, 437, 495, 506, 512, 703, 713
sex, 250, 256, 274, 429, 771
sheep, 449, 494, 512, 658, 694-695, 809, 837; sealing of, 516, 524, 559, 599, 613-614. *See also* Good Shepherd

sign (of cross), 228, 333, 344, 355, 459, 524, 540, 700, 753, 760-761, 774
signum. *See* seal
sin, 155, 254, 457, 496, 598-599, 604, 623. *See also* original sin; post-baptismal sin
singing, 481, 499-518, 606, 649, 694-695, 699, 755
sinlessness of children, 308, 364, 367-368, 372, 494, 512, 545, 629-630
sinlessness of Christ, 105, 481, 642-643. *See also* incarnation; purification of waters
size of baptismal fonts, 64-65, 441, 542-543, 633, 637, 660-661, 669, 769, 821, 836, 848; for children, 2, 824, 832-834, 838, 845, 849-850, 852. *See also* amount of water
sponsors, 340, 366-367, 487, 536, 579-580, 721, 779; for infants, 578, 630, 722-723, 805
sprinkling (aspersion), 45-47, 59, 60-62, 70, 438; contrasted with baptism, 273-274, 338, 341n.23, 456; substitute for immersion, 129, 355, 770, 838, 858
stain, 367-369, 378, 509-510, 558, 612
submersion. *See baptizō*; immersion
substitutes for baptism, 258, 338, 579. *See also* immersion
symbolo, 7, 332, 352, 396; *redditio symboli*, 475, 626, 768, 783-784; *traditio symboli*, 475, 636, 768, 772, 782-783. *See also* creeds, *specific creeds*
syntaxis, 722. *See also* adherence

temper (metal), 42, 245, 554
temperature of water, 8, 35-36, 68, 74, 649, 844, 846
temptations, 314, 741, 733, 777
three, 252, 329, 610, 665; days, 316, 410, 426
time appropriate for baptism, 180, 303, 329, 364, 699, 762, 855; any time, 345, 583; Pasch, 618, 652, 760, 780. *See also* delay of baptism; liturgical calendar
tinguere, 229, 338, 341, 657, 770, 775, 778, 852
tomb, 442, 542n.38, 556, 594, 706, 820
tradition (custom), 591, 679-680; appealed to as authoritative, 384-386, 397, 760, 801-802, 813; from Christ and apostles, 238, 421-422, 502, 710; lacking Biblical authority, 394, 584, 767

Index of Subjects | 953

Trinitarian doctrine, 116-118, 136, 450, 456
Trinitarian formula, 133-135, 342, 396, 508, 541n.36, 672-673
Trinity, 504, 518, 585, 642, 652; in name of, 505, 551, 585, 705, 800
triple immersion, 31, 75, 231, 331-332, 341-342, 466, 638, 643, 668, 705, 723, 855

unity, 152, 209-210, 306, 385, 646, 800-802

Valentinus, 107, 278-290, 310n.11, 311n.17, 311n.20, 318-199, 384, 703, 799n.38
validity of baptism, 349n.45, 395-396, 621, 675, 799-801; of clinical baptism, 355-357, 382, 851
vicarious baptism, 154, 277, 280-281, 299
virgin birth, 307, 347, 644-645
vow. *See* adherence; oath

washing, 108, 122, 150, 238, 534; *louō*, 25, 60, 67, 230, 267-268, 270; *niptō*, 60-61, 139, 270; *pluneō*, 60, 62, 746
water, 142, 211, 247, 277, 300-302, 306, 416, 439, 499, 529, 751, 853; amount of, 64, 71, 81, 205, 357, 834, 840, 860; living (running), 71n.676, 77, 202-204, 256, 466; praise of, 334, 482, 514-515; temperature of, 8, 35-36, 68, 74, 649, 844, 846. *See also* baptisteries; bath; Old Testament figures of baptism; purification of water
water baptism, 90, 153-154, 171, 175, 176-177, 270, 290-392, 294, 387, 407-408, 484-485, 556, 691, 746-747
water supply, 26, 65, 70-71, 179, 204-205, 250, 341, 432-434, 468, 621, 633, 748, 824, 837, 844; living (running) water, 62, 202-204, 256, 466
womb, 484, 504, 512, 666-667, 712, 737, 763-764, 773-774, 819-820. *See also* birth; church; regeneration
women administering baptism. *See* administrator
women, baptism of, 75, 79-81, 179, 230, 330, 366, 466, 567-568, 580-581, 770-771, 785, 836, 852
word, 312, 342, 461-462, 621-622, 785-786, 803
worthiness of candidate: conferred by baptism, 297, 409, 461, 471, 659; to receive baptism, 228, 238-239, 329, 366, 419-420, 422, 466, 521, 587, 771. *See also* baptism available to all; grace; scrutinies